A Practical Guide to Construction Adjudication

A Practical Guide to Construction Adjudication

James Pickavance
Partner
Eversheds LLP

WILEY Blackwell

This edition first published 2016
© 2016 James Pickavance (apart from Chapter 19 © Tony Jones, Chapter 20 © Michael Humphreys, Chapter 22 © Peter Wood and Phillip Greenham, Chapter 23 Dermot McEvoy, Chapter 24 © Philip Koh, Chapter 25 © Tómas Kennedy-Grant and Chapter 26 © Steven Cannon)

Registered Office
John Wiley & Sons Ltd, The Atrium, Southern Gate, Chichester, West Sussex, PO19 8SQ,
United Kingdom

Editorial Offices
9600 Garsington Road, Oxford, OX4 2DQ, United Kingdom.
The Atrium, Southern Gate, Chichester, West Sussex, PO19 8SQ, United Kingdom.

For details of our global editorial offices, for customer services and for information about how to apply for permission to reuse the copyright material in this book please see our website at www.wiley.com/wiley-blackwell.

The right of the author to be identified as the author of this work has been asserted in accordance with the UK Copyright, Designs and Patents Act 1988.

All rights reserved. No part of this publication may be reproduced, stored in a retrieval system, or transmitted, in any form or by any means, electronic, mechanical, photocopying, recording or otherwise, except as permitted by the UK Copyright, Designs and Patents Act 1988, without the prior permission of the publisher.

Designations used by companies to distinguish their products are often claimed as trademarks. All brand names and product names used in this book are trade names, service marks, trademarks or registered trademarks of their respective owners. The publisher is not associated with any product or vendor mentioned in this book.

Limit of Liability/Disclaimer of Warranty: While the publisher and author(s) have used their best efforts in preparing this book, they make no representations or warranties with respect to the accuracy or completeness of the contents of this book and specifically disclaim any implied warranties of merchantability or fitness for a particular purpose. It is sold on the understanding that the publisher is not engaged in rendering professional services and neither the publisher nor the author shall be liable for damages arising herefrom. If professional advice or other expert assistance is required, the services of a competent professional should be sought.

Library of Congress Cataloging-in-Publication Data

Pickavance, James, author.
  A practical guide to construction adjudication / James Pickavance.
     pages cm
  Includes bibliographical references and index.
  ISBN 978-1-118-71795-0 (pbk.)
1. Construction contracts–Great Britain. 2. Arbitration and award–Great Britain. 3. Construction contracts.
4. Arbitration and award. I. Title.
  KD1641.P525 2016
  343.4107′8624–dc23
                                                                                                    2015024795

A catalogue record for this book is available from the British Library.

Wiley also publishes its books in a variety of electronic formats. Some content that appears in print may not be available in electronic books.

Set in 10/12.5pt MinionPro by Aptara Inc., New Delhi, India

1   2016

Foreword

As Sir Rupert Jackson aptly commented, the mass of authorities on adjudication once formed an impenetrable jungle.

Since an illuminating path through this jungle has been created by the well-known work of my colleague, Mr Justice Coulson, it might be asked why there is a need for another book on the subject. I think that the reader of this valuable work by James Pickavance will soon find the answer.

Part 1 of this book, whilst fully supported by references to decided cases, is very much directed towards the practitioner who has to advise his or her client on a construction dispute and then conduct or defend proceedings brought by way of adjudication. To this end it provides a clear route map together with helpful checklists at the conclusion of each chapter. It is this different approach that I think readers will find so helpful. The guidance in relation to insolvency and administration is particularly valuable.

As an added benefit, there is Part 2 – which deals with adjudication in other jurisdictions. I know of no other similarly comprehensive guide and it is a fascinating and illuminating source of reference.

The final bonus is a comprehensive index of over 550 reported cases on adjudication, sorted into numerous subject headings that follow the subject headings in the main work.

This book does not set out to be a rival to existing works but to complement them. That is a role that I have no doubt that readers will find that it amply fulfils.

The Hon Mr Justice Edwards-Stuart
Judge in Charge of the Technology and Construction Court
London
August, 2015

Acknowledgements

I have sought the assistance of a number of individuals who have been kind enough to comment on, or write, sections or chapters, discuss issues and assist with various jobs.

In particular, my father and my uncle, with formidable experience in the industry, as adjudicators and as authors, have been of immeasurable assistance throughout this project. James Bowling of 4 Pump Court, provided me with erudite comments on insolvency, enforcement, set-off, adjudication strategy and losing the right to challenge the adjudicator's jurisdiction. Malcolm and Michael Harris of Harris Consulting, who between them have taken part in over 400 adjudications either representing parties or as adjudicators, have provided me with helpful insight that has been woven into several chapters of the book. Phillip Burton's technical prowess has allowed me to convert a vast spreadsheet into Appendix 8 and 9. Michael Mendelblat of Herbert Smith Freehills, kindly spent time reviewing part of an early edition and acted as a sounding board for ideas as the book took shape. Michael Conroy Harris of Eversheds helped produce the model forms. The Chartered Institute of Building, in particular Saleem Akram, offered and continue to offer vociferous support for the idea and production of this book.

Finally, thanks go to the authors of the chapters on jurisdictions other than England & Wales: Tony Jones of Brechin Tindal Oatts for Scotland, Michael Humphreys QC for Northern Ireland, Peter Wood and Phillip Greenham of Minter Ellison for Australia, Dermot McEvoy of Eversheds for Ireland, Philip TN Koh of Mah-Kamariyah & Philip Koh for Malaysia, Tómas Kennedy-Grant QC for New Zealand and Steven Cannon of Eversheds for Singapore. Although I have edited these chapters to a greater or lesser extent, any credit must go entirely to the authors. I have been very fortunate indeed that they agreed to contribute to this book.

James Pickavance
Hackney, London
September 2015

Contents

Foreword	v
Acknowledgements	vii

Part I   The United Kingdom

1	**Introduction**	**3**
	1.1 Overview	3
	1.2 Background to statutory adjudication in the UK	4
	1.3 Statutory adjudication regimes	5
	1.4 Use of case law in this part	6
2	**Adjudication in a nutshell**	**9**
3	**Deciding to adjudicate**	**13**
	3.1 Overview	13
	3.2 Do I have a claim?	14
	3.3 Is it worth it?	15
	3.3.1 *In a nutshell*	*15*
	3.3.2 *Amount in dispute*	*15*
	3.3.3 *Likely recovery*	*16*
	3.3.4 *Professional fees*	*16*
	3.3.5 *Resources*	*17*
	3.3.6 *Relationships*	*17*
	3.4 Is adjudication the right forum?	18
	3.4.1 *In a nutshell*	*18*
	3.4.2 *Advantages*	*18*
	3.4.3 *Disadvantages*	*21*
	3.4.4 *Statistics*	*24*
	3.5 Other forms of 'rapid' dispute resolution	24
	3.5.1 *In a nutshell*	*24*
	3.5.2 *Early neutral evaluation*	*24*
	3.5.3 *Expert determination*	*25*
	3.5.4 *Mediation*	*26*
	3.5.5 *Fast-track arbitration*	*27*
	3.5.6 *Statutory demand or winding-up petition*	*29*

		3.5.7	Part 8 claim	29
		3.5.8	Summary judgment	29
	3.6	Adjudication on behalf of, or against, an insolvent party		30
		3.6.1	In a nutshell	30
		3.6.2	Why do it?	30
		3.6.3	Trigger for insolvency	31
		3.6.4	Liquidation	33
		3.6.5	Voluntary or compulsory administration	37
		3.6.6	Administrative receivership	38
		3.6.7	A company voluntary arrangement (CVA)	38
		3.6.8	Bankruptcy	39
		3.6.9	Individual voluntary arrangement (IVA)	39
		3.6.10	Problems enforcing the adjudicator's decision	39
	3.7	Who to involve		40
		3.7.1	In a nutshell	40
		3.7.2	In-house lawyers	40
		3.7.3	External lawyers	41
		3.7.4	Claims consultants	41
		3.7.5	Experts	41
		3.7.6	Project team	42
	3.8	Checklist: considering whether or not to adjudicate		42
4	**Statutory adjudication**			43
	4.1	Overview		43
	4.2	Old or new act		44
	4.3	Existence and terms of a contract		44
		4.3.1	In a nutshell	44
		4.3.2	Contract formation and terms	45
		4.3.3	Contract terminated	46
		4.3.4	Void or voidable contract	46
		4.3.5	Choice of terms	47
		4.3.6	Incorporation of terms	47
	4.4	Construction contract		49
		4.4.1	In a nutshell	49
		4.4.2	Carrying out, arranging, providing labour for construction operations (Act s. 104(1))	49
		4.4.3	Consultants and advisers (Act s. 104(2))	50
		4.4.4	Contracts of employment (Act s. 104(3))	50
		4.4.5	Construction operations and other matters (Act s. 104(5))	50
		4.4.6	Application of the Act to contracts (Act s. 104(6))	51
		4.4.7	Ancillary agreements	52
	4.5	Construction operations		55
		4.5.1	In a nutshell	55
		4.5.2	Definition of construction operations (Act s. 105(1))	55
	4.6	Excluded construction operations		58
		4.6.1	In a nutshell	58
		4.6.2	Approach to interpreting the exclusion provisions at section 105(2) of the Act	59

	4.6.3	Court's approach to applying the exclusions at subsection 105(2)	59
	4.6.4	Drilling and extraction (Act s. 105(2)(a) and (b))	60
	4.6.5	Assembly, installation, erection, demolition in connection with certain activities (Act s. 105(2)(c))	60
	4.6.6	Manufacture, delivery, installation (Act s. 105(2)(d))	62
4.7	Excluded agreements		62
	4.7.1	In a nutshell	62
	4.7.2	Residential occupier (Act s. 106(1)(a) and (2))	63
	4.7.3	Exclusion Order (2009 Act, s. 106A; 1996 Act, s. 106(1)(b))	64
4.8	Contract in writing		66
	4.8.1	In a nutshell	66
	4.8.2	2009 Act	67
	4.8.3	1996 Act only applies to agreements in writing (1996 Act s. 107(1))	68
	4.8.4	'In writing' (1996 Act s. 107(2))	68
	4.8.5	An agreement made 'otherwise than in writing' (1996 Act s. 107(3))	69
	4.8.6	An agreement 'evidenced in writing' (1996 Act s. 107(4))	70
	4.8.7	'An exchange of written submissions in adjudication proceedings' (1996 Act s. 107(5))	70
	4.8.8	Scenarios	71
4.9	Checklist: What form of adjudication am I subject to?		74

5 Contractual and ad hoc adjudication 75

5.1	Overview		75
5.2	Contractual adjudication		75
	5.2.1	In a nutshell	75
	5.2.2	What is a contractual adjudication?	76
	5.2.3	Treatment of contractual adjudications by the court	77
5.3	Ad hoc adjudication		79
	5.3.1	In a nutshell	79
	5.3.2	Ad hoc adjudication by choice	79
	5.3.3	Ad hoc jurisdiction by mistake	80
	5.3.4	Ad hoc jurisdiction on issues	82

6 Adjudication procedure 83

6.1	Overview		83
6.2	Scheme		84
	6.2.1	In a nutshell	84
	6.2.2	Does the Scheme apply and the failure to comply with section 108(1)–(4) (Act s. 108(5) and 114(4))	84
	6.2.3	Why choose the Scheme?	86
	6.2.4	Scheme variants	87
6.3	Contractual procedures		88
	6.3.1	In a nutshell	88
	6.3.2	JCT	89
	6.3.3	ICE/ICC	90
	6.3.4	IChemE	91
	6.3.5	NEC	92

	6.3.6	TeCSA	93
	6.3.7	CIC	94
	6.3.8	CEDR Solve	95
	6.3.9	Bespoke rules	96
6.4	Checklist: What adjudication procedure am I subject to?		96

7 Preconditions and restrictions to statutory adjudication — 97
- 7.1 Overview — 97
- 7.2 Is there a dispute? — 98
  - 7.2.1 *In a nutshell* — 98
  - 7.2.2 *Court's approach* — 98
  - 7.2.3 *A claim must have been made* — 99
  - 7.2.4 *The meaning of 'dispute' (Act s.108(1))* — 100
  - 7.2.5 *The point at which to assess whether or not there is a dispute* — 102
  - 7.2.6 *Time period following a claim until a dispute is formed* — 102
  - 7.2.7 *Ambush* — 104
  - 7.2.8 *Scenarios* — 104
- 7.3 More than one dispute — 108
  - 7.3.1 *In a nutshell* — 108
  - 7.3.2 *More than one dispute (Act s. 108(1))* — 109
  - 7.3.3 *The Scheme (Scheme p. 8)* — 111
- 7.4 Substantially the same dispute (Scheme p. 9) — 111
  - 7.4.1 *In a nutshell* — 111
  - 7.4.2 *Substantially the same dispute* — 112
- 7.5 Does the dispute arise 'under' the contract (Act s. 108(1))? — 115
  - 7.5.1 *In a nutshell* — 115
  - 7.5.2 *Meaning of 'under' the contract* — 115
- 7.6 More than one contract — 117
  - 7.6.1 *In a nutshell* — 117
  - 7.6.2 *More than one contract (Act s. 108(1))* — 118
  - 7.6.3 *Scheme (Scheme p. 8(2))* — 119
- 7.7 Commencing an adjudication 'at any time' — 119
  - 7.7.1 *In a nutshell* — 119
  - 7.7.2 *Act (Act s. 108(2)(a))* — 119
  - 7.7.3 *Conclusivity clauses* — 121
  - 7.7.4 *Statutory limitation* — 122
  - 7.7.5 *Insolvent party* — 122

8 Adjudication strategy — 123
- 8.1 Overview — 123
- 8.2 Commencing the adjudication process — 123
  - 8.2.1 *Choosing the right time to start* — 123
  - 8.2.2 *Getting in there first* — 124
- 8.3 More than one adjudication — 125
  - 8.3.1 *Multiple adjudications during the project* — 125
  - 8.3.2 *Concurrent adjudications* — 125
- 8.4 Choosing the dispute to refer — 126

		8.4.1	Appropriate expertise	126
		8.4.2	Pecuniary and declaratory claims	127
		8.4.3	Contractual interpretation	128
		8.4.4	'Smash and grab'	129
		8.4.5	'Cherry-picking'	136
		8.4.6	Large-scale adjudications	137
		8.4.7	Without prejudice correspondence	139
	8.5	Deploying arguments		139
		8.5.1	Save the best until last	139
		8.5.2	Reverse ambush	140
	8.6	Assessing the other party's willingness and ability to pay		141
		8.6.1	Securing assets before the adjudication	141
		8.6.2	Can the other party pay?	142
	8.7	Removing procedural uncertainty		142
		8.7.1	Taking a jurisdiction point early	142
9	**Initiating the adjudication**			**144**
	9.1	Overview		144
	9.2	A precis on jurisdiction and natural justice		145
	9.3	Notice of adjudication		146
		9.3.1	In a nutshell	146
		9.3.2	The Scheme (Scheme p. 1(2) and (3))	147
		9.3.3	Practical considerations	147
	9.4	Checklist: Before serving the notice of adjudication – referring party		151
	9.5	Checklist: On receiving the notice of adjudication – responding party		151
	9.6	Appointing the adjudicator		152
		9.6.1	In a nutshell	152
		9.6.2	Timing (Act s. 108(2)(b), Scheme p. 7)	152
		9.6.3	Appointment procedure (Scheme p. 2, 3, 5 and 6)	153
		9.6.4	Inoperable procedure or defective appointment	155
		9.6.5	Appointment by an ANB	156
		9.6.6	Choosing the right ANB where one is not specified	158
		9.6.7	Forum shopping	160
		9.6.8	Appointment of an individual named in the contract	161
		9.6.9	Nominated or appointed adjudicator too busy, unwilling or unable to act	162
		9.6.10	Natural person and no conflict of interest (Scheme, p. 4)	163
		9.6.11	Objections to the appointed adjudicator (Scheme, p. 10)	163
		9.6.12	A party's assessment of an adjudicator's capability	164
		9.6.13	The prospective adjudicator's assessment of whether he should accept the appointment	166
		9.6.14	Post appointment before the dispute is referred	167
		9.6.15	Adjudicator's agreement	167
		9.6.16	Revoking the adjudicator's appointment (Scheme p. 11)	170
	9.7	Checklist: Appointing the adjudicator – referring party		171
	9.8	Checklist: Appointing the adjudicator – responding party		171
	9.9	Checklist: Accepting the appointment – adjudicator		172

10 The adjudication — 173

- 10.1 Overview — 173
- 10.2 Referral notice — 174
  - 10.2.1 In a nutshell — 174
  - 10.2.2 Timing (Act s. 108(2)(b)) — 174
  - 10.2.3 Scheme (Scheme p. 7) — 175
  - 10.2.4 Practical considerations and strategy — 177
  - 10.2.5 Actions for the adjudicator once the dispute is referred — 180
- 10.3 Response — 181
  - 10.3.1 In a nutshell — 181
  - 10.3.2 Timing — 182
  - 10.3.3 Practical considerations and strategy — 182
- 10.4 Reply, rejoinder and sur-rejoinder — 184
  - 10.4.1 In a nutshell — 184
  - 10.4.2 Practical considerations and strategy — 184
  - 10.4.3 Parallel correspondence — 186
- 10.5 Meetings — 186
- 10.6 Other matters — 188
  - 10.6.1 In a nutshell — 188
  - 10.6.2 Communicating with the other party and with the adjudicator during the adjudication — 189
  - 10.6.3 Pressure from the parties or the adjudicator — 190
  - 10.6.4 Set-off and abatement — 191
  - 10.6.5 Dropping a head of claim during the adjudication — 194
  - 10.6.6 Withdrawing from the adjudication entirely — 195
  - 10.6.7 Privilege — 195
  - 10.6.8 Disclosure of documents — 198
  - 10.6.9 Settlement offers — 199
  - 10.6.10 Staying adjudication proceedings — 199
  - 10.6.11 Confidential nature of adjudication (Scheme p. 18) — 200
  - 10.6.12 Service of documents and notices (Act s. 115) — 200
  - 10.6.13 Reckoning of time (Act s. 116) — 201
- 10.7 Adjudicator's powers and duties — 201
  - 10.7.1 In a nutshell — 201
  - 10.7.2 Duty to act impartially (Act s. 108(2)(e) and Scheme p. 12(a)) — 201
  - 10.7.3 Power to take the initiative (Act s. 108(2)(f) and Scheme p. 13) — 202
  - 10.7.4 Power to make requests or directions (Scheme p. 14 and 15) — 204
  - 10.7.5 Power to seek assistance (Act s. 108(2)(f) and Scheme p. 13(f)) — 205
  - 10.7.6 Duty to consider relevant information and provide it to the parties (Scheme p. 17) — 206
  - 10.7.7 Scope of what the adjudicator can decide (Scheme p. 20(a) and (b)) — 207
  - 10.7.8 Power to award interest (Scheme p. 20(c)) — 208
  - 10.7.9 Power to award damages — 209
  - 10.7.10 Adjudicator's immunity (Act s. 108(4), Scheme p. 26) — 209
  - 10.7.11 Adjudicator resignation (Scheme p. 9) — 210
- 10.8 Checklist: Managing the adjudication – the adjudicator — 212

11 The decision — 214

- 11.1 Overview — 214
- 11.2 What is the adjudicator required to do? — 214
  - *11.2.1 In a nutshell* — 214
  - *11.2.2 Purpose and nature of the decision* — 215
  - *11.2.3 Structure, format and content of the decision* — 216
  - *11.2.4 Reasons* — 217
- 11.3 On receiving the decision — 218
- 11.4 Timing — 219
  - *11.4.1 In a nutshell* — 219
  - *11.4.2 Act and Scheme (Act s. 108(2)(c) and (d) and Scheme p.19)* — 219
  - *11.4.3 Rigidity of the time limit* — 222
  - *11.4.4 Decision made and decision communicated* — 222
  - *11.4.5 Responding to the adjudicator's request for an extension* — 223
- 11.5 Effect and compliance — 223
  - *11.5.1 In a nutshell* — 223
  - *11.5.2 Temporary finality (Act s. 108(3), Scheme p. 23)* — 224
  - *11.5.3 Compliance with the decision (Scheme p. 21)* — 225
  - *11.5.4 Delaying compliance by contract* — 225
  - *11.5.5 Insurance claims* — 226

12 Post decision — 227

- 12.1 Overview — 227
- 12.2 Adjudicator's costs — 228
  - *12.2.1 In a nutshell* — 228
  - *12.2.2 2009 Act and 2011 Scheme (2009 Act s. 108A; 2011 Scheme p. 25)* — 228
  - *12.2.3 1996 Act and 1998 Scheme (1998 Scheme p. 25)* — 228
  - *12.2.4 Liability for fees* — 229
  - *12.2.5 Reasonableness of fees and expenses* — 231
  - *12.2.6 Lien on the decision* — 232
  - *12.2.7 Payment of fees when the decision is in breach of natural justice* — 232
  - *12.2.8 Award of adjudicator's costs* — 232
  - *12.2.9 Payment of fees on paying party's insolvency* — 233
- 12.3 Parties' costs — 233
  - *12.3.1 In a nutshell* — 233
  - *12.3.2 2009 Act (s. 108A)* — 233
  - *12.3.3 1996 Act* — 234
  - *12.3.4 The Late Payment of Commercial Debt (Interest) Act 1998* — 235
- 12.4 Apportioning costs — 237
  - *12.4.1 In a nutshell* — 237
  - *12.4.2 Timing* — 237
  - *12.4.3 Assessment* — 238
- 12.5 Correcting errors in the decision — 239
  - *12.5.1 In a nutshell* — 239
  - *12.5.2 The 2009 Act and 2011 Scheme (2009 Act s. 108(3)(A); 2011 Scheme p. 22A)* — 239
  - *12.5.3 The 1996 Act and 1998 Scheme* — 240

12.6	Setting off against the decision		241
	12.6.1	In a nutshell	241
	12.6.2	General rule and exceptions	241
	12.6.3	Contractual right to set off	243
	12.6.4	Later interim or final certificate	244
	12.6.5	Issuing a withholding or pay less notice	244
	12.6.6	Setting off liquidated damages	245
	12.6.7	Set off permitted but not quantified in the decision	246
	12.6.8	Set-off not formulated before the adjudication	247
	12.6.9	Adjudication rules prevent set-off in enforcement proceedings	247
	12.6.10	Multiple adjudications	247
	12.6.11	Litigation on foot	248
	12.6.12	Arbitration award	248
	12.6.13	Other arguments for set-off	248

13 Enforcement: options and procedure — 249

13.1	Overview		249
13.2	Key statements of principle and the court's policy		249
	13.2.1	Principles of enforcement	249
	13.2.2	Enforcement for contractual adjudications	252
13.3	TCC summary enforcement procedure		252
	13.3.1	In a nutshell	252
	13.3.2	Nature of summary judgment applications in adjudication	253
	13.3.3	Options for commencing the claim	256
	13.3.4	Commencing the claim	256
	13.3.5	Directions	260
	13.3.6	Responding to the claim	260
	13.3.7	Submission of cost budgets	261
	13.3.8	Hearing bundle and skeletons	261
	13.3.9	Extent of the evidence to be submitted	262
	13.3.10	Judgment in default and setting aside	262
	13.3.11	Representation	263
	13.3.12	Timetable to a decision	264
	13.3.13	The decision	264
	13.3.14	The effect of the court's decision	265
	13.3.15	Setting aside a summary judgment	266
	13.3.16	Costs: basis of assessment	266
	13.3.17	Costs: assessment of the bill of costs	269
	13.3.18	Costs: ATE insurance and conditional fee arrangements	272
	13.3.19	Costs: interest	272
	13.3.20	Costs: settlement reached before summary judgment	273
	13.3.21	Appealing a judgment of the court	273
	13.3.22	Staying enforcement proceedings where there is an arbitration agreement (s. 9 Arbitration Act 1996)	274
13.4	Other procedures for enforcement		276
	13.4.1	In a nutshell	276
	13.4.2	Pre-emptory order (Scheme p. 23(1) and 24)	276
	13.4.3	Mandatory injunction	277

	13.4.4	Statutory demand	278
	13.4.5	Scotland	280
13.5	Complying with an order of the court		280
	13.5.1	In a nutshell	280
	13.5.2	Time for payment	280
	13.5.3	Extending the time for payment	281
	13.5.4	Failing to comply	281
13.6	Checklist: Avoiding the consequences of an adjudicator's decision		284

14 Enforcement: insolvency, stay and severability — 285

14.1	Overview		285
14.2	Insolvency avoids summary judgment		286
	14.2.1	In a nutshell	286
	14.2.2	Liquidation	287
	14.2.3	Administration	287
	14.2.4	Administrative receivership	289
	14.2.5	CVA	289
	14.2.6	Individual insolvency or bankruptcy	290
14.3	Stay of execution		290
	14.3.1	In a nutshell	290
	14.3.2	Court's discretion to order a stay of execution	291
	14.3.3	Insolvency proceedings pending or not concluded	293
	14.3.4	Financial difficulty	296
	14.3.5	Imminent resolution of other proceedings	298
	14.3.6	Manifest injustice	299
	14.3.7	Other circumstances in which an application for a stay has failed	299
	14.3.8	Partial stay	300
	14.3.9	Conditions imposed on granting the stay	301
	14.3.10	Severability	301

15 Final determination — 304

15.1	Overview		304
15.2	Finalising the adjudicator's decision		305
	15.2.1	In a nutshell	305
	15.2.2	Adjudicator's decision made final by contract	305
	15.2.3	Adjudicator's decision made final by agreement	306
	15.2.4	Adjudicator's decision made final by the passing of time	306
15.3	Adjudication and other proceedings		307
	15.3.1	In a nutshell	307
	15.3.2	Final determination at the same time as enforcement proceedings	307
	15.3.3	Final determination at the same time as adjudication	308
	15.3.4	Final determination without complying with the adjudicator's decision	309
	15.3.5	Final determination in breach of the contractual dispute resolution procedure (including an agreement to adjudicate)	309

15.4	Commencement, onus of proof and costs		312
	15.4.1	In a nutshell	312
	15.4.2	Cause of action and limitation period for commencing final proceedings	312
	15.4.3	Delaying the final determination	314
	15.4.4	Onus of proof in subsequent proceedings	315
	15.4.5	Final decision different to adjudicator's decision	315
	15.4.6	Recovery of adjudication costs as part of the costs of a final determination	315

16 The adjudicator's jurisdiction 319

16.1	Overview		319
16.2	When to think about jurisdiction		319
16.3	Options when a jurisdictional issue arises		320
	16.3.1	In a nutshell	320
	16.3.2	Option 1: Determination from the court	321
	16.3.3	Option 2: Determination by the adjudicator	324
	16.3.4	Option 3: Determination from another adjudicator	326
	16.3.5	Option 4: Reserve the position and proceed with the adjudication	327
	16.3.6	Option 5: Withdraw	328
	16.3.7	Option 6: Injunction	329
16.4	Losing the right to challenge the adjudicator's jurisdiction		331
	16.4.1	In a nutshell	331
	16.4.2	Waiver	332
	16.4.3	No reservation or late reservation	333
	16.4.4	Abandoning the reservation	334
	16.4.5	Initial consent before objection	335
	16.4.6	Approbation and reprobation	335
	16.4.7	Consequence of losing the right: ad hoc jurisdiction	338
16.5	Threshold jurisdiction challenges		338
	16.5.1	In a nutshell	338
	16.5.2	No contract	339
	16.5.3	Contract is not a construction contract	339
	16.5.4	Construction contract is not in writing	340
	16.5.5	No dispute	340
	16.5.6	More than one dispute	341
	16.5.7	Substantially the same dispute	341
	16.5.8	Dispute not under the contract	342
16.6	Process jurisdiction challenges		342
	16.6.1	In a nutshell	342
	16.6.2	Incorrect parties named	343
	16.6.3	Adjudicator not correctly appointed	344
	16.6.4	Referral notice served out of time	347
	16.6.5	Arguments outside the scope of the dispute	347
	16.6.6	Defective service	348
	16.6.7	New material during the adjudication	348
	16.6.8	Other procedural improprieties	349

16.7	Decision based jurisdiction challenges		349
	16.7.1	In a nutshell	349
	16.7.2	Lien over the decision	350
	16.7.3	Failure to reach the decision within the required timescale	350
	16.7.4	Signing the decision	351
	16.7.5	Sufficiency of written reasons	351
	16.7.6	Scope of the decision	353
	16.7.7	Errors	357
	16.7.8	Correcting minor errors in the decision	360
16.8	Checklist: Jurisdiction – the parties		360
16.9	Checklist: Jurisdiction – the adjudicator		361

17 Natural justice   362

17.1	Overview		362
	17.1.1	What is it?	362
	17.1.2	Materiality	363
17.2	When to think about natural justice		364
17.3	Options when a natural justice point arises		364
17.4	Bias and apparent bias		366
	17.4.1	In a nutshell	366
	17.4.2	Actual bias	367
	17.4.3	Apparent bias	368
	17.4.4	Prior involvement in the project or in a separate dispute	369
	17.4.5	Appointment of the same adjudicator	370
	17.4.6	Communication between the adjudicator and one party: pre-appointment	371
	17.4.7	Communication between the adjudicator and one party: post-appointment	373
	17.4.8	Evidence	373
	17.4.9	Failure to make information available to the parties	375
	17.4.10	Failure to carry out a site visit	375
	17.4.11	Organisation of meetings and hearings	376
	17.4.12	Quasi-mediator	376
	17.4.13	Without prejudice communications	377
	17.4.14	Preliminary view	377
17.5	Procedural fairness		378
	17.5.1	In a nutshell	378
	17.5.2	Referring party's conduct pre-adjudication	379
	17.5.3	Abuse of process	380
	17.5.4	Ambush/no opportunity or insufficient opportunity to respond	380
	17.5.5	Christmas claims	382
	17.5.6	Dispute is too large or complex	382
	17.5.7	Failing to address an issue, part of a submission or evidence	384
	17.5.8	Failure to permit a further submission or information	389
	17.5.9	Failure to follow the agreed procedure	390
	17.5.10	Adjudicator's timetable unfair	391
	17.5.11	Documents received late or not at all	391

	17.5.12	Failure to inform the parties about an approach taken or methodology used	392
	17.5.13	Failure to inform the parties about advice from a third party	395
	17.5.14	Failure to inform the parties about use of own knowledge and expertise	395
	17.5.15	Failure to inform the parties about preliminary view	397
	17.5.16	Sufficiency of reasons	398
17.6	Checklist: Natural justice – the parties and the adjudicator	399

18 Further grounds for resisting enforcement — 400
18.1 Overview — 400
18.2 Fraud or deceit — 401
18.3 Duress — 402
18.4 UTCCR — 403
18.5 Human Rights Act — 404

19 Scotland: Tony Jones — 406
19.1 Overview — 406
19.2 Differences between the Scheme and the Scottish Scheme — 408
    19.2.1 1998 Scheme and 1998 Scottish Scheme — 408
    19.2.2 2011 Scheme and 2011 Scottish Scheme — 410
19.3 Enforcement of an adjudicator's award — 411
    19.3.1 In a nutshell — 411
    19.3.2 Enforcement procedure — 412
    19.3.3 Counterclaims — 414
    19.3.4 The Scottish courts' approach to jurisdictional challenges — 415
    19.3.5 The Scottish courts' approach to natural justice challenges — 416
    19.3.6 Miscellaneous points — 417
19.4 Issues of divergence between England and Wales and Scotland — 418
    19.4.1 In a nutshell — 418
    19.4.2 Failure to comply with subsections 108(1)–(4) of the Act — 418
    19.4.3 Adjudicator's decision out of time — 419
    19.4.4 Parties' costs under the 1996 Act — 419
    19.4.5 Insolvency — 420
    19.4.6 Approbation and reprobation — 422
    19.4.7 The size and nature of the claim — 422
    19.4.8 Abuse of process — 423
    19.4.9 The adjudicator taking advice from a third party or using his own knowledge — 424
    19.4.10 Human Rights Act — 425

20 Northern Ireland: Michael Humphreys QC — 427
20.1 Overview — 427
20.2 Enforcement of adjudicators' awards — 429
    20.2.1 The writ of summons — 430
    20.2.2 The application for summary judgment — 431
    20.2.3 The hearing of the application — 432

	20.2.4	Incidence of costs	433
	20.2.5	Taxation of costs	433
	20.2.6	Enforcement of judgments	434
20.3	An alternative remedy – declaratory relief		434
20.4	Judicial consideration		435
	20.4.1	In a nutshell	435
	20.4.2	No construction contract	435
	20.4.3	No dispute	436
	20.4.4	Setting off against an adjudicator's decision	437
	20.4.5	Financial difficulty of the paying party	437
	20.4.6	Insufficient time to respond	439
	20.4.7	Abuse of process	439

Part II   International

21   Introduction   443

22   Australia: Peter Wood and Phillip Greenham   446

22.1	Overview		446
	22.1.1	Initial introduction in NSW	446
	22.1.2	Rollout across the remaining states	447
	22.1.3	East-west coast divide	448
	22.1.4	Consequences of the divide	448
22.2	Requirements for commencing an adjudication		449
	22.2.1	Construction contract	449
	22.2.2	Construction work	450
	22.2.3	Claimable variations and excluded amounts in Victoria	451
	22.2.4	Reference date	451
	22.2.5	Time limits	452
	22.2.6	Who may refer a dispute under a construction contract to adjudication?	453
22.3	Adjudication process		453
	22.3.1	Appointment of the adjudicator	453
	22.3.2	Conduct of the adjudication	455
22.4	Determination, effect and costs		456
	22.4.1	Form of the decision	456
	22.4.2	Effect of the decision	456
	22.4.3	Costs	457
22.5	Enforcement		458
	22.5.1	Process for enforcement	458
	22.5.2	Express rights of appeal	458
	22.5.3	Judicial review of adjudication determinations	459

23   Ireland: Dermot McEvoy   461

23.1	Overview	461
23.2	Requirements for commencing an adjudication	462

23.3 Adjudication process	464
23.3.1 Notice of adjudication	*464*
23.3.2 Appointment of an adjudicator	*465*
23.3.3 Powers and duties of an adjudicator	*467*
23.4 Determination, effect and costs	469
23.5 Enforcement	470
23.6 Conclusion	471

24 Malaysia: Philip Koh — 473

24.1 Overview	473
24.2 Requirements for commencing the adjudication process	474
24.2.1 What contracts are caught by the 2012 Act?	*474*
24.2.2 Retrospective effect of the 2012 Act	*478*
24.3 Adjudication process	478
24.3.1 Step 1: Payment claim	*479*
24.3.2 Step 2: Initiation of adjudication	*479*
24.3.3 Step 3: Appointment	*479*
24.3.4 Step 4: Submissions	*480*
24.3.5 Step 5: The adjudicator	*480*
24.4 Administration of the adjudication	481
24.5 Determination, effect and costs	482
24.5.1 Form and timing of the decision	*482*
24.5.2 Effect of the decision	*482*
24.5.3 Costs	*483*
24.6 Enforcement	484
24.6.1 Suspension or a reduction in the pace of work	*484*
24.6.2 Secure direct payment from principal	*485*
24.7 Conclusion	485

25 New Zealand: Tómas Kennedy-Grant QC — 487

25.1 Overview	487
25.2 Requirements for commencing an adjudication	488
25.3 Adjudication process	490
25.4 Determination, effect and costs	493
25.4.1 Rights of a non-respondent owner	*496*
25.5 Enforcement	496
25.5.1 Judicial review	*499*
25.6 Proposed amendments	500

26 Singapore: Steven Cannon — 501

26.1 Overview	501
26.2 Requirements for commencing an adjudication	502
26.2.1 What contracts are caught by the 2004 Act?	*502*
26.2.2 Contracting out, the date of execution of the contract and contracts made in writing	*503*
26.3 Payment regime	504

	26.3.1	The right to progress payments	504
	26.3.2	The payment regime	504
	26.3.3	The crystallisation of a dispute and the dispute settlement period	507
26.4	Adjudication process		508
	26.4.1	The role of the Singapore Mediation Centre	508
	26.4.2	Notice of an intention to adjudicate	508
	26.4.3	The adjudication application	509
	26.4.4	The role of the adjudicator	512
26.5	Determination, effect and costs		515
	26.5.1	The adjudicator's determination	515
	26.5.2	The costs of the adjudication	516
	26.5.3	Adjudication review applications	517
	26.5.4	The effect of an adjudicator's determination	517
26.6	Enforcement		518
	26.6.1	Enforcement of the adjudicator's determination	518
	26.6.2	Setting aside the adjudicator's determination	518
26.7	Conclusion		520

Appendices

Appendix 1 – The 1996 Act as amended   523

Appendix 2 – The 1998 Scheme as amended   530

Appendix 3 – Glossary (UK only)   538

Appendix 4 – Model forms   542

Appendix 5 – Summary comparison of UK adjudication rules   561

Appendix 6 – Details of UK adjudicator nominating bodies   570

Appendix 7 – Comparison of UK and international statutory regimes   578

Appendix 8 – Case index: by subject matter   584

Appendix 9 – Alphabetical case index   678

Index   709

Part I
The United Kingdom

Chapter 1
Introduction

1.1 Overview

[1.01]　Construction adjudication can be defined as an interim dispute resolution procedure by which the parties submit their dispute to an independent third party for a decision.

[1.02]　In the UK, adjudication is available as a right for parties to a construction contract, following the enactment of the Housing Grants Construction and Regeneration Act 1996 (the **1996 Act**).[1] Unless the timetable has been extended, within a comparatively short period of time, parties will have a decision from an adjudicator, which save for in limited circumstances the courts will enforce. The mandatory and expedited nature of the process were the principal reasons why it was catapulted to the number-one method of dispute resolution in the construction industry no more than a year after the 1996 Act was passed and it is likely to retain its dominance for the foreseeable future, particularly as amendments made to the 1996 Act in 2011 widen the scope of its application.

[1.03]　The short timescale means that once an adjudication has commenced, there is very little time in which to learn or remind oneself about process and procedure. One needs to know quickly what to do, when to do it and, just as importantly, check that the other party and the adjudicator are following the right steps and, if not, what to do about it.

[1.04]　This part of the book aims to facilitate this, by providing a straightforward narrative of the process and procedure of adjudication. So far as it is possible to do, topics are presented in the order one would expect to encounter them. The procedure is interpreted and explained by reference to case law and enveloped with guidance on how to approach an issue, suggestions on what to do or not to do in certain situations, drafting tips and checklists at key points. In essence, this part of the book is a practical guide on construction adjudication in the United Kingdom.

[1.05]　There are three legal jurisdictions in the United Kingdom: England and Wales, Scotland and Northern Ireland. England and Wales is by far the largest economy of those jurisdictions and, no doubt at least partly for this reason, adjudication is more

---

[1] *http://www.legislation.gov.uk/ukpga/1996/53/part/II.* Accessed 1 September 2015.

A Practical Guide to Construction Adjudication, First Edition. James Pickavance.
© 2016 James Pickavance. Published 2016 by John Wiley & Sons, Inc.

prevalent. Therefore, the majority of this part will explain the adjudication process by reference to the rules that apply in England and Wales. Although the primary legislation applies equally in each jurisdiction, secondary legislation does not enjoy the same uniformity. Furthermore, judicial precedent set in England and Wales, Northern Ireland and Scotland does not bind the courts in the other countries (although it is of persuasive influence). The result is a divergence of opinion on certain matters relating to adjudication. Accordingly, the key differences in legislation, procedure and judicial interpretation in Scotland and Northern Ireland are addressed separately in Chapters 19 and 20 respectively.

1.2 Background to statutory adjudication in the UK

[1.06] In the 1970s and 1980s, payees[2] in the construction industry often struggled to ensure that they were remunerated in a timely fashion for the work they had done. The House of Lords decision of *Gilbert-Ash (Northern) Ltd v Modern Engineering (Bristol) Ltd*[3] in the early 1970s did not help. The decision effectively enabled payers to avoid paying payees merely by advancing a cross-claim. If the payee wished to contest the payer's position, the only way it could compel the payer to pay was either by a decision of the court or by an arbitral tribunal. Both litigation and arbitration would (and still do) take months at best, more likely years to reach a conclusion. Commercial intimidation was rife, with the result that thousands of firms were forced out of business. What the industry needed was a dedicated enforceable fast-track dispute process.[4]

[1.07] Soon after the recession of the early 1990s, Sir Michael Latham was commissioned by the government and industry organisations to review procurement and contractual arrangements in the UK construction industry, with the aim of tackling payment and other issues. In 1994, he published a paper called *Constructing the Team*, which set out 30 recommendations for how to tackle the problems faced. Recommendation 25 was that Parliament should enact legislation to ensure that the payer paid the whole sum applied for unless it notified the payee of its contrary intention within a fixed period of time, specifying the reasons why. If there was no notification, the payee would be entitled to the amount applied for, regardless of any reason the payer had for not paying. The aim was to ensure that a payee received money to which it was entitled expeditiously without having to embark on lengthy and expensive litigation. Recommendation 26 was that where parties do fall into dispute, they have available to them a dispute resolution process that facilitates a quick and inexpensive platform for hearing the dispute, and that results in an impartial decision to which the parties must comply forthwith. To that end, adjudication should be the 'normal process of dispute resolution'.

---

[2] The payee is the party receiving money (typically the contractor or subcontractor). The payer is the party paying (typically the employer or contractor).
[3] [1974] A.C. 689.
[4] JCT DOM 1 had an adjudication procedure in it, but any decision of the adjudicator was capable of being stayed, pending arbitration proceedings.

Those recommendations were, more or less, taken up by Parliament and drafted into the 1996 Act.

[1.08] The 1996 Act is one of the most important pieces of legislation for the building and civil engineering industry in recent times. It has now served the construction industry for over 17 years. The huge reliance that is placed on adjudication, together with the court's robust attitude to the enforcement of adjudicators' decisions are evidence that many of Sir Michael Latham's recommendations have been implemented successfully (although critics will say that the tens of thousands of adjudications and the 600+ reported court decisions evidence the fact that the legislation has failed in one of its goals, which was to reduce conflict in the industry).

[1.09] Perhaps the best statement which summarises the intent behind statutory adjudication can be found in a frequently cited extract of the decision of Mr Justice Dyson in *Macob Civil Engineering Ltd v Morrison Construction Ltd*.[5]

> The intention of Parliament in enacting the Act was plain. It was to introduce a speedy mechanism for settling disputes in construction contracts on a provisional interim basis, and requiring the decisions of adjudicators to be enforced pending the final determination of disputes by arbitration, litigation or agreement ... It is clear that Parliament intended that the adjudication should be conducted in a manner which those familiar with the grinding detail of the traditional approach to the resolution of construction disputes apparently find difficult to accept. But Parliament has not abolished arbitration and litigation of construction disputes. It has merely introduced an intervening provisional stage in the dispute resolution process. Crucially, it has made it clear that decisions of adjudicators are binding and are to be complied with until the dispute is finally resolved.

[1.10] The implementation of a regime whereby disputing parties could have an interim binding decision on a disputed issue within a few weeks was, and still is, a revolution that has transformed the landscape of construction disputes.

1.3 Statutory adjudication regimes

[1.11] In England and Wales, the 1996 Act came into operation on 1 May 1998.[6] It applies automatically to all contracts within its scope on or after that date and cannot be contracted out of.

[1.12] For a number of reasons, Parliament decided that certain changes should be made to the adjudication and payment provisions of the 1996 Act. After seven years and three public consultations, the 1996 Act was amended by Part 8 of the Local Democracy, Economic

---

[5][1999] BLR 93, per Dyson J at [14].
[6]SI 1998 No. 650 (C.13). Housing Grants Construction and Regeneration Act 1996 (England and Wales) Commencement No. 4) Order 1998. *http://www.legislation.gov.uk/uksi/1998/650/contents/made*. Accessed 1 September 2015.

Development and Construction Act 2009.[7] This book refers to the amended 1996 Act as the **2009 Act**. In England and Wales, the 2009 Act came into force on 1 October 2011.[8]

[1.13] Where there is a difference between a section in the 1996 Act and a section in the 2009 Act, they shall be distinguished and referred to accordingly. Where there is no difference, the reference shall be to the "**Act**". At the time of writing, it is estimated that around 80% of all adjudications arise out of contracts to which the 2009 Act applies. This percentage will continue to increase, making the provisions of the 1996 Act less and less relevant.

[1.14] In addition to primary legislation, each UK jurisdiction has enacted secondary legislation. Part 1 of this legislation is in essence a set of rules, which will either be chosen or imposed on the parties, by which parties and the adjudicator conduct the adjudication. In England and Wales, the legislation is called the Scheme for Construction Contracts (England and Wales) Regulations 1998[9] (the **1998 Scheme**) and was brought into force on 1 May 1998, on the same day as the 1996 Act. In order to align this instrument with changes brought in by the 2009 Act, in England, the 1998 Scheme was amended by the Scheme for Construction Contracts (England and Wales) Regulations 1998 (Amendment) (England) Regulations 2011, which also came into operation on 1 October 2011.[10] This book refers to the amended Scheme as the **2011 Scheme**. Where there is a difference between the paragraphs in the 1998 Scheme and the 2011 Scheme, they shall be distinguished and referred to accordingly. Where the paragraph is the same, the reference shall be to the **Scheme**.

[1.15] Thus, there are in effect two regimes: the 'old' regime which was brought into force in May 1998 and the 'new' regime which was brought into force in October 2011. In the main, the differences between the old and new regimes, at least in relation to the scope of the Act and the adjudication provisions, are not particularly extensive. Where there are differences between the two regimes, they will be highlighted in the relevant sections of this book.

1.4 Use of case law in this part

[1.16] The courts of England and Wales, Scotland and Northern Ireland have generated a significant body of case law arising out of the construction adjudication, in particular the interpretation of the statutory adjudication frameworks in those jurisdictions. England has generated by far the largest amount (around 85%), followed by Scotland, then

---

[7] http://www.legislation.gov.uk/ukpga/2009/20/part/8. Accessed 1 September 2015.
[8] SI 2011 No. 1597 (W. 185) (C.61). The Local Democracy, Economic Development and Construction Act 2009 (Commencement No. 2) (Wales) Order 2011. http://www.legislation.gov.uk/wsi/2011/1597/contents/made. Accessed 1 September 2015.
[9] SI 1998 No. 649. http://www.legislation.gov.uk/uksi/1998/649/made. Accessed 1 September 2015.
[10] SI 2011 No. 2333. http://www.legislation.gov.uk/uksi/2011/2333/contents/made. Accessed 1 September 2015. The amendments to the Scheme were enacted in Wales by the Scheme for Construction Contracts (England and Wales) Regulations 1998 (Amendment) (Wales) Regulations 2011 SI 2011 No. 1715 (W.194). http://www.legislation.gov.uk/wsi/2011/1715/contents/made. Accessed 1 September 2015.

Introduction 7

Northern Ireland. Although judicial precedent in each of these three jurisdictions does not bind the others, it is persuasive and is routinely referred to by counsel and judges.

[1.17] Court judgments are a vital component of understanding the rules and procedures of adjudication. In addition to providing the parties to a particular dispute with a determination of their issues, judgments provide the public with a body of opinion on how the law is to be interpreted, given a particular set of facts. Unless overturned, the views expressed by the judges are binding both on the parties to the dispute and anyone thereafter. These binding opinions, layered on top of one another over time, have gradually closed down areas of ambiguity in the process and procedure or have defined issues that are not expressly dealt with by legislation.

[1.18] In the usual way, this part of the book cites cases and extracts from court judgments in support of statements made. However, the presentation of those cases is perhaps different from many other books in three respects.

[1.19] Invariably there are several cases, sometimes as many as 50, addressing the same topic. While some of those cases will espouse new points of principle, most will apply existing principles to the particular facts of the case. Rather than cite and summarise every single case or a topic in the body of this book, the number of cases cited is limited to a small selection that evidence a point of principle or exemplify a common factual scenario. However, there will be times when the reader needs to analyse every single decision on a topic. For that situation, Appendix 8 provides a case list of all reported court decisions that could be found since the 1996 Act was brought into force that address the subject of adjudication. The cases have been categorised into the topics they address. For ease of reference, those topics mirror exactly those addressed under each of the headings in Chapters 1–18 and appear in the same order. In theory at least, most if not all of the reported cases on any topic addressed in this book should be contained in the list.[11] Appendix 8 therefore represents the most comprehensive published list of cases available from one source, numbering around 560.[12] This number of cases, by comparison with other areas of law, is a phenomenal volume of case law, particularly given the comparatively short space of time in which it has been produced.[13]

---

[11] In its 2013/2014 annual report, the TCC reported that there were 60 adjudication enforcement cases commenced in the TCC between October 2013 and 30 September 2014. See https://www.judiciary.gov.uk/wp-content/uploads/2015/05/technology-construction-court-ar-2013-14.pdf. Accessed 1 May 2015. Over the same period, the author was able to identify 31 reported cases. Whilst much of the difference is likely to be accounted for by discontinued cases or ex tempore judgments for example, there will be some instances where a written judgment has been handed down but not published.
[12] This excludes those cases relating to the payment provisions of Part II of the Act and Part 2 of the Scheme. Taking those into account, the total number of published cases rises to around 650.
[13] Coulson J, speaking extra-judicially, has commented that the popularity of adjudication was such that, in its first 10 years, it generated the equivalent of roughly 100 years of case law. It is notable, for example, that the arguments advanced to support or resist enforcement are very significantly more sophisticated now than they were in the early authorities.

[1.20] All decisions arise out of a series of facts and circumstances, unique to that case. Where a party seeks to rely on the court's decision as support for the submissions in its case, it is important to ensure that the facts of the dispute in hand marry up sufficiently with the facts of the dispute in the court judgment. If they do not, a party may argue that the circumstances of a decided case are distinguishable from the present facts, such that the conclusions reached in the decided case do not apply. However, consistent with the purpose of this book, which is to act as a practical guide to adjudication and not as a case book, the facts and circumstances of cases cited in this part are invariably not set out, or if they are, they are set out succinctly. This has the happy benefit of allowing each topic to be dealt with in fewer words.

[1.21] All the citations in the main body of the book, and in Appendix 8, refer not only to the name of the case and the neutral citation[14] but also the paragraph number or numbers of the judgment relevant to the issue in hand. This should allow the reader to expedite the identification of the relevant part of the decision. This may only save a minute or two, but in the context of the compressed adjudication timetable, every minute counts. For reasons explained below, the paragraph numbering is taken from the judgments published by the British and Irish Legal Information Institute (**Bailii**)[15] or where the case is not available on Bailii, at adjudication.co.uk.

[1.22] What are the different ways one can access court judgments? The 'traditional' route is via one of a number of law reports. Judgments relating to construction adjudication are, for the most part, reported in at least one of the following: Adjudication Law Reports, the All England Law Reports, the Building Law Reports, the Construction Industry Law Letter, the Construction Law Journal or the Construction Law Reports. Many of these reports not only provide the text of the judgments, but also offer thoughtful and interesting commentary on the issues raised, written by highly regarded construction law practitioners. All of these reports are available in hard copy and online, but none of them are freely available. Furthermore each report is selective as to which judgments it chooses to report (generally those it considers are important or offer something 'new') and so one will not find a complete record of all adjudication cases from any of those sources.

[1.23] Two of the most easily accessible, definitive, online and free sources of court judgments relating to adjudication are the websites Bailii.org and the adjudicator nominating body, adjudication.co.uk. Both websites are refreshingly free of bells and whistles. At the time of writing, all but a few of the judgments referred to in this book are contained on one of these two websites. Bailii is the more well-known and 'official' of the two sites, and judgments are typically posted on the site within a few days of being issued. However, it is generally easier to search for cases on adjudication.co.uk because it contains only cases that relate to the Act (whereas Bailii has a much wider remit) and it also contains the judgments of a number of unreported decisions not available on Bailii. Furthermore, although it already contained head notes for some judgments, in late 2014, head notes were added for many more judgments, courtesy of the law firm CMS Cameron McKenna LLP.

---

[14] Neutral citations were adopted as standard form in the High Court from early 2002. Before then, cases were cited by reference to one or more Law Reports. Citations in this book are made accordingly.
[15] www.bailii.org. Accessed on 1 September 2015.

Chapter 2
Adjudication in a nutshell

[2.01] The idiom 'I can't see the wood for the trees' is one that will be familiar to most. Particularly in adjudication, where timescales are short and decisions often need to be made quickly, it is all the more important that concepts and procedural matters are understood as easily as possible. This book aims to achieve this by providing straightforward explanations on each topic succinctly, but without losing key points of detail. In addition, every chapter has an overview, and most second-level sections within each chapter commence with an 'in a nutshell' sub-section to offer the reader a quick summary of what follows. However, for those new to construction adjudication, it may assist, as a starting point, to read the following short chapter, which provides a high-level overview of the process with cross references to the relevant chapters.

[2.02] Adjudication is a procedure that takes place over a relatively short period of time pursuant to which a dispute between parties is submitted to an independent determiner who, having received submissions from each party, makes a decision.

[2.03] There are three forms of adjudication: statutory, contractual and ad hoc. In this book, statutory adjudication means the form of adjudication that must be adhered to where the Act applies to the contract between the parties. The Act will apply where certain conditions of the Act are met, such as whether the contract between the parties in dispute is a 'construction contract' as defined by the Act. Where the Act applies, the right to adjudicate is mandatory and cannot be contracted out of (Chapter 4). Contractual adjudication refers to the form of adjudication where the Act does not apply, but nevertheless the parties have agreed a mechanism in their contract by which they can adjudicate disputes. An ad hoc adjudication refers to a form of adjudication where the parties have agreed, or are deemed to have agreed to submit their dispute, without reservation, to adjudication, thereby giving an adjudicator ad hoc jurisdiction to decide the dispute in circumstances where the statutory adjudication regime does not apply and where there is no pre-existing contractual agreement to adjudicate (Chapter 5). Part 1 of this book addresses all three forms of adjudication, albeit that the main focus of attention lies with statutory adjudication.

[2.04] The form of the adjudication is a separate matter to the procedure, or rules, by which the adjudication is to be conducted. This book describes two types of adjudication procedure in the UK: Scheme adjudications and contractual adjudications. In both cases,

---

A Practical Guide to Construction Adjudication, First Edition. James Pickavance.
© 2016 James Pickavance. Published 2016 by John Wiley & Sons, Inc.

the procedures are nothing more than a set of rules that both parties and the adjudicator are required to follow. A Scheme adjudication is one governed by the rules set out in the Scheme for Construction Contracts which is a statutory instrument. A contractual adjudication procedure refers to any other adjudication procedure, whether it is contained within a standard form of contract or an industry body publication, or is drafted by the parties. Part 1 of this book explains both forms of adjudication procedure, but attention is mainly directed to Scheme adjudications, because that is by far the most common type of adjudication procedure adopted (Chapter 6).

[2.05] Where the contract between the parties is caught by the Act and therefore the form of adjudication is statutory, before a referring party (the claiming party) is entitled to commence the adjudication, it must have satisfied a number of preconditions. For example, there must be an extant dispute between the parties. The referring party may only refer a single dispute. The dispute must not be the same or substantially the same as one already decided. The dispute must be contractual, in other words it must arise under the contract. The dispute must arise under one contract, not more than one contract, unless the parties agree. Where these preconditions are met, the referring party has an unfettered right to refer a dispute to adjudication at any time (Chapter 7).

[2.06] The adjudication process is commenced by serving a notification of the intention to refer the dispute to adjudication on the other party (the 'notice of adjudication'). The other purpose of the notice of adjudication is to outline who the parties are, what the dispute is about and what the referring party wants. Usually at the same time that the notice of adjudication is served, the referring party will request the appointment of an adjudicator. Where the form of adjudication is statutory, the adjudicator must be appointed within seven days of the notice of adjudication being served, otherwise the adjudication process will be invalidated. Depending on the terms of the contract and the applicable adjudication rules, the request will be made of an individual named in the contract, or a third-party organisation, commonly known as an adjudicator nominating body. Before accepting the appointment, the prospective adjudicator must satisfy himself that, as a minimum, he has the requisite expertise to decide the dispute, that he has the capacity to take on the appointment and that he has no conflict of interest (Chapter 9).

[2.07] Although the adjudication process commences when the notice of adjudication is served on the responding party, the adjudicator will not have jurisdiction to preside over the dispute until it is referred to him. This is done in a document called the referral notice. It is at that point that the adjudication is 'live', and unless the adjudicator resigns, the parties will be locked into the process until the adjudicator communicates his decision. Where the Act applies, it must be served within seven days of the date of receipt of the notice of adjudication. The responding party's defence is contained in a document called the response. The deadline for service of the response will either be dictated by the applicable adjudication rules or more likely by the adjudicator. Should the adjudicator permit it, the referring party will serve a further submission, called the reply, the responding party will respond with the rejoinder and the referring party will respond to that with the surrejoinder. The adjudicator may call for a meeting between the parties, a site visit or a telephone conference at any time. The adjudication rules and the Act (where it applies) will prescribe certain powers and duties on the adjudicator. Throughout the adjudication, the adjudicator must ensure that he exercises those powers and duties properly (Chapter 10).

[2.08] The adjudicator's primary objective is to provide the parties with a decision on the dispute referred to him. In statutory adjudication, this must be done within 28 days of the date of receipt of the referral notice, unless the timetable for the adjudication is extended. The decision must be communicated in writing and is usually, but not always, accompanied with an explanation as to how and why the decision was reached. Although there is normally no fixed rule, the adjudicator will usually order that the terms of his decision are complied with in seven or fourteen days (Chapter 11).

[2.09] The parties' liability for the fees of an adjudicator is joint and several, even where the adjudicator resigns, or where the decision is not enforced. Generally, the only circumstances in which a party may not have to pay an adjudicator's fees are where the adjudicator has acted in bad faith, has been fraudulent, or has breached the rules of natural justice or where a party withdraws from an adjudication very early having raised a valid jurisdictional challenge, or where the party is insolvent. The adjudicator will normally have discretion to allocate his fees as he sees fit. The parties' costs are generally borne by themselves unless some other agreement is reached after the notice of adjudication has been served. However, if the adjudication is pecuniary, and the Late Payment of Commercial Debts (Interest) Act 1998 applies, the debtor may be liable for the fees of both parties and those of the adjudicator. Both parties should check the decision meticulously to ensure that there are no typographical or clerical infelicities. If there are, then the adjudicator can correct these and issue a revised decision. Although the general rule is that adjudication decisions should stand alone, parties to a statutory adjudication may in limited circumstances set off an adjudication decision against a cross-claim or counterclaim. The ability to set off in a contractual adjudication depends on the wording of the contract and the terms of the adjudicator's decision (Chapter 12).

[2.10] The losing party to an adjudication sometimes decides that it does not wish to comply with the decision made by the adjudicator because it perceives it has good grounds for doing so. Where the losing party does not comply with the terms of the decision, the winning party must seek to enforce the decision. There are a number of methods available, but by far the most common is to commence a claim in the Technology and Construction Court and make a summary judgment application to enforce the adjudicator's decision (Chapter 13).

[2.11] Even where the court holds that the adjudicator's decision is valid, there are ways in which the paying party can avoid the consequences of that decision, temporarily or permanently. These include where either party is insolvent, near insolvent or in financial difficulty. Where one of these situations exists, the defendant may either avoid summary judgment entirely, or receive an order for a stay of execution, or to put it another way, a suspension of the consequences of the decision. Sometimes, a court may hold that part of an adjudicator's decision is valid and the other part is not. In this case the court may enforce the valid part so that the winning party to an adjudication may derive at least some benefit from the result (Chapter 14).

[2.12] An adjudicator's decision made pursuant to a statutory adjudication is only temporarily binding until it is finally determined by litigation, arbitration or by agreement between the parties. In the vast majority of cases, however, a party will take no further action at all and then, by default, the adjudicator's decision is the one that ultimately determines the dispute (Chapter 15).

[2.13] The adjudicator's jurisdiction refers to the existence and extent of the adjudicator's powers to decide the scope of the dispute legitimately referred to him. An adjudicator's powers are derived from the Act (where the adjudication is statutory) and the procedural rules governing the adjudication. Where the adjudicator does not exercise his powers and duties correctly or does not decide the dispute referred to him, he will have breached the boundaries of his jurisdiction. Similarly, the adjudicator will be found to have no jurisdiction *ab initio* if he was improperly appointed, either because there are preconditions of referring a dispute to adjudication that were not met or because the appointment of the adjudicator was defective. *Ultra vires* jurisdiction is one of the two main reasons why an adjudicator's decision may be determined invalid (Chapter 16).

[2.14] The other main reason why a decision may be overturned is because the adjudicator has breached the rules of natural justice. In adjudication, natural justice has two limbs: bias and procedural fairness. Bias has been described as an attitude of mind, which prevents the decision-maker from making an objective determination of the issues to be resolved. Where an adjudicator is shown to have a bias towards either party, then his decision will be a nullity. Procedural fairness - or the right to a fair hearing as it is sometimes known – is relevant to the way in which the adjudication is conducted. In essence, where the adjudicator does not conduct the proceedings in a way that allows both parties the opportunity to put forward their own case and respond to the other, he will be found to have breached the rules of natural justice and the decision will not be enforced (Chapter 17).

[2.15] There are other, less putative, reasons why an adjudicator's decision may not be enforced. The maxim 'fraud unravels all' applies equally to the enforcement of adjudication proceedings as to litigation or arbitration. The defence of duress is another reason why the court may decline to enforce an adjudicator's award. The Unfair Terms in Consumer Contracts Regulations 1999 applies when a company wishes to contract with a consumer. The legislation bestows certain protections on the consumer which need to be adhered to in the event such parties wish to incorporate adjudication provisions into the contract. If they are not adhered to, the adjudication provisions will be struck out. Finally, a failure to comply with the Human Rights Act 1998 may lead to an adjudicator's decision not being enforced (Chapter 18).

Chapter 3
Deciding to adjudicate

3.1 Overview

[3.01] Conflicts arise many times during the lifecycle of a construction project. The vast majority of these are resolved amicably between the parties. One party will either convince the other party that its interpretation is correct or the parties will settle on an agreed interpretation. But in some cases, a conflict cannot be resolved merely by discussion or negotiation. Sometimes parties will feel so strongly about their position, or feel that there is something to be gained from not reaching a consensus, that they will need to refer their conflict to a structured form of dispute resolution, where normally an independent third party will either assist the parties in trying to reach a consensus or, having appraised both parties' positions, make a decision for them.

[3.02] There are a large number of dispute resolution forums, ranging from quick non-binding voluntary and consensual processes like mediation, to more formal processes like litigation or arbitration. In the latter, the parties are bound by a long chain of procedural steps, culminating in a hearing and a decision that binds the parties. The time and costs involved with litigation and arbitration mean that a dispute is rarely suited to those processes as a first step, if at all. More often they are seen as a last resort, once other alternative means of resolving disputes have been exhausted. Indeed, the Civil Procedure Rules, which govern the conduct of litigation in England and Wales, require that parties at the very least consider alternative forums for resolving disputes before or sometimes during a court claim. It is also common for parties to recognise that litigation or arbitration is a last resort and include escalation clauses in their contract requiring (or at least recommending) that the parties undertake various steps such as exchange of information, meetings between directors and an alternative form of dispute resolution to see if they can resolve matters before either one commences litigation or arbitration proceedings.

[3.03] Although adjudication is by far the most common method of alternative dispute resolution in the construction industry, it may not be the most suitable method. Most contracts do not force parties to refer disputes to adjudication; they merely state that parties may refer a dispute to adjudication should they wish. In that case, and subject to other contractual requirements, a party wishing to formalise a dispute must choose whether adjudication or another form of dispute resolution is the most suitable.

A Practical Guide to Construction Adjudication, First Edition. James Pickavance.
© 2016 James Pickavance. Published 2016 by John Wiley & Sons, Inc.

[3.04] This chapter provides an overview of the key considerations one might have recourse to in order to reach the point of deciding to formalise a dispute and, if so, whether it should be referred to adjudication. They are as follows.

(1) Do I have a good case? This will entail a 'cold towel' assessment, possibly incorporating the advice of external advisers, as to whether the case is sufficiently strong to formalise a dispute (Section 3.2).
(2) Is it worth it? This should entail, as a minimum, an assessment of whether there is a benefit (financial or otherwise) to referring the dispute to formal dispute resolution versus the cost of doing so, both direct (e.g. legal advisers and third-party experts) and indirect (e.g. relevant, people pulled away from productive tasks and seconded to dealing with the dispute). This sort of assessment is commonly called a cost–benefit analysis (Section 3.3).
(3) What method of dispute resolution should I use? This may be adjudication, or it may be something else (Section 3.4 and 3.5).
(4) Where adjudication is the preferred method, if either party is insolvent, can I still adjudicate (Sections 3.5 and 3.6)?
(5) Whom do I involve and are they available (Section 3.7)?

3.2 Do I have a claim?

[3.05] Determining whether there is a legal and factual basis for a claim, and if so whether it is sufficiently strong, should be the very first step in the process of deciding whether or not to formalise a dispute. If the case has no real prospect of success, all other things being equal, the sensible approach must surely be either to accept the opponent's view or reach as good a compromise as possible. The emphasis is on whether the claim, or elements of it, is **sufficiently** strong that it merits referral to adjudication or similar. It will rarely, if ever, be the case that the prospects of success are a 'sure thing' or a 'dead loss', otherwise there would be no dispute in the first place. It will almost always be somewhere in between. It is surprising how often this essential first step is missed, and parties end up in dispute without any proper consideration as to whether the fight is one they should take up. It is this part – correctly identifying the issues – which is invariably the hardest. It is also the most important. It is a truism that a party that starts off by asking the wrong questions is unlikely to get to the right answers.

[3.06] At a very basic level, the preliminary analysis can be split into three parts: law, facts and application. The first part entails establishing the scope of the contractual or other relevant relationship between the parties and identifying the rights and obligations of the parties that are relevant to the matters in dispute. For instance, what terms and conditions of the contract are relevant to and support, or are adverse to, the claim. The second part entails ascertaining the facts. Gathering evidence to develop the factual picture is crucial, time-consuming, and often fraught with practical difficulty. Typically it involves mapping out what has happened in respect of the events or matters in dispute, and gathering documents (such as letters, emails and reports) or other

Deciding to adjudicate

information (such as witness statements) that tell the story. The final part entails applying the law to the facts. In other words, working out whether what has happened has led the would-be defendant to stray outside its obligations such that the would-be claimant has suffered some form of loss which, pursuant to the terms of the contract or otherwise, it is permitted to recoup from the defendant.

[3.07] At the end of the exercise, if it has been carried out properly, it should be possible to take a considered view on whether the claim is strong or weak. Following this preliminary analysis, and having taken into account other factors, such as those identified in the next section, if it is decided that the dispute should be formalised, most of the time from then until the conclusion of whatever dispute process is chosen will be spent fleshing out the initial analysis into detailed submissions, which are supported by evidence collated for the purpose. This is by far the most time-consuming part of dispute resolution. It is one of the principal reasons why it is so important to understand the procedural aspects of the dispute resolution procedure as well as possible so as to minimise the distraction from preparing the substantive case.

[3.08] Even at the initial analysis stage, it will be necessary to involve individuals from within the business who were or are involved with the subject matter in dispute. It may also be necessary or desirable to engage external assistance such as solicitors and consultants, who will have the legal expertise and experience to carry out the analysis on behalf of the company and (just as important) to give pointers as to what evidence needs to be gathered.

3.3 Is it worth it?

3.3.1 In a nutshell

[3.09] The second stage in deciding whether or not to formalise a dispute is to assess whether the dispute is 'worth it'. This entails assessing whether the redress sought, pecuniary or declaratory, is sufficiently large or important to formalise a dispute. It also requires weighing wider commercial considerations, such as the impact on the company, in terms of the time and expense of engaging others in the process, the diversion of resources away from normal, profitable business to dealing with the dispute, and the effect on any ongoing relationship with the other party.

3.3.2 Amount in dispute

[3.10] If the dispute relates to money, consider whether the value of the dispute is sufficiently high such that the award of money will provide a material financial benefit that outweighs the cost involved in achieving that success. What is 'sufficiently high' will depend on the context. To a small subcontractor, £10,000 may be a significant sum but that amount may be immaterial to an international contractor. Sometimes, a party will feel so aggrieved by the other party's position on a disputed issue, that it will formalise the dispute at whatever the cost. This rarely makes commercial sense.

[3.11] Generally, there is a fairly close link between the amount in dispute and the cost of recovery when deciding whether to prosecute a claim. The size of the claim versus the costs to be incurred may also inform the choice of procedure and what resources are deployed. For example, adjudicating over a £10,000 debt using lawyers and experts will rarely be worth it, given that adjudication is usually a 'no costs' environment. It might, however, be worth informally mediating.

3.3.3 Likely recovery

[3.12] Almost always, there is a significant difference between the value of the claim advanced to the other party and the claimant's internal assessment of the claim's true value. Presumably, the rationale behind this is that a party will want to recover as high a sum as possible, and so where there is even a small chance of recovery on a particular aspect of the claim, the party chooses to 'throw it in'. Furthermore, the value of the amount claimed at the outset will serve as the claimant's stake in the ground, representing the amount it wishes to recover. This is sometimes known as 'goal-posting', and some take the view that the higher/lower the starting figure the better the recovery or pay out will be at the conclusion of whatever dispute process is chosen.

[3.13] Before the start of any adjudication, the party and/or its advisers should carry out a detailed analysis of each element of its case, evaluating in money terms what the likely recovery of each of those elements might be. One way to do this is to assess each element within a range, selecting a value that represents a worst case outcome, likely outcome or best case outcome; or to put it another way low, medium or high. For example, a party might consider that its claim for disallowed costs articulated to the contractor at £300,000 will in fact yield a recovery of £100,000 at its lowest, most likely £200,000 and at the most £300,000. Once the analysis of each element of the claim is done, this can be fed into the overall assessment of whether or not to formalise the dispute.

3.3.4 Professional fees

[3.14] Very often, early involvement of lawyers and experts is essential, particularly if a claim is large and/or complex. If that is required, then, as described earlier, there will be an initial assessment of the merits of the claim which (if the claim is strong enough) will be followed by a period of claim development, which will include an explanation of the various ways in which the claim might be put. It is therefore quite common to incur considerable expense before the claim is ready. There are further (often considerable) costs associated with the dispute resolution procedure itself.

[3.15] It is important to obtain an estimate of costs from the advisers as to what their fees might be, or even to negotiate a fixed fee. These costs can then be fed into the financial assessment of the viability of formalising the dispute. The estimate or fixed fee should contain a written explanation of what it includes and does not include. For example, the estimate may be given on the basis that the dispute procedure will only last for a particular number of days, or that the scope of the dispute is limited. It is important for a client to carefully review any caveats to the estimate before accepting it. It is also important to understand that the case will evolve as more time is spent on it and particularly when the other side makes its case. Understandably any estimate or fixed fee is unlikely to encompass developed areas of the dispute that it was not reasonable to foresee at the outset.

3.3.5 Resources

[3.16] The amount of internal resource required by a party to prepare its case and engage in dispute resolution can be considerable. The dispute will involve a number of people from the project team; witness statements may be required; documents need to be located and organised, and so on. If the project is ongoing (or if personnel are now profitably deployed on other projects), the company should consider whether it is feasible or desirable to divert these individuals away from that project. This is particularly important in adjudication, where someone may need to be involved in providing evidence or other substantial input at very short notice with no real prospect of an extension of time being available. Where possible, the time and tasks undertaken by members of staff who are directed away from the business should be accurately recorded because in certain circumstances the cost of this time may be recoverable. Again, this factor (and the likely recoverability of any costs associated with it) should then be fed into the overall assessment of whether or not to formalise the dispute.

3.3.6 Relationships

[3.17] Although it is not always the case, more often than not the other party will not welcome the act of formalising a dispute. Accordingly, it may lead to a deterioration of relationships between the parties, both at a management level and between those working on the ground. The result may be that communication between the parties becomes more turgid and abrasive, causing the parties to quickly move away from working in a collaborative manner to searching out opportunities for further claims.

[3.18] That said, addressing a disputed issue during the course of the project can have the effect of 'lancing the boil' in relation to that dispute, following which the parties continue and arrange their affairs accepting whatever decision was reached. In the context of adjudication, non-anecdotal evidence is hard to come by, but it certainly seems that, as a general rule, (a) parties tend to accept adjudicator's decisions as final, even though they have a right to open them up subsequently, and (b) a series of adjudications during the course of the project, even if fought bitterly at the time, more often than not will produce an outcome more acceptable and cheaper than saving up a basket of disputes for the final account.

3.4 Is adjudication the right forum?

3.4.1 In a nutshell

[3.19]   Once the legal, factual and quantitative assessment has been undertaken, a party will be in a position to know whether or not to formalise the dispute. The next step is to decide what dispute resolution forum is appropriate, be it adjudication or something else. This section summarises what are commonly thought of as the advantages and disadvantages of adjudication.

3.4.2 Advantages

[3.20]   **Speed**. This is one of adjudication's greatest strengths. Once the adjudication process is commenced (which occurs when the referring party serves the notice of adjudication), unless the timetable is extended, the parties will have a decision in their hands within 35 days. Compared to litigation, arbitration or indeed most forms of dispute resolution, adjudication is a rapid process.

[3.21]   **Continuity**. Where disputes arise during the course of the works, resolving them can jeopardise or even halt the progress of the project. At best, they will serve to direct key resources in the project away from the business of completing the work. Because the adjudication process is so quick, this distraction is contained to a short period of time, which allows the project to continue in an uninterrupted way as much as possible.

[3.22]   **Cash flow**. Improvement in cash flow for contractors and subcontractors was one of the main reasons that statutory adjudication was introduced. Contractors, subcontractors and suppliers usually operate on low margins of profit, and need regular cash coming into the business to be able to fund their operations. The Act ensures this, not only by making regular interim payments by payers to payees mandatory,[1] but also by ensuring that where a legitimate application for payment is not paid, the payee can initiate a process which will force the payer to pay in a short space of time.

[3.23]   **Temporarily binding**. Statutory adjudication provides an interim binding resolution of the dispute. In other words, once a decision has been given by an adjudicator, provided the decision is not invalidated by the court, it will bind the parties until such time as it is finally resolved in litigation or arbitration. However, it is unusual for parties, who are in receipt of a valid adjudication decision, to advance the dispute further. This fact further underlines the success and importance of adjudication.

> It is relatively unusual for the parties to a building contract to raise proceedings at the conclusion of the contract covering the same ground as the adjudicator's awards, and I understand that the same is true of arbitration. Generally speaking, therefore, the decisions of the adjudicator provide in practice the last word on the parties' rights and obligations. This clearly reflects the

---

[1] This is addressed principally by sections 110 and 111 of the Act, which are outside of the remit of this book.

Deciding to adjudicate 19

success of adjudicators in providing fair and rational solutions to construction disputes. It also no doubt reflects the fact that the parties to construction contracts do not want their disputes to be the subject of over-elaborate procedures, which are time-consuming and expensive and divert resources away from the conduct of the parties' businesses.[2]

[3.24]   This is a unique aspect to adjudication, which separates it from other forms of dispute resolution. The temporarily binding nature of an adjudicator's decision is considered further at Section 11.5.1.

[3.25]   **Cost**. Although it depends on the nature of the disputed matters, adjudication is usually far cheaper than litigation[3] or arbitration. This is even more so where the adjudication timetable is not extended, because the fees that the parties, its advisers and the adjudicator can accrue are limited by time. This cost-effectiveness balances out the financial inequalities sometimes found between employer and contractor or contractor and subcontractor. Furthermore, the costs incurred by a party are normally irrecoverable from the other, so that the losing party will not be required to pay the winning party's costs.[4] In this sense, the financial exposure that accompanies a referral to adjudication is reduced. This is different from litigation or arbitration, where the judge or tribunal has jurisdiction to award costs as he or they may determine, which includes allocating the winning party's costs to the losing party.

[3.26]   **Flexibility**. Although it depends on the form of adjudication, the adjudication rules and the contract, adjudication is flexible as to what type of dispute may be adjudicated. Parties may be in dispute about the assessment of a payment application. They may be in dispute about a particular provision of the contract, or the liability for alleged defective work. Alternatively, there may be a dispute about the award of an extension of time or prolongation costs. All of these sorts of disputes may be, and regularly are, resolved via adjudication. There is also flexibility as to the adjudication procedure. Parties are free to agree whatever adjudication procedure they like, although when the Act applies to the contract, there are certain minimum requirements that must be in place. See Section 5.2.2.

[3.27]   **Privacy**. Unlike court proceedings, but as with arbitration and many forms of alternative dispute resolution, adjudication proceedings are private. This means that the submissions made by the parties, any hearings and the adjudicator's decision are not accessible by the public. However, where an adjudicated dispute is subject to enforcement proceedings in the court, the judgment of the court will be made publicly available and will contain details of the dispute. Furthermore, any documents or submissions served as part

---

[2] *Costain Limited v Strathclyde Builders Limited* [2003] ScotCS 316, per Lord Drummond Young at [9].

[3] CPR Part 8 litigation can be quick and cost-effective, but it is not available where there is a substantive dispute on the facts. It is therefore comparatively rare that a dispute on a construction project will be amenable to Part 8. See Section 3.5.7.

[4] Although see Chapter 12, which explains the circumstances in which costs may be recoverable from the other party in adjudication and also Section 15.4.6, which explains when costs incurred in an adjudication may be recoverable if the dispute progresses to a final determination.

of the enforcement proceedings may be released to a non-party upon application to the court.

[3.28] **Familiarity**. Adjudication has become by far the most common method of resolving construction disputes. Whereas parties may not be familiar with the details of an early neutral evaluation, or an expert determination, they are much more likely to be familiar with the process of adjudication. While familiarity is certainly not everything, there is perhaps, in this case, something to be said for 'better the devil you know'.

[3.29] **At any time**. Sometimes, dispute resolution provisions in contracts require parties to adhere to a tiered dispute resolution procedure. For instance, the procedure may require disputes to be referred to the contract administrator first, then to the company directors, then to mediation, before finally being resolved by litigation or arbitration. All of this will take time and cost money, and until the dispute reaches a court or arbitral tribunal, whatever decision is made may not bind the parties. Where the Act applies, it provides that parties may adjudicate disputes 'at any time'. This means what it says. Parties may adjudicate during the project or after it, or while another form of dispute resolution is in progress. The right to adjudicate at any time is examined further at Section 7.7.

[3.30] **Tried and tested process**. Statutory adjudication has been available since 1998. Over that time, there have been over 560 clear, well-written reported court judgments offering guidance on almost every aspect of adjudication, from matters such as when an adjudicator is likely to act in excess of the jurisdiction given to him, to the interpretation of the provisions of the Act and the Scheme. While there may be other forms of dispute resolution procedure that are as tried and tested (mediation for example), no other form of alternative dispute resolution has received the same level of attention in the courts.

[3.31] **Choice of decision-maker**. Parties to a written construction contract will usually make provision for adjudication within it. Where they do this, it is common for the parties to agree that a third-party organisation, known as an adjudicator nominating body, will appoint an adjudicator. However, if the parties wish to have more control over the appointment, they can name an adjudicator or a panel of adjudicators from which the parties must choose if disputes are referred to adjudication. Sometimes, parties will agree that certain types of dispute will be referred to adjudicators with particular qualifications. For example, the contract might provide that disputes over the legal interpretation of the contract are to be referred to a list of adjudicators whose primary profession is a solicitor or barrister, or that disputes over the assessment of payment applications are referred to an adjudicator whose professional background is quantity surveying. In this regard, the parties have the flexibility to agree what they wish.

[3.32] **Speed and certainty of enforcement**. It may sometimes be the case (although it is comparatively rare) that the losing party in a dispute refuses to comply with the decision. If this occurs, the victor can commence a claim in the Technology and Construction Court to enforce the adjudicator's decision and simultaneously file an application for an order that the claim is summarily dealt with. Consistent with the speed of the adjudication process, the court has developed a fast track procedure for adjudication enforcements, which means that, from the date of the application, the court will reach a decision and publish its judgment usually in no more than eight weeks. Furthermore, the grounds on which the courts will refuse to enforce an adjudicator's decision, or not summarily enforce compliance with it, are limited. The policy of the court is that the losing party will only avoid the consequences of a decision in clear-cut cases. The procedures for enforcing adjudicator's decisions are addressed at Chapter 13.

3.4.3 Disadvantages

[3.33] Every form of dispute resolution has its downsides and adjudication is no exception. What follows are some of the characteristics of adjudication generally thought of as disadvantages or limitations of the process.

[3.34] **Speed**. While the speed of adjudication can be a benefit to parties, it can also be a curse. This is particularly so for the responding party who will have considerably less time to prepare its case than the referring party, although once the response is served, the balance shifts back to the referring party, who typically will be given even less time than the responding party to prepare its reply. The limitations imposed by the speed of the process also inevitably impact upon the quality of the submissions made, the evidence submitted and thus the quality of the decision reached; see below.

[3.35] **Quality of submissions and evidence**. The tight timescales mean that the referring party (for the reply submission and thereafter) and the responding party have little time to prepare detailed, well thought out, clear submissions, and the adjudicator is unable to conduct the sort of thorough, exhaustive examination of the disputed issues that one might expect of a judge in litigation or a tribunal in arbitration. This aspect of adjudication has repeatedly led to the process being described as 'rough and ready'. Critics argue, with some justification, that the risk of a poor decision increases where the dispute is complex, or document heavy.

[3.36] **Quality of adjudicators**. It is said all too often that the adjudicator did or did not do something which prejudiced a party, or that the adjudicator did not properly consider the issues in dispute in his decision. It is certainly right that a number of court decisions dealing with adjudication matters reveal that the adjudicator has acted in error in some way. However, as statutory adjudication has matured since 1998, so too has the experience and skill of adjudicators. Today's adjudicators, at least those that hold positions on major adjudicator nominating body panels are, in the vast majority, construction professionals or lawyers (and sometimes both) who hold a vast amount of experience in dealing with all manner of construction disputes, certainly those involving time, money and defects. While it does not automatically follow that experience will mean that a correct decision is given, it certainly improves the odds. Furthermore, the adjudicators have grown more and more familiar in resolving disputes in a short space of time and more familiar with dealing with the adjudication process.

[3.37] Nevertheless if the adjudicator is overwhelmed and, as a result, issues a decision that is wrong, the losing party is more likely to refer the dispute to litigation or arbitration,[5] which means the dispute ultimately will cost more money and take more time to resolve. As a general rule, parties have therefore become choosier about the scale of disputes referred to adjudication. Disputes about everything in dispute, so called 'kitchen sink adjudications' are less common than they once were. Parties instead, as a general rule, break up issues where they can, in order to make them more amenable to the adjudication process.

[3.38] **Quality of adjudicator nominating bodies (ANBs).** In the early years after statutory adjudication was introduced, the adjudicators on the panels of some ANBs were perhaps not at the level of competence the parties wished them to be. ANBs have responded to the criticisms levelled at them. Most ANBs now conduct interviews for each prospective adjudicator. Some ANBs publish criteria that a prospective adjudicator needs to meet, even to be considered by the ANB. For instance, TeCSA require adjudicators to demonstrate that they satisfy 13 published criteria both in their first interview for the panel and in subsequent *vivat* interviews, which are conducted periodically, and peer review specimen decisions.

[3.39] **Large disputes.** It is said that statutory adjudication is unsuitable for large disputes, where for instance there are many subissues and volumes of documents. Where a dispute of this nature is referred to adjudication and the timetable is not extended to accommodate it, the risk of a poor decision by the adjudicator increases and so parties have learnt to avoid referring such disputes to adjudication. Some further thoughts on large-scale adjudications are set out at Section 8.4.6.

[3.40] **Temporary binding nature.** The fact that an adjudicator's decision is not, without agreement, permanently binding on the parties may well lead some parties to conclude that adjudicating a dispute is a waste of time and money, and they would much rather choose a different method of resolving their dispute, such as litigation, arbitration or expert determination, which will provide a final decision with a limited right of appeal. That said, the vast majority of adjudications provide a decision that both parties accept and so, in effect, the decision becomes final. That is so even when either or both parties can identify clear flaws in the decision. There appears to be a significant premium placed by the parties on an adjudication as closure, even if the outcome is not one that they had wished for.

[3.41] **Irrecoverable costs.** Depending on the form of adjudication and the type of procedure, the adjudicator does not normally have the power to direct the payment of the professional costs incurred by one party to another, unless the parties agree to give him that power. This is different from litigation or arbitration, where the judge or tribunal has the power to allocate the parties' costs as he sees fit. While this may be seen as an advantage, because absent a contrary agreement a party will only ever pay its own costs, depending

---

[5] Although it is thought that a very small percentage of all disputes referred to adjudication are ever referred to final determination.

on the size of the dispute and the time period over which the adjudication runs, those irrecoverable costs can be considerable.[6]

[3.42] **Ambush**. A dispute must have crystallised between the parties before it can be referred to adjudication. Where the Act applies, this is not a high threshold to overcome.[7] A referring party may spend as long as it wants preparing a claim before commencing an adjudication. Often therefore the responding party will be caught off-guard by the referring party and will not even have begun the process of preparing to defend the claim brought against it, such as identifying key people, document gathering, instructing experts and taking witness statements. Where this is the case, it will usually be a significant challenge to ensure that the defence is prepared in time. This is sometimes used by the referring party to its advantage, who will try to ensure that the adjudication is commenced at a time that causes the greatest inconvenience to the responding party. This approach does not always have the intended effect, because if the responding party considers that it has not had sufficient time for its defence and that the decision is wrong, it may litigate or arbitrate. This approach is considered further at Section 8.2.

[3.43] **No automatic right to interest**. The adjudicator has no freestanding power to award interest on money he decides should be paid. This power only exists if (a) it is expressly stated in the contract; (b) the entitlement to interest exists under statute; (c) it is included in the adjudication procedure adopted by the parties (as it may be in contractual adjudications); or (d) interest is one of the issues referred to the adjudicator as forming part of the dispute. See section 10.7.8 for more detail.

[3.44] **No joinder provisions**. Unless the parties agree, statutory adjudication is not available where there is a dispute involving parties engaged under separate contracts. This may arise, for instance, where there are issues of design and workmanship or there are claims by the employer against the contractor and subcontractor. To resolve such a dispute in adjudication, the employer will, unless the other parties consent, have to commence two adjudications. This issue can be avoided by drafting a provision which allows a dispute between parties engaged under different contracts to be dealt with in one adjudication.

[3.45] **No non-contractual claims**. Statutory adjudication is only available for disputes arising 'under the contract'. Thus, for example, where an employer has a claim in common law for negligence against the contractor, or the cause of action is negligent misstatement, it will not be able to pursue that claim through adjudication.

[3.46] **Evidence not under oath**. Evidence, either factual or expert, given either written or orally, does not have to be given with a statement of truth, or under oath. Evidence given in court or arbitration proceedings must be under oath. It is important to note, however, that what is said in adjudications is confidential but not privileged, so reference may be had to it in subsequent proceedings, even if it was not made under oath.

---

[6] Op. cit. No. 4.
[7] See Section 7.2.3.

3.4.4 Statistics

[3.47] The Centre for Dispute Resolution published a report in October 2014 entitled *'Research analysis of the progress of adjudication based on returned questionnaires from adjudicator nominating bodies (ANBs) and from a sample of adjudicators'.*[8] The report is thought to be the only one of its kind and is based on data taken from across the UK. In the two years up to April 2014 the report shows that:

- referring parties were successful[9] in two-thirds of cases;
- around one half of all adjudications concerned payment, 6% concerned variations or defective work and 15% concerned extensions of time;
- the disputed amount in 70% of adjudications was less than £250,000; and
- of all adjudications, 35% were brought by the main contractor against the employer, whereas only 7% of all adjudications were brought by the employer against the contractor. Most adjudications (36%) were brought by the subcontractor against the main contractor.

[3.48] These statistics give some indication of the sorts of disputes that are referred to adjudication, and by whom, and may assist in the consideration of whether adjudication is the right forum in which to formalise the dispute.

3.5 Other forms of 'rapid' dispute resolution

3.5.1 In a nutshell

[3.49] Although adjudication is by far the most common form of alternative dispute resolution in the construction industry, there are many other procedures that offer an expedited path to resolving a dispute. Each has its own strengths and weaknesses and may be more or less suited to a particular dispute, but most are aligned with adjudication in that they are quick and reasonably cheap when compared to litigation or arbitration. While this book concerns construction adjudication, it is thought to be helpful to provide a brief summary of some other forms of rapid alternative dispute resolution.

3.5.2 Early neutral evaluation

[3.50] Early neutral evaluation (**ENE**) is a non-binding dispute resolution process whereby a neutral party is retained to provide a non-binding evaluation on the merits of a dispute.

[3.51] The parties usually undertake it jointly, although one party can use it where it wishes to privately and independently evaluate the merits of its case with a third party. Typically,

---

[8] http://www.cdr.uk.com/documents/Report13_001.pdf. Accessed 1 September 2015. One of the authors of this report, Jane Milligan, was also the co-author of all previous editions of the report (nos 1–12) published by Glasgow Caledonian University. See http://www.gcu.ac.uk/ebe/businessservices/adjudicationreports. Accessed 1 September 2015.
[9] Albeit the report does not define 'success'.

the third-party evaluator will not engage the parties in discussion or debate (as he might in mediation); rather the evaluation will be a paper-based exercise, and the decision of the evaluator will be communicated, usually in writing, although sometimes in conference.

[3.52] As the name suggests, this mechanism is sometimes deployed early on in a dispute, before significant costs have been incurred. Where parties are in the initial stages of debating the dispute, the opinion of a mutually respected neutral party (a senior lawyer or retired judge for instance) can assist the parties with a realistic appraisal of their case.

[3.53] ENE can also form part of litigation. The *Technology and Construction Court Guide* provides[10] that the parties can seek an appropriate order from the assigned judge, either at the first case management conference or at any time prior to the commencement of the trial. The evaluation is usually undertaken by another judge (although sometimes by the assigned judge, in which case they will take no further part in the proceedings). Proceedings are stayed while the ENE is carried out. Usually, the evaluator will give reasons in writing, and the decision will not bind the parties.

[3.54] The principal disadvantages of an ENE are that the process is non-binding and so parties can simply ignore an opinion with which they disagree. It can also polarise positions in negotiation if one party perceives it is 'right' in light of the expert's evaluation. Unlike adjudication, the process is not underpinned by statute, there are usually no rules or procedures that either the parties or the evaluator are required to adhere to, and the evaluation can be less rigorous owing to the brevity of the submissions normally put to the evaluator.

3.5.3 Expert determination

[3.55] Expert determination is a process by which an independent third-party expert is appointed by the parties pursuant to the contract between them to decide a dispute. It thus shares many common features with adjudication. Indeed, it is possible to think of adjudication as statute-backed, mandatory interim binding expert determination. Where the parties' contract is not a 'construction contract' to which the Act applies, and so adjudication is not mandatory, but the contract nonetheless contains an exclusively contractual adjudication clause, then the process is even more akin to expert determination.

[3.56] As well as being part of the interim binding adjudication regime in the sense described above, final expert determination can be used for construction disputes, although it is more commonly used for accounting, valuation and technical engineering disputes wherein the parties anticipate that specific expertise of the decision-maker will be critical, and they wish to subcontract that dispute to someone for a quick and definitive answer. The parties are able to select the expert determiner who, as the name suggests, is likely to be an expert in the subject matter of the dispute. The process avoids the need for parties to appoint a dispute resolver (arbitrator, adjudicator, judge) and also an expert or experts on the subject matter in dispute.

---

[10] TCC Guide, 2014, third edition, section 7.5.

[3.57]   Unlike statutory adjudication, binding expert determination is only available if the contract between the parties provides for it or the parties otherwise agree. The exact remit of the expert's authority and the procedure will be set out in the contract and in the expert's terms of appointment. The expert has no residual powers beyond those expressly granted by the contracting parties.

[3.58]   One of the benefits, but also one of the main drawbacks, of expert determination is that the decision is usually final, unless it can be shown that the expert materially departed from his instructions, or committed fraud, or was partial.[11] This means that if the expert gets it wrong, the parties may be stuck with the decision. Statutory adjudication is different in that, while the adjudicator's decision will be temporarily binding, it is open to the parties to refer the dispute to litigation or arbitration if they perceive the decision was wrong. Like adjudication, expert determination is confidential.

3.5.4 Mediation

[3.59]   Mediation is a structured settlement negotiation facilitated by a neutral third party, the mediator, who has no decision-making power. The style of mediators can vary from pure facilitators who assist the parties in their negotiations to evaluators who express views on merits and outcomes to encourage settlement.

[3.60]   The principal advantages of mediation are:

- A third-party mediator is introduced, who typically spends at least a part of the mediation process engaged in shuttle diplomacy between parties located in separate rooms. This enables parties to appraise their cases with the mediator in confidence.
- The focus of the process is upon the interests of the parties rather than their legal rights. Factors such as business relationships, external commercial pressures, reputational issues or personal emotions normally play a bigger part.
- The process is conciliatory and the outcome consensual. This is in contrast to the contentious approach in adjudication and the imposition of a solution by an adjudicator.

[3.61]   While most mediators follow a broadly standard template, the procedure is entirely flexible, to suit the parties and the dispute. The mediation is confidential, usually lasts no more than a day and is therefore relatively cheap. Even when mediations are unsuccessful (i.e. a settlement is not achieved on the day of the mediation itself) the process will always provide an opportunity for the parties to focus on the issues in dispute and consider the true economic costs and risks of the dispute. It will also provide an opportunity to re-establish lines of communication that can be severed as the dispute escalates. Furthermore, it is not at all uncommon for a settlement to result in the two weeks or so after an unsuccessful mediation, as the parties each weigh the offers made and the points

---

[11] For this reason it is common practice for parties to agree that an expert's decision is binding except in the case of 'manifest error', which gives parties wider grounds to avoid a 'bad' decision.

advanced by the other side. An unsuccessful mediation can still therefore result in a settlement.

[3.62] The Technology and Construction Court offers a form of mediation during litigation, which it calls the Court Settlement Process.[12] Following a request from the parties, the assigned judge or another Technology and Construction Court judge will hold a case settlement conference at which the judge will act as a mediator. The case is stayed while the court settlement process takes place. If no settlement is achieved then the case proceeds as before.

[3.63] Clearly, mediation is significantly different from adjudication. There are normally no agreed rules or procedures in mediation, at least until the parties agree to mediate. The mediator will not issue a decision and usually will not offer an opinion as to which party's case is to be preferred (unless asked to do so, in which case a facilitative mediation can become an evaluative one). Mediations sometimes require parties to submit pleadings or submissions setting out their case and what they want from the mediation, either to the other party and the mediator, or just to the mediator (or both; it is not uncommon for the mediator to request a confidential briefing note, in addition to the open position papers setting out key points or likely concessions which can be made for the mediator's information alone). A party to a mediation can discontinue its involvement in the process at any time, normally without consequence.

3.5.5 Fast-track arbitration

[3.64] Fast-track arbitration is very similar in structure and outcome to traditional arbitration. As the name suggests, the key difference is that each step of the process is more limited in time and scope, with the result that an award will be issued within a much shorter time period. Three fast-track arbitration procedures have been published by different institutions, intended for use with construction disputes in the UK.

- The Society of Construction Arbitrators 100 Day Arbitration Procedure 2004[13] has the stated purpose of remedying the fact that the costs of some adjudications are becoming prohibitive and the resulting decision is not final and binding.
- The Society of Construction Arbitrators Construction Industry Model Arbitration Rules 1998 (**CIMAR 1998**).[14] These rules have also been published as part of the JCT 2011 suite of contracts,[15] and they contain two different options: a documents-only procedure for disputes where no hearing is required, and a short hearing procedure for when the matters in dispute can be determined principally by the arbitrator inspecting work, materials or machinery.

---

[12] TCC Guide, 2014, third edition, section 7.6.
[13] http://www.constructionarbitrators.org/rules/100-day. Accessed 1 September 2015.
[14] www.constructionarbitrators.org/rules/cimar. Accessed 1 September 2015.
[15] www.jetltd.co.uk/docs/JCT-CIMAR-2011.pdf. Accessed 1 September 2015

- The ICE Arbitration Procedure 2012,[16] also has two options: a short procedure for disputes with a value of less than £50,000, where submissions are made only on paper, and an expedited procedure for disputes with a value of between £50,000 and £250,000.

[3.65] All these procedures limit the time period in which the arbitrator's award is to be issued, with a view to striking a balance between ensuring that the dispute is dealt with quickly and enabling claims to be developed. The name of the SCA 100 Day Procedure is perhaps misleading, because the 100 days starts from either the date of the statement of defence or the date on which the arbitrator gives his directions, which means that the total duration of the proceedings is slightly longer. The ICE Expedited Procedure and the CIMAR 1998 both anticipate an overall duration, from commencement to award, of 2–3 months. The longer timetable reduces the risk of ambush that is inherent with adjudication, and this risk is further reduced in the SCA procedure by a clause that provides that a party may not commence arbitral proceedings until at least 28 days after it has communicated its claim to the other party. While the Act provides that a dispute must have crystallised before it may be adjudicated, the period of crystallisation is much shorter, commonly no more than a few days.

[3.66] All procedures, with the exception of the ICE Short Procedure, provide for a hearing. The timescale of the hearing ranges from one day for the CIMAR 1998 Short Hearing Procedure, to 10 working days for the SCA 100 Day Arbitration Procedure. The occurrence of a hearing in an adjudication is, in contrast, entirely at the adjudicator's discretion. As a result, they happen comparatively infrequently and furthermore might be better described as meetings, to reflect their typically less structured nature.

[3.67] The arbitrator has jurisdiction to allocate costs (both party and arbitrator) between the parties in all forms of fast-track arbitration. Where the parties adjudicate, the adjudicator will only have the power to award party costs if they both agree that he has that power after the adjudication has commenced,[17] although they may agree that he can determine the apportionment of his own costs between the parties before the adjudication (usually in the contract). While the costs of a fast-track arbitration are likely to be considerably higher than adjudication, the winning party will have the majority of its costs paid by the losing party.

[3.68] Parties may use fast-track arbitration to obtain a final and binding award after a dispute has been determined by adjudication. This may be appropriate in circumstances where both parties feel dissatisfied with the adjudicator's decision, for example if the decision is clearly wrong either in fact or law. The same submissions and documents could be provided to the arbitrator to minimise cost, and in effect the process could operate as an efficient and cheaper way of appealing a bad adjudication decision than if the parties commenced litigation or arbitration.

---

[16] http://www.ice.org.uk/Information-resources/Document-Library/ICE-Arbitration-Procedure. Accessed 1 May 2015.
[17] Although there is a question mark over whether this is the case under the 2009 Act. See Section 12.3.

3.5.6 Statutory demand or winding-up petition

[3.69] This is not a dispute resolution method, but it is sometimes used as a way of obtaining money, where there is no opportunity to contest the amount owed and there are no counter claims. Even the threat of winding-up may pressurise the payer into making payment, and is quick and cheap (usually it can be commenced by simply serving a statutory demand, which does not need to be formally issued, and attracts no court fee). However, using the threat or fact of winding-up proceedings as a tactical form of debt collection in this way is heavily discouraged by the courts, and can backfire. Furthermore, the prudent payee will know that a statutory demand or winding-up petition will not result in the company being deemed insolvent, where it can show that there are genuine outstanding cross-claims or other disputes, which might reduce or extinguish the amount claimed.[18] For this reason, winding-up petitions are often unsuccessful and rarely deployed by a creditor. Statutory demands are considered in the context of enforcing an adjudicator's decision at Section 13.4.4.

3.5.7 Part 8 claim

[3.70] Commencing a claim in accordance with the rules set out in Part 8 of the Civil Procedure Rules is another way in which a claim brought in the court can be dealt with relatively swiftly. The timescales for obtaining a judgment from the court are far quicker than a 'normal' CPR Part 7 claim, and so for certain claims, it can be seen as a real alternative to adjudication. Indeed, in some ways, it is preferable to adjudication. The parties obtain a final decision that binds them, the court's fees are low when compared to the fees typically charged by an adjudicator and the court has jurisdiction to allocate the parties' costs as it sees fit. However, the major limitation is that Part 8 claims are only available if there is no substantial dispute of fact.[19] Thus, it will be suitable where there is a dispute concerning the proper construction of the contract documents, where the answer depends only on an interpretation of contractual wording but it will not include pecuniary or technical disputes (which comprise the vast majority of all construction disputes). Nevertheless, resolving contractual issues of principle can have a significant bearing on substantial disputes concerning time and money, and so parties may seek a final determination of the contractual issues through the CPR Part 8 procedure, before adjudicating their disputes over time and money. In *Liberty Mercian Ltd v Dean & Dyball Construction*,[20] the parties referred issues concerning the sectional completion schedule and the validity of the liquidated damages provision. Once the court had ruled on those issues, the parties were then free to refer the outstanding time and money claims to the adjudicator.

3.5.8 Summary judgment

[3.71] A claim may be commenced in the court using either the procedure set out in CPR Part 7 or Part 8. Whichever route is followed, it is open to either party to make an

---

[18] *Shaw v MFP Foundations & Piling Ltd* [2010] EWHC 9 (Ch), per Davies J at [47–62].
[19] CPR rule 8.1(2)(a).
[20] [2008] EWHC 2617 (TCC), per Coulson J at [11–12].

application for summary judgment of the claim or a particular issue. One issue where summary judgment is thought to be of particular use is in circumstances where the payer in a construction contract has failed to pay an amount applied for and has not issued a notice of its intention to withhold some or all of the amount applied for. In this situation, which is described in more detail at section 8.4.4, a payee may often choose to commence an adjudication to recover the amount owed to it. Whilst that approach will almost certainly yield a decision in the referring party's favour, if the responding party chooses not to comply with the adjudicator's decision, the referring party must then commence a claim in the court and make an application for summary judgment of the adjudicator's decision.[21]

[3.72] Provided that the contract provides that disputes are to be finally resolved via litigation, it is suggested that a far better approach would be to avoid adjudication altogether and proceed directly to commencing a claim in the court and an application for summary judgment. The claimant will save the (up to) five weeks it would have spent referring the matter to adjudication and the costs associated with it. It will also recover most, if not all of its professional costs incurred in the litigation from the losing party. This approach was approved in the case of *Galliford Try Building Ltd v Estura Ltd*,[22] where this issue arose and where the judge explained that the time taken to obtain an adjudicator's award is roughly the same as the time taken to obtain an order for summary judgment.

3.6 Adjudication on behalf of, or against, an insolvent party

3.6.1 In a nutshell

[3.73] In the vast majority of cases, parties to an adjudication will be solvent and capable of absorbing the costs of the adjudication process as well as the consequences of whatever conclusion the adjudicator reaches on the substantive dispute. However, exceptionally, an insolvent party may wish to commence adjudication proceedings, or a solvent party will want to commence adjudication proceedings against an insolvent party. Where this is the case, there are certain legal hurdles to be overcome before the adjudication can be commenced. However, where the adjudication does proceed, then where one of the parties is insolvent and in the throes of an insolvency procedure, enforcing the decision of an adjudicator by way of summary judgment application can be very difficult, if not impossible. In short, adjudication does not marry well with an insolvent party.

3.6.2 Why do it?

(A) On behalf of an insolvent party

[3.74] The motivation for an insolvent party commencing an adjudication is likely to be relatively straightforward. It may have a claim for money against another party which, if successful, may serve to reduce or extinguish its own financial difficulties.

---

[21] See Chapter 13.
[22] [2015] EWHC 412 (TCC), per Edwards-Stuart J at [43].

(B) Against an insolvent party

[3.75] Intuitively, it would seem to be pointless to adjudicate against a party that has no money and where its assets are likely to be distributed to others. However, there are some circumstances in which it may be necessary to commence proceedings. For example, it may be that the insolvent party provided some form of third-party performance security or insurance, but that security or insurance is not triggered until matters are resolved in adjudication or by way of court order. Where the insolvency procedure is voluntary and may lead to the rescue of the company, the referring party may consider that the chances of the responding party being rescued are sufficiently good to merit pursuing a claim in adjudication and obtaining a decision in its favour which, once the party is rescued, it will be obliged to comply with. Another reason may be that the referring party wishes to substantiate a claim as an unsecured creditor in the insolvency so that the claim ranks higher than it otherwise would in the list of creditors, although as discussed below, such eventuality can only occur with the consent of the company or appointed insolvency practitioner.

3.6.3 Trigger for insolvency

[3.76] Section 123 of the Insolvency Act 1986 is the starting point for companies. It sets out the rules for determining when a company can be categorised as being unable to pay its debts. It provides:

> (1) A company is deemed unable to pay its debts—
> (a) if a creditor (by assignment or otherwise) to whom the company is indebted in a sum exceeding £750 then due has served on the company, by leaving it at the company's registered office, a written demand (in the prescribed form) requiring the company to pay the sum so due and the company has for 3 weeks thereafter neglected to pay the sum or to secure or compound for it to the reasonable satisfaction of the creditor, or
> (b) if, in England and Wales, execution or other process issued on a judgment, decree or order of any court in favour of a creditor of the company is returned unsatisfied in whole or in part, or
> ...
> (c) if it is proved to the satisfaction of the court that the company is unable to pay its debts as they fall due.
> (2) A company is also deemed unable to pay its debts if it is proved to the satisfaction of the court that the value of the company's assets is less than the amount of its liabilities, taking into account its contingent and prospective liabilities.
> (3) The money sum for the time being specified in subsection (1)(a) is subject to increase or reduction by order under section 416 in Part XV.

[3.77] Once one of these tests is satisfied, the company is insolvent in law.

[3.78] Section 1(a) refers to the statutory demand procedure. For a company, the failure to comply with a statutory demand is simply one way of establishing insolvency. Unlike bankruptcy, where anything less than personal service of the statutory demand will generally not do, the formalities surrounding service of a statutory demand on a company are relatively liberal. That is because an unanswered and unsatisfied demand for payment made by way of letter will, in practical terms, often have broadly the same evidentiary effect as expiry of statutory demand, because what the court is concerned with under section 123 is the debtor's unexplained failure to pay what appear to be undisputed debts, and both routes establish the answer to the question. See for example *Cornhill Insurance plc v Improvement Services Ltd*,[23] where, consistent with that approach, it was held that a petition under section 123 would 'go' on the basis of unanswered solicitor's correspondence demanding payment, without a formal statutory demand first being served.

[3.79] Section 1(b) flows from the failure to comply with a judgment or order of the court.

[3.80] Section 1(e) is commonly referred to as the 'cash flow test'. This is a commercial test where the courts look to see if, on the evidence, the company is paying its debts as they fall due. If not, the company is insolvent, and the fact that its assets may exceed its liabilities is irrelevant. The test is concerned with presently due debts and those falling due from time to time in the 'reasonably near future'.[24]

[3.81] Section 2 is often referred to as the balance sheet test. The balance sheet test is, in most cases, less important than the cash flow position, because a company is insolvent if it refuses to pay an unanswerable debt even if the court is satisfied it has the resources to do so. In *Cornhill Insurance plc v Improvement Services Ltd*,[25] reference to accounts showing very substantial assets did not impress the judge; what mattered was that the debtor was refusing to use those assets to pay its admitted debts. Whether the debts can be met as they fall due is usually what matters to the Companies Court; reference to solvency in the long run, as evidenced in balance sheet accounts, will often not be conclusive. Companies Court judges are usually Keynesian: in other words, the long run doesn't matter; in the long run we are all dead.

[3.82] One important point to note is that the effect of a winding-up order made under section 123 is that it relates back to the date upon which the petition is presented. In other words, a winding-up order made on 1 May against a petition presented on 1 January winds the company with effect from 1 January, not 1 May.[26] Further, a winding-up order automatically voids any disposition of property that takes place between the date of the petition being presented and the date of the winding-up order.[27] Accordingly, the enforceability or otherwise of an adjudicator's decision which is published during the life of a presented, but as-yet-unresolved petition is a precarious thing; for this reason, the court may stay enforcement of a decision reached in that period, pending the Companies Court decision on whether or not to wind up.[28]

---

[23] [1986] 1 WLR 114.
[24] *BNY Corporate Trustee Services Ltd v Eurosail* [2013] UKSC 28.
[25] [1986] 1 WLR 114.
[26] Subsection 129(2) Insolvency Act 1986.
[27] Section 127 Insolvency Act 1986.
[28] *Alexander & Law Ltd v Coveside (21BPR) Ltd* [2013] EWHC 3949 (TCC), per Coulson J at [18–22].

3.6.4 Liquidation

[3.83] If companies cannot keep operating as a going concern, it may voluntarily or by order of the court go into liquidation. Liquidation is process whereby the assets of a company are realised and distributed to creditors in satisfaction of the debt that is owed, and in the order of priority as set out in the Insolvency Act 1986. Following the end of liquidation, the company is dissolved.

[3.84] Adjudicating where one of the parties is in liquidation is problematic. Rule 4.90 of the Insolvency Rules applies where the company has gone into liquidation. One of the effects of the rule is what might be termed 'automatic self-executing insolvency set-off' which provides that as at winding-up, there was an automatic and immediate consolidation of all claims and cross-claims between the parties, such that there was only one debt owed either from or to the winding-up. Since an adjudicator can only be appointed in relation to one dispute under one contract, unless all of those claims arise under one contract and in one dispute (two conditions that need to be met in statutory adjudication),[29] the adjudicator will not have jurisdiction to resolve the dispute.

[3.85] Further, an enforceable adjudicator's decision, even though only intended to be temporarily binding, would (if enforceable) be a debt, and as such just as capable of claimed from the liquidator or proved for in the winding-up; but there would be little or no prospect of getting the money back later if the decision turned out to be wrong on the facts because the company would be dissolved. This issue was considered in detail in *Enterprise Managed Services v Tony McFadden Utilities*,[30] where Coulson J set out his reasons why a claim under Rule 4.90 could not be pursued.

> First, in the present case, there were four Sub-Contracts between TML and Enterprise. Under the Act, an adjudicator can only deal with one dispute under one contract: see *Fastrack v. Morrison* [2000] BLR 168. Thus, absent agreement, an adjudicator could never undertake the necessary task under Rule 4.90 if there was more than one contract between the parties.
>
> Secondly, as noted in Stein v. Blake, if (as here) the responding party has a cross-claim and considers that it would be entitled to the net balance from the claiming party (the assignees), then it would be necessary for them to join the assignors, in this case the liquidators of TML. As I have said, the Deed of Assignment in the present case envisages just that course. But again, that could not happen in adjudication because it is not possible to have a tripartite adjudication.
>
> Thirdly, I consider that, on its face, Rule 4.90 envisages that the account will be taken and the balance decided in one set of proceedings where the result would be final and binding. It seems to me that that is the inescapable effect of the words used, particularly in sub-rules 4.90(3) and (4). It is also, I think, what Lord Hoffmann had in mind in Stein v Blake when he referred to the taking of the 'single account'. Again, therefore, that would rule out adjudication, because the results could only be obtained piecemeal, contract by contract, and could only ever be temporarily binding… There is what I perceive to be a fundamental clash between the certainty

---

[29] See Sections 7.3 and 7.6.3.
[30] [2009] EWHC 3222 (TCC), per Coulson J at [62–79].

and finality envisaged by the full Rule 4.90 process and, to use the vernacular, the temporary, quick-fix solution offered by construction adjudication under the Act. How can a decision that, if challenged, is of a temporary nature only, and would relate just to an element of the chose in action, have any role in or relevance to the taking of a final account under the Insolvency Rules?'

[3.86] Further, in *Hart Investments Ltd v Fidler & Anor*,[31] the same judge refused to enter judgment where the company was insolvent, given that it would enshrine the decision in an enforceable judgment, which would bind the liquidation, even though it might very well be an inaccurate statement of the parties' rights.

[3.87] It follows from the above that (absent the consent of the liquidator to accept the outcome as being relevant to, or part of, the taking of the account of mutual credits and debits under Rule 4.90) adjudication by or against a company in winding-up will not generally be possible.

[3.88] There are three forms of liquidation: compulsory liquidation, member's voluntary liquidation and creditors' voluntary liquidation.

(A) Compulsory liquidation

[3.89] A company enters compulsory liquidation following a court order to wind up a company. The compulsory liquidation procedure commences when a petition for winding-up is presented at the court, usually by a creditor. There are a number of grounds upon which a petition may be made, but the most common one is that a company cannot pay its debts. The petition is followed by a court hearing at which the judge either issues a winding-up order, or dismisses the petition. Once a winding-up order is made, an official receiver is appointed as liquidator, and the process of realising the company's assets and paying the creditors begins. The process concludes when the company is dissolved, which occurs three months after the company is liquidated.

[3.90] In order to commence legal proceedings[32] against a company that is in compulsory liquidation, the court has to give permission.[33] This permission is granted sparingly, because the general philosophy is that once a company is wound up, the resolution of all claims by and upon the winding-up is a matter for the liquidator to deal with via the creditor submitting a proof of debt.

[3.91] The grounds upon which the court will give permission to commence proceedings, the existence of a winding-up order notwithstanding, were outlined by the Court of Appeal in the non-adjudication case of *Bourne v The Charit-Email Technology Partnership LLP*.[34]

---

[31] [2006] EWHC 2857 (TCC), per Coulson J at [70–75].
[32] This term has been taken to include adjudication proceedings. A *Straume (UK) Ltd v Bradlor Developments Ltd* [1999] CILL 1520, per Behrens J at [9–12].
[33] See subsection 130(2) and Schedule B7 of the Insolvency Act 1986.
[34] [2009] EWHC 1901 (Ch).

(1) The court's discretion to grant a credit permission to commence proceedings is broad and unfettered.
(2) The court will not investigate the merits of the proposed proceedings, other than to satisfy itself that there is a genuine dispute and an arguable claim.
(3) Permission will be refused if the issues can conveniently be decided in the liquidation, because it will ordinarily be quicker and less expensive for matters to be dealt with that way. Therefore the liquidator's stance may be relevant. So for example in *A Straume v Bradlor Developments*[35] the judge refused permission to bring a claim against the company in liquidation, because the liquidator had already started an adjudication to decide the same question. The judge thought that the outcome of that adjudication would assist the parties in agreeing the amount due to or from the company without duplicate litigation over the issue.
(4) Where the claim is a proprietary one, permission may be granted more readily, because a valid proprietary claim is a claim upon assets that are not available for the benefit of the creditors in the winding-up generally.
(5) When considering whether or not to grant permission, the court will be alive to the fact that the insolvency practitioner is appointed to deal with the assets and liabilities of the company, not to run litigation.
(6) Subject to the overriding objective in the Civil Procedure Rules and the obligation to deal with cases justly and proportionally to what is at stake, the court will adopt the primary objective of achieving an orderly resolution of all matters arising in the winding-up for the benefit of the creditors as a whole.

[3.92] A related procedural question is, of course – to which court should permission be sought – the Technology and Construction Court (which maintains principal jurisdiction over adjudication enforcement business) or the Companies Court or Bankruptcy Court in the Chancery Division (which maintains principal jurisdiction over insolvency business)? The short answer is that all these court have jurisdiction, because they are 'the Court' for the purposes of giving permission to commence proceedings.

[3.93] That is not to say that the application can be issued in either the Technology and Construction Court or the Chancery Division and either will deal with the application without question; either may, if it feels it appropriate, refuse to exercise its discretion to hear the application and, if appropriate, transfer it to the other if it considers that it is better equipped to deal with the facts of a particular application.[36]

(B) Members voluntary liquidation (MVL)

[3.94] A company enters into an MVL where the members of the company pass a special resolution for its winding-up. This form of liquidation is only available where the company is solvent. The company's directors must provide a statutory declaration of solvency which

---

[35] [2000] BCC 333.
[36] See the guidelines on the grant of permission in administration set out by HHJ Thornton QC in *Joinery Plus Ltd (In Administration) v Laing Ltd* [2003] EWHC 3513 (TCC) at [108].

provides, among other things, that the company's assets mean that it is possible to pay the company's creditors in full. Once the special resolution is passed, the MVL process is deemed to commence, and a liquidator is simultaneously appointed. The process is concluded in the same way as a compulsory liquidation.

[3.95] The director's statutory declaration must certify that all claims have been met, or will be met, from the liquidation of the company's assets.[37] Unless the company's directors can be certain that it can meet the cost of the claim or potential claim out of the assets of the company, then the company is unlikely to be able to commence an adjudication while an MVL is on foot. However, there is no automatic stay on proceedings while an MVL is taking place and so a company may commence proceedings against a company in MVL. That said, the court may order that any particular proceedings are stayed pursuant to its discretionary power at section 112(1) of the Insolvency Act 1986.

(C) Creditors' voluntary liquidation (CVL)

[3.96] As with an MVL, a company enters into a CVL when its members pass a special resolution for its winding-up. However, unlike an MVL, a CVL is not contingent on the solvency of the company. It will usually occur when the company realises that its liabilities exceed its assets or that it cannot pay its debts as they fall due. Furthermore, after the shareholders' meeting, the creditors convene a meeting to vote on the appointment of a liquidator. At that point, the CVL commences. It concludes in a similar way to a compulsory liquidation.

[3.97] A CVL imposes no automatic stay on any proceedings commenced by or against the company. Thus an adjudication can be brought, or continued during a CVL. However, if the liquidator refuses to accept that the adjudicator's decision represents the sum finally payable from the insolvent company to the creditor,[38] then he is entitled to reject it, and the court will not interfere with that decision because, as discussed above, an adjudicator's decision is generally outwith the taking of a single, final and permanent account under Insolvency Rule 4.90. If the liquidator does reject it, the aggrieved creditor can appeal the liquidator's decision to the Companies Court. The Companies Court will then consider afresh whether to reject or admit the proof. If the disputes underlying the liquidator's rejection are factually or legally complex, the Companies Court might adjourn the appeal, pending a final determination. The final determination would be binding on the CVL as to the issues decided and the proof for the amount claimed (i.e. the adjudicator's decision)[39] would have to be allowed by the liquidator.

---

[37] Section 89 Insolvency Act 1986
[38] For example, because there were cross-claims that the adjudicator could not consider, or because the liquidator thinks that the adjudicator has simply erred in his judgment.
[39] Subject to any cross-claims which the insolvent company had which were not made the subject of the final determination.

Deciding to adjudicate 37

3.6.5 Voluntary or compulsory administration

[3.98] Administration can be defined as a procedure under the Insolvency Act 1986 where a company may reorganise its assets or realise its assets[40] under the protection of a statutory moratorium.[41] The company is put into administration, and an insolvency practitioner is appointed as the company's administrator. The administrator effectively takes over the company with a view to reorganising it into a viable entity, or selling and realising the value of the company's assets for the benefit of its secured and unsecured creditors. Where the company cannot be rescued as a going concern, it will then be put into liquidation (wound up) at the end of the administration.

[3.99] There are two types of administration. The first is a compulsory or court administration, which is enacted by order of the court following an application by a creditor to the court for an administration order. The second is a voluntary administration, which can only be agreed by either the company's directors or qualified floating charge holders.[42] Once the administrator is in a position to distribute the assets of the company, he must issue a notice of distribution to the creditors.[43]

[3.100] A party may not commence or continue an adjudication[44] against a company that is in administration unless permission is given from the court or the administrator,[45] who can accept the claim by admitting proofs of debt from the creditor. This permission is granted sparingly. The court may grant permission either where the proof has not yet been formally dealt with by the administrator or it may give permission in lieu of hearing an appeal from the rejection of a proof. The administrator cannot make a distribution while there is an outstanding appeal unless it will not have any effect on the amount of the dividend to be paid to the creditor on the proof under appeal.

[3.101] Guidelines were laid down in *Joinery Plus Ltd (In Administration) v Laing Ltd*[46] as to whether permission would be granted to commence or continue adjudication against a company in administration. Relevant considerations included whether the granting of permission prejudices other creditors, whether the creditor is secured or unsecured, the conduct of the parties and whether the claim was proprietary in nature.[47] The general philosophy is that proofs of a debt or claim are intended to be dealt with via the

---

[40] Paragraph 3, Schedule B1, Insolvency Act 1986.
[41] Paragraphs 42 and 43, Schedule B1, Insolvency Act 1986.
[42] Paragraphs 10 to 34, Schedule B1, Insolvency Act 1986.
[43] Paragraph 78, Schedule B1, Insolvency Act 1986.
[44] The restriction is against legal proceedings, a term that has been taken to include adjudication proceedings. See *A Straume (UK) Ltd v Bradlor Developments Ltd* [1999] CILL 1520, per Behrens J at [9–12].
[45] See subsection 11(3), 130(2) and Schedule B7 of the Insolvency Act 1986.
[46] [2003] EWHC 3513 (TCC), per Thornton J at [108]. See also the Court of Appeal in *In Re: Atlantic Computers* [1992] Ch 505.
[47] For example, a claim to the release of a retention fund withheld under a building contract can, depending on the wording of the contract, be a proprietary claim to delivery up of trust moneys. Permission for proceedings might be granted more readily for such a claim since a fund held on trust would not form part of the insolvent company's assets available for distribution to the other creditors in any event.

administrator who ought not to be diverted into expensive and time-consuming litigation. In that case, the court had to consider whether Laing should be granted permission to adjudicate against Joinery Plus. Applying the facts to the guidance it had set out,[48] permission was refused.

3.6.6 Administrative receivership

[3.102] Administrative receivership is a procedure available to certain types of secured creditor. It allows such a creditor to appoint an administrative receiver who will take over the running of the company in order to realise the value of whatever property (e.g. a factory) is secured against the debt (e.g. a loan). The administrative receivership concludes when the debt is repaid or all the company's assets have been sold. If the company continues, management is handed back to the directors. More often, however, administrative receivership leads to liquidation. Since the revisions to the Insolvency Act 1986 to create 'out of court' voluntary administration (where the directors or charge holders can place the company into administration via a simple written notice), administrative receiverships are comparatively rare.

[3.103] The appointment of the administrative receiver does not create an automatic statutory moratorium, and so other creditors may begin or continue any legal action against the company, which may include adjudication.

3.6.7 A company voluntary arrangement (CVA)

[3.104] A CVA can be defined as an arrangement between the company and its creditors. Essentially, it is a way of settling the debts it has with its creditors by only paying a proportion of what is owed and by determining the manner and timing of which payments will be made. The arrangement binds all creditors if, at a meeting of the shareholders and creditors, the majority agree.

[3.105] There is a 28-day optional moratorium available for small companies,[49] while a CVA proposal is being considered.[50] While a moratorium is in place, no legal proceedings (including adjudication proceedings) may be commenced against the company.

[3.106] However, if there is no moratorium or after the moratorium expires, a company subject to a CVA, while bound by the terms of the CVA, can otherwise carry on business. It follows that the company can sue and be sued albeit that, if sued by a creditor for debts or other claims arising before the CVA, it may be subject to the CVA provisions and there may be a limited recovery.[51]

---

[48] Op. cit. No. 44 at [102–121].
[49] Turnover no greater than £6.5 million, assets no greater than £3.3 million, no more than 50 employees.
[50] Section 1A and Schedule A1, Insolvency Act 1986.
[51] *Westshield Ltd v Whitehouse* [2013] EWHC 3576 (TCC), per Akenhead J at [20].

3.6.8 Bankruptcy

[3.107] Where an individual is insolvent, creditors or the individual may take steps to seek an order declaring bankruptcy pursuant to which the individual's assets are realised and distributed among the creditors. The process commences with the presentation of a bankruptcy petition to the court,[52] although the bankruptcy commences on the date of the order of the court.[53] Once the court gives the order, an official receiver is appointed who either acts as or appoints a trustee in bankruptcy, who will realise the value of the assets in the individual's possessions and distributes it among the creditors.

[3.108] Pursuant to section 285(3) of the Insolvency Act 1986, once a bankruptcy order is made, the commencement or continuation of adjudication[54] for any debt forming part of the bankruptcy requires the permission of the court. Subject to permission being given, proceedings are treated as the working out of the mutual credits and debits due to or from the bankrupt's estate. Therefore, adjudication can commence or continue, but the trustee in bankruptcy is joined in the proceedings.[55]

3.6.9 Individual voluntary arrangement (IVA)

[3.109] An IVA is a voluntary arrangement between an individual's creditors and the individual to either settle the debts or come to some sort of compromise. Once an IVA proposal is put forward and approved by at least 75% of the creditors at a creditors' meeting, it binds every creditor who was entitled to vote at and had notice of the meeting.[56] Creditors will not be bound by the terms of the IVA in relation to debts created afterwards.[57]

[3.110] A party intending to enter into an IVA can seek an interim order from the court staying any extant adjudication proceedings. The interim order results in an automatic stay of the adjudication against the debtor and it can only be lifted by the court.[58]

3.6.10 Problems enforcing the adjudicator's decision

[3.111] It is one thing commencing an adjudication on behalf of or against a company that is insolvent, alleged to be insolvent, or even in financial difficulty. However, it is quite another to enforce that decision in the court against the losing party where the losing party refuses to comply with the adjudicator's decision. Whether or not it is possible to

---

[52] Section 265 of the Insolvency Act 1986.
[53] Section 278 of the Insolvency Act 1986.
[54] In *A Straume (UK) Ltd v Bradlor Developments* [2000] BCC 333 the court decided that adjudication was within the meaning of 'other proceedings' for the purposes of subsection 11(3) of the Insolvency Act 1986 (now incorporated in paragraph 43(6) of Schedule B1 as set out in Schedule 16 to the Enterprise Act 2002).
[55] *Stein v Blake* [1995] UKHL 11, [1996] AC243.
[56] Subsection 260(2)(b) Insolvency Act 1986.
[57] *Re Goldspan Ltd* [2003] BPIR 93 (Ch).
[58] Subsection 252(2) Insolvency Act 1986.

enforce the decision depends on a number of factors, which are analysed in Sections 14.2 and 14.3.

[3.112] Very broadly, it is unlikely that a court will give summary judgment to enforce an adjudicator's decision where the winning or losing party is insolvent, because the effect of doing so would be to create a court judgment which the insolvency practitioner appointed to deal with the assets simply could not ignore. It would thus have to be paid to or from the insolvency, but there would be little or no prospect of getting the money back if it later transpired that the adjudicator got it wrong; enforcement therefore would in effect turn an interim decision into a final one, which is not what the Act intended. However, where the winning or losing party is not formally insolvent, but merely in financial difficulty (even to the point where there is a winding-up petition presented but not yet determined),[59] then the court will ordinarily give judgment, although it may stay execution of that judgment until such time as the financial difficulties abate, or the dispute is finally resolved via litigation or arbitration.

3.7 Who to involve

3.7.1 In a nutshell

[3.113] Assembling the right team to assist with the dispute process is paramount. While the underlying facts of a dispute will (or should) play the biggest part in determining the outcome of a dispute, having the right professionals available is likely to radically improve the party's chances of success, particularly in the compressed timescale of adjudication. Whether and to what extent it is necessary to involve external solicitors, barristers and expert witnesses in addition to internal management, legal counsel and members of the project team familiar with the issues will always depend on the nature, scale and value of the dispute.

3.7.2 In-house lawyers

[3.114] Many medium or large companies will have an in-house legal team who have expertise in construction law matters and experience with adjudication. Where this is the case, a member or a number of members of that team may either manage the adjudication on behalf of the company, and in so doing appoint external advisers to assist, or they may run the adjudication themselves. As a minimum, it is sensible to involve in-house lawyers at least in a dispute-management capacity, because: they are likely to be familiar with the details of the project out of which the dispute arose; they will understand the business and its objectives much better than external teams; they are likely to have a relationship with members of the commercial and management team involved in the project; and other than the time they divert from their usual duties, they will not involve the company in any additional expense.

---

[59] *Alexander & Law Ltd v Coveside (21BPR) Ltd* [2013] EWHC 3949 (TCC), per Coulson J at [18–22].

3.7.3 External lawyers

[3.115] External lawyers, be they solicitors or barristers, are sometimes instructed to assist with or conduct the adjudication process. Experienced law firms or chambers will have a wealth of experience not only about the adjudication process, but also about the legal issues and the subject matter in dispute. Generally, external lawyers are instructed where there is no in-house legal function or it is insufficiently resourced, or it does not have experience with construction and/or adjudication. External lawyers are more likely to be instructed where the scale and/or value of the dispute is large.

3.7.4 Claims consultants

[3.116] Claims consultants have come to prominence in the past three decades, partly due to the rise in popularity of alternative forms of dispute resolution, such as adjudication. As a very general rule, claims consultant companies are a mix of practising or non-practising lawyers and industry professionals (quantity surveyors, architects, planners). More often than not, they will have had hands-on experience in the construction industry before turning to claims consultancy. Their charge-out rates can be (but are not necessarily) lower than those of law firms. For these reasons, in addition to claims consultants' experience with adjudication, companies will employ them to assist with claims that arise during the course of a project and to prepare for and conduct the adjudication.

[3.117] One possible drawback of employing claims consultants relates to the question of privilege. Legal advice from claims consultants will not attract legal advice privilege where those consultants are not legally qualified, or are retained to provide something other than legal advice, such as advice on claims or project management.[60] Thus, any sensitive information committed to permanent form (usually a written document) such as an assessment of the weakness of its client's case, or reference to 'smoking gun' evidence, may well fall to be disclosed to the other party in the event that the dispute is not resolved by adjudication and proceeds to litigation or arbitration. While it is true that the majority of disputes that are referred to adjudication proceed no further, for those disputes that do, this could present difficulties. Privilege is considered further at Section 10.6.7.

3.7.5 Experts

[3.118] There may be technical matters in dispute that necessitate external expertise. For example, an expert may be required to understand the metal fatigue properties of a particular steel member in a dispute concerning whether the structure is fit for its purpose. In that case, it can be useful to instruct an expert witness who has the expertise to know whether the steel is adequate and can prepare an independent report to be submitted as part of the

---

[60] *Walter Lilly & Co Ltd v Mackay* [2012] EWHC 649 (TCC), per Akenhead J at [15–19]. Although it may, of course, attract litigation privilege, i.e. that the material was created or gathered in contemplation of litigation. In that regard, see Section 10.6.7.

adjudication, which explains the relevant technical issues as well as his opinion and the reasons for it. Experts are particularly important where the success of a case relies heavily on the interpretation of technical information. Not only will this assist the adjudicator in his understanding, but he is also likely to attribute more evidential weight to the expert's report than he would to a technical submission made by the party itself.

[3.119] The number of experts required will depend. For instance, if there is a dispute over the entitlement to a period of an extension of time, it may be that only a programming or delay expert is required. However, if there is a dispute as to an extension of time, disruption and prolongation costs, it may be necessary to employ a delay expert to assess the extension of time claim and a quantum expert to value the costs flowing from that extension.

3.7.6 Project team

[3.120] Those responsible for delivering the project will be the best source of information to understand the factual background to the issues in dispute. The relevant individuals should be identified as early as possible in order to ascertain their availability to assist over the period it is anticipated that the adjudication will run for. It is helpful to map out who is best placed to speak about or assist with which issues and then interview those individuals to obtain as much information as possible. Depending on the scale of the dispute, it may be prudent to prepare witness statements for those individuals, not only for the purpose of submitting them in the adjudication, but also to preserve the knowledge retained by those individuals in written form before the individuals move off the project or before memories fade.

3.8 Checklist: considering whether or not to adjudicate

> (1) Is the legal and factual basis for my claim sound (section 3.2)?
> (2) All things considered, will the benefit of formalising the dispute (financial or otherwise) outweigh the cost (section 3.3)?
> (3) Having considered the advantages and disadvantages of adjudication, are there any drawbacks to the process that make it worthwhile to consider other options (section 3.4)?
> (4) If yes, having considered those other options, is adjudication the right forum for the dispute (section 3.5)?
> (5) Is the other party insolvent or near insolvent and if so how does this impact on my decision to adjudicate (section 3.6)?
> (6) Who should I involve (section 3.7)?

Chapter 4
Statutory adjudication

4.1 Overview

[4.01]   There are three forms of adjudication: statutory, contractual and ad hoc. The statutory adjudication regime will apply where the contract between the parties falls within the scope of the Act. A contractual adjudication is one in which the contract is outside of the scope of the Act, but the parties have nevertheless agreed to adjudicate their disputes by inserting an adjudication procedure into the contract. An ad hoc adjudication is one in which the parties have agreed, or are deemed to have agreed to submit their dispute, without reservation, to adjudication thereby giving an adjudicator ad hoc jurisdiction to decide the dispute in circumstances where the Act does not apply and where there is no pre-existing contractual agreement to adjudicate.

[4.02]   The three forms of adjudication are different in a number of respects. For instance, while it is a requirement in statutory adjudication for the dispute to arise under the contract, that need not be the case in a contractual adjudication, if the contractual rules permit the referral of non-contractual disputes. The normal period within which an adjudicator is required to reach a decision on the dispute that has been referred to him is 28 days in statutory adjudication, but the normal period may be shorter or longer in contractual adjudication, depending on what the parties agree.

[4.03]   The various differences mean it is important to determine, as early as possible, which form of adjudication is applicable. There are countless cases where the parties have erred in this regard, with the result that the adjudicator's decision is rendered void by the court. This wastes costs and time and means that the parties are no further forwards in resolving the dispute.

[4.04]   This chapter examines the requirements that need to be met in order for the contract to fall within the scope of the Act. In a nutshell, where there is a contract between two parties that falls within the meaning of what the Act terms a construction contract and – where the contract is entered into before 1 October 2011 – it is a contract made in writing, the

---

A Practical Guide to Construction Adjudication, First Edition. James Pickavance.
© 2016 James Pickavance. Published 2016 by John Wiley & Sons, Inc.

Act will apply. This precis can be expanded into a five-stage analysis, so that it is necessary to:

(1) determine whether the 1996 Act or 2009 Act applies (Section 4.2);
(2) establish there is a binding contract between the parties and the terms of that contract (Section 4.3);
(3) check whether the works required by the contract are within the scope of works listed in section 104 and 105(1) of the Act (Section 4.4);
(4) check whether the works required by the contract are excluded by virtue of section 105(2) and 106 of the Act (Sections 4.5 to 4.7); and
(5) where the 1996 Act applies (and not the 2009 Act), ensure that the whole contract is recorded in writing (Section 4.8).

[4.05] Other than the procedurally distinct nature of each form of adjudication, why else is it important whether or not the Act applies to the contract? The answer is that where the Act applies, it gives either party an immutable right to refer a dispute to adjudication at any time. This right is a fundamental component of the statutory adjudication regime and is likely to be the main reason why adjudication is more popular than any other form of dispute resolution in the construction industry.

[4.06] Where the Act does not apply, the parties may still adjudicate pursuant to a contractual or ad hoc form of adjudication. These forms are considered at Chapter 5.

4.2 Old or new act

[4.07] Changes to the 1996 Act were introduced by the Local Democracy Economic Development and Construction Act 2009 and brought into force in 2011. This book refers to the amended 1996 Act as the 2009 Act. In relation to adjudication, the changes impact on the scope of the 2009 Act's application, and certain procedural rules, so it is important to know whether the 1996 Act or the 2009 Act is the one that applies to the contract between the parties. Determining this is straightforward. Where the contract is dated 30 September 2011 or earlier, it will be caught by the 1996 Act. Where the contract is dated 1 October 2011 or later, it will be caught by the 2009 Act. A copy of those provisions relevant to adjudication in the 1996 Act as amended by the Local Democracy, Economic Development and Construction Act 2009 is contained at Appendix 1.

4.3 Existence and terms of a contract

4.3.1 In a nutshell

[4.08] Adjudication of any kind is only available to parties where a binding contract exists between them. Much of the time, there will be a detailed written agreement which has been signed and dated by both parties making it clear that there is a binding contract. However, sometimes the terms of the agreement will be less formally recorded and it will be necessary to review the contemporaneous documents to determine what, if anything, has been agreed.

[4.09] Adjudication will not be available where a contract is void, although it may remain available where the contract has been terminated. It is not unusual for parties to argue that different contract conditions apply. Although this is not normally relevant to the question of whether a contract exists, it can impact on the applicable adjudication procedure.

4.3.2 Contract formation and terms

[4.10] Any form of adjudication is only available where there is a contractual agreement between two or more parties.[1] It is trite law that a contract is formed when an offer has been made that has been accepted in return for some consideration (usually payment) and that both intend to enter into a binding agreement.

[4.11] Where the value of the works is significant and both parties want to particularise their rights and obligations, they will ordinarily agree the terms of their engagement in writing. Those terms range from one of the many standard form construction contracts to bespoke one-page terms and conditions. In all cases, in order for there to be a binding contract, the essential terms must be present. In the context of an agreement for construction works, the essential terms are the identity of the parties, the scope of work, the price, and the time for completion.[2]

[4.12] However, surprisingly frequently, building projects proceed without the parties ever getting round to executing a formal contract. It then becomes necessary to analyse the correspondence, minutes of meetings and so forth, in order to ascertain whether a contract was ever concluded. Where performance has been rendered, the court will lean in favour of finding a contract.[3]

[4.13] Adjudicators and the court repeatedly face the question of whether or not a contract has formed and if so what its terms are. It has been debated whether it is permissible for the court to decide this question in the context of a CPR 24 application to enforce an adjudicator's decision.[4] The Court of Appeal has given this answer:

> The factual matrix is key to understanding what the parties must have intended by the words they used. But it far from follows that the need to know what that matrix was requires a full trial with discovery, evidence and cross-examination of witnesses. If there is no actual conflict of evidence on a relevant point of background matrix, it is only when there really are reasonable grounds for supposing that a fuller investigation of the facts as to the background might make a difference to construction that the court should decline to construe the contract on a summary judgment (including strike out) application.

---

[1] S. 106 of the Act.
[2] *ERDC Group Ltd v Brunel University* [2006] EWHC 687 (TCC), per Lloyd J at [28].
[3] Chitty on Contracts 29th Edition at paragraph 2-026
[4] As to which, see section 13.

The court should not be over-astute to decline to deal with the construction of a contract summarily merely on the basis that something relevant to the matrix might turn up if there were a full trial. Most disputes as to 'pure' construction of a contract will be suitable for summary determination because the factual matrix necessary for its construction will itself be determinable on that application.[5]

[4.14] A case where it may be more difficult for the court to grant summary judgment is where the grounds for the contract formation are put forward based on a course of dealing between the parties. This requires a detailed analysis of that course of dealing, in terms of any written and oral exchanges. In such instance, the court has refused summary judgment, ordering that the issue is resolved at a full trial.[6]

[4.15] Instances where the court has been asked to determine the existence and terms of a contract in the context of adjudication enforcement proceedings are listed at Appendix 8. The answer is always highly dependent on the factual circumstances. Some of the putative issues that have arisen under the banner of contract formation are summarised below.

4.3.3 Contract terminated

[4.16] Whereas the primary obligations of performance cease when a contract is terminated, obligations of an ancillary nature, such as adjudication provisions, will normally survive. In so far as there are disputes arising out of the contract post-termination, the adjudication provisions normally remain operative just as much as an arbitration clause would remain operative.[7] The position may be different, however, where the adjudication arises from a contract that falls outside the scope of the Act (i.e. contractual adjudications). In that case, parties may agree to terminate their ability to adjudicate together with other contractual provisions.[8]

4.3.4 Void or voidable contract

[4.17] Where a contract is found to be void or it is found to be voidable and the innocent party elects, the Act will not apply because the law holds that there was never a contract in existence at all. This may be so where the contract is entered into by mistake, or where the terms are too uncertain. A void contract is different from a voidable contract. A voidable contract has all the necessary elements in it to make it a valid contract, but because of a fundamental flaw in it, the innocent party is entitled to elect whether it rescinds,[9] or

---

[5] *Khatri v Co-operative Centrale Raiffeisen-Boerenleenbank BA* [2010] EWCA Civ 397, per Jacob LJ at [4–5].
[6] *Rupert Cordle v Vanessa Nicholson* [2009] EWHC 1314, per Tearle J at [13–19].
[7] *A&D Maintenance and Construction Ltd v Pagehurst Construction Services Ltd* (2000) 16 Const LJ 199, per Glennie at [18–19].
[8] *Lanes Group plc v Galliford Try Infrastructure Ltd* [2011] EWHC 1234 (TCC), per Akenhead J at [23–26].
[9] *Barr Ltd v Law Mining Ltd* [2001] ScotCS 152 per Lord MacFadyen at [18].

affirms the contract. Where the contract is rescinded, the parties are put back in the position they were before the contract was entered into, so that the contract no longer exists. Voidable contracts in the context of adjudication have been considered in the context of duress[10] and fraud.[11]

4.3.5 Choice of terms

[4.18]   While it is not relevant to the question of whether a contract exists between the parties, a conundrum sometimes faced by the courts is to determine which contract governs the relationship between the parties, where the two parties allege that different contract conditions apply. Not only can this have an impact on the parties' rights and obligations, but also where the two sets of conditions contain a different adjudication procedure, if the parties followed the procedure under the wrong conditions, the court may determine that the adjudicator's decision is a nullity. Again, the court will conduct a detailed analysis of the factual background to ascertain which set of conditions applies.

4.3.6 Incorporation of terms

[4.19]   Determining whether provisions or terms are incorporated into a contract is not always straightforward. This may arise in respect of an individual term, or it may arise where a contract, letter of intent,[12] or purchase order or document purports to incorporate the terms of another contract. This was the case in *Imtech Inviron Ltd v Loppingdale Plant Ltd*,[13] where Loppingdale contended that the adjudication provisions in a framework agreement were incorporated into a subcontract between the parties. If that was right, those adjudication provisions provided for the appointment of one of three named adjudicators. In the event, a non-named adjudicator was appointed to decide the dispute. Loppingdale contended that this meant the adjudicator did not have jurisdiction to decide the dispute and therefore the adjudicator's decision should not be enforced. The court held that the framework agreement terms were not incorporated into the subcontract and therefore the adjudicator did have jurisdiction. In reaching its decision, it cited an extract from a non-adjudication Commercial Court case[14] which provides very useful guidance in this context:

> Where parties are in dispute as to what they have agreed, the task of the Court is to determine from the communications that passed between them in the context in which those communications were made what reasonable persons in their position would regard them as having intended to agree. Where those parties agree the essential terms of a contract and also that their contract shall include the terms of a previous contract or contracts between them the Court may have to determine which provisions of which contract(s) they meant to incorporate. If the

---

[10] *Capital Structures plc v Time & Tide Construction Ltd* [2006] EWHC 591, per Wilcox J at [16–30].
[11] *Speymill Contracts Ltd v Eric Baskind* [2010] EWCA Civ 120, per Jackson LJ at [36].
[12] *Twintec Ltd v Volkerfitzpatrick Ltd* [2014] EWHC 10 (TCC), per Edwards-Stuart J at [43–47].
[13] [2014] EWHC 4006 (TCC), per Edwards-Stuart J at [28–29].
[14] *Habas Sinai v Sometal SAL* [2010] EWHC 29 (Comm), per Clarke J at [46–49]

Court is able to decide what those provisions were, it should not, in my judgment, be astute to impose any special rules which limit the ability of the parties validly to agree what, on ordinary principles of construction, they would be taken to have agreed.

If terms which are said to have been agreed are particularly onerous or restrictive of rights that would otherwise arise, it may be necessary, if they are to be enforceable, for the party seeking to rely upon them to show that notice of their existence appropriate to their content was given to the party potentially affected by them. Where the term in question ('the offending term') was included in a previous contract, but without such notice being given, it may be that general words incorporating terms of the previous contract (including the offending term) in a later contract are insufficient to incorporate the offending term. But an arbitration clause such as the present is not usually some form of onerous term to which special attention must be drawn: see: Streford v Football Association [2007] EWCA Civ 238. The fact that such an arbitration clause ousts the jurisdiction of the court does not, in a single contract case, mean that it requires some extraordinary method of incorporation.

I accept that, if the terms of an earlier contract or contracts between the parties are said to have been incorporated it is necessary for it to be clear which terms those were. But, like Langley J, I do not regard this to be the position only if the terms said to be incorporated include an arbitration or jurisdiction clause. Whenever some terms other than those set out in the incorporating document are said to be incorporated it is necessary to be clear what those terms are. Since arbitration clauses are not terms which regulate the parties' substantive rights and obligations under the contract but are terms dealing with the resolution of disputes relating to those rights and obligations it is also necessary to be clear that the parties did intend to incorporate such a clause. But, if a contract between A and B incorporates all the terms of a previous contract between them other than the terms newly agreed in the later contract, there should be no lack of clarity in respect of what is to be incorporated.

There is a particular need to be clear that the parties intended to incorporate the arbitration clause when the incorporation relied on is the incorporation of the terms of a contract made between different parties, even if one of them is a party to the contract in suit. In such a case it may not be evident that the parties intended not only to incorporate the substantive provisions of the other contract but also provisions as to the resolution of disputes between different parties, particularly if a degree of verbal manipulation is needed for the incorporated arbitration clause to work. These considerations do not, however, apply to a single contract case.

[4.20] In *Harding (t/a M J Harding Contractors) v Paice and Springall*,[15] the court had to consider whether or not the contract provided for adjudication. In that case, the parties had deleted the reference to adjudication in the articles of agreement, but had left in the adjudication provisions in the main terms and conditions. The court found that on analysis of the particular terms of that contract, adjudication was provided for and therefore the adjudicator had jurisdiction to decide the dispute.

---

[15] [2014] EWHC 4819 (TCC) per Ramsey J at [31–38].

4.4 Construction contract

4.4.1 In a nutshell

[4.21] In order for a contract to fall within the scope of the Act, it must be a construction contract. A construction contract is defined at section 104. It describes the nature of the agreements that may be described as construction contracts. In broad terms, a construction contract means an agreement for (a) the carrying out, (b) arranging for the carrying out, or (c) providing his own labour or the labour of others for the carrying out of construction operations in England, Wales and Scotland. It can also mean an agreement for architectural design and surveying work or providing advice in relation to construction operations. The precise wording and the court's interpretation of each of the subsections of section 104 are examined below. The nature of the work carried out under those agreements is encapsulated in the term 'construction operations'. This term is defined at section 105(1) and analysed in the next section.

4.4.2 Carrying out, arranging, providing labour for construction operations (Act s. 104(1))

[4.22] Subsection 104(1) of the Act provides:

> In this Part a "construction contract" means an agreement with a person for any of the following—
>
> (a) the carrying out of construction operations;
> (b) arranging for the carrying out of construction operations by others, whether under sub-contract to him or otherwise;
> (c) providing his own labour, or the labour of others, for the carrying out of construction operations.

[4.23] This subsection encapsulates the actual carrying out of construction operations (doing the work), arranging for it to be carried out by others (supervising the work or contracting with others to do the work) and performing construction operations via labour only contracts. For example, a contract administrator or project manager's contract will fall within the scope of this subsection because that person or company 'arranges' for the carrying out of the construction operations by means of advising on consultations required, orchestrating tenders, programming, certifying and controlling finances.[16]

[4.24] The use of the phrase 'carrying out' means that this subsection applies even if the construction operations are not completed, properly or at all.[17]

---

[16] *Diamond (Gillies Ramsay) v PJW Enterprises* [2002] ScotCS 340, per Lady Paton at [45].
[17] *Savoye and Savoye Ltd v Spicers Ltd* [2014] EWHC 4195 (TCC), per Akenhead J at [36(b)].

[4.25] The fact that the contract is retrospective, in effect does not prevent it from being a contract falling within the scope of this subsection. Often contracts are finalised after works have commenced and the contract is backdated to some earlier date.[18]

4.4.3 Consultants and advisers (Act s. 104(2))

[4.26] Subsection 104(2) of the Act provides:

> References in this Part to a construction contract include an agreement—
> (a) to do architectural, design, or surveying work, or
> (b) to provide advice on building, engineering, interior or exterior decoration or on the laying-out of landscape, in relation to construction operations.

[4.27] This subsection is intended to capture consultants, such as architects and quantity surveyors, carrying out work in connection with construction operations, rather than the doing, or the arranging of the construction operations themselves. The performance of contract administration services qualifies as surveying work within the meaning of subsection 104(2)(a),[19] while the giving of factual evidence by an architect, designer or surveyor at an arbitral hearing does not fall within the scope of this subsection because it is not the doing of architectural, design or surveying work.[20]

4.4.4 Contracts of employment (Act s. 104(3))

[4.28] Subsection 104(3) of the Act provides:

> References in this Part to a construction contract do not include a contract of employment (within the meaning of the Employment Rights Act 1996).

[4.29] The Employment Rights Act 1996 defines a contract of employment as a contract of service or apprenticeship, whether express or implied, or in writing.[21] There are no reported cases dealing with this subsection.

4.4.5 Construction operations and other matters (Act s. 104(5))

[4.30] Subsection 104(5) of the Act provides:

> Where an agreement relates to construction operations and other matters, this Part applies to it only so far as it relates to construction operations.

---

[18] *Parkwood Leisure Ltd v Laing O'Rourke Wales and West Ltd* [2013] EWHC 2665 (TCC), per Akenhead J at [22].
[19] *Diamond (Gillies Ramsay) v PJW Enterprises* [2002] ScotCS 340, per Lady Paton at [47].
[20] *Fence Gate Ltd v James R Knowles Ltd*, Const Law R: (2001) 84, per Gilliland J at [6–14].
[21] Subsection 230(2).

[4.31] Some agreements contain both construction operations falling within the scope of Act together with either other non-construction related activities or construction operations excluded from the scope of the Act. Where this is the case, subsection 104(5) has the following effect:

> Where a contract relates both to construction operations and to other activities, the contract is to be treated as severable between those parts which relate to construction operations and those parts which relate to other activities and that Part II and the provisions for adjudication are to apply to the contract only in so far as the contract relates to construction operations.[22]

[4.32] Reservations have been expressed as to the operability of a provision that permits only part of the contract to be adjudicated. This is because it may be that the subject matter of the contract is so intertwined that it cannot be separated out.[23] There are cases where the court has been unable to sever an adjudicator's decision that dealt with both matters outside and inside the scope of the Act.[24]

[4.33] It is suggested that the vast majority of contracts for construction work will not also deal with non-construction related activities. What is more likely is that the contract will relate to construction operations and that 'other matters' will comprise excluded construction operations falling within the scope of section 105(2). Where it is impossible to disentangle the two types of operation, the court may, depending on the extent of the excluded operations, rule that the contract as a whole is not one falling within the scope of the Act. However, that does not necessarily mean that the parties are precluded from adjudicating a dispute. If the contract contains an operable adjudication procedure, the parties may proceed to adjudicate disputes arising out of both construction operations and excluded construction operations on the basis that the form of adjudication is contractual and not statutory. See Chapter 5.

[4.34] Where this issue arises during an adjudication, the adjudicator should try to issue a decision that is capable of severance, so that if a court holds that part of the contract is excluded from the Act with the consequence that the part of the decision relating to the excluded operations is unenforceable, the court will be able to save the other part of the decision that is a 'construction contract'.

4.4.6 Application of the Act to contracts (Act s. 104(6))

[4.35] Subsection 104(6) of the Act provides:

> This Part applies only to construction contracts which—
> (a) are entered into after the commencement of this Part, and
> (b) relate to the carrying out of construction operations in England, Wales or Scotland.

---
[22] *Fence Gate Ltd v James R Knowles Ltd* Const Law R: (2001) 84, per Gilliland J at [7].
[23] *North Midland Construction V AE & E Lentjes Ltd* [2009] EWHC 1371 (TCC), per Ramsay J at [40–74].
[24] *Cleveland Bridge (UK) Ltd v Whessoe-Volker Stevin Joint Venture* [2010] EWHC 1076 (TCC), per Ramsey at [105].

[4.36] The Act was brought into force on 1 May 1998 and so subsection 104(6)(a) is likely to be of little relevance now. In relation to subsubsection (b), the completed buildings or structures that are the product of the construction operations must be in England, Wales or Scotland.[25] This excludes offshore operations.

4.4.7 Ancillary agreements

[4.37] If the parties enter into an agreement that is a construction contract and then subsequently enter into an ancillary agreement, is that second agreement one to which the Act applies? In all cases, the question is whether the ancillary agreement is a construction contract. In order to address this it is necessary to determine first whether the ancillary agreement is connected to the first agreement or whether it is a standalone agreement.[26] Where it is connected, it will be treated as forming part of the original construction contract and will therefore fall within the scope of the Act. Where it is a standalone agreement, then it is necessary to determine whether the subject matter of the second agreement means it is a construction contract within the meaning of the Act. If it is, the parties can adjudicate any dispute arising out of that contract according to the applicable adjudication rules applying to the second agreement. If it is not, then the parties will not be able to adjudicate matters under the second agreement, unless it contains an operable contractual adjudication procedure.

[4.38] The question of whether an ancillary agreement is connected to the first will always turn on a comparison of the nature of the activities required by the contract against the activities falling within the meaning of construction contract under the Act. Sometimes it may be relatively obvious, because the ancillary agreement will be stated to be a variation to the original agreement which itself was for the performance of construction operations. In other cases, the scope of the dispute resolution procedure in the first agreement may be wide enough to encapsulate the ancillary agreement. Thus, where the dispute resolution procedure allows disputes to be resolved that arise 'out of or in connection with' the contract, this may well be wide enough to extend to ancillary agreements. Indeed, it has been held that this phrase is to be given a very wide application and denotes any link at all.[27] However, where the disputes provision is only said to encapsulate disputes arising 'under' the contract, then it is unlikely to encapsulate standalone ancillary agreements.[28]

[4.39] The question of whether an ancillary agreement falls within the scope of the Act has arisen in a variety of contexts. They include novation agreements, settlements, collateral warranties, agreements connected through the Contracts (Rights of Third parties) Act 1999 and framework contracts. Each of these scenarios is briefly examined now.

---

[25] *Staveley Industries plc v Odebrecht Oil & Gas*, Unreported, 28 February 2001, per Havery J at [10]. The Act also applies in Northern Ireland, albeit it is brought into effect through different primary legislation. See Chapter 20.
[26] *McConnell Dowell Constructors (Aust) Pty Ltd v National Grid Gas plc* [2006] EWHC 2551 (TCC), per Jackson J at [42].
[27] *AMEC Group v Thames Water Utilities* [2010] EWHC 419 (TCC), per Coulson J at [29].
[28] *L Brown &Sons Ltd v Crosby Homes (North West) Ltd* [2005] EWHC 3503 (TCC), per Ramsey J at [49–55].

(A) Novation agreements

[4.40] Novation agreements may be construction contracts. However, it will depend on the connection between the novated contract and the original construction contract. In the case of *Yarm Road Ltd v Costain Ltd*,[29] the novation agreement provided 'the substitute subcontractor undertakes to perform the subcontract and to be bound by the terms thereof in every way, as if the substitute subcontractor were a party to the subcontract in lieu of the original subcontractor.' That was sufficient to ensure that the novated agreement fell within the scope of the Act (in that case section 104(1)(a)).

[4.41] Where an agreement is entered into before 1 October 2011 (the date of the coming into force of the Act) and the novation agreement is entered into on or after 1 October 2011, parties need to ensure that the novation agreement complies with the provisions of the 2009 Act.

(B) Settlement agreements

[4.42] A standalone settlement agreement that settles disputes between parties through the payment of money is unlikely to be considered a construction contract within the meaning of the Act. However, where that agreement required construction operations to be carried out, then it will fall within the scope of the Act. There are a number of cases where the courts have found that settlement agreements are, or are not, construction contracts and these are listed under this subsection heading at Appendix 8. In *Melville Dundas Ltd v Hotel Corporation of Edinburgh Ltd*,[30] the court distinguished between settlement agreements that were independent of the original contract and those that flowed from the original contract, because for example they purported to agree a sum due pursuant to the original contract's terms. In this case, the settlement agreement was divisible between standalone items of dispute that were not referable to the contract and items that were settled pursuant to the provisions of the contract.

(C) Collateral warranties

[4.43] Collateral warranties may be construction contracts; it depends on the wording. In *Parkwood Leisure Ltd v Laing O'Rourke Wales and West Ltd*[31] the collateral warranty preceded the obligation placed on Laing with the words 'warrants, acknowledges and undertakes'. The court concluded that the 'undertaking' was not merely warranting or guaranteeing a past state of affairs. The defendant was undertaking the works would be completed (at a future date) in accordance with the contract. It was therefore a contract 'for the carrying out of construction operations by others'. The court noted that not all collateral warranties would be covered by the Act, although it is thought that the wording

---

[29] *Yarm Ltd v Costain Ltd*, Unreported, 30 July 2001, per Harvey J at [20].
[30] [2006] CSOH 136, per Lord Drummond Young at [30–33].
[31] [2013] EWHC 2665 (TCC), per Akenhead J at [22].

of the collateral warranty in this case is not unusual. A 'strong pointer' in favour would be whether there is an undertaking to complete work that was not already complete. A pointer against might be that the works are completed and the contractor is simply warranting a past state of affairs.

(D) Contracts (Rights of Third Parties) Act 1999

[4.44] Although rights against third parties may be, and typically are, secured by a collateral warranty, they may also be secured by the Contracts (Rights of Third Parties) Act 1999 (the **1999 Act**). The court has considered the extent to which the rights of a third party enforceable under the 1999 Act can be determined by adjudication under an express term contained within the agreement between the original contracting parties.

[4.45] In *Hurley Palmer Flatt Ltd v Barclays Bank plc*,[32] Barclays plc (the client) appointed HPF (the engineer) to provide mechanical and electrical engineering design services. The deed of appointment contained a provision for adjudication pursuant to the Scheme. Subsequently, Barclays Bank plc (the third party) commenced an adjudication, and HPF issued CPR 8 proceedings shortly thereafter seeking declarations that Barclays Bank was not entitled to commence adjudication proceedings as a third party and therefore the adjudicator did not have jurisdiction to hear the dispute. The court awarded HPF its declarations. It said that notwithstanding the presence of adjudication provisions in the deed of appointment to facilitate adjudication between the parties to the appointment, this did not extend to third parties. Unless there was express drafting bestowing the right to adjudicate on the third party, the third party may not rely adjudication.

[4.46] Furthermore, since the Scheme applied, subparagraph 1(1) refers to a party to a construction contract being able to give written notice to refer disputes to adjudication. Barclays Bank, the third party was not a party to a construction contract. Subparagraph 1(2) states that the notice of adjudication should be given to every other party to the contract. Barclays Bank was not party to the contract. In applying these subparagraphs to the facts of the case, the court held that adjudication was not available to Barclays Bank.

(E) Framework contracts

[4.47] Framework contracts may not always fall within the scope of the Act if the agreement provides for further 'call-off' contracts to be entered into. The call-off contract containing the detail of the construction operations to be performed will be a construction contract, but the framework agreement will not be.[33]

---

[32] [2014] EWHC 3042 (TCC), per Ramsey J at [20–54].
[33] *Amec Group Ltd v Thames Water Utilities Ltd* [2010] EWHC 419 (TCC), per Coulson J at [14].

4.5 Construction operations

4.5.1 In a nutshell

[4.48] Subsection 105(1) defines the term construction operations. Activities falling within the meaning of construction operations will, provided they are part of a construction contract (section 104) and are not excluded (subsection 105(2) and section 106), fall within the scope of the Act. The range of activities is wide and encapsulates almost the entire spectrum of what a lay person might ordinarily consider construction activity to be. If one bears that fact in mind, then although sections 105 and 106 may appear convoluted at first reading (and even second or third reading), it is submitted that the task of determining whether or not the activities are construction activities is made more straightforward.

4.5.2 Definition of construction operations (Act s. 105(1))

[4.49] Subsection 105(1) of the Act provides:

> In this Part "construction operations" means, subject as follows, operations of any of the following descriptions—
>
> (a) construction, alteration, repair, maintenance, extension, demolition or dismantling of buildings or structures forming, or to form, part of the land (whether permanent or not);
>
> (b) construction, alteration, repair, maintenance, extension, demolition or dismantling of any works forming, or to form, part of the land, including (without prejudice to the foregoing) walls, roadworks, power-lines, telecommunication apparatus, aircraft runways, docks and harbours, railways, inland waterways, pipe-lines, reservoirs, water-mains, wells, sewers, industrial plant and installations for purposes of land drainage, coast protection or defence;
>
> (c) installation in any building or structure of fittings forming part of the land, including (without prejudice to the foregoing) systems of heating, lighting, air-conditioning, ventilation, power supply, drainage, sanitation, water supply or fire protection, or security or communications systems;
>
> (d) external or internal cleaning of buildings and structures, so far as carried out in the course of their construction, alteration, repair, extension or restoration;
>
> (e) operations which form an integral part of, or are preparatory to, or are for rendering complete, such operations as are previously described in this subsection, including site clearance, earth-moving, excavation, tunnelling and boring, laying of foundations, erection, maintenance or dismantling of scaffolding, site restoration, landscaping and the provision of roadways and other access works;
>
> (f) painting or decorating the internal or external surfaces of any building or structure.

[4.50] Broadly, it can be seen that subsection 105(1) is split into two. Subsections (a) to (c) refer to the carrying out of various types of work that form or will form part of the land, whereas subsections (d) to (f) provide for certain ancillary operations. That said, unpicking the exact meaning of each of these subsections can appear like – and often is – a daunting task not only for the parties, but also for the court. By way of example, in *Savoye and Savoye Ltd v Spicers Ltd*[34] the judge received three rounds of written submissions, attended a site visit and heard oral submissions from the parties before he could decide, in an application for summary judgment, whether the works were inside or outwith the Act. Mercifully, in that case and a number of others the court has provided helpful guidance on the meaning of particular words or phrases in subsection 105(1) and has considered in numerous scenarios whether particular operations fall within or outside the scope of the subsection.

[4.51] Reference to the word 'construction' in subsections (a), (b) and (d) has been held to extend more widely than merely building something. It means putting together or bringing together of different elements to create for instance a building. As a noun, it covers things like houses, offices, commercial premises, factories and warehouses.[35]

[4.52] The word 'structure' referred to in subsections (a), (c), (d) and (f) has been held to mean something which has been placed, built, arranged or prepared. In other words,

> …it has a connotation as having a function of supporting or servicing something else; thus, steelwork for a building is structural and a structure. A house or office building is a structure; Nelson's Column is a structure. Things within a building may be a separate structure such as a mezzanine floor or steelwork to support heavy machinery…[36]

[4.53] The fact that the structure can move or has moving parts does not mean that it cannot be considered to be a structure. Thus, a windmill or a turntable is a structure. A floating pontoon, which is permanently in position as a landing stage beside a pier is a structure even though it moves up and down with the tide and is occasionally removed for repairs or cleaning. Equipment can be a structure although, of course, not all equipment is a structure.[37]

[4.54] The structure need not be built of man-made materials. The court has held[38] that a structure built into the ground made out of clay and rock, intended to receive landfill was a structure forming part of the land within the meaning of subsection 105(1)(a) and that a cover constructed to be placed over the top of the landfill, while not forming part of the land, enabled the completion of the works that did form part of the land and so fell within the definition at subsection 105(1)(e).

[4.55] Machinery or equipment can be a structure, works or a fitting within the meaning of subsection 105(1)(a)–(c). Particularly if it is all part of one system, one should have regard to the installation as a whole, rather than each individual component. The fact that

---

[34] [2014] EWHC 4195 (TCC).
[35] *Savoye and Savoye Ltd v Spicers Ltd* [2014] EWHC 4195 (TCC), per Akenhead J at [16].
[36] Ibid at [17].
[37] Ibid at [17–19].
[38] *Coleraine Skip Hire Ltd v Ecomesh Ltd* [2008] NIQB 141, per Weatherup J at [14–15].

some substantial and heavy pieces of machinery or equipment are more readily removable than others does not necessarily mean that the structure does not form part of the land.[39]

[4.56] Subsection 105(1)(c) refers to 'forming part of the land', while subsections 105(1)(a) and (b) refer to 'forming, or to form, part of the land'. The distinction between the present and future in the latter phrase recognises a stage in the works in question before they actually form part of the land and a mutual intention that they will form part of the land.[40] The test is whether the particular structure or fittings will, when completed, attach to the land (e.g. a wall) or attach to something else that is attached to the land (e.g. a light attached to a wall).[41] Attached in this sense will usually mean physically attached in some way, but it may, depending on the facts, be enough for the object to rest on the land under its own weight.[42] However, there is at least one example where an object that was attached to the land by nails and screws was not held to form part of the land.[43]

[4.57] In determining whether something forms part of the land, it is useful to use as a guide the meaning of fixture or fixtures in the sense understood in land or property law cases[44] and the judge in *Savoye and Savoye Ltd v Spicers Ltd* helpfully summarised a number of those cases in his judgment.[45]

[4.58] Another helpful pointer is whether or not the object or installation can be easily removed. If it cannot be removed without serious damage or destruction, it is a likely to be considered as forming part of the land.[46]

[4.59] Ultimately, whether something does or does not form part of the land is a question of fact and degree. One also needs to consider the purpose of the object or installation attaching.

> Purpose is to be determined objectively and not by reference simply to what one or other party to the contract, by which the object was brought to or installation brought about at the site, thought or thinks. Primarily, one looks at the nature and type of object or installation and considers how it would be or would be intended to be installed and used. One needs to consider the context, objectively established. If the object or system in question was installed to enhance the value and utility of the premises to and in which it was annexed, that is a strong pointer to it forming part of the land.[47]

[4.60] The reference to the land means the land where the construction operation is taking place, not the land where items are being prepared or manufactured.[48]

---

[39] Op. cit. No. 35 at [36(h)].
[40] Op. cit. No. 35 at [20].
[41] *Gibson Lea Retail Interiors Ltd v Makro Ltd* [2001] BLR 407, per Seymour J at [15].
[42] Op. cit. No. 35 at [36(f)].
[43] *Gibson Lea Retail Interiors Ltd v Makro Ltd* [2001] BLR 407, per Seymour J at [20–24].
[44] Op. cit. No. 35 at [24].
[45] [2014] EWHC 4195 (TCC), per Akenhead J at [26–34].
[46] [2014] EWHC 4195 (TCC), per Akenhead J at [36(k)].
[47] Op. cit. No. 35 at [36(g)].
[48] *Staveley Industries plc v Odebrecht Oil & Gas*, Unreported, 28 February 2001, per Havery J at [10].

[4.61] Example of objects or installations which, on the facts, were held to fall within the definition of this section include carpets[49] (105(1)(c)), crane and labour hire[50] (105(1)(e)), installation of lighting and blackout screens, the provision of irrigation feed units, construction of a water collection system[51] (105(1)(c)), certain scaffolding works,[52] the maintenance and repair of heating systems[53] (105(1)(a)) and a conveyor belt system built to collect, box, label and deliver goods to a loading bay.[54] Cleaning the surfaces of farm buildings and structures to provide a grease-free clean surface to which could be applied disinfectant was not works that formed part of the land, but they were works for the purpose of restoring the farm to working order after the foot and mouth outbreak. Accordingly they fell within section 105(1)(d).[55] The removal of contaminated material from the farm constituted works that were integral or preparatory to, or for rendering complete, the overall cleaning process within subsection 105(1)(e).[56]

[4.62] Works held to fall outside the definition include shop fittings (where they do not amount to fixtures)[57] and the provision of factual evidence in a dispute hearing or assistance provided to a party at that hearing where the subject matter in dispute is construction operations.[58]

4.6 Excluded construction operations

4.6.1 In a nutshell

[4.63] Subsection 105(2) lists types of work that would otherwise fall within the definition of construction operations at subsection 105(1), but are excluded pursuant to this subsection.

[4.64] As with subsection 105(1), applying this section to determine whether activities in a contract are excluded can at first seem a little daunting. It would be a fair assessment that the careful incorporation and exclusion of works within the definition of construction operations is not easy to decipher. Mercifully however, the excluded operations are reasonably limited. Taking it at its simplest, unless the contract relates to oil and gas, minerals, nuclear processing, power generation, water or effluent treatment, chemicals, pharmaceuticals, steel, food, drink, supply or artistic works, one need not consider this subsection at all.

---

[49] *Green (Barrie) v G W IBS Ltd & G&M Floorlayers Ltd* [2001] AdjLR 07/18, per Grannum J at [27].
[50] *Baldwins Industrial Service plc v Barr Ltd* [2002] EWHC 2915 (TCC), per Kirkham J at [22–23].
[51] *Hortimax Ltd v Hedon Salads Ltd*, (2004) 24 Const LJ 47, per Gilliland J at [4].
[52] *Palmers Ltd v ABB Power Construction Ltd*, [1999] BLR 426, per Thornton J at [20–23].
[53] *Nottingham Community Housing Assoc v Powerminster Ltd* [2000] BLR 309, per Dyson J at [14].
[54] Op cit. No. 34 at [44–45].
[55] *Ruttle Plant Hire Ltd v Secretary of State for the Environment, Food and Rural Affairs* [2004] EWHC 2152 (TCC), per Thornton at [275–286].
[56] Ibid.
[57] *Gibson Lea Retail Interiors Ltd v Makro Ltd* [2001] BLR 407, per Seymour J at [15].
[58] *Fence Gate Ltd v James R Knowles Ltd* [2002] All ER (D) 34 (May), per Gilliland J at [6].

4.6.2 Approach to interpreting the exclusion provisions at section 105(2) of the Act

[4.65]   The intention of subsection 105(2) is to exclude a specific activity from the operation as a whole. For example, 'drilling for ... oil and natural gas', excluded by s.105(2)(a), would be 'construction ... of any works ... including wells' within s.105(1)(b) and also 'operations which form an integral part of, or are preparatory to, or are for rendering complete, such operations ... including excavation, tunnelling and boring' within s.105(1)(e). Mr Justice Ramsey[59] provided the following further examples.

> A contract which was just for the manufacture and delivery to site of drilling equipment would be excluded by section 105(2)(d)(i) unless the contract also provided for the installation of the equipment. If it did then the "installation ... of plant and machinery" would be an excluded operation under section 105(2)(c) but the manufacture or delivery to site of the equipment would not. I see no reason why the word "drilling" needs inherently to include the manufacture or delivery to site of drilling equipment or its assembly and installation on site. Those matters have been dealt with in a particular way under section 105(2)(c) and (d).

> Equally in relation to section 105(2)(b) "extraction (whether by underground or surface working) of minerals; tunnelling or boring, or construction of underground works, for this purpose" would cover the tunnelling, boring, construction of underground works and extraction operations. Otherwise, depending on the primary activity at the site, assembly and any installation of the machinery might also be excluded under section 105(2)(c) and, depending on whether installation was included, manufacture or delivery to site of equipment to extract minerals might also be excluded under section 105(2)(d). I see no reason why operations for the extraction of minerals should be taken to include manufacture and delivery to site of equipment or machinery and assembly or installation of that plant or machinery on site when those other subsections deal with those matters.

[4.66]   For the purpose of identifying whether or not operations fall within one of the exceptions at subsection 105(2), it is important to read the subsection as a whole and also, in the context of subsection 105(1) and section 104. The nature of the operations can quite easily span more than one of these subsections, leading to the conclusion that the operations are excluded or not.

4.6.3 Court's approach to applying the exclusions at subsection 105(2)

[4.67]   Where the question of excluded construction operations arises, it is now settled law that the correct approach is not to conduct a minute analysis of the work to see what is excluded and what is not. One must look at the nature of the work broadly, and conduct a straightforward and common sense analysis as to whether the works fall within or

---

[59] *North Midland Construction plc v AE & E Lentjes Ltd* [2009] EWHC 1371 (TCC), per Ramsay J at [40–74].

outside the scope of the Act.[60] In *North Midland Construction v AE & E Lentjes Ltd*,[61] Ramsey J said:

> I do not consider that it was the intention of the Act for there to be a minute analysis to find an item which arguably was a construction operation or was within the exclusion, so as to defeat the purpose of giving or excluding the rights of the Act to what on a straightforward and common sense analysis is a contract for construction operations within section 105(1) or excluded operations under section 105(2).

[4.68] In so far as there is any question of interpretation as to whether the operations that are the subject of an agreement are excluded, those operations listed at subsection 105(2) should be construed narrowly.[62]

[4.69] It will always be a question of fact, when looking at the works as a whole, as to whether an element of the work is material enough to render it outside of the scope of the Act. For instance, the court held that a portion of the works, which in itself comprised 18% by value of the final account, were sufficiently material to be excluded from the Act by virtue of subsection 105(2).[63]

4.6.4 Drilling and extraction (Act s. 105(2)(a) and (b))

[4.70] Subsections 105(2)(a) and (b) of the Act state the following operations are not construction operations:

(a) drilling for, or extraction of, oil or natural gas;
(b) extraction (whether by underground or surface working) of minerals; tunnelling or boring, or construction of underground works, for this purpose.

[4.71] These subsections are clear enough in their meaning. Perhaps as a result, there are no reported cases dealing with these subsections.

4.6.5 Assembly, installation, erection, demolition in connection with certain activities (Act s. 105(2)(c))

[4.72] Subsection 105(2)(c) of the Act states the following operations are not construction operations:

> assembly, installation or demolition of plant or machinery, or erection or demolition of steelwork for the purposes of supporting or providing access to plant or machinery, on a site where the primary activity is—

---

[60] *Cleveland Bridge (UK) Ltd v Whessoe-Volker Stevin Joint Venture* [2010] EWHC 1076 (TCC), per Ramsey at [32].
[61] [2009] EWHC 1371 (TCC), per Ramsay J at [40–68].
[62] *North Midland Construction v AE & E Lentjes Ltd* [2009] EWHC 1371 (TCC), per Ramsay J at [40–74].
[63] *Cleveland Bridge (UK) Ltd v Whessoe-Volker Stevin Joint Venture* [2010] EWHC 1076 (TCC), per Ramsey at [30–36].

Statutory adjudication 61

(1) nuclear processing, power generation, or water or effluent treatment, or
(2) the production, transmission, processing or bulk storage (other than warehousing) of chemicals, pharmaceuticals, oil, gas, steel or food and drink.

[4.73] These provisions are aimed at excluding particular operations in specific industries. The exclusion is limited to particular operations where the primary activity is one of those listed, rather than excluding all operations.[64]

[4.74] The phrase 'on a site' in the first paragraph of the subsection means the site as a whole and not just the area were the operations were actually performed.[65] The word 'is' does not mean that the primary activity has to be occurring at the time of the operation in question. It can be taken to mean, 'will be'.[66] The words 'plant and machinery' are more likely to be in the form of components or items of plant than the whole industrial plant.[67] Plant, however, is to be distinguished from the place or setting in which the business is carried on.[68]

[4.75] Where there is more than one activity on site, determining the nature of the 'primary activity' requires consideration of various things. For instance, who owns the site? Where there are two activities on site and the freeholder's activity is not excluded but the lease-holder's activity is excluded, this may favour the view that the primary activity is that of the freeholder. What is the purpose of the site? Where part of the site is given over to a company so that it may build and maintain a power generation plant, for example (excluded), but the purpose of that power generation plant is to service a paper mill (not excluded), the paper mill is likely to be considered the primary activity. What is the total percentage area of the excluded activity? If it is a small percentage area and the vast majority of the site is taken up by a non-excluded activity, then that is likely to be the primary activity. Ultimately it will be a matter of overall impression, rather than detailed examination, to determine the nature of the primary activity.[69]

[4.76] Operations held to fall within the scope of this exclusion are the construction of steelwork to the pipejacks and the pipebridges,[70] assembly and installation of pipework linking machinery at a bulk storage and processing plant for pharmaceuticals,[71] the supply and installation of insulation and cladding to pipework and boilers,[72] the growing of cucumbers,[73] the supply of scaffolding to provide temporary access and support to the structural

---

[64] *North Midland Construction v AE & E Lentjes Ltd* [2009] EWHC 1371 (TCC), per Ramsay J at [26].
[65] *ABB Zantingh Limited v Zedal Business Services Limited* [2001] BLR 66, per J Bowsher QC, at [33].
[66] *ABB Power v Norwest Holst Engineering Ltd* (2000) 77 ConLR 20, per Lloyd J at [17–20].
[67] *North Midland Construction v AE & E Lentjes Ltd* [2009] EWHC 1371 (TCC), per Ramsay J at [20].
[68] *Hortimax Ltd v Hedon Salads Ltd* (2004) 24 Const LJ 47, per Gilliland J at [8].
[69] *Laker Vent Engineering Ltd v Jacobs E&C Ltd* [2014] EWHC 1058 (TCC), per Ramsey J at [66–71].
[70] *Cleveland Bridge (UK) Ltd v Whessoe-Volker Stevin Joint Venture* [2010] EWHC 1076 (TCC), per Ramsey J at [33].
[71] *Homer Burgess Limited v Chirex (Annan) Limited* (No. 1) (1999) ConLR 245, per Lord MacFayden at [38–44].
[72] *ABB Power v Norwest Holst Engineering Ltd* (2000) 77 ConLR 20, per Lloyd J at [16].
[73] *Hortimax Ltd v Hedon Salads Ltd* (2004) 24 Const LJ 47, per Gilliland J at [5–20].

frame within which plant was located during the process of erection,[74] and pipework and equipment to boilers providing steam to a petrochemical plant on a neighbouring site.[75] All these decisions are based on the specific facts and circumstances of the case.

[4.77] Where a contract for the installation of fixtures in a building or structure relates to, but is not integrated into plant on a site where the primary activity was one within section 105(c)(ii), then it may not fall within the exclusion.[76]

4.6.6 Manufacture, delivery, installation (Act s. 105(2)(d))

[4.78] Subsection 105(2)(d) of the Act states the following operations are not construction operations:

> manufacture or delivery to site of—
>
> (i) building or engineering components or equipment,
> (ii) materials, plant or machinery, or
> (iii) components for systems of heating, lighting, air-conditioning, ventilation, power supply, drainage, sanitation, water supply or fire protection, or for security or communications systems,

[4.79] The purpose of this section is to exclude from construction operations the mere manufacture or delivery at site of components, except under a contract that also provides for their installation. This is because the Act is aimed at construction operations, and not mere contracts for the supply of goods.

[4.80] The authorities contain no successful attempts to argue that construction operations fall within this exception, but there are a number of failed attempts. These include the supply and installation of joinery items,[77] the supply and installation of insulation and cladding to pipework and boilers (although this fell within the exception at 105(2)(c),[78] crane and labour hire[79] and a contract for groundwork and drainage work.[80]

4.7 Excluded agreements

4.7.1 In a nutshell

[4.81] Whereas subsection 105(2) is aimed at the exclusion of construction operations, section 106 targets the exclusion of agreements. Subsection 106(1)(a) and (2) exclude agreements

---

[74] *Palmers Ltd v ABB Power Construction Ltd* [1999] BLR 426, per Thornton J at [24–42].
[75] *Petition of Mitsui Babcock Energy Services Ltd* [2001] ScotCS 150, per Milligan at [13–17].
[76] *Comsite Projects Ltd v Andritz AG* [2003] EWHC 958 (TCC), per Kirkham J at [29–39].
[77] *Millers Specialist Joinery Company Ltd v Nobles Construction Ltd* [2001] CILL 1770, per Gilliland J at [11].
[78] *ABB Power v Norwest Holst Engineering Ltd* (2000) 77 ConLR 20, per Lloyd J at [16].
[79] *Baldwins Industrial Service plc v Barr Ltd* [2002] EWHC 2915 (TCC), per Kirkham J at [22–23].
[80] *Edenbooth Ltd v Cre8 Developments Ltd* [2008] EWHC 570 (TCC), per Coulson J at [6–7].

with a residential occupier, where the agreement principally relates to operations on a dwelling which one of the parties to the contract (who has to be a natural person) occupies, or intends to occupy, as his residence.

[4.82] Subsection 106A of the 2009 Act permits the exclusion of any or all of the sections of the Act. This replaced subsection 106(1)(b) of the 1996 Act, which permits the Secretary of State to exclude further matters from the scope of the 1996 Act.

[4.83] The Construction Contracts (England and Wales) Exclusion Order 1998 (SI 1998/648) excludes agreements relating to highways, planning, NHS developments, certain other developments, PFI, certain finance and insurance. The Construction Contracts (England) Exclusion Order 2011 (SI 2011/2332) was also enacted, which provides a further exclusion in relation to PFI projects.

4.7.2 Residential occupier (Act s. 106(1)(a) and (2))

[4.84] Subsection 106(1)(a) and (2) exclude the application of the Act to residential occupiers:

> (1) This Part does not apply—
>   (a) to a construction contract with a residential occupier (see below)
>   ...
> (2) A construction contract with a residential occupier means a construction contract which principally relates to operations on a dwelling which one of the parties to the contract occupies, or intends to occupy, as his residence.
> In this subsection "dwelling" means a dwelling-house or a flat; and for this purpose—
> "dwelling-house" does not include a building containing a flat; and
> "flat" means separate and self-contained premises constructed or adapted for use for residential purposes and forming part of a building from some other part of which the premises are divided horizontally.

[4.85] This provision is aimed at ensuring that the Act does not apply where individuals instruct others to carry out work to their home (be it a house or flat). The purpose of this provision was helpfully described by Coulson J in this way:[81]

> Section 106 was intended to protect ordinary householders, not otherwise concerned with property or construction work, and without the resources of even relatively small contractors, from what was, in 1996, a new and untried system of dispute resolution. It was felt that what might be the swift and occasionally arbitrary process of construction adjudication should not apply to a domestic householder. In this way, s.106 excluded adjudication in respect of construction works carried out for those who occupied and would continue to occupy as their home the property that was the subject of the works (even if they had to move out when those works were carried out), or who had bought the property and intended to live there when the construction works were completed.

---

[81] *Westfields Construction Limited v Clive Lewis* [2013] EWHC 376, per Coulson J at [10; 58–60].

[4.86] The term 'intends to occupy' in subsection 106(2) has been held to connote an ongoing process which is to be assessed by reference to the occupier's present and future intent. It cannot be tested by reference to a single snapshot in time. 'Occupies' indicates that the homeowner occupies and will remain at (or intends to return to) the property.[82] A person cannot occupy (for the purpose of the Act), more than one property at once. The Act will only apply to the property that a person principally occupies, or intends to occupy. Whether an individual occupies will be a matter of fact given all the circumstances.[83]

[4.87] Subject to the foregoing paragraph, this section applies to individuals and not companies. It will therefore not apply to property development companies. Given the relative frequency with which residential properties are bought through a company as a way of managing an individual's tax liability, this rule is of some importance.[84]

[4.88] Parties may agree in their contract to adjudicate disputes, notwithstanding the exclusion at section 106.[85] In this case, the form of adjudication will be contractual,[86] rather than statutory (in other words, it will not be governed by the Act). All that is necessary is for the contract to contain an operable adjudication regime written or incorporated into the contract. For instance, in the context of residential works, the JCT produces a standard form contract, snappily entitled the 'JCT Standard Form of Building Contract for a Home Owner/Occupier Who has Appointed a Consultant to Oversee the Work', which has within it an adjudication agreement that the courts have accepted as valid.[87] Where this has been done, there are cases where residential occupiers have challenged the validity of the adjudication provisions on the basis that they fall foul of the Unfair Terms in Consumer Contracts Regulations 1999 (UTCCR). Those cases are considered as part of the section on UTCCR, at Section 18.4. In such cases, to avoid falling foul of UTCCR, the company engaging with the residential occupier will, inter alia, be required to draw the consequences of the adjudication process specifically to the individual's attention. Provided that this is done, the court will uphold the adjudication provisions.

4.7.3 Exclusion Order (2009 Act, s. 106A; 1996 Act, s. 106(1)(b))

[4.89] Subsection 106A of the 2009 Act provides as follows:

> (1) The Secretary of State may by order provide that any or all of the provisions of this Part, so far as extending to England and Wales, shall not apply to any description of construction contract relating to the carrying out of construction operations (not being operations in Wales) which is specified in the order.
>
> (2) The Welsh Ministers may by order provide that any or all of the provisions of this Part, so far as extending to England and Wales, shall not apply to any description of construction

---

[82] *Westfields Construction Limited v Clive Lewis* [2013] EWHC 376, per Coulson J at [11; 58–60].
[83] *Westfields Construction Limited v Clive Lewis* [2013] EWHC 376, per Coulson J at [9; 58–60].
[84] *Edenbooth Ltd v Cre8 Developments Ltd* [2008] EWHC 570 (TCC), per Coulson J at [8–13].
[85] *Lovell Projects Limited v Legg and Carver* [2003]BLR 452, per Moseley J, at [1].
[86] Contractual adjudications are considered at section 5.2.
[87] *Malcolm Charles Contracts Ltd v Mr Crispin and Mrs Zhang* [2014] EWHC 3898 (TCC), per Carr J at [82–83].

contract relating to the carrying out of construction operations in Wales which is specified in the order.
(3) The Scottish Ministers may by order provide that any or all of the provisions of this Part, so far as extending to Scotland, shall not apply to any description of construction contract which is specified in the order.
(4) An order under this section shall not be made unless a draft of it has been laid before and approved by resolution of-
   (a) in the case of an order under subsection (1), each House of Parliament;
   (b) in the case of an order under subsection (2), the National Assembly for Wales;
   (c) in the case of an order under subsection (3), the Scottish Parliament.

[4.90] Subsection 106A allows the Secretary of State to exclude all **or part** of Part II of the Act.

[4.91] Subsection 106(1)(b) of the 1996 Act provides:

(1) This Part does not apply—
...
(b) to any other description of construction contract excluded from the operation of this Part by order of the Secretary of State.

[4.92] This provision allowed the Secretary of State the power to exclude all of Part II of the 1996 Act (an all-or-nothing approach). It is thought that Parliament considered that this provision was too restrictive and that the Secretary of State should have a wider power, which is why subsection 106A was introduced in the 2009 Act.

[4.93] Pursuant to subsection 106(1)(b) of the 1996 Act, the Secretary of State passed the Construction Contracts (England and Wales) Exclusion Order 1998 (SI 1998/648). This extends the scope of excluded agreements as follows:[88]

- an agreement under section 38 (power of highway authorities to adopt by agreement) or section 278 (agreements as to execution of works) of the Highways Act 1980(1);
- an agreement under section 106 (planning obligations), 106A (modification or discharge of planning obligations) or 299A (Crown planning obligations) of the Town and Country Planning Act 1990(2);
- an agreement under section 104 of the Water Industry Act 1991(3) (agreements to adopt sewer, drain or sewage disposal works);
- an externally financed development agreement within the meaning of section 1 of the National Health Service (Private Finance) Act 1997(4);
- a contract entered into under the private finance initiative, within the meaning of the Order. Note that this only includes the top-level agreements with the government authority. It does not include the construction contracts for the performance of the works;
- a finance agreement within the meaning of the Order; and

---
[88] http://www.legislation.gov.uk/uksi/1998/648/made/data.pdf. Accessed on 1 September 2015.

- development agreements. The case of *Captiva Estates Ltd v Rybarn Ltd (in Administration)*[89] considered whether the granting of options for the grant of leases for 7 out of 28 flats in the development and a car park meant that the contract fell within this provision. The court referred to the wording of the exclusion, which states that a development agreement 'includes provision for the grant or disposal of a relevant interest in the land on which takes place the principle construction operations to which the contract relates.' The court held that the granting of an option for a lease fell within this wording. The interesting point on this case is that it illustrates that the scope of the Order with regard to development agreements is wide, and provides parties with a way of avoiding the Act so long as there is an option relating to a relevant interest in a minority part of a development.

[4.94] The Secretary of State amended the 1998 Exclusion Order by the Construction Contracts (England) Exclusion Order 2011 (SI 2011/2332) (the 2011 Exclusion Order).[90] The 2011 Exclusion Order applies to all contracts entered into on or after 1 October 2011. It states at paragraph 3:

> Private finance initiative subcontracts
>
> A construction contract is excluded from the operation of section 110(1A) of the Act if it is a contract pursuant to which a party to a relevant contract has sub-contracted to a third party some or all of its obligations under that contract to carry out, or arrange that others carry out, construction operations.

4.8 Contract in writing

4.8.1 In a nutshell

[4.95] For contracts entered into on or after 1 October 2011, there is no need for the contract to be in writing in order for it to fall within the scope of the 2009 Act. In other words, regardless of whether the contract is oral, partly oral, or varied orally, the 2009 Act will still apply, provided that the other conditions set out in this chapter are fulfilled.

[4.96] For contracts entered into before 1 October 2011, section 107 of the 1996 Act requires that, in order to fall within the scope of the 1996 Act, the construction contract must be in writing, by an exchange of communication in writing, or evidenced in writing. What those words have been held to mean is examined in this section, but a helpful starting point is perhaps the following extract from Ward LJ's judgment in *RJT Consulting Engineers Ltd v DM Engineering (NI) Ltd*,[91] which is the leading case in this area.

---

[89] [2005] EWHC 2744 (TCC), per Wilcox J at [10–18].
[90] http://www.legislation.gov.uk/uksi/2011/2332/made/data.pdf. Accessed on 1 September 2015.
[91] [2002] EWCA Civ 270, per Ward LJ at [19].

What has to be evidenced in writing is, literally, the agreement, which means all of it, not part of it. A record of the agreement also suggests a complete agreement, not a partial one.

[4.97] Where the 1996 Act applies, this is the final hurdle[92] in determining whether or not a contract falls within the scope of the 1996 Act. No doubt because of the length of the provision and the frequency with which contracts are concluded or varied orally, this section has given rise to scores of disputes since the 1996 Act was introduced. Sections 4.8.3–4.8.8 recite and interpret the subsections of section 107 and review some putative issues that have arisen. The cases dealing with these subsections are all listed in Appendix 8, by reference to the subsection of section 107 that they apply and by reference to a particular scenario.

4.8.2 2009 Act

[4.98] Construction contracts entered into on or after 1 October 2011 do not need to be in writing in order to fall within the scope of the 2009 Act. This means that oral or partly oral construction contracts fall within the scope of the 2009 Act.[93]

[4.99] While procrastination as to the benefits or otherwise of the deletion of section 107 of the 1996 Act are now academic, it is instructive to refer to a quote taken from *RJT Consulting Engineers Ltd v DM Engineering (NI) Ltd*.[94]

> writing is important because it provides certainty. Certainty is all the more important when adjudication is envisaged to have to take place under a demanding timetable. The adjudicator has to start with some certainty as to what the terms of the contract are.

[4.100] Notwithstanding this compelling explanation as to why section 107 was inserted, the driving force behind the amendments appears to have been that section 107 was acting as a barrier to a significant part of the industry. There is a vast array of construction work pursuant to partly written and partly oral agreement or without any written agreement at all. Often, work is carried out by small companies or one-man-bands who need prompt payment from their employers and who need quick and cheap access to justice.

[4.101] The absence of this requirement means that adjudicators, now more than ever, have to determine issues about the formation and terms of contracts in addition to the legal and technical issues in the substantive dispute. Determining contractual issues may involve the adjudicator hearing witness evidence at an oral hearing to allow the credibility of the conflicting accounts to be tested.

---

[92] See the overview to this chapter for a list.
[93] This is explained in more detail at Section 4.8.
[94] [2002] EWCA Civ 270, per Ward LJ at [12].

4.8.3 1996 Act only applies to agreements in writing (1996 Act s. 107(1))

[4.102] Subsection 107(1) of the 1996 Act provides:

> The provisions of this Part apply only where the construction contract is in writing, and any other agreement between the parties as to any matter is effective for the purposes of this Part only if in writing.
>
> The expressions "agreement", "agree" and "agreed" shall be construed accordingly.

[4.103] The purpose behind this introductory provision was explained in this way.[95]

> Section 107(1) limits the application of the Act to construction contracts which are in writing or to other agreements which are effective for the purposes of that part of the Act only if in writing. This must be seen against the background which led to the introduction of this change. In its origin it was an attempt to force the industry to submit to a standard form of contract. That did not succeed but writing is still important and writing is important because it provides certainty. Certainty is all the more important when adjudication is envisaged to have to take place under a demanding timetable. The adjudicator has to start with some certainty as to what the terms of the contract are.

[4.104] For a contract to be in writing for the purpose of the 1996 Act, it must contain the 'material'[96] terms of a contract. These are the identity of the parties, price, time for performance and scope of work.[97] However, where the price is not expressly stated in the agreement, but reference is made to another document, such as a costings book that does not form part of the contract, then that may be sufficient, depending on the certainty of the words used.[98]

[4.105] The 1996 Act does not prescribe any requirements as to the time the agreement in writing needs to be evidenced, nor is there a requirement that the evidence needs to have been communicated by one party to another.[99]

4.8.4 'In writing' (1996 Act s. 107(2))

[4.106] Subsection 107(2) of the 1996 Act provides:

> There is an agreement in writing—
> (a) if the agreement is made in writing (whether or not it is signed by the parties),
> (b) if the agreement is made by exchange of communications in writing, or
> (c) if the agreement is evidenced in writing.

---

[95] *RJT Consulting Engineers Ltd v DM Engineering* (NI) *Ltd* [2002] BLR 217 CA, per Ward LJ at [12].
[96] *Lloyd Projects Ltd v John Malnick* [2005] AdjLR 07/22, per Kirkham J at [55].
[97] *Hart v Investments Ltd v Fidler* [2006] EWHC 2857 (TCC), Coulson J, at [60].
[98] *Murray Building Services v Spree Developments* [2004] AdjLR 07/30, per Raynor J at [11–15].
[99] *Westdawn Refurbishments Ltd v Roselodge Ltd* [2006] AdjLR 04/24, per McCahill J at [22].

[4.107] The Court of Appeal has interpreted this subsection as follows:[100]

> Section 107(2) gives three categories where the agreement is to be treated in writing. The first is where the agreement, whether or not it is signed by the parties, is made in writing. That must mean where the agreement is contained in a written document which stands as a record of the agreement and all that was contained in the agreement. The second category, an exchange of communications in writing, likewise is capable of containing all that needs to be known about the agreement. One is therefore led to believe by what used to be known as the eiusdem generis rule that the third category will be to the same effect namely that the evidence in writing is evidence of the whole agreement.

[4.108] In the majority of cases, parties will agree between them the terms of a contract in writing. That contract will – provided it contains all the essential terms of a contract – be a contract in writing within the meaning of subsection 107(2)(a). From time to time, contracts are agreed not on the basis of a single 'formal' contract, but by an exchange of letters or emails. Where all the essential terms of contract are contained in those exchanges, there will be a contract in writing within the meaning of subsection 107(2)(b). Finally, the parties may agree the terms of the contract orally, begin work, and then at some stage later record the terms of the oral agreement in writing, be it in a formal contract, meeting minutes or something else. It is then necessary to analyse the relevant documents in order to ascertain whether it can be said that a contract was evidenced from those documents. It if can, then there will be a contract evidenced in writing within the meaning of 107(2)(c).

4.8.5 An agreement made 'otherwise than in writing' (1996 Act s. 107(3))

[4.109] Subsection 107(3) of the 1996 Act provides:

> Where parties agree otherwise than in writing by reference to terms which are in writing, they make an agreement in writing

[4.110] This provision might apply to a circumstance where parties agree the terms of a contract in a framework agreement or call-off contract, where the nature of the work to be done is unchanged. The essential terms of the contract may already be pre-agreed and the parties bind themselves to them when, either by an exchange of written communication, orally or by their conduct, they commit to be bound by them in respect of work to be done.

[4.111] Where an oral agreement is made, it will not be possible for the parties to assimilate that agreement into a previously agreed written agreement so as to assert that the oral agreement is in writing. In that case, the oral agreement will, save where it is permitted within the contract (such as a variation of work), constitute an oral variation of the previous written contract and will not be an agreement to which the 1996 Act applies.[101]

---

[100] *RJT Consulting Engineers Ltd v DM Engineering (NI) Ltd* [2002] BLR 217 CA, per Ward LJ at [13].
[101] *Carillion Construction Ltd v Devonport Royal Dockyard Ltd* [2003] BLR 79, per Bowsher J at [32].

4.8.6 An agreement 'evidenced in writing' (1996 Act s. 107(4))

[4.112] Subsection 107(4) of the 1996 Act provides:

> An agreement is evidenced in writing if an agreement made otherwise than in writing is recorded by one of the parties, or by a third party, with the authority of the parties to the agreement.

[4.113] The court has said:[102]

> What is contemplated is, thus, a record (which by subsection (6) can be in writing or a record by any means) of everything which has been said. Again it is a record of the whole agreement.

[4.114] This subsection works hand in hand with subsection 107(2)(c), which states that an agreement may be 'evidenced in writing' to fall within the scope of the 1996 Act. The evidence documenting the existence of a contract need not be contained all in one document, nor is there a requirement for when the evidence needs to be made.[103]

[4.115] However, the section is not expressed to be a definition setting out what was meant by the words 'evidenced in writing'. Its intention is only to state that an agreement will be evidenced in writing where it has been recorded by a person with the authority of the parties. It does not limit the way in which an agreement may be evidenced in writing to those ways set out in the clause. This subsection is intended to widen the ambit of what is to be regarded as an agreement evidenced in writing, not restrict it.[104]

[4.116] This provision would apply, as it did in *Connex South Eastern Ltd v MJ Building Services Group plc*,[105] where the parties reach a binding agreement in a meeting, and minutes were taken of the agreement. Those minutes constitute evidence within the meaning of this subsection and subsection 107(2)(c).

4.8.7 'An exchange of written submissions in adjudication proceedings' (1996 Act s. 107(5))

[4.117] Subsection 107(5) of the 1996 Act provides:

> An exchange of written submissions in adjudication proceedings, or in arbitral or legal proceedings in which the existence of an agreement otherwise than in writing is alleged by one party against another party and not denied by the other party in his response constitutes as between those parties an agreement in writing to the effect alleged.

---

[102] *RJT Consulting Engineers Ltd v DM Engineering (NI) Ltd* [2002] BLR 217 CA, per Ward LJ at [15].
[103] *PT Building v ROK Build Ltd* [2008] EWHC 3434, per Ramsey J at [41].
[104] *Millers Specialist Joinery Company Ltd v Nobles Construction Ltd* [2001] CILL 1770, per Gilliland J at [13].
[105] [2004] EWHC 1518 (TCC), per Havery J at [24].

[4.118] What is meant by the expression 'an exchange of written submissions in adjudication proceedings, or in arbitral or legal proceedings' is a reference to written submissions made in the current adjudication proceedings, or to any arbitral or legal proceedings (presumably either on foot or prior).[106] It is not a reference to prior adjudication proceedings.[107] The subsection may also apply to court enforcement proceedings.[108]

[4.119] This subsection is drafted so as to prevent a responding party, who has accepted the adjudicator's jurisdiction notwithstanding the absence of a clear contract in writing, from going back on its concession.[109]

4.8.8 Scenarios

[4.120] In addition to considering each of the subsections of section 107 separately, it may also be helpful to consider some putative scenarios in which section 107 has been applied. Selected cases are cited in each scenario and the remainder are listed at Appendix 8.

(A) Oral Contracts

[4.121] Oral contracts are outside the scope of the 1996 Act. Given the relative frequency with which contracts are agreed orally, it is unsurprising that there are a number of court decisions seeking to interpret the meaning of section 107. Care must be taken to ascertain whether the oral agreement was later evidenced in writing. If so, pursuant to subsection 107(4), it will constitute a contract in writing. The court offered the following guidance:

> It is always necessary to determine whether a so-called agreement made orally was in reality expected or intended to be binding as between the parties. Thus, the parties having discussed and agreed something orally might later have reduced their agreement into writing in such a way as to supersede the earlier oral agreement. A later oral agreement may not be binding; for instance, it may lack consideration or otherwise may not be intended to be binding.[110]

[4.122] By way of example, in *Millers Specialist Joinery Company Ltd v Nobles Construction Ltd*,[111] the court found that although the contract had been agreed orally, the essential terms were later recorded in a letter between the parties. The letter was therefore a contract in writing for the purpose of the 1996 Act.

---

[106] *Naylor Construction Services Ltd v Acoustafoam Ltd* [2010] All ER (D) 138, per Grant J at [49].
[107] *Glendalough Associated SA v Harris Calnan Construction Co Ltd* EWHC 3142 (TCC), per Edwards-Stuart J at [34].
[108] *Sprunt Limited v London Borough of Camden* [2011] EWHC 3191(TCC), per Akenhead J at [41].
[109] *SG South v Swan Yard (Cirencester)* [2010] EWHC 376 (TCC), per Coulson J at [11–12].
[110] *Allen Wilson Joinery Ltd v Privetgrange Construction Ltd* [2008] EWHC 2802 (TCC), per Akenhead J at [27].
[111] [2001] CILL 1770, per Gilliland J at [12–13].

(B) One or more terms not agreed, or agreed orally

[4.123] There are a number of cases where one party alleges that not all of the essential terms were in writing, because one of the essential terms has not been agreed at all or because it was agreed orally.[112]

[4.124] There need only be all the essential terms in writing for a contract to be formed. The fact that the terms of the contract, as evidenced in writing, are vestigial, being two lines' worth, does not matter for the purposes of the 1996 Act.

(C) Oral variations

[4.125] Variations permitted by the contract, such as a variation to the scope of work are within the confines of the written agreement and fall within the scope of the 1996 Act.[113]

[4.126] There is a view by some that a contract will fall outside of the scope of the 1996 Act when there is an oral variation that is fundamental (i.e. not trivial) to the terms of the main contract. This is incorrect, it is submitted. In *RJT Consulting Engineers Limited v DM Engineering (NI) Limited*,[114] Lord Justice Ward pointed out that adjudication would be 'emasculated' if an adjudicator appointed in relation to a dispute under a contract could be deprived of jurisdiction simply by a subsequent oral variation to an otherwise written contract.[115] In *Carillion Construction Limited v Devonport Royal Dockyard*,[116] HHJ Bowsher QC held that an oral variation did indeed take the contract outside the scope of the Act. It is submitted that this is wrongly decided. Subsequent variations, in whatever form, do not affect the adjudicator's jurisdiction provided only that there remains a 'founding' construction contract satisfying section 107 for the adjudicator to be appointed under. This is consistent with the court's approach to construing adjudicator's jurisdiction over alleged settlement agreements where, properly analysed, it can be said that what is alleged is simply that the parties have varied a 'section 107 contract' to fix a given price or settle a particular dispute. See the approach of Ramsey J in *L. Brown & Sons Ltd v Crosby Homes (North West) Ltd*,[117] which is consistent with this analysis.

[4.127] Arguments to the contrary – namely that there must **at all times** be a contract in writing, and that section 107 ceases to apply to any agreement once it is **subsequently** the subject of an alleged oral variation – are based on a misreading of *RJT*, it is submitted. Not only did Ward LJ say precisely the opposite (see above), but it is also important to remember that what the Court of Appeal was dealing with in *RJT* was a situation where there was no clear written contract at all, merely swathes of documents which might be said to

---

[112] *Euro Construction Scaffolding Ltd v SLLB Construction Ltd* [2008] EWHC 3160 (TCC), per Akenhead J at [30].
[113] *Carillion Construction Ltd v Devonport Royal Dockyard* [2003] BLR 79, per Bowsher J at [31–35].
[114] [2002] BLR 217 CA, per Ward LJ at [11].
[115] See also *Dean and Dyball Construction Ltd v Kenneth Grubb* [2003] EWHC 2465, per Seymour J at [16].
[116] [2003] BLR 79, per Bowsher J at [31–35].
[117] [2005] EWHC 3503 (TCC), per Ramsey J at [49–55]

Statutory adjudication 73

evidence a contract, which is a different situation altogether (and the mischief that section 107 was trying to catch, because it was thought that adjudicators should not be required to spend a significant amount of the 28-day referral period working out what the contract was in the first place).

(D) Trivial terms

[4.128] A failure to record in writing trivial or minor details will not normally exclude the contract from the scope of the 1996 Act.[118] Whether a contractual right or obligation is trivial is to be assessed objectively in the context of the contract as a whole and the parties concerned. There is no fixed rule in this regard: what may be trivial in one contract may not be in another.[119]

(E) Implied terms

[4.129] Terms implied by statute (such as fitness for purpose) do not convert an otherwise written construction contract into a partly oral contract. Most construction contracts contain implied terms, and it would be an odd state of affairs if an implied term took what was otherwise a 1996 Act compliant contract outside of the scope of the 1996 Act.[120] There is a question as to whether terms not implied by statute, such as a term arising through a previous course of dealing, or terms implied to give the contract business efficacy, or a term that needs to be implied into an agreement so that it is a binding contract should move a contract outside of the scope of the 1996 Act. While there are *obiter dicta* remarks to suggest that such terms would move a contract outside of the scope of the 1996 Act,[121] the current law[122] is that these types of implied terms are not to be distinguished for the purposes of determining whether a contract is writing.

(F) Letters of intent

[4.130] A letter of intent can amount to a construction contract in writing, providing all the essential terms required for a contract to exist are in writing and the work falls within the scope of the Act. The essential terms are the identity of the parties, the scope of work, the price and the time for completion.[123] All the terms were not in writing in *RJT*

---

[118] *Westdawn Refurbishments Ltd v Roselodge Ltd* [2006] AdjLR 04/24, per McCahill J at [22].
[119] *Allen Wilson Joinery Ltd v Privetgrange Construction Ltd* [2008] EWHC 2802 (TCC), per Akenhead J at [27].
[120] *Rok Buildings Ltd v Bestwood Carpentry Ltd* [2010] EWHC 1409 (TCC), per Akenhead J at [29].
[121] *Galliford Try Construction Ltd v Michael Heal Associates Ltd* [2003] EWHC 2886 (TCC), per Seymour J at [29].
[122] *Allen Wilson Joinery Ltd v Privetgrange Construction Ltd* [2008] EWHC 2802 (TCC), per Akenhead J at [28–30].
[123] *Glendalough Associated SA v Harris Calnan Construction Co Ltd* [2013] EWHC 3142 (TCC), per Edwards-Stuart J at [47].

Consulting Engineers Ltd v DM Engineering (Northern Ireland) Ltd[124] and *Bennett (Electrical) Services Ltd v Inviron Ltd*,[125] but were in writing in *Harris Calnan Construction Co Ltd v Ridgewood (Kensington) Ltd*.[126] In the last case, the judge said that the letter of intent demonstrated that there was a complete agreement as to the parties, and the adjudicator had been right to conclude, 'there was nothing left to be said'.

[4.131] Certain letters of intent are headed 'subject to contract'. Save in exceptional circumstances, an arrangement made subject to contract means that exchange of a formal written contract is a condition precedent to legal liability, meaning that a contract will not be said to be formed.[127]

4.9 Checklist: What form of adjudication am I subject to?

> Before commencing the task of preparing the necessary papers and submissions for commencing adjudication, it is important to establish what form of adjudication the parties will be subject to. Is the form of adjudication statutory (i.e. does the Act apply to the contract between the parties), or contractual (i.e. where the Act does not apply)? A consideration of the following list of questions should provide an answer.
>
> (1) Does the 1996 Act or 2009 Act apply (Section 4.2)?
> (2) Is there a binding contract between the parties (Section 4.3)?
> (3) Are the works required by the contract are within the scope of works listed in section 104 and 105(1) of the Act (Section 4.4)?
> (4) Are the works required by the contract excluded by virtue of section 105(2) and 106 of the Act (Section 4.5–4.7)?
> (5) Where the 1996 Act applies (and not the 2009 Act), is the whole contract in writing (section 4.8)?
>
> If the answer to the question 2 is no, adjudication will not be available at all. If the answer to any of questions 1, 3, 4 or 5 is no, then provided the contract has an operable adjudication procedure, the form of adjudication will be contractual (section 5.2). If the answer to all these questions is yes, the Act will apply and the form of adjudication will be statutory.

---

[124] [2002] EWCA Civ 270, per Ward LJ at [18].
[125] [2007] EWHC 49 (TCC), per Wilcox J at [29–32].
[126] [2007] EWHC 2738 (TCC) per Coulson J at [10–12].
[127] *Bennett (Electrical) Services Ltd v Inviron Ltd* [2007] EWHC 49, per Wilcox J at [15].

Chapter 5
Contractual and ad hoc adjudication

5.1 Overview

[5.01] There are three forms of adjudication: statutory, contractual and ad hoc.

[5.02] The form of adjudication may be termed statutory where the contract between the parties is governed by the Act. At its simplest, a contract will be governed by the Act where the subject matter falls within the meaning of 'construction contract' as defined by the Act, the subject matter is not excluded by one or more exclusion provisions, and for contracts dated before 1 October 2011, the whole contract is in writing.

[5.03] Contractual adjudication means adjudication where the contract is outside of the scope of the Act, but the parties have nevertheless agreed to adjudicate their disputes by inserting an adjudication procedure into the contract.

[5.04] Ad hoc adjudication means adjudication where the parties have agreed, or are deemed to have agreed, to submit their dispute, without an effective reservation, to adjudication thereby giving an adjudicator ad hoc jurisdiction to decide the dispute in circumstances where the Act does not apply and where there is no pre-existing contractual agreement to adjudicate.

[5.05] This chapter examines the circumstances where the parties can be said to have agreed or submitted to a contractual or ad hoc form of adjudication and explains some of the key features of both forms. The circumstances giving rise to statutory adjudication are examined in Chapter 4.

5.2 Contractual adjudication

5.2.1 In a nutshell

[5.06] An adjudication can be said to be contractual where the contract agreed by the parties is not one that falls within the scope of the Act, but nonetheless the parties have agreed in their contract a mechanism by which they can adjudicate disputes. Beyond providing a method of resolving disputes, inserting or referring to an adjudication procedure into

---

A Practical Guide to Construction Adjudication, First Edition. James Pickavance.
© 2016 James Pickavance. Published 2016 by John Wiley & Sons, Inc.

[5.07] Where the form of adjudication is contractual, none of the provisions of the Act apply. So for instance, there will be no right to refer a dispute to adjudication 'at any time',[1] unless the adjudication rules provide that right. It will also not be necessary for the agreement between the parties (where that agreement is entered into before 1 October 2011) to be entirely in writing as required by section 107 of the Act.

[5.08] The approach of the court when considering contractual and statutory forms of adjudication is likely to be the same.

5.2.2 What is a contractual adjudication?

[5.09] The Act makes adjudication mandatory for contracts that fall within its scope. While a contract may fall outside the scope of the Act, in other words the subject matter is not a construction operation (subsection 105(1) of the Act) or if it is an excluded construction operation or agreement (subsection 105(2) and section 106 of the Act), should parties wish to provide for disputes to be referred to adjudication as part of the contract's dispute resolution mechanism, this is perfectly permissible.[2] For example, a contract for the drilling for, or extraction of, oil or natural gas would ordinarily be exempt from the provisions of the Act owing to subsection 105(1)(a), but if the parties to that contract wish to adjudicate disputes, all they need do is either insert into the contract or refer to a set of adjudication rules that allows them to do this. This form of adjudication can be described as 'contractual' as opposed to 'statutory'. This is the term used by HHJ Thornton QC in *Steve Domsalla (trading as Domsalla Building Services) v Kenneth Dyason*,[3] although it may be thought apt to mislead; 'statutory' adjudications are ultimately contractual in nature too; either the parties insert their own adjudication mechanism into their contract or the Scheme applies as a set of mandatory implied terms; see subsection 114(4) of the Act.

[5.10] Contracts for operations within the scope of the Act must contain an adjudication procedure which complies with certain rules as to the timing and conduct of the adjudication, pursuant to subsections 108(1)–(4);[4] in the event that they do not so comply, the contractual adjudication provisions are void and the Scheme applies. However, contracts that are outside of the scope of the Act, but nevertheless contain a mechanism in the contract for adjudicating disputes are not so restricted. In effect, a purely voluntary contractual adjudication regime inserted by the parties is simply an agreement to be temporarily bound by an interim expert determiner pending litigation or arbitration. Indeed, adjudication

---
[1] See subsection 108(1).
[2] *Lovell Projects Limited v Legg and Carver* [2003] BLR 452, per Moseley J at [1].
[3] [2007] EWHC 1174 (TCC) at [98].
[4] Although the Act specifically contemplates contracts which 'straddle' construction operations and non-construction operations, in which event only disputes about the former are subject to mandatory statutory adjudication. See section 4.4.5.

Contractual and ad hoc adjudication

as a whole can be thought of in these terms; the only differences are that for statutory adjudication, provision for such interim-binding expert determination is mandatory and there are certain mandatory preconditions that must be met before the adjudication can be commenced.

[5.11] One such mandatory precondition for all contracts entered into prior to 1 October 2011 is that the 1996 Act excludes contracts that are not wholly in writing or evidenced in writing pursuant to section 107. However, parties to a contract entered into before that date that is partly oral, or which is later varied orally, may still adjudicate their disputes if there is a functioning adjudication procedure contained within the written part of the contract. This was the case in *Treasure & Son Ltd v Martin Dawes*,[5] where an oral variation to the JCT 1998 form of contract took it outside of the scope of the Act, but because the contract contained an adjudication procedure, the parties were still entitled to adjudicate the dispute. To put it another way, by inserting an adjudication procedure into the contract, it does not matter whether the requirements for statutory adjudication are met, because the adjudication procedure acts as a safety net allowing the adjudication to proceed as a contractual form of dispute resolution.

[5.12] Similarly in *Dean & Dyball v Kenneth Grubb Associates*,[6] the court found that because the contract contained a clause permitting disputes to be adjudicated under the CIC model adjudication procedure, it was open to the parties to adjudicate their dispute on that basis, whether or not the requirements of section 107 (in that case) had been met. In *Linnett v Halliwells*,[7] the court said:

> Where the parties have provided for adjudication in their contract by the provisions of Clause 41A then there is an express provision which contains an enforceable adjudication provision. On that basis it does not matter, in my judgment, whether [the underlying] agreement is made in writing, orally or partly orally and in writing.

5.2.3 Treatment of contractual adjudications by the court

[5.13] There is a question over how the courts will consider challenges to the decisions of adjudicators where the adjudication is a voluntary contractual regime in the sense described above, as opposed to a mandatory statutory adjudication. In *Steve Domsalla t/a Domsalla Building Services v Kenneth Dyason*,[8] Thornton J referred to a governing principle of statutory adjudication which allows adjudicators to make errors of law or fact in arriving at or in the decision. This is commonly referred to as the 'unreviewable error doctrine'. The judge said that the unreviewable error doctrine:

> arises because of the statutory underpinning of adjudication and so as to give effect to the statutory policy of maintaining a contractor's cash flow. A consumer contract is not subject to that

---

[5] [2007] EWHC 2420 (TCC), per Akenhead J at [31].
[6] [2003] EWHC 2465, per Seymour J at [16–18].
[7] [2009] EWHC 319, per Ramsey J at [108].
[8] [2007] EWHC 1174 (TCC), per Thornton J at [99].

statutory policy and, instead, is subject to the law of contract as it exists in the absence of the provisions of the HGCRA.

[5.14] Taking this argument further, it can be said that Parliament ordained that the Act, together with the policies and motivations on which it was founded, would only ever apply to carefully defined categories of work. The Act is not supposed to apply in any way to work falling outside of its scope, and indeed parties to contracts not within the scope of the Act may well not wish to be subject to the same policies and interests under which the Act was formed. For contractual adjudications, the bargain struck between the parties as recorded in the terms of the contract should be foremost in the court's mind, over and above any considerations or policies that are applied in the context of statutory adjudication.

[5.15] However, this line of argument seems to have found little traction with the courts since *Domsalla*, who have tended towards the view that the principles and policies underpinning contractual and statutory adjudications should be the same. Thus in the Scottish case of *Fleming Builders Ltd v Forrest or Hives*[9] the court could see:

> ...no justification for a distinction between the way in which the Court will approach the decision of an adjudicator who has dealt with a dispute under the Act and the Scheme, and the way in which the Court will deal with an adjudicator who has dealt with a dispute under this contract.

[5.16] In *RWE Npower plc v Alstom Power Ltd*,[10] the court sought to limit the effect of that part of the judgment in *Domsalla*. The parties entered into a contract, the subject of which fell outside of the scope of the Act. The contract contained a dispute resolution procedure that referred disputes to adjudication with the rules of the Scheme to apply. The court held that an informed bystander would conclude that, by choosing to incorporate the Scheme as opposed to bespoke provisions, the parties must have intended to import into the contract the Parliamentary intention underlying the Scheme unless there are background matters or wording that compels a different conclusion. Similarly in *Lovell Projects Limited v Legg and Carver*,[11] the court determined that the adjudication was one to which the Act did not apply. However, because the contract contained similar provisions modelled on the Act, 'the principle [that an adjudicator's decision must be paid without set-off] applies to this contract to the same extent as it applies to contracts falling within the ambit of the Act.'

[5.17] The judge in *Amec Group Ltd v Thames Water Utilities Ltd*[12] arguably went further. Coulson J said that there is 'no difference in principle in the status of a decision provided by an adjudicator pursuant to the Act, and a decision provided pursuant to a contractual mechanism,' although it is unclear whether the judge was referring to contractual

---

[9] [2008] ScotCS CSOH_103, per Lord Menzies at [105].
[10] [2009] EWHC 1192 (QB), per Havelock-Allan J at [84–89].
[11] [2003] BLR 452, per Moseley J at [36–41].
[12] [2010] EWHC 419 (TCC), per Coulson J at [24].

adjudications outside of the scope of the Act, or to adjudications subject to the Act which are governed by contractual rules.

[5.18] Thus, it would seem that any argument to the effect that contractual adjudication should be treated differently from statutory adjudication might be difficult to win. It might be said that there are good reasons for such a difficulty. Adjudication is now well-established (and overwhelmingly popular) part of the dispute resolution machinery for the construction industry, underpinned by a very substantial body of case law setting out when an adjudicator's decision will and will not be enforced. There is a compelling argument for saying that parties who voluntarily sign up to adjudication must be taken to have agreed that they would take those principles as they find them; and that applying the same principles across the board promotes certainty of outcome, which is obviously highly desirable and reduces the scope for dispute.

5.3 Ad hoc adjudication

5.3.1 In a nutshell

[5.19] An adjudication is said to be 'ad hoc' where the parties have agreed, or are deemed to have agreed to submit their dispute, without reservation, to adjudication thereby giving an adjudicator ad hoc jurisdiction to decide the dispute in circumstances where the Act does not apply and where there is no pre-existing contractual agreement to adjudicate. Whether or not the courts will enforce an ad hoc adjudication will depend on the nature of the agreement and the timing and scope of any reservation on that agreement.

5.3.2 Ad hoc adjudication by choice

[5.20] The conferring of ad hoc jurisdiction on an adjudicator to decide a dispute between two parties in circumstances where there is no pre-existing contractual agreement to adjudicate is perfectly permissible. In *Nordot Engineering Services v Siemens*,[13] Gilliland J said:

> If parties with their eyes open enter into an agreement to the effect that 'The adjudicator will decide this question and we will be bound by his decision', why should the court not give effect to that agreement? There can be no public policy against that and the mere fact that the system of adjudication is established by statute does not, it seems to me, make any difference.

[5.21] The parties will need to agree between them the rules of the adjudication that they will follow before the adjudication can commence. Provided that the adjudication commences without objection from either party as to the validity of the adjudicator's jurisdiction to determine the dispute, neither party will be able to argue that the adjudicator's

---

[13] [2001] CILL 1778, per Gilliland J at [17].

decision should not be enforced on the basis that the adjudicator did not have jurisdiction to preside over the dispute.

[5.22] Where the contract between the parties is not a construction contract within the meaning of the Act, evidently it is unnecessary to adhere to the requirements of the Act when agreeing the precise wording of the rules that will govern the adjudication. In *Khurana and another v Webster Construction Ltd*,[14] Khurana was a residential owner and therefore the contract between the parties fell outside of the scope of the Act. There were no adjudication provisions in the contract. The parties fell into dispute and, partly as a result of poor dispute resolution provisions in the contract, they decided to adjudicate. The parties decided to adopt the rules of the Scheme, except that they agreed, contrary to paragraph 23 of the Scheme and section 108(3) of the Act, that the adjudicator's decision would be final and binding. Khurana subsequently commenced court proceedings to in effect overturn an adjudicator's decision. The court dismissed the court action, holding that while the decision of an adjudication in a statutory form of adjudication is only temporarily binding, it was perfectly permissible for the parties to agree that the adjudicator's decision in this instance was final and binding.

5.3.3 Ad hoc jurisdiction by mistake

[5.23] The validity of the adjudicator's jurisdiction to determine a dispute is less clear where the decision to adjudicate the dispute was, either by one or both parties, made on the erroneous belief that the Act applied to the contract and therefore the right to adjudicate was mandatory. Where the Act does not apply and there is no contractual agreement to adjudicate, the right to adjudicate will not exist unless the parties agree. That agreement may be express, or it may be implied by conduct. Where agreement is found, the parties will have conferred ad hoc jurisdiction on the adjudicator to decide the dispute. The court's view on what action or inaction is necessary to express or imply agreement seems to have developed since the coming into force of the 1996 Act. The early authorities suggest that it was not particularly onerous to confer jurisdiction to the extent that it may even occur before or at the start of the adjudication. For example, a letter confirming a party's agreement to the identity of the adjudicator and the rules of the adjudication,[15] or one that states 'we will, however, abide by your decision in this matter'[16] was, on the facts, enough to demonstrate an intent to expressly grant ad hoc jurisdiction on the adjudicator.

[5.24] In *Project Consultancy Group v Trustees of the Gray Trust*,[17] the Trustees had communicated as follows:

> The Act cannot apply and your Notice of Reference to Adjudication is invalid. We suggest that in the circumstances adjudication is inappropriate and enquire whether you intend to

---

[14] [2015] EWHC 758 (TCC), per Davies J at [35–36].
[15] *Galliford Try Construction Ltd v Michael Heal Associates Ltd* [2003] EWHC 2886, per Seymour J at [39–44].
[16] *Nordot Engineering Services Ltd v Siemens plc* [2001] CILL 1778, per Gilliland J at [11–30].
[17] [1999] BLR 377, per Dyson J at [10–15].

withdraw the Reference. If however your client proceeds with adjudication, our client shall dispute the Adjudicator's jurisdiction. If the Adjudicator makes a decision notwithstanding the objection to jurisdiction, our clients will not comply with any award made on the basis that it was made without jurisdiction. These issues will be placed before the Court should your client issue any application for enforcement of the Adjudicator's award. Without prejudice to the above, if you proceed with the adjudication, we reserve our clients' rights generally, and in particular to appear and present their case to the Adjudicator.

[5.25] The court noted that the Trustees had 'stated in the clearest terms' that they objected to the adjudicator's jurisdiction and that it has maintained its jurisdictional objection throughout the adjudication.

[5.26] In the Court of Appeal case of *Thomas-Fredric's (Construction) Ltd v Wilson*,[18] Brown LJ referred to the first instance decision of Gilliland J, in which he stated (agreeing with the decision in *Project Consultancy*) that it is possible for there to be an ad hoc submission to the jurisdiction of the adjudicator, but that this depends on the fair reading and interpretation of the correspondence which passed between the parties. The judge relied on a letter from Thomas which said 'We will, however, abide by your decision in this matter and will comply with whatever direction you deem appropriate' to assert that this conveyed a 'clear and... unequivocal' submission to the adjudicator's jurisdiction and that Thomas was 'agreeing to be bound by that decision (subject to any later challenge)'.

[5.27] However, Brown LJ said that it was 'impossible to conclude from these facts and documents that the appellant was submitting to the jurisdiction of the adjudicator in the full sense', concluding that the position was very similar to that taken by the Trustees in *Project Consultancy*. In giving his decision, Brown LJ summarised the position on ad hoc jurisdiction in two propositions:[19]

(1) If a defendant to a Part 24(2) application has submitted to the adjudicator's jurisdiction in the full sense of having agreed not only that the adjudicator should rule on the issue of jurisdiction but also that he would then be bound by that ruling, then he is liable to enforcement in the short term, even if the adjudicator was plainly wrong on the issue.
(2) Even if the defendant has not submitted to the adjudicator's jurisdiction in that sense, then he is still liable to a Part 24(2) summary judgment upon the award if the adjudicator's ruling on the jurisdictional issue was plainly right.

[5.28] More recent authorities tend not to have found that there was an ad hoc agreement except where the terms of the agreement are clear. For instance, an email from a party stating that it was unrepresented and unfamiliar with the adjudication process was not enough to give the adjudicator jurisdiction.[20] However, each case is fact and context specific.

[5.29] Where a party does not consider that the adjudicator has jurisdiction to preside over the dispute, but is not prepared to 'bet the ranch' on that conclusion, it may agree to take

---

[18] [2003] EWCA Civ 1494, per Brown LJ at [29–34].
[19] Ibid at [33].
[20] *Clark Electrical Ltd v JMD Developments (UK) Ltd* [2012] EWHC 2627 (TCC) per Behrens J at [24; 32–37].

part in an adjudication, but under the protest that it does not or may not consider that the adjudicator has jurisdiction to decide the dispute because the Act does not apply to the contract and there is no contractual adjudication mechanism in the contract. The protest is termed 'reserving the position' on the adjudicator's jurisdiction and, if done correctly, will mean that the protesting party can challenge the adjudicator's jurisdiction after the adjudication has taken place and, if the challenge is successful, the adjudicator's decision will be nullified. To reserve the position on the adjudicator's jurisdiction, the party must communicate the reservation to the adjudicator and the other party at the outset of the adjudication (preferably in writing) and then maintain it (i.e. keep repeating the reservation in any submission made) throughout the adjudication. If the reservation is not adequate, because the wording of the reservation does not suffice or it is not made in time, the agreement between the parties to adjudicate is enforceable and the parties will be bound by the adjudicator's decision as if the Act applied, whether in fact it applied or not.[21] The concept of reservation of jurisdiction is discussed in further detail at Section 16.3.5.

5.3.4 Ad hoc jurisdiction on issues

Ad hoc jurisdiction not only arises in the context of whether the adjudicator has jurisdiction to decide the dispute at all, but also where there is an issue or argument raised during the adjudication by one of the parties that is outside of the scope of the dispute referred to the adjudicator in the notice of adjudication. This may be termed an 'issue-based' ad hoc jurisdiction matter. The point is the same: did the other party by its express or implied actions agree that the issue could be addressed by the adjudication, thereby conferring ad hoc jurisdiction on him to decide it. If so, that new issue will form part of the scope of the dispute in the adjudication and the adjudicator will have jurisdiction to make a decision on it. Consider Sections 16.4, 16.6.5 and 16.7.6, which address the attempted widening of the scope of dispute, either by the parties or the adjudicator, and the ways in which a party may lose the right to challenge jurisdiction.

---

[21] *Maymac Environmental Services v Faraday* (2000) 75 ConLR 101, per Toulmin J at [50].

Chapter 6
Adjudication procedure

6.1 Overview

[6.01]   The different forms of adjudication described in Chapters 4 and 5 are a separate matter to the procedure, or rules, by which the adjudication is to be conducted. This book categorises adjudication procedures into two types: Scheme and contractual.

[6.02]   A Scheme adjudication procedure is one in which the procedure chosen by, or imposed on, the parties is that of the 1998 Scheme or 2011 Scheme.[1] The parties may expressly elect to adopt the rules of the Scheme by making reference to them in their contract. They may do this whether the form of adjudication is statutory (i.e. where the Act applies), contractual (i.e. where it does not), or ad hoc. However, where the form of adjudication is statutory and either the parties make no reference to adjudication in the contract, or the contract contains an adjudication procedure that does not comply with certain requirements set out in the Act, the Scheme rules will be implied into the contract; as if it had been part of the contract from the beginning.

[6.03]   A contractual adjudication procedure is one in which the procedure chosen is something other than the Scheme. In contrast to the Scheme rules a contractual adjudication procedure will never be imposed on parties. It must either be agreed in the parties' contract, or agreed as part of an ad hoc reference. The procedure may form part of a standard form contract (such as the NEC3 adjudication procedure), or one may be written by an industry body (such as the rules published by the Technology and Construction Solicitors Association) or the parties may draft a bespoke procedure.

[6.04]   Adjudications conducted under the Scheme rules are by far the most common type of adjudication used in the construction industry. It is therefore important to examine the Scheme rules and the court's interpretation of those rules in some detail. Rather than provide an explanation of the Scheme in isolation, each paragraph of the Scheme is addressed in context at the relevant part of the adjudication process in the relevant chapter in this book. In case the reader wishes to see the rules in their entirety, the 1998 Scheme as

---

[1] The 1998 Scheme and 2011 Scheme are collectively referred to as 'the Scheme', where there is no difference between the two sets of rules in relation to the point being made.

A Practical Guide to Construction Adjudication, First Edition. James Pickavance.
© 2016 James Pickavance. Published 2016 by John Wiley & Sons, Inc.

amended by the 2011 Scheme, are set out in full at Appendix 2. In relation to the Scheme procedure, this chapter is limited to a brief explanation of when the Scheme applies, the reasons why parties may wish to choose the Scheme and some amendments to the Scheme frequently drafted into construction contracts. The remainder of this chapter considers the key characteristics of the common contractual adjudication procedures. Appendix 5 contains a table comparing the provisions of the 1998 and 2011 Schemes and all the contractual adjudication procedures referred to in this chapter. Appendix 8 lists all those court judgments where the contractual adjudication procedures discussed in this chapter applied in the adjudication.

6.2 Scheme

6.2.1 In a nutshell

[6.05] The 1998 Scheme was brought into force in England and Wales on 1 May 1998, the same day as the 1996 Act. The original intention of the 1998 Scheme was to act as a fall-back set of rules that would apply where the parties had failed to draft their contract in a way that complied with the 1996 Act. However, the Scheme has become the set of rules that most parties choose to adopt. In 2011, the 1998 Scheme was amended to take account of the changes to the 1996 Act. The 2011 Scheme was brought into force on 1 October 2011.

[6.06] Both the 1998 Scheme and the 2011 Scheme comprise two parts. Part I – Adjudication: this provides for the selection and appointment of an adjudicator, and sets out the rules under which the adjudicator and the parties are to carry out and conduct the adjudication. Part II – Payment: this makes provision with respect to payments under a construction contract where either: the contract fails to make provision, or the parties fail to agree the amount of any instalment or stage payments for work done; the intervals at which such payments become due; failure to provide an adequate mechanism in the contract for determining either what payments become due under the contract or when they become due; failure to provide for a final date for payment; failure to provide for the issue of a payment notice; and failure to make provision for the period in which a pay less notice is to be issued. This book is only concerned with Part I – Adjudication.

6.2.2 Does the Scheme apply and the failure to comply with section 108(1)–(4) (Act s. 108(5) and 114(4))

[6.07] If there is no reference to adjudication in the contract and the contract is one to which the Act applies, the 1998 Scheme or the 2011 Scheme (depending on the date of the contract) will be imported into the contract, and the parties must follow the rules in the Scheme for any adjudication.

[6.08] If there are provisions relating to adjudication in the contract, then the 1998 Scheme or the 2011 Scheme may still apply in two situations. Where the Act does not apply to the contract, the provisions may expressly incorporate the rules of the Scheme because the parties have elected expressly that they wish those rules to apply. Alternatively, where the Act does apply, the parties may decide that they prefer to adopt a contractual adjudication procedure instead of the Scheme. Where this is done, the contractual procedure **must** as a minimum contain the eight requirements set out in subsections 108(1)–(4) of the Act as part of it. The requirements are as follows:

(1) A party must be able to give notice of its intention to refer a dispute to adjudication (the 'notice of adjudication') 'at any time' (subsection 108(2)(a)).
(2) The adjudication timetable in the contract must provide that both the appointment of an adjudicator and the referral of the dispute to the adjudicator occur within seven days of the date of the notice of adjudication (subsection 108(2)(b)).
(3) The dispute must be decided within 28 days of it being referred to the adjudicator or a longer period as agreed between the parties (subsection 108(2)(c)).
(4) The adjudicator must be permitted to extend the 28-day period for the decision by up to 14 days if the referring party consents (subsection 108(2)(d)).
(5) The adjudicator must be under a duty to act impartially (subsection 108(2)(e)).
(6) The adjudicator must be given the power to take the initiative in ascertaining the facts and the law (subsection 108(2)(f)).
(7) The adjudicator's decision must be said to be binding until finally determined by legal proceedings, arbitration or agreement. The parties may agree to accept the decision of the adjudicator as finally determining the dispute (subsection 108(3)).
(8) The adjudicator shall not be liable for anything that is done or not done as an adjudicator, unless the act or omission is in bad faith (subsection 108(4)).

[6.09] If this is done, the contractual procedure becomes determinative of the parties' rights and obligations in respect of adjudication, and neither the Act nor the Scheme will be implied to fill any gaps.[2] It does not matter if the procedure contains additional or different provisions from those contained in the Scheme, provided that the mandatory terms listed above are included and are not fettered in any way.

[6.10] If the contract fails to reproduce the eight mandatory requirements, either because there is no reference to the provisions at all or in part because the reproduction is imperfect, or because other provisions conflict, restrict or amend the mandatory requirements, the contractual provisions are struck out **in their entirety** and the rules of the Scheme apply **in their entirety** in place.[3] This occurred in *Banner Holdings Ltd v Colchester Borough Council*,[4] where the court held that all of the Scheme should replace the express terms of the contract pertaining to adjudication because there was a clause in the contract that sought to fetter the types of dispute that could be referred to adjudication.

---

[2] Subsection 108(5) of the Act. *David McLean Housing Contractors Ltd v Swansea Housing Association Ltd* [2001] EWHC 830 (TCC), per Lloyd J at [5–7].
[3] Regulation 2 of the Scheme and *Sprunt Ltd v London Borough of Camden* [2011] EWHC 3191 (TCC), per Akenhead J at [28–31].
[4] [2010] EWHC 139 (TCC), per Coulson J at [41–46].

[6.11]   Subsection 114(4) of the Act provides that where the Scheme applies in default of contractual provision agreed by the parties, its provisions have effect as implied terms of the contract concerned.[5]

[6.12]   Express adjudication provisions – as opposed to leaving matters to be implied under the Scheme – also have the useful function that, if a dispute arises later as to whether the Act applies, the whole dispute nevertheless remains adjudicable. Otherwise, statutory adjudication under the Scheme is only permissible in respect of such elements of the contract as fall within the Act, which can create problems on enforcement if a dispute has been referred containing both 'adjudicable' and 'non-adjudicable' elements.[6]

6.2.3 Why choose the Scheme?

[6.13]   If the contract is already agreed, then a decision on which adjudication procedure applies is obsolete. Otherwise, consideration should be given to which adjudication rules are most suitable for the parties. There are many reasons why parties may choose to adopt the Scheme as the rules by which they conduct an adjudication. What follows are just three reasons in favour of adopting the Scheme which may be relevant to the decision-making process.

(1) The Scheme is familiar. By far the majority of adjudications conducted in the UK are governed by or closely follow the rules of the Scheme. This means that where the Scheme is proposed, the parties should be familiar with how it operates and therefore more amenable to agreeing to adopt it in the contract.

(2) The Scheme provides certainty. Both the 1998 Scheme and the 2011 Scheme were the subject of extended debate (albeit not as extensive as the debates leading to the 1996 Act and the 2009 Act), leading up to their enactment. On one view, this means that each and every sentence of every paragraph has been examined in the finest detail to ensure that it makes sense and accommodates the needs of those who are likely to use it. Furthermore the rules of the Scheme have repeatedly been considered by the courts. Of the 550 or so court decisions on adjudication matters at least half of those relate to disputes arising from the conduct of Scheme adjudications. This means that the parties are able to look to court judgments to determine how the court has interpreted a particular provision or how it might decide a particular issue more than any other set of procedural rules.

(3) The Scheme is uncontroversial. As with the 1996 Act and the 2009 Act, the 1998 Scheme and 2011 Scheme represent what might be termed a compromise of the views from a variety of industry bodies and lobbyists from across the construction sector and by both the House of Commons and the House of Lords. As a result, while not everyone's views were accommodated in the instrument finally enacted, it will

---

[5]Subsection 114(4) and *VHE Construction plc v RBSTB Trust Co Ltd (as trustee of the Mercury Property Fund)* [2000] BLR 187, per Hicks J at [37].
[6]See for example *Cleveland Bridge (UK) Limited v Whessoe-Volker Stevin Joint Venture* [2010] EWHC 1076 (TCC), per Ramsey J at [62–77]. See also Sections 4.4.5 and 5.2.2.

be seen by most as a document that provides a fair, neutral set of rules by which adjudications are to be conducted. As such, adopting the 1998 or 2011 Scheme in a contract will more likely be viewed as uncontroversial, whereas an attempt to adopt other rules may not be viewed in the same way.

6.2.4 Scheme variants

[6.14] Provided that the rules remain compliant with the Act,[7] it is perfectly open to parties to agree that the 1998 Scheme or 2011 Scheme is adopted, subject to a list of amendments, deletions or additions. This is commonplace. Precisely what changes are made will depend on what the parties wish to achieve, but some of the amendments more frequently seen are as follows:

(A) Joinder

[6.15] The Scheme does not permit parties engaged under separate contracts to take part in the same adjudication. Where the project involves a number of different parties, such as employer, contractor, subcontractors, quantity surveyor, project manager and so on, the parties to a contract (say the employer and contractor) may wish to ensure that if a dispute arises involving them as well as other parties (the subcontractor and the architect), they can be included in the same adjudication. The following clause may facilitate this intent:

> The Parties irrevocably agree that if any adjudication proceedings commenced under this Contract raise issues which are substantially the same as, or relate to issues arising in any adjudication under or in connection with any contracts between the Employer and any of the professional consultants employed by the Employer in connection with the Works or any part thereof, the Contractor agrees to be joined as a party to such adjudication proceedings or to allow the relevant professional consultant to be joined as a party to adjudication proceedings under this Contract.

(B) Nominating body

[6.16] The default position under the Scheme is that the parties may approach any adjudication nominating body to select an adjudicator. Parties may wish to select a particular nominating body who they feel is better at pairing adjudicators with the subject matter in dispute, or who have more adjudicators on its panel with a particular skill (e.g. legal or. architectural). The clause may read as follows:

> The Technology and Construction Solicitors Association shall be the nominating body for the purposes of paragraph 2(1)(b) of the Scheme.

---

[7] See Section 6.2.2.

(C) Reasons

[6.17] The Scheme does not require that the adjudicator gives reasons unless one of the parties asks for them.[8] While the request can be made during the adjudication, often this is dealt with in the contract.

> The Adjudicator shall give detailed reasons for his decision.

6.3 Contractual procedures

6.3.1 In a nutshell

[6.18] In this book, a contractual adjudication procedure refers to an adjudication where the procedure chosen by the parties is not the Scheme. It may be a procedure contained in a standard form contract, or it may be a standalone procedure produced by an industry body, or it may be a bespoke procedure drafted by the parties. Contractual adjudication procedures may be used in any form of adjudication.

[6.19] Why might parties elect to adopt a procedure that is not the Scheme? The Scheme rules are the result of a concatenation of opinion from the many different individuals and organisations that lobbied on what provisions should or should not be included. They may not, therefore, represent the best interests of a particular party. The putative standard form and standalone contractual adjudication procedures are as follows.

Standard form

- ICE
- IChemE (Grey Book)
- JCT 1998 suite rules[9]
- NEC 2[10] and NEC 3

Standalone procedures

- CIC
- CEDR
- TeCSA
- RICS[11]
- RIBA

[6.20] Except where the contract or the rules are no longer published (as indicated), the rules published by each of these institutions have undergone a number of revisions. Importantly, they have all published a new version of the rules since the coming into

---

[8] Paragraph 22.
[9] No longer published.
[10] No longer published.
[11] No longer published.

Adjudication procedure 89

[6.21] Where the Act applies to the contract and where the parties agree a contractual adjudication procedure, that procedure must comply with subsections 108(1)–(4) of the Act, or else they will be replaced entirely by the rules of the 1998 Scheme or 2011 Scheme (subsection 108(5) of the Act).

[6.22] Although each of the contractual adjudication procedures listed above is compliant with the Act, they are all significantly different from the rules of the 1998 Scheme or the 2011 Scheme. Many of the rules contained in the Scheme simply do not appear in other rules, or they appear in a significantly varied form. There are a number of additional rules on matters such as costs and enforcement, the adjudicator's decision and powers of the adjudicator, and the order in which the Scheme sets out its rules is for the most part not followed by the other rules.

[6.23] Appendix 5 contains a table comparing the Scheme and 2011 Scheme rules to the ICE, IChemE, JCT 1998, NEC 3, CIC, CEDR and TeCSA adjudication rules and the following subsections outline some of the more important differences between the Scheme and each of these procedures.

6.3.2 JCT

[6.24] The JCT was one of the few companies responsible for drafting and publishing standard form construction contracts who, around the time the Act was brought into force, decided to embed its own adjudication rules within its contracts. All of the JCT 1998 contracts contains a detailed adjudication procedure that parties are required to follow. There are also adjudication cases arising out of the JCT 1980's forms, where the contract was signed after May 1998 and the 1998 suite adjudication provisions were incorporated into them. In the 2005 revision of the contract suite, the JCT decided to remove its own rules and replace them with those of the Scheme.[12] The same applies in all later revisions and editions.

[6.25] The 1998 suite is no longer in print (although it is understood the JCT still offers the contracts for purchase) and although a number of companies and practitioners chose to continue using the 1998 editions for a while after the 2005 suite was published, most made the switch to the 2005 suite fairly quickly. This means that the chance of adjudications being conducted on the basis of the 1998 rules grows ever more remote.

[6.26] However, it is helpful to provide an overview of the 1998 rules, because they have received no small amount of consideration by the court. Even where the parties have chosen an adjudication procedure that is not the JCT 1998 rules, where the procedure they have chosen contains the same or similar provisions to the JCT 1998 (as they often do – see

---

[12] Clause 9.2.

Appendix 5), it may be helpful to turn to the court's interpretation of the JCT 1998 provisions to understand how they have been interpreted. Over 100 court judgments relate to adjudicated disputes where the rules of the adjudication were the 1998 rules.[13] These judgments are listed in the case subject index under this section heading at Appendix 8. Where the judgment deals with one or more issues in this book, it is listed under the relevant section heading(s) at Appendix 8.

[6.27] The JCT procedure omits a number of provisions found in the 1998 Scheme. They are paragraph 3 (request to include notice of adjudication), 8 (multiple disputes), 9 (adjudicator resignation), 10 (objection to appointment), 11 (revocation of appointment), 14 (compliance with directions), 16 (legal representation), 17 (considering relevant information), 18 (confidentiality) and 24 (Arbitration Act (Scheme only)).

[6.28] The JCT procedure adds a number of provisions not found in the 1998 Scheme. They are: rules in the JCT procedure that are in addition to those of the Scheme include the following.

- 41A.2.1: no adjudicator shall be nominated under the relevant procedures, who will not execute the JCT Adjudication Agreement.
- 41A.4.2: methods of delivery of the referral notice and supporting information.
- 41A.5.5.1: the adjudicator may use his own knowledge and experience to ascertain the facts and law.
- 41A.5.7: requiring each party to bear its own costs, subject to the adjudicator directing that one party may be responsible for the costs of opening up or testing, if required.

[6.29] All other rules of the Scheme contain comparable provisions in the JCT rules.

6.3.3 ICE/ICC

[6.30] The Institution of Civil Engineers' Conditions of Contract (now rebranded as the Infrastructure Conditions of Contract (ICC)) are a family of standard conditions of contract typically used for civil engineering works. They incorporate the ICE adjudication procedure. The 1997 edition was drafted to satisfy the requirements of section 108 of the Act. The ICE published a second edition in 2010, which it updated in October 2011 to comply with the 2009 Act. At the time of writing, the 2011 updated edition was freely available from the ICE's website and the 1997 edition is available for purchase.[14] Within the 1997 edition, there is a 'simple issue procedure' which is said to be intended for disputes of less than £50,000, with the adjudicator's fees capped at £3000 plus VAT.[15] There are at least 15 court judgments relating to disputes where the adjudication procedure agreed

---

[13] There are over 160 court judgments where the contract between the parties was a JCT form. The online version of the database at Appendix 8 permits users to search court judgments by the form of contract. See the introduction to Appendix 8 for more detail.
[14] www.ice.org.uk
[15] At charge-out rates for most adjudicators, this will amount to something like 10–20 hours' work. Therefore, it will not be a suitable procedure for anything but the most simple of adjudications.

Adjudication procedure 91

between the parties was the ICE adjudication procedure. These judgments are listed in the case subject index under this section heading at Appendix 8. Where the judgment deals with one or more issues in this book, it is listed under the relevant section heading(s) at Appendix 8.

[6.31] The ICE 2011 procedure omits a number of the rules of the Scheme and the 2011 Scheme, namely paragraphs 5 (reference to nominating body), 10 (objection to appointment), 11 (revocation of appointment), 14 (compliance with directions), 16 (legal representation), 17 (considering relevant information), and 24 (Arbitration Act (Scheme only)). The rules contained in the ICE 2011 procedure that are in addition to the Scheme are:

- 1.1 and 1.2: Introductory provisions concerning the procedure and the purpose of adjudication and the form of contract to be used by the adjudicator.
- 1.5: Use of adjudicator's own knowledge and experience.
- 1.7: Directions on payment pursuant to an adjudicator's decision.
- 5.2: Power of the adjudicator to determine any question regarding his own jurisdiction.
- 5.4: Deadline for the service of the response.
- 5.7: Joinder of additional parties.
- 6.3: Liability for the fees of legal or technical adviser (not the adjudicator), where the adjudicator fails to reach a decision in time.
- 6.5: Requirement each party to bear their own costs.
- 6.6: Parties entitled to the relief and remedies set out in the decision regardless of whether the dispute is to be referred to legal proceedings or arbitration.
- 7.1: Unless the Parties agree, the Adjudicator shall not be appointed arbitrator in any subsequent arbitration. No Party may call the Adjudicator as a witness in any legal proceedings or arbitration concerning the subject matter of the adjudication.
- 7.3: No liability for the ICE.
- 7.4: Address for service is determined by the contract, or if none, the principal place of business or registered office. Any agreement required by the procedure shall be evidenced in writing.
- 7.5: The procedure shall be interpreted in accordance with the law of the contract.

[6.32] All other rules of the Scheme contain comparable provisions in the ICE procedure. The ICE adjudication procedure can be used as a standalone adjudication procedure even if the contract is not one of the ICE standard conditions of contract.

6.3.4 IChemE

[6.33] The IChemE Grey Book 3rd edition (as amended in 2012) procedure omits a number of the rules of the Scheme and the 2011 Scheme namely paragraphs 5 (reference to nominating body), 8 (multiple dispute), 10 (objection to appointment), 14 (compliance with directions), 16 (legal representation), 17 (considering relevant information) and 24 (Arbitration Act (Scheme only)). The rules contained in the IChemE procedure that are in addition to the Scheme are:

- 1.1 and 1.10: Introductory provisions concerning the procedure, incorporation of the current edition and conflict between contract and procedure.
- 1.6: The procedure shall be interpreted in accordance with the law of the country where the site is situated.
- 1.7: The Adjudicator shall not be appointed arbitrator in any subsequent arbitration. No Party may call the Adjudicator as a witness in any legal proceedings or arbitration concerning the subject matter of the adjudication.
- 1.9: No liability for the IChemE.
- 2.4: Time periods to exclude bank holidays.
- 4.4: Form of adjudicator's contract to be used.
- 7.7: If the parties reach an agreement on any part of the matter under dispute, they shall notify the adjudicator requesting that the adjudicator terminates the relevant part of the adjudication.
- 8.5: Requirement for each party to bear their own costs.
- 8.10: Power of the court and arbitrator.
- 8.11: The adjudicator shall inform the parties if he intends to destroy the documents sent to him in relation to the adjudication.

[6.34] All other rules of the Scheme contain comparable provisions in the IChemE procedure. The IChemE adjudication procedure can be used as a standalone adjudication procedure even if the contract is not one of the IChemE standard conditions of contract.

6.3.5 NEC

[6.35] The NEC 2 suite of contracts was first published in 1995. Option Y(UK)2 was published in April 1998 in an attempt to comply with the Act, but in 2001 the court found that the provisions were non-compliant.[16] The NEC rectified this through an amendment shortly thereafter.

[6.36] The NEC 3 suite was published in 2005. It revamped the dispute resolution provisions, offering what it called Option W1 and Option W2. Option W1 is for use with any contract to which the Act does not apply, and Option W2 is for use where the Act applies. Both Options, in common with the 2nd edition, include provisions for the reference of a dispute to adjudication and then to the tribunal, as identified in Contract Data Part One. The major change was that the provisions contained within the Option Y(UK)2 which involved referring the dispute to a 'matter of dissatisfaction' procedure before adjudication were deleted so that the procedure complied with section 108(2)(a) of the Act. The other major change was that clause W2 3(3) was inserted to allow a matter disputed under a subcontract to be referred to the main contract adjudicator at the same time providing the subcontractor agrees to such a reference.

[6.37] The NEC 3 was updated again in 2011 to reflect the changes to the 1996 Act. In relation to adjudication procedure, the provision allowing for correction of slips was revised in

---

[16] *John Mowlem & Co plc v Hydra-Tight & Co plc* (2001) 17 Const LJ 358, per Toulmin J at [41–42].

[6.38] Option W1 and W2 are available to purchase from the NEC as part of one of its suite of contracts.[17] The author has recorded 12 court judgments relating to disputes where the adjudication procedure agreed between the parties was an NEC adjudication procedure. These judgments are listed in the case subject index under this section heading at Appendix 8. Where the judgment deals with one or more issues in this book, it is listed under the relevant section heading(s) at Appendix 8.

[6.39] The NEC 3 2011 procedure omits a number of rules of the Scheme, namely paragraphs 4 (identity of adjudicator), 10 (objection to appointment), 16 (legal representation), 17 (considering relevant information), 21 (compliance with decision) and 24 (Arbitration Act (Scheme only)). The rules contained in the NEC 3 procedure that are in addition to the Scheme are:

- W2.2(1): Adjudicator is to be appointed under the NEC Adjudicator's Contract.
- AC 3(1): Advance payment.
- W2.3(6): Copies of communications.
- AC 4(2) and 2(1): Optional and compulsory resignation of the adjudicator.
- AC 4(1) and 3(3): Revocation of the adjudicator's appointment and liability for fees.
- W2.3(9): Project Manager to proceed as if the matter is not under dispute, until a decision is given by the adjudicator.
- W2.3(11): Time limit for challenging the decision of an adjudicator.
- W2.4(2): Time limit for referring dispute to final determination (four weeks).
- W2.3(12): Time limit for correction of mistakes is 14 days.
- W2.4(1): Reference of dispute to an arbitral tribunal.
- AC 3.5, 3.7, 3.8: Time limit for payment of adjudicator's fees.
- W2.4(5): The adjudicator may not be a witness in subsequent proceedings.
- W2.1(2): Time periods to exclude bank holidays.

6.3.6 TeCSA

[6.40] The Technology and Construction Solicitors Association (TeCSA), or the previously named ORSA, produces a standalone adjudication procedure. It has so far produced six iterations, in April 1998 (version 1.2), January 1999 (version 1.3), October 2002 (version 2.2), March 2011 (version 3.0), May 2011 (version 3.1), October 2011 (version 3.2) and most recently 2015 (version 3.2.1). At the time of writing, all versions of the rules are freely available to download on the TeCSA website.[18] It is important that parties cite the version of the rules on which they wish to rely, should they decide to use the TeCSA rules to adjudicate disputes under their contract. There are at least ten court judgments relating to disputes where the adjudication procedure agreed between the parties was a

---

[17] www.neccontract.com.
[18] www.tecsa.org.uk.

version of the TeCSA procedure. These judgments are listed in the case subject index under this section heading at Appendix 8. Where the judgment deals with one or more issues in this book, it is listed under the relevant section heading(s) at Appendix 8.

[6.41] The TeCSA v.3.2.1 omits a number of rules of the Scheme, namely paragraphs 4 (identity of adjudicator), 9 (resignation of the adjudicator), 10 (objection to appointment), 11 (revocation of adjudicator's appointment), 17 (considering relevant information), 21 (compliance with decision) and 24 (Arbitration Act (Scheme only)). The rules contained in the TeCSA v.3.2.1 procedure that are in addition to the Scheme are:

- 5.1: Deemed receipt of the notice of adjudication.
- 8: The Chairman of TeCSA may appoint the same adjudicator, notwithstanding the fact that he was appointed in another adjudication under the same contract.
- 10: More than one such notice of adjudication may be given in respect of disputes arising out of the same contract.
- 11: The scope of the adjudication shall be the matters identified in the notice of adjudication and any further matters agreed by the parties or included by the adjudicator so that the adjudication is effective and/or meaningful.
- 12: The adjudicator may decide his own jurisdiction and as to the scope of the adjudication.
- 20.1: The adjudicator may not request advance payment.
- 20.2: An obligation that the adjudicator may not receive submissions unless they are given to all parties.
- 22: The referring party shall be solely liable for the adjudicator's fees if it wrongly or invalidly commenced an adjudication.
- 24: The adjudicator's fees are capped at £1750 per day.
- 25: Adjudicator's jurisdiction to award the parties' costs after the notice of adjudication has been given, if the parties agree.
- 32: Liability of nominating body excluded.
- 34: The adjudicator may not be a witness in subsequent proceedings.
- 35: governing law clause.

6.3.7 CIC

[6.42] The Construction Industry Council (CIC) has published five editions of its 'model adjudication procedure' in February 1998 (1st edition), November 1998 (2nd edition), October 2003 (3rd edition), April 2007 (4th edition) and October 2011 (5th edition). These rules are available to purchase from the CIC website,[19] with the exception of the first edition, which can be downloaded free of charge. It is important that parties cite the edition of the rules on which they wish to rely, should they decide to use the CIC rules to adjudicate disputes under their contract.

---

[19] www.cic.org.uk/publications.

[6.43] The fourth edition of the CIC model adjudication procedure was published in March 2007 following HHJ Havery QC's decision in *Epping Electrical Company Limited v Briggs and Anor*,[20] in which he held that the third edition did not comply with section 108 of the Act.

[6.44] There are at least 13 court judgments relating to disputes where the adjudication procedure agreed between the parties was an edition of the CIC rules, all of them listed in Appendix 8. The fifth edition of the CIC contains rules are the same or similar to those contained in the Scheme save for paragraphs 4 (identity of adjudicator), 5 (nominating body), 11 (revocation of adjudicator's appointment), 16 (legal representation), 17 (considering relevant information) and 24 (Arbitration Act (Scheme only)). The rules contained in the fifth edition that do not appear in the Scheme include the following.

- 3: Use of adjudicator's own knowledge and experience.
- 29: Ability of the adjudicator to allocate the parties' costs.
- 30: Liability for fees in the event of a failed adjudication.
- 34: The adjudicator may not be a witness or arbitrator in subsequent proceedings.

6.3.8 CEDR Solve

[6.45] CEDR Solve has published editions of its adjudication rules in 1998 (1st edition), February 2002 (2nd edition) and September 2008 (3rd edition). Only the third edition is freely available from the CEDR Solve website.[21] Again, it is important that parties cite the edition of the rules on which they wish to rely, should they decide to use the CIC rules to adjudicate disputes under their contract.

[6.46] There are only two court judgments relating to disputes where the adjudication procedure agreed between the parties was an edition of the CEDR rules. The third edition of the CEDR omits a number of paragraphs of the Scheme namely paragraphs 4 (identity of adjudicator), 10 (objection to the appointment), 11 (revocation of adjudicator's appointment), 14 (compliance with directions), 16 (legal representation), 18 (confidentiality) and 24 (Arbitration Act (Scheme only)). The additions to the CEDR rules over those of the Scheme are:

- 12: Other parties may be joined, subject to the consent of all parties.
- 16, 28–30: The parties may mediate the dispute once the adjudicator has reached a decision. The rules provide that the adjudicator is to withhold his decision to allow the parties to settle the dispute via mediation, or if no settlement is reached, deliver his decision thereafter.
- 18: Slip rule with a time limit of 5 days.
- 22: All parties shall bear their own costs.

---

[20] [2007] EWHC 4 TCC, per Havery J at [19–20].
[21] www.cedr.com.

6.3.9 Bespoke rules

[6.47] Parties can and often do draft entirely bespoke adjudication provisions into their contract. By contrast to Scheme rules, standard forms or industry body rules, agreeing bespoke adjudication rules brings with it an increased risk that the rules will not comply with the provisions of the Act, where that is required. It also increases the risk that the bargaining powers of one of the parties will play a role in shaping the terms of the procedure. For example, an employer in a particularly strong bargaining position may wish to reduce the likelihood of adjudications being brought against it and so may demand the incorporation of rules that discourage the contractor from referring disputes to adjudication. There are examples where the referring party has been made responsible for all costs of the adjudication (although this is no longer permitted), or the volume of documents that a referring party can submit to adjudication is limited. There may, however, be more neutral reasons behind bespoke rules such as to direct the order or timing of submissions, the format of hearings and so on.

6.4 Checklist: What adjudication procedure am I subject to?

> As well as determining what form of adjudication the parties will be subject to (see Section 4.9), it is also necessary to determine what adjudication procedure the parties are required to follow. A consideration of the following questions will provide an answer.
>
> (1) Is there, expressly or by reference, an adjudication procedure in the contract? If not, and the form of the adjudication is statutory, the rules of the adjudication will be those of the 1998 Scheme (for contracts dated 30 September 2011 or earlier) or the 2011 Scheme (for contracts dated 1 October 2011 or later) (Section 6.2.2).
> (2) If there is an adjudication procedure, is it the 1998 or 2011 Scheme or something else (Section 6.3)? If it is the 1998 or 2011 Scheme, those rules will apply.
> (3) If the procedure is not the 1998 or 2011 Scheme, does it comply with subsections 108(1)–(4) of the Act (Section 6.2.2)?
> (4) If yes, those rules will be determinative of the parties' rights. If not, those rules will be replaced wholesale by the 1998 Scheme (if contract is dated before 1 October 2011) or the 2011 Scheme (if it is dated on or after that date).

Chapter 7
Preconditions and restrictions to statutory adjudication

7.1 Overview

[7.01] Where the contract is a construction contract within the meaning of the Act,[1] before a party can refer a dispute to adjudication, certain preconditions must be met. In addition, the nature of the dispute that can be referred to adjudication is restricted. These preconditions and restrictions are succinctly set out in subsection 108(1) of the Act.

> A party to a construction contract has the right to refer **a dispute** arising **under the contract** for adjudication under a procedure complying with this section.
>
> For this purpose 'dispute' includes any difference.[2]

[7.02] The effect of subsection 108(1) may be summarised as follows:
(1) There must be a dispute. This means that the referring party must have put forward a claim to the other party, and that party must have denied the claim, either expressly or by its conduct, such that a dispute has crystallised. In other words, there needs to be some disagreement between the parties that the adjudication will resolve (Section 7.2).
(2) The referring party may only refer one dispute in an adjudication at any one time, unless the other party agrees (Section 7.3).
(3) The dispute must not be substantially the same as a dispute already decided in a previous adjudication or otherwise (Section 7.4).
(4) The dispute must arise under the contract. In essence, the basis of the claim upon which the referring party relies must derive from the contract between the parties. It is not possible to adjudicate non-contractual claims, such as a claim in negligence under common law (Section 7.5).
(5) The dispute must arise under one contract, not more than one contract, unless the parties agree. Sometimes the parties will have a number of contracts between them

---
[1] If the 1996 Act applies, the construction contract must also be in writing.
[2] Emphasis added.

A Practical Guide to Construction Adjudication, First Edition. James Pickavance.
© 2016 James Pickavance. Published 2016 by John Wiley & Sons, Inc.

relating to the same or different projects, but they will only be entitled to refer a dispute arising out of one of those contracts. Subject to the contractual wording, a single contract may encapsulate connected agreements, such as a settlement agreement or variation so that it is possible to adjudicate disputes arising under those connected agreements (Section 7.6).

[7.03] Where these preconditions and restrictions are addressed, subsection 108(1) of the Act provides that a party has a right to refer a dispute to adjudication 'at any time' (Section 7.7).

7.2 Is there a dispute?

7.2.1 In a nutshell

[7.04] For there to be a dispute, within the meaning of subsection 108(1) of the Act, a claim must have been made and a dispute must have subsequently crystallised. A simple illustration of what this means is as follows. A wall to a house has been painted white by the contractor. The employer writes a letter stating that the wall should have been painted black. That letter constitutes a claim. The contractor writes back, stating that the wall has been correctly painted white. This response constitutes a denial of the claim, and at that point a dispute has formed, or crystallised, as to the correct colour of the wall.

[7.05] However, how, when and what claim is made and how, when and what response is given (if any) leads to a huge spectrum of scenarios that are invariably much more convoluted than this example and so determining whether or not there is a 'dispute' is not always straightforward. This precondition has led to a host of cases where the losing party to an adjudication has sought to resist the enforcement of the adjudicator's decision on the grounds that there was no 'dispute' within the meaning of the Act and therefore the adjudicator had no jurisdiction *ab initio* to preside over the adjudication. In addition to the guidance set out in this section, the question of the existence and extent of a dispute is considered at Sections 16.5.5, 16.7.6 and 17.5.4.

7.2.2 Court's approach

[7.06] The court's approach to deciding disputes as to whether a dispute has crystallised has evolved since the Act came into force, but it might now be summarised in this way.

(1) Where there is a challenge to the adjudicator's jurisdiction to preside over an adjudication (where one has not been commenced) or a challenge to the validity of an adjudicator's decision (where an adjudication has commenced) on the basis that there is no dispute between the parties in relation to the subject matter referred or to be referred, the courts will try to infer the existence of a dispute in relation to that subject matter so that the adjudication may proceed or the adjudicator's decision is valid. This is in line with the court's policy to avoid interfering with the right to refer disputes to adjudication and to try to enforce adjudicator's decisions wherever possible.

(2) The court's approach when identifying whether there is a dispute is to 'adopt a rigorous and common sense approach'.[3]
(3) The court should not 'adopt an over legalistic analysis of what the dispute between the parties are; instead it will determine in broad terms what the disputed claim, assertion or position is'.[4]
(4) In other words, it is not necessary for 'each and every such fact, and each and every element of the claim, to have been identified and put forward to the opposite party for it to consider and have an opportunity to formulate a response in detail'.[5]
(5) 'One should look at the essential claim which has been made and the fact that it has been challenged as opposed to the precise grounds upon which it has been rejected or not accepted'.[6] This approach reflects the tight time constraints of the process and the difficulties that an adjudicator faces.
(6) It will not therefore 'give a narrow meaning to the word dispute which would in turn permit a responding party to introduce uncertainties which might be difficult for an adjudicator to deal with. Otherwise, there is a risk that the purpose of [the Act] may be defeated'.[7]
(7) The court should 'look to the substance of the claims identified and denied and not to the descriptive labels variously attached by lay persons and professionals'.[8]
(8) 'It is necessary to differentiate between the substance of the dispute which is then referred to adjudication and the evidence needed to support or contest that disputed claim. The fact that some of the evidence has not been formally or informally submitted by the claiming party before the adjudication is not, and is certainly not necessarily, in itself determinative of the ambit of the referred dispute'.[9]

[7.07]   With this guidance in mind, the following sections set out the court's interpretation of the words 'claim', 'dispute' and 'difference' before outlining some examples of 'no dispute' situations that have been placed before the courts together with a summary of some of the reported cases on each scenario.

7.2.3 A claim must have been made

[7.08]   The first component required for there to be a dispute is the existence of a claim. The term 'claim' for these purposes does not mean a formal claim document. It need be nothing more than an assertion or the adoption of a position. The fact that a claim has been made does not mean there is a dispute. The two words have different meanings.[10]

---

[3] *All in One Building and Refurbishments Ltd v Makers UK Ltd* [2005] EWHC 2943 (TCC), per Wilcox J at [21–22].
[4] *Allied P&L Ltd v Paradigm Housing Group Ltd* [2009] EWHC 2890 (TCC), per Akenhead J at [30].
[5] *Dean & Dyball v Kenneth Grubb Associates* [2003] EWHC 2465, per Seymour J at [42].
[6] *Cantillon Ltd v Urvasco Ltd* [2008] EWHC 282 (TCC), per Akenhead J at [55].
[7] *Cowlin Construction Ltd v CFW Architects (A Firm)* [2002] EWHC 2914 (TCC), per Kirkham J at [88].
[8] *All in One Building and Refurbishments Ltd v Makers UK Ltd* [2005] EWHC 2943 (TCC), per Wilcox J at [21–22].
[9] *Bovis Lend Lease Ltd v The Trustees of the London Clinic* [2009] EWHC 64 (TCC), per Akenhead J at [47].
[10] *Edmund Nuttall Ltd v R G Carter Ltd* [2002] EWHC 400 (TCC), per J Seymour at [34].

[7.09] The claim must be communicated to the other party.[11] Merely an assertion by the claiming party that it was obvious that if the claim had been communicated to the other party, then it would have been rejected will not, without more, amount to a claim. Although the claim does not need to be in writing, it is good practice for it to be so. The claim should be made in writing to the intended respondent, setting out in clear terms what is being sought, the basis for the claim and the relief sought.

[7.10] The claim need not necessarily be detailed. After all, the details of almost all claims develop as the formalised dispute progresses.[12] However, in so far as it is possible, it is important that letters are sent or an adequate paper trail is produced to establish that a claim has been made and what the basis of that claim is because if, on later examination, that document trail does not address a particular aspect of the claim which is referred to adjudication, the responding party may well raise the objection that there was no dispute in relation to that matter because it was never informed of the claim against it.

[7.11] If the case presented is so nebulous and ill-defined that the responding party cannot sensibly understand what claim is being made against it, much less respond to it, then it will not constitute a claim that is capable of giving rise to a dispute.[13]

7.2.4 The meaning of 'dispute' (Act s.108(1))

[7.12] What does it mean for there to be a dispute? The courts have held that the word dispute should be given its normal meaning and there is no special meaning ascribed to it.[14] Once the existence of a communicated claim has been established, one must consider whether there are any restrictions or stipulations on the subject matter or the nature of the response that may preclude a conclusion that a dispute has formed.

[7.13] Disputes can arise in a variety of ways. The Act imposes no qualification or limitation upon the nature, scope and extent of the disputes that can be referred to adjudication under a construction contract,[15] and no doubt because of this there is no set formula that the court has laid out to determine whether a dispute has or has not arisen.

[7.14] The dispute may relate to future as well as to past events.[16] It may be very wide and cover a myriad of issues; on the other hand, it may be very narrow and involve one or more limited and discrete issues. There may be a dispute arising out of all or part of a small or large contract of small or large value in relation to a claim for money or a declaration.

[7.15] The scope of the dispute that crystallises before the adjudication depends on the relevant history of the exchanges between the two parties. The extent of that dispute may not

---

[11] *Allied P&L Ltd v Paradigm Housing Group Ltd* [2009] EWHC 2890 (TCC), per Akenhead J at [30].
[12] *Cowlin Construction Ltd v CFW Architects (A Firm)* [2002] EWHC 2914 (TCC), per Kirkham J at [88].
[13] *VGC Construction Ltd v Jackson Civil Engineering Ltd* [2008] EWHC 2082 (TCC), per Akenhead J at [50–57].
[14] *AMEC Civil Engineering Ltd v Secretary of State for Transport* [2004] EWHC 2339, per Jackson J at [68].
[15] *Banner Holdings Ltd v Colchester Borough Council* [2010] EWHC 139 (TCC), per Coulson J at [39].
[16] *Allied P&L Limited v Paradigm Housing Group Limited* [2009] EWHC 2890, per Akenhead J at [29].

simply be determined by the scope of the dispute referred to adjudication in the notice of adjudication, which may be deliberately narrower in scope. It must be construed against the underlying factual background.[17]

[7.16] Although the basis of the claim referred to adjudication needs to have been advanced before the start of the adjudication, the arguments deployed by the responding party in defence of the claim are not so limited. It is entitled to make any defence to the claim put forward, whether or not it has been raised before, provided it is within the scope of the dispute referred. This is not an expansion of the scope of the dispute as such; rather it is a widening of the arguments advanced within it.

[7.17] The scope of the dispute may be expanded if the parties, expressly or by their conduct, allow it to be extended during the adjudication. For instance, if the responding party makes submissions on an issue that is outside the scope of the dispute and the referring party does not challenge the permissibility of those submissions, then the referring party will be taken to have accepted by conduct that the dispute has expanded to include that issue.

[7.18] Finally, the dispute referred to adjudication might include issues which are not expressly stated to fall within the scope of the dispute, but which are integral to, or follow on from, the dispute as referred. By way of example, if a claim did not seek a declaration for interest, a claim for interest may well form part of the dispute because it is integral. Whether or not other issues fall within the scope of the dispute is to be determined by analysing what the essential dispute referred is.[18]

(A) The nature of the response

[7.19] Following the communication of a claim, not all forms of action or inaction by the responding party will mean that a dispute has formed, but most will.

[7.20] An express written denial of a claim made by a party is the clearest example of when it can be said that a dispute has formed. However, the respondent may prevaricate, thus giving rise to the inference that he does not admit the claim. The respondent may simply remain silent for a period of time, which will likely give rise to the same inference.[19]

[7.21] The rejection or non-acceptance does not need to be in writing or to be in any form or necessarily be detailed.[20]

[7.22] If the response to a claim is a request for some further information, particularly in circumstances where the claiming party has offered to provide that information, a dispute may not arise until later or at all.[21]

---

[17] *Stirling v Westminster Properties Scotland Ltd* [2007] ScotCS CSOH_117, per Lord Drummond Young at [9].
[18] *Allied P&L Limited v Paradigm Housing Group Limited* [2009] EWHC 2890, per Akenhead J at [29].
[19] *AMEC Civil Engineering Ltd v Secretary of State for Transport* [2004] EWHC 2339, per Jackson J at [68].
[20] *Allied P&L Ltd v Paradigm Housing Group Ltd* [2009] EWHC 2890 (TCC), per Akenhead J at [30].
[21] *Carillion Construction Ltd v Devonport Royal Dockyard Ltd* [2003] BLR 79, per Bowsher J at [51–55].

[7.23] Where there is negotiation and discussion between the parties, this has been held to be more consistent with the existence of a dispute – albeit an as yet unresolved dispute – than with the absence of a dispute.[22] Each case will turn on its own facts, which includes considering 'whether or not the parties are in continuing and genuine discussions in order to try to resolve the dispute.'[23]

(B) The meaning of the word 'difference'

[7.24] Subsection 108(1) states that the word 'dispute' includes any difference. It has been said that a difference is 'less hard-edged than "dispute" alone'.[24] However, it is unlikely to add any further complexity to the question of whether the section 108(1) test has been satisfied. Instead, it reduces the scope for arguments over whether an adversarial position between the two parties will fall within the scope of the Act.[25]

7.2.5 The point at which to assess whether or not there is a dispute

[7.25] The relevant point at which to assess whether a dispute has arisen is immediately before the service of the notice of adjudication.[26] This comparatively simple point can cause difficulty because of the changing nature of disputes. A dispute will often evolve over time and so if by the time that the adjudication process is initiated the amount previously in issue has been reduced and the arguments on any given issue have been modified or limited, it will usually be the dispute as developed which is capable of being referred to adjudication.[27]

[7.26] For the reasons articulated in the previous section, the extent of the crystallised dispute immediately before the notice of adjudication may not encapsulate the whole dispute that the adjudicator is required to decide. For example, the dispute may expand by mutual agreement between the parties (express or implied) during the adjudication. In that case, the point to assess the crystallisation of that expanded part of the dispute will be at the point in time that one party seeks to introduce it.

7.2.6 Time period following a claim until a dispute is formed

[7.27] Where the failure to respond at all is relied on as grounds for asserting that there is a dispute, the period of time that has elapsed after the claim being made is relevant to the

---

[22] *Collins (Contractors) Ltd v Baltic Quay Management (1994) Ltd* [2004] EWCA Civ 1757, per Clarke LJ at [64].
[23] *CIB Properties Ltd v Birse Construction* [2004] EWHC 2365 (TCC), per Toulmin J at [19].
[24] *AMEC Civil Engineering Ltd v Secretary of State for Transport* [2005] EWCA Civ 291, per May LJ at [31].
[25] *CIB Properties Ltd v Birse Construction* [2004] EWHC 2365 (TCC), per Toulmin J at [16].
[26] *Dean & Dyball v Kenneth Grubb Associates* [2003] EWHC 2465, per Seymour J at [41].
[27] *Herbosch-Kiere Marine Contractors Limited v Dover Harbour Board* [2012] EWHC 84 (TCC), per Akenhead J at [23]. See also Section 7.2.8(H).

[7.28] question of whether a dispute has formed. If a claim is made today, can it be said a dispute has arisen tomorrow, or will the claimant need to wait until next week, or next month? If an insufficient period of time elapses between the claim being made and the serving of the notice of adjudication, the court will find that there is no dispute.

[7.28] In *AMEC Civil Engineering Ltd v Secretary of State for Transport*,[28] the Court of Appeal offered this guidance.

> Unlike the arbitration context, adjudication is likely to occur at an early stage ... but there is the different concern that parties may be plunged into an expensive contest, the timing provisions of which are tightly drawn, before they, and particularly the respondent, are ready for it. In this context there has been an understandable concern that the respondent should have a reasonable time in which to respond to any claim.

[7.29] What constitutes a reasonable time will depend on the facts and circumstances of each case. However, it is highly unlikely that a dispute will be said to have crystallised in circumstances where the referring party first gave notice to the responding party of its claim at precisely the same time as it referred that claim to adjudication.[29] In *Beck Interiors Ltd v UK Flooring Contractors Ltd*,[30] Akenhead J found that one working day was not a sufficient period, but five days probably was. In that case, the claim had been made five days before the notice of adjudication was issued, but four of those days were public holidays. The judge held that this was not a sufficient period of time.

[7.30] Where the details of the claim are well known and it is obviously controversial, a very short period of time may suffice before it can be said a dispute has formed. Where the claim is notified to an agent of the respondent who has a legal duty to consider the claim independently and then give a considered response, a longer period of time may be required before it can be inferred that a dispute has arisen. For instance, where a claim has been submitted and discussions ensue between the contractor and the contract administrator, a reasonable time must be allowed for the contract administrator to prepare a response before it can be concluded that a dispute has arisen. However, a reasonable period is unlikely to extend to delays arising from the contract administrator's failure to assess a claim because he complains there is a paucity of supporting documentation. A reasonable time will constitute the period that the contract administrator needs to prepare a response, regardless of the inadequacies of the claim.[31]

[7.31] If the claimant states 'I want a response by the end of the day', that deadline will not curtail what would otherwise be a reasonable time for responding.[32] Equally, if a contract prescribes a time when a payment becomes due then, while that is likely to be material, it

---

[28] [2004] EWHC 2339, per Jackson J at [68].
[29] *Enterprise Managed Services Ltd v Tony McFadden Utilities Ltd* [2009] EWHC 3222 (TCC), per Coulson J at [83–90].
[30] [2012] EWHC 1808 (TCC) per Akenhead J at [26].
[31] *Gibson (Banbridge) Ltd v Fermanagh District Council* [2013] NIQB 16, per Weatherup J at [6–20].
[32] *AMEC Civil Engineering Ltd v Secretary of State for Transport* [2004] EWHC 2339, per Jackson J at [68].

is not determinative as to whether a dispute has arisen[33] although where a claimant puts forward a claim, the contract prescribes a period for response, and the claimant seeks to refer a claim to adjudication before the expiry of that period, a dispute may not be said to have formed.[34] For instance, a contractor may advance an extension of time claim and the contract provides that the contract administrator has a fixed period within which to evaluate it. In that case, the court has held that a dispute will not crystallise until the end of that period, or until the contract administrator arrives at a decision that is different from the claim made by the contractor.[35]

7.2.7 Ambush

[7.32] The term 'ambush' is commonly used in the context of adjudication. Ambush is not a term of art,[36] rather it is a way of describing the situation where the responding party believes it has not had sight of the claim (or part of it) at all, or there has been an insufficient time to consider and respond to the claim, such that a dispute has not formed. It follows that a claim from a party that it has been ambushed can be equiparated with a claim that there is 'no dispute'. Whether or not the responding party has been 'ambushed' will be a question of fact in each case.

7.2.8 Scenarios

[7.33] There are an almost infinite number of factual scenarios in which a dispute can be said to have formed. However, there are particular scenarios that have arisen before the courts on numerous occasions that it is thought helpful to highlight. Rather than cite all the cases relevant to each scenario, a small selection of cases is outlined in the following sections. A full list of cases is provided at Appendix 8.

(A) Exchange of correspondence as evidence of dispute

[7.34] An exchange of letters or emails is by far the most common way in which a dispute may be evidenced. Sometimes, the circumstances are straightforward, namely, there having been a series of exchanges concerning one or more issues between the parties which yields no compromise, and subsequently the referring party draws these issues together in a 'claim' letter. That letter commonly concludes with the phrase, 'and in respect of the aforementioned matters, the referring party considers that a dispute has crystallised between the parties'. Where a responding party sees those words, or a similar form of words, it would be well advised to begin preparing its defence as a matter of priority, because more often than not, those words signal that the referring party is poised to

---

[33] *All in One Building and Refurbishments Ltd v Makers UK Ltd* [2005] EWHC 2943 (TCC), per Wilcox J at [25].
[34] *Hitec Power Protection BV v MCI Worldcom Ltd* [2002] EWHC 1953, per Seymour J at [86-88].
[35] *R Durtnell & Sons Ltd v Kaduna Ltd* [2003] EWHC 517 (TCC), per Seymour J at [42-43].
[36] *Edmund Nuttall Ltd v RG Carter Ltd* [2002] EWHC 400 (TCC), per Bowsher J at [8].

strike. Where the responding party responds with anything other than a full admission, a dispute will have crystallised.

[7.35] In *PT Building v ROK Build Ltd*,[37] the parties had agreed to enter into discussions regarding the proper valuation of variations. PT Building issued a notice of adjudication and ROK claimed that there was no dispute because of the ongoing discussions. However, it was clear from correspondence exchanged between the parties that ROK's valuation was at odds with that of PT Building and so the court said at that point, which was three weeks prior to the issue of the notice of adjudication, a dispute had formed.

[7.36] Commonly, the claim will develop from the point at which the dispute first crystallised to the point at which the dispute was referred to adjudication. The question then is whether the developed dispute had been communicated to the responding party and a dispute had formed. In *Bovis Lend Lease Ltd v The Trustees of the London Clinic*,[38] the court had to consider whether the quantum of a loss and expense claim had crystallised into a dispute. The referring party had submitted two quantum reports, the second of which was materially different from the first in that it contained actual instead of estimated costs. However, the court said that the claims were essentially the same and so that was enough.

[7.37] In *Cowlin Construction Ltd v CFW Architects (A Firm)*,[39] the parties had ceased to work together by August 2001. At a meeting on 28 August 2001, Cowlin had notified to CFW a claim of about £8000 in respect of 'direct cost contras'. There was then a hiatus until March 2002, when CFW responded indicating that they had notified their insurers and asked Cowlin for further substantiation. Cowlin responded on 11 March providing what it described as full supporting documentation. CFW then complained that Cowlin had not explained the basis of its claim. Cowlin said it had. The court held that in circumstances where Cowlin had not given particulars of their claim, it was not good enough for Cowlin simply to say, as they did, that CFW knew what their claim was all about so there was no need for Cowlin to explain it. However, by the date of Cowlin's demand for a substantive response, which was almost eight weeks after the claim was made, the court said that CFW had sufficient opportunity to indicate broadly their response to Cowlin's claim. It did not matter in this case that CFW was only aware of the 'bare bones' of the claim: that was enough.

(B) Demand for payment, payment certificate, withholding notice as evidence of dispute

[7.38] The dispute need not arise out of correspondence exchanges between the parties; it may flow from a demand for payment or interim payment certificates.

---

[37] [2008] EWHC 3434 (TCC), per Ramsey J at [48–50].
[38] [2009] EWHC 64 (TCC), per Akenhead J at [55–65].
[39] [2002] EWHC 2914 (TCC), per Kirkham J at [84–89].

[7.39] In *Working Environments Ltd v Greencoat Construction Ltd*,[40] Working Environments had put in its Application No. 10 for payment on 24 November 2011 for a net sum of £488,153.45. Greencoat largely rejected that application and certified that only a net sum of £16,686.36 was due. Working Environments' consultants confirmed that they did not accept that assessment. It was therefore absolutely clear that there was a dispute as to whether £488,153.45 was due or £16,686.36 or something in between. The court did not accept that there could not be a dispute about an interim valuation of work until after the valuation falls due for payment.

[7.40] In *Ringway Infrastructure Services Ltd v Vauxhall Motors Ltd*,[41] Ringway submitted application for payment No. 11. The application, which had not been the subject of a withholding notice, became due on 24 May 2007. Since nothing had been paid, there was clearly a dispute. Ringway chose to rely on the operation of clause 30.3.3 and 30.3.5 of their JCT 1998 form of contract, which in effect required Vauxhall to issue a withholding notice or else pay the amount due. Vauxhall argued that those arguments had not been raised before and therefore there was no dispute. The court held that just because the Ringway decided to rely on two clauses as the basis for their payment, it did not mean that that argument was not encompassed by the overall claim which it had made under Interim Application No. 11. Since the Interim Application had been made under clause 30.3, it was open to Ringway to rely upon all the various provisions within that subclause to justify its entitlement for payment.

[7.41] In *Orange EBS Ltd v ABB Ltd*,[42] there was a dispute over the final account. ABB contended that because the adjudication was commenced during the final account process and not after it, a dispute could not yet have crystallised. Although the issue was complicated by a claim that there had been a repudiatory breach which brought the contract to the end which, according to Orange, meant that the timings of the contract procedure were no longer relevant, the court found that a dispute had nevertheless crystallised at the point at which negotiations had come to an end, which was mid-way through the final account process.

(C) Without prejudice material

[7.42] Without prejudice correspondence will not normally prevent the crystallisation of a dispute. The privilege attaches to the content of the exchanges rather than to the fact that they took place. Therefore, if the parties engaged in without prejudice negotiations in respect of a notified claim, and those negotiations did not result in the claim being admitted, there will be a dispute, certainly at the conclusion of the failed negotiations and possibly during them, provided a sufficient period of time has passed.[43]

---

[40] [2012] EWHC 1039 (TCC), per Akenhead J at [26–30].
[41] [2007] EWHC 2421 (TCC), per Akenhead J at [80–90].
[42] [2003] EWHC 1187 (TCC), per Kirkham J at [37–43].
[43] *RWE Npower plc v Alstom Power Ltd* [2009] EWHC 1192 (QB), per Havelock-Allan J at [48–55].

(D) Document not served correctly

[7.43] Where a document, such as a payment application, is not served in the manner required by the contract or the manner agreed between the parties and where the referring party relies on the contents of that document to allege that a dispute has crystallised, a dispute is unlikely to have formed. It will not matter for these purposes whether or not the recipient has challenged part or all of the content of the document where such challenge would ordinarily crystallise the dispute.[44]

(E) Wrong party

[7.44] Where a party that is not a party to the construction contract under which the dispute is said to have formed refers the dispute to adjudication, there will be no dispute between the parties because for there to be a dispute, one party to the contract must raise a claim and the other party must deny it. In *Enterprise Managed Services Ltd v Tony McFadden Utilities Ltd*,[45] Enterprise owed a sum of money to TML. TML made a claim against Enterprise before going insolvent. The liquidators assigned the balance of the monies owed to TML to Tony McFadden Utilities Limited. Utilities then later gave notice of its claim against Enterprise at the same time as serving the notice of adjudication. It argued that because a dispute had crystallised between TML and Enterprise, it had also crystallised between Utilities and Enterprise. The court did not accept this. It said that a dispute must crystallise between the parties to the contract.

(F) Claim abandoned

[7.45] Where the original claim has been abandoned and then the claimant attempts to refer the abandoned claim to adjudication there will be no dispute. However, it will be necessary to consider whether the claiming party was intending to abandon its claim or merely to temporarily suspend or put it into abeyance. If it is the latter, then it is likely there will be a dispute capable of adjudicating.[46] In *Edmund Nuttall Ltd v R G Carter Ltd*,[47] Carter argued that the claim was a 'dead duck' because Nuttall had turned its attention to a claim being prepared by one of its advisers, Mr Caletka, rather than to the claim that was referred to adjudication (the May claim). The court held that just because another claim was being investigated by Mr Caletka that did not mean the May claim was a dead duck. 'Viewed objectively it was very much a live mallard, even if, unknown to anyone save perhaps Mr Caletka, it was about to be transformed into the swan of the Caletka Report.'

---

[44] *Palmac Contracting Ltd v Park Lane Estates Ltd* [2005] EWHC 919 (TCC), per Kirkham J at [15–20].
[45] *Enterprise Managed Services Ltd v Tony McFadden Utilities Ltd* [2009] EWHC 3222 (TCC), per Coulson J at [80–90].
[46] *VGC Construction Limited v Jackson Civil Engineering Ltd* [2008] EWHC 2082, per Akenhead J at [49].
[47] [2002] EWHC 400 (TCC), per Seymour J at [38].

(G) Dispute settled or compromised

[7.46] Parties may settle or compromise matters that are disputed between them. In that case, where the settlement is binding on the parties, they will be barred from subsequently referring those matters to adjudication, or any other form of dispute resolution. Where a party does try to refer a dispute to adjudication that is alleged to be settled or compromised, the question of whether or not there is a dispute will be addressed by reference to the construction of the settlement or compromise agreement and, to the extent appropriate, other documents.[48]

(H) Creep between crystallisation and referral

[7.47] Sometimes the dispute that has crystallised by the date of the notice of adjudication is 'developed' by the referring party in the referral, such that it is alleged to have creeped outside the scope of the dispute that had crystallised in the notice of adjudication. Whether the allegation is correct will be a question of fact in each case.

[7.48] In *Lidl UK GmbH v RG Carter Colchester Ltd*,[49] the question before the court was what was the precise scope of the dispute referred by the notice of adjudication: was it confined to the question of whether Lidl was in principle entitled to deduct or demand liquidated damages after 27 June 2011 (Section 1) and 6 July 2011 (Section 2), or did it extend to determining, in addition, the amount of any such damages? Carter contended that there was no dispute in relation to the amount of damages. The court held that the wording of the notice of adjudication left it open to the adjudicator to determine not only the question of entitlement to pro-rata LADs, but also the amount of them.

[7.49] In *OSC Building Services Ltd v Interior Dimensions Contracts Ltd*,[50] Interior argued that the referral expanded the scope of the dispute as set out in the notice of adjudication. It said that the adjudicator only had jurisdiction to decide on non-payment against IDC's certification but not to determine the value of OSC's final account. OSC said that when the notice of adjudication and referral notice were read in context with the relevant documents there was no expansion of the dispute in the referral notice as contended. The court agreed with OSC.

7.3 More than one dispute

7.3.1 In a nutshell

[7.50] The right to use statutory adjudication as a means of resolving a dispute is restricted in that only one dispute may be referred within one adjudication. Where there is more than

---
[48] *Shepherd Construction Limited v Mecright Limited* [2000] BLR 489.
[49] [2012] EWHC 3138, per Edwards-Stuart J at [49–53].
[50] [2009] EWHC 248 (TCC), per Ramsey J at [9–15].

one dispute, these must be referred in separate adjudications. If more than one dispute is referred under the same adjudication and the Act applies, that referral and consequently the adjudicator's decision will be held to be invalid.

7.3.2 More than one dispute (Act s. 108(1))

[7.51] Parties participating in a statutory adjudication may only refer a single dispute to the adjudicator. A single dispute does not necessarily mean a single issue. As long as the issues are connected, then they can be characterised as a single dispute.

> It is to be noted that the HGCRA refers to a "dispute" and not to "disputes". Thus, at any one time, a referring party must refer a single dispute, albeit that the Scheme allows the disputing parties to agree, thereafter, to extend the reference to cover "more than one dispute under the same contract" and "related disputes under different contracts"… The dispute is whatever claims, heads of claims, issues or contentions or causes of action that… the referring party has chosen to crystallise into an adjudication reference.[51]

[7.52] While more than one dispute in the same adjudication is not permitted, there is nothing to preclude two disputes being referred in two separate adjudications to the same adjudicator at the same time.[52] While this may seem unfair on the responding party, it is consistent with the right to refer a dispute to adjudication 'at any time'.[53] However, there is of course an increased risk that in such circumstances, the adjudicator will consider he does not have the capacity to preside over two adjudications simultaneously or he may ask the parties to extend the timetable of one or both adjudications to allow him sufficient time.[54]

[7.53] In certain circumstances, where only part of an adjudicator's decision is rendered invalid, the court may sever the invalid part from the rest of the decision so that the valid part of the decision may be enforced.[55] However, where two disputes are referred within a single adjudication and the adjudicator proceeds to a decision on both disputes his decision on both disputes will be invalid. It will not be possible to sever the decision, so that the decision on one dispute survives and the other does not because there is no way of knowing which part of the decision to sever. That is so, even if the structure of the adjudicator's decision lends itself to severance.[56]

---

[51] *Fastrack Contractors Ltd v Morrison Construction Ltd* [2000] EWHC Technology 177, per Thornton J at [20].
[52] *Vision Homes Ltd v Lancsville Construction Ltd* [2009] EWHC 2042 (TCC), per Clarke J at [70–71].
[53] See subsection 108(2)(a) of the Act and section 7.7.
[54] *Willmott Dixon Housing Limited (formerly Inspace Partnerships Limited) v Newlon Housing Trust* [2013] EWHC 798 (TCC), per Ramsey J at [68–76].
[55] See Section 14.4 for an explanation of severability.
[56] *Bothma (t/a DAB Builders) v Mayhaven Healthcare Ltd* [2006] EWHC 2601 (QB), per Havelock-Allan J at [26].

[7.54] In *Witney Town Council v Beam Construction*,[57] Akenhead J reviewed the case law concerning this topic and provided clear guidelines to assist in determining whether there is a single dispute or multiple disputes.

> A dispute can comprise a single issue or any number of issues within it. However, a dispute between parties does not necessarily comprise everything which is in issue between them at the time that one party initiates adjudication; put another way, everything in issue at that time does not necessarily comprise one dispute, although it may do so.
>
> What a dispute in any given case is will be a question of fact albeit that the facts may require to be interpreted. Courts should not adopt an over legalistic analysis of what the dispute between the parties is, bearing in mind that almost every construction contract is a commercial transaction and parties cannot broadly have contemplated that every issue between the parties would necessarily have to attract a separate reference to adjudication.
>
> The Notice of Adjudication and the Referral Notice are not necessarily determinative of what the true dispute is or as to whether there is more than one dispute. One looks at them but also at the background facts.
>
> Where on a proper analysis, there are two separate and distinct disputes, only one can be referred to one adjudicator unless the parties agree otherwise. An adjudicator who has two disputes referred to him or her does not have jurisdiction to deal with the two disputes.
>
> Whether there are one or more disputes again involves a consideration of the facts. It may well be that, if there is a clear link between two or more arguably separate claims or assertions, that may well point to there being one dispute. A useful if not invariable rule of thumb is that, if disputed claim No 1 cannot be decided without deciding all or parts of disputed claim No 2, that establishes such a clear link and points to there being only one dispute.

[7.55] There is a spectrum of circumstances where it might be said that there is more than one dispute. For example, the notice of adjudication may refer disputed issues concerning both:

- the amount of the final account and an interim payment dispute;[58]
- claims under the contract as well as claims for variations;[59]
- damages for negligent misstatement and the validity of a novation agreement; and[60]
- the correct identity of the employer under the contract, and how much that employer owed to the contractor.[61]

---

[57] [2011] EWHC 2332 (TCC), per Akenhead J at [38].
[58] *Costain Ltd v Wescol Steel Ltd* [2003] EWHC 312 (TCC), per Havery J at [11–13].
[59] *Dalkia Energy and Technical Services Ltd v Bell Group UK Ltd* [2009] EWHC 73 (TCC), per Coulson J at [89–92].
[60] *Hillcrest Homes Ltd v Beresford & Curbishley Ltd* [2014] EWHC 280 (TCC), per Raynor J at [60].
[61] *Michael John Construction Ltd v Golledge & Ors* [2006] EWHC 71 (TCC), per Coulson J at [51–53].

[7.56] Determining whether, on the facts, there is more than one dispute will require a careful examination of the notice of adjudication, the referral notice and the surrounding circumstances and for the results of that examination to be set against the guidance laid down inter alia in *Witney Town*.

7.3.3 The Scheme (Scheme p. 8)

[7.57] Where the Scheme applies, subparagraph 8(1) provides:

> The adjudicator may, with the consent of all the parties to those disputes, adjudicate at the same time on more than one dispute under the same contract.

[7.58] The Scheme extends the ambit of the Act by permitting the parties to refer more than one dispute in the same adjudication, provided all parties consent.

[7.59] This provision must be aimed at situations where the parties agree to refer more than one dispute before the dispute is referred to the adjudicator because paragraph 20 of the Scheme addresses the situation where an agreement is made to expand the scope of an adjudication once it is in progress.[62] Also, if two disputes were referred to him in the same adjudication and the agreement had not yet been made between the parties, the appointment would be defective.

[7.60] Where the parties reach an agreement under subparagraph 8(1), subparagraph 8(3) provides that the parties may agree to extend the period within which the adjudicator may reach a decision in relation to all or any of the disputes. Subparagraph 8(4) provides that where an adjudicator ceases to act because a dispute is to be adjudicated on by another person, that adjudicator's fees and expenses shall be determined in accordance with paragraph 25 of the Scheme. The courts have considered neither subparagraph 8(3) nor 8(4).

7.4 Substantially the same dispute (Scheme p. 9)

7.4.1 In a nutshell

[7.61] Parties to a contract may adjudicate more than one dispute during the lifetime of a project. Where they do so, an adjudicator must not address matters already decided in an earlier adjudication. If he does so, his decision (or at least part of it) will be a nullity. Whether or not a decision treads on the toes of an earlier decision is a matter of fact and degree, and can require a careful analysis of the scope of the earlier decision to determine the boundaries of what was decided. Where the adjudicator discovers that a dispute he presides over is the same or substantially the same as a previous dispute already decided, he should resign immediately.

---

[62] *Mecright Ltd v TA Morris Developments Ltd*, Unreported, 21 June 2001, per Seymour J at [34–35].

7.4.2 Substantially the same dispute

[7.62] Not infrequently, this issue arises where a party is dissatisfied with a decision in a previous adjudication and attempts to commence a fresh adjudication on the same or similar matters. For example, it may seek to adjudicate an aspect of the final account that has already been adjudicated following an interim certificate. Or it may seek to claim extensions of time, liquidated damages and prolongation costs, the duration and value of which have already been determined by an adjudicator.

[7.63] There are a number of reasons why a party cannot adjudicate a dispute already decided. The Act requires that a dispute is referred to adjudication, but a 'dispute' cannot exist under the contract if the matter has already been submitted to and decided by an adjudicator.[63] Further, subsection 108(3) binds the parties to an adjudicator's decision until it is finally determined by legal proceedings, by arbitration or by agreement, not until the decision is re-adjudicated.[64]

[7.64] Where the Scheme applies, it deals with this situation expressly at subparagraph 9(2), providing that the adjudicator must resign if the dispute is the same or substantially the same as one that has previously been referred to adjudication and a decision made.[65]

[7.65] What is important is not that the same dispute was referred, but that there had been a decision on that dispute. If that was not the case, a party could refer a number of questions or issues to adjudication under the umbrella of one dispute, invite the adjudicator to decide only one or two of them, knowing that this would shut the door to the other party from subsequently referring the undecided issues to another adjudicator. Clearly this is not what the Act or Scheme contemplates.[66]

[7.66] Whether or not the later decision is enforced depends on whether, as a matter of fact and degree, the subsequent dispute was the same or substantially the same as that decided in the earlier adjudication. There can be a reasonably fine line between being permitted to refer successive disputes to adjudication and ensuring that the later adjudication does not trespass on the earlier decision. However, generally speaking, the court has found that subsequent decisions are sufficiently distinct from previous decisions such that they should be enforced.[67] The court has indicated that it will give considerable weight to the decision of the adjudicator and it will only embark on a jurisdictional enquiry where there were real grounds for concluding that the adjudicator had erred in deciding

---

[63] *Vertase F.L.I. Ltd v Squibb Group Ltd* [2012] EWHC 3194 (TCC), per Edwards-Stuart J at [46–50]
[64] Ibid.
[65] *Quietfield Ltd v Vascroft Construction Ltd* [2006] EWCA Civ 1737, per Dyson LJ at [45].
[66] *Harding (t/a M J Harding Contractors) v Paice and Springall* [2014] EWHC 3824 (TCC), per Edwards-Stuart J at [41–46].
[67] However, there are recent examples where the courts have declined to enforce on this basis. See *Carillion Construction Ltd v Smith* [2011] EWHC 2190 (TCC), per Akenehead J at [46–68].

Preconditions and restrictions to statutory adjudication

that there was no substantial overlap.[68] It has given the following detailed and helpful guidance:[69]

(1) One needs to consider what is and was the ambit and scope of the disputed claims which is being and was referred to adjudication. That of course will vary from dispute to dispute. One has however to take a reasonably broad brush approach in determining what the referred claims were. The reason for this is to avoid repeat references to adjudication of what is essentially the same dispute.

(2) The fact that different or additional evidence, be it witness, expert or documentary, over and above what was relied upon in the earlier adjudication, is deployed in the later claim to be referred to a second or later adjudication, will not usually alter what the essential dispute is or has been. The reason is that evidence alone does not generally alter what is the essential dispute between the parties. One needs to differentiate between the essential dispute and the evidence required to support or undermine one party's or the other's case or defence.

(3) The fact that different or additional arguments to support or enhance a claiming party's position are deployed in the later adjudication will not usually of itself mean that it is a different dispute to that which was referred earlier. Again, the reason is that different or even better arguments that are deployed in a later adjudication do not usually create an essentially different dispute.

(4) The fact that the quantum is different or is claimed on a different quantification basis in the later reference to adjudication from that claimed in the earlier adjudication is not necessarily a pointer to the referred disputes being in substance different. If for example in Adjudication A the referring party claims for the value of 100 m^3 of supplying and installing concrete, £20,000, at a rate of £200 per cubic metre, a claim for the same concrete work on a time plus materials basis in Adjudication B is essentially the same claim, albeit put on a different basis. There is nothing to stop the referring party in the subsequent arbitration or litigation claiming on each alternate basis but the claim is a claim for payment for the supply and installation of concrete.

(5) One should be particularly cautious about being over-awed in the exercise of comparison of two sets of documents purporting to set out the disputed claims for two adjudications by the amount or bulk of the detail, evidence, analysis, submissions or annexures attached to either.

(6) It is legitimate to look at the expressed motivation by the party in the later adjudication for bringing it and the given reasons for the basis of formulation of the later adjudication claim.

(7) One must bear in mind that Notices of Adjudication and Referral Notices are not required to be in any specific form; they may be more or less detailed and they may or may not be drafted by people with legal expertise. They do not need to be interpreted as if they were contracts, pleadings or statutes.

(8) One strong pointer as to whether disputes are substantially the same is whether essentially the same causes of action are relied upon in the earlier and later Notices of Adjudication and Referral Notices. One must bear in mind that one dispute (like one Claim in Court proceedings) may encompass more than one cause of action.

[7.67] The previous adjudicator's decision only becomes relevant to a subsequent adjudication in so far as the earlier decision relates to matters that were within the scope of the dispute referred to the adjudicator to decide. That part of the decision (which may be all of

---

[68] *Sherwood & Casson Ltd v Mackenzie* [1999] EWHC 274 (TCC), per Thornton J at [30–31].
[69] *Carillion Construction Ltd v Smith* [2011] EWHC 2190 (TCC), per Akenehead J at [46–68].

it) is binding and cannot be raised or adjudicated upon again in any later adjudication (although it can of course be challenged in a final determination). In contrast, any decision or part of a decision which can be described as not deciding the dispute as referred or as expanded effectively within the adjudication process, is not binding and can be raised or adjudicated upon again in any later adjudication. An example might be where an adjudicator offers an *obiter* opinion on a point or topic which is not part of the dispute over which he has jurisdiction.[70]

[7.68] The courts have concluded that two adjudications relating to the same matters but a different dispute is permissible.[71] To put it another way, a party is entitled to refer the same subject matter to a second adjudication, provided the cause or causes of action on which it relies are different from the first. However, where an adjudicator decided that a head of claim was valid in principle but failed for lack of proof of the correct amount, it is not open to the receiving party to plead a different calculation of quantum to a second adjudication.[72]

[7.69] Where an adjudicator makes a decision and that decision is put before the same or another adjudicator in a second adjudication and the adjudicator has regard to it, that is permitted. In *Arcadis UK Ltd v May and Barker Ltd (t/a Sanofi)*,[73] the legal basis of the first adjudication was very similar to the second adjudication, which meant that it was helpful for the second adjudicator to consider the legal analysis of the first. The court said that was permissible, stating that the first adjudicator's findings on what the contract meant were 'at the very least germane... and persuasive'.

[7.70] In certain circumstances, a sum of money can be recovered in a subsequent adjudication even though an attempt to recover the same sum failed in an earlier adjudication. Thus, a referring party may seek to recover sums claimed to be due to them after the certificate of practical completion had been issued but before the expiry of the defects liability period relying on an interim valuation, but that claim may be thwarted by grounds set out in a withholding notice, which identify defective works. The referring party may subsequently claim the same amount of money, after the end of the defects liability period in circumstances where the responding party has not claimed that there are any defects. The sum of money may be the same as that set out in the valuation relied on in the first adjudication, but the basis of the claim from the referring party is contractually different.[74]

[7.71] A distinct, but related point arises where a party could have raised a particular argument on an issue in an adjudication, but chose not to do so. Is that party then entitled to raise the argument on the same issue in a subsequent adjudication? Where the Scheme applies, the answer would appear to be yes. In the Northern Irish case of *Mel Davidson*

---

[70] *Redwing Construction Ltd v Charles Stewart* [2010] EWHC 3366 (TCC), per Akenhead J at [27].
[71] *Holt Insulation Ltd v Colt International Ltd* [2001] EWHC 451 (TCC), per Mackay J at [22].
[72] *Birmingham City Council v Paddison Construction Ltd* [2008] EWHC 2254 (TCC), per Kirkham J at [24–29].
[73] [2013] EWHC 87 (TCC), per Akenhead J at [31–36].
[74] *Bell Building Projects Ltd v Carfin Developments Ltd* [2010] Scots CA 296 09, per Taylor at [14].

Construction v Northern Ireland Housing Executive,[75] the court said it could see 'nothing in the nature of the Scheme which permits the adjudicator, in such circumstances, to refuse to decide a matter referred for decision.'

[7.72] Where the adjudicator finds that the dispute referred is the same or substantially the same as one which has previously been adjudicated, the appropriate course of action is to resign.[76] However, the Scheme makes no provision for the resignation of an adjudicator where the dispute that he is to decide has previously been referred to adjudication but no decision has been taken in that adjudication.[77] Therefore, a situation may arise where one adjudication is started a week after the other and the second adjudication relates to substantially the same as the first. While the court will not enforce the second adjudication, it is not incumbent on the adjudicator to resign.

[7.73] Appendix 8 provides a list of those cases where the principles relating to the issue of substantially the same dispute were debated and also separate lists of those cases where the courts have decided that the dispute in the second adjudication was, or was not, the same or substantially the same as the dispute in the first adjudication.

7.5 Does the dispute arise 'under' the contract (Act s. 108(1))?

7.5.1 In a nutshell

[7.74] Where the Act applies to the contract between the parties, subsection 108(1) provides that a dispute referred to adjudication must arise under the contract. This means that the ground or grounds for relief upon which the referring party relies must derive from the contract between the parties. The contract may be the original contract signed between the parties, or it may be a connected contract, such as a settlement agreement or variation. A dispute said to arise from a contract that is found to be void, will not be a dispute under the contract, because the contract is held to have never existed.

7.5.2 Meaning of 'under' the contract

[7.75] Statutory adjudication is only available for disputes arising 'under' the contract. In other words, the cause of action must have arisen from the contract between the parties pursuant to which one party fails to honour a term or terms of that contract by non-performance or interference with the other party's performance. This includes things like a failure to provide access on time, a delay giving rise to a claim for an extension of time or a claim for the cost of certain works. It may also, depending on the existence and

---

[75] [2014] NIQB 110, per Weatherup J at [19–21].
[76] Paragraph 9(4) of the Scheme.
[77] *Vision Homes v Lancsville Construction Ltd* [2009] EWHC 2042, per Clarke J at [70].

wording of the contract, include a claim for professional negligence,[78] or an order for rectification,[79] restitution[80] and specific performance.[81]

[7.76] Since the adjudicator's power flows from the contract, he is also entitled to determine a question as to whether a particular term has been incorporated into an agreement[82] as well as disputes arising out of variations made to the original terms of the contract,[83] a question as to which of two separate sets of contract conditions applied to the parties (provided that both sets gave him jurisdiction to do so),[84] or the entitlement to and award of damages if the breach of contract is proved.[85] The contract out of which the dispute arises must of course be between the parties to the adjudication. Therefore, where the adjudicator decides a question of costs based on a mechanism in a contract which is later found not to be the contract between the parties, he will have exceeded his jurisdiction.[86]

[7.77] Statutory adjudication is not available for non-contractual claims. For example, where an employer has a claim in common law for negligence against the contractor, or the cause of action is negligent misstatement, or misrepresentation under the Misrepresentation Act 1967,[87] it will not be able to pursue that claim through adjudication. However, where the referring party refers a claim to adjudication pursuant to a payment application and the responding party's defence is that the contract was induced by fraudulent misrepresentation or that the certificate on which the claiming party relies was procured by fraud, it is likely that the adjudicator will have jurisdiction to consider that defence, because the responding party is not limited to the defences it may deploy.[88]

[7.78] It is a common feature of the commercial world and the construction sector that contracts entered into between parties may be assigned. In *Devon County Council v Celtic Composting Systems Ltd*,[89] Celtic had assigned the benefit of the contract that it had entered into with the employer, Devon County Council, to Knowles. Consistent with the terms of the assignment, Celtic launched an adjudication conducted by Knowles in

---

[78] *Gillies Ramsay Diamond v PJW Enterprises Ltd* [2002] ScotCS 340, per Paton J at [67–70].
[79] *Christiani & Nielsen Ltd v The Lowry Centre Development Company Ltd* [2000] AdjLR 06/16, per Thornton J at [38–45].
[80] *ISG Retail Ltd v Castletech Construction Ltd* [2015] EWHC 1443 (TCC), per Edwards-Stuart J at [13–28].
[81] *Multiplex Constructions (UK) Ltd v Mott MacDonald Ltd* [2007] EWHC 20 (TCC), per Jackson J at [43–48].
[82] *RG Carter Ltd v Edmund Nuttall Ltd*, Unreported, 21 June 2000, per Thornton J at [25].
[83] *Ballast plc v The Burrell Company (Construction Management) Ltd* [2001] ScotCS 159 per Lord Reed at [42]. Whether the variation has to be written or not will depend on whether the contract is subject to the 1996 Act. See Section 4.8.
[84] *Dalkia Energy and Technical Services Ltd v Bell Group UK Ltd* [2009] EWHC 73 (TCC), per Coulson J at [42].
[85] *Gillies Ramsay Diamond and Gavin Ramsay and Philip Diamond v PJW Enterprises Ltd* [2003] ScotCS 354, per Clarke LJ at [21]. See also Section 10.7.9.
[86] *Adonis Construction v O'Keefe Soil Remediation* [2009] EWHC 2047 (TCC), per Clarke J at [49–50].
[87] *Hillcrest Homes Ltd v Beresford & Curbishley Ltd* [2014] EWHC 280 (TCC), per Raynor J at [47–53].
[88] *SG South Limited v Kings Head Cirencester LLP* [2009] EWHC 2645, per Akenhead J at [19]. See also Section 18.1.
[89] [2014] EWHC 552 (TCC), per Stuart-Smith J at [25].

which the remedies sought required that any monies due should be paid not to Celtic but to Knowles. The court held that:

> The contract provides that what may be referred to adjudication is disputes arising under the contract; To my mind, Celtic's arrangements with Knowles about who will receive the money; although notice of that assignment was given to Devon is not something which arises under the contract within the meaning of the Act or the contract itself. To my mind, it is quite different from the sort of dispute which is to be referred to adjudication, which is matters arising as to entitlement under the contract and by that I mean substantive entitlement as a result of work carried out and any allegations of breach of obligation and so on.

[7.79] Can there be a dispute under the contract when the contract has been terminated or it is held to be void? Where a contract has been terminated, the matters referred to the adjudicator remain disputes 'under' the contract. Statutory adjudication, and where they exist, contractual provisions in relation to adjudication, remain available just as much as an arbitration clause would remain operative.[90] Where a contract is found to be void, the law holds that it was never in existence and therefore there can be no dispute under the contract. This is considered in more detail at Section 4.3.

[7.80] A dispute arising under an agreement that is ancillary to the original construction contract, such as a settlement agreement, variation agreement, or collateral warranty must itself be a construction contract and the dispute must arise under the contract if the parties wish to adjudicate their dispute within statutory bounds. Therefore, a dispute about the terms of a settlement agreement that settles payment issues under the main contract is not a dispute 'under' the construction contract.[91] See Section 4.4.7 for more on ancillary agreements.

7.6 More than one contract

7.6.1 In a nutshell

[7.81] Where the Act applies to the contract between the parties, section 108(1) provides that the parties may only refer a dispute under a single contract. Where disputes arising under more than one contract are referred to an adjudicator in a single adjudication, the adjudicator will not have jurisdiction to decide them. However, if there is more than one contract and the contracts are connected, then it may still be possible to adjudicate within the statutory framework.

---

[90] *A&D Maintenance and Construction Ltd v Pagehurst Construction Services Ltd* (2000) 16 Const LJ 199, per Glennie at [18–19]. Cross refer to Section 4.3 for more cases.
[91] *Shepherd Construction Limited v Mecright Limited* [2000] BLR 489, per Lloyd J at [16–18]. However, see *Westminster Building Company Ltd v Andrew Beckingham* [2004] EWHC 138 (TCC), per Thornton J at [22–28] where different circumstances led to the court concluding that the adjudicator could consider an alleged settlement agreement although the court decided that it was in fact a variation to the main contract. Cross refer to Section 4.4.7 for more cases.

7.6.2 More than one contract (Act s. 108(1))

[7.82] The starting position is that a dispute referred to adjudication must arise under one contract, not more than one contract. Typically, a dispute will arise out of one contract in respect of one project. However, sometimes the parties will have entered into a number of contracts for different works on the same or different projects. In order that those contracts can be considered as one contract for the purpose of the Act, they must be connected in some way. For instance, the court has found that an adjudicator has jurisdiction to hear a dispute where that dispute arises from the original contract and subsequent variations of that contract,[92] or from a framework agreement and a series of call-off contracts.[93] In the latter example, this was justified on the basis that the contractual adjudication mechanism applied to 'any dispute or difference arising out of or in connection with' the framework agreement and that this was enough to capture the call-off contracts.

[7.83] One example of a case where the courts have held that the adjudicator did not have jurisdiction is *Enterprise Managed Services Ltd v Tony McFadden Utilities Ltd*.[94] There, the referring party sought to bring their claim under one of four contracts that existed between the parties. However, because of the nature of the claim[95] it was necessary to consider all four contracts. Therefore, the court readily concluded that the adjudicator did not have jurisdiction to decide the dispute.

[7.84] In *Viridis UK Ltd v Mulalley & Company Ltd*[96] the contractor issued a number of separate orders to the subcontractor for certain elements of the works. Viridis argued that the first order, order 24, was agreed between the parties, and the additional five orders agreed were essentially call-offs from that first order. The court held that the parties never reached agreement on payment terms, liquidated damages (LDs) and survey costs for order 24. The subsequent orders the contractor issued were not variations or orders placed under an 'overarching framework contract'. Furthermore, the work that was the subject of the dispute that was referred to adjudication was carried out by the subcontractor under orders 51, 62 and 77, which meant that there was more than one contract, which in turn meant the adjudicator did not have jurisdiction.

[7.85] Where there is a dispute about which contract applies in circumstances where it was contended that a series of contracts had been entered into, then provided that an adjudicator is properly appointed under a contract about which there is or can be no dispute, then he may also have jurisdiction to resolve jurisdictional issues if they are coincidentally part of the substantive dispute referred to him.[97]

---

[92] *Air Design (Kent) Ltd v Deerglen (Jersey) Ltd* [2008] EWHC 3047 (TCC) per Akenhead J at [21–24].
[93] *Amec Group Limited v Thames Water Utilities Ltd* [2010] EWHC 419 (TCC), per Coulson J at [35–39].
[94] [2009] EWHC 3222 (TCC), per Coulson J at [62].
[95] Rule 4.90 of the Insolvency Rules 1986 applied, which among other things requires that all the contracts between the parties are considered.
[96] [2014] EWHC 268 (TCC), per Stephen Davies J at [58–68].
[97] *Air Design (Kent) Ltd v Deerglen (Jersey) Ltd* [2008] EWHC 3047 (TCC), per Akenhead J at [22], *Camillin Denny Architects v Adelaide Jones & Company Limited* [2009] EWHC 2110, per Akenhead J at [28–31], *Supablast v Story Rail Limited* [2010] EWHC 56 (TCC), per Akenhead J at [29].

7.6.3 Scheme (Scheme p. 8(2))

[7.86]   Where the Scheme applies, subparagraph 8(2) provides:

> The adjudicator may, with the consent of all the parties to those disputes, adjudicate at the same time on related disputes under different contracts, whether or not one or more of those parties is a party to those disputes.

[7.87]   An important word in this subparagraph is 'related'. The Scheme is intended to cover situations where there are related disputes under different contracts, whether or not the parties to those contracts are the same. Those disputes may be concerned with the same facts, or substantially the same facts, or some of the same facts, or they might even be about the same provision in a contract. Where consent is given by the parties, it must be 'real and informed'.[98]

[7.88]   Where the parties reach an agreement under subparagraph 8(2), subparagraph 8(3) provides that the parties may agree to extend the period within which the adjudicator may reach a decision in relation to all or any of the disputes. Subparagraph 8(4) provides that where an adjudicator ceases to act because a dispute is to be adjudicated on by another person, that adjudicator's fees and expenses shall be determined in accordance with paragraph 25 of the Scheme.

7.7 Commencing an adjudication 'at any time'

7.7.1 In a nutshell

[7.89]   Where the contract is one to which the Act applies and is subject to the preconditions and restrictions of the Act being met,[99] subsections 108(1) and 108(2)(a) the Act provide a mandatory right for parties to a construction contract to adjudicate a dispute 'at any time'. This means that a party can commence adjudication during or after a project, or it can commence two or more adjudications simultaneously, or concurrently with another form of dispute resolution. There are, however, some limitations on this right, which can either be imposed contractually or are imposed by statute.

7.7.2 Act (Act s. 108(2)(a))

[7.90]   Subsection 108(2)(a) of the Act provides:

> The contract shall enable a party to give notice at any time of his intention to refer a dispute to adjudication

[7.91]   This provision permits a referring party to commence an adjudication at any time. Where the Act applies, any contractual provision that fetters this right will result in the entire

---
[98] *Pring & St. Hill Ltd v C J Hafner t/a Southern Erectors* [2002] EWHC 1775 (TCC), per Lloyd J at [13–22]
[99] Refer to the overview to this chapter for a summary.

adjudication provisions of the contract being replaced by those of the Scheme.[100] This includes a requirement that the dispute is referred first to mediation,[101] or that a notice of dissatisfaction is issued first. As it was put by Ramsey J in *City Basements Ltd v Nordic Construction UK Ltd*:[102]

> Whilst dispute avoidance and the early resolution of disputes by informal contact is obviously of great benefit to the construction industry, it is not a precursor to adjudication.

[7.92] The Scheme does not use the words 'at any time' in its procedure, although that omission has been held not to fetter the requirements of the Act.[103]

[7.93] The impact of the right to adjudicate at any time has a fundamental impact on the way in which parties react to disputes that arise. Many contracts contain multi-tiered dispute resolution procedures. These procedures comprise a number of options for resolving disputes, and typically one option must be undertaken or at least attempted before the parties can move on to the next option. For instance, the procedure may require an engineer to make a decision, then if that fails the parties may refer the dispute to the board of directors, if that fails the parties may refer the dispute to mediation and if that fails the dispute may be referred to arbitration. Statutory adjudication cuts through multi-tiered procedures, such that any party to a contract may commence an adjudication at any time, regardless of what stage the multi-tiered process is at, although by contrast the parties may provide that a dispute may not be referred to another form of dispute resolution before it is referred to adjudication.[104]

[7.94] It follows that unless the rules of the other form of dispute resolution prohibit it, adjudication can be conducted concurrently with any other form of dispute resolution, including litigation,[105] arbitration[106] or mediation.[107] This approach can be sensible, particularly where the parties are litigating or arbitrating, because if the adjudication resolves the dispute, it will bring to an end otherwise long and expensive proceedings. In litigation, subject to the particular circumstances, a court will try to facilitate a stay of proceedings to encourage an alternative means of resolving the dispute, including adjudication.[108] Where the parties' contract makes adjudication mandatory prior to a final dispute resolution process, then the court are even more likely to grant a stay.[109]

---

[100] See Section 6.2.2.
[101] *Ericsson AB v Eads Defence and Security Systems Limited* [2009] EWHC 2598 (TCC), per Akenhead J at [49–60].
[102] [2014] EWHC 4817 (TCC), per Ramsey J at [28].
[103] *Herschell Engineering Ltd v Breen Property Ltd* [2000] BLR 272, per Dyson J at [18].
[104] *Enterprise Managed Services Ltd v East Midland Contracting Ltd* [2008] EWHC 727 (TCC), per Davies J at [32–36].
[105] *Mentmore Towers Ltd v Packman Lucas Ltd* [2010] EWHC 457 (TCC), per Edwards-Stuart J at [22].
[106] *Herschell Engineering Ltd v Breen Property Ltd* [2000] BLR 272, per Dyson J at [18–20].
[107] *Ericsson AB v EADS Defence and Security Systems Ltd* [2009] EWHC 2598 (TCC), per Akenhead J at [49–60].
[108] *Cubitt Building & Interiors Ltd v Richardson Roofing (Industrial) Ltd* [2008] EWHC 1020 (TCC), per Akenhead J at [72].
[109] *DGT Steel and Cladding Ltd v Cubitt Building and Interiors Ltd* [2007] EWHC 1584, per Coulson J at [12 and 21].

7.7.3 Conclusivity clauses

[7.95] While it is right that parties are free to adjudicate their dispute at any time, contracts can in effect limit this right by only permitting the parties to adjudicate a dispute within a fixed period of time. For instance, the JCT 1998[110] and 2005[111] contracts provide that the final certificate shall have effect in any proceedings under or arising out of or in connection with the contract as conclusive evidence of the matters listed in the certificate unless adjudication proceedings are commenced within 28 days of its issue. This has been held[112] as legitimately limiting the rights of the parties to adjudicate disputes (in relation to matters contained within the certificate) to those commencing within the time period stipulated. For these purposes, the commencement of an adjudication is signified by the issue of the notice of adjudication.[113] Where the notice of adjudication is validly served, but the referral notice is invalidly served, then the right to adjudicate is not lost provided that the adjudication is restarted expeditiously.[114]

[7.96] If the contents of the certificate are challenged within the allotted time, that does not have the effect of nullifying the certificate, so that further proceedings may be commenced after the deadline. Furthermore, depending on the wording of the certificate, challengers may need to choose which form of dispute resolution they wish to use. They may not commence two identical disputes in different forums within the requisite period. In *The Trustees of the Marc Gilbard 2009 Settlement Trust v OD Developments and Projects Ltd*,[115] the parties entered into a JCT 2005 contract containing a conclusivity clause in respect of the Final Certificate. The clause required that the parties refer matters dealt with by the Final Certificate to dispute resolution within 28 days. The contractor duly commenced Part 7 proceedings within the 28-day period, but then those proceedings were stayed by the parties for the next 13 months. The contractor, frustrated with the progress of the litigation, commenced an adjudication. The Trustees objected on the basis that it was only open to the parties to commence one form of dispute resolution within the 28-day period. The judge agreed. He was in 'no doubt' that just because the contractor had got a 'foot in the door' by commencing court proceedings did not also entitle it to commence another set of proceedings (in this case adjudication) at the same time, nor did it entitle the contractor to commence that second set of proceedings some 12 months after the 28-day period. The judge rejected the suggestion that this result fettered the contractor's right to adjudicate at any time. The contractor could have adjudicated had it so wished, provided that it did so within the 28-day period. Furthermore, it could have adjudicated and then litigated (the contract provided for a further 28-day period after the conclusion of an adjudication to commence court proceedings), but instead the contractor chose to refer the dispute straight to court proceedings.

---

[110] Clause 30.9.
[111] Clause 1.10.
[112] *Tracy Bennett v FMK Construction Ltd* [2005] EWHC 1268 (TCC), per Havery J at [18].
[113] *University of Brighton v Dovehouse Interiors Ltd* [2014] EWHC 940 (TCC), per Carr J at [40–52].
[114] *University of Brighton v Dovehouse Interiors Ltd* [2014] EWHC 940 (TCC), per Carr J at [75–98].
[115] [2015] EWHC 70 (TCC), per Coulson J at [22–40].

[7.97] The permissibility of conclusivity clauses is reflected in the Scheme at subparagraph 20(a), which provides that the adjudicator may decide that any decision taken or any certificate given by any person referred to in the contract may be opened up, revised and reviewed by the adjudicator unless the contract states that the decision or certificate is final and conclusive.

7.7.4 Statutory limitation

[7.98] A dispute resolved by adjudication is subject to the same rules on limitation as a dispute brought in any other forum. While there is nothing to stop a referring party commencing a dispute where the limitation period on the claim has expired, a limitation defence must be taken into account by the adjudicator. If he fails to do so, then any payment made pursuant to his award would give rise to a claim for restitution.[116] Refer to Section 15.4.2 for more detail on this and for relevant case law.

7.7.5 Insolvent party

[7.99] Adjudication proceedings are 'other proceedings' within the meaning of subsection 11(3)(d) of the Insolvency Act 1986 and therefore leave may be required by the court or the appointed insolvency practitioner to commence an adjudication by or against an insolvent company depending on the type of insolvency the company has entered into.[117] Section 3.6 addresses the ability to adjudicate by or against an insolvent party in more detail and together with Appendix 8, refers to the relevant cases.

---

[116] *Connex South Eastern Ltd v MJ Building Services Group plc* [2004] EWHC 1518 (TCC), per Havery J at [33–34].
[117] *Straume Ltd v Bradlor Development Ltd* [1999] CILL 1520, per Behrens at [9–16].

Chapter 8
Adjudication strategy

8.1 Overview

[8.01] Strategising in dispute resolution is always important, but perhaps no more so than with adjudication, where the tight timescale and the temporarily binding nature of the decision means that if the wrong strategy is adopted, there will be little, if any, opportunity to correct it before the consequences of that error are felt in the adjudicator's decision. When should the notice of adjudication be served? Should the entire dispute be referred in one adjudication, or should it be broken into more than one? If more than one, should this be commenced concurrently or successively? How should the scope of the dispute be framed in the notice of adjudication? What follows are some legal and process-focused considerations that may be relevant to a referring or responding party before or during an adjudication.

8.2 Commencing the adjudication process

8.2.1 Choosing the right time to start

[8.02] Deciding when to commence an adjudication may be driven by financial, commercial or project-related factors. For instance, a party may desperately need the money it considers is owed to it as soon as possible, and so has no choice but to start the adjudication process immediately. Alternatively, there may be contractual timing restrictions that require that an adjudication must be commenced within a few weeks or it may not be commenced at all. However, if there are no imminent pressures on commencing, a vital factor in choosing the right time to start will be the availability of key people during the adjudication. The adjudication timetable is normally very tight, and if key people are unavailable to address the legal and factual arguments advanced by the other party, the chances of success in that adjudication will plummet.

[8.03] For the referring party, all of the work to prepare the notice of adjudication and referral notice should be complete before the notice of adjudication is served. Furthermore, since the notice of adjudication defines the scope of the dispute referred to adjudication and the referral document is merely an expansion of the issues identified in the notice of adjudication, it is strongly recommended that the referral notice is drafted first, and

---

A Practical Guide to Construction Adjudication, First Edition. James Pickavance.
© 2016 James Pickavance. Published 2016 by John Wiley & Sons, Inc.

the (much shorter) notice of adjudication is drafted afterwards, almost as an executive summary. This will ensure that the notice of adjudication covers everything that it needs to and that there are no gaps.

[8.04] The referring party's work will usually not end with the service of the referral notice. It will still have to work on submissions for the reply and possibly the sur-rejoinder. In a non-extended timetable, the referring party is likely to have, at most, three or four days to prepare the reply and one or two days for the sur-rejoinder. Those involved in the dispute are likely to be working full time (and then some) during these periods to prepare or assist with the preparation of submissions. Therefore, when selecting the date on which the notice of adjudication is to be served, the referring party should have mapped out when it considers it likely that the further submissions will be due and should ensure that the relevant people are available for the periods leading up to them. Very often the dates when these further submissions are due will change from what has been anticipated, but this approach means that all that can be done is done.

[8.05] It is important to focus the notice of adjudication and the referral notice on the key issues in dispute. A failure to do so can materially increase the amount of work to be done in the later stages of the dispute, which increases costs, diverts resources and increases uncertainty of outcome. If the dispute initially referred is poorly focused, then the result will be that the subissues in the dispute will proliferate, with the reply and any sur-rejoinder getting longer and longer to cope with new issues and subissues as they arise. This is the opposite of what should happen. A properly thought through and well presented, tightly focused referral notice will likely decrease the workload in the later stages of the dispute and lead to a concise reply and sur-rejoinder that focuses in on the key issues.

8.2.2 Getting in there first

[8.06] There is undoubtedly truth in the view held by most adjudication protagonists that the adjudication process is heavily loaded in favour of the referring party. Invariably, the referring party will have had many weeks or months to prepare a detailed, well-considered referral notice, witness statement(s) and expert reports. While the responding party may sometimes anticipate the referral of the adjudication to some extent and begin preparing its defence before the notice of adjudication is served, in the vast majority of cases it will not, and in a statutory adjudication with an unextended timetable, it is only likely to have 14 days to do so. The benefits of being first extend beyond preparation time. The referring party controls the scope of the dispute in the notice of adjudication and so, through careful drafting of the notice of adjudication, it can avoid placing disputed issues before the adjudicator that have a low prospect of success. It can also limit the extent of the submissions and supporting evidence placed before the responding party by providing a skeleton referral notice with a view to avoiding 'showing its colours' until it has seen what the responding party's defence is (see Section 8.5.1). The referring party also controls the timetable to some extent because it has the unilateral right to extend the timetable from 28 to 42 days. For these reasons, being the referring party is usually better than being the responding party and because of that, if one party senses the other party is planning to commence an adjudication, that party should consider whether it is in a position to commence one first. It is likely that the advantages outweigh the additional weight of bearing the burden of proof in relation to the allegations made.

[8.07] That being said, there is a clear tension between being first and being prepared. It is wise to wait until one's case is fully prepared before issuing the notice of adjudication because there is only seven days between serving the notice of adjudication and the referral notice. A reasonable portion of that time will be taken up appointing the adjudicator. This means that ensuring that the notice of adjudication is complete, and that the referral notice and any evidence collation or preparation is either complete or very nearly complete, is probably more important than getting in there first.

8.3 More than one adjudication

8.3.1 Multiple adjudications during the project

[8.08] Because adjudication is comparatively simple and quick, parties will often use it as the primary method of resolving disputes when negotiations reach an impasse. Where there are lots of issues on projects (as there often are) it can lead to numerous adjudications as the project progresses.

[8.09] On the one hand, this can be effective. It may be strategically or commercially prudent for the referring party to seek interim binding decisions by referring discrete legal points, or confined issues of disputed fact; or to sample five out of, say, fifty disputed issues with the same or similar legal basis in an attempt to gain a feel for how all fifty issues might be decided.

[8.10] On the other hand, the more adjudications there are, the more combative the parties will become, and the greater the risk that one or both parties will be dissatisfied with one or more of the decisions increases, which in turn may drive a party towards expensive litigation or arbitration in an attempt to reverse the decision. Furthermore, since the parties' costs of adjudication are normally not recoverable unless the parties agree otherwise (which invariably they do not), multiple adjudications can make for an expensive way of resolving all the disputes.

[8.11] Where this approach is followed, one rule that is particularly susceptible to falling down on is that the referring party is not entitled to refer the same or substantively the same dispute to adjudication more than once, nor is it entitled to raise an issue in a subsequent adjudication that it could have raised in a previous one. Section 7.4 provides more detail on this.

8.3.2 Concurrent adjudications

[8.12] Adjudications involve an intense period of work for both the professional advisors and the project teams. One tactic sometimes used by a referring party is to commence two or more adjudications at once or within a short space of time, in order to make life as difficult as possible for the other side. In statutory adjudication, this is permissible, since the Act provides that an adjudication may be commenced at any time.[1] It may also be permitted in contractual adjudication, depending on the rules of the adjudication and the terms of the contract. The compressed timescale of adjudication means that this approach will place the responding party under a considerable amount of pressure to prepare a defence to the disputes within the time available, draining resource from its project and its legal teams and will also mean that the quality of the defences is likely to be poorer. A referring party may perceive that the tactic will increase the chances of securing several 'wins' in a short space of time, providing cash (if the dispute relates to money) and importantly a morale boost to its team.

[8.13] Preparation is vital if this strategy is deployed. In particular, it is prudent to ensure that the disputes referred arise out of discrete issues and that the notices of adjudications are drafted so as to limit the scope of the dispute. Where this tactic can backfire is if one or more of the notices of adjudication are drafted widely, so as to permit the responding party to bring in a range of defences that the referring party may not be prepared to address.[2] Where this happens, and where no extension to the timetable is granted, the referring party can find it almost impossible to deal with those defences in the three or four days it will have to draft the reply.

[8.14] There are additional risks to this strategy. While the court is unlikely to take the view that the referring party unfairly ambushed the responding party, it will feel like an ambush. Rather than being a genuine attempt to resolve disputes between the parties, the responding party is likely to view this as a tactic aimed at securing a win, not by reason of the merits of its case, but as a result of the inability of the responding party to respond properly. Not only will this almost certainly lead to deterioration in relationships, but also the responding party is much more likely to bring final proceedings with the aim of overturning the adjudication decisions. In so doing, the responding party will have the time it needs to prepare the claim, and will now also have the benefit of having the arguments and evidence lodged by the referring party in the adjudication.

8.4 Choosing the dispute to refer

8.4.1 Appropriate expertise

[8.15] One of the benefits of adjudications is that the parties have a degree of autonomy over who is selected as the adjudicator. The degree of autonomy depends on the terms of the contract and the cooperation of the parties. It normally makes sense for the appointed adjudicator to have experience in the legal or technical issues in dispute. However, a dispute may encompass different technical or legal issues that are sufficiently varied that

---

[1] See Section 7.7.2.
[2] See Section 9.3.3(B) and Section 6.7.3(B) for more information on drafting the notice of adjudication and the ability of the responding party to raise any defence to the claim respectively.

Adjudication strategy

they do not readily lend themselves to being resolved by a single adjudicator. It may be better to refer different issues to different adjudicators whose expertise lies with the relevant issue. For example, an adjudicator with a background in programming may be better placed to decide a dispute about an extension of time, whereas an adjudicator with a background in law may be better placed to determine a dispute about the interpretation of a contractual provision.

[8.16] If a referring party were to combine both of these issues in one adjudication and a programming expert was appointed as an adjudicator, for example, the risk of the adjudicator reaching a poor or even wrong decision on the legal issue increases. Parties can deal with this in the contract by agreeing the appointment of an adjudicator or by listing different panels of adjudicators for different types of dispute. In practice however, provided the issues are not unusual in the context of construction disputes, most adjudicators appointed to the panels of adjudication nominating bodies are experienced and knowledgeable enough to be able to deal with the putative legal and technical issues that arise.

8.4.2 Pecuniary and declaratory claims

[8.17] Most commonly, the reason a claim is made is to obtain an award of money payable to it by the other party. This may involve the assessment of an interim application, a final account, the valuation of defects, the quantum assessment of a disallowed cost, or prolongation costs flowing from an extension of time. Clearly pecuniary claims are attractive because, if successful, the immediate result is money in the bank for the successful party.

[8.18] However, money claims may open the door to a much wider dispute. For instance, where the claim is in respect of an amount applied for in an interim certificate, because the calculation of the amount due is often calculated on a cumulative basis, the payer may be able to counter the claim for money with a series of counterclaims and cross-claims.

[8.19] As an alternative, it may be appropriate to refer a dispute to adjudication seeking certain declarations which, if upheld by the adjudicator, would cement the other party's legal liability in respect of a particular issue and subsequently lead, either inexorably or at least in likelihood, to a liability in quantum. Declaratory claims are suited to adjudications on issues such as extensions of time, contractual interpretations (such as the effectiveness of a time bar clause), technical issues (such as whether an item of work is or is not defective), whether particular work is included in the contract price or is an additional item and whether the other party is in breach of contract. The principal advantage of this approach is that it closes down the other party's opportunity to raise counter arguments that do not relate to the scope of the declaration sought.

[8.20] However, the obvious shortcoming with a declaratory claim is that very often the result will not achieve the end goal that the victor ultimately seeks. For instance, a declaration from the adjudicator that the contractor has breached the contract in failing to proceed regularly and diligently, thus causing delay on the project will not give the employer an immediate tangible benefit. It will then need to commence a further set of proceedings to recover whatever loss it has suffered consequent to that failure.

[8.21] A declaratory adjudication may not provide the adjudicator with sufficient information to enable him to measure the financial importance of the dispute referred to him. For example, he may be asked to interpret a clause in a contract, without being made aware that a very large sum of money turns on his interpretation. That can bring with it a risk of an unsatisfactory result. This problem can be circumvented, by overtly drawing attention to the financial importance of the declaration.

[8.22] A further problem with a declaratory adjudication is that the adjudicator, in making his declaration, can sometimes choose a form of words that is different from what the referring party would have wished, or worse still is open to interpretation. So it is important to assist the adjudicator by providing a form of words for the redress sought. Care should be taken not to close down the adjudicator's options too far, however. Should he decide that the form of words offered is not suitable, he may wish to use alternative wording. The best way to address this might be to offer the form of words, or in the alternative 'such other declaration as the adjudicator sees fit'. If the declarations only go to hypothetical, rather than real situations, or the adjudicator decides that the dispute between the parties is really a question of fact, then of course he may decline to grant declarations at all.

8.4.3 Contractual interpretation

[8.23] Putting aside contractual misfeasance, the entitlement to additional payment under the contract usually flows from a relatively small number of clauses. Understanding the precise scope and meaning of clauses entitling a variation, an extension of time and disallowed cost is always important. In a project of any scale, it may well be that the outcome of a number of claims turns on the precise scope and meaning of the clause. For example, there may be a dispute as to the scope of a compensation event clause. The employer may argue a narrow interpretation of the clause and rely on that interpretation to justify the project manager's rejection of the contractor's notification. The contractor may argue a wide interpretation, which if correct, would permit the compensation event. Where the exact meaning is disputed between the parties, it can be very helpful to refer that dispute to an adjudicator.

[8.24] Referring a dispute of this nature can be effective early on, or towards the end of the project. Early on in the project, the parties can agree quite amicably to adjudicate a point of law or contractual interpretation so that they may have clarity on what the position is for the remainder of the project. Conversely, towards the end of a project, or after it has completed, two or three adjudications on contractual points of principle may well settle a range of disputed issues and mean that the parties reach agreement on the remaining issues without recourse to further dispute resolution.

8.4.4 'Smash and grab'

[8.25] If there was ever an issue that strikes at the heart of the Act, then this is one. For this reason and that the legal issues in question are complex, the following explanation is more involved than those given in other parts of this chapter.

[8.26] Where the Act applies, and a payee makes an application for payment, if the payer wishes to pay less than the amount applied for but does not issue a withholding or pay less notice within the time required by the contract, subject to a debate about whether the amount applied for is due,[3] the payee will be entitled to the amount applied for, regardless of whether or not the payer considers, legitimately or otherwise, that the amount to be paid should be less. Where, in the absence of a withholding or pay less notice, the payer does not pay the full amount by the final date for payment, the payee may commence an adjudication to recover the sums due. This type of adjudication is sometimes known as a 'smash and grab' adjudication, because it is (in theory) a sure-fire way obtaining an award in the payee's favour and arises out of a technical argument based on the failure to issue a withholding or pay less notice and not on any argument as to whether the contractor was entitled to the sums applied for. What is more, since the amendments were introduced to the Late Payment of Commercial Debts (Interest) Act 1998 in March 2013, where that act applies, it may be possible for the payee to recover all the costs of the adjudication from the payer.[4]

[8.27] Historically and notwithstanding the strong legal footing of such a claim, adjudicators have been reticent to grant the referring party what it seeks because the claim does not get to the heart of the matter. Therefore, adjudicators have often latched on to the smallest crumb of evidence, such as any argument that the withholding or pay less notice was issued, or good reasons why it was not, in order to reject the claim wholesale or look behind the payment application notice and issue a decision on the correct value of the work that is the subject of the application. Where such morsels are not available the most likely outcome has always been that the adjudicator will enforce the failure to issue a withholding notice with an award in the payee's favour.[5]

[8.28] However, rather than pay the sum determined as due by the adjudicator, it has up until recently, been common practice for the responding party in the first adjudication to commence a second adjudication, either before or soon after the first adjudicator's decision, which seeks a determination of the value of the work carried out that was the subject of the application in the first adjudication. If the adjudicator in the second adjudication decided that the value of the works done was less than the amount applied for, then the referring party in the second adjudication (the responding party and payer in the first adjudication), would then set-off one adjudicator's decision from the other with the effect that the amount it ultimately paid was the true value of the works and not the sum

---

[3] Section 10.6.4 addresses the position with regard to set off and abatement.
[4] See Section 12.3.4 for further information on this point.
[5] *Harding (t/a MJ Harding Contractors) v Paice and another* [2014] EWHC 3824 (TCC), per Edwards-Stuart J at [30–37] for a recent decision upholding the effect of a failure to issue a pay less notice.

applied for. While this might seem an overall fair result, it may be seen as effectively neutering one of the central functions of the Act, which is to ensure that the payer pays the amount applied for forthwith in circumstances where a valid withholding or pay less notice is not in place. The neutering effect of the valuation adjudication was the reason that the editors of the Building Law Reports in the case of *Urang Commercial Ltd v Century Investments Ltd*[6] used to suggest that enforcement cases essentially arising from the failure to issue a withholding or pay less notice are rare.

[8.29] A recent quartet of cases has shone a light on the issue of smash and grab adjudications and in particular the ability of the paying party in the first adjudication to commence a second valuation adjudication. The question that has been at the heart of each of these cases is whether a party to a construction contract can challenge a payment notice in circumstances where it hasn't served the relevant pay less notice when it is said the payment notice is wrong or must the payer pay it forthwith.

[8.30] Before considering these cases, and although it is not within the scope of this book to address the statutory payment regime in detail, it is helpful to refer to certain aspects of the payment regime now.

(1) The payment regime under the 1996 Act and the 2009 Act are fundamentally different. Under the 1996 Act, section 110 permitted parties to a construction contract to agree whatever mechanism they deemed appropriate in order to calculate the amount due. However, pursuant to the 2009 Act, section 110A provides that the payer, payee or specified person issue a payment notice in accordance with the provisions of that section. Parties are no longer free, as they once were, to agree the mechanism to calculate the amount due, because the amount due is the amount in the payment notice. The payment notice should equate to the sum that is properly due, but in fact it is the author's assessment of what sum is due, which may be different from the amount properly due for a variety of reasons, because the author considers that the payee is entitled to payment that it is not in fact entitled to, because there has been a mistake or a divergence of views.

(2) It follows that because the payment mechanisms under the 1996 Act and the 2009 Act are different, decisions of the court decided under the 1996 Act in relation to this issue are of limited assistance.

(3) It is trite that the 1996 Act sets out what the parties must do with regard to payment. To the extent that the contract provides for a mechanism that is different from the legislation, the contractual provisions are invalid.

(4) Section 111 of the 1996 and 2009 Acts does not differentiate between the type of payment to which they apply. Thus, it applies to a single lump sum payment, payments in instalments (interim payments or interim payments on account), final payment or payments upon termination.

(5) Section 111(1) of the 2009 Act, which deals with the requirement to pay the notified sum, provides:

---
[6] [2011] EWHC 1561.

Subject as follows, where a payment is provided for by a construction contract, the payer must pay the notified sum (to the extent not already paid) on or before the final date for payment.

This provision does not expressly address the question of whether a party to a construction contract must pay the notified sum where it considers that it is wrong. It may be taken to mean either that the payer must pay the notified sum but is free to start its own proceedings to challenge it if it wishes, or that the obligation to pay the notified sum means what it says and that this can't be diluted by the payer seeking to achieve some different outcome before paying the sum.

[8.31] With that background in mind, it is now appropriate to turn to the quartet of cases.

[8.32] The first three cases were all decided by Edwards-Stuart J within four months of each other, they were all employer/contractor disputes and the contracts were all based on the JCT form. In *Harding t/a MJ Harding Contractors v Paice and Springall*,[7] the contractor terminated the contract (a JCT IFC 2011 form) and then issued a post termination final account valuation as required by the contract. It is relevant that the contract between the parties in this case provided that the employer was to pay the 'amount properly due in respect of the account'. This wording, it is submitted, is contrary to the requirement of the 2009 Act, which requires the payer to pay the amount in the payment notice. There is no question that the payer should only pay the amount 'properly due'.

[8.33] In any event, the employer (Paice and Springall) failed to issue a pay less notice, Harding commenced an adjudication for the full amount applied and was awarded the full amount. The employer then commenced a second adjudication seeking a valuation of the works that were the subject of the valuation. Harding made an application to the court for an injunction on the basis that the second adjudicator had no jurisdiction because unless a valid pay less notice had been served, then the amount applied for was due and could not ever be undone. Harding also argued that as a matter of fact the scope of the first adjudication included an assessment of the merits of the application, but the adjudicator decided that he did not need to address that point because of the failure to issue a pay less notice.

[8.34] The court disagreed, holding that the adjudicator's decision that the amount applied for was to be paid did not mean that the paying party was precluded for all time from commencing further proceedings to determine the value of the works. It also confirmed that where the adjudicator does not make a decision on an issue or issues, in this case the true value of the amount applied for, it is open for either party to raise those issues in a second adjudication. It seems to have been a relevant consideration to the court that the application in question related to the final account, not an interim application although it is questionable whether this distinction between types of payment is important for the reasons adumbrated earlier.

---

[7] [2014] EWHC 3824 (TCC) per Edwards-Stuart J at [30–37].

[8.35] The second case is that of *ISG Construction Ltd v Seevic College*.[8] There, under a JCT 2011 design and build form, the contractor issued an interim application for payment (albeit after practical completion), the employer did not issue a pay less notice nor did it pay and so the contractor commenced a 'smash and grab' adjudication. The contractor obtained an award in its favour for £1.1 million based on the employer's failure to issue a pay less notice. Before the conclusion of the first adjudication, the employer commenced a second adjudication and asked the adjudicator to value the contractor's works in respect of the same amount applied for in the first application. The second adjudicator valued the works at £315,000 and awarded a repayment of around £700,000 to the employer. In the event, the employer had not paid the £1.1 million and so there was nothing to repay. As a result, the contractor commenced proceedings to enforce the adjudicator's first decision and a declaration that the second adjudication was invalid because the second adjudicator lacked jurisdiction. The court enforced the first adjudicator's decision and declined to enforce the second adjudication for the following reasons.

- The contract provides no mechanism for repayment of sums from the contractor to the employer. The only mechanisms for payment under the contract were through interim applications or the Final Statement.
- The employer is not entitled to demand a valuation of the contractor's work on any other date than the valuation dates for interim applications.
- If the employer fails to serve any notices in time it must be taken to be agreeing the value stated in the application, right or wrong.
- If an employer that failed to serve a payment or pay less notice against an interim application could then refer to adjudication the value of that interim application (which may require a payment to the contractor or a repayment by the contractor), that would 'completely undermine' the statutory payment regime.
- The second adjudicator was asked to decide the same dispute as the first, which meant he lacked jurisdiction.

[8.36] Therefore, in contrast to *Harding*, in *ISG* the judge prohibited the subsequent valuation adjudication. Four observations may be made:

(1) The mechanism for payment in the contract in *Harding* is different and, it is submitted, defective. The mechanism in *ISG* appears compliant with the 2009 Act.
(2) The application in *ISG* was interim and not final. While again this seems to have been relevant to the court, it is submitted that this distinction is not relevant.
(3) The relief sought in the second adjudication was repayment, which was clearly prohibited (at that stage) under the contract.
(4) In part, the court found support for its conclusion in the case of *Watkin Jones & Son Ltd v Lidl UK GmbH (No. 2)*,[9] although for the reasons explained, it is thought that the decisions of the court on the 1996 Act are of limited, if any, applicability.

---

[8] [2014] EWHC 4195 (TCC), per Edwards-Stuart J at [22–33; 42–53].
[9] [2002] EWHC 183 (TCC), per Lloyd J at [16–26].

[8.37] Perhaps the most surprising and draconian of those observations is that interim applications that have not been the subject of a valid pay less notice cannot in themselves be challenged. In effect, the value of the application is unimpeachable.

[8.38] The decision was supported (albeit by the same judge) in the next case on this issue, *Galliford Try Building v Estura Ltd*.[10] In this case, the contractor issued an interim application, the employer's agent neglected to serve a pay less notice in time and the contractor commenced an adjudication for the value of the application. Estura commenced a second adjudication seeking a declaration as to the valuation of the amount in the interim application, which it considered to be some £4 million less. The second adjudicator resigned on the basis that, in line with the *ISG* decision (which had been issued six days after the commencement of the second adjudication), it was not open to him to value the amount in the interim application. Galliford commenced enforcement proceedings and the court enforced the adjudicator's decision, declining to entertain any of Estura's jurisdictional objections.

[8.39] In giving its judgment, the court held that where there is a dispute, as in this case, as to the correct amount owing in an alleged ambiguous interim application, it was open to the paying party to challenge the adjudicator's decision on that issue in a final determination. Thus, the court said that if the paying party commenced Part 8 proceedings, then it may well be the case that the court arrives at a different decision to the adjudicator at the same time, or soon after the adjudication enforcement proceedings.[11] To be clear, the court did not say that Part 8 can be used to determine the true value of the sum applied for in an interim application where no pay less notice has been issued. The court's view, as in *ISG*, is that an unchallenged interim payment application is permanent. Furthermore, if one accepts that all types of payment are the same under the Act, it may be said that this case and *ISG* is support for the view that any unchallenged payment becomes permanent.

[8.40] Whilst it may be possible to correct overpayments in subsequent interim applications or a final account, if the overpayment falls towards the end of the project, such as in a final payment application, and the overpayment is not capable of being recouped in later applications, this could cause real difficulties. Indeed, it is understood that the recent practice of payees is that post practical completion, they submit an application for payment, then keep updating the application with a minor change and resubmitting it in the hope that on one cycle the payer will miss the pay less notice. This is exactly what happened the most recent case on this issue, *Caledonian Modular Ltd v Mar City Developments Ltd*,[12] where the contractor submitted application number 15 on 30 January 2015 and subsequently submitted an updated application which the contractor sought to argue was a new application. Although a pay less notice was issued against the 30 January 2015 application, one was not issued against the later submission. The contractor commenced a smash and grab adjudication, the adjudicator awarded the contractor over £1.5 million, the employer failed to pay and so the contractor sought to enforce. The court rejected the

---

[10] [2015] EWHC 412 (TCC), per Edwards-Stuart J at [44–52].
[11] [2015] EWHC 412 (TCC), per Edwards-Stuart J at [50–51].
[12] [2015] EWHC 1855 (TCC), per Coulson J at [30–53].

validity of the later application for various reasons,[13] but in relation to the tactic deployed by the contractor, Coulson J said this:

> I consider that the suggestion that the documents of 13 February give rise to an undisputed entitlement to over £1.5 million defies common sense, and would be contrary to the purpose of the notice provisions in the 1996 Act. It is simply not permissible for a contractor to make a claim for £1.5 million (interim application 15 on 30 January); to have it knocked back through the payless notice mechanism; to update that same claim 8 days later by adding one small variation worth £6,000; and then, by reason of that update alone, miraculously to become entitled to the £1.5 million, despite the fact that the claim for the vast bulk of that sum had already been the subject of the valid payless notice.
>
> Such a sequence would make a mockery of the notice provisions under the Act and the Scheme. It would encourage a contractor to make fresh claims every few days in the hope that, at some stage, the employer or his agent will take his eye off the ball and fail to serve a valid payless notice, thus entitling the contractor to a wholly undeserved windfall. The whole purpose of the Act and the Scheme is to create an atmosphere in which the parties to a construction contract are not always at loggerheads. I consider that the claimant's approach would achieve the opposite result.

[8.41] Returning to *Galliford*, whilst an unchallenged interim application may be unimpeachable, the court held that an overpayment could be corrected in the final account. However, the court recognised that the final account may be some time away. Alternatively, an overpayment may also, in effect, be corrected in subsequent interim applications. Most standard form construction contracts provide that the assessment of the amount due at each interim application is calculated on a cumulative basis so that the whole account is revalued at each assessment. Therefore, if an overpayment is made to a contractor pursuant to interim application No. 1 (because, for instance, the payer failed to issue a withholding or pay less notice setting out the lower amount it calculated was due and was therefore forced to pay the full amount), the employer can in effect recoup that overpayment through its assessment of interim application No. 2 by reducing the amount that would otherwise be due to the contractor for the work done pursuant to interim application No. 2 to take account of the overpayment made on interim application No. 1. However, it is suggested that there are at least two problems:

(1) The JCT does not expressly permit negative declarations.[14] Therefore, if there is an overpayment of £4 million, the next interim application is only £1 million, it may be argued that the most the payer can do is value the application at £0 and not −£3 million. Even if a negative declaration is possible, the contract does not permit repayment of that amount until the final account stage.

(2) Given the repayment prohibition, the payer may not recoup the overpayment until interim application No. 3 or No. 4 if the value of the work done in interim

---

[13] Ibid at [47–48].

[14] Under the standard form, it is not open to the payer to demand a payment back from the payee to take account of an erroneous overpayment. Interim payments are made from the payer to the payee (see 4.7.1 JCT 2011 DB for example) – there is no facility for the payee to make payments to the payer, until the final account process. See *ISG Construction Ltd v Seevic College* [2014] EWHC 4195 (TCC), per Edwards-Stuart J at [14].

Adjudication strategy

application No. 2 is less than the overpayment in interim application No. 1. This may be a particular problem (as in this case) where the overpayment occurs at the end of the project where most, if not all the work has been done.

[8.42] The limitations expressed on the ability to recoup overpayments appear to be driven by the wording of the particular contract in question, as opposed to any mandatory requirements of the Act. Therefore, employers would be well advised to ensure that their contracts provide that if there is an overpayment in an interim application, this can be corrected in a subsequent application by the issue of a negative declaration and repayment at that stage.

[8.43] In addition to contractual wording that permits the payer to recoup overpayments, what other options might there be available that may lead to avoiding paying or at least recovering the money quickly?

(1) If the contract contains provisions that permit an adjudicator, arbitrator or the court to open up, review or revise certificates, it may be argued this provides a contractual basis upon which the overpayment may be correct. However, if it is accepted that the permanent effect of an unchallenged application is imported into the contract by virtue of the Act, it is doubtful this argument could succeed. Indeed, adjudication procedure in *ISG* and *Galliford* was the Scheme, which contains such a provision at paragraph 20(a) and yet it does not appear that the employer relied on this in argument.

(2) It may be possible to succeed on a claim for restitution to recover the money, although in circumstances where there is express wording that prohibits repayment, it is thought this claim is unlikely to succeed.

(3) Where the amount applied for is incorrect in that it arises from a clerical error, it may be possible to rely on section 110A of the 2009 Act to assert that the application is invalid. Section 110A provides that the payee, payer, or specified person's notice is the sum that the relevant entity 'considers to be or to have been due'. The argument may be made that a notice containing a sum that is arrived at in error is not considered due.

(4) Another argument might be that the notice (either the application notice or certificate) is in some way defective such that the failure to serve a pay less notice is immaterial.[15] For instance, the contents of the notice may not comply with the requirements of the contract, the notice may have been issued early or late, it may have been submitted fraudulently, or the person who issued or authorised the notice does not have the authority to do so.

(5) In the event the payee commences court proceedings and obtains summary judgment in its favour, it may now be possible to argue a stay of execution. As explained in detail at section 14.3, a stay of execution suspends the consequences of all or part of the adjudicator's decision. In what must have seemed like a clutching at straws, the final argument presented by Estura was that the court should stay the execution

---

[15] *Caledonian Modular Ltd v Mar City Developments Ltd* [2015] EWHC 1855 (TCC), per Coulson J at [30–53].

of the adjudicator's decision. A stay is generally only available where the payee is near insolvent or in financial difficulty. However, in this case, the court granted a stay of £2.5 million on grounds that there was a risk of manifest injustice. The stay of execution argument is considered further at section 14.3.6.

8.4.5 'Cherry-picking'

[8.44]   Where there is a large and unagreed financial claim comprising many subissues (as is typical in a final account dispute), then picking out for determination the issues where negotiations prove to be the most intractable either commercially or legally can smooth the way to an overall settlement on the remaining items. It may also prove strategically prudent to choose the issues where the claimant's case is the strongest and refer those to adjudication, rather than refer the entire suite of disputed issues.

[8.45]   Sometimes known as cherry-picking, or sampling, this approach is perfectly permissible in adjudication. In *Fastrack Contractors Ltd v Morrison Construction Ltd*,[16] the judge referred to it as 'pruning':

> In some cases, a referring party might decide to cut out of the reference some of the pre-existing matters in dispute and to confine the referred dispute to something less than the totality of the matters then in dispute. So long as that exercise does not transform the pre-existing dispute into a different dispute, such a pruning exercise is clearly permissible. However, a party cannot unilaterally tag onto the existing range of matters in dispute a further list of matters not yet in dispute and then seek to argue that the resulting 'dispute' is substantially the same as the pre-existing dispute.

[8.46]   In *St Austell Printing Company Ltd v Dawnus Construction Holdings Ltd*,[17] instead of referring the whole of the interim application for determination, the referring party selected items from within the application to refer. The judge said that approach:

> is not only permissible, but it is a process that is to be encouraged. Claims advanced in adjudication should be those claims which the referring party is confident of presenting properly within the confines of that particular jurisdiction. What if, in my example, the claim for loss and expense is recognised by the referring party as being very difficult to sustain. What if he in fact decides that he no longer intends to pursue it? It would be a nonsense if he had to include such a claim in his notice of adjudication merely because that claim formed part of his original interim application.
>
> ...
>
> Mr Jinadu argues that their liability was to pay on the basis of the whole of interim application 19, not just what they called the 'cherry-picked' elements. In my view, that submission ignores Fastrack. It also seems to flout common sense. This was Dawnus' application for payment and, since there is nothing anywhere to say that there had been an earlier overpayment to Dawnus, or any counterclaim, it must follow that, if the adjudicator had been obliged to consider the

---

[16] [2000] All ER (D) 11, per Thornton J at [23].
[17] [2015] EWHC 96 (TCC), per Coulson J at [25–33].

entirety of the interim application, he would either have found that further sums were due to Dawnus or, at the very least, that their entitlement was not less than the sum which he found to be due. In other words, this is a sterile objection.

[8.47] If this approach is deployed, it must be remembered that the responding party is entitled to raise whatever defence it wishes, provided it falls within the scope of the dispute. Care should be taken therefore to ensure that the scope of the dispute referred to adjudication is worded so that, so far as possible, it limits the scope of the responding party's defence in the desired way. In *Pilon Limited v Breyer Group plc*,[18] the referring party sought to limit the scope of the adjudication. The adjudicator acceded to this curtailment and, in so doing, refused to consider a significant portion of the responding party's case. The court held that the adjudicator was wrong to do this. It said the responding party was not limited to issues expressly set out in the notice of adjudication. It is entitled to raise, and the adjudicator must consider, any defence put forward, whether or not it has been raised before, provided it is within the scope of the adjudication and, in respect of a defence relating to money, the appropriate withholding or pay less notices have been given.

[8.48] The case of *Gary Kitt and EC Harris LLP v The Laundry Building Ltd and Etcetera Construction Services Ltd*[19] is a perfect example of where the referring party attempted to cherry-pick, but failed entirely. It commenced an adjudication on the final account. It said in the notice of adjudication that there were numerous items within the final account that 'are not required to be opened up by the adjudicator.' The Laundry Building disagreed and raised the purportedly excluded matters in the adjudication and the adjudicator considered them. The referring party challenged the decision on the basis that the adjudicator had decided matters outside the scope of the dispute referred to him. The judge firmly disagreed. He noted that 'it would be illogical, if not ludicrous' if the notice of adjudication could exclude particular defences that were within the scope of the dispute.

[8.49] Part of the difficulty in this case was that the referring party had drafted an ambiguous notice of adjudication. On the one hand it sought a decision on the final account, yet on the other it sought to exclude part of the final account from the adjudicator's consideration. The other problem lay with what the referring party was asking the adjudicator to do. The judge said that the referring party could have asked the adjudicator to decide the value of certain items (i.e. the *Dawnus* approach). If it had done this, it would have successfully contained the dispute as it had intended. But because the referring party sought payment from the adjudicator, it was then open to the responding party to raise a defence that no sum is due because the final account has been overvalued and because of various set-offs.

8.4.6 Large-scale adjudications

[8.50] A party may consider referring a dispute to adjudication that is 'large' in terms of either the number of issues it contains or the volume of documentation that is provided in

---

[18] [2010] EWHC 837 (TCC), per Coulson J at [24–31].
[19] [2014] EHWC 4250 (TCC), per Akenhead J at [26–28].

support. The classic example of this is where the referring party refers the entire final account of a project to adjudication. It has been repeatedly said that adjudication is not suited for such large claims. In *William Verry (Glazing Systems) Ltd v Furlong Homes Ltd*,[20] the court held that while 'kitchen sink' final account adjudications are not prohibited by the Act:

> there is little doubt that composite and complex disputes such as this cannot easily be accommodated within the summary procedure of adjudication. A Claimant should think very carefully before using the adjudication process to try and obtain some sort of perceived tactical advantage in final account negotiations and, in so doing, squeezing a wide-ranging final account dispute into a procedure for which it is fundamentally unsuited.[21]

[8.51] Nevertheless, there may be good reasons why a referring party feels it must refer a large dispute to adjudication. It may be that several issues cannot easily be separated, either because they are part of a common factual matrix or that there is one legal principle binding those issues together. A more sinister motive might be that a referring party, aware that the other party may not be as prepared for dispute as it is, triggers a large-scale adjudication with the aim of increasing its chance of obtaining a favourable decision because the responding party will not have time to pull together a strong defence.

[8.52] Notwithstanding the reasons or perceived benefits, the size of the dispute may simply not lend itself to being resolved within an unextended timeframe. If there are files upon files of information coupled with difficult or complex issues, the adjudicator will probably ask for additional time. Where consent is not given, he should resign. Where the adjudicator does not ask for more time, though he may not say it, the adjudicator is more likely to find shortcuts in his analysis so that a decision can be reached. This may increase the susceptibility of his decision-making process and the decision to a challenge that it was reached outside of the bounds of the adjudicator's jurisdiction and/or that the adjudicator has breached the rules of natural justice because he has not addressed the dispute put to him or he has not considered material parts of the submissions or evidence.

[8.53] If the referring party does decide to commence a large-scale adjudication, it should ensure that the referral notice is as clear and the supporting documents as well organised as possible. In particular, it greatly aids the referring party's case to provide references to the documents relied upon and to state how that document evidences or proves the point that the referring party is seeking to make. Simply providing a bundle of documents for the referring party to read without stating how such documents are relied upon does little to assist the referring party's case.[22]

[8.54] Costs are a further consideration. The longer the adjudication, the more likely there is to be an extended timetable which in turn will generate greater expense in professional fees. Where party costs are irrecoverable in whole or in part from the other party, that fact must surely play a significant factor in deciding whether it is appropriate to refer the dispute to adjudication.

---

[20] [2005] EWHC 138 (TCC). See also *Enterprise Managed Services Ltd. V Tony McFadden Utilities Ltd* [2009] EWHC 3222 (TCC), per Coulson J at [90–99].
[21] Ibid at paragraph 11.
[22] See Section 6.3 for more information on timetable and extensions.

8.4.7 Without prejudice correspondence

[8.55] The without prejudice rule applies to exclude from evidence all negotiations genuinely aimed at settlement, whether oral or in writing.[23] Generally, any correspondence between the parties in advance of the adjudication that is without prejudice may not be shown to the adjudicator.[24] Although without prejudice documentation commonly contains the words 'without prejudice' at the top of the document, this is not necessary in order for a document to be classed as without prejudice. Determining the privileged nature of a document is a matter of substance, not form. Care should be taken therefore to ensure that any information that a party may wish the adjudicator to see is not captured by without prejudice privilege. For instance, a party may wish to refer to the details of a particular letter or the appended documents in the adjudication. If the exchange is made on without prejudice basis, while the fact the letter exists may be made known to the adjudicator, the content will not be disclosable.

[8.56] Without prejudice correspondence will not normally prevent the crystallisation of a dispute. The without prejudice material would be admissible to prove the fact of the dispute, including in front of the adjudicator if he was otherwise asked to resign, since the without prejudice rule cannot be used by a party to further a submission designed to mislead a court or tribunal. It could also be deployed in adjudication enforcement proceedings to the same effect. If the parties are engaged in without prejudice negotiations in respect of a notified claim, and those negotiations do not result in the claim being admitted, there will be a dispute.[25] Section 7.2 considers the requirements for crystallisation of a dispute further.

[8.57] Subject to certain exceptions, once privilege applies to the information it can only be removed with both parties' consent. For example, it is not permissible for one party to use the fact that the other party has offered to settle for less than the value of the claim, as evidence before the adjudicator that the offeree considers its claim to be worth less than it contends in the adjudication.

8.5 Deploying arguments

8.5.1 Save the best until last

[8.58] If the referring party is unsure what defences the responding party might raise, or what evidence it has, it may sometimes limit the amount of detail in the referral notice or leave open the basis of its claim. The responding party will set out its defence and evidence in the response and then the referring party can draft the reply that most

---

[23] *Rush & Tompkins Ltd. v Greater London Council* [1989] A.C. 1280, per Lord Griffiths.
[24] There are various exceptions to this rule. For example, without prejudice communications which arguably have led to a prior binding settlement of a particular claim are admissible to prove, or disprove the fact of that agreement, or its proper construction. The precise scope of without prejudice privilege is outside the scope of this book. See for example *Foskett on the Law & Practice of Compromise,* 7th ed., 2010.
[25] *RWE Npower plc v Alstom Power Ltd* [2009] EWHC 1192 (QB), per Havelock-Allan J at [48–55].

adequately addresses the responding party's position. If the timetable has not been extended, the responding party will only have a few days to respond to the points made in the reply, which may mean it is not able to deal satisfactorily with the arguments just raised by the referring party. However, if new arguments are raised in the reply not previously seen by the responding party, or for example an expert report is served, the adjudicator should provide sufficient time to the responding party to address those submissions.

[8.59] Generally, this tactic is ill-advised; an adjudicator will not thank a referring party for new submissions late into the process because he will have that much less time to consider them and it will increase the chance that he may give less weight or pay less consideration to the evidence. Furthermore, though a right of reply is usually given, it is not automatic. It would be fairly disastrous if the referring party held back its key points for the reply, only to be denied the opportunity to serve one.

8.5.2 Reverse ambush

[8.60] During a project, the employer may refuse to certify that any sum at all is due, refuse to certify certain heads of claim, and/or underpay on amounts applied for without giving reasons. What is more, it will not articulate the reasons for the refusal to certify or pay in full. This may go on for several months until the payee commences an adjudication seeking payment of the total unpaid sums. Not knowing what the payer's case is, the payee's (now the referring party's) notice of adjudication and referral notice will invariably be limited to not much more than a demand for payment. In the response, the payer (now the responding party), having anticipated and prepared for commencement proceedings to recover the sums claimed, will suddenly unveil a series of particularised defences. Unless the timetable is extended, this will leave the referring party with very little time in which to prepare the reply that deals with all the issues. Although the referring party is entitled to extend the whole timetable by 14 days, this still may not be enough time to prepare a robust reply. As a result, the responding party may achieve a better outcome than if it had articulated the reasons for not paying in advance of the adjudication, leaving the referring party more time to prepare its claim.

[8.61] Quite understandably, if a payer adopts this approach, it will be considered in a very negative light by the payee. Although there may conceivably be some advantage to the payer in the short term, unless it is able to drive the payee out of business before it can mount a successful claim, it can expect to have to pay back any money it receives in an adjudication in subsequent proceedings. Moreover, the responding party risks that the referring party will be successful in the adjudication, which will thwart the purpose of the strategy.

[8.62] In its purest form, this tactic will only succeed for contracts governed by the 1996 Act prior to amendment. Indeed, the fact that the paying party could derail the payment process and starve the payee of cash flow by simply failing to cooperate in the certification regime in this way was one of the major drivers behind the amendments to the 1996 Act. This is because in its original form the 1996 Act did not make it mandatory for the

Adjudication strategy 141

parties' contract to say what would happen if the payer failed to issue a payment notice (section 110 notice)[26] certifying what sums are due. Therefore, without such a certificate, no sums became certified as due, and it was (arguably) not necessary for the payer to issue a withholding notice where he wished to pay less than the amount applied for. The payee would, in effect, have to start an adjudication for valuation of the whole of the amount in question, without the benefit of a certificate, and the payer would be entitled to run any defences it wanted to the value claimed, the absence of any withholding notice(s) notwithstanding. However, under the 2009 Act, the payer's ability to engineer this situation has been significantly curtailed. Following the 2009 Act, if the payer does not issue a payment notice certifying what sum is due, the payee is entitled to issue what is known as a default notice[27] certifying the sum due. Once the sum is certified under the payer's certificate or, in default of that, under the payee's default notice, then the payer has to issue a pay less notice a fixed number of days before the final date for payment setting out any grounds for paying less than the sum due.[28] If it does not do so, it will be required to pay the amount in the payment notice or default notice.[29]

[8.63] However, the reverse ambush can still be executed, at least in modified form. The paying party can deliberately under-certify amounts applied for without giving reasons (reasons are only required in pay less notices), and in the meantime start preparing its response to an adjudication over the amount certified which the payee will inevitably commence disputing the value. For all the reasons already stated, this is likely to still be seen in a negative light by the referring party and the adjudicator.

8.6 Assessing the other party's willingness and ability to pay

8.6.1 Securing assets before the adjudication

[8.64] The referring party may be concerned that the responding party will try to dissipate or charge its assets before an adjudicator issues an award against it. In that case, the referring party can make an application to the court for an injunction order freezing some or all of the assets of the responding party. The application will be made pursuant to section 37 of the Supreme Court Act and CPR 25.

[8.65] There are a number of factors that the court will consider, including whether it has jurisdiction, whether the exercise of that jurisdiction would be just and convenient, whether the applicant's case has a reasonable prospect of success, that there is no reasonable prospect of recovery if it succeeds and finally whether the applicant is willing to give a cross-undertaking in damages for any loss suffered by the defendant should the applicant

---
[26] So named because the requirement for the notice is stipulated at section 110 of the 1996 Act.
[27] Section 110B of the 2009 Act.
[28] Section 111 of the 2009 Act.
[29] Contracts which provide for a payee to apply for payment in advance of a payer's certificate have the added advantage that a timely application for payment will 'self-execute' as the certified amount without more; see sections 110A and 110B of the 2009 Act.

not succeed in the adjudication. Given the draconian nature of the order, the threshold for success is high and therefore applications of this nature are rare. For an example of a case of where an *ex parte* freezing injunction application was granted in advance of an adjudication, see *Pynes Three Ltd v Transco Ltd*.[30]

8.6.2 Can the other party pay?

[8.66] Where the claim is financial, before commencing an adjudication, both parties are well advised to carry out an assessment of the other party's financial health to determine whether or not it is solvent and, in the case of the referring party, whether the responding party can satisfy the claim made against it (if the claim is for money). If either party is insolvent or in financial difficulty, then it may not be possible, or there may be no point in commencing the adjudication, as explained in Section 3.6. If the adjudication does proceed to a decision, the paying party does not pay and the winning party seeks to enforce the decision in court, there is a risk that the court will either decline to enforce the adjudicator's decision at all,[31] or enforce the decision and subject it to a stay of execution.[32] In either case, the adjudication will have yielded no benefit.

[8.67] If the responding party falls insolvent during the adjudication, then depending on the rules of the adjudication, the referring party will be liable for all the adjudicator's fees. See for example paragraphs 11, 25 of the 1998 Scheme and paragraphs 9(4), 11(1), 25 of the 2011 Scheme.

8.7 Removing procedural uncertainty

8.7.1 Taking a jurisdiction point early

[8.68] There may be uncertainty about whether or not the Act applies to the contract and therefore whether the right to adjudicate a dispute exists. This uncertainty might be harboured by the referring party before it issues a notice of adjudication or by the responding party when it receives the notice of adjudication. There may, for example, be an issue as to whether there was a contract in writing,[33] or whether the contract is exempt from the Act. Proceeding with an adjudication in light of such uncertainty is a risk: if on an application to enforce an adjudicator's decision the courts find that the Act does not apply, it will not enforce the decision and both parties will most likely have wasted their costs and those of the adjudicator to obtain a decision that is useless.

[8.69] In such circumstances, commencing an action in the court to seek a decision on whether or not the Act applies can be sensible. If the court decides that it does apply, the parties can then proceed to adjudicate the substantive dispute without a concern as to whether or

---

[30] [2005] EWHC 2445 (TCC), per Thornton J at [4–22].
[31] See Section 14.2.
[32] See Section 14.3.
[33] Where the contract is dated before 1 October 2011.

not the right to adjudicate exists. Furthermore, unless the application is obviously inappropriate, it is likely that the judge will order that costs follow the event. In other words, whoever wins the substantive dispute pays for the costs of the application to determine the applicability of the Act. Further detail on this approach is set out at Section 16.3.2.

[8.70] Where the opportunity to refer a matter to the court does not avail itself, either because the referring party does not consult with the responding party or the referring party does not agree, the responding party can make an application for an injunction restraining the referring party from commencing or continuing with the adjudication. More often than not, these applications are refused because (a) the threshold for an injunction application to succeed is high; and (b) it is generally considered that an injunction would, except in the most clear cut of cases, fetter the referring party's right to adjudicate at any time. Section 16.3.7 discusses this option in more detail.

Chapter 9
Initiating the adjudication

9.1 Overview

[9.01]   The start of the adjudication is normally signified by the referral of the dispute to the adjudicator. Before then, two steps are required to initiate the adjudication. They are the service of the notice of adjudication and the appointment of an adjudicator to preside over the dispute.

[9.02]   The very first step in the process is the service of the notice of adjudication on the other parties to the adjudication. Broadly, the notice of adjudication is the document that notifies the other party of the intention to commence an adjudication and outlines what disputed matters will form the scope of the dispute to be decided. There are normally requirements for what a notice of adjudication should contain and these vary depending on which adjudication procedure applies. Where the applicable rules are the Scheme, the notice of adjudication will contain brief details of the dispute, the parties involved, what the dispute is and what remedy is sought. Great care should be taken when drafting the notice of adjudication to ensure that it addresses these requirements and also encapsulates precisely the scope of the dispute that the referring party intends to refer (Section 9.3). Before serving the notice of adjudication, the referring party should ensure that it has done all that is necessary to prepare for the commencement of the adjudication (Section 9.4). Once the notice of adjudication is received, the responding party should take steps to check that the referring party is entitled to commence the adjudication and it should begin the process of preparing its defence as expeditiously as possible (Section 9.5).

[9.03]   Usually at the same time that the notice of adjudication is served, the referring party will also request the appointment of an adjudicator. Where the form of adjudication is statutory, the adjudicator must be appointed within seven days of the notice of adjudication being served, and any attempt to appoint the adjudicator after that time is prohibited. Depending on the terms of the contract and the applicable adjudication rules, the request will be made of an individual named in the contract, or an adjudicator nominating body named in the contract, or an adjudicator nominating body of its choosing. Where the choice of the adjudicator is at the behest of an adjudicator nominating body, the referring party will normally make some form of representation as to which

---

A Practical Guide to Construction Adjudication, First Edition. James Pickavance.
© 2016 James Pickavance. Published 2016 by John Wiley & Sons, Inc.

Initiating the adjudication 145

individual should be appointed, or what sorts of legal and technical skills the appointed person should possess. Although the responding party may object to the referring party's representations and to an adjudicator nominating body's nomination, failure of the nominating body to take heed of that objection will not in itself invalidate the appointment (Sections 9.6.2–11).

[9.04] When an individual is approached with a request for an appointment, it is incumbent upon that individual to satisfy himself that, as a minimum, he has the requisite expertise to decide the dispute, that he has the capacity to take on the appointment and that he has no conflict of interest. There may be additional stipulations that adjudicator nominating bodies require adjudicators to meet, both before the individual is appointed to the adjudicator nominating body panel and before he accepts the appointment (Sections 9.6.12–13).

[9.05] Post appointment, and before the referral of the dispute to him, the adjudicator should attempt to agree his terms of appointment with the parties. It is also good practice for him to confirm directly with the parties that he has done so, and state the deadline by when he expects to receive the referral notice and the deadline for his decision. An adjudicator's appointment may be revoked by the parties at any time and he shall, save for limited circumstances, be entitled to be remunerated for the work he has done (Sections 9.6.14–16).

9.2 A precis on jurisdiction and natural justice

[9.06] In so far as it is possible to do so, it is vital that the adjudicator and the parties understand the concepts of the adjudicator's jurisdiction and the rules of natural justice before or as soon as possible after the adjudication process is initiated. The reason is simple: the two main causes[1] as to why an adjudicator's decision will be nullified by a court are that the adjudicator had no jurisdiction or where the adjudicator has breached the rules of natural justice. Therefore, all those involved in an adjudication must be equipped to know what to do and what not to do at the appropriate times, to identify where a party or the adjudicator strays into forbidden territory and to have the knowledge to react accordingly. The following paragraphs briefly define jurisdiction and natural justice and outline some relevant considerations. A more detailed review of these concepts is contained at Chapters 16 and 17.

[9.07] The adjudicator's jurisdiction is essentially the boundaries within which he is required to operate, as is determined by the Act (where it applies), by adjudication rules and by the scope of the dispute. Very broadly, the adjudicator will have exceeded this jurisdiction either because the provisions of the Act (where applicable) and/or adjudication rules

---

[1] Insolvency, fraud, duress, a breach of the Human Rights Act and the Unfair Terms of Consumer Contracts Regulations are also reasons. Insolvency is considered at Chapter 14 and the remaining reasons are considered at Chapter 18.

[9.08] Natural justice has two limbs. The first requires that both parties must have a reasonable opportunity to present their case, and the second requires that nobody may be a judge in their own cause. In other words, a party has a right to hear and respond to the case against it and the adjudicator must act in an unbiased manner.

[9.09] Where a party knows or suspects the adjudicator has exceeded his jurisdiction or breached the rules of natural justice, it may raise a challenge, either to the adjudicator if the adjudication is still on foot or to the court, either during the adjudication or in defence to a claim to enforce the adjudicator's decision. Why would a party want to do this? In certain circumstances it might not. It may well be that such excess or breach is not problematic in the eyes of the would-be challenger or that it may even work in a party's favour. However, the more likely scenario is that the excess or breach will adversely affect the party such that a challenge is desirable. By way of example, a responding party may raise an issue that falls outside the scope of the dispute referred to the adjudicator. The referring party will not have prepared to deal with the issue and furthermore it may adversely affect its chances of success in the dispute it referred. The best course of action will be to challenge the adjudicator's jurisdiction to consider the extraneous issue on the basis that it falls outside the scope of the dispute referred to him. Another example might be that after the adjudicator has issued his decision, the losing party learns that the adjudicator has shared his thoughts on a particular issue with the other party, but not with the losing party, thus prejudicing the ability of the uninformed party to consider and if necessary make submissions on what was discussed. Again, the best course of action will be to raise a challenge that, in communicating with only one party and/or formulating a methodology without giving both parties the opportunity to comment, he breached the rules of natural justice and therefore the adjudicator's decision should not be enforced.

[9.10] Raising a challenge with the adjudicator as soon as it becomes apparent is vital, particularly where the challenge goes to the adjudicator's jurisdiction. Where the innocent party knew, or ought to have known about circumstances that give rise to a challenge but failed to take action at the time, it may be taken to have irrevocably waived its right to raise a challenge on that issue later.

9.3 Notice of adjudication

9.3.1 In a nutshell

[9.11] The notice of adjudication is the first document that will be served (by the referring party). Its purpose is twofold: it initiates the adjudication process[2] and defines the scope

---

[2] *University of Brighton v Dovehouse Interiors Ltd* [2014] EWHC 940 (TCC), per Carr J at [40–52]. The point in time when the adjudication is initiated may be important where there are time bar or statutory limitation issues. However, the adjudication itself does not normally commence until the dispute is referred to the adjudicator. See Section 9.6.14.

Initiating the adjudication 147

of the dispute. It is, in many ways, the most important document in any adjudication. The purpose and function of the notice of adjudication was further described by HHJ Lloyd QC in *Griffin & Anor v Midas Homes Ltd:*[3]

> The purpose of such a notice [is] first, to inform the other party of what the dispute is; secondly, to inform those who may be responsible for making the appointment of an adjudicator, so that the correct adjudicator can be selected; and finally, of course, to define the dispute of which the party is informed, to specify precisely the redress sought, and the party exercising the statutory right and the party against whom a decision may be made so that the adjudicator knows the ambit of his jurisdiction.

[9.12] The notice of adjudication requires careful thought and drafting, not only to ensure that it complies with the adjudication rules, but also so that the scope of the dispute referred to adjudication is defined in the way the referring party intends.

9.3.2 The Scheme (Scheme p. 1(2) and (3))

[9.13] Where the Scheme applies, subparagraph 1(2) and (3) state:

> (2) The notice of adjudication shall be given to every other party to the contract.
> (3) The notice of adjudication shall set out briefly—
>   (a) the nature and a brief description of the dispute and of the parties involved,
>   (b) details of where and when the dispute has arisen,
>   (c) the nature of the redress which is sought, and
>   (d) the names and addresses of the parties to the contract (including, where appropriate, the addresses which the parties have specified for the giving of notices).

[9.14] Failure to comply with the requirements for the notice of adjudication in the Scheme or other adjudication rules may invalidate the adjudication, depending on the circumstances.[4]

9.3.3 Practical considerations

(A) Drafting

[9.15] The notice of adjudication should comply strictly with the terms of the adjudication rules. Provided it does this, the precise form of the notice of adjudication is likely to be

---

[3] [2000] 78 Con LR 152.
[4] *Primus Build Ltd v Pompey Centre Ltd* [2009] EWHC 1487 (TCC), per Coulson J at [14–15]. See also *Aveat Heating Ltd v Jerram Falkus Construction Ltd* [2007] EWHC 131 (TCC), per Havery J at [23]. As to incorrect names of parties, see *Mrs Sandra Williams trading as Sanclair Construction v Abdul Noor trading as India Kitchen* [2007] EWHC 3467 (TCC), per Hickinbottom J at [73–75]. See Sections 16.6.2, 16.6.6 and 16.6.8 for more here.

immaterial; for instance a notice of adjudication written in the form of a letter will still constitute a notice of adjudication.[5]

[9.16] The notice of adjudication should be as concise as possible, ensuring that the scope of the dispute is clearly and accurately defined. There is a balance between providing sufficient details of the dispute and providing too much detail. A detailed notice of adjudication will give the responding party more of an indication of what the referral notice is likely to contain, which means it will be easier to hone the preparation of its defence in advance of receiving the referral notice. This may not be in the referring party's interests.

[9.17] The referring party should have thought very carefully about the arguments that the responding party is likely to raise because this will more than likely affect the way the notice of adjudication (and the referral notice) is framed.

[9.18] Consider whether to summarise the legal basis of any defence already communicated by the responding party. This can be helpful for the adjudicator in that he can see from the outset the likely extent of the parties' arguments. It can also serve to steer the responding party down a particular line of argument that the referring party will (or should) have anticipated and prepared for.

[9.19] The notice of adjudication should set out, usually at the end, exactly what relief is sought by identifying exactly what the referring party wants the adjudicator to decide. If the referring party wishes the adjudicator to award it a sum of money, it may seek a declaration as to the legal entitlement for that money and a further declaration for the sum itself. That said, not all adjudication rules require the notice of adjudication to set out the details of the relief. For instance, the DOM2 rules of adjudication[6] require that the relief is set out in the referral notice instead, which has been held to be permissible.[7]

[9.20] If the referring party wishes to claim interest, that claim should be made clear. There is no freestanding power to award interest and so if it is not claimed, unless the adjudication rules permit it, the adjudicator will have no jurisdiction to award it.[8]

[9.21] If the referring party wishes the adjudicator to apportion his fees in a particular way, this should also be made clear. Most adjudication rules, including the Scheme, bestow this power on the adjudicator in any event.

[9.22] The dispute set out in the notice of adjudication must have crystallised. In other words, the claim being referred must either have been rejected entirely, or not responded to. The threshold that must be reached in order for it to be said that a dispute has crystallised is relatively low. Furthermore, it is not necessary for each and every detail of the dispute referred to adjudication to have crystallised. Provided the dispute referred is broadly the same as the one that has crystallised, that is enough. Section 7.2 provides further detail on this area.

---

[5]*Chamberlain Carpentry & Joinery Ltd v Alfred MacAlpine Construction Ltd* [2002] EWHC 514 (TCC), per Seymour J at [16–19].
[6]Which are very similar to the JCT 1998 rules.
[7]*Jerome Engineering Ltd v Lloyd Morris Electrical Ltd* [2002] CILL 1827, per Cockroft at [20].
[8]See Section 10.7.8.

Initiating the adjudication

[9.23] Unless the adjudication rules permit or the parties agree to the referral of multiple disputes in one notice of adjudication, the notice of adjudication should refer only to one dispute. If the adjudication notice refers to disputes, then the notice of adjudication will be invalid. However, a single dispute may embrace a number of issues. Section 7.3 considers this further.

[9.24] It is important that there are no errors in the notice of adjudication. Such errors cannot be remedied either in the referral notice or by serving an amended notice of adjudication once the adjudication has started, particularly where those amendments are material.[9] If the mistake is noticed before the referral notice has been served, the referring party should simply not serve the referral notice by the deadline. In that case, the notice of adjudication will lapse, the adjudication itself will not commence, and the referring party is free to serve an amended notice of adjudication with the mistake rectified. If the mistake is noticed after the referral notice has been served, the referring party is stuck with it. If the mistake is one that affects the jurisdiction of the adjudicator it may well serve to invalidate any decision the adjudicator makes.

[9.25] Appendix 4 contains a model form notice of adjudication containing the essential components of a notice of adjudication that complies with the Scheme. This can be downloaded in soft copy from the publisher's website.[10]

(B) Scope of the notice of adjudication

[9.26] The notice of adjudication is the primary document that defines the scope of the dispute that the adjudicator is required to decide. This is consistent with subparagraph 7(1) of the Scheme, which dictates that the dispute (as already crystallised) is to be referred to the adjudicator within seven days.[11] However, the scope of the dispute may also be determined by documents referred to within the notice of adjudication,[12] by reference to prior communications between the parties on the issues in dispute[13] and also by new issues introduced during the adjudication, which are expressly or impliedly accepted as forming part of the scope of adjudication.[14] Thus, when either party wishes to challenge the adjudicator's jurisdiction to consider all or part of a submission or challenge the adjudicator's jurisdiction because he purportedly decided something outside the scope of the dispute, it is likely that a number of documents will need to be considered in order to 'assemble' the scope of the dispute before concluding whether something is outside of it.

---

[9] *Vision Homes Ltd v Lancsville Construction Ltd* [2009] EWHC 2042 (TCC), per Clarke J at [51–57].
[10] *http://onlinelibrary.wiley.com*. Accessed 1 May 2015.
[11] *Carillion Construction Ltd v Devonport Royal Dockyard Ltd* [2005] EWCA Civ 1358 per Chadwick LJ at [22].
[12] *Chamberlain Carpentry & Joinery Ltd v Alfred MacAlpine Construction Ltd* [2002] EWHC 514 (TCC), per Seymour J at [17].
[13] *Gary Kitt and EC Harris LLP v The Laundry Building Ltd and Etcetera Construction Services Ltd* [2014] EHWC 4250 (TCC), per Akenhead J at [24].
[14] See Section 16.3.

[9.27] The dispute outlined in the notice of adjudication may be widely or narrowly drawn. There is a balance to be struck between the two. On one view, since adjudication is intended to be a quick, summary and only temporarily binding procedure, it is wise for the notice of adjudication to define the dispute narrowly. This will give a clearer focus for the adjudicator and is more likely to mean that he will be able to consider the issues in more depth and arrive at a better-thought-out decision within the time available. If the dispute is defined too widely, it will enable the responding party to raise defences or cross-claims which the referring party did not anticipate. This could increase the complexity and cost of the adjudication and may reduce the prospect of a successful result for the referring party.

[9.28] However, restricting the scope of the wider dispute between the parties into a narrow artificial formulation that is done with the intention of excluding legitimate defences is transparent and is an approach that may well fail. In *Pilon Limited v Breyer Group plc*,[15] the referring party sought to limit the scope of the adjudication. While the adjudicator agreed with the limitation on scope, and declined to consider a large part of the responding party's defence, the court did not. It held that the responding party was not limited to issues expressly set out in the notice of adjudication. It is entitled to defend itself with any legitimate defences to a claim for money, provided those defences are within the scope of the dispute that is outlined in the notice of adjudication. Indeed, in *Gary Kitt and EC Harris LLP v The Laundry Building Ltd and Etcetera Construction Services Ltd*,[16] the judge noted that 'it would be illogical, if not ludicrous' if the notice of adjudication could exclude particular defences that were within the scope of the dispute.

[9.29] One of the most frequently contested issues before the court at enforcement proceedings is whether the adjudicator decided the dispute that was referred to him. If he failed to address all parts of the dispute referred in his decision, or he addressed issues that did not form part of the referred dispute, then the decision is likely to be found to be made in excess of his jurisdiction, or in breach of natural justice. This is explored further at Sections 16.6.5 and 16.6.6 in the context of the adjudicator's jurisdiction and 17.5.7 in the context of natural justice.

[9.30] Care should be taken not to overly restrict the scope of relief that the referring party seeks. If the claim is for a specific sum of money or a specific number of weeks' extension of time, the notice of adjudication should of course make clear the sum of money or the extension sought, but also give the adjudicator scope to award something different should he see fit. If it does not offer this flexibility, then the adjudicator has two choices: award the sum or extension claimed, or award nothing. This can easily be dealt with in the notice of adjudication by adding the words 'such other sum as he sees fit' or 'such other extension of time as he sees fit' at the end of the relevant item of redress sought.

---

[15] [2010] EWHC 837 (TCC), per Coulson J at [24–31].
[16] [2014] EHWC 4250 (TCC), per Akenhead J at [26–28].

9.4 Checklist: Before serving the notice of adjudication – referring party

Before the adjudication process is initiated, the referring party should ensure that it is ready for the adjudication in all respects. It should have considered the following:

(1) Where the form of adjudication is statutory, the answer to the first four questions below must be 'yes' and the last question 'no':
- Is there a 'dispute' within the meaning of the Act (Section 7.2)?
- Is the dispute a single dispute arising out of one contract (Sections 7.3 and 7.6)?
- Is the dispute different from a dispute already decided (Section 7.4)?
- Is the dispute 'under' the contract (Section 7.5)?
- Is commencement of the adjudication time-barred (Section 7.7)?

(2) Where the form of adjudication is contractual or ad hoc, have all the preconditions of commencing an adjudication set out in the adjudication rules been complied with (Section 5.2)?
(3) Is everyone needed for the adjudication ready and available at and around the anticipated period for the reply and sur-joinder (Section 3.7)?
(4) When is the best time to commence the adjudication (Section 8.2)?
(5) What scope of dispute should be referred (Section 8.4)?
(6) Is there a risk that the other party will dissipate its assets (8.6.1)?
(7) If the claim is for money, can the other side pay (Section 8.6.2)?
(8) Is there a risk that an adjudicator may not have jurisdiction to consider the dispute? If so, is it worth addressing that risk before the adjudication commences (Section 8.7.1)?
(9) Does the notice of adjudication comply with the provisions of the rules of the adjudication (Section 9.3.2)?
(10) Does the notice of adjudication 'frame' the dispute as intended (Section 9.3.3)?
(11) Is the referral notice ready or nearly ready (Section 10.2.2)?

9.5 Checklist: On receiving the notice of adjudication – responding party

As soon as the responding party receives the notice of adjudication, there are a number of actions that need to be completed as soon as possible.

(1) Determine the form and type of adjudication and ensure that the referring party's initiation of the adjudication is permitted (Sections 4–6)?
(2) If the form of the adjudication is statutory, have all the statutory preconditions and restrictions been met (Chapter 7)?
(3) If the form of the adjudication is contractual, have all the contractual preconditions been met (Section 5.2)?
(4) Where the Act applies, if the adjudication rules are other than the Scheme, do they comply with subsections 108(1)–(4) of the Act (Section 6.2.2)?

> (5) Are there any threshold jurisdictional issues? If so, consider whether it is appropriate to raise a challenge. If proceeding with the adjudication, maintain the reservation throughout and after the adjudication (Section 8.7.1).
> (6) Have potential factual witnesses been notified as soon as the notice of adjudication is received, are relevant documents assembled and has a decision been taken early on whether or not to involve external advisers (Section 3.7)?
> (7) Draft a skeleton argument for the response and prepare a schedule for what needs to be done and by when.

9.6 Appointing the adjudicator

9.6.1 In a nutshell

[9.31] Once the notice of adjudication is served, the referring party needs to take steps to secure the appointment of an adjudicator. It has seven calendar days (excluding bank holidays) from the date the notice of adjudication is served to do this. The contract or adjudication rules will often dictate whether a specific named person in the contract, a person from a list of names in the contract or a particular adjudicator nominating body ('ANB') is to be approached.

[9.32] Where the contract says nothing about the method of appointment, depending on the adjudication rules, the referring party may be entitled to approach any ANB or individual with a request for the appointment of an adjudicator. Careful thought should be applied to determine which ANB or individual is the most suitable.

[9.33] Once an adjudicator is identified, he will usually circulate his terms of engagement to the parties. These should be carefully considered by both parties to ensure that they are acceptable and do not breach the adjudication rules or the Act.

9.6.2 Timing (Act s. 108(2)(b), Scheme p. 7)

[9.34] Section 108(2)(b) provides:

> The contract shall provide a timetable with the object of securing the appointment of the adjudicator and referral of the dispute to him within 7 days of such notice

[9.35] Where the Scheme applies, paragraph 7 provides:

> (1) Where an adjudicator has been selected in accordance with paragraphs 2, 5 or 6, the referring party shall, not later than seven days from the date of the notice of adjudication, refer the dispute in writing (the 'referral notice') to the adjudicator.
> (2) A referral notice shall be accompanied by copies of, or relevant extracts from, the construction contract and such other documents as the referring party intends to rely upon.

Initiating the adjudication

(3) The referring party shall, at the same time as he sends to the adjudicator the documents referred to in paragraphs (1) and (2), send copies of those documents to every other party to the dispute.

[9.36] Very often (but not always) these provisions have the effect that the adjudicator is appointed and the referral notice is served on the adjudicator and the respondent simultaneously on the seventh day. Both provisions are considered in the context of the timing for serving the referral notice at Sections 10.2.2 and 10.2.3. However, one thing that it is critical to grasp is that in the context of appointing an adjudicator, seven days is not a long time, particularly where there are issues with the appointment. Therefore, the referring party, the prospective adjudicator and, if appropriate, the appointing body, should waste no time in requesting or accepting the appointment. To facilitate this, all written communications should be transmitted by instantaneous methods, such as email or fax and not by post, courier or DX and, wherever possible, a response to any communication should be given on the same day.

9.6.3 Appointment procedure (Scheme p. 2, 3, 5 and 6)

[9.37] Whatever the adjudication rules, they must contain an operable mechanism by which to appoint an adjudicator.

[9.38] Where the Scheme applies, paragraphs 2, 3, 5 and 6 set out the procedure to follow for appointing an adjudicator.

2.(1) Following the giving of a notice of adjudication and subject to any agreement between the parties to the dispute as to who shall act as adjudicator—

(a) the referring party shall request the person (if any) specified in the contract to act as adjudicator, or

(b) if no person is named in the contract or the person named has already indicated that he is unwilling or unable to act, and the contract provides for a specified nominating body to select a person, the referring party shall request the nominating body named in the contract to select a person to act as adjudicator, or

(c) where neither paragraph (a) nor (b) above applies, or where the person referred to in (a) has already indicated that he is unwilling or unable to act and (b) does not apply, the referring party shall request an adjudicator nominating body to select a person to act as adjudicator.

(2) A person requested to act as adjudicator in accordance with the provisions of paragraph (1) shall indicate whether or not he is willing to act within two days of receiving the request.

(3) In this paragraph, and in paragraphs 5 and 6 below, an "adjudicator nominating body" shall mean a body (not being a natural person and not being a party to the dispute) which holds itself out publicly as a body which will select an adjudicator when requested to do so by a referring party.

3. The request referred to in paragraphs 2, 5 and 6 shall be accompanied by a copy of the notice of adjudication.

5.(1) The nominating body referred to in paragraphs 2(1)(b) and 6(1)(b) or the adjudicator nominating body referred to in paragraphs 2(1)(c), 5(2)(b) and 6(1)(c) must communicate the selection of an adjudicator to the referring party within five days of receiving a request to do so.

(2) Where the nominating body or the adjudicator nominating body fails to comply with paragraph (1), the referring party may—

(a) agree with the other party to the dispute to request a specified person to act as adjudicator, or

(b) request any other adjudicator nominating body to select a person to act as adjudicator.

(3) The person requested to act as adjudicator in accordance with the provisions of paragraphs (1) or (2) shall indicate whether or not he is willing to act within two days of receiving the request.

6.(1) Where an adjudicator who is named in the contract indicates to the parties that he is unable or unwilling to act, or where he fails to respond in accordance with paragraph 2(2), the referring party may—

(a) request another person (if any) specified in the contract to act as adjudicator, or

(b) request the nominating body (if any) referred to in the contract to select a person to act as adjudicator, or

(c) request any other adjudicator nominating body to select a person to act as adjudicator.

(2) The person requested to act in accordance with the provisions of paragraph (1) shall indicate whether or not he is willing to act within two days of receiving the request.

[9.39] Subparagraph 2(1) makes a distinction between a 'specified nominating body' and an 'adjudicator nominating body'. The former is clearly intended to refer to the nominating body specified in the contract between the parties and the latter denotes a wider class of nominating bodies where the contract is silent. The distinction between the 'specified nominating body' and the 'adjudicator nominating body' is maintained in paragraphs 5 and 6.[17] It is perhaps self-evident that the specified nominating body cannot be one of the parties to the contract and it is at least arguable that it should not be connected to the parties in any material way. In *Sprunt Ltd v London Borough of Camden*,[18] the contract provided that Camden was entitled to nominate the adjudicator. The judge held that this was not permissible.

> What Camden would have is not a judge in its own cause but the right to nominate a judge in its own cause and that strikes against the policy of the act of having actually and ostensibly impartial adjudicators.

[9.40] Under the Scheme, the application for nomination of an adjudicator must be made by the referring party after and not before the notice of adjudication is issued, otherwise the

---

[17] *Sprunt Ltd v London Borough of Camden* [2011] EWHC 3191 (TCC), per Akenhead J at [44–51].
[18] Ibid.

appointment will be invalid.[19] However, where the adjudication rules are not those of the Scheme, then this rule may of course not apply.[20]

[9.41] A person requested to act as adjudicator is required to indicate whether or not he is willing to do so within two days of receiving the request – subparagraphs 2(2), 5(3) and 6(2). That request is made on the basis of the dispute set out in the notice of adjudication. The short time period within which the person approached to act as adjudicator has to respond makes it all the more important that the notice of adjudication should be clear as to the nature of dispute so that the adjudicator can decide easily whether he has sufficient time to adjudicate the dispute and that the dispute is within his expertise and competence.[21]

[9.42] It is implicit in subparagraph 2(1)(b), as it is explicit in paragraph 6, that the unwillingness or inability of the specified person to act should be indicated to all parties.[22]

9.6.4 Inoperable procedure or defective appointment

[9.43] Where the Act applies to the contract and the adjudication procedure is inoperable or it contains a defective adjudicator appointment process such that an adjudicator cannot be appointed, the Scheme will replace the agreed procedure wholesale, pursuant to subsection 108(5) of the Act.[23] The same applies if there are no appointment rules at all. If the Act does not apply and the appointment procedure is inoperable, then this may preclude the parties from adjudicating their dispute entirely because the Act will not function to replace the procedure.

[9.44] There are a variety of ways in which the validity of an adjudicator's appointment has been contested. These are addressed in Chapters 16 and 17 and include:

- defective appointment of adjudicator, because the rules make the appointment impossible, the correct rules were followed incorrectly, or the incorrect rules were followed (Section 16.6.3);
- the prior involvement of adjudicator with the parties or in the project giving rise to actual or apparent bias (Section 17.4.4);
- the appointment of the same adjudicator either in the same dispute where the first adjudication was not enforced or on a different dispute on the same project, or in two disputes commencing simultaneously (Section 17.4.5).

---

[19] *IDE Contracting v RG Carter Cambridge Ltd* [2004] EWHC 36 (TCC), per Havery J at [9–11].
[20] *Palmac Contracting Ltd v Park Lane Estates Ltd* [2005] EWHC 919 (TCC), per Kirkham J at [30–36].
[21] *Carillion Construction Ltd v Devonport Royal Dockyard Ltd* [2005] EWCA Civ 1358, Chadwick LJ at [21].
[22] *IDE Contracting v RG Carter Cambridge Ltd* [2004] EWHC 36 (TCC), per Havery J at [9–11].
[23] See Section 6.2.2.

9.6.5 Appointment by an ANB

[9.45] Where an adjudicator or adjudicators are not named in the contract between the parties, the appointment of an adjudicator may be made in three ways. The contract or adjudication rules may provide for the appointment via a named ANB (such as TeCSA). This is probably the most common occurrence where the contract contains provisions relating to adjudication. Alternatively, where the contract is silent, the adjudication rules (such as the Scheme) can provide that, as a default, the referring party may approach any ANB to appoint an adjudicator. Finally, the contract or adjudication rules may not refer to the concept of an ANB at all, but instead refer to a particular entity (such as TeCSA) that is to appoint the adjudicator.

[9.46] Whatever the method, the referring party should comply with the appointment procedure in the adjudication rules as well as any further rules laid down by the ANB. The ANB rules will not normally be set out in the adjudication procedure, rather they will be available from the ANB, usually on its website. The procedure will determine what forms of documents need to be submitted and whether there is any administration fee to pay. Typically, there will be a form to fill in, which requires at least the names of the parties, a description of the dispute and a list of adjudicators who may be conflicted. It will also be a requirement that a copy of the notice of adjudication is provided so that the ANB and the potential adjudicator can glean what the dispute is about.

[9.47] Subject to the ANB's rules, the referring party may also wish to make further representations to allow the ANB to more readily identify who the right adjudicator might be. For example:

- The skills required of the adjudicator. Is it preferable or essential that the adjudicator is well versed in interim payment claims? Should the adjudicator be a lawyer or quantity surveyor or architect? Should the adjudicator be a certain level of seniority? Is there a limit on the hourly rate that the parties are prepared to pay?
- Are there are any adjudicators that should not be appointed because they have a genuine conflict of interest?

[9.48] Regardless of whether the ANB's appointment procedure expressly requires it, the referring party should, and the ANB should ensure that the responding party is provided with a copy of the form of appointment at the same time as it is received by the ANB so that it has an opportunity to make its own representations, or respond to those made by the referring party.

[9.49] Clearly there are limits to the nature of the representations made by either party to the ANB. There is no better example of where the referring party overstepped the mark than in *Eurocom Ltd v Siemens plc*.[24] In that case, Eurocom's advisers, Knowles Ltd, applied to the RICS for the nomination of an adjudicator in what would be the second adjudication between the parties. The RICS nomination form contains two boxes. The first box

---

[24] [2014] EWHC 3710 (TCC), per Ramsey J at [57–79].

Initiating the adjudication 157

allows the applicant to specify any guidelines it wishes RICS to take account of. The second box asked the referring party to name anyone who might have a conflict of interest. In this case, the form was completed as follows:

> We would advise that the following should not be appointed:

> Mr Leslie Dight and Mr. Nigel Dight of Dight and partners; Mr. Slamak Soudagar of Soudagar associates; Rob Tate regarding his fees – giving rise to apparent bias; Peter Barns for dispute of a minimum fees charge and apparent bias; Additionally Keith Rawson, Mark Pontin, J R Smalley, Jamie Williams, Colin Little, Christopher Ennis and Richard Silver, Mathew Molloy who has acted previously or anyone connected with Fenwick Elliott solicitors who have advised the Referring Party.

[9.50] RICS neither shared the form with Siemens, nor sought its view before appointing an adjudicator.

[9.51] Siemens asked for a copy of the application form three days into the adjudication. RICS provided it 39 days into the adjudication (which ran to day 60). Upon receipt of the form, Siemens asked Eurocom and Knowles to explain what the alleged conflicts of interest were. In particular, it queried the basis of the alleged conflict of Mr Molloy, who had been named as one of those conflicted on the basis that he had acted previously. The RICS approach where there is a series of adjudications under one contract is to nominate the same adjudicator 'because of potential savings in costs and time'. No explanation as to the alleged conflicts were given and the adjudicator subsequently awarded in Eurocom's favour.

[9.52] Siemens resisted enforcement on the basis that the adjudicator's appointment was invalid because Knowles had fraudulently misrepresented the position with regard to the conflicted adjudicators. Specifically, Knowles knew that the adjudicators it had listed were not conflicted, but listed them as conflicted because it suited their client not to have those individuals appointed. The court did not go so far as to find that Knowles had fraudulently misrepresented the position, but it did say:

> the evidence gives rise to a very strong prima facie case that Mr Giles [of Knowles] deliberately or recklessly answered the question as to whether there were conflicts of interest so as to exclude adjudicators who he did not want to be appointed. Indeed he says in paragraph 9 of his first witness statement that that was the reason he mentioned those people in that box. It is very difficult to understand how Mr Giles, as a non-practicing barrister, could otherwise complete that box in that way.

> Again this is supported by Mr Giles' explanation of the reason he included Mr Molloy within that box. I find it very difficult to accept his explanation as to a fresh mind which, as I have said, is not justified by the facts. It seems much more likely that the reason for including Mr Molloy was that Eurocom did not want Mr Molloy to be appointed because of the result of the First Adjudication being unfavourable to Eurocom in deciding that Eurocom owed money to Siemens.

[9.53] The court went on to say that a party applying for a nomination should not act dishonestly, and any party that did so would be in breach of an implied term to act honestly. Eurocom (through Knowles) breached this implied term and this was sufficient to mean that the adjudicator did not have jurisdiction.

[9.54] In *CSK Electrical Contractors Ltd v Kingwood Electrical Services Ltd*,[25] the court considered a situation in which the application for the appointment contained the sentence 'it is preferred that any of the adjudicators in the attached list are not appointed'. CSK submitted that they included this sentence in error and in any event, there was no attached list of preferred adjudicators. Because of this, the fraud identified in Eurocom did not arise in this case, the court declined to overturn the adjudicator's decision on this ground. However, it did say that the circumstances in which a stated preference for an adjudicator to be appointed or not appointed would amount to misrepresentation 'would never be very straightforward'.

[9.55] If the referring party contacts an adjudicator directly, it will not invalidate the subsequent appointment if that contact is unilateral and where the contact is only to check on availability.[26] In almost all other circumstances, unilateral contact brings with it a risk of breach of natural justice. The safe approach is therefore to copy any written communication with an ANB or adjudicator to the other party, or if the communication was made over the telephone, to record a note of the conversation after the telephone call and circulate it to the parties. See Section 17.4.7 for a discussion on the circumstances in which unilateral contact may breach the rules of natural justice.

9.6.6 Choosing the right ANB where one is not specified

[9.56] Where the contract between the parties and the adjudication rules do not specify an ANB body then, subject to the rules of the adjudication, it is open to the referring party to select which ANB it wishes to approach to appoint the adjudicator.

[9.57] There is an unhelpfully long list of ANBs and much longer list of adjudicators that sit on panels of each. A list of recognised ANBs in the United Kingdom is as follows:[27]

- Adjudication.co.uk
- Association of Independent Construction Adjudicators
- Centre for Effective Dispute Resolution
- Chartered Institute of Arbitrators
- Chartered Institute of Arbitrators (Scotland)
- Chartered Institute of Building
- Construction Conciliation Group
- Construction Confederation

---

[25] [2015] EWHC 667 (TCC), per Coulson J at [9–13].
[26] *Makers UK Ltd v London Borough of Camden* [2008] EWHC 1836 (TCC), per Akenhead J at [35(3)].
[27] The Adjudication Society lists most of these bodies. http://www.adjudication.org/links-adjudicator-nominating-bodies. Accessed 1 May 2015.

- Construction Industry Council
- Construction Plant-hire Association
- Dispute Board Federation
- Dispute Resolution Board Foundation
- Institution of Chemical Engineers
- Institution of Civil Engineers
- Institution of Electrical Engineers
- Institution of Mechanical Engineers
- Law Society of Scotland
- Nationwide Academy of Dispute Resolution
- RICS – Dispute Resolution Service
- Royal Incorporation of Architects in Scotland
- Royal Institute of British Architects
- Royal Institution of Chartered Surveyors
- Royal Society of Ulster Architects
- Technology and Construction Court Bar Association
- Technology and Construction Solicitors Association

[9.58] The Centre for Dispute Resolution published a report in October 2014 entitled 'Research analysis of the progress of adjudication based on returned questionnaires from adjudicator nominating bodies (ANBs) and from a sample of adjudicators'.[28] The research data is taken from across the UK. In the two years up to April 2014 the report shows that:

- The total number of requests for appointments from ANBs, though generally in decline from 2001 (2,000) to 2012 (1,100), has seen an increase of around 20% up to April 2014. The reasons for the decline are not given, but there has been a trend over the past 10 years for parties to turn away from appointing adjudicators via ANBs and towards listing an adjudicator or adjudicators in the contract between them. The recent increase is likely to be connected to the recovery in the economy.
- The Technology and Construction Bar Association, the Chartered Institute of Arbitrators, the Royal Institution of Chartered Surveyors have the largest number of adjudicators on their panel.[29] This may mean that parties are more likely to find an adjudicator who has the skill set suited for the dispute.
- 65% of adjudicators on the panels of those ANBs interviewed were either quantity surveyors or lawyers. The remainder were made up of civil engineers, architects, builders, building surveyors, construction consultants and structural engineers.

---

[28] http://www.cdr.uk.com/documents/Report13_001.pdf. Accessed 1 September 2015. One of the authors of this report, Jane Milligan, was also the co-author of all previous editions of the report (no.s 1–12) published by Glasgow Caledonian University. See http://www.gcu.ac.uk/ebe/businessservices/adjudicationreports. Accessed 1 September 2015.

[29] Note that the figures in the report do not accord with those in Appendix 6, although Appendix 6 does show that TeCSA, CIArb and RICS have the most adjudicators. Since the data in Appendix 6 was obtained directly from the ANBs in around June 2015, it is suggested that this reflects the true position.

[9.59] While it may be right that in the early years after statutory adjudication was introduced, some adjudicators on the panels of some ANBs were perhaps not at the level of competence the parties wished them to be, ANBs have responded to that criticism. ANBs now conduct interviews for each prospective panel adjudicator. Some ANBs publish criteria that a prospective adjudicator needs to meet even to be considered by the ANB.[30] Some require candidates to attend courses and sit exams and many conduct periodic refresher examinations to ensure that the adjudicators remain at the required level.

[9.60] ANBs do this because they are keen to carve out a reputation for having top-tier adjudicators on their panels. On one view, where an ANB has a good reputation, more parties will agree in their contract to refer requests for appointment to the ANB, which means that the adjudicators on the panel receive more adjudications that perhaps they would through other ANBs, which means more adjudicators try to win a position on the panel of that ANB, which means that the ANBs are able to be choosier about their panel members.

[9.61] Appendix 6 contains a table setting out some details for the ANBs listed, which may assist parties in deciding which ANB to approach. Some factors that it may be appropriate to consider are:

- the specialism of the body – the weighting of the expertise of adjudicators on some ANBs reflects the specialism of the body. For example, one might consider that an adjudicator on the panel of the Institute of Civil Engineers would be more appropriate for a civil engineering dispute than an adjudicator from the Nationwide Academy of Dispute Resolution;
- the experience of the adjudicators sitting on the panel;
- the price of the appointment – some ANBs have fees of up to £500 to appoint an adjudicator; others have fees of £100. In low-value disputes, this difference may be material.

9.6.7 Forum shopping

[9.62] What happens when the referring party does not like the adjudicator that has been appointed by an ANB? In *Lanes Group plc v Galliford Try Infrastructure Ltd (t/a Galliford Try Rail)*[31] an ANB appointed an adjudicator with whom Galliford's solicitors had previously had a 'robust clash'. Galliford did not serve the referral notice, then issued a further notice of adjudication and applied to the ANB for another adjudicator. A different adjudicator was appointed and decided the dispute. The adjudicator reached a decision in Galliford's favour and Lanes contested the validity of the decision on the basis that Galliford's 'forum shopping' for the right adjudicator was an abuse of process. Lanes lost at first instance and appealed. On appeal, Lanes argued that if a reference was not progressed, then the right to have it decided by adjudication was lost. The court held that

---

[30] For instance, TeCSA requires adjudicators to demonstrate that they satisfy 13 published criteria http://www.tecsa.org.uk/tecsa-adjudication-service. Accessed 1 September 2015.
[31] [2011] EWCA Civ 1617, per Jackson LJ at [35–43].

Galliford's approach was 'not an appealing one'. However, it was persuaded that its actions were permissible because:

- once a notice of adjudication has been served, adjudications may not be pursued for a variety of reasons. There is no authority indicating that in such circumstances the right to adjudicate a dispute is lost forever; and
- adjudications may be restarted in a number of circumstances. It cannot be right to suggest that the entitlement to adjudicate is lost if service does not take place for this reason.

[9.63] The court rejected an argument that there could be an abuse of process in relation to adjudication,[32] and although it described Galliford's approach to 'forum shopping' as 'never attractive', it decided that Galliford was entitled to take the action it did and therefore the second adjudicator had jurisdiction.

[9.64] The concept of forum shopping has previously been taken further than simply choosing adjudicators. In *Vision Homes Ltd v Lancsville Construction Ltd*,[33] the parties commenced two adjudications on the same issue concurrently. The court held, 'unhappily', that in Scheme adjudications there was nothing to prevent this. It only prevents a party referring a dispute to adjudication that has already been decided. Therefore, in theory at least, a responding party who is unhappy with the identity of the adjudicator can commence an adjudication on the same dispute with a different adjudicator. Since parties are precluded from referring a dispute to adjudication that has already been decided in an earlier adjudication (see Section 7.4), presumably the adjudicator who reaches a decision first will render the other adjudicator's decision a nullity.

9.6.8 Appointment of an individual named in the contract

[9.65] The biggest disadvantage of placing the appointment of an adjudicator in the hands of an ANB is the uncertainty of who will be appointed. Notwithstanding the ability of a party to make representations, the choice of adjudicator is solely at the discretion of the ANB. Another disadvantage of using an ANB is the additional cost. Not only will the referring party incur the administrative fee charged by the ANB, but where the parties have engaged external advisers to present them the parties will incur additional costs as a result of the advisers engaging in the ANB's appointment.[34] For these reasons, parties sometimes list an adjudicator to whom all adjudications are referred so that they have certainty as to who the adjudicator will be. This is perfectly permissible[35] and indeed increasingly common practice.

[9.66] While listing an individual to whom all adjudications are referred avoids the issues outlined, problems can arise where the named individual is unable or unwilling to act as

---

[32] See also Section 17.5.3 which discusses abuse of process further.
[33] [2009] EWHC 2042 (TCC), per Clarke J at [70].
[34] The administrative fees for the various ANBs are listed at Appendix 6.
[35] *John Mowlem & Co plc v Hydra-Tight Ltd* (2001) 17 Const LJ 358, per Toulmin J at [23].

adjudicator when a dispute is referred to him and there is no fallback provision in the contract to secure the appointment of someone else. In that case, the appointment procedure will be inoperable and, where the Act applies to the contract, the rules of the Scheme will be substituted into the contract wholesale, which will then permit the referring party to approach any ANB (see Section 16.6.2). A further disadvantage of listing an individual to whom all adjudications are referred is that parties are unlikely to be able to predict the nature of the disputes that will arise at the point in time when the contract is drafted. It may well be therefore that the named adjudicator is available and willing to act, but does not have the expertise to decide the dispute in question. For these reasons, it is suggested that the approach of naming a single individual is to be avoided.

[9.67] A better approach is to list a number of adjudicators to whom any dispute can be referred, or to list adjudicators to whom a particular type of dispute can be referred. For example, a contract may list the names of five individuals each under the headings of legal, quantum and programming so that a dispute concerning a legal issue will be referred to an adjudicator in the legal list and so on. The wording of the contract should determine the precise scope of dispute that is to fall within each area, the course of action if a dispute spans more than one area and insofar as the appointment requires the agreement of the parties, if they do not agree, what is to be done about it.

[9.68] Where an individual or individuals are named in the contract, it will not be possible to approach an ANB to appoint an adjudicator, unless the appointment procedure permits it.

9.6.9 Nominated or appointed adjudicator too busy, unwilling or unable to act

[9.69] If the adjudicator, appointed by an ANB or selected by the parties, thinks that he may not be able to produce a decision within the relevant period (because of other commitments), or he is unwilling to act, he should make that plain to the parties at the outset. The parties should then follow the mechanisms in the contract or the adjudication rules to seek the appointment of an alternative adjudicator.

[9.70] Where such mechanism does not exist, the adjudication procedure will be inoperable, and where the Act applies, the Scheme will be imported wholesale in place of the existing rules.[36] Then, the parties are free to appoint the adjudicator through an ANB in accordance with paragraph 2 of the Scheme. If the Act does not apply to the contract, the parties may be precluded from referring their disputes to adjudication at all, unless they agree a variation to the rules that corrects the appointment mechanism.

---

[36] See Sections 6.2.2 and 16.6.3.

9.6.10 Natural person and no conflict of interest (Scheme, p. 4)

[9.71] Where the Scheme applies, paragraph 4 provides:

> Any person requested or selected to act as adjudicator in accordance with paragraphs 2, 5 or 6 shall be a natural person acting in his personal capacity. A person requested or selected to act as an adjudicator shall not be an employee of any of the parties to the dispute and shall declare any interest, financial or otherwise, in any matter relating to the dispute.

[9.72] Although the Act provides no such stipulation, the Scheme provides that the adjudicator must be a natural person. The reason for this is simple enough; the role of an adjudicator must be carried out by one person, as opposed to a panel, team, or partnership. That does not mean that the individual cannot work within a company or partnership, nor does it mean that he may not address the parties on firm letterhead or solicit assistance from his team members, so long as he alone retains his decision-making responsibility, or that the company cannot administer his fees and recover them for him.[37]

[9.73] If the named or appointed adjudicator thinks there is a potential conflict of interest, he should consider whether it would be appropriate to accept any appointment or consider making a declaration to the parties inviting them to comment. If a material conflict is subsequently uncovered and the adjudicator has continued or continues to a decision, there is a strong risk that the decision will be held to be unenforceable on natural justice grounds. Section 17.4.2 addresses this further. If the adjudication rules require that the adjudicator should have no conflict (as with the Scheme), then the decision will also fail on jurisdictional grounds.

[9.74] The referring party should be particularly alive to this issue before the adjudicator is appointed. If the adjudicator or ANB flags a potential conflict and the referring party wants to continue using the adjudicator, it should ensure that at the very least it has the written unqualified agreement from the other party that such conflict will not affect the validity of the decision. Even then, this is not a fail-safe because that agreement will not necessarily override the decision of the court that the conflict is fatal and that the adjudicator's decision is therefore a nullity.

9.6.11 Objections to the appointed adjudicator (Scheme, p. 10)

[9.75] When a person is appointed as adjudicator, either party (although usually the responding party) may wish to object. For example, the same adjudicator may have presided over a series of adjudications under the same contract and the responding party feels, rightly or wrongly, that the decisions he previously made have been unsatisfactory.

[9.76] Where the Scheme applies, paragraph 10 provides:

> Where any party to the dispute objects to the appointment of a particular person as adjudicator, that objection shall not invalidate the adjudicator's appointment nor any decision he may reach in accordance with paragraph 20.

---

[37] *Faithful & Gould Ltd v Arcal Ltd and Ors*, Unreported, 1 June 2001, per Wood J at [2].

[9.77]   The purpose of this clause is to ensure that a party cannot stymie the progress of the appointment process because it disagrees with who has been appointed. Equally, where an objection is raised, paragraph 10 does not diminish the effect of that objection for the purpose of any later jurisdictional objection to the appointment. Paragraph 10 concerns the consequences of appointment, not the jurisdiction of the adjudicator.[38]

[9.78]   If a party objects to the appointed person, it should send an email to the ANB immediately setting out clearly and succinctly what the legal and factual basis for the objection is. The email should be copied to the other side. It is then a matter for the ANB whether it accepts the objection and appoints someone other than the individual or selection of individuals proposed or decides that the objection is spurious and follows the referring party's proposal. Where the grounds of the objection are sensible (not, for example, 'I have met the adjudicator and I don't like him') the ANB may respond to the objection by appointing someone else. As a general rule, where the objection is long-winded and the basis is convoluted, it is less likely to gain traction.

9.6.12 A party's assessment of an adjudicator's capability

[9.79]   Where a party is considering whether or not to appoint a particular individual as an adjudicator or to accept the appointment of an adjudicator by an ANB without objection, it is suggested that it should undergo a careful information-gathering exercise to determine whether or not that individual is capable. There are numerous ways of doing this.

- *Word of mouth* – Often this can be one of the best ways to obtain information about an individual's capability because the information will (normally) be obtained first hand. However, some care should be taken as to the weight attached to the recommendation. Comments may be tainted by whether the advisor won or lost their adjudication, or by a particular action or inaction by an adjudicator which the advisor particularly liked or disliked.
- *Adjudicator's CV* – These can be obtained from the ANB, from the organisation the adjudicator works for, or by asking the adjudicator directly. CVs will normally give a reasonably good indication of a person's experience but again care should be taken because the contents of the CV are likely to represent the best foot forward.
- *Articles or books* – A number of adjudicators publish articles or books. The content of these publications will give an indication of a person's expertise, writing style, analytical ability, an opinion on whatever matter has been written on. Publications can be located through an internet search or a paid-for online or hard copy journal.
- *Court judgments* – Many if not most of the court decisions addressing adjudication will name the adjudicator in the case. Reading the judge's comments about the adjudicator's case management skills or the accuracy or quality of his decision can be revealing. The easiest way to search for judgments where a particular adjudicator has been

---

[38] *Pring & St Hill Ltd v C J Hafner T/A Southern Erectors* [2002] EWHC 1775 (TCC) per Lloyd J at [17].

named is to use an online searchable case database. The most accessible ones available are adjudication.co.uk and Bailii.[39]
- *The number of the ANB panels the adjudicator is on* – While this is a rather crude way of determining an adjudicator's capability, the very fact that adjudicators are appointed to a number of ANB panels is probably a positive measure of that individual's competence. All the main ANBs now have strict criteria for assessing individuals who wish to be appointed to a panel and regularly test the competency of adjudicators in interviews.

[9.80] What does it mean to be a 'capable' adjudicator? It is suggested it means three things: the possession of excellent technical ability, procedural competence and the possession of excellent case management skills. Each of these is considered briefly now.

(A) Technical ability

[9.81] Technical ability encompasses knowledge, experience and current-awareness.

- *Knowledge* – a good adjudicator should be able to understand complex legal and factual scenarios and identify and analyse the key issues. While the range of construction disputes is wide, as a bare minimum one would expect all adjudicators to be familiar with the major standard forms of construction contract in the UK and the treatment within those forms of valuation and payment, time, loss and expense, defective work and termination.
- *Experience* – experience both in terms of knowledge of the subject matter and experience in the particular area of dispute is helpful because it allows the adjudicator to quickly grasp the factual issues.
- *Current-awareness* – it is important that adjudicators keep up to date with developments in adjudication and construction law.

(B) Understanding of the procedure

[9.82] The adjudicator needs to be fully aware of the procedural requirements and pitfalls that are common in adjudication. This will require, as a minimum, an in-depth knowledge of the 1996 Act, the 2009 Act, the 1998 Scheme and the 2011 Scheme and a working knowledge of standalone and standard form adjudication rules. He needs to be fully aware of how to determine jurisdictional challenges, as well as of the requirements of natural justice. He needs to know, or know where to look for, case law that has addressed any procedural issue that he is likely to face during the adjudication. He must be well versed in how to write decisions.

---

[39] *www.bailii.org*. Accessed 1 September 2015.

(C) Case management skills

[9.83] The timescales involved in adjudication are very tight, and so in order to conduct an adjudication effectively, within the timetable, the adjudicator must have tight control over the way in which the adjudication is run. Decisions on timetable or challenges to jurisdiction for example, must be made quickly. The adjudicator should be proactive in dealing with any issues that could cause delay. A poorly managed adjudication may lead to the adjudicator unnecessarily requesting an extension of time, which will irritate the parties and cause additional expense.

[9.84] An experienced adjudicator is likely to have a greater appreciation of how to manage the adjudication process effectively.

9.6.13 The prospective adjudicator's assessment of whether he should accept the appointment

[9.85] Many of the considerations that an adjudicator ought to have before accepting a request to be appointed as adjudicator have already been outlined in this chapter. They include whether:

- he has sufficient capacity to take on the adjudication. The adjudicator should not make his assessment based on the normal statutory timescales; rather he should make allowance for the fact that the timetable may be extended by at least by 14 days. Research shows that around half of all adjudications are completed on an extended timetable.[40]
- he is capable of deciding the dispute. All he will have is the notice of adjudication and any information contained on forms of appointment or covering letters. Nevertheless, this will give him a good indication of what issues are likely to arise. The subject matter of the dispute should broadly fall within the scope of the individual's professional practice, although that is not to say that the adjudicator must be an expert in all technical aspects. For instance, where the referring party outlines in the notice of adjudication that it seeks an extension of time, that does not mean the adjudicator must be a delay expert in order to consider the dispute, merely that he understands and is experienced in the concept of delay and extensions of time in the context of construction projects.
- There is any conflict of interest. Refer to Section 9.6.10.

[9.86] Where the adjudicator's appointment is procured via an ANB, often the ANB will ask the adjudicator to confirm that he fulfils a number of criteria before accepting the appointment. For example, the RICS list 10 criteria that adjudicators must confirm they meet before accepting the appointment, which include those points bulleted in the previous paragraph. Among other things, they must confirm that they attended an RICS-approved

---

[40]Trushell, Milligan and Cattanach, *Research analysis of the progress of adjudication based on returned questionnaires from adjudicator nominating bodies (ANBs) and from a sample of adjudicators.* October 2012. http://www.gcu.ac.uk/ebe/businessservices/adjudicationreports. Accessed 1 September 2015. Data is taken from the survey conducted in 2012.

9.6.14 Post appointment before the dispute is referred

[9.87] Where the Scheme applies, and in fact pursuant to most adjudication rules, the appointed adjudicator will not be seized of jurisdiction until the dispute is referred to him, or in other words the referral notice is served.[41] Before his appointment commences, he has no power in the proceedings at all and may not direct the parties. However, where the acceptance of the appointment occurs before the deadline for the service of the referral notice, an adjudicator will often make contact with the parties to confirm the date by when he expects the dispute to be referred, the applicable adjudication rules, the method by which he prefers communication to be made and the address(es) for communication. He may even provide a set of directions for how the adjudication will proceed. While those directions will have no effect before receipt of the referral notice, once it is served, those directions become operative and will bind the parties.[42]

[9.88] Sometimes, the responding party will object to the adjudication proceeding on grounds that the appointed adjudicator has no jurisdiction to preside over it. The referring party may accept the objection and decline to serve the referral notice, or both parties may agree to refer the jurisdictional objection to the court for determination before the adjudication is commenced.[43] Where neither of those things are done, it is a matter for the adjudicator whether he considers the objections, and if he does consider them how he reacts. However, it is suggested that, as a minimum, he should read the objections, and if he is able to conclude beyond reasonable doubt that those objections are valid, he should resign and notify the parties in writing immediately.

[9.89] Will the adjudicator be entitled to fees for any time he has spent after the appointment but before the dispute is referred to him? Some ANBs deal with this by inserting a clause on the appointment form that states that, in the event the adjudication does not commence, the adjudicator will be remunerated for any time he has spent. A similar clause may be drafted into the adjudication rules agreed between the parties, or into the adjudicator's agreement. If there is no express provision, an adjudicator may be able to formulate a claim based on unjust enrichment, although since the adjudicator will not have decided the dispute, it is arguable that there is no 'enrichment' of the parties for the adjudicator to rely on.

9.6.15 Adjudicator's agreement

[9.90] In addition to other draft directions or communications post appointment, the adjudicator will also send his terms of appointment to both parties for them to agree.

---

[41] *Ecovision Systems Ltd v Vinci Construction UK Ltd* [2015] EWHC 587 (TCC), per Havelock-Allan J at [60].
[42] Ibid.
[43] See Section 8.7.1.

[9.91] Given the time period between appointment and referral of the dispute is at most a matter of a few days, the adjudicator's terms may not be agreed before the dispute is referred to him. However, many adjudicators' agreements[44] will provide that unless the referring party accepts the terms of appointment before the dispute is referred, he will resign.

[9.92] The agreement must be considered next to the adjudication rules in order to determine the full extent of the adjudicator's rights. The precise terms of an adjudicator's appointment vary considerably from one adjudicator to the next. However, a model form adjudicator's appointment is contained at Appendix 4, which can be downloaded in soft copy from the publisher's website.[45] The adjudicator's agreement may include the following provisions:

- The fee rate of the adjudicator, normally expressed as an hourly rate, but sometimes as a daily rate or even a lump sum. Research shows that over 70% of adjudicators charge more than £175 per hour and 33% charge more than £200 per hour.[46]
- Where the adjudicator is part of an organisation and may wish to utilise members of staff to assist him, a fee rate for those individuals.
- Where the individual is part of an organisation, although it will be appropriate for him to enter into the agreement with the parties in his own name, where appropriate, he should ensure that it is clear that the contract between him and the parties specifies that the agreement is between his organisation and the parties and not between the parties and him personally.[47]
- The basis on which payment is to be made. This may include interim payments or an advance payment,[48] but not payment of his entire fee before the decision is given.[49] For a further discussion on the payment of the adjudicator's fees and the effect of the exercise of a demand for fees before the decision is given, see Sections 12.2 and 16.7.2 respectively. Note that where the adjudicator is found to have acted in bad faith or fraudulently,[50] or the decision is found to be in breach of the rules of natural justice,[51] or his appointment is revoked because of misconduct,[52] he will not be entitled to his fees.
- That the parties are jointly and severally liable for the adjudicator's fees.
- An exclusion of liability for anything done by the adjudicator acting in that capacity.

---

[44] Including the JCT standard form adjudicator's agreement.
[45] http://onlinelibrary.wiley.com. Accessed 1 September 2015.
[46] Trushell, Milligan and Cattanach, *Research analysis of the progress of adjudication based on returned questionnaires from adjudicator nominating bodies (ANBs) and from a sample of adjudicators*. October 2012. http://www.gcu.ac.uk/ebe/businessservices/adjudicationreports. Accessed 1 September 2015. Data is taken from a survey conducted in 2012.
[47] *Stork Technical Services (RBG) Ltd v Marion Howitson Ross* [2015] CSOH 10A, per Lord Tyre at [21–23]
[48] Although see the arguments put forward in *Stork Technical Services (RBG) Ltd v Marion Howitson Ross* [2015] CSOH 10A, per Lord Tyre at [24–35] and the judge's comments at [38].
[49] *Cubitt Building & Interiors Limited v Fleetglade Limited* [2006] EWHC 3413 (TCC), per Coulson J at [77–81].
[50] *Stubbs Rich Architects v WH Tolley & Son Ltd* [2001] AdjLR 08/8, per Lane J at [10–21].
[51] *PC Harrington Contractors Ltd v Systech International Ltd* [2012] EWCA Civ 1371, per Dyson LJ at [23–37; 42–46].
[52] Scheme, paragraph 11(2).

- An ability for the adjudicator to withdraw from the adjudication where he becomes unavailable. While this clause might seem draconian on the parties, it is rare for an adjudicator to exercise this right because he will appreciate the expense and inconvenience it will cause the parties, and it means he will miss out on the opportunity to earn more fees.
- A 'cancellation fee' should the adjudication not proceed for reasons unconnected with the adjudicator. The adjudicator will want to include this provision on the basis that if he cannot proceed to a decision, then he has lost the opportunity to earn fees that he otherwise would have earned. Parties may resist this provision because they are unwilling to agree an *ex gratia* payment on speculative earnings.
- That the adjudicator will comply with whatever adjudication rules are agreed between the parties.
- That the adjudicator will employ any external assistance he considers necessary in order to arrive at a decision. This is consistent with the statutory right at section 108(2)(f) of the Act.
- The adjudicator may wish to visit the site, or conduct meetings, or hold a hearing as he sees fit. Again this accords with the powers the Act bestows on him.
- A discount on the fees owed where payment is made within a (short) stipulated period following the issue of the decision. Even where only a small discount of say 5% is offered, this can be a very effective way of obtaining payment from the parties soon after the decision is communicated.

[9.93] Parties can and often do negotiate the terms of the appointment with the adjudicator. Whether or not the adjudicator agrees to negotiate will depend on the terms of the negotiation, the time available to negotiate and where the balance lies between the adjudicator wanting the appointment and the parties wanting that particular individual as its adjudicator.

[9.94] The referring party is likely to be keen for the adjudicator to be appointed by the deadline because it was the one who initiated proceedings and it will want to get on with it. The referring party is therefore likely to be the party which responds positively to the adjudicator's terms and conditions and may do so unilaterally if the responding party is slow to react or raises an objection to the appointment. In such circumstances it is not uncommon for the adjudicator's agreement to be executed only by the referring party and the adjudicator. This can raise questions as to the liability of the responding party for the fees and expenses of the adjudicator.[53] Even when the responding party signs the adjudicator's terms and conditions, it may wish to state expressly that it is signing without prejudice to any objections it may have as to the adjudicator's jurisdiction.

[9.95] Where the adjudicator does not seek to agree written terms of appointment, provided the adjudication rules state that the adjudicator has a right to be paid then, he will, subject to any contrary intention, be able to rely on the Contracts (Rights of Third Parties) Act 1999 to assert his right to be paid.[54]

---

[53] *Linnett v Halliwells LLP* [2009] EWHC 319, per Ramsey J at [37–38].
[54] *Cartwright v Fay*, 9 February 2005, per Rutherford J at [10–11].

9.6.16 Revoking the adjudicator's appointment (Scheme p. 11)

(A) The 2011 Scheme

[9.96]   Paragraph 11 of the 2011 Scheme provides:

> (1) The parties to a dispute may at any time agree to revoke the appointment of the adjudicator. The adjudicator shall be entitled to the payment of such reasonable amount as he may determine by way of fees and expenses incurred by him. Subject to any contractual provision pursuant to section 108A(2) of the Act, the adjudicator may determine how the payment is to be apportioned and the parties are jointly and severally liable for any sum which remains outstanding following the making of any such determination.
> (2) Where the revocation of the appointment of the adjudicator is due to the default or misconduct of the adjudicator, the parties shall not be liable to pay the adjudicator's fees and expenses.

[9.97]   Subparagraph 11(1) provides that parties may together revoke the adjudicator's appoint at any time, provided that they pay his fees. The second part of the subparagraph is consistent with subparagraph 9(1) and paragraph 25 of the 2011 Scheme. It is explained in the context of subsection 108A of the Act at Section 12.3.2.

[9.98]   With regard to subparagraph 11(2), in *Stubbs Rich Architects v WH Tolley & Son Ltd*,[55] the court found that the adjudicator's claim for fees could be challenged if he had acted in bad faith. On the facts of the case, there was no such evidence. In *Dr Peter Rankilor v Perco Engineering Services Ltd and Another*,[56] the court in *obiter dicta* said it would be surprising if the adjudicator would be entitled to his costs if the decision he reached was found to be a nullity. Indeed, these comments were ratified in the Court of Appeal case of *PC Harrington Contractors Ltd v Systech International Ltd*[57] where the court held that where an adjudicator produces a decision that is unenforceable due to a breach of the rules of natural justice, then his costs should not be paid. Section 12.2.7 considers this last case further.

(B) The 1998 Scheme

[9.99]   Where the 1998 Scheme applies, subparagraph 11(1) is amended as follows:

> (1) The parties to a dispute may at any time agree to revoke the appointment of the adjudicator. The adjudicator shall be entitled to the payment of such reasonable amount as he may determine by way of fees and expenses incurred by him. The parties shall be jointly and severally liable for any sum which remains outstanding following the making of any determination on how the payment shall be apportioned. ~~Subject to any contractual provision pursuant~~

---

[55] [2001] AdjLR 08/8, per Lane J at [10–21].
[56] [2006] AdjLR 01/27, per Gilliland J at [33].
[57] [2012] EWCA Civ 1371, per Dyson LJ at [23–37; 42–46].

Initiating the adjudication

~~to section 108A(2) of the Act, the adjudicator may determine how the payment is to be apportioned and the parties are jointly and severally liable for any sum which remains outstanding following the making of any such determination.~~

9.7 Checklist: Appointing the adjudicator – referring party

Not only is it important that, where possible, the right adjudicator is appointed for the dispute, but also that the appointment procedure is complied with. If the procedure is not followed, there is a risk that any decision the appointed adjudicator gives will be held to be invalid.

(1) Do the contract or the adjudication rules dictate who should be appointed and how?
(2) Are the rules governing the appointment operable (Section 9.6.4)?
(3) Where the appointment is to be selected by the referring party or agreed between the parties, does the adjudicator have the necessary experience and expertise in the subject matter of the dispute (Section 9.6.12)?
(4) Where the appointment is via an ANB and there is a choice of ANB to approach, which ANB is the most appropriate for the dispute (Section 9.6.6)?
(5) Where appointment is via an ANB, have adequate representations been made as to the type of adjudicator required (Section 9.6.5)?
(6) Have the adjudication rules and the rules of the ANB been followed with regard to the appointment (Sections 9.6.3 and 9.6.4)?
(7) Has the communication with an adjudicator or ANB been copied to the responding party (Section 9.6.4)?
(8) Does the proposed adjudicator have a conflict of interest (Section 9.6.10)?
(9) Where an adjudicator appointed by an ANB is unsatisfactory, is it worth letting the notice of adjudication lapse (Section 9.6.7)?
(10) Are the adjudicator's proposed terms and conditions of appointment acceptable and appropriate? For instance, the parties should consider rejecting any term that requires payment of final fees as a precondition to release of the decision (Section 9.6.15)?

9.8 Checklist: Appointing the adjudicator – responding party

(1) Consider whether or not to respond to any stipulations by the referring party to the ANB, as to the individual or sort of individual that should be appointed (Section 9.6.5).
(2) Consider whether to object to the appointment of an adjudicator by an ANB (Section 9.6.11). In particular, does the adjudicator have a conflict of interest (Section 9.6.10)?

> (3) Are the adjudicator's proposed terms and conditions of appointment acceptable and appropriate? For instance, the parties should consider rejecting any term that requires payment of final fees as a precondition to release of the decision (Section 9.6.15).
> (4) Ensure that when signing the adjudicator's terms and conditions, there is a stipulation that the agreement is without prejudice to any objections that it may have now or in the future as to the adjudicator's jurisdiction.
> (5) Have the adjudication rules and the rules of the ANB been followed with regard to the appointment (Sections 9.6.3 and 9.6.4)?

9.9 Checklist: Accepting the appointment – adjudicator

> Where an individual is approached with a request for an appointment as adjudicator, he needs to ensure that he is in a position to accept that appointment. The following considerations are relevant.
>
> (1) Do I have any actual or perceived conflict of interest with the parties or with the subject matter in dispute? If there is, it should be disclosed to both parties at the outset and the individual should either decline to accept the appointment or request a confirmation that the disclosed matter is not material (Section 9.6.10).
> (2) Am I sufficiently skilled to deal with the subject matter in dispute? It is not necessary to be an expert in the matters, but you should have experience of them (Section 9.6.12).
> (3) Do I have the capacity to deal with the dispute? Although the full extent of time you will need to spend on the adjudication and the timetable for the adjudication will not be apparent from the notice of adjudication, based on previous experience, you should ensure that there is sufficient time for you to act as adjudicator. As a precaution, assume that the adjudication will run for a minimum of 42 days from the date of the referral.
> (4) If the appointment request is via an ANB, ensure that any other prerequisites to the appointment made by the ANB are satisfied.
> (5) As soon as possible, and in any event within the timescale stated in the request, communicate to the parties (and the ANB where appropriate) that you accept or decline the appointment in principle, subject to concluding the terms of the appointment.
> (6) The terms of the appointment should be sent to both parties, at the same time as confirming the appointment in principle. The parties should be given a deadline to agree the appointment, which if possible is earlier than the date the referral notice is due to be served (Section 9.6.15).

Chapter 10
The adjudication

10.1 Overview

[10.01] Although the adjudication process is initiated when the notice of adjudication is served on the responding party, the adjudicator will not be seized of jurisdiction to preside over the dispute until it is referred to him. It is at that point that the adjudication is 'live', and unless the adjudicator resigns, the parties will be locked into the process until the adjudicator communicates his decision.

[10.02] The referral notice is the document that sets out the details of the referring party's claim. Where the Act applies, it must be served within seven days of the date of receipt of the notice of adjudication. The content of the referral notice is at the discretion of the referring party and will depend entirely on the nature of the dispute, but there are a number of guidelines that, if followed, can improve the quality of the submission (Section 10.2). The responding party's defence is contained in a document called the response. The deadline for service of the response will either be dictated by the applicable adjudication rules or more likely by the adjudicator when he sets the adjudication timetable (Section 10.3). Should the adjudicator permit it, the referring party will serve a further submission called the reply, the responding party will respond with the rejoinder and the referring party will respond to that with the sur-rejoinder (Section 10.4). The adjudicator may call for a meeting between the parties, a site visit or a telephone conference at any time (Section 10.5).

[10.03] Asides from the oral or written substantive arguments, there are other matters to consider during an adjudication. These include how to respond to pressure applied by a party or by the adjudicator, communications during the adjudication, dropping a head of claim, withdrawing from an adjudication entirely, the applicability of privilege in adjudication, the treatment of settlement offers, whether it is possible to adjudicate at the same time as another form of dispute resolution, the confidentiality of adjudication proceedings and, absent any rules in the contract, the service of documents and the reckoning of time (Section 10.6).

[10.04] The adjudication rules usually prescribe certain powers and duties on the adjudicator and, where the Act applies, the powers and duties of the adjudicator will include as a minimum those set out at subsection 108(2) of the Act. If the adjudicator exceeds the

---

A Practical Guide to Construction Adjudication, First Edition. James Pickavance.
© 2016 James Pickavance. Published 2016 by John Wiley & Sons, Inc.

limits of these powers and duties, either party can successfully challenge the validity of a decision on the basis that the adjudicator exceeded his jurisdiction or breached the rules of natural justice (Section 10.7).

10.2 Referral notice

10.2.1 In a nutshell

[10.05] The referral notice is the document that sets out the referring party's case in detail. It is the equivalent of the statement of case in an arbitration or the particulars of claim in litigation. The Act and the Scheme provide a deadline by which the referral notice is to be served and this must be complied with strictly. Typically, the referral notice is served shortly after the adjudicator's appointment. The content of the referral notice is, subject to any conditions imposed by the applicable adjudication rules, at the discretion of the referring party and will depend entirely on the nature of the dispute.

10.2.2 Timing (Act s. 108(2)(b))

[10.06] The referral notice should be sent to the adjudicator within seven days of the date of the notice of adjudication. Section 108(2)(b) provides:

> The contract shall provide a timetable with the object of securing the appointment of the adjudicator and referral of the dispute to him within 7 days of such notice

[10.07] This rule is sometimes misinterpreted to mean that the referral notice cannot be served until the seventh day after receipt of the notice of adjudication. This is incorrect. After the notice of adjudication has been served and as soon as the adjudicator has been appointed, the referring party may serve the referral notice.

[10.08] Unless there is no time, the referring party should have prepared its referral notice in advance of serving the notice of adjudication, so as to ensure the referral notice is ready in time. In practice, it always makes sense for the referral notice to be the first document drafted. This allows the drafter to be clear on the exact scope and the arguments of the claim that are to be advanced in the adjudication which will then make it easier for him to draft the notice of adjudication, which will be a summary of the referral notice and will be entirely consistent with the referral notice. For the reasons adumbrated in Section 9.3, it is unwise for the referring party to seek to compensate for deficiencies in the notice of adjudication in the referral notice.

[10.09] Some contractual procedures (i.e. those other than the Scheme) require that the referring party serves a final draft copy of the referral notice with the notice of adjudication, including all the supporting documents it intends to rely on. The rules require that the referring party is still required to submit the referral notice within seven days of the date of the notice of adjudication being received, but this is to be identical to the final draft form. This is a useful way for a responding party to reduce the impact of being caught off guard, because it will have sight of the details of the referring party's case for up to seven days longer.

[10.10] There is some debate as to whether failure to comply with the seven-day period in all circumstances will mean that the adjudicator's decision will be unenforceable. Sometimes the giving of the referral notice, or the provision of documents that are supplementary to the referral notice, will not occur within seven days through no fault of the referring party. For example, time may have been used up in approaching several adjudicators, none of whom were able or willing to act. The wording of the Act, s. 108(2)(b) of the Act arguably supports this, since it requires the contractual timetable to have 'the object of' referral within seven days from the notice of adjudication. The courts have historically demonstrated some support for this position. In *William Verry Ltd v North West London Communal Mikvah*[1] the court held that the parties may agree a longer period than seven days if they wish. In *Cubitt Building & Interiors Ltd v Fleetgate Ltd*,[2] the court considered the effect of a referral notice served after the seven days. In that case, the rules of the adjudication were the standard adjudication provisions found in an amended JCT 1998 form. The court said that the timing provision[3] had to be interpreted in a 'sensible and commercial way' and so based on an interpretation of the clause and subclauses and because, on the facts of that case, the late service of the referral notice was essentially the result of delays caused by the adjudicator nominating body, the service of the referral notice on the eighth day was effective.

[10.11] Notwithstanding these decisions, it is submitted that the correct view (which has judicial support) is that the seven-day period is mandatory, and that any lateness in serving the referral notice itself will invalidate the adjudication.[4] However, a small margin of delay is permitted for the supporting documents.[5]

[10.12] If the dispute is not referred to the adjudicator within seven days, though it may seem irksome, the best way forward is to restart the adjudication (by not serving the referral notice and reserving a 'fresh' notice of adjudication on the responding party), rather than continue and risk an unenforceable decision.

10.2.3 Scheme (Scheme p. 7)

(A) 2011 Scheme

[10.13] Where the 2011 Scheme applies, paragraph 7 provides:

---

[1] [2004] EWHC, 1300, per Thornton J, at [18–30.]
[2] [2006] EWHC 3143, per Coulson J at [41–47].
[3] Clause 41A.
[4] *Hart Investments Ltd v Fidler* [2006] EWHC 2857 (TCC), per Coulson J at [51].
[5] *Linnett v Italia Wells LLP* [2009] EWHC 319 (TCC), per Coulson J at [88–106].

(1) Where an adjudicator has been selected in accordance with paragraphs 2, 5 or 6, the referring party shall, not later than seven days from the date of the notice of adjudication, refer the dispute in writing (the 'referral notice') to the adjudicator.
(2) A referral notice shall be accompanied by copies of, or relevant extracts from, the construction contract and such other documents as the referring party intends to rely upon.
(3) The referring party shall, at the same time as he sends to the adjudicator the documents referred to in paragraphs (1) and (2), send copies of those documents to every other party to the dispute. Upon receipt of the referral notice, the adjudicator must inform every party to the dispute of the date that it was received.

[10.14] The court has referred to subparagraph 7(1) of the Scheme as 'a fundamental provision in the process of adjudication' where failure to comply with it takes the process outside the Scheme and renders the decision unenforceable. This is distinct, the court says, from subparagraph 7(2), which refers to an associated procedural requirement.[6] Thus, a short delay in serving the accompanying documents is unlikely to invalidate the adjudication. Where there is disconnect between the date of receipt for the referral notice and the supporting documents, then for the purpose of the commencement of the adjudication and the beginning of the 28-day period, it starts on the date of receipt of the referral notice.[7] Nevertheless, the failure to provide accompanying documents can render the referral notice so deficient that the entire adjudication process is invalid, for instance where no documents are served with the referral notice at all, or they are served several days late.[8] Subparagraph 7(3) makes it expressly clear when the 'clock starts' for the purpose of calculating the date by when the decision should be communicated.

(B) 1998 Scheme

[10.15] The 1998 Scheme is the same as the 2011 Scheme, save for the omission of the final sentence at the end of paragraph 7(3).

> Upon receipt of the referral notice, the adjudicator must inform every party to the dispute of the date that it was received.

[10.16] It is submitted that the omission of this sentence makes little difference to the function of this subsection. The court has held that where the 1998 Scheme applies, time starts to run for the purpose of calculating the decision date from the date of receipt of the referral notice.[9]

---

[6]*KNN Coburn LLP v GD City Holdings Ltd* [2013] EWHC 2879 (TCC), per Stuart-Smith J at [21–26].
[7]Ibid.
[8]*PT Building Services Ltd v ROK Build Limited* [2008] EWHC 3434 (TCC), per Ramsey J at [52–55].
[9]*Aveat Heating Ltd v Jerram Falkus Construction Ltd* [2007] EWHC 131 (TCC), per Havery J at [10].

10.2.4 Practical considerations and strategy

(A) Drafting

[10.17] A model form referral notice is contained at Appendix 4, which can be downloaded in soft copy from the publisher's website.[10]

[10.18] The referral notice should set out the referring party's case in full. Often this will include an overview of the case and the redress sought, the relevant contractual provisions relied on, the factual background to the dispute and claims, the legal basis for making the claim and a detailed statement of the redress sought.

[10.19] A focused chronology of events is appropriate more often than not, although if it is a long chronology, it may be better to consign it to the supporting documents and cherry-pick events to insert into the submission.

[10.20] The scope of the dispute set out in the referral notice should be consistent with the notice of adjudication. While a fairly loose rein has been given by the courts in this regard, where the referral notice widens the dispute and the adjudicator decides the dispute based on that expanded scope, at least the part of the decision that deals with those matters and possibly the decision as a whole will be unenforceable.

[10.21] It is easy to be verbose, but in circumstances where the adjudicator is fixed with a limited amount of time to read the submissions he will likely become irritated, bored or both should he find that the submission is not directed at the issues. Any jargon or technical terminology should be explained in the submission or in an appended definitions list so that the adjudicator can easily get to grips with the issues in dispute. Producing a submission that is concise, easy to read, directed and puts across the key points in a compelling way does take time, but the adjudicator will not only be grateful for a submission drafted in this way, but it may well be more disposed to the substantive arguments.

[10.22] The referring party should consider the background and experience of the adjudicator. If the adjudicator is not a lawyer, it may be appropriate to attach more emphasis to legal concepts and arguments. Equally, if the adjudicator is a lawyer or a non-lawyer unfamiliar with the subject matter or technical issues in dispute, the technical evidence will need careful explanation.

[10.23] It is appropriate in a referral notice to use persuasive language, aimed at trying to convey the sentiment of the party to the adjudicator. There may not be the opportunity to make oral representations to the adjudicator, so the persuasion that attaches to oral advocacy, to a degree, needs to be distilled into written form.

[10.24] The responding party will most likely have set out reasons why it does not agree with the claim, in correspondence before the adjudication. The referring party should consider addressing these defences in its referral. This will force the responding party to put forward arguments as to why the referring party's submissions are incorrect and in addition

---

[10] *http://onlinelibrary.wiley.com*. Accessed 1 May 2015.

(or if there are no such arguments available) come up with alternative defences to the claim. Either way, the referring party will then usually have a right of reply in which it can respond to those arguments and alternative defences. In short, it will benefit from two bites of the cherry. Furthermore, if it is done well, the referring party will have steered the responding party down a line of defence that the referring party would prefer it to follow and that it has anticipated. There is, however, a balance to be struck between dealing with the defence and focusing on the claim.

[10.25] It is likely to be helpful for the adjudicator if the referring party summarises in a list at the start of the referral notice the issues it believes the adjudicator needs to address. Provided that the adjudicator agrees with the list, he will find it a useful tool to guide him through the submission and to refer to when writing his decision.

[10.26] Finally, the referring party must not only set out its case, but must also prove it.[11] Making a bare assertion without some form of evidence in support will not persuade the adjudicator that, on the balance of probabilities, the referring party's case is to be preferred.

(B) Accompanying documents

[10.27] Within the referral notice, refer to contemporaneous documentation in support of statements made, and make it clear exactly how the document referred to supports the point being made.

[10.28] As a very rough guide, the sorts of documents that may be relevant are relevant extracts from the construction contract (which includes extracts from the employers requirements, contractor's proposals, the works information and the like), measured account details, variations, contractual notices, correspondence (including emails, attendance notes, letters and faxes) and meeting and progress minutes.

[10.29] Referring parties will sometimes serve files upon files of supporting information. While there is normally no limit on the amount of documentation that may be submitted, the more information that the adjudicator has to wade through, the less thorough his examination is likely to be, which brings with it a risk that the decision will be wrong. There is a further risk that he will consider that there is too much information to deal with within the time, and unless he is given an extension, he may feel forced to resign. Therefore, it is advisable to ensure that the supporting material has been carefully edited so that only the relevant documentation is attached. The referring party or its advisers should consider how long it took them to read and digest the material, consider the time available to the adjudicator, and curtail the supporting documentation accordingly.

[10.30] By and large, the most straightforward way of bundling the documentation is chronologically, although it may also be sensible to compile the documentation into packages.

---

[11] *SGL Carbon Fibres Ltd v RBG Ltd* [2012] CSOH 19, per Lord Glennie at [21–27].

The adjudication

For instance, where the dispute is around a number of compensation events or relevant events, packaging the documentation to support the claim in respect of each item may be more straightforward.

[10.31] To assist the adjudicator, paginate or tabulate the bundle of supporting documents and provide references to the page or tab numbers in the referral notice.

[10.32] The referring party should try to ensure that the contemporaneous documentation served with the referral notice has been seen by the responding party before. This is particularly so where the documents are fundamental to the issues or the basis of the dispute. If there are documents that are new to the responding party, it will undoubtedly raise a jurisdictional or natural justice challenge on the basis that a dispute has not crystallised, because it has not had sight of the documents that form the basis of the referring party's claim before the adjudication was commenced.[12] While this challenge rarely succeeds, it is best to avoid this risk altogether because: (a) the referring party and its advisers will have to spend time responding to the challenge during the adjudication; (b) there is a risk that the adjudicator may agree with the challenge and resign; and (c) even if he does not, the responding party may refuse to comply with the adjudicator's decision, in which case the referring party will incur further time and expense bringing enforcement proceedings before the court.

(C) Witness evidence

[10.33] Consider whether witness evidence is to be included and, if so, whether that should be factual, expert or both. This should be prepared long before the referral notice is served, because it will take time for the relevant individuals to prepare statements or reports. Witness evidence can be extremely persuasive and can enhance the strength of a party's case considerably. However, consider the consequence of showing the witness's hand in the adjudication. Evidence may come to light in the adjudication or subsequently that may cause the witness to change his position. Where this happens, the other party will inevitably make a meal of the witness's adjusted position, seeking to highlight differences in fact or opinion in an attempt to undermine credibility. The witness should carefully consider the wording of his statement to (so far as possible) protect his integrity against this eventuality.

[10.34] If it is decided that factual witness evidence is required, the following considerations are relevant.
(1) Factual witness evidence is provided in order that the witness can verify certain facts or events. The statements should be based on the witness's own first-hand knowledge, wherever possible. It is generally not appropriate for witnesses to offer any opinion, such as 'I think the contractor got it wrong' or hearsay, such as 'I overheard Sam saying the contractor got it wrong'. Although there is no rule in adjudication

---
[12] See Section 7.2.

that requires the witness evidence to be limited in this way, experienced adjudicators will discount or at least attach less weight to opinion or hearsay evidence given by factual witnesses.

(2) As a very general rule, the preparation of a witness statement can be broken into three stages. First, the scope of what the witness can cover should be determined. To do that, the dispute should be broken down into topics, and the witness asked whether he has first-hand experience of each topic. Second, either the witness will write it down or a professional adviser will interview the witness to obtain a 'warts and all' account of what he knows. This working draft document should refer to contemporaneous evidence, where possible, to support what is being said. Finally, the witness statement is honed so that it focuses on the aspects of the witness's knowledge that are particularly pertinent to the dispute.

(3) Generally, it is helpful for the witness statement to be written in numbered paragraphs.

(4) In adjudication, there is no requirement to sign a statement of truth, unlike in court proceedings. However, where there is a signed statement of truth, the adjudicator may well attach more evidential weight to the statement than he would if the statement was made without one. However, there may be concerns about the veracity of the witness evidence such that he does not wish to certify the statement as true.

(5) The witness will normally include exhibits as evidence to support the statements made. Reference to the exhibits should be identified in bold and inserted either in parenthesis or in the margin at the appropriate point. The usual way of labelling exhibits is to use to the witness's initials as a prefix, and then number each document separately (e.g. **[JAP-1]**).

(6) Consider whether the exhibits to the witness statements are collated in a separate file or files for each witness, or whether the exhibits for all witnesses are collated together or whether the exhibits for all witnesses and the documents referred to in the referral notice are collected together. Documents that are already contained in one part of the bundle should not be duplicated in another part.

10.2.5 Actions for the adjudicator once the dispute is referred

[10.35] As soon as the adjudicator receives the referral notice, he should do at least three things. The first is to take account of the nature of the dispute before him. He will now have sight of the referral notice as well as the notice of adjudication and will be able to reassess (he will have done this already before accepting the appointment, although only on the basis of the notice of adjudication and the ANB application notice, if any, and representations from the parties) the type of the dispute, its complexity and size (both in value and the volume of documentation) and decide whether he has the capability to preside over the adjudication. If he now considers he does not, he should notify the parties and resign immediately. The second is to consider whether he can resolve the dispute within the allotted time, in a manner that does broad justice to the parties. If not, the best course of action is to ask the parties for whatever further time he needs. Often, an adjudicator will put pressure on the parties to agree to the extension by proclaiming that unless the extension is given, he will resign. In *Bovis Lend Lease Ltd v The Trustees of the London Clinic*,[13] Akenhead J said:

> there is a sensible school of thought which suggests that in those circumstances an adjudicator can in effect decline to accept the appointment on the grounds that justice cannot be done or the adjudicator can simply say to the claiming party words to the effect: 'Unless you agree to an extension of time I will not be able to produce my decision within 28 days.' Indeed, that is commonly what adjudicators will do and it is a very rare case when the claiming party does not accede to some extension of time accordingly.

[10.36] The final action (which will take account of the first two) is to communicate a set of directions to the parties, which will include the timetable upon which the adjudication will proceed. He may have communicated a set of directions before receipt of the referral, in which case those directions will become operative on receipt of the referral, unless the adjudicator directs otherwise.[14] This will typically include a deadline (both a date and time) for the response and for any submissions, such further submissions will only be permitted on application to the adjudicator. He should indicate that any further submissions should only relate to new points not addressed by the relevant party's prior submission. If further submissions are required, notwithstanding the initial deadline date given, it is common for a party to request an extension to the timetable to allow time for further submissions, and for the referring party and adjudicator to agree. Where the adjudicator has been given jurisdiction to allocate costs, he may set aside some time in the timetable to receive submissions and make a decision.[15] Ordinarily, he will not determine whether a site visit, hearing or meeting is required at least until after the response is served.

10.3 Response

10.3.1 In a nutshell

[10.37] The response is the first document setting out the responding party's defence to the claim set out in the notice of adjudication and the referral notice. While there is sometimes an opportunity for further submissions, these are usually only permitted in respect of new points raised by the referring party. Therefore it is important for the responding party to raise all its defences in this document. The deadline for service of the response will either be dictated by the applicable adjudication rules or by the adjudicator when he sets the adjudication timetable. The responding party is entitled to bring any defence within the scope of the dispute, whether or not it has been raised before. However, where the defence is that the amount claimed is worth less, or there are amounts to be deducted from the amount claimed, it is normally a requirement that the responding party has

---

[13] [2009] EWHC 64 (TCC), per Akenhead J at [51].
[14] *Ecovision Systems Ltd v Vinci Construction UK Ltd* [2015] EWHC 587 (TCC), per Havelock-Allan J at [60].
[15] See Section 12.2 and 12.3.

served a valid withholding notice or pay less notice in respect of the amount it wishes to reduce or deduct from the claim.

10.3.2 Timing

[10.38] Where the Scheme applies, the adjudicator sets the period in which the responding party must serve the response. In a non-extended timetable, this is usually, although not always, seven days from the date of the referral notice. The responding party is not automatically entitled to serve the response unless the adjudicator permits. It would, however, be highly unusual and probably in breach of his jurisdictional powers and the rules of natural justice, if the adjudicator did not allow the response. Other adjudication rules expressly make provision for the service of the response, and provide a time within which it will be served.

[10.39] If the responding party needs more time to serve the response, it should write to the adjudicator (copying in the other party) and request it. The request should be accompanied by reasons why more time is needed. It may be, for instance, that the referring party has served evidence that the responding party has not seen before and needs time to consider. Or it may be that the key people needed are on holiday. Clearly, where the dispute is relatively simple and the volume of documents reasonably light, a request for an extension is more likely to fall on deaf ears. If the responding party fails to ask for more time and then later challenges the decision in enforcement proceedings on grounds of natural justice, the challenge will stand little chance.[16]

[10.40] If the request for extra time requires an extension to the adjudication timetable as a whole, consent will need to be obtained first from the referring party.[17] If the referring party refuses, the adjudicator may take the view that he cannot properly consider the case unless the responding party is given the time, and threaten to resign. This can be an effective way for the adjudicator to strong-arm the referring party into consenting.

10.3.3 Practical considerations and strategy

(A) Drafting, accompanying documents and witness evidence

[10.41] A model form response is contained at Appendix 4, which can be downloaded in soft copy from the publisher's website.[18]

[10.42] Many of the same considerations apply to the response as they do to the referral notice. The response document should be concise, to the point and persuasive. It should set out a detailed defence to the factual and legal basis of the referring party's case. It is often helpful for the response to structure the submission in the same way as the referral notice,

---

[16] See Section 17.3.
[17] See Section 11.4.
[18] http://onlinelibrary.wiley.com. Accessed 1 May 2015.

on a paragraph-by-paragraph or at least section-by-section basis, so that the adjudicator can see, side by side, the referring party's assertion and the responding party's response to that assertion. However, it may well be that the responding party considers parts of the referral notice to be irrelevant, or not appropriate to address, or that the order of topics in the referral notice is unfavourable, in which case such an approach will need to be moderated. See Section 10.2.4(A).

[10.43] Only essential documents should be appended to the response. Where some of those documents are also appended to the referral notice, it is unnecessary to also append them to the response. A cross-reference to the page number(s) or tab(s) in the referring party's bundle will suffice. Consider the comments made at Section 10.2.4(B) with regard to the accompanying documents to the referral notice.

[10.44] The responding party's witnesses (factual and expert) will invariably have much less time than the referring party to prepare statements. It should arguably apply an even greater level of caution than the referring party might when preparing witness evidence. Consider Section 10.2.4(C).

(B) Scope of the defence

[10.45] Subject to two provisos, the responding party is entitled to raise, and the adjudicator must consider, any defence, regardless of whether that defence was raised in advance of the adjudication.[19] This is perhaps the best tool in the responding party's armoury and is in contrast to the referring party's claim, which must have been raised with the responding party in advance of it being referred to adjudication.[20]

[10.46] The first proviso is that the defence raised must of course fall within the scope of the dispute. Where the defence is outside the scope of the dispute, the adjudicator must exclude it, or risk exceeding his jurisdiction. However, adjudicators should tread carefully before deciding to exclude a defence. As further set out in Sections 16.7.6 and 17.5.7, there are a number of cases in which the adjudicator has been found to act in excess of his jurisdiction or in breach of the rules of natural justice because he failed to consider part or all of a defence.

> an adjudicator should think very carefully before ruling out a defence merely because there was no mention of it in the claiming party's notice of adjudication. That is only common sense: it would be absurd if the claiming party could, through some devious bit of drafting, put beyond the scope of the adjudication the defending party's otherwise legitimate defence to the claim.[21]

[10.47] The second proviso is that the defence must be permissible in law or in fact. A common example of an impermissible defence is a set-off which had not been raised before and

---

[19] *William Verry (Glazing Systems) Ltd v Furlong Homes Ltd* [2005] EWHC 138, per Coulson J at [49].
[20] See Section 7.2.
[21] *Pilon Limited v Breyer Group plc* [2010] EWHC 837 (TCC), per Coulson J at [16].

was therefore not the subject matter of the appropriate contractual or statutory withholding notice requirements. Set-off is addressed further at Section 10.6.4. The fact that the defence is impermissible does not prevent the adjudicator from having the jurisdiction from considering it, but it clearly does not mean that he is required to accept it.[22]

[10.48] Raising defences that have never before been raised during the evolution of the dispute may be viewed with scepticism by the adjudicator and so therefore it is advisable that new defences are accompanied by sound evidence in support, if the adjudicator is to be persuaded of the responding party's position.

[10.49] If the responding party chooses not to advance a particular defence, he cannot raise that defence in a subsequent adjudication.[23] Furthermore, even though the adjudicator may privately consider that a defence not raised would be effective, he must not make a finding based on that defence, unless he has raised his thoughts with the parties and has provided them with sufficient opportunity to comment. If he does not do this, the adjudicator runs a real risk of breaching the rules of natural justice.[24]

[10.50] Some adjudication rules entitle the adjudicator to take into account other matters. So for instance the Scheme provides at paragraph 20 that the adjudicator may consider matters outside the scope of the dispute if they are under the contract and are necessarily connected with the dispute. This will include defences and cross-claims. See Sections 10.7.7 and 10.7.8.

10.4 Reply, rejoinder and sur-rejoinder

10.4.1 In a nutshell

[10.51] The reply is the submission containing the referring party's answer to the response, the rejoinder is the responding party's answer to the reply and the sur-rejoinder is the response to the rejoinder. The entitlement to serve these submissions and the extent of what they address is variable and to an extent dictated by the adjudicator.

10.4.2 Practical considerations and strategy

[10.52] The reply, rejoinder and sur-rejoinder will be needed if the prior submission raises substantive new facts or arguments that have not been addressed, whether they are raised in a submission, the supporting documents or witness statements. There is no provision in the Scheme for the referring party to issue a reply or sur-rejoinder, or for the responding party to issue the rejoinder. Usually the adjudicator will not make express provision for

---

[22] *Roland Horne v Magna Design Building Ltd and Marcus Build Décor Ltd* [2014] EWHC 3380 (TCC), per Akenhead J at [14].
[23] *Working Environments Ltd v Greencoat Construction Ltd* [2012] EWHC 1039 (TCC), per Akenhead J at [24].
[24] See Section 17.5.14.

further submissions beyond the response in his timetable. Therefore, the relevant party must seek leave from the adjudicator to serve a further submission. If a request is not made, then the prejudiced party is unlikely to be able to claim after the adjudication that the adjudicator should have allowed a further submission.

[10.53] It is common practice among adjudicators to grant the referring party permission to serve the reply and usually, but less frequently, the rejoinder and sur-rejoinder. Sometimes this may be because there are substantive new arguments or evidence that need to be addressed in reply or in the rejoinder, and the adjudicator's directions permit a further submission, but only in so far as the submission responds to something not already dealt with.[25] However, more often than not further submissions are granted out of a fear by the adjudicator that if he does not grant permission for a party to serve an additional submission, that party will mount a successful challenge that by refusing a further submission, it is not being afforded the opportunity to respond to the case being put to it and therefore the adjudicator is acting in breach of the rules of natural justice. Whether this argument succeeds depends on a number of factors such as the opportunity of the party to make the submission previously, whether the arguments that a party seeks a right of reply to are substantive new points and whether the adjudicator considers there is sufficient time left in the adjudication process for a party to make the decision and then for him to consider that submission before the deadline for his decision. See Section 17.5 for more detail on this point.

[10.54] However, it is to be remembered that the courts will only entertain material breaches of natural justice and therefore, only where it is plain that there is a substantive new argument made and that a right of reply to that argument should have been allowed, will the court find the adjudicator has erred. It is therefore submitted that adjudicators should pause for careful thought on whether a further submission is really warranted. In many ways, even allowing the referring party a right of reply and thus a second bite of the cherry is unreasonable; it will already have had months to prepare its referral notice, as compared to the few weeks that the responding party will have had to prepare its response. Why then should the referring party be given a further opportunity to put forward its case? Permitting further submissions will also eat into the time the adjudicator has to consider the parties' submissions and make a decision. Therefore, only where the referring party has clearly demonstrated that there are substantive new lines of argument in defence should the adjudicator permit a reply.

[10.55] Parties should also avoid leaping to the conclusion that a further submission is in its favour. It is generally not helpful for parties to repeatedly request that they have the last word and less helpful still for those submissions to be lengthy. Further, each successive submission can give the impression that the party concerned is either not as well prepared as it might be or that it does not have confidence in the case presented in earlier submissions. If a further submission is made, the content of the submission should be limited as much as possible.

---

[25] *GPS Marine Contractors Ltd v Ringway Infrastructure Services Ltd* [2010] EWHC 283 (TCC), per Ramsey J at [102].

[10.56] As the submissions increase in number, it can become a difficult or at least a time-consuming task for the adjudicator and the parties to track through the submissions to work out what has been said about each issue. This can be prevented in two ways. Where possible, the party that is responding to a submission should either mirror the paragraph numbering used in the previous submission (so that paragraph 11 of the rejoinder responds to paragraph 11 of the reply) or indicate at the start of each paragraph or section heading which paragraph, paragraphs or sections are being responded to. Alternatively, or in addition, the parties can distil submissions into a Scott Schedule. A Scott Schedule is a way of tabulating submissions on different elements or items of claim in a spreadsheet. It is particularly useful where the claim consists of a number of separate items, such as disputed items of payment, items of defective works or a number of variations or compensation events. The spreadsheet can be a useful means of recording each party's position against a particular item. The schedule should be submitted to the adjudicator in soft copy so that if he wishes, he can add his own columns to set out his financial findings and reasons for the decision he reaches against each item.

10.4.3 Parallel correspondence

[10.57] Sometimes in adjudication, in addition to setting out their case in formal submissions, the parties will also make submissions through correspondence with the adjudicator. This may start with an exchange of letters on a request for an extension to the timetable, but then develop into substantive issues and spiral out of control as one party considers it must address representations made by the other party. A party may also try to shoehorn further submissions into a letter where the adjudicator has made it clear that there are to be no more 'formal' submissions.

[10.58] Unless this is controlled, the adjudicator may very quickly find himself faced with the job of piecing together the arguments made in submissions and the arguments set out in letters written by the parties in order to establish the extent of each party's case. Adjudicators can try to address this problem by making it clear at the outset that the parties are only permitted to advance arguments on the substance of the case within the body of the formal submissions and that any arguments advanced in correspondence will be disregarded. Depending on how and when this is done, however, the adjudicator runs the risk of breaching the rules of natural justice because he failed to consider a material part of a party's case. Section 17.5.7 considers this issue further in the context of failing to address an issue or part of a submission and Section 17.5.8 considers it in the context of failing to allow a further submission or information.

10.5 *Meetings*

[10.59] Many adjudications are decided on paper submissions alone. However, a meeting, which may take the form of an informal meeting, a telephone or video conference, a hearing or a site visit, may be requested by the adjudicator. The meeting may be used to inspect the site or clarify procedural matters, or it may be used if the adjudicator wishes to hear from the parties' representatives or witnesses. Not only are meetings beneficial for the adjudicator, but they can also benefit the parties in that each party will feel like it has had an opportunity to vocalise its complaints and hear directly from the other party. This may lead to a settlement of the dispute before the adjudicator reaches his decision, but if not, it may at least increase the likelihood that the parties accept the adjudicator's decision when it comes. The Centre for Dispute Resolution published a report in October 2014 entitled 'Research analysis of the progress of adjudication based on returned questionnaires from adjudicator nominating bodies (ANBs) and from a sample of adjudicators'.[26] It found that while most adjudications are a paper-only exercise, 30% of all adjudications involve an interview, meeting or conference call with the parties.

[10.60] The Act implicitly permits the adjudicator to hold meetings in that it provides that the adjudicator may take the initiative in ascertaining the facts and the law.[27] Where the Scheme applies, it expressly provides that the adjudicator may hold meetings and carry out site visits or inspections.[28] Where there is a meeting and where the Scheme applies, subparagraph 16(2) of the Scheme provides that a party may not be represented by more than one person, unless the adjudicator permits otherwise.

[10.61] The way in which a party prepares for a meeting will be dictated by the adjudicator, who will normally outline in advance the procedure he expects to follow, the issues he would like to cover and who he would like to attend. Parties should try to obtain as much detail from the adjudicator as to why he is calling the meeting, precisely what issues he wants to address or what questions he wants to have answered and how procedurally he will conduct it. Similarly, it is good practice for the adjudicator to make clear what his intentions are for the meeting, either by way of a list of questions, a schedule or an agenda. If the meeting is to take the form of a hearing, he may wish to hear submissions from the referring party and the responding party on a particular point, and he may request that one or more witnesses attend the hearing to be questioned by him or by the parties. He may decide to 'face off' the parties, their legal advisers, factual or expert witnesses on particular issues; a procedure known as hot-tubbing. Because the adjudicator enjoys a high level of flexibility, everyone who attends the hearing needs to be fully prepared.

[10.62] In so far as the adjudicator seeks oral submissions from the parties, those submissions should be limited to the issues in dispute. It is tempting for the adjudicator to stray outside the scope of the dispute or for the parties to try to shoehorn new arguments or material into their oral submissions. Where this happens, objection should be taken immediately, with the aim of ensuring that the adjudicator strikes out the extraneous issue raised. If he does not, and it is obvious that the new material forms part of his decision, the new material may invalidate the decision (or at least the part dealing with new issue) on grounds that the dispute he decided was not the dispute referred to him and therefore he

---

[26] http://www.cdr.uk.com/documents/Report13_001.pdf. Accessed 1 September 2015. One of the authors of this report, Jane Milligan, was also the co-author of all previous editions of the report (no.s 1–12) published by Glasgow Caledonian University. See http://www.gcu.ac.uk/ebe/businessservices/adjudicationreports. Accessed 1 September 2015.
[27] Subsection 108(2)(f) of the Act.
[28] Paragraph 13 of the Scheme.

acted outside of his jurisdiction. A successful objection in these circumstances is likely to be contingent on the objecting party (a) maintaining the objection and (b) not accepting the new material as part of the adjudication. These issues are explored in some detail at Section 16.4. If the adjudicator does not strike out the new point, then he should give the other party sufficient opportunity to consider and respond to the issue, either at the meeting or afterwards. Failure to do this may amount to a breach of natural justice.[29]

[10.63] One important feature of adjudication is that witnesses are not under oath. In court proceedings, for example, factual and expert witnesses can face criminal prosecution, through contempt of court proceedings, if they make false statements.[30] There are no such consequences for false statements in adjudication proceedings, meaning that a witness can lie, without fear of reprisal. Therefore, oral evidence that is unsupported by evidence should be treated with caution. If the oral evidence is recorded on a transcript and it is later found to be wrong, where legal proceedings are commenced, the transcript may be used to damage the credibility of the witness during those proceedings.

10.6 Other matters

10.6.1 In a nutshell

[10.64] Beyond procedural requirements concerning the content, timing and requirements for service of the various submissions, there are a number of other matters to which it is important to adhere or which should be considered.

- When communicating with the adjudicator, always include all other parties to the adjudication in those communications.
- Adjudication can be a highly volatile environment; consider guidance on how to deal with pressure from the adjudicator or, as an adjudicator, dealing with pressure from one or both parties.
- The responding party may wish to reduce the amount claimed by the referring party by way of set-off. Whether or not it is entitled to do that as a matter of law is dependent on the nature of the set-off, whether provisions of the 1996 Act or 2009 Act (as applicable) have been complied with (the rules differ on this issue) and what the contract says.
- The referring party is entitled to drop heads of claim raised in the notice of adjudication if it wishes and, provided certain condition are met, reformulate the claim in a different adjudication. It may also stop the adjudication itself commencing, provided that it has not served the referral notice.
- Privilege is the right to withhold a document from inspection by another party or by the court. The three types of privilege important in the context of adjudication are legal, without prejudice and litigation privilege. The question of the applicability of legal privilege and without prejudice privilege over documents produced for the

---

[29] See Section 17.5.7.
[30] Civil Procedure Rule 32.14.

purpose of adjudication proceedings is reasonably straightforward. However, whether or not litigation privilege applies is less so.
- The adjudicator has no power to order disclosure of documents during an adjudication, although if he requests a document or class of documents and they are not provided, he may draw inference from that refusal.
- Settlement offers are regularly made during adjudication. The court rules regarding settlement offers do not apply in adjudication. However, the question of whether a settlement offer has been made, and if so at what amount, can be relevant to the question of allocation of costs by the adjudicator. Parties may stay adjudication proceedings while settlement discussions are being held or for any other reason. Where a stay is sought after the dispute has been referred to the adjudicator, his permission must be sought.
- An adjudication may commence or continue during litigation or arbitration and vice versa. Documents or information produced for adjudications under the Scheme will be confidential if the party supplying information or documents indicates that to the adjudicator, although there may be confidentiality provisions in the contract that bind the parties in any event.
- Finally, where the Act applies, it provides rules for the service of documents where the contract does not expressly provide them. It also provides rules for the reckoning of time.

10.6.2 Communicating with the other party and with the adjudicator during the adjudication

[10.65] While parties may communicate between themselves without including the adjudicator, if either party wishes to communicate with the adjudicator before or during the course of the adjudication, the other party should be included. Equally, the adjudicator should communicate with both parties. A typically clear and concise summary was given by Akenhead J in *Makers UK Ltd v The Mayor and Burgesses of the London Borough of Camden*[31] as to how the parties should communicate with each other and with the adjudicator before, during and after an adjudication:

> (1) It is better for all concerned if parties limit their unilateral contacts with adjudicators both before, during and after an adjudication; the same goes for adjudicators having unilateral contact with individual parties. It can be misconstrued by the losing party, even if entirely innocent.
> (2) If any such contact, it is felt, has to be made, it is better if done in writing so that there is a full record of the communication.
> (3) Nominating institutions might sensibly consider their rules as to nominations and as to whether they do or do not welcome or accept suggestions from one or more parties as to the attributes or even identities of the person to be nominated by the institutions. If it is to be permitted in any given circumstances, the institutions might wish to consider whether notice of the suggestions must be given to the other party.

---

[31] [2008] EWHC 1836 (TCC) per Akenhead J at [36].

[10.66] Cases where a party has argued that unilateral contact invalidates the adjudicator's decision are considered at Sections 17.4.6 and 17.4.7.

10.6.3 Pressure from the parties or the adjudicator

[10.67] In a small number of cases, a party or its representatives consider that it is in their client's best interest to intimidate or bully the adjudicator to achieve their desired outcome in the dispute or on a particular point. They may use inappropriate language, repeatedly lodge spurious challenges to the adjudicator's jurisdiction insisting that he acts or does not act in a certain way, challenge the procedure adopted by the adjudicator as unfair, continue to serve submissions until the 11th hour, or threaten to withdraw from the adjudication or report him to his professional institution and/or sue him.

[10.68] Perhaps this approach is short-sighted when one considers that the adjudicator has been charged with deciding the dispute between the parties and that his answer, provided it is made within jurisdiction and natural justice, will bind the parties whether or not that answer is right or wrong. If an adjudicator feels a party or its representatives are applying undue pressure, he may not feel as disposed to that party's case as he otherwise might. He may feel that the reason the party is applying undue pressure has its foundation in the fact that the party's case is poor and so its only option is to try to exercise whatever leverage it can by whatever means.

[10.69] The way to deal with intimidation tactics will depend on the circumstances, but there are some things an adjudicator can do to help minimise the opportunity:

- The adjudicator should set a clear timetable for the adjudication and stick to it. The timetable should spell out the consequences to the parties of failing to comply.
- When a jurisdictional issue arises, the adjudicator should explain exactly how he intends to deal with it and respond quickly (not leaving it to when he writes his decision).
- The adjudicator should always engage professionally with the parties and avoid emotive or inflammatory language.
- Where something is not clear, the adjudicator should ask the parties to explain it.
- Where more time is needed, the adjudicator should give the parties a clear choice. Either agree the extension or expect resignation. It is not advisable to continue under the original timetable if the extension is refused, unless a party or the parties have reasonably explained to the adjudicator why he has enough time and that explanation is recorded in writing.

[10.70] Adjudicators as well as parties' representatives are capable of exerting pressure. However, there is a difference between the appropriate use of clear firm directions and intimidation or abuse to achieve a particular result. Adjudicators should be very careful indeed not to appear biased, which may be the inference drawn if intimidation was levied on a party. In fact, it is difficult to see any circumstance where the adjudicator may he feel he is relieved of his obligation to act fairly and in an unbiased as between the parties. Moreover the adjudicator will have obligations to his professional institution. For example the Royal

Institution of Chartered Surveyors produces a guidance note[32] and rightly 'expects the highest standards from those on its panel of adjudicators'.

10.6.4 Set-off and abatement

[10.71] Where a claimant and a defendant have a liability to each other, the general principle is that a defence arises where one obligation is deducted from the other. This can be characterised as a set-off or an abatement. Such defence is available absent clear words to the contrary in the contract.[33] Set-off or abatement commonly arises in four ways.

- The payer[34] argues that the sum applied for should not be paid because it is worth less, either as a result of a defect making the item less valuable, or an erroneous valuation, or where the amount applied for is a mistake. This is called abatement. In that case, the payer's assertion is not based on a distinct cross-claim[35] for money, but instead on the assertion that the payee's claim for money should be reduced because it worth less than the sum claimed.[36]
- The payer argues that the amount claimed should be reduced by a cross-claim, where the cross-claim is so closely connected that it would be manifestly unjust to enforce payment without taking into account the cross-claim. This is called equitable set-off. In this case, the payer will claim a sum of money that is separate from, though connected with, the sum claimed by the payee.
- The payer may seek to reduce the claim through a cross-claim that is unconnected with the amount claimed. There may be a sum owed to it in respect of a matter unconnected with the subject matter of the dispute, or it may be a sum owed under a different contract entirely that it wishes to offset against the sums claimed by the referring party. This is known as an independent or legal set-off. It is only permissible where it is for a liquidated sum which arises due and payable prior to the date of the sum claimed.
- A contractual set-off is a matter of the parties' express agreement. Here the parties may agree what they like, so for example, unliquidated claims or estimates of future liability arising under other contracts may, if the language of the set-off clause permits it, be deducted from the sums otherwise due.

---

[32] *Surveyors Acting as Adjudicators in the Construction Industry*, 2012, 3rd edition, www.rics.org/uk/knowledge/professional-guidance/guidance-notes/surveyors-acting-as-adjudicators-in-the-construction-industry. Accessed 1 September 2015.

[33] *Gilbert-Ash (Northern) Ltd v Modern Engineering (Bristol) Ltd* [1974] A.C. 689.

[34] In other words, the paying party, usually either the employer or the contractor. The payee is the receiving party, usually the contractor or subcontractor.

[35] A cross-claim can be taken to mean any claim that seeks to reduce the claimant's or the referring party's claim. A cross-claim can be used defensively, as an abatement or a set-off, it can be used as a counter-attack or counterclaim, or any other type of claim that competes with the claimant's or referring party's claim. See *Set-Off in Adjudication*, Winser, 30 Const. L.J., Issue 2 at [103–113].

[36] *Mondel v Steel* (1841) 8 M&W 858, per Parke B. The reasons for the development of distinct common law rules of abatement and equitable rules permitting cross-claims for defects are mostly of historical interest only, but the fact that they are two separate doctrines means that a contractual exclusion of set-off rights will not affect the ability to abate; see e.g. *Acsim (Southern) v Danish Contracting* (1989) 47 BLR 55.

[10.72] The following example illustrates the differences. A contract requires the contractor to install a roof. Work proceeds and during the finishing stage the roof leaks and is found on inspection to be defective. The contractor claims for the full value of installing the roof in his application for payment, refusing to acknowledge that there are any defects and refusing to correct the defective work. The contractor also claims loss and expense because he claims the employer changed the roofing tiles from those originally specified which took longer to install.

[10.73] The employer argues that the roof installed was never executed in accordance with the contract and therefore some or all of the sums claimed by the contractor are not owed to the contractor because the roof is not worth what has been claimed. The employer issues a certificate of payment setting out his (lower) value of the work properly carried out. This is an abatement.

[10.74] In addition, the employer has obtained quotations from other roofing contractors to put the works right. This is going to cause the employer additional costs in removing and replacing the poorly installed roof. Furthermore, the works inside the building will come to a standstill until the building is made watertight, causing delay to completion of the main contract works. As a result, the employer puts the contractor on notice of his intention to recover liquidated damages for the delay. The employer issues a withholding or pay less notice setting out the full breakdown of the additional costs incurred or likely to be incurred arising from the delay and the cost of fixing the roof. This is an equitable set-off.

[10.75] Thirdly, the employer previously advanced to the contractor an entirely separate loan repayable on demand to enable the contractor to purchase materials. The employer is entitled to set off the amount of the loan as a due and immediately repayable debt. This is a legal or independent set off, permissible because it is for a liquidated sum due and payable before the contract sum became due.

[10.76] Lastly, the employer notes that there is an express provision in the contract for recovery of losses caused by the contractor to the employer on a completely unrelated, separate contract between the parties because of a breach of contract by the contractor. This contract was completed two years ago. Relying on the contract, the employer includes a full breakdown of the loss arising on the other contract in his withholding or pay less notice for the current contract. This is an unconnected cross-claim for an unliquidated sum. It is only capable of set-off by virtue of the contractual set-off clause.

[10.77] The common law position as regards the ability to set off sums against amounts due is adjusted by virtue of the payment provisions in the Act. In summary, the 1996 Act prohibits a payer from setting off against sums **certified** as due, unless a withholding or pay less notice is served within a fixed period of time indicating the intention to set off and the reasons for doing so. Under the 2009 Act the payee is afforded a further right to self-certify in the absence of the necessary certificate from the payer (by virtue of a default notice),[37] and the payer must then serve its pay less notice against that self-certification or

---
[37] Section 110B of the 2009 Act.

The adjudication

no set-off is permissible. The right to self-certify given to payees under the 2009 Act stems from one perceived shortcoming in the 1996 Act, namely that the payer is able to abate sums from the application for payment, where that application has **not** been certified as due, because all claims and cross-claims could be considered if in the absence of a certificate the payee was forced to adjudicate for valuation. The 2009 Act was a response to payers' 'gaming' of the 1996 Act's provisions by refusing to certify anything, creating the arguably perverse situation where the payer was in a better position if it breached its obligation to certify than it was if it followed the contract.[38] Although the payment provisions are outside the scope of this book, it is useful to explain this distinction in a little more detail.

[10.78] Where an amount is applied for by a payee and a sum has been certified as due[39] (usually by the contract administrator or project manager), unless the payer issues to the payee a notice within a fixed period setting out its intention to pay less than the certified amount and reasons and calculations why,[40] subject to a situation where the payee is insolvent,[41] the payer is required to pay that amount regardless of any claim that it may subsequently consider it has to reduce or extinguish the amount.[42] If it does not, the payee is entitled to commence an adjudication to recover that amount and/or suspend further work.[43] The notice is called a withholding notice under the 1996 Act or pay less notice under the 2009 Act and the rules governing its issue and effect are set out at section 111. The critical point here is that the amount applied for has been certified as due. Where this has been done, there is no defence of set-off available under the 1996 or 2009 Act.

[10.79] However, the position is different under the 1996 Act and 2009 Act, where sums are claimed by the payee, but not certified as 'due'. This may arise where the contract does not require a third-party certifier, or it does but the certification has not been done. Pursuant to the 1996 Act, there is a requirement for the payer to certify sums due, known as a subsection 110(a) notice, but the 1996 Act provides no consequences on the payer for failing to comply with this requirement. Thus, where a sum is not certified as due, it can be said that it is merely 'claimed' by the payee. In this case, where the payer contends that the amount claimed by the payee should not be paid because it claims an abatement, it is not necessary for there to be a withholding notice in place in order for the payer to pay a reduced amount.

[10.80] Where the payer contends that the amount claimed should not be paid because of an equitable set-off or unconnected matter, it is less clear whether, under the 1996 Act, a valid withholding notice is required. On the one hand, it is not necessary because the sums claimed are not 'due' and are therefore not capable of being subject to a withholding

---

[38] This tactic is discussed further at Section 8.5.2.
[39] Section 110 of the Act.
[40] Section 111 of the Act.
[41] *Urang Commercial Ltd v Century Investments Ltd, Eclipse Hotels Luton Ltd* [2011] EWHC 1561 (TCC), per Edwards-Stuart J at [22–24].
[42] *Imtech Inviron Ltd v Loppingdale Plant Ltd* [2014] EWHC 4109 (TCC), per Edwards-Stuart J at [47–53].
[43] Section 112 of the Act.

notice.[44] On the other hand, there is a line of authorities where it has been made reasonably clear that where there is a certificate, a withholding notice must be in place if the payer is to lawfully reduce the amount claimed by set-off.[45]

[10.81] The position is different under the 2009 Act because the ability of the payer to avoid certifying sums applied for as due has been removed as discussed above. If the payer fails to certify as due an amount applied for within a fixed period of time, the payee may step into the shoes of the payer and certify its own application as due.[46] Once the sum is so certified, if the payer does not issue a pay less notice within the time prescribed in the contract, it is not entitled to abate, or apply any cross-claim to the amount applied for to reduce or extinguish the amount certified. It must pay it.

[10.82] Parties and adjudicators therefore need to be astute about these provisions of the 1996 Act and the 2009 Act in order to determine whether or not the a payer is entitled to reduce the amount claimed, either by an abatement or a set-off or by virtue of an unconnected cross-claim.

10.6.5 Dropping a head of claim during the adjudication

[10.83] Where a referring party has advanced a number of heads of claim, which together comprise the dispute, and then subsequently decides to drop one or more of those heads for whatever reason, it is entitled to do so. The court has held that this is permissible because:[47]

(i) There is nothing in the Act or the Scheme which suggests that any such restriction is intended.
(ii) Adjudication is an informal process which arrives at an interim resolution of disputes pending final determination by litigation or arbitration. It would be contrary to the statutory purpose to prohibit a party from withdrawing from such a process any claim which it did not wish to pursue.
(iii) If there were such a restriction, it would have the bizarre consequence that parties would be forced to press on with bad claims in adjudication. This would lead to wastage of costs and resources on the part of all parties. In my view, this simple consideration outweighs all the policy arguments which have been urged in Mr Blackburn's skeleton argument.
(iv) In John Roberts Architects Ltd v Park Care Homes [2006] BLR 106, the Court of Appeal stated obiter that a referring party could discontinue an adjudication. See the judgment of Lord Justice May at page 109.

[10.84] Once the claim is withdrawn, the referring party can reformulate it and advance it under a new adjudication, provided it can show that the reformulated claim is a different dispute

---

[44] *SL Timber Systems v Carillion* [2001] ScotCS 167, per Lord MacFayden at [18–23].
[45] *Rupert Morgan Building Services (LLC) Ltd v Jervis & Anor* [2003] EWCA Civ 1563, per Jacob LJ at [4–16].
[46] Section 110B of the 2009 Act.
[47] *Midland Expressway Ltd v Carillion Construction & Ors* [2006] EWHC 1505 (TCC), per Jackson J at [99–108].

from the dispute that was decided in the first adjudication. If the adjudicator decides on the claim, then the party is precluded from challenging that decision in a subsequent adjudication. This includes deploying different arguments that could have been raised first time around.[48] Section 7.4 addresses this in more detail.

10.6.6 Withdrawing from the adjudication entirely

[10.85] Sometimes a referring party may wish to withdraw from the adjudication entirely. Where it wishes to do this before the referral notice is served, all it needs to do is not serve the referral notice. In that case, the adjudication will not commence[49] and the referring party is free to issue another notice of adjudication in respect of the same dispute at a later time. If it withdraws after it has served the referral notice, the adjudication will already have commenced and the adjudicator should proceed to reach a decision in any event. Therefore, once the referral notice is served, unless there is an issue that goes to the adjudicator's jurisdiction and a party decides it is appropriate to withdraw,[50] by and large the best course of action is to remain engaged in the process until its conclusion.

[10.86] When the referring party withdraws from an adjudication entirely before the decision is given, the question can arise as to whether the referring party has any liability to pay the adjudicator or the other party's costs. The answer will depend on the form and type of adjudication. Sections 12.2 and 12.3 discuss this point further.

10.6.7 Privilege

[10.87] Privilege is the right to withhold a document from inspection by another party or by the court. There are different types of privilege: legal advice privilege, litigation privilege and without prejudice privilege are the most relevant in the context of adjudication. The question is whether these types of privilege apply in the context of documents produced for the purpose of, or in connection with, adjudication proceedings.

(A) Legal advice privilege

[10.88] Legal advice privilege attaches to:

> all communications made in confidence between solicitors [or other lawyers] and their clients for the purpose of giving or obtaining legal advice[51]

---

[48] *Benfield Construction Ltd v Trudson (Hatton) Ltd* [2008] EWHC 2333 (TCC) per Coulson J at [20–56].
[49] The adjudication itself does not commence until the dispute is referred to the adjudicator, albeit that the process starts once the notice of adjudication is served.
[50] See Section 16.3 for options on how a party may respond to a jurisdictional issue.
[51] *Three Rivers DC v Bank of England (Disclosure) (No. 4)* [2004] UKHL 48, per Lord Roger at [50].

[10.89] Any confidential communications between a lawyer and a client for the purpose of giving or receiving legal advice will be privileged. This means that legal advice given by lawyers to clients in relation to an adjudication (as well as communications from the clients seeking such advice) will be protected from inspection either during or subsequent to an adjudication.

[10.90] The custodian of this form of privilege falls to qualified and practising solicitors or barristers, whether they are employed in private practice or within a company. This form of privilege does not extend to legal advice given to clients by other professionals, such as accountants[52] or claims consultants, where those claims consultants are retained to provide claims and project management services.[53] Legal advice given by such individuals may fall within litigation privilege (but see below).

[10.91] It has become commonplace for parties to adjudication to use claims consultants to prepare their case and to conduct the adjudication on their behalf. However, where the consultant is not a qualified practising lawyer, any information committed to permanent form, such as an assessment of the client's case, or reference to 'smoking gun' evidence, whether that is recorded in emails, letters, meeting minutes or tape recordings will fall to be disclosed to the other party in the event that the dispute is not resolved by adjudication and proceeds to litigation or arbitration, and the party cannot successfully claim litigation privilege. While it is true that the majority of disputes that are referred to adjudication proceed no further, for those disputes that do, this could present real difficulty.

(B) Litigation Privilege

[10.92] Litigation privilege allows a client to withhold from inspection communications between either the client or his solicitor (on the one hand) and a third party (on the other) which are confidential, and were made for the dominant purpose of litigation which was reasonably in contemplation at the time the communications were made.[54] The scope of the privilege is wide and can include documents such as draft expert reports and witness statements.

[10.93] In order for a document to be protected from inspection under this type of privilege, it must have been created for the dominant purpose of litigation that was reasonably in contemplation at the time it was made. The question therefore is whether adjudication falls within the definition of 'litigation'.

[10.94] The House of Lords in *Re L*[55] considered that litigation privilege 'is essentially a creature of adversarial proceedings'[56] and refused to apply it to other types of proceedings, which are more inquisitorial in nature. Adjudication must therefore be shown to be adversarial

---

[52] *R (Prudential plc and another) v Special Commissioner of Income Tax and another* [2013] UKSC 1.
[53] *Walter Lilly & Co Ltd v Mackay* [2012] EWHC 649 (TCC), per Akenhead J at [15–19].
[54] *Starbev GP Ltd v Interbrew Central European Holding BV* [2013] EWHC 4038.
[55] [1996] 2 W.L.R. 395.
[56] Ibid. (per Lord Jauncey).

in order to attract litigation privilege. In an excellent paper written by Adrian Bell,[57] he argues that the similarities in terms of formality and procedure between adjudication and arbitration (which is treated as being adversarial) mean that adjudication should be seen as sufficiently adversarial to attract litigation privilege.

[10.95] Mr Justice Akenhead in *Walter Lilly*[58] left open the possibility that 'advice and other communications given by claims consultants in connection with adjudication proceedings are privileged'. He said that when deciding whether or not adjudication should be held to fall within the scope of 'litigation' so as to attract litigation privilege, 'consideration might have to be given to issues of policy'.

[10.96] As explained in *Three Rivers v Bank of England*,[59] the policy reason for allowing litigation privilege in adversarial proceedings is that 'in such a system each party should be free to prepare his case as fully as possible without the risk that his opponent will be able to recover the material generated by his preparations.' Arguably, similar concerns would apply in the adjudication context.

[10.97] It seems there is a compelling argument that litigation privilege should be available in relation to documents created in preparation for an adjudication. However, as yet, the issue is unresolved by the courts. There exists a risk therefore that documents created for the purpose of an adjudication (other than those protected by legal advice privilege) would fall to be disclosed in the event the parties sought to resolve the adjudicated dispute or a similar dispute in litigation if they are not protected by another form of privilege. In order to minimise the risk that this uncertainty creates, where communications take place between non-lawyers, it is advisable to exercise caution in how and when those communications are recorded before and during an adjudication and to avoid referring to such communications in submissions.

(C) Without prejudice privilege

[10.98] The without prejudice rule applies to exclude from evidence all negotiations genuinely aimed at settlement, whether oral or in writing.[60] In the context of litigation, it means that any correspondence written with this intention in mind may be withheld from inspection by the other party or by the court.

[10.99] In *Ellis Building Contractors Limited v Vincent Goldstein*,[61] Mr Justice Akenhead confirmed that without prejudice communications are privileged and should not be referred to in any legal or quasi-legal proceedings, including adjudication, and he expressed the court's desire to discourage reliance on without prejudice material in adjudication. The issue of without prejudice privilege is considered further at Section 17.4.13.

---

[57] *The Role of Privilege in Adjudication*, Adrian Bell, paper presented to the Society of Construction Law, April 2013.
[58] *Walter Lilly & Co Ltd v Mackay* [2012] EWHC 649 (TCC).
[59] *Three Rivers DC v Bank of England (Disclosure) (No. 4)* [2004] UKHL 48, per Lord Roger at [52].
[60] *Rush & Tompkins Ltd. v Greater London Council* [1989] A.C. 1280, per Lord Griffiths.
[61] [2011] EWHC 269 (TCC), at [25].

The question of whether and, if so, how the adjudicator takes account of offers made without prejudice save as to costs is considered in Section 10.6.9.

10.6.8 Disclosure of documents

[10.100] In litigation and domestic arbitration in England and Wales, parties are usually required by the court or tribunal to disclose non-privileged documents which support or are adverse to their or the other party's case.[62] Unlike litigation or arbitration, there is no provision in the Act or the Scheme that requires a party to comply with an order for disclosure from the adjudicator, or that compels an adjudicator to accede to a party request for disclosure.[63] However, where the adjudicator does make a request for documents and this is refused, he is entitled to draw inferences from that refusal.[64] Within the bounds of his jurisdiction and the rules of natural justice, there is no control on the level of inference that the adjudicator may draw. Therefore, unless there is a good reason not to disclose documents the adjudicator requests, a party should comply. A good reason to refuse a disclosure request might be that there are provisions in the contract that preclude the provision of information after a certain period of time. So, for example, a clause prohibiting the provision and receipt of further information, documentation or details about direct loss and expense after the six-month period following practical completion, may preclude the disclosure of such documents to the adjudicator. However, the clause would need to be expressed in clear and unambiguous language.[65]

[10.101] Can parties obtain disclosure of documents in some other way? CPR 31.16 provides that parties may apply to the court for an order that documents are disclosed before court proceedings are commenced. An order will be granted where it can be shown that it is desirable in order to dispose fairly of the anticipated proceedings, to assist the dispute to be resolved without proceedings or to save costs. Although there are no reported examples of a CPR 31.16 succeeding before or during an adjudication, it is in theory possible to obtain disclosure via this route provided the test is met.

[10.102] In *PHD Modular Access Services Ltd v Steele GmbH*,[66] the parties had already undergone six adjudications and were about to commence a seventh. PHD made an application for pre-action disclosure pursuant to CPR 31.16. The court was clear that CPR 31.16 should not be used as some sort of procedural support and a tactical weapon for the purposes of adjudication. It said that there must be a real prospect, if not a certainty or likelihood, of proceedings between the parties. Pre-action disclosure should not be common or standard and should not always be available simply because an issue has arisen between the parties that may result in litigation. Given, that the applicant had been successful in a number of adjudications already, the court said it would be odd if PHD was seriously contemplating court proceedings, and there was no indication that Steele

---

[62] CPR 31.6.
[63] *CIB Properties Ltd v Birse Construction Ltd* [2004] EWHC 2365 (TCC), per Toulmin J at [196].
[64] Scheme, paragraph 15.
[65] *Skanska Construction UK Ltd v ERDC Group Ltd & Anor* [2002] ScotCS 307, per Lady Paton at [29–32].
[66] [2013] EWHC 2210 (TCC), per Akenhead J at [8–24].

intended to so. The court therefore found that PHD had not shown a realistic prospect that proceedings would be instituted. It also found that the classes of documents sought were 'impossibly wide'. Furthermore, the court said that it should not normally interfere with the parties' contractual relationship where the contract does not give either party a right to see the other's documents.

10.6.9 Settlement offers

[10.103] Parties may make offers to each other to settle the dispute during the adjudication. This may be because a party has a clearer understanding of its potential liability under the dispute and it wishes to crystallise that liability without incurring additional expenses from its professional advisers and from the adjudicator and avoid the risk of a poor decision from the adjudicator. In litigation, settlement offers are known as Part 36 offers because the rules that dictate the terms on which the offer is made and the consequences of that offer being accepted or rejected are set out in Civil Procedure Rule 36.

[10.104] This rule does not apply in the context of adjudication proceedings although parties are of course free to make settlement offers as they wish. Offers are often made without prejudice save as to costs, which means that any details of the offer are not to be shared with the adjudicator except for the purpose of assessing costs. How and when the adjudicator considers without prejudice save as to costs offers is considered at Section 12.4.1.

10.6.10 Staying adjudication proceedings

[10.105] Subject to any contrary provision in the adjudication rules, the parties may agree to stay (or pause) adjudication proceedings at any time. Where this is done before the dispute is referred to the adjudicator, the agreement need only be between the parties themselves. Where it is done after that point, the adjudicator must also agree. There are many reasons why the parties may wish to stay proceedings, but it is commonly done where the parties wish to negotiate a settlement, or where there is a challenge to the adjudicator's jurisdiction that the parties wish to refer to the court or third party to resolve. Staying proceedings has the benefit that the parties can put aside the adjudication and focus on the purpose of the stay. It also has the benefit that the adjudicator will not continue to incur fees.

[10.106] Where the parties (and the adjudicator) agree a stay, the terms of the stay should be carefully prescribed. The terms might provide for things like the responsibility for costs incurred during the stay, the period of the stay or the precise circumstances in which the stay will be lifted. Sometimes a stay will continue for a month or even longer. In that case, the adjudicator will not know at the commencement of the stay whether he will have capacity to reengage in the adjudication once the stay is lifted. Therefore, he will usually impose a condition that the stay will only be lifted upon written confirmation that he is available to continue with the adjudication.

10.6.11 Confidential nature of adjudication (Scheme p. 18)

[10.107] Paragraph 18 of the Scheme provides:

> The adjudicator and any party to the dispute shall not disclose to any other person any information or document provided to him in connection with the adjudication which the party supplying it has indicated is to be treated as confidential, except to the extent that it is necessary for the purposes of, or in connection with, the adjudication.

[10.108] This paragraph does not automatically impose confidentiality on the adjudication information or documents. The party supplying information must indicate that it requires information to be treated as confidential before it will be treated as such.

[10.109] The paragraph also has the meaning that information disclosed may only be used in the adjudication, or in connection with the adjudication. 'In connection with' is probably wide enough to include enforcement proceedings. However, if either party wishes to advance the dispute beyond adjudication to a final determination, where this paragraph has been activated, it seems they are precluded from relying on any information disclosed in the adjudication in the arbitration or litigation on the basis that 'any other person' must include a judge or tribunal. That said, it cannot be taken to override the parties' general obligation of disclosure, as prescribed by the Civil Procedure Rules.

[10.110] If this paragraph is not activated, does it mean that the parties are free to disclose information provided to them to others? It depends on the terms of the contract between the parties. The vast majority of standard form construction contracts contain wide-ranging confidentiality clauses that prohibit the disclosure of information to other parties.

10.6.12 Service of documents and notices (Act s. 115)

[10.111] Often a construction contract will determine the methods by which written communications are to be made and when the communication is deemed to be received. Where there are no such provisions, then the terms of section 115 of the Act apply. They provide:

> (1) The parties are free to agree on the manner of service of any notice or other document required or authorised to be served in pursuance of the construction contract or for any of the purposes of this Part.
> (2) If or to the extent that there is no such agreement the following provisions apply.
> (3) A notice or other document may be served on a person by any effective means.
> (4) If a notice or other document is addressed, pre-paid and delivered by post—.
>   (a) to the addressee's last known principal residence or, if he is or has been carrying on a trade, profession or business, his last known principal business address, or.
>   (b) where the addressee is a body corporate, to the body's registered or principal office, it shall be treated as effectively served.
> (5) This section does not apply to the service of documents for the purposes of legal proceedings, for which provision is made by rules of court.

(6) References in this Part to a notice or other document include any form of communication in writing and references to service shall be construed accordingly.

[10.112] It is important that the parties comply with the terms of the contract, or else section 115, when serving submissions on one another. Cases where it has been argued that the defective service of a document as part of the adjudication process has rendered the adjudicator's decision invalid are considered in at Sections 16.6.4 and 16.6.6.

10.6.13 Reckoning of time (Act s. 116)

[10.113] Section 116 provides:

(1) For the purposes of this Part periods of time shall be reckoned as follows.
(2) Where an act is required to be done within a specified period after or from a specified date, the period begins immediately after that date.
(3) Where the period would include Christmas Day, Good Friday or a day which under the Banking and Financial Dealings Act 1971 is a bank holiday in England and Wales or, as the case may be, in Scotland, that day shall be excluded.

[10.114] The effect of this provision is that the time period between (a) the notice of adjudication and both the appointment of the adjudicator and the referral notice of the dispute to him;[67] and (b) the receipt of the referral notice and the deadline for the decision (whether extended or not)[68] shall be determined in accordance with this section of the Act. The calculation of any other time period will be determined by reference to the adjudication rules or by the contract, or by the adjudicator.

10.7 Adjudicator's powers and duties

10.7.1 In a nutshell

[10.115] Where the Act applies to the contract, the powers and duties of the adjudicator will include as a minimum those set out at section 108(2) of the Act. Where the Scheme applies, those powers and duties are supplemented by paragraphs 12 to 17. If the adjudicator exceeds the limits of these powers and duties, either party can successfully challenge the validity of a decision on the basis that the adjudicator exceeded jurisdiction or breached the rules of natural justice.

10.7.2 Duty to act impartially (Act s. 108(2)(e) and Scheme p. 12(a))

[10.116] Subsection 108(2)(e) of the Act provides

The contract shall impose a duty on the adjudicator to act impartially.

---
[67] Subsection 108(2)(b).
[68] Subsection 108(2)(c).

[10.117] Where the Scheme applies, subparagraph 12(a) provides:

> The adjudicator shall act impartially in carrying out his duties and shall do so in accordance with any relevant terms of the contract and shall reach his decision in accordance with the applicable law in relation to the contract.

[10.118] The provisions of the Act and the Scheme are the gateway to one of the fundamental requirements imposed on the adjudicator, which is to act impartially, or in an unbiased way. Bias falls into two categories, actual bias and apparent bias. There are very few reported cases of actual partiality or bias, although there are a number relating to apparent bias.[69] The requirement to act impartially is probably wider than bias and extends to the obligation to observe the rules of natural justice, which also encompasses procedural fairness.[70] The concepts of bias and procedural fairness as they apply to adjudication are examined in detail in Chapter 17. Cases dealing specifically with subparagraph 12(a) of the Scheme are listed at Appendix 8.

[10.119] In addition to the requirement for impartiality, subparagraph 12(a) of the Scheme also requires the adjudicator to decide the case in accordance with the applicable law. That has been held to mean that he should decide it in accordance with the proper law of the contract and not on some other basis such as his own idea of an equitable solution. His decision will be enforced if it is made in accordance with the applicable law but that law is applied erroneously.[71]

10.7.3 Power to take the initiative (Act s. 108(2)(f) and Scheme p. 13)

[10.120] Subsection 108(2)(f) of the Act provides:

> The contract shall enable the adjudicator to take the initiative in ascertaining the facts and the law.

[10.121] Where the Scheme applies, paragraph 13 provides:

> The adjudicator may take the initiative in ascertaining the facts and the law necessary to determine the dispute, and shall decide on the procedure to be followed in the adjudication. In particular he may—
>
> (a) request any party to the contract to supply him with such documents as he may reasonably require including, if he so directs, any written statement from any party to the contract supporting or supplementing the referral notice and any other documents given under paragraph 7(2),
>
> (b) decide the language or languages to be used in the adjudication and whether a translation of any document is to be provided and if so by whom,

---

[69] *Sprunt Ltd v London Borough of Camden* [2011] EWHC 3191 (TCC), per Akenhead J at [47]. See Section 17.4.
[70] *RSL (South West) Ltd v Stansell Ltd* [2003] EWHC 1390 (TCC), per Seymour J at [31]. See Section 17.5.
[71] *Diamond (Gillies Ramsay) v PJW Enterprises Judicial* [2003] ScotCS 354, per Lord Clarke at [39].

(c) meet and question any of the parties to the contract and their representatives,
(d) subject to obtaining any necessary consent from a third party or parties, make such site visits and inspections as he considers appropriate, whether accompanied by the parties or not,
(e) subject to obtaining any necessary consent from a third party or parties, carry out any tests or experiments,
(f) obtain and consider such representations and submissions as he requires, and, provided he has notified the parties of his intention, appoint experts, assessors or legal advisers,
(g) give directions as to the timetable for the adjudication, any deadlines, or limits as to the length of written documents or oral representations to be complied with, and
(h) issue other directions relating to the conduct of the adjudication.

[10.122] The Act provides the adjudicator with the power to take the initiative in ascertaining both the law and the facts, but it does not expand on the scope of that initiative. Paragraph 13 of the Scheme embellishes the scope of that basic power, providing a non-exhaustive list of actions the adjudicator may take. The adjudicator is entitled to be proactive and adopt an inquisitorial role, seeking evidence and other material which he considers appropriate to enable him to properly understand the dispute, or indeed limit the volume of submissions or evidence that the parties are permitted to submit. The adjudicator's powers may in some circumstances override the adjudication rules agreed by the parties. For example, the parties may agree to limit the length of the referral notice and supporting documents to 20 pages, but if the adjudicator decides pursuant to paragraph 13(a) that he wishes to see more documents, he will be entitled to receive them.[72]

[10.123] The actively inquisitorial role of an adjudicator is different from the role of a judge, whose role is passive in that he decides the dispute on the basis of the facts presented. This means that the adjudicator may make site visits and obtain legal or expert advice or interview relevant personnel, but only in the presence of both parties and/or their representatives. The adjudicator may conduct meetings, or hold telephone conferences at his convenience.[73] That said, an adjudicator will rarely, if ever, conduct a grass roots investigation of the case before him; there is unlikely to be time to do little more than probe the evidence put before him. He must also exercise care when he conducts his investigations to ensure that his decision-making process is based on the materials and arguments put before him, or if not, that any new materials and arguments generated by the adjudicator or a third party are placed before both parties, and that both parties have sufficient time to make submissions on the new information. Sections 17.5.12 to 17.5.15 debate this further.

[10.124] Subparagraph 13(g) of the Scheme allows the adjudicator to set a timetable for the adjudication, although he is only entitled to do this once the dispute has been referred to him.[74] As outlined in Section 10.2.5, he should devise a plan for how the adjudication

---

[72] *London & Amsterdam Properties Ltd v Waterman Partnership Ltd* [2003] EWHC 3059 (TCC), per Wilcox J at [96–116].
[73] *Discain Project Services Ltd v Opecprime Development Ltd (No. 2)* [2001] BLR 285, per Bowsher J at [22–23].
[74] The adjudicator is not empowered until that point. See Section 9.6.14.

should be conducted. He may wish to engage the parties in this process before finalising the timetable, in order to flush out any issues or objections early on.

[10.125] While the adjudicator's investigatory powers are wide, he must always act within the boundaries of his jurisdiction and the rules of natural justice.[75] Where he strays outside these restrictions, he (or rather his decision) will not be absolved by relying on subsection 108(2)(f) of the Act or paragraph 13 of the Scheme. The various circumstances in which action or inaction pursuant to his inquisitorial powers may lead to him straying outside the boundaries of his jurisdiction or being in breach of the rules of natural justice are examined in Chapters 16 and 17. Cases dealing specifically with paragraph 12(a), subsection 108(2)(f) and paragraph 13 are listed in Appendix 8.

10.7.4 Power to make requests or directions (Scheme p. 14 and 15)

[10.126] Where the Scheme, applies paragraphs 14 and 15 provide:

> 14. The parties shall comply with any request or direction of the adjudicator in relation to the adjudication.
> 15. If, without showing sufficient cause, a party fails to comply with any request, direction or timetable of the adjudicator made in accordance with his powers, fails to produce any document or written statement requested by the adjudicator, or in any other way fails to comply with a requirement under these provisions relating to the adjudication, the adjudicator may-
>   (a) continue the adjudication in the absence of that party or of the document or written statement requested,
>   (b) draw such inferences from that failure to comply as circumstances may, in the adjudicator's opinion, be justified, and
>   (c) make a decision on the basis of the information before him attaching such weight as he thinks fit to any evidence submitted to him outside any period he may have requested or directed.

[10.127] Thus, the parties are required to comply with the adjudicator's requests made or directions given during the adjudication. The consequence of failing to do this is, as a minimum, the drawing of adverse inference by the adjudicator against the incompliant party, although it is good practice for the adjudicator to warn the party that such inference might be drawn.[76]

[10.128] However, if the adjudicator has directed that a submission should be served by a particular date or that a submission should not be served at all, non-compliance by the party against whom the direction is made may entitle the adjudicator to disregard the submission. However, this must be balanced against the terms of paragraph 17 of the Scheme

---

[75] *McAlpine PPS Pipeline Systems Joint Venture v Transco plc* [2004] EWHC 2030 (QB), per Toulmin J at [141–148].
[76] *Balfour Beatty Engineering Services (HY) Ltd v Shepherd Construction Ltd* [2009] EWHC 2218 (TCC), per Akenhead J at [72].

which provide a mandatory requirement that the adjudicator shall consider any relevant information submitted to him by any of the parties.[77] The adjudicator should ensure that he is on firm ground before he makes the decision to disregard submissions or witnesses.

[10.129] The adjudicator's powers under paragraph 15 do not extend to curing fatal jurisdictional errors or natural justice breaches. For example, if the referring party fails to serve the referral notice within the required time limit, the adjudication at that point will probably be doomed[78] and the adjudicator cannot (or should not) continue with the adjudication. The safe approach for an adjudicator who receives a submission or information late is to either seek more time to deal with it and where the relevant party fails to accede the request, explain to the parties that there is insufficient time to consider the submission properly or at all and resign. See Section 17.5.8 (failure to allow a further or final submission) for more detail on this point.

10.7.5 Power to seek assistance (Act s. 108(2)(f) and Scheme p. 13(f))

[10.130] Section 108(2)(f) of the Act provides:

> The contract shall [include provision in writing so as to][79] ... enable the adjudicator to take the initiative in ascertaining the facts and the law.

[10.131] The Scheme provides at subparagraph 13(f) that the adjudicator may:

> Obtain and consider such representations and submissions as he requires, and, provided he has notified the parties of his intention, appoint experts, assessors or legal advisers.

[10.132] Together, these provisions give the adjudicator a fairly wide-ranging remit to appoint others to assist him in his role. The adjudicator may appoint a delay analyst to analyse competing delay analyses submitted by the parties or he may instruct a barrister to provide an opinion on the interpretation of a clause in the contract. It probably also extends to the ability of the adjudicator to obtain the assistance of staff (where the adjudicator is part of an organisation) to help with carrying out his role. For instance, there may be administrative tasks that need to be done (photocopying, organising a meeting room) or there may be some legal research that the adjudicator wishes to have done. In both cases this is perfectly acceptable and may well benefit the parties because certain tasks may be performed quicker and/or cheaper than if the adjudicator undertook them himself. However, the adjudicator should always ensure that:

- the parties are informed beforehand and are given an opportunity to object. Although the adjudicator is not required to obtain consent from the parties before he employs assistance, it is prudent for the adjudicator to outline any course of action before undertaking it;

---

[77] See Section 10.7.6.
[78] Although there may be some leeway in the timing. See Section 10.2.2.
[79] Inserted by the LDEDC.

- the reason for the assistance is clearly explained;
- any information obtained is shared with the parties and that time is allowed for them to consider and make submissions on it. It may be appropriate to allow for a meeting at which the adjudicator and the third party can meet with the parties to review and debate whatever has been produced;
- he always retains the task of evaluating both parties' case and deciding the dispute.

[10.133] Where any of these things are not done, the adjudicator runs a real risk of breaching natural justice (see Section 17.5.13). As a matter of good practice, adjudicators should always carefully consider whether the third-party assistance materially benefits the parties. Neither party will thank the adjudicator if he incurs significant additional costs on third-party assistance and indeed, the adjudicator will be more at risk of having his fees challenged on the grounds that they are unreasonable.[80]

10.7.6 Duty to consider relevant information and provide it to the parties (Scheme p. 17)

[10.134] Where the Scheme applies, paragraph 17 provides:

> The adjudicator shall consider any relevant information submitted to him by any of the parties to the dispute and shall make available to them any information to be taken into account in reaching his decision.

[10.135] The Scheme requires the adjudicator to consider any relevant information submitted by the parties to the dispute.[81] The corollary is that if the adjudicator decides that material is irrelevant, even if that conclusion has been reached by an erroneous analysis of the facts or the law such that if he had carried out the correct analysis he would have realised the material was relevant, that action will not undermine the adjudicator's jurisdiction (only in so far as he will not have breached paragraph 17 of the Scheme), although he may breach the rules of natural justice by failing to consider submissions or materials put forward.[82] Whether or not it is a breach will depend on whether the failure is material.[83]

[10.136] Paragraph 17 also provides that the adjudicator should make available to the parties any information not provided by the parties that the adjudicator will take into account when reaching the decision. The parties should also be allowed time to make submissions on that information. Where the adjudicator fails to comply with the terms of this paragraph, he is likely to be in breach of the rules of natural justice and, by not complying with paragraph 17 of the Scheme, will have acted outside the boundaries of his jurisdiction.

[10.137] Sections 16.6.7 (new material during the adjudication), 17.5.7 (failing to address all or part of a submission or supporting evidence), 17.5.12 (failure to inform a party about

---

[80] See Section 12.2.5.
[81] Paragraph 17.
[82] See Section 17.5.7.
[83] *Carillion Construction Ltd v Devonport Royal Dockyard Ltd* [2005] EWHC 778 (TCC), per Jackson J at [81–82].

an approach taken or methodology used), 17.5.8 (failure to permit a further submission or information), 17.5.13 (failure to inform the parties about advice from a third party) and 17.5.14 (use of own knowledge and expertise) all discuss scenarios where the failure to comply with the requirements captured by paragraph 17 can lead to a breach of jurisdiction or natural justice.

10.7.7 Scope of what the adjudicator can decide (Scheme p. 20(a) and (b))

[10.138] Where the Scheme applies, subparagraphs 20(a) and (b) provide:

> The adjudicator shall decide the matters in dispute. He may take into account any other matters which the parties to the dispute agree should be within the scope of the adjudication or which are matters under the contract which he considers are necessarily connected with the dispute. In particular, he may—
>
> (a) open up, revise and review any decision taken or any certificate given by any person referred to in the contract unless the contract states that the decision or certificate is final and conclusive,
>
> (b) decide that any of the parties to the dispute is liable to make a payment under the contract (whether in sterling or some other currency) and, subject to section 111(4) of the Act, when that payment is due and the final date for payment,

[10.139] The adjudicator must decide the matters in dispute. In order to do that, he must determine the scope of the dispute. The notice of adjudication, the documents referred to in the notice of adjudication, defences raised by the responding party and new issues introduced, expressly or implicitly, during the adjudication define this. However, paragraph 20 of the Scheme provides the adjudicator with a way of dealing with matters that are not within the scope of the submission documents. He may also take into account any matter arising under the contract which he considers is necessarily connected with the dispute.[84] The Scheme does not say that he **must** take into account matters connected with the dispute, merely that he **may** do this. However, it may be that the matters that are necessarily connected with the dispute referred to the adjudicator are necessary for him to determine, so that he can decide the original dispute referred to him.[85]

[10.140] Subparagraph 20(a) also provides that the adjudicator may decide that any decision taken or any certificate given by any person referred to in the contract may be opened up, revised and reviewed by the adjudicator. Thus, the adjudicator can correct errors in interim certificates, final certificates, extensions of time and so on. On one reading of this subparagraph, the adjudicator only has jurisdiction under this subparagraph where a certificate has been issued – he cannot issue one himself. However, the court has held that an adjudicator can consider whether or not a certificate should have been issued and,

---

[84] *Mecright Ltd v TA Morris Developments Ltd*, Unreported, 21 June 2001, per Seymour J at [23–25].
[85] *Northern Developments (Cumbria) Ltd v J & J Nichol*, Unreported, 24 January 2000, per Bowsher J at [35–36].

if a missing certificate was due, he can determine the sum that would have been payable had the certificate been issued properly.[86]

[10.141] The power in the first half of subparagraph 20(a) is limited by the second half of subparagraph 20(a), because the adjudicator may not open up, revise and review if the contract states that the decision or certificate is final and conclusive. In other words, if the construction contract provides that particular decisions or certificates are to be final and conclusive (for example, an engineer's certificate as to the amount of payment due, or a main contractor's decision on the exercise of a right of set-off) then those certificates or decisions cannot be altered by the adjudicator, and are effectively non-adjudicable. This might seem contrary to one of the purposes of the Act because the parties have in effect contracted to remove the right to adjudicate by agreeing that there can be no dispute about such decision or certificate. Section 7.7.3 discusses this point further.

[10.142] Paragraph 20 does not create or modify a right or liability under the contract except in one respect. Subparagraphs 20(b) and 21 provide that the adjudicator may determine the time for compliance with his decision. This may alter the time within which a payment might otherwise have had to be made under the contract. The reason the adjudicator is permitted to do this is that the Scheme is an implied term of the contract and as part of the contractual scheme it can modify the ordinary contractual relationship.[87] The purpose of this rule is to thwart reliance on a contractual clause that entitles the paying party to avoid paying for an extended period of time.

[10.143] Paragraph 20 of the Scheme ties in with the question of what the dispute is and also whether the decision given by the adjudicator relates to that dispute. These issues are considered in Sections 7.2 and 16.7.2 respectively.

10.7.8 Power to award interest (Scheme p. 20(c))

[10.144] The adjudicator has no freestanding power to award interest under the Act. However, the Scheme gives the adjudicator the power to award interest at subparagraph 20(c). This states:

> The adjudicator shall decide the matters in dispute. He may take into account any other matters which the parties to the dispute agree should be within the scope of the adjudication or which are matters under the contract which he considers are necessarily connected with the dispute. In particular, he may—
>
> ...

---

[86] *Vaultrise Ltd v Paul Cook* [2004] Adj.C.S. 04/06 at [7].
[87] *David McLean Housing Contractors Limited v Swansea Housing Association Limited* [2002] BLR 125, per Lloyd J at [16].

(c) having regard to any term of the contract relating to the payment of interest decide the circumstances in which, and the rates at which, and the periods for which simple or compound rates of interest shall be paid.

[10.145] The courts have interpreted subparagraph 20(c) to mean that the adjudicator only has power to decide questions as to interest if (a) there is a right under the contract, or in law to do so and it is claimed; or (b) those are questions which the parties to the dispute have agreed should be within the scope of the adjudication; or (c) those are questions which the adjudicator considers to be 'necessarily connected' with the dispute.[88]

[10.146] If the referring party wishes interest to be one of the matters in dispute, then it should consider the following:

- Make interest one of the issues in dispute. Before the adjudication commences, refer to it in correspondence.
- Make interest one of the issues that the adjudicator has to decide. This can be done in the notice of adjudication and the referral notice.
- Check the contract terms. If the contract provides a right to award interest on the disputed sum, then the adjudicator has jurisdiction to do so.
- If there is no contractual right to interest, check whether the debt is a qualifying debt within the meaning of the Late Payment of Commercial Debts (Interest) Act 1998. If it is, then the adjudicator will have jurisdiction to decide on interest.
- Where the contract does include a rate for interest and/or it falls within the scope of the Late Payments of Commercial Debts (Interest) Act 1998, check whether the rate of interest in the contract is a 'substantial remedy' within the meaning of the act. If it is not, it may be possible to increase it.
- Set out the rate at which it should be calculated and calculate the amount owed so that the adjudicator can see it.

10.7.9 Power to award damages

[10.147] Adjudicators will normally have the power to award damages. The reason is that the statutory references to adjudication of 'a dispute under the contract' (section 108(1)) and of 'any dispute under the contract' (Scheme, paragraph 1) must comprehend a dispute that arises from a breach of contract. Thus, if a breach is proved, the adjudicator must have the power to award damages, otherwise the Scheme would be unworkable.[89]

10.7.10 Adjudicator's immunity (Act s. 108(4), Scheme p. 26)

[10.148] Section 108(4) provides:

---

[88] *Carillion Construction Ltd v Devonport Royal Dockyard Ltd* [2005] EWCA Civ 1358 per Chadwick LJ at [89–94]. Confirmed in *Partners Projects Ltd v Corinthian Nominees Ltd* [2011] EWHC 2989, per Edwards-Stuart J at [33–34].
[89] *Gillies Ramsay Diamond v PJW Enterprises Ltd* [2003] ScotCS 354, per Clerk LJ at [17–21].

The contract shall also provide that the adjudicator is not liable for anything done or omitted in the discharge or purported discharge of his functions as adjudicator unless the act or omission is in bad faith, and that any employee or agent of the adjudicator is similarly protected from liability.

[10.149] Where the Scheme applies, paragraph 26 provides:

> The adjudicator shall not be liable for anything done or omitted in the discharge or purported discharge of his functions as adjudicator unless the act or omission is in bad faith, and any employee or agent of the adjudicator shall be similarly protected from liability.

[10.150] This immunity has no effect on third parties and so if an adjudicator's decision directs that a building is safe to inhabit, it is inhabited and then the building falls down, the adjudicator may be liable to the third parties for any personal injury or physical damage. Such a risk should be covered by insurance, and the adjudicator should seek an indemnity for third-party liability from the referring party. The adjudicator's immunity will also not extend to an entitlement to recover his fees where he issues a decision which is later found to be invalid because the adjudicator breached the rules of natural justice. This point and the cases associated with it are dealt with at Section 12.2.

10.7.11 Adjudicator resignation (Scheme p. 9)

(A) 2011 Scheme

[10.151] Where the 2011 Scheme applies, paragraph 9 provides:

> (1) An adjudicator may resign at any time on giving notice in writing to the parties to the dispute.
> (2) An adjudicator must resign where the dispute is the same or substantially the same as one which has previously been referred to adjudication, and a decision has been taken in that adjudication.
> (3) Where an adjudicator ceases to act under paragraph 9(1)-
>   (a) the referring party may serve a fresh notice under paragraph 1 and shall request an adjudicator to act in accordance with paragraphs 2 to 7; and
>   (b) if requested by the new adjudicator and insofar as it is reasonably practicable, the parties shall supply him with copies of all documents which they had made available to the previous adjudicator.
> (4) Where an adjudicator resigns in the circumstances referred to in paragraph (2), or where a dispute varies significantly from the dispute referred to him in the referral notice and for that reason he is not competent to decide it, the adjudicator shall be entitled to the payment of such reasonable amount as he may determine by way of fees and expenses reasonably incurred by him. Subject to any contractual provision pursuant to section 108A(2) of the Act, the adjudicator may determine how the payment is to be apportioned and the parties are jointly and severally liable for any sum which remains outstanding following the making of any such determination.

The adjudication

[10.152] Under the 2011 Scheme, the adjudicator may resign at any time by giving the parties written notice (subparagraph 9(1)). Thus, the adjudicator may resign if he becomes unavailable or ill. The adjudicator should resign if, during the adjudication, it becomes apparent that the dispute will be incapable of being decided fairly within the statutory (or extended) timetable. That is also the appropriate course of action where a material conflict of interest becomes apparent. Resignation is also appropriate where there is a jurisdictional challenge which the adjudicator accepts is valid.

[10.153] The adjudicator must also resign if it transpires that the dispute is the same or substantially the same as one that has previously been referred to and decided by adjudication (subparagraph 9(2)). It follows that the parties are not entitled to refer a dispute that is the same or substantially the same as one already decided. This issue and the relevant case law is examined in more detail at Section 7.4.

[10.154] If the adjudicator resigns or fails to reach a decision, and the referring party starts a new adjudication with a different adjudicator, subparagraph 9(3)(b) stipulates that the new adjudicator may request copies of all the documents that were made available to the previous adjudicator. The parties should comply with this request as far as it is possible to do so.[90]

[10.155] The circumstances provided in the first sentence of subparagraph 9(4) in which the adjudicator is entitled to his fees if he resigns are limited to two scenarios. The first is where the dispute is the same or substantially the same as a previously decided dispute. The second is where the dispute evolves from that referred to the adjudicator in the referral to the extent that he is no longer competent to decide it. Where these two scenarios do not occur, the adjudicator is not entitled to any remuneration.[91] This provision is therefore of considerable import to the adjudicator and, in practice, is likely to influence his decision as to whether or not he should continue in the face of a challenge to his jurisdiction or the exercise of natural justice.

[10.156] The second sentence of subparagraph 9(4) is consistent with the amendment made to subparagraph 11(1) and paragraph 25 of the 2011 Scheme and concerns the ability of the adjudicator to apportion his fees. Section 12.3.2 discusses the amendment further.

(B) The 1998 Scheme

[10.157] Paragraph 9 of the 1998 Scheme is the same as the 2011 Scheme, save for the following deletion to subparagraph (4):

> Where an adjudicator resigns in the circumstances referred to in paragraph (2), or where a dispute varies significantly from the dispute referred to him in the referral notice and for that reason he is not competent to decide it, the adjudicator shall be entitled

---

[90] See also paragraph 19(2)(b) of the Scheme.
[91] This is subject to the terms of the adjudicator's agreement, which may provide an entitlement for interim payment, or payment if he resigns come what may. See Section 9.6.15.

to the payment of such reasonable amount as he may determine by way of fees and expenses reasonably incurred by him. ~~Subject to any contractual provision pursuant to section 108A(2) of the Act, the adjudicator may determine how the payment is to be apportioned and the parties are jointly and severally liable for any sum which remains outstanding following the making of any such determination.~~

10.8 Checklist: Managing the adjudication – the adjudicator

> The adjudicator's task of conducting an adjudication efficiently, effectively, fairly and in accordance with the adjudication rules is not always an easy task. Consider the following guidelines.
>
> (1) Always have the Act (if it applies to the contract) and the relevant adjudication rules by your side. Continually refer to these documents to try to ensure that you are acting within the rules (Section 10.7).
> (2) Review the notice of adjudication to satisfy yourself that you know what the scope of the dispute is. As the adjudication progresses and submissions are served, cross check the content of those submissions with the scope of the dispute. If in your view part or all of a submission strays outside the scope of the dispute, consider raising your view with the parties.
> (3) Continually assess whether the existing timetable provides sufficient time to decide the dispute. If not, write to the parties asking for more time, giving reasons why you need it. Once the dispute is referred, you will have sight of the referral notice as well as the notice of adjudication and will be able to reassess the type of the dispute, its complexity and size and decide whether you can resolve the dispute within the allotted time in a manner that does broad justice to the parties. This assessment should be made as quickly as possible after each submission is made.
> (4) Communicate a timetable early in the process. Request or make decisions on changes to the timetable clearly. Either before or very soon after the referral notice is served, you should communicate a set of directions to the parties, which will include the timetable upon which the adjudication will proceed. This will typically include a deadline (both a date and time) for the response and reply. Where a party requests permission to serve an additional submission, or requests further time to serve a submission, it is good practice to request short submissions from either party, setting a deadline (of usually no more than a day each) before making the decision. If a party serves a submission you have not authorised, provided the timetable you have given clearly prohibits that submission, you are entitled to refuse to consider it (Section 17.5.8).
> (5) Communicate the need for a hearing or site visit as early as possible, providing the detail of exactly what you want to cover as soon as possible. The more structure that can be provided, the better. For instance, an agenda is helpful, a list of questions to be answered, witnesses that you would like to question or particular parts of the site you want to visit (Section 10.5).

(6) Read each submission carefully as soon as possible after it is received. It is not good practice to put everything to one side until the last few days. This will cause you to rush your analysis and you will probably have lost the opportunity to ask questions or request a hearing or a site visit.
(7) Avoid being dragged into the 'high drama' that can often accompany adjudications. Do not submit to pressure tactics from either party, communicate in a professional and fair-handed way (Section 10.6.1).
(8) Always communicate with all parties (Section 10.6.2).

Chapter 11
The decision

11.1 Overview

[11.01] The adjudicator's primary objective is to provide the parties with a decision on the dispute referred to him. In statutory adjudication, this must be done within 28 days of the date of receipt of the referral notice, unless the timetable for the adjudication is extended (Section 11.4). The structure, content and detail of an adjudicator's decision can vary enormously (Section 11.2). There are usually no hard and fast rules that the adjudicator is required to follow, with the exception that he must ensure that it is responsive to the dispute he has been asked to decide. Some but not all adjudication rules require that the adjudicator must give reasons for his decision when asked. This is sensible: when done properly, it forces the adjudicator into a methodical evaluation of the parties' arguments and it allows the parties to satisfy themselves that the decision arrived at is the right one (Section 11.3).

[11.02] The decision of an adjudicator binds the parties. Although there is often no fixed rule, the adjudicator will usually order that the terms of his decision are complied with in seven or fourteen days. In the majority of cases, the losing party will accept the decision of the adjudicator and do whatever is needed to comply with it. Accepting the decision does not necessarily spell the end for the losing party. It may advance the dispute to court proceedings or arbitration so that the disputed issues can be re-evaluated and a final determination obtained (Section 11.5). Where this is done, the adjudicator's decision becomes obsolete. However, this is comparatively rare. It is estimated that less than 10% of all disputes resolved by adjudication are finally determined by litigation or arbitration which, on one view at least, is testament to the success of the process.

11.2 What is the adjudicator required to do?

11.2.1 In a nutshell

[11.03] Unless the adjudicator resigns, he must decide the dispute referred to him. His decision must be communicated in writing. There is usually no requirement for the adjudicator's decision to be in a particular style or form, and as a result they vary enormously. That

A Practical Guide to Construction Adjudication, First Edition. James Pickavance.
© 2016 James Pickavance. Published 2016 by John Wiley & Sons, Inc.

said, all adjudicators would benefit from adhering to the '3Cs' mantra when writing a decision: clear, concise and cogent. If the adjudicator, having weighed the evidence and having applied the relevant law to the issues in hand, produces a 3Cs decision, the decision is much more likely to be right and more likely to be one that the parties are satisfied with, whether or not the dispute is decided in their favour. This section provides some suggestions on how one might go about producing a 3Cs decision. A model form adjudicator's decision is contained at Appendix 4 and can be downloaded in soft copy from the publisher's website.[1]

11.2.2 Purpose and nature of the decision

[11.04] An adjudicator is appointed to decide whether, in the circumstances of a dispute, a particular right or rights exist and should be enforced. Unless the parties specifically agree otherwise, an adjudicator is not appointed to adapt the terms of the contract or to vary, add to, or take away from the terms of the contract. Like a contract administrator, an adjudicator must apply the terms of the contract as they stand, but unlike a contract administrator, decisions of an adjudicator are more immediately enforceable.[2]

[11.05] Although the adjudicator makes a decision as a judge or arbitrator would, there is clearly a difference, as acknowledged by Chadwick LJ in *Carillion Construction Ltd v Devonport Royal Dockyard Ltd*[3]

> The task of the adjudicator is not to act as arbitrator or judge. The time constraints within which he is expected to operate are proof of that. The task of the adjudicator is to find an interim solution which meets the needs of the case.

[11.06] The scope of the distinction was developed in *Austin Hall v Buckland Securities*[4] where the court stated:

> Legal proceedings result in a judgment or order that in itself can be enforced. If the decision at the end of legal proceedings is that money should be paid, a judgment is drawn up that can be put in the hand of the Sheriff or Bailiff and enforced. That is not the case with an adjudicator. The language of the 1996 Act throughout is that the adjudicator makes a decision. He does not make a judgment. Nor does he make an "award" as an arbitrator does though he can order that his decision be complied with. Proceedings before an arbitrator are closer to court proceedings because an award of an arbitrator can in some circumstances be registered and enforced without a judgment of the court. But the decision of an adjudicator, like the decision of a certifier, is not enforceable of itself. Those decisions, like the decisions of a certifier, can be relied on as the basis for an application to the court for judgment, but they are not in themselves enforceable.

---

[1] http://onlinelibrary.wiley.com. Accessed 1 May 2015.
[2] *KNS Industrial Services (Birmingham) Ltd v Sindall Ltd (2000)* 75 ConLR 71, per Lloyd J at [28]. Although see Section 10.7.7.
[3] [2005] EWCA Civ 1358, per Chadwick LJ at [86].
[4] [2001] All ER (D) 137, per Buckland J at [14].

[11.07] There are circumstances in which an adjudicator may decline to make a decision. He may do this, for instance, where it is not possible for an adjudicator to reach a fair and impartial decision on a complex issue.[5] Similarly, where it would be extremely difficult for the adjudicator, or other party, to deal with the case within the time allowed, then 'an adjudicator, acting impartially and in accordance with the principles of natural justice, ought in such circumstances to inform the parties that a decision could not properly reasonably and fairly be arrived at within the time and invite the parties to agree further time. If the parties were not able to agree more time, then an adjudicator ought not to make a decision at all and should resign.'[6]

[11.08] Where the decision is marked 'draft for comment', without any limitations on the nature of the comments that may be provided, there is a real chance the court will consider that the adjudicator has not produced a binding decision. In contrast, a decision marked 'draft for comment' which clearly indicates that what is invited is suggested linguistic emendations or calculation errors, rather than alterations of substance, will constitute a binding decision.[7]

11.2.3 Structure, format and content of the decision

[11.09] Neither the Act nor the Scheme prescribe any requirements for the structure and format of the decision, merely that it must be responsive to the scope of the dispute. While each adjudicator will have his own style, it is worth ensuring the following.

- The decision should be signed and dated. That said, unless the adjudication rules require it (the Scheme does not), it is not necessary for an adjudicator's decision to be signed in order for it to be enforceable.[8] However, it is good practice to do so.
- The paragraphs of the decision should be numbered.
- References to documents should be cross-referenced to the bundles of documents provided.
- The decision should be divided into sections, with an index inserted at the front.
- The views of the adjudicator should be written in the first person.

[11.10] The content of adjudicators' decisions varies enormously. Some adjudicators take the view that only a very short decision is required, regardless of the size or complexity of the decision. It may be that the adjudicator does not have the time to provide a detailed and logical decision. But remember that the parties and their representatives will have worked incredibly hard to prepare and advance their case on the dispute, the outcome of which may have a profound effect on their businesses going forwards. While it is right that an adjudicator's decision is in theory only interim, in the vast majority of cases the

---

[5] *CIB Properties Ltd v Birse Construction Ltd* [2004] EWHC 2365 (TCC), per Toulmin J at [197].
[6] *Balfour Beatty Construction Ltd v The Mayor and Burgesses of the London Borough of Lambeth* [2002] EWHC 597 (TCC), per Lloyd J at [36].
[7] *Simons Construction Ltd v Aardvark Developments Ltd* [2003] EWHC 2474 (TCC), per Seymour J at [22–25]. See also Section 12.5.
[8] *Treasure & Son Ltd v Martin Dawes* [2007] EWHC 2420 (TCC), per Akenhead J at [45–48].

parties accept it as final, either because they are broadly satisfied with the outcome or because they simply cannot afford to advance to litigation or arbitration.

[11.11] For these reasons, and since the adjudicator will be reimbursed for the time he spends doing it, it is suggested that it is incumbent on adjudicators to spend time and effort providing a clear, concise, cogent decision that explains in a logical step-by-step fashion how he arrived at his answer. Not only will this allow the parties to understand how the adjudicator has dealt with their arguments, but it will also assist the adjudicator in his analysis. While the adjudicator may think he knows what the answer is in his head, rehearsing the relevant provisions of the contract, the facts and the parties' arguments in writing will always aid the adjudicator's consideration and will invariably lead to an improved, possibly different decision to the one he may have formulated in his mind.

[11.12] To that end, it is suggested that the following points should be addressed in the body of the decision, as a minimum:

- the names and addresses of the parties
- the form and type of adjudication
- the basis and terms on which the adjudicator has been appointed
- the background to the project and the dispute
- the scope of the dispute and the issues to be decided, with express reference to any new issues that have expanded the scope of the dispute as set out in the notice of adjudication
- the relief sought by the referring party
- the source and decision of any challenges to the adjudicator's jurisdiction or any allegations of breach of natural justice
- whether a meeting or hearing took place and if so, broadly what occurred
- the relevant contractual terms
- the parties' submissions
- the decision, which is responsive to the scope of the dispute and the relief sought
- reasons for the decision, whether or not they are requested or required
- the award of the adjudicator's and party costs (if party costs are a matter to be decided)
- a short summary of the decision and the award on costs.

[11.13] Often the clearest way to deal with the parties' submissions and the adjudicator's decision is to break the dispute into issues and set out the submissions and the decision on each issue under subheadings. This mirrors the clarity with which judges in the Technology and Construction Court now write decisions, and it makes the submissions and the decision much easier to reconcile.

11.2.4 Reasons

[11.14] The Act does not require the adjudicator to give reasons for the decision. Where the Scheme applies, paragraph 22 provides:

> If requested by one of the parties to the dispute, the adjudicator shall provide reasons for his decision.

[11.15] The Scheme only requires reasons to be given if one of the parties asks the adjudicator to do so. In practice, most adjudicators give reasons for their decision of their own volition. This is sensible: a reasoned decision, provided that there is not an obvious and fundamental error of fact or law, is more likely to be accepted by the parties as a final resolution of the dispute. Furthermore, where there are interested parties that were not party to the adjudication, a reasoned decision provides them with an understanding of how the adjudicator has decided the disputed issues. The question of whether the failure to provide reasons at all, or a paucity of reasoning amounts to the adjudicator stepping outside of the boundaries of his jurisdiction or breaching the rules of natural justice is examined in more detail at Sections 16.7.5 and 17.5.16 respectively.

11.3 On receiving the decision

[11.16] Upon receiving a decision, both parties should of course examine it to determine precisely what has been decided. The overriding point to remember is that it is the decision of the adjudicator that binds the parties, not his reasoning or findings. However, determining what the adjudicator's decision is may not be as straightforward as turning to the back page to read his conclusions. It may be necessary to pick through the decision to understand the full extent of the binding determinations the adjudicator has made.

[11.17] Many, if not most adjudications relate to money. To that end, the adjudicator's decision may comprise a declaration that a particular sum is due, together with related declarations in relation to the amount of interest and questions of costs. The decision of the adjudicator in that regard is reasonably clear. However, it becomes less clear when there are several points in the path to the decision. For example, if the adjudicator is asked for a decision on the amount of prolongation costs the referring party is entitled to, he must necessarily determine (if it has not already been determined) what extension of time the referring party is due before he can determine the amount of prolongation costs – one is inseparably connected to the other. In this case, both the decision on the extension of time and prolongation costs will form part of the decision and will bind the parties unless a final determination amends the decision (or unless the referring party argues in a subsequent adjudication that it is entitled to a further extension on different grounds). In other words, an adjudicator's decision will comprise (a) the award; and (b) any other findings in relation to the rights of the parties that form an essential component of or basis for that award.

[11.18] The separation between the award itself and the findings of the adjudicator was illustrated in *Hyder Consulting Ltd v Carillion Construction (UK) Ltd*.[9] The court held that the adjudicator acted within the rules of natural justice when he based his award on material submitted by the parties even though, using his knowledge and experience, he rejected both parties' submissions and made his own calculations. The award (which remained binding) was to be distinguished from the adjudicator's reasoning and 'findings' (which were not binding).

---

[9] [2011] EWHC 1810 (TCC), per Edwards-Stuart J at [35–38].

[11.19] Almost as important as the award itself is an assessment of whether that award, and the adjudicator's path to it, is legitimate. In other words, the decision should be examined to ensure that it is given within the boundaries of the jurisdiction afforded to the adjudicator and within the rules of natural justice. There are a number of complaints made (usually by the losing party), which may only become apparent upon reading the decision itself. The following examples are dealt with in more detail in the sections referred to.

- The decision contains matters outside of the scope the dispute (Section 16.7.2).
- The decision is not responsive to the relief sought by the referring party in the notice of adjudication (Section 16.7.6).
- There is a failure to address all or part of a submission or evidence in the decision (Section 17.5.7).
- There is a failure to inform the parties and allow them to comment upon a methodology used by the adjudicator or advice sought from a third party (Sections 17.5.12 and 17.5.13).

11.4 Timing

11.4.1 In a nutshell

[11.20] The Act, the Scheme and all standard form and industry body adjudication rules require that the adjudicator must reach his decision no more than 28 days after the date of receipt of the referral notice. This deadline may be extended to 42 days by the referring party, or longer by both parties. There is a distinction to be made between reaching the decision and communicating it to the parties. It is an absolute rule that the decision must be reached within the requisite deadline. However, the decision may be communicated past the deadline, provided it is communicated as soon as reasonably possible.

11.4.2 Act and Scheme (Act s. 108(2)(c) and (d) and Scheme p.19)

[11.21] Subsections 108(2)(c) and (d) of the Act provide:

> (2) The contract shall—
> (c) require the adjudicator to reach a decision within 28 days of referral or such longer period as is agreed by the parties after the dispute has been referred.
> (d) allow the adjudicator to extend the period of 28 days by up to 14 days, with the consent of the party by whom the dispute was referred.

[11.22] Where the 2011 Scheme applies, paragraph 19 provides:

> (1) The adjudicator shall reach his decision not later than-
> (a) twenty eight days after receipt of the referral notice mentioned in paragraph 7(1), or
> (b) forty two days after receipt of the referral notice if the referring party so consents, or

(c) such period exceeding twenty eight days after receipt of the referral notice as the parties to the dispute may, after the giving of that notice, agree.
(2) Where the adjudicator fails, for any reason, to reach his decision in accordance with paragraph (1)
   (a) any of the parties to the dispute may serve a fresh notice under paragraph 1 and shall request an adjudicator to act in accordance with paragraphs 2 to 7; and
   (b) if requested by the new adjudicator and insofar as it is reasonably practicable, the parties shall supply him with copies of all documents which they had made available to the previous adjudicator.
(3) As soon as possible after he has reached a decision, the adjudicator shall deliver a copy of that decision to each of the parties to the contract.

[11.23] Where the 1998 Scheme applies, subparagraph 19(1) is amended as follows:

(1) The adjudicator shall reach his decision not later than-
   (a) twenty eight days after the date of the referral notice mentioned in paragraph 7(1), or
   (b) forty two days after the date of the referral notice if the referring party so consents, or
   (c) such period exceeding twenty eight days after the referral notice as the parties to the dispute may, after the giving of that notice, agree.

[11.24] The difference between subparagraph 19(1) of the 1998 Scheme and the 2011 Scheme is that the 2011 Scheme refers expressly to time running from the date of receipt of the referral notice. However, this amendment is thought to be unnecessary, since the court had already determined that where the Act applies, the time period within which the adjudicator must reach his decision is 28 days from the date of receipt of the referral notice.[10]

[11.25] Therefore, it may be said that regardless of whether the 1996 Act, the 2009 Act, the 1998 Scheme or the 2011 Scheme applies, the rule is that the adjudicator is required to reach his decision no later than 28 days after the date of receipt of the referral notice. There are two exceptions to this. The first is where the referring party allows the adjudicator to extend the period from the service of the referral notice to the decision by up to 14 days.[11] The responding party has no entitlement to challenge the referring party's position at all, although it may well make submissions to the adjudicator in an attempt to persuade him of its view. The request for additional time may come from either party or from the adjudicator. The adjudicator will ask for extra time where he feels that he cannot reach a decision on the dispute within the usual time frame. The referring party does not have to grant the adjudicator's request, but usually it will consent because otherwise the adjudicator may conclude that he cannot decide the dispute within the time available and will resign, an action which is invariably not in the referring party's interests. The second exception is where both parties consent to give the adjudicator an extension of more than 14 days to decide the dispute. The extension can be any length of time and requires the agreement of both parties.[12]

---

[10] *Aveat Heating Ltd v Jerram Falkus Construction Ltd* [2007] EWHC 131 (TCC), per Havery J at [3].
[11] Subsection 108(2)(d) of the Act and paragraph 19(1)(b) of the Scheme.
[12] Subsection 108(2(c) of the Act and paragraph 19(1)(c) of the Scheme.

Again, this extension is usually given either where the adjudicator asks for more time to decide the dispute or where the parties require more time to prepare submissions, or both.

[11.26] Subsections 108(2)(c) and (d) may therefore be described as permissive subsections. Neither the parties nor the adjudicator (as appropriate) are bound to agree to an extension of time beyond the 28 days. Should either party not agree to a further extension of time after the dispute has been referred, the time limit for the adjudicator's decision is, therefore, 28 days or, if the referring party has unilaterally agreed an extension, up to 42 days from the date of receipt of the referral notice.[13]

[11.27] Research shows that less than half of all statutory adjudications are completed within 28 days. In around 40% of cases, the timetable is extended to 42 days and in around 15% of cases it is extended for a longer period.[14]

[11.28] Just because a party has agreed to an extension of time does not necessarily mean that it agrees to further extensions of time. It will depend in each case on the circumstances in which the initial extension of time is agreed. In some cases, a party may have expressly agreed to further extensions of time, or that may be inferred from its conduct. There will be other cases where no inference can be drawn, for example, where a defendant has made it clear that the initial extension of time is agreed without prejudice to any further extensions.[15]

[11.29] Subparagraph 19(2) of the Scheme concerns the situation where an adjudicator may not, for whatever reason, be able to produce his decision within the stipulated time limits. It enables either party to require the adjudication to start anew with a different adjudicator. Accordingly, where the adjudicator has not proceeded expeditiously to produce a decision, either party may effectively dismiss the adjudicator and substitute another. This is supported by subparagraph 11(2), which provides that if the adjudicator defaults, for example, by failing to decide the dispute on time, the parties can revoke the adjudicator's appointment, restart the adjudication and avoid paying the adjudicator's fees and expenses.

[11.30] The Civil Procedure Rules on the method and timing of service of submissions and communications do not apply to adjudication.[16] Sections 115 and 116 of the Act address the service of notices and the reckoning of time.[17]

---

[13] *CIB Properties Ltd v Birse Construction* [2004] EWHC 2365 (TCC), per Toulmin J at [25–26].
[14] Trushell, Milligan and Cattanach, *Research analysis of the progress of adjudication based on returned questionnaires from adjudicator nominating bodies (ANBs) and from a sample of adjudicators*. October 2012. http://www.gcu.ac.uk/ebe/businessservices/adjudicationreports. Accessed 1 September 2015. Data is taken from a survey conducted in 2012.
[15] *Ibid*.
[16] *Cubitt Building & Interiors Ltd v Fleetglade Ltd* [2006] EWHC 3413 (TCC), per Coulson J at [35].
[17] See Sections 10.6.12 and 10.6.13.

11.4.3 Rigidity of the time limit

[11.31] The adjudicator must adhere strictly to the deadline, be it 28 days or longer. Case law generally supports the view that if the decision is not reached within the requisite period, the result is catastrophic in that a decision issued subsequently will be deemed unenforceable and, probably, a nullity by the courts.[18] It is not sufficient, for example, to show that provided neither party suffered prejudice, a late decision can stand.[19] In light of this, it is good practice for the adjudicator to confirm with the parties (and if this is not done, for the parties to find out) exactly when the decision is due so that there are no misunderstandings.

[11.32] The argument has been made that the adjudicator's decision is not just due on the day of the deadline, it is due at the same time in the day when the referral notice was received. For example, if the dispute is referred at 09.00 and a decision is reached at 17.00, 28 days later, it is arguably out of time. However, the court has held that as a general rule, parts of a day are not to be taken into account in determining whether a decision has been delivered on time.[20] The position may be different if there are express words requiring the decision to be delivered by a particular time, either in the adjudication rules or in the directions given by the adjudicator.

11.4.4 Decision made and decision communicated

[11.33] The Scheme differentiates between the reaching of the decision (subparagraph 19(1) and (2)) and the delivery to the parties of a copy of that decision (subparagraph 19(3)).[21] It may occur that the adjudicator reached and wrote the decision by the 27th day, but failed to communicate it to the parties until the 29th day. In that case, the courts have held that an adjudicator's decision will be valid provided *the decision* is reached in time and delivered[22] as soon as possible thereafter. However, the leeway is small. In *Lee v Chartered Properties (Building) Ltd*,[23] Akenhead J held that the adjudicator's decision was unenforceable on the facts because the adjudicator had not delivered the decision within the time allowed. The adjudicator informed the parties that he had reached the decision in time (on Friday afternoon), but delayed sending the final written document until Monday afternoon. The court held that the adjudicator's decision must be delivered 'as soon as possible' after it was reached. Coulson J in *Cubitt Building & Interiors Ltd v*

---

[18] See for example *Cubitt Building & Interiors Limited v Fleetglade Ltd* [2006] EWHC 3413 (TCC), per Coulson J at [75–76]. It has been said that the decision of Jackson J in *M. Rohde Construction v Nicholas Markham-David* [2006] EWHC 814 (TCC) at [31] suggests that the deadline is not mandatory, but it is suggested that this is not the preferred view.
[19] *AC Yule & Son Ltd v Speedwell Roofing & Cladding Ltd* [2007] EWHC 1360 (TCC), per Coulson J at [30].
[20] *Aveat Heating Ltd v Jerram Falkus Construction Ltd* [2007] EWHC 131 (TCC), per Havery J at [13].
[21] *Barnes & Elliott Ltd v Taylor Woodrow Holdings Ltd* [2003] EWHC 3100 (TCC), per Lloyd J at [3–27].
[22] This has been held to mean delivered and received as opposed to just sent. See *Mott MacDonald Ltd v London & Regional Properties Ltd* [2007] EWHC 1055 (TCC), per Thornton J at [79–85].
[23] [2010] EWHC 1540 (TCC), per Akenhead J at [32].

Fleetglade Ltd[24] said that the time between the decision being reached and communicated should be 'a matter of hours.'

[11.34] When is a decision 'reached'? The case of *Mott MacDonald Ltd v London & Regional Properties Ltd*[25] suggests that a decision is reached when it has been drafted but not checked for typographical errors or other mistakes. This view is reinforced (though not in that judgment) by the fact that the adjudicator benefits from the application of the slip rule, which permits amendments to be made to the decision for a period after it is communicated that arise from mistakes or errors. In *Lee v Chartered Properties (Building) Ltd*,[26] the court said that if a decision was written in longhand, but had not been typed up, then if typing it up meant the decision would be given after the 28th day, it should be faxed or emailed to the parties in longhand form.

11.4.5 Responding to the adjudicator's request for an extension

[11.35] The adjudicator can normally assess the prospects of his being able to reach a decision within the 28 days once he has sight of the referral notice, or if not then, certainly after he receives the response. If he considers that he cannot meet the timetable, he should at once seek either the referring party's or both parties' consent to an extension, depending on the length of the extension he requires. Similarly, if any party is concerned that the adjudicator may not meet the deadline, it should raise its concern with the adjudicator in good time. When the adjudicator asks for more time, the parties should respond plainly and promptly to the request. If the relevant party or parties do not respond at all, there is a strong case for saying that it, or they, accepted by their silence.[27] In *KNN Coburn LLP v GD City Holdings Limited*,[28] the referral notice was sent to the adjudicator on 31 January 2013 and he produced his decision on 1st March 2013 which was longer than the 28 day period allowed, if only by a day. The court concluded that there was no application to extend time but that the responding party in the adjudication had acquiesced in the adjudicator's timeline that he had made clear at the outset of the adjudication. Thus, the decision was still valid.

11.5 *Effect and compliance*

11.5.1 In a nutshell

[11.36] The legitimate decision of an adjudicator will bind the parties in accordance with its terms, until such time as the decision is reversed or altered either by agreement between

---

[24] [2006] EWHC 3413 (TCC), per Coulson J at [26–28; 68–76; 82–92].
[25] [2007] EWHC 1055 (TCC), per Thornton J at [79–85].
[26] [2010] EWHC 1540 (TCC), per Akenhead J at [25–33].
[27] *AC Yule & Son Ltd v Speedwell Roofing & Cladding Ltd* [2007] EWHC 1360 (TCC), per Coulson J at [14–22].
[28] [2013] EWHC 2879 (TCC), per Stuart-Smith J at [28–35].

the parties or by a court judgment or arbitral award. Attempts to delay the effect of the decision are unlikely to be successful.

11.5.2 Temporary finality (Act s. 108(3), Scheme p. 23)

[11.37] Subsection 108(3) of the Act provides:

> The contract shall provide that the decision of the adjudicator is binding until the dispute is finally determined by legal proceedings, by arbitration (if the contract provides for arbitration or the parties otherwise agree to arbitration) or by agreement.

[11.38] Where the 2011 Scheme applies, paragraph 23 provides:

> The decision of the adjudicator shall be binding on the parties, and they shall comply with it until the dispute is finally determined by legal proceedings, by arbitration (if the contract provides for arbitration or the parties otherwise agree to arbitration) or by agreement between the parties.

[11.39] The 1998 Scheme contains an additional subparagraph 23(1):

> (1) In his decision, the adjudicator may, if he thinks fit, order any of the parties to comply peremptorily with his decision or any part of it.

[11.40] Subparagraph 23(1) of the 1998 Scheme is considered at Section 13.4.2. It has been relied on very rarely.

[11.41] Subsection 108(3), paragraph 23 of the 2011 Scheme and subparagraph 23(2) of the 1998 Scheme are concerned with the relationship between an adjudicator's decision and subsequent arbitration or litigation of the same dispute. While they do pave the way for enforcement of the adjudicator's decision, should that prove necessary, neither the Act nor the Scheme makes any provision for enforcement or requires the contract to contain terms making such provision in any particular form.

[11.42] The decision of an adjudicator is intended to provide a similar degree of compliance by the parties as a court or arbitration judgment might. However, the decision is not 'final' but is 'interim'.[29] The decision of an adjudicator may therefore be said to be of a temporarily binding nature. The temporary finality is an absolutely critical part of adjudication and enables the winning party to receive the benefit of the adjudicator's decision, often cash, as soon as possible, although clearly the decision only binds if it is valid.[30] The temporarily binding nature of the decision does not mean that the dispute has been finally resolved, unless the parties agree that it does. Thus, where the contract requires there to be a dispute before it can be referred to resolution by the chosen method set out in the contract, the fact that the dispute has been the subject of an adjudicator's decision

---

[29] *William Verry Ltd v The Mayor and Burgesses of the London Borough of Camden* [2006] EWHC 761 (TCC), per Ramsey J at [24].
[30] *Homer Burgess Ltd v Chirex (Annan) Ltd (No. 1)* (1999) 71 ConLR 245, per Lord MacFadyen at [32–35].

does not mean that there is no longer a dispute. The dispute remains in existence until it is resolved in a final determination or by agreement.[31]

[11.43] The temporary finality of an adjudicator's decision also applies to circumstances in which the parties pursue multiple adjudications. In that case, the terms of an adjudicator's valid decision in a previous adjudication will bind any adjudicator in subsequent adjudications. The issues contested in a previous adjudication may also preclude the parties from re-raising those issues in subsequent adjudications. However, the court will carefully examine the issues and material that the adjudicator was asked to consider before deciding that he had no jurisdiction to consider it.[32] Refer to Sections 11.3 and 16.5.7 for further discussion on this point.

[11.44] In the event the dispute is resolved by subsequent legal proceedings, arbitration or by agreement and it is determined or agreed that some or all of the sums awarded in the adjudication should not have been paid, those sums must be repaid. Although the Act and subparagraph 23(2) of the Scheme do not say this in such terms, that must be the intention of these provisions.[33]

[11.45] An adjudication decision creates a debt that may, for example, form the basis of a statutory demand. The status of the debt arising out of an adjudication judgment for the purposes insolvency proceedings falls to be treated in the same way as a judgment or order, and the court will not normally go behind it.[34]

11.5.3 Compliance with the decision (Scheme p. 21)

[11.46] Where the Scheme applies, paragraph 21 provides:

> In the absence of any directions by the adjudicator relating to the time for performance of his decision, the parties shall be required to comply with any decision of the adjudicator immediately on delivery of the decision to the parties in accordance with this paragraph.

[11.47] The parties are required to comply with the adjudicator's decision immediately upon it being delivered to them, unless the adjudicator directs otherwise. In practice, the adjudicator will normally direct that compliance with the decision shall be within seven or fourteen days or in accordance with a period for payment stated in the contract.

11.5.4 Delaying compliance by contract

[11.48] Some parties try to limit the effectiveness of an adjudicator's decision by inserting a clause into the contract that delays the consequences of the decision (such as the payment of

---

[31] *Trustees of the Harbours of Peterhead v Lilley Construction Ltd* [2004] ScotCS 91, per Lord Mackay at [15–21].
[32] *Quietfield Ltd v Vascroft Contractors Ltd* [2006] EWHC 174 (TCC), per Jackson J at [32–43].
[33] *Aspect Contracts (Asbestos) Ltd v Higgins Construction plc* [2013] EWCA Civ 1541, per Longmore LJ at [9].
[34] *George Parke v The Fenton Gretton Partnership* [2001] CILL 1713, per Boggis J at [14 and 29].

money) until some later date. For instance, they may contract that any sums awarded pursuant to an adjudicator's decision should be paid into a stakeholder account where the money will stay until the dispute is finally resolved by litigation, arbitration or by agreement. These sorts of provisions are unlikely to succeed on the grounds that they do not comply with paragraphs 20, 21 and 23 of the Scheme, or sections 108(1) and 108(3) of the Act. Certainly, such clauses are contrary to the policy of the Act.[35]

11.5.5 Insurance claims

[11.49] In circumstances where a company is insured and there is a resolution for the voluntary winding-up of that company, then where that company is liable to a third party and the terms of the insurance policy cover that liability, pursuant to section 1 of the Third Parties (Rights Against Insurers) Act 1930, the benefit of that insurance passes to the third party. However, it has been held that an adjudicator's decision will not create an established liability for the purpose of the 1930 Act.[36] The liability under the policy will not be established until the adjudication award is enforced by a court.

---

[35] *Pioneer Cladding v John Graham Construction Limited* [2013] EWHC 2954 (TCC), per Coulson J at [4–8].
[36] *Galliford (UK) Ltd v Markel Capital Ltd* [2003] EWHC 1216 (QB), per J Behrens QC at [44–47].

Chapter 12
Post decision

12.1 Overview

[12.01] This chapter is concerned with the rules on payment of the adjudicator and party costs of the adjudication, the circumstances in which it is permissible to amend the decision once it has been issued and the ability of the losing party to set off sums against the amount awarded by the adjudicator.

[12.02] Parties will invariably be jointly and severally liable for the adjudicator's fees even where the adjudicator resigns, or where the decision is not enforced. The only circumstances in which a party may not have to pay an adjudicator's fees are where it withdraws from an adjudication very early, having raised a valid jurisdictional challenge, or where it is insolvent or unless the adjudicator has acted in bad faith, has been fraudulent or has breached the rules of natural justice.

[12.03] Where the 1996 Act applies, the parties' costs are borne by themselves unless some other agreement is reached after the notice of adjudication has been served. The position is probably the same where the 2009 Act applies, although this is a matter of some debate.

[12.04] Both parties should check the decision meticulously to ensure that there are no typographical or clerical infelicities. If there are, then the adjudicator can correct these and issue a revised decision. There is no time limit imposed in the Act and the 1998 Scheme, although the courts have determined that it must be done in a short period of time. Where the 2011 Scheme applies, the time limit is five days.

[12.05] Although the general rule is that adjudication decisions should stand alone, parties may set off an adjudication decision against another payment provided that other payment is a natural consequence of the decision and the other payment has been the subject of a withholding or pay less notice. The court may also set off one adjudication decision against another in limited circumstances or against a court decision or tribunal award.

A Practical Guide to Construction Adjudication, First Edition. James Pickavance.
© 2016 James Pickavance. Published 2016 by John Wiley & Sons, Inc.

12.2 Adjudicator's costs

12.2.1 In a nutshell

[12.06] The adjudicator's costs will be shared equally between the parties, unless the adjudication rules provide otherwise. The Scheme provides that the adjudicator may apportion his costs as he sees fit. Where an apportionment has been made, the court is unlikely to adjust the apportionment, except where the decision is rendered unenforceable, in which case the apportionment will not apply and the parties will bear the costs equally. The adjudicator will still be entitled to his fees where his decision is wrong, not within jurisdiction or where he has had to resign because the dispute is the same as one previously decided, subsequent to him accepting that the appointment the dispute has evolved outside his area of competence or the parties revoke his appointment. In all other cases (including where his decision is nullified as a result of a breach of natural justice), he will not be entitled to his fees. The adjudicator's fees must be reasonable, but that rule is given a considerable margin of appreciation by the court in favour of the adjudicator.

12.2.2 2009 Act and 2011 Scheme (2009 Act s. 108A; 2011 Scheme p. 25)

[12.07] Section 108A of the 2009 Act provides:

> (1) This section applies in relation to any contractual provision made between the parties to a construction contract which concerns the allocation as between those parties of costs relating to the adjudication of a dispute arising under the construction contract.
> (2) The contractual provision referred to in subsection (1) is ineffective unless-
>   (a) it is made in writing, is contained in the construction contract and confers power on the adjudicator to allocate his fees and expenses as between the parties, or
>   (b) it is made in writing after the giving of notice of intention to refer the dispute

[12.08] Where the 2011 Scheme applies, paragraph 25 provides:

> The adjudicator shall be entitled to the payment of such reasonable amount as he may determine by way of fees and expenses reasonably incurred by him. Subject to any contractual provision pursuant to section 108A(2) of the Act, the adjudicator may determine how the payment is to be apportioned and the parties are jointly and severally liable for any sum which remains outstanding following the making of any such determination.

[12.09] In short, the 2009 Act provides that the parties may agree in their contract that the adjudicator has the power to allocate his fees and expenses. Where the 2011 Scheme applies, section 108A of the 2009 Act is reflected at paragraph 25.

12.2.3 1996 Act and 1998 Scheme (1998 Scheme p. 25)

[12.10] The 1996 Act is silent on the adjudicator's entitlement to payment of his fees and who pays them. Therefore, unless the adjudication rules allow for it or the parties agree, the adjudicator does not have jurisdiction to allocate his costs.[1] Where the 1998 Scheme applies, paragraph 25 provides:

> The adjudicator shall be entitled to the payment of such reasonable amount as he may determine by way of fees and expenses reasonably incurred by him. The parties shall be jointly and severally liable for any sum which remains outstanding following the making of any determination on how the payment shall be apportioned.

[12.11] The second sentence in the 1998 Scheme was replaced with the second sentence of the 2011 Scheme. This was in order to align the paragraph with section 108A of the 2009 Act.

[12.12] Thus, both the Scheme and the 2011 Scheme allow the adjudicator to determine how his costs are to be apportioned.

12.2.4 Liability for fees

[12.13] Liability for fees is normally expressed in two places. In the adjudication rules and in the adjudicator's terms of appointment.

[12.14] Whether an adjudicator is appointed via express or implied contractual provisions, absent any term to the contrary, the parties are jointly and severally liable for the adjudicator's fees and expenses.[2] The fact that the parties are so liable means that the adjudicator can sue either party for his fees, at his discretion. However, where the adjudicator has directed that one party is liable for his fees, that party refuses to pay and so the adjudicator sues the other party in order to recover his fees, that party must have a legal entitlement pursuant to the tripartite adjudicator's agreement, contractually, to recover what it has been required to pay the adjudicator from the non-paying party. Alternatively, at common law, where two parties owe a common liability to pay a sum and the party who is not primarily liable discharges that liability, that party has an entitlement to recover the amount it paid from the other party to avoid unjust enrichment. A further alternative may lie with the Civil Liability (Contribution) Act 1978 which provides that any person liable in respect of any damage suffered by another person may recover contribution from any other person liable in respect of the same damage,[3] although generally this avenue of recourse is only available for claims in negligence.

[12.15] In *Gary Kitt and EC Harris LLP v The Laundry Building Ltd and Etcetera Construction Services Ltd*,[4] the claimant relied on the joint and several liability rule to recover the adjudicator's fees from Laundry, notwithstanding that the adjudicator directed in the adjudication that Etcetera should pay his fees. Laundry joined Etcetera as a Part 20 defendant in the proceedings claiming that it was liable for whatever sum Laundry was required to pay. The court held that the adjudicator was entitled to his fees (there had

---

[1] *Aveat Heating Ltd v Jerram Falkus Construction Ltd* [2007] EWHC 131 (TCC), per Havery J at [25].
[2] *Linnett v Halliwells LLP* [2009] EWHC 319 (TCC), per Ramsey J at [37–38].
[3] Section 1(1).
[4] [2014] EHWC 4250 (TCC), per Akenhead J at [34].

been challenges to the validity of the adjudicator's decision which were dismissed), that Laundry was entitled to pay them but that Etcetera should reimburse Laundry accordingly.

[12.16] The joint and several liability arises even if one party does not sign the adjudicator's terms and conditions of appointment (which is often the case where the responding party raises a jurisdictional challenge), provided both parties participate in the adjudication. However, in those circumstances, one party may be bound to pay a fixed fee or fees calculated at a particular hourly rate which was expressly agreed, while the other party may only be bound to pay a reasonable fee as a matter of implication.[5] In practical terms this may not make any difference.

[12.17] Where the adjudication rules differ from the contract between the parties in that the adjudication rules permit him to allocate his fees as he sees fit and the contract provides that the adjudicator's fees should be apportioned equally, subject to any express wording on hierarchy in either document, the contract will take precedence.[6]

[12.18] Where, before the start of the adjudication, the responding party makes an assertion of lack of jurisdiction and withdraws, taking no further part in the adjudication proceedings and leaving the adjudicator and the other party to proceed at their risk, in the absence of any express or implied agreement with the adjudicator to do anything, it would be difficult to make the responding party liable for the fees and expenses of the adjudicator in the event that assertion is borne out. However, if the responding party reserves its position on jurisdiction and then proceeds with the adjudication, it will be liable for its share of the fees.[7]

[12.19] Under the Scheme, the adjudicator is entitled to be paid his fees and expenses even if:

- the adjudicator's decision is wrong;
- the adjudicator's decision is found to be invalid because it was not made within the boundaries of his jurisdiction;
- the adjudicator ceases to act where there are multiple disputes and one of the disputes is to be adjudicated by another adjudicator (subparagraph 8(4));
- the adjudicator resigns because the dispute is:
  ○ the same or substantially the same as a previous dispute where a decision has been given (subparagraph 9(2));
  ○ different from the dispute referred in the referral notice and he is not competent to decide it (subparagraph 9(4));
- the parties revoke the adjudicator's appointment (subparagraph 11(1)), unless the revocation is due to the adjudicator's default (such as a failure to reach a decision within 28 days) or misconduct (subparagraph 11(2)).

---

[5] *Fenice Investments Inc v Jerram Falkus Construction Ltd* [2011] EWHC 1678 (TCC), per Waksman J at [19].
[6] *Interserve Industrial Services Ltd v Cleveland Bridge UK Ltd* [2006] EWHC 741 (TCC), per Jackson J at [54–63].
[7] *Linnett v Halliwells LLP* [2009] EWHC 319 (TCC), per Ramsey J at [43–53].

[12.20] The adjudicator is not entitled to any remuneration if he resigns for any other reason.[8] This provision is therefore of considerable import to the adjudicator and, whether it should or not, in practice is likely to influence his decision as to whether or not he should continue in circumstances where there is not a clear cut case for him to resign.

[12.21] The parties are only liable for the adjudicator's expenses incurred by him during the course of the adjudication. Any expenses incurred after he has given his decision will not, prima facie, be recoverable, although if the adjudicator incurs costs correcting errors in his decision, those costs will probably be recoverable.[9]

12.2.5 Reasonableness of fees and expenses

[12.22] Where the Scheme applies, subparagraph 12(b) provides:

> The adjudicator shall avoid incurring unnecessary expense.

[12.23] Adjudicator's costs can be significant. If the adjudicator is a solicitor, barrister, architect or accountant, fees can be as much as £700 per hour. For anything other than the most menial of adjudications, the adjudicator is likely to spend at least 30 hours which, at a high charge out rate, means the adjudicator's bill will be considerable. Can the time the adjudicator records be subject to challenge? The Scheme and a number of other adjudication rules limit the recovery of fees and expenses to those that are reasonable. In *Fenice Investments Inc v Jerram Falkus Construction Ltd*,[10] the court considered what was meant by 'reasonable' in the context of adjudication. It said there should be a 'a considerable "margin of appreciation" given to the adjudicator', for the following reasons:

(1) The work has to be undertaken at considerable speed, and sometimes with moving targets in the sense of what the core issues underlying the adjudication are, or become; by analogy, where work is done by solicitors on an urgent basis, this is frequently advanced as a reason why the Court should award more than the guideline rate of costs;
(2) Routine satellite litigation about an adjudicator's costs could not have been intended by the framers of s108 or the Scheme and would be a discouragement to potential adjudicators to act in this important process.

[12.24] The court held that the reasonableness of hourly rates can vary considerably and may depend on the adjudicator's seniority and experience. Where the adjudicator sets out his hourly rate and a party does not complain about the rate at that time, any later complaint that the rate was excessive is unlikely to provoke much sympathy.

---

[8] Paragraph 9(4) of the Scheme. PC *Harrington Contractors Ltd v Systech International Ltd* [2012] EWCA Civ 1371, per Davis LJ at [26].
[9] *Barrie Green v GW Integrated Building Services Ltd & Anor*, Unreported, 18 July 2001, per Grannum J at [25].
[10] [2011] EWHC 1678 (TCC), per Waksman J at [32–38].

[12.25] The more common challenge relates to the time spent on a particular task or in relation to the adjudication as a whole. Again, the court will give the adjudicator leeway because of the tight timescales of the process and also where the Scheme applies, paragraph 20 expressly entitles him to take into account 'matters under the contract which he considers are necessarily connected with the dispute.'

[12.26] Notwithstanding this, where there is a question of the reasonableness of the adjudicator's fees, the burden of proof is on the adjudicator to demonstrate they are reasonable.

12.2.6 Lien on the decision

[12.27] The adjudicator is not entitled to exercise any lien on his decision, such as the payment of his fees. See Section 16.7.2 for more detail.

12.2.7 Payment of fees when the decision is in breach of natural justice

[12.28] The Court of Appeal in *PC Harrington Contractors Ltd v Systech International Ltd*[11] held that where an adjudicator produces a decision that is unenforceable due to a breach of the rules of natural justice, his fees should not be paid. The adjudicator's decision was unenforceable because he had failed to consider part of the subcontractor's defence. In refusing to enforce the first instance decision, the Court decided that the adjudicator's duty was to produce an enforceable decision and there was no entitlement to be paid if he did not do so, even in respect of services performed by him which were preparatory to making the decision.

[12.29] Following this decision, many adjudicators have sought to amend their terms of appointment so that they provide for payment in all circumstances (although this may itself pose problems under section 3 of the Unfair Contract Terms Act 1977) or, at the very least, interim payments.

12.2.8 Award of adjudicator's costs

[12.30] Where the adjudicator is empowered to apportion his fees between the parties, the court is highly unlikely to unpick that apportionment on the basis that would be 'an extremely difficult task for a tribunal that has not heard the same arguments as the adjudicator.'[12]

[12.31] Where the decision of an adjudicator is only enforceable in part, the court may sever the enforceable part from the unenforceable part, if it is possible to do so.[13] Where the court decides that severance is possible and where the adjudicator has power to apportion his

---

[11] [2012] EWCA Civ 1371, per Dyson LJ at [23–37; 42–46].
[12] *Castle Inns (Stirling) Ltd trading as Castle Leisure Group v Clark Contracts Ltd* [2005] CSOH 178, per Lord Drummond Young at [17].
[13] See Section 14.4.

fees, in the absence of a division of the adjudicator's overall fees to each issue in dispute by the adjudicator, again a court is likely to find it difficult to assess what amount of the adjudicator's fees belongs to the good part of a decision and what part belongs to the severed part. This is because one cannot second guess how the adjudicator might have apportioned his fees. For this reason, where the court orders that the decision is to be severed, it will enforce the good part of the decision, but will not enforce the bad part of the decision and the adjudicator's apportionment of his costs. With regard to the adjudicator's costs, the result is that the parties will share his costs equally.[14]

12.2.9 Payment of fees on paying party's insolvency

[12.32] If the losing party is insolvent, it may escape liability for payment of the adjudicator's fees notwithstanding the fact that the adjudicator has ordered it to pay all his fees. In this case, because the Scheme requires that payment of the adjudicator's fees is joint and several, the winning party will be required to pay them.

12.3 Parties' costs

12.3.1 In a nutshell

[12.33] The 2009 Act contains specific provisions governing the allocation of parties' costs in advance of the adjudication, which probably also serve to preclude any attempt to allocate the parties' costs in advance of the adjudication. However, where the date of the contract is after March 2013 and where the The Late Payment of Commercial Debt (Interest) Act 1998 applies, the referring party, if successful, will probably be able to recover all its costs from the losing party. While this rule conflicts with the provisions of the 2009 Act, it is likely to prevail.

[12.34] The 1996 Act does not contain provisions preventing pre-allocation of party costs. However, the courts have held that parties are nonetheless precluded from making any provision in their contract as to the allocation of the parties' costs of the adjudication. This can only be done once the adjudication has commenced.

12.3.2 2009 Act (s. 108A)

[12.35] Section 108A of the 2009 Act provides:

> (1) This section applies in relation to any contractual provision made between the parties to a construction contract which concerns the allocation as between those parties of costs relating to the adjudication of a dispute arising under the construction contract.
> (2) The contractual provision referred to in subsection (1) is ineffective unless-

---

[14] *Beck Interiors Ltd v UK Flooring Contractors Ltd* [2012] EWHC 1808 (TCC), per Akenhead J at [25].

(a) it is made in writing, is contained in the construction contract and confers power on the adjudicator to allocate his fees and expenses as between the parties, or

(b) it is made in writing after the giving of notice of intention to refer the dispute.

[12.36] This clause is intended to mirror the common law position in *Yuanda (UK) Co Ltd v WW Gear Construction Ltd*[15] (although the amendments were the subject of consultation before that decision). Thus, for contracts entered into on or after 1 October 2011, the parties are precluded from relying on any contractual provision that concerns the allocation as between the parties of costs relating to the adjudication of a dispute arising under the construction contract **unless** that agreement is made in writing after the service of the notice of adjudication.

[12.37] It has been argued that the wording of section 108A does the opposite of what was intended, which is to legitimise clauses that permit the allocation of party costs before the adjudication commences, because there is no limitation in the clause which means it only applies to the allocation by the adjudication of his fees and expenses.[16] While the drafting of section 108(A) certainly might have been clearer, the likelihood is that a court will uphold Parliament's intention to outlaw pre-allocation of party clauses, particularly in light of Coulson J's comments in *Leander Construction Limited v Mulalley and Company Limited*.[17]

[12.38] The fact that the parties may not agree the allocation of their costs before the adjudication commences probably does not mean that they may not, in their contract, give the adjudicator the power to award costs as he sees fit. Such a provision would not be an agreement made between the parties to allocate the party costs as such, rather it is an agreement to place the task of allocating in the hands of the adjudicator.

[12.39] The changes made by section 108A have flowed through into the 2011 Scheme at paragraphs 9,[18] 11(1),[19] and 25,[20] which all concern payment to the adjudicator or the allocation of the parties' costs. The amendments provide the adjudicator with discretion to apportion his fees, provided they are compliant with subsection 108A(2).

12.3.3 1996 Act

[12.40] The 1996 Act does not contain any rules as to the payment of parties' costs. The original intention was that each party should bear its own costs of an adjudication so that parties could exercise control over and have foreseeability of the professional fees. Some parties originally interpreted this omission to mean that parties could agree in advance, either in the original contract or at the outset of the adjudication, who is to be responsible for all the costs and expenses of adjudication. Provisions to this effect are known as Tolent

---

[15] [2010] EWHC 720 (TCC), per Edwards-Stuart J at [51].
[16] For further discussion, see Dominic Helps' excellent article at Constr. L.J. 2011, 27(7), 575–593.
[17] [2011] EWHC 3449 (TCC), er Coulson J at [11–12].
[18] See Section 9.7.11(B).
[19] See Section 8.5.17(B).
[20] See Section 11.2.2.

clauses, following the case of *Bridgeway Construction Ltd v Tolent Construction Ltd*[21] which supported the use of such a clause.

[12.41] However, the decision in Tolent came under considerable criticism and is now unlikely to be followed since the decision in *Yuanda (UK) Co Ltd v WW Gear Construction Ltd*.[22] Edwards-Stuart J held that a Tolent clause in the parties' contract conflicted with section 108 of the Act because its effect was to inhibit the right to refer a dispute to adjudication 'at any time'. Therefore, in England, any agreement before the adjudication commences as to the allocation of parties' costs, save for a reference which permits the adjudicator to allocate costs, is likely to be ineffective.

[12.42] It may be possible to apportion parties' costs in the contract between them in another way. In *Balfour Beatty v Speedwell Roofing and Cladding Ltd*,[23] the contract provided that 'where the referring party is awarded in the aggregate a sum less than 50% of the amount claimed he shall reimburse the other party the legal costs and expenses which the non-referring party incurred in the adjudication'. Although it is not clear from the judgment whether the contract between the parties was one to which the 1996 Act applied, the judge did not adversely comment on the provision. In that case, Balfour Beatty sought recovery of costs in five adjudications, two of which the defendant lost and three of which it withdrew from. The defendant argued that because it withdrew, there was no 'award', and therefore it was not liable for Balfour's costs. The court held that this was an artificial analysis. If Speedwell withdrew, then it would in effect be awarded nothing, which would trigger the operation of the clause.

[12.43] Where the adjudicator is empowered to award parties' costs between them, he will need to carefully consider when and how that is done. See Section 12.4.1.

12.3.4 The Late Payment of Commercial Debt (Interest) Act 1998

[12.44] The Late Payment of Commercial Debts (Interest) Act 1998 (the **LPCDA**)[24] allows a creditor to charge interest at a rate of 8% per annum above the base rate of the Bank of England on a debt owed. Further, a fixed sum of up to £100 is also chargeable by a creditor as compensation for recovering the debt.[25] This sum only applies (a) where statutory interest is implied into the contract; and (b) once statutory interest begins to run.

[12.45] The scope of application of the LPCDA is limited. It only applies to contracts for the supply of goods and services where the purchaser and supplier are acting in the course of business, but this means it will apply to construction contracts within the meaning of the Act.[26] The LPCDA will only imply a rate of interest and permit a fixed sum of

---

[21] (2000) CILL 1662, per Mackay J at [28–36].
[22] [2010] EWHC 720 (TCC), per Edwards-Stuart J at [51].
[23] [2010] EWHC 840 (TCC), per Edwards-Stuart J at [22–24].
[24] 1998 Chapter 20. http://www.legislation.gov.uk/ukpga/1998/20. Accessed 1 September 2015.
[25] Section 5A LPCDA.
[26] Clearly it will not apply to residential home owners contracting in their personal capacity.

compensation to be charged if the contract does not provide a substantial remedy on a debt.[27] All standard form construction contracts contain detailed provisions as to the payment of interest on a debt and so for those contracts the LPCDA will not apply. Furthermore, the LPCDA will only apply to what is termed a qualifying debt,[28] which means a debt created by virtue of an obligation under a contract to which the LPCDA applies to pay the whole or any part of the contract price. Therefore, it will apply to a contractual right to claim a sum of money, but will not apply to a claim for damages for breach of contract, for instance. Where the LPCDA applies, its provisions are mandatory and cannot be contracted out of.

[12.46] The Late Payment of Commercial Debts Regulations 2013 (the **LPCDR**)[29] came into force on 16 March 2013, in order to comply with European Directive 2011/7/EU on combatting late payment in commercial transactions. The LPCDR has, among other things, radically changed the nature of the compensation available under the LPCDA. It inserts the following provision section 5A[30] of the LPCDA:

> (2A) If the reasonable costs of the supplier in recovering the debt are not met by the fixed sum, the supplier shall also be entitled to a sum equivalent to the difference between the fixed sum and those costs.

[12.47] In other words, (a) where the LPCDA applies; (b) where statutory interest is implied into the contract; and (c) once statutory interest begins to run, the costs incurred in pursuing and collecting a legitimate unpaid debt, even if the debt is disputed, are payable by the debtor.

[12.48] Applying these provisions in the context of adjudication, the position with regards to recovering a debt used to be that where the LPCDA applied to a debt, the referring party could claim statutory interest and a fixed sum in compensation, and the adjudicator could decide that interest and the fixed sum was payable. However, the LPCDR extends the referring party's rights much further. For contracts dated after 16 March 2013 and where the LPCDA applies to a debt, the new provisions entitle the referring party to recover its costs in the adjudication in full from the responding party.

[12.49] What ability is there under this regime for a would-be debtor to recover the costs of proceedings if a creditor pursues a claim for a debt but in defence of the claim, either in the same adjudication or in subsequent proceedings, the debtor raises a set-off which partially or entirely extinguishes the debt? Unless there has been an agreement between the parties after the notice of adjudication has been served, it would seem there is no recourse, because pre-allocation of costs before the commencement of an adjudication is prohibited by the 2009 Act. Therefore, the LPCDA appears to permit a one-way street with regard to recovery of costs arising from the pursuit of a debt.

---

[27] Subsection 8(1) LPCDA.
[28] Subsection 3(1) LPCDA.
[29] SI 2013 No. 395. The Late Payment of Commercial Debts Regulations 2013. http://www.legislation.gov.uk/uksi/2013/395/introduction/made. Accessed 1 September 2015.
[30] Implementing Article 6 of the aforementioned directive.

[12.50] What is more, clause 5A(2A) of the LPCDA conflicts with section 108A of the 2009 Act because the former amounts to a pre-allocation of party costs before the commencement of the adjudication. It also arguably conflicts with subsection 108(2)(a) of the Act, namely the right to refer a dispute 'at any time', if one applies the same logic as was deployed in *Yuanda (UK) Co Ltd v WW Gear Construction Ltd*[31] where the court considered pre-allocation of costs. However, this conflict is resolved when one considers the hierarchy of European and member state legislation. In *Thoburn v Sunderland City Council and Others*,[32] the Court of Appeal said this.

> The present state of our domestic law is such that substantive Community rights prevail over the express terms of any domestic law, including primary legislation, made or passed after the coming into force of the ECA, even in the face of plain inconsistency between the two. This is the effect of Factortame (No 1) [1990] 2 AC 85.[33]

[12.51] Thus, notwithstanding the intentions of section 108A, given that the changes to the LPCDA were enacted as a result of a European directive it would appear that where the LPCDA applies, its provisions and any other conflicting provision in the Act are overridden.

12.4 Apportioning costs

12.4.1 In a nutshell

[12.52] Where the adjudicator has been given the power to determine how his own costs and/or the parties' are to be apportioned, he has complete discretion as to how that is done. Unlike litigation or arbitration, there are no rules or judicial precedent that guide the basis on which an adjudicator should assess the costs, or the factors he should take into account when considering the claim submitted. However, it is suggested that the principles applied in court proceedings can broadly be applied in adjudication. Generally speaking, the adjudicator should seek submissions from both parties as to how they consider costs should be apportioned. Although there is some debate as to when this should be done, it is suggested that it is done before the deadline for the decision, be it 28 days from receipt of the referral notice or later.

12.4.2 Timing

[12.53] If the adjudicator has the power to apportion costs, at what point should he make that assessment? The court has held that once the adjudicator has given his decision, he is functus officio, which means 'the adjudicator has no status or function in relation to the adjudication once his decision has been published and, subject to a limited power to

---

[31] [2010] EWHC 720 (TCC), per Edwards-Stuart J at [51].
[32] [2002] EWHC 195 (Admin), per Laws LJ at [61].
[33] See also subsection 2(1) of the European Communities Act 1972.

correct errors in that decision, has no further role to play in the dispute or its adjudication.'[34] Therefore, the adjudicator ought to make his decision on the award of his costs before he communicates his decision. He may or may not seek submissions from either party, although it will always be advisable for him to do so in order to demonstrate that he has acted in a fair manner. He should direct that those submissions are sent to him after the date for the last submission and before the deadline for his decision.

[12.54] The position is complicated where parties have made without prejudice save as to costs offers and one or both parties wish the adjudicator to consider those offers before making his award on costs. Clearly he cannot do this before he has reached his decision because knowledge of the content of those offers would result in a real risk that his decision would be influenced as a result, which in turn may lead to a claim that the adjudicator was biased.[35] The court has held that he cannot do it after he has delivered his decision, since he would be functus officio.

[12.55] Adjudicators have sought to circumvent this problem by ensuring that they reach a decision on the substantive dispute and on costs before the deadline for the decision. They will provide a timetable, which allows sufficient time after the decision has been reached and communicated and before the deadline to consider submissions and make his decision on costs. Alternatively, the adjudicator may seek an extension to the timetable of a few days in order to deal with costs. Or, he may reach their decision, but not deliver it to the parties, then consider submissions on costs, reach a decision on costs and then deliver both the decision on the dispute and on the costs together.

12.4.3 Assessment

[12.56] In court proceedings, the general rule is that costs follow the event. In other words, whichever party loses pays the majority of the costs of the proceedings. Although it varies, where there are no special circumstances, the court will order that costs are assessed on a standard basis, which generally means the losing party pays 60–80% of the costs of the proceedings. Sometimes, the losing party will have acted in an unsatisfactory manner. It may have tried to manipulate the proceedings. It may have no defence at all to the claim brought. In those cases, the court may order that costs are paid on an indemnity basis, which generally means the losing party pays 85–100% of the costs of the proceedings. It is suggested that these basic principles that are applied in court proceedings should also be applied in adjudication proceedings. See Section 13.3.16 which outlines the court's consideration of the basis of costs assessment in the context of adjudication enforcement proceedings. It is submitted there is no reason why the principles outlined there cannot apply in the adjudication itself.

[12.57] Where the adjudicator has jurisdiction to allocate the parties' costs, he should consider if the costs claimed by the winning party are reasonable and proportionate. The

---

[34] *Joinery Plus Ltd (In Administration) v Laing Ltd* [2003] EWHC 3513 (TCC) per Thornton J at [42].
[35] See Section 17.4.13.

CPR determines[36] that costs are proportionate if they bear a reasonable relationship to:

(a) the sums in issue in the proceedings;
(b) the value of any non-monetary relief in issue in the proceedings;
(c) the complexity of the litigation;
(d) any additional work generated by the conduct of the paying party; and
(e) any wider factors involved in the proceedings, such as reputation or public importance.

[12.58] Although of course the CPR does not apply in adjudication proceedings, it is suggested that this guidance may be applied nonetheless. Accordingly, if the winning party has incurred £100,000 in costs on a dispute valued at £100,000, it is highly unlikely that the incursion of those costs is proportionate to the value of the dispute. In the context of adjudication enforcement proceedings reasonableness of proportionality of costs is considered at Section 13.3.17.

[12.59] Adjudicators usually dictate that parties' costs are payable within seven or fourteen days from the date of the award.

12.5 Correcting errors in the decision

12.5.1 In a nutshell

[12.60] For a short period after the decision has been communicated, the adjudicator may correct genuine or patent mistakes in the decision. The scope of this rule, known as the slip rule, is relatively confined and does not extend to permitting the adjudicator to change the substance of what he decided, even if he considers that what he decided was wrong.

12.5.2 The 2009 Act and 2011 Scheme (2009 Act s. 108(3)(A); 2011 Scheme p. 22A)

[12.61] Where the 2009 Act applies, subsection 108(3)(A) provides:

> The contract shall include provision in writing permitting the adjudicator to correct his decision so as to remove a clerical or typographical error arising by accident or omission.

[12.62] Thus, the adjudication rules adopted by the parties must contain a provision allowing the adjudicator to correct infelicities in his decision. This rule is commonly known as the slip rule. The subsection does not set out a time limit for slip rule corrections, although paragraph 22A of the 2011 Scheme states that any correction must be made within five days of the decision and that the adjudicator must deliver the corrected decision as soon as possible. It provides:

---

[36] CPR 44.3(5).

(1) The adjudicator may on his own initiative or on the application of a party correct his decision so as to remove a clerical or typographical error arising by accident or omission.
(2) Any correction of a decision must be made within five days of the delivery of the decision to the parties.
(3) As soon as possible after correcting a decision in accordance with this paragraph, the adjudicator must deliver a copy of the corrected decision to each of the parties to the contract.
(4) Any correction of a decision forms part of the decision.

[12.63] Presumably the parties are free to specify what matters fall within the scope of this new rule if they wish, provided that whatever is agreed does not conflict with or extend beyond the scope of the new section of the Act, or the requirement to reach a decision within 28 days. That said, the decision as to whether a particular point or part of the decision is wrong and should be amended lies with the adjudicator alone. Whether he identifies the error himself or the error is pointed out to him by one or both of the parties, if he decides that there is no error and decides not to make a correction, that is the end of the matter and the decision incorporating the alleged error will be enforced.

12.5.3 The 1996 Act and 1998 Scheme

[12.64] There is nothing in the 1996 Act or 1998 Scheme that permits the adjudicator to revisit the decision once it has been made. However, the courts have held that an adjudicator is permitted to amend his decision within a reasonable time after it has been issued in order to correct genuine mistakes or accidental clerical errors (for example, a typographical or mathematical error or omission).[37] The slip rule does not permit the adjudicator to reconsider the substance of the decision, it merely allows the adjudicator to give effect to his original intention.[38] It is not licence to change the substance of what has been decided. It is of 'very limited and narrow application': it enables an adjudicator to correct only genuine mistakes that failed to give effect to the adjudicator's first thoughts.[39] One recorded example entailed the adjudicator misreading a spreadsheet, which gave him an incorrect balance. As a result, he found for the claimant, however had he read the figures correctly, he would have found for the defendant. The court accepted this was a genuine slip, which the adjudicator corrected within a matter of a few days.[40]

[12.65] The adjudicator may amend the decision without permission from the parties, although the revised decision must be delivered to the parties. Either party can notify the

---

[37] *Bloor Construction (UK) Ltd v Bowmer & Kirkland (London) Ltd* [2000] BLR 314 per Toulmin, J at [28–43].
[38] *ROK Building Ltd v Celtic Composting Systems Ltd (No. 2)* [2010] EWHC 66 (TCC), per Akenhead J at [30–31].
[39] *CIB Properties v Birse* [2004] EWHC 2365 (TCC), per Toulmin, J at [35].
[40] *Coleraine Skip Hire Ltd v Ecomesh Ltd* [2008] NIQB 141, per Weatherup J at [25–26].

adjudicator of an error, although if the adjudicator decides that it is not an error, that is an end to the matter and the original decision stands.[41]

[12.66] The correction must be made within a reasonable time.[42] What is reasonable will depend on the facts. Certainly a few days is permissible, but 21 days will not be.[43] Parties are advised to read the decision carefully as soon as it is issued and if they consider there is an error, notify the adjudicator at the earliest opportunity.

[12.67] Where a party asks the adjudicator to correct a decision, it may be taken to have acceded to the adjudicator's jurisdiction to determine the dispute, thereby waiving its right to challenge the decision on grounds that the adjudicator lacked jurisdiction, that is unless the request for a correction is accompanied by an express reservation as to the jurisdiction of the adjudicator. See Section 16.3 for an explanation of how and when to reserve the position on the adjudicator's jurisdiction.

12.6 Setting off against the decision

12.6.1 In a nutshell

[12.68] The general rule is that compliance with an adjudicator's decision will not be affected by any other right or claim. The exception is that where there is a set-off or cross-claim that flows from or is closely connected to the adjudicator's decision, it may be possible to take that set-off or cross-claim into account when determining the amount due to the payee. There are various situations in which the courts have considered whether set-off against the adjudicator's decision is permitted and these are considered in the following sections.

12.6.2 General rule and exceptions

[12.69] The decision of an adjudicator that money must be paid gives rise to a statutory and/or a contractual obligation on the paying party to comply with that decision within the time period prescribed.

[12.70] Sometimes, the losing party tries to avoid paying the sum awarded by the adjudicator by claiming that it has a set-off or other cross-claim that partly or entirely reduces the amount awarded.[44] For contracts within the scope of the Act, the general position is that the obligation to comply with an adjudicator's decision means 'comply, without recourse to defences or cross-claims not raised in the adjudication.'[45] In so far as the set-off or cross-claim is within the scope of the dispute, it should be raised in the adjudication and the adjudicator either allows or disallows it; it is not appropriate for the losing party to

---

[41] *Bouygues (UK) Ltd v Dahl-Jensen (UK) Ltd* [2000] BLR 49, per Buxton LJ at [16–19].
[42] *YCMS Ltd v Grabiner* [2009] EWHC 127 (TCC), per Akenhead J at [50].
[43] Ibid.
[44] See Chapter 10, footnote 35 for the meaning of cross-claim.
[45] *VHE Construction PlC v RBSTB Trust Co Ltd* [2000] B.L.R. 187, per Hicks J at [55–56].

raise the same set-off or cross-claim after the decision or to raise new ones which could have been but were not raised.[46] Should a party have a claim that does not form part of the dispute that has been decided, it should be resolved separately either by another adjudication or in another forum.

[12.71] The general rule is subject to certain exceptions, which have been summarised by Grant J in *Naylor Construction Services Ltd v Acoustafoam Ltd*:[47]

> a defendant can only set off a sum against an amount an Adjudicator has decided will be paid to a referring party:
>
> (a) If it 'follows logically' from the Adjudicator's decision that the defendant is entitled to recover a specific sum in respect of the matters now raised by the defendant; that is to adopt the language of Jackson J in Balfour Beatty v Serco; and/or
> (b) If it is 'the natural corollary of the Adjudicator's decision' that the defendant is entitled to recover a specific sum in respect of the matters now raised by the defendant; that is to adopt the language of Ramsay J in Ledwood v Whessoe Oil.

[12.72] Whether or not it follows logically or is the natural corollary of the adjudicator's decision is a question of fact. It will be necessary to work out what exactly the adjudicator has decided. For that purpose the decision must be interpreted, both from the words used and taking into account the context of the dispute.[48] Evidently, where the adjudicator has already, in the course of the adjudication, considered the substance of the particular set-off, the losing party cannot seek to set up the same set-off as a reason for not paying the sum ordered by the adjudicator.[49] Furthermore, it is not open to a party who asserts a claim that has not yet materialised (such as a pending decision in another adjudication) to set that future sum off against the adjudicator's decision.[50] The set-off will only be permitted where the calculation of the set-off is 'not disputed or indisputable'.[51]

[12.73] A losing party's attempt to set off sums against the sum awarded by the adjudicator has arisen in a number of circumstances. They include whether the unsuccessful party is entitled to set off:

- pursuant to a contractual right;
- following the issue of a withholding or pay less notice against the sum the adjudicator has decided it should pay;
- following the issue of a later interim or final certificate;
- liquidated and ascertained damages against the adjudicator's decision;
- where the amount of the set-off is not quantified;
- where the set-off was not formulated before the start of the adjudication;

---

[46] *ROK Building Ltd v Celtic Composting Systems Ltd* [2009] EWHC 2664 (TCC), per Akenhead J at [18].
[47] [2010] All ER (D) 138, per Grant J at [58].
[48] *Rok Building Ltd v Celtic Composting Systems Ltd* [2009] EWHC 2664 (TCC), per Akenhead J at [20].
[49] *Ferson Contractors Ltd v Levolux AT Ltd* [2003] EWCA Civ 11, per Mantell LJ at [29–30].
[50] *Interserve Services Ltd v Cleveland Bridge UK Ltd* [2006] EWHC 741, per Jackson J at [43].
[51] *Ledwood Mechanical Engineering Ltd v Whessoe Oil and Gas Ltd* [2007] EWHC 2743, per Ramsey J at [37].

- where the adjudication rules prevent set-off in enforcement;
- the decision of another adjudicator in a separate adjudication against the adjudication;
- the decision of a court judgment against the adjudication;
- the decision of an arbitration award against the adjudication.

[12.74] These scenarios are considered in the following sections.

12.6.3 Contractual right to set off

[12.75] Most construction contracts will contain a clause permitting the paying party to set off or deduct sums certified as due. Whether or not this contractual right prevails will depend on the wording of the clause, the nature of the adjudicator's decision and the form of adjudication.

[12.76] For example, where an adjudicator directs that a sum was payable in accordance with the terms of the contract as opposed to determining that a specific sum is due, the paying party may be able to deploy that part of the contract payment machinery which allows it to issue a withholding or pay less notice to set off sums that it is entitled to but that do not form part of the adjudication.[52]

[12.77] However, clear words are required in order to permit such a course of action, and the courts will construe any attempt to thwart the consequences of an adjudicator's decision with considerable scepticism. In circumstances where the adjudicator's decision does not permit a set-off but the contract nevertheless contains a clause which would otherwise permit a set-off or cross-claim pursuant to an adjudicator's decision, the relevant clause will normally be overridden. This does not mean that the clause will be struck out, rather that it will be read as not applying to monies due by reason of an adjudicator's decision.[53]

[12.78] Whether or not the position is different where the form of adjudication is contractual as opposed to statutory is unclear. The courts have indicated that the policy of enforcement of decisions under either form of adjudication should be the same,[54] although there are examples where the form of adjudication was contractual, the adjudicator awarded a specific sum as due (as opposed to directing a sum was payable in accordance with the terms of the contract) and the court permitted the losing party to set off against that sum because there was wording in the contract that permitted it.[55]

[12.79] A clause requiring the parties to 'submit to summary judgment/decree and enforcement in respect of all such decisions' was sufficient to preclude any arguments, subject to a valid decision, that the amount of the adjudicator's decision should not be paid in full.[56]

---

[52] *R&C Electrical Engineers Ltd v Shaylor Construction Ltd* [2012] EWHC 1254 (TCC), per Edwards-Stuart J at [80–83].
[53] *Ferson Contractors Ltd v Levolux AT Ltd* [2003] EWCA Civ 11, per Mantell LJ at [30] followed by *William Verry Ltd v The Mayor and Burgesses of the London Borough of Camden* [2006] EWHC 761 (TCC), per Ramsey J at [28].
[54] See Section 5.2.2.
[55] *Parsons Plastic Ltd v Purac Ltd* [2002] BLR 334, per Pill LJ at [14–15].
[56] *Ferson Contractors Ltd v Levolux AT Ltd* [2003] EWCA Civ 11, per Longmore LJ at [32–34].

[12.80] Even if the contract and the adjudicator's decision permits set-off, whether in fact the unsuccessful party is entitled to set off will normally depend on whether it issues a withholding or pay less notice against the sum certified as due from the adjudicator. The requirement to issue such notice may also apply to contracts outside of the ambit of the Act, depending on the wording of the contract.[57]

12.6.4 Later interim or final certificate

[12.81] The enforcement of an adjudicator's decision cannot be avoided because it has been overtaken by an interim[58] or final[59] certificate issued after the date of the decision. If later certificates could impact on the enforceability of an adjudicator's decision, it would defeat the whole purpose of adjudication, which is to provide a binding and temporarily enforceable decision and cash flow to the winning party.

[12.82] However, payment mechanisms in most construction contracts value the works on a cumulative basis, so that the entire account is taken into account at each payment application. Subject to the terms of the contract, this enables the parties to, in effect, correct earlier applications and certifications to take account of mistakes, omissions, overpayments and so on. Therefore, in respect of the same item or items of work, where the amount certified as due in a later interim certificate is less than the amount certified as due by the adjudicator in respect of an earlier interim certificate and the adjudicator's decision on the earlier interim certificate arrives at the same time or after the later interim certificate, the effect will be that the payer will only pay the lesser sum. Section 8.4.5 considers the status of interim applications and a tactic sometimes deployed by payees, known as a 'smash and grab' adjudication.

12.6.5 Issuing a withholding or pay less notice

[12.83] The question of whether the losing party is entitled to withhold sums claimed by it against the sum awarded by the adjudicator depends on the nature of the adjudicator's decision. In cases where the adjudicator did not order immediate payment, but instead gave a declaration as to the proper operation of the contract, or ordered that the sum due should be paid, but only as part of, and pursuant to, the existing contract machinery, then it may be possible to set off sums against an adjudicator's decision.[60] So, where the adjudicator did not order payment, but instead ordered that an invoice should be issued so that the contractual machinery for the payment of such invoices could be set in motion, it was permissible for the paying party to issue a withholding notice against that sum in line with the requirements of the contract.[61] In *Conor Engineering Ltd v Constructions*

---

[57] *Lovell Projects Ltd v Legg & Carver* [2003] BLR 452, per Moseley J at [36–41].
[58] *MJ Gleeson Group plc v Devonshire Green Holding Ltd* [2004] AdjLR 03/19, per Gilliland J at [8–12].
[59] *William Verry Ltd v The Mayor and Burgesses of the London Borough of Camden* [2006] EWHC 761 (TCC), per Ramsey J at [36–44].
[60] *Beck Interiors Ltd v Classic Decorative Finished Ltd* [2012] EWHC 1956 (TCC) per Coulson J at [11].
[61] *Shimizu Europe Ltd v LBJ Fabrications Ltd* [2003] EWHC 1229 (TCC), per Kirkham J at [13–32].

Industrielles de la Mediterranée SA,[62] the particular wording of the contract and the nature of the decision permitted the losing party to issue a withholding notice within seven days of the date of the decision. In the event, the withholding notice was not served within the time and so, notwithstanding a claim to set off liquidated damages, the court enforced the adjudicator's award.

[12.84] The issue of a notice to withhold or pay less in a subsequent application cannot affect the question of what amount was properly payable under the earlier application, as decided by the adjudicator. The fact that the withholding notice for the later application was given before the adjudicator issued his decision does not affect the binding force of the decision.[63] However, as described in the subsection above, the monetary effect of the adjudicator's decision is likely to be neutered in the event the subsequent payment cycle is completed before the adjudicator's decision, because the payer can probably make an adjustment which takes account of the overpayment.

12.6.6 Setting off liquidated damages

[12.85] Where the adjudicator has awarded the contractor an extension of time and prolongation costs arising from that extension of time, the employer is likely to have a cross-claim for liquidated damages where the extension of time awarded does not reflect the entire delay. Whether the employer is entitled to set off the liquidated damages will be determined from an analysis of what the adjudicator had decided and from the particular circumstances of the case. The principle was outlined by Jackson J in *Balfour Beatty Construction v Serco Ltd*[64] as follows:

> (a) Where it follows logically from an adjudicator's decision that the employer is entitled to recover a specific sum by way of liquidated and ascertained damages, then the employer may set off that sum against monies payable to the contractor pursuant to the adjudicator's decision, provided that the employer has given proper notice (insofar as required).
>
> (b) Where the entitlement to liquidated and ascertained damages has not been determined either expressly or impliedly by the adjudicator's decision, then the question whether the employer is entitled to set off liquidated and ascertained damages against sums awarded by the adjudicator will depend upon the terms of the contract and the circumstances of the case.

[12.86] It will only follow logically where it is evident that the adjudicator has assessed the entire extension of time claim and there is no other reason preventing liquidated damages from becoming due. That may not always be the case. In *Balfour Beatty Construction v Serco Ltd*,[65] the adjudicator had granted an extension of time, but left open whether further extensions might be due. As a result, Jackson J could not say that it unquestionably followed from the adjudicator's decision that liquidated damages claimed were applicable

---

[62] [2004] EWHC 899 (TCC), per Blunt J at [41–50].
[63] *MJ Gleeson Group plc v Devonshire Green Holding Ltd* [2004] AdjLR 03/19, per Gilliland J at [8–12].
[64] *Balfour Beatty Construction v Serco Ltd* [2004] EWHC 3336, per Jackson J [53].
[65] Ibid.

to the balance of delay. A similar result followed in *Squibb Group Ltd v Vertase F.L.I. Ltd*,[66] albeit in different circumstances and with different reasons given. However, in *David McLean Housing Contractors Ltd v Swansea Housing Association Ltd*,[67] the court determined that on the facts the liquidated damages sum 'reflects the adjudicator's view about the extension of time that was sought by the claimant so the claimant is bound to accept that conclusion in these proceedings since it was part of the dispute which it referred.' In *Thameside Construction Co Ltd v Stevens*,[68] Mr and Mrs Stevens sought to set off a sum from the amount awarded by the adjudicator in relation to construction works on their home. They argued that the adjudicator's decision was the equivalent of an interim certificate against which they were entitled to set off their claim for liquidated damages. Rather than rely on the *Balfour Beatty v Serco* argument, they relied on the argument that the adjudicator had awarded that a sum was payable in accordance with a clause of the contract and so they were entitled to operate the contractual machinery to withhold sums against that amount. The court concluded that it would be absolutely wrong to construe, or interpret the decision as permitting the loser to set off the obviously disputed claim for liquidated damages. The decision was not one where the adjudicator was declaring that a sum should be paid in accordance with the contract, but directed payment to be made. Accordingly, set-off was not available.

[12.87] The right to set off liquidated damages will be contingent upon the employer giving a proper and timely notice (a withholding or pay less notice) to withhold the sum of money in question.[69] However, where the employer fails to issue a notice on the application for payment that is the subject of the adjudication, but has issued a notice on a subsequent application before the date of the adjudicator's decision, then that later notice may be considered a viable set-off against the sums otherwise awarded as due. In that particular case, the entitlement to recover liquidated damages arose as a debt under the contract.[70] There are numerous other cases where the question of whether the employer is entitled to deduct liquidated damages has arisen and these are listed in Appendix 8.

12.6.7 Set off permitted but not quantified in the decision

[12.88] In at least one case,[71] the court refused to enforce a decision of the adjudicator because, while the adjudicator had decided that the defendant was entitled to set off its cross-claims against sums due to the claimant, those sums had not been quantified by him owing to jurisdictional issues. In other words, the decision of the adjudicator did not give rise to an immediate right to payment of the amounts claimed by the claimant, because it did not take account of the set-off, which had yet to be valued.

---

[66] [2012] EWHC 1958 (TCC) per Coulson J at [19–27].
[67] [2004] EWHC 3336 (TCC), per Jackson J at [25–35].
[68] [2013] EWHC 2071 (TCC), per Akenhead J at [30–33].
[69] *Balfour Beatty Construction v Serco Ltd* [2004] EWHC 3336, per Jackson J [4–55].
[70] *David McLean Housing Contractors Ltd v Swansea Housing Association Ltd* [2004] EWHC 3336 (TCC), per Jackson J at [25–35].
[71] *Geris Handelsgesellschaft v Les Constructions Industrielles de la Mediterrannée S.A.* [2005] EWHC 499, per Lloyd J at [30–37].

12.6.8 Set-off not formulated before the adjudication

[12.89] Where the set-off has not been formulated before the start of the adjudication, it has been said that it is 'at the very least difficult, if not in fact impossible' for an unsuccessful party to set off a non-particularised cross-claim against the amount an adjudicator has determined as payable.[72]

12.6.9 Adjudication rules prevent set-off in enforcement proceedings

[12.90] Sometimes the rules of the adjudication will expressly prevent set-off or deductions of any kind from the adjudicator's decision in enforcement proceedings. Whether or not this is sufficient to prevent the awarded amount being reduced or extinguished will again depend on the words of the contract and the nature of the adjudicator's decision. Where there is a contractual right to set off, and the adjudicator has preserved that right of set-off in his decision, then set-off may be permitted on the basis that the unsuccessful party merely seeks to exercise a contractual right, rather than exercise its right to set off in enforcement proceedings.[73]

12.6.10 Multiple adjudications

[12.91] Where there have been multiple adjudications between the parties, the courts are reluctant to set off one decision against another, favouring instead to ensure that the winning party receives the benefit of the decision as soon as possible. In *Interserve Services Ltd v Cleveland Bridge UK Ltd*,[74] Jackson J said 'where the parties to a construction contract engage in successive adjudications ... at the end of each adjudication, absent special circumstances, the losing party must comply with the decision.'

[12.92] Notwithstanding this, there are examples where the court has set one decision off against the other. In *HS Works Ltd v Enterprise Managed Services Ltd*,[75] the court set out a number of guidelines for considering when to set off one adjudicator's decision against another adjudicator's decision:

- Both adjudicators' decisions must be valid.
- Both decisions must be capable of being enforced or given effect to.
- If those two conditions are met, the court should enforce the decisions, provided separate proceedings have been brought by each party to enforce each decision.
- It is a matter for the court's discretion how each decision is enforced (that is, whether one decision should be set off against the other).

---

[72] *Naylor Construction Services Ltd v Acoustafoam Ltd* [2010] All ER (D) 138, per Grant J at [59–61].
[73] *R and C Electrical Engineers Ltd v Shaylor Construction Ltd* [2012] EWHC 1254 (TCC), per Edwards-Stuart J at [83–84].
[74] [2006] EWHC 741 per Jackson J at [43].
[75] [2009] EWHC 729 (TCC), per Akenhead J [40].

[12.93] In that case, the adjudication awards were set off against each other on the basis that 'it would be pointless, at least administratively, for Enterprise to hand over the net sum due (allowing for the belated payment) pursuant to the First Adjudication decision to be followed by HSW having to hand back all or the bulk of what had just been paid to it to Enterprise.'[76]

[12.94] The cases seem to show that only where the adjudications are decided is there any prospect of succeeding on a case of set-off. Where there is one adjudication decision and the other adjudication decision is yet to be issued, the courts will not entertain a set-off defence.

12.6.11 Litigation on foot

[12.95] The same principles apply where the adjudicator has issued a decision and there are legal proceedings in the court which are set for trial in the near future. In one case, where the adjudicator's decision was issued in March and a trial between the same parties on a different dispute was scheduled for July, even though the enforcement hearing was not until June, the court still ordered the losing party to comply with the adjudicator's decision forthwith.[77]

12.6.12 Arbitration award

[12.96] In Workspace Management Ltd v YJL London Ltd,[78] Coulson J held that the contractor was entitled to set off an adjudicator's decision in its favour against sums it was obliged to pay the employer under an arbitrator's interim (or provisional) award relating to the same contract. The court also held that the arbitrator's award did not 'trump' the adjudicator's decision because the arbitrator's award was interim (or provisional).

12.6.13 Other arguments for set-off

[12.97] Claims for defective works,[79] the application of a pain/gain assessment to sums determined to be due[80] or counterclaims referred to an arbitration[81] are in themselves unlikely to usurp the general rule on set-off.

---

[76] Ibid at [48–55].
[77] *Hillview Industrial Developments (UK) Ltd v Botes Building Ltd* [2006] EWHC 1365 (TCC), per Toulmin J at [27–28].
[78] [2009] EWHC 2017 (TCC), per Coulson J [28–37].
[79] *Harlow & Milner Ltd v Linda Teasdale (No. 1)* [2006] EWHC 54 (TCC), per Coulson J at [9].
[80] *Ledwood Mechanical Engineering Ltd v Whessoe Oil and Gas Ltd & Anor* [2007] EWHC 2743 (TCC), per Ramsey J at [30–38].
[81] *DG Williamson v Northern Ireland Prison Service* [2009] NIQB 8, per McLaughlin J at [31].

# Chapter 13
Enforcement: options and procedure

13.1 Overview

[13.01] The losing party to an adjudication sometimes decides that it does not wish to comply with the decision of the adjudicator because it perceives it has good grounds for doing so. Usually, this will be made reasonably apparent by the losing party's actions (for example by writing to the adjudicator or winning party) or inaction (for example by failing to pay money by the required date). A losing party is not required to comply with the adjudicator's decision if it plans to contest its enforceability.[1]

[13.02] Where the losing party does not comply with the decision, the winning party must seek to enforce it by obtaining a court order. There is no method of enforcement set out in the Act or Scheme. The winning party must choose either to commence a claim in the Technology and Construction Court and make a summary judgment application to enforce, or (less commonly) seek a pre-emptory order, a mandatory injunction or issue a statutory demand. Where the winning party is successful, the losing party will be ordered to comply with the terms of the adjudicator's decision. It will also be liable for the majority of the costs of the enforcement proceedings and, where the adjudicator's award was one of money, for interest on the awarded sum.

[13.03] This chapter sets out in detail the procedure for enforcing an adjudicator's decision in the Technology and Construction Court (Section 13.3) as well as giving an overview of the rules and procedure for enforcing a decision by other means (Section 13.4). It deals with the rules for complying with an order from the court and the consequences and options available to the enforcing party where the other party fails to comply with that order (Section 13.5).

13.2 Key statements of principle and the court's policy

13.2.1 Principles of enforcement

[13.04] The first enforcement case ever to come to the court under the Act was *Macob Civil Engineering Ltd v Morrison Construction Ltd*.[2] In that case, it was alleged that there

---

[1] *Alstom Signalling Ltd v Jarvis Facilities Ltd (No. 2)* [2004] EWHC 1285 (TCC), per Lloyd J at [19–20].
[2] [1999] EWHC 254 (TCC), per Dyson J at [22].

A Practical Guide to Construction Adjudication, First Edition. James Pickavance.
© 2016 James Pickavance. Published 2016 by John Wiley & Sons, Inc.

had been a procedural error by the adjudicator. Dyson J dismissed the challenge on policy grounds, finding that to do otherwise would be to allow a 'coach and horses' to be driven through the legislation. He commented that, by imposing a provisional and speedy dispute resolution procedure on the construction industry, Parliament clearly intended an element of 'rough justice', and a process in which mistakes and injustices were more or less bound to happen.

[13.05] The principles set out in that case were elaborated in *Carillion Construction Ltd v Devonport Royal Dockyard*.[3] At first instance, Jackson J made the following comments:

- The adjudication procedure does not involve the final determination of the parties' rights (unless the parties so agree).
- The court has repeatedly emphasised that adjudicators' decisions must be enforced, even if they result from errors of procedure, fact or law.
- Where an adjudicator acts in excess of jurisdiction or in serious breach of the rules of natural justice, the court will not enforce the decision.
- Judges must be astute to examine technical defences with a degree of scepticism consistent with the policy of the Act. Errors of law, fact or procedure by an adjudicator must be examined critically before the court accepts that such errors constitute an act in excess of jurisdiction or a breach of the rules of natural justice.

[13.06] The Court of Appeal approved[4] the first instance decision and, in doing so, Chadwick LJ further described the approach that the courts should apply to enforcement. Although there are tens of court judgments that address the court's approach to enforcement (see Appendix 8), the following extract is probably the clearest and certainly the most frequently cited of all.

> 85 The objective which underlies the Act and the statutory scheme requires the courts to respect and enforce the adjudicator's decision unless it is plain that the question which he has decided was not the question referred to him or the manner in which he has gone about his task is obviously unfair. It should be only in rare circumstances that the courts will interfere with the decision of an adjudicator. The courts should give no encouragement to the approach adopted by DML in the present case; which (contrary to DML's outline submissions, to which we have referred in paragraph 66 of this judgment) may, indeed, aptly be described as 'simply scrabbling around to find some argument, however tenuous, to resist payment'.
>
> 86 It is only too easy in a complex case for a party who is dissatisfied with the decision of an adjudicator to comb through the adjudicator's reasons and identify points upon which to present a challenge under the labels 'excess of jurisdiction' or 'breach of natural justice'. It must be kept in mind that the majority of adjudicators are not chosen for their expertise as lawyers. Their skills are as likely (if not more likely) to lie in other disciplines. The task of the adjudicator is not to act as arbitrator or judge. The time constraints within which he is expected to operate are proof of that. The task of the adjudicator is to find an interim solution which meets the needs

---

[3] [2005] EWHC 778 (TCC) per Akenhead J at [80].
[4] [2005] EWCA Civ 1358.

of the case. Parliament may be taken to have recognised that, in the absence of an interim solution, the contractor (or sub-contractor) or his sub-contractors will be driven into insolvency through a wrongful withholding of payments properly due. The statutory scheme provides a means of meeting the legitimate cash-flow requirements of contractors and their subcontractors. The need to have the 'right' answer has been subordinated to the need to have an answer quickly. The scheme was not enacted in order to provide definitive answers to complex questions. Indeed, it may be open to doubt whether Parliament contemplated that disputes involving difficult questions of law would be referred to adjudication under the statutory scheme; or whether such disputes are suitable for adjudication under the scheme. We have every sympathy for an adjudicator faced with the need to reach a decision in a case like the present.

87 In short, in the overwhelming majority of cases, the proper course for the party who is unsuccessful in an adjudication under the scheme must be to pay the amount that he has been ordered to pay by the adjudicator. If he does not accept the adjudicator's decision as correct (whether on the facts or in law), he can take legal or arbitration proceedings in order to establish the true position. To seek to challenge the adjudicator's decision on the ground that he has exceeded his jurisdiction or breached the rules of natural justice (save in the plainest cases) is likely to lead to a substantial waste of time and expense—as, we suspect, the costs incurred in the present case will demonstrate only too clearly.

[13.07] Cases on enforcement are replete with attempts by parties disappointed by an adjudicator's decision to avoid the enforcement of that decision – attempts that are usually found to be more inventive than successful. That said, the right to enforce an adjudicator's decision is not absolute. The court's policy on enforcement only applies to decisions that are valid, in that they were decisions which the adjudicator was authorised to make. Accordingly, the right to enforce an adjudicator's decision is always qualified or contingent. Moreover subsection 108(3) of the Act states that the decision is binding until the dispute is finally determined by legal proceedings, which means that the parties must comply with a valid decision until such time as it is overturned in final proceedings.

[13.08] Where the dispute is about money, the rubric 'pay now; argue later' is often used when describing the court's policy on enforcement,[5] although strictly this catchphrase probably more accurately refers to the requirements of sections 110 and 111 of the Act, which impose a requirement on a party to pay without set-off or deduction sums due on interim certificates unless various procedural notices are given in time: so-called withholding or pay less notices. Absent compliance with that interim valuation notice regime, a paying party must truly 'pay now, argue later', although it can of course invoke adjudication seeking compensation for the value of the cross-claims it failed to raise in time in its notices, meaning that the 'later' may come relatively soon. Adjudication is perhaps more accurately described, not as 'pay now, argue later', but as 'argue now at speed, pay now if the adjudicator decides you must, and have any more full, detailed, final and forensic argument later if you wish' – although clearly any such description is not pithy enough to catch on.

---

[5] *Alstom Signalling Ltd v Jarvis Facilities Ltd (No. 2)* [2004] EWHC 1285 (TCC), per Lloyd J at [19–20].

[13.09] Where a court determines that an adjudicator's award is a nullity, either because he in some way acted outside of his own jurisdiction, or he breached the rules of natural justice, the parties are entitled to commence a fresh adjudication as if the original adjudication had never taken place. Where the adjudication is conducted in accordance with the Scheme, subparagraph 9(2) (which prevents the same or similar disputes being referred to adjudication twice) will not apply.[6]

13.2.2 Enforcement for contractual adjudications

[13.10] It would seem that the policy adopted by the court for adjudications governed by the Act (statutory adjudication) is the same as for adjudications falling outside of the Act (contractual adjudication). See Section 5.2.3.

13.3 TCC summary enforcement procedure

13.3.1 In a nutshell

[13.11] By far the most commonly used method of enforcing an adjudicator's decision in England and Wales is to commence a claim (usually in the Technology and Construction Court (TCC)[7] and at the same time make an application for summary judgment. Acknowledging that the timescale of statutory adjudication was set with the aim of resolving disputes quickly, the TCC moulded a similarly rapid procedure for enforcing adjudicators' decisions, the details of which are contained at section 9 of the TCC Guide.[8] The process is reasonably straightforward and will usually result in a decision from the court in no more than eight weeks from the commencement of the claim. The parties' costs incurred in bringing a summary judgment application are heavily scrutinised, particularly solicitor's fees. Solicitors should therefore be in a position to justify each hour they have spent.

[13.12] It is worth noting at the outset that the TCC enforcement procedure is entirely organic and judge-made; it has no statutory underpinning, because of the (some might say curious) decision by Parliament to include no enforcement regime in either the Act itself or the Scheme. The TCC judges have accordingly fashioned the enforcement procedure from the materials that they had to hand under the Civil Procedure Rules. The result nevertheless is a flexible and effective system that works well.

[13.13] It is important to note in particular that it is difficult, if not impossible in the vast majority of cases, to derail or extend the timetable for adjudication enforcement in any material

---

[6] *Joinery Plus Ltd (In Administration) v Laing Ltd* [2003] EWHC 3513 (TCC), per Thornton J at [97].
[7] Section 1.3.6 TCC Guide.
[8] TCC Court Guide, Second Edition, Third Revision, 30 April 2014. http://www.justice.gov.uk/downloads/courts/tech-court/tec-con-court-guide.pdf. Accessed on 1 September 2015. It has been noted that the TCC Guide is merely that. It is designed to set out in simple terms how the TCC can answer or assist the parties to resolve their disputes. It is not designed to define the TCC's jurisdiction in every case. See *Vitpol Building Service v Michael Samen* [2008] EWHC 2283 (TCC) per Coulson J at [13–15].

Enforcement: options and procedure 253

way save where the parties agree, and attempts to do so normally meet with a swift and robust judicial response. TCC judges in particular are used to – and will deal in a common sense and not overly precious way with – parties' attempts to get the last word in by serving evidence out of time or without permission. Adjournments of enforcement hearings to cope with such late flurries of material are rare, save where the parties agree, and judges normally rightly perceive material served at the 11th hour as likely to be peripheral to the two fundamental issues on enforcement, viz. whether the adjudicator had, or was given, jurisdiction to carry out a valid adjudication and, if he was, whether the decision should nevertheless not be enforced because they have gone about the process in a materially unfair or seemingly biased way, giving rise to a breach of natural justice.

13.3.2 Nature of summary judgment applications in adjudication

[13.14] CPR Part 24 sets out the rules and procedure where a party wishes to apply for summary judgment. If summary judgment is ordered, it represents an early knock-out blow for the claimant, who obtains a decision on the claim without having to proceed to a full trial.

[13.15] Either party may apply for summary judgment of its claim. In an action to enforce an adjudicator's decision, it will almost always be made by the party who won the adjudication. However, claims for negative declarations by the losing party are not unknown, and the court will entertain such claims where they have real utility. In *PC Harrington Contractors Ltd v Tyroddy Construction Ltd*,[9] the court declared three materially identical decisions, arising under different contracts between the same parties, and over which the same adjudicator had been appointed, to each be unenforceable, because it was clear that the adjudicator had fallen into the same jurisdictional error in each one, and there were another five adjudications on materially the same point over which the same adjudicator had already been appointed. It was also clear that the defendant to the declarations was asserting that the three decisions were valid. As well as declaring the first three decisions unenforceable, the court also gave declarations on the proper construction of the contract to assist the adjudicator as to how to deal properly with the same point arising in the remaining five referrals he had to decide.

[13.16] At the hearing, pursuant to CPR Part 24.2 the court will grant summary judgment if it considers that the defendant has no real prospect of successfully defending the claim or issue, or to put it another way, there is no real live triable issue between the parties. The defendant's prospects of success must be realistic as opposed to merely fanciful. This means that some credible evidence or basis has to be advanced, albeit that, at this stage, it does not have to be proved on the balance of probabilities.[10] The summary judgment application takes the form of an assessment of the merits of the defendant's objections to the adjudicator's decision. It is not a trial, or a mini-trial.[11]

---

[9] [2011] EWHC 813 (TCC), per Akenhead J at [22–27].
[10] *A.T. Stannard Ltd v James Tobutt and Thomas Tobutt* [2014] EWHC 3491 (TCC), per Akenhead J at [14].
[11] *Fileturn Ltd v Royal Garden Hotel Ltd* [2010] EWHC 1736 (TCC), per Edwards-Stuart J at [7].

[13.17] CPR 24 is, of course, not a mechanism purely for enforcing adjudicator's decisions; it was designed for use in conventional litigation and is effectively being pressed into service for the purpose of adjudication enforcement.[12] In the context of conventional litigation, CPR 24 applications are comparatively rare; it will only be sought in a very strong case, where the applicant can, in effect, say that either (a) the respondent's case is so fanciful on the facts that it can be dismissed out of hand (obviously a difficult submission to sustain in all save the clearest cases); or (b) that even assuming all the points the respondent takes are valid, the applicant is nevertheless bound to win. Obviously few cases fulfil those criteria. The respondent only needs to find a single material point on which it has an arguable case and summary judgment will not be granted.

[13.18] Why then is summary judgment, which is so difficult to achieve in other contexts, so readily granted in relation to adjudication enforcement? It is suggested there are at least four reasons.

[13.19] First, the nature of the subject matter. The court is not conducting a review or an appeal from the adjudicator's substantive reasoning. It simply has to decide whether the decision is enforceable. Second, the grounds upon which the court will impugn enforceability are very narrow indeed; in essence there are only two – whether the adjudicator acted in excess of his jurisdiction and, if he did not, whether his decision should nevertheless not be enforced because he did something materially unfair in how he conducted matters or produced his decision. Third, the relative ease with which the material to be reviewed to answer those questions can be identified; threshold points are essential matters of procedure (for instance, was the referral made within 7 days of the notice of adjudication, or was the decision delivered in 28 days?) or even if more involved (for instance, was there a contract for construction operations?) they normally will not involve significant factual disputes. If threshold jurisdiction is established (or conceded) then establishing whether the adjudicator conducted the adjudication in a materially unfair way is invariably a case of reviewing the decision, its reasoning and the parties' relevant submissions. Fourth and last, is policy: from the outset the courts have taken the view that adjudication is 'rough justice' and, in particular in relation to claims of breach of natural justice, it is only in the very clearest cases of unfairness that the court will decline to enforce.[13]

[13.20] The result of those four factors is that, in adjudication hearings, it is perhaps easier to arrive at a conclusion that the defendant's (the losing party's) resistance to the claimant's

---

[12] This was initially at the suggestion of Dyson J, as he then was, in *Macob v Morrison, supra*, in one of the first reported enforcement cases. As noted above, and the report of the judgment makes clear, until this guidance was given it is clear that the parties were unsure as to what tools to use to enforce, because the Act and the Scheme contained no regime to compel compliance; the claimant in *Macob* in fact sought declarations as to the amounts owing.

[13] This point has less force in relation to 'threshold' points, where judges have (to their sometimes evident regret) been compelled to accept unsympathetic technical points as depriving a decision of enforceability; see e.g. *Primus Build v Pompey Centre* [2009] EWHC 1487 (TCC), per Coulson J at [35]. But even where a decision has been reached in an unfair way and that unfairness only infects part of the decision, judges have sometimes expressed dissatisfaction, or at least misgivings, about their inability to enforce the unaffected parts – see *Pilon v Breyer Group* [2010] EWHC 837 (TCC), per Coulson J at [66].

claim to enforce is indeed fanciful, since there are a limited number of grounds on which the defendant to enforcement proceedings can successfully argue that the adjudicator's decision should not be enforced, or at least that there is a realistic prospect of being able to argue that the decision should not be enforced, and all the material is available to the court to decide those grounds there and then.

[13.21] Thus, it might be said that a party applying for summary judgment of an adjudicator's decision has a rather lower hurdle to overcome in order for the summary judgment to be granted than might be the case on conventional CPR 24 application.[14] This is not, in itself, particularly remarkable or a sign of any inconsistency of judicial approach, it is submitted. There are plenty of areas of the law where, for a variety of reasons, the courts take a robust line and in effect insulate a particular class of claims, or a particular bundle of rights arising, from what are properly considered extraneous matters or collateral disputes, which will simply be disregarded because to do so abets a useful general commercial purpose. Actions to enforce a dishonoured cheque, for example, are equally amenable to summary judgment in the vast majority of cases for the simple reason that a commercial policy decision has always been taken to treat that particular class of contracts as enforceable as if it were cash. So too with claims under on-demand bonds for similar reasons; and so too with the very limited grounds upon which arbitrator's decisions can be challenged under sections 66–68 of the Arbitration Act 1996. Adjudication enforcement can be seen as simply another example in the same vein.

[13.22] The general position with regard to the hearing of evidence at summary judgment applications is that the court will not permit substantial disputes of fact to be resolved. So for example, in *Beck Interiors Ltd v Dr Mario Luca Russo*,[15] Beck sought to enforce the decision of the adjudicator pursuant to a guarantee provided by Dr Russo for sums due under the contract. However, there was a conflict of factual evidence as to the effectiveness of the guarantee which could not be resolved at the summary judgment hearing, which led the court to conclude that there were real prospects that Dr Russo could successfully defend the claim against him. However, the courts have shown a willingness to adopt a more flexible approach to oral evidence in summary judgment applications for adjudication, than it might in other types of summary judgment applications. In *Able Construction (UK) Ltd v Forest Property Development Ltd*,[16] the court allowed oral submissions on behalf of the applicant because there was an issue that could only be resolved by oral submissions, and the issue was short and self-contained and hearing it would allow the court to decide on the summary judgment application, rather than adjourn it.

---

[14] *Canary Riverside Development (Private) Ltd v Timtec International Ltd*, 19 Const LJ 283, per Oliver J at [28–29].
[15] [2009] EWHC 3861 (QB), per Ramsey J at [42–45].
[16] [2009] EWHC 159 (TCC), per Coulson J at [15].

13.3.3 Options for commencing the claim

[13.23]   A party may apply to the TCC to enforce an adjudicator's decision by issuing a claim in accordance with the rules of either CPR Part 7 or Part 8, together with an application for summary judgment in accordance with CPR Part 24.

[13.24]   Issuing a claim in the TCC under CPR Part 7 is normally the appropriate procedure if the enforcement proceedings seek a judgment that awards money or where there is a mix of declaratory[17] and monetary issues.[18] If the enforcement proceedings raise a question that is unlikely to involve a substantial dispute of fact and no monetary judgment is sought (because, for example, the adjudicator's award was for declaratory relief only), the appropriate procedure is normally to bring a claim for a declaration under CPR Part 8.[19]

[13.25]   Where a party commences a claim through the CPR Part 8 procedure and there is a dispute about the suitably of that procedure to the nature of the claim, the court has the discretion to either convert the hearing into a Part 7 hearing,[20] or hear parts of the application that are suitable for Part 8 and then give directions for how the remaining parts are to be dealt with.[21]

[13.26]   One attraction of commencing an action through the Part 8 procedure is that it may provide a way of obtaining a final determination of the dispute, effectively 'leap-frogging' the adjudication enforcement process in place of a summary judgment. This is discussed further in Section 15.3.

13.3.4 Commencing the claim

[13.27]   Ordinarily, parties to litigation in the TCC must have complied with the Pre-Action Protocol for Construction and Engineering Disputes (the **Protocol**).[22] However, it is not necessary to comply with the Protocol where the claimant intends to make an application for summary judgment to enforce an adjudicator's decision.[23]

[13.28]   The lack of any formal requirement to comply with the Protocol before commencing adjudication enforcement proceedings notwithstanding, it is a question of fact in each case as to whether to preface any enforcement proceedings with correspondence with the other side. If, for example, the other side has made numerous and detailed challenges to jurisdiction during the adjudication and has taken part under protest, or if it set out

---

[17] An example of a declaratory decision may be a determination of the meaning of a particular clause in the contract, or a decision on whether the actions or inaction of a party were in breach of contract. A declaratory decision will not award money.
[18] Section 9.2.1, TCC Guide.
[19] Section 9.2.1, TCC Guide.
[20] *William Verry Ltd v North West London Communal Mikvah* [2004] EWHC 1300 (TCC), per Thornton J at [3].
[21] *Bovis Lend Lease Ltd v Triangle Development Ltd* [2002] EWHC 3123 (TCC), per Thornton J at [20–24].
[22] https://www.justice.gov.uk/courts/procedure-rules/civil/protocol/prot˙ced. Accessed 1 September 2015.
[23] Paragraph 1.2 of the Protocol.

its reasons for refusing to take part at the outset and then withdrew, it may be perfectly plain that there is no point in further correspondence and reasonable to move straight to enforcement proceedings.

[13.29] If on the other hand the adjudication appears to have gone off without any jurisdictional dispute but the other side then refuse to comply with the outcome, it may be worthwhile for the challenger to write to the other party setting out the reasons why the decision has not yet been complied with, seeking a response within a suitably short time frame (say five or seven days). If a response is not given within the time frame or the response is not satisfactory, it will be reasonable to commence proceedings.

[13.30] The claimant should lodge in the appropriate registry or court centre the following three documents:

- claim form
- application notice for summary judgment and abridgment of time for service of the acknowledgement of service
- witness statement in support of the application.

[13.31] Each document should be clearly marked as being a 'paper without notice adjudication enforcement claim and application for the urgent attention of a TCC judge'.[24] For documents where there is no obvious place to write this, such as an application notice or claim form, a 'text box' or similar inserted into the electronic draft works perfectly well. In witness statements and the particulars, the header or the footer is a good place to make the point clearly but to otherwise keep it out of the way.

(A) Claim form

[13.32] The claim form should, in accordance with CPR Part 7, identify:[25]

- the construction contract that complies with the requirements of the Act;
- brief details of the dispute;
- the basis of the adjudicator's jurisdiction;
- the procedural rules under which the adjudication was conducted;
- the adjudicator's decision;
- the relief sought;
- the grounds for relief;
- where the relief sought is money, in monetary claims, a claim for interest from the date on which the adjudicator's decision was due to have been complied with; and
- that the claimant has not complied with the Protocol because it intends to make an application for summary judgment of the claim.

---

[24] Section 9.2.5, TCC Guide.
[25] Section 9.2.3, TCC Guide.

[13.33] It is important that documents lodged with the court are clearly paginated or otherwise ordered in a way that is easily navigable; there are few things that annoy judges more than badly prepared papers. Remember too that the file as presented will go straight before a judge for him to make an order on paper, setting out directions, so making it easy for him to locate the relevant documents is particularly important.

[13.34] It is also important that the details of the claim articulated on the claim form are the same as the claim decided by the adjudicator. In *Redworth Construction v Brookdale Healthcare*,[26] HHJ Havery QC said that a party had elected to put its case on contract formation in one way before the adjudicator and could not therefore reprobate that decision by arguing on enforcement that the adjudicator's threshold jurisdiction could be justified by an entirely different case for contract formation. However, on the facts of the case in *Nickleby FM v Somerfield Stores*,[27] Akenhead J expressly disagreed with that approach, holding that there was no election in putting the case for formation in one way in the adjudication and then changing that analysis on enforcement. The election argument favoured by HHJ Havery QC in *Redworth* was based on cases in court, where the court had previously upheld a particular model of contract formation argued for such that there was a finding of fact on it. By contrast, an adjudicator considering a threshold point of jurisdiction about contract formation was simply making a non-binding enquiry into his jurisdiction, and so there was no binding election in putting that case one way in the adjudication and in another way on enforcement.

(B) Application notice

[13.35] The application notice[28] is made on CPR Form N244 and should set out clearly the procedural directions that are being sought. Those directions should be based on the standard directions in Appendix F of the TCC Guide. The application notice will apply for:

- an abridgement (i.e. a shortcut) of time for the various procedural steps required to be taken under the CPR; and
- summary judgment under CPR Part 24.

[13.36] It should also set out the time estimate for the hearing of the application.[29] All but the simplest contested enforcement hearing is likely to take half a day, and hearings taking a day are not unknown if multiple, discrete jurisdictional points are taken. In an extreme case, hearings of more than a day may occur. In *MBE Electrical Contractors Ltd v Honeywell Control Systems Ltd*[30] for example, it is clear that the judge only had time to deal with one of the jurisdictional objections (whether there should be a stay to arbitration), and gave judgment on that issue alone, with directions for the remaining issues to be tried subsequently. This case is very much the exception; the TCC generally strives to

---

[26] [2006] EWHC 1994 (TCC), per Havery J at [38–41].
[27] [2010] EWHC 1976 (TCC), per Akenhead J at [27–33].
[28] Section 9.2.4, TCC Guide.
[29] Section 9.2.10, TCC Guide.
[30] [2010] EWHC 2244 (TCC), per Akenhead J at [39].

deal with all matters quickly and in a single hearing, but for that to occur the parties need to give accurate time estimates. In MBE Electrical, the judge appears to criticise the elaborateness of the parties' submissions, which no doubt contributed to the case going part-heard.[31]

(C) Witness statement

[13.37] The claim form and application notice should normally be supported by a witness statement setting out the evidence relied on in support of both the adjudication enforcement claim and the associated procedural application.[32] Where the claimant is represented by a law firm, the witness statement will usually (but not always) be from the claimant's solicitor. As a minimum, the following documents should be exhibited to the witness statement:

- the notice of adjudication
- the adjudicator's agreement
- the relevant procedural rules and copies of any provisions of the Act relied upon[33]
- the adjudicator's decision.

[13.38] If the other side has taken a jurisdictional point already which is relevant to explaining the story (e.g. because it was raised and dealt with by the adjudicator), then of course it can be useful to summarise the objection and exhibit the key documents. But avoid explaining the other side's case in detail, and be careful not to say too much about why it is wrong. Setting up a case to knock it down is rarely required, and if the point is to be persisted with, then of course the other side will raise it in their response, presenting the chance to deal with it in reply. There is also the risk that the claimant will give away points for nothing, and thus enable the defendant to better prepare (or even amend) their jurisdictional objection to meet the points the claimant has pre-emptively taken.

[13.39] Avoid 'loading' the exhibit with every conceivable document, if at all possible. It annoys judges, and excessively long and detailed bundles may be penalised in costs.

[13.40] Generally restrict the witness statement to a brief summary of the facts as set out above and the key issue, plus an explanation of any factual matters that the witness statement can and should speak to that do not come out clearly in the documents. For instance, if the adjudicator said something relevant to enforcement, or to a jurisdictional challenge that the other side have already raised in a procedural hearing but there was no transcript of the hearing, it would certainly be something that should go in the witness statements. Avoid the temptation to give a running narrative of what the correspondence says; it annoys the judge, takes time (and is therefore expensive), and is often penalised with non-recovery of costs of such work on the ground that it was not required.

---

[31] Ibid, per Akenhead J at [2].
[32] Section 9.2.4, TCC Guide.
[33] Section 9.3.1, TCC Guide.

13.3.5 Directions

[13.41] A TCC judge will ordinarily provide directions in connection with the procedural application within three working days of receipt of the application notice at the courts.[34] Those directions will address:[35]

- that the claim form, supporting evidence and court order providing for the hearing are to be served on the defendant as soon as practicable, or sometimes by a particular date;
- the abridged period of time in which the defendant must file an acknowledgement of service;
- the time for service by the defendant of any witness statement(s) in opposition to the relief being sought (which will usually only be required if there is to be a hearing to decide the summary judgment application). In the event a witness statement or statements is or are required, the directions will provide the time for the service of those statements (usually 14 days from the date of the order). The defendant's witness statement(s) should set out its response to the claimant's application, including details as to why the application for summary judgment should be refused and any evidence in support;
- an early return date for the hearing of the application for summary judgment (usually no more than 28 days from the date of the order) and a note of the time required or allowed for that hearing;
- the relief the claimant seeks; and
- the defendant's liberty to apply to vary the terms of the order made.

[13.42] The TCC Guide[36] provides an example of the draft directions that may be given at Appendix F to the Guide. It is important for both parties to comply with the dates set by the court. In any event, but particularly in summary enforcement proceedings, the court is likely to disregard late submissions and will have little sympathy for applications to extend deadline dates. In *City Basements Ltd v Nordic Construction*,[37] Nordic made an application for relief from sanctions pursuant to CPR 3.9 four days after the deadline for the defence, so that it could serve a witness statement that it said it forgot to serve. Nordic did not pursue the application, but the judge nevertheless referred to it in his judgment and made it clear that in summary enforcement proceedings it is imperative to keep to the timetable and that there would have been 'no question' of granting the relief sought.

13.3.6 Responding to the claim

[13.43] On receipt of the claim documents, the defendant may proceed in one of four ways. It can admit the claim and comply forthwith with the adjudicator's decision. It might

---

[34] Section 9.2.5, TCC Guide.
[35] Sections 9.2.6–9.2.8, TCC Guide.
[36] Section 9.2.9, TCC Guide.
[37] [2014] EWHC 4817 (TCC), per Ramsey J at [7–12].

Enforcement: options and procedure 261

do this because, having considered the claimant's particulars, it now considers it has no defence to the enforcement action, or it may have forgotten or neglected to comply with the adjudicator's decision. Admitting the claim is likely to bring with it a demand from the claimant that its costs of commencing the enforcement action are paid and that if the adjudicator's decision was an award of money, interest is paid on the amount awarded from the due date up until the date it is paid.

[13.44] The second option is to try to settle the dispute with the other party, typically at an amount lower than the amount the adjudicator awarded. This may be a prudent course of action for the claimant because it wants to avoid incurring further professional fees or there is some uncertainty as to whether the adjudicator's award is valid. The prudent approach for the parties where a settlement is agreed is to ensure that it encompasses everything: the dispute, costs and interest. Problems can arise where elements are not included in the settlement. See Section 13.3.20 for further details.

[13.45] The third (and most common) is to serve a defence within the time period allowed by the judge's directions and then proceed to the enforcement hearing.

[13.46] Finally, the defendant may simply do nothing, refusing to acknowledge the claim or engage with the claimant or the court. This course of action is invariably a mistake – it will most likely lead to an application by the claimant for judgment in default together with an application that the defendant pays all the claimant's professional costs. Judgment in default is considered at Section 13.3.10.

13.3.7 Submission of cost budgets

[13.47] Unless the court directs otherwise, cost budgets are not required for enforcement proceedings, because in the TCC cost budgets do not have to be submitted until seven days before the first Case Management Conference.[38] Since all directions in enforcement proceedings are invariably made on paper without a hearing, no such Case Management Conference will take place.

13.3.8 Hearing bundle and skeletons

[13.48] In the absence of specific directions from the court, the parties should lodge, by 4 pm one clear working day before the hearing, a bundle containing the documents that will be required at the hearing.[39] This will normally include all the submissions and the decision in the adjudication, contractual and contemporaneous documentation and details of the costs incurred by both parties in bringing or defending the summary judgment application.

[13.49] The parties should also file and serve skeleton arguments and copies of any authorities that are to be relied on (preferably as an agreed joint bundle). The skeleton should set out why the adjudicator's decision is or is not enforceable. For a hearing that is expected

---
[38] CPR 3.13.
[39] Section 9.3.2, TCC Guide

to last half a day or less, the skeletons should be provided no later than 1 pm on the last working day before the hearing. For a hearing that is estimated to last more than half a day, the skeletons should be provided no later than 4 pm one clear working day before the hearing.[40]

13.3.9 Extent of the evidence to be submitted

[13.50] This is highly dependent on the issues raised at enforcement. However, because by their nature the enforcement proceedings are intended to be summary, it will invariably be the right approach to limit the extent of the evidence as far as possible. It is unlikely to be appropriate to conduct a detailed analysis of the submissions in the adjudication as well as inter-party correspondence.[41] The court has held that this kind of analysis is invariably not appropriate on an application to enforce, just as it would not be appropriate on an application for permission to appeal against an arbitrator's award under section 69 of the Arbitration Act 1996. As a very general rule of thumb, the greater the detail that a defendant invites the court to consider in resisting an application of this kind, the less likely it must be that it is the kind of plain case necessary to avoid an enforcement order. Indeed, the TCC Guide guidance on the conduct of adjudication enforcement proceedings stresses at Appendix C that the volume of documents should be relevant and kept to a minimum. One instance of where the bundle was both voluminous and largely irrelevant was in *NAP Anglia Ltd v Sun-Land Development Co. Ltd*,[42] where the judge remarked at length at the disorganised, voluminous, irrelevant documentation served in the proceedings.

13.3.10 Judgment in default and setting aside

[13.51] If and when it becomes clear that it is likely that a defendant is not going to participate in enforcement proceedings for one reason or another, then the best course of action for the claimant will be to make an application for judgment in default.[43] The rules and procedure for an application for judgment in default are set out at CPR 13. The point at which to proceed on this basis will usually be when an acknowledgement of service is not served within any abridged time. Of course, if an acknowledgment of service is lodged before any judgment in default is obtained, then matters may have to proceed along the usual course.

[13.52] The main benefit of making an application for judgment in default is the time and cost saving when set against an enforcement application and hearing. However, it is worth noting that if the claimant's enforcement claim seeks any relief other than monetary relief (e.g. declarations) then there will still need to be a short hearing before a judge at which the judge will scrutinise the relief sought before granting it; unlike a monetary claim, it is not possible to just enter judgment in default by purely administrative steps.

---

[40] Section 9.3.2, TCC Guide
[41] See *CG Group Ltd v Breyer Group plc* [2013] EWHC 2722 (TCC), per Akenhead J at [31(e)].
[42] [2011] EWHC 2846 (TCC), per Edwards-Stuart J at [81–82].
[43] *Coventry Scaffolding Company (London) Ltd v Lancsville Construction Ltd.* [2009] EWHC 2995 (TCC), per Akenhead J at [13–18]. See also Section 9.2.12, TCC Guide.

[13.53] If there is a good reason why the acknowledgment of service has not been filed, the defendant is protected by the right it has to apply to the court to have the judgment in default set aside. In essence, where the applicant can show that there is a real prospect of successfully defending the claim, the court will normally exercise its discretion to set aside the judgment in default.[44] The court exercised its discretion in *M Rohde Construction v Nicholas Markham-David*.[45] The judge said that, in determining whether to set aside, he was required to consider (a) the prejudice suffered by the claimant if the judgment was set aside; (b) the prejudice which the defendant would suffer if it was not set aside; (c) the interests of justice; and (d) all the circumstances of the case. All of these factors were to be considered having regard to the overriding objective set out in Part 1 of the Civil Procedure Rules. Notwithstanding the fact that in that case the claimant made its application four years after judgment in default (although for most of that time it had been unaware of the judgment entered against it), there was a triable issue and therefore it was right to set the judgment aside.

13.3.11 Representation

[13.54] Almost always, each party to an adjudication enforcement hearing is represented by a firm of solicitors and an advocate, who may be a solicitor from the instructed firm or (more usually) a barrister. The solicitor will ordinarily be responsible for everything other than the drafting of the skeleton and the advocacy at the hearing. Whereas solicitors are usually instructed in advance of an adjudication, advocates may only be instructed where there is to be an enforcement action.

[13.55] That said, there is often advantage in instructing an advocate sooner rather than later, when he can not only consider the merits of the arguments being run, but also advise on any further points that might be taken, and the evidence that should be adduced in support. The danger of instructing the advocate late on is that his ability to advise on further points and mould the case appropriately will be seriously curtailed. At best, such action will be done in haste and at further cost. At worst, it may simply be too late to run that alternative or better case.

[13.56] A further point is that a party may lose an unnoticed but good argument to challenge a decision simply by taking a step which recognises its validity before that defence is recognised; a later attempt to go back on that step and challenge enforcement may then be rejected by the court as an attempt to 'approbate and reprobate' the decision. See Section 16.4.6 for more on this point.

[13.57] Before selecting an advocate to instruct, it is worthwhile researching which advocates are experienced with adjudication enforcement hearings. It may also be advantageous to select an advocate who has had experience (preferably recent) of the grounds on which enforcement of the adjudicator's decision is being resisted. The case law on this area is detailed, develops very quickly, and is inherently specialist in nature. Details of how to

---

[44] CPR 13.3(1).
[45] [2006] EWHC 814 (TCC), per Jackson J at [40–51].

search for advocates with experience of enforcement hearings or of particular issues are set out in the introduction to Appendix 8.

[13.58] The parties should also be mindful of the size of their legal team, particularly if the amount of the decision is comparatively modest. In some cases, the court's written judgment reveals that two barristers (a Queen's Counsel and a Junior) and a firm of solicitors have represented a party. While the sums at stake and the complexity of the issues in hand may justify such weighty representation, it will be very much the exception rather than the norm for two reasons. First, the courts are unlikely to be convinced by anything other than straightforward arguments as to why an adjudicator's decision should be nullified or stayed. Second, the courts adopt a niggardly approach towards the percentage of costs a successful party is entitled to recover from the losing party. Where a party, as a result of a party being represented by numerous lawyers, incurs substantial fees, it may find that it is unable to recover a substantial proportion of them from the other party should its application or defence be successful. See Section 13.3.16 for more detail on the assessment of costs.

13.3.12 Timetable to a decision

[13.59] The court will endeavour to list an application to enforce an adjudicator's decision 28 days from the issued date of the claim form,[46] although it can sometimes take up to six weeks. Where the claimant has issued a summary judgment application at the same time as the claim form, the judge will give the defendant 14 days to put in a response witness statement. There may be a further short period (under a week) for a reply witness statement. After that, bundles are exchanged and skeleton arguments submitted and the hearing can take place within another week to two weeks. In some hearings, the judge will give a decision at the hearing and will not commit it to writing. However, where the judge considers it necessary to do so, judgment will be reserved and handed down in writing, usually no more than two weeks after the hearing.

13.3.13 The decision

[13.60] The court has three options:

(1) grant the application for summary judgment (i.e. enforce the decision);
(2) reject the application for summary judgment, and strike out or otherwise dismiss the claim (i.e. hold the decision unenforceable); or
(3) reject the application for summary judgment and give permission to defend the claim at trial.

[13.61] The court will give reasons for the decision, sometimes in an *ex tempore* judgment, but mostly (if matters are more complex or of wider importance) in a written judgment.

[13.62] In the vast majority of cases, the court will take one of the first two options, because it can make a decision one way or another – either it will grant summary judgment or it will

---

[46]Section 9.2.8, TCC Guide and *Pochin Construction Ltd v Liberty Property (G.P.) Ltd* [2014] EWHC 2919 (TCC), per Akenhead J at [5].

reject it and strike out or otherwise dismiss the whole of the claim, and that will be the end of the case. This is not always expressly stated in the resulting minute of order, but where the claimant's summary judgment application fails in full, because for instance the court makes a finding as a matter of fact that there has in fact been a breach of natural justice or because of a positive finding that the adjudicator lacked jurisdiction, then it follows that not only the application, but also the whole of the claim fails, it is submitted. It is difficult to see how there could be a trial over such issues given that the judge has already rejected them in dismissing the summary judgment application.

[13.63] Permission will only be given where the evidence before the court does not allow the judge to come to a decision on a particular issue. Acknowledging the function of adjudication to resolve the dispute quickly and the court's policy on enforcement, permission to defend will rarely be given.

13.3.14 The effect of the court's decision

[13.64] The outcome of adjudication decisions can of course be 'challenged' in subsequent high court or arbitral proceedings; that is in their very nature. But, of course, it is misleading to speak in any technical sense of 'challenging' the adjudicator's decision by subsequent litigation or arbitration; what the court is doing is finally deciding the underlying dispute.

[13.65] However, where, on an application for summary judgment, the court issues a decision granting or declining summary judgment, it is not open to an arbitrator in a subsequent arbitration hearing, or a court (of equal or lower standing) in subsequent litigation, or an adjudicator in subsequent adjudications to impugn the terms of that judgment, since it is binding for being *res judicata*. It is only in the most exceptional circumstances that a party in subsequent proceedings would be permitted to adduce further material relevant to an issue already decided by the court. Thus, in *Michael John Construction Ltd v St Peter's Rugby Football Club*,[47] Michael John Construction tried to reopen an issue relating to the identity of the parties to the contract. The arbitrator allowed the club to submit additional evidence on the issue of who was the employer and then found that he had jurisdiction to hear the claim. The court found that the arbitrator did not have the jurisdiction to do this, which invalidated the arbitrator's decision.

[13.66] It is not always a straightforward matter to determine from the judgment which parts of it are findings of the court that bind the parties and which are general observations or a summary of the facts presented to the court; it is, after all, the decision which binds the parties, not the reasons. Similar issues can arise when the court is trying to determine whether a dispute referred to adjudication is similar to or the same as one that has been decided in a previous adjudication.[48] Therefore, in the event that a losing party to an adjudication wishes to challenge the adjudicator's decision by referring the dispute to litigation or arbitration, it is good practice to sift through the court's decision in order to extract the findings made by the court so that the party knows the limits of what has already been decided.

---

[47] [2007] EWHC 1857 (TCC), per Wilcox J at [35–46].
[48] See Section 16.5.7.

[13.67] This can be very important, because it is obvious that notwithstanding the ostensibly temporary nature of an enforceable adjudicator's decision, the decision, if wrong, can have a major and permanent impact on the parties' rights.

[13.68] To take a simple example, if the adjudicator decided that the contract machinery had broken down irretrievably so that 'time was at large' (as contractors often argue, in order to escape LADs deduction, and also to avoid the burden of having to make formal extension of time applications), the employer's rights to terminate the contractor's employment under the contract for delay may be limited to a situation if the contractor committed a repudiatory breach in failing to complete within reasonable time. That position would remain unless and until that decision was overturned, which would be unlikely to happen before either termination or practical completion. It would probably be of very little use to the employer to seek a final determination of the 'time at large' point after the works had finished or after he had terminated at common law; a final determination by the court or arbitrator of that point could not 'put the clock back' in any practical way. On the other hand if the employer successfully resisted enforcement of that decision and went on to terminate pursuant to the contract machinery (which permitted termination where the contractor was X weeks in culpable delay), the contractor could not be heard to say that such action was not permissible.

[13.69] This example demonstrates that it can be essential to establish what the adjudicator has decided and what the court has upheld, because in practical terms it may not always prove possible to unwind the consequences of a court's finding one way or the other.

13.3.15 Setting aside a summary judgment

[13.70] In limited circumstances and always at the court's discretion, a party may make an application to set aside a summary judgment.[49] The court's discretion will normally be exercised in accordance with CPR 3.9(1) which is headed 'relief from sanctions'. That rule lists a number of factors including whether the application for the relief sought has been made properly and whether there is a good explanation for the failure. It has been held[50] that failure to make an application to set aside promptly after summary judgment (the guidance given is that 30 days after judgment will be too long) will scupper it. Given the high importance that the court attaches to swift enforcement of adjudicator's decisions, it is unlikely that, save in the most truly exceptional of cases, the court will permit judgment on an enforcement hearing to be set aside.

13.3.16 Costs: basis of assessment

(A) Standard or indemnity

[13.71] The costs of any enforcement application are at the discretion of the court, within the guidelines set out at CPR Part 44.3 and 44.4. The general rule that costs follow the event

---

[49] CPR 24, PD 8.
[50] *Nageh v Richard Giddings & Another* [2006] EWHC 3240 (TCC), per Coulson J at [11–14].

will usually apply to the costs of the enforcement proceedings. This means, subject to the following, that the successful party will obtain an order from the court that the professional costs it has incurred preparing for and participating in the proceedings are paid either entirely or in the majority by the losing party.

[13.72] In the context of adjudication enforcement proceedings, the court applies one of two bases to assess the costs: standard or indemnity.[51] If costs are ordered to be assessed on the standard basis, the costs judge will only allow costs to be recovered which are proportionate and either reasonably incurred or reasonable in amount. Costs which are disproportionate in amount may be disallowed or reduced even if they were reasonably or necessarily incurred.[52] Where there is any doubt as to whether costs comply with these requirements, that doubt will be resolved in favour of the paying party. Note that the court's approach to the assessment of costs on a standard basis has altered to this stricter method of assessment for cases commenced after 1 April 2013.[53]

[13.73] If costs are ordered to be assessed on the indemnity basis, costs will only be recovered which are reasonably incurred and reasonable in amount. The test of proportionality does not arise as there is a presumption of proportionality in favour of the receiving party.[54] This shifts the burden onto the paying party to show that the costs being claimed by the winning party are unreasonable. While this increases the likelihood that the paying party will have to pay a higher percentage of the winning party's costs, unreasonable costs will still be penalised.[55]

[13.74] The court has absolute discretion over which basis it assesses costs under, although by far the most common method of assessment is on the standard basis. The court need not choose one or the other method, it may split the costs so that some are paid on an indemnity basis and the remainder on a standard basis.[56] As a general rule, the assessment of costs on a standard basis tends to reduce a costs bill by 25–30%, while the indemnity costs bill usually tends to reduce the costs bill by as little as 5–10%.

[13.75] The imposition of indemnity costs will be made where the paying party has conducted itself in a particularly egregious way before or during the proceedings. In other words, there has to be something to take the case out of the norm, although it is not necessary for the circumstances to be so extraneous that they amount to a lack of moral probity.[57] So, where the judge considered that the defendant had no defence to the claim for enforcement, or where a summary judgment application is made and then before the hearing the court is told that the application will not be contested, it will award costs on that basis.[58] Equally, it will award indemnity costs where the defendant did not comply

---

[51] CPR 44.4(1).
[52] CPR 44.3 and PD 44.6.
[53] See in particular CPR 44.3(2)(a) and CPR 44.3(5), amended on 1 April 2013.
[54] CPR 44.3 and PD 44.6.
[55] *Gipping Construction Ltd v Eaves Ltd* [2008] EWHC 3134 (TCC), per Akenhead J at [13–19].
[56] *O'Donnell Developments Ltd v Build Ability Ltd* [2009] EWHC 3388 (TCC), per Ramsey J at [58–69].
[57] *Eurocom Ltd v Siemens plc*, Unreported, 12 February 2015, per Ramsey J at [4].
[58] *Gray & Sons Builders (Bedford) Ltd v Essential Box Company Ltd* [2006] EWHC 2520 (TCC), per Coulson J at [7–13].

with the adjudicator's decision and then did not defend the enforcement proceedings at all,[59] or agreed to pay the awarded sum a few days before the enforcement hearing,[60] or where an application for summary judgment is deemed to be opposed unreasonably, because the respondent advances a number of spurious defences that it drops shortly before the enforcement hearing.[61] Other circumstances may include time spent on vexatious submissions or issues, whether part of the claim (such as the application for a stay) was dropped at the start of or during the hearing,[62] whether defences that the adjudicator was without jurisdiction or breached the rules of natural justice had little merit,[63] a failure to take up without prejudice offers to settle the dispute[64] and where there was a strong prima facie case of fraud.[65] In *Savoye and Savoye Ltd v Spicers Ltd*,[66] Akenhead J helpfully recited some principles that have been identified in cases outside the context of adjudication for when indemnity costs might be awarded.

(B) Summary or detailed assessment

[13.76] Costs will either be assessed summarily (either at the hearing or by the same judge in his judgment) or subjected to a detailed assessment, a process that requires the parties to follow the procedure set out in CPR 47 and the associated practice direction. In the overwhelming majority of enforcement cases, costs are assessed summarily, owing to the fact that the hearing rarely lasts more than a day and the costs claimed are rarely substantial enough to merit the time, effort and cost associated with a detailed assessment. In the rare case where detailed assessment is ordered, the court's standard practice is to order a payment on account pending detailed assessment for the minimum amount it thinks the claimant will recover; typically a payment on account in the range of 30–50% of the claimed costs might be expected.

(C) Issue based and proportionate based assessments

[13.77] Although relatively unusual, it is open to the court in appropriate cases to order costs on an 'issues' basis, that is, by awarding each party its costs of and occasioned by its success on individual issues in the litigation. Although the courts are moving against issue based cost orders, such an order will be made where a party had pursued a defence unreasonably.[67] It is also open to the court to make a 'proportionate costs order'. This approach

---

[59] *Pochin Construction Ltd v Liberty Property (G.P.) Ltd* [2014] EWHC 2919 (TCC), per Akenhead J at [10–13].
[60] *Wates Construction Ltd v HGP Greentree Allchurch Evans Ltd* [2005] EWHC 2174 (TCC) per Coulson J at [7–10].
[61] *O'Donnell Developments Ltd v Build Ability Ltd* [2009] EWHC 3388 (TCC), per Ramsey J at [67].
[62] *Allied P&L Ltd v Paradigm Housing Group Ltd* [2009] EWHC 2890 (TCC), per Akenhead J at [48–55].
[63] *CG Group Ltd v Breyer Group plc* [2013] EWHC 2959 (TCC), per Akenhead J at [2].
[64] *CG Group Ltd v Breyer Group plc* [2013] EWHC 2959 (TCC), per Akenhead J at [4–5].
[65] *Eurocom Ltd v Siemens plc*, Unreported, 12 February 2015, per Ramsey J at [4].
[66] *Savoye and Savoye Ltd v Spicers Ltd* [2015] EWHC 33 (TCC), per Akenhead J at [5–10].
[67] *Eurocom Ltd v Siemens plc*, Unreported, 12 February 2015, per Ramsey J at [4].

involves determining which party has been successful overall in the proceedings and, taking into account the issues upon which each party has been successful, fixing the percentage proportion of its overall costs to those issues. The approach the court should take when making a proportionate costs order was described by Akenhead J in *Enterprise Managed Services Ltd v Tony McFadden Utilities Ltd*.[68]

13.3.17 Costs: assessment of the bill of costs

[13.78] Where costs are assessed summarily, the judge is required to apply the two-stage approach explained in *Lownds v Home Office*.[69] First, he should assess whether, on a global approach, the costs claimed were proportionate, having regard to the various considerations identified in CPR Part 44.5(3). Having concluded that the costs claimed were, overall, not disproportionate, the judge must satisfy himself that 'each item should have been reasonably incurred and the cost for that item should have been reasonable' (see CPR Part 44.4(2)).[70] In practice, that means the court will make an assessment as to whether the rates used, the hours spent and therefore the amount claimed in costs by the winning party's professional advisers are reasonable. If it considers that they are not, it will reduce the sums claimed, either by ordering that a percentage of the amount claimed is paid or by ordering an ascertained sum. The court has offered the following guidance on what sorts of matters it will have regard to when assessing proportionality and reasonableness of costs in an adjudication enforcement case.[71]

(a) The relationship between the amount of costs claimed for and said to have been incurred and the amount in issue. Thus, for example, if the amount in issue in the claim was £100,000 but the costs claimed for are £1 million, absent other explanations the costs may be said to be disproportionate.

(b) The amount of time said to have been spent by solicitors and barristers in relation to the total length of the hearing(s). For example, if 3,000 hours of lawyers time is incurred on a case which involves only a one day hearing, that might well point to a disproportionate incurrence of time spent.

(c) In the context of time spent, the Court can have regard to the extent to which the lawyers for the party claiming costs and the party itself has incurred cost and spent time before the Court proceedings in connection with any other contractual dispute resolution machinery agreed upon between the parties. Here, for instance, there was provision for adjudication, in which the parties were required to pay their own costs of that process. If and to the extent that the work in connection with the adjudication duplicates the work done in the Court proceedings, or, put another way, if the same issue arises and was addressed in the Court proceedings as in the adjudication, it may be disproportionate to expend anew what is repetitious effort and time in the later proceedings.

(d) The extent to which the case is a test case or in the nature of a test case.

---

[68] [2010] EWHC 1506 (TCC), per Akenhead J at [7–14].
[69] [2002] EWCA Civ 365 at [31].
[70] *Bryen & Langley Ltd v Martin Boston* [2005] EWCA Civ 973, per Rimer LJ at [48–55].
[71] *Savoye and Savoye Ltd v Spicers Ltd* [2015] EWHC 33 (TCC), per Akenhead J at [17].

(e) The importance of the case to either party. If for instance an individual or a company is being sued for everything which he, she or it is worth, it may not be disproportionate for that individual to engage a QC even if the amount in issue is objectively not very large.

[13.79] Further factors that the court will consider are whether the claim was complicated, time spent on submissions, the length of the hearing, the sums in dispute, the fee rate charged by solicitors and barristers, issues that were not decided in favour of the party that was overall successful, whether part of the claim (such as the application for a stay) was dropped at the start of or during the hearing, whether the volume of documentation submitted by the claimant was excessive,[72] the existence of without prejudice offers to settle the claim[73] and whether such offers were in the full amount of the judgment sum, but were proposed to be paid in instalments, rather than in one amount.[74] In making an assessment of reasonableness, the court should not simply compare the winning party's costs with those of the losing party and, if they are the same, assume the winning party's costs are reasonable and award them.[75]

[13.80] In *Allied P&L Ltd v Paradigm Housing Group Ltd*,[76] Akenhead J set out what the court considers a reasonable level of costs:

> It is rare in the TCC in London that relatively simple contested summary adjudication enforcement applications cost more than £15,000 to £20,000 and often on the simpler applications it is less than £10,000.

[13.81] In *Imtech Inviron Ltd v Loppingdale Plant Ltd*,[77] Edwards-Stuart J said:

> It is my experience that the costs incurred by a claimant in applications to enforce adjudicators' awards range, typically, from about £15,000 to about £25,000, or perhaps a little more, excluding court fees.
>
> ...
>
> It is also a matter of common observation that the costs of a claimant in an application [to summarily enforce an adjudicator's decision], will, all other things being equal, be higher than those incurred on behalf of a defendat. The difference is usually between about 20% and 30%, depending on the circumstances. This is because the claimant's solicitors have additional tasks, such as that of preparing the application and the bundles of documents that are required to support it, liaising with the court about possible hearing dates, preparing the bundles of documents for the hearing and so on.

---

[72] *Mead General Building Ltd v Dartmoor Properties Ltd* [2009] EWHC 200 (TCC), per Coulson J at [24–27].
[73] *Jacques (t/a C & E Jacques Partnership) v Ensign Contractors Ltd* [2009] EWHC 3383 (TCC), per Akenhead J at [54–60].
[74] *Gray & Sons Builders (Bedford) Ltd v Essential Box Company Ltd* [2006] EWHC 2520 (TCC), per Coulson J at [14–20].
[75] *Bryen & Langley Ltd v Martin Boston* [2005] EWCA Civ 973, per Rimer LJ at [48–55].
[76] [2009] EWHC 2890 (TCC), per Akenhead J at [47].
[77] [2014] EWHC 4109 (TCC), per Edwards-Stuart J at [3–5].

[13.82] In *Jacques and another (t/a C&E Jacques Partnership) v Ensign Contractors Ltd*,[78] Akenhead J expressed surprise at the level of the employer's costs (some £27,000) for what he described as a relatively simple claim and application for summary judgment. The employer's costs were summarily assessed at £20,000.

[13.83] Each case will turn on its own facts and so while parties should certainly be mindful of the judges' dicta in the above cases, they do not set a hard and fast rule or a 'tariff' of recoverable costs.[79] Indeed, in the same year as *Allied* and *Jacques*, Akenhead J summarily assessed costs in another case at £45,000.[80] More recently, the same judge has assessed costs at £96,000 (albeit reduced from a claimed £202,000).[81]

[13.84] In *Devon County Council v Celtic Bioenergy Ltd*[82] the court considered costs incurred in a claim for declaratory relief and an earlier injunction hearing. In relation to the injunction, Devon served a schedule of costs 18 minutes late. Celtic sought to penalise Devon for the late service. The court held that the Devon's delay was 'trivial' and said of Celtic's conduct that 'the substantive irrelevance of the failure, and the complete absence of any disadvantage to Celtic' meant that no deduction should be made. In relation to the claim for declaratory relief, the court held that:

> To incur costs in excess of £60,000 for a 2.5 hour application such as this is clearly disproportionate by a significant margin, even allowing for the fact that the hearing eventually took just under 4 hours ... I do not accept that it required over 28 hours of solicitors' time and over 100 hours of Knowles' time (or anything like it) to prepare Celtic's case for the hearing.

[13.85] Furthermore, Knowles' costs were significantly reduced because the rate it was charging was well beyond the Grade A London rate, notwithstanding the fact that Knowles were neither solicitors nor did they practise in London. The court cut Celtic's claim in half, before applying a reduction of 30% to take account of the fact that it had succeeded in its claim. It was entitled to recover the remaining 70% from Devon.[83]

[13.86] Where a claim is admitted in full before the hearing, the court may order in certain circumstances that the defendant (who admitted the claim) is only required to pay a fixed fee of £100, pursuant to CPR 45.1. However, except in the clearest of circumstances, such an order is unlikely in proceedings to enforce an adjudicator's decision.[84]

---

[78] [2009] EWHC 3383, per Akenhead J at [54–60].

[79] But there is some suggestion that with the advent of formal costs budgeting – for which the TCC operated the pilot scheme – judges are now becoming more interventionist and purposive in relation to costs, and that the relevant factors to be taken into account on costs budgeting mean that they are (at the very least) more comfortable with the idea of fixing costs not merely by reference to the complexity of the issues raised but also to the value of the case, which might be said to come close to a tariff-type structure.

[80] *Balfour Beatty Engineering Services (HY) Ltd v Shepherd Construction Ltd* [2009] EWHC 2218 (TCC), per Akenhead at [84–86].

[81] *Savoye and Savoye Ltd v Spicers Ltd* [2015] EWHC 33 (TCC), per Akenhead J at [18–25].

[82] [2014] EWHC 309 (TCC), per Stuart-Smith J at [8–11].

[83] [2014] EWHC 309 (TCC), per Stuart-Smith J at [14–19].

[84] *Amber Construction Services Ltd v London Interspace HG Ltd* [2007] EWHC 3042 (TCC), per Akenhead J at [18–25].

13.3.18 Costs: ATE insurance and conditional fee arrangements

[13.87] After the event (ATE) insurance is a type of legal expenses insurance policy that provides cover for the legal costs incurred in the pursuit or defence of dispute. Conditional fee arrangements (CFA) are agreements between solicitors or barristers and their clients, providing for an uplift, or success fee, should certain criteria within the agreement be met. The main benefit of ATE insurance and CFAs is that the party who has secured such an arrangement will, depending on the terms of the arrangement and the outcome of the dispute, pay less in legal fees than it otherwise would. The court has considered the rules relating to CFAs and ATEs and has provided guidance on how the costs arising from such arrangements should be assessed.[85]

> It needs to be borne in mind that the large majority of reported cases on adjudication enforcements are successful and indeed in almost every case the claimants are sufficiently confident to pursue summary judgment applications on the basis that there is no realistic defence. It must follow that courts, particularly the TCC which deals with virtually all such cases, will think long and hard about allowing substantial CFA mark-ups, particularly when there is a summary judgment application by the party with the CFA. It is important that claimants do not use CFAs and ATE insurance primarily as a commercial threat to defendants. It is legitimate for the Court to ask itself whether, in any particular case, a CFA or ATE Insurance was a reasonable and proportionate arrangement to make.

[13.88] In that case, the successful party had procured both ATE insurance and a CFA. The court only allowed 20% of the insurance premium and a 20% uplift in the solicitor's costs.

[13.89] Important changes to the Civil Procedure Rules means that the cost of ATE insurance and CFA insurance is not recoverable from the losing party, where the agreement was reached after 1 April 2013.[86]

13.3.19 Costs: interest

[13.90] Where money is claimed, the court has discretion[87] to award interest on the amount awarded by the court from the date the cause of action arose to the date it is paid. In the context of adjudication, the cause of action is said to arise on the date the adjudicator ordered payment to be made. The court may also apply a punitive rate of interest where the defendant to the enforcement proceedings can show no good reason why the sum ordered has not been paid.[88]

---

[85] *Redwing Construction Ltd v Charles Wishart* [2011] EWHC 19 (TCC), per Akenhead J at [15].
[86] http://www.justice.gov.uk/civil-justice-reforms/main-changes. Accessed on 1 May 2015.
[87] Section 35A of the Senior Courts Act 1981.
[88] See the Late Payment of Commercial Debts (Interest) Act 1998 and *Able Construction (UK) Ltd v Forest Property Development Ltd* [2009] EWHC 159 (TCC), per Coulson J at [20].

[13.91] Where the adjudicator decides the rate and amount of interest the losing party must pay it. The court will not interfere with that decision, even if it is wrong in fact or in law.[89]

13.3.20 Costs: settlement reached before summary judgment

[13.92] Sometimes, only when the winning party commences enforcement proceedings will the losing party agree to pay part or the entire amount awarded by the adjudicator. Clearly, the sensible course of action is to ensure that the settlement sum relates to the disputed issues and all related costs, such as the costs of the enforcement proceedings. But who is liable for costs if they do not form part of the settlement?

[13.93] This was the case in *Rokvic v Peacock*,[90] where Peacock agreed to pay and did pay Miss Rokvic a sum in settlement of the claim, provided she discontinued proceedings. Crucially however, the settlement did not include the costs of the enforcement proceedings, and the court rules provide that discontinuance 'does not affect proceedings to deal with any question of costs'.[91] The costs issue came before the court. It noted that the general position is that under CPR 38.6(1), a claimant who discontinues is liable for the defendant's costs, unless the court orders otherwise. However, the court held that the rule did not apply in this case where the whole reason the claimant discontinued was because the defendant agreed to pay a sum to settle the dispute. The court held that the defendant was liable to pay the claimant's costs, which in the circumstances it reduced from a claimed amount of £17,000 to £5,500.

[13.94] A similar position was reached in *Southern Electric v Mead Realisations*.[92] Mead had been ordered to pay around £125,000. It could not pay it within seven days of the adjudicator's decision as ordered and so Southern Electric commenced enforcement proceedings. Subsequently, Mead offered to pay the amount owing in tranches, which Southern Electric accepted. The question then was who was liable for the cost of the court proceedings. The court held that by offering to make a final balance payment, Mead had offered to pay interest and any other ancillary relief that the claimant was seeking (the claim form and particulars of claim expressly claimed costs). Therefore, the defendant's offer included the claimant's costs of the proceedings.

13.3.21 Appealing a judgment of the court

[13.95] The details of the process and legitimate basis of the right to appeal are outside the scope of this book. Suffice to say that the losing party to a summary judgment application may

---

[89] *McConnell Dowell Constructors (Aust) Pty Ltd v National Grid Gas plc (formerly Transco plc)* [2006] EWHC 2551 (TCC), per Jackson J at [48].
[90] [2014] EWHC 3729 (TCC), per Akenhead J at [7–10].
[91] CPR 38.5(3).
[92] [2009] EWHC 2947 (TCC), per Akenhead J at [13–19].

consider that the judgment is wrong. In that case, it has a right to make an application to appeal to (usually) the next level of court in the court hierarchy. An appeal may only be brought with the permission of the court in which the decision was given, or by application to the next court in the hierarchy. A court will only allow the appeal (in other words reverse the decision of the lower court) where the decision of the lower court was either (a) an error of law, fact or of the court's discretion; or (b) unjust because of a serious procedural or other irregularity in the proceedings in the lower court. The procedure for appeals is set out in CPR 52 and its practice directions. It is worth noting that while appeals are not unheard of, they are rare. The grounds for appeal will need to be robust and well thought out in order for permission to be granted. While permission to appeal is usually made some time after the summary judgment application, not infrequently the losing parties' representatives will make an application for appeal to the TCC judge immediately at the end of the summary judgment application hearing. This can be a risky, and for the most part has been unsuccessful. There is perhaps no better demonstration of a botched attempt to appeal during a summary judgment application hearing than in *Beck Peppiatt Ltd v Norwest Holst Construction Ltd*.[93]

13.3.22 Staying enforcement proceedings where there is an arbitration agreement (s. 9 Arbitration Act 1996)

[13.96] Where parties have entered into an agreement to finally resolve disputes by arbitration and one party commences High Court proceedings to enforce an adjudicator's decision, there are cases where the other party has applied to the court for a stay of those proceedings pursuant to section 9 of the Arbitration Act 1996. Section 9 provides:

> (1) A party to an arbitration agreement against whom legal proceedings are brought (whether by way of claim or counterclaim) in respect of a matter which under the agreement is to be referred to arbitration may (upon notice to the other parties to the proceedings) apply to the court in which the proceedings have been brought to stay the proceedings so far as they concern that matter.
>
> …
>
> (4) On an application under this section the court shall grant a stay unless satisfied that the arbitration agreement is null and void, inoperative, or incapable of being performed.
>
> …

[13.97] Clearly, in order for a section 9 application to be successful at all, there has to be a binding arbitration agreement.[94] That aside, the courts have generally not granted a stay where

---

[93] [2003] EWHC 822 (TCC), per Forbes J at [22].
[94] *Walter Llewllyn & Sons Ltd and Rok Building Ltd v Excel Brickwork Ltd* [2010] EWHC 3415 (TCC), per Akenhead J at [21–25].

the court proceedings are for the purpose of enforcing an adjudicator's decision, since to do so would delay the enforcement of an adjudicator's decision. The court has offered this helpful guidance on how it should address such situations.[95]

> One has in the last-mentioned provisions what appears to me to be a clear articulation of the "pay now, argue later" policy which underlies Part II of the Construction Act and the Scheme itself. That policy would be stultified if a reference to arbitration under clause 30.3 were to put a brake, whether permanently or otherwise, on the carrying through of the adjudication process to enforcement. Honeywell is free to take any points which are open to it in the arbitration, but this does not entitle it to set on one side the Scheme which is part and parcel of the agreement into which it entered. Objections as to the adjudicator's jurisdiction, if they are to bar enforcement of his award, will have to be made in the enforcement proceedings. Questions which relate to the merits of the dispute must be left to the arbitration. In that way, proper weight is given both to the arbitration clause and to the importation of the Scheme into the contract.

[13.98] The cases that have addressed this point are listed in Appendix 8. There does not, as yet, appear to have been any reported case in which a party has been successful in obtaining a stay of adjudication enforcement proceedings to arbitration. The policy reasons for that reluctance are clear: the TCC wants to enforce adjudication decisions summarily to uphold the 'pay now, argue later' philosophy behind the Act. Permitting the parties to contract out of rapid, certain and clear TCC enforcement and into enforcement via arbitration, which is typically slower and where the arbitrator does not usually have power to grant summary judgment (merely an expedited procedure) would substantially frustrate that.

[13.99] That said, the jurisprudential basis for essentially ignoring a widely drawn arbitration clause in favour of TCC enforcement is not brilliantly clear.[96] Indeed, there is some suggestion in the very earliest case on adjudication enforcement that a sufficiently widely drawn arbitration clause would indeed be apt to 'catch' adjudication enforcement. In *Macob Civil Engineering v Morrison Construction Ltd,* Dyson J appears to have rejected the claimant's wider argument that the validity of an adjudicator's decision could never be a matter for the arbitrator, holding that 'there can be no objection in principle to the parties to a construction contract giving an arbitrator the power to decide such questions'.[97] Dyson J went on to find that in order to invoke a stay to arbitration, the losing party must necessarily be indicating that there was indeed a decision in existence capable of being referred; thus it could not approbate and reprobate the decision, and had to pay it.

---

[95] *MBE Electrical Contractors Ltd v Honeywell Control Systems Ltd* [2010] EWHC 2244 (TCC), per Langan J at [26–37].
[96] See the commentary to this effect by the editors of the Building Law Reports in *MBE Electrical Contractors Ltd v Honeywell Control Systems Ltd* [2010] BLR 561.
[97] [1999] BLR 93, per Dyson J at [24].

[13.100] This reasoning is hard to follow, it is submitted; a party does not refer decisions to arbitration, it refers disputes to arbitration, including logically a dispute about whether there is an enforceable decision at all. It may also be worth noting in this context that Dyson J appeared to base his reasoning on the stay application at least in part by analogy to some public law cases which had not been the subject of argument, which held in effect that an invalid and *ultra vires* decision was nonetheless 'a decision' for the purpose of the legislation.[98] But that is not the way in which subsequent cases have characterised unenforceable adjudicators' decisions, and it is not consistent with the Act or the Scheme, by which such unenforceable decisions must logically, it is suggested, be nullities. If an unenforceable decision was nonetheless 'a decision' for the purposes of section 108, as Dyson J suggested, it would, by definition, bind the parties pending litigation or arbitration. Such analysis leads to the startling conclusion that a decision can both be unenforceable for the purposes of the defendant complying with it, but also existing and valid for the purposes of stopping the disappointed claimant who has failed to enforce it from starting again under a fresh referral. That seems very unlikely to be the correct characterisation of an invalid decision, and it finds no support in the subsequent cases.

[13.101] This issue seems to be troubling enough to have persuaded the draftsman of the JCT contracts – the most popular suite of standard form contracts – to carve out adjudication enforcement from the otherwise widely drawn standard form of arbitration clause. It is suggested that this is the right approach for any construction contract.

13.4 Other procedures for enforcement

13.4.1 In a nutshell

[13.102] Although by far the most common method of enforcing an adjudicator's decision – and the method repeatedly endorsed by the court – is to commence a claim via the CPR Part 7 or Part 8 procedure and raise an application for summary judgment, there are three other options. They are to make an application to the court for a pre-emptory order, a mandatory injunction or a winding-up order.

13.4.2 Pre-emptory order (1998 Scheme p. 23(1) and 24)

[13.103] Where the Scheme applies, subparagraph 23(1) provides:

> In his decision, the adjudicator may, if he thinks fit, order any of the parties to comply peremptorily with his decision or any part of it.

[13.104] Paragraph 24 of the Scheme provides:

---
[98] Ibid at [20–22].

Section 42 of the Arbitration Act 1996 shall apply to this Scheme subject to the following modifications—
- (a) in subsection (2) for the word "tribunal" wherever it appears there shall be substituted the word "adjudicator",
- (b) in subparagraph (b) of subsection (2) for the words "arbitral proceedings" there shall be substituted the word "adjudication",
- (c) subparagraph (c) of subsection (2) shall be deleted, and
- (d) subsection (3) shall be deleted.

[13.105] These provisions mean that an adjudicator (acting in a Scheme adjudication) may order the parties to comply with its decision straightaway and without objection (paragraph 23) and that the court must enforce such an order (paragraph 24).

[13.106] It has been noted that a decision will not be peremptory which does not on its face state that it is made as a peremptory order, regardless of whether it states it is to be complied with forthwith.[99] This right has been exercised very rarely and has been viewed with some scepticism by the court.[100] Both subparagraph 21(1) and 24 have been deleted in the 2011 Scheme.

13.4.3 Mandatory injunction

[13.107] An injunction is an order of the court which either prohibits a person or company from taking a particular action (a prohibitory injunction) or requires him or it to take a particular action (a mandatory injunction). Where a party is in receipt of an adjudicator's decision which it wishes to enforce on another party, it can apply for a mandatory injunction, which if ordered will compel the other party to comply with the adjudicator's decision. The right to injunct another person or company arises under subsection 37(1) of the Senior Courts Act 1981.

[13.108] The most well-known example is in *Macob Civil Engineering Ltd v Morrison Construction Ltd*.[101] In that case, Dyson J said that it would rarely be appropriate to grant such injunctive relief, and inappropriate where the decision was merely an order to pay money. He said it was 'difficult to see why the failure to pay in accordance with an adjudicator's decision should be more draconian than for failure to honour a money judgment entered by the Court'. In *Multiplex Constructions (UK) Ltd v Mott MacDonald Ltd*, the court could see 'no basis' on which a mandatory injunction will be available where a party seeks to enforce an adjudicator's decision through a summary judgment application.[102]

[13.109] Thus, the more obvious and common remedy remains to grant a simple money judgment under CPR 24. That is not, however, to say that there are not ever circumstances where an injunction might be used to enforce an adjudicator's decision. For example, a claim

---

[99] *MBE Electrical Contractors Ltd v Honeywell Control Systems Ltd* [2010] EWHC 2244 (TCC), per Langan J at [38].
[100] *Macob Civil Engineering v Morrison Construction Ltd* [1999] BLR 93, per Dyson J at [31–40].
[101] [1999] BIR 93.
[102] [2007] EWHC 20 (TCC), per Jackson J at [47].

to have the court grant a final mandatory injunction might be still be appropriate where, for example, the adjudicator has ordered the losing party to execute documents which he has refused to sign despite a contractual term obliging him to do so (e.g. the giving of a bond, or providing a collateral warranty in agreed form to a funder), or where the adjudicator has ordered the losing party to create a separate, proprietary fund as agreed (e.g. in relation to retention monies). In such situations, a mandatory injunction compelling compliance might legitimately be sought, because no effective monetary relief under CPR 24 would be available

[13.110] Injunctive relief is sometimes sought where parties seek to stop adjudication proceedings commencing or proceeding. This issue is addressed at Section 16.3.7.

13.4.4 Statutory demand

[13.111] An adjudication decision that a sum of money is to be paid creates a debt which, if it is over £750 (£5,000 in the case of an individual), can in theory be enforced by issuing a statutory demand.[103] The creditor may present a petition to court for either a bankruptcy or winding-up order if after 21 days, a statutory demand claiming the debt which is equal to or exceeds £750/£5,000 is not paid, secured (an agreement reached for payment), or set aside.[104]

[13.112] While a statutory demand has been used successfully to enforce an adjudicator's decision,[105] this route is unlikely to be effective because the statutory demand will be set aside if:

- there was a genuine triable cross-claim;[106] and/or
- the debt was disputed on grounds which appear substantial.[107]

[13.113] Both such grounds are permissible and will be entertained by the insolvency court (at least in principle) even if the dispute has been raised in TCC enforcement proceedings and dismissed. That is because there is a fundamental difference between TCC proceedings to enforce decisions on a 'pay now, argue later' basis (where the court is solely concerned with the enforcement of the decision to promote cash flow) and proceedings either in bankruptcy or winding-up, where the court is of necessity deciding whether to permit a permanent and final insolvency procedure to get underway on the basis of a debt which derives from a procedure which is only interim binding. Generally speaking, and for understandable reasons, the court will permit that to occur.

[13.114] However, the court will not blindly accept that there are cross-claims or that there are substantial grounds for disputing the debt, such that a debtor under a decision can ignore it with impunity. The debtor has to demonstrate that the grounds or cross-claims are

---

[103] See paragraph 12.3 of the Insolvency Proceedings Practice Direction.
[104] Refer to the Insolvency Act 1986 for more detail.
[105] *Guardi Shoes Ltd v Datum Contracts* [2002] CILL 1934, per Ferris J at [15–22].
[106] *Shaw and another v MFP Foundations Piling Ltd* [2010] EWHC 9 (Ch), per J Davies at [47–62].
[107] *Lacontha Foundation v GBI Investments Ltd* [2010] EWHC 37(Ch), per Warren J at [79–84].

genuine. That means the debtor needs to be seen to pursue the cross-claim in adjudication or some other dispute resolution forum where possible. In *Company No. 1299 of 2001, Re A*,[108] it was held that if the debtor had foregone a 'reasonable opportunity' to adjudicate his alleged cross-claims, the court may allow the petition to proceed; the failure or refusal to get on with the alleged cross-claim was seen as a strong evidential signpost to the conclusion that the cross-claim was simply not bona fide. For similar reasons, the cross-claim must be well articulated. An unwilling debtor seeking to raise 'a cloud of objections' in order to claim the debt is disputed will not prevail over a creditor with a good debt.[109]

[13.115] There are examples of where a statutory demand has been successful to enforce an adjudicator's decision. In *Jamil Mohammed v Dr Michael Bowles*,[110] Dr Bowles used a statutory demand to enforce the adjudicator's decision, and attempts by Mohammed to set it aside were refused. The registrar decided that the nature of that debt was the binding contractual obligation on Mohammed to pay the sum quantified by the adjudicator's decision, unless and until varied by arbitration or legal proceedings. She did not accept that the debt was disputed on substantial grounds, or any other kind. As a result she dismissed the application to set aside the statutory demand, ordered Mohammed to pay Dr Bowles' costs and confirmed that Dr Bowles may petition the court forthwith. The registrar seems to have been persuaded in particular by the fact that it was open to Mohammed to seek a declaration of non-liability from the relevant specialist division, i.e. the TCC, but that he had declined to do so. This approach is consistent with *Company No. 1299 of 2001, Re A*,[111] in that it is a relevant factor for the insolvency court to take into account the genuineness of the debtor's disputes, and any failure on his part to take the obvious steps to make good those alleged disputes.

[13.116] By and large, because it is relatively straightforward to set aside a statutory demand, this approach is not recommended over the summary judgment enforcement procedure which offers a more robust approach to enforcement. The courts have made clear that a statutory demand is not the preferred option.

> It is unfortunate that this court finds itself in the position of having to exercise that function because it is ill equipped to do so in the expert manner of the TCC. It must do so, it seems to me, not by exercising the function that the TCC would exercise but by exercising its discretion in accordance with well established principles applicable to this jurisdiction. This is, as I have remarked, a summary jurisdiction. The jurisdiction to make a winding up order has potentially draconian consequences and is therefore exercised with caution. The winding up jurisdiction is not and never has been the proper forum for the determination of disputed claims.
>
> In by-passing the TCC filter process and proceeding directly to winding up the petitioning creditors have assumed the risks attendant on invoking this jurisdiction. They have adopted

---

[108] [2001] C.I.L.L. 1745 Ch D, per Donaldson J at [14–20].
[109] *Towsey v Highgrove Homes Ltd* [2013] BLR 45, per Baister R at [37].
[110] Unreported, 11 March 2003, per Derrens Ms at [31–35].
[111] [2001] C.I.L.L. 1745 Ch D, per Donaldson J at [14–20].

what has been called 'a high risk strategy' (per Hoffmann J, as he then was, in Re A Company (No 0012209 of 1991) [1992] 1 WLR 351).[112]

[13.117] Similarly, in *Alexander & Law Limited v Coveside (21 BPR) Limited*,[113] Coulson J emphasised that the TCC jurisdiction to deal with enforcement, and the Companies Court jurisdiction to wind up 'ought to be kept very separate'.[114] In that case, Coulson J declined to resist enforcement just because there was a winding-up petition presented, but not determined as at the date of the adjudication enforcement hearing.

13.4.5 Scotland

[13.118] The equivalent to an application for summary judgment in Scotland is a summary decree, the test for which has been described by Lord MacFadyen in *The Construction Centre Group Ltd v The Highland Council*[115] and by judicial review, the appropriateness of which for enforcing an adjudicator's decision was debated in *Vaughan Engineering Ltd v Hinkins & Frewin Ltd*.[116] Both of these procedures are explained in more detail in Chapter 19.

13.5 Complying with an order of the court

13.5.1 In a nutshell

[13.119] Generally speaking, an order of the court takes effect from the date upon which it is made, not the date upon which the order is drawn up and sealed by the court subsequently. The default position is that all orders must be completed within 14 days of the order being made. In the High Court, the parties are responsible for agreeing and drawing up the order for approval by the judge; in many County Courts the court will draw up the order itself. The court retains a general jurisdiction to revise or correct its order in any way it thinks appropriate up until the point at which the order is sealed. After the order is sealed, then the judge's power is limited only to amending the terms of the order to correct any administrative errors in the way in which the order is expressed; any substantive revisions to the order can only be sought by way of appeal.

13.5.2 Time for payment

[13.120] Unless the judge orders otherwise, the default position is that a party must comply with a judgment or order for the payment of an amount of money (including costs) within

---

[112] *Towsey v Highgrove Homes Ltd* [2013] BLR 45, per Baister R at [42–43].
[113] [2013] EWHC 3949 (TCC).
[114] Ibid, per Coulson J at [22].
[115] [2002] ScotCS CSOH_354, per Lord MacFayden at [2–3].
[116] [2003] ScotCS 56, per Lord Clarke at [31–35].

14 days of the date of the judgment or order. This rule applies to adjudication summary enforcement proceedings.[117] However, given the fact that most adjudicators' decisions are expressed for compliance forthwith and the losing party has failed to do so for some considerable period by the time the enforcement hearing comes on, it is not at all unusual for the court to order payment within a shorter period.

13.5.3 Extending the time for payment

[13.121] The court may exercise its discretion to extend the time for payment. The following factors will apply when the court decides whether to exercise its discretion to extend the time to pay beyond 14 days. First, the application by the paying party should be supported by proper evidence. Second, the parties should try to resolve the issue between them and only if that is not possible should they seek an order from the court. If the court is asked to make an order, it is unlikely that mere inability to pay will suffice to justify an extension. Often, the paying party may not know whether or not it can meet the 14 day deadline until a day or two before the payment deadline. In such cases, the court will normally allow the paying party to make a separate application to extend the time for payment at that point.[118]

[13.122] Payment will usually be made by the debtor (the loser), although it can be made by a third party, provided that such payment is authorised by the debtor or receives subsequent ratification. The case of *Treasure & Sons Ltd v Dawes*[119] is an example of this where, in stark contrast to the usual flow of finances within families, the judgment debt Mr Dawes was liable for was paid off by his son and daughter. Treasure argued that the debt was not discharged because Mr Dawes himself had not paid it. This was dismissed by the court on the basis that there was actual evidence of the authority and because Treasure had not repaid the money to Mr Dawes's siblings, instead choosing to use some of it to pay the adjudicator's fees.

13.5.4 Failing to comply

[13.123] Where a party to a summary judgment application fails to comply with the terms of the order given by the court, there are a number of options available to the other party to ensure that the terms of the order are met. Those options depend on the particular circumstances of the case, but also on whether the order pertains to the payment of money or whether it is declaratory in nature.

[13.124] The court's approach where a party fails to comply with a summary judgment order has been made clear: it will do what it can to make the respondent comply with the terms

---

[117] CPR Part 40.11.
[118] *Gipping Construction Ltd v Eaves Ltd* [2008] EWHC 3134 (TCC), per Akenhead J at [10–12].
[119] [2008] EWHC 2181 (TCC), per Coulson J at [27].

of that order as soon as possible. Thus, in *Harrow & Milner v Mrs Linda Teasdale (No. 3)*,[120] the court said this:

> Standing back from the authorities for a moment, it is worth considering what the effect would be if I acceded to the defendant's request not to make the order for sale because of the ongoing arbitration. It would mean that any unsuccessful party in adjudication would know that, if they refused to pay up for long enough, and started their own arbitration, they could eventually render the adjudicator's decision of no effect. It would be condoning, in clear terms, a judgment debtor's persistent default, and its complete refusal to comply with the earlier judgment of the Court. For those reasons, it is a position which I am simply unable to adopt.

(A) Failing to comply with a money judgment

[13.125] Once that judgment is made, CPR 70.2 states that any of the methods set out in PD 70 can be used to enforce the judgment. The appropriate method to use will depend upon the assets that the judgment debtor has.

- Executing against goods is the appropriate method where the other party has sufficient assets to cover the judgment. It involves the court issuing a writ of fieri facias in the High Court[121] or a warrant of execution in the County Court[122] commanding an enforcement officer to seize and sell a judgment debtor's goods. This is known as an order of sale.[123]
- A third-party debt order[124] can be obtained if there are sums owed to a judgment debtor that are in the hands of a third party, such as a bank, so that they are frozen and seized for the benefit of the judgment creditor.[125]
- A charging order[126] can be used where the other party has a beneficial interest in land, securities or certain other assets. A charging order of itself does not realise funds to satisfy a judgment debt, an order for the sale of the property under CPR 73.10 is needed. Therefore, a charging order is appropriate where the other party has an interest in land, and other (quicker) enforcement methods are not sufficient to cover the judgment debt. The applicant must first apply for an interim charging order. If that is granted, it can apply for a final charging order.[127]
- An attachment of earnings order[128] provides that a proportion of a judgment debtor's earnings is deducted by his employer and paid to the judgment creditor until the judgment debt is paid. It is only available against individuals and in the county court,

---

[120] [2006] EWHC 1708 (TCC), per Coulson J at [8–26].
[121] RSC Orders 46 and 47.
[122] CCR Order 26.
[123] *Harlow & Milner Ltd v Mrs Linda Teasdale* [2006] EWHC 1708 (TCC), per Coulson J at [8–26].
[124] CPR 72.
[125] *Kier Regional Ltd (t/a Wallis) v City and General (Holborn) Ltd & Ors (No. 2)* [2008] EWHC 2454 (TCC), per Coulson J at [51–71].
[126] CPR 73.
[127] *Harlow & Milner Ltd v Teasdale (No. 2)* [2006] EWHC 535 (TCC), per Coulson J at [5–13].
[128] CCR Order 27.

although a judgment can be transferred from the High Court to a county court for the purposes of obtaining an order.
- The appointment of a receiver by way of equitable execution can be used.[129] Subsection 37(1) Senior Courts Act 1981 gives courts the power to appoint a receiver in all cases in which it appears to the court to be just and convenient to do so.
- A winding-up petition against a losing company[130] or a creditor's bankruptcy petition against a losing individual[131] can be made if the order to pay money is worth over £750 (£5,000 in the case of an individual), or if the order to pay money has not been satisfied in whole or in part by one of the above forms of execution. Such a petition might put pressure on a losing party to pay. However, as discussed above, generally speaking the Companies Court or the Bankruptcy Court will be hesitant to wind up a company or make a person bankrupt on the strength of only an interim binding decision where it is clear that the debtor under that decision (and the judgment enforcing it) are disputed on genuine grounds, and where the debtor has not foregone the opportunity to take reasonable steps to bring that dispute on (by commencing litigation or arbitration over the issues decided by the adjudicator).

(B) Failing to comply with a declaration

[13.126] In some cases, an applicant to enforcement proceedings may seek a declaration from the court that the adjudicator's decision is valid, rather than a determination of an amount due. This may be so where the relief sought from the adjudicator was also a declaration, for example as to the meaning of a particular contract clause or the applicability of liquidated damages, because such a declaration is desirable to bind the parties so that they can focus on resolving other issues.

[13.127] Where court's order is a declaration, rather than an award of money, the options for enforcing compliance listed above will not be available. In circumstances where the losing party continues to act in a manner that is inconsistent with the declaration, the winning party may commence proceedings seeking injunctive relief from the court. If the losing party does not comply with the injunction, this will constitute a contempt of court, which may lead to criminal sanctions for the person or directors of the company against whom the injunction is sought[132] or a sequestration of goods,[133] if the order granting the injunction contained a penal notice.[134]

---

[129] CPR 69.
[130] Sections 122–124 Insolvency Act 1986 and Part 4 of the (amended) Insolvency Rules 1986.
[131] Sections 267–271 Insolvency Act 1986 and Part 6, Chapter 2 of the (amended) Insolvency Rules 1986.
[132] CPR 81.4.
[133] CPR 81.20.
[134] CPR 81.9.

13.6 Checklist: Avoiding the consequences of an adjudicator's decision

> There are a number of grounds on which the consequences of an adjudicator's decision can be delayed, reduced or avoided altogether.
>
> (1) There may be an entitlement to set off sums against the sum awarded by the adjudicator (Section 12.6).
> (2) If the winning party is insolvent, it is unlikely that it will be able to enforce the adjudicator's decision at all (Section 14.2).
> (3) If the winning party is near insolvent or in financial difficulty, then while a court is likely to grant summary judgment enforcing the adjudicator's decision, the court is also likely to stay the enforcement of that summary judgment until such time as the financial impecuniosity alleviates (Section 14.3).
> (4) If the adjudicator did not have the jurisdiction to decide the dispute he did, his decision will not be enforced (Chapter 16).
> (5) If the adjudicator acted in breach of the rules of natural justice, his decision will not be enforced (Chapter 17).
> (6) The adjudicator and/or the parties were fraudulent (Section 18.1).
> (7) The adjudicator and/or the parties acted under duress (Section 18.3).
> (8) In Scotland, the adjudicator's decision is in breach of the Human Rights Act 1998 (Section 18.5).
>
> Invariably, where one of the above challenges is made, a prerequisite to a successful challenge is that the issue was raised in the adjudication. Where the challenge goes to the jurisdiction of the adjudicator, the challenger must reserve and maintain its position (Section 16.3 and 16.4).
>
> For certain types of dispute, it may be possible to avoid the consequences of the adjudicator's decision by commencing a Part 8 claim for a final determination of the issues decided by the adjudicator. Where this is possible, the adjudicator's decision is effectively leap-frogged in favour of the decision by the court (Section 15.3).

Chapter 14
Enforcement: insolvency, stay and severability

14.1 Overview

[14.01] Even where the court holds that the adjudicator's decision is valid, the losing party may temporarily or permanently avoid the consequences of that decision where the court determines that the party is insolvent or in financial difficulty.

[14.02] The court will not enter a judgment (pursuant to an application for summary judgment to enforce an adjudicator's decision or otherwise) where either party is insolvent,[1] because a judgment either for or against the insolvent company would be binding on both parties in working out the assets to be distributed, and might well amount to an inaccurate statement of the parties' rights.

[14.03] In the case of winding-up and bankruptcy, there is automatic self-executing insolvency set-off, such that from the onset of bankruptcy or winding-up, the law deems there to be only a single consolidated debt due in one direction or the other. Litigation or arbitration can be used to work out what that debt is (or work out what part of that debt is), but adjudication, being a temporarily binding phenomenon, cannot.[2] Automatic self-executing insolvency set-off does not apply to all forms of formal insolvency. For example, it does not apply in administration unless and until the administrator decides to declare a distribution – but in any event the effect of a supervening administration order, regardless of whether a distribution is declared, is to render adjudication enforcement inappropriate.[3]

[14.04] It is suggested therefore that while the effect of self-executing insolvency set-off provides a further reason as to why enforcement cannot be granted where there is formal insolvency, the true, broader justification for the rule is that explained by Coulson J in *Hart Investments Ltd v Fidler & Anor*,[4] where he said that entry of judgment should be declined because it might involve the court making a binding but inaccurate statement of the parties' rights to which the appointed insolvency practitioner would have to

---

[1] Section 3.6 provides a definition of corporate insolvency and a description of the main insolvency procedures.
[2] *Enterprise Managed Services Ltd v Tony McFadden Utilities Ltd* [2009] EWHC 3222 (TCC), per Coulson J at [61–79].
[3] *Straw Realisations (No. 1) Ltd (formerly known as Haymills (Contractors) Ltd (in administration)) v Shaftsbury House (Developments) Ltd* [2010] EWHC 2597 (TCC), per Edwards-Stuart J at [89–97].
[4] [2006] EWHC 2857 (TCC), per Coulson J at [73–75].

A Practical Guide to Construction Adjudication, First Edition. James Pickavance.
© 2016 James Pickavance. Published 2016 by John Wiley & Sons, Inc.

pay heed. Although never expressly stated in the cases, such a broader approach (where there was formal insolvency but no self-executing insolvency set-off) would be obviously permissible on the basis that under CPR 24.2(b), the court can decline summary judgment on the basis that there is a 'compelling reason' as to why the case or issue should be disposed of at trial, rather than by way of summary judgment (Section 14.2).

[14.05] Sometimes, in addition to the claimant's application for summary judgment to enforce the adjudicator's decision, the defendant will also make a cross-application for an order that summary judgment, if granted, should be stayed. Commonly known as a stay of execution, such an order will suspend the consequences of the adjudicator's decision according to the terms of the order. The court's general policy is to not grant a stay of execution, since to do so would delay getting money into the hands of the person or company to whom it is owed as quickly as possible. Stays tend to be limited to situations of near insolvency or financial hardship on the part of the payee, where the court concludes that through no fault of the paying party, if it were to pay it would be unlikely to ever see its money again if the effect of the adjudicator's decision was later reversed in litigation or arbitration (Section 14.3). However, the court may grant a stay of execution of the judgment in circumstances where to do otherwise would risk 'manifest injustice'.[5]

[14.06] Severability is the idea that where a part of the adjudicator's decision is found to be unenforceable, it can be severed from the other part, which is found to be enforceable. The effect is that the winning party to an adjudication may derive at least some benefit from the result, as opposed to nothing at all (Section 14.4).

14.2 Insolvency avoids summary judgment

14.2.1 In a nutshell

[14.07] Where there is a situation of insolvency, the importance given to enforcing adjudication decisions subject to the Act effectively gives way to the rights of creditors set out under the Insolvency Act 1986 (the **Insolvency Act**) and the Insolvency Rules 1986 (the **Insolvency Rules**).

[14.08] It is important to distinguish between two different situations, the first being where formal insolvency has already occurred before the adjudicator's decision is produced. In such circumstances, the effect of the supervening insolvency event is, by and large, to derail the adjudication and stop it in its tracks; invariably one party or the other will call on the adjudicator to resign, and he should resign (save in very limited circumstances, e.g. where the formal insolvency event is not one that would provide a defence to enforcement, such as a CVA). That should stop any decision being produced at all. The second situation is more common: formal insolvency occurs after the decision is produced and it then becomes relevant in the context of the court's decision as to whether to enforce.

---

[5] *Hillview Industrial Developments (UK) Ltd v Botes Building Ltd* [2006] EWHC 1365 (TCC), per Toulmin J at [33].

Most of the case law is concerned with this second situation. However, because the principles are invariably the same, the effect of insolvency upon an adjudicator's decision (whether that insolvency occurs before or after the decision is produced) is dealt with in this section.

14.2.2 Liquidation

[14.09] Rule 4.90 of the Insolvency Rules applies where the company has gone into liquidation at any time before the court comes to consider enforcement. It states:

> (1) This rule applies where, before the company goes into liquidation there have been mutual credits, mutual debts or other mutual dealings between the company and any creditor of the company proving or claiming to prove for a debt in the liquidation.
> (2) An account shall be taken of what is due from each party to the other in respect of the mutual dealings and the sums due from one party shall be set off against the sums due from the other.
> (3) …
> (4) Only the balance (if any) of the account is provable in the liquidation. Alternatively (as the case may be) the amount shall be paid to the liquidator as part of the assets.

[14.10] The effect of this rule is that where there are claims or cross-claims between parties, one of which is in liquidation, a summary judgment application to enforce an adjudicator's decision will be refused.[6] All claims and cross-claims will then be resolved in the liquidation, where full account can be taken of the balance struck. The cases have made it clear that rule 4.90 debars enforcement, and so the effect of formal insolvency prior to a decision means that invariably the decision will not be enforceable (the principal exception being where the nature of the formal insolvency procedure is a voluntary arrangement, where the arrangement and its terms are merely relevant to the granting of a stay of execution). The result is that unless the parties (including the party now controlled by an insolvency practitioner appointed) agree to the outcome of the adjudication being finally binding, supervening insolvency either during the adjudication or at any time prior to an enforcement hearing is to stop the adjudication dead in its tracks.

14.2.3 Administration

[14.11] Where administrators are appointed by the court, no proceedings may be commenced or continued against the company without the consent of the administrators or the leave of the court and subject to such terms as the court imposes in granting leave.[7] This

---

[6] *Bouygues (UK) Ltd v Dahl-Jensen (UK) Ltd* [2000] EWCA Civ 507, per Buxton LJ at [29–36]. See also the detailed analysis justifying the rule in *Enterprise Managed Services Ltd v Tony McFadden Utilities Ltd* [2009] EWHC 3222 (TCC), per Coulson J at [61–79]. Note also the broader considerations for declining enforcement, outlined at paragraph 14.03, which it is submitted provide grounds for refusing summary judgment even without reference to Insolvency Rule 4.90.
[7] Subsection 11(3)(d) of the Insolvency Act.

requirement covers proceedings to enforce a decision and also an application for summary judgment if the proceedings are already on foot.[8] The circumstances in which permission to commence or continue proceedings against a company in administration are addressed at Section 3.6.5. Therefore, where administration occurs during an adjudication, the effect will be to derail the adjudication unless and until permission or consent is obtained.

[14.12] Subject to permission being obtained (either for the purposes of continuing an adjudication against the company or for the purposes of seeking enforcement where the administration order post-dates the decision), the question of whether the court will decline to give judgment against the company in administration or will give judgment to enforce the decision subject to a stay of execution is determined on a case-by-case basis. The fundamental objective of an administration order is different from a winding-up. The intention is to rescue the company as a going concern and it is possible therefore that the company may emerge as a trading entity. There may therefore be circumstances in which it would be appropriate to hold the company in administration bound by the adjudicator's decision, the administration order notwithstanding. Therefore the general approach is that enforcement will be refused, but that it may nevertheless be granted where (a) the administrator has not declared a distribution (because if he does, the situation is the same as with bankruptcy and winding-up, self-executing insolvency set-off taking effect); and (b) the adjudicator's decision has become final, either by agreement of the parties or operation of the contract.[9] Where those two conditions are fulfilled, then the decision has become binding and it will operate on the administration by way of summary judgment, subject only to a stay (because the creditor under that decision will only be entitled to a dividend against the value of the debt thereby created, not to execute for the debt in full).

[14.13] These principles were developed by Edwards-Stuart J in *Straw Realisations (No. 1) Ltd v Shaftsbury House (Developments) Ltd*:[10]

> 3. I consider that if a party is in administration and a notice of distribution has been given, an adjudicator's decision will not be enforced.
> 4. If a party is in administration, but no notice of distribution has been given, an adjudicator's decision which has not become final will not be enforced by way of summary judgment. In my view, this follows from the decision in Melville Dundas as well as being consistent with the reasoning in Integrated Building Services v PIHL.
> 5. If the circumstances are as in paragraph (4) above but the adjudicator's decision has, by agreement of the parties or operation of the contract, become final, the decision may be enforced by way of summary judgment (subject to the imposition of a stay). I reach this conclusion because I do not consider that the reasoning of the majority in Melville Dundas extends to this situation.

---

[8] *Joinery Plus Ltd (In Administration) v Laing Ltd* [2003] EWHC 3513 (TCC), per Thornton J at [102–120].
[9] See for example under the NEC standard forms, where the adjudicator's decision becomes binding unless proceedings in respect of its subject matter are commenced within a certain period.
[10] [2010] EWHC 2597, per Edwards-Stuart J at [89].

6. There is no rule of English law that the fact that a party is on the verge of insolvency ('vergens ad inopiam') triggers the operation of bankruptcy set-off: see Melville Dundas, per Lord Hope at paragraph 33. However, the law in Scotland appears to be different on this point (perhaps because the Scottish courts do not enjoy the power to grant a stay in such circumstances).

7. If a party is insolvent in a real sense, or its financial circumstances are such that if an adjudicator's decision is complied with the paying party is unlikely to recover its money, or at least a substantial part of it, the court may grant summary judgment but stay the enforcement of that judgment.

14.2.4 Administrative receivership

[14.14] Administrative receivership is defined at Section 3.6.6. While the appointment of administrative receivers does not necessarily that mean a company is insolvent, it is taken as evidence of such.[11] Until such time as the company is declared insolvent by the administrative receiver, it is likely that the court will grant an order for summary judgment, but stay the consequences of the adjudicator's decision until the outcome of the administrative receiver's exercise.[12]

14.2.5 CVA

[14.15] A company subject to a CVA,[13] while bound by the terms of the CVA, can otherwise carry on business and it can also commence or participate in adjudication proceedings. A CVA occurring prior to the adjudicator's decision being published will not, therefore, deprive the adjudicator of jurisdiction. The nature of a CVA is further described at Section 3.6.7. Where that company participates in adjudication proceedings and the adjudicator decides it has to pay money, then where that company has cross-claims against the other party, depending on the terms of the CVA then this may be sufficient for the court to refuse summary judgment.[14] However, there is authority that a company subject to a CVA will not be able to use that as grounds for refusing judgment or for granting a stay of execution.[15] The outcome will depend on the particular facts of the case.

[14.16] In *Tate Building Services Ltd v B & M McHugh Ltd*,[16] Tate had agreed as part of the CVA it had entered into to pay its creditors around 50% of the total monies owed. Six months later, it adjudicated against the contractor, McHugh, for a sum of £300,000 and

---

[11] *Melville Dundas Limited (in receivership) and others George Wimpey UK Limited and others* [2007] UKHL 18, per Lord Hoffman at [14].
[12] *Rainford House Ltd v Cadogan Ltd* [2001] EWHC 18 (TCC), per Seymuor J at [15–20] and *Baldwins Industrial Services plc v Barr Ltd* [2002] EWHC 2915 (TCC), per Kirkham J at [35–40].
[13] For an explanation of the meaning of a CVA, see Section 3.6.7.
[14] *Westshield Ltd v Whitehouse* [2013] EWHC 3576 (TCC), per Akenhead J at [20–33].
[15] *Mead General Building Ltd v Dartmoor Properties Ltd* [2009] EWHC 200 (TCC), per Coulson J at [12–20].
[16] [2014] EWHC 2971 (TCC), per Edwards-Stuart J at [37–43].

the adjudicator ordered McHugh to pay £270,000. McHugh refused to pay, Tate commenced an action to enforce the decision and McHugh applied for a stay of execution. The court agreed to grant summary judgment, but stayed the execution of £75,000 of the total sum. The judge appears to have been influenced to a great extent by the evidently underhand approach of Tate and its inability to provide evidence to support its claimed financial position.

14.2.6 Individual insolvency or bankruptcy

[14.17] Individual insolvency and bankruptcy are described at Sections 3.6.8 and 3.6.9. Section 323 of the Insolvency Act, which is applicable in an individual insolvency or bankruptcy, applies in the same way as Rule 4.90 of the Insolvency Rules. Thus, where there are claims or cross-claims between parties, a summary judgment application to enforce an adjudicator's decision will be refused where one of the parties goes bankrupt after the decision is produced. For the same reasons, any adjudication which is ongoing as at the date upon which one of the parties is made bankrupt will result in an unenforceable decision and so the adjudicator should resign (unless of course the Trustee in Bankruptcy and the other party agree to treat the decision as final).

14.3 Stay of execution

14.3.1 In a nutshell

[14.18] If both parties are solvent but the evidence shows that the enforcing party is unlikely to be able to repay the sums awarded, the defendant may make a cross-application to the court for a stay of execution in the event judgment is granted, or, to put it another way, a suspension of the consequences of the decision. Stays tend to be limited to situations of near insolvency or financial hardship on the part of the payer, although there are other circumstances in which a stay has exceptionally been granted.

[14.19] Evidence is required to demonstrate that the risk of the claimant being unable to repay the sum awarded by the adjudicator is sufficiently great to warrant a stay of execution. Unless the evidence is compelling, the court is unlikely to grant a stay because it would 'cut across [the principles of enforcement] if a losing party could avoid enforcement of the decision simply by pleading poverty'.[17]

[14.20] While there are a set of principles that have been developed by the courts, 'this is an area which is particularly fact sensitive, and each case must be considered in the light of its own particular facts and all the surrounding circumstances'.[18]

---

[17] *Volker Stevin Ltd v Holystone Contracts Ltd* [2010] EWHC 2344 (TCC), per Coulson J at [27].
[18] *Partner Projects Limited v Corinthian Nominees Limited* [2011] EWHC 2989 (TCC), per Edwards-Stuart at [51].

14.3.2 Court's discretion to order a stay of execution

[14.21] CPR 83.7[19] provides that where there are special circumstances which render it inexpedient to enforce a judgment or order to pay money, the court may stay the execution either absolutely or for a fixed period. In the case of adjudication, the court will give summary judgment of an adjudicator's decision (provided it is valid), but suspend the enforcement, or consequences of that decision, by granting a stay of execution. The leading case on this issue is *Wimbledon Construction Company 2000 Ltd v Derek Vago*,[20] where the court said this:

> In an application to stay the execution of summary judgment arising out of an Adjudicator's decision, the Court must exercise its discretion under Order 47 with considerations a) and b) firmly in mind (see **AWG**).[21]
>
> The probable inability of the claimant to repay the judgment sum (awarded by the Adjudicator and enforced by way of summary judgment) at the end of the substantive trial, or arbitration hearing, may constitute special circumstances within the meaning of Order 47 rule 1(1)(a) rendering it appropriate to grant a stay (see **Herschell**).[22]
>
> ...
>
> If the claimant is in insolvent liquidation, or there is no dispute on the evidence that the claimant is insolvent, then a stay of execution will usually be granted (see **Bouygues**[23] and **Rainford House**[24]).
>
> Even if the evidence of the claimant's present financial position suggested that it is probable that it would be unable to repay the judgment sum when it fell due, that would not usually justify the grant of a stay if:
>
> (i) the claimant's financial position is the same or similar to its financial position at the time that the relevant contract was made (see **Herschell**); or
>
> (ii) The claimant's financial position is due, either wholly, or in significant part, to the defendant's failure to pay those sums which were awarded by the adjudicator (see **Absolute Rentals**).[25]

[14.22] As can be seen from the quoted extract, these principles are derived from previously decided cases.

[14.23] The court's discretion as to the terms of the stay is largely unfettered. It may therefore consider it appropriate to order the stay to take effect and then continue only upon terms. If, for example, the court thought that there was a real risk of an inability to repay when the

---

[19] Formerly RSC Order 47(1)(a), CPR Schedule 1 and also CPR 50. Although the stay jurisdiction has now been taken up into the CPR itself, the material wording (and thus the test) remains the same in the transposition, and it is submitted that the case law on RSC Order 47(1)(a) will continue to be relevant and relied upon by judges.
[20] [2005] EWHC 1086 (TCC), per Coulson J at [26].
[21] *AWG Construction Services Ltd v Rockingham Motor Speedway Ltd* [2004] EWHC 888 (TCC), per Toulmin J at [185–188].
[22] *Herschell Engineering Ltd v Breen Property Ltd* [2000] AdjLR 07/28, per Lloyd J at [3–20].
[23] *Bouygues (UK) Ltd v Dahl-Jensen (UK) Ltd* [2000] EWCA Civ 507, per Chadwick LJ at [29–36].
[24] *Rainford House Ltd v Cadogan Ltd* [2001] BLR 416, per Seymour J at [15–20].
[25] *Absolute Rentals Ltd v Gencor Enterprises Ltd* (2001) 17 Const LJ 322, per Wilcox J at [17].

matter was finally determined, but that it was also concerned that the loser was dragging its feet over the appointment of arbitrators or the service of proceedings, it could make it a condition of the stay that appointment of arbitrators or service of the claim form take place within a fixed period of time. It can therefore be of assistance to show the court that not only is there a risk of non-repayment at final determination, but also that everything possible is being done to bring that final determination on as quickly as possible.

[14.24] Sound evidence of the claimant's likely inability to repay is absolutely crucial if an application for a stay of execution is to be successful. Evidence of insolvency proceedings, past and future accounts, the type and amount of any security held over the company's assets, evidence of the (lack of) turnover and credit ratings are all likely to be important.

[14.25] That said, there is no obligation on the claimant to disclose this information. A submission that the claimant had to do so because there was 'reverse burden of proof' applicable on such an application was expressly rejected by Coulson J in *Pilon Ltd v Breyer Group plc*,[26] although in *Alexander & Law Ltd v Coveside (21BPR) Ltd*[27] the same judge accepted that there was an 'asymmetry of [the] evidence' available to the applicant and the respondent, with the respondent necessarily knowing more about his own financial affairs than the applicant did, and that the court could, where appropriate, draw inferences from what was not in evidence. In other words, where the applicant gets its case for inability to repay 'off the ground' on the evidence available to it, the burden of persuasion then shifts to the respondent to produce its own evidence to rebut that picture – and that if, armed with more information than is available to the applicant, it declines to do so, the court may draw the appropriate inference that such additional evidence as it might employ would help rather than hinder the applicant.

[14.26] It may be helpful to instruct an accounting expert to provide an opinion on the company's financial health.[28] Although a full-scale expert report is plainly outside the scope of the application, any accountant giving evidence as to solvency or insolvency should of course bear CPR 35 strongly in mind. In *Alexander & Law Ltd v Coveside (21BPR) Ltd*,[29] for example, Coulson J rejected accountancy evidence deployed in resistance to the application on the basis that it was, 'peppered with errors and advocacy', and that rather than being an objective assessment of the trading future of the company:

> their cash-flow analysis is actually no such thing. All [the accountants] appear to have done, is to accept [the director's] general assurance that [future] trading would be at the same level as before, and then plugged into their calculations turnover figures from previous years. ... such a bland assumption is unhelpful.

[14.27] The party resisting stays of execution (i.e. the party trying to enforce the adjudicator's decision) on the basis that it is not impecunious is well advised not to attempt to mislead

---

[26] [2010] EWHC 837 (TCC), per Coulson J at [46–47].
[27] [2013] EWHC 3949 (TCC), per Coulson J at [24–36].
[28] *FG Skerritt Ltd v Caledonian Building Systems Ltd* [2013] EWHC 1898 (TCC), per Ramsey J at [12].
[29] [2013] EWHC 3949 (TCC), per Coulson J at [24–36].

the court with overly rosy assertions of its trading history or future; not surprisingly, attempts to mislead the court tend to encourage the judge in his conclusions that the company cannot repay. In both *Alexander & Law Ltd v Coveside (21BPR) Ltd*[30] and *Pilon Ltd v Breyer Group plc*,[31] Coulson J seems to have been encouraged to grant a stay on the basis that the picture of solvency with which he was being presented was probably inaccurate for being partial, and based in part on assertion rather than objectively balanced evidence. A cynic might suggest that, given there is no general duty of disclosure on such applications, sometimes the difference between presenting a misleading picture and presenting an accurate one lies merely in being caught out. In *Coveside*, for example, it appears that Coulson J had more, rather than less evidence upon which to base his conclusions because the claimant was being compelled in parallel Companies Court proceedings to give more full disclosure than it might otherwise have liked, and Coulson J had regard to that evidence. At least in theory, dishonest evidence to see off a stay application can see the directors committed for contempt of court; see the discussion in *Berry Piling Systems v Sheer Projects*.[32]

[14.28] By staying execution, the court retains a general jurisdiction over that order, so that it is possible to apply to lift even a general, unfettered stay at some future point if the circumstances warrant it, for example, as a result of a very significant upturn in trading profits by award of unanticipated contracts, or evidence that the claimant has done nothing to get on with a final determination for a long period of time. On this latter example, while the analogy is not perfect, it is submitted that a party losing an adjudication enforcement hearing but succeeding in obtaining a stay of execution will (absent insolvency making the stay effectively final) be in a position broadly similar to that of a party who obtains a freezing order. In other words, it will be under a general duty to get on with the proceedings, which it claims will vindicate its position, and that a failure to prosecute those proceedings may persuade the court not to extend to him the continued protection of the stay.

14.3.3 Insolvency proceedings pending or not concluded

[14.29] An explanation of various forms of insolvency proceedings is set out at Section 3.6. Where the payee is demonstrably insolvent, summary judgment will not be given. However, where insolvency proceedings are pending or not concluded, subject to the nature of those proceedings, this will not normally preclude judgment being given in the claimant's favour (subject to the validity of the adjudicator's decision of course), but it may be enough to persuade the court to exercise its discretion to stay the enforcement of that judgment until such time as it can be demonstrated that the claimant is solvent.[33]

---

[30] [2013] EWHC 3949 (TCC), per Coulson J at [24–36].
[31] [2010] EWHC 837 (TCC), per Coulson J at [47–62; 64].
[32] [2013] EWHC 347 (TCC).
[33] *Alexander & Law Ltd v Coveside (21BPR) Ltd* [2013] EWHC 3949 (TCC), per Coulson J at [24–36].

[14.30] For the paying party, the effect of the court declining to enforce a decision can be very different from the imposition of a stay. The stay may only be granted for a limited period and may have attached to it a number of conditions that need to be met. By contrast, where the court declines to enforce an adjudicator's decision, the paying party will never have to comply with the terms of what the adjudicator decided although such a refusal will, logically, be to the effect that the decision is a nullity, and absent a debarring insolvency event, the referring party will be able to start its claim again.

(A) Liquidation

[14.31] Where the paying party is shown to be insolvent, but not yet in liquidation, summary judgment will still be given (assuming the decision is valid), but a stay of execution will be granted either permanently or until such time as it can be determined that the company will not go into liquidation.[34]

[14.32] If a petition for winding-up had been presented for an order for compulsory liquidation and was due to be heard in the near future, then the court is likely to stay the execution of the decision until the petition is heard, provided there is sufficient evidence of the payee's inability to repay the debt following a final determination.[35] If the winding up order was granted at the hearing, then presumably the stay will persist, although it will probably cease to have any relevance.

[14.33] There appears to be no case directly on point but, in the case of a company which is subsequently wound up, it is submitted that in line with the cases where no stay was granted, the effect of the supervening winding-up order will be to render the judgment in the creditor's favour on the adjudicator's decision irrelevant, because under self-executing insolvency set-off what matters is the underlying debt, not the adjudicator's temporary binding assessment of it, and so the stay will cease to have any practical relevance from that date; see *Stein v Blake*[36] as to the effect of litigation over rights determining the single account due for insolvency set-off, and the explanation in *Enterprise Managed Services Ltd v Tony McFadden Utilities Ltd*,[37] as to why adjudication cannot be treated in the same way. The stay will then cease to have any effect because the judgment will cease to have any effect (unless of course the insolvency practitioner decides to accept it).

[14.34] If the company is not wound up, then stay will be lifted and the defendant will be required to comply with the adjudicator's decision.[38]

[14.35] Where a company indicates it wishes to enter an MVL, then it would appear that the court may grant either a partial or full stay until the company has in fact done so and

---

[34] *FG Skerritt Ltd v Caledonian Building Systems Ltd* [2013] EWHC 1898 (TCC), per Ramsey at [29–32].
[35] *Alexander & Law Ltd v Coveside* (21BPR) Ltd EWHC 3949 (TCC), per Coulson J at [18–46].
[36] [1996] AC 243.
[37] [2009] EWHC 3222 (TCC), per Coulson J at [83–90]
[38] *Harwood Construction Ltd v Lantrode Ltd* 24 November 2000, unreported, per Seymour J at [10–20].

the directors have signed the statutory declaration of solvency. In *Maguire & Co v Mar City Developments*,[39] the adjudicator awarded the contractor £130,000. The contractor then decided it would enter an MVL on the basis of accountancy evidence that it said showed that it was solvent on a balance sheet test (i.e. it could repay if required to do so). The court held that summary judgment should be entered in the contractor's favour, but that only 60% of that sum should be paid by the employer within 21 days.

[14.36] Execution of the remaining 40% would be stayed until such time as the contractor had in fact entered an MVL and the directors had made the required declaration of solvency. At that stage, the contractor could apply to the court for the stay to be lifted. This is a correct and logical outcome, it is submitted: the directors of the winning contractor could hardly be heard to say that they were entitled to summary judgment in full while at the same time as saying they were winding up the business because they could only achieve balance sheet (as opposed to cash flow) solvency.

(B) Administration

[14.37] The question of whether a stay will be ordered depends on the stage the company is in the administrative process. As discussed at Section 14.2.3, it would appear that unless the adjudicator's decision has become final (either by agreement or by operation of an express contractual term) and unless a notice of distribution has been issued, no judgment will be given at all, but if both those requirements are fulfilled, judgment will be entered and subjected to a stay.

(C) Administrative receivership

[14.38] When a company is in administrative receivership, that seems to be sufficient grounds for a stay. See Section 14.2.4 for more details. If the administrative receivership had not commenced but was pending, then it seems likely the court would take that into account in determining whether or not to grant a stay.

(D) CVA

[14.39] The fact that a claimant (to an application to stay execution) was subject to a CVA was a relevant factor for the court to take into account when considering an application to stay enforcement of the judgment. Whether the existence of the CVA means that the court should refuse either summary judgment or a stay of execution will depend on the facts.[40]

---

[39] [2013] EWHC 3503 (TCC), per Edwards-Stuart J at [22–29].
[40] *Mead General Building Ltd v Dartmoor Properties Ltd* [2009] EWHC 200 (TCC), per Coulson J at [12–20].and *Westshield Ltd v Whitehouse* [2013] EWHC 3576 (TCC), per Akenhead J at [20–33].

14.3.4 Financial difficulty

[14.40] The payee (i.e. the party to whom money will be paid – invariably the claimant in enforcement proceedings) may not have entered or been placed in insolvency proceedings. It may, however, be possible for the payer (i.e. the party paying money or the defendant in enforcement proceedings) to be able to demonstrate that the payee's financial circumstances are such that it would be unable to repay the judgment sum, and persuade the court to exercise its power to stay the execution of the judgment it has given.

[14.41] On the whole, applications for a stay of execution on the basis of financial difficulty have rarely been successful because strong evidence will be required to usurp the fundamental proposition that adjudicator's decisions must be complied with forthwith. Each case will turn on its own facts, applying the principles set out at Section 14.3.2 and the further guidance below. Appendix 8 lists the cases where an application for a stay based on financial difficulty has been successful or unsuccessful.

[14.42] The payee's financial position must be considered at the time the adjudicator's decision may be overturned. That exercise involves the court making an informed estimate as to when it is likely that a judgment will be given that would result in the relevant liability arising. In *Berry Piling Systems Ltd v Sheer Projects Ltd*,[41] for example, that time was when an arbitrator gave an award, estimated to be some 12–18 months in the future.

[14.43] Where the payer asserts it has cross-claims that, if successful, would result in the payee repaying the amount awarded in the adjudicator's decision, even if the payee is impecunious, then a stay may not be granted where the payer cannot show that it has diligently pursued those cross-claims.[42]

[14.44] Where the payer claims that the payee will not be able to repay the sums awarded in the summary judgment application in the event the decision is reversed in final proceedings, where the payee's financial position is the same or similar to that when it entered into the contract out of which the right to adjudication arose,[43] then that is a factor against granting a stay.[44] Part of the logic of this is that if a party chooses to contract with a company which is in the same or similar financial difficulties at the time of the contract as it is at the time of a later judgment against that company, that is part of the background to the commercial transaction and should not be used as grounds to prevent payment or enforcement of a judgment against it; the payer can be said to have 'contracted for the result'. However, that reasoning will not apply where the payee is found to

---

[41] [2012] EWHC 241 (TCC), per Edwards-Stuart J at [15–17].
[42] *AWG Construction Services Ltd v Rockingham Motor Speedway Ltd* [2004] EWHC 888 (TCC) per J Toulmin at [187].
[43] Where the form of adjudication is statutory or contractual, the date where the right arose will be the same date as the contract. Where the form of the adjudication is ad hoc, the date where the right arose will be the date of the adjudication agreement.
[44] *Air Design (Kent) Ltd v Deerglen (Jersey) Ltd*. [2008] EWHC 3047 (TCC) per Akenhead J at [26].

have misled the payer as to its true financial position at the time the contract was entered into, by false representations that its financial position was better than it otherwise was.[45]

[14.45] Where the payee is in financial difficulties, but it can show that (a) its financial difficulties arise from the failure of the payer to pay the monies ordered by the adjudicator to be paid; and/or (b) the withholding of those monies is likely to make the payee's financial position significantly worse (for example, by pushing the payee into liquidation), then the court will not be so willing to impose a stay.[46]

[14.46] Where both parties are in financial difficulty, such as where one party is in receivership and the other party is shown to have made losses over the past few years of trading, then to avoid the risk that either party would be unable to repay money in a subsequent arbitration or litigation, the payer is likely to be granted a stay of execution; however, the impecunious payee may be required to pay a sum of money into court, pending final resolution of the matter.[47]

[14.47] Where the payer is undertaking a project or development, and the success of that development determines whether or not the payer will remain solvent, that fact, together with the payer's other financial circumstances, may be taken into account.[48]

[14.48] Where the payer claims that the payee will not be able to repay the judgment debt should the dispute be decided differently in final proceedings, it is perfectly open to a payee to adduce evidence to counter that allegation. So, where a parent company guarantee,[49] insurance policy[50] or bond[51] is offered, that may well be sufficient to convince the court that a stay of execution is not necessary.

[14.49] Where the payer contracted with the payee knowing that the payee was in financial difficulty partly as a result of the insolvency of a third party who owed the payee money, this is likely to weigh against the granting of a stay.[52]

[14.50] Where a payer claims that it is technically insolvent, but insolvency proceedings have not been commenced, the court will consider its conduct, in particular whether it has been trading.[53]

---

[45] *Pioneer Cladding Ltd v John Graham Construction* [2013] EWHC 2954 (TCC), per Coulson J at [9-38].
[46] *Rainford House Ltd v Cadogan Ltd* [2001] BLR 416, per Seymour J at [15-20].
[47] *Rodgers Contracts (Ballynahinch) Ltd v Merex Construction Ltd* [2012] NIQB 94, per Weatherup J at [23-24].
[48] *Barry D Trentham Ltd v Lawfield Investments Ltd* [2002] ScotCS 126, per Lord Drummond Young at [13-15].
[49] *Avoncroft Construction Ltd v Sharba Homes (CN) Ltd* [2008] EWHC 933 (TCC), per Kirkham J at [21-29].
[50] *Sutton Services International Ltd v Vaughan Engineering Services Ltd* [2013] NIQB 63, per Weatherup J at [20].
[51] *McConnell Dowell Constructors (Aust) Pty Ltd v National Grid Gas plc (formerly Transco plc)* [2006] EWHC 2551 (TCC), per Jackson J at [50-54].
[52] *True Fix Construction Ltd v Apollo Property Services Group Ltd* [2013] EWHC 2524 (TCC), per Ramsey J at [26-33].
[53] *Partner Projects Ltd v Corinthian Nominees Ltd* [2011] EWHC 2989 (TCC), per Edwards-Stuart J at [55].

[14.51] There has been an *obiter dicta* remark[54] in one enforcement case where it was suggested that if the adjudicator's decision was unquestionably correct, then the financial status of the payee would not be considered at all and the court would decline to order a stay of execution. However, there is no case with a *ratio decideni* to that effect, although it is submitted that this approach is right. If the payer could not make out any realistic case that it would, in fact, ever be entitled to the repayment of any money because it was clear to the court that the adjudicator had obviously got the answer right, and there were no other claims to be taken into account, then there would be no likely future final determination in the other direction which required the interim protection of a stay.

14.3.5 Imminent resolution of other proceedings

[14.52] If separate court proceedings are on foot to determine the dispute between the parties at the same time as the summary judgment application, and those proceedings are close to being concluded, where there is doubt as to whether the payee in the summary judgment proceedings will be able to repay the amount awarded in the summary judgment application in the event that the parallel court proceedings decide against that party, a stay may be granted.[55] The same may be true where there are arbitral proceedings that are close to being heard.[56]

[14.53] In *William Verry Ltd v North West London Communal Mikvah*,[57] the adjudicator erroneously failed to consider a variety of matters, but was held with some hesitation to have just 'but only just' acted within jurisdiction. The court exceptionally gave the losing party six weeks to pursue a further adjudication dealing with 'other matters' (defects) so that the results of both adjudications could be considered together. However, it is difficult to see how such decision was arrived at, given the 'pay now argue later' mantra on which the Act is founded. This decision has not been followed since. Furthermore, in *Alexander & Law Ltd v Coveside (21BPR) Ltd*,[58] Coulson J expressly rejected any suggestion that there could be a 'near miss' theory justifying a stay. If the decision was enforceable, it decided the dispute pending litigation or arbitration, any expressed reservations about its correctness by the court or the adjudicator himself notwithstanding.

[14.54] In *Workspace Management Ltd v YJL London Ltd*,[59] arbitration proceedings were occurring at the same time as the enforcement proceedings. A decision in the arbitration was 'apparently imminent'. It was clear that the result of the arbitration proceedings would have an effect on the overall financial liability of the parties and a stay was therefore applied for until the arbitration decision was handed down. The court was not required to deal with the application for a stay of execution because of the other issues. However,

---

[54] *Anrik Ltd v AS Leisure Properties Ltd* [2010] EWHC 441 (TCC), per Edwards-Stuart J at [29–35].
[55] *Herschell Engineering Ltd v Breen Property Ltd* (2000) 70 Con LR 1, per Dyson J at [23].
[56] *Kier Regional Ltd v City and General (Holborn) Ltd* [2008] EWHC 2454 (TCC), per Coulson J at [68–71].
[57] *William Verry Ltd v N W London Communal Mikvah* [2004] EWHC 1300 (TCC), per J Thornton QC at [54–60].
[58] [2013] EWHC 3949 (TCC), per Coulson J at [13–14].
[59] [2009] EWHC 2017 (TCC), per Coulson J at [40–44].

Enforcement: insolvency, stay and severability

if it had been required to deal with it, the judge said he would have been persuaded to exercise his discretion in favour of a stay.

14.3.6 Manifest injustice

[14.55] In *Galliford Try Building v Estura Ltd*,[60] the court ordered that Estura was liable to pay £4 million which was an amount that had been determined as payable by the adjudicator because Galliford submitted an application for payment and Estura had failed to issue a pay less notice. The details of the case and the reasons why court made the decision it did are considered further at Section 8.4.4, but in parallel with the application for summary judgment, Estura made an application for a stay of execution, in the event summary judgment was awarded. Estura argued for a stay on grounds that there would be manifest injustice if it was forced to pay £4 million because it had failed to issue a pay less notice in circumstances where it would be unable to challenge the merits of the application and recover any overpayment due. Furthermore, there was a risk that Galliford would walk off site and/or delay the final account process indefinitely and there was also a strong risk that Estura would go insolvent if it was forced to pay £4 million. The court held that in 'exceptional' cases, a stay could be granted where there was a risk of manifest injustice. While it ruled out that a stay of the entire amount owed was appropriate because Galliford had done nothing wrong, it ruled that a stay of £2.5 million of the £4 million was appropriate, until further financial information came to light which supported the lifting of the stay or until the Final Statement. The court took five factors into account, namely that:

(1) The enforcement amount should not stifle Estura from pursuing its rights.
(2) Galliford should not be placed in a worse position than if the application for payment had been properly valued.
(3) Estura should not be in a better position than if the application had been properly valued (it was suggested that £1.3 million was due).
(4) The recovery of the judgment sum should not remove the incentive to complete the project.
(5) Estura was withholding £900,000 in liquidated damages.

[14.56] The judge made it clear that the application of manifest injustice to a stay of execution was very much the exception rather than the rule. This case is the first time manifest injustice has succeeded in support of an application for a stay of execution.

14.3.7 Other circumstances in which an application for a stay has failed

[14.57] Other than the instances mentioned above, there are unlikely to be any other grounds upon which a stay of execution can be successfully argued. A number of other grounds have been put forward, all of them have failed. These include a stay of execution:

- pending the decision in a cross adjudication;[61]

---

[60] [2015] EWHC 412 (TCC), per Edwards-Stuart J at [53–55; 78–101].
[61] *Avoncroft Construction Ltd v Sharba Homes Ltd* [2008] EWHC 933 (TCC), per Kirkham J at [27].

- to allow the parties to mediate;[62]
- where there is an existing cross-claim being pursued and the size of the cross-claim is considerably larger than the amount on which a stay is sought;[63]
- where a threat is made by the winning party to wind up the company once payment has been made, which if carried out would deprive the losing party of the opportunity to recover some or all of the money paid by proceeding to a final determination of the dispute and obtaining a decision awarding less than the amount awarded by the adjudicator;[64]
- subject to Section 14.3.5, where there are existing arbitration or litigation proceedings;[65]
- where the matter will be referred to arbitration or litigation proceedings;[66]
- where the company seeking the stay is a dormant company;[67]
- because of the illness or non-attendance of the one of the parties at the time of the enforcement hearing.[68]

14.3.8 Partial stay

[14.58] The court has jurisdiction to order a partial stay of execution if it considers that there is a real risk that the payee would not be able to repay the judgment sum in full. In *Jacques and another (t/a C&E Jacques Partnership) v Ensign Contractors Ltd*,[69] Akenhead J, relying on the decision of *Wimbledon v Vago*,[70] ordered a stay of approximately 50% of the judgment sum to reflect the financial state of the employer.

[14.59] In *NAP Anglia v Sun-Land Development*,[71] the court ordered a partial stay of execution of the judgment sum due to the payee's financial position. Edwards-Stuart J considered the guidelines in *Wimbledon v Vago* and held that a partial stay of execution was appropriate for sums in excess of £65,000 because:

- the current financial position of NAP could not be attributable to Sun-Land's failure to pay the sum awarded by the adjudicator; and
- NAP was in a less healthy financial position than when it entered into the contract with Sun-Land, but the financial position was not so bad as to preclude NAP repaying a significant part of the adjudicator's decision.

---

[62] *Balfour Beatty Construction Ltd v Modus Corovest (Blackpool) Ltd* [2008] EWHC 3029 (TCC), per Coulson J at [14–21].
[63] *Knight Build Ltd v Urvasco Ltd* [2008] EWHC 3056 (TCC), per Ramsey at [50].
[64] Ibid at [48–49].
[65] *DGT Steel and Cladding Ltd v Cubitt Building and Interiors Ltd* [2007] EWHC 1584 (TCC), per Coulson J at [51].
[66] Ibid.
[67] *Westshield Civil Engineering Ltd v Buckingham Group Contracting Ltd* [2013] EWHC 1825 (TCC), per Akenhead J at [30–35].
[68] *AJ Brenton t/a Manton Electrical Components v Jack Palmer* [2001] AdjLR 01/19 per Havery J at [8].
[69] [2009] EWHC 3383, per Akenhead J at [35–39].
[70] [2005] EWHC 1086 (TCC), per Coulson J at [26].
[71] [2011] EWHC 2846 (TCC), per Edwards-Stuart J at [68–72].

14.3.9 Conditions imposed on granting the stay

[14.60] Where the court grants a stay, it will sometimes attach conditions to the order, principally for the purpose of protecting the party against whom the order was made (the payee). In principle, a payer is entitled to be provided with security that is equivalent to the security it would have had based on the payee's financial position at the time when the relevant contract was made. Such security might be provided by a bond[72] or guarantee which provides sufficient security for the repayment of the judgment sum.[73]

[14.61] The court may order that the sum awarded by the adjudicator is paid into court.[74] It may also order that the stay is imposed for a limited period (a month perhaps) on the basis that the payer undertakes to commence arbitral or court proceedings within that period in respect of matters which are the subject of the adjudicator's decision.[75]

14.3.10 Severability

[14.62] Severability is a concept that has developed markedly since the passing of the 1996 Act. In short, it espouses the idea that where a part of the adjudicator's decision is found to be unenforceable, it can be severed from the other part, which is found to be enforceable. The effect is that the winning party to an adjudication will derive at least some benefit from the result, as opposed to nothing at all.

[14.63] It had formerly been considered settled law that if an adjudicator was in breach of the rules of natural justice or acted outside of the boundaries of jurisdiction, the decision would be unenforceable in its entirety.[76]

[14.64] This rule was put in doubt with Akenhead J's *obiter* comments in *Cantillon Ltd v Urvasco Ltd*.[77] In that case, the court concluded that the bad parts of an adjudicator's decision could be severed from the good, provided the adjudicator had determined two or more disputes (where the adjudication rules allow it) and the successful challenge went only to one of those disputes. The effect of the decision in *Cantillon v Urvasco* was thought to be limited because adjudications dealing with more than one dispute are rare and challenges to adjudicators' decisions on grounds of a breach of natural justice are even rarer.

[14.65] In *Quartzelec Ltd v Honeywell Control Systems Ltd*,[78] the whole of the adjudicator's decision was held unenforceable for failing to consider 'the omissions defence' which,

---

[72] *McConnell Dowell Constructors (Aust) Pty Ltd v National Grid Gas plc (formerly Transco plc)* [2006] EWHC 2551 (TCC), per Jackson J at [52–53].
[73] *FG Skerritt Ltd v Caledonian Building Systems Ltd* [2013] EWHC 1898 (TCC), per Ramsey J at [35].
[74] *Rainford House Ltd v Cadogan Ltd* [2001] EWHC 18 (TCC), per Seymour J at [20].
[75] *Baldwins Industrial Services plc v Barr Ltd* [2002] EWHC 2915 (TCC), per Kirkham J at [35–40].
[76] See for example *Farebrother Building Services Ltd v Frogmore Investments Ltd* [2001] CILL 1762, per Gilliland J at [32]; *CSC Braehead Leisure Ltd and Capital & Regional (Braehead) Ltd v Laing O-Rourke Scotland Ltd* [2008] CSOH 119, per Lord Menzies at [38–40]; *RSL (South West Ltd) v Stansell Ltd (No. 1)* [2003] EWHC 1390 (TCC), per Seymour J at [38].
[77] [2008] EWHC 282 (TCC), per Akenhead J at [63].
[78] [2008] EWHC 3315 (TCC), per David J at [39–42].

even if it had been considered and accepted by the adjudicator in full, could only have provided the losing party with a partial defence worth about £36,000 against a liability otherwise found by the adjudicator of £135,000. That notwithstanding, Davies J held that the whole of the decision was unenforceable and that severance of a single dispute to allow enforcement of the £99,000 otherwise obviously due in any event was not possible. Disquiet about this result was expressed by Coulson J in *Pilon Ltd v Breyer Group plc*,[79] where he presaged Edwards-Stuart J's approach in the *Working Environments*[80] case, saying

> I acknowledge that it may soon be time for the TCC to review whether, where there is a single dispute, if it can be shown that a jurisdiction/natural justice point is worth a fixed amount which is significantly less than the overall sum awarded by the adjudicator, severance could properly be considered...

[14.66] Between 2009 and 2012, in addition to *Pilon*, there were at least 10 court decisions that dealt in some way with the question of severability. A number of them dealt with the question of whether it is possible to sever a single dispute, but none displaced the rule laid down in *Cantillon*. All of these cases are listed at Appendix 8. However, 2012 heralded three decisions that developed this area of law.

[14.67] In *Working Environments Ltd v Greencoat Construction Ltd*,[81] the employer listed 12 items in its withholding notice for withholding money. The court found that items 11 and 12 were new items in respect of which a dispute had not crystallised. Instead of rendering the whole decision unenforceable, it severed the decision in respect of items 11 and 12 because the adjudicator's decision in relation to those two items was outside his jurisdiction. It is noteworthy that the total sum for items 11 and 12 was small in comparison to the claim as a whole.

[14.68] In *Beck Interiors Ltd v UK Flooring Contractors Ltd*,[82] the adjudicator decided two issues, namely sums due for increased costs of completing carpeting work and a liquidated damages claim. The court decided that only the claim for the carpeting work fell within the scope of the adjudication and that the liquidated damages claim was a new and unauthorised introduction. The court severed decision on the liquidated damages claim, noting that it was possible to do so because they had been presented and decided as two separate issues.

[14.69] In *Lidl UK GmbH v R G Carter Colchester Ltd*,[83] the court, having considered Working Environments and Beck, said that:

> where a single dispute or difference has been referred, it will generally be difficult to show that the reasoning in relation to the part of the decision that it is being sought to sever had no impact

---

[79] [2010] EWHC 837 (TCC), per Coulson J at [39–42].
[80] Op. cit. No. 78.
[81] [2012] EWHC 3138 (TCC), per Edwards-Stuart J at [61].
[82] [2012] EWHC 1808 (TCC), per Akenhead J at [32–33].
[83] [2012] EWHC 3138, per Edwards-Stuart J at [57–61].

on the reasoning leading to the decision actually reached, or that the actual outcome would still have been the same. If this is the case, the part cannot safely be severed from the whole. However, where, in the case of the referral of a single dispute additional questions are brought in and adjudicated upon, there should be no reason in principle why any decision on those additional questions should not be severed provided that the reasoning giving rise to it does not form an integral part of the decision as a whole.

[14.70] Thus, in relation to a single dispute, a useful doctrine of severability has developed that may salvage an enforceable decision (albeit only in part) from the ruins of a successful jurisdictional or natural justice challenge. However, there is at least an argument that for the time being, this doctrine is limited to circumstances where additional issues are brought into the adjudication, as opposed to the question of where the single dispute originally referred to adjudication is unenforceable in part.

[14.71] Note that a party will only be entitled to object to the 'bad' part of the adjudicator's decision where it has adequately reserved its position on the jurisdiction of the adjudicator. Where it has not done so, it may be taken to have waived its right to object, and the court will not sever the decision.[84]

[14.72] Where the court decides to sever part of a decision and where the adjudicator has apportioned his fees between the parties, in the absence of a division of that apportionment by the adjudicator between what is now the severed and non-severed parts of the decision, a court will not try to second guess how the adjudicator might have apportioned his fees between those parts. In other words, the court will sever the substantive decision, but decline to enforce the adjudicator's decision on how his fees are to be apportioned. The effect is that both parties will bear the adjudicator's fees equally.[85]

[14.73] Where a jurisdictional or natural justice issue arises during the adjudication which, if found valid, may give rise to a severable decision, it is advisable to ask the adjudicator to give a decision capable of severance. This can be achieved by asking the adjudicator (either as part of the main decision or as an alternative) to address each issue separately and separately allocate an award of the fees and expenses of the adjudicator to those issues. This may then improve the prospect of the court deciding that the adjudicator's decision is one capable of severance.

---

[84] *Allied P&L Ltd v Paradigm Housing Group Ltd* [2009] EWHC 2890 (TCC), per Akenhead at [44].
[85] *Beck Interiors Ltd v UK Flooring Ltd* [2012] EWHC 1808 (TCC), per Akenhead J at [33].

Chapter 15
Final determination

15.1 Overview

[15.01] An adjudicator's decision made pursuant to a statutory adjudication is binding which means that providing the decision is valid, it must be complied with in accordance with the terms set out therein. But it is only temporarily binding in that the adjudicator's decision may subsequently be replaced by the decision of a court or arbitral tribunal, or by an agreement reached between the parties, but it may be made permanent by wording in the contract that prohibits the referral of the adjudicated dispute to final proceedings once a period of time has elapsed without a given step or steps being taken. In the vast majority of cases, however, the parties will simply take no action at all and then, by default, the adjudicator's decision is the one that ultimately determines the dispute (Section 15.2).

[15.02] Parties may litigate or arbitrate a dispute before, during or after that dispute is being adjudicated. In other words, there is no bar to adjudication for a temporary result being obtained in parallel with final dispute resolution. Obviously, to have any utility, the adjudication must conclude prior to the court giving judgment or the arbitrators rendering their award, otherwise such a judgment or award will finally decide the dispute, and any subsequent adjudicator's decision on it will then be a nullity. (Section 15.3).

[15.03] The underlying dispute notwithstanding, the paying party under an adjudicator's decision has the benefit of a 'fresh' limitation period of 6 or 12 years (depending on whether the contract was under hand or seal) within which to advance the adjudicated dispute to a final determination. The law holds that while the underlying dispute can become time-barred, the limitation period in respect of those parts of the dispute lost in the adjudication is effectively extended. The litigation or arbitration is not affected by the decision in the adjudication – the losing party does not have to persuade the judge that the adjudicator was wrong in order to win at trial. However, compliance with the adjudicator's decision can sometimes have an effect as to where the burden of persuasion might lie. The fees in respect of the adjudicator during the adjudication will not be recoverable as part of the final proceedings. Even if the court or arbitrator reaches a different conclusion from the adjudicator and thus finally determines the dispute differently, that will not entitle the ultimately successful party to claim repayment of any adjudicator's fees he was ordered to pay as a result of his losing the adjudication. Whether or not a party's costs are recoverable depends on the circumstances (Section 15.4).

A Practical Guide to Construction Adjudication, First Edition. James Pickavance.
© 2016 James Pickavance. Published 2016 by John Wiley & Sons, Inc.

15.2 Finalising the adjudicator's decision

15.2.1 In a nutshell

[15.04] An adjudicator's decision made pursuant to a statutory adjudication is only temporarily binding. However, parties may agree to settle the dispute finally by way of a separate agreement either on the same or different terms as set out in the adjudicator's decision.

[15.05] Where the form of adjudication is statutory, an agreement between the parties that the decision of the adjudicator is final and binding may only be made after the start of the adjudication. Thus it may be made at the time of referring the dispute, or after the decision has been received. But the parties cannot agree in the original contract itself to accept the decision of the adjudicator as final, for that would be contrary to the express terms of section 108(3) of the Act. Provisions in contractual adjudication schemes set out in standard forms such as the NEC3, which make an adjudicator's decision finally binding unless notice of disputation is given within a certain period after the decision is rendered do not offend this rule, it is submitted.

[15.06] The finally binding nature of the decision in those circumstances arises not from a prior agreement, but from the subsequent failure or refusal of the losing party to give the relevant notice of disputation in time. Generally speaking, where a party is under a duty to elect in this way within a certain period of time, the failure to take a required step where there is a right or duty to do so is treated in law as a positive act in its own right, to which the parties may permissibly assign significance in advance.

15.2.2 Adjudicator's decision made final by contract

[15.07] Where the Act applies, it is not permissible for the contract between the parties to prescribe that the adjudicator's decision be final and binding. What is permissible is for the parties to agree that the decision is final and binding after the decision has been given (typically by way of a settlement agreement), or for the contract to stipulate that if the adjudicator's decision is not challenged within the fixed period, then it becomes final and binding (so-called conclusivity clauses).[1] In the latter case, the time limits within which final proceedings must be brought are generally construed strictly.[2] The time runs from the date of the decision of the adjudicator. It does not refer to any earlier ruling or decision which the adjudicator may make during the adjudication.[3]

[15.08] Not infrequently, parties that are the subject of such contractual provisions will seek to determine disputes during the project through adjudication and will then refer a dispute to final determination after completion. The defendant will sometimes challenge the

---

[1] See for example *Midland Expressway Ltd v Carillion Construction* [2006] EWHC 1505 (TCC), per Jackson J at [85–89].
[2] *LaFarge (Aggregates) Ltd v Newham LBC* [2005] EWHC 1337, per Cooke J at [17–30].
[3] *Midland Expressway Ltd & Ors v Carillion Construction Ltd & Ors (No. 3)* [2006] EWHC 1505 (TCC), per Jackson J at [85–89].

tribunal's jurisdiction to hear the dispute on the basis that the dispute that is being referred has already been decided in adjudication and is now final.[4] Whether or not that is the case will depend on the facts and on the wording of the contract. The court will examine the exact nature and scope of the dispute referred to adjudication. It will not conduct an over-elaborate or over-analytical construction of references to adjudication and therefore – and as a very general rule – it will try to find that the dispute referred to the courts is one that it has jurisdiction to hear.[5] Consider Section 7.7.3, which provides further detail on conclusivity clauses.

15.2.3 Adjudicator's decision made final by agreement

[15.09] The court will not enforce the decision of an adjudicator in circumstances where the parties have settled the dispute. That settlement may occur before the adjudication, during it or after the adjudicator's award and before the enforcement hearing.[6]

[15.10] The settlement may relate to any part of the dispute, or all of it. If the settlement comes after the adjudicator has issued his decision, it may relate not only to the decision on the dispute referred, but also to part of it, or to any process of reasoning adopted in the course of reaching the decision.[7] See Section 7.2.8(G), which addresses settlement before the adjudication, Section 10.6.9, which addresses settlement during an adjudication and Section 13.3.20, which addresses the cost consequences of settling after the commencement of enforcement proceedings.

15.2.4 Adjudicator's decision made final by the passing of time

[15.11] There exists circumstances where an adjudicator's decision can become final by the simple passing of time, because the parties are obliged to arrange their affairs on the basis of that binding decision, and, in so doing, they may be compelled to act on certain grounds and in certain ways that cannot be undone later.

[15.12] For example, where the adjudicator reaches a binding decision that parts of the contract are not operable, that certain documents are not incorporated into it, or even that the contract needs to be rectified, then the parties will have to organise their behaviour accordingly, unless and until they get a contrary ruling from the court. If the adjudicator decides that the contract termination mechanism only permits termination on 28 days' written notice, a party wishing to terminate will have to give that notice. It will not be possible to give a different form of notice and then have that retrospectively vindicated by a subsequent court decision.

---

[4] See for example *Castle Inns (Stirling) Limited t/a Castle Leisure Group v Clark Contracts* [2007] CSOH 21, per Drummond Young L at [12–20].
[5] *Westshield Civil Engineering Ltd v Buckingham Group Contracting Ltd* [2013] EWHC 1825 (TCC), per Akenhead J at [18–26].
[6] *Bracken and another v Billinghurst* [2003] EWHC 1333 (TCC), per Wilcox J at [28–30].
[7] *RSL (South West Ltd) v Stansell Ltd (No. 1)* [2003] EWHC 1390 (TCC), per Seymour J at [37].

15.3 Adjudication and other proceedings

15.3.1 In a nutshell

[15.13] Parties may litigate or arbitrate a dispute before, during or after that dispute is adjudicated. Where the dispute is adjudicated, the parties will normally be required to comply with the adjudicator's decision forthwith, notwithstanding a decision to litigate or arbitrate.

15.3.2 Final determination at the same time as enforcement proceedings

[15.14] Where the nature of the dispute between the parties does not involve a substantial dispute of fact (thus the procedure is invariably unavailable for monetary disputes), either party may commence a claim in the court to resolve the dispute through CPR Part 8 proceedings. The time period between commencing Part 8 proceedings and the case being heard by the court is short, so that if a losing party to an adjudication commences Part 8 proceedings as soon as the adjudicator issues his decision, then those proceedings are likely to reach a hearing at the same time as the enforcement proceedings. Where there are two actions, one commenced by the winning party and another commenced by the losing party, then where it is appropriate to do so, the court will join the proceedings and hear them together.

[15.15] The effect of taking this course of action is to leapfrog enforcement of the adjudicator's decision and proceed straight to a final determination of the dispute, thus neutering the effect of the adjudicator's decision. Part 8 proceedings used in this way amount to a preemptive strike to defeat the application to enforce.

[15.16] Seeking a final determination at the same time as an enforcement hearing is in one sense difficult to digest because it renders the adjudication useless and goes against one of the key policies of the Act, which is to enforce adjudicator's decisions as quickly as possible. However, the court has justified it in this way:[8]

> Any other conclusion would be verging on the absurd: to allow the application to enforce the decision and then to set it aside (assuming the defendant had its tackle in order to do so). The decision is binding only in so far as the dispute has not been finally determined. The Act does not say when the final determination may take place. In my judgment the Act does not lead to any such technical absurdity, nor is it permissible under the Civil Procedure Rules as it is directly contrary to the overriding objective and other provisions of Part 1. Once the court is seized of the case it has to take a course which saves expense and is expeditious. To proceed first to deal with the application for summary judgment, to allow it and then to track back and to determine the dispute that gave rise to it is not consistent with the principles of Part 1 of the CPR and it is not in the interests of both parties, when they can be satisfied in an expeditious and less expensive way.

---
[8] *Alstom Signalling Ltd v Jarvis Facilities Ltd* (No. 2) [2004] EWHC 1285 (TCC), per Lloyd J at [19–20].

[15.17] It is acknowledged that those cases where Part 8 is available to be used in this way will be relatively rare because most adjudications are about issues of fact which will not be capable of being finally determined in a court before the application for summary judgment is heard.[9] However, examples might include the determination of the meaning of a clause in a contract, or the effect of a novation agreement.[10]

[15.18] The final determination through Part 8 proceedings need not be limited to situations where the entire dispute is susceptible to being resolved in that way. If there is part of the dispute that can be isolated and determined by the court, then the court has jurisdiction to decide that part. One such example can be found in the case of *Geoffrey Osborne Ltd v Atkins Rail Ltd*,[11] although it is worth noting that the court was persuaded to grant Part 8 relief in this case to correct part of an adjudicator's decision because it was common ground between the parties that the adjudicator had made an error, albeit one not going to jurisdiction. The debate thus centred on whether as a matter of policy the court should grant a declaration to correct that error, or whether it should enforce the decision in full on the basis that enforceable adjudicators decisions should be enforced without further analysis. Given that this was an unusual case where the parties agreed there was an error, and what the financial implications of that error were, it is perhaps not surprising that the court enforced – but at the same time gave a Part 8 ruling – to correct the error.

[15.19] Part 8 proceedings are of course only available in this context where the contract provides for court proceedings and not arbitration as the method of finally resolving disputes.[12]

[15.20] The ability to use Part 8 proceedings to shortcut final proceedings may also be used even if an application for summary judgment is refused and the defendant is given leave to defend. That is what happened in *Leeds City Council v Waco UK Ltd*,[13] where Waco was not granted its summary judgment application, Leeds was given permission to defend at full trial but at the same time ordered to pay Waco the sum of £500,000 awarded by the adjudicator pending the resolution of the dispute. Rather than wait until the resolution of the full trial, Leeds commenced Part 8 proceedings seeking a declaration that the adjudicator's decision was wrong. The court granted the declaration and ordered Waco to pay back the money. The decision pursuant to the Part 8 proceedings would have been obtained much quicker than if the parties had proceeded to full trial under the Part 7 procedure.

15.3.3 Final determination at the same time as adjudication

[15.21] Is it permissible for parties to adjudicate and litigate at the same time? The answer is yes.[14] Subject to the provisions of the contract between the parties and unless a party is

---

[9] *Caledonian Modular Ltd v Mar City Developments Ltd* [2015] EWHC 1855 (TCC), per Coulson J at [12–13].
[10] *Hillcrest Homes Ltd v Beresford & Curbishley Ltd* [2014] EWHC 280 (TCC), per Raynor J at [81–96].
[11] *Geoffrey Osborne Ltd v Atkins Rail Ltd* [2009] EWHC 2425 (TCC), per Edwards Stuart J at [10–18].
[12] *Laker Vent Engineering Ltd v Jacobs E&C Ltd* [2014] EWHC 1058 (TCC), per Ramsey J at [124–129].
[13] [2015] EWHC 1400 (TCC) at [63–66].
[14] *Twintec Ltd v Volkerfitzpatrick Ltd* [2014] EWHC 10 (TCC), per Edwards-Stuart J at [7].

estopped or has waived its right to do so, final proceedings in relation to a dispute that is the subject of an adjudication (or otherwise) may be commenced at any time. It has been argued that pursuing two forms of dispute resolution simultaneously may amount to an abuse of process. However, in the context of statutory adjudication, this has been rejected[15] on the basis that the Act provides that parties may adjudicate their dispute 'at any time'.

15.3.4 Final determination without complying with the adjudicator's decision

[15.22] Subject to the circumstances outlined in Section 15.3, the losing party to an adjudication must comply with the terms of the decision before commencing litigation or arbitration proceedings in respect of the same dispute. In *Anglo Swiss Holdings Ltd v Packman Lucas Ltd*,[16] Anglo Swiss commenced High Court proceedings, notwithstanding the fact that they had not complied with the terms of an adjudicator's decision, or the terms of a court order to enforce the adjudicator's decision. The court held that Anglo had simply ignored the contractual and statutory requirement that they should honour the adjudicator's decision. It ordered both a stay of the High Court proceedings until such time as Anglo Swiss complied with the terms of the adjudicator's decision and that a sum of £50,000 was paid into court as security for costs, because there was reason to believe that it would be unable to pay Packman's costs should the court find against Anglo Swiss.

[15.23] Notwithstanding the clear position set out in Anglo Swiss, one should not always assume that a court will enforce an adjudicator's decision where proceedings to finally determine the same dispute have been initiated. In the case of *Cygnet Healthcare plc v Higgins City Limited*,[17] the parties had agreed an ad hoc arbitration to determine a dispute and at the same time, Cygnet commenced an adjudication on the same dispute. A decision was given by the adjudicator in Cygnet's favour, which it then tried to enforce. The court held that in circumstances where a dispute has been the subject of an adjudicator's decision and where the parties had already agreed to finally determine the dispute via ad hoc arbitration and where (in this case) because of a dispute as to the terms of the contact it could not be said that there was a clear statutory entitlement to adjudication, it would be 'inappropriate' to embark upon a consideration of the validity of the adjudicator's decision, let alone to determine whether or not it should be enforced.

15.3.5 Final determination in breach of the contractual dispute resolution procedure (including an agreement to adjudicate)

[15.24] Where the Act applies, referring a dispute to statutory adjudication is not mandatory, albeit that the right to adjudicate at any time is. However, the parties may agree in their

---

[15] *Connex South Eastern Ltd v MJ Building Services Group plc* [2004] EWHC 1518 (TCC), per Havery J at [35].
[16] [2009] EWHC 3212 (TCC), per Akenhead J at [25–31].
[17] (2000) 16 Const LJ 394, per Thornton J at [20–27] [100–108].

[15.25] For instance, in *Impresa Castelli SpA v Cola Holdings Ltd*,[18] the conditions of contract contained an elaborate code for the adjudication and arbitration of disputes. This provided that certain disputes (including whether the works were carried out in accordance with the contract) arising prior to practical completion, could not be referred to arbitration, but they could be referred to adjudication. Following that adjudication, the same dispute could be referred to arbitration after practical completion. The disputes that could be referred to adjudication before practical completion could not be referred to adjudication after practical completion. Impresa said that the counterclaim put forward by Cola was a matter that was to be referred to adjudication before practical completion, but since it hadn't been, it could not now be arbitrated. On the facts, this argument was rejected but this is one example of how dispute resolution procedures can control the referral of disputes.

[15.26] In *DGT Steel and Cladding Ltd v Cubitt Building and Interiors Ltd*,[19] the question for the court was in what circumstances, if any, should a temporary stay be granted to restrain court proceedings until an adjudication of the underlying dispute has taken place? The court reviewed a number of authorities and derived the following principles that related to circumstances in which there was a binding agreement to adjudicate before litigation:

(a) The court will not grant an injunction to prevent one party from commencing and pursuing adjudication proceedings, even if there is already court or arbitration proceedings in respect of the same dispute: see **Herschell v Breen**[20]

(b) The court has an inherent jurisdiction to stay court proceedings issued in breach of an agreement to adjudicate (see Cape Durasteel), just as it has with any other enforceable agreement for ADR; see **Channel Tunnel Group**,[21] **Cott**[22] and **Cable & Wireless**.[23]

(c) The court's discretion as to whether or not to grant a stay should be exercised in accordance with the principles noted above.[24] If a binding adjudication agreement has been identified then the persuasive burden is on the party seeking to resist the stay to justify that stance; see **Cott** and **Cable & Wireless**.

[15.27] In that case, the court determined that there was a binding agreement to adjudicate and further that there was no good reason for the court not to exercise its inherent jurisdiction[25] to stay the proceedings.[26]

---

[18] [2002] EWHC 1363 (TCC), per Thornton J at [100–108].
[19] [2007] EWHC 1584 (TCC), per Coulson J at [5–12].
[20] *Herschell Engineering Ltd v Breen Property Ltd (No. 2)* [2000] AdjLR 07/28, per Lloyd J at [3–20].
[21] *Channel Tunnel Group Ltd v Balfour Beatty Construction Ltd* [1993] AC 334.
[22] *Cott UK Ltd v FE Barber Ltd* [1997] 3 All ER 540.
[23] *Cable & Wireless PLC v IBM United Kingdom Ltd* [2002] EWHC 2059 (Comm).
[24] Which are that there is a 'presumption in favour of the parties' agreement to adjudicate, putting the persuasive burden on the party resisting the stay to show good reasons for their stance.'
[25] Subsection 49(3) of the Senior Courts Act 1981.
[26] *DGT Steel and Cladding Ltd v Cubitt Building and Interiors Ltd.* [2007] EWHC 1584 (TCC), per Coulson J at [51].

[15.28] In the Northern Irish case of *Sam Abbas and Anthony Hayes (t/as AH Design) v Rotary (International) Ltd*,[27] there was a mandatory provision in the consultancy agreement requiring the parties to refer the disputes to adjudication. Rotary had commenced court proceedings and so Sam Abbas made an application for a stay of those proceedings until the parties had submitted their dispute to adjudication. The first question for the court was whether, in the context of some poor drafting, adjudication was provided for under the contract. Interpreting the provisions of the contract, the court found that it was. The second question for the court was whether the adjudication provisions were clear enough to be enforceable. The court found that they were. Finally the court was asked to consider whether a stay was appropriate. Notwithstanding the mandatory provision in the consultancy agreement, because (a) an element of the claim was not the subject of the consultancy agreement; and (b) the claimant had previously had the opportunity to refer the dispute to adjudication but chose not to, the court declined to grant a stay.

[15.29] A stay was granted in *Peterborough City Council v Enterprise Managed Services*.[28] In that case, the parties had entered into a contract based on the FIDIC Silver Book. The contract, which was not one to which the Act applied, required that the parties must refer disputes to a dispute adjudication board before referring it to litigation. Following an unsuccessful mediation, Peterborough commenced court proceedings without referring the dispute to adjudication. This was followed by an application for the appointment of an adjudicator by Enterprise and an application for a stay of the court proceedings. The court had sympathy with Peterborough's submissions, which in essence were that adjudication was pointless because the dispute was too complex, that it would require extensive disclosure in order to be resolved and that it was not suited to the 'rough and ready' process of adjudication. However, noting that there is a presumption in favour of leaving the parties to resolve their disputes in the manner provided for by their contract, the court held that a stay was appropriate.

[15.30] Where a party has adjudicated a dispute and wishes to refer the same dispute to either litigation or arbitration, it must have complied with any other prerequisite steps required by the dispute resolution procedure. In *J.T.Mackley v Gosport Marina Ltd*,[29] the contract (an ICE form) required that a decision of the engineer was a condition precedent to the entitlement of a party to a contract to refer a dispute to arbitration. The parties had adjudicated the dispute and then Gosport referred the dispute to arbitration. The court held that the Act:

> makes it plain ... that arbitration is only available as a means of challenging the decision of an adjudicator if the relevant contract so provides or an ad hoc arbitration agreement is made. Where it is sought to rely on an arbitration clause in the relevant contract, it seems to me to be obvious that the ability to do so, and the terms upon which such may be done, fall to be determined under the relevant arbitration clause.

---

[27] [2012] NIQB 41, per Weatherup J at [10–26].
[28] [2014] EWHC 3193 (TCC), per Edwards-Stuart at [37–43].
[29] [2002] EWHC 1315, per Seymour J at [35–38].

[15.31] Therefore, notwithstanding the adjudication, the parties had to refer the dispute to an engineer for a decision before they could arbitrate.

[15.32] In *Cubitt Building & Interiors v Richardson Roofing (Industrial) Ltd*,[30] the contract between the parties was a construction contract within the meaning of the Act and therefore both parties had a right to adjudicate. The court held that in certain circumstances it may be appropriate to build time into the court or arbitration proceedings to allow the parties to adjudicate, where it considered that adjudication would resolve the dispute, but that building extra time into the timetable is different from an order for a stay. The court said that a stay was unlikely to be appropriate where there was merely a discretionary right to adjudicate because the party who started the proceedings was entitled to have them resolved as quickly as possible and should not be forced into an adjudication when it did not want to.

[15.33] In all cases, whether the agreement to adjudicate is mandatory or discretionary will depend on the exact wording of the dispute resolution provisions in the contract.

15.4 Commencement, onus of proof and costs

15.4.1 In a nutshell

[15.34] The time period within which to litigate or arbitrate the same dispute following an adjudication will be 6 or 12 years, commencing from the date of compliance with the adjudicator's decision by the losing party.

[15.35] The onus of proof in the litigation or arbitration will not be affected by the decision in the adjudication.

[15.36] The fees in respect of the adjudicator during the adjudication will not be recoverable as part of the final proceedings, and the parties' fees are unlikely to be recoverable also.

15.4.2 Cause of action and limitation period for commencing final proceedings

[15.37] What is the effect of an adjudicator's decision on the nature and date of accrual of the cause of action (and therefore the date of limitation) where a losing party to a statutory adjudication subsequently commences court proceedings to seek a final determination of the matters determined by the adjudicator? This was answered in the Supreme Court decision of *Aspect Contracts (Asbestos) Ltd v Higgins Construction Plc*.[31] Whilst the answer can be condensed to a sentence and this issue rarely arises in practice, because Aspect is the only case on the subject of construction adjudication to reach the Supreme

---

[30] [2008] EWHC 1020 (TCC), per Akenhead J at [72].
[31] [2015] UKSC 38, per Lord Mance at [18–33].

Court and because the arguments raised and the Courts reasoning is interesting, it is perhaps worth considering the case in a little detail.

[15.38] The facts in brief were that the adjudicator had ordered Aspect to pay Higgins damages for breach of contract. After the expiry of the limitation period for claims under the contract and in tort, Aspect commenced a claim in the court in an attempt to recover the money it had paid to Higgins pursuant to the adjudicator's decision. The court considered whether:

(1) there was an implied term which permitted Aspect to commence proceedings to recover the overpayment;
(2) the correct route by Aspect should be a claim for a negative declaration; and
(3) there was a claim in restitution.

[15.39] In relation to the first question, the court held that the imposition of an implied term is a 'necessary legal consequence' of the Scheme that Aspect must have a directly enforceable right to recover any overpayment that the adjudicator's decision can be shown to have led. Thus, the implied term gave Aspect a new and independent cause of action, commencing from the deadline date for compliance with the adjudicator's decision by the losing party. The court accepted the policy factors in favour of imposing the implied term, namely that it encourages the use of adjudication, it creates certainty entitlement to a final determination and payment, it corrects the imbalance between the parties' access to final determination and that an adjudicator's decision is provisional. In relation to the limitation period, the court referred to authority which held that a claim to enforce a contractual entitlement is a claim founded on contract and in that case it fell within the scope of section 5 of the Limitation Act 1980, which means the payer has six years from the date of payment to bring its claim for a final determination and repayment. Furthermore, in the event it is awarded repayment, the payer is entitled to interest on that sum from the date the obligation to pay arose.

[15.40] In relation to the second argument, Higgins argued that no implied term was necessary to give a route into court because the paying party had available to it a claim for a declaration of non-liability, or a negative declaration, and it could use that to secure a final determination. Higgins said that if the court made such a declaration it has an inherent jurisdiction to order repayment. Finally, it said that the limitation period for such a declaration of non-liability is the same as the limitation period applying to a claim of liability. In other words, claim for a negative declaration had a six year limitation period running from the date when Aspect did not breach the contract and as such, Aspect was out of time. The court did not agree with Higgins. It said there is no inherent right to claim a negative declaration, it is a matter for the court's discretion. The court's jurisdiction does not include a power to order anyone to do anything simply in consequence of a declaration being made. What is needed is a cause of action independent from the declaration. Finally, the court said it was not appropriate to apply the limitation act to a claim for a negative declaration.

[15.41] Restitution, or unjust enrichment as it is otherwise known, is a remedy that seeks to reverse an unjust enrichment (in this case the overpayment), by restoring the relevant benefit or enrichment to the claimant. The general position is that a payment made where there is an obligation to make the payment cannot be regarded as unjust enrichment on the basis that the payee was entitled to it. Thus, a payment made in compliance with an adjudicator's decision is a payment made pursuant to a contractual obligation to comply with a decision. However, the Supreme Court held that if and to the extent the contractual basis on which the payment was made falls away in the final determination, because the tribunal or court decided there was no entitlement, an overpayment is retrospectively established. The final determination displaces the adjudication and leads to the overpayment amounts to a failure of consideration. A failure of consideration for a payment means that the state of affairs contemplated as the basis or reason for the payment has failed to materialise, or if it did exist, has failed to sustain itself. Thus, the failure of consideration paves the way for a claim for unjust enrichment even though when the payment was made it was made pursuant to a contractual obligation.

[15.42] For a payee in an adjudication (the winner), the decision in Aspect means that it may be faced with recovery proceedings at any time within six years from the date payment is made from the payer. It is thought that whilst such instances are likely to be rare, where they do occur, the payee may find limitation problems of its own. By the time recovery proceedings are brought, the payee in the adjudication may well be time barred from bringing its own proceedings, whether by counterclaim or otherwise, to challenge the claim being made against it in final determination.

15.4.3 Delaying the final determination

[15.43] Parties to a contract falling within the scope of the Act may adjudicate a dispute at any time. Any term of a contract that seeks to fetter that right will be struck out by the court. This has been interpreted quite broadly. Obvious fetters (such as a 'no adjudication until practical completion') are clearly void, but so too are more subtle forms of control or inhibition, such as terms of a contractual adjudication regime requiring one party to pay all the costs of the referral.[32]

[15.44] This applies equally to the right to challenge the enforcement of a decision by an adjudicator in the courts or otherwise. However, parties may agree in their contract that any final determination of a dispute is to be delayed until such time as prescribed in the contract. Thus, in *Enterprise Managed Services Ltd v East Midlands Contracting Ltd*,[33] the subcontract prohibited the parties from commencing any action or proceedings other than adjudication arising out of or in connection with the subcontract until 'the main contract works have been certified substantially or practically complete'. In the particular circumstances of that case, the court allowed the subcontractor to commence a claim in the court. However, it acknowledged that it is open to the parties to agree a moratorium on claims in their contract until a stipulated point in time.

---

[32] *Yuanda (UK) Co. Limited v WW Gear Construction Limited* [2010] EWHC 720 (TCC) per Edwards-Stuart J at [42–51].
[33] [2007] EWHC 727 (TCC), per Davies J at [32–36].

15.4.4 Onus of proof in subsequent proceedings

[15.45] The general principle is that the adjudicator's decision does not affect the onus of proof in subsequent arbitration or litigation of the dispute, which was the subject of the decision.[34] The subsequent proceedings do not involve any reconsideration of the adjudicator's decision, but are entirely freestanding.[35] That said, parties will of course argue points made in their favour in an adjudicator's decision, and a court or arbitrator may well take account of those points if it so wishes. If the court or arbitrator decides the dispute before the adjudicator's decision has been enforced, the adjudicator's decision is no longer effective.[36]

[15.46] This principle was cast into some doubt in *Walker Construction (UK) Ltd v Quayside Homes Ltd and Others*.[37] In *obiter dicta*, Lady Justice Gloster stated that she had 'real difficulty' with the proposition that an adjudicator's decision had no impact on subsequent proceedings. She observed that the defendant in the court proceedings (the successful party in the adjudication) has no reason to bring court proceedings to claim payment as it has already been paid. Further, because the decision of the adjudicator is binding 'until the dispute or difference is finally determined' by the court, she suggested that the onus of proof should rest with the claimant to adduce evidence and prove that the adjudicator's decision was wrong. While these comments are *obiter*, they re-open what was previously a settled area of law.

15.4.5 Final decision different to adjudicator's decision

[15.47] Once a final decision is made by the court or tribunal, the adjudicator's decision will cease to be binding. If the court's decision on the dispute is at variance with the adjudicator's decision, that variance will have to be dealt with, so for instance if the court awards a lesser sum than the adjudicator, sums must be repaid. While the Act does not expressly deal with the basis for this repayment, the right arises either because of an implied term in the parties' contract or a restitutionary obligation based on unjustified enrichment. Where the parties' contract remains extant at the point of judgment, the obligation to repay will more naturally arise out of an implied term of the contract, rather than out of an extra-contractual restitutionary obligation.[38]

15.4.6 Recovery of adjudication costs as part of the costs of a final determination

[15.48] What is the position as regards the liability to pay the parties' costs and adjudicator's fees of adjudication, where the dispute that was the subject of the adjudication is taken

---

[34] *City Inn Ltd v Shepherd Construction Ltd* [2001] ScotCS 187, per Lord Macfadyen at [54–58].
[35] *Castle Inns (Stirling) Ltd v Clark Contracts Ltd* [2005] CSOH 178, per Lord Drummond Young at [13].
[36] *Alstom Signalling Ltd v Jarvis Facilities Ltd* (No. 2) [2004] EWHC 1285 (TCC), per J Lloyd at [20].
[37] [2014] EWCA Civ 93, per Gloster LJ at [58–64].
[38] *Castle Inns (Stirling) Ltd trading as Castle Leisure Group v Clark Contracts Ltd* [2005] CSOH 178, per Lord Drummond at [13–14].

forwards to and decided by litigation or arbitration? Is the winning party entitled to recover the costs of the adjudication as well as the costs of the litigation or arbitration from the other party?

[15.49] The position as to the recoverability of such costs and fees must be considered in three parts: first, the recovery of money spent in prosecuting an adjudication as damages, second the extent to which a court can order repayment of any adjudicator's fees ordered payable by one party where it overturns/finally decides the adjudicator's decision and order return of other monies; and third the recovery of a party's fees and expenses incurred in an adjudication as costs of the subsequent litigation or arbitration.

[15.50] As to the first – adjudication costs as recoverable damages – a party can claim against another party to the construction project adjudication costs as damages if it can show that the adjudication and its associated costs were a foreseeable consequence of a breach of contract. This situation was considered in *National Museums and Galleries on Merseyside v AEW Architects and Designers Limited*.[39] There, the museum claimed as damages the adjudicator's fee, its own expenses and its expert's fee, all of which amounted to around £120,000 as incurred in an earlier adjudication with the contractor from the defendant architect. The court accepted that the fees were recoverable as damages in principle, but the issue centred around the reasonable foreseeability of the museum incurring the fees and whether, as a matter of causation, it could be said that the architect's breaches of contract (including liability for design) caused the adjudication with the contractor and the museum's associated costs.

[15.51] Akenhead J held that it was foreseeable that the contractor may refer a dispute, which could include a dispute over the scope of its design liability. Concerning causation, the architect contended that as the museum knew that it could not recover its costs in the adjudication (even if it was successful), and fought the adjudication knowing this (and that it could not recover those costs from the contractor in subsequent proceedings), there was no reason why it should recover its costs now, 'this being a backdoor method of cost recovery'. The court decided the costs were recoverable as follows:

> If AEW had done its job properly in the first place, it is inconceivable that there would have been any adjudication in relation to the design responsibility of the Contractor because the issue simply would not have arisen... Adjudication is a fact of life now in construction contracts... It was within the bounds of reasonable foreseeability that there could be adjudication in circumstances such as arose here. There was a sufficient causative link between the defaults of AEW and this adjudication.

[15.52] The court's view was that the causative link could only have been severed if the museum had acted unreasonably or its solicitors had negligently advised it that it had an arguable defence in the adjudication (in which case that negligent advice would have been the

---

[39] EWHC 2403 (TCC), per Akenhead J at [124–130].

[15.53] It is important to note that in the *AEW* case, the claim was to recover as damages the money which A (the museum) had to spend defending an adjudication commenced by B (the contractor) from C (the architect). In this kind of tripartite situation it is possible to see how A's costs of the adjudication spent fighting with B were recoverable from C. It was inherent in C's retainer as a professional for the museum project that C was to represent and advise A in relation to the performance of A's contract with B and, if C did so negligently, that might expose A to additional cost, including the cost of an adjudication which would not have occurred but for C's poor performance.

[15.54] It is also important to distinguish that tripartite situation from the more normal 'bipartite' situation – i.e. where A and B simply disagree about the proper construction of the construction contract, or about B's rights under it to further payment. That can and regularly does occur without any negligence on the part of C or any other member of the professional team, and under construction contracts where there is no independent third-party contract administrator, project manager or the like. In that bipartite situation, it is difficult to see how in causation the adjudicator's fees and the costs spent could be recovered in subsequent litigation as damages. It is suggested that the basis of claiming them as damages as per the *AEW* decision would not apply.

[15.55] As to the second topic, it is obviously fundamental to the court's jurisdiction over the dispute that it can order one party to repay to another sums that the adjudicator found due, if it finally decides the dispute in a different way from that decided by the adjudicator. However, it is suggested that the adjudicator's decision as to who should pay his fees is fundamentally a case management decision for him within jurisdiction, and that unlike his substantive decision on the merits, an adjudicator's decision as to who should pay his fees is not subject to review by the court subsequently (absent perhaps fraud). Any other approach risks very strange results. For example, it is difficult to see why a party should be able to overturn not only the adjudicator's substantive decision, but also his allocation of fees where (for example) it may have argued its case in a fundamentally different way at trial, but that would be a logically permissible outcome if adjudicator's fees could be reclaimed as part of the overturning of his decision by a final determination. Permitting the adjudicator's fees to be recovered upon ultimate success at trial would also be inconsistent with the general irrecoverability of fees in adjudication,[40] and the fact that the final determination by the court is not an appeal from the adjudicator. This view is consistent with the characterisation of that part of the adjudicator's decision concerning fees in *Fenice Investments v Jerram Falkus*,[41] it is submitted.

[15.56] Second, there may be an arguable case that some of the costs incurred investigating and formulating the claim, or costs incurred preparing witness statements and expert reports,

---

[40] But see the discussion in relation to the Late Payment of Commercial Debts (Interest) Act 1998 at Section 12.3.4 regarding the potential recoverability of fees in adjudication where that Act applies.
[41] [2011] EWHC 1678 (TCC), per Waksman J at [22].

may be recoverable if such statements and reports were of utility in the action as ultimately constituted.

[15.57] As to the third part – adjudication costs claimed – this is within the court's jurisdiction owing to the broad discretion to award costs given to it by section 51 of the Senior Courts Act 1981. Whether and to what extent fees spent in an adjudication are **in fact** recoverable under section 51 is a matter for detailed assessment by a costs judge (absent agreement of the parties). It is possible to see how, in principle, £1 spent in an adjudication formulating a claim and proving it saves £1 on the same work when the dispute is finally sent to litigation or arbitration, so that the first £1 spent in the adjudication can easily be said to be costs of the final dispute in a very real sense. That is potentially so both on the facts and in principle, since the adjudication, being only temporarily binding until final determination in litigation or arbitration, must in some way have that final determination in mind, even if only as a contingency. It is a question of fact and discretion for the judge in each case whether adjudication expenses can be recovered subsequently as the costs of litigation over the same issue. However, proving that on the facts may not be straightforward, particularly if no detailed records are kept, and/or in the not uncommon situation where the final form and detail of the claim has developed very significantly between the adjudication and the litigation.

[15.58] It seems that the position may be different in Scotland, at least in respect of adjudicator's fees. There, the court has held that the recovery of the adjudicator's fees is unlikely for three reasons. The adjudicator's decision cannot be challenged on the basis of any error and so final proceedings do not examine what the adjudicator decided, rather they examine the dispute afresh. Second, although a party can indirectly challenge an adjudicator's decision by court or arbitral proceedings, subsection 108(3) provides that only relates to the dispute or difference and the adjudicator's fees are not part of that dispute or difference. Finally, there is the practical difficulty of reconsidering the adjudicator's decision on such a matter. Final proceedings contrast to adjudication in that they entail a full and detailed examination of the dispute, and the judge has a significantly better opportunity to come to a carefully reasoned decision. Additional facts may emerge, or additional arguments may be developed. Therefore, one cannot determine that the adjudicator's decision is 'wrong', such that his fees should be paid by the eventual loser, and therefore it would not be appropriate to allow the winning party to recover whatever adjudicator fee and expenses it paid.[42]

[15.59] Although *Castle Inns* did not deal with party costs, one might argue that absent any contractual agreement to the contrary, the position as to the recovery of adjudicator's fees is also likely to apply to the parties' costs. The general position is that if there is no provision in the contract dealing with the recovery of costs of such as costs in a subsequent action on the same dispute, then the costs are irrecoverable and cannot form part of the assessment of costs following a decision in litigation or arbitration.

---

[42] *Castle Inns (Stirling) Ltd trading as Castle Leisure Group v Clark Contracts Ltd* [2005] CSOH 178, per Lord Drummond at [15–17].

Chapter 16
The adjudicator's jurisdiction

16.1 Overview

[16.01] Jurisdiction can be taken to mean the extent or range of judicial power. In the context of adjudication, jurisdiction means the existence and extent of the adjudicator's powers to decide the scope of the dispute legitimately referred to him. An adjudicator's powers are derived from the Act (only where the adjudication is statutory) and the procedural rules governing the adjudication. The scope of the dispute is determined by the notice of adjudication, which can include documents referred to within the notice of adjudication, and any expansion of that dispute by new issues introduced during the adjudication that the parties expressly or impliedly agree form part of the dispute. Typically, an adjudicator's jurisdiction commences when the dispute is referred to him and ends when he reaches his decision.

[16.02] Where the adjudicator does not exercise his powers and duties correctly or does not decide the dispute referred to him, he will have breached the boundaries of his jurisdiction. Similarly, the adjudicator will be found to have no jurisdiction *ab initio* if he was improperly appointed, either because there are preconditions of, or limits to, referring a dispute to adjudication that were not complied with or because the appointment of the adjudicator was defective. The consequence for an adjudicator who is not seized of jurisdiction or who breaches the boundaries of his jurisdiction is that the adjudication is invalidated and it follows that any decision the adjudicator reaches will be worthless.

[16.03] This chapter provides guidance on when to think about jurisdictional issues (Section 16.2), the available options for how to react when a jurisdictional issue arises (Section 16.3), the circumstances in which the ability to challenge the jurisdiction of an adjudication may be lost (Section 16.4) and some putative threshold (Section 16.5), process (Section 16.6) and decision-based (Section 16.7) jurisdictional challenges.

16.2 When to think about jurisdiction

[16.04] The short answer is: all the time. Jurisdictional issues arise before the adjudication starts, during it and at the point the decision is made. Indeed, it is perhaps useful to

A Practical Guide to Construction Adjudication, First Edition. James Pickavance.
© 2016 James Pickavance. Published 2016 by John Wiley & Sons, Inc.

compartmentalise any consideration of the adjudicator's jurisdiction in this way, if only to limit the number of issues one needs to consider.

[16.05] Jurisdictional issues occurring before the adjudication commences may be termed 'threshold' jurisdiction issues because where such an issue is found to apply, the adjudicator will not have jurisdiction to accept the appointment at all, or to put it another way, the referring party will not be permitted to commence an adjudication.

[16.06] Jurisdictional points arising during the adjudication most commonly involve a failure by either a party or the adjudicator to comply with the rules of the adjudication, or an unauthorised attempt by one party to widen the scope of the dispute in the adjudication by introducing extraneous matters into a submission.

[16.07] Jurisdictional points arising in the decision itself most commonly involve a claim that the adjudicator has decided something that was not part of the dispute referred to him, or has not decided part of the dispute that was referred to him. They also include issues around the timing of the decision, the reasons given for the decision, and errors in the decision. It is always important for both parties to scrutinise the decision, beyond the summary the adjudicator will typically include on the final page, to determine whether there are any issues within it that merit a challenge to his jurisdiction.

16.3 Options when a jurisdictional issue arises

16.3.1 In a nutshell

[16.08] Where the jurisdictional issue arises in the adjudicator's decision, if a party (invariably the losing party) wishes to challenge the adjudicator's jurisdiction, it has only one option, which is to refuse to comply with the consequences of the adjudicator's decision, wait for the other party to commence proceedings to enforce the decision, and then raise the challenge as a defence to those proceedings. However, where the jurisdictional issue arises before or during the adjudication, there are a number of other options available.

- A party may reserve its position on the adjudicator's jurisdiction and, having made the reservation, continue to participate in the adjudication. This is by far the most common option chosen. The main benefit of it is that it allows the aggrieved party to put forward its case in full, while still keeping open the possibility of challenging the adjudicator's jurisdiction later. If the decision of the adjudicator is not favourable, having reserved its position and maintained the reservation, it can seek to avoid the consequences of the decision by arguing in enforcement proceedings that the adjudicator did not have the jurisdiction to decide the dispute.
- A party may refer the issue to the court for determination. Here, the parties will usually (but not always) agree to stay the adjudication process (if it has begun) to enable them to seek a final and binding determination from the court on whether the adjudicator has jurisdiction. The advantage of using this approach is that the parties benefit from a binding decision on the jurisdictional matter. If the court determines the adjudicator has no jurisdiction, they can avoid the expense of the adjudication

(partially or entirely depending on the point at which the determination is sought) and either choose another form of dispute resolution or, if it is possible, address the jurisdictional point before commencing, or continuing the adjudication.
- A party may seek a determination from the adjudicator. Invariably, where a jurisdictional issue arises during the adjudication, the adjudicator will (or should) investigate it in any event. If as a result of that investigation he determines that he does not have jurisdiction to act, he must resign. Otherwise, he may continue. Whether the adjudicator's determination binds the parties will depend first on whether the adjudication rules provide for this. Most do not, but there are some that do. If the rules do not provide for it, the parties may nevertheless agree to be bound by the decision. That agreement may be express, or it may be implied. If a party does not wish to be bound by the decision, it should reserve its position on the adjudicator's jurisdiction and maintain that reservation.
- A party may refer a challenge to another adjudicator for a decision. This option may be preferable where the parties wish to choose a particular individual to decide the jurisdictional issue, or they wish to keep the costs of deciding the jurisdictional matter as low as possible. However, the second adjudicator's decision will not bind the parties unless they agree to be bound.
- A party may withdraw from the adjudication entirely. This option may be chosen where a party considers that the issue giving rise to a challenge on the adjudicator's jurisdiction is so clear that there is no point participating or continuing to participate in the adjudication. Where it is done before the adjudication commences, the aggrieved party will avoid incurring any expense in the adjudication if its challenge is later found to be valid. Where the other party and the adjudicator do not agree the challenge is valid, they may commence or continue with the adjudication and the adjudicator may produce a decision. Assuming the aggrieved party will not comply with that decision, the other party must enforce it. Provided the aggrieved party has reserved its position, it can raise the jurisdictional issue as a defence to a claim to enforce the adjudicator's decision. If its challenge to the adjudicator's jurisdiction fails, the adjudicator's decision will bind. It will not have had any opportunity to put forward its case on the adjudicated dispute, it will have to comply with the adjudicator's decision and it will have to commence litigation or arbitration proceedings to try to reverse the adjudicator's decision, a process that will invariably be more expensive than if it had participated in the adjudication and won.
- A party may make an application for an injunction. Where the adjudicator's jurisdiction is in question and in circumstances where the consequences of an invalid adjudicator's decision cannot be remedied by damages, it may be appropriate to make an application for an injunction. However, the threshold to overcome in order for the application to be successful is high and there are only a few cases where this approach has succeeded.

16.3.2 Option 1: Determination from the court

[16.09] A party may resolve an issue concerning the adjudicator's jurisdiction through the court by commencing proceedings that seek a declaration that, in light of a certain issue or issues, the adjudicator does (or does not) have jurisdiction to determine the dispute. This can be done before or, subject to the applicable adjudication rules,[1] during the adjudication. The court has jurisdiction to hear such claims.[2]

[16.10] Proceedings can be brought through the procedures set out in either CPR Part 7 or Part 8.

- Where there is a substantial dispute of fact, the claim should be brought under CPR Part 7. This may include a dispute about whether there was a binding contract between the parties, or about whether the contract was in writing and the permissible scope of the adjudication, including issues such as whether there is a pre-existing dispute between the parties.[3]
- Cases may be suitable for the CPR Part 8 procedure if there is no substantial dispute of fact.[4] This may include a dispute concerning the proper construction of the contract documents, which body is the correct nominating body or the correct application of the Act.

[16.11] Where possible, a party should use the Part 8 procedure, because it is generally quicker and cheaper than the Part 7 procedure. The court has on occasion stretched the rules in relation to the nature of claims that are ordinarily permissible under the Part 8 procedure. In *Vitpol Building Service v Samen*,[5] the parties disagreed about the terms of their contract. Vitpol sought declarations under CPR Part 8 to resolve this issue before adjudication proceedings were commenced. Samen argued that the CPR Part 8 procedure was inappropriate because there were disputes of fact that needed to be addressed in oral evidence. The court rejected this stating that it was content to agree a hybrid between Parts 7 and 8 so as to ensure that any necessary oral evidence can be accommodated within the final hearing. However, there will be limits to the extent of factual evidence the courts will allow.[6]

[16.12] Whichever route is followed, the court will endeavour to resolve the matter quickly. While it depends on the nature of the claim, the court will usually hear such cases within a few weeks from the issued date of the claim form, with a decision either being given at the hearing or up to a week afterwards.

[16.13] The TCC Guide recognises proceedings of this sort, describing them as 'other proceedings arising out of adjudication'.[7] The TCC Guide does not set out a full procedure for adjudication business other than for enforcement applications, but paragraph 9.1.3 recognises that, ordinarily, such business will also be taken rapidly to reflect the mandatory 28-day adjudication procedure in the Act. Paragraph 9.4.2 of the TCC Guide states

---

[1] See *Re W.H. Malcolm Ltd* [2010] CSOH 152, per Lady Smith at [24–27] where an amended TeCSA procedure prohibited either party from making an application to the court in relation to the conduct of the adjudication.
[2] CPR 40.20.
[3] See also Paragraph 9.4.1 of the TCC Guide.
[4] CPR rule 8.1(2)(a).
[5] [2008] EWHC 2283 (TCC), per Coulson J at [13–19].
[6] *Forest Heath DC v ISG Jackson Ltd* [2010] EWHC 322 (TCC), per Ramsey J at [28–48].
[7] Section 9.4, TCC Guide.

that an application for other adjudication business will be 'immediately assigned to a named judge', who will usually require the parties to attend a case management conference (CMC) within two working days of the case being assigned to that judge. At the CMC, the judge will give the necessary directions to ensure the 'speedy resolution' of the dispute.

[16.14] An advantage of referring a jurisdictional issue to the court before or during the adjudication is that it decides the issue early on, which may save costs.[8] While the parties will incur costs bringing/defending the claim, they would incur the costs anyway where the losing party refused to comply with the decision, on grounds that the adjudicator does not have jurisdiction and the winning party brings proceedings to enforce the decision. Where the jurisdictional issue is decided early on, if the court's decision is that the adjudicator does not have jurisdiction, the parties can then refrain from commencing the adjudication, or not continue it further.

[16.15] While a party may readily commence a claim in the court before the adjudication, commencing one during the adjudication can present difficulties. It will distract the parties from giving full attention to the adjudication which, given the tight timescales, is likely to have a material impact on the quality of submissions. Furthermore, the court claim is unlikely to be heard before the conclusion of the adjudication or at least until it is well advanced.[9] Therefore, the sensible approach is for the parties to agree to stay the adjudication pending the outcome of the court case. This gives the parties the ability to properly focus on the court claim.[10] The court's approach to such proceedings is that its discretion to interfere with the adjudication will be exercised 'very sparingly' and that the appropriateness of such intervention will be 'very much the exception rather than the rule'. Its view is that, wherever possible, the adjudication process is allowed to operate free from the intervention of the court.[11] There must be a clear-cut case. If not, the court is unlikely to intervene, postponing the argument until enforcement stage.[12] Nevertheless, there are numerous situations where the court has permitted these sorts of claims. They include where it was alleged that there was a breach of natural justice,[13] where the parties wish to clarify the meaning of a contract clause,[14] whether the adjudicator has jurisdiction to determine the dispute under the contract agreed between the parties,[15] whether there was a contract in writing,[16] whether the dispute referred was the same or substantially

---

[8] *The Dorchester Hotel Ltd v Vivid Interiors Ltd* [2009] EWHC 70 (TCC), per Coulson J at [12].
[9] *WW Gear Construction Ltd v McGee Group Ltd* [2012] EWHC 1509 (TCC), per Edwards-Stuart J at [23–28].
[10] *ABB Zantingh Ltd v Zedal Building Services Ltd* [2001] BLR 66, per Bowsher J at [13].
[11] *Dorchester Hotel Ltd v Vivid Interiors Ltd* [2009] EWHC 70 (TCC) per Coulson J at [12–17].
[12] *Aceramais Holdings Ltd v Hadleigh Partnerships Ltd* [2009] EWHC 1664 (TCC), per Kirkham J at [46].
[13] *The Dorchester Hotel Ltd v Vivid Interiors Ltd* [2009] EWHC 70 (TCC), per Coulson J at [12].
[14] *WW Gear Construction Ltd v McGee Group Ltd* [2012] EWHC 1509 (TCC) at [16–28].
[15] *Dalkia Energy and Technical Services Ltd v Bell Group UK Ltd* [2009] EWHC 73 (TCC), per Coulson J at [7–12].
[16] *Glendalough Associated SA v Harris Calnan Construction Co Ltd* [2013] EWHC 3142 (TCC), per Edwards-Stuart J at [56].

the same as one decided previously[17] and what the correct adjudication nomination procedure was.[18] Further examples can be found in the cases listed at Appendix 8.

[16.16] The court's judgment on jurisdiction is final and binding (subject to the right of appeal). If the adjudication proceeds, a later challenge to the enforceability of the adjudicator's decision on grounds of jurisdiction will be unsuccessful unless a different jurisdictional point arises to those decided by the court.

[16.17] Where details of the dispute in an ongoing adjudication have been discussed in a judgment of the court, the court may order that the judgment is neither published nor shown to the adjudicator until the adjudicator's decision has been given, so as not to prejudice the adjudicator's decision-making process.[19] However, at some point later, the court decision will be published (unless, in light of the adjudicator's decision, the parties and the judge agree that it is not to be published) and become a matter of public record. The parties may not want any details of the dispute to be known publicly, and so this may be a reason not to resolve a jurisdictional issue using this method.

16.3.3 Option 2: Determination by the adjudicator

[16.18] Where the adjudicator has been appointed and where the parties identify an issue that goes to the adjudicator's jurisdiction, it is appropriate to raise the matter with the adjudicator and ask him for a ruling. Indeed, the adjudicator himself may flag the issue. In either case, the adjudicator can, and indeed should, investigate it. Unless the rules dictate otherwise, there is no obligation for the adjudicator to invite the parties to make representations to him on matters of jurisdiction.[20] However, in practice, adjudicators should do this because the parties will inevitably provide the adjudicator with detailed reasons for their respective positions which will assist him in reaching a conclusion.

[16.19] If, as a result of that investigation, he determines that he has no jurisdiction, then where the issue is one that deprives him of jurisdiction entirely, the proper course of action is for him to resign. If he decides otherwise, he should carry on to a decision. It may be that the issue is one that does not deprive him of jurisdiction entirely but relates to certain isolated issues. For example, there may be a question as to whether an argument advanced by one party falls within the scope of the dispute referred to the adjudicator. In that case, he may rule that he has no jurisdiction on that argument, but still continue to a decision on the remaining part of the dispute.

[16.20] Whether or not the adjudicator's decision binds the parties will depend first of all on the rules of the adjudication. Most, including the Scheme, do not permit the adjudicator to

---

[17] *Carillion Construction Ltd v Stephen Andrew Smith* [2011] EWHC 2910 (TCC), per Akenhead J at [1].
[18] *Bovis Lend Lease Ltd v Cofley Engineering Services* [2009] EWHC 1120 (TCC), per Coulson J at [2].
[19] *Glendalough Associated SA v Harris Calnan Construction Co Ltd* [2013] EWHC 3142 (TCC), Edwards-Stuart J at [56].
[20] *Amec Capital Projects Ltd v Whitefriars City Estates Ltd* [2004] EWCA Civ 1418, per Dyson LJ at [41].

rule on his own jurisdiction.[21] However, some do and in those cases where the adjudicator makes a determination, it will bind the parties, and the court is unlikely to interfere with what the adjudicator has decided.[22]

[16.21] Where the adjudication rules do not give the adjudicator power to issue a binding decision on his own jurisdiction and where there is an issue which, if found to be correct, would otherwise deprive the adjudicator of jurisdiction to determine the dispute at all, or an issue that the adjudicator does not have jurisdiction to address, the parties may consent to give the adjudicator that jurisdiction. It may be, for example, that the contract is not one that falls within the scope of the Act, but the parties nevertheless desire for their dispute to be determined by an adjudicator. Or it may be that the responding party raises an issue in its defence which is outside of the scope of the dispute, but the parties decide the issue should be determined by the adjudicator. In either case, where the parties agree to do so, they can give the adjudicator ad hoc jurisdiction to decide the dispute, or the issue. That agreement may be given expressly, usually in writing to the adjudicator and the other party. It may also be implied. The process that the court will follow to determine if there has been an implied agreement has been described in this way:[23]

> For there to be an implied agreement giving the adjudicator such jurisdiction, one needs to look at everything material that was done and said to determine whether one can say with conviction that the parties must be taken to have agreed that the adjudicator had such jurisdiction. It will have to be clear that some objection is being taken in relation to the adjudicator's jurisdiction because otherwise one could not imply that the adjudicator was being asked to decide a non-existent jurisdictional issue which neither party had mentioned.

[16.22] Implied consent is invariably demonstrated by the actions or inaction of a party. So, where the objector proceeds with the adjudication and it responds to the claims made both in the notice of adjudication and the referral notice, there is likely to be an implied agreement from that party that it accepts the jurisdiction of the adjudicator.[24] Similarly, where the parties have exchanged correspondence or submissions and that correspondence or those submissions demonstrate that the parties are willing to address issues which would otherwise form a valid jurisdictional challenge, a court will be likely to find an implied agreement that the parties agreed to be bound by the jurisdiction of the adjudicator.

[16.23] In the overwhelming majority of cases, the parties will not agree to be bound by the result of the adjudicator's investigation. Where a party referring the jurisdictional matter to the adjudicator does not wish to be bound, it should be made clear in writing that whatever

---

[21] See for example *Nordot Engineering Services Ltd v Siemens plc* (unreported), 04/00 QBD (TCC) Salford DR.
[22] *Farebrother Building Services Ltd v Frogmore Investments Ltd* [2001] CILL 1762, per Gilliland J at [27–32].
[23] *Aedifice Partnership Ltd v Shah* [2010] EWHC 210 (TCC), per Akenhead J at [21].
[24] *OSC Building Services Ltd v Interior Dimensions Contracts Ltd* [2009] EWHC 248 (TCC), per Ramsey J at [22–24].

decision the adjudicator reaches is provisional and non-binding, and that the right to challenge this decision in any enforcement proceedings is reserved. The act of reserving the position on the adjudicator's jurisdiction is explained in detail in Section 16.3.5. Where it does this, it will subsequently be entitled to raise the jurisdictional challenge in defence to a claim to enforce the adjudicator's decision.[25] Where it does not do this, it may lose its right to challenge the adjudicator's jurisdiction. This is explained further in Section 16.4.

[16.24] Often there can be disagreement about whether the parties agreed to allow the adjudicator to determine his own jurisdiction,[26] or agreed to be bound by his decision. The position will always be determined by applying the basic principles outlined in this section and Section 16.4 to the particular facts of the case. There are numerous cases where this issue has arisen. They are listed under this section heading at Appendix 8.

16.3.4 Option 3: Determination from another adjudicator

[16.25] The parties may agree to refer the dispute on jurisdiction to a second adjudicator. Again, this is generally only done before or at the start of the adjudication process.

[16.26] Why might one pursue this route instead of commencing a claim in the court (option 1)? One reason is that it may be cheaper for the parties because the adjudication process is less formal, and because in court proceedings counsel are usually retained. Further, unlike court proceedings, the adjudication will be private. Finally, courts operate at a reduced capacity for a period during Christmas (three weeks), Easter (two weeks) and summer (nine weeks) and so if parties are in need of a decision on jurisdiction during this time, the courts may not be able to provide it at all, or at least not as quickly as in term time.[27]

[16.27] This option should only be followed if both parties and the adjudicator agree to stay the first adjudication while the second adjudication is concluded because (a) if the second adjudicator concludes the adjudicator in the first adjudication has no jurisdiction and it has continued, costs will have been wasted; and (b) the party referring the jurisdictional issue to the second adjudicator is unlikely to get a decision before the first adjudication concludes.

[16.28] Furthermore, the parties should agree to be bound by the second adjudicator's decision on jurisdiction, otherwise there is little point in it. Should a party not agree to be finally bound by the second adjudicator's decision on jurisdiction, it should reserve and maintain its position in respect of the first adjudicator's jurisdiction (as explained in Section 16.3.5).

---

[25] *Pegram Shopfitters Limited v Tally Weijl (UK) Limited* [2003] EWCA Civ 1750, per May LJ at [10].
[26] *Christiani & Nielsen Ltd v The Lowry Centre Development Company Ltd*, Unreported, 29 June 2000, per Thornton J at [14–20].
[27] The courts will normally entertain urgent applications during these periods, at its discretion.

[16.29] Unlike seeking a determination from the court, parties will not be able to recover costs incurred in referring the matter to the second adjudicator, unless they agree that the adjudicator has the power to allocate costs.

16.3.5 Option 4: Reserve the position and proceed with the adjudication

[16.30] Where a party does not, or may not, accept the jurisdiction of the adjudicator, as a minimum, the appropriate action is to reserve its position on the adjudicator's jurisdiction. Indeed, the act of reserving the position can be, and often is, done as a matter of course. Even if there is no apparent issue with the adjudicator's jurisdiction, a party will often reserve the position on the adjudicator's jurisdiction, in case an issue becomes apparent at a later stage, which arose and could have been identified earlier. The reservation must be maintained, which means that once it has been raised, it must be repeated whenever submissions are made and until the jurisdiction is resolved or until a decision is made not to pursue it.

[16.31] Having reserved the position, the party continues to participate in the adjudication until its conclusion. Once the decision is given, if the party does not wish to abide by the decision on grounds that the adjudicator lacked the jurisdiction to decide the dispute, it may (having reserved the position and maintained it), refuse to comply with the decision. The other party may then commence proceedings to enforce the adjudicator's decision and the jurisdictional issue can be raised in defence. However, if the challenger failed to reserve the position at all or at the appropriate time, or failed to maintain it, it will have no grounds to contest the adjudicator's decision.

[16.32] There are two types of reservation: specific and general. A specific reservation deals with a particular issue the complaining party points to as the reason why the adjudicator does not have jurisdiction. An example might be that the adjudicator does not have jurisdiction to hear the dispute because there is 'no dispute' within the meaning of the Act. A general reservation is broader in nature and might read something like 'the responding party reserves its right to raise any jurisdictional issue arising now or in due course and the responding party's participation in the adjudication is without prejudice to this right'. However, if the reservation is so indefinite and nebulous such that it is meaningless, then it could be ineffective. Meaningless reservations do not extend to a reservation as to 'further jurisdiction issues which we have not yet had time or opportunity to investigate': this reservation was held to be sufficient both in terms of the matters the party had investigated and those it had not.[28]

[16.33] If a specific reservation is made on one ground only and that ground is subsequently found to be invalid, the party will be taken to have acceded to the jurisdiction on all other grounds and it will not be permitted to raise a challenge on those other grounds later.[29]

---

[28] *GPS Marine Contractors Ltd v Ringway Infrastructure Services Ltd* [2010] EWHC 283 per Ramsey J at [35–41].
[29] *Aedifice Partnership Ltd v Shah* [2010] EWHC 210 (TCC), per Akenhead J at [33].

[16.34] The timing of the initial reservation is important. As soon as the issue is identified, or could have been identified, the reservation should be made. That may be when the notice of adjudication is issued, during the adjudication or on receiving the decision, depending on the nature of the issue. In *R Durtnell & Sons Ltd v Kaduna Ltd*,[30] the court held that Kaduna had not waived its right to raise a question about the adjudicator's jurisdiction by not reserving its position during the adjudication, because the issue only became apparent once the decision had been issued. While there may be some flexibility between the point at which the objection could have been raised and the point at which it was in fact raised before that party can be taken to have waived its right to reserve the position on jurisdiction, that flexibility is unlikely to amount to much more than a few days.[31]

[16.35] The form of the reservation will usually be made in writing to the adjudicator and the other party, either as part of a submission or by way of separate communication. A valid reservation can also be found where it can be shown there is 'unequivocal conduct' which demonstrates that the party intended to reserve its position.[32] The consequences of a party not reserving its position timeously or maintaining the reservation is that it may be said to have waived its right to challenge whatever jurisdictional issue arose. This is explored further in Section 16.4.

[16.36] Akenhead J has neatly summed up the principles of reserving the position on jurisdiction as follows:[33]

> A clear reservation can, and usually will, be made by words expressed by or on behalf of the objecting party. Words such as 'I fully reserve my position about your jurisdiction' or 'I am only participating in the adjudication under protest' will usually suffice to make an effective reservation; these forms of words while desirable are not absolutely essential. One can however look at every relevant thing said and done during the course of the adjudication to see whether by words and conduct what was clearly intended was a reservation as to the jurisdiction of the adjudicator. It will be a matter of interpretation of what was said and done to determine whether an effective reservation was made. A legitimate question to ask is: was it or should it have been clear to all concerned that a reservation on jurisdiction was being made?

[16.37] A disadvantage of reserving the position as to jurisdiction, continuing with the adjudication and then refusing to comply with the decision and defending enforcement proceedings is that if the jurisdictional challenge is found to be valid and the adjudicator's decision is therefore held to be a nullity, both parties will have wasted the costs incurred in participating in the adjudication and the parties will not have resolved the dispute between them.

16.3.6 Option 5: Withdraw

[16.38] A party who considers it has a robust case that the adjudicator has no jurisdiction may withdraw from the adjudication entirely. Provided that the reason for the withdrawal is clearly stated and maintained in any subsequent correspondence with the other party or

---

[30] [2003] EWHC 517 (TCC), per Seymour J at [46].
[31] *All Metal Roofing v Kamm Properties Ltd* [2010] EWHC 2670 (TCC), per Akenhead J at [21].
[32] *CJP Builders Ltd v William Verry Ltd* [2008] EWHC 2025 (TCC), per Akenhead J at [72].
[33] *Aedifice Partnership Ltd v Shar* [2010] EWHC 2016 (TCC), per Akenhead J at [21].

the adjudicator, the basis of the withdrawal can be raised as a defence to a claim to enforce the adjudicator's decision. The main benefit to this strategy is that the withdrawing party will not have to incur its own potentially irrecoverable costs as a result of proceeding with the adjudication. Further, a party who challenges the jurisdiction of the adjudicator at the outset and refuses to participate will not be jointly and severally liable with the other party for the adjudicator's fees, although if that party asks the adjudicator to make a non-binding decision on the jurisdictional matter, it will be liable further.[34]

[16.39] While there are cases where this strategy has been deployed,[35] it is high-risk because if the withdrawing party is wrong about its challenge, it will have missed the opportunity to present its case. In all probability, the adjudicator is likely to find for the other party, and the withdrawing party will be required to comply with the adjudicator's decision until such time as the decision is altered or reversed by court or arbitral proceedings. This will almost certainly be far more costly and time-consuming than if the withdrawing party participated in the adjudication and obtained a favourable (or more favourable) result.

16.3.7 Option 6: Injunction

[16.40] In the context of a jurisdictional challenge in adjudication, an application for an interim injunction can be made to halt the commencement or progress of an adjudication. The application notice and accompanying evidence should be compiled and submitted in accordance with the general rules on interim applications in CPR Part 23 and the specific provisions on injunctions in CPR Part 25, together with the accompanying practice directions. Only in truly exceptional cases should the application be made ex parte. Almost always the appropriate course is to serve the papers on the other party and then allow the court to fix a date that suits both parties. It is likely to be appropriate for the applicant to give a cross undertaking in damages.

[16.41] The court must be satisfied that the applicant has a real prospect of succeeding in its claim for a permanent injunction at trial; the court must consider whether damages would or would not be an adequate remedy for the applicant if it was refused an injunction and whether damages would be an inadequate remedy for the respondent if the injunction was granted; finally, if damages would not be an adequate remedy, the court needs to consider where the 'balance of convenience' lies.[36]

[16.42] In the round, this test is difficult to meet in the context of adjudication (or at all) and indeed the court has said that a party should not be prevented from pursuing its right to adjudication save in the most exceptional of circumstances.[37] As a result, there are only a few examples of where an injunction has been sought and even fewer where one has been granted. Therefore, seeking an injunction to restrain the commencement or continuation of an adjudication should only be done where there is a clear-cut case in

---

[34] See Section 12.2.4.
[35] *IDE Contracting Ltd v R G Carter Cambridge Ltd* [2004] EWHC 36 (TCC) per Havery J at [3].
[36] *American Cyanamid v Ethicon Ltd* [1975] AC 396.
[37] *Twintec Ltd v Volkerfitzpatrick Ltd* [2014] EWHC 10 (TCC), per Edwards-Stuart J at [69].

favour of granting the injunction. If there is doubt as to whether an application for an injunction will be successful, other options should be considered.

[16.43] Before making the application it is important that all the necessary available evidence is gathered so that the court can make an informed decision. If the claimant does not do this, the court may adjourn the application.[38]

[16.44] Examples of successful injunction applications include:

- *Twintec Ltd v Volkerfitzpatrick Ltd*,[39] where Edwards-Stuart J granted an injunction restraining Volkerfitzpatrick from continuing with an adjudication because it had appointed the adjudicator incorrectly. He said 'I am unable to see how it would be either just or convenient to permit an adjudication to continue in circumstances where the decision of the adjudicator will be incapable of enforcement.'[40]
- *ABB Power Construction Ltd v Norwest Holst Engineering Ltd*,[41] where Lloyd J granted a mandatory order restraining the referring party from continuing with the adjudication and from taking any steps to enforce any decision made by the adjudicator after concluding that the contract was not a construction contract.
- *John Mowlem & Co plc v Hydra-Tight & Co plc*,[42] where the court held that the adjudicator appointed by the Institution of Civil Engineers did not have jurisdiction to act. The court granted an injunction restraining Hydra-Tight from taking any substantive step in the adjudication or seeking to enforce or implement any decision which the appointed adjudicator may make without the agreement of Mowlem.
- *Mentmore Towers Ltd and others v Packman Lucas Ltd*,[43] where the claimants issued three notices of adjudication in relation to disputes concerning overpayments. The defendants applied for an injunction to prevent the claimants from taking any further steps in those adjudications. The court could see no reason why a referral to adjudication that is unreasonable or oppressive should not be restrained by application of the same principles that would apply to an application made on similar grounds for the stay of the same claim made by litigation. The court concluded that the injunction to restrain the adjudications should be granted. The courts have said 'again and again' that adjudicator's awards should be strictly enforced unless there has been some excess of jurisdiction or breach of natural justice. 'That is the "pay now argue later" approach the underlines the legislative purpose.'

[16.45] Unsuccessful injunction applications include:

- *Workplace Technologies plc v E Squared Ltd and Mr J Riches*,[44] where an injunction was sought to restrain a party initiating an adjudication where the terms of the contract

---

[38] *Lanes Group plc v Galliford Try Infrastructure Ltd (No. 2)* [2011] EWHC 1234 (TCC), per Akenhead J at [3–6].
[39] [2014] EWHC 10 (TCC), per Edwards-Stuart J at [88–89].
[40] Ibid at [63].
[41] [2000] EWHC Technology 68, Lloyd J at [21].
[42] [2001] 17 Const LJ 358, per Toulmin J at [50 et seq.].
[43] [2010] EWHC 457 (TCC), per Edwards-Stuart J at [29–38].
[44] HT 00 34, per Wilcox J at [45–55].

and therefore the right to adjudicate was uncertain. Speaking generally, the court said that in most adjudication cases it would be difficult to satisfy the threshold test of there being a serious question to be tried and therefore the balance of convenience lay with allowing the adjudication process to continue. In this case, if the court granted the injunction without determining the issue of the date of the contract then it inexorably followed that it may be interfering in a valid adjudication to its detriment. This would frustrate the right to adjudicate.

- *Aceramais Holdings Ltd v Hadleigh Partnerships Ltd*,[45] where disputes arose and the matter was referred to adjudication by Hadleigh. Aceramais failed to participate in the adjudication, but shortly after it had been commenced, Aceramais initiated court proceedings seeking an injunction to stop the adjudication. Its contention was that there was no contract in writing. Among other things, the judge refused to grant Aceramais the injunction and was critical of its approach. It was noted that discretionary relief should only be exercised sparingly, and that the parties should argue an adjudicator's decision at enforcement stage as opposed to asking the court to intervene beforehand.
- *Ericsson AB v EADS Defence & Security Systems Ltd*,[46] where there were two applications for interim injunctions. Ericsson sought to prevent EADS from terminating the agreement, at least before the adjudication had taken place and EADS sought an order preventing Ericsson from taking any further steps in the adjudications, seeking a declaration that any decision would be invalid because the parties had agreed to mediate the disputes. Akenhead J refused both applications each for separate reasons.
- *T Clarke (Scotland) Ltd v MMAXX Underfloor Heating Ltd*,[47] where the court held that while a 'cloud of suspicion hangs over [the defendant's] conduct', in order to grant the interdict (this was a Scottish case) it is necessary for the initiation of legal proceedings to be 'so unjustifiable as to be an abuse of legal process' and even in that event, the court's 'drastic' power to dismiss a claim should be exercised sparingly. Despite the defendant's behaviour, the court found it had not acted unreasonably and oppressively and so refused the application. It is suggested that the threshold one must overcome in Scotland is higher than it is in England.

16.4 Losing the right to challenge the adjudicator's jurisdiction

16.4.1 In a nutshell

[16.46] Where the adjudicator acts outside of the boundaries of his jurisdiction and the adjudication proceeds to a conclusion, then depending on the nature of the ultra vires act, then either the adjudicator's decision is doomed, or the issue can be isolated and struck out so that the 'good' part of the decision survives. Either party has a right to object if the adjudicator acts outside his jurisdiction. However, a party may waive its right to challenge the adjudicator's jurisdiction. A waiver will be found where a party fails to reserve

---
[45] [2009] EWHC 1664, per Kirkham J at [40].
[46] [2009] EWHC 2598 (TCC), per Akenhead J at [34–60].
[47] [2014] ScotCS CSOH 62, per Lord Woolman at [16–23].

its position on the adjudicator's jurisdiction either at all or too late, where a reservation is made but it is later abandoned, and where a party approbates and reprobates.

16.4.2 Waiver

[16.47] Waiver is the foundation for any argument that a party has lost its right to challenge the jurisdiction of the adjudicator.

[16.48] Waiver can be defined as the giving up of a legal or procedural right, either by choosing between two inconsistent alternatives (waiver by election) or by conduct (waiver by estoppel) showing that a particular entitlement will not be pursued. In either case, the waiver may be made expressly, or it may be implied. The law of waiver by election and waiver by estoppel is complicated, and what follows may be characterised as a simplification for the purposes of this book. There is, however, a useful line of Court of Appeal authority[48] which debates the distinction between the two types of waiver and provides clear and detailed guidance in this area.

[16.49] Waiver by election only applies where there is a choice to make. It is concerned with the reaction of X when faced with conduct by Y, or a particular factual situation which has arisen, which entitles X to exercise or refrain from exercising a particular right to the prejudice of Y. In order to waive by election, there must be a choice or election to be made, the electing party must be aware or be taken to be aware of the choice and the electing party must, viewed objectively, have unequivocally made a choice. In contrast to waiver by estoppel, waiver by election does not require that the other party relied on the election for it to bind. Once made, the election represents a permanent decision and the electing party will not later be permitted to resile from that position.

[16.50] Waiver by estoppel applies in a much broader context than waiver by election. It can apply to any situation where the waiving party has a right, contractual or otherwise. Known sometimes as promissory estoppel or equitable estoppel,[49] it is the most common way in which a party may waive its rights. As with waiver by election, waiver by estoppel can only arise when the thing being waived has manifested and there must be an unambiguous statement or conduct that demonstrates that the waiving party has given up a right or obligation. There are three key differences to waiver by election. First, the estopping conduct may occur before or after the time for the relevant performance. Second, a party waiving its right does not need to know it has a right to waive. Therefore, if objectively it is held that a party has waived its right, a waiver by estoppel will have occurred. Finally,

---

[48] *Kammins Ballroom Co v Zenith Investments* [1971] AC 850; *Motor Oil Hellas (Corinth) Refineries SA v Shipping Corporation of India* [1990] 1 Lloyd's Rep 391; *Kosmar Villa Holidays plc v Trustees of Syndicate 1243* [2008] EWCA Civ 147; *Persimmon Homes (South Coast) v Hall Aggregates (South Coast) Ltd* [2009] EWCA Civ 1108.

[49] It is argued by some that there are distinctions between waiver by estoppel, promissory estoppel and equitable estoppel and equitable forbearance, but for present purposes they will be treated as one. In relation to adjudication jurisdiction, the essence of matters is an unequivocal representation that the other party relies upon and which cannot then be undone or otherwise resiled from.

the estoppel will only prevent the waiving party from relying upon the waived right if the other party relied upon the waiver having taken place, therefore making it inequitable for the waiving party to go back on the waiver. If there has been no such reliance, there will be no estoppel.

[16.51] In short, therefore, the essential components that need to be met in order for waiver by estoppel to apply are (a) words or conduct by the waiving party; (b) which are intended to be relied upon; and (iii) are actually relied upon by the other party (with time, money and resource expended by it).[50] For example, where a jurisdictional issue could have been identified from the referral notice, but the responding party did not object to the jurisdictional issue and indeed addressed it in its response, then where the referring party served the reply and did not raise the jurisdictional challenge until 14 days after the service of the response, the responding party will have waived its right to object to the adjudicator's jurisdiction.

[16.52] Applying the concept of waiver by estoppel to jurisdictional objections, Akenhead J said this:[51]

> It goes, almost without saying, that the failure prior to the adjudicator's decision to make a jurisdictional objection which it was open to a party to make during the adjudication, can be taken as a waiver of jurisdiction because in effect the party later wishing to raise the jurisdictional objection has actively participated in the adjudication, as if the adjudicator had jurisdiction, the other party has been entitled to rely upon that unqualified participation and has itself relied upon that in continuing to take part, to make submissions, and to incur costs and management time in the adjudication (to its detriment if there are always was a good jurisdictional challenge).

[16.53] An example of waiver by estoppel occurred where the responding party sought to argue on enforcement that the application to the RICS for the nomination of an adjudicator was inconsistent with the adjudication rules, which required the nomination to be carried out by the chairman of TeCSA. However, the responding party wrote to the referring party encouraging it to secure a nomination through RICS. The court found that as a result of that action, the responding party was estopped from raising a complaint as to the validity of the adjudicator's jurisdiction on the grounds that the adjudicator had been wrongly appointed.[52]

16.4.3 No reservation or late reservation

[16.54] Where a party fails to reserve, or delays reserving, its position on the adjudicator's jurisdiction, there is a real risk that it will be held to have given up, or waived its right to challenge the adjudicator's jurisdiction.

---

[50] *Brims Construction Ltd v A2M Development Ltd* [2013] EWHC 3262 (TCC), per Akenhead J at [30].
[51] *Brims Construction Ltd v A2M Development Ltd* EWHC 3262 (TCC), per Akenhead J at [27].
[52] *CJP Builders Ltd v William Verry Ltd* [2008] EWHC 2025 (TCC), per Akenhead J at [73–74].

even if the jurisdictional challenge is made relatively late on in the adjudication proceedings but before the decision, there can still have been an effective prior waiver by the party which challenges jurisdiction at a late stage where it has had the opportunity to but failed to take the relevant jurisdictional point at an earlier stage, if and to the extent that the other party has continued (positively) to participate (spend time, cost and resource) in the adjudication. What however is needed is some activity (such as the service of a Response without qualification) by the party which later seeks to challenge jurisdiction which amounts objectively to an assertion or representation that it is participating without reservation.[53]

[16.55] In practice, a party should reserve its position on the adjudicator's jurisdiction at each and every stage of the adjudication to avoid waiving its right. The reservation can be made specific if the objection is known, or it can be general, or a specific objection can be made together with a general objection, where the former is without prejudice to the latter. Section 16.3.5 considers this further.

16.4.4 Abandoning the reservation

[16.56] A party may make a reservation, but fail to maintain that reservation throughout the adjudication. Such failure will amount to an abandonment of the reservation and a loss of the right to raise a jurisdictional challenge later.[54] Whether a reservation has been maintained or whether it is properly treated as having been abandoned is fact and context specific and may arise in two ways.

[16.57] First, a party may make a jurisdictional objection and then fail to maintain the objection because the ground for reservation appears to have been cured to its satisfaction. For example, a responding party may reserve its position in the response over its ability to deal with a new claim in the time available, asserting that no dispute has arisen over it. If directions were then given and time extended following which it made further submissions on the point without continuing to reserve, it will be taken to have withdrawn the reservation.

[16.58] The second possibly is that a party may alter the wording of its original reservation in a subsequent reservation such that the first reservation is properly treated as abandoned. For example, an initial reservation made in the response may be framed in general terms, but a subsequent development of the reservation made in the rejoinder may make it clear that the only real jurisdictional complaint concerned the improper appointment of the adjudicator. If the responding party later seeks to challenge jurisdiction on the entirely different ground that the contract was not a construction contract, the court is likely to find that only the narrow challenge to jurisdiction had been made. It is a question of fact, taking into account the language used and the context, as to whether successive challenges are to be taken as separate and concurrent, or whether the later challenges are to be taken as a refinement or clarification or the earlier ones, cutting down their scope. A party wishing to reserve its position widely would therefore be well advised to make

---

[53] *Brims Construction Ltd v A2M Development Ltd* EWHC 3262 (TCC), per Akenhead J at [27].
[54] *Hortimax Ltd v Hedon Salads Ltd* (2004) 24 Const LJ 47, per Gilliland J at [21–38].

16.4.5 Initial consent before objection

[16.59] Where a party consents or affirms the adjudicator's jurisdiction and then later challenges it, the initial consent or election will most likely permanently waive the party's right to challenge the adjudicator's jurisdiction, notwithstanding the later objection. Thus, where a party accepts the jurisdiction of the adjudicator by making a submission to the adjudicator and the other party and then continues to engage in correspondence with them before raising its objection at some point later, that party was found to have waived its right to object to the jurisdiction of the adjudicator.[55]

16.4.6 Approbation and reprobation

[16.60] Where a party approbates and reprobates or 'blows hot and cold', it will adopt a position or act in a certain way, but then later act in a way which contradicts the original adoption or act. Where this occurs, provided that the other party has taken a benefit[56] from the original adoption or act, the later contradiction will serve to extinguish the original adoption or act such that the party can no longer rely on it.

[16.61] In the context of maintaining a right to challenge the jurisdiction of the adjudicator, provided the party's actions either during or after the adjudication do not conflict with a reservation on the adjudicator's jurisdiction, it will not be found to fall foul of this rule, and the party will retain its right to raise a challenge in defence to an application to enforce the adjudicator's decision. However, where they are inconsistent, the right to challenge may evaporate.

[16.62] This issue generally (though not exclusively) arises after the adjudicator has given his decision. The losing party will act in a certain way that contradicts the reservation on the adjudicator's jurisdiction made before or during the adjudication. The concept of approbation and reprobation was first discussed in the context of adjudication *Macob Civil Engineering v Morrison Construction Ltd*,[57] where the court held:

---

[55] *Cowlin Construction Ltd v CFW Architects (A Firm)* [2002] EWHC 2914 (TCC), per Kirkham J at [59–68].
[56] What amounts to a benefit is described in *R Durtnell & Sons Ltd v Kaduna Ltd* [2003] EWHC 517 (TCC), per Seymour J at [46], although see *AMEC Group Ltd v Thames Water Utilities Ltd* [2010] EWHC 419 (TCC), per Coulson J at [94–98].
[57] [1999] BLR 93, per Dyson J at [29]. But it is suggested that this reasoning, as applied to the particular circumstances before Dyson J, is problematic. He appears to be saying that a party who complains that a decision reached in breach of natural justice sufficient to engage the arbitration clause cannot also say that the adjudicator's decision is a nullity incapable of enforcement. This appears to be because Dyson J took the view that a decision reached in breach of natural justice is still 'a decision' for the purposes of the 1996 Act and the Scheme, but that is not the approach taken in subsequent authorities.

what the defendant could not do was to assert that the decision was a decision for the purposes of being the subject of a reference to arbitration but was not a decision for the purposes of being binding and enforceable pending any revision by the arbitrator. In so holding, I am doing no more than applying the doctrine of approbation and reprobation or election… Once the defendant elected to treat the decision as one capable of being referred to arbitration, he was bound also to treat it as a decision which was binding and enforceable unless revised by the arbitrator.

[16.63] Generally, the court will not easily find that a party who has adequately reserved its position will reprobate it by its actions.

the test for approbation is high… the approbatory acts must be so strong and express, that no reasonable construction can be put on them, other than that they were performed by the party from his approbation[58]

[16.64] Nevertheless, there are numerous examples of where this rule has been put to the test. They include:

- making a part or full payment of the adjudicator's fees and the sum awarded by the adjudicator.[59] If the responding party makes a payment in respect of the adjudicator's fees, the responding party should make clear that the payment is made subject and without prejudice to its objection to jurisdiction and without admission;
- reliance on the terms of an adjudicator's decision in a subsequent adjudication;[60]
- accepting a cheque in payment. However, 'if the acceptance is intended to be qualified so that the payment is accepted generally on account of that party's entitlement to payment, and it is clear from the surrounding circumstance objectively determined that the acceptance of the cheque was qualified in that way, the accepting party will not be taken to have fully and finally accepted or approbated or settled the underlying obligation or the situation giving rise to that obligation';[61]
- seeking a correction to the adjudicator's decision pursuant to the slip rule. It would appear that this will not amount to an act of approbation where the party seeking a correction has reserved its position on the adjudicator's jurisdiction.[62] However, the court has made *obiter dicta* remarks to the contrary;[63]
- commencing arbitration or litigation proceedings. However, issuing a notice of dissatisfaction in order to preserve the right to refer the dispute to arbitration or litigation

---

[58] *Highlands and Islands Authority Ltd v Shetland Islands Counsel* [2012] ScotCS CSOH 12, per Lord Menzies at [60].
[59] *Wales and West Utilities Ltd v PPS Pipeline Systems GmbH* [2014] EWHC 54 (TCC), Akenhead J at [42–44].
[60] *Linnett v Halliwells LLP* [2009] EWHC 319, per Ramsey J at [112–117].
[61] *Joinery Plus Ltd (In Administration) v Laing Ltd* [2003] EWHC 3513 (TCC), per Thornton J at [92–96].
[62] *Laker Vent Engineering Limited v Jacobs E&C Limited* [2014] EWHC 1058 (TCC), per Ramsey J at [33–36].
[63] *Shimizu Europe Ltd v Automajor Ltd* [2002] EWHC 1571 (TCC), per Seymour J at [30].

in circumstances where a failure to do so will result in the adjudicator's decision being final is unlikely to amount to an approbation;[64]
- putting forward one argument during an adjudication and a different argument in enforcement proceedings. This was the position in *Galliford Try Construction Ltd v Michael Heal Associates Ltd*.[65] The court, *obiter dicta*, concluded that Galliford was:

> playing fast and loose with the process of adjudication, shifting its ground opportunistically to meet the challenge of the moment. No Court can be expected to treat phlegmatically a case in which a successful party to an adjudication comes before it saying, 'I know that I succeeded in the adjudication on a basis which I now recognise was wrong in law, but the adjudicator decided what he was asked to decide and it is just tough luck for the Defendant.' That attitude seems to come very close an abuse of the process of adjudication.

- raising an objection, by way of jurisdictional challenge to the second adjudicator or by way of interim injunction, to the commencement of a second adjudication in circumstances where the dispute is the same as the first adjudication. In *PT Building Services Ltd v Rok Build Ltd*,[66] the losing party to the first adjudication raised jurisdictional challenges to its enforceability; those challenges were such as to leave the successful claimant sufficiently worried that it decided to re-refer the dispute rather than enforce. The losing party then used the previous decision on topic to persuade the second adjudicator to resign. Unsurprisingly, the court held that by deploying the first decision to persuade the second adjudicator to resign, the losing party had debarred itself from arguing subsequently that the first decision was unenforceable – it had relied on that decision to precisely the opposite effect;
- seeking to rely on the first adjudicator's decision, in a second adjudication, while challenging the adjudicator's jurisdiction in the first adjudication;[67]
- relying on the terms of the decision as support for subsequent payment applications or as support for a withholding or pay less notice;[68]
- commencing proceedings to enforce the adjudicator's decision and, at the same time, commencing proceedings under CPR Part 8 for a final declaration that the adjudicator made an error that the court should correct. In *Pilon Ltd v Breyer Group plc*,[69] Coulson J held that such as approach would 'amount to the clearest possible case of approbation and reprobation';
- issuing an interim certificate by reference to the adjudicator's decision and making payment pursuant to that certificate. In *Thameside Construction Co Ltd v Stevens*,[70]

---

[64] *Highlands and Islands Authority Ltd v Shetland Islands Counsel* [2012] ScotCS CSOH 12, per Lord Menzies at [54–60].
[65] [2003] EWHC 2886 (TCC), per Seymour J at [52].
[66] [2008] EWHC 3434 (TCC), per Ramsey J at [28].
[67] *Linnett v Halliwells LLP* [2009] EWHC 319 (TCC), per Ramsey J at [112–117].
[68] *Amec Group Ltd v Thames Water Utilities Ltd* [2010] EWHC 419 (TCC), per Coulson J at [94–98]. Note the comments on this point were made *obiter dicta*.
[69] [2010] EWHC 837 (TCC), per Coulson J at [35].
[70] [2013] EWHC 2071 (TCC), per Akenhead J at [13; 27].

Akenhead J noted that the losing party had properly conceded that it could not challenge the validity of the decision where it had issued an interim certificate by reference to it and paid the sum shown on that certificate.

16.4.7 Consequence of losing the right: ad hoc jurisdiction

[16.65] What is the consequence of losing the right to object to the adjudicator's jurisdiction? It means that the adjudicator's jurisdiction is expanded such that he now has power to act or not act in a particular way, or determine an issue where he otherwise would not. His jurisdiction can therefore be described as ad hoc[71] in respect of that action or issue.

> If the party does not raise any objection and participates in the adjudication then, even if there is a defect in the jurisdiction of the adjudicator, that party will create an ad-hoc jurisdiction for the adjudicator and lose the right to object to any decision on jurisdictional grounds. If a party raises only specific jurisdictional objections and those jurisdictional objections are found by the court to be unfounded then that party is precluded from raising other grounds which were available to it, if it then participates in the adjudication. That participation amounts to a waiver of the jurisdictional objection and confers ad-hoc jurisdiction.

16.5 Threshold jurisdiction challenges

16.5.1 In a nutshell

[16.66] Threshold jurisdiction issues go to 'questions relating to the ability to set in train an adjudication process at all'.[72] The issues giving rise to these sorts of challenges are typically requirements that need to be met or issues that need to be avoided before the parties are permitted to refer a dispute to the adjudicator. These issues are often termed threshold jurisdictional issues because if they are not overcome, they act as a bar to the commencement of an adjudication. The following sections analyse the putative threshold jurisdiction issues. They are:

(1) no contract;
(2) contract is not a construction contract;
(3) construction contract is not in writing;
(4) no dispute;
(5) dispute settled;
(6) dispute not under the contract;
(7) more than one dispute;
(8) substantially the same dispute.

---

[71] *GPS Marine Contractors Ltd v Ringway Infrastructure Services Ltd* [2010] EWHC 283 (TCC), per Ramsey J at [37].
[72] *RG Carter Ltd v Edmund Nuttall Ltd*, Unreported, 21 June 2000, per Thornton J at [18].

[16.67] They are all issues that arise in the context of statutory adjudication and may arise, depending on the wording of the contract, in contractual adjudication.

16.5.2 No contract

[16.68] Adjudication is a form of dispute resolution borne from contract whether it is implied in the contract[73] or expressly provided for and so it follows that the parties must have reached a binding agreement between them in order to adjudicate. Where there is no binding agreement, the adjudicator will have no jurisdiction to decide any dispute between the parties. There are numerous examples of where the court has conducted a factual analysis to determine whether or not a contract formed between the parties. Often that analysis is required where the parties' agreement is said to have formed via an exchange of correspondence, or it has been recorded in meeting minutes or in some other informal way. Not infrequently, construction projects are concluded without the parties ever reaching agreement on all material terms, with the effect that a contract cannot be said to have formed. In those situations, the contractor may have an entitlement to be paid on a *quantum meruit* or *quantum valebat* basis, but the parties will not have an entitlement to adjudicate disputes, because no contract exists.

[16.69] Where a contract has been terminated or determined, although it depends on the form of adjudication and the wording of the contract, it is likely that the contract survives to the extent that the parties may adjudicate any dispute. A contract that is held to be void, either because it has been rescinded or there has been duress or fraud, is one that in the eyes of the law never existed at all. As such, any dispute between the parties cannot be resolved via adjudication. Section 4.3 debates this topic further and the cases that have had to address this issue are listed at Appendix 8 under that section.

16.5.3 Contract is not a construction contract

[16.70] The contract between the parties must be a construction contract, as defined by the Act, in order for the provisions of the Act to apply. This is explained in detail in Chapter 4, but in broad terms, a construction contract is defined by section 104 of the Act as pertaining to construction operations, which itself is defined at subsection 105(1) of the Act. Subsection 105(2) of the Act excludes certain activities that would otherwise fall within the definition at subsection 105(1). Those exclusions relate to works involving oil and gas, minerals, nuclear processing, power generation, water or effluent treatment, chemicals, pharmaceuticals, steel, food, drink, supply or artistic works. Further exclusions are identified in section 106 in respect of residential occupiers, and reference is made to the Construction Contracts (England and Wales) Exclusion Order 1998, an instrument that excludes agreements for certain types of work. If only part of the contract falls within the

---

[73] As it will be where the contract is caught by the Act and there are no adjudication provisions in the contract. See Section 6.2.

scope of the Act, it is still permissible for disputes arising out of that part of the contract to be adjudicated within the statutory framework.

[16.71] If the Act does not apply and the contract does not contain an operable adjudication procedure, adjudication will be unavailable as an automatic right. However, where the contract contains or makes reference to an operable adjudication procedure, the parties may still adjudicate any dispute within the confines of that procedure. An adjudication conducted in those circumstances may be termed a contractual adjudication (see Section 5.2). Parties may even be able to adjudicate a dispute where neither the Act applies nor is there a pre-existing contractual agreement to adjudicate. In this case, the parties may agree, or be deemed to agree to submit their dispute to adjudication on an ad hoc basis. In that case, the adjudication is termed an ad hoc adjudication (see Section 5.3).

16.5.4 Construction contract is not in writing

[16.72] Where the contract is dated earlier than 1 October 2011, section 107 of the 1996 Act provides that a construction contract must be made in writing, by an exchange of communication in writing, or be evidenced in writing in order for the provisions of the 1996 Act to apply to it. The court has interpreted this provision strictly, holding that the whole contract must be in writing. Reported cases when this section has been considered tend to fall into one of a handful of scenarios, including where the contract is oral, it is the subject of an oral variation, where one or more terms were not agreed in writing, where trivial terms are not agreed in writing, whether an implied term means an agreement is not in writing and whether a letter of intent can constitute a construction contract in writing. The meaning of section 107, together with the position on each of these scenarios is debated in Section 4.8. Section 107 will, of course, not apply where the contract falls outside the scope of the Act.

16.5.5 No dispute

[16.73] Where the Act applies, it requires that the referring party must be in dispute with the responding party before it is entitled to commence adjudication proceedings in an attempt to resolve it. In essence, this means that the referring party must have made a claim and the responding party must have acted in a way other than to admit the claim in full. Even where the Act does not apply, the contractual adjudication procedure prescribed by the contract will almost certainly require that a dispute has formed before an adjudication can commence.

[16.74] The court's approach to determining challenges of this nature is to infer the existence of a dispute where possible. This is in line with the court's policy to support the process of adjudication and to enforce an adjudicator's decision unless there is a clear reason not to.

[16.75] A challenge that there is no dispute usually materialises at two points. The first is at the outset of the adjudication. The referring party will commence an adjudication in respect of allegedly disputed matters and the responding party will raise a complaint that those matters are not disputed, with the effect that the adjudicator does not have jurisdiction to decide the dispute at all. This is often referred to as an ambush because the responding party was not aware that there was a dispute on the issue or issues that have been set out in the notice of adjudication.

[16.76] The second will arise from an attempt to expand the dispute during the adjudication (usually in a submission) such that the expanded part of the dispute had not crystallised prior to the start of the adjudication.[74] This second complaint goes hand in hand with a complaint that the extraneous matter is outside of the scope of the dispute referred to the adjudicator.

[16.77] The answer on both of these scenarios is simple – the dispute must have crystallised before the adjudicator has jurisdiction to consider it.[75] Refer to Section 7.2 for full details on this subject.

16.5.6 More than one dispute

[16.78] The Act permits only one, not multiple disputes to be referred to an adjudicator at any one time. This makes perfect sense: if an adjudicator were simultaneously bombarded with five adjudications at once, then within the statutory timescale given to reach a decision, it is unlikely there would be sufficient time to decide them at all or properly.

[16.79] Provided that where there are a group of issues, they can be properly characterised in the notice of adjudication as one dispute, and the notice of adjudication does not refer to 'disputes' plural, the adjudicator will have jurisdiction to decide the dispute. For example, a dispute over monies owed may be characterised as one dispute, although it will usually be made up of a number of issues. Alternatively, there may be a claim for an extension of time which is claimed as a result of a number of separate events.

[16.80] Section 7.3 addresses this issue in more detail.

16.5.7 Substantially the same dispute

[16.81] Once matters in dispute have been decided by an adjudicator, they may not be re-adjudicated, and any attempt to re-adjudicate the same matters already decided will render the second adjudicator's decision invalid. In the same vein, an adjudicator in a subsequent adjudication must not alter any part of a previous adjudicator's decision. There are a number of reasons why this is the case. A precondition of commencing an adjudication is that there is a dispute. A dispute cannot exist under the contract if the matter has already been submitted to and decided by an adjudicator. Subsection 108(3) binds the parties to an adjudicator's decision until it is finally determined by legal proceedings, by arbitration or by agreement. There is nothing that permits the decision to be

---

[74] For an example of this, see *Beck Interiors Ltd v UK Flooring Contractors Ltd* [2012] EWHC 1808 (TCC) per Akenhead J at [28–31].
[75] Paragraphs 7.08–7.12 provide more detail.

re-adjudicated. Where the Scheme applies, subparagraph 9(2) provides that the adjudicator must resign if the dispute is the same or substantially the same as one that has previously been referred to adjudication and a decision made.

[16.82] There is a reasonably fine line between being permitted to refer successive disputes to adjudication and ensuring that the scope of a subsequent adjudicator's decision does not address matters decided by a previous adjudicator. However, generally speaking, the courts have found in favour of enforcing subsequent decisions. It will give considerable weight to the decision of the adjudicator and it will only embark on a jurisdictional enquiry where there were real grounds for concluding that the adjudicator had erred in deciding that there was no substantial overlap.

[16.83] Section 7.4 addresses this issue in more detail.

16.5.8 Dispute not under the contract

[16.84] Statutory adjudication is only available for contractual claims. Therefore, common law negligence or misrepresentation under the Misrepresentation Act 1967, for instance, cannot be adjudicated. The most common issue under this head is whether a dispute under an ancillary or connected agreement is a dispute 'under' the original construction contract, or a dispute arising under the ancillary or connected agreement. Where it is the former, then the parties may adjudicate pursuant to the terms of the original contract. Where the dispute arises under the ancillary contract or connected agreement, the subject matter of that contract about which there is a dispute must fall within the scope of the Act in order for a statutory adjudication right to exist.

[16.85] The 'dispute' may arise under more than one contract, but those contracts have to be connected in some way. An example might be a framework agreement and a call-off contract.

[16.86] Sections 7.5 and 7.6 expand on these issues.

16.6 Process jurisdiction challenges

16.6.1 In a nutshell

[16.87] The adjudicator's jurisdiction is dictated by the Act (where it applies) and the applicable adjudicator's rules. Both provide a framework within which the adjudicator must operate during the adjudication process. The process starts with the issue of the notice of adjudication and concludes when the adjudicator communicates his decision. Within that time frame there are a number of issues that have arisen which have given rise to jurisdictional challenges. They can be described as follows:

(1) incorrect parties named in the notice of adjudication
(2) adjudicator was not correctly appointed
(3) referral notice served out of time

(4) arguments outside the scope of the dispute
(5) change to the relief claimed
(6) defective service
(7) other procedural improprieties
(8) new material during the adjudication
(9) a submission that contains matters outside the scope of the dispute as set out in the notice of adjudication.

[16.88] They are all issues that arise in the context of statutory adjudication and may arise, depending on the wording of the contract, in contractual adjudication.[76]

16.6.2 Incorrect parties named

[16.89] Surprisingly frequently, the name of one or both parties recorded in the notice of adjudication will not be the name of the party who entered into the contract, either because there was a clerical error made when the name was written or there was a genuine belief that proceedings could be brought by the non-party, or brought against it. Since the Act provides that only parties to a construction contract may adjudicate, on the face of it, where the wrong party is recorded, the adjudicator will not have jurisdiction to decide the dispute. However, this is one issue where the courts have adopted a less rigid approach.

[16.90] The authorities demonstrate that the courts will need to see compelling evidence that a party to the adjudication is not the party named in the contract before it will entertain a challenge on the adjudicator's jurisdiction. Thus, in *Andrew Wallace Ltd v Artisan Regeneration Ltd*,[77] the contract was with Mr Wallace and yet his company sought to enforce the adjudicator's decision. The court found that, on a review of the contemporaneous evidence, it was clear that the responding party knew the contract was with the company and not the individual and so the decision was enforced. In *Total M&E Services Ltd v ABB Building Technologies Ltd (formerly ABB Stewarts Ltd)*,[78] notwithstanding the fact that the referring party had referred the dispute under the name Total Mechanical and Engineering Services Limited, a different name from the name of the party of the contract and a different company, the court found that the mis-description had no real effect because the parties were aware of the true identities of the contracting parties and no-one could be misled. However, the court said that where there are similar company names, as for instance in a group of companies or where there are subsidiaries with overlapping management systems, a precise description of the referring party is more likely to be critical.

[16.91] An example of where an adjudicator's decision was not enforced was in *Estor Ltd v Multifit (UK) Ltd*.[79] There, the contract was with the Ginger Group (the parent of Estor) and Hub Design Ltd. Hub had subcontracted its work to Multifit. In the adjudication, Estor

---

[76] As to the distinction, see section 5.
[77] [2006] EHWC 15, per Kirkham J at [33–40].
[78] [2002] EWHC 248 (TCC), per Wilcox J at [17–23].
[79] [2009] EWHC 2565 (TCC), per Akenhead J at [41–42].

took the point that Multifit was not the party to the contract. The court found that there was a realistic prospect that Estor could establish that Multifit was not the party to the contract and so the decision was not enforced.

[16.92] An adjudication decision against one joint debtor alone ought not, as a matter of principle, to be enforceable against another joint debtor who has not been served with, and taken no part in, the adjudication proceedings.[80]

[16.93] In at least one case,[81] the losing party to the adjudication challenged the application to enforce on the basis that the adjudication had taken place between the wrong parties because it was contended that there had been a novation of all rights and obligations from one company to another, and the referring party had in error commenced a claim against the pre-novation company instead of the post-novation company, where its rights now lay. Although in this instance the court enforced the adjudicator's decision on the basis that the paucity and late receipt of evidence did not support the defendant's claim for novation, there was an acceptance that had the defendant's claim been supported, the adjudicator's decision would be invalid.

16.6.3 Adjudicator not correctly appointed

[16.94] The ways in which an adjudicator may be appointed to preside over an adjudication are discussed in detail at Section 9.6. If the rules governing the appointment of an adjudication cannot be followed or are not followed correctly, there is a risk that the courts will hold the adjudicator did not have the jurisdiction to decide the dispute. There are three common scenarios:

- The adjudication rules make the appointment impossible.
- The correct set of rules are followed incorrectly.
- The incorrect set of rules are followed.

(A) The adjudication rules make an appointment impossible

[16.95] The adjudication rules will normally prescribe a primary method by which an adjudicator is appointed, but if that method cannot be followed for some reason, there is usually also an alternative method of appointing the adjudicator such that, come what may, an adjudicator will be appointed. In the event the parties are not able to appoint via the primary method and there is no alternative, what then? It is suggested that the unworkability of the rules leads to one of three outcomes.

- The parties agree the appointment of an adjudicator on an ad hoc basis.
- Where the Act applies to the contract, the adjudication rules are replaced wholesale by the Scheme.

---

[80] *Belgrave Developments (Poole) Ltd v Vaughan & Anor*, Unreported, 30 June 2005, per Blunt R at [86–89].
[81] *A.T. Stannard Ltd v James Tobutt and Thomas Tobutt* [2014] EWHC 3491 (TCC), per Akenhead J at [18].

- Where the Act does not apply and there is no agreement, adjudication is unavailable.

[16.96] Sometimes, a defect in the procedure which, on a strict interpretation, would lead to an unworkable appointment procedure will be overlooked by the court. In *Amec Capital Projects Ltd v Whitefriars Ltd*,[82] Amec contended that provisions in the contract failed because the nominated adjudicator did not exist because the contract called for the appointment of a Mr George Ashworth, when in fact the name of the individual was Mr Geoffrey Ashworth. The court decided that Amec was trying to take advantage of a 'misnomer', which it would not allow, and it therefore imported the name of Geoffrey in place of George. Amec also argued that because Mr Ashworth had died before the dispute could be referred to him, the particular wording of the appointment procedure (in that case JCT) was impossible to operate. On that point, the court agreed but rather than scupper the adjudication, it accepted that the rules of the Scheme could apply in place of the contractual rules.

(B) The correct set of rules are followed incorrectly

[16.97] The rules of appointment may not be followed properly, such that the adjudicator is appointed ultra vires. The courts will separate failures that go to a fundamental aspect of the appointment affecting the whole adjudication, such as the use of the wrong ANB[83] or the appointment of the wrong adjudicator and a minor procedural failure, such as the failure to provide certain documents to the adjudicator as part of his appointment. In the former case, the decision is unlikely to be enforced whereas in the latter case it is likely to be. For example, in *Vision Homes Ltd v Lancsville Construction Ltd*,[84] a notice of adjudication was issued together with a request to an ANB for the appointment of an adjudicator. The notice of adjudication was subsequently abandoned in favour of a second notice of adjudication because the first notice of adjudication did not deal with a minor point that the referring party had omitted. However, the request to the ANB was not renewed. The court found that the adjudicator was improperly appointed and therefore lacked jurisdiction to decide the dispute.

[16.98] Where the referring party attempts to influence the appointment of a particular adjudicator by acting dishonestly, then that appointment is likely to be invalid. The court has held that there is an implied term that parties enter contracts on the basis that they will act honestly and so, where the referring party completes an ANB application form and lists individuals as conflicted from appointment knowing that they are not conflicted, that will amount to a dishonest act that will render the appointment invalid.[85]

---

[82] [2004] EWHC 393 (TCC), per Toulmin J at [85–109].
[83] See for example *Lead Technical Services Ltd v CMS Medical Ltd* [2007] EWCA Civ 316, per Moses LJ at [18].
[84] [2009] EWHC 2042 (TCC), per Clarke J at [56–57].
[85] *Eurocom Ltd v Siemens plc* [2014] EWHC 3710 (TCC), per Ramsey J at [57–79].

(C) The incorrect set of rules are followed

[16.99] There may be a dispute between the parties as to which set of adjudication provisions apply. This very often occurs where the parties aver that a different contract governs their agreement and the rules of adjudication set out or referred to within each contract are also different. In circumstances where it is shown that the adjudicator was appointed pursuant to the wrong set of rules, it will be a matter of fact whether or not his decision is invalid. Thus, in *Lead Technical Services Ltd v CMS Medical Ltd*,[86] there was a dispute about which form of contract applied. Each form contained different adjudication rules. The court held that a decision as to which contract (and therefore rules) applied was sufficiently uncertain that it was not possible to say at summary judgment that the adjudication procedure adopted was the right one and so the adjudicator's decision was not summarily enforced. Similarly, where the adjudicator was appointed pursuant to the rules of the Scheme in circumstances where one party argued that the contract agreed was the JCT Prime Cost contract (incorporating the JCT adjudication provisions), or in the alternative that no written construction contract was agreed and the other party argued that its own set of conditions applied (which incorporated the Scheme), the court was not able to satisfactorily resolve the contractual dispute at summary enforcement proceedings sufficiently to conclude that there was no real prospect of the defendant being able to argue counter to the decision made against it. Therefore, it declined to enforce the adjudicator's decision.[87]

[16.100] In *Dalkia Energy and Technical Services Ltd v Bell Group UK Ltd*,[88] there was no dispute as to the existence of a construction contract between the parties, but instead there was a dispute as to whether Bell's standard terms were incorporated or not. If they were, the adjudication rules set out in those standard terms applied and if they were not, the Scheme applied. The adjudicator decided that Bell's standard terms were incorporated and therefore the appointment was to be made in accordance with those terms.

[16.101] These cases and others were considered in the case of *Ecovision Systems Ltd v Vinci Construction UK Ltd*.[89] In that case, there was a dispute as to whether the TeCSA, Scheme or NEC adjudication rules applied and, in the event, the adjudicator had been appointed using the wrong set of rules. Addressing the question of whether the adjudicator had jurisdiction to determine which set of rules to adopt, the court held that the adjudicator did not have such jurisdiction. It said:[90]

> even where it is common ground that a construction contract exists under which there is a right to claim adjudication, the adjudicator has no power to determine what rules of adjudication apply if there is a dispute about those rules and the dispute affects (i.e. makes a material difference as to) the procedure for appointment, the procedure to be followed in the adjudication or

---

[86] [2007] EWCA Civ 316, per Moses LJ at [18].
[87] *Pegram Shopfitters Ltd v Tally Weijl (UK) Ltd* [2003] EWCA Civ 1750, per May LJ at [30–34].
[88] [2009] EWHC 73 (TCC), per Coulson J at [38–46].
[89] [2015] EWHC 587 (TCC), per Havelock-Allan J at [70–78; 83–93].
[90] Cf. *Dalkia Energy and Technical Services Ltd v Bell Group UK Ltd* [2009] EWHC 73 (TCC), per Coulson J at [38–46].

the status of the decision. Specifically I hold that there is no rule that the Court will not interfere with an adjudicator's conclusion as to a matter affecting his jurisdiction when considering whether to enforce a decision by summary judgment.

[16.102] Even though the adjudicator is appointed pursuant to the wrong procedure, that does not mean that the adjudication will be held to have never existed. Provided that the notice of adjudication was otherwise valid, then the adjudication will be held to have been commenced, albeit that the adjudicator may not have been properly appointed, thus rendering his decision a nullity.[91] This may be important where the contract contains a conclusivity clause which prohibits the referral of a dispute to adjudication after a certain number of days.

16.6.4 Referral notice served out of time

[16.103] Where the Act applies, the referral notice must be sent to the adjudicator within seven days of the date of the notice of adjudication. If it is served late, that is likely to be fatal to the adjudication. The courts have shown some flexibility with regard to the deadline for service of the supporting documents, but the flexibility is unlikely to amount to more than one or two days. Section 10.2.2 addresses this issue in more detail.

16.6.5 Arguments outside the scope of the dispute

[16.104] The general rule is that the scope of the dispute lies primarily in the notice of adjudication. The scope of the dispute may also be determined by documents referred to in the notice of adjudication, by reference to prior communications between the parties, and by new issues introduced during the adjudication, which are expressly or implicitly accepted as forming part of the dispute.[92]

[16.105] It should be remembered that the responding party is entitled to raise any defence or cross-claim it wishes provided that defence falls within the scope of the dispute. Where a cross-claim is raised, not only must it fall within the scope of the dispute but also, where it relates to money, it should be the subject of a valid withholding or pay less notice.[93]

[16.106] What is not permitted by either party is the introduction of new arguments outside the scope of the dispute. Each submission should be carefully considered to ensure that it does not creep outside the boundaries of the dispute. Where it does, the party in receipt of the decision should carefully consider how to proceed in accordance with the guidance of Section 16.3. Where the adjudicator decides to deal with an out-of-scope argument in his decision, provided the aggrieved party has not lost its right to challenge the adjudicator's jurisdiction to determine that argument, it may raise it in defence during any enforcement proceedings to defeat the validity of the decision. This is addressed at Section 16.7.6.

---

[91] *University of Brighton v Dovehouse Interiors Ltd* [2014] EWHC 940, per Carr J at [77–78].
[92] See Section 9.3.3.
[93] See Section 10.3.3.

[16.107] This argument is in effect a 'no dispute' challenge, because the issues raised have not been the subject of a dispute before (in that one party makes a claim and the other party rejects the claim or does not admit it).[94]

16.6.6 Defective service

[16.108] The adjudication rules will generally prescribe a procedure by which documents are to be served. Where this is not done, and where the Act applies, section 115 of the Act dictates the permissible methods of service. Whether the rules of service are contained in the adjudication procedure or whether section 115 applies, they should be followed. Where they are, even if the other party does not receive documents and as a result does not participate in an adjudication, a complaint that it did not receive the documents is likely to fall on deaf ears.[95]

[16.109] In *Primus Build Ltd v Pompey Centre Ltd*,[96] the court found that the referring party had complied with the rather unusual requirement to affect 'personal delivery' of the notice of adjudication, but it said that had that not been the case, it would have had no hesitation in rendering the adjudicator's decision invalid.

[16.110] In *Costain v Wescol*,[97] the court found that the failure to serve documents by first-class post, as required by the adjudication rules, did not invalidate the adjudicator's decision, although in that case there was a clause in the rules stating that a failure to comply with certain procedural requirements shall not invalidate the decision of the adjudicator.

[16.111] Care should be taken where a party knows that the other party will not receive documents served by the agreed method, but knows how to reach that party and serve the documents on it by other means. In that case, it should attempt to deliver the documents by those means, or risk a claim of bad conduct by the other party, which in turn may lead to the adjudicator's decision being nullified.[98]

16.6.7 New material during the adjudication

[16.112] In exercising the powers afforded to him, the adjudicator will often ask questions or seek information in relation to matters that form part of the dispute from one or both of the parties during the adjudication. In these circumstances, it is plain that the adjudicator is acting within his jurisdiction and, in so far as the information asked for in some way enables him to answer the questions put to him, he is entitled to – indeed obliged to – ask for it. Both parties should be kept appraised of the adjudicator's requests and given some opportunity to review and comment on the material. The issue of the scope of the adjudicator's jurisdiction in relation to new material is sometimes raised hand in hand

---

[94] See Section 7.2.
[95] *Nageh v Richard Giddings & Another* [2006] EWHC 3240 (TCC), per Coulson J at [26].
[96] [2009] EWHC 1487 (TCC), per Coulson J at [9–26].
[97] *Costain Ltd v Wescol Steel Ltd* [2003] EWHC 312 (TCC), per Havery J at [14–18].
[98] *M Rohde Construction v Nicholas Markham-David* [2006] EWHC 814 (TCC), per Jackson J at [32–38].

with a claim that the adjudicator breached the rules of natural justice, in particular that he did not give one or both parties sufficient time to deal with it in a further submission.[99] See Section 17.5.8.

16.6.8 Other procedural improprieties

[16.113] A party should ensure at all times that the adjudicator and the other party comply with the rules of the adjudication (be they the Scheme or contractual rules). Where this does not happen, the other party may complain that the adjudicator reached his decision having followed an incorrect procedure and therefore is outwith his jurisdiction. However, the courts have distinguished between directory and mandatory rules, such that not all breaches of the adjudication rules will result in the courts determining that the adjudicator's decision is unenforceable. It seems likely that where the Scheme rule uses the word 'shall', that rule is far more likely to be mandatory. An example of a directory rule is paragraph 1 of the Scheme. This paragraph determines the requirements for the content of the notice of adjudication. However, provided the notice of adjudication is sufficient for the purpose of selecting an adjudicator and commencing the adjudication, it may not matter that parts of paragraph 1 are not complied with.[100] For instance, the failure of the notice of adjudication to set out the contractually specified address for the giving of notices, contrary to subparagraph 1(3)(d) of the Scheme did not invalidate it because on the facts of that case it was not a 'fundamental non-compliance'.[101]

[16.114] The court may endeavour to interpret the rules in a way that allows the adjudicator's decision to be enforced, even in light of a procedural impropriety. For example, in *London & Amsterdam Properties Ltd v Waterman Partnership Ltd*,[102] the adjudication rules prescribed that the referral notice would only be 20 pages. London & Amsterdam served a referral notice of over 1000 pages. Waterman argued that the adjudicator had no jurisdiction because London & Amsterdam had not served a referral notice (as defined by the adjudication rules) as required by the rules. The court decided that the adjudicator had jurisdiction to act as he did, where he accepted the first 20 pages of the referral notice as the referral notice and accepted the rest through the powers given to him at paragraph 13(a) of the Scheme, which empowers him to request any documents he may reasonably require.

16.7 Decision based jurisdiction challenges

16.7.1 In a nutshell

[16.115] The primary task of an adjudicator is to deliver a decision on the dispute referred to him. He must deliver his decision within the required time, and the content of the decision

---

[99] *Volker Stevin Ltd v Holystone Contracts Ltd* [2010] EWHC 2344 (TCC), per Coulson at [10–14].
[100] *Aveat Heating Ltd v Jerram Falkus Construction Ltd* [2007] EWHC 131 (TCC), per Havery J at [15–17; 23].
[101] *University of Brighton v Dovehouse Interiors Ltd* [2014] EWHC 940 (TCC), per Carr J at [62–68].
[102] [2003] EWHC 3059 (TCC), per Wilcox J at [96–116].

must comply with the rules of the adjudication and must relate to the matters in dispute. The following subsections outline scenarios arising in the lead-up to the decision, or in the decision itself, that may demonstrate that the adjudicator has acted outside, or has failed to exhaust, his jurisdiction.

(1) lien over the decision
(2) failure to reach a decision within the required time
(3) signing the decision
(4) sufficiency of written reasons
(5) scope of the decision
(6) errors of law
(7) errors of fact
(8) correcting errors

16.7.2 Lien over the decision

[16.116] Where the Act applies, it is not open to an adjudicator to impose a lien on his decision, or in other words impose conditions that need to be met by one or both parties before he issues it. To do so would 'frustrate or impede the progress of the statutory arrangements for resolving these contractual disputes.'[103] The authorities are all concerned with a request by the adjudicator for payment of his fees before his decision is given,[104] but the rule extends to any reason for holding the decision back.[105] Where he imposes a lien, he acts in excess of his jurisdiction, and the decision will not be enforced. However, depending on the terms of adjudication rules or the adjudicator's agreement, the adjudicator may be entitled to an advance payment, or interim payments during the adjudication. See Section 9.6.15.

16.7.3 Failure to reach the decision within the required timescale

[16.117] An adjudicator is required to reach a decision within the period allotted to him. Where the Act applies and where no extension has been given, that period is 28 days from the date of receipt of the referral notice. Where the decision is not reached in time, it will be reached outside the adjudicator's jurisdiction and will be invalid. The cases distinguish between the act of reaching a decision and communicating that decision to the parties. It is clear that if a decision is not reached within the requisite period, be it 28 days or an extended time, then it will not be enforced.[106] There is some leeway for a decision

---

[103] *St Andrews Bay Development Ltd v HBG Management Ltd and Mrs Janey Milligan* [2003] ScotCS 103, per Lord Wheatley at [19].
[104] *Mott MacDonald Ltd v London & Regional Properties Ltd* [2007] EWHC 1055 (TCC), per Thornton, at [75–78].
[105] *Cubitt Building & Interiors Ltd v Fleetglade Ltd* [2006] EWHC 3413, per Coulson J at [77–81].
[106] See for example *Cubitt Building & Interiors Limited v Fleetgate Ltd* [2006] EWHC 3413 (TCC), per Coulson J at [76].

to be communicated after the 28-day period, but that communication must be made as soon as possible. If it is communicated more than a day after the requisite period, the decision will likely be held to be invalid. See Section 11.4 for a fuller explanation on this topic.

16.7.4 Signing the decision

[16.118] Does the failure by the adjudicator to sign the decision invalidate it? In *Treasure & Son v Martin Dawes*,[107] the adjudicator did not sign his decision. The adjudication rules placed no requirement on the adjudicator to sign it. The defendant to the enforcement proceedings argued that such a term could be implied and that the failure to sign meant that the decision had not been reached within the requisite time period and was therefore unenforceable. The court held that such a term could not be implied into the adjudication rules. It said that while it is the case that a decision signed by the adjudicator will clearly demonstrate as a matter of evidence that it is his decision, the adjudication provisions are still operable if it can be demonstrated as a matter of evidence that a decision was the decision of the particular adjudicator issued at a particular time. Accordingly, subject to there being evidence of the decision being that of the adjudicator, it seems unlikely that the failure by the adjudicator to sign his decision will render it invalid, whether the rules require it or not, although of course it is good practice to do so.

16.7.5 Sufficiency of written reasons

[16.119] Certain adjudication rules, including the Scheme, do not require the adjudicator to give reasons unless he is asked to do so. Where a request is made, unless the rules say otherwise, a brief statement of reasons will suffice. The reasons must be intelligible and must show that the adjudicator has considered the issues before him and reached his decision on those issues for reasons explained in his decision.[108] But the reasons need not be explained in great detail, nor does the adjudicator need to refer to each document or each submission put before him. However, where those reasons are insufficient to demonstrate that the adjudicator has dealt with the dispute, the adjudicator's decision may not be enforced.[109]

[16.120] One of the few cases where the courts declined to enforce a decision because of the inadequacy of the reasons given was *Thermal Energy Construction Ltd v AE & E Lentjes UK Ltd*.[110] Here the court held that the adjudicator's failure to give reasons caused

---

[107] [2007] EWHC 2420 (TCC), per Akenhead J at [45–48].
[108] *Atholl Developments (Slackbuie) Ltd, Re Application for Judicial Review* [2010] CSOH 94, per Lord Glennie at [17].
[109] *Carillion Construction Ltd v Devonport Royal Dockyard* [2005] EWHC 778 (TCC), per Jackson J at [81] supported on appeal (EWCA Civ 1358, per Chadwick LJ at [80]).
[110] [2009] EWHC 408 (TCC), per Davies J at [29].

'substantial prejudice'. In that case the responding party had raised a counterclaim and set-off argument. The judge found that:

> there is simply no express reference at all [in the decision] to this point being one of the issues which the Adjudicator recognised he had to decide, nor is it the subject of any express reference [in the decision] as being an issue which he has in fact decided, nor is it even included in the summary of items decided or the summary of the decision.[111]

[16.121] Accordingly, the decision was not enforced. Possibly the clearest judicial guidance on this topic was given by Akenhead J in *Balfour Beatty Engineering Services (HY) Ltd v Shepherd Construction Ltd*.[112]

(a) The decision needs to be intelligible so that the parties, objectively, can know what the adjudicator has decided and why.

(b) A decision which is wholly unreasoned but which is required to be reasoned is not a decision for the purposes of the Scheme or under contractual machinery which requires a reasoned decision. It would therefore not be enforceable as such.

(c) Because the Courts have said time and again that the decision cannot be challenged on the grounds that the adjudicator answered the questions, which he or she was required to address wrongly, the fact that the reasons given are, demonstrably or otherwise, wrong in fact or in law or even in terms of emphasis will not give rise to any effective challenge.

(d) The fact that the adjudicator does not deal with every single argument of fact or law will not mean that the decision is necessarily unreasoned. He or she should deal with those arguments which are sufficient to establish the route by which the decision is reached.

(e) The failure to give reasons is not a breach of natural justice.

(f) The reasons can be expressed simply. If the reasons are so incoherent that it is impossible for the reasonable reader to make sense of them, it will not be a reasoned decision.

(g) Adjudicators are not to be judged too strictly, for instance by the standards of judges or arbitrators, in terms of the reasoning. This reflects the fact that decisions often have to be reached in a short period of time and adjudicators are often not legally qualified. It certainly reflects the fact that there has not been a full judicial or arbitral type process.

(h) The fact that reasoning in a decision is repetitive, diffuse or even ambiguous does not mean that the decision is unreasoned.

[16.122] Refer to Section 11.2.4 for a general discussion on providing reasons with a decision and Section 17.5.16 for a discussion of whether failure to give reasons amounts to a breach of the rules of natural justice.

---

[111] Paragraph 25.
[112] [2009] EWHC 2218 (TCC) at [48].

16.7.6 Scope of the decision

(A) Principle

[16.123] This is possibly the most common jurisdictional challenge raised, certainly in the context of decision-based challenges. The principal rule on this topic is this: the adjudicator must deliver a decision that is responsive to the dispute and the questions referred to him to decide. Provided he does this, even if he makes a mistake, that decision will be enforceable. In other words, the scope of his decision must marry with the scope of the dispute. This accords with section 108 of the Act and subparagraphs 9(2) and 23 of the Scheme.[113]

[16.124] In order to determine whether or not the adjudicator has produced a decision that is responsive to the dispute, it is first necessary to determine what the dispute was between the parties. This can be done by reviewing the relevant exchanges between the parties. Next, it is necessary to determine whether all or part of that dispute was referred to adjudication, by analysing the scope of the dispute referred to adjudication as defined by the notice of adjudication. Next, one should analyse the submissions between the parties in order to determine whether there was an agreement, express or implied, to expand the scope of the dispute during the adjudication. In this regard, it is helpful to draw up a bullet point list of those issues in dispute. Finally, one should review the adjudicator's decision, to determine whether what has been decided directly responds to the issues in dispute. One can do this by writing the paragraph number(s) of the decision next to each item in the list of issues. If one is able to assign all the paragraphs that relate to the adjudicator's decision to one or more of the disputed issues that form part of the adjudication, then the adjudicator's decision is likely to be made within jurisdiction. The court has offered the following further guidance:

> (i) To determine the scope and ambit of any given dispute, the Court needs to analyse the relevant exchanges between the parties.
>
> (ii) It is open to a party which wishes to proceed to adjudication to refer only part of the crystallised dispute. Primarily, one must construe the Notice of Adjudication to determine the extent to which all or part of the crystallised dispute is being referred to adjudication.
>
> (iii) It is open to the defending party to adjudication to run any factual or legal defence to the disputed claim which is being referred (see e.g. Cantillon Ltd v Urvasco Ltd [2008] BLR 250 at Paragraph 54).
>
> (iv) However, none of the post-Notice of Adjudication documentation generated in an adjudication will alter the scope or ambit of the dispute referred, save by agreement or by operation of waiver or estoppel (see e.g. Lidl UK GmbH v RG Carter Colchester Ltd [2012] EWHC 3138 (TCC))[114]

---

[113] *Quietfield Ltd v Vascroft Construction Ltd* [2006] EWCA Civ 1737, per May LJ at [33].
[114] *Wales and West Utilities Ltd v PPS Pipeline Systems GmbH* [2014] EWHC 54 (TCC), Akenhead J at [27].

[16.125] The broad interpretation given to the word 'dispute'[115] and the court's policy of enforcing adjudicator's decisions means challenges raised on this basis are normally doomed. Nevertheless, sometimes an adjudicator will accidentally decide a matter that is not part of the dispute. He may even make a conscious decision to do this because, for example, he considers the dispute as defined by the notice of adjudication is too narrow in scope and it is thought that there is an opportunity for resolving a wider dispute. Where he does this, the decision (or at least the extraneous part of it[116]) will be a nullity.

[16.126] Equally, an adjudicator may fail to decide the whole dispute referred to him. In *RBG Ltd v SGL Fibers Ltd*,[117] the Outer House of the Court of Session refused to enforce an adjudicator's decision because the adjudicator had failed to exhaust his jurisdiction. The court found that, when assessing a contractor's claim for payment under several invoices, the adjudicator should have considered the employer's allegation that it had overpaid the contractor earlier in the project.

[16.127] However, in considering whether the scope of the adjudicator's decision is within his jurisdiction, the court will not consider whether the adjudicator expressly dealt with every single item of claim. Where there are both large and small items making up a claim, it may be sufficient for the adjudicator only to consider the large items.[118] The failure of the adjudicator to exhaust his jurisdiction is considered hand in hand with a claim that the adjudicator breached the rules of natural justice by failing to consider an issue, part or all of a submission, or evidence put before him. These issues are considered at Sections 17.5.7 and 17.5.8.

[16.128] Where the Scheme applies, the court will, in some cases, enforce a decision that reflects the full extent of the adjudicator's findings, even if that goes beyond the strict literal wording of the notice of adjudication. However, this will only be permitted where the adjudicator's findings are a necessary precursor to, or follow inevitably and logically from, the decision.[119] This aligns with paragraph 20 of the Scheme, which permits the adjudicator to 'take into account any other matters which the parties to the dispute agree should be within the scope of the adjudication or which are matters under the contract which he considers are necessarily connected with the dispute.'[120]

[16.129] There are a large number of cases where one party has sought to argue that the scope of the decision exceeds or fails to exhaust the adjudicator's jurisdiction. Broadly, most of the cases can be divided into one of the following categories:

- applications for payment, certification and final account
- delay and prolongation
- contractual interpretation.

---

[115] See Section 7.2.4.
[116] Refer to section 14.4 on the subject of severability.
[117] [2010] CSOH 77, per Menzies J at [28].
[118] *AMEC Group v Thames Water Utilities* [2010] EWHC 419 (TCC), Coulson J at [87–91].
[119] *Workspace Management Ltd v YJL London Ltd* [2009] EWHC 2017, per Coulson J at [20–27].
[120] *A&D Maintenance and Construction Ltd v Pagehurst Construction Services Ltd* [1999] 64 Con LR, per Glennie at [21–22].

[16.130] A sample of cases where one of these issues has been raised are discussed in the following sections. For the sake of brevity, and because the court's determination on this issue is particularly fact sensitive, the reminder of the cases are listed at Appendix 8. Appendix 8 also contains a separate lists for (a) cases where the issue was something other than one of the categories listed above; (b) all those the court decided that the adjudicator has exceeded his jurisdiction; (c) all those cases the court decided that the adjudicator had not exceeded his jurisdiction; and (d) cases where the adjudicator failed to exhaust his jurisdiction.

(B) Applications for payment, certification and final account

[16.131] Disputes arising out of interim applications, the existence, timing and content of the architect or project manager's certification, and competing views of the quantification of a final account constitute the most common source of all disputes on construction projects. Given the complicated nature of the documents in these disputes, it is not surprising that there are challenges based on whether all or part of the matters contained within them form part of the dispute referred. In *Brims Construction v A2M Development Limited*[121] the dispute concerned the failure by A2M to pay the amount to which Brims was entitled, as it had applied for. A2M challenged the decision on the basis that the adjudicator made a decision based in part on an alternative argument not raised by Brims in the notice of adjudication. The court held that the failure to mention this argument was not material because it was simply an alternative way of putting the case. In *J G Walker Groundworks Ltd v Priory Homes (East) Ltd*,[122] the question arose whether the adjudicator had jurisdiction to determine whether or not JGW/28 was an interim or final application, and then decide the amount owed. The court held on analysis that the adjudicator did have the necessary jurisdiction and so enforced his decision. In *Roe Brickwork Limited v Wates Construction Limited*,[123] the adjudicator the adjudicator adopted a method of calculation that was consistent with the method adopted by the claimant, save for one minor respect. The adjudicator did not share the difference with the parties and give them an opportunity to comment. The court found that although the adjudicator did deviate from the case put to him, the deviation was not material.

(C) Delay and prolongation

[16.132] The presentation of delay and prolongation claims can be complicated, such that the adjudicator unknowingly or otherwise falls into the trap of deciding the dispute on a basis not reflected in either party's case. In *Balfour Beatty Engineering v Shepherd Construction Limited*,[124] the adjudicator applied certain factors concerning an extension of time claim in part of his decision. The court found that these factors were part of Balfour

---

[121] EWHC 3262 (TCC), per Akenhead J at [29].
[122] [2013] EWHC 3723 (TCC), per Edwards-Stuart J at [20–30].
[123] [2013] EWHC 3417 (TCC), per Edwards-Stuart J at [23–37].
[124] [2009] EWHC 2218, per Akenhead J at [49–62].

Beatty's alternative case, which was either encompassed in the dispute in the first place or brought within the ambit of the dispute during the adjudication itself. In *Herbosch-Kiere Marine Contractors Limited v Dover Harbour Board*,[125] the adjudicator adopted an entirely separate method of assessing the quantum payable from an extension of time under a wreck removal contract, which did not form any part of the dispute referred. The court held the adjudicator had exceeded his jurisdiction because 'in essence, and doubtless for what he believed were good and sensible reasons, the adjudicator has gone off "on a frolic of his own" in using a method of assessment which neither party argued and which he did not put to the parties.'

[16.133] In *WSP CEL Limited v Dalkia Utilities Services plc*[126] the defendant contended that the adjudicator, by considering certain claims as compensation events, acted without jurisdiction because they were listed as items of loss and expense in the notice of adjudication and not compensation events. The court found that the referring party's declaration 'as to the amount payable to the referring party whether pursuant to the consultancy services contract, by way of damages for breach of contract, by way of quantum meruit or otherwise at law' was wide enough to enable the adjudicator to consider the claims as compensation events. The claims were incorporated on the basis that they were claims in relation to the amount payable pursuant to the consultancy services contract. The court said that the fact that some claims expressly referred to them as being claims for compensation did not preclude other claims from being pursued as compensation events, provided that the terms of the notice of adjudication were broad enough, as they were in this case.

(D) Contractual interpretation

[16.134] Where the responding party chooses to rely on a contractual argument in defence of the claim brought against it, that argument will fall within the list of arguments raised in the dispute, and the referring party is then entitled to counter the defence raised in the reply. In *Viridis UK Ltd v Mulalley & Company Ltd*,[127] Mulalley raised a question as to the validity of a termination notice in the response, which Viridis then responded to in the reply. The adjudicator addressed the issue in his decision, deciding that the notice was invalid. Mulalley contended that the issue was outside the adjudicator's jurisdiction because it was not part of the dispute as outlined in the notice of adjudication. The court disagreed, stating that it could not accept Mulalley's submission that because Viridis had not specifically contested the validity of the termination prior to the notice of adjudication the adjudicator had no jurisdiction to consider it once the defendant raised the termination as a defence. Where the parties argue that different construction contracts govern the rights and obligations between them, then provided that issue is a matter referred to the adjudicator, it is within his jurisdiction to decide.[128]

---

[125] [2012] EWHC 84 (TCC), per Akenhead J at [34].
[126] [2012] EWHC 2428, per Ramsey J at [90–93].
[127] [2014] EWHC 268 (TCC), per Davies J at [100–105].
[128] *Dalkia Energy and Technical Services Ltd v Bell Group UK Ltd* [2009] EWHC 73 (TCC), per Coulson J at [38–44].

16.7.7 Errors

(A) Principle

[16.135] The court has repeatedly held that where an adjudicator makes an error in arriving at his decision, provided that error is within the boundaries of the jurisdiction given to him, it will uphold his decision.[129] In other words, 'if he answered the right question in the wrong way, his decision will be binding. If he has answered the wrong question, his decision will be a nullity.'[130] The proper mechanism for disputing the alleged error is to commence litigation or arbitration proceedings.[131] However, where the error impinges on the adjudicator's jurisdiction or finds the adjudicator in breach of the rules of natural justice, then the decision may be held to be invalid. The invalidity stems from the fact that, as a consequence of the error, he acted outside of the jurisdiction given to him or acted in breach of natural justice, not that the error per se invalidated the decision.

[16.136] The court has offered the following guidelines:[132]

(1) The precise question giving rise to the dispute that has been referred to the adjudicator must be identified.
(2) If the adjudicator has answered that referred question, even if erroneously or in the wrong way, the resulting decision is both valid and enforceable. If, on the other hand, the adjudicator has answered the wrong question, the resulting decision is a nullity.
(3) In determining whether the error is within jurisdiction or is so great that it led to the wrong question being asked and to the decision being a nullity, the court should give a fair, natural and sensible interpretation to the decision and, where there are reasons, to the reasons in the light of the disputes that are the subject of the reference. The court should bear in mind the speedy nature of the adjudication process which means that mistakes will inevitably occur. Overall, the court should guard against characterising a mistaken answer to an issue that lies within the scope of the reference as an excess of jurisdiction.
(4) A mistake which amounts to a slip in the drafting of the reasons may be corrected by the adjudicator within a reasonable time but this is a limited power that does not extend to jurisdictional errors or errors of law.
(5) In deciding whether an error goes to jurisdiction, it is pertinent to ask whether the error was relevant to the decision and whether it caused any prejudice to either party.
(6) A wrong decision as to whether certain contract clauses applied; or whether they had been superseded by the statutory Scheme for Adjudication; or as to whether a particular sum should be evaluated as part of, or should be included in the arithmetical. Computation of, the Final Contract Sum in a dispute as to what the Final Contract Sum was do not go to jurisdiction.
(7) However, where the claim that was considered by the adjudicator was significantly different in its factual detail from the claim previously disputed and referred, the resulting decision was one made by reference to something not referred, was without jurisdiction and was unenforceable since the adjudicator had asked and answered the wrong question.

---

[129] *Macob Civil Engineering Ltd v Morrison Construction Ltd* [1999] BLR 93, per Dyson J at [19].
[130] *Bouygues UK Ltd v Dahl-Jensen UK Ltd* [2000] EWCA Civ 507, per Buxton LJ at [12–13].
[131] *Shimizu Europe Ltd v Automajor Ltd* [2002] BLR 113 per Seymour J at [23].
[132] *Joinery Plus Ltd (In Administration) v Laing Ltd* [2003] EWHC 3513 (TCC), per Thornton J at [51].

[16.137] An error may lead to a breach of natural justice because, for instance, the adjudicator may make an error that causes him not to consider a substantial part of a submission, or he may make unilateral contact with one party, or he may use his own knowledge when making his decision without giving the parties an opportunity to comment on that knowledge. Natural justice is considered further in Chapter 17.

[16.138] In the context of the adjudicator's jurisdiction, the courts have categorised errors as either of law, or of fact.

(B) Errors of law

[16.139] Errors of law will include circumstances where the adjudicator has interpreted the contract or applied the law incorrectly. In almost all of the cases in which the argument has been advanced that an adjudicator's error of law invalidated his decision, the argument has failed.

- In *GPS Marine Contractors Ltd v Ringway Infrastructure Services Ltd*,[133] the adjudicator held that a method statement was not a contract document as the parties intended, but a letter of intent. Ramsey J held that the adjudicator was entitled to hold this view and that it did not invalidate the decision.
- An error in interpreting the precise nature of the contractual payment machinery to assess what was due was, on the facts, held to be an error that the adjudicator was permitted to make.[134]
- In *C&B Scene Concept Design Ltd v Isobars Ltd*,[135] the parties had referred a dispute to adjudication. The adjudicator relied on clause 30.3 of the JCT form in arriving at his decision, which concerned the mechanics of the payment process. The court of first instance held that clause 30.3 did not apply to the agreement between the parties but that the provisions of the Scheme were implied into the contract. As a result, the adjudicator exceeded his jurisdiction and the court rendered his decision invalid. However, the Court of Appeal said that the scope of the dispute referred to the adjudicator was the employer's obligation to make payment in respect of certain applications for payment. In order to determine this dispute the adjudicator had to resolve as a matter of law whether clause 30.3 applied or not, and if it did, what was the effect of failure to serve a timeous withholding notice by the employer? Even if the adjudicator was wrong on both these points, it did not affect his jurisdiction and so the adjudicator's decision, though wrong, was upheld. In effect, this decision is authority for the argument that the construction of contractual terms, however erroneous, gives rise to a question of law within jurisdiction if that issue of construction arises as a necessary step along the route that the adjudicator must travel in order to determine the question that has been referred to adjudication.[136]

---

[133] [2010] EWHC 283 (TCC), per Ramsey J at [56–68].
[134] *Allen Wilson Shopfitters v Buckingham* [2005] EWHC 1165 (TCC), per Coulson J at [28–30].
[135] [2002] EWCA Civ 46, per Sir Stuart-Smith LJ at [21–32.]
[136] *Joinery Plus Ltd (In Administration) v Laing Ltd* [2003] EWHC 3513 (TCC), per Thornton J at [61].

- An error of law as to the finding of professional negligence was not one which invalidated the adjudicator's decision.[137]

[16.140] There are some examples where the error of law was found to be one that affected the adjudicator's jurisdiction and that error was such that it was fatal to the validity of his decision.

- An allegation that variations had been instructed by or on behalf of the respondents otherwise than in the form stipulated in the JCT conditions, and that the respondents had in bad faith prevented the issue of certificates were not errors of law which the adjudicator was permitted to make, rather they were issues which fell within the scope of the dispute that the adjudicator had to decide. In refusing to deal with those issues, he acted without jurisdiction.[138]
- Where the parties contend that different contractual conditions form the basis of the agreement between them, each set of conditions contains different adjudication rules and a different procedure for appointment, where the adjudicator is appointed through the adjudication rules under one set of conditions and it is subsequently determined that the other set of contractual conditions applies, then the adjudicator will have been wrongly appointed and his decision will be invalid.[139]

(C) Errors of fact

[16.141] As with errors of law, intra vires errors of fact will not render a decision unenforceable.

- The adjudicator may mistake the names of the parties and issue a decision against the wrong parties. Whether or not that decision will be enforced will turn on an assessment of the factual circumstances of the use of the incorrect name and whether a challenge was raised by the parties at the time, rather than on the fact that an error was made by the adjudicator.[140]
- In *Bouygues (UK) Ltd v Dahl-Jensen (UK)*,[141] the adjudicator erred because he considered the gross figures without having regard to retention. This resulted in a payment being due to Dahl-Jensen in circumstances where, had he not made the error, they would have been the paying party. Notwithstanding this fundamental calculating error, the Court of Appeal held that the adjudicator had not exceeded his jurisdiction, he had merely given a wrong answer to the question which was referred to him.
- In *Shimizu Europe Limited v Automajor Limited*,[142] the adjudicator held that a claim for a particular variation worth £161,996 was not in fact a variation at all. However, he awarded that sum to the contractor because he thought that the parties were

---
[137] *London & Amsterdam Properties Ltd v Waterman* [2003] EWHC 3059, per Wilcox J at [189–209].
[138] *Ballast plc v The Burrell Company (Construction Management) Ltd* [2001] ScotCS 159, per Lord Reed at [40–42]. See also Section 16.7.6. on scope of decision.
[139] *Pegram Shopfitters Ltd v Tally Wiejl (UK) Ltd* [2003] EWCA Civ 1750, per May LJ at [30–34] and *Ecovision Systems Ltd v Vinci Construction UK Ltd* [2015] EWHC 587 (TCC) at [82].
[140] *Thomas-Fredric's Construction Ltd v Keith Wilson* [2003] EWCA Civ 1494, per Brown LJ at [16; 26–31].
[141] [2000] EWCA Civ 507, per Buxton LJ at [14–20].
[142] [2002] BLR 113 per Seymour J at [23–25].

agreed that there could be no challenge to that head of claim. The court held that if there was a mistake, the position was no different from that in Bouygues, and the award was enforced.
- An error in calculating the full worth of a claim by failing to add some items to it was an error of calculation that would not, as a matter of principle, affect the enforceability of the decision.[143]

16.7.8 Correcting minor errors in the decision

[16.142] Adjudicators are entitled to correct minor errors in their decision within either a reasonable or fixed time after the decision, depending on the applicable adjudication rules. Where the court agrees that the nature of the correction and the time in which it was done was intra vires, the court will not interfere with that correction, even if the correction itself contains a further slip or even an error of fact or law.[144] This matter is dealt with in more detail at Section 12.5.

16.8 Checklist: Jurisdiction – the parties

> Before the adjudication is commenced, and throughout, it is necessary to consider whether or not the adjudicator has acted, or will act, in excess of his jurisdiction, or in other words outside of the boundaries within which the adjudicator is required to operate. The boundaries are determined by the Act (where the form of adjudication is statutory or ad hoc), the adjudication rules and the scope of the dispute. Consider the following:
>
> (1) Where the form of adjudication is statutory, have all the necessary preconditions for commencing an adjudication been met (Section 16.5)?
> (2) Where the form of adjudication is contractual, have all the preconditions of commencing an adjudication set out in the adjudication rules been complied with (Section 5.2)?
> (3) If so, has the adjudicator failed to follow the provisions of the Act and/or adjudication rules? If so, was that failure minor or material (for example Section 16.6.8)?
> (4) Has the adjudicator, or will the adjudicator, address a matter that is outside of the scope of the dispute he has been asked to decide (Section 16.7.6)?
> (5) Where a jurisdictional issue arises, what is the best method of addressing it (Section 16.3)?
> (6) Have you or the other party acted or failed to act in a way that will lead to the loss of the right to challenge the jurisdictional issue (Section 16.4)?

---

[143] *AMEC Group Ltd v Thames Water Utilities Ltd* [2010] EWHC 419 (TCC), per Coulson J at [87–92].
[144] *O'Donnell Developments Ltd v Build Abbey Ltd* [2009] EWHC 3388 (TCC), per Coulson J at [20–55].

16.9 Checklist: Jurisdiction – the adjudicator

Challenges to the adjudicator's jurisdiction are common. Although most challenges are baseless, it is necessary for the adjudicator to tread carefully. Consider the following steps.

(1) When a party raises a challenge to your jurisdiction, although there is no obligation for you to respond to the challenge at all, it is best practice to do so because it avoids any allegation that you have failed to conduct the adjudication properly and, during the adjudication least, concludes the issue so that the adjudication can proceed without further distraction or, if the challenge is valid, end as soon as possible. Accordingly, write to the parties advising them what you intend to do. Do not ignore it.

(2) If, having considered the challenge, it leads you to a conclusion beyond reasonable doubt that you have acted outside your jurisdiction, the appropriate course of action is to resign forthwith.

(3) However, in the vast majority of cases, it will be appropriate for you to seek submissions from either party on the jurisdictional issue, stipulating deadlines (usually of no more than a day) for when each submission should be made by. Once your have received the response submission, the challenger will invariably seek to make a further submission. Whether you allow that will depend on the circumstances, but to avoid rounds of submissions, adjudicators often stipulate that no more than one submission from each party will be considered.

(4) The submissions should be considered quickly and a view formed as to whether you continue or resign. Very often, there will not be a clear-cut answer as to whether the jurisdictional issue is valid or not. In those cases, adjudicators usually continue with the adjudication. Whatever the view, it should be communicated to the parties together with a brief explanation. The view will either bind the parties if the adjudication rules allow for it or the parties have agreed. However, the usual position is that your view will not bind the parties (Section 16.3.3).

Chapter 17
Natural justice

17.1 Overview

17.1.1 What is it?

[17.01] Natural justice is founded on two principles, which are encapsulated in the maxims: *audi alteram partem* and *nemo judex in causa sua*. Literally these mean 'hear the alternative party too' and 'no one may be a judge in their own cause'. In other words, a party has a right to a fair hearing in that it is entitled to hear the case against it and have the opportunity to respond to it, and the adjudicator must not be biased. The requirement to comply with these rules applies in adjudication and in most other forms of dispute resolution that involve an independent third party decision maker.

[17.02] The right to a fair hearing or procedural fairness, as it is sometimes known, is relevant to the way in which the adjudication is conducted. In essence, where the adjudicator does not conduct the proceedings in a way that allows both parties the opportunity to put forward their own case and respond to the other, he will be found to have breached the rules of natural justice and the decision will not be enforced. 'Fairness' is given a restrictive meaning as equiparated to what one might consider to be fair and unfair in layman's parlance. For instance, one might consider that it is unfair to allow a party to rely on an adjudicator's decision that is wrong in law or fact or that an adjudicator who does not review all the evidence submitted by one party acts unfairly. In the forum of adjudication, however, neither of these examples is likely to be classed as unfair so as to amount to a breach of natural justice.

[17.03] Bias has been described as an attitude of mind, which prevents the decision-maker from making an objective determination of the issues to be resolved. Where an adjudicator is shown to have a bias towards either party, his decision will be a nullity. In practice findings of actual bias are rare because of the difficulties in proof. What is more common are cases of apparent bias which will be found to occur where a fair-minded and informed observer, having considered the facts, concludes that there was a real possibility, or real likelihood of bias.

[17.04] It is sometimes said that the law of bias or impartiality is distinct from the law of natural justice, but the two issues are very often considered under the umbrella of natural

---

A Practical Guide to Construction Adjudication, First Edition. James Pickavance.
© 2016 James Pickavance. Published 2016 by John Wiley & Sons, Inc.

justice, both by legal professionals and by the courts, and so this chapter follows that practice.

17.1.2 Materiality

[17.05] The court has held that the principles of natural justice are not to be regarded as diluted for the purposes of the adjudication process. In an individual case, however, they must be judged in the light of such matters as timetable restraints, the provisional nature of the decision and any concessions or agreements made by the parties as to the nature of the process in a particular case.[1] In effect, this means that the goalposts of what might amount to a breach of natural justice in other circumstances are shifted in adjudication. Only in instances where it is clear that there is actual or apparent bias, or a party's right to a fair hearing has been impinged, such that it is likely to have had a significant effect on the outcome of the adjudication, will there be a breach of natural justice. As Bowsher J put it in *Discain Project Services Ltd v Opecprime Development Ltd*:[2]

> one has to recognise that the adjudicator is working under pressures of time and circumstance which make it extremely difficult to comply with the rules of natural justice in the manner of a Court or an Arbitrator. Repugnant as it may be to one's approach to judicial decision making, I think that the system created by [the Act] can only be made to work in practice if some breaches of the rules of natural justice which have no demonstrable consequence are disregarded.

[17.06] Thus, there is a materiality threshold which must be overcome before an action or inaction will be ultra vires. Perhaps the clearest guidance on what is meant by 'material' in this context has been given by Akenhead J in *Cantillon Ltd v Urvasco Ltd*.[3]

(a) It must first be established that the Adjudicator failed to apply the rules of natural justice;
(b) Any breach of the rules must be more than peripheral; they must be material breaches;
(c) Breaches of the rules will be material in cases where the adjudicator has failed to bring to the attention of the parties a point or issue which they ought to be given the opportunity to comment upon if it is one which is either decisive or of considerable potential importance to the outcome of the resolution of the dispute and is not peripheral or irrelevant.
(d) Whether the issue is decisive or of considerable potential importance or is peripheral or irrelevant obviously involves a question of degree which must be assessed by any judge in a case such as this.
(e) It is only if the adjudicator goes off on a frolic of his own, that is wishing to decide a case upon a factual or legal basis which has not been argued or put forward by either side, without giving the parties an opportunity to comment or, where relevant put in further evidence, that the type of breach of the rules of natural justice with which the case of

---

[1] *Try Construction Ltd v Eton Town House Group Ltd* [2003] EWHC 60 (TCC), per Wilcox J at [50].
[2] [2000] AdjLR 08/09, addendum to judgment, page 1, paragraph 4.
[3] [2008] EWHC 282 (TCC), per Akenhead J at [57].

Balfour Beatty Construction Company Ltd -v- The Camden Borough of Lambeth was concerned comes into play. It follows that, if either party has argued a particular point and the other party does not come back on the point, there is no breach of the rules of natural justice in relation thereto.

17.2 When to think about natural justice

[17.07] As with the adjudicator's jurisdiction, parties should be alive to possible breaches of natural justice throughout the adjudication. However, with a few limited exceptions, the majority of natural justice challenges will materialise during the adjudication or in the decision itself, and are most frequently challenged after the parties have the decision from the adjudicator. This is in contrast to jurisdictional challenges where there are a number of issues, described as threshold jurisdictional issues, which can arise before or at the outset of an adjudication.

17.3 Options when a natural justice point arises

[17.08] Where a suspected breach of natural justice does arise, a party may choose to react in one of a number of ways. It may seek a determination from the court,[4] seek a determination from another adjudicator, withdraw from the adjudication or apply for an injunction preventing the continuance of the adjudication. These options are described in detail in the context of jurisdictional challenges at Sections 16.3.2, 16.3.4, 16.3.6 and 16.3.7 respectively and the procedural guidance set out there applies equally in the context of natural justice. However, contrary to jurisdictional challenges, it is not open to a party to seek a determination from the adjudicator who is suspected of breaching natural justice, since to do so would allow the adjudicator to determine his own suspected wrong.

[17.09] Where the breach is discovered during the adjudication, by far the most common option adopted is to participate in the adjudication until its conclusion. Once the decision is given, a party may raise the challenge in enforcement proceedings. This approach is echoed in case law: whereas there are scores of cases in respect of challenges to the adjudicator's jurisdiction made before or during the adjudication, there are almost none in respect of challenges arising out of a suspected breach of natural justice.

[17.10] It is always advisable to raise a suspected breach of natural justice with the adjudicator and the other party as soon as it is discovered. Not only will the notification serve as evidence, should the issue arise in enforcement proceedings, but it also provides the adjudicator with the opportunity to consider the suspected breach and, if he agrees with it, resign. In some circumstances, failing to raise an issue that has given, or is about to give, rise to a breach of natural justice may act as a waiver to raising it later.

---

[4]*Dorchester Hotel Ltd v Vivid Interiors Ltd* [2009] EWHC 70 (TCC), per Coulson J at [18–22].

[17.11] However, the application of waiver in the context of the adjudicator's jurisdiction[5] is not one that directly transposes to natural justice. A party may only waive its right in respect of a natural justice challenge if, once it knows or is taken to know about the grounds for the challenge, it acts in a way that clearly and unequivocally demonstrates that it does not intend to rely on that natural justice challenge. The court has put it in this way:[6]

> In principle a party may waive a failure by an adjudicator to comply with the rules of natural justice, although the natural justice challenge differs in important respects for a challenge to the jurisdiction of an adjudicator. For there to be a waiver it is evident that a party must be aware of or be taken to be aware of the right of challenge to the adjudicator's decision. The second step requires a clear and unequivocal act which, with the required knowledge, amounts to waiver of the right.
> …
> In the case of a natural justice challenge the party has to know or be taken to know that the grounds for a natural justice challenge have arisen. However there has then to be some clear and unequivocal act by that party to show that it does not intend to rely on that natural justice challenge before there can be a waiver

[17.12] In *Bovis Lend Lease Ltd v The Trustees of the London Clinic*,[7] the court held that where a party complains that it has insufficient opportunity to respond to submissions or other material, it will be more difficult (though certainly not impossible) to criticise the adjudicator for not allowing more time after the event, and in *CSK Electrical Contractors Ltd v Kingwood Electrical Services Ltd*,[8] the judge found that the payment of the adjudicator's fees and the seeking of corrections to the adjudicator's decision were each sufficient to amount to unequivocal acts.

[17.13] Therefore, there is an additional hurdle of actual or imputed knowledge of the right to challenge on natural justice grounds and furthermore there must be a clear and unequivocal act that amounts to a waiver. However, the current law in adjudication does not make it at all clear where the dividing line is drawn in each of these steps. Therefore, as already stated, it is suggested that the safest course of action is to raise the challenge as soon as it materialises, and maintain that challenge in any submission to the adjudicator, just as one would maintain a jurisdictional challenge.

[17.14] In the Scottish case of *Costain Ltd v Strathclyde Builders Ltd*,[9] the adjudicator informed both parties that he intended to seek advice from a legal adviser. The parties neither asked to be told what was to be discussed nor did they seek an opportunity to comment on those discussions. In addition, no objection was taken to the procedure proposed by the adjudicator. Strathclyde said that the adjudicator had breached the rules of natural justice by failing to share the information he obtained from the legal advisers and to allow

---
[5] See Section 16.3.5
[6] *Farrelly (M & E) Building Services Ltd v Byrne Brothers (Formwork) Ltd* [2013] EWHC 1186 (TCC), per Ramsey J at [27–36].
[7] [2009] EWHC 64 (TCC), per Akenhead J at [68].
[8] [2015] EWHC 667 (TCC), per Coulson J at [20–22].
[9] [2003] ScotCS 352, per Lord Drummond Young at [30–33].

them time to comment. Costain said Strathclyde was barred from making such a claim because, by failing to raise the issue during the adjudication, it had acquiesced. The court said this:

> In some cases there might be considerable force in such an argument. If parties or their representatives lead an adjudicator to believe that the procedure that he intends to follow is fair, the appropriate conclusion may be that the procedure was indeed fair, because there was an opportunity to object to it which was not taken. Nevertheless, two further considerations are in my opinion relevant. In the first place, for reasons already discussed, I consider the role of natural justice to be of the greatest importance. Consequently I would be reluctant to derogate from the audi alteram partem rule except in a case where the procedure proposed by the adjudicator was clearly accepted as fair, whether expressly or by implication. In the second place, if too much importance is attached to a failure to object to a proposed procedure, that may place an undue burden on the parties' advisers. In particular, the significance of a proposed procedure may not be immediately apparent. Moreover, the rapid time limits that apply in an adjudication affect the parties and their advisers as well as the adjudicator, and there may not be a great deal of time to consider the full implications of the procedure that has been proposed. For these reasons I am of the opinion that it is only in a clear case that acquiescence, in the sense in which that concept is used by the pursuer, should be relevant to the issue of whether there has been a breach of the principles of natural justice.

17.4 Bias and apparent bias

17.4.1 In a nutshell

[17.15] The following sections further outline what is meant by the terms 'bias' and 'apparent bias' before outlining the position in law on some of the putative issues encountered in the context of a challenge to the enforceability of an adjudicator's decision on grounds of apparent bias. A list of those issues is as follows.

  (1) adjudicator's prior involvement in the project or dispute
  (2) appointment of the same adjudicator
  (3) communication between the adjudicator and one party: pre-appointment
  (4) communication between the adjudicator and one party: post-appointment
  (5) adjudicator's treatment of evidence
  (6) failure to make information available to the parties
  (7) failure to carry out a site inspection
  (8) organisation of meetings as hearing
  (9) adjudicator acting as a quasi-mediator
  (10) disclosure of without prejudice communications to the adjudicator
  (11) adjudicator reaching a preliminary view.

[17.16] For each issue, the principles that give rise to the challenge are set out together with a summary of some cases that exemplify the application of those principles in a given factual scenario. A list of all the cases (or at least all that could be found) on each issue is contained at Appendix 8.

17.4.2 Actual bias

[17.17] Actual bias means a direct or pecuniary material interest in the outcome of the adjudication. This may include where an adjudicator has a direct or indirect financial stake in either the parties or their representatives, or a personal friendship between the adjudicator and one of the parties. The Court of Appeal in *Re Medicaments*[10] said that actual bias applied:

> where a judge had been influenced by partiality or prejudice in reading his decision, and where it had been demonstrated that a judge is actually prejudiced in favour of or against a party...

[17.18] Where it applies, paragraph 4 of the Scheme requires that:

> A person requested or selected to act as an adjudicator shall not be an employee of any of the parties to the dispute and shall declare any interest, financial or otherwise, in any matter relating to the dispute.

[17.19] Where the adjudicator is found to be biased, the court will hold that any decision he produces is a nullity. Therefore, if the adjudicator considers that he has any interest which might arguably create more than a fanciful prospect of an allegation of bias being successful, that interest should be drawn to the attention of both parties at the earliest opportunity. The adjudicator should make clear that if either party objects as a result, he will resign. If this is not done and the connection emerges during or after the adjudication, this is far more likely to lead one or both parties to suspect that the adjudicator is biased and not only may the losing party use this as a basis for challenging the validity of the decision, but both parties can avoid paying the adjudicator's fees, and there is a strong argument that the adjudicator is held liable to pay the parties' costs on grounds that the adjudicator acted in bad faith by accepting the appointment and failing to disclose the conflict.[11]

[17.20] Although the circumstances giving rise to bias may be clear, proving that an adjudicator is actually biased may be difficult.[12] The party who asserts this needs to demonstrate, as a matter of fact, that the adjudicator is actually prejudiced in favour of or against a party. It is for this reason that a challenge that the adjudicator is biased is very rarely deployed; rather the challenge is made on the basis that there is a real possibility or appearance of bias. Commonly termed 'apparent bias', this is sufficient for an adjudicator's decision to be nullified.

---

[10] [2001] 1 WLR 700, per Phillips L at [37–38].
[11] Subsection 108(4) of the Act.
[12] *Lanes Group plc v Galliford Try Infrastructure Ltd* [2011] EWCA Civ 1617, per Jackson LJ at [46].

17.4.3 Apparent bias

[17.21] The test for apparent bias was set out by Lord Phillips in *Re Medicaments*[13] and affirmed by Lord Hope in the House of Lords case of *Magill v Porter*.[14] It is known as the fair-minded and informed observer test.

> The court must first ascertain all the circumstances which have a bearing on the suggestion that the judge was biased. It must then ask whether those circumstances would lead a fair-minded and informed observer to conclude that there was a real possibility, or a real danger, the two being the same, that the tribunal was biased.

[17.22] What is meant by 'fair-minded and informed observer' was explained in the case of *Gillies v Secretary of State for Work and Pensions*.[15]

> The fair-minded and informed observer can be assumed to have access to all the facts that are capable of being known by members of the public generally, bearing in mind that it is the appearance that these facts give rise to that matters, not what is in the mind of the particular judge or tribunal member who is under scrutiny. It is to be assumed ... that the observer is neither complacent nor unduly sensitive or suspicious when he examines the facts that he can look at. It is to be assumed too that he is able to distinguish between what is relevant and what is irrelevant, and that he is able when exercising his judgment to decide what weight should be given to the facts that are relevant.

[17.23] The meaning of fair-minded observer was more recently considered in *Lanes Group plc v Galliford Try Infrastructure Ltd*:[16]

> The fair minded observer must be assumed to know all relevant publicly available facts. He or she must be assumed to be neither complacent nor unduly sensitive or suspicious. He or she must be assumed to be fairly, because he or she is able 'to distinguish between what is relevant and what is irrelevant, and when exercising his judgment to decide what weight should be given to the facts that are relevant'.

[17.24] In what situations might a fair-minded observer conclude that there is a 'real possibility' or 'real danger' of bias? In the context of adjudication, there are a number of putative instances that the courts have addressed this. However, detailed guidance given outside the context of adjudication by the Court of Appeal in *Locabail (UK) Ltd v Bayfield Properties Ltd*[17] is perhaps a useful starting point (if a little long-winded) when considering whether a circumstance, action or inaction would lead a fair-minded observer to consider that an adjudicator was biased.

---

[13] [2001] 1 WLR 700, per Phillips L at [85].
[14] [2001] UKHL 67, per Hope L at [95–105].
[15] [2006] 1 UKHL 2, per Hope L at [17].
[16] [2011] EWCA Civ 1617, per Jackson LJ at [44–52].
[17] [2000] QB, 451 at [25].

It would be dangerous and futile to attempt to define or list the factors which may or may not give rise to a real danger of bias. Everything will depend on the facts, which may include the nature of the issue to be decided. We cannot, however, conceive of circumstances in which an objection could be soundly based on the religion, ethnic or national origin, gender, age, class, means or sexual orientation of the judge. Nor, at any rate ordinarily, could an objection be soundly based on the judge's social or educational or service or employment background or history, nor that of any member of the judge's family; or previous political associations; or membership of social or sporting or charitable bodies; or Masonic associations; or previous judicial decisions; or extra-curricular utterances (whether in text books, lectures, speeches, articles, interviews, reports or responses to consultation papers); or previous receipt of instructions to act for or against any party, solicitor or advocate engaged in a case before him; or membership of the same Inn, circuit, local Law Society or chambers (KFTCIC v. Icori Estero SpA (Court of Appeal of Paris, 28 June 1991, International Arbitration Report. Vol. 6 #8 8/91)). By contrast, a real danger of bias might well be thought to arise if there were personal friendship or animosity between the judge and any member of the public involved in the case; or if the judge were closely acquainted with any member of the public involved in the case, particularly if the credibility of that individual could be significant in the decision of the case; or if, in a case where the credibility of any individual were an issue to be decided by the judge, he had in a previous case rejected the evidence of that person in such outspoken terms as to throw doubt on his ability to approach such person's evidence with an open mind on any later occasion; or if on any question at issue in the proceedings before him the judge had expressed views, particularly in the course of the hearing, in such extreme and unbalanced terms as to throw doubt on his ability to try the issue with an objective judicial mind (see Vakauta v. Kelly (1989) 167 CLR 568); or if, for any other reason, there were real ground for doubting the ability of the judge to ignore extraneous considerations, prejudices and predilections and bring an objective judgment to bear on the issues before him. The mere fact that a judge, earlier in the same case or in a previous case, had commented adversely on a party or witness, or found the evidence of a party or witness to be unreliable, would not without more found a sustainable objection. In most cases, we think, the answer, one way or the other, will be obvious. But if in any case there is real ground for doubt, that doubt should be resolved in favour of recusal. We repeat: every application must be decided on the facts and circumstances of the individual case. The greater the passage of time between the event relied on as showing a danger of bias and the case in which the objection is raised, the weaker (other things being equal) the objection will be.

17.4.4 Prior involvement in the project or in a separate dispute

[17.25] One way in which it might be said that the adjudicator exhibits apparent bias is through a prior knowledge of the project or a connection with either party in a previous dispute. The test will be whether such prior knowledge leads a fair-minded observer to conclude that there was a real danger of bias. Whether or not the answer is in the affirmative will always depend on the facts.

[17.26] In *Andrew Wallace Ltd v Jeff Noon*,[18] the adjudicator had acted as mediator in an entirely separate dispute involving one of the parties to this adjudication, but otherwise

---

[18] [2009] BLR 158, per Grant J at [24–28].

was entirely unconnected with the subject matter of this adjudication, which was concluded only two days before he was appointed adjudicator in this adjudication. The Royal Institute of British Architects appointed the adjudicator, and the form of enquiry he was required to fill in asked the potential adjudicator to disclose whether he had any current relationship with either party, or connection with the subject matter of the proceedings. The court held that the adjudicator had no current relationship towards either of the parties to this adjudication, nor did he have any connection with the subject matter of the dispute.

[17.27] In *London & Amsterdam Properties Ltd v Waterman Partnership Ltd*,[19] the adjudicator was found to have prior involvement with the project on which there was now a dispute and on which he had been appointed adjudicator because he had previously been appointed adjudicator on an earlier dispute on a separate issue. The waters were slightly muddied by the fact that the adjudicator said he did not recall any knowledge that may be relevant to the particular issues to the current dispute. The court held that the prior knowledge in this case did not lead to apparent bias. The knowledge or information that the adjudicator had was not central to the decision he made in the current dispute and therefore there was not a real risk of bias.

[17.28] In *Fileturn Ltd v Royal Garden Hotel Ltd*,[20] Royal Garden resisted enforcement of the adjudicator's decision on the basis of the adjudicator's apparent bias. It argued that there was a pre-existing relationship between Mr Sliwinski, the adjudicator, and Fileturn's representative in the adjudication, Mr Silver of Always Associates. In that case, Mr Silver had requested the appointment of Mr Sliwinski on about 12 occasions, although there was no evidence that this was known to Mr Sliwinski. Always Associates had acted for one of the parties in 5–10% of the adjudications conducted by Mr Sliwinski. Also, Mr Sliwinski was formerly a co-director of Always Associates, although he had left six years before the adjudication. Based on these facts, Edwards-Stuart J held that it was 'inherently unlikely' that a fair-minded and informed observer would conclude that Mr Sliwinski was biased.

[17.29] The takeaway point for adjudicators is that they must always disclose at an early stage any information that they consider may affect their impartiality.

17.4.5 Appointment of the same adjudicator

[17.30] Instances where the appointment of the same adjudicator in a subsequent adjudication may lead to a breach of the rules of natural justice may arise in three ways: the appointment of the same adjudicator on the same dispute, the appointment of the same adjudicator on a different dispute on the same project and the appointment of the same adjudicator in two adjudications commenced simultaneously.

[17.31] The first scenario may arise because the adjudication was abandoned halfway through or the adjudicator's decision was found to be a nullity by the court, or (exceptionally)

---

[19] [2003] EWHC 3059 (TCC) per Wilcox J at [85–95].
[20] [2010] EWHC 1736 (TCC), per Edwards-Stuart J at [20–33].

the court decided that the dispute needed to be reheard. In any circumstance, the mere fact that an adjudicator has previously considered the dispute is not of itself sufficient to justify a conclusion of apparent bias. Nor is it sufficient if, in the first adjudication, the adjudicator had made adverse comment against one party's case, although if the adjudicator made an extremely hostile remark about a party, the position might well be different because it would arguably demonstrate a bias against the party. It is also unlikely to be sufficient where the adjudicator lacked jurisdiction or breached the rules of natural justice in the first adjudication, or that legal advice obtained in the first adjudication was deployed in the second adjudication.[21]

[17.32] Often, adjudicators are appointed in a number of different disputes between the same parties arising from the same contract. A challenge in this situation has been that an adjudicator's decision should not be enforced on the basis that, as a result of his prior involvement, he must be biased. However, the mere fact that an adjudicator had already decided earlier issues under a contract is not enough to justify a conclusion of apparent bias in a subsequent adjudication.[22] In *RG Carter Ltd v Edmund Nuttall Ltd (No. 2)*,[23] the same adjudicator was appointed for a fifth time, against the request of the referring party, to decide the dispute. Carter made an application to set aside the appointment on the grounds of bias, because he had decided the previous disputes, and in particular, one of these decisions had not been enforced because the adjudicator lacked jurisdiction. The court held that the adjudicator could not be considered biased merely because he had decided previous disputes under the same contract and had been acting in excess of the boundaries of jurisdiction on one of them.

[17.33] In *Willmott Dixon Housing Limited (formerly Inspace Partnerships Limited) v Newlon Housing Trust*,[24] it was suggested that appointing the same adjudicator to preside over two adjudications proceeding at the same time meant that the adjudicator was incapable of dealing with each dispute in an unbiased manner. The court found 'there is nothing in the [adjudication rules] or otherwise to prevent a party from giving two notices of adjudication, each relating only to one dispute and for each of those adjudications then to be referred to the same adjudicator.'

17.4.6 Communication between the adjudicator and one party: pre-appointment

[17.34] The referring party may strive to obtain the appointment of a particular individual as adjudicator because it perceives that individual to be more sympathetic to the merits of its case. In certain circumstances, it may be tempting to engage with the adjudicator or ANB without involving the other party to the dispute. This will normally lead to allegations of bias from the other party. The simplest way to avoid the possibility of an

---

[21] *AMEC Capital Projects Ltd v Whitefriars City Estates Ltd (No. 3)* [2004] EWCA Civ 1418, per Dyson J at [19–33].
[22] *Michael John Construction Ltd v Richard Hentry Golledge and others* [2006] EWHC 71 (TCC), per Coulson at [65–70].
[23] [2002] EWHC 400 (TCC), per Seymour J at [29].
[24] [2013] EWHC 798 (TCC), per Ramsey J at [68–76].

adjudicator's decision being overturned is for all communication to or from the adjudicator to be in the presence of, or copied to, all parties in the adjudication at the time of the communication. If in exceptional circumstances that is not possible, a detailed record of the communication should be circulated to all parties soon after it takes place.

[17.35] In *Amec Capital Projects Ltd v Whitefriars City Estates Ltd*,[25] the referring party's solicitor called the adjudicator, who had presided over a previous adjudication between the parties, in which it was determined that the adjudicator did not have jurisdiction. The solicitor wished to appoint the same adjudicator again. The solicitor explained that he did this to save time and costs because the adjudicator would be familiar with the case. The Court of Appeal, in overturning the court of first instance, held that the adjudicator would have likely drawn the conclusion that the matter was being referred back to him to save time and costs and that the prefatorial contact could not be construed as an attempt to persuade the adjudicator to reach the same decision as on the previous occasion.

[17.36] In *Makers UK Limited v London Borough of Camden*,[26] the referring party's solicitor undertook a search of RIBA panel members to identify which one he thought was best suited to the dispute. Before RIBA was contacted regarding the appointment of an adjudicator, Mr Harris was called by the referring party's solicitor to confirm his availability. When the RIBA was later contacted and the referring party requested that Mr Harris act, no mention was made of this telephone call. The responding party lost the adjudication and challenged enforcement on the grounds of bias. Akenhead J held that the solicitor's contact with Mr Harris and the failure of the referring party and Mr Harris to mention this before Mr Harris's appointment did not amount to bias. Nevertheless, Akenhead J said that it was better for all concerned if parties limit their unilateral contacts before, during and after adjudication, and that the same was true for an adjudicator having unilateral contact with the individual parties. He correctly observed that such contact 'can be misconstrued by the losing party, even if entirely innocent'.

[17.37] An example of where pre-adjudication contact led to a finding of apparent bias is *Paice and Springall v Matthew Harding (t/a M J Harding Contractors)*.[27] There, the contractor held an hour-long telephone conversation with the adjudicator's practice manager, wherein they discussed substantive matters that related to the forthcoming adjudication. The practice manager outlined the content of that conversation to the adjudicator soon afterwards. The adjudicator decided not to communicate the details of that conversation to the claimants, neither when he was told about it, nor when he was specifically asked about it in an email during the adjudication, some three months later. The court found that the adjudicator's deliberate decision not to disclose the content of the conversation was sufficient to amount to an act of apparent bias. It was no defence to argue that the conversation took place two months before the commencement of the adjudication, nor was it a defence to argue that the conversation took place between the contractor

---

[25] [2004] EWCA Civ 1418, per Dyson LJ at [33–35].
[26] [2008] EWHC 1836, per Akenhead J at [33–36].
[27] [2015] EWHC 661 (TCC), per Coulson J at [32–45].

and the adjudicator's practice manager and not the adjudicator himself. However, the court also held that had the adjudicator disclosed the content of conversations during the adjudication when he was asked, even though three months had elapsed, he would have exonerated himself at that point.

17.4.7 Communication between the adjudicator and one party: post-appointment

[17.38] The message with regard to contact between one party and the adjudicator post-appointment is the same as it is pre-appointment: it should be avoided. The leading case is *Discain Project Services Ltd v Opecprime Development Ltd*.[28] The adjudicator's decision was challenged on the basis that a central issue in the case had been discussed only with one party's representative on the telephone, although the content of those conversations was subsequently communicated to the other party. Bowsher J refused to enforce the adjudicator's decision holding that there was a very serious risk of bias.

[17.39] Conversely in *Dean & Dyball Construction Ltd v Kenneth Grubb Associates Ltd*,[29] notwithstanding the fact that the adjudicator conducted separate interviews with the parties and their respective experts, the court still enforced the adjudicator's decision. The judge said natural justice does not necessarily require that evidence from witnesses for one party be taken in the presence of the opposite party or its representatives. It may be sufficient for a tribunal taking evidence from the witnesses for one party simply to communicate the event to the other party and give it an opportunity to deal with it. In doing so, it is not necessary to communicate verbatim what went on, merely the substance of what the witnesses have said to which the tribunal is minded to attribute importance. Further, in relation to the detail of which it was unaware, there was no suggestion that the adjudicator actually took that into account in his decision.

[17.40] Adjudicators can avoid falling into the trap of unilateral communications by refusing to engage in them. If a party calls the adjudicator he should interrupt the caller at the outset to insist that he calls back in conference with the other party. If a party writes to the adjudicator without copying the other party, the adjudicator should forward the communication to the other party before responding. However, if for some reason there is contact between the adjudicator and only one party, then the adjudicator and the party should record what was said and send the record to the other party as soon as possible.

17.4.8 Evidence

[17.41] Where it is evident that the adjudicator has placed significant weight on a particular aspect of the evidence but has not made it clear that he would do so and did not seek representations from the parties, he may be found to be biased. In *A&S Enterprises Ltd v Kema Holdings Ltd*,[30] a witness had declined to make himself available for interview.

---

[28] [2001] EWHC 435 (TCC), per Bowsher J [20–23 and 69].
[29] [2003] EWHC 2465 (TCC), per Seymour J at [48–54].
[30] [2004] EWHC 3365 (QB), per Seymour J at [36–41].

In his decision, the adjudicator described that witness as playing 'a crucial role in the events leading to the dispute'. The court found that, given the importance the adjudicator placed on the witness, he ought to have given the defendant an opportunity to make the witnesses available for questioning. Without making clear that he would be influenced to a significant degree by whether he had or had not heard from the witness in circumstances where there was no suggestion that it was an important matter, the adjudicator failed to comply with the requirements of natural justice.

[17.42] Adjudicators are permitted to draw adverse inference against a party as a result of the non-production of documents or the failure of a witness to appear without necessarily being subject to criticism for doing so.[31] However, depending on the significance of the inference, it may be appropriate for an adjudicator to give advance notice of at least the possibility of drawing such an adverse inference. Where he does this, he cannot be subject to criticism if he then draws an inference.[32]

[17.43] It may be that, unbeknown to the adjudicator, a party provides documents to the adjudicator and not to the other party. The position here seems to be that where the adjudicator has no reason to believe that the documents have not been provided to the other side, this will not amount to a breach of natural justice. So, where one party provided a witness statement to the adjudicator as part of its submissions, but failed to provide it to the other party, that did not amount to a breach of natural justice.[33] However, in that case, the adjudicator did not rely on the witness statement in his decision, nor did it form part of the adjudicator's decision. It seems more likely that a court would find that the rules of natural justice had been breached where the adjudicator had relied on the document when making his decision, because the affected party will not have had an opportunity to make representations in relation to the unseen material.

[17.44] It may not be a breach of natural justice where the adjudicator takes a party's evidence on face value without seeking substantiation to verify whether the evidence is correct. In *Aveat Heating Ltd v Jerram Falkus Construction Ltd*,[34] it was submitted that the adjudicator in asking the claimant for a schedule of its costs and expenses and in awarding £12,044.25 by way of costs and expenses without having received any substantiation showed a real danger that he was biased and did not comply with the principles of natural justice. The court was not satisfied that this amounted to a breach of natural justice.

[17.45] Nevertheless, the way information or evidence is dealt with by the adjudicator to support his decision can give rise to a complaint of bias. In *Barr Ltd v Klin Investment Ltd*,[35] it was submitted that the adjudicator had construed the withholding notice by reference to the employer's knowledge at the time of the notice, which did not form part

---

[31] See Section 6.11.5.
[32] *Balfour Beatty Engineering Services (HY) Ltd v Shepherd Construction Ltd* [2009] EWHC 2218 (TCC), per Akenhead J at [72].
[33] *CRJ Services Ltd v Lanstar Ltd (trading as CSG Lanstar)* [2011] EWHC 972 (TCC), per Akenhead J at [31–32].
[34] [2007] EWHC 131 (TCC), per Havery J at [25].
[35] [2009] ScotCS CSOH 104, per Lord Glennie at [43–48].

of the employer's arguments and was not put to the contractor to enable him to comment. This amounted to an act of apparent bias by making a decision which was prejudicial against the contractor without allowing the contractor to comment. Lord Glennie rejected both contentions. As to the contention in relation to apparent bias, whether one took the employer's complaints singly or together, there was nothing in them that would lead any fair-minded and informed observer to conclude that there was a real possibility that the adjudicator was biased. The adjudicator attempted to construe the further withholding notice according to its terms and against the background of the knowledge that the contractor had. Even if those reasons were wrong it was not incumbent upon an adjudicator to put his proposed findings of fact to the parties to give them an opportunity of commenting on them. While if the adjudicator took account of something within his own knowledge without the parties having been made aware of that, he should give them an opportunity of commenting, that was not so in the instant case. The adjudicator heard the parties, read their submissions and was fully entitled to proceed to a decision without giving a further opportunity for the parties to comment on his findings.

17.4.9 Failure to make information available to the parties

[17.46]   Where the adjudicator fails to make information he has obtained from one party or by himself available to the other party to comment and make submissions on, the decision may not be enforced on grounds of apparent bias. In *Woods Hardwick Ltd v Chiltern Air-Conditioning Ltd*,[36] the adjudicator obtained information from Woods Hardwick and Chiltern's subcontractors without telling Chiltern or telling it what information he had been given. The court held that the failure to make the information obtained available to Chiltern meant that he was not acting impartially and therefore the decision was not upheld. This complaint is invariably coupled with the complaint that a party or parties have been the subject of procedural unfairness because the adjudicator obtained information from a third party and then failed to allow the parties the opportunity to comment on it. See Section 17.5.13.

17.4.10 Failure to carry out a site visit

[17.47]   At least one attempt has been made to nullify an adjudicator's decision on the basis that his failure to carry out a site inspection meant that he had breached the rules of natural justice. In *Gipping Construction Ltd v Eaves Ltd*,[37] the court found that the adjudicator's failure to carry out a site inspection did not amount to a breach of natural justice on the basis that (a) there was no obligation to carry out such inspection because a site visit is a matter of discretion in the circumstances; and (b) the adjudicator believed in good faith that he had sufficient information for him to reach his decision.

---

[36] [2001] BLR 23, per Thornton J at [37–39].
[37] [2008] EWHC 3134 (TCC), per Akenhead J at [7–9].

17.4.11 Organisation of meetings and hearings

[17.48] A challenge to the adjudicator's impartiality on grounds that he requested a meeting or hearing be held at one of the parties' offices and that he refused to move the date because one of the parties' representatives was on holiday does not amount to apparent bias on the part of the adjudicator.[38]

[17.49] In *Vaultrise Ltd v Paul Cook*,[39] the defendant to enforcement proceedings argued that he was under severe disadvantage by not having legal representation at a hearing between the parties. The hearing date had been set when the defendant and his legal adviser were unavailable. However, there had been no objections during the hearing, the matter only being raised after the hearing. While paragraph 16 of the Scheme entitles a party to legal representation at hearings, in this case the defendant took over two weeks to object to the hearing date. The court took the view that during this time he could have instructed other legal representation. The court enforced the adjudicator's decision.

17.4.12 Quasi-mediator

[17.50] While an adjudicator's role may be described as inquisitional, actively engaging the parties, he must always remain impartial. In *Glencot Development & Design Co Ltd v Ben Barrett & Son (Contractors) Ltd*,[40] midway through the adjudication, the adjudicator went to and fro between each party in private sessions, as if acting as a mediator. It was not made clear to the other party what he heard or learned in these sessions. Glencot argued he was under no obligation to report it and furthermore the content was 'without prejudice' and confidential. The court found that those private discussions could have conveyed material or impressions that subsequently influenced his decision. Although the adjudicator sought consent from both parties before acting in this way, the court said that a fair-minded observer would still conclude there was a danger of bias.

[17.51] Provided that the adjudicator acts in a way that does not mean he falls foul of the rules of natural justice (or indeed place him outside the limits of his jurisdiction), then he can conduct a facilitative or mediation style process. The CEDR adjudication rules give the adjudicator the power to mediate the dispute,[41] but only after he has reached his decision in the adjudication. The decision is then put 'on ice' and the adjudicator turns into a mediator. If the mediation does not resolve the dispute, or on the request of one of the parties, the decision is released. The TeCSA adjudication rules also provide that the adjudicator may facilitate an agreement during the adjudication at a certain time.[42]

---

[38] *Barrie Green v GW Integrated Building Services Ltd & Anor* [2001] AdjLR 07/18, per Grannum J at [30–38].
[39] [2004] Adj.C.S. 04/06 at [4–6].
[40] HT00/401 13 Feb 2001, per Lloyd J at [23–25].
[41] Rule 28.
[42] Rule 19 (xiii).

17.4.13 Without prejudice communications

[17.52] Parties will frequently engage in without prejudice settlement communications before or during the adjudication. Mere knowledge by the adjudicator that these communications are happening is unlikely to have any effect on the viability of his decision. Adjudicators are generally commercially aware, and will know that offers may be made for sound commercial reasons which are not necessarily reflective of the true position on liability. For instance, the court noted in *Specialist Ceiling Services Northern Ltd v ZVI Construction (UK) Ltd*[43] that the adjudicator was 'unfazed by the knowledge that there had been without prejudice negotiations', and that he approached the adjudication 'in an even handed manner'. It concluded that the adjudicator's decision could stand. Similarly in *Volker Stevin Ltd v Holystone Contracts Ltd*,[44] the court concluded that, on the facts, the adjudicator's knowledge of without prejudice material did not nullify the decision.

[17.53] However, where the details of without prejudice communications are deliberately or inadvertently disclosed by one party to the adjudicator, there is a greater risk that any decision from the adjudicator will be nullified by the court, although the test is, as always, whether a reasonable and fair-minded observer would conclude that there was a real possibility of bias. The court has offered the following guidance.[45]

(a) Obviously, such material should not be put before an adjudicator. Lawyers who do so may face professional disciplinary action.
(b) Where an adjudicator decides a case primarily upon the basis of wrongly received "without prejudice" material, his or her decision may well not be enforced.
(c) The test as to whether there is apparent bias present is whether, on an objective appraisal, the material facts give rise to a legitimate fear that the adjudicator might not have been impartial. The Court on any enforcement proceedings should look at all the facts which may support or undermine a charge of bias, whether such facts were known to the adjudicator or not.

[17.54] Provided the adjudicator can put the without prejudice material out of mind, then it is appropriate to proceed with the adjudication. If otherwise, he should resign.

[17.55] Where there is a deliberate attempt to sabotage the adjudication by placing prejudice material in front of the adjudicator, the court is likely to lean in favour of enforcing the decision where it can.

17.4.14 Preliminary view

[17.56] It will often be the case that the adjudicator forms a preliminary view on some or all of the evidence presented to him. This can in some cases lead to a court declining to enforce the

---
[43] [2004] BLR 403, per Grenfall J at [8–26].
[44] [2010] EWHC 2344, per Coulson J at [20–25].
[45] *Ellis Building Contractors Ltd v Goldstein* [2011] EWHC 269, per Akenhead J at [29].

adjudicator's decision. In *Lanes Group plc v Galliford Try Infrastructure Ltd*,[46] Waksman J declined to enforce the adjudicator's decision, holding that there was apparent bias by the adjudicator because he served a preliminary views document that was very similar to the final decision before the responding party had served the response. It therefore appeared to the judge that the adjudicator had formed a view without taking cognisance of the responding party's arguments. On appeal, Jackson LJ reversed Waksman J's judgment on the basis that there was no real danger of bias, saying that a fair-minded observer:

> would characterise the Preliminary View as a provisional view, disclosed for the assistance of the parties, not as a final determination reached before Mr Atkinson had considered Lanes' submissions and evidence.[47]

[17.57] He said that Mr Atkinson's decision was not tainted by 'apparent bias or apparent predetermination'. This view was reinforced by the rough and ready nature of adjudication and the fact that an adjudicator's decision is not final and binding on the parties. He also drew an analogy with judges, who set out their provisional view at an early stage, giving the parties an opportunity to comment on it and correct errors in the judge's thinking or to concentrate on matters that may be influencing the judge.

[17.58] The nature of this challenge is also often put on the basis of procedural unfairness[48] and is sometimes connected with the issue of the adjudicator deploying is own (a) methodology or approach;[49] or (b) knowledge and expertise[50] and in either case failing to allow the parties to consider and make submissions.

17.5 Procedural fairness

17.5.1 In a nutshell

[17.59] Broadly, procedural fairness requires that both parties must be given some opportunity to put forward submissions and respond to the other and the adjudicator is required to consider those submissions. Where procedural fairness is not observed, the adjudicator will be found to have breached natural justice and his decision will be invalid. 'Fairness' is given a restrictive meaning as equiparated to what one might consider fair and unfair in layman's parlance. For instance, while the timescales inherent in the adjudication process may seem unfair, they are not in breach of the rules of natural justice. In all cases, the assessment of whether the adjudicator has acted or not acted in a procedurally fair way will be determined by reference to the material effect of the action or inaction. In other words, is the conduct in question serious enough to merit invalidating the

---

[46] [2011] EWHC 1679 (TCC), per Waksman J at [34–79].
[47] [2011] EWCA Civ 1617, per Jackson LJ at [57].
[48] See Section 17.5.15.
[49] See Section 17.5.12.
[50] See Section 17.5.14.

adjudicator's decision? The following sections outline some of the issues that are most commonly encountered in the context of a challenge to the enforceability of an adjudicator's decision on grounds of procedural unfairness. Those issues are as follows:

(1) the referring party's conduct pre-adjudication
(2) abuse of process
(3) ambush/no opportunity or insufficient opportunity to respond
(4) Christmas claims
(5) dispute is too large or complex
(6) failing to address an issue, part of a submission or supporting evidence
(7) failure to permit a further submission or information
(8) failure to follow the agreed procedure
(9) adjudicator's timetable unfair
(10) failure to allow a site visit or meeting
(11) documents received late or not at all
(12) failure to inform the parties about an approach taken or methodology used
(13) failure to inform the parties about advice from a third party
(14) failure to inform the parties about the use of own knowledge and experience
(15) indication of preliminary view
(16) sufficiency of written reasons.

[17.60] For each issue, the principles that give rise to the challenges are set out, together with a select number of cases. A list of all cases (or at least all that could be found) on each issue is contained at Appendix 8.

17.5.2 Referring party's conduct pre-adjudication

[17.61] The question has arisen as to whether the conduct of the referring party prior to the service of the notice of adjudication renders the whole process unfair and puts the responding party at an unacceptable disadvantage. This claim was put on behalf of Birse in the case *CIB Properties Ltd v Birse Construction Ltd*.[51] Birse alleged that CIB, who had instructed Shadbolt & Co as its solicitors, had among other things (a) prepared for the adjudication in secret; (b) failed to refer to the possibility of an adjudication in correspondence with Birse; (c) given a false impression that it was prepared to enter into meaningful discussion after the commencement of the adjudication; (d) refused or had been dilatory in answering Birse's questions; and (e) had delayed in providing key information. In such circumstances, Birse argued that the adjudicator was required to extend the timetable for the adjudication to at least 100 days, and the fact that he did not do so rendered his decision unfair.

[17.62] The court held that CIB's conduct before the notice of adjudication did not render the whole process unfair. In the circumstances, Birse had 15 weeks in total to respond

---

[51] [2004] EWHC 2365 (TCC), per Toulmin J at [176–179; 190–193].

to the claim. Furthermore, prior to the service of the notice of adjudication, Birse was aware that there was a possibility of a referral to adjudication of part or all the claim.

[17.63] Provided that the referring party's conduct is lawful and the issue referred to adjudication meets the preconditions required by the Act and/or adjudication rules (as appropriate), it seems unlikely that 'sharp tactics' will ever, in themselves, lead to a successful claim that the adjudicator breached the rules of natural justice.

17.5.3 Abuse of process

[17.64] Abuse of process has been explained as 'using [a] process for a purpose or in a way significantly different from its ordinary and proper use'.[52] Abuse of process is a concept that is well understood in the context of litigation. It applies in various contexts, such as the commencement of vexatious proceedings, attempts to re-litigate decided issues (*res judicata*) and pursuing a claim for an improper purpose. In circumstances where it can be shown that there is abuse of process, the court has power to strike out the claim.[53]

[17.65] While numerous attempts have been made to apply abuse of process to adjudication, none have been successful. Neither the Act nor the Scheme gives the adjudicator power to strike out a claim for abuse of process, although it has been suggested that such power could be bestowed on an adjudicator if the adjudication rules so dictated.[54] In *Connex South Eastern Ltd v M.J. Building Services Group plc*,[55] the Court of Appeal held that the referring party's delay in referring a dispute to adjudication 15 months after a cause of action arose did not amount to an abuse of process because no such concept existed in adjudication. Nor was it an abuse of process to have adjudication and litigation proceedings in relation to the same claim run concurrently. In *Dalkia Energy and Technical Services v Bell Group UK Ltd*,[56] the court found that the taking of points before the adjudicator which were palpably wrong, if not misleading, and the delays concerning the commencement of Part 8 proceedings while an adjudication was ongoing, did not amount to an abuse of process.

17.5.4 Ambush/no opportunity or insufficient opportunity to respond

[17.66] As unfair as it may seem, time, or rather lack of it, is not something that will normally lead to a successful challenge on grounds that the adjudicator has acted in a procedurally unfair way. The adjudication timetable is restrictive, and a party, most often the responding party, may consider that it does not have time to properly deal with the information

---

[52] *Attorney General v Barker* [2000] 1 F.L.R. 759.
[53] CPR 3.4.
[54] *Benfield Construction Ltd v Trudson (Hatton) Ltd* [2008] EWHC 2333 (TCC), per Coulson J at [56].
[55] [2005] EWCA Civ 193, per Dyson LJ at [38–45].
[56] [2009] EWHC 73, per Coulson J at [13–31].

placed before it. This may arise because it is thought that the claim or defence is too big, too complex, or the supporting documents too voluminous to deal with in the time available. In those cases, the affected party will complain that it has been ambushed or that it has insufficient time to respond, and that the adjudicator, by failing to extend the timetable to allow sufficient time to consider the material, breached the rules of natural justice.

[17.67] But for all the problems and frustrations that lack of time might cause, the short timetable in adjudication is one of its greatest assets and is one of the key bases upon which the Act was founded. Providing the adjudicator himself considers that he has sufficient time to consider the material placed before him and provides a party with a reasonable opportunity to respond to submissions or evidence relied upon by the other party,[57] any perceived unfairness arising from lack of time will invariably not meet the threshold for a successful challenge to the adjudicator's decision based on breach of natural justice.[58] Only where new material or arguments are legitimately introduced and the adjudicator refuses any or sufficient additional time for a response will a breach of natural justice claim gain traction.[59] The test is whether the ambush or lack of time causes the receiving party substantial prejudice. Substantial prejudice is likely to be caused in instances where the material goes to one or more fundamental issues in the dispute, and the receiving party has not had sufficient time to consider and respond to the information.

[17.68] In *AWG Construction Services Ltd v Rockingham Motor Speedway Ltd*,[60] the referring party changed the basis of its claim in the reply, which meant that the responding party only had a few days to consider what was in effect an entirely new case. The court found that the responding party had insufficient time to respond to the claim, and held that the adjudicator's decision was unenforceable on this and other grounds. In *London and Amsterdam Properties Limited v Waterman Partnership Ltd*,[61] the referring party delayed the submission of a substantial proportion of its quantum evidence until the reply, which left the responding party with very little time to deal with it. The court held that the evidence should have been provided with the referral notice, particularly as it went to one of the key issues in dispute and refused to grant summary judgment as a result.

[17.69] Where an adjudicator considers that he or a party has insufficient time to consider material, he should inform the parties that a decision cannot reasonably and fairly be arrived at within the time and invite the parties to agree further time. If the parties cannot agree, then an adjudicator ought not to make a decision at all and should resign.

---

[57] *Bovis Lend Lease Ltd v The Trustees of the London Clinic* [2009] EWHC 64 (TCC), per Akenhead J at [66–68].
[58] *CIB Properties Ltd v Birse Construction Ltd.* [2004] EWHC 2365 (TCC), per Toulmin J at [180].
[59] *RSL (South West) Ltd v Stansell Ltd* [2003] EWHC 1390 (TCC), per Seymour J at [32–33]. See also Section 17.5.8.
[60] [2004] EWCH 888, per Toulmin J at [154–170].
[61] [2003] EWHC 3059 (TCC) per Wilcox J at [178–186].

[17.70] A claim of ambush, or 'no dispute' as it is also known, also arises in the context of jurisdictional challenges and is considered further at Sections 7.2 and 16.5.5.

17.5.5 Christmas claims

[17.71] For contracts governed by the Act, parties may refer a dispute to adjudication at any time.[62] Where the referring party issues a notice of adjudication on or before a public holiday, such as Christmas, where the adjudicator proceeded with the adjudication without extending the timetable to take account of the holiday period,[63] the responding party may claim that he has breached the rules of natural justice. This claim will not succeed.[64] Notwithstanding this, many adjudicators will often circumvent such sharp tactics either by declining the appointment or by accepting only on the grounds that the timetable is extended to reflect the holiday period.

17.5.6 Dispute is too large or complex

[17.72] A proportion of disputes referred to adjudication are large by value and/or documentary volume, or are particularly complex from a legal or technical perspective. Defending such claims within the statutory timescales can place an almost impossible strain on the responding party.

[17.73] For example, if the referring party, who will have invariably had months to prepare its claim, serves on the adjudicator 100 files of information and a 300-page referral notice, then the responding party will have an enormous task ahead of it to deal with that material within the period allowed for the response. Even worse, the referring party may prepare a concise referral notice (such as a claim for monies due), but the responding party may respond with a complex range of defences that the referring party has not seen before or prepared for.[65] Within normal timescales, the referring party would only have a few days at most to respond.

[17.74] While much has been made of the unsuitability of adjudications for large-scale, complex or 'kitchen sink' disputes, the simple point is that if Parliament wanted to restrict the application of statutory adjudications to smaller disputes, it could have (and arguably should have) done so. The fact that it did not must presumably indicate that it is Parliament's intention that adjudication is suitable for all sizes of dispute. Where the adjudicator decides that it is possible to deal with the matter and goes on to produce a decision, the courts have never invalidated that decision simply because it was too big or too complicated. There is perhaps no better example of this issue in *CIB Properties Ltd v Birse*

---

[62] See Section 7.7.
[63] Albeit time should be allowed for bank holidays, unless the contract provides otherwise. See section 116 of the Act.
[64] *Bovis Lend Lease Ltd v The Trustees of the London Clinic* [2009] EWHC 64 (TCC), per Akenhead J at [51].
[65] See Section 8.5.

Construction Ltd.[66] In that case, the claim made was for over £12 million plus VAT and interest. Also, 49 files accompanied the referral notice, containing 24 expert reports on defects, 18 level arch files of reports on quantum and 16 witness statements. A further 52 files were served in relation to a separate part of CIB's claim and a further 55 files served by the parties during the course of the adjudication. In that case, the parties had agreed to extend the adjudication timetable to around three months, but nevertheless Birse complained in the enforcement proceedings that this was not enough time given the size and complexity of the claim.

[17.75] The court held that this did not amount to a breach of natural justice because Birse had a period of time within which to make its response, and in the course of the extended adjudication it had a full opportunity to undertake investigations and to put its substantive case to the adjudicator within the limits imposed by the adjudication process, and it did so. The judge considered whether there could ever be an adjudication case that was so complex that it was unsuitable for adjudication. He decided that there was nothing to preclude this. Referring to section 108(1) and (2) of the Act, he said a party to a construction contract has a right to refer any dispute or difference to adjudication and the adjudicator has a duty to deliver a decision on such dispute, provided he can discharge that duty impartially and fairly within the time limit stipulated in the Act, or if extended by the parties. A defendant is not bound to agree to extend time beyond the time limits laid down in the Act even if such a refusal renders the task of the adjudicator to be impossible.[67]

[17.76] In *Amec Group Limited v Thames Water Utilities Ltd*,[68] Coulson J summarised the law as follows:

(a) The mere fact that an adjudication is concerned with a large or complex dispute does not of itself make it unsuitable for adjudication: see CIB v. Birse.
(b) What matters is whether, notwithstanding the size or complexity of the dispute, the adjudicator had: (i) sufficiently appreciated the nature of any issue referred to him before giving a decision on that issue, including the submissions of each party; and (ii) was satisfied that he could do broad justice between the parties (see CIB v. Birse).
(c) If the adjudicator felt able to reach a decision within the time limit then a court, when considering whether or not that conclusion was outside the rules of natural justice, would consider the basis on which the adjudicator reached that conclusion (HS Properties). In practical terms, that consideration is likely to amount to no more than a scrutiny of the particular allegations as to why the defendant claims that the adjudicator acted in breach of natural justice.
(d) If the allegation is, as here, that the adjudicator failed to have sufficient regard to the material provided by one party, the court will consider that by reference to the nature of the material; the timing of the provision of that material; and the opportunities available to the parties, both before and during the adjudication, to address the subject matter of that material.

---

[66] [2004] EWHC 2365 (TCC), per Toulmin J at [180].
[67] Ibid at [199].
[68] [2010] EWHC 419 (TCC), per Coulson J at [60].

[17.77] Generally, if the adjudicator accepts the appointment, accepts that a decision can be reached within the timescale afforded and proceeds to a decision, that decision will not be found to be in breach of the rules of natural justice. However, if the adjudicator decides at any point that the material cannot be dealt with in the time, he should ask the parties for an extension of time. If one is not granted, or it is not granted in full, the appropriate action is to resign. If the adjudicator indicates that there is too much material, but then carries on to a decision, there is a real risk that the courts will hold that there has been a breach of natural justice because the adjudicator may be held to have admitted that he cannot deal with the dispute in the allocated time in a manner that does broad justice to the parties.

[17.78] In Scheme adjudications, the adjudicator is not powerless to control the amount of information submitted to him. Paragraph 13 of the Scheme allows him to appoint experts, assessors or legal advisers to assist him, limit the length of written documents and issue other directions relating to the conduct of the adjudication. Provided that the adjudicator exercises these powers properly, he can to some extent control the flow of information submitted. Paragraph 13 is considered further at Section 10.7.

[17.79] The question of whether the referring party should submit a large dispute to adjudication requires careful consideration. One approach is to agree with the other party beforehand that it wishes to adjudicate the dispute and agree between them an extended timetable that is suitable for the size of the dispute. This will allow the responding party time to prepare its case and provide both parties and the adjudicator with more time to consider the merits of the case. This is likely to lead to 'better' submissions and a 'better' decision which in turn should increase the chance that both parties will accept that decision as final. Section 8.4.6 considers the merits of referring large-scale disputes to adjudication further.

17.5.7 Failing to address an issue, part of a submission or evidence

(A) Principle

[17.80] Where the adjudicator fails to address an issue, part of a submission or evidence, there is a risk he breaches the rules of natural justice. The courts place emphasis on the extent of the adjudicator's failure in this regard. If the adjudicator is found only to have failed to address a minor issue, or subissue in the adjudication, then the courts are unlikely to hold that the adjudicator breached the rules of natural justice.[69] If, however, the adjudicator is found not to have addressed – deliberately or otherwise – whole parts of a defence or claim, such that the innocent party has been prejudiced as a result, that is likely to amount to a breach of natural justice.[70]

[17.81] The law on this issue is summarised in *Pilon Ltd v Breyer Group plc*.[71]

---

[69] *Balfour Beatty Construction Northern Ltd v Modus Corovest (Blackpool) Ltd* [2008] EWHC 3029, per Coulson J at [44–50].
[70] *Thermal Energy Construction Ltd v AE and E Lentjes UK* [2009] EWHC 408, per Davies J at [25–26].
[71] [2010] EWHC 837, per Coulson J at [22].

The adjudicator must attempt to answer the question referred to him. The question may those issues in order to answer the question then, whether right or wrong, his decision is enforceable: see ***Carillion v Devonport***.[72]

If the adjudicator fails to address the question referred to him because he has taken an erroneously restrictive view of his jurisdiction (and has, for example, failed even to consider the defence to the claim or some fundamental element of it), then that may make his decision unenforceable, either on grounds of jurisdiction or natural justice: see ***Ballast***,[73] ***Broadwell***,[74] and ***Thermal Energy***.[75]

However, for that result to obtain, the adjudicator's failure must be deliberate. If there has simply been an inadvertent failure to consider one of a number of issues embraced by the single dispute that the adjudicator has to decide, then such a failure will not ordinarily render the decision unenforceable: see ***Bouygues***[76] and ***Amec v TWUL***.[77]

It goes without saying that any such failure must also be material: see ***Cantillon v Urvasco***[78] and ***CJP Builders Limited v William Verry Limited***.[79] In other words, the error must be shown to have had a potentially significant effect on the overall result of the adjudication: see ***Kier Regional Ltd v City and General (Holborn) Ltd***.[80]

A factor which may be relevant to the court's consideration of this topic in any given case is whether or not the claiming party has brought about the adjudicator's error by a misguided attempt to seek a tactical advantage. That was plainly a factor which, in my view rightly, Judge Davies took into account in ***Quartzelec***[81] when finding against the claiming party.

[17.82] While it may be a breach of natural justice not to consider a defence or an important aspect of it, the breach must always be material, which means that an express or apparent failure to consider and address every single aspect of the defence will not amount to a breach of natural justice, so long as the omission was ancillary to the main thrust of what was decided.[82]

[17.83] The failure may occur in the adjudicator's treatment of the responding party's defence. The adjudicator will fail to consider an issue or argument in the defence because either he believes the responding party is not entitled to raise the defence (because for instance no withholding notice was given), or because the defence is outside the scope of the dispute referred to adjudication. The key point to remember is that provided the defence is within

---

[72] [2005] EWHC 778 (TCC), per Jackson J at [81].
[73] [2001] ScotCS 159, per Reed J at [39–43].
[74] [2006] ADJ CS 04/21, per Raynor J at [17].
[75] [2009] EWHC 408 (TCC), per Davies J at [21–30].
[76] [2000] BLR 49, per Dyson J at [35].
[77] [2010] EWHC 419 (TCC), per Coulson J at [81–88].
[78] [2008] EWHC 282 (TCC), per Akenhead J at [57].
[79] [2008] EWHC 2025 (TCC), per Akenhead J at [78–86].
[80] [2006] EWHC 848 (TCC), per Jackson J at [39–44].
[81] [2008] EWHC 3315 (TCC), per Davies J at [27–33].
[82] *HS Works Ltd v Enterprise Managed Services Ltd* [2009] EWHC 729, per Akenhead J at [51].

the scope of the dispute and it is a defence permitted in law, the responding party is generally entitled to raise any points in its defence to the claims that would amount in law or in fact to a defence to the claim, regardless of whether those points have been raised in previous correspondence or discussions prior to referring the dispute to adjudication.[83]

[17.84] In *Jacques and another (t/a C&E Jacques Partnership) v Ensign Contractors Ltd*,[84] the judge gave the following guidance on whether, and if so how, the adjudicator should deal with the responding party's defences:

(a) The Adjudicator must consider defences properly put forward by a defending party in adjudication.

(b) However, it is within an adjudicator's jurisdiction to decide what evidence is admissible and, indeed, what evidence is helpful and unhelpful in the determination of the dispute or disputes referred to that adjudicator. If, within jurisdiction, the adjudicator decides that certain evidence is inadmissible, that will rarely (if ever) amount to a breach of the rules of natural justice. The position is analogous to a court case in which the Court decides that certain evidence is either inadmissible or of such little weight and value that it can effectively be ignored: it would be difficult for a challenge to such a decision on fairness grounds to be mounted.

(c) Even if the adjudicator's decision (within jurisdiction) to disregard evidence as inadmissible or of little or no weight was wrong in fact or in law, that decision is not in consequence impugnable as a breach of the rules of natural justice.

(d) One will need in most and possibly all 'natural justice' cases to distinguish between a failure by an adjudicator in the decision to consider and address a substantive (factual or legal) defence and an actual or apparent failure or omission to address all aspects of the evidence which go to support that defence. It is necessary to bear in mind that adjudication involves, usually, the exchange of evidence and argument over a short period of time and the production of a decision within a short time span thereafter. It is simply not practicable, usually, for every aspect of the evidence to be meticulously considered, weighed up and rejected or accepted in whole or in part. Primarily, the adjudicator, needs to address the substantive issues, whether factual or legal, but does not need (as a matter of fairness) to address each and every aspect of the evidence. The adjudicator should not be considered to be in breach of the rules of natural justice if the decision does not address each aspect of the evidence adduced by the parties.

[17.85] Where it is alleged that the adjudicator failed to consider an issue, part of a submission or evidence, the allegation is often coupled with a failure to comply with paragraphs 17 and 20 of the Scheme (where the Scheme applies), namely that the adjudicator is required to consider any relevant information submitted to him by the parties[85] and the adjudicator is required to decide the matters in dispute.[86] This also brings with it a complaint that the adjudicator has committed a jurisdictional error because

---

[83] *William Verry (Glazing Systems) Ltd v Furlong Homes Ltd* [2005] EWHC 138, per Coulson J at [49].
[84] [2009] EWHC 3383, per Akenhead J at [26].
[85] See Section 10.7.6.
[86] See Section 10.7.7.

the scope of the adjudicator's decision is outside, or does not exhaust, the adjudicator's jurisdiction.[87]

[17.86] The following sections summarise some key cases where the court has held that the failure to address an issue, evidence or part of a submission led, or did not lead, to a breach of natural justice. A full list of cases on this matter is contained in Appendix 8.

(B) Examples leading to a breach

[17.87] In *Buxton Building Contractors Ltd v Governors of Durand Primary School*,[88] the adjudicator's decision revealed that he had not considered the responding party's cross-claim: the validity of the project manager's certificate of payment or the validity of a withholding notice. Even though the referring party agreed that he should not look at the relevant documents, his failure to do so amounted to him making a decision which was 'intrinsically unfair' and so the decision was held to be invalid.

[17.88] In *Pilon Ltd v Breyer Group plc*[89] the adjudicator erred in failing to take into account part of Breyer's defence, which claimed an overpayment in respect of part of the work. While the defence was not expressly dealt with in the notice of adjudication, its wording gave the adjudicator the jurisdiction to consider what further sums should be paid to Pilon and that issue, of necessity, involved a consideration of the part of Breyer's defence relating to the overpayment. The court held this to be a material error and one which caused it to decide that the adjudicator's decision was invalid. In *Paul Boardwell v k3D Property Partnership Ltd*,[90] the court found that the adjudicator's erroneous decision not to consider a counterclaim because he thought he did not have jurisdiction to do so was a material breach of natural justice. In *Thermal Energy Construction Ltd v AE & E Lentjes UK Ltd*,[91] the adjudicator failed to consider the responding party's defence at all. On the facts, the court found that the adjudicator's decision in that regard amounted to a breach of natural justice.

[17.89] Finally, in *Whyte and Mackay Ltd v Blyth & Blyth Consulting Engineers Ltd*,[92] the responding party contended in the response that even if it was at fault in producing a design which did not specify piling, there was no causative link with any damage to the buildings, nor to costs claimed by the referring party. Such loss and damage would have occurred in any event. The adjudicator appeared to ignore this argument in his decision which, if correct, would have amounted to a complete defence. As a result, the court refused to enforce his decision.

---

[87] See Section 16.7.6.
[88] [2004] EWHC 733, per Thornton J at [16–21].
[89] [2010] EWHC 837 (TCC), per Coulson J at [24–31].
[90] Unreported, 21 April 2006, per Raynor J at [17].
[91] [2009] EWHC 408 (TCC), per Davies J at [21–30].
[92] [2013] CSOH 54, per Lord Malcolm at [30–35].

(C) Examples not leading to a breach

[17.90] In *Letchworth Roofing Company v Sterling Building Company*,[93] the adjudicator had declined to consider a counterclaim because it had not been the subject of a valid withholding notice. The court agreed with the adjudicator's decision. A similar position was reached albeit in different circumstances in *Urang Commercial Ltd v (1) Century Investments Ltd (2) Eclipse Hotels (Luton) Ltd*.[94] In *Humes Building Contracts Ltd v Charlotte Homes (Surrey) Ltd*[95] the adjudicator refused to consider the defendant's claims that the claimant's work was defective. Those claims amounted to £135,916.48 and, if correct, would have reduced the amount of any award in favour of the claimant significantly. However, the adjudicator rejected this claim (and any balance of the claim for liquidated damages) because he concluded wrongly that a withholding notice was necessary. The court agreed with the adjudicator, although it held the decision invalid on other grounds.

[17.91] In *AMEC Capital Projects Ltd v Whitefriars City Estates Ltd (No. 3)*,[96] the court found that the adjudicator's decision not to refer to arguments raised in a jurisdictional challenge did not breach the rules of natural justice because the adjudicator did not have jurisdiction to rule on his own jurisdiction. Lord Justice Dyson at paragraph 41 stated:

> A more fundamental question was raised as to whether adjudicators are in any event obliged to give parties the opportunity to make representations in relation to questions of jurisdiction... The reason for the common law right to prior notice and an effective opportunity to make representations is to protect parties from the risk of decisions being reached unfairly. But it is only directed at decision which can affect parties' rights. Procedural fairness does not require that parties should have their rights to make representations in relation to decisions which do not affect their rights, still less in relation to "decisions" which are nullities and which cannot affect their rights. Since the "decision" of an adjudicator as to his jurisdiction is of no legal effect and cannot affect the rights of the parties, it is difficult to see the logical justification for a rule of law that an adjudicator can only make a "decision" after giving the parties an opportunity to make representations.

[17.92] The court did state that it is appropriate for an adjudicator to allow both parties to make representations before coming to a conclusion about his jurisdiction.

[17.93] In *Gillies Ramsay Diamond and Gavin Ramsay and Philip Diamond v PJW Enterprises Ltd*,[97] the adjudicator failed to refer to any of the legal authorities submitted by the parties in his decision. The court found that while the adjudicator is under a duty to consider any information validly submitted by the parties, he is not required to analyse every part of those submissions in his decision. The presumption will be in favour

---

[93] [2009] EWHC 1119 (TCC), per Coulson J at [17–34].
[94] [2011] EWHC 1561 (TCC), per Edwards-Stuart at [30–37].
[95] Unreported, 4 January 2007, per Gilliland J at [20–28].
[96] [2004] EWCA Civ 1418, per Dyson LJ at [38–43].
[97] [2003] ScotCS 354, per Lord MacFadyen at [26–28].

of the adjudicator having considered the information, except in the plainest of cases. In *Kier Regional Ltd (t/a Wallis) v City & General (Holborn) Ltd*,[98] the court considered whether or not the adjudicator's refusal to consider the two expert reports meant that he had breached the rules of natural justice. The court thought that the adjudicator should have taken the reports into account, but did not on balance consider the error was one which would invalidate the decision. At worst the adjudicator had made an error of law which caused him to disregard two pieces of relevant evidence. However, this was not enough to invalidate the adjudicator's decision. Finally, in *Viridis UK Ltd v Mulalley & Company Ltd*[99] the defendant to the enforcement proceedings argued that it was evident from the adjudicator's global rejection of the contra-charges that the adjudicator must have failed to consider and address the argument that the defendant failed to issue test certificates and if he had done so he would have deducted 10% from the claimant's claim. The court held that the adjudicator was not obliged to state all of his reasons for rejecting this particular item of contra-charge. It held that it was enough that he made it clear that he had considered all of the documents and submissions supplied by the defendant, that he was aware that the defendant was relying on the various contra-charges, including the certificate defence, and that he had considered those contra-charges and rejected them.

17.5.8 Failure to permit a further submission or information

[17.94] As the adjudication clock keeps ticking, parties will have less and less time to respond to the other party's latest missive, and the adjudicator will have less time to consider it. Sometimes the adjudicator will not permit a party to present a further submission. As with the failure to consider an issue or part of a submission, whether or not the exclusion of that further submission by the adjudicator is considered a breach of natural justice will depend on the extent to which the deliberate or inadvertent exclusion of material relates to a subissue or some critical matter, but it also relates to whether the adjudicator had permitted a further submission and how much time is left before the adjudicator is required to reach his decision.

[17.95] There is no inherent entitlement for parties to serve as many submissions as they wish, unless the contract or the relevant adjudication rules expressly permit it.[100] Save for an express rule to the contrary, the adjudicator is entitled to limit the number of rounds of submissions from each party. Where the adjudicator has not made provision in the timetable for the service of a further submission, the timetable was not challenged at the time and then later a party served a further submission after the conclusion of the submissions period in the timetable, there is probably no requirement to consider it, regardless of what it contains, and certainly no requirement to consider it where there is

---

[98] [2006] EWHC 848 (TCC), per Jackson J at [39–44].
[99] [2014] EWHC 268 (TCC), per Stephen Davies J at [88–99].
[100] *Amec Group Ltd v Thames Water Utilities Ltd* [2010] EWHC 419 (TCC), per Coulson J at [65].

nothing new in the submission to which the further submission responds.[101] However, where the adjudicator excluded an entire submission because it was late, he erroneously believed that he did not have the jurisdiction to consider it and there was ample time left for him to consider it before reaching his decision, that is likely to amount to a breach of natural justice. This was the case in *CJP Builders Ltd v William Verry Ltd*,[102] where the adjudicator determined that the rules of the adjudication (DOM 2) did not give him power to extend the time for the service of the response, so he refused to consider it. The court found that the adjudicator was wrong and that he did have the jurisdiction. As a result of his actions, the adjudicator had failed to consider the responding party's response and had materially breached the rules of natural justice. The decision was not enforced.

[17.96] In *Balfour Beatty Construction Northern Ltd v Modus Corovest (Blackpool) Ltd*,[103] Modus contended that the adjudicator wrongly considered Balfour Beatty's reply, without permitting a rejoinder from Modus. However, the timetable set by the adjudicator made no allowance for the rejoinder. Modus did not challenge the timetable at any point, and in the enforcement hearing it was unable to identify any new points it would have made in the rejoinder. The court held that the adjudicator had not breached the rules of natural justice. In *GPS Marine Contractors Ltd v Ringway Infrastructure Services Ltd*,[104] the responding party served the rejoinder, which the adjudicator failed to take account of. The reply was served two days before the due date for the decision and there was no provision in the adjudicator's timetable for the rejoinder. The court found that the adjudicator's decision not to consider the rejoinder was correct and upheld his decision.

[17.97] The best course of action for an adjudicator is to set out a clear timetable at the outset of the adjudication, with a date by which any new material can be provided, with the express warning that any material sent thereafter will not be considered unless the parties consent to an extension of the period for reaching his decision.

17.5.9 Failure to follow the agreed procedure

[17.98] Can a failure to follow the agreed adjudication procedure amount to a breach of natural justice? The answer lies in the extent of the failure and the circumstances in which the mistake is made. For example, if the adjudicator calls a hearing, natural justice may not necessarily require that a party be given an opportunity to cross-examine witnesses for the opposite party, although it may do, especially if the credibility of a witness is an issue. Nor may it require that evidence from witnesses for one party be taken in the presence of the opposite party or its representatives, provided the evidence is communicated to the

---

[101] *Balfour Beatty Construction Northern Limited v Modus Corovest (Blackpool) Ltd* [2008] EWHC 2029, per Coulson J at [54–57] and *GPS Marine Contractors Ltd v Ringway Infrastructure Ltd* [2010] EWHC 283, per Ramsey J at [102–109].
[102] [2008] EWHC 2025 (TCC), per Akenhead J at [78–86].
[103] [2008] EWHC 2029, per Coulson J at [54–57].
[104] [2010] EWHC 283, per Ramsey J at [102–109].

other party and the other party has an opportunity to deal with it. However, where the adjudicator acts contrary to the rules and in a way that substantially affects the ability of a party to advance its case and respond to the other party's case, a court is most likely to hold that the decision is invalid.[105]

17.5.10 Adjudicator's timetable unfair

[17.99] In *NAP Anglia Ltd v Sun Land Development Co Ltd*,[106] the defendant argued on enforcement that the adjudicator's timetable was unfair and therefore he was in breach of the rules of natural justice. The complaint seemed to stem from the fact that the defendant had received less time than it had asked for and the claimant had received the same or more time than it had asked for. Furthermore, the adjudicator gave the last word to the claimant, without allowing a response from the defendant. The court found the defendant's case to be entirely without merit. It said that provided the adjudicator gave both parties sufficient time to respond to the case put to them, that was enough. The fact that the adjudicator cut off the defendant's ability to respond to the claimant's sur-rejoinder was entirely proper.

17.5.11 Documents received late or not at all

[17.100] What is the position where the responding party fails to receive the referring party's submissions, either on time or not at all? This was the case in *M Rhode v Markham-David (No. 2)*.[107] Mr Rhodes delivered the notice of adjudication and subsequent submissions to the last known address of Mr Markham-David. As it turned out, Mr Markham-David no longer lived at that address and did not receive any of the documents served on him. Furthermore, the adjudicator made very little attempt to engage Mr Markham-David in the proceedings or to keep him informed as to the progress of the adjudication, notwithstanding the fact that he knew Mr Markham-David had not been served with the notice of adjudication or the appointment of the adjudicator's terms. The court found this unsatisfactory, holding that it was incumbent on the adjudicator to take reasonable steps to establish where the responding party is resident, and that the appropriate documentation has been validly served and brought to his attention. The court held the adjudicator's actions so unfair as to fatally compromise the validity of the proceedings.

[17.101] In *Hughes (JW) Building Contractors Ltd v GB Metalwork*,[108] although GB's solicitors had correctly served its clients notice of adjudication and referral notice, Hughes's solicitors failed to provide Hughes with GB's notice of adjudication, referral notice and supporting documents. Hughes was notified of this failure, albeit late in the adjudication process, and was given the opportunity by the adjudicator to raise the matter with him

---

[105] *Dean & Dyball Construction Ltd v Kenneth Grubb Associates Ltd* [2003] EWHC 2465 (TCC), per Seymour J at [53].
[106] [2011] EWHC 2846 (TCC), per Edwards-Stuart J at [13–24].
[107] [2007] EWHC 1408 (TCC).
[108] Unreported, 3 October 2003, per Forbes J at [18–37].

if Hughes felt it was necessary to do so. Hughes was able to submit a detailed response. The court held that Hughes had sufficient opportunity to make submissions and so it enforced the adjudicator's decision.

17.5.12 Failure to inform the parties about an approach taken or methodology used

[17.102] The adjudicator must decide the dispute on the basis of material that has been put before him by the parties, and the parties must have had some opportunity to make submissions on it. It follows that where the adjudicator wishes to adopt an approach or methodology to determine a material issue in the dispute that the parties have not advanced, he must share this with the parties and allow them the chance to address him on it. Where he fails to do this, he is likely to be in breach of natural justice. In *ABB Limited v BAM Nuttall Limited*,[109] the court put it in this way:

> The reference in the [Cantillon Ltd v Urvasco Ltd [2008] BLR 250] case to a breach of the rules being material where the adjudicator has not, prior to his or her decision, identified to the parties a point or issue "which is either decisive or of considerable potential importance to the outcome of the resolution of the dispute and is not peripheral or irrelevant" should not be treated as requiring statutory or contractual rules of interpretation to construe what was meant in the decision. If the adjudicator relies upon such a point or issue (either of fact or of law) and his whole decision stems from his finding on that point or issue, it will be decisive. A point or issue might well be of considerable potential importance to the outcome if it is not decisive of the whole decision but if it goes to important parts of the decision. Even if an adjudicator's breach of the rules of natural justice relates only to a material or actual or potentially important part of the decision, that can be enough to lead to the decision becoming wholly unenforceable essentially because the parties (or at least the losing party) and the Court can have no confidence in the fairness of the decision making process.

[17.103] In order to establish whether or not there has been a failure under this head, it will be necessary to establish firstly the basis on which the parties have put their case, followed by the approach taken or methodology adopted by the adjudicator to decide it. Where the adjudicator has stepped outside the foundation of the parties' arguments, it will be necessary to consider the terms on which the adjudicator engaged with the parties to understand whether the new method or approach set out in his decision was one which he shared and sought submissions on.

[17.104] The court will be slow to pick holes in the minutiae of the adjudicator's actions. So, for instance, when the adjudicator invited the parties to address him on the effect of a clause and directed that any submissions should be filed, that did not mean that he was barring the parties from producing any further evidence. Part of the submissions could have been an evidential submission.[110]

---

[109] [2013] EWHC 1983 (TCC), per Akenhead J at [5].
[110] *Brims Construction Ltd v A2M Development Ltd* [2013] EWHC 3262 (TCC), per Akenhead J at [31].

[17.105] The adjudicator is not required to share every last thought with the parties before reaching his decision, either because it is not practical or because the thought is not something that will materially affect the parties' case.[111] The threshold is one of materiality, and the court will always endeavour to support the adjudicator's actions and his resulting decision where it can.

[17.106] Where the adjudicator provided the parties with an opportunity to comment on a method or approach, but the parties did not take the opportunity, the adjudicator will not be found at fault.[112] The opportunity to make submissions on a new point need not last for very long; that is the consequence of the time pressures of adjudication.

[17.107] The adjudicator must ensure that his approach or methodology has been seen by the parties, and they have at least some time to consider it. So long as that is done, the adjudicator may reach whatever decision he wishes.[113] His decision may not directly align with one or other of the party's contentions; it may be a 'development and exposition' of the parties' contentions and still be within the boundaries of natural justice.[114] So, where the adjudicator was required to establish the rate to apply to value compensation events, a question arose as to whether a prospective or retrospective analysis was required. The adjudicator sought submissions from the parties as to the 'switch date', or the point at which the basis of the assessment changed from prospective to retrospective. He then proceeded to a decision without further recourse to the parties. The defendant contended that the adjudicator should have reverted to the parties to ask for further submissions on other clauses which also impacted the question. The court found that the adjudicator had done enough, and reached the decision that he did by applying his own expertise legitimately.[115] Similarly, where an adjudicator has heard full argument on the construction of a particular clause or set of provisions in a contract and reaches a different conclusion to that arrived at in the submissions, there is no obligation upon him to canvass that view with the parties before reaching and issuing his decision.[116]

[17.108] However, there are limits to the extent to which the adjudicator can 'develop' the parties' arguments. It can be tempting for the adjudicator to make a party's case for it, where his expertise leads him to foresee that the basis of a claim advanced by a party will fail, but a different basis for the claim may succeed.[117] Indeed, the actively inquisitorial role of an adjudicator requires him to take the initiative in ascertaining the facts and the law.[118]

---

[111] See Section 17.5.15.
[112] *Cantillon Ltd v Urvasco Ltd* [2008] EWHC 282 (TCC), per Akenhead J at [76].
[113] *Roe Brickwork Ltd v Wates Construction Ltd* [2013] EWHC 3417 (TCC), per Edwards-Stuart J at [22].
[114] *Vision Homes Ltd v Lancsville Construction Ltd* [2009] EWHC 2042 (TCC), per Clarke J at [64–70].
[115] *Farrelly (M&E) Building Services Ltd v Byrne Brothers (Formwork) Ltd* [2013] EWHC 1186 (TCC), per Ramsey J at [58–64].
[116] *Hyder Consulting Ltd v Carillion Construction (UK) Ltd* [2011] EWHC 1810 (TCC), per Coulson J at [71–74].
[117] See Section 17.5.14.
[118] Subsection 108(2)(f) of the Act.

However, the adjudicator may not go off 'on a frolic of his own'.[119] Clearly, there is a line to be drawn between the adjudicator applying his own expertise to a dispute, and developing a case beyond the boundaries of that presented to him, but it may not always be crystal clear where that line is.

[17.109] Although the weight of authority on this issue has found the adjudicator's conduct to be *intra vires*, there are instances where the court has refused to enforce the adjudicator's decision. For example, where the adjudicator uses a reference guide to determine the value of certain works done and the reference guide had not been used by either party to calculate the value of the works, he will breach natural justice if he does not share this with the parties.[120] Similarly, the adjudicator is not permitted to adopt a delay analysis technique and an approach to valuing the cost flowing from that delay which was not advanced by either party,[121] or create his own as-built programme and then derive his own critical path[122] in reaching his decision. It is impermissible for an adjudicator to decide an issue concerning the liability of an issue, such as the liability to pay overtime on a basis not presented by the parties. This was so, even though the adjudicator claimed that the issue was raised at a hearing during the adjudication.[123] Where the adjudicator rejected a claim because he considered that a withholding notice was required and not issued, the court found that not only was the adjudicator wrong about that, but also that he was in breach because neither party had made any submissions on the requirement for a withholding notice, nor were they given any opportunity to comment.[124]

[17.110] Where the adjudicator relies on material that the parties have agreed should be ignored, he will act in breach of natural justice. So where the adjudicator rejected the referring party's claim for loss of profit based on a construction and management fee percentage stated in the contract and relied on material that the parties had agreed should be ignored, to calculate a figure which represented its actual loss of profit, the court invalidated the decision.[125]

[17.111] The challenge that an adjudicator failed to inform the parties about an approach taken will usually go hand in hand with a challenge that the adjudicator's decision was outside the scope of the dispute and therefore the adjudicator lacked jurisdiction.

---

[119] *Farrelly (M&E) Building Services Ltd v Byrne Brothers (Formwork) Ltd* [2013] EWHC 1186 (TCC), per Ramsey J at [61].
[120] *Roe Brickwork Limited v Wates Construction Limited* [2013] EWHC 3417 (TCC), per Edwards-Stuart J at [23].
[121] *Herbosch-Kiere Marine Contractors Ltd v Dover Harbour Board* [2012] EWHC 84 (TCC), per Akenhead J at [24–34].
[122] *Balfour Beatty Construction Ltd v The Mayor & Burgesses of the London Borough of Lambeth* [2002] EWHC 597 (TCC), per Lloyd J at [28–39].
[123] *Ardmore Construction Ltd v Taylor Woodrow Construction Ltd* [2006] CSOH 3, per Lord Clarke at [43–48].
[124] *Humes Building Contracts Ltd v Charlotte Homes (Surrey) Ltd*, Unreported, 4 January 2007, per Gilliland J at [20–28].
[125] *Primus Build Ltd v Pompey Centre and Another* [2009] EWHC 1487, per Coulson J at [36–44].

17.5.13 Failure to inform the parties about advice from a third party

[17.112] Adjudication procedures often permit adjudicators to seek advice or assistance from others. The Scheme provides at subparagraph 13(f) that the adjudicator may:

> obtain and consider such representations and submissions as he requires, and, provided he has notified the parties of his intention, appoint experts, assessors or legal advisers.

[17.113] However, where an adjudicator seeks advice from a third party and fails to advise the parties and/or permit them the opportunity to comment on any material or opinion the third party provides, the decision that he provides is unlikely to be enforced[126] where the failure is of material consequence.[127] Conceivably, it may be possible to argue that a party acquiesced its position, with the effect that the adjudicator may not be required to share information with the parties. However, merely not asking the adjudicator to share with the parties whatever report or documentation the third party produced is insufficient.[128]

[17.114] In *RSL (South West) Ltd v Stansell Ltd*,[129] the adjudicator had placed reliance in the decision upon the final report of a planning expert that had not been circulated to the parties (albeit an earlier draft report had been circulated). Mr Justice Seymour QC refused to enforce the decision:

> It is absolutely essential, in my judgment, for an adjudicator, if he is to observe the rules of natural justice, to give the parties to the adjudication the chance to comment upon any material, from whatever source, including the knowledge or experience of the adjudicator himself, to which the adjudicator was minded to attribute significance in reaching his decision.[130]

17.5.14 Failure to inform the parties about use of own knowledge and expertise

[17.115] Invariably, adjudicators are experts in their field, be it law, architecture, quantity surveying, delay analysis or some other area of construction. As part of their role, they are required to apply that expertise and knowledge when considering the contentions of the parties and arriving at a decision. However, where an adjudicator's own knowledge and experience is used to decide matters (provided those matters are material to the decision), and that knowledge and experience does not form part of, or fall out of, the parties' submissions, the adjudicator is required to put that before the parties and invite them to comment on it unless (a) the knowledge and experience is used when deciding a contention placed before the adjudicator by the parties; and/or (b) the adjudicator arrives at an

---

[126] *Highlands and Islands Airports Ltd v Shetland Islands Council* [2012] CSOH 12, per Menzies L at [31–34].
[127] *Balfour Beatty Construction Ltd v The Mayor & Burgesses of the London Borough of Lambeth* [2002] EWHC 597 (TCC), per Lloyd J at [41].
[128] *BAL (1996) Ltd v Taylor Woodrow Construction Ltd*, Unreported, 23 January 2004, per Wilcox J at [31–38].
[129] [2003] EWHC 1390 (TCC).
[130] At [32].

intermediate position for which neither party was contending.[131] Whether or not the adjudicator's actions amount to a breach of natural justice is a question of fact and degree in each case. The Scottish court in *Re Mr & Mrs Jack Paton,*[132] offered the following guidance, which it is submitted would apply equally in England, Wales and Northern Ireland.

> an adjudicator may use his own knowledge and experience in deciding disputed matters before him.
>
> …if the adjudicator uses such knowledge and experience to decide a contention placed before him by the parties he does not require to obtain their further comments thereon.
>
> The mere fact that the adjudicator arrives at an intermediate position for which neither party was contending does not of itself mean that said conclusion must be referred to parties for their comments.
>
> However, if he uses his own knowledge and experience to decide matters not advanced by parties then if these matters are of materiality in reaching his decision it would be his duty in order to comply with the rules of natural justice to revert to parties for their comments.

[17.116] The issue of the adjudicator using his own expertise and knowledge is often considered with the issue of the adjudicator failing to inform the parties about an approach or method taken (see Section 17.5.12). Although in themselves these are distinct issues, they can overlap so that, for instance, an adjudicator will use his own expertise in adopting an approach not contended for by either party. This is reflected in the overlap of cases listed in Appendix 8.

[17.117] In *Hyder Consulting (UK) Ltd v Carillion Construction Ltd,*[133] Carillion was seeking to resist enforcement of an adjudicator's decision in favour of one of their consultants (Hyder) on the East London Line railway project. They contended that the adjudicator had acted in breach of the rules of natural justice in that he had not put his method of calculation of the target cost to the parties before adopting it in his decision. In response, Hyder said that having rejected both parties' primary position, it was inevitable that the adjudicator would have to carry out his own calculation. He had only used information provided to him as part of the adjudication in reaching his conclusion. The court agreed. The adjudicator had adopted an interpretation of the agreement which was different from the submissions put forward by each of the parties; this did not amount to a breach of the rules of natural justice as the adjudicator had only drawn on information which the parties had seen. The application to enforce was granted.

[17.118] In *Rankilor (Dr Peter) & Perco Engineering Service Ltd v Igoe (M) Ltd*[134] the complaint made by Igoe was that the adjudicator made findings of fact and reached conclusions based upon his own expert assessment of a laboratory analysis of soil which

---

[131] *Miller Construction (UK) Limited v Building Design Partnership Limited* [2014] CSOH 80, per Lord Malcolm at [13–18].
[132] [2010] CSOH 40, per Lord Bannatyne at [72].
[133] [2011] EWHC 1810 (TCC), per Edwards-Stuart at [72].
[134] Unreported, 27 January 2006, per Gilliland J at [28–32].

had been produced by Igoe when such findings and conclusions had not been contended for by either Igoe or Perco and when Igoe had had no opportunity to comment upon those findings or conclusions. The court found that the adjudicator had not breached the rules of natural justice because the adjudicator was entitled to use his expert knowledge as an engineer to calculate from the information supplied by Igoe the density of the soil, applying a well-known formula and other conventional mathematical components to arrive at his answer.

[17.119] Finally, in *SGL Carbon Fibres Ltd v RBG Ltd*,[135] RBG contended that, in respect of productivity calculations that were used to value the claim, the adjudicator made his decision on the basis of assumptions derived from his own experience, without providing the parties with a proper opportunity of making submissions to him about the course he proposed to adopt or as to the relevance of his experience or as to the assumptions upon which he proposed to proceed. The court said that while the adjudicator is obliged to apply his experience and knowledge to the matters in dispute, in doing so he must not 'add to the evidence led by the parties; or to use it to explore for himself, and introduce into his decision making process, matters upon which the parties have not focused their attention and upon which they have led no evidence', unless the parties see that evidence and have chance to comment on it. In this case, the court found that the adjudicator had given the parties the opportunity to comment, but it had been an insufficient period of time. On each occasion, the parties were given a day or less to comment, which the judge considered to be insufficient. On the last occasion, the time for responding (less than a day) ended on the morning that the adjudicator was to produce his full decision, and so the court questioned whether in fact the adjudicator would have considered and taken on board comments received before issuing his decision.

17.5.15 Failure to inform the parties about preliminary view

[17.120] An adjudicator may form an early view on the evidence presented or how he intends to decide the case before the final decision is actually made. In cases where the adjudicator's view already falls within the view of one of the parties, then the adjudicator does not need to communicate that view, because the parties are already aware of it. If, however, the adjudicator forms a view that is different from any of the views that the parties hold and one which they could not have reasonably anticipated, then that view must be communicated when it is made and the parties must be given the opportunity to consider and make submissions on it.[136] This view might be formed on the basis of written documents, or video imagery,[137] or on the basis of a hearing held between the parties,[138] or on a view of the law, which had not been argued by, or put to, either party.[139]

---

[135] [2011] CSOH 62, per Lord Glennie at [11–13; 28–36].
[136] *Shimizu Europe Ltd v LBJ Fabrications Ltd* [2003] EWHC 1229 (TCC), per Kirkham J at [45].
[137] *Berry Piling Systems Ltd v Sheer Project Ltd* [2012] EWHC 241 (TCC), per Edwards-Stuart J at [10–14].
[138] *Ardmore Construction Ltd v Taylor Woodrow Construction Ltd* [2006] CSOH 3, per Lord Clarke at [43–48].
[139] *Humes Building Contracts Ltd v Charlotte Homes (Surrey) Ltd* [2007] AdjLR 01/03, per Gilliland J at [20–28].

[17.121] Where the adjudicator assesses the quantum for a particular claim and decides to reduce the quantum by a percentage, but does not share that view with the parties before reaching his final decision, then that in itself is unlikely to be the subject of a successful challenge. So, a 20% reduction in quantum claim for defects may be perfectly acceptable. It is 'precisely the kind of exercise which one would expect the adjudicator ... to undertake', particularly where he is under tight timescales and is required to deal with a mass of further evidence and submissions.[140]

[17.122] The nature of this challenge is also put forward on the basis of apparent bias[141] and is often connected with the issue of the adjudicator deploying is own (a) methodology or approach;[142] or (b) knowledge and expertise[143] and in either case failing to allow them to consider and make submissions. For instance, where the adjudicator has expertise in the subject matter or area of law in dispute, then it will not be a breach of natural justice if the adjudicator simply brings that experience to bear in weighing the facts and law with which he is presented by the parties. The important point is that his experience is used to weigh up the materials provided and not reach a provisional conclusion on the basis of information that is in his mind alone.

17.5.16 Sufficiency of reasons

[17.123] Claimants in enforcement proceedings have more than once attempted to argue that a failure to give adequate reasons amounts to a breach of natural justice. While this challenge may succeed on the basis that the adjudicator exceeded his jurisdiction,[144] it will not succeed on the basis of a breach of natural justice. In *Multiplex Construction (UK) Ltd v West India Quay Development Company (Eastern) Limited* Jackson J said:[145]

> I do not, however, consider that a criticism of a failure to give reasons or adequate reasons is a breach of the rules of natural justice in the context of an adjudication.

[17.124] This was later supported in *Balfour Beatty Engineering Services (HY) Ltd v Shepherd Construction Ltd*[146] where the court held that the 'failure to give reasons is not a breach of natural justice.'

[17.125] However, it may be that a party wishes to advance a challenge that the adjudicator failed to give adequate reasons on natural justice grounds as a support for other natural justice

---

[140] *Carillion Construction Ltd v Devonport Royal Dockyard Ltd* [2005] EWHC 778 (TCC), per Jackson J at [114–115].
[141] See Section 17.4.14.
[142] See Section 17.5.12.
[143] See Section 17.5.14.
[144] See Section 16.7.5.
[145] [2006] EWHC 569 (TCC), per Jackson J at [34–36].
[146] [2009] EWHC 2218 (TCC), per Akenhead J at [49].

challenges, such as the decision demonstrates the adjudicator did not refer to a particular argument or give weight to a particular piece of evidence.

17.6 Checklist: Natural justice – the parties and the adjudicator

> Natural justice is founded on two principles, which are encapsulated in the maxims: *audi alteram partem* and *nemo judex in causa sua*. Literally these mean 'both parties must have a reasonable opportunity to present their case' and 'nobody may be a judge in their own cause'. In other words, a party has a right to hear the case against it and have the opportunity to respond to it, and the adjudicator must act in an unbiased manner. Consider the following questions to determine whether or not there is a natural justice issue and, if so, what to do about it.
>
> (1) Has the adjudicator had any prior involvement with the project or the parties (Sections 17.4.4 and 17.4.5)?
> (2) Has the adjudicator communicated with one party only, and failed to relay the substance of that communication to the other party (Sections 17.4.6 and 17.4.7)?
> (3) Has the adjudicator conducted the adjudication or dealt with evidence in a way that leads the fair-minded observer to believe that there was a risk that he was being biased (Sections 17.4.8–17.4.14)?
> (4) Has the adjudicator given each party a reasonable opportunity to present its case and to address the opponent's case (Sections 17.5.4, 17.5.10 and 17.5.11)?
> (5) Has the adjudicator considered all the material issues, submissions and evidence (Section 17.5.7 and 17.5.8)?
> (6) Has the adjudicator failed to follow the applicable adjudication rules and, if so, is that failure material (Section 17.5.9)?
> (7) Has the adjudicator presented facts, information or preliminary views found or formed by him to both parties and given them an opportunity to make submissions (Sections 17.5.12–17.5.15)?
> (8) If there is a suspected breach of natural justice, what is the best way of challenging it (Section 17.3)?

Chapter 18
Further grounds for resisting enforcement

18.1 Overview

[18.01] Although the adjudicator's jurisdiction and natural justice are the most common grounds relied on to render an adjudicator's decision invalid, fraud, duress and violation of the Unfair Terms in Consumer Contracts Regulations 1999 (the **UTCCR**) and the Human Rights Act 1998 (the **HRA**) have also been relied on by defendants in adjudication enforcement proceedings, albeit far less frequently.

[18.02] The defence of fraud or deceit may be raised as a defence to a claim in the adjudication or as a defence to the enforcement of an adjudicator's decision. However, there needs to be clear evidence of the fraud and deceit and, where the defence is in relation to the claim in the adjudication and it was not raised in the adjudication where it could have been, it will not be a defence to enforcement.

[18.03] The defence of duress may also lead to the court declining to enforce an adjudicator's award. As with fraud and deceit, the test for duress leads to a relatively high threshold to overcome in order to succeed. There is only one example of where this defence has been successful.

[18.04] The purpose of the UTCCR is to ensure that whenever a consumer enters into a contract to buy goods or services from a company, the terms on which that contract is made are not unfair to the consumer. Often, the UTCCR is raised in the context of domestic residential works where the contractor is alleged to have agreed with the consumer adjudication provisions. The question that has been raised is whether agreeing an adjudication procedure with a residential occupier falls foul of the UTCCR. Generally, the courts have found that it does not.

[18.05] The HRA is a statute that enshrines into legislature certain fundamental rights and freedoms that individuals in the UK have access to. In the context of adjudication, two arguments have been put before the courts. The first is that the adjudication system as a whole is flawed in that it falls foul of Article 6 of the HRA, which concerns the right to a fair trial. This argument has failed for a variety of reasons. The second argument is that an adjudicator's decision falls foul of Article 1, Protocol 1. This concerns the right of a natural or legal person to enjoy his possessions. This argument was raised and succeeded in a Scotland, but it has not been tested in England and Wales.

A Practical Guide to Construction Adjudication, First Edition. James Pickavance.
© 2016 James Pickavance. Published 2016 by John Wiley & Sons, Inc.

18.2 Fraud or deceit

[18.06] In the context of adjudication, fraud or deceit may be considered in two respects: first, whether it can be used as a basis for a claim or defence in the adjudication, and second, whether it can be used as a defence to an application for the enforcement of an adjudicator's decision.

[18.07] As to the first, it is unclear whether a claiming party can refer a claim to adjudication based on the tort of fraud or deceit, since such a claim does not arise 'under' the contract.[1] However, fraud or deceit can be raised as a defence to a claim in adjudication, provided that it is a real defence to whatever the claims are. Furthermore, it is open to parties in adjudication to argue that the other party's witnesses are not credible by reason of fraudulent or dishonest behaviour, albeit that as a result of there being no requirement for witnesses to sign statements of truth, there will be no recourse available against the witnesses themselves.

[18.08] The maxim 'fraud unravels all'[2] was thought to apply to the enforcement of adjudicator's decisions as it does in litigation or arbitration. Thus, in *Pro-Design Limited v New Millennium Experience Company Limited*[3] a lighting subcontractor sought to enforce an adjudicator's decision against a main contractor. It was alleged in the enforcement proceedings that the claimant was a fraudulent vehicle, being a company owned and operated by an employee of the defendant. The court refused to grant summary judgment for the claimant on the basis of the adjudicator's award. In *Andrew Wallace Limited v Artisan Regeneration Limited*[4] the claimant sought to enforce an adjudicator's award that the claimant should be paid architectural fees of £128,845. The defendants, who had employed the claimant, advanced several lines of defence including allegations of fraud. Kirkham J rejected the allegations as untenable. She added that the court's enforcement of the decision would not constitute assistance in the perpetration of a fraud. The facts upon which the fraud allegation was based emerged after the date of the adjudication. However, the judge concluded that on the evidence the defendant had no real prospect of establishing its allegation of fraud.

[18.09] However, the position now appears to be that while it is perfectly legitimate to raise the defence of fraud or deceit in adjudication enforcement proceedings, whether the defence will succeed is dependent on (a) clear and unambiguous evidence in support, which is needed in order to satisfy the 'real prospect of success' test for summary judgment;[5] and (b) demonstrating that the fraudulent behaviour, acts or omissions could not reasonably have been raised during the adjudication.[6]

---

[1] *SG South Limited v Kings Head Cirencester LLP* [2009] EWHC 2645, per Akenhead J at [19].
[2] *Pearson v Dublin Corporation* [1907] AC 351.
[3] [2001] Adj L.R. 09/26, per Mackay J at [6–11].
[4] [2006] EWHC 15 (TCC), per Kirkham J at [44–52].
[5] See Section 13.3.2.
[6] *Speymill Contracts Ltd v Eric Baskind* [2010] EWCA Civ 120, per Jackson LJ at [36].

[18.10] In *SG South Limited v Kings Head Cirencester LLP*[7] the defendant employer raised allegations of fraud in adjudication proceedings. The defendant failed to establish any factual basis for his allegations. Akenhead J summarised the legal position as follows:

> Some basic propositions can properly be formulated in the context albeit only of adjudication decision enforcements:
>
> (a) Fraud or deceit can be raised as a defence in adjudications provided that it is a real defence to whatever the claims are; obviously, it is open to parties in adjudication to argue that the other party's witnesses are not credible by reason of fraudulent or dishonest behaviour.
>
> (b) If fraud is to be raised in an effort to avoid enforcement or to support an application to stay execution of the enforcement judgment, it must be supported by clear and unambiguous evidence and argument.
>
> (c) A distinction has to be made between fraudulent behaviour, acts or omissions which were or could have been raised as a defence in the adjudication and such behaviour, acts or omissions which neither were nor could reasonably have been raised but which emerge afterwards. In the former case, if the behaviour, acts or omissions are in effect adjudicated upon, the decision without more is enforceable. In the latter case, it is possible that it can be raised but generally not in the former.

[18.11] The reality is that this test will make it difficult to raise fraud or deceit for the first time in enforcement proceedings and therefore defendants should ensure that if there are such arguments available, they are deployed during the adjudication.

[18.12] A question that remains unanswered is the extent of knowledge to be attributed to the defendant at the time of the adjudication such that it could or could not have raised the defence. Thus, in *Andrew Wallace*, the defendant argued that the fraudulent manuscript amendments to the contract were not picked up before enforcement because of a change of personnel. Is this an oversight that (applying the test in *SG South*) could reasonably have been identified and deployed during the adjudication? Kirkham J did deal not with the question in that way, choosing instead to focus on whether the defendant had met the test for summary judgment. It is suggested this remains an area still to be settled.

18.3 Duress

[18.13] The defence of duress is another reason why the court may decline to enforce an adjudicator's award. In *Capital Structures plc v Time & Tide Construction Ltd*,[8] the judge recited the ingredients of actual duress, which are that:

> there must be pressure (a) whose practical effect is that there is compulsion on or a lack of practical choice for the victim; (b) which is illegitimate; and (c) which is a significant cause in

---

[7] [2009] EWHC 2645, per Akenhead J at [20].
[8] [2006] EWHC 591, per Wilcox J at [16–30].

inducing the claimant to enter into the contract. See Universe Tankships Inc. of Monrovia v. International Transport Workers Federation 1983 AC 366,400 b-L and Dimskol Shipping 6 S.A v. ITWF 1992 AC 152, 165G.

[18.14] Where duress is found, the contract is voidable, which means that if proper steps are taken to avoid the agreement from which the adjudicator's jurisdiction derives, the adjudicator has no jurisdiction in an adjudication.

[18.15] The judge prefaced his decision in *Capital Structures* by saying that 'imaginative and strange interpretation of facts and events arising in the commercial rough and tumble of the construction industry should not be allowed to found weak challenges of the adjudicator's jurisdiction.' However, on the facts of this case, he could see that there was an arguable case, 'albeit shadowy' as to economic duress.

18.4 UTCCR

[18.16] Where a seller or supplier[9] wishes to use standard contract terms with a consumer[10] and the parties wish to incorporate adjudication provisions into the contract, it is necessary to have regard to the regulations set out in the UTCCR. The UTCCR aims to ensure that whenever a consumer enters into a contract to buy goods or services from a company, the terms on which that contract is made are not unfair to the consumer.

[18.17] Often this arrangement will occur in relation to domestic residential works. In those circumstances, the Act will not apply[11] and so unless the agreement between the parties contains an adjudication procedure, the parties will be unable to adjudicate any disputes. However, notwithstanding its exclusion from the Act, often one or both of the parties will want to incorporate adjudication provisions into the Act, or the standard form contract that the parties agree will already contain adjudication provisions, such as the JCT 1998 forms.

[18.18] Where there are such adjudication provisions, it has been argued on behalf of the consumer that such provisions breach Regulation 5 of the UTCCR. This holds that contractual terms shall be regarded as 'unfair' if, contrary to the requirements of good faith, they create a significant imbalance in the parties' rights and obligations arising under the contract, to the detriment of the consumer. The assessment of fairness is prescribed at Regulation 6, examples of unfairness are contained at Schedule 2 and the consequences of an unfair term, which include that the term is not binding on the consumer, are set out at Regulation 8.

[18.19] Although there are cases that have been decided in favour of, and against, upholding an adjudicator's decision made pursuant to an agreement similar to the one outlined in the foregoing paragraphs, generally the courts have found that the adjudication provisions

---

[9] Any natural person acting for purposes relating to his trade, business or profession.
[10] A natural person who is acting outside his trade, business or profession.
[11] These are excluded by section 106.

do not fall foul of the Regulations. Factors to consider when determining whether or not adjudication provisions are fair include whether:

- they have been imposed on the consumer in circumstances which justify the conclusion that the supplier has fallen short of the requirements of fair dealing;[12]
- they were specifically brought to the attention of the consumer;[13]
- they created a 'significant imbalance' to the parties' rights and obligations contrary to the requirements of good faith;[14]
- the adjudication terms are couched in plain and intelligible language;[15]
- the consumer was provided with competent and objective advice as to the meaning of the provisions;[16] and
- the provisions do not significantly exclude or hinder the consumer's right to take legal action or other legal remedy or restrict the evidence available to him.[17]

18.5 Human Rights Act

[18.20] The Human Rights Act 1998 (the **HRA**) is a statute that, in its words, gives 'further effect to rights and freedoms guaranteed under the European Convention on Human Rights'.[18] Put another way, it enshrines into legislature certain fundamental rights and freedoms that individuals domiciled in the UK have access to.

[18.21] In England and Wales, the argument has been advanced that the adjudication system as a whole is flawed because it falls foul of Article 6 of the HRA. The complaint is that the statutory requirement that the adjudicator shall reach a decision within 28 days is manifestly unfair and is particularly unfair when the only liberty given to the adjudicator to extend that time is a liberty to extend the time by 14 days but only with the consent of the party by whom the dispute was referred. Further, the adjudication is not a public forum. Article 6(1) of the HRA requires that:

> In the determination of his civil rights and obligations or of any criminal charge against him, everyone is entitled to a fair and public hearing within a reasonable time by an independent and impartial tribunal established by law. Judgment shall be pronounced publicly but the press and public may be excluded from all or part of the trial in the interest of morals, public order or national security in a democratic society, where the interests of juveniles or the protection of the private life of the parties so require, or to the extent strictly necessary in the opinion of the court in special circumstances where publicity would prejudice the interests of justice.

---

[12] See regulation 5(ii) and *Bryen & Langley Ltd v Martin Boston* [2005] EWCA Civ 973, per Rimer LJ at [39-47].
[13] *Picardi v Cuniberti & Cuniberti* [2002] EWHC 2923 (TCC), per Toulmin J at [127].
[14] *Bryen & Langley Ltd v Martin Rodney Boston* [2004] EWHC 2450, per Seymour J at [37].
[15] *Westminster Building Co Ltd v Beckingham* [2004] EWHC 138 (TCC), per Thornton J at [31].
[16] *Director General of Fair Trading v First National Bank plc* [2001] UKHL 52, per Bingham LJ at [p. 494].
[17] *Lovell Projects Ltd v Legg & Carver* [2003] 1 BLR 452, per Moseley J, at [27].
[18] Introductory text to the HRA.

[18.22] The court analysed the position in detail in *Austin Hall Building Ltd v Buckland Securities Ltd* and held[19] that the system of adjudication does not breach the requirements of adjudication. While a number of points were considered, three are addressed here. The first is that an adjudicator acting under the Act is not a public authority and is therefore not bound by the HRA. Second, even assuming that the adjudicator is a public authority and that the HRA (in particular Article 6(1)) applies to his conduct, it is covered by subsection 6(2) of the HRA, which states:

> Subsection (1) does not apply to an act if as the result of one or more provisions of primary legislation, the authority could not have acted differently.

[18.23] Thus, in order to comply with the 28-day time limit provided by statute, the adjudicator could not have acted differently in imposing the time limits that he imposed on the parties. Third, the court concluded that adjudication proceedings were not legal proceedings and did not result in a judgment that, without further procedural steps, could be enforced. Further reason as to why Article 6 does not apply is that adjudication proceedings are only provisional and therefore do not finally determine the parties' rights.[20]

[18.24] There is another argument that has been advanced in Scotland, namely that, in certain circumstances, an adjudicator's decision should not be enforced because of Article 1, Protocol 1 of the HRA. This is addressed at Section 19.4.10.

---

[19] [2001] BLR 272, per Bowsher J at [13–48].
[20] *Elanay Contracts v The Vestry* [2001] BLR 33, per Havery J at [16–17].

Chapter 19
Scotland: Tony Jones[1]

19.1 Overview

[19.01] The Treaty of Union in 1707 created the political union that is Great Britain and merged both the Scottish and English Parliaments to create a new Westminster Parliament endowed with exclusive legislative competence over Great Britain. From that point on, as a general rule,[2] primary legislation created by that Parliament applied in Scotland, just as it did in England and Wales. However, such primary legislation could and often did have different dates upon which it came into force. Often provisions, in so far as they related to Scotland, were commenced by virtue of separate UK statutory instrument. A further change arrived with the Scotland Act 1998, which established the Scottish Parliament as a devolved legislature. The result is that in specifically devolved areas the power to legislate is under the control of the Scottish Parliament. Furthermore the Scottish Parliament can, even in the context of UK-wide legislation, have control over the statutory instrument that brings acts of the Westminster Parliament into force and control over the content[3] and enactment of delegated legislation. As a result, the date when acts come into force and the content and coming into force of statutory instruments sometimes differ between England and Wales and Scotland. Statutory adjudication is one example of this.

[19.02] Part II of the 1996 Act was brought into operation in Scotland on 1 May 1998.[4] The 1998 Scheme was introduced in Scotland by the Scheme for Construction Contracts (Scotland) Regulations 1998 (the **1998 Scottish Scheme**)[5] and came into operation in Scotland on the same day as Part II of the 1996 Act. There are a number of material differences

---

[1] Tony Jones is a solicitor advocate and head of commercial dispute resolution at Brechin Tindal Oatts, in Edinburgh. Tony was assisted by Emma Harris and Garry Borland QC. Emma Harris is a construction specialist based in Scotland. Garry Borland's practice spans commercial contracts, commercial property, company law and insolvency, construction and engineering and energy.
[2] The position is in fact rather more complicated than this general rule belies, but for present purposes it is unnecessary to explore this further.
[3] In so far as the content is consistent with the primary legislation.
[4] SI 1998 No. 894, Housing Grants Construction and Regeneration Act 1996 (Scotland) (Commencement No. 5) Order 1998. http://www.legislation.gov.uk/uksi/1998/894/made. Accessed 1 September 2015.
[5] SI 1998/687. http://www.legislation.gov.uk/uksi/1998/687/contents/made. Accessed 1 September 2015.

A Practical Guide to Construction Adjudication, First Edition. James Pickavance.
© 2016 James Pickavance. Published 2016 by John Wiley & Sons, Inc.

between the 1998 Scottish Scheme and the 1998 Scheme, which are highlighted in this chapter.

[19.03] Part 8 of the 2009 Act was brought into force in Scotland by the Local Democracy, Economic Development and Construction Act 2009 (Commencement No. 2) (Scotland) Order 2011.[6] Amendments to the 1998 Scottish Scheme were introduced by the Scheme for Construction Contracts (Scotland) Amendments Regulations 2011 (the **2011 Scottish Scheme**).[7] Again, the 2011 Scottish Scheme is different from the 2011 Scheme. In Scotland, the effective date for the 2009 Act and the 2011 Scottish Scheme is 1 November 2011,[8] one month after the effective date in England and Wales. In this chapter, when referring to a paragraph of the relevant scheme, where there is a difference between the paragraph in the 1998 Scottish Scheme and the 2011 Scottish Scheme, they will be distinguished and referred to accordingly. Where the paragraph is the same, the reference shall be to the 'Scottish Scheme'.

[19.04] It was guaranteed by the Treaty of Union in 1707 that, amongst other things, Scotland would retain its laws, customs and courts and consequently Scotland is and always has been a distinct legal jurisdiction from England and Wales. Scots law owes much to civil or Roman law but is sometimes viewed as a hybrid, or 'mixed', legal system as it draws upon both civil law and common law elements. Whilst the consequences of Union, including the right of appeal in civil cases to the House of Lords, exerted great common law influences upon Scots law, and continues to do so, the Scottish legal system remains different in a great many respects from the English system. In the context of adjudication, this means that sometimes the Scottish courts have interpreted the statutory adjudication rules and procedures in different ways from the English courts.[9] Furthermore, if one requires to use Scottish Courts the court rules and procedures that one must follow – for example, to enforce the award of an adjudicator – are quite different as between the two countries.

[19.05] Therefore, it is thought appropriate to highlight and describe the key differences between the applicable legislation and the courts' interpretation of that legislation in England and Wales, on the one hand, and in Scotland, on the other. In that regard, this chapter will divide into the following sections.

(1) Differences between the Scheme and the Scottish Scheme.
(2) Enforcement of an adjudicator's award. In particular:

---

[6]SSI 2011 No. 291. http://www.legislation.gov.uk/ssi/2011/291/made. Accessed 1 September 2015.
[7]SSI 2011 No. 371. http://www.legislation.gov.uk/ssi/2011/371/contents/made. Accessed 1 September 2015.
[8]SSI 2011 No. 291, Local Democracy, Economic Development and Construction Act 2009 (Commencement No. 2) (Scotland) Order 2011. http://www.legislation.gov.uk/ssi/2011/291/made. Accessed 1 September 2015.
[9]Efforts have been made to minimise such divergence where possible, in order to avoid confusion among end users. See for instance *Improving Adjudication in the Construction Industry: a Consultation Document January 13, 2003*. http://www.scotland.gov.uk/Publications/2003/01/16130/16352. However, notwithstanding these efforts, differences still exist and further divergences materialise each year. It is submitted that this is the inevitable and unavoidable consequence of two legal systems.

- enforcement procedure;
- counterclaims;
- the Scottish courts' approach to jurisdictional challenges;
- the Scottish courts' approach to natural justice challenges; and
- miscellaneous points.

(3) Issues of divergence between England and Wales and Scotland. In particular:
- failure to comply with subsection 108(1)–(4) of the Act;
- adjudicator's decision out of time;
- parties' costs under the 1996 Act;
- insolvency;
- approbation and reprobation;
- abuse of process;
- the adjudicator taking advice from a third party or using his own knowledge; and
- the Human Rights Act.

[19.06] Where a party is faced with an adjudication in Scotland, regard should be had to the rules, procedures, explanation and guidance offered in Chapters 1–17, except on the matters addressed in this chapter. Where the reader wishes to identify the cases relevant to a particular topic within this chapter, check the equivalent section within Chapters 1–17 and then the appropriate section in Appendix 8.

19.2 Differences between the Scheme and the Scottish Scheme

19.2.1 1998 Scheme and 1998 Scottish Scheme

[19.07] The 1998 Scottish Scheme differs from the 1998 Scheme at paragraphs:

(1) 9(4) – payment of fees where the adjudicator resigns
(2) 11(1) – revoking the adjudicator's appointment
(3) 20 – the adjudicator making a decision
(4) 24 – section 42 of the Arbitration Act
(5) 25 – payment of the adjudicator's fees

[19.08] In each of the following sections, the relevant provisions are quoted and shown as amended from the 1998 Scheme. The shaded grey denotes deleted text and the double underlined text denotes added text.

(A) Subparagraph 9(4)

[19.09] Paragraph 9 concerns the entitlement of the adjudicator to resign at any time (9(1)); the requirement to resign where the decision is the same or substantially the same as one which has previously been referred to adjudication and a decision has been taken in that adjudication (9(2)); the appointment of a new adjudicator in such circumstances (9(3)); and the adjudicator's entitlement to payment of his fees and expenses if he resigns for the reason set out in subparagraph 9(2) (9(4)). It is this last subparagraph that is different. As amended from the 1998 Scheme, it reads as follows:

> Where an adjudicator resigns in the circumstances <u>mentioned</u> referred to in paragraph (2), or where a dispute varies significantly from the dispute referred to him in the referral notice and for that reason he is not competent to decide it, that adjudicator's shall be entitled to the payment of such reasonable amount as he may determine by way of fees and expenses reasonably incurred by him. The parties shall be jointly and severally liable for any sum which remains outstanding following the making of any determination on how the payment shall be apportioned <u>shall be determined and payable in accordance with paragraph 25.</u>

[19.10] The changes appear to make no material difference to the meaning of subparagraph 9(4). The subject matter of paragraph 9 of the 1998 Scheme is considered in more detail at Sections 7.4 and 10.7.11.

(B) Subparagraph 11(1)

[19.11] Subparagraph 11(1) concerns the entitlement of the parties to revoke the appointment of the adjudicator. The 1998 Scheme and the 1998 Scottish Scheme differ as follows:

> The parties to a dispute may at any time agree to revoke the appointment of the adjudicator. The adjudicator shall be entitled to the payment of such reasonable amount as he may determine by way of fees and expenses incurred by him. The parties shall be jointly and severally liable for any sum which remains outstanding following the making of any determination on how the payment shall be apportioned <u>and in such circumstances the fees and expenses of that adjudicator shall, subject to subparagraph (2), be determined and payable in accordance with paragraph 25.</u>

[19.12] As with subparagraph 9(4), when paragraph 11(1) of the 1998 Scottish Scheme is considered, the changes make no material difference. The subject matter referred to in paragraph 11 of the 1998 Scheme is considered further at Section 9.6.16.

(C) Paragraph 20

[19.13] This paragraph concerns the duty on the adjudicator to decide the matters in dispute and the scope of what matters he may take into account when so deciding. The paragraph has been amended as follows:

> (1) The adjudicator shall decide the matters in dispute <u>and may make a decision on different aspects of the dispute at different times.</u>
> (2) He may take into account any other matters which the parties to the dispute agree should be within the scope of the adjudication or which are matters under the contract which he considers are necessarily connected with the dispute…

[19.14] The introduction of the wording at subparagraph (1) appears to be consistent with the view that a single dispute may comprise a number of parts, and with the adjudicator's power in paragraph 13 to decide on the procedure to be followed in the adjudication. Whether the dispute referred to adjudication is categorised as one or more than one dispute is debated at Section 7.3. Paragraph 20 of the 1998 Scheme is considered further at Sections 10.7.7 and 10.7.8.

(D) Paragraph 24

[19.15] Paragraph 24 provides that section 42 of the Arbitration Act 1996 shall apply to the 1998 Scheme subject to certain amendments. This paragraph does not appear in the 1998 Scottish Scheme, but is instead replaced with the following:

> Where a party or the adjudicator wishes to register the decision for execution in the Books of Council and Session, any other party shall, on being requested to do so, forthwith consent to such registration by subscribing the decision before a witness.

[19.16] An explanation of this paragraph is provided at Section 19.3.6(B) below.

(E) Paragraph 25

[19.17] Paragraph 25 concerns the right of the adjudicator to receive reasonable remuneration. As compared to the 1998 Scheme, it reads as follows:

> (1) The adjudicator shall be entitled to the payment of such reasonable amount as he may determine by way of fees and expenses incurred by him and the parties shall be jointly and severally liable for any sum which remains outstanding following the making of any determination on how the payment shall be apportioned to pay that amount to the adjudicator.
> (2) Without prejudice to the right of the adjudicator to effect recovery from any party in accordance with subparagraph (1), the adjudicator may by direction determine the apportionment between the parties of liability for his fees and expenses.

[19.18] The slightly different text in the 1998 Scottish Scheme does not appear to materially affect the principal content and meaning in this context, which can be taken from paragraph 25 of the 1998 Scheme. Paragraph 25 of the 1998 Scheme is considered further at Section 12.2.

19.2.2 2011 Scheme and 2011 Scottish Scheme

[19.19] By virtue of the 2011 Scottish Scheme no amendments were made to paragraphs 1 to 21 of Part I of the 1998 Scottish Scheme. This was in contrast to the changes made in England and Wales to the 2011 Scheme. Thus, there was in Scotland no amendment to refer to time running from the date of receipt of the referral[10] and also no amendments to subparagraphs 9(4) and 11(1) to take account of section 108A of the Act which concerns

---

[10] See Section 10.2.3.

pre-allocation of costs.[11] However, subparagraph 25(2) of the 1998 Scottish Scheme is amended by the 2011 Scottish Scheme as follows:

> (2) Without prejudice to the right of the adjudicator to effect recovery from any party in accordance with subparagraph (1), the adjudicator may determine the apportionment between the parties of liability for the payment of his fees and expenses <u>and such determination shall be binding upon the parties unless any effective contractual provision in terms of section 108A(2)(4) of the Act applies.</u>

[19.20] This amendment has the same effect as the amendments to subparagraphs 9(4), 11(1) and paragraph 25 of the 1998 Scheme made by the 2011 Scheme.

[19.21] A new paragraph 22A is inserted into the 1998 Scottish Scheme by the 2011 Scottish Scheme (as it was England), enshrining the 'slip rule' into legislation. The new paragraph 22A provides:

> (1) The adjudicator may on his own initiative or on the request of a party correct his decision so as to remove a clerical or typographical error arising by accident or omission.
> (2) Any correction of a decision shall be made within 5 days of the date upon which adjudicator's decision was delivered to the parties.
> (3) Any correction of a decision shall form part of a decision.

[19.22] However, the Scottish version of the slip rule differs from that applicable in England in that there is no reference to the adjudicator delivering his corrected decision to the parties as soon as possible, as there is in the 2011 Scheme.

19.3 Enforcement of an adjudicator's award

19.3.1 In a nutshell

[19.23] The TCC Court Guide includes at section 9 an expedited procedure for enforcement of adjudicators' decisions. The settled position in England is that so long as the adjudicator acts within his jurisdiction, asks himself the correct question and complies with the rules of natural justice, then the decision will be enforced, even if it is wrong in fact or in law. The English courts take a robust approach to enforcing a party's contractual and statutory right to be paid sums awarded by an adjudicator and only in the most exceptional of cases will they delve into the underlying merits of the claim.

[19.24] Although the basic principles behind enforcing the decision of an adjudicator are the same in Scotland as they are in England, the rules concerning the commencement of court proceedings and the procedure for enforcement are completely different. There is also another method of enforcing a decision, namely by registering an adjudicator's

---

[11] See Section 12.3.2.

decision in the Books of Council and Session. Finally, a party may challenge the adjudicator's decision by a process known as judicial review.

19.3.2 Enforcement procedure

[19.25] In Scotland, an adjudicator's decision is normally enforced by raising a Commercial Court action (or 'commercial action') in the Court of Session.[12] Raising the action as a commercial action allows the party seeking enforcement to invoke the quicker and less procedurally formal process offered by the Commercial Court – as compared to so-called 'ordinary actions'. The procedure is under the control of a Lord Ordinary (the commercial judge) who will take a proactive approach to case management with a view to ensuring the resolution of the case in an expedited manner.

[19.26] In a commercial action in the Court of Session, the initiating writ is called a summons. Unlike in an ordinary action, the pleadings in a commercial action are usually in a relatively abbreviated form, giving notice of the parties to the action, the orders sought and the essential elements of the case. In an adjudication enforcement case, the key elements of the case to be addressed will be: the contractual arrangements from which the dispute emerged; what the dispute was; the reference to adjudication; the adjudicator's decision; and the fact that, in the normal case, payment has not been made in accordance with the adjudicator's decision. The key documents in the adjudication process, together with the adjudicator's decision, are also normally referred to in the court pleadings. In that connection, there must be appended to the summons a schedule listing any documents initially founded on or adopted as incorporated in the pleadings.[13] Detailed averments are not generally required in the summons.

[19.27] Once drafted, the summons is lodged for signetting. This is the process whereby the court authorises service of the summons, and this step is normally a formality. A commercial action registration form (Form CA1) must also be completed, lodged in process,[14] and a copy served with the summons. The registration form identifies the parties, the nature of the case and the pursuer's legal advisers, including proposed counsel.

[19.28] There is a 21-day period of notice after service of the summons before the action can be lodged for calling.[15] However, a motion can be lodged at court at the same time as the summons, requesting that the court reduce this 21-day period. In adjudication enforcement actions, the normal practice is for the pursuer[16] to seek to have the period reduced

---

[12] On the coming into force of the Courts Reform (Scotland) Act 2014, section 39(1), the jurisdiction of the Court of Session in this context will relate to claims for payment in excess of £100,000. On the 2014 Act coming into force, claims below that level will have to be raised in the Sheriff Court. The procedure in the Sheriff Court is not considered here. However new procedural rules are in the process of being drafted for both the Court of Session and Sheriff Courts and an aim of that exercise is to minimise differences.
[13] See the Rules of the Court of Session 1994 ('RCS'), r 47.3(3). Cf RCS, r 27.1(1)(a), which requires such documents to be lodged as productions when the summons is lodged for calling.
[14] This is, in essence, the file held by the court, comprising all the papers relevant to the case.
[15] Calling is the procedural step which brings the action formally into court following service.
[16] In other words, the claimant.

to seven days. While there is strictly speaking no guarantee that such an application will be granted, the relevant period is now almost invariably reduced by the court to seven days in keeping with the policy of expediting adjudication enforcement proceedings.

[19.29] A defender has three days from the date the action is lodged for calling to enter appearance in the proceedings.[17] Defences must be lodged within seven days after the summons is lodged for calling.[18] There must be appended to the defences a schedule listing any documents initially founded on or adopted as incorporated in them.[19] Any such documents must be lodged at the time the defences are lodged. Like the summons, defences should normally be relatively brief and should set out the key grounds (and their basis) on which enforcement is resisted. The defender must complete a Form CA1 and lodge it in process, or complete the process copy, with the relevant information required of a defender.

[19.30] After defences have been lodged, a preliminary hearing before the court will normally be fixed within 14 days.[20] At the preliminary hearing there should be a discussion of the key issues in the case and of the steps required to resolve them. In advance of the preliminary hearing, the parties should lodge a document setting out briefly the issues which they contend require judicial determination. If possible, that document should be a joint list of issues agreed by the parties.

[19.31] It is open to the commercial judge at the preliminary hearing to allow the parties an opportunity to adjust their respective pleadings. The period for adjustment must be made out by reference to the circumstances of the case. In an adjudication enforcement case, the court will normally wish any adjustment period to be short: no more than a few weeks for each party at the most. Where adjustment is allowed, it is normally carried out by revising an electronic copy of the summons or defences or other document, intimating the revised copy to the other party, and thereafter lodging the revised copy with the court. Where adjustment is carried out on more than one occasion, successive sets of adjustments should be differentiated from the original pleadings and any earlier adjustments.

[19.32] The commercial judge may continue the preliminary hearing, fix a date for a procedural hearing (to determine further substantive procedure) or simply allocate a date for a substantive hearing to determine the case.

[19.33] In the normal course of events, the pursuer, who is seeking enforcement of the adjudicator's decision, should enrol a motion for summary decree.[21] An application for summary decree is in essence the equivalent to an application for summary judgment in England and Wales. This is the usual procedural vehicle in the Court of Session by which a pursuer will seek the enforcement of an adjudicator's decision. The

---

[17] See RCS, r 17.1. By entering appearance, the defender intimates his involvement in the action. Entering appearance does not imply acceptance of the jurisdiction of the court: RCS, r 17.2.
[18] RCS, r 18.1(2).
[19] RCS, r 47.6(2).
[20] RCS, r 47.8(2).
[21] Refer to RCS, chapter 21, for the summary decree procedure.

date and time when the summary decree motion will be heard falls to be fixed by the judge, having heard parties' counsel.[22] The pursuer may, at any time during the dependence of an action after defences have been lodged, apply for summary decree 'on the ground that there is no defence to the action, or a part of it, disclosed in the defences.'[23]

[19.34] An application for summary decree may take a number of forms, one of which is a motion 'to grant decree in terms of all or any of the conclusions of the summons.'[24] The court may grant summary decree 'if satisfied that there is no defence to the action disclosed.'[25]

[19.35] The test for summary decree was definitively addressed by the House of Lords in *Henderson v 3052775 Nova Scotia Limited*.[26] The basic test which the court must apply is to ask whether if it is satisfied, first, that there is no issue raised in the defences or other documents available to the court which can only properly be resolved at proof (trial) and, second, that, on the asserted facts that have been clarified in this way, the defender has no defence to all, or any part, of the action. In other words, the judge must be satisfied that the defender's defence must fail.

[19.36] The alternative to proceeding by way of summary decree motion would be for the case to proceed to a legal debate hearing,[27] either with or without a procedural hearing beforehand. At a debate hearing, the parties can argue whether they have a proper legal basis for their respective legal positions. In the context of adjudication enforcement, there is in essence little substantive difference, in terms of the format of the hearing, between a summary decree application and a debate.

[19.37] Since a judge is not normally concerned with the underlying merits of an adjudicator's decision, a proof (or trial) is very rarely fixed. Only in exceptional circumstances, where there is a relevant dispute in relation to the underlying facts, would a proof be ordered.[28]

19.3.3 Counterclaims

[19.38] In a commercial action, if a defender wishes to lodge a counterclaim, it requires the leave of the court.[29] When deciding whether to allow a counterclaim to be lodged, 'a commercial judge will wish to consider, amongst other things, the impact of such additional

---

[22] RCS, r 47.8(1).
[23] RCS, r 21.2(1).
[24] RCS, r 21.2 (2)(a). The conclusions are the section of the pleadings where the pursuer identifies the orders it seeks from the court. The conclusions are the equivalent of the relief section of English pleadings.
[25] RCS, r 21.2(4)(a).
[26] 2006 SC (HL) 85, per Lord Rodger of Earlsferry at [19].
[27] A debate is similar to a hearing of preliminary issues in England.
[28] An example, relating to allegations of breach of the rules of natural justice, is *Ardmore Construction Limited v Taylor Woodrow Construction Limited*, [2006] CSOH 3.
[29] RCS, r 47.7.

procedure upon the efficient determination of the main action.'[30] It is very rare indeed for leave to be granted to lodge a counterclaim in an adjudication enforcement action.

[19.39]   One case where it was allowed was *Whyte and Mackay Limited v Blyth & Blyth Consulting Engineers Limited*.[31] Lord Malcolm acknowledged that the court had a discretion to refuse leave for the counterclaim to be lodged, but decided in the somewhat special circumstances of the case that leave could be granted without disrupting determination of the enforcement element of the case. But it must be emphasised that it will likely only be in the most special circumstances that the court will grant such leave in an adjudication case.

19.3.4 The Scottish courts' approach to jurisdictional challenges

[19.40]   In *Carillion Construction Limited v Devonport Royal Dockyard Limited*,[32] Jackson J stated at first instance that the courts should be astute to examine technical defences with a degree of scepticism consonant with the policy of the Act – that policy being that an adjudicator's decision should generally be enforced.

[19.41]   On appeal,[33] the Court of Appeal accepted that statement of principle and added:

> The objective which underlies the Act and the statutory scheme requires the courts to respect and enforce the adjudicator's decision unless it is plain that the question which he has decided was not the question referred to him or the manner in which he has gone about his task is obviously unfair. It should be only in rare circumstances that the courts will interfere with the decision of an adjudicator. The courts should give no encouragement to the approach adopted by [the appellant] in the present case; which ... may, indeed, aptly be described as 'simply scrabbling around to find some argument, however tenuous, to resist payment'.

[19.42]   That approach has been followed in Scotland in cases such as *Atholl Developments (Slackbuie) Limited, petitioner*,[34] where Lord Glennie said:

> Where the Adjudicator has exceeded his jurisdiction, or failed to exhaust his jurisdiction, or where there has been a breach of natural justice, the court will interfere, but it will only do so in the plainest of cases.

[19.43]   In *SW Global Resourcing Limited v Morris and Spottiswood Limited*,[35] Lord Hodge stated that the court is 'hostile' to technical arguments put up by defenders with a view to resisting enforcement of adjudicators' decisions.

---

[30] Macfadyen et al, *Court of Session Practice*, at F3 [433].
[31] *Whyte and Mackay Limited v Blyth & Blyth Consulting Engineers Limited* [2012] CSOH 89.
[32] [2005] EWHC 778 (TCC), per Jackson J at [80].
[33] [2005] EWCA Civ 1358, per Chadwick LJ at [85].
[34] [2010] CSOH 94, per Lord Glennie at [17]. See also at *RBG Limited v SGL Carbon Fibres Limited* [2010] CSOH 77, per Lord Menzies at [28].
[35] [2012] CSOH 200, per Lord Hodge at [34].

[19.44] This approach has been strongly endorsed at an appellate level in Scotland. An Extra Division of the Inner House[36] of the Court of Session, in the case of *Charles Henshaw & Sons Limited v Stewart & Shields Limited*,[37] specifically stated[38] that it will only be in the plainest of cases that the court will uphold a challenge to an adjudicator's decision based on a submission that he exceeded his jurisdiction. Moreover, the Scottish appellate courts have also made it clear that provided an adjudicator has answered the question put to him, his decision is not reviewable by the court on the ground that he answered the question incorrectly – whether as a matter of law or on the basis of the facts.[39]

[19.45] Three further points should be noted. The first is that in Scotland the scope of the adjudication is defined by the relevant notice of adjudication together with any ground founded upon by the responding party to justify its position in defence of the claim made.[40]

[19.46] The second, and related, point is that if a responding party in adjudication proceedings raises a line of defence to a claim made against it, the adjudicator must deal with it and cannot ignore it.[41] If he does not deal with such a line of defence, the adjudicator may be regarded as having failed to exhaust his jurisdiction, rendering his decision invalid.

[19.47] The third point is that the reasons given by an adjudicator for his decision must make sense to a reasonable reader. If they do not, the court may conclude that his decision is not supported by any reasons at all, and on that basis the decision may be rendered invalid.[42]

19.3.5 The Scottish courts' approach to natural justice challenges

[19.48] The seminal Scottish case on the subject of natural justice in construction adjudication is *Costain Limited v Strathclyde Builders Limited*,[43] where Lord Drummond Young examined this area of law in detail. The overriding principle, he said, is that in adjudication proceedings each party must be given a fair opportunity to meet the case being made against it and to present its own case. He also observed that a challenge based on a breach of the rules of natural justice might succeed in Scotland if the party making the challenge can demonstrate that there was merely a possibility that the breach caused injustice. It might be thought therefore that the threshold to be overcome in Scotland is lower than in England, where the test is that the breach of natural justice is material.[44]

---

[36] The Scottish equivalent to the Court of Appeal in England.
[37] [2014] CSIH 55.
[38] See Lady Smith, giving the opinion of the court, at [4] and [17].
[39] *Gillies Ramsay Diamond, petitioners*, 2004 SC 430, per the Lord Justice Clerk (Gill) at [38–41].
[40] *Construction Centre Group Limited v Highland Council*, 2002 SLT 1274, per Lord Macfadyen at [19]. Cf *Pilon Limited v Breyer Group plc*, [2010] EWHC 837 (TCC), per Coulson J at [25–26].
[41] *Connaught Partnerships Limited v Perth & Kinross Council*, [2013] CSOH 149, per Lord Malcolm at [19].
[42] *Gillies Ramsay Diamond*, supra, at [31]; *Connaught Partnerships*, supra, at [21]; and *Miller Construction (UK) Limited v Building Design Partnership Limited*, [2014] CSOH 80, per Lord Malcolm at [4].
[43] 2004 SLT 102, per Lord Drummond Young at [20–24].
[44] See Section 17.1.2.

[19.49] However, the Scottish appellate courts[45] have stressed that, as with jurisdictional challenges, it will only be in very limited cases, where there is a clear and consequential breach of natural justice, that the court will refuse to enforce an adjudicator's decision.

19.3.6 Miscellaneous points

(A) Judicial review

[19.50] In Scotland, where the unsuccessful party wishes to challenge the decision of the adjudicator on the grounds that the adjudicator exceeded his jurisdiction or was guilty of some form of misconduct, then an application for judicial review can be made.[46] In this way, the losing party in an adjudication can take the imitative, and seek to have the adjudicator's decision struck down by the court.[47]

(B) Registering a decision

[19.51] Paragraph 24 of the 1998 Scottish Scheme provides:

> Where a party or the adjudicator wishes to register the decision for execution in the Books of Council and Session, any other party shall, on being requested to do so, forthwith consent to such registration by subscribing the decision before a witness.

[19.52] The Books of Council and Session are a court register[48] for the registering of documents whereby, providing the consent of the parties is given, the document can in some circumstances become the equivalent of a court decree. An official extract of the document must be obtained so that recovery of the debt can take place, if necessary, on the basis of the document.

[19.53] Paragraph 24 may superficially seem of more utility than the 'usual' method of enforcement because there is no need to commence proceedings in the court to enforce the adjudicator's decision. However, where the agreement of the parties is not obtained in advance of the decision (in the contract, adjudication procedure or by the parties during the adjudication), it is unlikely that the losing party would agree to register the decision after the event. Paragraph 24 requires the parties to consent on request, but that does not mean that the other party is forced to accede to the request (and furthermore failure to accede to such a request will not be taken as deemed acceptance). If the successful party

---

[45] See *Charles Henshaw & Sons Limited*, supra, per Lady Smith at [17].
[46] The appropriateness of this as a way of enforcing an adjudicator's decision was debated in *Vaughan Engineering Ltd v Hinkins & Frewin Ltd* 2003 SLT 428, per Lord Clarke at [31–35]. For the applicable court rules, see RCS, chapter 58.
[47] See, for example, *Atholl Developments (Slackbuie) Limited*, supra; cf *W H Malcolm Limited, petitioner*, [2010] CSOH 152.
[48] Register of Deeds (which is nowadays maintained by the Keeper of the Registers of Scotland) was and is still usually cited as 'The Books of Council and Session'.

wishes to enforce the award via this route, it will be necessary to seek an order from the court ordaining the relevant party to sign a consent to registration. If the debt is disputed, it would be incumbent on the party from which payment is sought to seek suspension or interdict of any steps taken to enforce the debt.

[19.54] This route for enforcement is very rarely followed in place of the quicker, more reliable methods of enforcement, via the courts, as outlined above.

19.4 Issues of divergence between England and Wales and Scotland

19.4.1 In a nutshell

[19.55] In the main, the approach to construction adjudication by the Scottish and English judiciaries is broadly aligned. However, there are some areas where there are divergences. When adjudicating in Scotland, it is therefore important to be aware of what these differences are. This section addresses the following topics:

(1) failure to comply with subsections 108(1)–(4) of the Act
(2) adjudicator's decision out of time
(3) parties' costs under the 1996 Act
(4) insolvency
(5) approbation and reprobation
(6) the size and nature of the claim
(7) abuse of process
(8) advice from a third party or use of his own knowledge
(9) the Human Rights Act.

19.4.2 Failure to comply with subsections 108(1)–(4) of the Act

[19.56] In England and Wales, where the contract is one to which the Act applies and the contract contains an adjudication procedure, it must replicate subsections 108(1)–(4) of the Act. If it does not, the rules will be replaced wholesale by those of the 1998 Scheme or the 2011 Scheme. The position has been underlined in a number of court decisions[49] and is addressed in further detail at Section 6.2.2.

[19.57] In Scotland, the position may be different. In *Profile Projects Limited v Elmwood (Glasgow) Limited*,[50] Lord Menzies concluded that an adjudication could be governed partly by the express provisions of the relevant contract and partly by the terms implied by the relevant statutory Scheme. His Lordship arrived at this conclusion by placing emphasis on section 114(4) of the Act.

---

[49] See Regulation 2 of the Scheme and, for example, *Sprunt Ltd v London Borough of Camden* [2011] EWHC 3191 (TCC), per Akenhead J at [28–31] and *Yuanda (UK) Co Limited v WW Gear Construction Ltd* [2010] EWHC 720 (TCC), per Edwards-Stuart J at [55–65].
[50] *Profile Projects Limited v Elmwood (Glasgow) Limited* [2011] CSOH 64, per Lord Menzies at [47–50]. See also *Ballast plc v The Burrell Company (Construction Management) Limited* 2001 SLT 1039; and *Hills Electrical and Mechanical plc v Dawn Construction Limited* 2004 SLT 477.

[19.58] Lord Menzies rejected the perceived difficulty that a 'mixed' form of adjudication procedure (part contract, part Scheme) would be a recipe for confusion and chaos.

19.4.3 Adjudicator's decision out of time

[19.59] The Act and the 1998 Scottish Scheme require that the adjudicator's decision must be reached within 28 days of receipt of the referral by the adjudicator, or such longer period as may be determined by either one or both parties (depending on the length of the extension required). In England and Wales, a distinction is drawn between reaching the decision and communicating it. In *Lee v Chartered Properties (Building) Limited*,[51] Akenhead J considered that decisions reached within time, but communicated after that period, will be valid, provided it can be shown they were delivered forthwith. This is considered further at Section 11.4.

[19.60] However, the position in Scotland is arguably stricter. The leading authority on time limits is *Ritchie Brothers (PWC) Limited v David Phillip (Commercials) Limited*.[52] The majority decision of the Inner House was that the 1998 Scottish Scheme's time limit provisions, in compliance with the Act, were mandatory, providing 'a clear time limit that leaves all parties knowing where they stand.'[53]

[19.61] A distinction was mooted, in argument by the pursuer's counsel, between the time limit for reaching a decision and the time limit for communicating it. The Lord Justice Clerk (Gill) declined to express a view on whether a decision reached within the relevant time limit, but communicated out of time, would remain valid because that was not the issue before the court.[54] It is unclear therefore whether the Scottish court would invalidate or uphold an adjudicator's decision that was made timeously but which was communicated out of time. However, the safest course for an adjudicator is obviously to reach his decision and communicate it within the statutory time limit.

19.4.4 Parties' costs under the 1996 Act

[19.62] In England, for contracts subject to the 1996 Act any agreement before the adjudication commences as to the allocation of parties' costs, save for references which permit the adjudicator to allocate costs, is likely to be ineffective. In *Bridgeway Construction Limited v Tolent Construction Limited*[55] Mackay J upheld the validity of a contract term which required the party serving the notice of adjudication to bear all the costs and expenses incurred by both parties in relation to the adjudication. That included all the

---

[51] *Lee v Chartered Properties (Building) Ltd* [2010] EWHC 1540 (TCC), per Akenhead J at [29–32].
[52] *Ritchie Brothers (PWC) Limited v David Phillip (Commercials) Limited* [2005] CSIH 32. This is another case to which the adjudication provisions of the Scottish equivalent of the Scheme applied.
[53] *Ritchie Brothers (PWC) Limited*, supra, at [14].
[54] Lord Justice Clerk at [22], the facts of *Ritchie* were distinguishable from the English case of *Barnes & Elliot Limited v Taylor Woodrow Holdings* [2003] EWHC 3100 (TCC), where the decision was reached in time, but communicated out of time.
[55] *Bridgeway Construction Limited v Tolent Construction Limited* [2000] CILL 1662, per Mackay J at [28–36].

legal costs and fees of experts. However, in *Yuanda (UK) Limited v WW Gear Construction Limited*,[56] Edwards-Stuart J held that a clause which rendered a contractor who made a reference to adjudication 'fully responsible for meeting and paying both his own and the Employer's legal and professional costs in relation to the Adjudication' was in conflict with the requirements of section 108 of Act. That was because its effect was to inhibit the right to refer a dispute to adjudication 'at any time'. This judgment has subsequently been followed by the English courts numerous times.

[19.63] The same issues in *Yuanda* were considered by Lord Menzies in the Scottish case of *Profile Projects Limited v Elmwood (Glasgow) Limited*.[57] Lord Menzies had to decide whether the term which required the referring party to pay the whole costs of the adjudication was compatible with the Act. Lord Menzies agreed with the decision in *Tolent* for two principal reasons, namely:

(1) it did not contradict any express or implied provision in the Act; and.
(2) the parties in *Profile Projects v Elmwood* might have been discouraged from referring a dispute to adjudication, but it could not be said that they had been disabled from doing so. According to Lord Menzies[58], it was only if a contractual term actually disabled a party from adjudicating that it would be in conflict with the terms of subsection 108(2)(a) of the Act.

[19.64] Thus, for contracts subject to the 1996 Act, the position in Scotland would appear to be that 'Tolent' type clauses are permitted. However, for contracts subject to the 2009 Act, such clauses are now probably prohibited by virtue of section 108A. Section 12.3 addresses the topic of pre-allocation of party costs in more detail.

19.4.5 Insolvency

[19.65] The courts in England have not, as a general rule, enforced the decision of an adjudicator in favour of a contractor which is demonstrably insolvent and unable to repay the sums to be paid in the event of further proceedings. In cases in which there is a probability, or at least a significant risk, that a contractor will be unable to repay the sum which the adjudicator had ordered to be paid, the court has exercised its discretion to grant summary judgment and then impose a stay of execution. Sections 14.2 and 14.3 address these points further.

[19.66] The balancing of accounts is a Scottish principle of law which requires the court to take account of any counterclaim or cross-claim in circumstances where a party seeking payment is insolvent. It is an equitable principle so that the court can regulate its operation to ensure fairness. The principle of balancing of accounts on bankruptcy is available not

---

[56] *Yuanda (UK) Co Limited v WW Gear Construction Limited* [2010] EWHC 720 (TCC), per Edwards-Stuart J at [43 and 51].
[57] *Profile Projects Limited v Elmwood (Glasgow) Limited* [2011] CSOH 64, per Lord Menzies, at [40–42].
[58] At [39–42].

only on bankruptcy or liquidation, but also when the party is on the verge of insolvency. It is noteworthy that there is no equivalent English concept to the balancing of accounts when a party is merely verging on insolvency.[59]

[19.67] The defence of balancing of accounts in bankruptcy can be deployed in Scotland against a claim to enforce an adjudicator's decision and, if successful, will mean that the adjudicator's decision will not be enforced or that it will be enforced subject to a stay of execution. The leading case is *Integrated Building Services Engineering Consultants Limited t/a Operon v PIHL UK Ltd*,[60] where the court held that the principle may be applied when an administrator is appointed to a company by the court under section 8 of the Insolvency Act 1986 as the inability or likely inability to pay its debts is a precondition of the administration order. Similarly, if the company itself or the holder of a floating charge appoints an administrator under Schedule B1 to the 1986 Act, the principle can be applied if there is sufficient prima facie evidence of insolvency. The basic reason for this is that if a creditor were unable to assert the principle of balancing accounts in bankruptcy in an insolvent administration, unfairness could result.

[19.68] The court in *Integrated* held that the Act does not exclude the principle of balancing of accounts in bankruptcy.[61] Nor will the court confine its application to circumstances in which it was pleaded before the adjudicator. It is available as a defence when the claimant seeks to enforce the adjudicator's decision in court proceedings – albeit it must be pled by the defender in that context. The entitlement to plead the principle arises from the pursuer's insolvency. The obligation to pay the sum due under the adjudicator's decision is a contractual obligation to implement the result of the provisional dispute resolution procedure. But that obligation does not supersede the right to assert the balancing of accounts principle on the claimant's insolvency. The decision in *Integrated* has subsequently been followed.[62]

[19.69] Thus, the result achieved by the Scottish principle is similar to that in England. It is simply achieved by different means.

[19.70] However, the limitations of the principle of balancing of accounts in the context of construction adjudication must be understood. It is very doubtful that allegations of insolvency, if seriously contested, would justify the application of the principle.[63] Hence it may be very difficult to apply the principle when a party's insolvency is not demonstrated by a formal legal act or process.[64] The Scottish courts will therefore be wary about refusing enforcement in the absence of clear or uncontested insolvency.[65] Even the uncontested

---

[59] *Straw Realisations (No. 1) Limited v Shaftsbury House (Developments) Limited*, per Edwards-Stuart J at [76 to 85]. In England and Wales, the Insolvency Rules only apply if one party is insolvent within the meaning of the Insolvency Acts.
[60] [2010] CSOH 80, per Lord Hodge at [22–30].
[61] See Lord Hodge's opinion at [28–30].
[62] See *Connaught Partnerships Limited (in administration) v Perth & Kinross Council* [2013] CSOH 149.
[63] *Integrated*, supra, at [28].
[64] *Integrated*, supra, at [34].
[65] *J&A Construction (Scotland) Limited v Windex Limited*, [2013] CSOH 170, per Lord Malcolm at [7].

fact that the party seeking enforcement is 'balance sheet insolvent' may not be sufficient to prevent the adjudicator's decision being enforced.[66]

19.4.6 Approbation and reprobation

[19.71] In English law, where a party adopts a particular position or acts in a certain way, but then later acts in a way which contradicts its original position or act, the party is said to be approbating and reprobating. Where this occurs, provided that the other party has acted on the basis of the original adoption or act, the later contradiction will serve to extinguish the original adoption or act, such that the first party can no longer rely on it.[67] This topic is addressed in further detail at Section 16.4.6.

[19.72] The doctrine of approbation and reprobation was initially developed in the area of wills, trusts and succession, albeit it has over the years found wider application. In the context of construction adjudication, the Scottish commercial court was persuaded to adopt and apply an approbate and reprobate analysis in the case of *Redding Park Development Company Limited v Falkirk Council*.[68]. On that basis, a party that had by its conduct indicated that it accepted the validity of an adjudicator's determination could not thereafter seek to argue that it was invalid.

19.4.7 The size and nature of the claim

[19.73] In England, the general position is that if the adjudicator accepts the appointment, accepts that a decision can be reached within the timescale afforded and proceeds to a decision, that decision will not be found to be in breach of the rules of natural justice.

[19.74] If at any point the adjudicator decides that he is unable to deal with the material within that timescale, he should ask the parties for an extension of time. If one is not granted, or it is not granted in full, the appropriate action is to resign. If the adjudicator does not do so but carries on to issue a decision, there is a real risk that the courts will hold that there has been a breach of natural justice.

[19.75] A recent case in Scotland has found that, in certain circumstances, the court will refuse to enforce an adjudicator's decision because of the size and nature of the claim. In *Whyte and Mackay Ltd v Blyth and Blyth Consulting Engineers Ltd*,[69] a claim in damages for professional negligence was intimated several years after completion of the building contract. The dispute was referred to adjudication and the adjudicator awarded the pursuers £3 million. The defenders resisted the application to enforce on the grounds that, due to the size and nature of the claim, it was unsuitable for adjudication and/or would be a

---

[66] *J&A Construction (Scotland) Limited*, supra.
[67] *PT Building Services Ltd v Rok Build Limited* [2008] EWHC 3434 (TCC), per Ramsey J at [58].
[68] *Redding Park Development Company Limited v Falkirk Council* [2011] CSOH 202, per Lord Menzies at [54–62]. See also *Highland and Islands Airports Limited v Shetland Islands Council*, supra, per Lord Menzies at [54–60].
[69] *Whyte and Mackay Limited v Blyth & Blyth Consulting Engineers Limited* [2012] CSOH 89, per Lord Malcolm at [36–47].

breach of Articles 1 and 6 of the First Protocol of the European Convention on Human Rights.

[19.76] As to the size and nature of the claim, Lord Malcolm failed to see how the adjudicator could have hoped to resolve it within the time available and without an inquiry into the full circumstances of the project. He said that to do so would involve evidence from key witnesses and appropriate submissions on the evidence and the law. The judge noted that while the summary enforcement procedure is in place to ensure swift enforcement of adjudicator's decisions, it is also there to ensure that adjudicators' decisions that ought not to be enforced, are not enforced. In this case, the court held that proceeding to adjudication in this case was unnecessary and inappropriate, and that the enforcement proceedings ought to be used to refuse enforcement of the decision. This was because the adjudicator was presented with a next-to-impossible task which even a judge would have struggled to deal with in six weeks given the complex issues of fact and law arising between the parties. He formed the conclusion that it would, in view of the defenders' Article 1 rights, be disproportionate and wrong to enforce the award.

[19.77] Thus, in certain circumstances, it would appear that where the size and nature of the claim places a draconian, unassailable burden on the adjudicator and he proceeds to a decision, that decision may be unenforceable.

19.4.8 Abuse of process

[19.78] Abuse of process has been explained as 'using [a] process for a purpose or in a way significantly different from its ordinary and proper use'.[70] While abuse of process is a familiar concept in litigation, despite repeated attempts, the English courts have never restrained an adjudication or overturned an adjudicator's decision on this basis. Abuse of process is considered further at Section 17.5.3.

[19.79] In Scotland, abuse of process was considered in the context of an application for an interim interdict[71] in *T Clarke (Scotland) Limited v MMAXX Underfloor Heating Limited*.[72] Against the background of the defender having raised multiple adjudications, the pursuer sought an interim interdict to restrain the defender from referring to adjudication any further disputes arising out of the same contract. In refusing to grant the pursuer an interdict, Lord Woolman noted[73] that a court would only deprive a party of the express right to adjudicate conferred by Parliament 'in the most exceptional circumstances'. While he did not say that the court would never make such an order, he indicated that 'it will hardly ever do so'.[74] The judge also observed that in circumstances where a party vexatiously pursued adjudication proceedings, it was open to the other party

---

[70] *Attorney General v Barker* [2000] 1 F.L.R. 759 at [19].
[71] Interdict is the Scottish equivalent of an injunction in England.
[72] *T Clarke (Scotland) Limited v MMAX Underfloor Heating Limited* [2014] CSOH 62.
[73] See his opinion at [17].
[74] *T Clarke (Scotland) Limited v MMAX Underfloor Heating Ltd* [2014] CSOH 62, per Lord Woolman at [17].

to commence an action for damages for abuse of process.[75] Lord Woolman's decision was upheld on appeal.[76] An Extra Division of the Inner House of the Court of Session laid particular emphasis on the fact that the pursuer was not just seeking to prevent the defender from persisting in a particular adjudication which had been embarked upon in bad faith or on an untruthful basis. Rather, the pursuer was seeking to prohibit the defender from referring **any** future dispute to adjudication, whether it was well vouched and brought on a legitimate basis. To allow that would be a 'drastic curtailment' of the defender's rights.[77] Curtailing the defender's rights in that way simply could not be justified in the circumstances of the case.

19.4.9 The adjudicator taking advice from a third party or using his own knowledge

[19.80] In England, where an adjudicator seeks advice from a third party and does not advise the parties and/or permit them the opportunity to comment on any material or opinion the third party provides, the decision that he provides is unlikely to be enforced[78] where the failure by the adjudicator is of material consequence.[79]

[19.81] In Scotland, the same basic position applies. However, the rule requiring disclosure of the advice would seem to extend to situations where third-party advice was informally received.[80] Furthermore, it may extend not only to the requirement to provide the advice to the parties for comment, but also to informing the parties what advice was sought, which may entail sharing the instructions given to the third party.[81]

[19.82] Equally, if an adjudicator intends to use his own knowledge and experience to add to the evidence led by the parties (or to fill the gaps in it), it is incumbent upon him to provide the parties with a full explanation of his intended approach, the nature of the experience he brings to bear which is relevant to the particular matters at issue, and the conclusions of fact or law to which that experience drives him, all in sufficient detail and at a time which enables them to comment sensibly and on an informed basis. The imminence of the final date for reaching a decision is not an excuse for not providing adequate time for comment.[82]

[19.83] The approach of the Scottish courts in the present context was usefully summarised by Lord Hodge in *Carillion Utility Services Limited v SP Power Systems Limited*,[83] where he said:

---

[75] *T Clarke (Scotland) Limited v MMAX Underfloor Heating Ltd* [2014] CSOH 62, per Lord Woolman at [23].
[76] [2014] CSIH 83.
[77] Lord Bracadale, giving the opinion of the court, at [35].
[78] *Highlands and Islands Airports Limited*, supra, per Menzies L at [31–34].
[79] *Balfour Beatty Construction Limited v The Mayor & Burgesses of the London Borough of Lambeth* [2002] EWHC 597 (TCC), per Lloyd J at [41].
[80] *Highlands and Islands Airports Limited*, supra, per Lord Menzies at [31–34].
[81] *Costain Limited*, supra, per Lord Drummond Young at [23–27].
[82] *SGL Carbon Fibres Limited v RGB Limited* [2011] CSOH 62, per Lord Glennie at [30–31].
[83] [2011] CSOH 139, per Lord Hodge at [25].

while the courts have warned parties against raising technical arguments and searching for breaches of natural justice to challenge an adjudicator's decision, the judges in the cases, to which I have referred, have been consistent in their approach. They have required an adjudicator to disclose to the parties information, which he has obtained from his own experience or from sources other than the parties' submissions, if that information is material to the decision which he intended to make. Whether the information is of sufficient potential importance to the decision is a question of degree which must be assessed on the facts of the particular case.

[19.84] Thus, the adjudicator should ask himself whether the relevant information is of potential importance for his decision. If there is any significant doubt about the matter, it should be presumed to be material and should be disclosed.[84]

19.4.10 Human Rights Act

[19.85] In England and Wales, the only basis on which a defence has been raised that an adjudicator's decision should not be enforced by virtue of the Human Rights Act 1998 (HRA) is, specifically, under reference to article 6 of the European Convention on Human Rights (ECHR). The latter provides the right to 'a fair and public hearing'. The courts have concluded that statutory adjudication does not conflict with this right.[85]

[19.86] Another argument that has been advanced in Scotland, far more recently than the first, is that in certain circumstances an adjudicator's decision should not be enforced because of article 1 of the first protocol to the ECHR (A1P1). The article reads as follows:

> (1) Every natural or legal person is entitled to the peaceful enjoyment of his possessions. No one shall be deprived of his possessions except in the public interest and subject to the conditions provided for by law and by the general principles of international law.
> (2) The preceding provisions shall not, however, in any way impair the right of a State to enforce such laws as it deems necessary to control the use of property in accordance with the general interest or to secure the payment of taxes or other contributions or penalties.

[19.87] The argument was raised in the Scottish case of *Whyte & Mackay Limited v Blyth & Blyth Consulting Engineers Limited*.[86] The pursuer sought to enforce an adjudicator's decision which required the defender to pay £3 million. The sums claimed principally related to defective foundations in a bottling plant leased by the pursuer. The circumstances were unusual in that, on the adjudicator's finding, the pursuer would not be out of pocket for some 20 years because the foundations were – for the time being – performing adequately. It was only when the lease expired and the pursuer required to return the plant to the lessor that it would be necessary to pay sums to rectify the foundations. Until then, only relatively modest sums would need to be expended by way of inspection of certain remedial works. Effectively, the adjudicator awarded the pursuer a fund in respect of

---

[84] See the approach of Lord Menzies in *Highland and Islands Airports Limited*, supra, at [33].
[85] See Section 18.5 for more detail. A similar argument was mounted in *Whyte & Mackay Limited v Blyth & Blyth Consulting Engineers Limited* [2013] CSOH 54, where it was rejected: per Lord Malcolm at [55–65].
[86] Supra, per Lord Malcolm at [37–54].

works it might have to carry out in 20 years' time. In these circumstances, the defender argued that to enforce the adjudicator's award would amount to a breach, inter alia, of A1P1.

[19.88] The court took the view that its power to refuse enforcement can provide a long stop safeguard if and when ECHR rights are violated.[87] The court was prepared to assume, for the purposes of that case, that enforcement would amount to an interference with the defender's entitlement to peaceful enjoyment of their possessions (i.e. its money) and the issue arising was whether such interference was justified.[88]

[19.89] Ultimately, the court took the view that it was unnecessary and inappropriate to proceed to adjudication in this case and that to enforce the award would result in an unfair and excessive burden being placed upon the defender.

[19.90] The Court of Appeal in England and Wales has since commented[89] on the case in such a way as to highlight that the case was based on a very unusual set of facts. In a well-argued paper written for the Society of Construction Law by Andrew Bartlett QC,[90] it was asserted that Lord Malcolm's decision is supported on the following bases.

(1) The inability to refer such a dispute to adjudication is not at odds with the statutory right to refer disputes to adjudication 'at any time'.[91]
(2) On the facts of the case, there was no public policy reason for interfering with the right to peaceful enjoyment of possessions, and given the court's discretion as whether to enforce an adjudicator's decision, in such a case it should not do so.
(3) Statutory adjudication was intended to ensure cash flow on projects, but it was not intended for a case such as this, where the claimant did not need a quick answer and swift access to funds.

---

[87] Supra, at [39].
[88] Supra, at [42].
[89] *Lindum Group Limited v Fernie and another* [2014] EWCA Civ 124. In *Bouygues E&S Contracting UK Ltd v Vital Energi Utilities Ltd* [2014] CSOH 115 Lord Malcolm himself commented that his intervention in Whyte & Mackay sprang from the adjudicator having "completely ignored a relevant line of defence" at [7].
[90] *The Limits of Adjudication: The Impact of the European Convention on Human Rights*. Paper Number D175, Society of Construction Law. December 2014.
[91] Subsection 108(2)(a) of the Act.

Chapter 20
Northern Ireland: Michael Humphreys QC[1]

20.1 Overview

[20.01] The partition of Ireland established Northern Ireland as a separate jurisdiction within the United Kingdom in 1921, following the coming into force of the Government of Ireland Act 1920. That act established the Northern Ireland Parliament which was the body responsible for the passing of legislation for Northern Ireland.

[20.02] In 1972, the Northern Ireland Parliament was prorogued by the Northern Ireland (Temporary Provisions) Act 1972, and legislative responsibility passed to the Secretary of State for Northern Ireland. This responsibility was exercised by Orders in Councils. In 1998, the Northern Ireland Act 1998 established the Northern Ireland Assembly which took over responsibility for legislation save for excepted and reserved matters. This responsibility was exercised in the form of primary acts.[2]

[20.03] Accordingly, the Northern Ireland Parliament introduced the Construction Contracts (Northern Ireland) Order 1997 (the **Order**)[3] and is the instrument through which the 1996 Act is enacted in Northern Ireland. It was brought into operation on 1 June 1999.[4] The changes to the 1996 Act were introduced by the Northern Ireland Assembly through the Construction Contracts (Amendment) Act (Northern Ireland) 2011 (the **2011 Act**)[5] and came into force in Northern Ireland on 14 November 2012.[6]

[20.04] There are no material differences between the English and Northern Irish legislation. Sections 104 to 107 of the 1996 Act concerning the scope of the 1996 Act are replicated

---

[1] Michael Humphreys QC was educated at Brasenose College, Oxford. He was called to the Bar of Northern Ireland in 1994 and took Silk in 2011. Michael practises in commercial law, specialising particularly in construction and public procurement. He is the Chair of the Commercial Bar Association and a member of the Commercial Court Liaison Committee.
[2] The legislative framework is more complicated than this, but it is unnecessary to explain this further.
[3] SI 1997 No. 274 (NI 1). *http://www.legislation.gov.uk/nisi/1997/274/contents*. Accessed 1 September 2015.
[4] SI 1999 No. 34 (C.4). *http://www.legislation.gov.uk/nisr/1999/34/contents/made*. Accessed 1 September 2015.
[5] *http://www.legislation.gov.uk/nia/2011/4/contents*. Accessed 1 September 2015.
[6] SI 2012 No. 367 (C. 34). The Construction Contracts (2011 Act) (Commencement) Order (Northern Ireland) 2012. *http://www.legislation.gov.uk/nisr/2012/367/introduction/made*. Accessed 1 September 2015.

A Practical Guide to Construction Adjudication, First Edition. James Pickavance.
© 2016 James Pickavance. Published 2016 by John Wiley & Sons, Inc.

in articles 3 to 6 of the 1997 Order; the right to refer disputes to adjudication enshrined by section 108 of the 1996 Act is found in article 7 of the Northern Irish legislation and section 114 and article 13 enable the making of the Scheme regulations. The amendments introduced in the Local Democracy, Economic Development and Construction Act 2009 which, inter alia, removed the requirement for the construction contract to be in writing in order to trigger the right to refer a dispute to adjudication, were effected in Northern Ireland by the 2011 Act.

[20.05] The 1998 Scheme was introduced in Northern Ireland by the Scheme for Construction Contracts in Northern Ireland Regulations (Northern Ireland) 1999 and came into operation on 1 June 1999.[7] The amendments to the 1998 Scheme were introduced by the Scheme for Construction Contracts in Northern Ireland (Amendment) Regulations (Northern Ireland) 2012 and came into operation on 14 November 2012.[8] As with the primary legislation, the secondary legislation is the same in England and Northern Ireland.

[20.06] It is estimated that there are around 100 construction adjudications per annum in Northern Ireland. The vast majority of these are final account claims advanced by subcontractors against main contractors. It is comparatively rare for disputes which arise during the currency of the contract to be referred to adjudication in this jurisdiction. The reasons for this may be twofold: first, a subcontractor does not want to harm relations by instigating formal dispute resolution procedures while work is ongoing and second, the prohibition against recovery of costs (unless the parties consent to the adjudicator making a costs award) acts as a disincentive to make referrals when only modest sums can be recovered. It therefore makes economic sense for one single referral to be made at the end of the contract works.

[20.07] It is striking that while statutory adjudication came into being in Northern Ireland in 1999, there are no reported judgments on the enforcement of adjudicators' awards until 2008. There may be a number of reasons for this. First, practitioners may have been unaware of, or unfamiliar with, the particular requirements of the adjudication regime. Second, most disputes may ultimately have settled either by acceptance of the adjudicator's decision or further agreement. Third, in keeping with most summonses under Order 14, applications for summary judgment were initially heard by Masters in the Queen's Bench Division, rather than being referred to the Commercial Judge for determination.

[20.08] It was not until January 2009, when the then Commercial Judge, McLaughlin J, delivered judgment in *D G Williamson v Northern Ireland Prison Service*[9] that the High Court gave detailed consideration to the questions surrounding enforcement of adjudicators' awards. The defendant in that action, seeking to resist enforcement of the award,

---

[7] SI 1999 No. 32. http://www.legislation.gov.uk/nisr/1999/32/contents/made. Accessed 1 September 2015.
[8] SI 2012 No. 365.
[9] (2009) NIQB 8.

advanced a number of arguments based on the claimed want of jurisdiction of the adjudicator and the existence of a substantial set-off against the plaintiff's claim. McLaughlin J cited with approval a number of the leading English authorities, including *Macob Civil Engineering v Morrison Construction*[10] and *Carillion Construction v Devonport Royal Dock Yard*,[11] and commented:

> I am satisfied that the starting point for a court dealing with a request for enforcement of the award of an Adjudicator is that it should work on the assumption that the award ought to be enforced, on a summary basis if necessary. The purpose of the legislation is to ensure speedy payment by dint of a summary process and, even where there is an error, to require the money to be paid and for the matter to be sorted out later when the contract disputes are settled finally by way of agreement, arbitration or litigation. I do not need to review at this stage the history of the legislation and the valiant attempts made to improve cash flow and payment practices in the construction industry. In this context it is worthy of note that the 1997 Order, and the 1996 Act, both outlaw the practice of 'pay when paid' clauses which were frequently operated by main contractors to withhold payments from sub-contractors where they had not themselves been paid. The essential ground upon which the defendants object to paying the award of the adjudicator, once the jurisdictional issues are set to the side, is that they have a large Counterclaim. That Counterclaim remains subject to proof. It may be accurately stated in the affidavits, or it may be under or overstated. The purpose of the arbitration is to find out what sum, if any, is due by way of restitution to the defendants. I am satisfied that process should take its own course and that there are no cogent reasons put before me which justify the court in refusing to follow the normal practice of enforcing the award of the adjudicator pending authoritative determination of all remaining disputes between the contracting parties.

[20.09] Since this judgment, the courts in Northern Ireland have seen an increase in the number of claims to enforce adjudicators' awards and, in the majority, the courts have so enforced.

[20.10] This chapter will address the procedures for enforcing an adjudicator's award in Northern Ireland and summarise the few reported cases that have been subject to that process. Where a party is faced with an adjudication in Northern Ireland, regard should be had to the rules, procedures, explanation and guidance offered in Chapters 1 to 17 above, except on matters of enforcement procedure and the topics addressed in the cases highlighted. Where the reader wishes to identify the reported cases relevant to a particular topic within this chapter, regard should be had to the equivalent section within Chapters 1 to 17 and then the appropriate section in Appendix 8.

20.2 Enforcement of adjudicators' awards

[20.11] If the statutory scheme is to provide an effective and expeditious route to ensure cash flow in the construction industry, it is essential that awards made by adjudicators are capable of enforcement through the Courts.

---

[10] (1999) BLR 93.
[11] (2005) EWCA Civ 1358.

20.2.1 The writ of summons

[20.12] Proceedings in the High Court of Justice to enforce an adjudicator's award are commenced by writ of summons issued in the Queen's Bench Division. Given that a summary judgment application under Order 14 of the Rules of the Court of Judicature (Northern Ireland) 1980 ('RCJ (NI) 1980') cannot be commenced unless and until a statement of claim has been served, it is standard practice to endorse the writ of summons with the statement of claim.

[20.13] If interest is sought, whether pursuant to contract, the Late Payment of Commercial Debts (Interest) Act 1998 or the court's discretion under section 33A of the Judicature (Northern Ireland) Act 1978, it is mandatory that the writ be endorsed with:

(1) the rate of interest claimed;
(2) the date from which interest is payable
(3) the amount of interest claimed to the date of the writ of summons;
(4) the claim for interest to date of judgment or sooner payment.[12]

[20.14] Any writ of summons seeking to enforce an award of an adjudicator must also be endorsed with the following words:

> In the opinion of the Plaintiff's Solicitor, this is a commercial action.

[20.15] There is no Technology & Construction Court in Northern Ireland. Instead, such actions come within the ambit of 'commercial actions', which are dealt with in a Commercial List within the Queen's Bench Division, under the control of the Commercial Judge, currently Mr Justice Weatherup. The provisions for entry into the List and case management are contained within Order 72 of the RCJ (NI) 1980 the Commercial List Practice Direction,[13] the Practice Note and the Pre-Action Protocol for Commercial Actions.[14]

[20.16] Order 72 rule 1(2) states:

> In this Order 'commercial actions' shall include any cause relating to business or commercial transactions and, without prejudice to the generality of the foregoing words, any cause relating to contracts for works of building or engineering construction, contracts of engagement of architects, engineers or quantity surveyors, the sale of goods, insurance, banking, the export or import of merchandise, shipping and other mercantile matters, agency, bailment, carriage of goods and such other causes as the Commercial Judge may think fit to enter in the Commercial List.

[20.17] Any action that seeks to enforce the award of an adjudicator arising out of a construction contract is therefore a commercial action. By virtue of Order 72 rule 3(1) it is mandatory for a plaintiff's solicitor, on the commencement of proceedings in a commercial action,

---

[12] Order 6, rule 2A-2D.
[13] 1/2000.
[14] Both issued on 21 December 2012, with effect from 1 January 2013.

to endorse this fact on the writ of summons and thereby seek entry into the Commercial List.

[20.18] The Practice Note envisages most interlocutory applications in Commercial Actions being determined by a Master of the High Court but the Practice Note specifically states:

> Applications for summary judgment on an Adjudicator's award under the Constructions Contracts (NI) Order 1997 as amended shall be made to the Commercial Judge.

[20.19] The Pre-Action Protocol for Commercial Actions requires parties to exchange detailed correspondence and engage in a meeting prior to the issue of proceedings. However, there is no obligation to comply with the Protocol when the proceedings:

> are for the enforcement of the decision of an Adjudicator to whom a dispute has been referred pursuant to the Construction Contracts (NI) Order 1997, as amended, or relate to the same or substantially the same issues as have been the subject of recent Adjudication under the Construction Contracts (NI) Order 1997, as amended, or some other formal alternative dispute resolution procedure.

[20.20] The Protocol provisions are excluded since they are perceived to be incompatible with the expedition provided by adjudication in general.

20.2.2 The application for summary judgment

[20.21] As a result of these various procedural measures, applications for summary judgment to enforce adjudicators' awards are now made to the Commercial Judge and dealt with by him under an expedited procedure.

[20.22] Order 14 of the RCJ (NI) 1980 lays down the procedure for applications for summary judgment. This provides that in any case where a statement of claim has been served, and a defendant has entered an appearance, a plaintiff may seek summary judgment on the grounds that the defendant has no defence to a claim, or part of a claim.

[20.23] Order 14 rule 2 requires the application to be made by summons, supported by a grounding affidavit verifying the facts upon which the claim is made, and stating that in the deponent's belief there is no defence to the claim. The grounding affidavit will generally set out the background to the dispute and exhibit the adjudicator's award. The defendant will be afforded an opportunity to file a replying affidavit which will set out the substance of any claim of want of jurisdiction or denial of natural justice or, frequently, the evidence relied upon to substantiate a claim that the plaintiff will be unable to repay the amount of the award at the ultimate end of the dispute resolution process. This will often necessitate a rejoinder affidavit from the plaintiff responding to the issues raised by the defendant.

[20.24] Once the summary judgment application has been filed, the court will swiftly list the case for directions. The target set by the court is to hear and determine such applications within 28 days of issue. The standard timetable permits:

(1) 10 days for the plaintiff to file its affidavit evidence;
(2) 10 days for the defendant to respond;
(3) a hearing date within 28 days.

[20.25] The court will also give directions as to the filing and exchange of skeleton arguments on any legal issues arising.

[20.26] Speaking extra-judicially, Weatherup J has commented:

> If the statutory scheme is to require the Adjudicator to make his decision within 28 days then the Court should attempt a timetable that permits any dispute on the Adjudicator's decision to be heard within the same period.[15]

[20.27] One important exception to the procedure is contained in Order 77 rule 5 of the RCJ (NI) 1980, whereby summary judgment is not available against the Crown. In the Northern Ireland context, Crown status extends to each of the departments of the devolved administration as well as the Northern Ireland Office. Importantly, the Northern Ireland Housing Executive is not a Crown body and is therefore subject to the summary judgment procedure. In order to circumvent this procedural difficulty, the plaintiff in *DG Williamson v Northern Ireland Prison Service*[16] pursued declaratory relief against the defendant on the basis that the Crown would comply with any declaration made by the court. It was agreed by the parties that the court could proceed to an expedited hearing of the trial of the action.

20.2.3 The hearing of the application

[20.28] While the court enjoys a power under Order 14 rule 4(3)(b) to order that a deponent attend to be examined on oath, such power is rarely exercised, and the hearing is conducted on the basis of the affidavit evidence, the skeleton arguments and submissions made by each party.

[20.29] At the hearing of such an application, if the court is satisfied that there is an issue or question in dispute which ought to be tried or there ought to be a trial for some other reason, then it may either dismiss the summons or give the defendant leave to defend with or without conditions and then give further directions as to the trial of the action.

[20.30] If judgment is entered in favour of the plaintiff on foot of a summary judgment application, the defendant may appeal as of right to the Court of Appeal.[17] If the application is dismissed, the plaintiff may only appeal with the leave of the judge or the Court of Appeal since such a decision is interlocutory, not final. If the defendant is given unconditional leave to defend, no party may appeal.[18]

---

[15] Address to the British & Irish Commercial Bar Association on 18 June 2014.
[16] (2009) NIQB 8.
[17] Judicature (NI) Act 1978, subsection 35(3).
[18] Subsection 35(2)(c).

20.2.4 Incidence of costs

[20.31] Under section 59 of the Judicature (NI) Act 1978 the court enjoys a discretion as to costs which is exercised within well-settled general principles. Order 62, rule 3 of the RCJ (NI) 1980 lays down some general rules:

> (1) Costs cannot be recovered without an Order of the court.
> (2) If the court sees fit to make any order as to costs, it shall order that costs follow the event except where it appears to the court that in the circumstances of the case some other order should be made as to the whole or any part of the costs.
> (3) The amount of costs which any party is entitled to recover is the amount allowed after taxation on the standard basis unless it appears to the court to be appropriate to order costs to be taxed on an indemnity basis.

[20.32] If a plaintiff succeeds on an Order 14 application for summary judgment, it will be entitled to its costs unless some exceptional circumstances apply. It is worth noting that under Order 62 rule 17(3) and Appendix 3 Part I of the RCJ (NI) 1980, very modest scale costs are payable on such an application unless the court otherwise orders. At the conclusion of a hearing therefore, the judge should be asked to order that costs are taxed in default of agreement, thereby disapplying rule 17(3).

20.2.5 Taxation of costs

[20.33] In a taxation of costs on the standard basis the Taxing Master allows a reasonable amount in respect of all costs reasonably incurred while on an indemnity basis all costs are allowed except insofar as they are unreasonable in amount or have been unreasonably incurred. In a standard basis taxation, any doubt resolves in favour of the paying party; in an indemnity basis taxation, the reverse is true.

[20.34] Order 62 Appendix 2 directs the Taxing Master to exercise his discretion in relation to the fixing of the amount of costs allowed by reference to:

> (a) the complexity of the item or of the cause or matter in which it arises and the difficulty or novelty of the questions involved;
> (b) the skill, specialised knowledge and responsibility required of, and the time and labour expended by, the solicitor or counsel;
> (c) the number and importance of the documents (however brief) prepared or perused;
> (d) the place and circumstances in which the business involved is transacted;
> (e) the importance of the cause or matter to the client;
> (f) where money or property is involved, its amount or value;
> (g) any other fees and allowances payable to the solicitor or counsel in respect of other items in the same cause or matter, but only where work done in relation to those items has reduced the work which would otherwise have been necessary in relation to the item in question.

20.2.6 Enforcement of judgments

[20.35] Judgments in Northern Ireland are enforceable in accordance with the provision of the Judgments Enforcement (Northern Ireland) Order 1981 (the **1981 Order**), the Judgments Enforcement Rules (NI) 1981 and Order 45 RCJ (1980). Under the 1981 Order, application is made by the judgment creditor to the Enforcement of Judgments Office (**EJO**) for registration of a judgment. The EJO then examines the financial circumstances of the debtor and determines the best means of enforcement. The functions of the EJO are exercised by a Master, who is a judicial officer.

[20.36] In the case of money judgments, the EJO can make a number of different orders:

(1) instalment orders[19]
(2) attachment of earnings orders when the debtor is in receipt of wages or a salary[20]
(3) seizure and sale of the debtor's goods[21]
(4) orders charging land[22]
(5) orders appointing a receiver[23]
(6) garnishee order, in the event a judgment debtor is owed money by third parties.[24]

[20.37] In determining which (if any) of these orders to make, the EJO has a number of procedural powers including the examination of debtors and the issuing of warrants. In the event that the EJO determines that the debtor is unable to pay it will issue a Certificate of Unenforceability.

[20.38] In the event of wilful default by a judgment debtor in compliance with an order made by the EJO, the court may exercise the powers conferred by articles 106–115 of the 1981 Order to commit a debtor to prison or to make a sequestration order.

[20.39] For consideration of the detail of the procedures entailed in an application to the EJO for enforcement, reference should be had to the specialist text on the subject, Capper on the Enforcement of Judgments in Northern Ireland.[25]

[20.40] A creditor may, in the alternative, issue and serve a statutory demand on the debtor under the provisions of the Insolvency (Northern Ireland) Order 1989.[26] Failure to pay a debt on foot of a statutory demand is conclusive evidence of an inability to pay on foot of which the creditor can issue a bankruptcy or winding-up petition.

20.3 An alternative remedy – declaratory relief

[20.41] Most commonly, the legal process is invoked by the successful party to an adjudication in order to secure payment of a sum of money awarded by the adjudicator. However,

---

[19] Article 30 of the 1981 Order.
[20] Article 73.
[21] Article 31.
[22] Article 46.
[23] Article 67.
[24] Article 69.
[25] SLS, 2004.
[26] Articles 103(1)(a) & 242(1)(a).

[20.42] An example of this approach can be found in the case of *Northern Ireland Housing Executive v Healthy Buildings (Ireland) Limited*.[27] The dispute arose out of an NEC3 contract for asbestos surveying services when the contractor claimed that a compensation event had arisen as a result of an instruction given by the employer as to the manner in which surveys were to be carried out. The employer claimed that no instruction had been issued under the contract and any claim to compensation was time barred under the contractual terms. The adjudicator found for the contractor on both issues and the employer then issued proceedings seeking a declaration that the adjudicator's decision was wrong in law. Both the findings and the reasoning of the adjudicator were upheld by Weatherup J and the employer appealed to the Court of Appeal. The Court of Appeal unanimously dismissed the appeal and upheld the decision of the adjudicator and the Commercial Judge. This procedure can therefore be invoked when, for instance, an adjudicator has made a determination relating to the construction of a contract or the date of practical completion.

20.4 Judicial consideration

20.4.1 In a nutshell

[20.43] There is an emerging body of case law in Northern Ireland in relation to the enforcement of adjudicators' awards. The decisions of the Courts of England and Wales are not strictly binding in Northern Ireland but are of strongly persuasive authority. However, it should be recognised that such decisions are routinely cited in commercial actions where there is little or no difference between the substantive law of the respective jurisdictions. There is, for instance, a well-settled practice that the Court of Appeal in Northern Ireland will generally follow a relevant decision of the Court of Appeal of England and Wales.[28] The following sections address the court's consideration of the following topics:

(1) construction contract
(2) no dispute
(3) setting off against an adjudicator's decision
(4) financial difficulty of the paying party
(5) insufficient time to respond
(6) abuse of process.

20.4.2 No construction contract

[20.44] In order for a contract to fall within the scope of the Order, it must be a construction contract. Section 4.4 addresses in more detail what is meant by a construction contract.

---
[27] (2014) NICA 27.
[28] *Beaufort Developments v Gilbert Ash* (1997) NI 142.

In *Coleraine Skip Hire Limited v Ecomesh Limited*[29] the defendant contractor undertook remediation works at a landfill site and obtained an adjudicator's award. The plaintiff employer sued for overpayment and the defendant counterclaimed for the amount of the adjudicator's award and applied for summary judgment on the counterclaim. The plaintiff challenged the jurisdiction of the adjudicator on the basis that the works did not involve 'construction operations'. The works in question involved placing a capping layer over an existing landfill cell and the creation of a new landfill cell to receive new waste material. 'Construction operations' are defined at article 4 of the 1997 Order[30] as including:

> (a) the construction or alteration of structures forming, or to form, part of the land
>
> ...
>
> (e) operations which form an integral part of, or are preparatory to, or are for rendering complete such operations.

[20.45] Weatherup J concluded that the landfill cell was a 'structure' which formed part of the land, and that while the capping layer was not a structure it did involve operations which formed an integral part of or were preparatory to or were for rendering complete the operations relating to the landfill cell. Thus the works came within the statutory definition, and the adjudicator had jurisdiction.

20.4.3 No dispute

[20.46] One of the preconditions that must be met before commencing a statutory adjudication is that there must be a dispute. For there to be a dispute, within the meaning of article 7(1) of the Order,[31] a claim must have been made and a dispute must have subsequently crystallised. If there is 'no dispute', any decision produced by the adjudicator will be a nullity. Section 7.2 addresses this in more detail. In *Gibson (Banbridge) Limited v Fermanagh District Council*[32] the plaintiff contractor applied for summary judgment to enforce an adjudicator's award of some £3m on foot of its final account claim. The defendant employer resisted on the ground that the adjudicator did not have jurisdiction because a 'dispute' had not crystallised at the date of the issue of the notice of adjudication. The works were completed in February 2008 and followed by the contractor's application for payment in April 2008. After further applications in February 2010 and again in October 2011 no payment had been made and notice of adjudication was issued in September 2012. Correspondence ensued, the contractor pressing for payment and the employer contending that the contractor had failed to provide the necessary documentation to permit a proper assessment of the claim.

---

[29] [2008] NIQB 141, per Weatherup J at [14–15].
[30] Equivalent to section 104 of the Act.
[31] Equvialent to section 108(1) of the Act.
[32] [2013] NIQB 16, per Weatherup J at [6–20].

[20.47] The contract in question was the ICE Engineering and Construction Contract Option C, which provided for a project manager to assess the amount due to the contractor at intervals of four weeks. The contractor was obliged to permit the project manager to inspect at any time within working hours his accounts and records. The employer claimed that it had been unable to make any assessment on the contractor's claim as a result of its failure to comply with this obligation. It had therefore not made any decision on the contractor's claim. The court held that where a claim has been submitted, the contract administrator was entitled to a reasonable time to prepare a response before it can be concluded that a dispute has arisen. However, regard had to be had to the terms of the contract and the specific obligations on each party. It was decided by the court that reasonable time had been afforded to the project manager to make the assessment after the inspections had taken place. If the supporting documentation was not sufficient to support the application for payment then this ought to have been reflected in the assessment. The contract did not permit undue delay in the making of a determination by reason of a failure to supply documentation. Following the initiation of the adjudication proceedings, the project manager assessed the claim at £300,000 but judgment was entered for the full amount of £3m awarded by the adjudicator. The plaintiff obtained judgment for the amount of the adjudicator's award.

20.4.4 Setting off against an adjudicator's decision

[20.48] The position in England is that the general rule is that compliance with an adjudicator's decision will not be affected by any other right or claim. The exception to the general rule is that where there is a set-off or cross-claim that flows from or is closely connected to the adjudicator's decision, then it may be possible to take that set-off or cross-claim into account. Section 12.6 provides further detail. In both *Charles Brand v Donegall Quay*[33] and *Henry Brothers (Magherafelt) v Brunswick (8 Lanyon Place)*[34] defences relying on claimed rights to set-off were rejected by Weatherup J. In *Charles Brand*, it was held that the limited exception to the general principle of no deduction found in the judgment of Jackson J in *Balfour Beatty v Serco*[35] had no application in circumstances where the notice procedures of the contract in relation to liquidated and ascertained damages had not been followed. In *Henry Brothers* the defendant had served a Schedule of Defects but no entitlement to any damages had been established. No right of set-off could therefore exist against the sum due on foot of the adjudicator's award.

20.4.5 Financial difficulty of the paying party

[20.49] Weatherup J followed the English law set out in *Wimbledon Construction v Derek Vago*[36] and granted a stay on the execution of a judgment in circumstances where the

---

[33] (2010) NIQB 67, per Weatherup J at [15–22].
[34] (2011) NIQB 102, per Weatherup J at [9–16].
[35] (2004) EWHC 3336, per Jackson J at [48–55].
[36] (2005) EWHC 1986 (TCC), per Coulson J at [12–26].

evidence was sufficient to justify a finding that the plaintiff would probably be unable to repay the amount of the adjudicator's award in the event that it is ultimately found that it is repayable. It should be noted that there is a slightly different juridical basis for the grant of such a stay in Northern Ireland. As Weatherup J summarised the position:

> Thus it may be stated that in Northern Ireland the probable inability of the plaintiff to repay the judgment sum awarded by the Adjudicator and enforced by way of summary judgment at the end of a substantive trial or arbitration hearing may constitute grounds to grant a stay of execution under Order 14 Rule 3(2) or the inherent jurisdiction of the Court.

[20.50] In *Sutton Services v Vaughan Engineering Services*[37] Weatherup J granted a partial stay of enforcement on the basis that the defendant paid £150,000 to the plaintiff forthwith, with the balance paid into court. He also issued directions to the effect that the defendant was obliged to issue its claim against the plaintiff in respect of defective works within three days. He also directed that he would review the operation of the stay as the defendant's claim progressed. In the event, it transpired that the plaintiff carried professional indemnity insurance for the type of loss allegedly sustained by its defective workmanship. The Judge directed that the balance of the adjudicator's award paid into court be released to the plaintiff on confirmation by the insurers that it would indemnify the plaintiff under the policy. The court stressed that the discretion to grant a stay, while it would be exercised in an appropriate case, could not be used to frustrate the purpose of the statutory scheme.

[20.51] In *Rogers Contracts v Merex Construction*[38] the commercial judge grappled with the problem of the exercise of the stay when both parties are in financial difficulties. On the one hand, the plaintiff was entitled to payment of the sums found to be due by the adjudicator but the evidence revealed that it may not be in financial position to repay this sum upon the outcome of a pending arbitration. Equally, however, it appeared that the defendant may not be able to pay the sum due at all. Weatherup J commented:

> The Adjudication system was introduced to maintain cash flow during construction disputes and, in general, payment should be made on the Adjudicator's award pending overall resolution of the contract dispute in Arbitration or litigation or by agreement. In the meantime the enforcement of the Adjudicator's award is by legal proceedings and by application for summary judgment. The present case produces the not uncommon result that three sets of proceedings arise, namely the Adjudication on an issue that produces an interim result, the referral of contract disputes to Arbitration that will produce an overall result and the legal proceedings required to enforce the Adjudicator's interim award in the meantime. When there are no grounds to resist judgment on the Adjudicator's award pending the Arbitration, the role of the Court concerns the interim arrangements for the handling of the amount of the award until such time as the decision of the Arbitrator issues.

---

[37] (2013) NIQB 63, per Weatherup J at [30–33].
[38] (2012) NIQB 94, per Weatherup J at [14–26].

[20.52] In order to balance the competing interests of the parties, the judge exercised his discretion to order the amount of the adjudicator's award to be paid into court with the parties to have liberty to apply to have the stay lifted and the monies released upon the outcome of the arbitration. Financial difficulty is considered further at Section 14.3.4.

20.4.6 Insufficient time to respond

[20.53] Provided both parties have some time to consider and respond to the case put to them, then time, or rather lack of it, is not something that will normally constitute procedural unfairness and therefore a breach of natural justice. This is considered further at Section 17.5.4.

[20.54] In *Gibson (Banbridge) Limited v Fermanagh District Council*,[39] there was a complaint by the employer that there had been a breach of the rules of natural justice. The Adjudicator had required the plaintiff to submit his supporting papers to the Adjudicator in seven days and the defendant to respond in a further seven days. The Adjudicator refused the defendant's application for an extension to 21 days to reply.

[20.55] It was decided that there was no breach of the rules of natural justice. The seven-day response could not be looked at in isolation. The claim had been pending for many months. The defendant had had the opportunity for extensive inspection of the records and had spent many days examining the records. The basic time for the adjudication process of 28 days from notice to decision served to demonstrate the expedition demanded by the process and consequently that many cases would necessarily have to be dealt with in a summary manner.

20.4.7 Abuse of process

[20.56] In *Mel Davidson Construction v Northern Ireland Housing Executive*[40] the contractor had been successful in obtaining an award of over £1.1m in respect of inflationary uplifts due under a response maintenance contract. Having been paid this sum, the contractor then made a claim for statutory interest of some £53,000 under the Late Payment of Commercial Debts (Interest) Act 1998 and referred this claim to a second adjudication. The employer resisted any such payments on the grounds that either this was the same or substantially the same dispute as had been previously referred to adjudication[41] or that the claim fell foul of the principle in *Henderson v Henderson*,[42] since the claim should have been included in the first adjudication and to seek to raise it in separate proceedings constituted an abuse of process. Weatherup J concluded that the second adjudication

---

[39] [2013] NIQB 16, per Weatherup J at [28–29].
[40] (2014) NIQB 110, per Weatherup J at [20].
[41] Paragraph 9(2) of the Scheme
[42] (1843) Hare 100

concerned a different dispute from the first and, in such circumstances, the principle in *Henderson v Henderson* did not operate. He held:

> Has the Adjudicator discretion to refuse to decide the case in the second adjudication, if he forms the opinion that the claim ought to have been made in the first adjudication? I think not. I see nothing in the nature of the Scheme which permits the Adjudicator, in such circumstances, to refuse to decide a matter referred for decision. The Scheme requires the Adjudicator to decide a claim if it possible for him to do so. There are instances where an Adjudicator has been unable to make a decision, possibly because the material presented is not sufficient to permit the decision to be made. That is not this case.

Part II
International

Chapter 21
Introduction

[21.01] The problems that beset the United Kingdom and led to the introduction of statutory adjudication are not confined to those jurisdictions. In every country around the world, the construction industry faces similar challenges. The working capital and regular cash flow demanded by smaller businesses is contrasted with the employer's desire to extend supply and payment chains and at the same time require high quality projects to be delivered in a timely and reliable manner. This tension repeatedly leads to disputes.

[21.02] Regulators and participants continually deliberate on how to address the disputes within the industry, in a way that allows the participants to arrange their affairs and relationships in the way that is most convenient to them. Different challenges are presented in each jurisdiction. Projects often comprise a blend of different people from various legal backgrounds and cultures all of whom have different expectations when it comes to resolving disputes. Although litigation and arbitration are the most familiar and utilised methods of resolving disputes, many have realised a need for a dispute resolution process that is quicker and less costly. One method that has attracted interest is mandatory adjudication.

[21.03] The United Kingdom was the first to legislate for adjudication in 1996 and others followed thereafter. Australia from 1997 to 2009, New Zealand in 2002, the Isle of Man in 2004, Singapore in 2005, Malaysia in 2012 and Ireland in 2013. Other countries are seriously considering whether to introduce statutory adjudication. They include Germany, Hong Kong, China and South Africa. No doubt by the next edition of this book, some or all of those countries will have a mandatory adjudication regime and even more countries will be considering it. The United Kingdom regime, though similar in many respects, is also fundamentally different to other jurisdictions. To take just two examples, the regimes in other Commonwealth countries do not operate as implied terms of the contract, they operate directly from statute and most other regimes only apply to disputes about payment, as opposed to any contractual dispute.

[21.04] Outside a statutory framework, in an enormous leap forwards for adjudication, the most utilised international standard form construction contract, FIDIC, contains a mandatory adjudication process. Adjudication was first introduced in 1996, in a document entitled 'Supplement to the 4th edition (1987) – Conditions of Contract for Works of Civil Engineering Construction – Reprint with Further Amendments 1992', and a dispute

---

A Practical Guide to Construction Adjudication, First Edition. James Pickavance.
© 2016 James Pickavance. Published 2016 by John Wiley & Sons, Inc.

adjudication board was adopted to replace the engineer's role in the resolution of disputes. In the wider revisions in 1999, dispute adjudication boards were introduced across most of the suite. Dispute adjudication board rules are also published by other institutions, such the International Chamber of Commerce and the Institute of Civil Engineers.

[21.05] While the detailed implementation of statutory and contractual regimes varies from market to market, the base concept remains the same – an accessible, inexpensive, timely mechanism to resolve payment disputes and maximise cash flow through a decision-making process that is binding on both parties, either until the completion of the contract or until it is revisited in final determination. The proliferation of mandatory alternative dispute resolution is a positive step in a wider, global trend of encouraging alternative and interim dispute resolution, particularly in the field of construction and engineering projects. It would seem that the use of adjudication to resolve construction disputes is gaining international acceptance and that there is an emerging trend towards its adoption as the preferred form of resolving disputes. In most jurisdictions where it has been introduced, mandatory statutory adjudication rapidly eclipsed all other forms of dispute resolution within the construction industry and, in theory at least, there is no reason why this should not continue to be the case wherever else it is introduced.

[21.06] Interesting as all that may be, why should practitioners and construction professionals be interested in statutory adjudication in jurisdictions other than their own? It is suggested there are at least three reasons.

[21.07] Within the construction sector, both legal practitioners and industry professionals increasingly operate on an international platform. Law firms and consultancy practices have offices in a number of foreign jurisdictions, or if they do not, they are engaged on matters in foreign jurisdictions. Most, if not all major construction companies carry out work in a multitude of jurisdictions. Therefore, providing these companies, firms and consultancies with a resource which provides detail on the availability, operation and distinguishing features of statutory adjudication in foreign jurisdictions may be of some assistance. Certainly, it must be attractive for lawyers, to have the knowledge that enables one to say to clients that one is familiar with a reliable (more or less) mandatory form of dispute resolution available in multiple jurisdictions that is successful and is likely to save time and money in resolving dispute.

[21.08] International jurisdictions who either have a statutory adjudication regime, are contemplating legislative amendments to that regime, or are considering introducing a statutory regime for the first time may wish to know the extent of the influence that the UK regime has had on its own, but also how the provisions of the Act and the Scheme have been treated by the courts. The overall success of the UK regime and the extensive and forensic judicial attention it has received over the past two decades surely makes it of interest to international practitioners, as a lesson of what to do – or what not to do.

[21.09] Finally, the jurisprudence in some of countries will be relevant to others. In particular, a number of the countries form part of the Commonwealth, where the decisions of the court are of persuasive influence in others. Even for those countries that are not part of the Commonwealth, all of the statutory regimes have similarities and so practitioners and professionals will benefit from an understanding of how arguments have been deployed by counsel and how the courts have been interpreted in different jurisdictions.

[21.10] The following chapters address the statutory regimes in Australia (Chapter 22), Ireland (Chapter 23), Malaysia (Chapter 24), New Zealand (Chapter 25) and Singapore (Chapter 26).

Chapter 22
Australia: Peter Wood and Phillip Greenham[1]

22.1 Overview

22.1.1 Initial introduction in NSW

[22.01] New South Wales (NSW) was the first Australian state or territory to introduce a statutory adjudication scheme. In the Second Reading Speech of the Building and Construction Industry Security of Payment Bill 1999 (NSW), the then Minister for Public Works and Services, Morris Iemma stated:

> The Building and Construction Industry Security of Payment Bill is a key component of the Government reform package for security of payment in the New South Wales construction industry. It follows the 15 February announcement by the Premier of the Government's intention to stamp out the unAustralian practice of not paying contractors for work they undertake on construction. It is all too frequently the case that small subcontractors – such as bricklayers, carpenters, electricians and plumbers – are not paid for their work. Many of them cannot survive financially when that occurs, with severe consequences for themselves and their families. The Government is determined to rid the construction industry of such unacceptable practices.[2]

[22.02] Consequently, the Building and Construction Industry Security of Payment Act 1999 (NSW) (**NSW Act**) was enacted by the NSW Parliament, commencing on 26 March 2000. The adjudication provisions contained in the NSW Act were based upon similar British provisions, namely the Housing Grants, Construction and Regeneration Act 1996, which commenced operating in England and Wales on 1 May 1998. However, the adjudication

---

[1] Peter Wood and Phillip Greenham are partners at Minter Ellison in Melbourne, Australia. Peter has practised construction, engineering and infrastructure law for over 20 years. He is recognised as a leading individual in the field of construction in Chambers Asia Pacific 2014. Phillip has practised construction, engineering and infrastructure law for over 30 years. He is former President of the Building Dispute Practitioners Society, Chairman of the Society of Construction Law Australia and is recognised as a leading individual in the field of construction in Chambers & Partners Global. Peter and Phillip were assisted in writing this chapter by Chris Hey and Tom Johnstone who are lawyers in the construction, engineering and infrastructure group at Minter Ellison, Melbourne.

[2] M Iemma, *New South Wales Hansard Articles*, Legislative Assembly, 29 June 1999, No. 16 <http://www.parliament.nsw.gov.au>.

A Practical Guide to Construction Adjudication, First Edition. James Pickavance.
© 2016 James Pickavance. Published 2016 by John Wiley & Sons, Inc.

regime set out in the NSW Act contained (and still contains) some notable differences to its UK counterpart. In particular, there is a divergence in the types of disputes regulated by the adjudication legislation, the appointment of an adjudicator and the ability of the adjudicator to investigate the issues that are in dispute.[3]

[22.03] Amendments were made to the NSW Act in 2002.[4] The amendments implemented a more efficient regime for the enforcement of payment claims by precluding a respondent from bringing a cross-claim or raising a defence to counter an application for summary judgment.

22.1.2 Rollout across the remaining states

[22.04] Following NSW's lead, all Australian states and territories have now introduced legislation providing for the statutory adjudication of construction disputes. The table below sets out the applicable adjudication legislation in each state and territory:

State/Territory	Legislation
New South Wales	Building and Construction Industry Security of Payment Act 1999 (NSW) (**NSW Act**)
Victoria	Building and Construction Industry Security of Payment Act 2002 (Vic) (**Vic Act**)
Queensland	Building and Construction Industry Payments Act 2004 (Qld) (**QLD Act**)
Western Australia	Construction Contracts Act 2004 (WA) (**WA Act**)
Northern Territory	Construction Contracts (Security of Payments) Act 2004 (NT) (**NT Act**)
Australian Capital Territory	Building and Construction Industry Security of Payment Act 2009 (ACT) (**ACT Act**)
South Australia	Building and Construction Industry Security of Payment Act 2009 (SA) (**SA Act**)
Tasmania	Building and Construction Industry Security of Payment Act 2009 (Tas) (**Tas Act**)

[22.05] Except for Western Australia (**WA**) and the Northern Territory (**NT**), the legislation is generally based, to varying degrees, on the NSW Act. However, no two state or territory

---

[3] For an in-depth comparison of the UK and Australian legislation see P Gerber and B Ong, 'Best Practice in Construction Disputes: Avoidance, Management and Resolution', Lexis Nexis Butterworth, Australia, 2013, Chapter 16.
[4] Building and Construction Industry Security of Payment Amendment Act 2002 (NSW).

security of payment regimes are the same. The result of this is that there are eight statutory adjudication Acts throughout Australia, which although based on the similar policy objectives of regulating payment in the building and construction industry, take vastly different approaches to achieve this.[5]

22.1.3 East-west coast divide

[22.06] The jurisdictions that have moved furthest away from the NSW adjudication model are NT and WA. While incorporating some aspects of the NSW Act, the NT and WA Acts have also modelled their adjudication regimes on the New Zealand and UK statutes. This has led certain commentators to broadly distinguish the 'west coast' model of statutory adjudication, comprising the NT and WA and the 'east coast' model of statutory adjudication comprising all remaining Australian states and territories.[6] For ease of reference, this chapter will adopt this terminology.

22.1.4 Consequences of the divide

[22.07] The differing success of the adjudication regimes throughout Australia has led a number of commentators to call for a uniform national approach to combating payment issues in the building and construction industry.[7] In 2003, the Honourable Terence Cole, as Federal Royal Commissioner released his report into the conduct and practices of the building and construction industry.[8] In the report, it was recommended that:

> National consistency in this area is important because it reduces the cost of businesses moving between jurisdictions and operating in different jurisdictions. It minimizes duplication and reduces the cost of education campaigns. It means that the cost of subcontractors and the cost

---

[5] P Vickery, Security of Payment Legislation in Australia, Differences between the States – Vive la Différence? *http://www.supremecourt.vic.gov.au/home/contact+us/speeches/speech+-+security+of+payment+legislation+in+australia* as at 23 October 2014.

[6] See J Coggins, R Fenwick Elliott and M Bell, 'Towards Harmonisation of Construction Industry Payment Legislation: A Consideration of the Success Afforded by the East and West Coast Models in Australia' (2010) 10(3) *AJCEB* 14; P Vickery, Security of Payment Legislation in Australia, Differences between the States – Vive la Différence?, < *http://www.supremecourt.vic.gov.au/home/contact+us/speeches/speech+-+security+of+payment+legislation+in+australia*> as at 23 October 2014 and P Gerber and B Ong, 'Best Practice in Construction Disputes: Avoidance, Management and Resolution', Lexis Nexis Butterworth, Australia, 2013, p. 363.

[7] See Zhang T, 'Why national legislation is required for the effective operation of the security of payment scheme' (2009) 25 BCL 376 and J Coggins, R Fenwick Elliott and M Bell, 'Towards Harmonisation of Construction Industry Payment Legislation: A Consideration of the Success Afforded by the East and West Coast Models in Australia' (2010) 10(3) *AJCEB* 14.

[8] Royal Commission into the Building and Construction Industry, *Final Report of the Royal Commission into the Building and Construction Industry* (2003).

of building are not inflated in those States and Territories where there is a higher risk that subcontractors will not get paid.[9]

[22.08] Despite the Federal Royal Commissioner's report, the states and territories are no closer to implementing a uniform approach to security of payment legislation. Instead, the divide has been further exacerbated by the raft of case law that has emerged in each jurisdiction, governing the interpretation of the relevant act. No doubt this fosters inefficiencies and uncertainty throughout the building and construction industry.

22.2 *Requirements for commencing an adjudication*

22.2.1 Construction contract

[22.09] In order to commence an adjudication there must be a construction contract. The existence of a construction contract has been held to be a precondition to a valid adjudication determination.[10]

[22.10] A construction contract is defined under the NSW Act as:

> a contract or other arrangement under which one party undertakes to carry out construction work, or to supply related goods and services, for another party.[11]

[22.11] Similar definitions of a construction contract are used in the other east coast jurisdictions.[12] In contrast, the WA legislative definition of construction contract (among other slight differences) replaces the word 'arrangement' with 'agreement' and the NT Act omits the words 'or other arrangement'. The phrase 'or other arrangement' has been the subject of much judicial consideration.[13] In *Machkevitch v Andrew Building Constructions*, McDougall J held that:

> the word "arrangement" denotes some engagement, or state of affairs, or agreement (whether legally enforceable or not) under which, perhaps among other things, one party undertakes to perform construction work for another.[14]

[22.12] The wording used in the west coast model suggests that such a broad interpretation of what constitutes a construction contract is not possible.

---

[9] Vol 8, p 255.
[10] *Brodyn Pty Ltd Time Cost and Quality v Davenport & Anor* at [53].
[11] NSW Act s. 4.
[12] See Vic Act s. 4, ACT Act schedule 2, QLD Act Schedule 2, SA Act s. 4, Tas Act s. 4.
[13] See for example *Okaroo Pty Limited v Vos Construction and Joinery Pty Limited and Anor* [2005] NSWSC 45; *Olbourne v Excell Building Corp Pty Ltd* [2009] NSWSC 349 at [25–28]; *Machkevitch v Andrew Building Constructions* [2012] NSWSC 546 at [14–30].
[14] [2012] NSWSC 546 at [29].

[22.13] In all Australian states and territories a construction contract can be written or oral, or partly written and partly oral.[15]

22.2.2 Construction work

[22.14] Central to the definition of construction contract is the concept that one party must have undertaken to carry out construction work. The NSW Act sets out an extensive list of the types of works that constitute construction work.[16] The types of work include:
(1) the construction, alteration, repair, restoration, maintenance, extension, demolition or dismantling of works, buildings or structures forming, or to form part of land;
(2) the installation in any buildings, structure or works of fittings forming, or to form part of land;
(3) the cleaning of building, structures or works to the extent hat it is relates to a construction, alteration, repair, restoration, maintenance or extension; and
(4) any operation which is an integral part of, is preparatory to or is for rendering complete any work referred to above.

[22.15] Works listed as forming part of land include road works, aircraft runways, railways, pipelines, wells and sewers among others. Expressly excluded from the definition of a construction contract are oil, gas and mining contracts.[17]

[22.16] In addition, pursuant to subsection 7(2) of the NSW Act, the security of payment regime does not apply to:
(1) contracts that form part of a loan agreement, guarantee or contract of insurance;[18]
(2) domestic building contract works (unless the building owner is in the business of building residences);[19] and
(3) contracts where the value of the contract is not ascertained by reference to the value of the work carried out or the value of the goods and services supplied.[20]

[22.17] The definition of the construction work in the NSW Act has been broadly adopted in all east coast jurisdictions.[21] In the west coast jurisdictions the definition of construction works extends to the off-shore construction of civil works, buildings or structures.[22] Further, the oil, gas and mining exclusion is extended to works that are incidental to the extraction of oil, gas or minerals such as the construction of a shaft, pit or quarry.[23]

---

[15] ACT Act s. 9; NT Act s. 9; NSW Act s. 7; QLD Act s. 3; SA Act s. 7; Tas Act s. 7; VIC Act s. 7; WA Act s. 7.
[16] See NSW Act s. 5(1).
[17] NSW Act s. 5(2).
[18] Vic Act s. 5(2)(a).
[19] Vic Act s. 7(2)(b).
[20] Vic Act s. 7(2)(c).
[21] ACT Act s. 7; QLD Act s. 10; SA Act s. 5; Vic Act s. 5.
[22] NT Act s. 6(1)(c); WA Act s. 4(3).
[23] WA Act s. 4(3) and NT Act s. 6(2).

[22.18] Given the detailed definitions of construction work under the Acts, and the divergence in approach in the jurisdictions, often a legal analysis will be required prior to commencing an adjudication to determine if the work in question falls within the ambit of the relevant Act. Such an outcome is clearly at odds with one of the key purposes of the legislation, which is to provide the efficient and timely resolution of payment disputes in the construction industry.[24]

22.2.3 Claimable variations and excluded amounts in Victoria

[22.19] The Victorian adjudication legislation further restricts the availability of adjudication, by excluding the following amounts from any disputes that are referred to adjudication:[25]
(1) variations that are not 'claimable variations';
(2) latent conditions;
(3) time-related costs and claims for damages; and
(4) losses arising from changes in regulatory requirements.

[22.20] 'Claimable variations' are defined in clause 10A of the Victorian adjudication legislation and include agreed variations and variations directed by the principal or head contractor where the contract sum is less than $5m or there is no dispute resolution clause in the contract. However, if the total disputed variation claims exceed 10% of the contract sum, they will only be 'claimable variations' where the contract sum is less than $150,000 or there is no dispute resolution clause in the contract.

[22.21] The Victorian amendments were introduced in 2006 as a means of avoiding the uncertainties experienced in other Australian jurisdictions.[26] However, ensuing case law such as *Seabay Properties Pty Ltd v Galvin Constructions Pty Ltd*[27] has shown that the Victorian amendments do not necessarily operate to restrict the rights of claimants as was intended.

22.2.4 Reference date

[22.22] A claimant under the SOP legislation will only be entitled to make a payment claim concerning a **reference date**.[28] The NSW Act defines a reference date as:[29]
(1) the date determined under the contract as the date on which a progress payment arises; or
(2) if not stated in the contract, the last day of each month commencing from the month in which **construction work** was first carried out.

---

[24] J Coggins et al. (2010) 'Towards harmonisation of construction industry payment legislation; a consideration of the success afforded by the East and West Coast models in Australia', *Australasian Journal of Construction Economics and Building*, 10 (3) 14–35, p. 19.
[25] Vic Act, s. 10B.
[26] *Victorian Hansard*, 9 February 2006, p 219, <http://www.parliament.vic.gov.au>.
[27] (2011) 27 BCL 244
[28] See Vic Act ss 9(1) and 14.
[29] NSW Act s. 8(2).

[22.23] In Victoria, the courts have held that a party that serves a payment claim prior to a reference date arising is not automatically prevented from relying on that payment claim.[30] This approach differs from that taken in NSW and Queensland where it has been held that a payment claim is not valid unless a reference date has arisen.[31]

[22.24] Claimants are precluded from serving more than one payment claim in respect of each reference date.[32] However, payment claims may include amounts that have been the subject of previous claims,[33] allowing parties to effectively bring repeat payment claims so long as new work has arisen in between the relevant reference dates. This clause has been the subject of some criticism.[34]

22.2.5 Time limits

[22.25] The Australian Capital Territory, NSW and Tasmanian jurisdictions permit claimants to serve a payment claim 12 months after the construction work to which the claim relates was carried out.[35] The period for bringing an adjudication in the other states and territories range from three months after a reference date arises[36] to six months after the construction work to which the claim relates was last carried out.[37]

[22.26] In the east coast jurisdictions, a respondent has up to 10 business days to serve a payment schedule after a payment claim has been served.[38] If the amount in the payment schedule is less than that in the payment claim, the respondent must indicate the reasons for this.[39] A claimant will be entitled to make an adjudication application where:
(1) the scheduled amount is less than the claimed amount;
(2) the respondent fails to pay the entirety of the scheduled amount; or
(3) the respondent does not provide a payment schedule and does not pay the entirety of the claimed amount by the due date.[40]

---

[30] *Metacorp Pty Ltd v Andeco Construction Group Pty Ltd* [2010] VSC 199.
[31] *Walter Construction Group Ltd v CPL (Surry Hills) Pty Ltd* [2003] NSWSC 266 at [52]-[60]; *Beckhaus v Brewarrina Council* [2002] NSWSC 960; and *F.K. Gardner & Sons Pty Ltd v Dimin Pty Ltd* [2007] 1 Qd. R 10.
[32] NSW Act s. 13(5).
[33] NSW Act s. 13(6).
[34] SOCLA, p35.
[35] NSW Act s. 13(4). Tas Act s. 17. ACT Act s. 15
[36] Vic Act s. 14(4).
[37] SA Act, s. 13(4).
[38] See NSW Act s. 14(4). Note the SA Act allows 15 business days to serve a payment schedule, s. 14(b)(ii).
[39] See NSW Act s. 14(3).
[40] See NSW Act s. 17(1). Note where the respondent fails to provide a payment schedule and fails to pay the claimed amount, the claimant may alternatively seek summary judgment in court for the debt due (s 15(2)(a)(i) of the NSW Act). If the claimant chooses to refer the amount to arbitration it must notify the respondent of its intention to apply for adjudication and give the respondent five days to serve a payment schedule (s17(2) of NSW Act).

[22.27]   If a claimant wishes to refer the payment schedule to adjudication, the claimant has 10 business days to serve an adjudication application after receipt of the payment schedule.[41] Under the east coast model, a respondent must serve an adjudication response within five business days of service, or two business days after an adjudicator accepts the application, whichever comes later.[42] The west coast model provides more time for a respondent to provide an adjudication response.[43]

22.2.6 Who may refer a dispute under a construction contract to adjudication?

[22.28]   The policy underlying the introduction of the NSW adjudication legislation was to 'stamp out the practice of not paying contractors for work they undertake on construction'.[44] In this regard, the legislation sought to:

> entitle certain persons who carry out construction work (or who supply related goods and services) to timely payment for the work they carry out and the goods and services they supply...[45]

[22.29]   Accordingly, the NSW legislation only entitles those persons who carry out construction work or supply related goods or services, to bring an adjudication application. Principals to a head contract or contractors to a subcontract are thus denied this avenue of redress.

[22.30]   This model has been adopted by each of the east coast jurisdictions. In contrast, both the NT and WA allow any party to a construction contract to apply under the applicable legislation to have a dispute adjudicated.[46] The model adopted by the west coast jurisdictions reflects the position in the UK.[47] By way of an example, this would entitle principals or head contractors to refer a dispute concerning their right to liquidated damages or rectification costs from the relevant contractor or subcontractor to adjudication.

22.3 Adjudication process

22.3.1 Appointment of the adjudicator

[22.31]   In both the east coast and west coast jurisdictions, parties are able to apply to an authorised nominating authority (**ANA**) to commence an adjudication. ANAs are professional

---

[41] See NSW Act s. 17(1). Note the SA Act allows 15 business days to serve a payment schedule, s. 17(3)(c).
[42] NSW Act s20(1). N.B. the ACT Act allows 10 business days (or 5 business days after the adjudicator accepts) and the Tas Act allows 7 business days (or 5 business days after the adjudicator accepts). Under the *Building and Construction Industry Payments Amendment Bill 2014* (QLD) the time limit to provide a response in complex payment claims will be increased to 15 business days.
[43] 14 days under s27 of the WA Act (s27) and 10 working days under s29 of the NT Act.
[44] M Iemma, *New South Wales Hansard Articles*, Legislative Assembly, 29 June 1999, No. 16 <http://www.parliament.nsw.gov.au>.
[45] Explanatory Note, *Building and Construction Industry Security of Payment Bill 1999 (No. 2)*
[46] s 25 of WA Act, s. 27 of NT Act.
[47] The Act, s. 108.

bodies or private companies authorised by the relevant minister to receive adjudication applications.[48] If an adjudication application is made to an ANA, the ANA is required to nominate an adjudicator to determine the matter. ANAs take a commission of the adjudicators fee (which is paid by the parties to the dispute) usually in the range of 10–40%.[49] In practice it is common for parties to specify the ANAs to which an adjudication application can be made.

[22.32] At the date of writing, the Building and Construction Industry Payments Amendment Bill 2014 (QLD) was before the Queensland Parliament. This bill abolishes ANAs. Instead, the Queensland Building and Construction Commission will have an adjudication registry to administer the QLD Act, monitor performance and appoint adjudicators based on skills, knowledge and experience.

[22.33] While in both models, the adjudicator may be appointed by an ANA, the west coast model also allows the parties to agree on the appointment of an adjudicator in the construction contract.[50] There is no equivalent right in the east coast jurisdictions.[51] The clear limitation to the approach adopted by the east coast states is that ANAs have a 'vested interest' in ensuring that adjudicators are pro contractor/subcontractor.[52] This is because contractors/sub contractors have the sole right of referring a dispute to adjudication and ANAs receive a commission from any such referrals.

[22.34] Adjudicators must have the 'qualifications, expertise and experience' prescribed in the regulations.[53] However, with the exception of Queensland, none of the east coast jurisdictions have prescribed the requisite 'qualifications, expertise and experience' of an adjudicator. It is therefore left to individual ANAs to regulate their own adjudicators.[54] The result of this self-regulation is that the competence and experience of individual adjudicators in the east coast jurisdictions differs markedly. This has led some commentators to propose that a formal training regime should be implemented so as to ensure that adjudicators have a better grasp of the issues at hand and are able to deliver a higher quality of service.[55]

[22.35] In Queensland, adjudicators must be registered under the Act and hold a certificate of adjudication from an authorised body. The west coast jurisdictions are even more stringent in their regulation of adjudicators. Not only must adjudicators be registered under the Act, but they must have:

---

[48] See NSW Act, s. 28(1)(a). Note in WA all ANAs stipulated in the regulations are construction or legal professional bodies or associations.
[49] SOCLA Report, p 31.
[50] WA Act s26(1)(c) and NT Act s. 28(1)(c).
[51] See for example s18(3) of the Vic Act.
[52] SOCLA, p33.
[53] See Vic Act s. 19.
[54] See for instance the South Australian Code of Conduct for Authorised Nominating Authorities which prohibits ANAs from nominating an adjudicator that has been found in a court of Australia to have made technical errors in performing adjudications unless it is satisfied those errors have been resolved.
[55] Zhang T, 'Why national legislation is required for the effective operation of the security of payment scheme' (2009) 25 *Building and Construction Law Journal* 376, 396.

(1) a degree in law, architecture, engineering or other construction-related field or be a registered builder;
(2) at least five years' experience in administering construction contracts or dispute resolution relating to construction contracts; and
(3) completed a training course.[56]

22.3.2 Conduct of the adjudication

[22.36] In the east coast jurisdictions, the adjudicator is limited in what it may consider in reaching its determination. Generally, the adjudicator may only consider:[57]
(1) the applicable SOP legislation;
(2) the terms of the construction contract;
(3) the payment claim and any documents provided by the claimant in support of the claim (including the claimant's submissions);
(4) the payment schedule and any documents provided by the respondent in support of the schedule (including the respondent's submissions); and
(5) the results of any inspection carried out by the adjudicator on any matter to which the claim relates.

[22.37] Adjudicators in the west coast jurisdictions are given far broader powers to investigate payment claims.

[22.38] Adjudicators are not bound by the rules of evidence and may request parties to make further submissions or to attend conferences with the adjudicator.[58] In addition, unless all the parties object, adjudicators may inspect the work that relates to the payment claim and engage experts to report on the matter in dispute.[59]

[22.39] While the east coast model also allows adjudicators to call a conference of the parties, the parties are not entitled to legal representation, except in Victoria where legal representation may be permitted by the adjudicator.[60] Given that parties generally seek legal advice in relation to the other steps in the adjudication process, such a distinction appears to be arbitrary and unhelpful to the parties.[61]

[22.40] In its Report on Security of Payment and Adjudication in the Australian Construction Industry, SOCLA conducted an analysis on court challenges made to the end of 2013. SOCLA's analysis found that roughly 80% of challenges resulted in the adjudicator's determination being quashed. Such a high proportion of determinations being quashed suggests that the current procedures available to adjudicators to assess applications are inadequate.

---

[56] WA Act s. 48(1) and WA Regs r 9. NT Act s. 52, NT Regs r11.
[57] See s. 22 of the NSW Act.
[58] s 32 WA Act, s. 34 NSW Act.
[59] Ibid.
[60] NSW Act s. 21, QLD Act s. 25, SA Act s. 21, ACT Act s. 23, Tas Act s. 24, Vic Act s. 25(5A).
[61] See criticism of the East Coast model in this regard in SOCLA Report p30.

22.4 Determination, effect and costs

22.4.1 Form of the decision

[22.41] Under both the east coast and west coast regimes the adjudicator is to determine:
(1) the amount of the progress payment (if any) to be paid by the respondent to the claimant; and
(2) the rate of interest payable on any such amount.[62]

[22.42] Each of the Australian jurisdictions provides that an adjudicator's determination must be in writing and include the reasons for the determination.[63] With the exception of Victoria, under the east coast model an adjudicator is not required to provide reasons if both of the parties request the adjudicator not to include reasons in the determination.[64]

[22.43] Generally, if an adjudicator determines that a respondent is required to pay an adjudicated amount, the respondent must pay that amount to the claimant within five business days, or the date specified in the adjudication.[65] However, in NSW the payment must be made within five business days of a determination and is not set by the adjudicator.[66] Conversely, the west coast model fixes the date for payment solely as specified in the adjudication.[67]

[22.44] Under both the east coast and west coast models, if an adjudicator's determination contains a mistake or accidental omission the adjudicator may correct the determination at the adjudicator's own initiative.[68]

22.4.2 Effect of the decision

[22.45] Given that payment claims generally occur on a regular basis under most construction contracts, a distressed project may result in a number of determinations. To counter the risk of inconsistent determinations, principles of issue estoppel have been held to apply to adjudication determinations under the NSW Act and the QLD Act. Just as a claimant is not entitled to resubmit claims previously determined by an adjudicator, until it finally receives an advantageous outcome, so a respondent is not entitled to resubmit deductions or set-offs on the basis of issues previously determined by an adjudicator or to re-agitate contentions as to invalidity, until it finally receives an advantageous outcome. In the decision of the NSW Court of Appeal in *DualCorp Pty Ltd v Remo Constructions Pty Ltd* (2009) 74 NSWLR 190, MacFarlan JA stated:

---

[62] WA Act s. 31(2)(b), NSW Act s. 22(1).
[63] WA Act s. 36, NSW Act s. 22(3).
[64] NSW Act s. 22(3)(b), QLD Act s. 26(3)(b), SA Act s. 22(3)(b), ACT Act s. 24(3)(b), TAS Act s. 25(4)(b).
[65] QLD Act s. 29(2), Vic Act s. 28M(2), SA Act s. 23(2), ACT Act s. 25, TAS Act s. 26(1).
[66] NSW Act s. 23(2).
[67] WA Act s. 39(1).
[68] WA Act s. 41(2), NSW Act s. 22(5).

> The view that the claimant once disappointed by an adjudicator can seek a different determination from another, or indeed from a succession of others, until a favourable decision is reached would in my view conflict with the policy of the Act to render adjudicators' determinations final on issues which they resolved, subject only to provisions of the Act conferring limited rights of correction of determinations.[69]

[22.46] Adjudication determinations are binding decisions made on an interim basis. Each of the models provides that the legislation does not affect the rights of a party under the contract, and that those amounts may be subsequently recovered in later court proceedings.[70] Thus, security of payment legislation provides for the flow of money during construction projects, but does not conclusively resolve the issues in dispute. In *Macob Civil Engineering Ltd v Morrison Construction Ltd*, Dyson J held that:

> The intention of Parliament in enacting the Scheme was to introduce a speedy mechanism for settling disputes in construction contracts on a provisional interim basis and requiring the decisions of adjudicators to be enforced pending the final determination of disputes. Accordingly even if there was challenge to the validity of the adjudicator's decision, it remained binding and enforceable until any challenge to it was finally determined.[71]

[22.47] In Western Australia, evidence of anything said or done in an adjudication is not admissible before an arbitrator or other person or a court or other body, except for the purposes of an application made to declare an adjudicator as disqualified or an appeal made under section 46 of the West Australian Act.[72]

22.4.3 Costs

[22.48] Parties to an adjudication under the east coast jurisdictions bear their own costs, subject to any contractual provision to the contrary. Under the west coast model the parties also bear their own costs in relation to the adjudication of the dispute, but if an appointed adjudicator is satisfied that a party to a payment dispute incurred costs of the adjudication because of frivolous or vexatious conduct on the part of, or unfounded submissions by, another party, the adjudicator may decide that the other party must pay some or all of those costs.[73]

[22.49] Under both the east coast and west coast models the claimant and respondent are jointly and severally liable to pay the adjudicator's fees and expenses.[74] In contrast to the west coast model, where the parties involved in a dispute are liable to pay the costs of an adjudication of the dispute in equal shares, under the east coast model the claimant and

---

[69] *DualCorp Pty Ltd v Remo Constructions Pty Ltd* (2009) 74 NSWLR 190 at [70].
[70] WA Act s. 45, NSW Act s. 26F.
[71] *Macob Civil Engineering Ltd v Morrison Construction Ltd* [1999] BLR 93 at [1].
[72] WA Act s. 45(3).
[73] WA Act s. 34.
[74] WA Act s. 44(5), NSW Act s. 29(2).

respondent may also be deemed liable to contribute to the payment of the adjudicator's fees in such proportions as the adjudicator may determine.[75]

22.5 Enforcement

22.5.1 Process for enforcement

[22.50] If the respondent fails to pay the whole or any part of the adjudicated amount to the claimant, the claimant may request the ANA to whom the adjudication application was made to provide an adjudication certificate,[76] which may be filed as a judgment for a debt in any court. To avoid a finding of contempt of court, the respondent is then required to pay the amount in the adjudication certificate. However, as discussed above, an aggrieved respondent is not precluded from ultimately recovering this amount and enforcing their common law rights following the completion of the relevant project. The Vic Act expressly provides that in subsequent court proceedings the court may make such orders as it considers appropriate for the restitution of any amounts paid under the Vic Act, and such other orders as it considers appropriate.[77]

[22.51] Under the west coast model, the applicant must apply for a summary judgment at common law, which may be thwarted if a defendant can demonstrate to the court that it can mount a reasonable defence by way of a cross-claim, in which case the only option left to the contractor will be to pursue its claim in relatively lengthy and costly court or arbitration proceedings.[78]

[22.52] In New South Wales, if the respondent commences proceedings to have the judgment set aside, the respondent, among other things, is required to pay into the court as security the unpaid portion of the adjudicated amount pending the final determination of those proceedings.[79]

22.5.2 Express rights of appeal

[22.53] Both west coast jurisdictions provide a limited right to appeal. A person who is aggrieved by a decision may apply to the State Administrative Tribunal for a review of the decision.[80] While generally, in any other circumstances, a decision or determination of an adjudicator on an adjudication cannot be appealed or reviewed,[81] the WA courts have

---

[75] NSW Act s. 29(3), VIC Act s. 45(4), TAS Act s. 37(3)(b), SA ACT s. 30(3), QLD Act s. 35(3), ACT Act s. 36(3)(b).
[76] NSW Act s. 24(1).
[77] VIC Act s. 47(3).
[78] P Gerber and B Ong, 'Best Practice in Construction Disputes: Avoidance, Management and Resolution', Lexis Nexis Butterworth, Australia, 2013, p. 381.
[79] NSW Act s. 25(4)(b).
[80] WA Act s. 46(1).
[81] WA Act s. 46(3).

adopted the reasoning of McLure J in *Perrinepod Pty Ltd v Georgiou Building Pty Ltd*,[82] who accepted that 's. 46(3) does not exclude judicial review of a decision or determination of an adjudicator made under s 31(2)(a) or (b) of the Act'.[83]

[22.54] In the ACT, parties are provided with an express legislative avenue for appeals from an adjudication determination. With the leave of the Supreme Court, or the consent of the parties, an appeal can be made to the Supreme Court on a question of law arising out of an adjudication, but there are narrow grounds for a grant of leave and the nature of the appeal decisions is confined.[84]

22.5.3 Judicial review of adjudication determinations

[22.55] Under the east coast model, the court may grant relief in the nature of certiorari to quash an adjudicator's decision on the basis of jurisdictional error.[85] That is, the decision is void unless the basic and essential requirements of the Act are met, including:
(1) there is a construction contract;
(2) a payment claim was served;
(3) there was an adjudication application;
(4) the application was referred to an eligible adjudicator who accepted the application; and
(5) there is a written determination by the adjudicator determining the adjudicated amount, the due date and the rate of interest payable.

[22.56] An adjudicator's determination may also be void if there was no bona fide attempt by the adjudicator to exercise the function of the adjudicator or if there was a substantial denial of natural justice.[86] A denial of natural justice will only be sufficient to render an adjudication determination void if the denial goes to an issue which is germane or material in the making of the adjudication. Furthermore, it has been held that the denial of natural justice must be one which should not only be germane or material to, but also actually affect the outcome of, the adjudicator's ultimate decision.[87]

[22.57] In Victoria, the position is that 'relief in the nature of certiorari, on all of the grounds available under the writ, including error on the face of the record, is not excluded either

---

[82] *Perrinepod Pty Ltd v Georgiou Building Pty Ltd* [2011] WASCA 217.
[83] Perrinepod Pty Ltd v Georgiou Building Pty Ltd [2011] WASCA 217 at [7] and [8].
[84] ACT Act s. 43.
[85] *Brodyn Pty Ltd t/as Time Cost and Quality v Davenport & Anor* [2004] NSWCA 394 at [53] and [55], followed in QLD by *Queensland Bulk Water Supply Authority v McDonald Keen Group Pty Ltd (In liq) & Anor* [2010] QCA 7 at [51].
[86] See *Hall Contracting Pty Ltd v MacMahon Contractors Pty Ltd* [2014] NTSC 20.
[87] Coggins J 'Breaches of natural justice in alternative dispute resolution of construction disputes' (2013) 29 *Building and Construction Law Journal* 247, 253 citing McDougall R, *An Examination of the Role and Content of Natural Justice in Adjudications under Construction Industry Payment Legislation* (2009), <http://www.lawlink.nsw.gov.au/lawlink/supreme_court/ll_sc.nsf/vwfiles/mcdougall110909.pdf/$file/mcdougall110909.pdf>.

expressly or by implication under the Act in Victoria'.[88] Vickery J, the judge in charge of the Victorian Supreme Court TEC List has reasoned that 'there is no error of law on the face of the record in simply making a wrong finding of fact... a finding of fact will only be open to challenge as erroneous in law if there is no probative evidence to support it.'[89] The basis for the difference in Victoria is based upon statutory interpretation of the Vic Act and s. 85 of the Constitution Act 1975 (Vic).

[22.58] In Queensland, the Supreme Court recently found that a part of an adjudication determination that is void for jurisdictional error can be severed from an otherwise valid determination.[90] However, it is unlikely that this case will assist with jurisdictional error in the form of a substantial denial of natural justice or procedural fairness or because the adjudicator did not exercise his function in good faith. Such jurisdictional error is much more likely to affect all aspects of the adjudication determination.[91]

[22.59] In contrast, the west coast model provides that certiorari does not lie to quash an adjudication determination.[92] Beech J in *O'Donnell Griffin Pty Ltd v John Holland Pty Ltd* held:

> on the proper construction of the Act, whether there has been compliance with s 26(1) is a matter for the adjudicator and for the State Administrative Tribunal on a review under s 46(1); it is not a matter for objective determination by the court. Apart from the reference to s 46(1), that was the approach taken by Mildren J in Independent Fire Sprinklers [32] – [50].[93]

[22.60] Under the east coast model nearly four out of five court challenges to an adjudicator's determination result in the adjudication determination being overturned, and this has been shown to be rising over the years.[94] The east coast model stands in stark contrast to the west coast model, which has far fewer challenges to an adjudicator's decision.[95]

---

[88] *Hickory Developments Pty Ltd v Schiavello (Vic) Pty Ltd* [2009] VSC 156 at [90] as confirmed by *Grocon Constructors v Planit Cocciardi Joint Venture (No. 2)* [2009] VSC 426 at [102].
[89] *Asian Pacific Building Corporation Pty Ltd v Aircon Duct Fabrication Pty Ltd* [2010] VSC 300 at [79].
[90] *BM Alliance Coal Operations Pty Ltd v BGC Contracting Pty (No. 2)* [2013] QSC 67 at [35]. This has been adopted in section 37 of Building and Construction Industry Payments Amendment Bill 2014 (QLD) amending s. 100 of the QLD Act.
[91] Creedon M and Dickson E, 'Jurisdictional error in adjudication decisions – what is the most convenient and satisfactory remedy?' (2013) 25(2) *Australian Construction Law Bulletin* 31.
[92] WA Act, see *O'Donnell Griffin Pty Ltd v John Holland Pty Ltd* [2009] WASC 19, NT ACT see *Independent Fire Sprinklers (NT) Pty Ltd v Sunbuild Pty Ltd* [2008] NTSC 46 at [50].
[93] *O'Donnell Griffin Pty Ltd v John Holland Pty Ltd* [2009] WASC 19 at [129].
[94] SOCLA, page 37.
[95] SOCLA, page 39 (where it is shown that from 2005 to 2013 a total of 24 determinations were upheld while only two determinations were quashed).

Chapter 23
Ireland: Dermot McEvoy[1]

23.1 Overview

[23.01] The 2013 Act[2] (the **2013 Act**) was enacted on 29 July 2013 but remains subject to a Ministerial commencement order before it becomes operative. Although this was anticipated for Spring 2015,[3] it now appears no date is imminent. Born out of the latest economic recession, in which the construction industry suffered markedly due to unprecedented financial and liquidity problems, the stated purpose of the 2013 Act is to regulate payments under construction contracts.

[23.02] Following a dramatic transition from boom to bust, where the Irish construction industry shrunk from €39 billion annual turnover to €7.5 billion annual turnover, the sector continues to face a tough challenge in seeking to return to sustainable activity. By regulating payments under construction contracts, the 2013 Act seeks to create a sustainable future for construction in Ireland. The 2013 Act seeks to achieve this by introducing mandatory payment provisions, the entitlement to stop work for non-payment and statutory adjudication for payment disputes.

[23.03] The model for statutory adjudication under the 2013 Act broadly follows the model introduced into the UK under the 1996 Act,[4] but has some notable differences. These differences will remain subject to clarification from the Irish courts or by subsequent amending legislation. The body of precedent that has developed under the UK model will be instructive in interpreting the 2013 Act, but no more.

[23.04] The 2013 Act will be complemented by a Code of Practice.[5] The Code of Practice has yet to be finalised and has been the subject of consultation with key industry stakeholders. It is understood that the final version will be published in advance of the commencement

---

[1] Dermot McEvoy is a partner at Eversheds in Dublin, Ireland. Dermot is a dispute resolution lawyer, specialising in construction and engineering, financial services and professional indemnity law. He is ranked as a leading individual in Chambers & Partners Global.
[2] No. 34/2013.
[3] Press release dated 20 October 2014 from the Department of Jobs Enterprise and Innovation.
[4] As amended by the Local Democracy, Economic Development and Construction Act 2009.
[5] Section 9 of the 2013 Act provides that the Minister for Jobs Enterprise and Innovation may prepare and publish a code of practice governing the conduct of adjudications.

A Practical Guide to Construction Adjudication, First Edition. James Pickavance.
© 2016 James Pickavance. Published 2016 by John Wiley & Sons, Inc.

of the 2013 Act.[6] The purpose of the Code of Practice is to provide guidelines on governance of adjudicators conduct under the 2013 Act.[7]

[23.05] The 2013 Act will apply to all construction contracts entered into after the date of the commencement order.[8] Importantly, the 2013 Act will apply irrespective of whether the parties purport to limit or exclude its application and/or where the applicable law of the contract is not Irish.[9] The term construction contract is widely defined, although there are some exclusions for low value works, suppliers, residential properties, employment and PPP contracts.

[23.06] The aim of this chapter is to explore the statutory framework of the Irish adjudication procedure and the key features provided for under the 2013 Act. The 2013 Act is divided into five sections:

(1) the requirements for commencing an adjudication
(2) the adjudication process
(3) the adjudicator's determination, the effect of the determination and costs
(4) the different methods and process of enforcement of an adjudicator's determination
(5) concluding comments.

23.2 Requirements for commencing an adjudication

[23.07] If a contract falls within the scope of the 2013 Act, the right to refer disputes to adjudication cannot be excluded.[10] This does not mean that parties must adjudicate their dispute, rather that they may adjudicate should they choose to do so.

[23.08] For a contract to fall within the scope of the 2013 Act, it must be a construction contract. For the purposes of the 2013 Act, a construction contract is an agreement, whether or not in writing, whereby a party is engaged to carry out, to arrange or to provide labour for construction operations.[11] Construction operations are widely defined. They include construction, alteration, repair, maintenance, extension or dismantling of buildings or structures, permanent or temporary, forming, or to form, part of land.[12] Further, a construction contract includes an agreement to provide ancillary services to the construction contract such as architectural, design, engineering and project management services.[13]

[23.09] The 2013 Act excludes certain operations from construction operations including the manufacture or delivery of building or engineering components or equipment and materials, plant or machinery.[14] The 2013 Act further excludes certain contracts from

---

[6] Press release dated 20 October 2014 from the Department of Jobs Enterprise and Innovation.
[7] Long Title, Code of Practice.
[8] Subsection 12(2) of the 2013 Act.
[9] Subsection 2(5) of the 2013 Act.
[10] Subsection 2(5)(b) of the 2013 Act.
[11] Subsection 1(1) of the 2013 Act.
[12] Subsection 1(1) of the 2013 Act.
[13] Subsection 1(2) of the 2013 Act.
[14] Subsection 1(3) of the 2013 Act.

the definition of construction contracts, for example, contracts with a value of less than €10,000; contracts in relation to private residents where the floor space is less than 200 m^2; contracts of employment within the meaning of the Organisation and Working Time Act 1997; and contracts between a State Authority and its partner in a PPP arrangement.[15]

[23.10] Before an adjudication may be commenced there must be a 'payment dispute' arising under a construction contract. It is notable that the 2013 Act limits the nature of the dispute to payment disputes. It is regrettable that the scope of the adjudication provisions is limited to payment disputes and does not extend to disputes regarding rights and obligations under construction contracts. However, the term payment dispute is widely defined; and adjudication may be invoked for 'any dispute relating to payment arising under the construction contract'.[16]

[23.11] The interpretation of what is a 'payment dispute' will be central to the application of the new statutory regime. Given the litigious nature of the construction sector in Ireland it is inconceivable that disputes and differences will not arise as between parties to the construction contract concerning (a) the meaning of a 'dispute', (b) the meaning of 'relating to', (c) the meaning of 'payment' and (d) the meaning of 'arising under'. This will undoubtedly lead to claims before the Irish courts and delays in processing payments on construction projects and by consequence to frustration of the intent of the 2013 Act.

[23.12] One interpretation is that a payment dispute might be limited to the payment provisions under the 2013 Act. These payment provisions are contained in sections 3, 4 and 5 of the 2013 Act and are broadly set out hereafter.

[23.13] The 2013 Act provides that a construction contract shall provide for the amount of each interim and the final payment to be made under the construction contract or for an adequate mechanism to determine those amounts.[17] The 2013 Act further provides that a construction contract shall provide for a payment claim date or an adequate mechanism for determining the payment claim date.[18] It is thought that the term 'adequate mechanism' will require interpretation and we might derive guidance from the UK's interpretation of the term. While many construction contracts already provide for these payment details, if a contract fails to do so, the 2013 Act sets out default intervals for stage payments of 30 days which will apply together with the default formula for calculating the amount of an interim payment due at a particular claim date.[19] In seeking payment under a construction contract, not later than five days after the payment claim date, a party may deliver a payment claim notice.[20] The notice should specify the following:

(1) the amount claimed
(2) the period, stage of work or activity to which the payment claim relates

---

[15] Subsection 2(1) of the 2013 Act.
[16] Subsection 6(1) of the 2013 Act.
[17] Subsection 3(1) of the 2013 Act.
[18] Subsection 3(2) 2013 Act.
[19] Schedule, of the 2013 Act.
[20] Subsection 4(1) of the 2013 Act.

(3) the subject matter of the payment claim
(4) the basis of the calculation of the amount claimed.[21]

[23.14] While a party can reply and withhold payment, importantly the 2013 Act provides payment cannot be withheld or made conditional on a third party payment.[22] The reply must specify the following:

(1) the amount proposed to be paid
(2) the reason or reasons for the difference between the amount if the payment claim notice and the amount proposed to be paid
(3) the basis on which the amount proposed to be paid is calculated.[23]

[23.15] The 2013 Act includes a right to suspend work for non-payment.[24] However, the suspension cannot continue once the dispute is referred to adjudication.[25] Therefore the party must continue work under the construction contract during the adjudication process. This return to work greatly dilutes the effect of the right to suspend work for non-payment and may in turn lead to parties not selecting adjudication for dispute resolution.

23.3 Adjudication process

23.3.1 Notice of adjudication

[23.16] The party seeking to commence an adjudication (the 'referring party') may exercise their right by serving on the other party (the 'responding party') at any time a notice of adjudication.[26] Although the term 'at any time' is not defined in the 2013 Act, by comparison with its interpretation in the UK, it may be taken to mean that a party may commence an adjudication irrespective of whether the construction contract provides for a multi-tiered dispute resolution process. Further, it may be taken to mean that this entitlement cannot be restricted to post practical completion or by having to complete other steps under the contract beforehand.

[23.17] The form or requirements of the notice of adjudication are not prescribed under the 2013 Act; and this is left to the Code of Practice which provides that the notice of adjudication shall include:

(1) details of how and when the contract, under which the payment dispute has arisen, was formed;
(2) a description of the payment dispute and of the parties involved;
(3) the name, address and contact details of each party to the payment dispute;
(4) the date of service of the notice of adjudication;

---

[21] Subsection 4(2) of the 2013 Act.
[22] Subsection 3(5) of the 2013 Act.
[23] Subsection 4(3) of the 2013 Act.
[24] Subsection 5(1) of the 2013 Act.
[25] Subsection 5(3) of the 2013 Act.
[26] Subsection 6(2) of the 2013 Act.

(5) the redress sought;

(6) copies of relevant payment claim notices and responses to payment claim notices, if any.[27]

[23.18] If the Irish courts follow their UK counterparts, the notice of adjudication will prove to be an important step in defining the extent of the dispute, that it is properly referred and that the issues in dispute are adequately set out in the notice of adjudication.

[23.19] The 2013 Act allows the adjudicator to deal with several payment disputes at the same time, where they arise under the same construction contract or indeed under related contracts.[28] It is not clear, however, whether this ability to deal with more than one payment dispute at the same time means that the referring party can refer more than one dispute at the same time with the originating notice or whether the referral of different disputes subject to separate notices can be brought together and dealt with by the same adjudicator at the same time. What is clear is that the provision to deal with several payment disputes at one time is in the interests of time and cost efficiency. Indeed, once an adjudicator has disposed of a dispute and issued a decision, it is not open to him to revisit that decision in any way other than to correct a clerical or typographical error arising by accident or omission.[29] As a matter of practicality we believe that best practice will be to issue a separate notice of adjudication for each payment dispute unless and until a court rules that one notice of adjudication may deal with more than one payment dispute or where amending legislation is passed clarifying this lacuna.

23.3.2 Appointment of an adjudicator

[23.20] Having served the notice of adjudication, the parties may, within five days beginning with the day on which the notice of adjudication is served, agree to appoint an adjudicator of their own choice or from the Panel of Adjudicators ('the Panel') appointed by the Minister for Jobs Enterprise and Innovation (the 'Minister').[30] While Subsection 8(1) allows the Minister appoint individuals to the Panel, we understand that the Minister has yet to undertake this exercise save for the appointment of the chair of the panel Dr. Nael Bunni on the 12th May 2015.[31] However when undertaken, the Panel will comprise individuals with experience and expertise in dispute resolution procedures under construction contracts[32] and shall be either a registered professional, a chartered member of the Institution of Engineers of Ireland, a barrister, a solicitor or a fellow of the Chartered Institute of Arbitrators.[33] It is understood that the selection of the panel shall be made

---

[27] Section 10, Code of Practice.
[28] Subsection 6(9) of the 2013 Act.
[29] Subsection 6(13) of the 2013 Act.
[30] Subsection 6(3) of the 2013 Act.
[31] It is understood that the Public Appointments Service will undertake a transparent recruitment process in advance of the commencement of the 2013 Act.
[32] Subsection 8(5) of the 2013 Act.
[33] Subsection 8(6) of the 2013 Act.

[23.21] In circumstances where the parties are in agreement as to the appointment of an adjudicator, the Code of Practice provides that the requested adjudicator shall respond within two days and either accept or decline the appointment. If the appointment is accepted the date on which that acceptance is notified in writing to the parties shall be the date on which the appointment is made.[34]

[23.22] Failing agreement to appoint an adjudicator of their own choice, the adjudicator shall be appointed by the chair of the Panel.[35] The Code of Practice provides that a request to the chair of the Panel for the appointment of an adjudicator shall be in writing and copied to the responding party and shall include:

(1) a copy of the notice of adjudication;
(2) a statement of when the notice of adjudication was served on the responding party and how this was done; and
(3) any information that it is considered will assist the chair in appointing an adjudicator with the appropriate expertise to deal with the payment dispute.[36]

[23.23] The Code of Practice provides that where the chair of the Panel is requested to appoint an adjudicator, that appointment should be made and notified to the parties within seven days after receipt of that request but no sooner than five days after the date of service of the notice of adjudication. The date on which that appointment is notified in writing to the parties shall be the date on which the appointment is made.[37]

[23.24] The referring party must refer the payment dispute to the adjudicator within seven days beginning with the day on which the appointment is made.[38] The Code of Practice provides that a referral notice must include:

(1) the contentions on which the referring party relies in support of its case on the payment dispute and the redress sought;
(2) copies of, or relevant extracts from, the construction contract(s) and such documents as the referring party intends to rely upon; and
(3) a copy of the notice of adjudication.[39]

[23.25] A copy of the referral notice must be supplied to the responding party at the same time as it is provided to the adjudicator.[40]

[23.26] The strict and tight time frames which are triggered by the service of the notice of adjudication give rise to the possibility of 'ambush' situations, where the referring party prepares its case in advance of referral. The UK experience suggests that the fact that the referring

---

[34] Section 13, Code of Practice.
[35] Subsection 6(4) of the 2013 Act.
[36] Section 12, Code of Practice.
[37] Section 14, Code of Practice.
[38] Subsection 6(5) of the 2013 Act.
[39] Section 16, Code of Practice.
[40] Section 17, Code of Practice.

party has had the opportunity to prepare in advance will not invalidate the adjudication procedure and the adjudicator will have jurisdiction to hear the dispute. We believe that any threat presented by such abuse will ultimately have to be managed by the adjudicators. Indeed, adjudicators will have in their armoury their own threat of withdrawal to ensure that fair procedures are observed and extensions required are agreed consensually as between the parties. Ultimately, this will evolve as the system of adjudication evolves in Ireland with a growing body of experienced adjudicators.

23.3.3 Powers and duties of an adjudicator

[23.27] The adjudicator must act impartially and comply with the Minister's Code of Practice.[41] The Code of Practice expands on the statutory requirement and provides that 'the adjudicator shall observe the principles of procedural fairness and act impartially and independently and without bias.'[42] It further provides that a person requested to act as adjudicator shall notify the parties of any conflict of interest or external factors that would give rise to a reasonable apprehension of bias; such a person shall decline the appointment unless satisfied it would be appropriate to accept.

[23.28] After appointment, the adjudicator shall immediately notify the parties of any such conflict or factors that arise during the course of the adjudication.[43] In Ireland, the issue of bias will have to be carefully monitored by the stakeholders. The sector is small, with a limited number of design, legal and construction professionals working within the sector, and they often tend to have existing close relationships – as such we believe that care needs to be taken to ensure full disclosure of existing relationships and full transparency at the time of making adjudicator appointments – this will help to avoid bias, or the perceptions of bias

[23.29] Importantly, the Code of Practice provides for the confidentiality of the adjudication procedure. It provides that any document or information supplied for, and/or disclosed in the course of, the adjudication will be kept confidential. It provides that an adjudicator will only disclose any document or information supplied if required to do so by law, or pursuant to an order of a court, or with the consent of all the relevant parties.[44]

[23.30] The Code of Practice provides that the adjudicator shall use reasonable endeavours to process the payment dispute between the parties in the shortest time and at the lowest cost.[45] It further provides that the adjudicator shall ensure that the procedure adopted is commensurate with the nature and value of the payment dispute and shall promptly notify the parties of any matter that will slow down or increase the cost of making a determination.[46]

---

[41] Subsection 6(8) of the 2013 Act.
[42] Section 3, Code of Practice.
[43] Section 4, Code of Practice.
[44] Section 5, Code of Practice.
[45] Section 1, Code of Practice.
[46] Section 2, Code of Practice.

[23.31] The adjudicator may take the initiative in ascertaining the facts and the law in relation to the payment dispute.[47] To that end, the Code of Practice provides that for the purposes of the adjudication the adjudicator may:
(1) request any reasonable supporting or supplementing documents pertaining to the payment dispute detailed in the referral notice and notice of adjudication;
(2) invite written submissions and evidence from both parties;
(3) meet jointly with, and question, the parties and their representatives;
(4) subject to obtaining any necessary consent from a third party or parties, make site visits and inspections or carry out tests;
(5) obtain and consider such representations and submissions as required, and provided that the parties have been notified, appoint experts, assessors or legal advisers;
(6) give directions as to the timetable for the adjudication, any deadlines or limits as to the length of written documents or oral representations; and
(7) issue other directions relating to the conduct of the adjudication.[48]

[23.32] These powers will need to be used sparingly and proportionately by adjudicators, by reference to the amounts in dispute and the limited time available for the operation of the process. Again the choice of adjudicator will be key to ensure that the powers are not abused.

[23.33] It should be noted that the adjudicator will not be liable for anything done or omitted in the discharge or purported discharge of his functions as adjudicator unless the act or omission is in bad faith.[49]

[23.34] The Code of Practice provides that the parties shall comply with a request or direction of the adjudicator made in accordance with the adjudication process.[50] It further provides that if, without showing sufficient cause, a party fails to comply with any request, direction or timetable of the adjudicator made in accordance with his powers, fails to produce any document or written statement requested by the adjudicator, or in any other way fails to comply with a requirement under these provisions relating to the adjudication, the adjudicator may:
(1) continue the adjudication in the absence of that party or of the document or written statement requested;
(2) draw such inferences from that failure to comply as circumstances may, in the adjudicator's opinion, be justified; and
(3) make a decision on the basis of the material properly provided.[51]

[23.35] Commentators have expressed concern that parties to the dispute may seek to put in question an adjudicator's bona fides depending on how he operates this aspect of the Code, and this will inevitably lead to judicial challenges being brought before the courts, causing further delays and uncertainty.

---
[47] Subsection 6(9) of the 2013 Act.
[48] Section 20, Code of Practice.
[49] Subsection 6(14) of the 2013 Act.
[50] Section 21, Code of Practice.
[51] Section 22, Code of Practice.

23.4 Determination, effect and costs

[23.36] One of the key features of adjudication is the short time frame within which the procedure is to be completed. This is fundamental to the key aim underpinning the 2013 Act, to ensure that monies flow promptly and that disputes about payment are resolved quickly. To that end, the adjudicator shall reach a decision within 28 days of the referral.[52] This may be extended, on consent of the referring party, by a period of 14 days.[53] While this might be perceived as overly restrictive, the Code of Practice supplements this provision by providing that 'the adjudicator shall reach a decision within 28 days of the date that a referral is made. This period can be extended by a further 14 days with the consent of the referring party *or such longer period as is agreed by the parties.*'

[23.37] The 2013 Act is silent on the form of the decision; importantly it does not provide for a requirement to provide reasons. The Code of Practice provides that the decision of the adjudicator shall be in writing and signed and dated by the adjudicator and, save where the parties agree otherwise in writing, the decision shall include the reasons for the decision.[54] It is regrettable that unlike other jurisdictions, the 2013 Act does not prescribe the matters to be considered by an adjudicator in determining a dispute. It is further regrettable that the 2013 Act does not prescribe the timing, form and substance of the decision. Rather the 'initiative' given to the adjudicator under the 2013 Act is ambiguous.[55]

[23.38] The decision of the adjudicator shall be binding until the payment dispute is finally settled by the parties or a different decision is reached on the reference of the payment dispute to arbitration or in proceedings initiated in court in relation to the adjudicator's decision.[56] This is a significant departure from the conciliation procedures under the Royal Institute of Architects of Ireland contracts and that under Engineers' Ireland contracts, where a conciliator's decision is not binding if one of the parties confirms its rejection of the decision in writing within 10 days.[57] This means that where an adjudicator decides that payment is due, such payment must be made up-front despite a referral to arbitration or the initiation of court proceedings. The reason for this is that adjudication is a way of protecting cash flow, both of contractors and of the wider supply chain.

[23.39] Each party shall bear its own legal and other costs incurred in connection with the adjudication.[58] It is noted that, in other jurisdictions, an adjudicator may order a party to pay the whole or part of the costs and expenses of another party if the adjudicator considers that the first-named party has caused those costs and expenses to be incurred unnecessarily by bad faith or allegations or objections that are without substantial merit.

---

[52] Subsection 6(6) of the 2013 Act.
[53] Subsection 6(7) of the 2013 Act.
[54] Section 23, Code of Practice.
[55] Subsection 6(9) of the 2013 Act.
[56] Subsection 6(10) of the 2013 Act.
[57] Conciliation procedures as referred to in Royal Institute of Architects of Ireland's Agreement and Schedule of Conditions of Building Contracts and in the Engineers Ireland Conciliation Procedure 2000 – Electronic version July 2011.
[58] Subsection 6(15) of the 2013 Act.

Despite comments and submissions to the Oireachtas[59] on the 2013 Act while at Bill stage to include the wording 'unless decided otherwise by the adjudicator' in the interests of ensuring prompt cooperation between the parties,[60] ultimately the Act was drafted on the basis that each party shall bears its own costs.

[23.40] The parties shall pay the amount of the fees, costs and expenses of the adjudicator in accordance with the decision of the adjudicator.[61] The Code of Practice provides that promptly after appointment, the adjudicator shall provide the parties with his proposed terms of appointment including the basis for his fees, costs and expenses.[62] It further provides that the adjudicator's fees, costs and expenses shall be reasonable in amount having regard to the amount in dispute, the complexity of the dispute, the time spent by the adjudicator and other relevant circumstances.[63]

23.5 Enforcement

[23.41] Where any amount due pursuant to the decision of the adjudicator is not paid in full within 7 days of the adjudicator's decision, the referring party has a right to suspend work for failure to comply with the adjudicator's decision.[64] The referring party must give notice in writing specifying the grounds on which it is intended to suspend work and the notice must be provided 7 days before the proposed suspension is to begin.[65] However, this right of suspension for non-payment of an adjudicator's decision is frustrated by the provision that the right to suspend work will cease if the decision is referred to arbitration or the courts.[66]

[23.42] A key characteristic of adjudication is that the decision of the adjudicator is intended to be binding in the interim. The decision of the adjudicator shall be enforceable by action, or by leave of the High Court, in the same manner as a judgment or order of that court with the same effect and, where leave is given, judgment may be entered in the terms of the decision.[67] The reference to 'leave of the court' for enforcement of an adjudicator's decision as a judgment of the High Court does not make clear how this would work in practice, and what factors the court would take into account in deciding whether to grant leave. Indeed, the entire question of how an adjudicator's decision can be enforced, if not complied with, remains very uncertain, and there is a real danger that a quick decision that payment is due may be undermined by a much longer process for enforcing that decision. If the Irish courts follow the approach taken by the UK courts, the enforceability of adjudicators' decisions will be strictly upheld, subject to very limited exceptions.

---

[59] The Irish parliament.
[60] Society of Chartered Surveyors Ireland, Comments and Submission on the Construction Contracts Bill 2010.
[61] Subsection 6(16) of the 2013 Act.
[62] Section 26, Code of Practice.
[63] Section 27, Code of Practice.
[64] Subsection 7(1) of the 2013 Act.
[65] Subsection 7(2) of the 2013 Act.
[66] Subsection 7(3) of the 2013 Act.
[67] Subsection 6(11) of the 2013 Act.

[23.43] It is regrettable that neither the 2013 Act nor the Code of Practice divested enforcement of disputes to a single court to facilitate speedy enforcement actions. It remains to be seen if the Irish courts will issue a practice direction on the matter. As Ireland does not have a specialist construction court available to hear challenges to adjudicators' decisions, it is arguable that the Commercial Division of the High Court is the appropriate jurisdiction for hearing all such claims, irrespective of the amounts in dispute. In the absence of nominating a specific court or judge to deal with disputes, the floodgates may open for unnecessary and sporadic judicial challenges and it is arguable that what is needed is delegation to a single court or judge as this will ensure a smooth transition and creation of a systematic and coherent body of judicial precedent from a single source.

[23.44] We anticipate that parties seeking enforceability of adjudicators' decisions will refer to the Commercial Division of the High Court. The Commercial Division can admit any claim with a monetary value in excess of €1,000,000; any claim arising from or in relation to arbitration and any claim of significant legal importance (in other words judicial discretion is allowed). On this basis it is arguable that claims for non-payment under the 2013 Act properly fall to the Commercial Division for determination, as it would in our view take a dim view of non-application of the provision of this important new legislation and for smaller disputes (say less than €250,000) the €5000 stamp duty requirement for the Commercial Division might even be waived.

[23.45] If disputes are admitted to the Commercial Division, judgment could be obtained very quickly (i.e. within six to eight weeks of issuing proceedings) and this would assist the implementation of the aims of the 2013 Act. Indeed, the Rules of the Superior Courts in Ireland, which include the Rules for the Commercial Court, might yet be amended to provide specifically that claims arising from adjudication decisions are automatically admitted to the Commercial Division of the High Court and that the normal stamp duty requirement of a payment of €5000 would be waived for claims less than €250,000 and staggered on a pro rata basis up to the normal threshold of €1m. What is needed is lobbying and consensus on the need for disputes to be referred into the Commercial Court.

[23.46] The power of adjudication under the 2013 Act is a statutory power and, therefore, subject to judicial review. Judicial review is primarily concerned with the decision-making process rather than with the substance of the decision. There is, however, a limited scope for review of the substance of a decision as well. Judicial review is governed by the Rules of the Superior Courts.

23.6 Conclusion

[23.47] It can be argued that given the wording of the 2013 Act and the Code of Practice that the success of adjudication of construction contracts in Ireland will very much depend on the quality of the adjudicators. While the Code of Practice provides that the adjudicator must comply with the Code of Practice, it does not impose a specific sanction on the adjudicator for failing to adhere to same.

[23.48] Unfortunately, practitioners do not have the benefit of an established body of case law to assist in the interpretation of the 2013 Act. As demonstrated elsewhere in this book, there has been, and continues to be, a plethora of case law from other jurisdictions on their corresponding legislation, which will assist in guiding the Irish system through this new process. There will, of course, be numerous elements of the 2013 Act that will require clarification through decisions of the Irish courts and no doubt this will lead to a period of uncertainty, contested adjudication decisions and expensive court challenges to enforcement actions.

[23.49] While there are complaints that the 2013 Act has come too late for many in the industry who suffered as a result of the latest economic recession, it will hopefully provide important protection for those operating in the construction industry in the future. The enactment of the 2013 Act is a very significant development for the administration of construction contracts in Ireland and, in particular, for the management and resolution of construction sector disputes. To be a success, the industry as a whole must welcome the process and see it as a final platform to resolving commercial disputes, thereby avoiding the traditional alternative dispute resolution procedures of mediation, conciliation and arbitration, and bypassing the courts too.

Chapter 24
Malaysia: Philip Koh[1]

24.1 Overview

[24.01] Particularly in the past decade, the Malaysian construction industry has been bedevilled by claims of delay in payments, which have resulted in hardships and even bankruptcies of contractors and subcontractors. While in the short term the 'pain' was felt by the payee, the negative impact of payment default reverberated throughout all sections of the industry, and constrained growth.

[24.02] The Construction Industry Payment And Adjudication Act 2012 (the **2012 Act**),[2] which came into effect on 15 April 2014, introduces a statutory adjudication process and payment rules that seek to balance the rights of parties who are entitled to payment for work done or services rendered under a construction contract in Malaysia. Malaysia joins a number of Commonwealth jurisdictions who have legislated to provide quick and clear access to justice by instituting a system of adjudication for expeditious resolution of disputed claims in the construction industry. The preamble to the 2012 Act provides that it is intended:

> to facilitate regular and timely payment, to provide a mechanism for speedy dispute resolution through adjudication, to price remedies for recovery of payments in the construction industry.

[24.03] In other words, the objective is to address the pervasive and prevalent culture of delayed payment or non-payment, which has long been lamented by those in the construction industry.

[24.04] The Kuala Lumpur Regional Centre for Arbitration (KLRCA) is the body appointed as the statutory adjudication authority pursuant to section 32 of the 2012 Act. The Construction Industry Payment and Adjudication Regulations 2014 (the **Malaysia**

---

[1] Philip TN Koh is the senior partner at Mah-Kamariyah & Philip Koh. Philip has served as an Adjunct Professor of Deakin University and as visiting Fulbright Scholar attached to the Harvard University Economics Department. He is appointed to the panel of arbitrators for the KLRCA and is an accredited KLRCA construction law adjudicator. Philip was assisted by Shi Ying Chai and Steven Cannon of Eversheds
[2] klrca.org/cipaa. Accessed 1 September 2015.

A Practical Guide to Construction Adjudication, First Edition. James Pickavance.
© 2016 James Pickavance. Published 2016 by John Wiley & Sons, Inc.

Regulations),[3] which came into force on the same day as the 2012 Act, set out the roles and responsibilities of the KLRCA in respect of adjudication matters, the competency standards for adjudicators, the appointment procedure and the amount and entitlement to fees. It also provides administrative support before and during adjudications.

[24.05] Certain key characteristics of the adjudication process are as follows:

(1) It applies to contracts for construction work carried out wholly or partly within the territory of Malaysia.
(2) There is a significant distinction between the nature of the regime in respect of (1) contracts where the employer is a private company or individual, and (2) where the employer is a government or government-linked entity.
(3) The right of either party to adjudicate a dispute is mandatory and does not require the consent of both parties.
(4) The right to adjudicate is only available in respect of a specific payment dispute under the payment regime.
(5) The appointment of the adjudicator is either secured by agreement or by application to the director of the KLRCA.
(6) An employer may raise a defence of set-off in the adjudication even if it did not notify the contractor of its intention when responding to the interim application for payment.
(7) The adjudicator must reach a decision within 45 working days from the receipt of the adjudication response or the reply if it is served, whichever is later.
(8) The decision is binding on the parties until the dispute is resolved via litigation, arbitration or by agreement between the parties.
(9) The High Court may stay enforcement proceedings where 'the subject matter of the adjudication decision is pending final determination by arbitration or the Court.' While it is unclear in what circumstances the High Court would decide to exercise such a discretion, this power, to a certain extent, would seem to undermine the 'pay now, argue later' intention of adjudication.

24.2 Requirements for commencing the adjudication process

24.2.1 What contracts are caught by the 2012 Act?

[24.06] Pursuant to section 2, the 2012 Act applies to:

- every construction contract relating to construction work;
- made in writing;
- carried out wholly or partly within the territory of Malaysia; and
- including a construction contract entered into by the Government.

[24.07] The 2012 Act and the Malaysia Regulations expand upon each of these aspects.

---
[3] Ibid.

(A) Every construction contract relating to construction work

[24.08] The term 'construction contract' is defined at section 4 of the 2012 Act as 'a construction work contract or a construction consultancy contract'.

[24.09] Section 4 goes on to define what is meant by construction work. The term is given a broad meaning and includes the construction, extension, installation, repair, maintenance, renewal, removal, renovation, alteration, dismantling or demolition of:

(a) any building, erection, edifice, structure, wall, fence or chimney, whether constructed wholly or partly above or below ground level;
(b) any road, harbour works, railway, cableway, canal or aerodrome;
(c) any drainage, irrigation or river control work;
(d) any electrical, mechanical, water, gas, oil, petrochemical or telecommunication work; or
(e) any bridge, viaduct, dam, reservoir, earthworks, pipeline, sewer, aqueduct, culvert, drive, shaft, tunnel or reclamation work.

[24.10] Section 4 also provides the meaning of 'construction consultancy contract', which is said to comprise of consultancy services in relation to construction work. This includes planning and feasibility study, architectural work, engineering, surveying, exterior and interior decoration, landscaping and project management services.

[24.11] The scope of section 4 is wide enough to include ancillary works, such as preparatory, temporary and procurement work. It also encapsulates supply control and the provision of workers for construction works.[4]

[24.12] The 2012 Act, however, does not apply to construction contracts entered into by a natural person for any construction work in respect of any building which is less than four stories high and is wholly intended for his occupation (in other words a residential construction contract).[5]

[24.13] However, the exclusion only applies where the building is the employer's principal place of occupation. It follows that it does not extend to the situation where the employer builds the residential building to sell, rent or lease.[6] Furthermore, the phrase 'wholly intended for his own occupation' has not been further explained or defined in the 2012 Act, and so how it will be interpreted by the courts is unclear.

[24.14] More issues of interpretation may arise where only part of the construction work is intended for personal occupation. For instance, what is the position where five residential buildings below four floors in height are built at the same time by an individual, and that individual intends to occupy one building and sell the other four buildings, but has not decided which building he will occupy? Does the 2012 Act apply to all of the buildings or does the individual have to choose which building is exempted? It remains a moot

---
[4] Ibid.
[5] Section 3 of the 2012 Act.
[6] Sundra Rajoo & Harbans Singh KS, *Construction Law in Malaysia*, (Thomson Reuters Malaysia Sdn Bhd, 2012) p. 568.

point whether this exemption is confined only to merely residential occupation or will also extend to business accommodation. However, the phrase 'wholly intended for his occupation' suggests that if a residential building is not exclusively for occupation then the legislation would be applicable.

(B) Made in writing

[24.15] The 2012 Act only applies to a construction contract 'made in writing'. Unlike legislation enacted in other jurisdictions, such as Singapore's Building and Construction Industry Security Payment Act 2004,[7] there is no provision in the 2012 Act that defines what 'made in writing' means. It is submitted that this omission will inevitably breed uncertainty as to exactly what is and is not within the meaning of the term. The term does not require that all construction contracts must be in a formal contract document to fall within the scope of the 2012 Act. The phrase should be given a broad meaning and should include partly oral contracts, but not settlement agreements, financing agreements and collateral warranties.[8]

[24.16] That said, the KLRCA has provided guidance[9] in an effort to provide some certainty. 'Construction contract in writing' is widely defined by KLRCA to cover (1) the contract is made in writing (whether or not it is signed by the parties); (2) the contract is made by exchange of communications in writing; (3) the contract is evidenced in writing; (4) where the parties agree otherwise than in writing by reference to terms which are in writing; and (5) where the terms of contract is recorded by one of the parties or by a third party with the authority of the parties to the contract.[10]

[24.17] It is KLRCA's position that this interpretation is binding – it notes that 'The KLRCA Guideline on Construction Contract in Writing shall apply to all adjudication cases commenced under CIPAA'. As it is unclear from where KLRCA derives its power to make binding interpretations of statute, it is likely that the High Court will be required to make a determination as to whether or not the KLRCA's interpretation applies.

[24.18] It is noted that the definition of 'construction contract in writing' by the KLRCA is of the provisions set out in section 107 of the 1996 Act in the UK. Practitioners who wish to gain further insight into precisely what is meant by this guidance may be assisted by UK case law. Section 4.8 of this book examines the meaning of section 107 of the 1996 Act in some detail.

---

[7] Subsection 4(3) Building and Construction Industry Security Payment Act 2004.
[8] C.K. Oon, *'Initiating And Defending Adjudication Cases Under Construction Industry Payment And Adjudication Act 2012 – Challenges And Pitfalls'*, [2013] 5 MLJ c, p 2.
[9] KLRCA CIPAA Circular 03 'Circular on KLRCA's Guidance on the Meaning of 'Construction Contract Made in Writing'. A copy of which can be found at <http://klrca.org/cipaa/#KLRCACIRCULARS>.
[10] Ibid. Although the KLRCA's Circular is not legally binding, judicial notice will, however, be taken of it and this will have persuasive effect on the adjudicator in making decision over this issue.

(C) Carried out wholly or partly within the territory of Malaysia

[24.19] This wording appears to encompass works that are being carried out on Malaysian territory, including off-shore works within Malaysian territorial waters. Construction contracts regarding oil and gas are expressly caught by the 2012 Act.

[24.20] More difficult issues may arise whereby only part of the work is carried out in Malaysian territory. For instance, if an EPC contractor has an engineering or administrative function in Malaysia but the physical works are to be carried out outside of Malaysian territory (whether in international waters or in another territory altogether) then difficult questions of private international law may arise.

[24.21] One can imagine circumstances whereby a Malaysian contractor is operating in (say) Iraq while the design function is being carried out in Malaysia and payment type issues arise. If the contract is subject to Malaysian law, and under the jurisdiction of a Malaysian Court, then there may be few practical difficulties in applying the 2012 Act. However, if the governing law is of a state other than Malaysia, or where the final forum for disputes is a court or arbitrator outside of Malaysia, then it is difficult to see how the 2012 Act will practically apply.

(D) Construction contract entered into by the government

[24.22] Section 2 of the 2012 Act specifically states that it applies equally to the private sector as well as to construction contracts entered into by the Federal Government of Malaysia. Although the definition of 'government construction contract' is not expressly provided in the 2012 Act, the implication is that the 2012 Act extends to construction contracts to which the Government is a party. The applicability of the 2012 Act to the Government of Malaysia is important. The purpose of this legislation would be undermined and eroded if the Government of Malaysia, being one of the largest employers in the country, was exempted from the 2012 Act. Therefore, it would be appropriate if the 2012 Act applies equally across the Malaysian construction industry for its benefit as a whole.

[24.23] Notwithstanding the application of the 2012 Act to the Government, there are a few exceptions. The Construction Industry Payment and Adjudication (Exemption) Order 2014, which came into force on the same day as the 2012 Act,[11] provides two categories of exemptions for government construction contracts.

[24.24] The first exemption relates to construction contracts for any construction works that either need to be carried out urgently and without delay due to natural disaster, flood, landslide, ground subsidence, fire and other emergency and unforeseen circumstances or that relate to the matters of national security or security-related facilities.[12] These categories of work are exempted from all provisions of the 2012 Act.[13]

---

[11] Op. cit. No. 2.
[12] Order 2 Construction Industry Payment and Adjudication (Exemption) Order 2014. A copy of which can be found at: <http://klrca.org/cipaa/#CONSTRUCTIONINDUSTRYPAYMENTANDADJUDICATION(EXEMPTION)ORDER20144>
[13] Regulation 2(1) of the Exemption Order.

[24.25] The second exemption is a temporary exemption, which applies from 15 April 2014 until 31 December 2015 and excludes government construction contracts for any construction work with a contract sum of MYR 20 million and below. This exemption only applies to part of the 2012 Act and replaces subsections 6(3), 7(2), 10(1), 10(2), 11(1) and 11(2) with provisions set out at regulation 2(3) of the Exemption Order. The amended provisions enable a longer period for service of certain documents, such as the payment response, adjudication response and adjudication reply.

24.2.2 Retrospective effect of the 2012 Act

[24.26] In the case of *UDA Holdings Bhd v Bisraya Construction Sdn Bhd*[14] and *Capital Avenue Development Sdn Bhd v Bauer (M) Sdn Bhd*,[15] Justice Mary Lim of the High Court of Malaysia determined that the 2012 Act was intended to apply retrospectively, subject to sections 2 and 41 of the Act.

[24.27] Section 41 is the saving provision considering only the effect upon court or arbitral proceedings extant as at the date the 2012 Act came into force. It provides that the 2012 Act shall not:

> affect any proceedings relating to any payment dispute under a construction contract which had been commenced in any court or arbitration before coming into operation of this Act.

[24.28] Thus, subject to sections 2 and 41, the 2012 Act applies to construction contracts falling within its scope which were entered into at any time. The impact of these High Court decisions is significant and has widened the operational scope of the legislation.

24.3 Adjudication process

[24.29] The 2012 Act offers a relatively simple and more expedient mechanism of dispute resolution when compared to arbitration or court proceedings in Malaysia. The procedure is generally informal with little opportunity for negotiations between the parties. The adjudicator is constrained to produce the written decision within a limited time frame, unless both parties agree otherwise.

[24.30] The entire process assures an adjudication decision no more than 100 days[16] from the day of service of the payment claim. This makes it a highly efficient mode of payment

---

[14] 24C-6-09/2014.
[15] 24C-5-09/2014.
[16] This assumes the following maximum time table (all in working days) (1) notice of adjudication; then (2) 10 days to seek to agree an adjudicator (s.21(a)); then (3) 5 days for nomination of adjudicator by KLRCA (s.23(1); then (4) 10 days for negotiation of terms of appointment (s.23(2); then (5) 10 days for the service of the Adjudication Claim (s.9(1)); then (6) 10 days for the service of the Adjudication Response (s.10(1)); then (7) 5 days for the service of the Adjudication Reply (s.11(1)); and finally (8) 45 days for the adjudicator's decision or such further time as agreed to by the parties (s.12(2)).

dispute resolution and facilitates cash flow liquidity within a construction project. In contrast with arbitration and court litigation which is 'argue first, pay later', the adjudication process related to payment disputes is akin to the concept 'pay first, argue later'.

[24.31] The process can be summarised within the following five steps.

24.3.1 Step 1: Payment claim

[24.32] The right of the receiving party to refer a dispute to adjudication only arises upon a dispute over a contractual payment which has first passed through the payment regime.

[24.33] The process commences with the payee serving a 'payment claim to non-paying party' (i.e. the payee), which states the amount claimed and the due date, the cause of action, the provision(s) the contract relied on, the description of the work or services to which the payment relates and a statement that is made under the 2012 Act.[17] A model form for a payment claim can be found at Schedule 1, Form 1 of the KLRCA Adjudication Rules and Procedure.

[24.34] Upon receiving the payment claim, the payee has an option as to whether to respond to the payment claim or not. The payee may admit or dispute wholly or partly on the amount disputed by serving a payment response within 10 working days, save in respect of a Government contract with a value of MYR 20 million or below, where the period for the service of the payment response is 30 days. A payee who fails to respond to a payment claim is deemed to have disputed the entire payment claim.[18]

24.3.2 Step 2: Initiation of adjudication

[24.35] The adjudication is initiated by the claimant serving a notice of adjudication which states the nature and description of the crystallised dispute[19] and the remedy sought, together with supporting documents. The claimant is entitled to serve the notice upon the expiry of the 10 days referred to in Step 1.[20] A model form can be found at Form 2 of Schedule 1 to the KLRCA Adjudication Rules and Procedure.

24.3.3 Step 3: Appointment

[24.36] Once the respondent has received the notice of adjudication,[21] the parties to the adjudication may by agreement, appoint the adjudicator.[22] If agreement cannot be reached within 10 days, the appointment shall be made by the director of KLRCA within 5 days of

---

[17] Section 5 of the 2012 Act.
[18] Subsection 6(4) of the 2012 Act.
[19] Subsection 27(1) of the 2012 Act.
[20] Subsection 8(1) of the 2012 Act.
[21] Subsection 8(2) of the 2012 Act.
[22] Section 21 of the 2012 Act sets out the process of appointing an adjudicator by the parties.

a request from either party, such request being made in an application form and accompanied by an administrative fee of MYR 400, being the Adjudicator Appointment Fee.[23]

[24.37] Once appointed, the adjudicator will propose and negotiate his terms (including fees chargeable) and, if negotiations conclude satisfactorily, he will notify his acceptance of the appointment within 10 working days. If the adjudicator rejects his appointment, or fails to indicate his acceptance within the 10 working day period, the parties may proceed to appoint another adjudicator by agreement or through the Director of the KLRCA.[24]

[24.38] Forms 4 to 6 of Schedule 1 to the KLRCA Adjudication Rules and Procedure are model forms for Step 3.

24.3.4 Step 4: Submissions

[24.39] The claimant shall, within 10 working days of accepting the appointment by the adjudicator, serve upon the respondent a written adjudication claim which contains the details of the dispute and the remedy sought.[25] The respondent will have 10 working days from the date of receipt of the claimant's claim to serve a response.[26] The claimant will then have five working days from the date of receipt of the response to submit a reply to the adjudication response together with any supporting documents.[27] Pursuant to Rules 5 and 6 of the KLRCA Rules, the relevant party must inform the KLRCA of the adjudication response and reply within seven working days of service.

[24.40] Sections 8 and 9 of the 2012 Act require the claimant to serve on the respondent the same set of supporting documents twice: one in the notice of adjudication and the other in the claim. In addition, section 9(2) further requires the serving to the adjudicator of 'a copy of the adjudication claim together with any supporting document within the time specified in section 9(1)'. It is submitted that this repetition, though required by the 2012 Act, is unnecessary.

24.3.5 Step 5: The adjudicator

[24.41] The appointed adjudicator reviews the documents submitted by the parties and ascertains the facts and law by hearing the parties' presentations. The 2012 Act and KLRCA Rules empower the adjudicator to make decisions and set his own procedures, provided this is consistent with the 2012 Act and Rules. The express rights, powers, duties and jurisdiction of the adjudicator are set out in detail in sections 24 to 27 of the 2012 Act.

---

[23] Section 23 of the 2012 Act and rule 3(2)(a) of the KLRCA Adjudication Rules and Procedure. A copy of which can be found at: http://klrca.org/downloads/cipaa/KLRCA_Adjudication_Rules_(as_of_1_August_2014).pdf.
[24] Sections 22 and 23 of the 2012 Act.
[25] Subsection 9(1) of the 2012 Act.
[26] Subsection 10(1) of the 2012 Act
[27] Section 11 of the 2012 Act.

[24.42] In the event of any non-compliance with the 2012 Act by the parties, it is clear that the adjudicator's power to conduct the adjudication to a decision is unaffected.[28] However, in the case of non-compliance, the adjudicator has considerable powers, including a power to 'set aside wholly or partly the adjudication proceedings', which would appear to be the equivalent to a court's power to strike out a claim. There is little guidance as to when an adjudicator may exercise such a power, and any decision to do so must be balanced against the adjudicator's obligation to comply with the principles of natural justice. The adjudicator also has additional powers to 'make any order dealing with the adjudication proceedings as the adjudicator deems fit' or to allow an amendment to any non-compliant document.[29]

24.4 Administration of the adjudication

[24.43] The KLRCA has been appointed as the adjudication authority by virtue of section 32 of the 2012 Act. Its functions are set out in that section and relate to the setting of competency standards for adjudicators, determining the standard terms of appointment and fees, providing administrative support for the conduct of adjudication and providing any function as may be required for the efficient conduct of adjudication. This role has been augmented by the Malaysia Regulations which provide the KLRCA with the following further responsibilities:

(1) maintaining a register of adjudicators;
(2) determining a code of conduct for an adjudicator;
(3) providing training and examinations for an adjudicator;
(4) determining fees for the services and expenses of an adjudicator; and
(5) receiving and holding any fees and expenses deposited by the parties in dispute on behalf of an adjudicator.[30]

[24.44] KLRCA has produced a considerable body of work in this regard, including schedules of fees and expenses, criteria/competency standards for an adjudicator and, perhaps most importantly, the KLRCA Adjudication Rules and Procedure (**KLRCA Rules**) which contains, inter alia, detailed provisions as to adjudication procedure.

[24.45] Pursuant to section 21 of the 2012 Act, the Director of the KLRCA is the default appointing authority if:

> upon request of either party in dispute if there is no agreement of the parties within 10 working days from the service of notice of adjudication by the claimant.

[24.46] The KLRCA will also act as a stakeholder for the adjudication fees payable to the adjudicators,[31] and for any adjudicated amount ordered by the court to be deposited with KLRCA by any party pursuant to an application for a stay.[32]

---

[28] Subsection 26(1) of the 2012 Act.
[29] Subsection 26(2) of the 2012 Act.
[30] Regulation 2 of the Malaysia Regulations.
[31] Subsection 19(4) of the 2012 Act.
[32] Subsection 16(2) of the 2012 Act.

[24.47] The appointment of KLRCA as the official adjudication authority is well received. Without doubt the KLRCA is well placed to perform this role, as it is already tasked with appointing mediators and arbitrators under the Arbitration Act 2005.

24.5 Determination, effect and costs

24.5.1 Form and timing of the decision

[24.48] Save where both parties agree to extend time, the adjudicator has 45 working days from the date of service of the adjudication response or reply to the adjudication response (whichever is later), or if no adjudication response is served, 45 working days from the date it was supposed to be served, to deliver his decision.[33]

[24.49] The decision shall be in writing and the adjudicator shall provide written reasons for his decision unless the requirement for reasons is dispensed with by agreement between the parties.[34] The decision shall determine the adjudicated amount and the time and manner the adjudicated amount is payable.[35]

24.5.2 Effect of the decision

[24.50] After the adjudication decision is delivered, by virtue of section 13 of the 2012 Act, it is binding unless:

(1) it is set aside by the High Court;
(2) subject matter of the decision is settled by a written agreement between the parties; or
(3) the dispute is finally decided by arbitration or the court.

[24.51] An application to set aside the adjudication decision may be made by the aggrieved party to the High Court relying on one or more of the following grounds:

(1) the adjudication decision was improperly procured through fraud or bribery;
(2) a breach of natural justice;
(3) the adjudicator was biased;
(4) the adjudicator exceeded his jurisdiction.[36]

[24.52] Any computational or typographical error may be corrected at any time on the adjudicator's own initiative or at the request of any party and shall not be a reason to set aside the adjudication decision.[37]

---

[33] Section 12 of the 2012 Act.
[34] Rule 10 of the KLRCA Rules and Section 12(4) of the 2012 Act.
[35] Subsection 12(5) of the 2012 Act.
[36] Section 15 of the 2012 Act.
[37] Subsection 12(7) of the 2012 Act.

[24.53] A party may apply to the High Court for a stay of an adjudication decision.[38] Subsection 16(2) of the 2012 Act provides that a High Court can:

(1) grant a stay of adjudication decision;
(2) order the adjudicated amount or part of it to be deposited with the director of the KLRCA; or
(3) make any order as it thinks fit.

[24.54] Can an adjudication proceed in parallel with a final determination? Section 37 provides that a reference to arbitration or the court in respect of a dispute being adjudicated will not affect the adjudication proceedings nor will bring it to an end. However, the adjudication proceedings will be terminated once the dispute being adjudicated is decided by arbitration or the court or settled between the parties by an agreement in writing.

24.5.3 Costs

(A) Party costs

[24.55] When an adjudicator makes a decision in relation to the costs for the adjudication proceedings, he shall order the costs to follow the event and shall fix the quantum of costs to be paid.[39] This provision overrides any other agreement reached between the parties.

(B) Adjudicator's fees and expenses

[24.56] The fees to be paid to an adjudicator are dictated by the Malaysia Regulations. However, the KLRCA is of the view that the schedule of fees under the Regulations may not be sufficiently remunerative to attract qualified and experienced individuals to act as adjudicators.[40]

[24.57] For this reason, the KLRCA suggests an alternative fee schedule which has been calculated taking into consideration the standard of professionalism expected of an adjudicator, the amount claimed in the adjudication dispute and the timeline which an adjudicator needs to complete the adjudication.

[24.58] The KLRCA Recommended Schedule of Fees may be adopted by the adjudicator and parties at any time during the discussions of the adjudicator's terms of appointment and fees.[41]

[24.59] An adjudicator may incur expenses as part of performing his duties. These expenses are to be borne by the parties as directed by the adjudicator. Although expenses are to be

---

[38] Subsection 16(1) of the 2012 Act.
[39] Subsection 18(1) of the 2012 Act.
[40] KLRCA CIPAA Circular 02 'Circular On KLRCA's Recommended Schedule of Fees (Amended as at 1 August 2014)'. A copy of which can be found at *http://klrca.org/cipaa/#KLRCACIRCULARS*.
[41] Ibid.

paid by the parties, the expenses incurred must be of reasonable value and submitted to the KLRCA for approval.[42]

[24.60] The parties are jointly and severally liable for the payment of the adjudicator's fees.[43] The adjudicator is also entitled to withhold his decision until such time as his full fees and expenses are deposited with the KLRCA.[44] He is even able to withhold beyond the time for the decision,[45] without prejudicing his entitlement to be paid.

24.6 Enforcement

[24.61] Where an unsuccessful party fails to comply with the terms of an adjudicator's decision, the other party may enforce the decision by applying to the High Court for an order as if it were a judgment or order of the High Court.[46] This means that the whole range of enforcement sanctions is available to the court including, inter alia, writ of seizure and sale, winding-up proceedings, bankruptcy, debtor summons and garnishee order.

[24.62] The enforcement of an adjudicator's decision is subject to the key proviso that the adjudication decision has not been stayed or set aside or overruled by arbitration or the court. A party may resist enforcement of adjudication decisions by pleading one of the grounds provided under section 16 of the 2012 Act as described in the previous section.

[24.63] Other than enforcement of the adjudication decision through the court, the 2012 Act offers additional ways of agreement. They are:

(1) suspension or reduction in the pace of work; and
(2) payment from the principal.

24.6.1 Suspension or a reduction in the pace of work

[24.64] If the adjudicated amount pursuant to an adjudication decision has not been paid wholly or partly after the receipt of the adjudicated decision, the successful claimant may suspend the performance or reduce the rate of progress of performance of any construction work or construction consultancy services in the construction contract in which the payment dispute arose.[47]

[24.65] The party intending to suspend or reduce the pace of performance shall provide and serve a written notice of intention to suspend performance or reduce the rate of progress of performance to the other party if the adjudicated amount is not paid within 14 calendar days from the date of receipt of the notice.[48] There is a further entitlement to

---

[42] Ibid.
[43] Subsection 19(3) of the 2012 Act.
[44] Subsection 19(5) of the 2012 Act.
[45] Subsection 19(5) and (6) of the 2012 Act.
[46] Section 28 of the 2012 Act.
[47] Subsection 29(1) of the 2012 Act.
[48] Subsection 29(2) of the 2012 Act.

recover any loss or expenses incurred as a result of the reduction in the rate of progress of performance from the other party.[49] Work shall resume in accordance with the contract within 10 working days upon the receipt of the adjudicated amount or the amount determined by the court or arbitration.[50]

[24.66] Prior to the enactment of the 2012 Act, suspension or go-slow by contractor was likely to amount to a breach of contract in the absence of a contractual provision permitting such action.[51]

24.6.2 Secure direct payment from principal

[24.67] The 2012 Act provides for the successful claimant to obtain or secure the payment of the adjudicated decision directly from the principal of the construction contract.[52] A written request for payment of the adjudicated amount may be served to its main contractor's principal if there is a failure to secure the adjudicated payment in his favour.

[24.68] The 'principal' is defined as 'a party who has contracted with and is liable to make payment to another party where that other party has in turn contracted with and is liable to make payment to a further person in a chain of construction contracts'. The definition of 'principal' referred in the 2012 Act does not limit the ultimate employer or developer or owner in the construction contract in which the payment dispute arose but is wide enough to encompass the main contractor or subcontractor who has entered into a construction contract with the losing party.

[24.69] The successful claimant may only exercise this remedy if the losing party has failed to pay the adjudicated amount, subject to the condition that the money is due or payable by the principal to the losing party at the time of receipt of the written request for payment of the adjudicated amount.[53]

24.7 Conclusion

[24.70] There is no single mechanism of dispute resolution that fits all circumstances. That said, the introduction of statutory adjudication and the creation of a specialist construction court has changed the Malaysian construction dispute resolution landscape. Even though there are clear difficulties with the drafting of the 2012 Act, overall it has been warmly welcomed in the Malaysian construction industry. It is believed that the 2012 Act is a positive milestone in forcing a paradigm shift in the Malaysian construction industry.

[24.71] While protagonists are sure that the 2012 Act will facilitate a transformation in the construction industry, the success of its implementation depends on the competency and

---

[49] Subsection 29(4)(c) of the 2012 Act.
[50] Subsection 29(4)(d) of the 2012 Act.
[51] *Kah Seng Construction Sdn Bhd v Se/sin Development Sdn Bhd* [1997] 1 CLJ SUPP 448 (HC).
[52] Section 30 of the 2012 Act.
[53] Subsection 30(5) 2012 Act.

integrity of the adjudicators, effective administration by the KLRCA and strong support from the judiciary. It is hoped that the 2012 Act will force a fundamental change in mind-set and attitude towards timely payment, in order to promote progressive change in the domestic business culture. Malaysia will take a justifiable pride in joining jurisdictions around the world in providing a statute-backed platform that ensures quick access to both payment and justice.

Chapter 25

New Zealand: Tómas Kennedy-Grant QC[1]

25.1 Overview

[25.01] New Zealand's security of payments legislation is contained in the Construction Contracts Act 2002 (the **2002 Act**), which came into force on 1 April 2003.[2] The purpose of the 2002 Act was to reform the law relating to construction contracts and, in particular, to facilitate regular and timely payments between the parties to a construction contract, provide for the speedy resolution of disputes arising under a construction contract, and provide remedies for the recovery of payments under a construction contract.[3] The 2002 Act prohibits conditional payment provisions in construction contracts,[4] provides a statutory regime for progress payments and the procedure for making and responding to payment claims,[5] and most importantly in the context of the present text, establishes a system of statutory adjudication of disputes arising out of construction contracts.[6] Finally, in the present context, it provides for the enforcement of adjudicators' determinations in a variety of manners.[7]

[25.02] In 1987, the Wages Protection and Contractors' Liens Act 1939, which (together with predecessor acts) had provided a measure of security for payments in the construction industry for almost a century, was repealed. It was not until 1999–2002 that progress was made in formulating a replacement scheme. The key factors that resulted in the adoption

---

[1] Tómas Kennedy-Grant QC has recently retired, after more than 50 years' experience in the fields of civil and commercial law and construction law. He was a Master of the High Court of New Zealand from 1992 to 2002, prior to which he acted as counsel and arbitrator. Since leaving the Bench he has practised as an arbitrator, adjudicator and mediator. He was elected as the inaugural President of the Society of Construction Law New Zealand.

[2] Sections 65, 81 and 82 came into force on the day after the date on which the 2002 Act received the Royal consent. A copy of the 2002 Act can be downloaded from the New Zealand Legislation website at *www.legislation.govt.nz*.

[3] Section 2.

[4] Section 13.

[5] Sections 14–24.

[6] Sections 25–71.

[7] Sections 72–79.

A Practical Guide to Construction Adjudication, First Edition. James Pickavance.
© 2016 James Pickavance. Published 2016 by John Wiley & Sons, Inc.

of the new scheme were the New Zealand Law Commission's Study Paper in 1999, recommending such an act,[8] agreement among the various parts of the construction industry on a group that would speak with one voice for the industry, and the succession of major construction company failures that occurred from 2000 onwards.

[25.03] Because there is no equivalent in New Zealand to the Adjudication Reporting Centre at Glasgow Caledonian University, there is no readily accessible record of the number of adjudications that have been held in New Zealand.[9] Estimates have been made of as many as 120 nationally in any one year; but the probability is that the number has fluctuated significantly from year to year. What is certain is that adjudication has replaced arbitration as the most common method of resolving construction disputes, particularly in relation to claims for payment under the contract, and that very few adjudication determinations have been relitigated in the courts or in arbitration. However, the 2002 Act has probably had its greatest effect simply by being in force and making parties to construction contracts think more carefully before they adopt intransigent or unreasonable positions.

[25.04] There are no up-to-date texts on the New Zealand legislation, but reference can be made to Bayley and Kennedy-Grant: A guide to the Construction Contracts Act[10] and to Chapter 28 of the shortly to be released online loose-leaf publication Kennedy-Grant and Weatherall on Construction Law (LexisNexis NZ, 2015).

[25.05] The following review of the 2002 Act and its operation is divided into seven sections:

(1) the requirements for commencing an adjudication;
(2) the adjudication process;
(3) the adjudicator's determination, the effect of the determination, and costs;
(4) the rights of a non-respondent owner;
(5) the different methods and processes of enforcement of an adjudicator's determination;
(6) judicial review; and
(7) proposed amendments.

25.2 Requirements for commencing an adjudication

[25.06] Before an adjudication may be commenced there must be a dispute or difference arising under a construction contract.[11]

[25.07] The 2002 Act does not limit the nature of the dispute in any way, although it does give, as an example of a dispute, a disagreement between the parties to a construction contract about whether or not an amount is payable under the contract or the reasons given

---

[8] *Protecting Construction Contractors* NZLC SP3.
[9] Clause 31 of the Construction Contracts Amendment Bill presently before Parliament seeks to remedy this situation.
[10] Rawlinsons Media Ltd, 2nd ed, 2009.
[11] Section 5 of the 2002 Act, definition of 'dispute'.

for non-payment of that amount. It is clear, however, that the scope of the adjudication provisions of the 2002 Act is not limited to what may be called money claims, but extends to any questions in dispute about the rights and obligations of the parties to the contract.[12] Whether or not a dispute exists has been held to be 'of an intensely factual nature'.[13]

[25.08] The 2002 Act, as presently worded (there are proposed amendments, as to which see the last part of this chapter), differentiates between commercial construction contracts and residential construction contracts. Both types of contract involve the carrying out of construction work as defined in the 2002 Act. A commercial construction contract is a contract in which none of the parties is a residential occupier of the premises that are the subject of the contract, whereas a residential construction contract is a contract in which one of the parties is the residential occupier of the premises that are the subject of the contract.[14] The 2002 Act only applies to construction contracts that relate to the carrying out of construction work in New Zealand.[15] The 2002 Act does not require the contract to be in writing.[16]

[25.09] Under the 2002 Act, construction work includes the physical aspects of the construction process on site, both in relation to building contracts and civil engineering contracts, and the pre-fabrication of customised components, whether carried out on the site or off site.[17] It does not include design.

[25.10] A dispute may not be referred to adjudication without the consent of the parties to the dispute if the parties have also agreed to refer disputes between them to arbitration and the arbitration is an international arbitration as defined in article 1(3) of Schedule 1 to the Arbitration Act 1996 or covered by the provisions of the Protocol on Arbitration Clauses (1923) or covered by the provisions of the ICSID Convention and is an arbitration to which the Arbitration (International Investment Disputes) Act 1979 applies.[18]

[25.11] The fact that the dispute is the subject of proceedings between the same parties in a court or tribunal is not a bar to referral to adjudication[19] nor does the 2002 Act prevent the parties to a construction contract from submitting the dispute to another dispute resolution procedure, whether or not the proceedings for the other dispute resolution procedure take place concurrently with an adjudication.[20] There is no provision in the 2002 Act for contractual adjudication of disputes arising under construction contracts.

---

[12] Subsection 48(1),(2) of the 2002 Act.
[13] *Willis Trust Co Ltd v Green* (High Court, Auckland, CIV 2006-404-809, 25/5/06, Harrison J).
[14] Section 5, definitions of *'commercial construction contract'* and *'residential construction contract'*.
[15] Section 9 of the 2002 Act.
[16] Subsection 9(c) of the 2002 Act.
[17] Section 6 of the 2002 Act.
[18] Subsections 25(3),(4) of the 2002 Act.
[19] Subsection 25(1) of the 2002 Act.
[20] Subsection 26(1). For other provisions applicable in those circumstances see subsection 26(2),(3)of the 2002 Act.

25.3 Adjudication process

[25.12] An adjudication may be commenced against a party to the relevant construction contract (termed 'the respondent') seeking an order for the payment of money under the contract and/or a determination of the rights and obligations of the parties under the contract.[21] Where the respondent owns the construction site, approval may be sought for the issue of a charging order in relation to the site.[22] Where the respondent is not the owner of the site but an associate of the owner, the adjudication may also be commenced against the non-respondent owner and approval sought for the issue of a charging order in relation to the site owned by that person.[23] However, approval for the issue of a charging order may not be sought against a respondent owner where that person is a residential occupier of the site nor may an adjudication be commenced, or approval for the issue of a charging order be sought, against a non-respondent owner who is a residential occupier of the site.[24] The procedure to be followed in an adjudication is prescribed in the 2002 Act and described in the remaining paragraphs of this section.

[25.13] An adjudication is initiated by the claimant serving notice of its intention to refer the dispute for adjudication (the notice of adjudication) on the other party or parties to the construction contract and on the non-respondent owner, where a determination of the non-respondent owner's liability and approval for the issue of a charging order in respect of the site owned by that owner are sought.[25] The requirements of the notice of adjudication are prescribed by the 2002 Act.[26] Where the notice is to be served on a residential occupier, the 2002 Act requires further information to be included in the notice.[27]

[25.14] Having served the notice of adjudication on the respondent and, if permitted, on a non-respondent owner, the claimant must select an adjudicator within the prescribed period after the notice of adjudication has been served.[28] Where a person has been chosen to act as adjudicator by agreement between the parties, whether initially or subsequently, the claimant must request that person to act as soon as practicable after the notice of adjudication has been served.[29] If the parties have not agreed on a person to act as adjudicator, the claimant must request a nominating body chosen by agreement between the parties to select a person to act.[30] If the person chosen by agreement is unwilling or unable to act and there has been no agreement as to a nominating body or if approval for the issue of

---

[21] Subsections 25(1), 38(1) and 48(1).
[22] Section 29.
[23] Subsections 25(1), 30, 38(1) and section 50 of the 2002 Act. The term 'associate' is defined in Section 6 of the 2002 Act.
[24] Section 31 of the 2002 Act. A 'residential occupier' is defined in Section 5 of the 2002 Act as an individual who is occupying, or intends to occupy, the premises that are the subject over the relevant contract as a dwellingplace.
[25] Subsection 28(1) of the 2002 Act.
[26] Subsection 28(2) of the 2002 Act.
[27] Subsection 61(1) of the 2002 Act. There is a prescribed form: Form 2 in Schedule 1 to the Construction Contracts Regulations 2003. The Regulations may be downloaded from the New Zealand Legislation website at *www.legislation.govt.nz*.
[28] Section 33 of the 2002 Act.
[29] Subsection 33(1)(a),(b) and (2)(a) of the 2002 Act.
[30] Subsection 33 (1)(c) of the 2002 Act.

a charging order is sought, the claimant must request an authorised nominating authority chosen by the claimant to select a person to act.[31] In each of these last two cases the request must be made within 5 working days after the notice of adjudication has been served or any further period that the parties may agree.[32]

[25.15] There is no restriction on who may act as a nominating body.[33] Authorised nominating authorities are authorised by the Minister responsible for the administration of the 2002 Act.[34]

[25.16] A person requested to act as an adjudicator must, within 2 working days of receiving the request, indicate whether he is willing and able to act[35] and, if he is willing and able to act, must then serve a notice of acceptance on the parties to the adjudication and, as the case may be, on the nominating body or authorised nominating authority.[36] A person is not eligible to be an adjudicator in relation to a construction contract if he is a party to that contract or if he does not meet any requirements relating to qualifications, expertise and experience that may have been prescribed by Order in Council (to date none have been prescribed).[37] A person requested to act as an adjudicator must disclose to the parties to the adjudication and, as the case may be, the nominating body or authorised nominating authority, any conflict of interest (whether financial or otherwise) and must not act as an adjudicator in that dispute unless all the parties to the adjudication agree.[38] The adjudicator's notice of acceptance must confirm that the person meets the eligibility criteria for adjudicators,[39] and a notice of acceptance which fails to do this has no effect.[40]

[25.17] Once the adjudicator has been appointed, the claimant must, within 5 working days of receiving the adjudicator's notice of acceptance, refer the dispute in writing (the adjudication claim) to the adjudicator and serve a copy of the adjudication claim and any accompanying documents on every other party to the adjudication.[41]

[25.18] The respondent and any relevant non-respondent owner is entitled to serve on the adjudicator a written response to the adjudication claim (the adjudication response) within 5 working days after receiving the claim or within any further time that the parties to the adjudication may agree or any further time that the adjudicator may allow if he considers that, in the circumstances, the additional time is reasonably required to enable the respondent to complete the written response.[42] The respondent must also serve a copy of

---

[31] Subsections 33(1)(d) and 63 of the 2002 Act.
[32] Subsection 33(2)(b) of the 2002 Act.
[33] Section 5 of the 2002 Act, definition of 'nominating body'.
[34] Section 5 of the 2002 Act, definition of 'authorised nominating authority' and Section 65 of the 2002 Act.
[35] Subsection 35(1) of the 2002 Act.
[36] Subsection 35(2) of the 2002 Act.
[37] Subsection 34(1) and (2) and section 82 of the 2002 Act.
[38] Subsection 34(3) of the 2002 Act.
[39] Subsection 35(4) of the 2002 Act.
[40] Subsection 35(5) of the 2002 Act.
[41] Section 36 of the 2002 Act.
[42] Subsection 37(1) as read with section 32 of the 2002 Act.

the adjudication response and any accompanying documents on the claimant and every other party to the adjudication.[43]

[25.19] An adjudicator must act independently, impartially and in a timely manner, avoid incurring unnecessary expense and comply with the principles of natural justice.[44] He must also disclose any conflict of interest to the parties to the adjudication and, if he has a conflict of interest, resign from office unless the parties agree otherwise.[45]

[25.20] An adjudicator's jurisdiction in relation to any dispute that has been referred to adjudication is limited to determining any questions in dispute about the rights and obligations of the parties under the contract and, where an amount of money is claimed, whether or not any of the parties to the adjudication (including non-respondent owners) are liable, or will be liable if certain conditions are met, to make a payment under the contract.[46] In addition, where approval is sought for the issue of a charging order against a respondent or non-respondent owner, the adjudicator has jurisdiction to determine that issue.[47] First instance decisions have upheld the right of an adjudicator to determine his jurisdiction in the first instance, subject to subsequent judicial review following the adjudicator's determination.[48]

[25.21] An adjudicator has extensive powers, including the power to conduct the adjudication in any manner that he thinks fit (subject, obviously, to also fulfilling his duty to comply with the principles of natural justice).[49] The parties to the adjudication are obliged to comply with any request or direction of the adjudicator made or given within the scope of his powers.[50] In the vast majority of cases the parties present their evidence in the form of witness statements, not affidavits. The power to call a conference of the parties is rarely used.

[25.22] An adjudication claim may be withdrawn if the claimant serves written notice of the withdrawal on the adjudicator, unless the respondent objects to the withdrawal and the adjudicator recognises a legitimate interest on the respondent's part in obtaining a determination in respect of the dispute. A claim may also be withdrawn if the parties agree.[51]

[25.23] If two or more adjudication proceedings are pending, the adjudicator may, with the written consent of all the parties to the various proceedings, determine them at the same time.[52]

---

[43] Subsection 37(3) of the 2002 Act.
[44] Subsection 41(a)-(c) of the 2002 Act.
[45] Subsection 41(d),(e) of the 2002 Act.
[46] Subsection 48(1),(2) as read with subsection 38(1)(a) of the 2002 Act.
[47] Sections 49 and 50 as read with subsection 38(1)(a) of the 2002 Act.
[48] *Patel v Pearson Ltd* (High Court, Wellington, CIV 2008-485-2571, 24/4/09, Miller J); *Origin Energy Resources (Kupe) Ltd v Tenix Alliance New Zealand Ltd* (High Court, Auckland, CIV 2010-404-106, 19/1/10, Potter J).
[49] Subsection 42(1) of the 2002 Act.
[50] Subsection 42(2) of the 2002 Act.
[51] Section 39 of the 2002 Act.
[52] Section 40 of the 2002 Act.

[25.24] Special provisions apply in respect of a notice of adjudication to be served on a residential occupier[53] and where the claimant seeks approval for the issue of a charging order in respect of a construction site.[54]

[25.25] A claimant may seek a fresh adjudication if no adjudicator's notice of acceptance is received or the adjudicator dies or becomes seriously ill or is otherwise unavailable for any reason or fails to determine the dispute within the prescribed period.[55]

[25.26] The parties to a dispute referred to adjudication may be represented by the representatives (whether legally qualified or not) that each party considers appropriate.[56]

[25.27] The Act provides for the confidentiality of the adjudication proceedings.[57]

25.4 Determination, effect and costs

[25.28] An adjudicator's decision is called a determination in the 2002 Act.[58] The 2002 Act prescribes the matters to be considered by an adjudicator in determining a dispute, and the timing, form and substance of the determination.

[25.29] In determining a dispute, an adjudicator is required and permitted to consider only the provisions of the 2002 Act, the provisions of the relevant construction contract, the adjudication claim, together with all submissions (including relevant documentation) that may have been made by the claimant, the respondent's response (if any), together with all submissions (including relevant documentation) that may have been made by the respondent, the report of the expert or experts appointed to advise on specific issues (if any), the results of any inspection carried out by the adjudicator, and any other matters that the adjudicator reasonably considers to be relevant.[59] An adjudicator's power to determine a dispute is not affected by the failure of the respondent to serve a response on the claimant or by the failure of any of the parties to make a submission or comment within the time allowed or provide specified information within the time allowed or comply with the adjudicator's call for a conference of the parties or do any other thing that the adjudicator requests or directs.[60] In any such situation, the adjudicator may draw any inferences from the failure that he thinks fit, determine the dispute on the basis of the information available to him, and give any weight that he thinks fit to any information provided outside any periods that he requested or directed.[61] It is, however, specifically provided in the 2002 Act that an adjudicator may not have regard to

---

[53] Section 62 and Form 2 in Schedule 1 to the Construction Contracts Regulations 2003.
[54] Section 63 of the 2002 Act.
[55] Section 66 of the 2002 Act.
[56] Subsection 67(1) of the 2002 Act.
[57] Section 68 of the 2002 Act.
[58] See, for instance, section 38 of the 2002 Act.
[59] Section 45 of the 2002 Act.
[60] Section 43 of the 2002 Act.
[61] Section 44 of the 2002 Act.

an adjudication response unless it is served on him before the end of the prescribed period.[62]

[25.30] An adjudicator is prohibited from determining a dispute until after the end of the period within which the respondent may serve an adjudication response.[63] He must determine the dispute within 20 working days after the end of that period or within 30 working days after the end of the period if the adjudicator considers that, even though the parties to the adjudication do not agree, further time for the determination of the dispute is reasonably required or within any further time that the parties to the adjudication agree.[64] He must give a copy of the determination to every party to the adjudication as soon as practicable after making the determination, subject to his right to require payment of his fees and expenses before doing so.[65]

[25.31] An adjudicator's determination must be in the form prescribed by Form 3 in Schedule 1 to the Construction Contracts Regulations 2003.[66] However, the 2002 Act provides that a failure to comply with this requirement does not affect the validity of the determination.[67]

[25.32] An adjudicator may, on his own initiative, and within 2 working days after the date on which a copy of the determination is given to the parties to the adjudication, correct in the determination any errors in computation, any clerical or typographical errors or any errors of a similar nature.[68] There is no other power of correction.

[25.33] If an amount of money under the relevant construction contract is claimed in an adjudication, the adjudicator must determine whether or not any of the parties to the adjudication are liable, or will be liable if certain conditions are met, to make a payment under the contract and any questions in dispute about the rights and obligations of the parties under the contract.[69] If an adjudicator determines that a party to the adjudication is liable, or will be liable if certain conditions are met, to make a payment, the adjudicator must also determine the amount payable or provisionally payable and the date on which that amount became or becomes payable and may determine that the liability of the party to the adjudication to make the payment depends on certain conditions being met.[70] If no amount of money under the relevant contract is claimed in the adjudication, the adjudicator must determine any questions in dispute about the rights and obligations of the parties under the contract.[71] An adjudicator is not required to determine a dispute

---

[62] Subsection 46(1)(b) of the 2002 Act.
[63] Subsection 46(1)(a) of the 2002 Act; and see paragraph 25.18 above.
[64] Subsection 46(2) of the 2002 Act.
[65] Subsections 46(3)-(4) and 57(6) of the 2002 Act.
[66] Subsection 47(1)(a) of the 2002 Act and Reg 6 of the 2003 Regulations.
[67] Subsection 47(2) of the 2002 Act. The effect of this provision has not been considered by the courts. Presumably, the determination would stand unless so defective in content as to amount to a nullity.
[68] Subsection 47(3) of the 2002 Act.
[69] Subsection 48(1) of the 2002 Act.
[70] Subsection 48(3) of the 2002 Act.
[71] Subsection 48(2) of the 2002 Act.

that has been withdrawn,[72] and if a dispute is settled by agreement between the parties before the adjudicator communicates his determination, the adjudicator must terminate the adjudication proceedings and, if requested by the parties, may record the settlement in the form of a determination on agreed terms.[73]

[25.34] The 2002 Act also prescribes the circumstances in which approval may be granted for the issue of a charging order over the construction site owned by the respondent or owned by a non-respondent owner.[74]

[25.35] An adjudicator's determination that a party to the adjudication is liable, or will be liable if certain conditions are met, to make a payment under the contract, is enforceable by recovery of the amount of the payment ordered as a debt due to the party in whose favour the order was made.[75] An adjudicator's determination about the parties' rights and obligations under a construction contract (whether or not a money order was also sought) is not enforceable.[76] However, the party in whose favour the determination is made may bring proceedings in any court to enforce that party's rights under the contract and the court must have regard to, but is not bound by, the adjudicator's determination.[77]

[25.36] The 2002 Act provides for the costs of the adjudication proceedings and for the adjudicator's fees.[78] In the normal course, the parties to an adjudication must meet their own costs and expenses and contribute to the adjudicator's fees and expenses in equal proportions.[79] An adjudicator may, however, order a party to pay the whole or part of the costs and expenses of another party or other parties if the adjudicator considers that the first-named party has caused those costs and expenses to be incurred unnecessarily by bad faith or allegations or objections that are without substantial merit.[80] Similarly, an adjudicator may order that a party pay the whole or a larger than equal part of his fees or expenses if, in the adjudicator's view, the adjudication claim, or, as the case may be, the adjudication response was without substantial merit or a party to the adjudication acted in a contemptuous or improper manner during the adjudication.[81] The 2002 Act does not permit the parties to agree that the adjudicator has jurisdiction to allocate his costs or the parties' costs depending on the outcome of the adjudication, as a judge or arbitral tribunal would. If an adjudication claim is withdrawn or terminated, or the dispute between the parties is resolved, an adjudicator is entitled to be paid the fees and expenses incurred in the adjudication up to and including, as the case may be, the date on which the adjudication claim was withdrawn or terminated or the adjudicator was notified that the dispute had been resolved.[82] An adjudicator is not entitled to be paid any fees or

---

[72] Subsection 48(4) of the 2002 Act.
[73] Subsection 48(5) of the 2002 Act.
[74] Sections 49, 50 of the 2002 Act.
[75] Subsections 58(1) and 59 of the 2002 Act.
[76] Subsection 58(2) of the 2002 Act.
[77] Subsections 58(3) and 61 of the 2002 Act.
[78] Subsections 56, 57 of the 2002 Act.
[79] Subsections 56(2) and 57(3)(a) of the 2002 Act.
[80] Subsection 56(1) of the 2002 Act.
[81] Subsection 57(3)(b) and (4) of the 2002 Act.
[82] Subsection 57(7) of the 2002 Act.

expenses in connection with an adjudication if he fails to determine the dispute within the prescribed period.[83]

25.4.1 Rights of a non-respondent owner

[25.37]   Where a claimant seeks a determination that a non-respondent owner is jointly and severally liable with the respondent to make a payment to the claimant and approval for the issue of a charging order in respect of the construction site owned by the non-respondent owner, the non-respondent owner is a party to the adjudication and has all the rights of a party.[84]

[25.38]   In addition, a non-respondent owner who has been found to be jointly and severally liable with the respondent to pay an amount may discharge his liability by paying the amount determined by the adjudicator to the claimant.[85] A non-respondent owner who does so may treat the payment as a payment to the respondent in reduction of any amount that the non-respondent owner owes, or may in future owe, to the respondent in connection with the construction work or, if he is unable to recover the amount in that way, may recover it from the respondent as a debt.[86] If a non-respondent owner has paid the amount determined by the adjudicator in this way, the subsequent setting aside of the adjudication's determination does not affect the rights conferred on the non-respondent owner by the 2002 Act.[87]

[25.39]   A non-respondent owner against whom an adjudicator has determined that he is jointly and severally liable with the respondent to make a payment to the claimant and has given approval for the issue of a charging order in respect of the construction site may apply to a District Court for a review of that determination and approval.[88] The procedure for seeking such a review and the powers of the District Court on such a review are prescribed by the 2002 Act.[89] An application for review by a non-respondent owner does not operate as a stay of the adjudicator's determination unless a District Court Judge, on application, so determines.[90]

25.5 Enforcement

[25.40]   The 2002 Act allows a party in whose favour an adjudicator has determined that another party must pay an amount under a construction contract to enforce the payment of that amount by suspending construction work under the contract,[91] or by application

---

[83] Subsection 57(5) of the 2002 Act; and see paragraph 25.30 above.
[84] Section 32 of the 2002 Act.
[85] Subsection 51(1) of the 2002 Act.
[86] Subsection 51(2) of the 2002 Act.
[87] Subsection 51(3) of the 2002 Act.
[88] Subsection 52(1) of the 2002 Act.
[89] Sections 53,54 of the 2002 Act.
[90] Section 55 of the 2002 Act.
[91] Section 52 of the 2002 Act.

to a District Court for entry of the determination as a judgment[92] or by recovering the amount of the determination as a debt.[93]

[25.41] The right to suspend construction work under the contract arises when a respondent fails to comply with an adjudicator's determination that it must pay the claimant an amount by a particular date, the claimant serves on the respondent a notice of its intention to suspend the carrying out of construction work under the contract, and the respondent fails to comply with the determination within 5 working days after the date of the claimant's notice.[94] A claimant who exercises the right to suspend construction work under the contract is not in breach thereby of the construction contract, is not liable for any loss or damage suffered by the respondent, or any person claiming through the respondent, is entitled to an extension of time to complete the contract (but is not entitled solely by reason of the 2002 Act to recover any costs incurred as a consequence of the extension of time), keeps its rights under the contract, including any right to terminate the contract, and may at any time lift the suspension even if the determination has not been complied with.[95]

[25.42] A party in whose favour an adjudicator has determined that another party to an adjudication is liable, or will be liable if certain conditions are met, to pay an amount of money under the construction contract and/or any costs and expenses incurred in the adjudication may apply to a District Court for the determination to be enforced by entry as a judgment.[96]

[25.43] The application must be made in the manner provided by the District Courts Rules 2014 and must be served on the party against whom the adjudicator's determination was issued either before or immediately after making the application to the court.[97] The party against whom enforcement is sought may apply to the court for an order that entry of the adjudicator's determination as a judgment be refused.[98] Such an application may only be made on the ground that the amount payable under the determination has been paid to the plaintiff by the defendant or that the contract to which the adjudicator's determination relates is not a construction contract to which the 2002 Act applies or that a condition imposed by the adjudicator in his determination has not been met.[99]

[25.44] If the party against which enforcement is sought takes no steps within 15 working days after the date on which a copy of the application to enforce the adjudicator's determination is served on him, the claimant is entitled to request the District Court to enter

---

[92] Section 73 of the 2002 Act.
[93] Section 59 of the 2002 Act.
[94] Subsection 72(1) of the 2002 Act.
[95] Subsection 72(2) of the 2002 Act. Further provisions applicable where a claimant exercises its rights under Section 72 are found in subsection 72(3)–(5) of the 2002 Act.
[96] Subsection 73(1),(2) of the 2002 Act.
[97] Subsection 73(3),(4) of the 2002 Act. See Rules 20.86–20.87 of the District Courts Rules 2014. The Rules can be downloaded from the New Zealand Legislation website at *www.legislation.govt.nz*
[98] Subsection 74(1) of the 2002 Act.
[99] Subsection 74(2) of the 2002 Act. See also Rule 20.88 of the District Courts Rules 2014.

the determination as a judgment as soon as practicable.[100] If the defendant does oppose entry of the determination as a judgment and the District Court is satisfied that one of the grounds just referred to is made out, the court must refuse the application to enforce the determination by entry as a judgment.[101] If, however, the District Court is not satisfied that any of the grounds just referred to is made out, the District Court must accept the application to enforce the determination by entry as a judgment and enter the determination as a judgment accordingly.[102] The District Court has the power to stay the judgment enforcing the determination on the same principles as apply to a stay application generally.[103]

[25.45] Where the adjudicator's determination includes approval for the issue of a charging order in respect of the site, the party in whose favour the order is made may apply for the issue of a charging order at the same time as it applies for entry of judgment. If it does so and its application is successful, the Registrar of the District Court must immediately issue a charging order in respect of the site.[104] The provisions of the District Courts Rules 2014 relating to charging orders apply to charging orders issued in accordance with the 2002 Act.[105]

[25.46] While adjudications under the 2002 Act are, generally speaking, working well and being completed promptly, there is dissatisfaction over the length of time it takes to enforce adjudicators' determinations, although there is no data available on the extent of the delay that is occurring.

[25.47] Although the 2002 Act is silent on the point there is, as one would expect, authority that a determination which is a nullity will not be enforced.[106] Breaches of natural justice are properly the subject of judicial review proceedings, as to which see Section 25.5.1.

[25.48] As noted in paragraph 25.40, a party which has been successful in an adjudication may also enforce any determination for the payment of money by action for the recovery of a debt. The 2002 Act provides that in any such proceedings the court must not give effect to any counterclaim, set-off, or cross-demand raised by any party to those proceedings other than a set-off or liquidated amount if judgment has been entered for that amount or there is not in fact any dispute between the parties in relation to the claim for that amount.[107] The courts have held that the provision applies not only where a party seeks to recover a debt by ordinary court proceedings (usually an application for summary judgment) but also where that party serves a bankruptcy notice or a statutory demand on the debtor.[108] There is first instance authority for the proposition that it also applies at

---

[100] Section 75 of the 2002 Act.
[101] Subsection 74(3) of the 2002 Act.
[102] Subsection 74(4) of the 2002 Act.
[103] District Courts Rules 2014 Rules 20.80 and 19.9.
[104] Section 76 of the 2002 Act.
[105] Section 78 of the 2002 Act. See also Rules 19.23–19.46 of the District Courts Rules 2014.
[106] *Stellar Projects Ltd v Nick Gjaja Plumbing Ltd* (High Court, Auckland, CIV 2005-404-6984, 10/4/06, Venning J). See also *Patel v Pearson Group Ltd* (High Court, Wellington, CIV 2008-485-2571, 24/4/09, Miller J).
[107] Section 79 of the 2002 Act.
[108] *Laywood v Holmes Construction (Wellington) Ltd* [2009] NZCA 35.

the stage of an application for an order staying the subsequent liquidation proceeding.[109] The question of whether it applies at the later stage of adjudication of bankruptcy or order to wind up a company has been left open.[110]

25.5.1 Judicial review

[25.49] The power of adjudication under the 2002 Act is a statutory power and, therefore, subject to judicial review under the Judicature Amendment Act 1972. An adjudicator's determination that an amount of money is owing by one party under a construction contract to another is binding on the parties to the adjudication and continues to be of full effect even though a party has applied for a judicial review of the determination.[111]

[25.50] In *Rees v Firth*[112] the Court of Appeal was required to consider the scope of judicial review, it being argued for the appellant that it was only those errors of law that go to the adjudicator's jurisdiction that can be the subject of judicial review in respect of an adjudicator's determination. The Court rejected that argument, holding (at paragraph [22]):

> We are satisfied that the CCA as a whole does not require judicial review be limited to instances of what might be classified as jurisdictional error. In our view, to hold that the availability of judicial review is limited in that way invites unproductive and diversionary debate about whether a particular error is or is not "jurisdictional". The key point, we think, is that the statutory context is such that a person who does not accept the adjudicator's determination should litigate, arbitrate or mediate the underlying dispute rather than seeking relief by way of judicial review of the determination. Such relief will be available only rarely.

[25.51] At paragraph [27] the court went on to say:

> The courts must be vigilant to ensure that judicial review of adjudicators' determinations does not cut across the scheme of the CCA and undermine its objectives. But this does not mean the judicial review must be limited to instances of "jurisdictional error". In principle, any ground of judicial review may be raised, but an applicant must demonstrate that the court should intervene in the particular circumstances, and that will not be easy in the purpose and scheme of the CCA. Indeed, we consider that it will be very difficult to satisfy the court that it is necessary. As an example, given that an important purpose of the CCA is to provide a mechanism to enable money flows to be maintained on the basis of preliminary and non-binding assessments of the merits, it is unlikely that errors of fact by adjudicators will give rise to successful applications for judicial reviews. In the great majority of cases where an adjudicator's determination is to be challenged, the appropriate course will be for the parties to submit the merits of the dispute to binding resolution through arbitration or litigation (or, of course, to go to mediation).

---

[109] *Gill Construction Co Ltd v Butler* (High Court, Wellington, CIV 2009-485-203, 2/11/09, Mallon J).
[110] *Laywood v Holmes Construction (Wellington) Ltd* [2010] NZHC 53.
[111] Subsection 60(a) of the 2002 Act. An application for judicial review may be brought at any time, although in the normal course it will not be brought until after the adjudicator has made his determination. See also paragraph 25.20 above.
[112] [2011] NZCA 668.

25.6 Proposed amendments

[25.52] The Construction Contracts Amendment Bill was introduced into Parliament in June 2013. It was referred to the Commerce Committee, which reported back in December 2013. The Bill had its second reading in March 2014. At the time of writing, it has not yet progressed beyond that stage; but it is anticipated that it will do so in the near future.[113]

[25.53] In addition to rearranging the order of the sections in the 2002 Act and making minor amendments to the wording of various sections, the Bill proposes a number of significant amendments to the 2002 Act, including repealing the distinction between commercial construction contracts and residential construction contracts, extending the scope of the 2002 Act to cover defined design or engineering work and defined quantity surveying work, in each case carried out in New Zealand,[114] repealing the distinction between money order determinations and their enforceability and rights and obligations determinations,[115] requiring an explanatory statement of the respondent's rights and obligations and of the adjudication process to be served in the case of every adjudication,[116] and removing any doubt that may have existed regarding whether a charging order could be sought where the premises that are the subject of a construction contract are owed by a family trust rather than an individual respondent.[117]

---

[113] The Bill may be downloaded from the New Zealand Parliament website at *www.parliament.nz*.
[114] Clause 6 of the Bill, amending section 6 of the 2002 Act.
[115] Clauses 20 and 21 of the Bill, amending s. 58 of the 2002 Act and inserting a new section 59A into the 2002 Act.
[116] Clause 12 of the Bill, amending section 28 of the 2002 Act.
[117] Clause 13 of the Bill, replacing section 31 of the 2002 Act.

Chapter 26
Singapore: Steven Cannon[1]

26.1 Overview

[26.01] An adjudication regime was introduced in respect of construction contracts in Singapore by the Building and Construction Industry Security of Payment Act (Cap 30B) of 2004 (the **2004 Act**). The 2004 Act came into force in part on 3 January 2005 and in full on 1 April 2005. The purpose of the 2004 Act is to:

> facilitate payments for construction work done or for related goods and services supplied in the building and construction industry, and for matters connected therewith.

[26.02] The provisions of the 2004 Act substantially draw upon the New South Wales Act of the same name enacted in 1999, although it does contain material differences. The underlying intention of the 2004 Act is similar to the 1996 Act in the UK and other similar acts in Australia, New Zealand, Malaysia and elsewhere, namely to deal with practices within the construction industry whereby contractors and subcontractors find themselves starved of cash by their counterparties up the contractual chain. Like the other acts, the 2004 Act introduces a payment and adjudication regime which is implied into all construction contracts for work to be carried out within the territory of Singapore.

[26.03] In common with the NSW and Malaysian acts, but at odds with the 1996 Act, there is an inextricable link between the interim payment regime and the adjudication regime. Adjudications must:

- only be commenced in respect of a specific progress payment applied for under the 2004 Act;
- only be commenced by the receiving party against the paying party (e.g. the contractor against the employer, or the subcontractor/supplier against the contractor);
- only be commenced within a very specific 7 day 'window' following the conclusion of the procedure for that progress payment;

---

[1] Steven specialises in International Arbitration and other forms of dispute resolution, with a particular expertise in construction and engineering disputes. He has for several years worked in South East Asia, based for some years in Eversheds' Singapore office.

A Practical Guide to Construction Adjudication, First Edition. James Pickavance.
© 2016 James Pickavance. Published 2016 by John Wiley & Sons, Inc.

- only involve a consideration by the adjudicator of issues specifically raised by the paying party in a valid payment response under the 2004 Act;
- be determined by a decision of the adjudicator within 14 days of the commencement of the adjudication.

[26.04] Accordingly, in comparison with other regimes (particularly the UK) the Singapore regime is fast, highly targeted in terms of disputes and substantially benefits the receiving party in many respects.

[26.05] Since the commencement of the 2004 Act, the Singapore High Court and Court of Appeal have had several opportunities to consider the provisions of the 2004 Act and have given guidance on how provisions of the 2006 Act are to be interpreted. It is clear that the Singapore courts have actively supported the legislative intention of the 2004 Act, frequently rejecting applications to challenge and set aside adjudicators' decisions.

[26.06] In addition to the 2004 Act, the government has enacted the 2006 Building and Construction Security of Payment Regulations (the **Regulations**). The Regulations provide further rules concerning the payment, adjudication procedure, eligibility criteria for adjudicators and the cost of adjudication proceedings.

26.2 Requirements for commencing an adjudication

26.2.1 What contracts are caught by the 2004 Act?

[26.07] The word 'contract' as used in the 2004 Act means a 'construction contract' or a 'supply contract'.

(A) Construction contract

[26.08] This is defined as an agreement where one party undertakes to carry out 'construction work', including 'the supply of goods and services', for one or more parties. It also includes an agreement where one party undertakes to supply services.

[26.09] What constitutes 'construction work' is identified at section 3. The definition is extremely wide, encompassing all works relating to building, civil engineering, power, process engineering, infrastructure, telecommunications and oil and gas – the key point is that the works must 'form, or are to form, part of the land'.

[26.10] The 2004 Act also embraces:

- site preparation activities (e.g. land reclamation, site clearance etc.);
- certain temporary works, including scaffolding;
- pre-fabrication of components to form part of any works, whether the fabrication is carried out on site or otherwise;
- site restoration and landscaping;

- provision of building services;
- cleaning of structures, if carried out in the course of the construction, alteration, repair, restoration, maintenance or extension of works; and
- internal or external painting and decorating.

[26.11] Section 3 also identifies the meaning of 'supply of goods and services'. 'Goods' means any materials or components that are to form part of any construction works, or used in connection with the carrying out of construction work, presumably to include materials used for temporary works. 'Services' embraces all likely forms of construction and engineering consultancy services, for example feasibility and planning services, site supervision, project management and professional engineering services (including architectural, design, surveying and quantity surveying services).

[26.12] 'Services' also includes 'the provision of labour to carry out construction work'. It is clear that this means labour-only subcontracting rather than an employer/employee relationship, itself specifically excluded by subsection 4(2)(b)(i).

[26.13] In addition to contracts of employment, the other exceptions to the application of the 2004 Act are:

- contracts relating to residential property which do not require the approval of the Commissioner of Building Control under the Building Control Act (Cap. 29);
- construction work carried out outside of Singapore; and
- such other contract or class of contract as may be prescribed.

26.2.2 Contracting out, the date of execution of the contract and contracts made in writing

[26.14] According to subsection 4(1) the 2004 Act applies to all contracts:

- 'made in writing';
- 'on or after 1 April 2005';
- 'whether or not the contract is expressed to be governed by the law of Singapore'.

(A) Made in writing

[26.15] The meaning of 'made in writing' is developed by section 4(3) to include written contracts which are unsigned, contracts made by exchanges of correspondence, and those made otherwise than in writing (for instance orally) but are either recorded by one party or an authorised third party or are made by reference to written terms.

[26.16] If a contract is not wholly made in writing (for instance some of the terms are oral and some are written), the contract shall be treated as made in writing if the matter in dispute between the parties is governed by the written element of the contract (s. 4(4)).

(B) Whether or not the contract is expressed to be governed by the law of Singapore.

[26.17] The clear intention of this provision is to avoid parties from 'contracting out' of the effect of the 2004 Act by choosing a governing law other than Singapore. The inability to contract out of the 2004 Act generally is set out at section 36.

(C) Government contracts

[26.18] Section 35 of the 2004 Act makes it plain that the 2004 Act binds the government.

26.3 Payment regime

[26.19] As the right to adjudication only arises in respect of a dispute that has crystallised through the operation of the payment regime, any analysis of the adjudication regime must first involve some consideration of the payment regime under the 2004 Act.

26.3.1 The right to progress payments

[26.20] Section 5 states:

> Any person who has carried out any construction work, or supplied any goods or services, under a contract is entitled to a progress payment.

[26.21] The value of each progress payment is to be calculated and valued in accordance with the terms of the contract (sections 6 and 7). If the contract does not have a valuation provision, the 2004 Act provides for a valuation process under subsection 7(2).

26.3.2 The payment regime

[26.22] The process is as follows:
  (1) The claiming party serves a payment claim (section 10).
  (2) The responding party serves a payment response (section 11).
  (3) If a dispute arises over the monies to be paid, or a payment response is not served, there is then a short disputes settlement period of 7 days (subsections 12 (2) to (5)).
  (4) Following the expiry of the 7-day disputes settlement period the claiming party may within a further 7 days make an adjudication application (sections 12 and 13).

(A) The payment claim

[26.23] Under section 10, a claimant is entitled to serve[2] a payment claim for a progress payment. This must be served either in accordance with the terms of the contract or at such time as is prescribed by the 2004 Act.

---

[2] As to effective service, see section 37 of the 2004 Act.

[26.24] Both the 2004 Act (subsection 10(3)) and the Regulations (reg. 5(2)) set out the contents of the payment claim. These include that the payment claim shall state the claimed amount calculated by reference to the period to which the payment claim relates and further must:

(a) be in writing;
(b) identify the contract to which the progress payment that is the subject of the payment claim relates; and
(c) contain details of the claimed amount, including—
   (i) a breakdown of the items constituting the claimed amount;
   (ii) a description of these items;
   (iii) the quantity or quantum of each item; and
   (iv) the calculations which show how the claimed amount is derived.

[26.25] There have been several cases on the issue of whether a payment notice is valid which have implications upon the enforceability of an adjudicator's decision. The following principles have been laid down by the High Court and Court of Appeal:

(1) The Act covers payment claims for both interim and final payments.[3]
(2) A contractor may submit a payment claim following a termination for breach;[4]
(3) The payment claim need not identify itself as such under the 2004 Act. If it satisfied all of the requirements of a payment claim then it will be valid.[5]
(4) Even if the payment claim does not satisfy all of the requirements of a payment claim then it will not necessarily be invalid. The court should examine as to whether any provisions which were not complied with was so important that it was the legislative purpose that the Payment Claim becomes invalid.[6]
(5) There is no compulsion within the 2004 Act for a contractor to make a monthly payment claim. However, it may not make more than one payment claim per month.[7]
(6) If the dispute between the parties have been the subject of a valid and enforceable settlement then the contractor is not entitled to serve a later payment claim.[8]
(7) The **existence** of a payment claim is a matter which goes to the heart of the jurisdiction of the adjudicator – if there was no payment claim at all, then there can be no payment claim dispute and therefore the adjudicator can have no jurisdiction.[9]
(8) It is the role of the court to consider whether the failure of the claimant to meet one (or more) of the provisions of the 2004 Act in respect of the contents of a payment

---

[3] *Tiong Seng Contractors (Pte) Ltd v Chuan Lim Construction Pte Ltd* [2007] SGHC 142; *Lee Wee Lick v Chua Say Eng* [2012] SGCA 63.
[4] *Sundo Engineering & Construction (S) Pte Ltd v Italcor Pte Ltd* [2010] SGHC 105.
[5] *Lee Wee Lick v Chua Say Eng* [2012] SGCA 63; *Admin Construction Pte Ltd v Vivaldi (S) Pte Ltd* [2013] SGHC 95.
[6] *Lee Wee Lick v Chua Say Eng* [2012] SGCA 63; *Australian Timber Products Pte Ltd v A Pacific Construction & Development Pte Ltd* [2013] SGHC 56.
[7] *Lee Wee Lick v Chua Say Eng* [2012] SGCA 63.
[8] *Admin Construction Pte Ltd v Vivaldi (S) Pte Ltd* [2013] SGHC 95.
[9] *RN & Associates Pte Ltd v TPX Builders Pte Ltd* [2012] SGHC 225; *Lee Wee Lick v Chua Say Eng* [2012] SGCA 63.

claim is a breach of such an essential condition as to result in the adjudication determination being invalid.[10]

(B) The payment response

[26.26] Pursuant to section 11 of the 2004 Act, upon receipt of a payment claim the employer must serve[11] a payment response within a short period of time:

- in accordance with the dates specified or determined in the contract, or within 21 days after the payment claim is served, whichever is the earlier;
- where there is no provision, within 7 days of service of the payment claim; or
- in the case of a supply contract by paying all of the claim by the due date, or such part as the employer agrees to pay (subsection 11(2)).

[26.27] The contents of the payment response are set out in the subsection 11(3) of the 2004 Act and rule 6(1) of the Regulations. The payment response shall:

- be in writing and addressed to the claimant (e.g. the contractor);
- identify the payment claim to which it relates;
- state the response amount (if any), and specifically shall state 'nil' where the employer does not intend to pay any amount;
- state, where the response amount is less than the claimed amount, the reason for the difference and the reason for any amount withheld and;
  - contain the amount that the respondent proposes to pay for each item constituting the claimed amount, the reasons for the difference in any of the items and the calculations which show how the amount that the respondent proposes to pay is derived; and
  - contain any amount that is being withheld, the reason for doing so and the calculations which show how the amount being withheld is derived;
- shall be made in such form and manner, and contain such other information or be accompanied by such documents, as may be prescribed.

[26.28] Under subsection 11(4), there is a limited opportunity for varying the payment response. To do so the respondent must use:

- the form prescribed by rule 6(2) of the Regulations and make the changes within either:
- the period that a Payment Response is to be provided under subsection 11(1); or
- the disputes settlement period under section 13.

[26.29] There is some assistance from the courts on the requirements and effect of the payment response.

---

[10] *Lee Wee Lick v Chua Say Eng* [2012] SGCA 63.
[11] As to effective service, see section 37 of the 2004 Act.

(1) The respondent is not permitted in the adjudication to raise 'any reason for withholding any amount, including but not limited to any cross claim, counterclaim and set off' unless that reason was included in the payment response (subsection 15(3)).
(2) Therefore a failure to serve a valid payment response bars the responding party from raising any positive defence in the adjudication.
(3) This bar extends to submissions both as to (1) the value of the account claimed; and (2) the raising of any defence of set-off.[12]
(4) The bar does not of itself create a breach of natural justice which would allow an adjudicator's decision to be impeached.[13]
(5) The exception to this bar, it seems, is that there is nothing to stop the responding party from drawing to the adjudicator's attention any patent errors on the face of the material provided to the adjudicator by the claiming party. This is because an adjudicator is still under an obligation to consider the claiming party's materials in assessing the value of the payment claim – the adjudicator cannot simply accept the claim at face value.[14]
(6) Further, the failure to issue a payment response does not prevent the responding party from raising issues regarding the validity of the payment notice.[15]
(7) The jurisdiction of the adjudicator arises from the payment response.[16]
(8) Even if a payment response is not served by the time for service under subsection 11(1), the respondent has a further opportunity to serve a payment response during the 7-day disputes settlement period – see subsection 12(2) and (4)(b). This provision is commensurate with the period provided to the respondent to vary the payment response under subsection 12(4)(b) and subsection 11(4).

26.3.3 The crystallisation of a dispute and the dispute settlement period

[26.30] The payment regime is connected to the adjudication regime by section 12 of the 2004 Act, which governs the entitlement of the claimant to make an adjudication application.

[26.31] A right to adjudicate arises in two ways:

- under subsection 12(1) where a payment response is issued but the claimant does not receive payment in accordance with the payment response by the due date;[17]
- under subsection 12(2) where:
  - the claimant disputes the payment response; or
  - the respondent fails to provide a payment response to the claimant within the period set out in subsection 11(1).

---

[12] *WY Steel Construction Pte Ltd v Osko Pte Ltd* [2013] SGCA 32.
[13] *Chip Hup Hup Kee Construction Pte Ltd v Ssangyong Engineering & Construction Co. Ltd* [2009] SGHC 237.
[14] *WY Steel Construction Pte Ltd v Osko Pte Ltd* [2013] SGCA 32 at [51] and [52].
[15] *JFC Builders Pte Ltd v LionCity Construction Co Pte Ltd* [2013] 1 SLR.
[16] *RN & Associates Pte Ltd v TPX Builders Pte Ltd* [2012] SGHC 225.
[17] For the calculation of the 'due date for payment' see section 8 of the 2004 Act.

[26.32] In both of these situations, the right of the claimant to make an adjudication application only arises where, by the end of the disputes settlement period, the dispute is not settled or the respondent does not provide the payment response.

[26.33] Under subsection 12(5) the 'dispute settlement period' means the period of 7 days after the date on which the payment response is required under subsection 11(1).

26.4 Adjudication process

[26.34] Following the conclusion of the payment process, and the expiry of the disputed settlement period, the right of the claimant to apply for the dispute to be adjudicated arises.

26.4.1 The role of the Singapore Mediation Centre

[26.35] The adjudication is administered by the Singapore Mediation Centre (SMC), the 'authorised nominating body' under section 28 of the 2004 Act. The Singapore Mediation Centre has published a number of documents further to its administrative obligations under subsection 28(4) of the 2004 Act including:

- a register of adjudicators;
- an adjudicator code of conduct;
- the Adjudication Procedure Rules (the **SMC Rules**);
- various forms including the Adjudication Application Form (AA-1), Adjudication Response Form (AR-1) and the Adjudication Review Application Form (ARA-1); and
- a fee schedule.

26.4.2 Notice of an intention to adjudicate

(A) The window for an adjudication application

[26.36] After the expiry of the disputes settlement period, the claimant has just **7 days** to make an adjudication application – see section 13(2). This is a very short window, and the adjudicator will not have jurisdiction in respect of the dispute if the adjudication application is made either before or after this 7-day period.

(B) The notice of an intention to adjudicate

[26.37] Prior to issuing the adjudication application, the claimant must first serve[18] a notice in writing notifying the respondent in the prescribed form of his intention to apply for adjudication of the payment claim dispute (subsection 13(2)). Rule 7(1) of the Regulations provide that such notice must include:

---

[18] As to effective service, see section 37 of the 2004 Act.

(a) the names and service addresses of the claimant and the respondent;
(b) the date of the notice;
(c) the particulars of the relevant contract, comprising—
   (i) the project title or reference, or a brief description of the project;
   (ii) the contract number or a brief description of the contract; and
   (iii) the date the contract was made;
(d) the claimed amount;
(e) the response amount (if any); and
(f) a brief description of the payment claim dispute.

[26.38] In *JFC Builders Pte Ltd v Lion City Construction Co Pte Ltd*,[19] it was found that a notice of an intention to adjudicate which was served before the end of the disputes settlement period (i.e. too early for the issue of an adjudication application) was not rendered invalid by that fact.

26.4.3 The adjudication application

[26.39] Following the service of the notice of an intention to adjudicate, and within the 7-day window, the claimant may apply for the adjudication of a payment claim dispute by lodging[20] the adjudication application with the Singapore Mediation Centre as authorised nominating body (section 13(1)).

[26.40] The contents of the adjudication application is governed by:

- subsection 13(3) of the 2004 Act;
- rule 7(2) of the Regulations;
- rule 2.3 of the SMC Adjudication Rules; and
- adjudication application form AA-1 at annex A to the SMC adjudication rules.

[26.41] The adjudication application shall be in form AA-1 and under rule 2.3 of the SMC Adjudication Rules, SMC is entitled to reject incomplete documents. The adjudication application 'shall be in writing address to the authorised nominating body requesting it to appoint and adjudicator'[21] and shall:

(a) contain the names and service addresses of the claimant, the respondent, the principal (if known) and the owner concerned;
(b) state whether the relevant contract is a construction contract or a supply contract;
(c) contain the particulars of the relevant contract, comprising—
   (i) the project title or reference, or a brief description of the project;
   (ii) the contract number or a brief description of the contract; and
   (iii) the date the contract was made;

---

[19] [2013] 1 SLR.
[20] As to effective lodging, see section 37 of the 2004 Act and rule 2 of the SMC Rules.
[21] Subsection 13 (b) of the 2004 Act.

(d) contain an extract of the terms or conditions of the contract that are relevant to the payment claim dispute; and
(e) be accompanied by a copy of the relevant notice of intention to apply for adjudication, a copy of the relevant payment claim and a copy of the payment response (if any) thereto.[22]

[26.42] Furthermore, the adjudication application is the claimant's opportunity to evidence its claim. Subsection 13(3)(e) of the 2004 Act provides that the adjudication application:

> may contain or be accompanied by such other information or documents (including expert reports, photographs, correspondences and submissions) as the claimant may consider to be relevant to the application.

[26.43] Finally, under subsection 13(3)(d) the adjudication application must be accompanied by such application fee as may be determined by the authorised body. The Singapore Mediation Centre publishes a fee schedule in this regard.

(A) The appointment of the adjudicator and other action by the authorised nominating body

[26.44] Upon receipt of the adjudication application, the authorised nominating body must:

- serve a copy on the respondent (subsection 13(4)(a));
- notify in writing the principal (i.e. the party above the responding party in the contractual chain) and the owner of the site of the existence of the application (subsection 13(4)(b)) in accordance with rule 7(3) of the Regulations. The information notified will include the value and brief details of the claim; and
- appoint within 7 days of receipt an adjudicator from the register of adjudicators and notify the appointment to the claimant, respondent, owner and principal (Section 14).

[26.45] The Regulations provide eligibility criteria for adjudicators for inclusion on the register of adjudicator (rule 11(1)) and in respect of a particular dispute (rule 11(2)). A person may not be appointed as adjudicator on a dispute if he is connected to a party or if he has assisted a party to prepare any document for, or has provided any advice to, the party in relation to the contract.

[26.46] Further, rule 4 of the SMC adjudication rules provides that an adjudicator must disclose 'any circumstances likely to create an impression of bias or prevent him from acting promptly'.

[26.47] In *Lee Wee Lick Terence v Chua Say Eng*,[23] the Court of Appeal considered the circumstances in which the court could decide that an adjudicator was wrongfully appointed. The court found that an adjudicator is not competent to decide whether he was validly

---

[22] Clause 7(2) of the Regulations.
[23] [2012] SGCA 63.

appointed to decide a matter – such a determination can only be made by the court on the application of the aggrieved party.[24]

(B) The response

[26.48] Section 15 of the 2004 Act provides that the respondent shall within 7 days of receiving a copy of the adjudication application, lodge[25] with the authorised nominating body a response to the adjudication (the 'response'). The response should be in the form AR-1 at Annex A of the SMC Adjudication Rules,[26] should be addressed to the nominating body and should refer to the correct adjudication application.[27] Under rule 8(1) of the Regulations it should also:

(a) refer to the relevant adjudication application by the adjudication application reference number assigned by the authorised nominating body;
(b) where the contract that is the subject of the payment claim dispute is a sub-contract, contain the date the main contract is made;
(c) contain details of the response amount (if any); and
(d) where the respondent intends to supplement the relevant payment response, contain the additional computations and justifications.

[26.49] Finally, the response is the Respondent's opportunity to persuade the adjudicator as to the merits of his case and

may contain or be accompanied by such other information or documents (including expert reports, photographs, correspondences and submissions) as the respondent may consider to be relevant to the application.[28]

[26.50] The authorised nominating body will serve a copy of the response on the claimant and notify the owner and principal in writing (subsection 15(4)).

[26.51] The courts have laid down the following principles regarding the response:

(1) As set out above, in Section 26.3.2(B) 'Payment response' above, the respondent is not permitted in the adjudication to raise 'any reason for withholding any amount, including but not limited to any cross claim, counterclaim and set off' unless that reason was included in the payment response (subsection 15(3)).
(2) This is subject to the minor exception set out in *WY Steel Construction Pte Ltd v Osko Pte Ltd*:[29] there is nothing to stop the responding party from drawing to the

---

[24] At [64].
[25] As to effective lodging please see section 37 of the 2004 Act and rule 2 of the SMC Adjudication Rules.
[26] Rule 2.3 of the SMC Adjudication Rules.
[27] Subsection 15(2) of the 2004 Act.
[28] Subsection 15(1)(d) of the 2004 Act.
[29] [2013] SGCA 32.

adjudicator's attention any patent errors on the face of the material provided to the adjudicator by the claiming party.

(3) The adjudicator need not consider any materials served by the respondent that were not included in the response. In *RN & Associates Pte Ltd v TPX Builders Pte Ltd*,[30] the adjudicator decided not to take into account three lever-arch files of material served after the response. As these documents were not served in accordance with subsection 15(3) the adjudicator was entitled to decide to exclude this material and the respondent had not proven that it had been substantially denied justice.

[26.52] Once the time for the lodging of the response has expired the adjudication commences.

26.4.4 The role of the adjudicator

[26.53] The adjudicator has a number of statutory obligations and powers.

(A) Rejection of non-compliant adjudication applications/responses

[26.54] Under subsection 16(2) of the 2004 Act, the adjudicator is obliged to reject:

- any adjudication application that is not made in accordance with subsection 13(3)(a)(b) or (c); and
- any response that is not lodged within the period referred to in subsection 15(1).

[26.55] Accordingly, it seems that although an adjudication application must be rejected out of hand if it is late, wrongly addressed or does not contain the information required under rule 7(2) of the Regulations, the adjudicator is entitled to consider any material submitted by the respondent as long as it is lodged on time. The main exception to this is the bar upon the respondent relying upon, or the adjudicator considering, any reasons for non-payment contained in the adjudication response which were not contained in a valid payment response.[31]

(B) Natural justice and avoiding unnecessary expense

[26.56] Subsection 16(3) of the 2004 Act imposes obligations of natural justice upon the adjudicator. In particular an adjudicator shall:

    (a) act independently, impartially and in a timely manner;
    (b) avoid incurring unnecessary expense; and
    (c) comply with the principles of natural justice.

---

[30] [2012] SGHC 225.
[31] Subsection 15(3) of the 2004 Act.

[26.57] The obligation to act 'independently and impartially' has not yet been considered by the court but is likely to only be grounds for setting aside any decision of the adjudicator, and only where actual or apparent bias is identified.

[26.58] As to compliance 'with the principles of natural justice' in the context of the parties being entitled to a fair process, the prescriptive nature of the payment and adjudication regimes under the 2004 Act appears to have prevented a significant number of attacks upon the process adopted by the adjudicator.

[26.59] For instance, in *WY Steel Construction Pte Ltd v Osko Pte Ltd*,[32] the Court of Appeal noted that a failure to issue a valid payment response under subsection 15(3) of the 2004 Act, or a failure to raise a reason for non-payment at that stage, curtailed the jurisdiction of the adjudicator to consider new arguments in the adjudication. This was Parliament's express intention, and the court found that the adjudicator's refusal to consider new arguments/material submitted in the adjudication could not be impeached on the grounds of natural justice. The respondent had not been deprived of a right to be heard; he had simply failed to exercise that right in raising the issue in a valid payment response.

[26.60] In *SEF Construction v Skoy Connected Pte Ltd*,[33] the court confirmed that it could set aside an adjudicator's decision on the basis of how the adjudication was conducted. This covered only the process, rather than the substance of the decision, but included whether the adjudicator had complied with the principles of natural justice. Indeed, the court described that 'affording natural justice is a fundamental requirement of the adjudication procedure'.

[26.61] However, the court went on to find that where a respondent had raised issues in an adjudication which the adjudicator had not expressly dealt with or disposed of in his decision, this did not amount to a breach of natural justice. In making this finding, the court was satisfied that the adjudicator had considered all of the submissions, although it was stated to be unfortunate that the adjudicator had not explicitly discussed his reasoning. The court said 'natural justice requires that the parties should be heard; it does not require that they be given responses on all submissions made'. The ability of the respondent to raise the same issues in a review adjudication – an opportunity which was not taken – was also a factor taken into account by the court.

[26.62] In *RN & Associates Pte Ltd v TPX Builders Pte Ltd*,[34] the respondent lodged the response but then submitted at a later time a further three bundles of material, asking the adjudicator to take these into account. The court found that these supplementary bundles were not submissions which formed part of the response, although they did seek to support defences validly raised in the response. The court found that the adjudicator, who had refused to take this new material into account, did not deny the respondent a fair process. The adjudicator was only compelled to consider the documents served in

---

[32] [2013] SGCA 32 at [51–52].
[33] [2009] SGHC 257.
[34] [2012] SGHC 225.

the response – although he **may** consider other material under subsection 16(4) (possibly only if he requested them[35]) his decision to do so was within his discretion.

[26.63] The court found that 'the right to have one's case heard is not a right to have the adjudicator consider all material which the parties think are relevant. The adjudicator may make a decision on what considerations are relevant.' The fact that the additional material was submitted after the 7-day period for the filing of the response weighed against consideration of the new material – this deadline is intended to prevent the process of the adjudication becoming protracted, and any challenge must be considered in that context. The respondent had no valid excuse for not filing this material on time. Furthermore the claimant had not seen these materials before the adjudication and would have had no practical opportunity to consider and respond to them.

(C) The conduct of the adjudication

[26.64] Subsection 16(4) of the 2004 Act sets out the adjudicator's powers in conducting an adjudication:

> Subject to subsection (3), an adjudicator may do all or any of the following in relation to an adjudication:
>
> (a) conduct the adjudication in such manner as he thinks fit;
> (b) require submissions or documents from any party to the adjudication;
> (c) set deadlines for the submissions or documents to be provided by any party and for the submissions or responses thereto by any other party;
> (d) appoint, after notifying the parties, an independent expert to inquire and report on specific issues relevant to the adjudication;
> (e) call a conference of the parties;
> (f) carry out an inspection of any construction work, construction site, goods or any other matter to which the adjudication relates;
> (g) issue such directions as may be necessary or expedient for the conduct of the adjudication.
>
> (5) Where an adjudicator has called for a conference of the parties to an adjudication, a party to the adjudication shall not be represented by more than 2 representatives (whether legally qualified or otherwise) unless the adjudicator permits otherwise.
>
> (6) The parties to an adjudication shall comply with any requirement made or direction issued by the adjudicator in accordance with this section.
>
> (7) An adjudicator's power to determine an adjudication application is not affected by the failure of —
>
> (a) the respondent to provide a payment response or lodge an adjudication response; or
> (b) any of the parties to comply with the adjudicator's call for a conference of the parties or any other requirement made or direction issued by the adjudicator,

---

[35] See [71] and [72].

and in the event of any such failure, the adjudicator may determine the application on the basis of the information and documents available to him.

(8) The determination of an adjudicator on any adjudication application shall be in writing.

[26.65] As identified by the court in *RN & Associates Pte Ltd v TPX Builders Pte Ltd*,[36] the majority of these powers are drafted as being adjudicator driven, rather than party driven. The parties may ask that the adjudicator holds a meeting, or requires the submission of further material, but ultimately it is the adjudicator who controls the process within, of course, the confines of his jurisdiction and the requirements of natural justice.

26.5 Determination, effect and costs

26.5.1 The adjudicator's determination

[26.66] The adjudicator must determine the dispute in the adjudication application within a strict timescale of:

- seven days after the time for service of the payment response if no payment response/response has been served, or the respondent has failed to pay the response amount by the due date (subsection 17(a)); or
- in any other case, within 14 days after the commencement of the adjudication or within such longer period as may have been requested by the adjudicator and agreed to by the claimant and the respondent (subsection 17(b)).

[26.67] In the determination, which must be made in writing[37] and be reasoned, the adjudicator 'shall ... determine':

    (a) the adjudicated amount (if any) to be paid by the respondent to the claimant;
    (b) the date on which the adjudicated amount is payable;
    (c) the interest payable on the adjudicated amount; and
    (d) the proportion of the costs of the adjudication payable by each party to the adjudication,

and shall include, in the determination, the reasons therefor.

[26.68] Subsections 17(3) and (4) constrain the adjudicator in the matters he may consider in making his determination:

> (3) Subject to subsection (4), in determining an adjudication application, an adjudicator shall only have regard to the following matters:
>
>   (a) the provisions of this Act;
>   (b) the provisions of the contract to which the adjudication application relates;

---

[36] Ibid.
[37] Subsection 16(8) of the 2004 Act.

(c) the payment claim to which the adjudication application relates, the adjudication application, and the accompanying documents thereto;
(d) the payment response to which the adjudication application relates (if any), the adjudication response (if any), and the accompanying documents thereto;
(e) the results of any inspection carried out by the adjudicator of any matter to which the adjudication relates;
(f) the report of any expert appointed to inquire on specific issues;
(g) the submissions and responses of the parties to the adjudication, and any other information or document provided at the request of the adjudicator in relation to the adjudication; and
(h) any other matter that the adjudicator reasonably considers to be relevant to the adjudication.

(4) In determining an adjudication application, an adjudicator shall not be bound by any payment response, or any assessment in relation to the progress payment, that is provided in the contract to be final or binding on the parties thereto, whether subject to any term or condition or otherwise.

[26.69] Under section 17(5) in making his determination the adjudicator must also take into account the outcome of earlier adjudications, including the valuation of particular works at that date.

[26.70] The determination is delivered by the authorised nominating body, which will also serve a notice on the principal and/or owner that the adjudication determination has been made.[38]

[26.71] Finally, subsection 17(6) the 2004 Act provides for a statutory 'slip rule', whereby the adjudicator may correct a clerical error, slip, omission or a 'defect of form.'

26.5.2 The costs of the adjudication

[26.72] The apportionment of the costs of the adjudication is dealt with at section 30 of the 2004 Act. The adjudicator shall when making his determination 'decide which party shall pay the costs of the adjudication and, where applicable, the amount of contribution by each party.' In this context 'costs' relates only to the fees and disbursements of the adjudicator and the authorised nominating body, rather than inter parties' costs.

[26.73] The costs as between the parties are borne by the parties themselves, subject to two exceptions:
(1) 'Where an adjudicator is satisfied that a party to an adjudication incurred costs of the adjudication because of frivolous or vexatious conduct on the part of, or unfounded submissions by, another party' the adjudicator may order the offending party to pay some or all of the innocent parties' costs.[39]

---

[38] Subsection 17(8) of the 2004 Act.
[39] Subsection 30(3) of the 2004 Act.

(2) Either party may include the whole or any part of its costs in any claim for costs in any proceeding before a court or tribunal.[40]

26.5.3 Adjudication review applications

[26.74] Should the respondent be dissatisfied with the determination of the adjudicator, and should the amount determined as payable exceed $100,000 over the sum admitted by the respondent,[41] there is a limited opportunity for the respondent to apply for a review of the determination. Such an application must be made to the authorised nominating body within 7 days of the respondent having been served with the adjudicator's decision.[42]

[26.75] The contents of the application are governed by s. 18(4) of the 2004 Act, rule 10 of the Regulations and the SMC Rules, and the procedures that apply may be found at section 19 of the 2004 Act and rule 10(3) of the Regulations. The review panel, to be appointed by the authorised nominating body, will consist of a single member if the difference between the adjudicated sum and the admitted amount is between $100,000 and $1m, and three members if it exceed $1m.

[26.76] However, it is a precondition of lodging such an application that the respondent first pays the determined sum.[43]

[26.77] The review panel will then determine the adjudication review application within 14 days after commencement of the review (or such longer period as may be agreed), and may either refuse the application or substitute their own determination.[44]

26.5.4 The effect of an adjudicator's determination

(A) The determination is binding

[26.78] The determination is binding upon the parties unless/until:

- leave of the court to enforce the adjudication is refused;
- the dispute is finally determined by the court or other tribunal under the applicable dispute resolution procedure; or
- the dispute is disposed of by settlement.[45]

[26.79] However, there is nothing to stop the substance of the adjudicator's determination being considered afresh in any subsequent final dispute resolution proceedings.[46]

---

[40] Subsection 30(4) of the 2004 Act.
[41] Rule 10(1) of the Regulations.
[42] Subsection 18(1) and (2) and subsection 19(2) of the 2004 Act.
[43] Subsection 18(3) of the 2004 Act.
[44] Subsection 17(4) and (5) of the 2004 Act.
[45] Subsection 21(1) of the 2004 Act.
[46] Subsection 21(3) and section 34 of the 2004 Act. Adjudication and other dispute resolution proceedings can proceed concurrently.

(B) Payment must be made as determined

[26.80] If payment is directed in the adjudicator's determination (or the adjudication review determination), it must be made within 7 days of the service of the determination upon the respondent, or such other date as determined by the adjudicator, whichever is the later.[47]

26.6 *Enforcement*

[26.81] Should the respondent fail to pay the adjudicated amount, the claimant may:

- serve a notice under section 25 of the 2004 Act that he intends to exercise a lien upon goods which are unfixed;[48]
- serve a notice under section 26, notifying an intention of suspend performance;[49]
- apply for payment from the principal of the respondent;[50] and/or
- apply to the court for the enforcement of the adjudicator's determination under section 27 of the 2004 Act.

26.6.1 Enforcement of the adjudicator's determination

[26.82] Leave of the court is required to enforce the adjudicator's determination in the same manner, and to the same effect, of a judgment or order of the court.[51] When an application is made, the claimant must also submit an affidavit stating that the sum determined has not been paid (in whole or in part) at the time the application was filed.

26.6.2 Setting aside the adjudicator's determination

[26.83] Under subsection 27(5), it is clear that the court has the power to set aside the adjudicator's determination, or any judgment obtained under section 27, upon application by the respondent. In making such an application the respondent shall pay into the court the unpaid portion of the determination, pending the final determination of those proceedings.

[26.84] The High Court, in *SEF Construction Pte Ltd v Skoy Connected Pte Ltd*,[52] set out the broad circumstances in which it will be prepared to consider whether a determination should be set aside:

---

[47] Subsection 22(1) of the 2004 Act.
[48] Subsection 23(1)(a) of the 2004 Act.
[49] Subsection 23(1)(b) of the 2004 Act.
[50] Section 24 of the 2004 Act.
[51] Subsection 27(1) of the 2004 Act.
[52] [2009] SGHC.

(1) The court cannot 'look into the parties' arguments before the adjudicator and determine whether the adjudicator arrived at the correct decision.'[53] If the adjudicator does make an error of fact or law in arriving at his adjudication determination, this error can be rectified in subsequent arbitration or court proceedings.[54]

(2) Instead, 'the court's role is limited to supervising the appointment and conduct of the adjudicator to ensure that the statutory provisions governing such appointment and conduct are adhered to and that the process of the adjudication, rather than the substance, is proper.'[55] A failure to comply with the 2004 Act 'will not be in truth an adjudicator's determination within the meaning of the Act; it will be void and not merely voidable.'[56]

(3) The court then listed the matters in which the court must concern itself in considering an application under subsection 27(5) of the 2004 Act:

(a) the existence of a contract between the claimant and the respondent, to which the Act applies (s. 4);
(b) the service by the claimant on the respondent of a payment claim (s.10);
(c) the making of an adjudication application by the claimant to an authorised nominating body (s.13);
(d) the reference of the application to an eligible adjudicator who agrees to determine the adjudication application (s. 14);
(e) the determination by the adjudicator of the application within the specified period by determining the adjudicated amount (if any) to be paid by the respondent to the claimant; the date on which the adjudicated amount is payable; the interest payable on the adjudicated amount and the proportion of the costs payable by each party to the adjudication (ss.17(1) and (2);
(f) whether the adjudicator acted independently and impartially and in a timely manner and complied with the principles of natural justice in accordance with s. 16(3); and
(g) in the case where a review adjudicator or panel of adjudicators has been appointed, whether the same conditions existed, mutatis mutandis, as under (a) to (f) above.[57]

(4) If the court finds that the answer to any of these questions is in the negative, then the adjudication determination and any judgment arising therefrom must be set aside.[58]

[26.85] Many of these grounds will find parallels in the other adjudication systems, and it is clear that the courts are willing to consider court decisions from other jurisdictions in the correct circumstances. It is of note that the Court of Appeal has taken a similar view on the enforcement of Interim Dispute Adjudication Board decisions under the FIDIC form of contract in *PT Perusahaan Gas Negara (Persero) TBK v CRW Joint Operation (Indonesia) [2014] SGHC 146*.

---

[53] Ibid at [41].
[54] Ibid at [42].
[55] Ibid at [42].
[56] Ibid at [43].
[57] Paragraph [45].
[58] Paragraph [46].

[26.86] Similarly, the courts have a residual power to stay the enforcement of an adjudication determination where it was necessary to do so to secure the ends of justice. For instance, a stay could be justified where there was clear and objective evidence of the claimant's insolvency and where the court was satisfied that, if the stay was not granted, the monies paid to the claimant would not be recoverable in subsequent arbitration/litigation. Factors to take into account are whether the claimant's financial distress was caused or contributed to by the respondent's failure to pay monies due, and whether the claimant's financial state is similar to its state at the date the contract was entered into.[59]

26.7 Conclusion

[26.87] By providing a targeted and swift interim dispute resolution method, inextricably linked to a strict payment regime, it appears that the 2004 Act has largely achieved its stated aims. The decisions of the High Court and Court of Appeal tend to support the clear intention of Parliament and the industry has been more than willing to avail itself of the rights created by the 2004 Act.

---

[59] *WY Steel Construction Pte Ltd v Osko Pte Ltd* [2013] SGCA 32.

Appendices

Appendix 1
The 1996 Act as amended

~~Deletions made by the Local Democracy, Economic Development and Construction Act 2009 are shaded in grey.~~

<u>Insertions made by the Local Democracy, Economic Development and Construction Act 2009 are double underlined.</u>

Introductory provisions

104 Construction contracts

(1) In this Part a "construction contract" means an agreement with a person for any of the following—
   (a) the carrying out of construction operations;
   (b) arranging for the carrying out of construction operations by others, whether under sub-contract to him or otherwise;
   (c) providing his own labour, or the labour of others, for the carrying out of construction operations.
(2) References in this Part to a construction contract include an agreement-
   (a) to do architectural, design, or surveying work; or
   (b) to provide advice on building, engineering, interior or exterior decoration or on the laying-out of landscape, in relation to construction operations.
(3) References in this Part to a construction contract do not include a contract of employment (within the meaning of the Employment Rights Act 1996).
(4) The Secretary of State may by order add to, amend or repeal any of the provisions of subsection (1), (2) or (3) as to the agreements which are construction contracts for the purposes of this Part or are to be taken or not to be taken as included in references to such contracts.
   No such order shall be made unless a draft of it has been laid before and approved by a resolution of each House of Parliament.
(5) Where an agreement relates to construction operations and other matters, this Part applies to it only so far as it relates to construction operations.
   An agreement relates to construction operations so far as it makes provision of any kind within subsection (1) or (2).

A Practical Guide to Construction Adjudication, First Edition. James Pickavance.
© 2016 James Pickavance. Published 2016 by John Wiley & Sons, Inc.

(6) This Part applies only to construction contracts which-
   (a) are entered into after the commencement of this Part, and
   (b) relate to the carrying out of construction operations in England, Wales or Scotland.
(7) This Part applies whether or not the law of England and Wales or Scotland is otherwise the applicable law in relation to the contract.

105 Meaning of "construction operations"

(1) In this Part "construction operations" means, subject as follows, operations of any of the following descriptions—
   (a) construction, alteration, repair, maintenance, extension, demolition or dismantling of buildings, or structures forming, or to form, part of the land (whether permanent or not);
   (b) construction, alteration, repair, maintenance, extension, demolition or dismantling of any works forming, or to form, part of the land, including (without prejudice to the foregoing) walls, roadworks, power-lines, telecommunication apparatus, aircraft runways, docks and harbours, railways, inland waterways, pipe-lines, reservoirs, water-mains, wells, sewers, industrial plant and installations for purposes of land drainage, coast protection or defence;
   (c) installation in any building or structure of fittings forming part of the land, including (without prejudice to the foregoing) systems of heating, lighting, air-conditioning, ventilation, power supply, drainage, sanitation, water supply or fire protection, or security or communications systems;
   (d) external or internal cleaning of buildings and structures, so far as carried out in the course of their construction, alteration, repair, extension or restoration;
   (e) operations which form an integral part of, or are preparatory to, or are for rendering complete, such operations as are previously described in this subsection, including site clearance, earth-moving, excavation, tunnelling and boring, laying of foundations, erection, maintenance or dismantling of scaffolding, site restoration, landscaping and the provision of roadways and other access works;
   (f) painting or decorating the internal or external surfaces of any building or structure.
(2) The following operations are not construction operations within the meaning of this Part—
   (a) drilling for, or extraction of, oil or natural gas;
   (b) extraction (whether by underground or surface working) of minerals; tunnelling or boring, or construction of underground works, for this purpose;
   (c) assembly, installation or demolition of plant or machinery, or erection or demolition of steelwork for the purposes of supporting or providing access to plant or machinery, on a site where the primary activity is—
      (i) nuclear processing, power generation, or water or effluent treatment, or
      (ii) the production, transmission, processing or bulk storage (other than warehousing) of chemicals, pharmaceuticals, oil, gas, steel or food and drink;

(d) manufacture or delivery to site of—
  (i) building or engineering components or equipment,
  (ii) materials, plant or machinery, or
  (iii) components for systems of heating, lighting, air-conditioning, ventilation, power supply, drainage, sanitation, water supply or fire protection, or for security or communications systems, except under a contract which also provides for their installation;
(e) the making, installation and repair of artistic works, being sculptures, murals and other works which are wholly artistic in nature.

(3) The Secretary of State may by order add to, amend or repeal any of the provisions of subsection (1) or (2) as to the operations and work to be treated as construction operations for the purposes of this Part.

(4) No such order shall be made unless a draft of it has been laid before and approved by a resolution of each House of Parliament.

106 Provisions not applicable to contract with residential occupier

(1) This Part does not apply—
  (a) to a construction contract with a residential occupier (see below), or
  (b) to any other description of construction contract excluded from the operation of this Part by order of the Secretary of State.

(2) A construction contract with a residential occupier means a construction contract which principally relates to operations on a dwelling which one of the parties to the contract occupies, or intends to occupy, as his residence.

In this subsection "dwelling" means a dwelling-house or a flat; and for this purpose- "dwelling-house" does not include a building containing a flat; and "flat" means separate and self-contained premises constructed or adapted for use for residential purposes and forming part of a building from some other part of which the premises are divided horizontally.

(3) The Secretary of State may by order amend subsection (2).

(4) No order under this section shall be made unless a draft of it has been laid before and approved by a resolution of each House of Parliament.

106A Power to disapply provisions of this Part

(1) The Secretary of State may by order provide that any or all of the provisions of this Part, so far as extending to England and Wales, shall not apply to any description of construction contract relating to the carrying out of construction operations (not being operations in Wales) which is specified in the order.

(2) The Welsh Ministers may by order provide that any or all of the provisions of this Part, so far as extending to England and Wales, shall not apply to any description of construction contract relating to the carrying out of construction operations in Wales which is specified in the order.

(3) The Scottish Ministers may by order provide that any or all of the provisions of this Part, so far as extending to Scotland, shall not apply to any description of construction contract which is specified in the order.
(4) An order under this section shall not be made unless a draft of it has been laid before and approved by resolution of-
   (a) in the case of an order under subsection (1), each House of Parliament;
   (b) in the case of an order under subsection (2), the National Assembly for Wales;
   (c) in the case of an order under subsection (3), the Scottish Parliament.

107 *Provisions applicable only to agreements in writing*

(1) The provisions of this Part apply only where the construction contract is in writing and any other agreement between the parties as to any matter is effective for the purposes of this Part only if in writing.
   The expression "agreement", "agree" and "agreed" shall be construed accordingly.
(2) There is an agreement in writing
   (a) if the agreement is made in writing (whether or not it is signed by the parties).
   (b) if the agreement is made by exchange of communications in writing, or
   (c) if the agreement is evidenced in writing.
(3) Where parties agree otherwise than in writing by reference to terms which are in writing, they make an agreement in writing.
(4) An agreement is evidenced in writing if an agreement made otherwise than in writing is recorded by one of the parties, or by a third party, with the authority of the parties to the agreement.
(5) An exchange of written submissions in adjudication proceedings, or in arbitral or legal proceedings in which the existence of an agreement otherwise than in writing is alleged by one party against another party and not denied by the other party in his response constitutes as between those parties an agreement in writing to the effect alleged.
(6) References in this Part to anything being written or in writing include its being recorded by any means.

Adjudication

108. Right to refer disputes to adjudication

(1) A party to a construction contract has the right to refer a dispute arising under the contract for adjudication under a procedure complying with this section.
   For this purpose "dispute" includes any difference.
(2) The contract shall include provision in writing so as to-
   (a) enable a party to give notice at any time of his intention to refer a dispute to adjudication;

(b) provide a timetable with the object of securing the appointment of the adjudicator and referral of the dispute to him within 7 days of such notice;
(c) require the adjudicator to reach a decision within 28 days of referral or such longer period as is agreed by the parties after the dispute has been referred;
(d) allow the adjudicator to extend the period of 28 days by up to 14 days, with the consent of the party by whom the dispute was referred;
(e) impose a duty on the adjudicator to act impartially; and
(f) enable the adjudicator to take the initiative in ascertaining the facts and the law.

(3) The contract shall provide <u>in writing</u> that the decision of the adjudicator is binding until the dispute is finally determined by legal proceedings, by arbitration (if the contract provides for arbitration or the parties otherwise agree to arbitration) or by agreement.

The parties may agree to accept the decision of the adjudicator as finally determining the dispute.

<u>(3A) The contract shall include provision in writing permitting the adjudicator to correct his decision so as to remove a clerical or typographical error arising by accident or omission.</u>

(4) The contract shall also provide <u>in writing</u> that the adjudicator is not liable for anything done or omitted in the discharge or purported discharge of his functions as adjudicator unless the act or omission is in bad faith, and that any employee or agent of the adjudicator is similarly protected from liability.

(5) If the contract does not comply with the requirements of subsections 1 to 4, the adjudication provisions of the Scheme for Construction Contracts apply.

(6) For England and Wales, the Scheme may apply the provisions of the Arbitration Act 1996 with such adaptations and modifications as appear to the Minister making the scheme to be appropriate.

For Scotland, the Scheme may include provision conferring powers on courts in relation to adjudication and provision relating to the enforcement of the adjudicator's decision.

<u>108A Adjudication costs: effectiveness of provision</u>

<u>(1) This section applies in relation to any contractual provision made between the parties to a construction contract which concerns the allocation as between those parties of costs relating to the adjudication of a dispute arising under the construction contract.</u>
<u>(2) The contractual provision referred to in subsection (1) is ineffective unless-</u>
  <u>(a) it is made in writing, is contained in the construction contract and confers power on the adjudicator to allocate his fees and expenses as between the parties, or</u>
  <u>(b) it is made in writing after the giving of notice of intention to refer the dispute to adjudication.</u>

Payment

[s.109–113]

Supplementary provisions

114 The Scheme for Construction Contracts

(1) The Minister shall by regulations make a scheme ("the Scheme for Construction Contracts") containing provision about the matters referred to in the preceding provisions of this Part.
(2) Before making any regulations under this section the Minister shall consult such persons as he thinks fit.
(3) In this section "the Minister" means-
   (a) for England and Wales, the Secretary of State, and
   (b) for Scotland, the Lord Advocate.
(4) Where any provisions of the Scheme for Construction Contracts apply by virtue of this Part in default of contractual provision agreed by the parties, they have effect as implied terms of the contract concerned.
(5) Regulations under this section shall not be made unless a draft of them has been approved by resolution of each House of Parliament.

115 Service of notices and communications

(1) The parties are free to agree on the manner of service of any notice or other document required or authorised to be served in pursuance of the construction contract or for any of the purposes of this Part.
(2) If or to the extent that there is no such agreement the following provisions apply.
(3) A notice or other document may be served on a person by any effective means.
(4) If a notice or other document is addressed, pre-paid and delivered by post-
   (a) to the addressee's last known principal residence or, if he is or has been carrying on a trade, profession or business, his last known principal business address, or
   (b) where the addressee is a body corporate, to the body's registered or principal office, it shall be treated as effectively served.
(5) This section does not apply to the service of documents for the purposes of legal proceedings, for which provision is made by rules of court.
(6) References in this Part to a notice or other document include any form of communication in writing and references to service shall be construed accordingly.

116 Reckoning periods of time

(1) For the purposes of this Part periods of time shall be reckoned as follows.
(2) Where an act is required to be done within a specified period after or from a specified date, the period begins immediately after that date.

(3) Where the period would include Christmas Day, Good Friday or a day which under the Banking and Financial Dealings Act 1971 is a bank holiday in England and Wales or, as the case may be, in Scotland, that day shall be excluded.

117 Crown application

(1) This Part applies to a construction contract entered into by or on behalf of the Crown otherwise than by or on behalf of Her Majesty in her private capacity.
(2) This Part applies to a construction contract entered into on behalf of the Duchy of Cornwall notwithstanding any Crown interest.
(3) Where a construction contract is entered into by or on behalf of Her Majesty in right of the Duchy of Lancaster, Her Majesty shall be represented, for the purposes of any adjudication or other proceedings arising out of the contract by virtue of this Part, by the Chancellor of the Duchy or such person as he may appoint.
(4) Where a construction contract is entered into on behalf of the Duchy of Cornwall, the Duke of Cornwall or the possessor for the time being of the Duchy shall be represented, for the purposes of any adjudication or other proceedings arising out of the contract by virtue of this Part, by such person as he may appoint.
...

146 Orders, regulations and directions

...

(2) Orders and regulations under this Act may contain such incidental, supplementary or transitional provisions and savings as the Secretary of State authority making them considers appropriate.
(3) ...
(a) orders and regulation subject to affirmative resolution procedure (see sections 104(4), 105(4), 106(4), 106A and 114(5), ...

Appendix 2
The 1998 Scheme as amended

Deletions made by the Scheme for Construction Contracts (England and Wales) Regulations 1998 (Amendment) (England) Regulations 2011 are shaded in grey.

Insertions made by the Scheme for Construction Contracts (England and Wales) Regulations 1998 (Amendment) (England) Regulations 2011are double underlined.

The Secretary of State, in exercise of the powers conferred on him by sections 108(6), 114 and 146(1) and (2) of the Housing Grants, Construction and Regeneration Act 1996, and of all other powers enabling him in that behalf, having consulted such persons as he thinks fit, and draft Regulations having been approved by both Houses of Parliament, hereby makes the following Regulations:

Citation, commencement, extent and interpretation

(1) (1) These Regulations may be cited as the Scheme for Construction Contracts (England and Wales) Regulations 1998 and shall come into force at the end of the period of 8 weeks beginning with the day on which they are made (the "commencement date").

(2) These Regulations shall extend only to England and Wales.

(3) In these Regulations, "the Act" means the Housing Grants, Construction and Regeneration Act 1996.

The Scheme for Construction Contracts

(2) Where a construction contract does not comply with the requirements of section 108(1) to (4) of the Act, the adjudication provisions in Part I of the Schedule to these Regulations shall apply.

(3) Where–
   (a) the parties to a construction contract are unable to reach agreement for the purposes mentioned respectively in sections 109, 111 and 113 of the Act, or

---

A Practical Guide to Construction Adjudication, First Edition. James Pickavance.
© 2016 James Pickavance. Published 2016 by John Wiley & Sons, Inc.

(b) a construction contract does not make provision as required by section 110 <u>or by section 110A of the Act</u>, the relevant provisions in Part II of the Schedule to these Regulations shall apply.

(4) The provisions in the Schedule to these Regulations shall be the Scheme for Construction Contracts for the purposes of section 114 of the Act.

The Scheme for Construction Contracts Part 1 – Adjudication

Notice of Intention to seek Adjudication

(1) (1) Any party to a construction contract (the "referring party") may give written notice (the "notice of adjudication") <u>at any time</u> of his intention to refer any dispute arising under the contract, to adjudication.
   (2) The notice of adjudication shall be given to every other party to the contract.
   (3) The notice of adjudication shall set out briefly–
      (a) the nature and a brief description of the dispute and of the parties involved,
      (b) details of where and when the dispute has arisen,
      (c) the nature of the redress which is sought, and
      (d) the names and addresses of the parties to the contract (including, where appropriate, the addresses which the parties have specified for the giving of notices).

(2) (1) Following the giving of a notice of adjudication and subject to any agreement between the parties to the dispute as to who shall act as adjudicator–
      (a) the referring party shall request the person (if any) specified in the contract to act as adjudicator, or
      (b) if no person is named in the contract or the person named has already indicated that he is unwilling or unable to act, and the contract provides for a specified nominating body to select a person, the referring party shall request the nominating body named in the contract to select a person to act as adjudicator, or
      (c) where neither paragraph (a) nor (b) above applies, or where the person referred to in (a) has already indicated that he is unwilling or unable to act and (b) does not apply, the referring party shall request an adjudicator nominating body to select a person to act as adjudicator.
   (2) A person requested to act as adjudicator in accordance with the provisions of paragraph (1) shall indicate whether or not he is willing to act within two days of receiving the request.
   (3) In this paragraph, and in paragraphs 5 and 6 below, an "adjudicator nominating body" shall mean a body (not being a natural person and not being a party to the dispute) which holds itself out publicly as a body which will select an adjudicator when requested to do so by a referring party.
   (3) The request referred to in paragraphs 2, 5 and 6 shall be accompanied by a copy of the notice of adjudication.

(4) Any person requested or selected to act as adjudicator in accordance with paragraphs 2, 5 or 6 shall be a natural person acting in his personal capacity. A person requested or selected to act as an adjudicator shall not be an employee of any of the parties to the dispute and shall declare any interest, financial or otherwise, in any matter relating to the dispute.

(5) (1) The nominating body referred to in paragraphs 2(1)(b) and 6(1)(b) or the adjudicator nominating body referred to in paragraphs 2(1)(c), 5(2)(b) and 6(1)(c) must communicate the selection of an adjudicator to the referring party within five days of receiving a request to do so.

(2) Where the nominating body or the adjudicator nominating body fails to comply with paragraph (1), the referring party may—

(a) agree with the other party to the dispute to request a specified person to act as adjudicator, or
(b) request any other adjudicator nominating body to select a person to act as adjudicator.

(3) The person requested to act as adjudicator in accordance with the provisions of paragraphs (1) or (2) shall indicate whether or not he is willing to act within two days of receiving the request.

(6) (1) Where an adjudicator who is named in the contract indicates to the parties that he is unable or unwilling to act, or where he fails to respond in accordance with paragraph 2(2), the referring party may—

(a) request another person (if any) specified in the contract to act as adjudicator, or
(b) request the nominating body (if any) referred to in the contract to select a person to act as adjudicator, or
(c) request any other adjudicator nominating body to select a person to act as adjudicator.

(2) The person requested to act in accordance with the provisions of paragraph (1) shall indicate whether or not he is willing to act within two days of receiving the request.

(7) (1) Where an adjudicator has been selected in accordance with paragraphs 2, 5 or 6, the referring party shall, not later than seven days from the date of the notice of adjudication, refer the dispute in writing (the "referral notice") to the adjudicator.

(2) A referral notice shall be accompanied by copies of, or relevant extracts from, the construction contract and such other documents as the referring party intends to rely upon.

(3) The referring party shall, at the same time as he sends to the adjudicator the documents referred to in paragraphs (1) and (2), send copies of those documents to every other party to the dispute. <u>Upon receipt of the referral notice, the adjudicator must inform every party to the dispute of the date that it was received.</u>

(8) (1) The adjudicator may, with the consent of all the parties to those disputes, adjudicate at the same time on more than one dispute under the same contract.
(2) The adjudicator may, with the consent of all the parties to those disputes, adjudicate at the same time on related disputes under different contracts, whether or not one or more of those parties is a party to those disputes.
(3) All the parties in paragraphs (1) and (2) respectively may agree to extend the period within which the adjudicator may reach a decision in relation to all or any of these disputes.
(4) Where an adjudicator ceases to act because a dispute is to be adjudicated on by another person in terms of this paragraph, that adjudicator's fees and expenses shall be determined in accordance with paragraph 25.

(9) (1) An adjudicator may resign at any time on giving notice in writing to the parties to the dispute.
(2) An adjudicator must resign where the dispute is the same or substantially the same as one which has previously been referred to adjudication, and a decision has been taken in that adjudication.
(3) Where an adjudicator ceases to act under paragraph 9(1)–
   (a) the referring party may serve a fresh notice under paragraph 1 and shall request an adjudicator to act in accordance with paragraphs 2 to 7; and
   (b) if requested by the new adjudicator and insofar as it is reasonably practicable, the parties shall supply him with copies of all documents which they had made available to the previous adjudicator.
(4) Where an adjudicator resigns in the circumstances referred to in paragraph (2), or where a dispute varies significantly from the dispute referred to him in the referral notice and for that reason he is not competent to decide it, the adjudicator shall be entitled to the payment of such reasonable amount as he may determine by way of fees and expenses reasonably incurred by him. The parties shall be jointly and severally liable for any sum which remains outstanding following the making of any determination on how the payment shall be apportioned. Subject to any contractual provision pursuant to section 108A(2) of the Act, the adjudicator may determine how the payment is to be apportioned and the parties are jointly and severally liable for any sum which remains outstanding following the making of any such determination.

(10) Where any party to the dispute objects to the appointment of a particular person as adjudicator, that objection shall not invalidate the adjudicator's appointment nor any decision he may reach in accordance with paragraph 20.

(11) (1) The parties to a dispute may at any time agree to revoke the appointment of the adjudicator. The adjudicator shall be entitled to the payment of such reasonable amount as he may determine by way of fees and expenses incurred by him. The parties shall be jointly and severally liable for any sum which remains outstanding following the making of any determination on how the payment shall be apportioned. Subject to any contractual provision pursuant to section 108A(2) of the Act, the adjudicator may determine how the payment is to be

apportioned and the parties are jointly and severally liable for any sum which remains outstanding following the making of any such determination.
(2) Where the revocation of the appointment of the adjudicator is due to the default or misconduct of the adjudicator, the parties shall not be liable to pay the adjudicator's fees and expenses.

Powers of the adjudicator

(12) The adjudicator shall—
   (a) act impartially in carrying out his duties and shall do so in accordance with any relevant terms of the contract and shall reach his decision in accordance with the applicable law in relation to the contract; and
   (b) avoid incurring unnecessary expense.
(13) The adjudicator may take the initiative in ascertaining the facts and the law necessary to determine the dispute, and shall decide on the procedure to be followed in the adjudication. In particular he may-
   (a) request any party to the contract to supply him with such documents as he may reasonably require including, if he so directs, any written statement from any party to the contract supporting or supplementing the referral notice and any other documents given under paragraph 7(2),
   (b) decide the language or languages to be used in the adjudication and whether a translation of any document is to be provided and if so by whom,
   (c) meet and question any of the parties to the contract and their representatives,
   (d) subject to obtaining any necessary consent from a third party or parties, make such site visits and inspections as he considers appropriate, whether accompanied by the parties or not,
   (e) subject to obtaining any necessary consent from a third party or parties, carry out any tests or experiments,
   (f) obtain and consider such representations and submissions as he requires, and, provided he has notified the parties of his intention, appoint experts, assessors or legal advisers,
   (g) give directions as to the timetable for the adjudication, any deadlines, or limits as to the length of written documents or oral representations to be complied with, and
   (h) issue other directions relating to the conduct of the adjudication.
(14) The parties shall comply with any request or direction of the adjudicator in relation to the adjudication.
(15) If, without showing sufficient cause, a party fails to comply with any request, direction or timetable of the adjudicator made in accordance with his powers, fails to produce any document or written statement requested by the adjudicator, or in any other way fails to comply with a requirement under these provisions relating to the adjudication, the adjudicator may-
   (a) continue the adjudication in the absence of that party or of the document or written statement requested,

(b) draw such inferences from that failure to comply as the circumstances may, in the adjudicator's opinion, justify, and

(c) make a decision on the basis of the information before him attaching such weight as he thinks fit to any evidence submitted to him outside any period he may have requested or directed.

(16) (1) Subject to any agreement between the parties to the contrary, and to the terms of paragraph (2) below, any party to the dispute may be assisted by, or represented by, such advisers or representatives (whether legally qualified or not) as he considers appropriate.

(2) Where the adjudicator is considering oral evidence or representations, a party to the dispute may not be represented by more than one person, unless the adjudicator gives directions to the contrary.

(17) The adjudicator shall consider any relevant information submitted to him by any of the parties to the dispute and shall make available to them any information to be taken into account in reaching his decision.

(18) The adjudicator and any party to the dispute shall not disclose to any other person any information or document provided to him in connection with the adjudication which the party supplying it has indicated is to be treated as confidential, except to the extent that it is necessary for the purposes of, or in connection with, the adjudication.

(19) (1) The adjudicator shall reach his decision not later than-

(a) twenty eight days after receipt of the referral notice mentioned in paragraph 7(1), or

(b) forty two days after receipt of the referral notice if the referring party so consents, or

(c) such period exceeding twenty eight days after receipt of the referral notice as the parties to the dispute may, after the giving of that notice, agree.

(2) Where the adjudicator fails, for any reason, to reach his decision in accordance with paragraph (1)

(a) any of the parties to the dispute may serve a fresh notice under paragraph 1 and shall request an adjudicator to act in accordance with paragraphs 2 to 7; and

(b) if requested by the new adjudicator and insofar as it is reasonably practicable, the parties shall supply him with copies of all documents which they had made available to the previous adjudicator.

(3) As soon as possible after he has reached a decision, the adjudicator shall deliver a copy of that decision to each of the parties to the contract.

Adjudicator's decision

(20) The adjudicator shall decide the matters in dispute. He may take into account any other matters which the parties to the dispute agree should be within the scope of the adjudication or which are matters under the contract which he considers are necessarily connected with the dispute. In particular, he may–

(a) open up, revise and review any decision taken or any certificate given by any person referred to in the contract unless the contract states that the decision or certificate is final and conclusive,

(b) decide that any of the parties to the dispute is liable to make a payment under the contract (whether in sterling or some other currency) and, subject to section 111(4)(9) of the Act, when that payment is due and the final date for payment,

(c) having regard to any term of the contract relating to the payment of interest decide the circumstances in which, and the rates at which, and the periods for which simple or compound rates of interest shall be paid.

(21) In the absence of any directions by the adjudicator relating to the time for performance of his decision, the parties shall be required to comply with any decision of the adjudicator immediately on delivery of the decision to the parties in accordance with this paragraph.

(22) If requested by one of the parties to the dispute, the adjudicator shall provide reasons for his decision.

22A.(1) The adjudicator may on his own initiative or on the application of a party correct his decision so as to remove a clerical or typographical error arising by accident or omission.

(2) Any correction of a decision must be made within five days of the delivery of the decision to the parties.

(3) As soon as possible after correcting a decision in accordance with this paragraph, the adjudicator must deliver a copy of the corrected decision to each of the parties to the contract.

(4) Any correction of a decision forms part of the decision.

Effects of the decision

(23) (1) In his decision, the adjudicator may, if he thinks fit, order any of the parties to comply peremptorily with his decision or any part of it.

(2) The decision of the adjudicator shall be binding on the parties, and they shall comply with it until the dispute is finally determined by legal proceedings, by arbitration (if the contract provides for arbitration or the parties otherwise agree to arbitration) or by agreement between the parties.

(24) Section 42 of the Arbitration Act 1996 shall apply to this Scheme subject to the following modifications-

(a) in subsection (2) for the word "tribunal" wherever it appears there shall be substituted the word "adjudicator",

(b) in subparagraph (b) of subsection (2) for the words "arbitral proceedings" there shall be substituted the word "adjudication",

(c) subparagraph (c) of subsection (2) shall be deleted, and

(d) subsection (3) shall be deleted.

(25) The adjudicator shall be entitled to the payment of such reasonable amount as he may determine by way of fees and expenses reasonably incurred by him. The parties

shall be jointly and severally liable for any sum which remains outstanding following the making of any determination on how the payment shall be apportioned. <u>Subject to any contractual provision pursuant to section 108A(2) of the Act, the adjudicator may determine how the payment is to be apportioned and the parties are jointly and severally liable for any sum which remains outstanding following the making of any such determination.</u>

(26) The adjudicator shall not be liable for anything done or omitted in the discharge or purported discharge of his functions as adjudicator unless the act or omission is in bad faith, and any employee or agent of the adjudicator shall be similarly protected from liability.

Appendix 3
Glossary (UK only)

This appendix provides definitions for the defined terms in this book, court defined terminology and some of the terminology commonly used in the context of adjudication and adjudication proceedings across the United Kingdom and then separately in England and Wales and Scotland.

1.1 United Kingdom

- **1996 Act** means Part 2 of the Housing Grants Construction and Regeneration Act 1996.
- **2009 Act** means Part 2 of the Housing Grants Construction and Regeneration Act 1996 as amended by Part 8 of the Local Democracy, Economic Development and Construction Act 2009 (the "LDEDC").
- **Act** is used to refer to both the 1996 Act and 2009 Act in circumstances where the provisions of both are identical or the statement applies equally to both acts.
- **Ad hoc adjudication** means a form of adjudication where the parties have agreed, or are deemed to have agreed to submit their dispute, without reservation, to adjudication thereby giving an adjudicator ad hoc jurisdiction to decide the dispute in circumstances where a statutory adjudication regime does not apply and where there is no pre-existing contractual agreement to adjudicate.
- **ANB** means adjudicator nominating body. This is an independent organisation whose purpose is to appoint an adjudicator to preside over a dispute within a short space of time when requested to do so.
- **Contractual adjudication** means adjudication where the Act does not exist or does not apply, but nevertheless the parties have agreed a mechanism by which they can adjudicate disputes.
- **Jurisdiction** means, in the context of adjudication, the existence and extent of the adjudicator's powers to decide the scope of the dispute legitimately referred to him.
- **LDEDC** means Part 8 of the Local Democracy, Economic Development and Construction Act 2009.
- **Natural justice** comprises two key rules: a party has a right to hear the case against it and have the opportunity to respond to it and the adjudicator must not be biased.

A Practical Guide to Construction Adjudication, First Edition. James Pickavance.
© 2016 James Pickavance. Published 2016 by John Wiley & Sons, Inc.

- **Notice of Adjudication** means the document that outlines what the dispute is about and the relief sought and that commences the adjudication process.
- **Referral notice** means the document that sets out the referring party's case in detail. It is the equivalent of the statement of case in an arbitration or the particulars of claim in litigation.
- **Rejoinder** means the document containing the responding party's response to the reply
- **Reply** means the document containing the referring party's response to the responding party's response.
- **Response** means the first document setting out the responding party's defence to the claim set out in the Notice of Adjudication and the Referral.
- **Statutory adjudication** means a form of adjudication governed by the Act. The Act will apply where certain conditions of the Act are met, including whether the contract between the parties in dispute is a 'construction contract' as defined by the Act. Where the Act applies, the right to adjudicate is mandatory and cannot be contracted out of.
- **Sur-rejoinder** means the document containing the referring party's response to the rejoinder.

1.2 England and Wales

- **1998 Scheme** means the Scheme for Construction Contracts (England and Wales) Regulations 1998.
- **2011 Scheme** means the Scheme for Construction Contracts (England and Wales) Regulations 1998 as amended by the Scheme for Construction Contracts (England and Wales) Regulations 1998 (Amendment) (England) Regulations 2011.
- **Court of Appeal** means the appellate court to which cases from the High Court (or exceptionally the County Court) are referred. Adjudication decisions that are appealed will be referred to the Civil Division of the Court of Appeal.
- **High Court** means, in the context of high value cases, the court of first instance. There are several divisions of the High Court. The Technology and Construction Court is the division through which claimants will commence proceedings to enforce an adjudicator's decision.
- **Injunction** means an equitable remedy in the form of a court order that compels a party to do or refrain from specific acts.
- **Judgment** means a decision by the court on the dispute referred to it.
- **Part 7 Claim** means the procedure for the commencement of a claim where the claimant seeks a judgment that awards money or where there is a mix of declaratory and monetary issues, where both entail a substantial dispute of fact.
- **Part 8 Claim** means the procedure to commence a claim where the dispute is unlikely to involve a substantial dispute of fact and no monetary judgment is sought.
- **Scheme** means either the 1998 Scheme or the 2011 Scheme
- **Summary judgment** means a procedure set out at CPR Part 24 pursuant to which the court may give summary judgment against a claimant or defendant on the whole of a

claim or on a particular issue if it considers that the claimant has no real prospect of succeeding on the claim or issue, or that defendant has no real prospect of successfully defending the claim or issue, and there is no other compelling reason why the case or issue should be disposed of at a trial.

1.3 Scotland

- **1998 Scottish Scheme** means the Scheme for Construction Contracts (Scotland) Regulations 1998.
- **2011 Scottish Scheme** means the 1998 Scottish Scheme as amended by the Scheme for Construction Contracts (Scotland) Amendments Regulations 2011.
- **Adjustment** means adjustment of the pleadings where the new material is indicated – usually by underlining, side-lining, a difference of typeface or otherwise – to alter the written pleadings of an action or its defence in its early stages.
- **Arrestment** means an attachment of property for the satisfaction of a debt.
- **Books of Council and Session** means the Registers of Deeds and Probative Writs in which, according to the directions they contain, deeds, etc. may be registered for preservation or preservation and execution.
- **By Order hearing** means a hearing of a case put out for the hearing at the instance of the court and not on the motion of a party.
- **Calling** means where the principal summons is returned to court after it has been served on the defender.
- **Commercial action** means civil proceedings defined in rules of court heard in a Commercial Court in the Court of Session or a specified Sheriff Court.
- **Conclusion of the Summons** means the statement of the precise order sought in a civil action in the Court of Session.
- **Court of Session** means the supreme civil court in Scotland, equivalent to the High Court in England and Wales.
- **Debate** means an intermediate step in procedure when legal points are considered in a civil action before the facts are determined, and which can result in the conclusion of a case or a part of it without evidence being led.
- **Decree** means the judgment of a court.
- **Defender** means a person against whom a civil action is raised. The word 'defendant' is not used in Scotland.
- **Enrol** means lodging a motion seeking an interlocutory order from the court.
- **Enter appearance** means the formal act whereby the defender in an action intimates his intention to defend.
- **Initial writ** means the document by which civil proceedings in the sheriff court are normally initiated.
- **Inner House** means the appellate division of the Court of Session. It is equivalent to the Court of Appeal in England and Wales.
- **Interdict** means a court order that compels a party to do or refrain from specific acts. The equivalent order in England and Wales is an injunction.

- **Judgment** means the decision of a court setting out its reasons for the decision. In the Court of Session it is called an 'Opinion'. In the Sheriff Court it is called a 'Note' attached to the interlocutor.
- **Judicial Review** means a remedy whereby the Court of Session may review and if necessary set aside or rectify the decision of public officials or bodies where no other form of appeal is available.
- **Motion** means an application made in court for an order during the course of court proceedings.
- **Ordinary action** means all sheriff court civil actions other than small claims, summary causes and summary applications; ordinary actions are subject to the Ordinary Cause Rules 1993 in the First Schedule to the Sheriff Courts (Scotland) Act 1907. A claim for £5000 or more must be by an ordinary action.
- **Petition** means a writ by which civil court proceedings are initiated, in which some administrative order of the court is required for something to be done which requires judicial authority. It is distinct from a summons in an action which is to enforce a legal right against a person (the defender). In the Court of Session civil causes are raised at first instance as either a summons or a petition as the case may be. In the sheriff court all civil proceedings are raised in the same way, whether petitions or not, that is by initial writ.
- **Petitioner** means one who presents a formal, written application to a court that requests action on a certain matter.
- **Proof** means an evidential hearing (similar to a trial).
- **Pursuer** means the person suing in a civil action seeking an order against a defender.
- **Scottish Scheme** means either the 1998 Scottish Scheme or the 2011 Scottish Scheme
- **Sheriff** means the judge who presides in the sheriff court.
- **Sheriff Principal** means a judge appointed to be in charge of a sheriffdom, and responsible for the speedy and efficient disposal of business. He is also a judge to whom a litigant may appeal a decision from a sheriff.
- **Sheriff Court** means a judicial court for civil and criminal cases, equivalent to a county court in England.
- **Signetting** means a summons in the Court of Session must have the signet or seal of the Sovereign bearing the Royal Court of Arms embossed upon it to authorise execution (that is service of the writ on a defender). The Keeper of the Signet is the Lord Clerk Register who on 3rd May 1976 granted a commission to the Principal Clerk of Session (and clerks authorised by him) to signet summonses; this was formerly done by members of the Society of Writers to HM Signet.
- **Summary Decree** means a final decision on part or all of a defence to an action or defence to a counterclaim on the basis that the defence does not in fact disclose a defence.
- **Summons** means the form of writ initiating an action in the Court of Session. It is issued in the name of the sovereign, containing a royal mandate to messengers-at-arms to cite the defender to the court.

Appendix 4
Model forms

1.1 Notice of adjudication

IN THE MATTER OF PART II OF THE HOUSING GRANTS, CONSTRUCTION AND REGENERATION ACT 1996 (AS AMENDED)

[✕AND PURSUANT TO [●ADJUDICATION PROCEDURE]] [1]

AND

IN THE MATTER OF A PROPOSED ADJUDICATION

BETWEEN:

[●NAME]

Referring Party

AND

[●NAME]

Responding Party

NOTICE OF INTENTION TO REFER A DISPUTE TO ADJUDICATION

To: The Responding Party

TAKE NOTICE that the Referring Party intends, pursuant to the Housing Grants, Construction and Regeneration Act 1996 (as amended) (the "Act") [✕ and in accordance with [●**ADJUDICATION PROCEDURE**]],[2] to refer to Adjudication the dispute of which particulars are set out in this Notice of Intention to Refer a Dispute to Adjudication.

The Parties

1.   The Referring Party, [●NAME], is a [●TYPE OF BUSINESS].[3]

---

[1]   Complete with the relevant procedure (i.e. the Scheme for Construction Contracts or other scheme agreed by the parties).
[2]   Specify the relevant procedure (i.e. the Scheme or otherwise).
[3]   Also state whether the Referring Party is a limited company or partnership.

A Practical Guide to Construction Adjudication, First Edition. James Pickavance.
© 2016 James Pickavance. Published 2016 by John Wiley & Sons, Inc.

2. The Responding Party, [●NAME], is a [●TYPE OF BUSINESS].[4]

The Contract

3. The contract was made on [●DATE] and is in the terms of [●IDENTIFY CONTRACT CONDITIONS AND CONTRACTUAL DOCUMENTS] (the "**Contract**").

4. The Contract is a construction contract for the purposes of the Act. The Referring Party is entitled to refer the dispute referred to below to Adjudication in accordance with the Act.

5. [✘The Contract does not satisfy the Act and therefore the Scheme for Construction Contracts implies provisions into the Contract for the resolution of the dispute by Adjudication][5].

6. The parties are engaged in a project for [●DESCRIBE PROJECT].

7. The Referring Party's role in the project was as [●IDENTIFY REFERRING PARTY'S ROLE IN PROJECT]. The Responding Party is required under the Contract to [● IDENTIFY RESPONDING PARTY'S ROLE IN PROJECT].

The Dispute

8. A dispute has arisen between the Referring Party and the Responding Party details of which are set out below.

9. Issues have arisen in respect of [●OUTLINE ISSUES FORMING PART OF THE DISPUTE].

10. As a result, there is a dispute as to [●IDENTIFY THE EXACT SCOPE OF THE DISPUTE (WHICH MAY NOT BE ALL THE DISPUTED ISSUES BETWEEN THE PARTIES) AND ANY CONTRACTUAL PROCEDURES WHICH ARE RELEVANT TO THE FORMATION OF A DISPUTE].

11. The location where the dispute arose is [●IDENTIFY LOCATION].

The Redress Sought by the Referring Party

12. The Referring Party seeks redress of the following nature: [●IDENTIFY NATURE OF REDRESS SOUGHT e.g. payment of the sum of £[●FIGURES] plus interest in respect of the loss and damage incurred by the Referring Party as a result of the breaches of contract referred to.]

13. The Referring Party seeks redress in the form of a decision of the Adjudicator that [●IDENTIFY DETAILS OF REDRESS SOUGHT. FOR EXAMPLE:

- payment by the Responding Party by [●DATE] of £[●FIGURES],[6] or such other sum as the Adjudicator sees fit; and
- interest at such rate and in such amount as the Adjudicator thinks fit; and
- any declaratory relief sought e.g. if a specified event is or is not a relevant event, or a declaration that the Responding Party is in breach of contract, or a declaration as to the meaning of a clause in the contract.
- the Referring Party is awarded an extension of time to the Date for Completion until [●DATE]; and
- the Referring Party is awarded damages of [●AMOUNT], or such other sum as the Adjudicator sees fit; and

---

[4] Also state whether the Referring Party is a limited company or partnership.
[5] Use where the contract has provisions that do not comply with the Act.
[6] Redress sought should include where relevant an order for payment of the sums in dispute or due under the Contract. Use wordssuch as "…or such other sum as the Adjudicator considers just and reasonable in all the circumstances".

- the Adjudicator orders the Responding Party to pay the Adjudicator's fees and expenses] [and to reimburse to the Referring Party the cost, to the Referring Party, of securing the Adjudicator's appointment][7].

Crystallisation of the Dispute

14. By letter dated [●DATE], the Referring Party wrote to the Responding Party seeking [●SET OUT PECUNIARY OR DECLARATORY CLAIM].

15. By letter of response dated [●DATE], the Responding Party expressly rejected the Referring Party's claim. The reasons for rejecting the claim are [●CONSIDER SUMMARISING THE DEFENCES].

16. The Responding Party has since refused to engage with the Referring Party on the question of [●DETAILS].

Appointment of Adjudicator

17. The Referring Party will apply to the [●NAME OF NOMINATING BODY] for the appointment of an Adjudicator OR [●ADJUDICATOR NAMED IN THE CONTRACT] to act as the Adjudicator in this dispute.

Relevant Addresses

18. The names and addresses of the parties [✂and the addresses which the parties have specified for the giving of notices][8] to the Contract are set out below:

Referring Party	Responding Party
[●FULL COMPANY DETAILS]	[●FULL COMPANY DETAILS]

19. The names and addresses of the parties' representatives:

Referring Party	Responding Party
[●REPRESENTATIVE'S DETAILS]	[●REPRESENTATIVE'S DETAILS]

Dated [●DATE]

....

[●REFERRING PARTY OR ITS REPRESENTATIVE]

---

[7] If the Adjudicator was appointed by a nominating body.
[8] Use where the contract specifies addresses.

1.2 *Referral*

IN THE MATTER OF AN ADJUDICATION

PURSUANT TO THE HOUSING GRANTS, CONSTRUCTION AND REGENERATION ACT 1996

[✂AND PURSUANT TO [●ADJUDICATION PROCEDURE]] [1]

BETWEEN:

[●NAME]

Referring Party

AND

[●NAME]

Responding Party

REFERRAL

The Parties

1. The Referring Party, [●NAME], is a [●TYPE OF BUSINESS].[2]
2. The Responding Party, [●NAME], is a [●TYPE OF BUSINESS].[3]

Introduction

3. [●SUMMARISE DISPUTE AND CLAIM.]
4. The Referring Party claims from the Responding Party the sum of £[●FIGURES], plus VAT for [●BRIEF DETAILS OF CLAIM], or such other amount as the Adjudicator shall decide.

---

[1] Complete with the relevant procedure (i.e. the Scheme for Construction Contracts or other scheme agreed by the parties).
[2] Also state whether the Referring Party is a limited company or partnership.
[3] Also state whether the Referring Party is a limited company or partnership.

5. These monies are due under the terms of the engagement of the Referring Party as [●ROLE] for [●WORKS OR SERVICES], full particulars of which are set out below.

6. The Referring Party also claims interest on the monies due pursuant to [✗clause [●NUMBER], of the Contract] [the Late Payment of Commercial Debts (Interest) Act 1998].

7. [✗The Referring Party seeks a declaration from the Adjudicator that [●IDENTIFY NATURE OF DECLARATORY RELIEF SOUGHT e.g. if a specified event is or is not a relevant event.]][4]

8. Where the context admits, capitalised terms in the Contract have the same meaning in this Referral.

The Contract

9. The Contract was made on [●DATE] and is in the terms of [●IDENTIFY CONTRACT CONDITIONS AND CONTRACTUAL DOCUMENTS] (the "**Contract**").

10. A copy of [✗relevant parts of] the Contract is at **Appendix 1**. [✗If the Adjudicator requires a complete copy of the Contract, this can be provided by the Referring Party.][5]

11. The Contract is a construction contract for the purposes of the Act. The Referring Party is entitled to refer the dispute referred to below to Adjudication in accordance with the Act.

12. [✗The Contract does not satisfy the Act and therefore the Scheme for Construction Contracts implies provisions into the Contract for the resolution of the dispute by adjudication].[6]

13. The Referring Party relies on the whole of the terms of the Contract for its true meaning intent and effect.

14. The following provisions are relevant to this dispute [●INSERT AND EXPLAIN RELEVANT CLAUSES].

15. In summary, the contractual position is as follows [●SUMMARISE THE CONTRACTUAL POSITION].

[✗Applications and Relevant Notices

16. [●SET OUT RELEVANT PAYMENT DETAILS, IN FULL IF APPROPRIATE, WHERE THE CONTRACT DOES NOT COMPLY WITH THE ACT AND THE TERMS THAT ARE CONSEQUENTLY IMPLIED BY THE ACT].[7]

The Facts

17. [●SET OUT FACTS AND, WHEN COMPLETING THIS SECTION, CONSIDER:

    For unpaid valuations claims:
    - ➢ has the payment become due?
    - ➢ has the final date for payment passed?
    - ➢ has the employer issued a Notice of Payment?
    - ➢ has the employer issued a Notice to Withhold Payment?
    - ➢ does the Notice to Withhold Payment comply with the requirements of the Act?
    - ➢ is the employer arguing set-off or abatement?
    - ➢ have the monies been certified for payment?

    For variation payment claims:

---

[4] Use where claiming declaratory relief.
[5] Insert the entire contract or relevant extracts as appropriate.
[6] Use where the contract has provisions that do not comply with the Act.
[7] Use where the dispute relates to payment notices or notices of withholding, either in whole or in part, if the adjudicator is likely to consider whether the application made was due under the terms of the contract and not simply whether the notices provisions have been complied with.

- what is the scope of the contract works?
- what was the nature of the change that was requested?
- is there a contractual mechanism for dealing with variations?
- was there a request or instruction for a variation?
- was the request made in accordance with the terms of the contract?
- was the change a sufficient departure from the original scope of works or was the change simply the contractor's way of doing the work?
- how have the variations been measured?

For extension of time claims:
- are there conditions precedent in the contract and have they been satisfied?
- what was the contractor's original planned progress?
- what events are alleged to have caused delay?
- precisely what effect did those events have on the contractor's planned progress?
- what does the as-built programme show?
- what methodology has been used to calculate any extension of time?
- how has any concurrent delay been dealt with?
- has the employer attempted to apply liquidated damages?
- what evidence is available to support the allegations made?
- has the contractor considered the practice set out in the Society of Construction Law's "Protocol for Determining Extensions of Time and Compensation for Delay and Disruption"?

For loss and expense claims:
- will the claim for loss and expense be a claim under the contract (have any conditions precedent in the contract been satisfied?) or will it be a common law claim for damages for breach of contract?
- has the contractor considered the practice set out in the Society of Construction Law's "Protocol for Determining Extensions of Time and Compensation for Delay and Disruption"?
- consider the recognised categories of loss and expense: prolongation costs, delay and disruption, head office overheads, loss of profit and finance charges – does the contractor have claims under every head?
- can a full cause and effect analysis be produced?]

Expert Evidence

18. Expert(s) were instructed on [●DATE]. The expert(s) produced an expert report on [●DATE], which is attached at [●**APPENDIX X**].

19. The **expert**(s) were instructed to provide an opinion on [●INSERT].

20. In his/her opinion [●SUMMARISE FINDINGS AND CONCLUSION].

Witness Evidence

21. The following witness(es) have prepared statement(s) setting out the facts and matters within their own knowledge, or where not within their own knowledge, true to the best of their knowledge and belief. The witnesses are [●LIST NAMES OF WITNESSES AND ROLES].

22. [[✂[●NAME] addresses the following issues: [●LIST ISSUES]

23. In particular, [●NAME] records the following:
    - SET OUT KEY POINT(S).] [8]

---

[8] Repeat for each witness.

The Claim

24. The claim by the Referring Party comprises the following issues [●SUMMARISE IN A LIST EACH OF THE ISSUES. THIS SHOULD, WHERE POSSIBLE, ALIGN WITH HEADS OF RELIEF]
25. [●IN RESPECT OF EACH ISSUE, EXPLAIN HOW THE APPLICATION OF THE CONTRACT TO THE FACTS SUPPORT THE RELIEF BEING SOUGHT.]

The Redress Sought by the Referring Party

26. The Referring Party seeks redress of the following nature: [●IDENTIFY NATURE OF REDRESS SOUGHT e.g. payment of the sum of £[●FIGURES] plus interest in respect of the loss and damage incurred by the Referring Party as a result of the breaches of contract referred to.]
27. The Referring Party seeks redress in the form of a decision of the Adjudicator that [●IDENTIFY DETAILS OF REDRESS SOUGHT e.g.

    - payment by the Responding Party by [●DATE] of £[●FIGURES];
    - a declaration from the Adjudicator that [●DETAILS OF DECLARATORY RELIEF SOUGHT]; and
    - interest at such rate and in such amount as the Adjudicator thinks fit; and
    - the Referring Party is awarded an extension of time to the Date for Completion until [●DATE]; and
    - the Adjudicator orders the Responding Party to pay the Adjudicator's fees and expenses] [✘and to reimburse to the Referring Party the cost, to the Referring Party, of securing the Adjudicator's appointment[9]].

Served this [●DATE] by [●NAME OF REFERRING PARTY OR ITS REPRESENTATIVE], [✘[solicitors][consultants][representative for the Referring Party.][10]

....
[●REFERRING PARTY OR ITS REPRESENTATIVE]

……..

APPENDICES

[●INSERT APPROPRIATE APPENDICES, INCLUDING:
APPENDIX 1: CONTRACT OR RELEVANT EXTRACTS
APPENDICES THAT SET OUT KEY INFORMATION SUCH AS

> ➢ measured account details, including variations
> ➢ contractual notices
> ➢ correspondence (including emails, attendance notes, letters, faxes)

APPENDICES THAT SET OUT ANY EXPERT REPORTS]

---

[9] Insert where appropriate.
[10] Where served by a representative, set out the capacity in which the representative is acting.

1.3 *Response*

IN THE MATTER OF AN ADJUDICATION

PURSUANT TO THE HOUSING GRANTS, CONSTRUCTION AND REGENERATION ACT 1996

[✂AND PURSUANT TO [●ADJUDICATION PROCEDURE]] [1]

BETWEEN:

[●NAME]

Referring Party

AND

[●NAME]

Responding Party

RESPONSE TO REFERRAL

Introduction

1. This Response [✂and its Appendices][2] answer the substantive issues raised in the Referral Notice served on the Responding Party on [●DATE].

2. Where the context admits, capitalised terms in the Contract have the same meaning in this Response.

3. It also generally adopts the headings of the Referral Notice but is not a "line by line response". As a result, if a particular sentence, paragraph or section of the Referral Notice is not specifically dealt with that is not to be taken as acceptance of that part of the Referral Notice. This Response is intended to be read as a whole.

4. The Response is structured as follows:

    - [Set out the structure of the Response and a list of the witness evidence appended].

---

[1] Complete with the relevant procedure (i.e. the Scheme for Construction Contracts or other scheme agreed by the parties).
[2] Use where it is appropriate to include materials by way of appendix.

Executive Summary

5. This section sets out a summary of the Responding Party's responses by reference to each of the heads of relief sought by the Referring Party. In each case, the Responding Party's detailed position is set out in the sections that follow.

- [SET OUT THE STRUCTURE OF THE RESPONSE AND A LIST OF THE WITNESS EVIDENCE APPENDED].

Background

6. [●SUMMARISE THE BACKGROUND TO THE PROJECT, THE PARTIES, ANY NOMENCLATURE THAT NEEDS EXPLAINING.]

The Contract

7. [✕Clauses [●REFERENCE] are [✕admitted/noted.]
8. [●REFER TO ADDITIONAL CLAUSES WHERE NECESSARY, CORRECT ERRORS IN INTERPRETATION MADE BY THE REFERRING PARTY.]

The Facts

9. [●SET OUT FACTS AND, WHEN COMPLETING THIS SECTION, CONSIDER:
   - ➢ the guidance set out in the model form Referral,
   - ➢ which sections of the Referral are correct and which are disputed. Ensure that all the facts that are disputed are addressed in the Response.]

Expert Evidence

10. Expert(s) were instructed on [●DATE]. The expert(s) produced an expert report on [●DATE], which is attached at [●APPENDIX X].
11. The expert(s) were instructed to provide an opinion on [●INSERT]
12. In his/her/their opinion [●SUMMARISE FINDINGS AND CONCLUSION, ADDRESSING REFERRING PARTY EVIDENCE].

Witness Evidence

13. The following witness(es) have prepared statement(s) setting out the facts and matters within their own knowledge, or where not within their own knowledge, true to the best of their knowledge and belief. The witnesses are [●LIST NAMES OF WITNESSES AND ROLES]
14. [[✕[●NAME] addresses the following issues: [●LIST ISSUES]
15. In particular, [●NAME] records the following:
    - [SET OUT KEY POINT(S), ADDRESSING REFERRING PARTY'S WITNESS(ES)] [3]

Response to the Claims

---

[3] Repeat for each witness.

16. The claim by the Referring Party comprises the following issues [●SUMMARISE IN A LIST EACH OF THE ISSUES. THIS SHOULD, WHERE POSSIBLE, ALIGN WITH HEADS OF RELIEF]
17. The Responding Party responds as follows:
    - [● SET OUT THE RESPONSE IS TO EA CH OF THE CLAIMS, APPLYING THE RELEVANT PARTS OF THE CONTRACT TO THE FACTS.]

Summary of Response to redress sought by the Referring Party

18. [✗Paragraphs [●REFERENCE] of the Referral are agreed.
19. Paragraphs [●REFERENCE] of the Referral are denied.
20. Paragraphs [●REFERENCE] of the Referral are noted.][4]
21. The Responding Party invites the Adjudicator to decide as follows:
22. [●IDENTIFY DETAILS OF WHAT IS REQUESTED]

Served this [●DATE] by [●NAME OF RESPONDING PARTY OR ITS REPRESENTATIVE], [✗[solicitors][consultants][representative] for the Responding Party.][5]

....
[●RESPONDING PARTY OR ITS REPRESENTATIVE]

…..

APPENDICES
[●APPEND RELEVANT MATERIALS]

---

[4] Work systematically through the redress sought.
[5] Where served by a representative, set out the capacity in which the representative is acting.

1.4 *Reply*

IN THE MATTER OF AN ADJUDICATION

PURSUANT TO THE HOUSING GRANTS, CONSTRUCTION AND REGENERATION ACT 1996

[✂AND PURSUANT TO [●ADJUDICATION PROCEDURE]] [1]

BETWEEN:

[●NAME]

Referring Party

AND

[●NAME]

Responding Party

REPLY TO RESPONSE

Introduction

1. This Reply [✂and its Appendices][2] answer the substantive issues raised in the Response Notice served on the Referring Party on [●DATE].

2. Where the context admits, capitalised terms in the Contract have the same meaning in this Reply.

3. This Reply also generally adopts the headings of the Referral Notice and the Response Notice but is not a "line by line reply". As a result, if a particular sentence, paragraph or section of the Response Notice is not specifically dealt with that is not to be taken as acceptance of that part of the Response Notice. This Reply is intended to be read as a whole.

---

[1] Complete with the relevant procedure (i.e. the Scheme for Construction Contracts or other scheme agreed by the parties).
[2] Use where it is appropriate to include materials by way of appendix.

Model forms

4. [✂Paragraphs [●REFERENCE] of the Response Notice are agreed.
5. Paragraphs [●REFERENCE] of the Response Notice are denied.
6. Paragraphs [●REFERENCE] of the Response Notice are noted.][3]

The Contract

7. [✂Clauses [●REFERENCE] are [✂admitted/noted].

Issues Raised in the Response

8. [✂The position in respect of [●DETAILS] is not relevant to this Adjudication.]
9. [✂The existence of any earlier alleged [●DETAILS e.g. any settlements] are not the subject of this Adjudication.]
10. [✂The position in respect of [●DETAILS] is not relevant to this Adjudication.]
11. [✂The Responding Party has raised [●DETAILS] in paragraphs [●DETAILS] of the Response that [is not][are not] part of this Adjudication and should be excluded.]
12. [✂The Referring Party's position is that the only material factor for consideration by the adjudicator on the issue before him is [●DETAILS e.g. limit to contractual issues.]
13. [✂The Responding Party has omitted the following provision of [●DETAILS] in the Contract extracts it has provided:
14. [✂●EXTRACT FROM CONTRACT]].[4]
15. [✂The parties are agreed that we need to focus on [●DETAILS e.g. meaning of particular words actually used in the Contract and to exclude pre-contract negotiations.]]

Conclusion

16. [●BRIEFLY SUMMARISE ISSUES ABOVE].

Ruling from the Adjudicator

17. The Referring Party invites the Adjudicator to decide as follows:
18. [●IDENTIFY e.g. to reject any specific requests made by the Responding Party in the Response].
19. [●IDENTIFY e.g. to find for specific redress requested by the Referring Party in the Referral].

Served this [●DATE] by [●NAME OF REFERRING PARTY OR ITS REPRESENTATIVE], [✂[solicitors][consultants][representative] for the Referring Party.][5]

…………………………………………………..

[●REFERRING PARTY OR ITS REPRESENTATIVE]

---

[3] Work through the Response, identifying those parts of it that can be agreed, have to be denied or are noted.
[4] Repeat as required.
[5] Where served by a representative, set out the capacity in which the representative is acting.

1.5 Decision

IN THE MATTER OF AN ADJUDICATION

PURSUANT TO THE HOUSING GRANTS, CONSTRUCTION AND REGENERATION ACT 1996

[✘AND PURSUANT TO [●ADJUDICATION PROCEDURE]] [1]

BETWEEN:

[●NAME]

Referring Party

AND

[●NAME]

Responding Party

ADJUDICATOR'S DECISION

[✘Insert an index if appropriate] [2]

The Contract

1. By a contract dated [●DATE] between the Referring Party and the Responding Party (the 'Contract') [●BRIEF DESCRIPTION OF CONTRACT].

The Appointment

---

[1] Complete with the relevant procedure (i.e. the Scheme for Construction Contracts or other scheme agreed by the parties).
[2] This will depend on the overall length of the Decision but is good practice.

2. A dispute arose between the parties and on [●DATE] [✗the [●NOMINATING BODY], a nominating body,][the parties] appointed me, [●NAME], as Adjudicator and I accepted the appointment.

3. The terms of my appointment are set out in an agreement which was sent to the parties on [●DATE].

The Procedure and Directions

4. The Contract provides that the [●INSERT NAME OF RELEVANT PROCEDURE] applies.

5. In accordance with the terms of that procedure, I wrote to the parties on [●DATE], setting out the directions for how the Adjudication should proceed. Those directions were [●INSERT].

6. [On [●DATE] [I/●PARTY] sought an extension to the deadline for [serving [●SUBMISSION] OR the date of the decision]. The parties made [further] submissions on [●DATE(S)]. Following those submissions, I gave further directions that [●INSERT].]

Background to the Project and the Dispute

7. The background to the project is as follows. [●INSERT BACKGROUND]

8. The dispute is [●SCOPE OF THE DISPUTE AND THE ISSUES TO BE DECIDED, WITH EXPRESS REFERENCE TO ANY NEW ISSUES THAT HAVE EXPANDED THE SCOPE OF THE DISPUTE AS SET OUT IN THE NOTICE].

[Challenges

9. On [●DATE] in a letter addressed to me, the [●PARTY] raised a challenge on the grounds that [●INSERT SOURCE OF CHALLENGE AND REASONS].

10. On [●DATE] I gave directions for how and when the parties should address me on that challenge.

11. On [●DATE], the [●OTHER PARTY] responded. [●INSERT RESPONSE TO CHALLENGE].

12. On [●DATE] I wrote to the parties setting out my decision on the challenge. I decided that I had not [acted in excess of my jurisdiction/breached the rules of natural justice] for the following reasons [●INSERT].]

[Hearing

13. ●IDENTIFY WHETHER A MEETING OR HEARING TOOK PLACE AND IF SO, BROADLY WHAT OCCURRED]

The Relevant Provisions of the Contract

14. [●IDENTIFY THE RELEVANT CONTRACTUAL PROVISIONS THAT ARE PERTINENT TO THE DECISION BEING MADE AND THE REASONING]

Summary of the Relief Sought

15. [●LIST OUT THE RELIEF SOUGHT BY THE REFERRING PARTY]

Issue 1 – Parties' Submissions

16. [●SUMMARISE THE RELEVANT PARTS OF THE PARTIES' SUBMISSIONS. TRY TO AVOID INCORPORATING REASONING INTO THE SUBMISSIONS. DECISIONS ARE EASIER TO READ IF THE REASONING IS KEPT SEPARATE FROM THE SUBMISSIONS]³

Issue 1 – Decision and Reasons

17. [●ANALYSE THE RELEVANT PARTS OF THE CONTRACT, THE FACTS AND THE PARTIES' SUBMISSIONS

18. Having carefully considered all the evidence and submissions (whether or not specifically referred to in this Decision) I, the said [●NAME], decide that [●DECISION *e.g. The claim [fails/succeeds]*] because:

19. [●REASON set out each reason as a separate bullet point]

Issue 2 – Parties' Submissions

20. [●As above]

Issue 2 – Decision and Reasons

21. [●As above]

Summary of Decision

22. [●SHORT SUMMARY OF THE DECISION TOGETHER WITH (IF APPLICABLE) THE DATE BY WHEN THE TERMS OF THE DECISION ARE TO BE MET.]

Fees

23. I have spent [●HOURS] engaged on this adjudication. As per the terms of my appointment, my fee rate is [●AMOUNT] per hour. In addition, and as notified to the parties, I have engaged [●NAME] who has spent [●HOURS] at [●AMOUNT] per hour. My expenses amount to [●AMOUNT]. The total of my fees is therefore [●AMOUNT] which I determine [shall be paid in full by [●NAME]/ shall be paid in the amount of [●AMOUNT] by [●PARTY] and [●AMOUNT] by [●PARTY]/ shall be paid [●PERCENT] by [●PARTY] and [●PERCENT] by [●PARTY].

Made by me this [●DATE]

....
[●NAME]
Adjudicator

---

[3] Any references to documents should be cross-referenced to the bundles of documents provided.

1.6 *Adjudicator's agreement*

DATE

(1)   [●ADJUDICATOR]

(2)   [●REFERRING PARTY]

(3)   [●RESPONDING PARTY]

Adjudicator's appointment

Relating to [●DETAILS]

THIS AGREEMENT is made the   day of

BETWEEN:

(1)   **[●ADJUDICATOR]** [✂(registered number [●NUMBER]), whose registered office is][of] [●ADDRESS] (the 'Adjudicator');

(2)   **[●REFERRING PARTY]** [✂(registered number [●NUMBER]), whose registered office is][of] [●ADDRESS] (the 'Referring Party); and

(3)   **[●RESPONDING PARTY]** [✂(registered number [●NUMBER]), whose registered office is][of] [●ADDRESS][1] (the 'Responding Party')

In this Agreement, the Referring Party and the Responding Party are the 'Parties' and a 'Party' is either of them.

BACKGROUND:

(A)   The Parties entered into a contract dated [●DATE] for [●BRIEF DETAILS OF CONTRACT], [✂ [a copy][extracts] of which [has][have][2] been given to the Adjudicator.

(B)   The Parties wish to appoint the Adjudicator on the terms and conditions set out in this Agreement.

IT IS AGREED THAT:

---

[1]   Complete details as appropriate for each party.
[2]   Complete as appropriate.

Appointment

1. The Parties appoint the Adjudicator to adjudicate a dispute referred to him under the Contract referred by either Party.

2. Unless terminated pursuant to this agreement, the Adjudicator's appointment under this Agreement shall continue until the Adjudicator has adjudicated the dispute referred to him and the Parties have complied with their obligations under this Agreement.

3. The Adjudicator may, as he see fit:

    - employ others to assist him;
    - visit any site relevant to the Contract;
    - conduct meetings; and
    - hold a hearing.

Adjudication Procedure

4. A Party may refer a dispute under the Contract to the Adjudicator in accordance with the adjudication procedure provided for in the Contract (the 'Adjudication Procedure').[3]

5. The Adjudicator shall comply with the Adjudication Procedure.

Adjudicator's Protection from Liability

6. The Adjudicator is not liable for anything done or omitted in the discharge or purported discharge of his functions as adjudicator unless the act or omission is in bad faith and any employee or agent of the Adjudicator is similarly protected from liability.

Confidentiality

7. The Adjudicator and the Parties shall keep confidential this Agreement, the Contract and any dispute referred to the Adjudicator under the Contract.

The Adjudicator's Fee

8. The fee to be paid to the Adjudicator shall be calculated on the basis set out in Schedule 1 (the Adjudicator's Fee').

9. The Parties are jointly and severally liable for the Adjudicator's Fee (which includes any expenses reasonably incurred by the Adjudicator) and undertake to pay the Adjudicator's Fee in equal shares.

10. The Adjudicator may invoice for the Adjudicator's Fee at the times specified in Schedule 1 and payment of any invoice is due 28 days from the date on which it is submitted.

Termination of the Adjudicator's Appointment

11. By a jointly issued notice, the Parties may terminate the Adjudicator's appointment at any time.

12. The Adjudicator may terminate his appointment by notice to the Parties.

13. On any termination of the Adjudicator's appointment, that amount of the Adjudicator's Fee properly incurred at that time shall be paid by the Parties.

---

[3] Consider if it is appropriate to include the Adjudication Procedure as a schedule to this Agreement.

Third Party Rights

14. The parties to this Agreement do not intend that any of its terms shall be enforceable under the Contracts (Rights of Third Parties) Act 1999 by any person not a party to it.

No Assignment

15. Neither the Adjudicator nor the Parties may assign or otherwise transfer any benefit, right or obligation under this Agreement.

Governing Law

16. This agreement and any dispute or claim arising out of or in connection with it or its subject matter or formation (including non-contractual disputes or claims) shall be governed by and construed in accordance with the law of England and Wales. The Parties irrevocably agree that the courts of England and Wales shall have exclusive jurisdiction to settle any dispute or claim arising out of or in connection with this agreement or its subject matter or formation (including non-contractual disputes or claims).

....

SCHEDULE 1

Adjudicator's Fees & Expenses

The Adjudicator's Fee is calculated as follows:

[●SET OUT DETAILS OF:

- *the fee rate of the Adjudicator, normally express ed as an hourly rate, but sometimes as a daily rate or even a lump sum*
- *the fee rate of any staff members who the Adjudicator wishes to use to assist him*
- *state any limitations (e.g. hours per day or time spent in preparation)*
- *whether or not travel time will be paid*]

The Adjudicator's Fee is to be paid on the following basis:

[●SET OUT DETAILS OF:

- *any retainer or advance payment*
- *any interim payments*
- *any cancellation fee should the Adjudication not proceed for reasons unconnected with the Adjudicator*
- *any discount for prompt payment*]

The Adjudicator's expenses shall include:

[●SET OUT DETAILS OF ANYTHING EXPRESSLY INCLUDED SUCH AS:

- ➤ telephone and other telecommunications costs
- ➤ hotel accommodation
- ➤ travel (stating any agreed mileage for car travel and whether other travel is to be first/business/economy etc.]

[✘ The Adjudicator may not recover the following expenses:

[●SET OUT DETAILS OF ANYTHING EXPRESSLY THAT IS EXPRESSLY EXCLUDED, IF ANYTHING]][4]

---

[4] Consider if anything should be expressly excluded, such as travel within a certain radius.

Appendix 5
Summary comparison of UK adjudication rules

A Practical Guide to Construction Adjudication, First Edition. James Pickavance.
© 2016 James Pickavance. Published 2016 by John Wiley & Sons, Inc.

	Subject matter	2011 Scheme[1] (adopted by JCT 05, 08 and TECBAR[2])	1998 Scheme	ICE 2011 procedure	NEC3 Option W2[3]	IChemE Grey Book 3rd edition (as amended in 2012)[4]	JCT 1998	TeCSA 2011 v3.1	CIC Model Adjudication Procedure 5th edition (2011)	CEDR Solve (2008)
1	Procedure to govern adjudication	–	–	1.1	W2.1(1)	1.1	–	3	–	–
2	Incorporation of current edition	–	–	–	–	1.1, 1.10	–	1.1	6	–
3	Purpose of adjudication	–	–	1.2	–	–	–	13	1	–
4	Conflict between contract and procedure	–	–	–	–	1.1	–	–	7	–
5	The Notice (given by)	1(1)	1(1)	2.1	W2.1(1)	3.1	Article 5, 41A.1, 41A.4.1	2, 9	8	1
6	The notice of adjudication (given to)	1(2)	1(2)	2.1, 3.1, 8.1(d)	W2.3(1)	3.1, 4.1	41A.4.1	2, 9	8	1
7	The notice of adjudication (contents)	1(3)	1(3)	2.1	W2.3(1)	3.1	41A.4.1	2	8	1
8	Multiple notices of adjudication	–	–	–	–	–	–	10	–	–

Rows 1–4 grouped under **General**; rows 5–8 grouped under **The Notice**.

[1] The Scheme for Construction Contracts 1998, as amended by the Scheme for Construction Contracts (England and Wales) Regulations 1998 (Amendment) (England) Regulations 2011 (SI 2011/2333)

[2] TECBAR Adjudication Rules 2012 adopt the 2011 Scheme (as amended from time to time) but include guidance notes on some paragraphs.

[3] As amended in 2011. References to AC paragraphs relate to paragraphs of the NEC 3 Adjudicator's Contract (which W2.2(1) requires the adjudicator to be appointed under).

[4] The number references are to the rule numbers cited in the 'IChemE Rules for the Conduct of Adjudications' as amended by the 16 January 2012 'Amendment to the Adjudication Rules' (which renumbers some of the rules).

	Subject matter	2011 Scheme (adopted by JCT 05, 08 and TECBAR)	1998 Scheme	ICE 2011 procedure	NEC3 Option W2	IChemE Grey Book 3rd edition (as amended in 2012)	JCT 1998	TeCSA 2011 v3.1	CIC Model Adjudication Procedure 5th edition (2011)	CEDR Solve (2008)
9	Appointment (procedure)	2(1)	2(1)	3.1–3.3	W2.3(1), W2.2(3)	4.1, 4.2, 4.3	41A.2	4, 5	10	1, 2
10	Appointment (time limit to reply)	2(2)	2(2)	3.1, 3.2	W2.3(1)	4.1	41A.2.2	4	10	1
11	Appointment (definition of ANB)	2(3)	2(3)	—	—	—	—	—	—	—
12	Request to include notice of adjudication	3	3	3.1, 3.3	W2.3(1)	4.1, 4.3	—	5.2, 2	10	1, 2
13	The adjudicator (natural person)	4	4	1.4	—	1.2	41A.2	—	—	—
14	The adjudicator (not an employee)	4	4	—	—	—	—	—	—	—
15	Nominating body (time limit to nominate)	5(1)	5(1)	—	W2.2(3)	—	41A.2.1	5.3	10	2
16	Nominating body (failure to nominate)	5(2)	5(2)	—	—	—	—	—	—	—
17	Nominating body (time limit to accept)	5(3)	5(3)	—	—	—	—	6.1, 6	—	2
18	Unable to act (procedure)	6(1)	6(1)	3.3, 3.4	W2.3(1), W2.2(3)	4.5	41A.3	5	10, 11	1, 2, 31
19	Unable to act (time limit for replacement)	6(2)	6(2)	—	—	—	—	6.1, 6	—	2
20	Adjudicator's contract	—	—	1.1	W2.2(1)	4.4 and Annex B	41A.2.2, 41A.2.1	—	12	—
21	Receipt of the notice of adjudication	—	—	—	—	—	—	5.1	—	—
	Appointing an Adjudicator									

(Continued)

		Subject matter	2011 Scheme (adopted by JCT 05, 08 and TECBAR)	1998 Scheme	ICE 2011 procedure	NEC3 Option W2	IChemE Grey Book 3rd edition (as amended in 2012)	JCT 1998	TeCSA 2011 v3.1	CIC Model Adjudication Procedure 5th edition (2011)	CEDR Solve (2008)
22	Referral	Referral notice (time limit)	7(1)	7(1)	4.1	W2.3(2)	5.1	41A.4.1	6, 6.2	14	3
23		Referral notice (contents)	7(2)	7(2)	4.1	W2.3(2)	5.1	41A.4.1	6.2, 2	14	3
24		Referral notice (copied to)	7(3)	7(3)	4.1, 8.1(d)	W2.3(2)	5.1	41A.4.1	6.2, 6	14	4[5]
25		Referral notice (date of referral)	7(3)	—	4.2	—	5.2	41A.5.1	7	15	5
26		Submissions deadline	—	—	5.4	W2.3(2)	—	41A.5.2	—	—	—
27		Advanced payment	—	—	—	AC3.1	—	—	—	—	—
28		Copies of communications	—	—	—	W2.3(6)	—	—	20.2	—	9
29		Delivery of referral	—	—	—	—	—	41A.4.2	—	—	—
30	Multiple Disputes	Multiple disputes (same contract)	8(1)	8(1)	5.7	W2.3(3)	—	—	8	22	12
31		Multiple disputes (separate contracts)	8(2)	8(2)	5.7	W2.3(3)	—	—	—	22	12
32		Multiple disputes (time periods)	8(3)	8(3)	—	—	—	—	—	—	—
33		Multiple disputes (fees and expenses)	8(4)	8(4)	—	—	—	—	—	—	—
34	Resignation	Resignation (may)	9(1)	9(1)	—	AC4.2	6.1	—	—	23	—
35		Resignation (must)	9(2)	9(2)	—	AC2.1	6.2	—	20.4	—	25, 26
36		Resignation (replacement)	9(3)(a)	9(3)(a)	3.3, 3.4	W2.2(3), W2.2(4)	6.3	—	—	11	27, 31

[5] On the face of it, paragraph 4 does not refer to the referral notice, but a number of documents related to the notice of adjudication and adjudicator appointment forms. This seems to be an error, as otherwise there would be no specific obligation to send a copy of the referral notice to the other party.

		Subject matter	2011 Scheme (adopted by JCT 05, 08 and TECBAR)	1998 Scheme	ICE 2011 procedure	NEC3 Option W2	IChemE Grey Book 3rd edition (as amended in 2012)	JCT 1998	TeCSA 2011 v3.1	CIC Model Adjudication Procedure 5th edition (2011)	CEDR Solve (2008)
37		Resignation (resubmit documents)	9(3)(b)	9(3)(b)	–	–	6.3	–	–	–	–
38		Resignation (fees and expenses)	9(4)	9(4)	–	–	6.5	–	–	–	26
39		Resignation (apportionment)	9(4)	9(4)	–	–	6.5, 8.6	–	–	–	23, 24, 26
40	Revocation	Objection	10	10	–	–	–	–	–	–	–
41		Revocation and fees	11(1)	11(1)	–	AC4.1, AC 3.3	6.4, 6.5	–	–	–	–
42		Revocation (misconduct)	11(2)	11(2)	–	–	–	–	–	13	–
43		Revocation (apportionment)	11(1)	11(1)	–	AC 3.2	6.5, 8.6	–	–	–	–
44	Adjudicator's Powers	Impartiality Avoid unnecessary expense	12(a) 12(b)	12(a) 12(b)	1.4	W2.2(2)	1.2	41A.5.5	14, 19	2	14
45		Adjudicator's powers (generally)	13(a)–(h)	13(a)–(h)	1.5, 5.2, 5.5, 5.6	W2.3(4), AC 2.3, AC 2.4	1.3, 7.1 – 7.5	41A.5.5	12, 17, 18	3	7
46		Compliance with directions	14	14	–	AC 2.4	–	–	–	18	–
47		Failure to comply	15	15	5.5(g)	W2.3(5)	7.4 (h) & (j)	41A.5.6	17	17(vii)	11

(*Continued*)

565

		Subject matter	2011 Scheme (adopted by JCT 05, 08 and TECBAR)	1998 Scheme	ICE 2011 procedure	NEC3 Option W2	IChemE Grey Book 3rd edition (as amended in 2012)	JCT 1998	TeCSA 2011 v3.1	CIC Model Adjudication Procedure 5th edition (2011)	CEDR Solve (2008)
	48	Legal representation (right)	16(1)	16(1)	—	—	—	—	20.3	—	—
	49	Legal representation (number)	16(2)	16(2)	—	—	—	—	—	—	—
	50	Considering relevant information	17	17	—	—	—	—	—	—	10
	51	Confidentiality	18	18	Para 4 – Adjudicator's Agreement	AC 2.5	7.8	—	33	Para 3 – adjudicator's contract[6]	—
	52	Law of the contract	—	—	—	—	—	—	—	21	—
Decision Time Limits	53	Decision time limits	19(1)	19(1)	5.1	W2.3(8)	8.1	41A.5.3	21	16	6
	54	Time limits (failure)	19(2)(a)	19(2)(a)	6.3, 3.3	W2.3(10)	8.3, 8.4	—	—	11, 25	31
	55	Time limits (failure)	19(2)(b)	19(2)(b)	—	—	—	—	—	—	—
	56	Time limits (notifying failure)	—	—	6.4	—	—	—	—	—	—
The Decision	57	Ignoring the dispute	—	—	—	W2.3(9)	—	—	—	—	—
	58	Delivering decision	19(3)	19(3)	6.1	W2.3(8)	8.1, 7.4(k)	41A.5.3	28	24	16, 28, 29
	59	Adjudicator's decision (scope)	20	20	5.2	W2.3(8)	7.3	—	11, 11.1, 11.2	20	15
	60	Adjudicator's decision (open up, revise, review)	20(a)	20(a)	5.3	W2.3(4)	7.6	41A.5.5.2	16	26	14

[6] Paragraph 3 of the terms and conditions attached to the procedure. This agreement is to be used to appoint the parties and the adjudicator otherwise agree (Rule 12 of the procedure).

		Subject matter	2011 Scheme (adopted by JCT 05, 08 and TECBAR)	1998 Scheme	ICE 2011 procedure	NEC3 Option W2	IChemE Grey Book 3rd edition (as amended in 2012)	JCT 1998	TeCSA 2011 v3.1	CIC Model Adjudication Procedure 5th edition (2011)	CEDR Solve (2008)
The Decision	61	Adjudicator's decision (ordering payment)	20(b)	20(b)	5.3	W2.3(7)	7.6, 8.9	—	—	—	20, 21
	62	Adjudicator's decision (interest)	20(c)	20(c)	6.2	—	8.2	41A.5.5.8	27	27	—
	63	Freedom to vary terms	—	—	5.3	—	—	—	—	—	—
	64	Compliance with decision	21	21	1.7	—	1.5	41A.7.2	—	5	20
	65	Payment provisions	—	—	1.7	—	—	—	—	—	—
	66	Reasons	22	22	6.1	W2.3(8)	8.7	41A.5.4	28	24	17
	67	Settlement	—	—	—	—	7.7	—	—	—	—
	68	Mediation	—	—	—	—	—	—	—	—	28, 29
	69	Mediator's fees and expenses	—	—	—	—	—	—	—	—	30
Slip Rule	70	Slip rule	22A(1)	—	6.7	—	8.8	—	29	28	18
	71	Slip rule (time limit)	22A(2)	—	6.7	W2.3(12)	8.8	—	30, 31	28	18
	72	Slip rule (delivering new copies)	22A(3)	—	—	—	8.8	—	—	28	—
	73	Slip rule (effect of corrections)	22A(4)	—	—	—	8.8	—	—	28	—
Costs and Enforcement	74	Peremptory compliance	—	23(1)	—	—	—	—	—	—	—
	75	Binding nature of decision	23(2)	23(2)	1.6, 6.6	W2.3(11)	1.4, 8.9	41A.7.1, 41A.7.3	15	4, 32	19
	76	Time limit for challenge	—	—	—	W2.3(11), W2.4(2)	—	—	—	—	—

(Continued)

		Subject matter	2011 Scheme (adopted by JCT 05, 08 and TECBAR)	1998 Scheme	ICE 2011 procedure	NEC3 Option W2	IChemE Grey Book 3rd edition (as amended in 2012)	JCT 1998	TeCSA 2011 v3.1	CIC Model Adjudication Procedure 5th edition (2011)	CEDR Solve (2008)
	77	Referring to the tribunal	—	—	—	W2.4(1)	—	—	—	—	—
	78	Subsequent adjudication	—	—	6.6	—	—	—	—	32	—
	79	Arbitration Act 1996	—	24	—	—	—	—	—	—	—
	80	Adjudicator's fees and expenses	25	25	Schedule to Adjudicator's Agreement (1, 2)	AC 1.4	—	41A.6.1, 41A.6.2	—	12	—
Costs and Enforcement	81	Adjudicator's fees and expenses (apportionment)	25	25	6.5	W2.3(8), AC 3.2	8.6	41A.6.1	22,23	30	23, 24
	82	Time limit for payment	—	—	Schedule to Adjudicator's Agreement (5)	AC 3.5, AC 3.7, AC 3.8	Fees and expenses Annex to Annex B[7]	—	—	—	—
	83	Fee cap	—	—	—	—	—	—	24	—	—
	84	Advance payments	—	—	—	AC3.1	—	—	20.1	—	—
	85	Failed adjudication (fees)	—	—	—	—	—	—	22	30	—
	86	Parties' costs	—	—	6.5	—	8.5	41A.5.7	20.5, 25	29, 31	22
	87	Referring party not required to pay all costs	—	—	—	—	—	—	26	—	—

[7] (which forms part of the Rules under Rule 2.3)

(Continued)

	Subject matter	2011 Scheme (adopted by JCT 05, 08 and TECBAR)	1998 Scheme	ICE 2011 procedure	NEC3 Option W2	IChemE Grey Book 3rd edition (as amended in 2012)	JCT 1998	TeCSA 2011 v3.1	CIC Model Adjudication Procedure 5th edition (2011)	CEDR Solve (2008)
88	Liability of adjudicator	26	26	7.2	W2.2(5)	1.8	41A.8	32	35, 36	32, 33
89	Adjudicator not to be a witness	–	–	7.1	W2.4(5)	1.7	–	34	34	–
90	Adjudicator not to become arbitrator	–	–	7.1	–	1.7	–	–	34	–
91	Powers of the court/arbitrator	–	–	–	W2.4(3)	8.10	Footnote [xx]	–	33	19
92	Arbitration procedure	–	–	–	W2.4(4)	–	–	–	–	–
93	Destruction of documents	–	–	Para 5 – Adjudicator's Agreement	AC 2.6	8.11	–	–	Para 4 – adjudicator's contract[8]	–
	Costs and Enforcement									
94	Liability of nominating body	–	–	7.3	–	1.9	–	32	–	32
95	Giving notices	–	–	7.4	–	–	–	–	–	–
96	Agreements to be in writing	–	–	7.4	–	–	–	–	–	–
97	Governing law	–	–	7.5	–	1.6	–	35	37	34
98	Time periods exclude bank holidays	–	–	–	W2.1(2)	2.4	–	–	–	–
99	Application to particular contracts	–	–	9.1	–	–	–	–	–	–
100	Architect's reasonable instructions	–	–	–	–	–	41A.5.8	–	–	–
	Miscellaneous									

[8] Paragraph 4 of the terms and conditions attached to the procedure. This agreement is to be used to appoint the adjudicator unless the parties and the adjudicator otherwise agree (Rule 12 of the procedure).

Appendix 6
Details of UK adjudicator nominating bodies

Name	Website and contact details	Number of adjudicators	Adjudicator professions	Fee & application method	Why choose me? (according to the ANB)
Association of Independent Construction Adjudicators	http://www.aica-adjudication.co.uk/ 0844 249 5353 enquiries@aica-adjudication.co.uk	64	Architects Barristers Building Surveyors Civil Engineers Quantity Surveyors	£300 (incl. VAT) Application form on website Return by post	A nationwide panel comprising the industry's top adjudicators. Adjudicators that are practising regularly and undertake disputes of any value. Named ANB in the JCT suite. Nominations guaranteed within 3 working days. Represents a range of professional disciplines. Application form available online. Competitive nomination fee of just £300 (free to NSCC members)
Centre for Effective Dispute Resolution (CEDR)	www.cedr.com/solve/constructadjud/ 020 7536 6060 adr@cedr.com	41	Accountants Architects Barristers Building Surveyors Chartered Builders Civil Engineers Electrical Engineers Solicitors Quantum Expert Quantity Surveyor Queens Counsel	No fee (unless the process is discontinued before a decision is issued. If decision not issued for any reason, £250 (excl. VAT) Complete application form on website, or PDF form provided by CEDR, or email covering letter and Notice	CEDR will endeavour to nominate the most appropriate available adjudicator on a case-by-case basis. We do not nominate adjudicators from a rota. CEDR offer a quick, efficient service managed by a CEDR Director who previously worked as the Senior Clerk of the construction law specialists barristers Keating Chambers. CEDR guarantee to nominate an adjudicator from the CEDR Panel within 2 working days of receipt of a referral notice and in more than 90% of cases we can nominate in less than 24 hours.

(*Continued*)

Name	Website and contact details	Number of adjudicators	Adjudicator professions	Fee & application method	Why choose me? (according to the ANB)
Chartered Institute of Arbitrators (CIArb)	http://www.ciarb.org/dispute-appointment-services/adjudication 020 7421 7444 Keisha Williams das@ciarb.org	80	Civil Engineers Engineers Quantity Surveyors Solicitors	£300 (excl. VAT) Application form on website Return by email, fax or post	CIArb's dispute appointment service ('DAS') provides a fast and cost-effective approach to resolving disputes. DAS operates Presidential Panels, which are panels made up of senior and experienced practitioners in arbitration, mediation and construction adjudication. DAS utilise the panels to identify and appoint members who are suitably qualified and experienced to assist in resolving your civil or commercial disputes. All individuals who form part of the panels are CIArb members and are either: Chartered Arbitrators, Accredited Mediators or Accredited Construction Adjudicators. If you, or your legal advisers, do not know of a dispute resolver (arbitrator, mediator, adjudicator or independent expert) to resolve a dispute, DAS can help to find you a suitably qualified practitioner with the right knowledge and experience. Search our members' directory or contact CIArb directly by email.

(*Continued*)

Name	Website and contact details	Number of adjudicators	Adjudicator professions	Fee & application method	Why choose me? (according to the ANB)
Chartered Institute of Building (CIoB)	http://www.ciob.org.uk/content/dispute-resolution 01344 630710 reception@ciob.org.uk	38	Architects Engineers Construction consultants Lawyers Project Managers Quantity surveyors	£300 (incl. VAT) Application form on website Return by email, fax or post	The adjudication panel is multi-skilled and highly specialised, ready to resolve any dispute. The CIOB is one of the forerunners of adjudication in the industry and, along with other professional institutions and the Construction Industry Council, sets criteria in order to establish high standards of competency for their adjudicators.
Construction Industry Council (CIC)	http://www.cic.org.uk/services/adjudications.php 020 7399 7403 LRussell@cic.org.uk	79	Pan industry	£348 (incl. VAT) Application form on website Return by post	CIC will appoint an adjudicator to act on your behalf within 5 working days of receipt of the request. Adjudicators will only be appointed if they have the appropriate technical background to deal with the dispute, are impartial to the parties involved in the dispute and are available immediately to take the case.
Construction Plant-hire Association (CPA)	http://www.cpa.uk.net/adjudicators-lists-and-forms/ 020 7796 3366 enquiries@cpa.uk.net	82	Architects Barristers Civil Engineers Quantity Surveyors Solicitors	£175 (excl. VAT) Application form on website Return by post	
Institution of Chemical Engineers (IChemE)	http://www.icheme.org/resources/forms_of_contract/dispute-resolution.aspx 01788 578214 contracts@icheme.org	14	Not publically available	£800 (excl. VAT). Applicants should write to the President of IChemE for a nomination	IChemE not only sets out the mechanisms for dispute resolution through its contracts, it also provides for the appointment on request of suitable persons to act as adjudicator, expert or arbitrator.

[1] April 2012 (Source: GCU Adjudication Reporting Centre Report No. 12)

Name	Website and contact details	Number of adjudicators	Adjudicator professions	Fee & application method	Why choose me? (according to the ANB)
Institution of Civil Engineers (ICE)	http://www.ice.org.uk/About-ICE/What-we-do/Dispute-resolution Brendan.VanRooyen @ice.org.uk 020 7665 2224	47	Architects Barristers Civil Engineers Quantity Surveyors Solicitors Structural Engineers	£350 (excl. VAT) Complete application form on website	ICE's Dispute Resolution Services offers a comprehensive suite of services, including Adjudication, Arbitration and Mediation to the construction and engineering industries. Our services cover all forms of contract including NEC3 and Infrastructure Conditions of Contract. We have 22 years' experience of proving remedies and facilitating collaboration under the NEC. Our highly skilled and experienced registered dispute professionals undergo some of the most rigorous assessments processes in the market.
Institution of Engineering and Technology (IET)	http://www.theiet.org/policy/dispute/ 01438 765 689 policy@theiet.org	15	All areas of electrical engineering (including ICT) and manufacturing	200 (excl. VAT)	The IET has a broad range of expertise in engineering and technology addressing areas such as software, computing, power distribution and generation, networking, manufacturing plant, intellectual property Information systems and mobile communications.
Institution of Mechanical Engineers (IMechE)	http://www.imeche.org/knowledge/industries/consultancy-and-dispute-resolution/adjudication/ 020 7973 1266 Sarah Rogers s_rogers@imeche.org	6	Chartered mechanical engineers	£250 (excl. VAT) Application form on website Return by post	The Institution maintains a list of trained and experienced adjudicators, who are capable of resolving disputes in the engineering and construction industries. The Institution's adjudicators are Chartered Engineers, who have undertaken further rigorous training in the procedures and practices of adjudication. The Institution will normally appoint an adjudicator within 24 hours of a request being made, and it is not unusual for the adjudicator to contact the parties on the same day he is appointed.

(Continued)

Name	Website and contact details	Number of adjudicators	Adjudicator professions	Fee & application method	Why choose me? (according to the ANB)
Royal Institution of Chartered Surveyors (RICS)	http://www.rics.org/uk/join/member-accreditations-list/dispute-resolution-service/ 020 7334 3806 drs@rics.org	114	Architects Barristers Building Surveyor Civil Engineers Quality Surveyors Solicitors Structural engineers	£382 (incl. VAT) Application form on website Return by email, fax or post	Why use RICS to appoint a dispute resolver? Speed and cost – Dispute resolution through DRS is generally a quicker and cheaper way to resolve disputes than going to court. Professionalism – chartered surveyors are highly trained professionals who understand property issues and are skilled in working with people who own, manage or rent property. They are governed by the rules and conduct laid down by RICS. Trained specialists – RICS members who provide dispute resolution services through DRS are specially selected and undergo continuous training. They must also maintain the highest professional standards. Costs – An administrative fee is charged to appoint the appropriate specialist, who will then set out the fees to be charged, which will generally be at an hourly rate. This can be a cost-effective approach as it ensures the efficient and speedy appointment of a dispute resolver.

Name	Website and contact details	Number of adjudicators	Adjudicator professions	Fee & application method	Why choose me? (according to the ANB)
Royal Incorporation of Architects in Scotland	http://www.rias.org.uk/services/panel-of-rias-experts/ 0131 229 7545 Maryse Richardson mrichardson@rias.org.uk	Not available	Not available	£250 (excl. VAT) Nomination requests are received by email and the enquirer receives an electronic form to complete	Upon formal request the Incorporation will nominate an adjudicator from a list of accredited senior members of the profession.
Royal Institute of British Architects	http://www.architecture.com/RIBA/Professional support/Professional standards/Adjudication.aspx 020 7307 3649 adjudication@riba.org	66	Architects Construction Consultants Construction Lawyers Engineers Surveyors	£240 (excl. VAT) £117.5 (incl. VAT) for disputes arising under JCT Building Contract for Home Owner/Occupier Application form on website Return by email, fax or post	RIBA maintains a panel of around 70 expert adjudicators. The panel is drawn from professionals across the industry including architects, surveyors, engineers, construction consultants and construction lawyers, allowing for every type of dispute to be dealt with by a specialist in the field. Once your application is received, the Adjudication Nomination Officer will approach a person on the RIBA list of adjudicators who has the relevant expertise to deal with the dispute. The Nomination Officer will ascertain whether the person approached: • has any connection with the parties or the subject matter of the dispute which would disqualify him or her as an adjudicator • would be able to take the case without delay.

(Continued)

Name	Website and contact details	Number of adjudicators	Adjudicator professions	Fee & application method	Why choose me? (according to the ANB)
Technology and Construction Court Bar Association (TCCBAR)	http://www.tecbar.org/dispute-resolution-appointments/adjudication.asp Daniel Jones djones@atkinchambers.com 0207 404 0102	125	Barristers	£75 (excl. VAT) Apply to the Clerk to the Chairman (Daniel Jones) Nomination form online	TECBAR members have instigated the growth of the adjudication jurisprudence through their involvement as advocates in enforcement procedures, and many of them have developed real expertise in the field. They have also been frequently appointed as adjudicators so that TECBAR is able to provide a showcase of experienced adjudicators who are able to accept instructions and to act on very short notice. The Adjudication Scheme Clerk has developed significant experience in the appointment of adjudicators so that the process can be as swift and trouble-free as possible.
Technology and Construction Solicitors Association (TeCSA)	http://www.tecsa.org.uk/adjudication 020 7421 1986 Simon Tolson stolson.TeCSA@fenwickelliott.com	80	Architects Barristers Engineers Project Manager Quantity Surveyor Solicitors	£250 (incl. VAT) Application form on website Return by post	TeCSA has been at the heart of the development of statutory adjudication since its introduction in 1996. It produced the first set of compliant adjudication rules. It was active in lobbying government on the nature and form of both the primary and secondary legislation and advised both government and industry bodies in connection with the recent review of its operation. TeCSA provides a broad service to its members and their clients for adjudication in many ways: It has its own adjudication rules that can be used in place of the Scheme. It maintains a multi-disciplinary list of adjudicators, many of whom are TeCSA trained, from which the Chairman makes appointments.

Appendix 7
Comparison of UK and international statutory regimes

Description	United Kingdom	Australia East Coast NSW	Australia West Coast WA	Ireland	Singapore	Malaysia	New Zealand
General							
The Act applies to construction contracts performed within the jurisdiction.	s.107	s.7	s.4; s.7	s.2(5)(a)	s.4(1)	s.2	s.9
The parties cannot 'contract out' of the Act.	s.108(6); s.109(3)	s.34	s.53	s.2(5)(b)	s.35	[ ][1]	s.12
The Act generally binds the government.	s.117	s.33	s.8		s.36	s.2	s.8
However, contracts for certain works are specifically excluded from the application of the Act.	s.105(2); s.109(1) s.106	s.5(2)	s.4(3)	s.2	s.4(2)	s.3	s.6(2)
Contracts caught by the Act							
Residential property	Exempted subject to 200 m^2 (s.105(2)(d))	Exempted	Not exempted	Exempted subject to 200 m^2	Exempted	Exempted	Partially exempted
Supply only contracts	Exempted (s.105(2)(d))	No exemption (s.5(1)(e)(iv))	No exemption (s.3 and 5(1)	s.1(3)	No exemption (s.3(1)(d)(v))	No exemption (s.4(B))	Not specifically exempted

[1] The Malaysian Act is silent on this issue, but it is assumed that contracting out is prohibited.

Description	United Kingdom	Australia East Coast NSW	Australia West Coast WA	Ireland	Singapore	Malaysia	New Zealand
Other exceptions	Contracts for (s.105(2)): Drilling for/extraction of oil and gas Extraction of minerals Nuclear processing, power generation or water treatment Production, processing or storage of chemicals, pharmaceuticals, oil, gas, steel, food or drink Artistic works	Contracts under loan and other financial agreements Contracts for (s.5): Drilling for/extraction of oil and gas Extraction of minerals	Work that is for (s.4(3)): Drilling for oil or natural gas Constructing or drilling for any mineral bearing Constructing any plant for oil, natural gas or any mineral bearing Wholly artistic works	If the value is less than €10,000 (s.2(a); Contracts of employment (s.2(2); State Authority and a Public private partnership (s.2(3)); contracts containing provisions in relation to activities outside the definition of construction contracts (2(4))	No additional exemptions under the Act	Government contracts for: Urgent works due to natural disaster, emergencies and other unforeseen circumstances National security, including police and military camps, power and water treatment plants	s.6(2) and 11
Do different rules apply to different contracts?	No exemptions	No exemptions	No exemptions	No exemptions	No exemptions	Government contracts where the contract sum is less than RM 20m (around USD 6.3m)	Other than above, no

[2] Arguably the Malaysian Act does not impose a right to progress payments, although it will apply a progress payment regime if no regime is agreed between the parties.

Description	United Kingdom	Australia East Coast NSW	Australia West Coast WA	Ireland	Singapore	Malaysia	New Zealand
The Payment Regime							
The contractor has a right to progress payments.	s.109	s.8	Div.3 of Sch 1	n/a	s.5	n/a	s.15
The value of the progress claim is subject to assessment by the Employer/contract administrator within a limited period.	s.110; s.111	s.14	Div.5 of Sch 1	n/a	s.11	s.6	s.21
A default payment regime is imported into the contract if one is not agreed	s.110	s.8(2); s.11	s.13 to 22	n/a	s.8(b); s.10–11	s.36	s.15
'Pay when paid' clauses are unenforceable.	s.113(1)	s.12	s.9	n/a	s.9	s.35	s.16–18
Is there an obligation on the paying party to issue a Payment Notice (or similar)?	Yes	Yes	Yes	n/a	Yes	Yes	No
Will the absence of a timely and complete notice dealing with valuation issues bar the paying party from raising new valuation issues in Adjudication?	No	Yes	No	n/a	Yes	No	Yes
Will the absence of a timely and complete notice raising a defence of set-off bar the paying party from raising grounds for withholding/set-off defences issues in Adjudication?	Yes	Yes	No	n/a	Yes	No	Yes
Even in the absence of timely and complete valuation/withholding notices, must the adjudicator still decide and determine the true value of the progress payment?	Yes	Yes	Yes	n/a	Yes	Yes	No

[2] Arguably the Malaysian Act does not impose a right to progress payments, although it will apply a progress payment regime if no regime is agreed between the parties.

Description	United Kingdom	Australia East Coast NSW	Australia West Coast WA	Ireland	Singapore	Malaysia	New Zealand
The Adjudication Regime							
Can 'any dispute' be referred, or just a 'payment dispute' over a particular progress payment?	Any Dispute (s.108(1))	Payment dispute (s.17(1))	Payment dispute (s.25)	Payment dispute (S.6(1)	Payment dispute (s.12)	Payment dispute (s.7(1))	Any dispute (s.25)
Who can commence an Adjudication?	Either party (s.108)	Receiving party only (s.17(1))	Either party (s.25)	a party to a construction contract S.6(1)	Receiving party only (s.12)	Receiving party only (s.8(1))	Either party (s.25)
Is there a restriction upon when an adjudication be commenced?	No – 'at any time' (s.108(2))	Yes – a 'window' (s.17(2))	Yes – a 'window' (s.26)	at any time S.6(2)	Yes – a 'window' (s.12–13)	Yes – but no 'window' (s.7(2))	No (s.25)
Is there a statutory period for the adjudication response by the defending party?	No	Yes (s.20(1))[3]	Yes (s.27)	No	Yes (s.15)[4]	Yes (s.10(1))	Yes (s.37)
Is there a statutory bar to raising issues in the adjudication if no adjudication response served?	No	Yes (s.21(3))	Yes (s.32(1))	No	Yes (s.16(2))	No	No (s.45)
Is there a statutory period for the service by the claimant of a reply to the adjudication response?	No	No	No	No	No	Yes (s.11)	No
By when must the adjudicator provide his decision following commencement (in calendar days)?	28 days s.108(2)(c)	14 days (s.21(3))	14 days (s.31(1))	Within 28 days of the Notice or such period as is agreed (s.6(6) or by 14 days at the adjudicators discretion s.6(7)	14 days (s.17(b))	Upto 133 days	Min. 30 working days (s.36(1); 37(1) and 46(2))

[3] The paying party may only issue a response where it has already issued a valid a Payment Schedule (s.20(2A)).
[4] As above, but the relevant section is (s.15(3)).

Description	United Kingdom	Australia East Coast NSW	Australia West Coast WA	Ireland	Singapore	Malaysia	New Zealand
A valid decision of the adjudicator is binding on an interim basis and will be (generally) enforced by the national courts	s.108(3)	s.23; s.25	s.43(2)	Yes s.6(10)	s.21(1); s.23(2); s.27	s.13; s.28	s.58, 59, 61
A party who is unhappy with the decision of the adjudicator may refer the same dispute to the courts/arbitration for a final decision.	s.108(3)	S.23(2)	s.45(1)	Yes s.6(10)	s.21	s.13	s.26
There is an additional right of unpaid party to suspend works.	s.112	s.24(1); s.15–16	s.42	Yes s.7(1)	s.23(1)(b)	s.29	s.59
The adjudicator must act independently, impartially and comply with the principles of natural justice.[5]	s.108(2)(f)		s.30	Yes s.6(8)	s.16(3)	s.24	s.41
The adjudicator has wide powers to set his own process within a limited period to reach a decision	s.108(2) s.108(2)(4)	s.21(4) s.21(3)	s.32(1); s.32(6)	Yes s.6	s.16(4) s.17	s.25; s.12(2)	s.42; s.46

[5] The obligation to comply with the rules of natural justice or rules with similar principles apply as a matter of law in most jurisdictions.

Appendix 8
Case index: by subject matter

This appendix contains a list of reported cases relevant to the subject of construction adjudication[1] that have been decided by the courts of England, Scotland and Northern Ireland since the 1996 Act came into force.

Around 550 cases are categorised into around 250 subjects. The subject headings align directly with the subject headings in Chapters 1 to 17 of this book. Every effort has been made to locate all reported cases and list all the cases that are relevant to a particular subject so that this appendix may act as close to a definitive resource as possible. That said, there will undoubtedly be mistakes and omissions, and readers are kindly requested to contact the author in this regard. There are cases relevant to most but not all subjects within those chapters. Where there are no cases relevant to a particular subject addressed in Chapters 1– 17, the subject heading does not appear here.

Each case is referenced with the case name, the neutral citation (or where that is not available a law report) and the relevant paragraph number(s) of the judgment.[2] The paragraph numbers are taken from the copy of the judgment on Bailii, or if not available, adjudication.co.uk.

Owing to the limitations of space, not all of the case details and categories of information can be shown in this appendix. However, there is an online database version of this appendix which can be accessed at www.eversheds.com/construction. In addition to the case name, neutral citation and paragraph number, this database displays and allows the users to search by judgment date, judgment year, law report, judge, counsel, type of proceedings, country, adjudication rules and form of contract. This is of course subject to this information being available within the text of the judgment itself, which sometimes it is not. This database also provides a weblink to the case judgment on Bailii and adjudication.co.uk so that the judgment can be accessed directly.

---

[1] There are cases cited in Chapters 1–19 of this book that do not directly relate to the subject of construction, such as cases on the law of privilege and the law of waiver. These cases are not contained within this index, although they are in the index at Appendix 9.

[2] Except for cases listed under Section 6.3, which have no paragraph numbers.

A Practical Guide to Construction Adjudication, First Edition. James Pickavance.
© 2016 James Pickavance. Published 2016 by John Wiley & Sons, Inc.

1 Introduction

1.2 Background to statutory adjudication in the UK

A Straume (UK) Ltd v Bradlor Developments Ltd [1999] CILL 1520 at [7–10]
A v B [2002] ScotCS 325 at [7–11]
AWG Construction Services Ltd v Rockingham Motor Speedway Ltd [2004] EWHC 888 (TCC) at [117–128]
Bouygues (UK) Ltd v Dahl-Jensen (UK) Ltd [2000] EWCA Civ 507 at [2]
C&B Scene Concept Design Ltd v Isobars Ltd [2001] CILL 1781 at [14–15]
C&B Scene Concept Design Ltd v Isobars Ltd [2002] EWCA Civ 46 at [23]
CIB Properties Ltd v Birse Construction [2004] EWHC 2365 (TCC) at [5–14]
Costain Ltd v Strathclyde Builders Ltd [2003] ScotCS 352 at [9]
Galliford Try Building v Estura Ltd [2015] EWHC 412 (TCC) at [37–39]
Gibson v Imperial Homes [2002] EWHC 676 (QB) at [45]
Integrated Building Services Engineering Consultants Ltd trading as Operon v PIHL UK Ltd [2010] CSOH 80 at [14–16]
Karl Construction (Scotland) Ltd v Sweeney Civil Engineering (Scotland) Ltd [2000] ScotCS 330 at [17; 19]
Lead Technical Services v CMS Medical Ltd [2007] EWCA Civ 316 at [3]
Macob Civil Engineering v Morrison Construction Ltd [1999] All ER (D) 143 at [14]
McAlpine PPS Pipeline Systems Joint Venture v Transco plc [2004] EWHC 2030 (TCC) at [115–123]
Pegram Shopfitters Ltd v Tally Wiejl (UK) Ltd [2003] EWCA Civ 1750 at [1–9]
Quietfield Ltd v Vascroft Construction Ltd [2006] EWCA Civ 1737 at [2]
Rainford House Ltd v Cadogan Ltd [2001] BLR 416 at [17–18]
RJT Consulting Engineers Ltd v DM Engineering (Northern Ireland) Ltd [2002] EWCA Civ 270 at [1]
Shaw v MEP Foundations Piling Ltd [2009] EWHC 493 (TCC) at [15]
Speymill Contracts Ltd v Eric Baskind [2010] EWCA Civ 120 at [30–31]
The Construction Centre Group Ltd v The Highland Council [2003] ScotCS 114 at [14]
Watson Building Services Ltd [2001] ScotCS 60 at [21–25]
Westdawn Refurbishments Ltd v Roselodge Ltd [2006] AdjLR 04/24 at [5]
William Naylor t/a Powerfloated Concrete Floors v Greenacres Curling Ltd [2001] ScotCS 163 at [2]
William Verry Ltd v The Mayor and Burgesses of the London Borough of Camden [2006] EWHC 761 (TCC) at [23–25]
Woods Hardwick Ltd v Chiltern Air Conditioning Ltd [2001] BLR 23 at [19–20]

3 Deciding to adjudicate

3.6 Adjudication on behalf of or against an insolvent party

3.6.4 Liquidation

> Cross refer to case Section 14.2.2

3.6.5 Administration

> Cross refer to case Section 14.2.3

3.6.6 Administrative receivership

> Cross refer to case Section 14.2.4

3.6.7 CVA

> Cross refer to case Section 14.2.5

4 Statutory adjudication

4.2 The existence and terms of a contract

4.3.2 Contract formed

> Bryen & Langley Ltd v Martin Boston [2004] EWHC 2450 (TCC) at [20–24]
> Bryen & Langley Ltd v Martin Boston [2005] EWCA Civ 973 at [26–38]
> Cowlin Construction Ltd v CFW Architects (A Firm) [2002] EWHC 2914 (TCC) at [70–74]
> David McLean Contractors Ltd v The Albany Building Ltd [2005] TCC101/05 at [10–14]
> Durham County Council v Jeremy Kendall (trading as HLB Architects) [2011] EWHC 780 (TCC) at [31–33]
> Fleming Buildings Ltd v Mr and Mrs Jane Forrest [2010] CSIH 8 at [20–24]
> Imtech Inviron Ltd v Loppingdale Plant Ltd [2014] EWHC 4006 (TCC) at [28]
> Irvin v Robertson [2010] EWHC 3723 (TCC) at [37–40]
> Malcolm Charles Contracts Ltd v Mr Crispin and Mrs Zhang [2014] EWHC 3898 (TCC) at [74–81]
> RC Pillar & Son v The Camber (Portsmouth) Ltd [2007] EWHC 1626 (TCC) at [16–21]
> Universal Music Operations Ltd v Flairnote Ltd & Others [2000] All ER (D) 1182 at [48–53]

4.3.2 No contract formed

Adonis Construction v O'Keefe Soil Remediation [2009] EWHC 2047 (TCC) at [32–42]
Bennett (Electrical) Services Ltd v Inviron Ltd [2007] EWHC 49 (TCC) at [14–19]
Galliford Try Construction Ltd v Michael Heal Associates Ltd [2003] EWHC 2886 (TCC) at [27]
GPN Limited (In Receivership) v 02 (UK) Limited [2004] EWHC 2494 (TCC) at [21–41]
Mast Electrical Services v Kendall Cross Holdings Ltd [2007] EWHC 1296 (TCC) at [37; 57; 71]
Rupert Cordle v Vanessa Nicholson [2009] EWHC 1314 at [13–19]
Viridis UK Limited v Mulalley and Company Limited [2014] EWHC 268 (TCC) at [80–82]

4.3.3 Contract terminated

A&D Maintenance and Construction Ltd v Pagehurst Construction Services Ltd (2000) 16 Const LJ 199 at [18–19]
Lanes Group plc v Galliford Try Infrastructure Ltd (No. 2) [2011] EWHC 1234 (TCC) at [23–26]

4.3.4 Void or voidable contract

Barr Ltd v Law Mining Ltd [2001] ScotCS 152 at [18; 30]
Capital Structures plc v Time & Tide Construction Ltd [2006] EWHC 591 (TCC) at [16–30]
Speymill Contracts Ltd v Eric Baskind [2010] EWCA Civ 120 at [36]

4.3.5 Incorporation of terms

Imtech Inviron Ltd v Loppingdale Plant Ltd [2014] EWHC 4006 (TCC) at [28–29]
Matthew J Harding (t/a M J Harding Contractors) v Paice and Springall [2014] EWHC 4819 (TCC) at [31–38]
Twintec Ltd v Volkerfitzpatrick Ltd [2014] EWHC 10 (TCC) at [44–47]

4.4 Construction Contract

4.4.2 Carrying out, arranging, providing labour for construction operations (Act s. 104(1))

Gillies Ramsay Diamond and Gavin Ramsay and Philip Diamond v PJW Enterprises Ltd [2003] ScotCS 343 at [16]
Gillies Ramsay Diamond v PJW Enterprises Ltd [2002] ScotCS 340 at [42–48]
Parkwood Leisure Ltd v Laing O'Rourke Wales and West Ltd [2013] EWHC 2665 (TCC) at [20–29]

Savoye and Savoye Ltd v Spicers Ltd [2014] EWHC 4195 (TCC) [36(b)].
Yarm Road Ltd v Costain Ltd [2001] AdjLR 07/30 at [20]

4.4.3 Consultants and advisers (Act s. 104(2))

Cowlin Construction Ltd v CFW Architects (A Firm) [2002] EWHC 2914 (TCC) at [73]
Fence Gate Ltd v James R Knowles Ltd [2002] All ER (D) 34 (May) at [6–14]
Gillies Ramsay Diamond and Gavin Ramsay and Philip Diamond v PJW Enterprises Ltd [2003] ScotCS 343 at [16]
Gillies Ramsay Diamond v PJW Enterprises Ltd [2002] ScotCS 340 at [42–48]
Parkwood Leisure Ltd v Laing O'Rourke Wales and West Ltd [2013] EWHC 2665 (TCC) at [20–29]

4.4.5 Construction operations and other matters (Act s. 104(5))

Cleveland Bridge (UK) Ltd v Whessoe-Volker Stevin Joint Venture [2010] EWHC 1076 (TCC) at [62–77; 91]
Fence Gate Ltd v James R Knowles Ltd [2002] All ER (D) 34 (May) at [7]
Gibson Lea Retail Interiors Ltd v Makro Self Service Wholesalers Ltd [2001] All ER (D) 333 (Jul) at [16; 24]
Homer Burgess Ltd v Chirex (Annan) Ltd (No. 1) (1999) 71 ConLR 245 at [35]
North Midland Construction V AE & E Lentjes Ltd [2009] EWHC 1371 (TCC) at [40–74]

4.4.6 Application of the Act to contracts (Act s. 104(6))

Christiani & Nielsen Ltd v The Lowry Centre Development Company Ltd [2000] AdjLR 06/16 at [21–28]
Earls Terrace Properties Ltd v Waterloo Investments Ltd [2002] CILL 1889 at [21–28]
Staveley Industries plc v Odebrecht Oil & Gas Services Ltd [2001] AdjLR 02/28 at [10–15]
Yarm Road Ltd v Costain Ltd [2001] AdjLR 07/30 at [20]

4.4.7 Ancillary agreements

Able Construction (UK) Ltd v Forest Property Development Ltd [2009] EWHC 159 (TCC) at [10–12]
AMEC Group Ltd v Thames Water Utilities Ltd [2010] EWHC 419 (TCC) at [29]
C&B Scene Concept Design Ltd v Isobars Ltd [2001] CILL 1781 at [24–30]
C&B Scene Concept Design Ltd v Isobars Ltd [2002] EWCA Civ 46 at [21–31]
Hurley Palmer Flatt Ltd v Barclays Bank plc [2014] EWHC 3042 (TCC) at [20–54]

Case index: by subject matter 589

L Brown & Sons Ltd v Crosby Homes (North West) Ltd [2005] EWHC 3503 (TCC) at [49–55]

Lathom Construction Ltd v Brian Cross & Anor [2000] CILL 1568 at [7–10]

McConnell Dowell Constructors (Aust) Pty Ltd v National Grid Gas plc (formerly Transco plc) [2006] EWHC 2551 (TCC) at [30–44]

Melville Dundas Ltd v Hotel Corporation of Edinburgh Ltd [2006] CSOH 136 at [30–33]

Parkwood Leisure Ltd v Laing O'Rourke Wales and West Ltd [2013] EWHC 2665 (TCC) at [26–31]

Shepherd Construction Ltd v Mecright Ltd [2000] BLR 489 at [16–18]

Westminster Building Company Ltd v Andrew Beckingham [2004] EWHC 138 (TCC) at [22–28]

Yarm Road Ltd v Costain Ltd [2001] AdjLR 07/30 at [20]

4.5 Construction operations

4.5.2 Definition of construction operations (Act s. 105(1))

ABB Power Construction Ltd v Norwest Holst Engineering Ltd (2000) 77 ConLR 20 at [10; 18]

Baldwins Industrial Services plc v Barr Ltd [2002] EWHC 2915 (TCC) at [12–14]

Barrie Green v GW Integrated Building Services Ltd & Anor [2001] AdjLR 07/18 at [27]

Cleveland Bridge (UK) Ltd v Whessoe-Volker Stevin Joint Venture [2010] EWHC 1076 (TCC) at [30–36]

Coleraine Skip Hire Ltd v Ecomesh Ltd [2008] NIQB 141 at [14–15]

Fence Gate Ltd v James R Knowles Ltd [2002] All ER (D) 34 (May) at [6]

Gibson Lea Retail Interiors Ltd v Makro Self Service Wholesalers Ltd [2001] All ER (D) 333 (Jul) at [15; 20–24]

Hortimax Ltd v Hedon Salads Ltd (2004) 24 Const LJ 47 at [4]

North Midland Construction plc v AE & E Lentjes UK Ltd [2009] EWHC 1371 (TCC) at [23–29]

Nottingham Community Housing Association Ltd v Powerminster Ltd [2000] BLR 309 at [13–21]

Palmers Ltd v ABB Power Construction Ltd [1999] All ER (D) 1273 at [20–23]

Ruttle Plant Hire Ltd v Secretary of State for the Environment, Food and Rural Affairs [2004] EWHC 2152 at [275–286]

Savoye and Savoye Ltd v Spicers Ltd [2014] EWHC 4195 (TCC) at [16–44]

Staveley Industries plc v Odebrecht Oil & Gas Services Ltd [2001] AdjLR 02/28 at [4–14]

4.6 Excluded construction operations

4.6.2 Approach to interpreting the exclusions provisions at section 105(2) of the Act

> North Midland Construction plc v AE & E Lentjes Ltd [2009] EWHC 1371 (TCC), per Ramsay J at [40–74]

4.6.3 The court's approach to applying the exclusions at section 105(2)

> ABB Power Construction Ltd v Norwest Holst Engineering Ltd (2000) 77 ConLR 20 at [9–21]
> Cleveland Bridge (UK) Ltd v Whessoe-Volker Stevin Joint Venture [2010] EWHC 1076 (TCC) at [44–61]
> North Midland Construction plc v AE & E Lentjes UK Ltd [2009] EWHC 1371 (TCC) at [40–68]
> Palmers Ltd v ABB Power Construction Ltd [1999] All ER (D) 1273 at [24–42]

4.6.5 Assembly, installation, erection, demolition in connection with certain activities (Act s. 105(2)(c))

> ABB Power Construction Ltd v Norwest Holst Engineering Ltd (2000) 77 ConLR 20 at [9–21]
> ABB Zantingh Ltd v Zedal Building Services Ltd [2001] BLR 66 at [19–35]
> Cleveland Bridge (UK) Ltd v Whessoe-Volker Stevin Joint Venture [2010] EWHC 1076 (TCC) at [44–61]
> Comsite Projects Ltd v Andritz AG [2003] EWHC 958 (TCC) at [29–39]
> Conor Engineering Ltd v Les Constructions Industrielles de la Mediterranée SA [2004] EWHC 899 (TCC) at [16–20; 32–33]
> Homer Burgess Ltd v Chirex (Annan) Ltd (No. 1) (1999) 71 ConLR 245 at [38–44]
> Hortimax Ltd v Hedon Salads Ltd (2004) 24 Const LJ 47 at [5–20]
> Laker Vent Engineering Ltd v Jacobs E&C Ltd [2014] EWHC 1058 (TCC) at [66–71]
> North Midland Construction plc v AE & E Lentjes UK Ltd [2009] EWHC 1371 (TCC) at [26–82]
> Palmers Ltd v ABB Power Construction Ltd [1999] All ER (D) 1273 at [24–42]
> Petition of Mitsui Babcock Energy Services Ltd [2001] ScotCS 150 at [13–17]

4.6.6 Manufacture, delivery, installation (Act s. 105(2)(d))

> ABB Power Construction Ltd v Norwest Holst Engineering Ltd (2000) 77 ConLR 20 at [9–16]
> Baldwins Industrial Services plc v Barr Ltd [2002] EWHC 2915 (TCC) at [15–23]
> Edenbooth Ltd v Cre8 Developments Ltd [2008] EWHC 570 (TCC) at [6–7]

Millers Specialist Joinery Company Ltd v Nobles Construction Ltd [2001] CILL 1770 at [11]
Nottingham Community Housing Association Ltd v Powerminster Ltd [2000] BLR 309 at [20]
Palmers Ltd v ABB Power Construction Ltd [1999] All ER (D) 1273 at [24–42]

4.7 Excluded agreements

4.7.2 Residential occupier (Act s.106(1)(a) and (2))

Allen Wilson Shopfitters and Builders Ltd v Buckingham [2005] EWHC 1165 (TCC) at [38]
Edenbooth Ltd v Cre8 Developments Ltd [2008] EWHC 570 (TCC) at [8–13]
Ken Biggs Contractors Ltd v Norman [2004] AdjLR 08/20 at [2–3]
Lovell Projects Ltd v Legg & Carver [2003] BLR 452 at [1]
Malcolm Charles Contracts Ltd v Mr Crispin and Mrs Zhang [2014] EWHC 3898 (TCC) at [82–83]
Picardi v Cuniberti [2002] EWHC 2923 (TCC) at [112–133]
Samuel Thomas Construction v J&B Developments [2000] CILL 1637 at [12–18]
Shaw v MEP Foundations Piling Ltd [2009] EWHC 493 (TCC) at [29–38]
Speymill Contracts Ltd v Eric Baskind [2009] No 9LV 22750 at [78]
Speymill Contracts Ltd v Eric Baskind [2010] EWCA Civ 120 at [10]
Westfields Construction Ltd v Lewis [2013] EWHC 376 (TCC) at [9–11; 58–60]

4.7.3 Exclusion order (2009 Act, s. 106A; 1996 Act, s. 106(1)(b))

Captiva Estates Ltd v Rybarn Ltd (In Administration) [2005] EWHC 2744 (TCC) at [10–18]

4.8 Contract in Writing

4.8.3 1996 Act only applies to agreements in writing (Act s.107(1))

Hart Investments Ltd v Fidler & Anor [2006] EWHC 2857 (TCC) at [55–64]
Lloyd Projects Ltd v John Malnick [2005] AdjLR 07/22 at [31–55]
Murray Building Services v Spree Developments [2004] AdjLR 07/30 at [11–15]
RJT Consulting Engineers Ltd v DM Engineering (Northern Ireland) Ltd [2002] All ER (D) 108 (Mar) at [5; 11]
RJT Consulting Engineers Ltd v DM Engineering (Northern Ireland) Ltd [2002] EWCA Civ 270 at [12]
Westdawn Refurbishments Ltd v Roselodge Ltd [2006] AdjLR 04/24 at [22]

4.8.4 In writing (1996 Act s.107(2))

Aceramais Holdings Ltd v Hadleigh Partnerships Ltd [2009] EWHC 1664 (TCC) at [7–34]
Ale Heavylift v MSD (Darlington) Ltd [2006] EWHC 2080 (TCC) at [85–88]
Branlow Ltd v Dem-Master Demolition Ltd [2004] ScotCS A904/03 at [24]
Carillion Construction Ltd v Devonport Royal Dockyard Ltd [2003] BLR 79 at [25–30]
Debeck Ductwork Installation Ltd v T&E Engineering Ltd [2002] AdjLR 10/14 at [5–15]
Hatmet Ltd v Herbert (t/a LMS Lift Consultancy) [2005] EWHC 3529 (TCC) at [20–28]
Millers Specialist Joinery Company Ltd v Nobles Construction Ltd [2001] CILL 1770 at [13]
Mott MacDonald Ltd v London & Regional Properties Ltd [2007] EWHC 1055 (TCC) at [49–52]
Naylor Construction Services Ltd v Acoustafoam Ltd [2010] All ER (D) 138 (Apr) at [25–32]
Nickleby FM Ltd v Somerfield Stores Ltd [2010] EWHC 1976 (TCC) at [29–31]
RJT Consulting Engineers Ltd v DM Engineering (Northern Ireland) Ltd [2002] EWCA Civ 270 at [13]
Trustees of the Stratfield Saye Estate v AHL Construction Ltd [2004] EWHC 3286 (TCC) at [48–49]

4.8.5 An agreement made otherwise than in writing (1996 Act s. 107(3))

Carillion Construction Ltd v Devonport Royal Dockyard Ltd [2003] BLR 79 at [23; 32]
RJT Consulting Engineers Ltd v DM Engineering (Northern Ireland) Ltd [2002] EWCA Civ 270 at [14]
Sprunt Ltd v London Borough of Camden [2011] EWHC 3191 (TCC) at [42]

4.8.6 An agreement evidenced in writing (1996 Act s. 107(4))

Concrete & Coating (UK) Ltd v Cornelius Moloney [2004] ADJ LR 12/06 at [1 to 8]
Connex South Eastern Ltd v MJ Building Services Group plc [2004] EWHC 1518 (TCC) at [24]
D G Williamson Ltd v Northern Ireland Prison Service [2009] NIQB 8 at [19–20]
Durham County Council v Jeremy Kendall (trading as HLB Architects) [2011] EWHC 780 (TCC) at [34]
Millers Specialist Joinery Company Ltd v Nobles Construction Ltd [2001] CILL 1770 at [12–13]
PT Building Services Ltd v ROK Build Ltd [2008] EWHC 3434 (TCC) at [31–42]
RJT Consulting Engineers Ltd v DM Engineering (Northern Ireland) Ltd [2002] EWCA Civ 270 at [15]
Sprunt Ltd v London Borough of Camden [2011] EWHC 3191 (TCC) at [42]

Case index: by subject matter 593

4.8.7 An exchange of written submissions in adjudication proceedings (1996 Act s. 107(5))

> A&D Maintenance and Construction Ltd v Pagehurst Construction Services Ltd (2000) 16 Const LJ 199 at [15]
> Ale Heavylift v MSD (Darlington) Ltd [2006] EWHC 2080 (TCC) at [88]
> Glendalough Associated SA v Harris Calnan Construction Co Ltd [2013] EWHC 3142 (TCC) at [18–37]
> Grovedeck Ltd v Capital Demolition Ltd [2000] All ER (D) 317 at [27–32]
> Mott MacDonald Ltd v London & Regional Properties Ltd [2007] EWHC 1055 (TCC) at [53–59]
> Naylor Construction Services Ltd v Acoustafoam Ltd [2010] All ER (D) 138 (Apr) at [43–52]
> RJT Consulting Engineers Ltd v DM Engineering (Northern Ireland) Ltd [2002] EWCA Civ 270 at [16; 24]
> SG South Ltd v Swan Yard (Cirencester) Ltd [2010] EWHC 376 (TCC) at [11–12]
> Sprunt Ltd v London Borough of Camden [2011] EWHC 3191 (TCC) at [41]
> Trustees of the Stratfield Saye Estate v AHL Construction Ltd [2004] EWHC 3286 (TCC) at [50–51]

4.8.8 Scenarios

> (A) *Oral contracts*
> All Metal Roofing v Kamm Properties Ltd [2010] EWHC 2670 (TCC) at [16–20]
> Allen Wilson Joinery Ltd v Privetgrange Construction Ltd [2008] EWHC 2802 (TCC) at [27; 31–32]
> Bennett (Electrical) Services Ltd v Inviron Ltd [2007] EWHC 49 (TCC) at [28]
> Cain Electrical Ltd v Richard Cox t/a Pennine Control Systems [2011] EWHC 2681 (TCC) at [31–36]
> Grovedeck Ltd v Capital Demolition Ltd [2000] All ER (D) 317 at [27–32]
> Lloyd Projects Ltd v John Malnick [2005] AdjLR 07/22 at [31–55]
> Millers Specialist Joinery Company Ltd v Nobles Construction Ltd [2001] CILL 1770 at [12–13]
> RJT Consulting Engineers Ltd v DM Engineering (Northern Ireland) Ltd [2002] All ER (D) 108 (Mar) at [11]
> RJT Consulting Engineers Ltd v DM Engineering (Northern Ireland) Ltd [2002] EWCA Civ 270 at [11–19]
> Sprunt Ltd v London Borough of Camden [2011] EWHC 3191 (TCC) at [36]
>
> (B) *One or more terms not agreed, or agreed orally*
> ART Consultancy Ltd v Navera Trading Ltd [2007] EWHC 1375 (TCC) at [13–20]
> Bennett (Electrical) Services Ltd v Inviron Ltd [2007] EWHC 49 (TCC) at [28]
> Cowlin Construction Ltd v CFW Architects (A Firm) [2002] EWHC 2914 (TCC) at [70–74]

Dean & Dyball Construction Ltd v Kenneth Grubb Associates Ltd [2003] EWHC 2465 (TCC) at [13–16]

Estor Ltd v Multifit (UK) Ltd [2009] EWHC 2108 (TCC) at [18–20]

Euro Construction Scaffolding Ltd v SLLB Construction Ltd [2008] EWHC 3160 (TCC) at [30]

Flannery Construction Ltd v M Holleran Ltd [2007] EWHC 825 (TCC) at [13–16]

Lead Technical Services v CMS Medical Ltd [2007] EWCA Civ 316 at [4; 17–20]

Linnett v Halliwells LLP [2009] EWHC 319 at [108]

Mast Electrical Services v Kendall Cross Holdings Ltd [2007] EWHC 1296 (TCC) at [42–71]

Murray Building Services v Spree Developments [2004] AdjLR 07/30 at [11–15]

T&T Fabrications Ltd (A Firm) v Hubbard Architectural Metal Work Ltd [2008] EWHC B7 (TCC) at [6–13]

Westdawn Refurbishments Ltd v Roselodge Ltd [2006] AdjLR 04/24 at [32–44]

(C) *Oral variations*

Adonis Construction v O'Keefe Soil Remediation [2009] EWHC 2047 (TCC) at [46]

Bennett (Electrical) Services Ltd v Inviron Ltd [2007] EWHC 49 (TCC) at [28]

Carillion Construction Ltd v Devonport Royal Dockyard Ltd [2003] BLR 79 at [31–35]

Linnett v Halliwells LLP [2009] EWHC 319 at [107–111]

Management Solutions & Professional Consultants Ltd v Bennett (Electrical) Services Ltd (No 1) [2006] EWHC 1720 (TCC) at [10–17]

Management Solutions & Professional Consultants Ltd v Bennett (Electrical) Services Ltd (No 2) [2006] EWHC 1720_2 (TCC) at [13–17]

Naylor Construction Services Ltd v Acoustafoam Ltd [2010] All ER (D) 138 (Apr) at [38–42]

ROK Building Ltd v Bestwood Carpentry Ltd [2010] EWHC 1409 (TCC) at [30–33]

Total M&E Services Ltd v ABB Building Technologies Ltd (formerly ABB Stewarts Ltd) [2002] EWHC 248 (TCC) at [29–34]

Treasure & Son Ltd v Martin Dawes [2007] EWHC 2420 (TCC) at [29–40]

(D) *Trivial terms*

Allen Wilson Joinery Ltd v Privetgrange Construction Ltd [2008] EWHC 2802 (TCC) at [27]

Westdawn Refurbishments Ltd v Roselodge Ltd [2006] AdjLR 04/24 at [22]

(E) *Implied terms*

Allen Wilson Joinery Ltd v Privetgrange Construction Ltd [2008] EWHC 2802 (TCC) at [28–31]

BSF Consulting Engineers Ltd v MacDonald Crosbie [2008] All ER (D) 171 (Apr) at [1–6]

Connex South Eastern Ltd v MJ Building Services Group plc [2004] EWHC 1518 (TCC) at [24]
Galliford Try Construction Ltd v Michael Heal Associates Ltd [2003] EWHC 2886 (TCC) at [29]
Rok Buildings Ltd v Bestwood Carpentry Ltd [2010] EWHC 1409 (TCC) at [29]

(F) *Letters of intent*
Adonis Construction v O'Keefe Soil Remediation [2009] EWHC 2047 (TCC) at [42–47]
Allen Wilson Shopfitters and Builders Ltd v Buckingham [2005] EWHC 1165 (TCC) at [12–21]
Bennett (Electrical) Services Ltd v Inviron Ltd [2007] EWHC 49 (TCC) at [14–19; 29–32]
Cubitt Building and Interiors Ltd v Richardson Roofing (Industrial) Ltd [2008] EWHC 1020 (TCC) at [40]
Glendalough Associated SA v Harris Calnan Construction Co Ltd [2013] EWHC 3142 (TCC) at [45–53]
Harris Calnan Construction Co Ltd v Ridgewood (Kensington) Ltd [2007] EWHC 2738 (TCC) at [9–12]
Mott MacDonald Ltd v London & Regional Properties Ltd [2007] EWHC 1055 (TCC) at [33–52]
RC Pillar & Son v The Camber (Portsmouth) Ltd [2007] EWHC 1626 (TCC) at [16–21]
RJT Consulting Engineers Ltd v DM Engineering (Northern Ireland) Ltd [2002] EWCA Civ 270 at [18]
Twintec Ltd v Volkerfitzpatrick Ltd [2014] EWHC 10 (TCC) at [43–47]

5 Contractual and ad hoc adjudication

5.1 Contractual adjudication

5.1.1 *Contractual adjudication*

AMEC Group Ltd v Thames Water Utilities Ltd [2010] EWHC 419 (TCC) at [24]
Bryen & Langley Ltd v Martin Boston [2005] EWCA Civ 973 at [2]
Dean & Dyball Construction Ltd v Kenneth Grubb Associates Ltd [2003] EWHC 2465 (TCC) at [16–18]
Fleming Buildings Ltd v Mr and Mrs Jane Forrest [2008] CSOH 103 at [105]
Linnett v Halliwells LLP [2009] EWHC 319 at [108]
Lovell Projects Ltd v Legg & Carver [2003] BLR 452 at [1; 36–41]
PP Construction Ltd v Geoffrey Osborne Ltd [2015] EWHC 325 (TCC) at [32]
RWE Npower plc v Alstom Power Ltd [2009] EWHC 1192 (QB) at [84–89]
Steve Domsalla (t/a Domsalla Building Services) v Kenneth Dyason [2007] EWHC 1174 (TCC) at [19; 98–99]

Treasure & Son Ltd v Martin Dawes [2007] EWHC 2420 (TCC) at [29–40]
Vitpol Building Service v Michael Samen [2008] EWHC 2283 (TCC) at [9]

5.2 Ad hoc adjudication

5.2.2 Ad hoc adjudication

Anrik Ltd v As Leisure Properties Ltd Unreported, 8 January 2010 at [12]
Christiani & Nielsen Ltd v The Lowry Centre Development Company Ltd [2000] AdjLR 06/16 at [23–29]
Clark Electrical Ltd v JMD Developments (UK) Ltd [2012] EWHC 2627 (TCC) at [24; 32–37]
Fence Gate Ltd v James R Knowles Ltd [2002] All ER (D) 34 (May) at [4–5]
Galliford Try Construction Ltd v Michael Heal Associates Ltd [2003] EWHC 2886 (TCC) at [39–44]
Harris Calnan Construction Co Ltd v Ridgewood (Kensington) Ltd [2007] EWHC 2738 (TCC) at [4–8]
Irvin v Robertson [2010] EWHC 3723 (TCC) at [13; 41]
Maymac Environmental Services Ltd v Faraday Building Services Ltd [2000] All ER (D) 1406 at [50]
Nordot Engineering Services Ltd v Siemens plc [2001] CILL 1778 at [11–30]
Parsons Plastics (Research & Development) Ltd v Purac Ltd [2002] EWCA Civ 459 at [9]
Parsons Plastics (Research and Development) Ltd v Purac Ltd [2001] AdjLR 08/13 at [15–16]
Project Consultancy Group v Trustees of the Gray Trust [1999] All ER (D) 842 at [14–15]
R Durtnell & Sons Ltd v Kaduna Ltd [2003] EWHC 517 (TCC) at [46–48]
RC Pillar & Son v The Camber (Portsmouth) Ltd [2007] EWHC 1626 (TCC) at [9–14]
Rossco Civil Engineering Ltd v Dwr Cymru Cyfyngedic [2004] EWHC HT-03–190 (TCC) at [74]
Steve Domsalla (t/a Domsalla Building Services) v Kenneth Dyason [2007] EWHC 1174 (TCC) at [20–21]
Thomas-Fredric's (Construction) Ltd v Wilson [2003] EWCA Civ 1494 at [27–34]
William Oakley & David Oakley v Airclear Environmental Ltd and Airclear TS Ltd [2002] CILL 1824 at [48–55; 69–72]

6 Adjudication procedures

6.2 Scheme

6.2.2 Does the Scheme apply and the failure to comply with section 108(1)–(4) (Act s. 108(5) and 114(4))

Anglian Water Services Ltd v Laing O'Rourke Utilities Ltd [2010] EWHC 1529 (TCC) at [21–32]
Aveat Heating Ltd v Jerram Falkus Construction Ltd [2007] EWHC 131 (TCC) at [4–9]
Ballast plc v The Burrell Company (Construction Management) Ltd [2001] ScotCS 159 at [28]
Banner Holdings Ltd v Colchester Borough Council [2010] EWHC 139 (TCC) at [41–45]
C&B Scene Concept Design Ltd v Isobars Ltd [2001] CILL 1781 at [1–15]
Cubitt Building & Interiors Ltd v Fleetglade Ltd [2006] EWHC 3413 (TCC) at [24–25]
Dalkia Energy and Technical Services Ltd v Bell Group UK Ltd [2009] EWHC 73 (TCC) at [65–77]
Hills Electrical & Mechanical plc v Dawn Construction Ltd [2003] ScotCS 107 at [18–20]
John Mowlem & Company plc v Hydra-Tight Ltd (2001) 17 Const LJ 358 at [35–50]
Lanes Group plc v Galliford Try Infrastructure Ltd [2011] EWHC 1035 (TCC) at [25]
Pegram Shopfitters Ltd v Tally Wiejl (UK) Ltd [2003] EWCA Civ 1750 at [3]
Pegram Shopfitters Ltd v Tally Wiejl (UK) Ltd [2003] EWHC 984 (TCC) at [27–30]
Pioneer Cladding Ltd v John Graham Construction Ltd [2013] EWHC 2954 (TCC) at [4–8]
Profile Projects Ltd v Elmwood (Glasgow) Ltd [2011] CSOH 64 at [47–50]
Sprunt Ltd v London Borough of Camden [2011] EWHC 3191 (TCC) at [28–31]
VHE Construction plc v RBSTB Trust Co Ltd (as trustee of the Mercury Property Fund) [2000] BLR 187 at [37]
Yuanda (UK) Co Ltd v WW Gear Construction Ltd [2010] EWHC 720 (TCC) at [55–65]

6.3 Contractual procedures

6.3.2 JCT

A Straume (UK) Ltd v Bradlor Developments Ltd [1999] CILL 1520
A&S Enterprises Ltd v Kema Holdings Ltd [2004] EWHC 3365 (QB)
Adonis Construction v O'Keefe Soil Remediation [2009] EWHC 2047 (TCC)
Allen Wilson Shopfitters and Builders Ltd v Buckingham [2005] EWHC 1165 (TCC)
AMEC Capital Projects Ltd v Whitefriars City Estate Ltd [2003] EWHC 2443 (TCC)
AMEC Capital Projects Ltd v Whitefriars City Estates Ltd (No 2) [2004] EWHC 393 (TCC)
AMEC Capital Projects Ltd v Whitefriars City Estates Ltd (No 3) [2004] EWCA Civ 1418
ART Consultancy Ltd v Navera Trading Ltd [2007] EWHC 1375 (TCC)
Austin Hall Building Ltd v Buckland Securities Ltd [2001] All ER (D) 137
Avoncroft Construction Ltd v Sharba Homes (CN) Ltd [2008] EWHC 933 (TCC)
Balfour Beatty Construction Ltd v The Mayor & Burgesses of the London Borough of Lambeth [2002] EWHC 597 (TCC)

Balfour Beatty Construction Northern Ltd v Modus Corovest (Blackpool) Ltd [2008] EWHC 3029 (TCC)
Barnes & Elliot Ltd v Taylor Woodrow Holdings Ltd & Anor [2003] EWHC 3100 (TCC)
Barr Ltd v Klin Investment Ltd [2009] ScotCS CSOH 104
Benfield Construction Ltd v Trudson (Hatton) Ltd [2008] EWHC 2333 (TCC)
Bennett v FMK Construction Ltd [2005] EWHC 1268 (TCC)
Bickerton Construction Ltd v Temple Windows Ltd [2001] AdjLR 06/26
Bloor Construction (UK) Ltd v Bowmer & Kirkland (London) Ltd [2000] BLR 314
Bovis Lend Lease Ltd v Cofely Engineering Services [2009] EWHC 1120 (TCC)
Bovis Lend Lease Ltd v The Trustees of the London Clinic [2009] EWHC 64 (TCC)
Bovis Lend Lease Ltd v Triangle Development Ltd [2002] EWHC 3123 (TCC)
Bracken and another v Billinghurst [2003] EWHC 1333 (TCC)
Branlow Ltd v Dem-Master Demolition Ltd [2004] ScotCS A904/03
Bryen & Langley Ltd v Martin Boston [2005] EWCA Civ 973
Cantillon Ltd v Urvasco Ltd [2008] EWHC 282 (TCC)
Capital Structures plc v Time & Tide Construction Ltd [2006] EWHC 591 (TCC)
Chamberlain Carpentry & Joinery Ltd v Alfred MacAlpine Construction Ltd [2002] EWHC 514 (TCC)
Charles Brand Ltd v Donegall Ltd [2010] NIQB 67
City Inn Ltd v Shepherd Construction Ltd [2001] ScotCS 54
CJP Builders Ltd v William Verry Ltd [2008] EWHC 2025 (TCC)
Collins (Contractors) Ltd v Baltic Quay Management (1994) Ltd [2004] EWCA Civ 1757
Costain Ltd v Wescol Steel Ltd [2003] EWHC 312 (TCC)
CPL Contracting Ltd v Cadenza Residential Ltd [2005] AdjLR 01/31
Cubitt Building & Interiors Ltd v Fleetglade Ltd [2006] EWHC 3413 (TCC)
Cubitt Building and Interiors Ltd v Richardson Roofing (Industrial) Ltd [2008] EWHC 1020 (TCC)
Dorchester Hotel Ltd v Vivid Interiors Ltd [2009] EWHC 70 (TCC)
Dumarc Building Services Ltd v Mr Salvador – Rico [2003] Adj.C.R. 01/31
Edmund Nuttall Ltd v R G Carter Ltd [2002] EWHC 400 (TCC)
Edmund Nuttall Ltd v RG Carter Ltd (No 2) [2002] BLR 359
Emcor Drake & Scull Ltd v Costain Construction Ltd & Skanska Central Europe AB (t/a Costain Skanska Joint Venture) [2004] EWHC 2439 (TCC)
FG Skerritt Ltd v Caledonian Building Systems Ltd [2013] EWHC 1898 (TCC)
Forest Heath District Council v ISG Jackson Ltd [2010] EWHC 322 (TCC)
Henry Brothers (Magherafelt) Ltd v Brunswick (8 Lanyon Place) Ltd [2011] NIQB 102
HG Construction Ltd v Ashwell Homes (East Anglia) Ltd [2007] EWHC 144 (TCC)
Image Decorations Ltd v Dean & Bowes (Contracts) Ltd [2004] ADJ CS 03/65
Impresa Castelli SpA v Cola Holdings Ltd [2002] EWHC 1363 (TCC)
Jamil Mohammed v Dr Michael Bowles [2002] 394 SD 2002
Jerome Engineering Ltd v Lloyd Morris Electrical Ltd [2002] CILL 1827
Joinery Plus Ltd (In Administration) v Laing Ltd [2003] EWHC 3513 (TCC)
Ken Biggs Contractors Ltd v Norman [2004] AdjLR 08/20
Kier Regional Ltd (t/a Wallis) v City & General (Holborn) Ltd [2006] EWHC 848 (TCC)

KNS Industrial Services (Birmingham) Ltd v Sindall Ltd (2001) 75 ConLR 71
L Brown & Sons Ltd v Crosby Homes (North West) Ltd [2005] EWHC 3503 (TCC)
Lathom Construction Ltd v Brian Cross & Anor [2000] CILL 1568
Letchworth Roofing Company v Sterling Building Company [2009] EWHC 1119 (TCC)
Linnett v Halliwells LLP [2009] EWHC 319
Lovell Projects Ltd v Legg & Carver [2003] BLR 452
Makers UK Ltd v The Mayor and Burgesses of the London Borough of Camden [2008] EWHC 1836 (TCC)
Melville Dundas Limited (in receivership) and others George Wimpey UK Limited and others [2007] UKHL 18
Michael John Construction Ltd v Golledge & Ors [2006] EWHC 71 (TCC)
Michael John Construction Ltd v St Peter's Rugby Football Club [2007] EWHC 1857 (TCC)
MJ Gleeson Group plc v Devonshire Green Holding Ltd [2004] AdjLR 03/19
Multiplex Constructions (UK) Ltd v West India Quay Development Company (Eastern) Ltd [2006] EWHC 1569 (TCC)
O'Donnell Developments Ltd v Buildability Ltd [2009] EWHC 3388 (TCC)
Orange EBS Ltd v ABB Ltd [2003] EWHC 1187 (TCC)
Outwing Construction Ltd v H Randell and Son Ltd [1999] BLR 156
Palmac Contracting Ltd v Park Lane Estates Ltd [2005] EWHC 919 (TCC)
Partner Projects Ltd v Corinthian Nominees Ltd [2011] EWHC 2989 (TCC)
Paul Broadwell v k3D Property Partnership Ltd [2006] Adj.C.S. 04/21
R Durtnell & Sons Ltd v Kaduna Ltd [2003] EWHC 517 (TCC)
Rainford House Ltd v Cadogan Ltd [2001] BLR 416
RG Carter Ltd v Edmund Nuttall Ltd Unreported, 21 June 2000
Ringway Infrastructure Services Ltd v Vauxhall Motors Ltd (No 2) [2007] EWHC 2507 (TCC)
Ringway Infrastructure Services Ltd v Vauxhall Motors Ltd [2007] EWHC 2421 (TCC)
RJ Knapman Ltd v Richards [2006] EWHC 2518 (TCC)
ROK Build Ltd v Harris Wharf Development Company Ltd [2006] EWHC 3573 (TCC)
RSL (South West Ltd) v Stansell Ltd (No 1) [2003] EWHC 1390 (TCC)
Samuel Thomas Construction v J&B Developments [2000] CILL 1637
SG South Ltd. v King's Head Cirencester LLP & Anor [2009] EWHC 2645 (TCC)
Simons Construction Ltd v Aardvark Developments Ltd [2003] EWHC 2474 (TCC)
Sindall Ltd v Solland and Others [2001] All ER (D) 370 (Jun)
Sir Robert McAlpine v Pring & St Hill Ltd [2001] All ER (D) 484 (Oct)
Speymill Contracts Ltd v Eric Baskind [2009] No 9LV 22750
Speymill Contracts Ltd v Eric Baskind [2010] EWCA Civ 120
Stirling (t/a M&S Contracts) v Westminster Properties Scotland Ltd [2007] CSOH 117
Stubbs Rich Architects v W H Tolley & Son Ltd [2001] AdjLR 08/08
Surplant Ltd v Ballast plc (T/A Ballast Construction South West) [2002] EWHC TC33/02
Tera Construction Ltd v Yuk Tong Lam [2005] EWHC 3306 (TCC)
Thomas Vale Construction PLC v Brookside Syston Ltd [2006] EWHC 3637
Treasure & Son Ltd v Martin Dawes [2007] EWHC 2420 (TCC)

Try Construction Ltd v Eton Town House Group Ltd [2003] EWHC 60 (TCC)
VHE Construction plc v RBSTB Trust Co Ltd (as trustee of the Mercury Property Fund) [2000] BLR 187
Vitpol Building Service v Michael Samen [2008] EWHC 2283 (TCC)
Watkin Jones & Son Ltd v Lidl UK GmbH (No 2) [2002] EWHC 183 (TCC)
Watkin Jones & Son Ltd v Lidl UK GmbH [2002] CILL 1834
Westminster Building Company Ltd v Andrew Beckingham [2004] EWHC 138 (TCC)
Westwood Structural Services Ltd v Blyth Wood Park Management Company Ltd [2008] EWHC 3138 (TCC)
Whiteways Contractors (Sussex) Ltd v Impresa Castelli Construction UK Ltd (2000) 75 ConLR 92
William Verry Ltd v North West London Communal Mikvah [2004] EWHC 1300 (TCC)
William Verry Ltd v The Mayor and Burgesses of the London Borough of Camden [2006] EWHC 761 (TCC)
WW Gear Construction Ltd v McGee Group Ltd [2012] EWHC 1509 (TCC)
YCMS Ltd (t/a Young Construction Management Services) v Grabiner & Anor [2009] EWHC 127 (TCC)

6.3.3 ICE/ICC

AMEC Group Ltd v Thames Water Utilities Ltd [2010] EWHC 419 (TCC)
AWG Construction Services Ltd v Rockingham Motor Speedway Ltd [2004] EWHC 888 (TCC)
Barr Ltd v Law Mining Ltd [2001] ScotCS 152
Gibson (Banbridge) Ltd v Fermanagh District Council [2013] NIQB 16
J.T.Mackley v Gosport Marina Ltd [2002] EWHC 1315
Lafarge (Aggregates) Ltd. v London Borough of Newham [2005] EWHC 1337 (Comm)
Lanes Group plc v Galliford Try Infrastructure Ltd [2011] EWCA Civ 1617
Lanes Group plc v Galliford Try Infrastructure Ltd (No. 2) [2011] EWHC 1234 (TCC)
Lanes Group plc v Galliford Try Infrastructure Ltd [2011] EWHC 1035 (TCC)
Lanes Group plc v Galliford Try Infrastructure Ltd [2011] EWHC 1679 (TCC)
Rankilor (Dr Peter) & Perco Engineering Service Ltd v Igoe (M) Ltd [2006] AdjLR 01/27
Scrabster Harbour Trust v Mowlem plc t/a Mowlem Marine [2005] CSOH 44
Supablast (Nationwide) Ltd v Story Rail Ltd [2010] EWHC 56 (TCC)
The Construction Centre Group Ltd v The Highland Council [2002] ScotCS CSOH_354
The Construction Centre Group Ltd v The Highland Council [2003] ScotCS 114
The Highland Council v The Construction Centre Group Ltd [2003] ScotCS 221
Vertase FLI Ltd v Squibb Group Ltd [2012] EWHC 3194
VGC Construction Ltd v Jackson Civil Engineering Ltd [2008] EWHC 2082 (TCC)
Westshield Civil Engineering Ltd v Buckingham Group Contracting Ltd [2013] EWHC 1825 (TCC)

6.3.5 NEC

ABB Ltd v Bam Nuttall Ltd [2013] EWHC 1983 (TCC)
Arcadis UK Ltd v May and Baker Ltd (t/a Sanofi) [2013] EWHC 87 (TCC)
Devon County Council v Celtic Composting Systems Ltd [2014] EWHC 552 (TCC)
Farrelly (M&E) Building Services Ltd v Byrne Brothers (Formwork) Ltd [2013] EWHC 1186 (TCC)
John Mowlem & Company plc v Hydra-Tight Ltd (2001) 17 Const LJ 358
McConnell Dowell Constructors (Aust) Pty Ltd v National Grid Gas plc (formerly Transco plc) [2006] EWHC 2551 (TCC)
Northern Ireland Housing Executive v Healthy Buildings Ltd [2013] NIQB 124
RBG Ltd v SGL Carbon Fibers Ltd [2010] CSOH 77
ROK Building Ltd v Celtic Composting Systems Ltd [2009] EWHC 2664 (TCC)
SGL Carbon Fibres Ltd v RBG Ltd [2011] CSOH 62
Stork Technical Services (RBG) Ltd v Marion Howitson Ross [2015] CSOH 10A
Volker Stevin Ltd v Holystone Contracts Ltd [2010] EWHC 2344 (TCC)
Wales and West Utilities Ltd v PPS Pipeline Systems GmbH [2014] EWHC 54 (TCC)
WSP Cel Ltd v Dalkia Utilities Services plc [2012] EWHC 2428 (TCC)

6.3.6 TeCSA

A v B [2002] ScotCS 325
Balfour Kilpatrick Ltd v Glauser International SA [2000] Adj.C.S. 07/27
Deko Scotland Ltd v Edinburgh Royal Joint Venture & Anor [2003] ScotCS 113
Farebrother Building Services Ltd v Frogmore Investments Ltd [2001] CILL 1762
FW Cook Ltd v Shimizu (UK) Ltd [2000] BLR 199
Lead Technical Services v CMS Medical Ltd [2007] EWCA Civ 316
R and C Electrical Engineers Ltd v Shaylor Construction Ltd [2012] EWHC 1254 (TCC)
Re W. H. Malcolm Ltd [2010] CSOH 152
Shimizu Europe Ltd v Automajor Ltd [2002] EWHC 1571 (TCC)
Shimizu Europe Ltd v LBJ Fabrications Ltd [2003] EWHC 1229 (TCC)
Thermal Energy Construction Ltd v AE & E Lentjes UK Ltd [2009] EWHC 408 (TCC)
Yuanda (UK) Co Ltd v WW Gear Construction Ltd [2010] EWHC 720 (TCC)

6.3.7 CIC

Bouygues (UK) Ltd v Dahl-Jensen (UK) Ltd [1999] All ER (D) 1281
Bouygues (UK) Ltd v Dahl-Jensen (UK) Ltd [2000] EWCA Civ 507
Bridgeway Construction Ltd v Tolent Construction Ltd [2000] CILL 1626
David McLean Contractors Ltd v The Albany Building Ltd [2005] TCC101/05
Epping Electrical Company Ltd v Briggs and Forrester (Plumbing Services) Ltd [2007] EWHC 4 (TCC)
Galliford (UK) Ltd t/a Galliford Northern v Markel Capital Ltd [2003] EWHC 1216 (QB)

Hillview Industrial Developments (UK) Ltd v Botes Building Ltd [2006] EWHC 1365 (TCC)
Interserve Industrial Services Ltd v Cleveland Bridge UK Ltd [2006] EWHC 741 (TCC)
John Roberts Architects Ltd v Parkcare Homes (No. 2) Ltd [2005] EWHC 1637 (TCC)
John Roberts Architects Ltd v Parkcare Homes (No. 2) Ltd [2006] EWCA Civ 64
Primus Build Ltd v Pompey Centre Ltd & Anor [2009] EWHC 1487 (TCC)
ROK Building Ltd v Celtic Composting Systems Ltd (No 2) [2010] EWHC 66 (TCC)
Willmott Dixon Housing Limited (formerly Inspace Partnerships Limited) v Newlon Housing Trust [2013] EWHC 798 (TCC)

6.3.8 CEDR Solve

Carillion Construction Ltd v Stephen Andrew Smith [2011] EWHC 2910 (TCC)
Stiell Ltd v Riema Control Systems Ltd [2000] ScotCS 174

7 Preconditions and limits to a statutory adjudication

7.2 Is there a dispute?

7.2.2 Court's approach

All in One Building and Refurbishments Ltd v Makers UK Ltd [2005] EWHC 2943 (TCC) at [20–22]
Allied P&L Ltd v Paradigm Housing Group Ltd [2009] EWHC 2890 (TCC) at [30]
Bovis Lend Lease Ltd v The Trustees of the London Clinic [2009] EWHC 64 (TCC) at [47].
Cantillon Ltd v Urvasco Ltd [2008] EWHC 282 (TCC) at [55]
Cowlin Construction Ltd v CFW Architects (A Firm) [2002] EWHC 2914 (TCC) at [88]
Dean & Dyball v Kenneth Grubb Associates [2003] EWHC 2465 at [42]
Enterprise Managed Services Ltd v Tony McFadden Utilities Ltd [2009] EWHC 3222 (TCC) at [82]
Sindall Ltd v Solland and Others [2001] All ER (D) 370 (Jun) at [12]

7.2.3 A claim must have been made

All in One Building and Refurbishments Ltd v Makers UK Ltd [2005] EWHC 2943 (TCC) at [26–29]
Allied P&L Ltd v Paradigm Housing Group Ltd [2009] EWHC 2890 (TCC) at [30]
AMEC Civil Engineering Ltd v Secretary of State for Transport [2004] EWHC 2339 (TCC) at [68]
Cowlin Construction Ltd v CFW Architects (A Firm) [2002] EWHC 2914 (TCC) at [84–86]

Edmund Nuttall Ltd v R G Carter Ltd [2002] EWHC 400 (TCC) at [34]
Ringway Infrastructure Services Ltd v Vauxhall Motors Ltd [2007] EWHC 2421 (TCC) at [55]
VGC Construction Ltd v Jackson Civil Engineering Ltd [2008] EWHC 2082 (TCC) at [50–57]

7.2.4 The meaning of 'dispute' (Act s. 108(1))

All in One Building and Refurbishments Ltd v Makers UK Ltd [2005] EWHC 2943 (TCC) at [17–19]
Allied P&L Ltd v Paradigm Housing Group Ltd [2009] EWHC 2890 (TCC) at [29–30]
AMEC Civil Engineering Ltd v Secretary of State for Transport [2004] EWHC 2339 (TCC) at [61–68]
AMEC Civil Engineering Ltd v Secretary of State for Transport [2005] EWCA Civ 291 at [25–30; 65]
AWG Construction Services Ltd v Rockingham Motor Speedway Ltd [2004] EWHC 888 (TCC) at [129–146]
Balfour Beatty Engineering Services (HY) Ltd v Shepherd Construction Ltd [2009] EWHC 2218 (TCC) at [41]
Banner Holdings Ltd v Colchester Borough Council [2010] EWHC 139 (TCC) at [39]
Beck Interiors Ltd v UK Flooring Contractors Ltd [2012] EWHC 1808 (TCC) at [16–19]
Beck Peppiatt Ltd v Norwest Holst Construction Ltd [2003] EWHC 822 (TCC) at [2–5]
Bovis Lend Lease Ltd v The Trustees of the London Clinic [2009] EWHC 64 (TCC) at [40–47]
Cantillon Ltd v Urvasco Ltd [2008] EWHC 282 (TCC) at [55]
Carillion Construction Ltd v Devonport Royal Dockyard Ltd [2003] BLR 79 at [51–55]
CIB Properties Ltd v Birse Construction [2004] EWHC 2365 (TCC) at [18–19; 189–190]
Collins (Contractors) Ltd v Baltic Quay Management (1994) Ltd [2004] EWCA Civ 1757 at [53–64]
Costain Ltd v Wescol Steel Ltd [2003] EWHC 312 (TCC) at [5–7]
Dean & Dyball Construction Ltd v Kenneth Grubb Associates Ltd [2003] EWHC 2465 (TCC) at [41–42]
Devon County Council v Celtic Composting Systems Ltd [2014] EWHC 552 (TCC) at [14–24]
Edmund Nuttall Ltd v R G Carter Ltd [2002] EWHC 400 (TCC) at [32–36]
Fastrack Contractors Ltd v Morrison Construction Ltd & Anor [2000] All ER (D) 11 at [20–29]
Gibson (Banbridge) Ltd v Fermanagh District Council [2013] NIQB 16 at [6–20]
Herbosch-Kiere Marine Contractors Ltd v Dover Harbour Board [2012] EWHC 84 (TCC) at [23]
Karl Construction (Scotland) Ltd v Sweeney Civil Engineering (Scotland) Ltd [2002] SLT 312P/872/00 at [18–26]
Ken Griffin (t/a K&D Contractors) v Midas Homes Ltd (2000) 78 ConLR 152 at [6–7]

Lee v Chartered Properties (Building) Ltd [2010] EWHC 1540 (TCC) at [19]
London & Amsterdam Properties Ltd v Waterman Partnership Ltd [2003] EWHC 3059 (TCC) at [134–146]
Lovell Projects Ltd v Legg & Carver [2003] BLR 452 at [32–33]
McAlpine PPS Pipeline Systems Joint Venture v Transco plc [2004] EWHC 2030 (TCC) at [128–148]
Orange EBS Ltd v ABB Ltd [2003] EWHC 1187 (TCC) at [25]
RG Carter Ltd v Edmund Nuttall Ltd Unreported, 21 June 2000 at [28–37]
Ringway Infrastructure Services Ltd v Vauxhall Motors Ltd [2007] EWHC 2421 (TCC) at [55]
ROK Build Ltd v Harris Wharf Development Company Ltd [2006] EWHC 3573 (TCC) at [21–23]
St Austell Printing Company Ltd v Dawnus Construction Holdings Ltd [2015] EWHC 96 (TCC) at [20]
Stirling (t/a M&S Contracts) v Westminster Properties Scotland Ltd [2007] CSOH 117 at [8–9]
Watkin Jones & Son Ltd v Lidl UK GmbH (No 2) [2002] EWHC 183 (TCC) at [9]
William Verry (Glazing Systems) Ltd v Furlong Homes Ltd [2005] EWHC 138 (TCC) at [29–35]
Willmott Dixon Housing Limited (formerly Inspace Partnerships Limited) v Newlon Housing Trust [2013] EWHC 798 (TCC) at [76]
Witney Town Council v Beam Construction (Cheltenham) Ltd [2011] EWHC 2332 (TCC) at [38]
Working Environments Ltd v Greencoat Construction Ltd [2012] EWHC 1039 (TCC) at [23–24; 26–30]

(B) The nature of the response
Allied P&L Ltd v Paradigm Housing Group Ltd [2009] EWHC 2890 (TCC) at [30]
AMEC Civil Engineering Ltd v Secretary of State for Transport [2004] EWHC 2339 (TCC) at [68]
Carillion Construction Ltd v Devonport Royal Dockyard Ltd [2003] BLR 79 at [51–55]
CIB Properties Ltd v Birse Construction [2004] EWHC 2365 (TCC) at [19]
Collins (Contractors) Ltd v Baltic Quay Management (1994) Ltd [2004] EWCA Civ 1757 at [64]

(C) The meaning of the word 'difference'
Allied P&L Ltd v Paradigm Housing Group Ltd [2009] EWHC 2890 (TCC) at [31]
AMEC Civil Engineering Ltd v Secretary of State for Transport [2005] EWCA Civ 291 at [31]
CIB Properties Ltd v Birse Construction [2004] EWHC 2365 (TCC) at [16]
Stirling (t/a M&S Contracts) v Westminster Properties Scotland Ltd [2007] CSOH 117 at [10]

7.2.5 The point at which to assess whether there is a dispute

Allied P&L Ltd v Paradigm Housing Group Ltd [2009] EWHC 2890 (TCC) at [40]

Dean & Dyball Construction Ltd v Kenneth Grubb Associates Ltd [2003] EWHC 2465 (TCC) at [41]

Herbosch-Kiere Marine Contractors Limited v Dover Harbour Board [2012] EWHC 84 (TCC) at [23]

ROK Build Ltd v Harris Wharf Development Company Ltd [2006] EWHC 3573 (TCC) at [21–23]

Surplant Ltd v Ballast plc (T/A Ballast Construction South West) [2002] EWHC TC33/02 at [17–20]

7.2.6 The time period following the claim until a dispute is formed

All in One Building and Refurbishments Ltd v Makers UK Ltd [2005] EWHC 2943 (TCC) at [25]

AMEC Civil Engineering Ltd v Secretary of State for Transport [2004] EWHC 2339 (TCC) at [78]

AMEC Civil Engineering Ltd v Secretary of State for Transport [2005] EWCA Civ 291 at [31, 36, 64]

Beck Interiors Ltd v UK Flooring Contractors Ltd [2012] EWHC 1808 (TCC) at [26–27]

Enterprise Managed Services Ltd v Tony McFadden Utilities Ltd [2009] EWHC 3222 (TCC) at [80–90]

Gibson (Banbridge) Ltd v Fermanagh District Council [2013] NIQB 16 at [6–20]

Hitec Power Protection BV v MCI Worldcom Ltd [2002] EWHC 1953 (QB) at [86–88]

Orange EBS Ltd v ABB Ltd [2003] EWHC 1187 (TCC) at [37–43]

R Durtnell & Sons Ltd v Kaduna Ltd [2003] EWHC 517 (TCC) at [42–43]

7.2.8 Scenarios

(A) Exchange of correspondence or documents as evidence of dispute

Allied P&L Ltd v Paradigm Housing Group Ltd [2009] EWHC 2890 (TCC) at [36–37]

AMEC Civil Engineering Ltd v Secretary of State for Transport [2004] EWHC 2339 (TCC) at [74–78]

AMEC Civil Engineering Ltd v Secretary of State for Transport [2005] EWCA Civ 291 at [32–35, 62]

Beck Interiors Ltd v UK Flooring Contractors Ltd [2012] EWHC 1808 (TCC) at [26]

Beck Peppiatt Ltd v Norwest Holst Construction Ltd [2003] EWHC 822 (TCC) at [19–21]

Bovis Lend Lease Ltd v The Trustees of the London Clinic [2009] EWHC 64 (TCC) at [54–65]

British Waterways Board (Judicial Review) [2001] ScotCS 182 at [6–7]

CIB Properties Ltd v Birse Construction [2004] EWHC 2365 (TCC) at [18–19; 189–190]

Collins (Contractors) Ltd v Baltic Quay Management (1994) Ltd [2004] EWCA Civ 1757 at [65]

Cowlin Construction Ltd v CFW Architects (A Firm) [2002] EWHC 2914 (TCC) at [84–89]
Dean & Dyball Construction Ltd v Kenneth Grubb Associates Ltd [2003] EWHC 2465 (TCC) at [37–45]
Discain Project Services Ltd v Opecprime Development Ltd (No 1) [2000] BLR 402 at [5–6]
Edmund Nuttall Ltd v R G Carter Ltd [2002] EWHC 400 (TCC) at [38–40]
HS Works Ltd v Enterprise Managed Services Ltd [2009] EWHC 729 (TCC) at [53]
JW Hughes Building Contractors Ltd v GB Metalwork Ltd [2003] EWHC 2421 (TCC) at [4–11]
Ken Griffin (t/a K&D Contractors) v Midas Homes Ltd (2000) 78 ConLR 152 at [16–22]
London & Amsterdam Properties Ltd v Waterman Partnership Ltd [2003] EWHC 3059 (TCC) at [117–134; 147–150]
Midland Expressway Ltd & Ors v Carillion Construction Ltd & Ors (No. 3) [2006] EWHC 1505 (TCC) at [90–91; 96–98]
Multiplex Constructions (UK) Ltd v Mott MacDonald Ltd [2007] EWHC 20 (TCC) at [35–42]
Orange EBS Ltd v ABB Ltd [2003] EWHC 1187 (TCC) at [30–36]
PT Building Services Ltd v ROK Build Ltd [2008] EWHC 3434 (TCC) at [48–50]
Sindall Ltd v Solland and Others [2001] All ER (D) 370 (Jun) at [12–15]
South West Contractors Ltd v Birakos Enterprises Ltd [2006] EWHC 2794 (TCC) at [15–18; 27–29]
Stirling (t/a M&S Contracts) v Westminster Properties Scotland Ltd [2007] CSOH 117 at [11–28]
Surplant Ltd v Ballast plc (T/A Ballast Construction South West) [2002] EWHC TC33/02 at [17–20]
William Verry Ltd v North West London Communal Mikvah [2004] EWHC 1300 (TCC) at [31–39]

(B) Demand for payment, payment certificate, withholding notice as evidence of dispute
All in One Building and Refurbishments Ltd v Makers UK Ltd [2005] EWHC 2943 (TCC) at [23–24]
Aveat Heating Ltd v Jerram Falkus Construction Ltd [2007] EWHC 131 (TCC) at [18–22]
City Basements Ltd v Nordic Construction UK Ltd [2014] EWHC 4817 (TCC) at [31–34]
Costain Ltd v Wescol Steel Ltd [2003] EWHC 312 (TCC) at [8–10]
CPL Contracting Ltd v Cadenza Residential Ltd [2005] AdjLR 01/31 at [8–15]
CSK Electrical Contractors Ltd v Kingwood Electrical Services Ltd [2015] EWHC 667 (TCC) at [6–7]
Discain Project Services Ltd v Opecprime Development Ltd (No 1) [2000] BLR 402 at [4]
Enterprise Managed Services Ltd v Tony McFadden Utilities Ltd [2009] EWHC 3222 (TCC) at [80–90]

Fastrack Contractors Ltd v Morrison Construction Ltd & Anor [2000] All ER (D) 11 at [33–40]
KNS Industrial Services (Birmingham) Ltd v Sindall Ltd (2001) 75 ConLR 71 at [18–21]
Lee v Chartered Properties (Building) Ltd [2010] EWHC 1540 (TCC) at [20]
Lovell Projects Ltd v Legg & Carver [2003] BLR 452 at [34–35]
Malcolm Charles Contracts Ltd v Mr Crispin and Mrs Zhang [2014] EWHC 3898 (TCC) at [34–41]
Midland Expressway Ltd v Carillion Construction Ltd & Ors (No. 2) [2005] EWHC 2963 (TCC) at [53–60]
Northern Developments (Cumbria) Ltd v J & J Nichol [2000] All ER (D) 68 at [29–31]
Orange EBS Ltd v ABB Ltd [2003] EWHC 1187 (TCC) at [37–43]
Redworth Construction Ltd v Brookdale Healthcare Ltd [2006] EWHC 1994 (TCC) at [48–49]
Ringway Infrastructure Services Ltd v Vauxhall Motors Ltd [2007] EWHC 2421 (TCC) at [75–78; 84]
St Austell Printing Company Ltd v Dawnus Construction Holdings Ltd [2015] EWHC 96 (TCC) at [17–21]
Working Environments Ltd v Greencoat Construction Ltd [2012] EWHC 1039 (TCC) at [26–30]

(C) Without prejudice material
RWE Npower plc v Alstom Power Ltd [2009] EWHC 1192 (QB) at [48–55]

(D) Document not served correctly
Palmac Contracting Ltd v Park Lane Estates Ltd [2005] EWHC 919 (TCC) at [15–21]

(E) Wrong party
A.T. Stannard Ltd v James Tobutt and Thomas Tobutt [2014] EWHC 3491 (TCC) at [18]
Discain Project Services Ltd v Opecprime Development Ltd (No 1) [2000] BLR 402 at [5–6]
Enterprise Managed Services Ltd v Tony McFadden Utilities Ltd [2009] EWHC 3222 (TCC) at [80–90]

(F) Claim abandoned
Edmund Nuttall Ltd v R G Carter Ltd [2002] EWHC 400 (TCC) at [38]
Enterprise Managed Services Ltd v Tony McFadden Utilities Ltd [2009] EWHC 3222 (TCC) at [61–79]
VGC Construction Ltd v Jackson Civil Engineering Ltd [2008] EWHC 2082 (TCC) at [49; 59]

(G) Dispute settled
Bracken and another v Billinghurst [2003] EWHC 1333 (TCC) at [28–30]
GPS Marine Contractors Ltd v Ringway Infrastructure Services Ltd [2010] EWHC 283 (TCC) at [41–44]
Joseph Finney plc v Gordon Vickers and Gary Vickers t/a Mill Hotel (A Firm) [2001]

AdjLR 03/07 at [30–40]
Lee v Chartered Properties (Building) Ltd [2010] EWHC 1540 (TCC) at [22]
McConnell Dowell Constructors (Aust) Pty Ltd v National Grid Gas plc (formerly Transco plc) [2006] EWHC 2551 (TCC) at [30–44]
Quality Street Properties (Trading) Ltd v Elmwood (Glasgow) Ltd [2002] CILL 1922 at [8–9]
Shepherd Construction Ltd v Mecright Ltd [2000] BLR 489 at [16–21]

(H) Creep between crystallisation and referral
Allied P&L Ltd v Paradigm Housing Group Ltd [2009] EWHC 2890 (TCC) at [41–42]
Beck Interiors Ltd v UK Flooring Contractors Ltd [2012] EWHC 1808 (TCC) at [28–31]
Lidl UK GmbH v RG Carter Colchester Ltd [2012] EWHC 3138 at [49–53]
OSC Building Services Ltd v Interior Dimensions Contracts Ltd [2009] EWHC 248 (TCC) at [9–15]

(I) Creep during adjudication
Bovis Lend Lease Ltd v The Trustees of the London Clinic [2009] EWHC 64 (TCC) at [47]
Dean & Dyball Construction Ltd v Kenneth Grubb Associates Ltd [2003] EWHC 2465 (TCC) at [45–47]
J and A Construction (Scotland) Ltd v Windex Ltd [2013] CSOH 170 at [15–19]
William Verry (Glazing Systems) Ltd v Furlong Homes Ltd [2005] EWHC 138 (TCC) at [35–39]

7.3 More than one dispute

7.3.2 More than one dispute (Act s. 108(1))

Balfour Kilpatrick Ltd v Glauser International SA [2000] Adj.C.S. 07/27 at [4]
Barr Ltd v Law Mining Ltd [2001] ScotCS 152 at [14–15; 25–27]
Bothma (t/a DAB Builders) v Mayhaven Healthcare Ltd [2007] EWCA Civ 527 at [7–13]
Bothma (t/a DAB Builders) v Mayhaven Healthcare Ltd [2006] EWHC 2601 (QB) at [26–34]
Chamberlain Carpentry & Joinery Ltd v Alfred MacAlpine Construction Ltd [2002] EWHC 514 (TCC) at [11–18]
Costain Ltd v Wescol Steel Ltd [2003] EWHC 312 (TCC) at [11–13]
Dalkia Energy and Technical Services Ltd v Bell Group UK Ltd [2009] EWHC 73 (TCC) at [89–92]
David McLean Housing Contractors Ltd v Swansea Housing Association Ltd [2001] All ER (D) 519 (Jul) at [8–12]
Enterprise Managed Services Ltd v Tony McFadden Utilities Ltd [2009] EWHC 3222 (TCC) at [61–79]

Fastrack Contractors Ltd v Morrison Construction Ltd & Anor [2000] All ER (D) 11 at [20]
GPS Marine Contractors Ltd v Ringway Infrastructure Services Ltd [2010] EWHC 283 (TCC) at [45–55]
Hillcrest Homes Ltd v Beresford & Curbishley Ltd [2014] EWHC 280 (TCC) at [54–60]
Imtech Inviron Ltd v Loppingdale Plant Ltd [2014] EWHC 4006 (TCC) at [30–34]
Lee v Chartered Properties (Building) Ltd [2010] EWHC 1540 (TCC) at [21]
Mecright Ltd v TA Morris Developments Ltd [2001] AdjLR 06/22 at [33–35]
Michael John Construction Ltd v Golledge & Ors [2006] EWHC 71 (TCC) at [26–28; 51–53]
Pring & St. Hill Ltd v C J Hafner t/a Southern Erectors [2002] EWHC 1775 (TCC) at [21–22]
PT Building Services Ltd v ROK Build Ltd [2008] EWHC 3434 (TCC) at [43–46]
RWE Npower plc v Alstom Power Ltd [2009] EWHC 1192 (QB) at [32–47]
Speymill Contracts Ltd v Eric Baskind [2009] No 9LV 22750 at [81–83]
TSG Building Services plc v South Anglia Housing Ltd [2013] EWHC 1151 (TCC) at [20–22]
Vision Homes Ltd v Lancsville Construction Ltd [2009] EWHC 2042 (TCC) at [70–71]
Willmott Dixon Housing Limited (formerly Inspace Partnerships Limited) v Newlon Housing Trust [2013] EWHC 798 (TCC) at [68–76]
Witney Town Council v Beam Construction (Cheltenham) Ltd [2011] EWHC 2332 (TCC) at [31–40]

7.3.3 More than one dispute (Scheme p. 8(1))

Bothma (t/a DAB Builders) v Mayhaven Healthcare Ltd [2007] EWCA Civ 527 at [4]
Bothma (t/a DAB Builders) v Mayhaven Healthcare Ltd [2006] EWHC 2601 (QB) at [26]
David McLean Housing Contractors Ltd v Swansea Housing Association Ltd [2001] All ER (D) 519 (Jul) at [8–12]
Mecright Ltd v TA Morris Developments Ltd [2001] AdjLR 06/22 at [34–35]
R Durtnell & Sons Ltd v Kaduna Ltd [2003] EWHC 517 (TCC) at [41]

7.4 Substantially the same dispute

7.4.2 Substantively the same dispute – principle

Arcadis UK Ltd v May and Baker Ltd (t/a Sanofi) [2013] EWHC 87 (TCC) at [31–36]
Balfour Beatty Engineering Services (HY) Ltd v Shepherd Construction Ltd [2009] EWHC 2218 (TCC) at [41]
Barr Ltd v Klin Investment Ltd [2009] ScotCS CSOH 104 at [31–34]
Bell Building Projects Ltd v Carfin Developments Ltd [2010] ScotSC 19 at [14]
Benfield Construction Ltd v Trudson (Hatton) Ltd [2008] EWHC 2333 (TCC) at [20–36]

Birmingham City Council v Paddison Construction Ltd [2008] EWHC 2254 (TCC) at [15–29]
Carillion Construction Ltd v Stephen Andrew Smith [2011] EWHC 2910 (TCC) at [53–57]
HG Construction Ltd v Ashwell Homes (East Anglia) Ltd [2007] EWHC 144 (TCC) at [31–40]
Holt Insulation Ltd v Colt International Ltd [2001] EWHC 451 (TCC) at [22]
HS Works Ltd v Enterprise Managed Services Ltd [2009] EWHC 729 (TCC) at [38]
Matthew Harding (t/a M J Harding Contractors) v Paice and Springall [2014] EWHC 3824 (TCC) at [41–46]
Prentice Island Ltd v Castle Contracting Ltd [2003] ScotCS 61 at [13–18]
Quietfield Ltd v Vascroft Construction Ltd [2006] EWCA Civ 1737 at [45–48]
Redwing Construction Ltd v Charles Wishart [2010] EWHC 3366 (TCC) at [25–27]
SGL Carbon Fibres Ltd v RBG Ltd [2011] CSOH 62 at [47]
Sherwood & Casson Ltd v Mackenzie [2000] CILL 1577 at [30–31]
Vertase FLI Ltd v Squibb Group Ltd [2012] EWHC 3194 at [46–50]

7.4.2 Substantively the same dispute – the same

Benfield Construction Ltd v Trudson (Hatton) Ltd [2008] EWHC 2333 (TCC) at [37–50]
Birmingham City Council v Paddison Construction Ltd [2008] EWHC 2254 (TCC) at [15–29]
Carillion Construction Ltd v Stephen Andrew Smith [2011] EWHC 2910 (TCC) at [58–67]
Eurocom Ltd v Siemens plc [2014] EWHC 3710 (TCC) at [118]
HG Construction Ltd v Ashwell Homes (East Anglia) Ltd [2007] EWHC 144 (TCC) at [96–104]
ISG Construction Ltd v Seevic College [2014] EWHC 4007 (TCC) at [34–41]
Paice and Springall v Matthew Harding (t/a M J Harding Contractors) [2015] EWHC 661 (TCC) at [62–64]
SGL Carbon Fibres Ltd v RBG Ltd [2011] CSOH 62 at [48]
Vertase FLI Ltd v Squibb Group Ltd [2012] EWHC 3194 at [46–50]
Watkin Jones & Son Ltd v Lidl UK GmbH [2002] CILL 1834 at [16–26]
William Naylor t/a Powerfloated Concrete Floors v Greenacres Curling Ltd [2001] ScotCS 163 at [8]

7.4.2 Substantively the same dispute – not the same

Arcadis UK Ltd v May and Baker Ltd (t/a Sanofi) [2013] EWHC 87 (TCC) at [31–36]
Balfour Beatty Engineering Services (HY) Ltd v Shepherd Construction Ltd [2009] EWHC 2218 (TCC) at [63–65]
Barr Ltd v Klin Investment Ltd [2009] ScotCS CSOH 104 at [35–40]
Bell Building Projects Ltd v Carfin Developments Ltd [2010] ScotSC 19 at [14]

Case index: by subject matter 611

>Bell Building Projects Ltd v Carfin Developments Ltd [2010] ScotSC 68 at [39–46]
>David McLean Contractors Ltd v The Albany Building Ltd [2005] TCC101/05 at [15–21]
>DGT Steel and Cladding Ltd v Cubitt Building and Interiors Ltd [2007] EWHC 1584 (TCC) at [33–38]
>Emcor Drake & Scull Ltd v Costain Construction Ltd & Skanska Central Europe AB (t/a Costain Skanska Joint Venture) [2004] EWHC 2439 (TCC) at [18]
>Holt Insulation Ltd v Colt International Ltd [2001] AdjLR 01/09 at [22]
>KNN Coburn LLP v GD City Holdings Ltd [2013] EWHC 2879 (TCC) at [41–43]
>Matthew Harding (t/a M J Harding Contractors) v Paice and Springall [2014] EWHC 3824 (TCC) at [41–46]
>Mel Davidson Construction v Northern Ireland Housing Executive [2014] NIQB 110 at [18–21]
>Michael John Construction Ltd v Golledge & Ors [2006] EWHC 71 (TCC) at [58–63]
>Mivan Ltd v Lighting Technology Projects Ltd [2001] Adj.C.S. 04/09 at [10]
>Quietfield Ltd v Vascroft Construction Ltd [2006] EWCA Civ 1737 at [39–44; 49]
>Quietfield Ltd v Vascroft Construction Ltd [2006] EWHC 174 (TCC) at [32–51]
>Re W. H. Malcolm Ltd [2010] CSOH 152 at [28]
>Redwing Construction Ltd v Charles Wishart [2010] EWHC 3366 (TCC) at [29–34]
>Sherwood & Casson Ltd v Mackenzie [2000] CILL 1577 at [32–37]
>Skanska Construction UK Ltd v ERDC Group Ltd & Anor [2002] ScotCS 307 at [28]
>SW Global Resourcing Limited v Morris & Spottiswood Limited [2012] CSOH 200 at [19–24]
>VHE Construction plc v RBSTB Trust Co Ltd (as trustee of the Mercury Property Fund) [2000] BLR 187 at [47–48]
>Vision Homes Ltd v Lancsville Construction Ltd [2009] EWHC 2042 (TCC) at [70–74]

7.5 Does the dispute arise 'under' the contract (Act s. 108(1))

7.5.2 The meaning of 'under' the contract

>Adonis Construction v O'Keefe Soil Remediation [2009] EWHC 2047 (TCC) at [49–50].
>Air Design (Kent) Ltd v Deerglen (Jersey) Ltd [2008] EWHC 3047 (TCC) at [22]
>AMEC Group Ltd v Thames Water Utilities Ltd [2010] EWHC 419 (TCC) at [29]
>Ballast plc v The Burrell Company (Construction Management) Ltd [2001] ScotCS 159 at [42]
>C&B Scene Concept Design Ltd v Isobars Ltd [2001] CILL 1781 at [24–30]
>C&B Scene Concept Design Ltd v Isobars Ltd [2002] EWCA Civ 46 at [21–31]
>Camillin Denny Architects Ltd v Adelaide Jones & Company Ltd [2009] EWHC 2110 (TCC) at [28–31]
>Capital Structures plc v Time & Tide Construction Ltd [2006] EWHC 591 (TCC) at [16–30]

Christiani & Nielsen Ltd v The Lowry Centre Development Company Ltd [2000] AdjLR 06/16 at [38–45]
Dalkia Energy and Technical Services Ltd v Bell Group UK Ltd [2009] EWHC 73 (TCC) at [42]
Devon County Council v Celtic Composting Systems Ltd [2014] EWHC 552 (TCC) at [25]
Discain Project Services Ltd v Opecprime Development Ltd (No 2) [2001] All ER (D) 123 at [43–48]
Gillies Ramsay Diamond and Gavin Ramsay and Philip Diamond v PJW Enterprises Ltd [2003] ScotCS 343 at [21]
Gillies Ramsay Diamond v PJW Enterprises Ltd [2002] ScotCS 340 at [67–70]
Hillcrest Homes Ltd v Beresford & Curbishley Ltd [2014] EWHC 280 (TCC) at [47–53]
ISG Retail Ltd v Castletech Construction Ltd [2015] EWHC 1443 (TCC) at [13–28]
L Brown & Sons Ltd v Crosby Homes (North West) Ltd [2005] EWHC 3503 (TCC) at [49–55]
Michael John Construction Ltd v Golledge & Ors [2006] EWHC 71 (TCC) at [54–57]
Multiplex Constructions (UK) Ltd v Mott MacDonald Ltd [2007] EWHC 20 (TCC) at [43–48]
Pegram Shopfitters Ltd v Tally Wiejl (UK) Ltd [2003] EWHC 984 (TCC) at [26; 30]
RG Carter Ltd v Edmund Nuttall Ltd Unreported, 21 June 2000 at [25]
SG South Ltd. v King's Head Cirencester LLP & Anor [2009] EWHC 2645 (TCC) at [19–37]
Shepherd Construction Ltd v Mecright Ltd [2000] BLR 489 at [16–18]
Speymill Contracts Ltd v Eric Baskind [2010] EWCA Civ 120 at [36]
Supablast (Nationwide) Ltd v Story Rail Ltd [2010] EWHC 56 (TCC) at [29]
Viridis UK Limited v Mulalley and Company Limited [2014] EWHC 268 (TCC) at [80–82]
Watson Building Services Ltd [2001] ScotCS 60 at [25]
Westminster Building Company Ltd v Andrew Beckingham [2004] EWHC 138 (TCC) at [22–28]

7.6 More than one contract

7.6.2 More than one contract (Act s. 108(1))

Air Design (Kent) Ltd v Deerglen (Jersey) Ltd [2008] EWHC 3047 (TCC) at [21–24]
AMEC Group Ltd v Thames Water Utilities Ltd [2010] EWHC 419 (TCC) at [35–39]
Charles Henshaw & Sons Ltd v Stewart & Shields Ltd [2014] CSIH 55 at [19]
Charles Henshaw & Sons Ltd v Stewart & Shields Ltd [2014] ScotSC 59 at [19–26]
Enterprise Managed Services Ltd v Tony McFadden Utilities Ltd [2010] EWHC 1506 (TCC) at [62]
GPS Marine Contractors Ltd v Ringway Infrastructure Services Ltd [2010] EWHC 283 (TCC) at [45–55]
Grovedeck Ltd v Capital Demolition Ltd [2000] All ER (D) 317 at [33–36]

Supablast (Nationwide) Ltd v Story Rail Ltd [2010] EWHC 56 (TCC) at [26–35]
Viridis UK Limited v Mulalley and Company Limited [2014] EWHC 268 (TCC) at [64–68]

7.6.3 More than one contract (Scheme p. 8(2))

Pring & St. Hill Ltd v C J Hafner t/a Southern Erectors [2002] EWHC 1775 (TCC) at [13–22]

7.7 Commencing an adjudication 'at any time'

7.7.2 Act (s.108(2)(a))

City Basements Ltd v Nordic Construction UK Ltd [2014] EWHC 4817 (TCC) at [28]
Connex South Eastern Ltd v M J Building Services Group plc [2005] EWCA Civ 193 at [38–42]
Connex South Eastern Ltd v MJ Building Services Group plc [2004] EWHC 1518 (TCC) at [33–34]
Cubitt Building & Interiors Ltd v Richardson Roofing (Industrial) Ltd [2008] EWHC 1020 (TCC) at [72]
Cygnet Healthcare plc v Higgins City Ltd (2000) 16 Const LJ 394 at [20–27]
DGT Steel and Cladding Ltd v Cubitt Building and Interiors Ltd [2007] EWHC 1584 at [12 and 21]
Enterprise Managed Services Ltd v East Midland Contracting Ltd [2008] EWHC 727 (TCC) at [32–36]
Ericsson AB v EADS Defence and Security Systems Ltd [2009] EWHC 2598 (TCC) at [49–60]
Herschell Engineering Ltd v Breen Property Ltd [2000] All ER (D) 559 at [15–20]
Mentmore Towers Ltd v Packman Lucas Ltd [2010] EWHC 457 (TCC) at [22]
Morphuse Framing Solutions Ltd v Bracknell Property Ltd, Unreported, 31 July 2014 at [23]
Profile Projects Ltd v Elmwood (Glasgow) Ltd [2011] CSOH 64 at [40]
The Mayor and Burgesses of the London Borough of Camden v Makers UK Ltd [2009] EWHC 605 (TCC) at [30–31]
Twintec Ltd v Volkerfitzpatrick Ltd [2014] EWHC 10 (TCC) at [67–73]
Willmott Dixon Housing Limited (formerly Inspace Partnerships Limited) v Newlon Housing Trust [2013] EWHC 798 (TCC) at [68–76]
WSP Cel Ltd v Dalkia Utilities Services plc [2012] EWHC 2428 (TCC) at [86–89]

7.7.3 Conclusivity clauses

Bennett v FMK Construction Ltd [2005] EWHC 1268 (TCC) at [15–20]
Cubitt Building and Interiors Ltd v Richardson Roofing (Industrial) Ltd [2008] EWHC 1020 (TCC) at [72–74]

Jerram Falkus Construction Ltd v Fenice Investments Inc (No 4) [2011] EWHC 1935 (TCC) at [28–37]

The Trustees of the Marc Gilbard 2009 Settlement Trust v OD Developments and Projects Ltd [2015] EWHC 70 (TCC) at [22–40]

University of Brighton v Dovehouse Interiors Limited [2014] EWHC 940 (TCC) at [40–52; 75–98]

8 Adjudication strategy

8.4 Choosing the right dispute to refer

8.4.4 Smash and grab

Caledonian Modular Ltd v Mar City Developments Ltd [2015] EWHC 1855 (TCC) at [30–53]

Galliford Try Building v Estura Ltd [2015] EWHC 412 (TCC) at [44–52]

ISG Construction Ltd v Seevic College [2014] EWHC 4007 (TCC) at [22–33; 42–53]

Leeds City Council v Waco UK Ltd [2015] EWHC 1400 (TCC) at [63–66]

Matthew Harding (t/a M J Harding Contractors) v Paice and Springall [2014] EWHC 3824 (TCC) at [25–37]

Morphuse Framing Solutions Ltd v Bracknell Property Ltd, Unreported, 31 July 2014 at [20–26]

Watkin Jones & Son Ltd v Lidl UK GmbH (No 2) [2002] EWHC 183 (TCC) at [16–26]

8.4.5 Cherry-picking

Ameycespa v Taimweser [2014] EWHC 4638 (TCC) at [31–33]

Fastrack Contractors Ltd v Morrison Construction Ltd & Anor [2000] All ER (D) 11 at [23]

St Austell Printing Company Ltd v Dawnus Construction Holdings Ltd [2015] EWHC 96 (TCC) at [25–33]

8.4.6 Large scale adjudications

Enterprise Managed Services Ltd v Tony McFadden Utilities Ltd [2009] EWHC 3222 (TCC) at [90–99]

William Verry (Glazing Systems) Ltd v Furlong Homes Ltd [2005] EWHC 138 (TCC) at [11]

8.4.7 Without prejudice correspondence

RWE Npower plc v Alstom Power Ltd [2009] EWHC 1192 (QB) at [48–55]

8.6 Assessing the other party's willingness and ability to pay

8.6.1 Securing assets before the adjudication

> Pynes Three Ltd v Transco Ltd [2005] EWHC 2445 (TCC) at [4–22]

9 Initiating the adjudication

9.3 The notice of adjudication

9.3.2 The Scheme (Scheme p. 1(2) and (3))

> Aveat Heating Ltd v Jerram Falkus Construction Ltd [2007] EWHC 131 (TCC) at [23]
> Ballast plc v The Burrell Company (Construction Management) Ltd [2001] ScotCS 159 at [29]
> D G Williamson Ltd v Northern Ireland Prison Service [2009] NIQB 8 at [23–24]
> Ecovision Systems Ltd v Vinci Construction UK Ltd [2015] EWHC 587 (TCC) at [79–81]
> Herschell Engineering Ltd v Breen Property Ltd [2000] All ER (D) 559 at [18]
> Lee v Chartered Properties (Building) Ltd [2010] EWHC 1540 (TCC) at [15–16]
> Primus Build Ltd v Pompey Centre Ltd & Anor [2009] EWHC 1487 (TCC) at [14–15]
> University of Brighton v Dovehouse Interiors Limited [2014] EWHC 940 (TCC) at [40–52; 62–68; 69–74]
> Westdawn Refurbishments Ltd v Roselodge Ltd [2006] AdjLR 04/24 at [53–54]
> Williams (t/a Sanclair Construction) v Noor (t/a India Kitchen) [2007] EWHC 3467 (TCC) at [73–75]

9.3.3 Practical considerations

> Ameycespa v Taimweser [2014] EWHC 4638 (TCC) at [31–33]
> Ballast plc v The Burrell Company (Construction Management) Ltd [2002] ScotCS 324 at [17–20]
> Cain Electrical Ltd v Richard Cox t/a Pennine Control Systems [2011] EWHC 2681 (TCC) at [31–33]
> Carillion Construction Ltd v Devonport Royal Dockyard Ltd [2005] EWCA Civ 1358 at [22]
> Chamberlain Carpentry & Joinery Ltd v Alfred MacAlpine Construction Ltd [2002] EWHC 514 (TCC) at [16–19]
> Fastrack Contractors Ltd v Morrison Construction Ltd & Anor [2000] All ER (D) 11 at [20]
> Gary Kitt and EC Harris LLP v The Laundry Building Ltd and Etcetera Construction Services Ltd [2014] EHWC 4250 (TCC) at [24]
> Jerome Engineering Ltd v Lloyd Morris Electrical Ltd [2002] CILL 1827 at [20]
> KNS Industrial Services (Birmingham) Ltd v Sindall Ltd (2001) 75 ConLR 71 at [21]

Letchworth Roofing Company v Sterling Building Company [2009] EWHC 1119 (TCC) at [17]
Mecright Ltd v TA Morris Developments Ltd [2001] AdjLR 06/22 at [21–34]
OSC Building Services Ltd v Interior Dimensions Contracts Ltd [2009] EWHC 248 (TCC) at [14]
Pilon Ltd v Breyer Group plc [2010] EWHC 837 (TCC) at [27]
Roland Horne v Magna Design Building Ltd and Marcus Build Décor Ltd [2014] EWHC 3380 (TCC) at [14]
St Austell Printing Company Ltd v Dawnus Construction Holdings Ltd [2015] EWHC 96 (TCC) at [25–33]
Tera Construction Ltd v Yuk Tong Lam [2005] EWHC 3306 (TCC) at [16]
Vision Homes Ltd v Lancsville Construction Ltd [2009] EWHC 2042 (TCC) at [51–57]
Witney Town Council v Beam Construction (Cheltenham) Ltd [2011] EWHC 2332 (TCC) at [38]

9.6 Appointing the adjudicator

9.6.3 Appointment procedure (Scheme p. 2, 3, 5 and 6)

Carillion Construction Ltd v Devonport Royal Dockyard Ltd [2005] EWCA Civ 1358 at [21]
IDE Contracting Ltd v RG Carter Cambridge Ltd [2004] EWHC 36 (TCC) at [9–11]
Lee v Chartered Properties (Building) Ltd [2010] EWHC 1540 (TCC) at [15–16]
Palmac Contracting Ltd v Park Lane Estates Ltd [2005] EWHC 919 (TCC) at [30–36]
Sprunt Ltd v London Borough of Camden [2011] EWHC 3191 (TCC) at [44–51]

9.6.5 Appointment by an ANB

CSK Electrical Contractors Ltd v Kingwood Electrical Services Ltd [2015] EWHC 667 (TCC) at [9–14]
Eurocom Ltd v Siemens plc [2014] EWHC 3710 (TCC) at [57–79]
Makers UK Ltd v The Mayor and Burgesses of the London Borough of Camden [2008] EWHC 1836 (TCC) at [29; 35]

9.6.7 Forum shopping

Cleveland Bridge (UK) Ltd v Whessoe-Volker Stevin Joint Venture [2010] EWHC 1076 (TCC) at [87–90; 93–106]
CSK Electrical Contractors Ltd v Kingwood Electrical Services Ltd [2015] EWHC 667 (TCC) at [9–14]
Eurocom Ltd v Siemens Plc [2014] EWHC 3710 (TCC) at [57–79]
Lanes Group plc v Galliford Try Infrastructure Ltd [2011] EWCA Civ 1617 at [35–43]
Lanes Group plc v Galliford Try Infrastructure Ltd [2011] EWHC 1035 (TCC) at [32]

Lanes Group plc v Galliford Try Infrastructure Ltd [2011] EWHC 1679 (TCC) at [21–53]

9.6.8 Appointment of an individual named in the contract

John Mowlem & Company plc v Hydra-Tight Ltd (2001) 17 Const LJ 358 at [23]

9.6.10 Natural person and no conflict of interest (Scheme, p. 4)

Faithful & Gould Ltd v Arcal Ltd and Ors. [2001] AdjLR 05/25 at [2]

9.6.11 Objections to a proposed appointment (Scheme, p. 10)

Pring & St. Hill Ltd v C J Hafner t/a Southern Erectors [2002] EWHC 1775 (TCC) at [17]

9.6.15 Adjudicator's agreement

Cartwright v Fay [2005] AdjLR 02/09 at [10–11]
Cubitt Building & Interiors Ltd v Fleetglade Ltd [2006] EWHC 3413 (TCC) at [77–81]
Linnett v Halliwells LLP [2009] EWHC 319 at [37–38]
PC Harrington Contractors Ltd v Systech International Ltd [2012] EWCA Civ 1371 at [23–37; 42–46]
Stork Technical Services (RBG) Ltd v Marion Howitson Ross [2015] CSOH 10A at [21–23; 38]
Stubbs Rich Architects v W H Tolley & Son Ltd [2001] AdjLR 08/08 at [10–21]

9.6.16 Revoking the appointment (Scheme p. 11)

Paul Jensen Ltd v Staveley Industries plc [2001] AdjLR 09/27 at [1–4]
PC Harrington Contractors Ltd v Systech International Ltd [2012] EWCA Civ 1371 at [23–37; 42–46]
Rankilor (Dr Peter) & Perco Engineering Service Ltd v Igoe (M) Ltd [2006] AdjLR 01/27 at [33]
Stubbs Rich Architects v W H Tolley & Son Ltd [2001] AdjLR 08/08 at [10–21]

10. The adjudication

10.2 The referral notice

10.2.2 Timing (Act s. 108(2)(b))

Aveat Heating Ltd v Jerram Falkus Construction Ltd [2007] EWHC 131 (TCC) at [10–11]

Carillion Construction Ltd v Devonport Royal Dockyard Ltd [2005] EWCA Civ 1358 at [22]
Cubitt Building & Interiors Ltd v Fleetglade Ltd [2006] EWHC 3413 (TCC) at [41–47]
Hart Investments Ltd v Fidler & Anor [2006] EWHC 2857 (TCC) at [40–54]
Lanes Group plc v Galliford Try Infrastructure Ltd (No. 2) [2011] EWHC 1234 (TCC) at [14–20]
Lanes Group plc v Galliford Try Infrastructure Ltd [2011] EWHC 1035 (TCC) at [20, 29]
Linnett v Halliwells LLP [2009] EWHC 319 at [88–106]
Pegram Shopfitters Ltd v Tally Wiejl (UK) Ltd [2003] EWHC 984 (TCC) at [30]
Ritchie Brothers (Pwc) Ltd v David Philp (Commercials) Ltd [2004] ScotCS 94 at [6–7]
William Verry Ltd v North West London Communal Mikvah [2004] EWHC 1300 (TCC) at [18–30]
Willmott Dixon Housing Limited (formerly Inspace Partnerships Limited) v Newlon Housing Trust [2013] EWHC 798 (TCC) at [46–56]

10.2.3 Scheme (Scheme p. 7)

Aveat Heating Ltd v Jerram Falkus Construction Ltd [2007] EWHC 131 (TCC) at [10–11]
Hart Investments Ltd v Fidler & Anor [2006] EWHC 2857 (TCC) at [40–54]
KNN Coburn LLP v GD City Holdings Ltd [2013] EWHC 2879 (TCC) at [21–26]
London & Amsterdam Properties Ltd v Waterman Partnership Ltd [2003] EWHC 3059 (TCC) at [96–116]
PT Building Services Ltd v ROK Build Ltd [2008] EWHC 3434 (TCC) at [52–55]

10.3 The response

10.3.2 Timing

CJP Builders Ltd v William Verry Ltd [2008] EWHC 2025 (TCC) at [78–86]
Ecovision Systems Ltd v Vinci Construction UK Ltd [2015] EWHC 587 (TCC) at [60]

10.3.3 Scope of the defence

Ameycespa v Taimweser [2014] EWHC 4638 (TCC) at [24–31]
Cantillon Ltd v Urvasco Ltd [2008] EWHC 282 (TCC) at [54–55; 69]
CJP Builders Ltd v William Verry Ltd [2008] EWHC 2025 (TCC) at [78–86]
Gary Kitt and EC Harris LLP v The Laundry Building Ltd and Etcetera Construction Services Ltd [2014] EHWC 4250 (TCC) at [25–28]
KNS Industrial Services (Birmingham) Ltd v Sindall Ltd (2001) 75 ConLR 71 at [21]
Pilon Limited v Breyer Group plc [2010] EWHC 837 (TCC) at [16]
Quartzelec Ltd v Honeywell Control Systems Ltd [2008] EWHC 3315 (TCC) at [27–30]

Roland Horne v Magna Design Building Ltd and Marcus Build Décor Ltd [2014] EWHC 3380 (TCC) at [14]
SG South Ltd. v King's Head Cirencester LLP & Anor [2009] EWHC 2645 (TCC) at [19]
Viridis UK Limited v Mulalley and Company Limited [2014] EWHC 268 (TCC) at [104–105]
William Verry (Glazing Systems) Ltd v Furlong Homes Ltd [2005] EWHC 138 (TCC) at [29–49]
Working Environments Ltd v Greencoat Construction Ltd [2012] EWHC 1039 (TCC) at [24]

10.6 Other matters

10.6.4 Set-off and abatement

Ale Heavylift v MSD (Darlington) Ltd [2006] EWHC 2080 (TCC) at [64–73]
Ameycespa v Taimweser [2014] EWHC 4638 (TCC) at [24–31]
Fleming Buildings Ltd v Mr and Mrs Jane Forrest [2008] CSOH 103 at [106–108]
Hart Builders (Edinburgh) Ltd v St Andrew Ltd [2002] A69/02 Edinburgh at [28–30]
Hart Builders (Edinburgh) Ltd v St Andrew Ltd [2003] ScotSC 14 at [12–14]
Harwood Construction Ltd v Lantrode Ltd [2001] AdjLR 11/24 at [9]
Imtech Inviron Ltd v Loppingdale Plant Ltd [2014] EWHC 4109 (TCC) at [25–32; 47–53]
ISG Construction Ltd v Seevic College [2014] EWHC 4007 (TCC) at [42–53]
KNS Industrial Services (Birmingham) Ltd v Sindall Ltd (2001) 75 ConLR 71 at [15–17]
Letchworth Roofing Company v Sterling Building Company [2009] EWHC 1119 (TCC) at [25–30]
Matthew Harding (t/a M J Harding Contractors) v Paice and Springall [2014] EWHC 3824 (TCC) at [30–36]
Millers Specialist Joinery Company Ltd v Nobles Construction Ltd [2001] CILL 1770 at [16–24]
Parsons Plastics (Research & Development) Ltd v Purac Ltd [2002] EWCA Civ 459 at [11–16]
Parsons Plastics (Research and Development) Ltd v Purac Ltd [2001] AdjLR 08/13 at [16–19]
PC Harrington Contractors Ltd v Tyroddy Construction Ltd [2011] EWHC 813 (TCC) at [21]
Rupert Morgan Building Services (LLC) Ltd v Jervis & Anor [2003] EWCA Civ 1563 at [4–16]
Sir Robert McAlpine v Pring & St Hill Ltd [2001] All ER (D) 484 (Oct) at [16–22]
SL Timber Systems Ltd v Carillion Construction Ltd [2001] ScotCS 167 at [18–23]
Solland International Ltd v Daraydan Holdings Ltd [2002] EWHC 220 (TCC) at [30–31]
Surplant Ltd v Ballast plc (T/A Ballast Construction South West) [2002] EWHC TC33/02 at [16–20]

Urang Commercial Ltd v (1) Century Investments Ltd (2) Eclipse Hotels (Luton) Ltd [2011] EWHC 1561 (TCC) at [22–29]

VHE Construction plc v RBSTB Trust Co Ltd (as trustee of the Mercury Property Fund) [2000] BLR 187 at [35–37]

Watkin Jones & Son Ltd v Lidl UK GmbH (No 2) [2002] EWHC 183 (TCC) at [16–26]

Whiteways Contractors (Sussex) Ltd v Impresa Castelli Construction UK Ltd (2000) 75 ConLR 92 at [29–33]

Woods Hardwick Ltd v Chiltern Air Conditioning Ltd [2001] BLR 23 at [10]

Working Environments Ltd v Greencoat Construction Ltd [2012] EWHC 1039 (TCC) at [31–35]

10.6.5 Dropping a head of claim or withdrawing

Benfield Construction Ltd v Trudson (Hatton) Ltd [2008] EWHC 2333 (TCC) at [20–56]

John Roberts Architects Ltd v Parkcare Homes (No. 2) Ltd [2005] EWHC 1637 (TCC) at [8–22]

John Roberts Architects Ltd v Parkcare Homes (No. 2) Ltd [2006] EWCA Civ 64 at [28–31]

Midland Expressway Ltd & Ors v Carillion Construction Ltd & Ors (No. 3) [2006] EWHC 1505 (TCC) at [99–106]

10.6.8 Disclosure

CIB Properties Ltd v Birse Construction [2004] EWHC 2365 (TCC) at [196]

PHD Modular Access Services Ltd v Seele GmbH [2011] EWHC 2210 (TCC) at [8–24]

Skanska Construction UK Ltd v ERDC Group Ltd & Anor [2002] ScotCS 307 at [29–32]

10.6.12 Service of documents and notices (Act s. 115)

M. Rohde Construction v Nicholas Markham-David (No 2) [2007] EWHC 1408 (TCC) at [12–16]

10.7 Adjudicator's powers and duties

10.7.2 Duty to act impartially (Act s. 108(2)(e) and Scheme p. 12(a))

Balfour Beatty Construction Ltd v The Mayor & Burgesses of the London Borough of Lambeth [2002] EWHC 597 (TCC) at [28–39]

Discain Project Services Ltd v Opecprime Development Ltd (No 1) [2000] BLR 402 at [9–11]

Gillies Ramsay Diamond and Gavin Ramsay and Philip Diamond v PJW Enterprises Ltd [2003] ScotCS 343 at [39]

Glencot Development & Design Co Ltd v Ben Barrett & Son (Contractors) Ltd [2001] All ER (D) 384 (Feb) at [14–20]
Mott MacDonald Ltd v London & Regional Properties Ltd [2007] EWHC 1055 (TCC) at [75–78]
RSL (South West Ltd) v Stansell Ltd (No 1) [2003] EWHC 1390 (TCC) at [31]
Sprunt Ltd v London Borough of Camden [2011] EWHC 3191 (TCC) at [47]

10.7.3 Power to take the initiative (Act s. 108(2)(f) and Scheme p. 13)

CIB Properties Ltd v Birse Construction [2004] EWHC 2365 (TCC) at [21]
Discain Project Services Ltd v Opecprime Development Ltd (No 2) [2001] All ER (D) 123 at [22–23]
GPS Marine Contractors Ltd v Ringway Infrastructure Services Ltd [2010] EWHC 283 (TCC) at [101–109]
London & Amsterdam Properties Ltd v Waterman Partnership Ltd [2003] EWHC 3059 (TCC) at [96–116]
McAlpine PPS Pipeline Systems Joint Venture v Transco plc [2004] EWHC 2030 (TCC) at [124; 141–148]
Pring & St. Hill Ltd v C J Hafner t/a Southern Erectors [2002] EWHC 1775 (TCC) at [34]
Costain Ltd v Strathclyde Builders Ltd [2003] ScotCS 352 at [20]
Volker Stevin Ltd v Holystone Contracts Ltd [2010] EWHC 2344 (TCC) at [10–14]

10.7.4 Power to make requests or directions (Scheme p. 14 and 15)

Balfour Beatty Engineering Services (HY) Ltd v Shepherd Construction Ltd [2009] EWHC 2218 (TCC) at [72]

10.7.6 Duty to consider relevant information and provide it to the parties (Scheme p. 17)

Britcon (Scunthorpe) Ltd v Lincolnfields Ltd [2001] AdjLR 08/29 at [14]
Buxton Building Contractors Ltd v The Governors of Durand Primary School [2004] EWHC 733 (TCC) at [18–21]
Carillion Construction Ltd v Devonport Royal Dockyard Ltd [2005] EWHC 778 (TCC) at [81–82]
Carillion Utility Services Ltd v SP Power Systems Ltd [2011] CSOH 139 at [23]

10.7.7 Scope of what adjudicator can decide (Scheme p. 20(a) and (b))

David McLean Housing Contractors Ltd v Swansea Housing Association Ltd [2001] All ER (D) 519 (Jul) at [15–16]
Fastrack Contractors Ltd v Morrison Construction Ltd & Anor [2000] All ER (D) 11 at [30]

Image Decorations Ltd v Dean & Bowes (Contracts) Ltd [2004] ADJ CS 03/65 at [1 to 7]
Mecright Ltd v TA Morris Developments Ltd [2001] AdjLR 06/22 at [23–25]
Northern Developments (Cumbria) Ltd v J & J Nichol [2000] All ER (D) 68 at [35–36]
Vaultrise Ltd v Paul Cook [2004] Adj. C.S. 04/26 at [7]
Watson Building Services Ltd [2001] ScotCS 60 at [25–26]

10.7.8 Power to award interest (Scheme p. 20(c))

Allen Wilson Joinery Ltd v Privetgrange Construction Ltd [2008] EWHC 2802 (TCC) at [33–37]
Carillion Construction Ltd v Devonport Royal Dockyard Ltd [2005] EWCA Civ 1358 at [89–94]
Carillion Construction Ltd v Devonport Royal Dockyard Ltd [2005] EWHC 778 (TCC) at [118–124]
Partner Projects Ltd v Corinthian Nominees Ltd [2011] EWHC 2989 (TCC) at [30–40]

10.7.9 Power to award damages

Gillies Ramsay Diamond and Gavin Ramsay and Philip Diamond v PJW Enterprises Ltd [2003] ScotCS 343 at [17–21]
Gillies Ramsay Diamond v PJW Enterprises Ltd [2002] ScotCS 340 at [49–54]

10.7.10 Adjudicator's immunity (Act s. 108(4) and Scheme p. 26)

Ballast plc v The Burrell Company (Construction Management) Ltd [2001] ScotCS 159 at [32]

11 The decision

11.2 What is the adjudicator required to do?

11.2.2 The purpose and nature of the decision

Allied London & Scottish Properties plc v Riverbrae Construction Ltd [1999] ScotCS 224 at [13]
Austin Hall v Buckland Securities [2001] All ER (D) 137 at [14]
Balfour Beatty Construction Ltd v The Mayor & Burgesses of the London Borough of Lambeth [2002] EWHC 597 (TCC) at [36]
Carillion Construction Ltd v Devonport Royal Dockyard Ltd [2005] EWCA Civ 1358 at [86]
CIB Properties Ltd v Birse Construction Ltd [2004] EWHC 2365 (TCC) at [197]

CSC Braehead Leisure Ltd and Capital & Regional (Braehead) Ltd v Laing O-Rourke Scotland Ltd [2008] CSOH 119 at [41–45]
Simons Construction Ltd v Aardvark Developments Ltd [2003] EWHC 2474 (TCC) at [22–25]
Systech International Limited v PC Harrington Contractors Limited [2011] EWHC 2722 (TCC) at [43]
Treasure & Son Ltd v Martin Dawes [2007] EWHC 2420 (TCC) at [45–48]

11.2.4 11.2.4 Reasons

Cross refer to case Section 15.7.5

11.3 On receiving the decision

Hyder Consulting Ltd v Carillion Construction (UK) Ltd [2011] EWHC 1810 (TCC) at [35–38]

11.4 Timing

11.4.2 Act (Act s. 108(2)(c) and (d))

AC Yule & Son Ltd v Speedwell Roofing & Cladding Ltd [2007] EWHC 1360 (TCC) at [5–6; 30]
Aveat Heating Ltd v Jerram Falkus Construction Ltd [2007] EWHC 131 (TCC) at [3]
CIB Properties Ltd v Birse Construction [2004] EWHC 2365 (TCC) at [25–26]
Cubitt Building & Interiors Ltd v Fleetglade Ltd [2006] EWHC 3413 (TCC) at [35]
Epping Electrical Company Ltd v Briggs and Forrester (Plumbing Services) Ltd [2007] EWHC 4 (TCC) at [19–20]
Letchworth Roofing Company v Sterling Building Company [2009] EWHC 1119 (TCC) at [13–16]
Ritchie Brothers (Pwc) Ltd v David Philp (Commercials) Ltd [2005] ScotCS CSIH_32 at [13; 22]
Simons Construction Ltd v Aardvark Developments Ltd [2003] EWHC 2474 (TCC) at [28]

11.4.2 Scheme (Scheme p. 19)

AC Yule & Son Ltd v Speedwell Roofing & Cladding Ltd [2007] EWHC 1360 (TCC) at [5–6]
Ballast plc v The Burrell Company (Construction Management) Ltd [2001] ScotCS 159 at [30]
Barrie Green v GW Integrated Building Services Ltd & Anor [2001] AdjLR 07/18 at [48]
Lee v Chartered Properties (Building) Ltd [2010] EWHC 1540 (TCC) at [25–26]

Ritchie Brothers (Pwc) Ltd v David Philp (Commercials) Ltd [2004] ScotCS 94 at [6–7; 10; 22–24]
Ritchie Brothers (Pwc) Ltd v David Philp (Commercials) Ltd [2005] ScotCS CSIH_32 at [8–20]
Simons Construction Ltd v Aardvark Developments Ltd [2003] EWHC 2474 (TCC) at [28]

11.4.3 Rigidity of the time limit

AC Yule & Son Ltd v Speedwell Roofing & Cladding Ltd [2007] EWHC 1360 (TCC) at [5–6; 30]
Aveat Heating Ltd v Jerram Falkus Construction Ltd [2007] EWHC 131 (TCC) at [3]
Barnes & Elliot Ltd v Taylor Woodrow Holdings Ltd & Anor [2003] EWHC 3100 (TCC) at [3–27]
Cubitt Building & Interiors Ltd v Fleetglade Ltd [2006] EWHC 3413 (TCC) at [26–28; 68–76; 82–92]
M. Rohde Construction v Nicholas Markham-David [2006] EWHC 814 (TCC) at [31]
Ritchie Brothers (Pwc) Ltd v David Philp (Commercials) Ltd [2004] ScotCS 94 at [9–10; 22–23]
Ritchie Brothers (Pwc) Ltd v David Philp (Commercials) Ltd [2005] ScotCS CSIH_32 at [8–20]
Simons Construction Ltd v Aardvark Developments Ltd [2003] EWHC 2474 (TCC) at [26–33]

11.4.4 Decision made and decision communicated

Aveat Heating Ltd v Jerram Falkus Construction Ltd [2007] EWHC 131 (TCC) at [9–10; 13]
Barnes & Elliot Ltd v Taylor Woodrow Holdings Ltd & Anor [2003] EWHC 3100 (TCC) at [3–27]
Cubitt Building & Interiors Ltd v Fleetglade Ltd [2006] EWHC 3413 (TCC) at [26–28; 68–76; 82–92]
Lee v Chartered Properties (Building) Ltd [2010] EWHC 1540 (TCC) at [25–33]
Mott MacDonald Ltd v London & Regional Properties Ltd [2007] EWHC 1055 (TCC) at [79–85]
St Andrews Bay Development Ltd v HBG Management Ltd and Mrs Janey Milligan [2003] ScotCS 103 at [15–22]

11.4.5 Responding to the adjudicator's request for an extension

AC Yule & Son Ltd v Speedwell Roofing & Cladding Ltd [2007] EWHC 1360 (TCC) at [14–22]
KNN Coburn LLP v GD City Holdings Ltd [2013] EWHC 2879 (TCC) at [28–35]

Case index: by subject matter

Letchworth Roofing Company v Sterling Building Company [2009] EWHC 1119 (TCC) at [13–16]

11.5 The effect and compliance

11.5.2 Temporary finality (Act s. 108(3), Scheme p. 23)

Aspect Contracts (Asbestos) Ltd v Higgins Construction plc [2013] EWCA Civ 1541 at [9–12]
Aspect Contracts (Asbestos) Ltd v Higgins Construction plc [2013] EWHC 1322 (TCC) at [38–39]
Austin Hall Building Ltd v Buckland Securities Ltd [2001] All ER (D) 137 at [34]
Ballast plc v The Burrell Company (Construction Management) Ltd [2001] ScotCS 159 at [14; 29]
Bouygues (UK) Ltd v Dahl-Jensen (UK) Ltd [2000] EWCA Civ 507 at [2; 26]
George Parke v The Fenton Gretton Partnership [2001] CILL 1713 at [14]
Gillies Ramsay Diamond and Gavin Ramsay and Philip Diamond v PJW Enterprises Ltd [2003] ScotCS 343 at [22–23; 40]
Homer Burgess Ltd v Chirex (Annan) Ltd (No. 1) (1999) 71 ConLR 245 at [32–35]
Macob Civil Engineering v Morrison Construction Ltd [1999] All ER (D) 143 at [18–23]
Millers Specialist Joinery Company Ltd v Nobles Construction Ltd [2001] CILL 1770 at [14]
Quietfield Ltd v Vascroft Construction Ltd [2006] EWHC 174 (TCC) at [32–43]
Solland International Ltd v Daraydan Holdings Ltd [2002] EWHC 220 (TCC) at [32]
Sprunt Ltd v London Borough of Camden [2011] EWHC 3191 (TCC) at [44]
Stiell Ltd v Riema Control Systems Ltd [2000] ScotCS 174 at [16–19]
The Construction Centre Group Ltd v The Highland Council [2002] ScotCS CSOH_354 at [8–11]
Trustees of the Harbours of Peterhead v Lilley Construction Ltd [2003] ScotCS 91 at [15–22]
VHE Construction plc v RBSTB Trust Co Ltd (as trustee of the Mercury Property Fund) [2000] BLR 187 at [38–55]
William Verry Ltd v The Mayor and Burgesses of the London Borough of Camden [2006] EWHC 761 (TCC) at [24]

11.5.3 Compliance with the decision (Scheme p. 21)

A v B [2002] ScotCS 325 at [6–11]
MBE Electrical Contractors Ltd v Honeywell Control Systems Ltd [2010] EWHC 2244 (TCC) at [30–31]
RSL (South West Ltd) v Stansell Ltd (No 1) [2003] EWHC 1390 (TCC) at [37]

11.5.4 Delaying compliance by contract

>Ferson Contractors Ltd v Levolux AT Ltd [2003] EWCA Civ 11 at [26–34]
>Pioneer Cladding Ltd v John Graham Construction Ltd [2013] EWHC 2954 (TCC) at [4–8]

11.5.5 Insurance claims

>Galliford (UK) Ltd t/a Galliford Northern v Markel Capital Ltd [2003] EWHC 1216 (QB) at [44–47]

12 Post-decision

12.2 Adjudicator's costs (2009 Act, s.108A; Scheme, p. 25)

>Aveat Heating Ltd v Jerram Falkus Construction Ltd [2007] EWHC 131 (TCC) at [25]
>Balfour Beatty Ltd v Speedwell Roofing and Cladding Ltd [2010] EWHC 840 (TCC) at [17–21]
>Barrie Green v GW Integrated Building Services Ltd & Anor [2001] AdjLR 07/18 at [53]
>Beck Interiors Ltd v UK Flooring Contractors Ltd [2012] EWHC 1808 (TCC) at [33]
>Cartwright v Fay [2005] AdjLR 02/09 at [10–11]
>Castle Inns (Stirling) Ltd trading as Castle Leisure Group v Clark Contracts Ltd [2005] CSOH 178 at [17]
>Epping Electrical Company Ltd v Briggs and Forrester (Plumbing Services) Ltd [2007] EWHC 4 (TCC) at [6–7]
>Faithful & Gould Ltd v Arcal Ltd and Ors. [2001] AdjLR 05/25 at [3–9]
>Fenice Investments Inc v Jerram Falkus Construction Ltd [2011] EWHC 1678 (TCC) at [16–62]
>Gary Kitt and EC Harris LLP v The Laundry Building Ltd and Etcetera Construction Services Ltd [2014] EHWC 4250 (TCC) at [34]
>Interserve Industrial Services Ltd v Cleveland Bridge UK Ltd [2006] EWHC 741 (TCC) at [54–63]
>Jacques (t/a C & E Jacques Partnership) v Ensign Contractors Ltd [2009] EWHC 3383 (TCC) at [40]
>Ken Griffin (t/a K&D Contractors) v Midas Homes Ltd (2000) 78 ConLR 152 at [23 et seq.]
>Linnett v Halliwells LLP [2009] EWHC 319 at [34–38; 59–85]
>London & Amsterdam Properties Ltd v Waterman Partnership Ltd [2003] EWHC 3059 (TCC) at [75–84]
>Paul Jensen Ltd v Staveley Industries plc [2001] AdjLR 09/27 at [1–4]
>PC Harrington Contractors Ltd v Systech International Ltd [2012] EWCA Civ 1371 at [23–37; 42–46]
>Prentice Island Ltd v Castle Contracting Ltd [2003] ScotCS 61 at [16–20]

Rankilor (Dr Peter) & Perco Engineering Service Ltd v Igoe (M) Ltd [2006] AdjLR 01/27 at [33]

Stubbs Rich Architects v W H Tolley & Son Ltd [2001] AdjLR 08/08 at [10–21]

Systech International Limited v PC Harrington Contractors Limited [2011] EWHC 2722 (TCC) at [39–49]

12.3 Parties' costs (2009 Act, s. 108A)

Balfour Beatty Ltd v Speedwell Roofing and Cladding Ltd [2010] EWHC 840 (TCC) at [22–24]

Bridgeway Construction Ltd v Tolent Construction Ltd [2000] CILL 1626 at [28–36]

Deko Scotland Ltd v Edinburgh Royal Joint Venture & Anor [2003] ScotCS 113 at [8–16]

Fenice Investments Inc v Jerram Falkus Construction Ltd [2011] EWHC 1678 (TCC) at [63–67]

John Cothliff Ltd v Allen Build (North West) Ltd [1999] CILL 1530 at [19–30]

John Roberts Architects Ltd v Parkcare Homes (No. 2) Ltd [2005] EWHC 1637 (TCC) at [8–22]

John Roberts Architects Ltd v Parkcare Homes (No. 2) Ltd [2006] EWCA Civ 64 at [28–31]

Leander Construction Limited v Mulalley and Company Limited [2011] EWHC 3449 (TCC) at [12]

Nolan Davis Ltd v Catton 2000 TCC No 590 at [30]

Northern Developments (Cumbria) Ltd v J & J Nichol [2000] All ER (D) 68 at [37–46]

Profile Projects Ltd v Elmwood (Glasgow) Ltd [2011] CSOH 64 at [38–46]

Total M&E Services Ltd v ABB Building Technologies Ltd (formerly ABB Stewarts Ltd) [2002] EWHC 248 (TCC) at [24–25]

Yuanda (UK) Co Ltd v WW Gear Construction Ltd [2010] EWHC 720 (TCC) at [38–66]

12.5 Correcting errors in the decision (2009 Act, s. 108(3)(A); 2011 Scheme, p. 22(A); 1996 Act and 1998 Scheme)

Bloor Construction (UK) Ltd v Bowmer & Kirkland (London) Ltd [2000] BLR 314 at [28–43]

Bouygues (UK) Ltd v Dahl-Jensen (UK) Ltd [1999] All ER (D) 1281 at [33–34]

Bouygues (UK) Ltd v Dahl-Jensen (UK) Ltd [2000] EWCA Civ 507 at [16–19]

CIB Properties Ltd v Birse Construction [2004] EWHC 2365 (TCC) at [28–35; 200–201]

Coleraine Skip Hire Ltd v Ecomesh Ltd [2008] NIQB 141 at [25–26]

Edmund Nuttall Ltd v Sevenoaks District Council [2000] AdjLR 04/14 at [12–18]

Joinery Plus Ltd (In Administration) v Laing Ltd [2003] EWHC 3513 (TCC) at [38–44]

O'Donnell Developments Ltd v Buildability Ltd [2009] EWHC 3388 (TCC) at [20–55]

PP Construction Ltd v Geoffrey Osborne Ltd [2015] EWHC 325 (TCC) at [21–36]

Redwing Construction Ltd v Charles Wishart [2010] EWHC 3366 (TCC) at [28; 35–39]
ROK Building Ltd v Celtic Composting Systems Ltd (No 2) [2010] EWHC 66 (TCC) at [30–31]
Shimizu Europe Ltd v Automajor Ltd [2002] EWHC 1571 (TCC) at [30]
Thermal Energy Construction Ltd v AE & E Lentjes UK Ltd [2009] EWHC 408 (TCC) at [31–36]
YCMS Ltd (t/a Young Construction Management Services) v Grabiner & Anor [2009] EWHC 127 (TCC) at [46–50; 57–60]

12.6 Setting off against the adjudicator's decision

12.6.2 eneral rule and exceptions

Ferson Contractors Ltd v Levolux AT Ltd [2003] EWCA Civ 11 at [30]
Geris Handelsgesellschaft GmbH v Les Constructions Industrielles de la Mediterranée S.A. [2005] EWHC 499 (TCC) at [37]
Naylor Construction Services Ltd v Acoustafoam Ltd [2010] All ER (D) 138 (Apr) at [62–64]
ROK Building Ltd v Celtic Composting Systems Ltd [2009] EWHC 2664 (TCC) at [17–18]
Squibb Group Ltd v Vertase FLI Ltd [2012] EWHC 1958 (TCC) at [10–18]
Thameside Construction Co Ltd v Stevens [2013] EWHC 2071 (TCC) at [16–24]
VHE Construction plc v RBSTB Trust Co Ltd (as trustee of the Mercury Property Fund) [2000] BLR 187 at [55–56; 65]
William Verry Ltd v The Mayor and Burgesses of the London Borough of Camden [2006] EWHC 761 (TCC) at [26–35]

12.6.3 Contractual right to set-off

Bovis Lend Lease Ltd v Triangle Development Ltd [2002] EWHC 3123 (TCC) at [67]
Ferson Contractors Ltd v Levolux AT Ltd [2003] EWCA Civ 11 at [26–34]
Fleming Buildings Ltd v Mr and Mrs Jane Forrest [2008] CSOH 103 at [107–108]
Interserve Services Ltd v Cleveland Bridge UK Ltd [2006] EWHC 741 at [43]
Ledwood Mechanical Engineering Ltd v Whessoe Oil and Gas Ltd [2007] EWHC 2743 [37]
Levolux A.T. Ltd v Ferson Contractors Ltd [2002] BLR 341 at [37–42]
Lovell Projects Ltd v Legg & Carver [2003] BLR 452 at [36–41]
Parsons Plastics (Research & Development) Ltd v Purac Ltd [2002] EWCA Civ 459 at [11–16]
Parsons Plastics (Research and Development) Ltd v Purac Ltd [2001] AdjLR 08/13 at [16–19]
R and C Electrical Engineers Ltd v Shaylor Construction Ltd [2012] EWHC 1254 (TCC) at [80–83]

Case index: by subject matter 629

ROK Building Ltd v Celtic Composting Systems Ltd [2009] EWHC 2664 (TCC) at [17–18; 25–29]

Thomas Vale Construction PLC v Brookside Syston Ltd [2006] EWHC 3637 at [49–52]

William Verry Ltd v The Mayor and Burgesses of the London Borough of Camden [2006] EWHC 761 (TCC) at [28]

12.6.4 Later interim or final certificate

MJ Gleeson Group plc v Devonshire Green Holding Ltd [2004] AdjLR 03/19 at [8–12; 16–22]

William Verry Ltd v The Mayor and Burgesses of the London Borough of Camden [2006] EWHC 761 (TCC) at [36–44]

12.6.5 Issuing a withholding or pay less notice

Beck Interiors Ltd v Classic Decorative Finishing Ltd [2012] EWHC 1956 (TCC) at [8–16]

Conor Engineering Ltd v Les Constructions Industrielles de la Mediterranée SA [2004] EWHC 899 (TCC) at [47–50]

MJ Gleeson Group plc v Devonshire Green Holding Ltd [2004] AdjLR 03/19 at [8–12].

Shimizu Europe Ltd v LBJ Fabrications Ltd [2003] EWHC 1229 (TCC) at [13–32]

The Construction Centre Group Ltd v The Highland Council [2002] ScotCS CSOH_354 at [19–24]

12.6.6 Setting off liquidated damages

A v B [2002] ScotCS 325 at [14–20]

Avoncroft Construction Ltd v Sharba Homes (CN) Ltd [2008] EWHC 933 (TCC) at [8–13]

Balfour Beatty Construction Ltd v Serco Ltd [2004] EWHC 3336 (TCC) at [48–55]

Balfour Beatty Construction Northern Ltd v Modus Corovest (Blackpool) Ltd [2008] EWHC 3029 (TCC) at [82–88]

Charles Brand Ltd v Donegall Ltd [2010] NIQB 67 at [15–19]

Conor Engineering Ltd v Les Constructions Industrielles de la Mediterranée SA [2004] EWHC 899 (TCC) at [47–50]

David McLean Contractors Ltd v The Albany Building Ltd [2005] TCC101/05 at [25–35]

David McLean Housing Contractors Ltd v Swansea Housing Association Ltd [2001] All ER (D) 519 (Jul) at [19–26]

Dumarc Building Services Ltd v Mr Salvador – Rico [2003] Adj.C.R. 01/31 at [11–15]

Edinburgh Royal Joint Venture, Petition of [2002] ScotCS P762/02 at [10–12]

Edmund Nuttall Ltd v Sevenoaks District Council [2000] AdjLR 04/14 at [34–36]

Henry Brothers (Magherafelt) Ltd v Brunswick (8 Lanyon Place) Ltd [2011] NIQB 102 at [9–16]
Lovell Projects Ltd v Legg & Carver [2003] BLR 452 at [36–41]
MJ Gleeson Group plc v Devonshire Green Holding Ltd [2004] AdjLR 03/19 at [13–15]
RJ Knapman Ltd v Richards [2006] EWHC 2518 (TCC) at [27–37]
RWE Npower plc v Alstom Power Ltd [2009] EWHC 1192 (QB) at [83–93]
Solland International Ltd v Daraydan Holdings Ltd [2002] EWHC 220 (TCC) at [30–35]
Squibb Group Ltd v Vertase F.L.I. Ltd [2012] EWHC 1958 (TCC), per Coulson J at [19–27]
Thameside Construction Co Ltd v Stevens [2013] EWHC 2071 (TCC) at [30–33]
The Construction Centre Group Ltd v The Highland Council [2003] ScotCS 114 at [16]
The Highland Council v The Construction Centre Group Ltd [2003] ScotCS 221 at [5 to 7]
VHE Construction plc v RBSTB Trust Co Ltd (as trustee of the Mercury Property Fund) [2000] BLR 187 at [65–67]

12.6.7 Set-off permitted but not quantified in the decision

Geris Handelsgesellschaft GmbH v Les Constructions Industrielles de la Mediterranée S.A. [2005] EWHC 499 (TCC) at [30–36]

12.6.8 Set-off not formulated before the adjudication

Naylor Construction Services Ltd v Acoustafoam Ltd [2010] All ER (D) 138 (Apr) at [59–61]

12.6.9 Adjudication rules prevent set-off in enforcement proceedings

R and C Electrical Engineers Ltd v Shaylor Construction Ltd [2012] EWHC 1254 (TCC) at [84–85]

12.6.10 Multiple adjudications

Bovis Lend Lease Ltd v Triangle Development Ltd [2002] EWHC 3123 (TCC) at [67]
Hart (t/a D W Hart & Son) v Smith & Anor [2009] EWHC 2223 (TCC) at [38–39; 43–46]
HS Works Ltd v Enterprise Managed Services Ltd [2009] EWHC 729 (TCC) at [38–40; 58–65]
Interserve Industrial Services Ltd v Cleveland Bridge UK Ltd [2006] EWHC 741 (TCC) at [39–47]
Morphuse Framing Solutions Ltd v Bracknell Property Ltd, Unreported, 31 July 2014 at [22–24]

Case index: by subject matter 631

JPA Design and Build Ltd v Sentosa (UK) Ltd [2009] EWHC 2312 (TCC) at [22–27]

YCMS Ltd (t/a Young Construction Management Services) v Grabiner & Anor [2009] EWHC 127 (TCC) at [63–64]

12.6.11 Litigation on foot

Hillview Industrial Developments (UK) Ltd v Botes Building Ltd [2006] EWHC 1365 (TCC) at [27–28]

Whyte and Mackay Ltd v Blyth & Blyth Consulting Engineers Ltd [2012] ScotCS CSOH_89 at [9]

12.6.12 Arbitration award

Workspace Management Ltd v YJL London Ltd [2009] EWHC 2017 (TCC) at [28–39]

12.6.13 Other arguments for set off

Balfour Beatty Ltd v Speedwell Roofing and Cladding Ltd [2010] EWHC 840 (TCC) at [25–28]

Charles Brand Ltd v Donegall Ltd [2010] NIQB 67 at [20–22]

D G Williamson Ltd v Northern Ireland Prison Service [2009] NIQB 8 at [31]

Harlow & Milner Ltd v Linda Teasdale (No 1) [2006] EWHC 54 (TCC) at [9]

Ledwood Mechanical Engineering Ltd v Whessoe Oil and Gas Ltd & Anor [2007] EWHC 2743 (TCC) at [30–38]

Total M&E Services Ltd v ABB Building Technologies Ltd (formerly ABB Stewarts Ltd) [2002] EWHC 248 (TCC) at [35–44]

Woods Hardwick Ltd v Chiltern Air Conditioning Ltd [2001] BLR 23 at [3; 10]

13 Enforcement: options and procedure

13.2 Key statements of principle and the court's policy

13.2.1 The principles of enforcement

Alstom Signalling Ltd v Jarvis Facilities Ltd (No 2) [2004] EWHC 1285 (TCC) at [19–20]

AMEC Group Ltd v Thames Water Utilities Ltd [2010] EWHC 419 (TCC) at [21]

Atholl Developments (Slackbuie) Ltd, Re Application for Judicial Review [2010] CSOH 94 at [17]

Balfour Beatty Construction Ltd v The Mayor & Burgesses of the London Borough of Lambeth [2002] EWHC 597 (TCC) at [27]

Barr Ltd v Law Mining Ltd [2001] ScotCS 152 at [9–10]

Bouygues (UK) Ltd v Dahl-Jensen (UK) Ltd [1999] All ER (D) 1281 at [35–36]
Bouygues (UK) Ltd v Dahl-Jensen (UK) Ltd [2000] EWCA Civ 507 at [2; 26]
Bovis Lend Lease Ltd v Triangle Development Ltd [2002] EWHC 3123 (TCC) at [25–27]
Cantillon Ltd v Urvasco Ltd [2008] EWHC 282 (TCC) at [53]
Carillion Construction Ltd v Devonport Royal Dockyard Ltd [2005] EWCA Civ 1358 at [84–87]
Carillion Construction Ltd v Devonport Royal Dockyard Ltd [2005] EWHC 778 (TCC) at [75–80]
Charles Henshaw & Sons Ltd v Stewart & Shields Ltd [2014] CSIH 55 at [17]
Farebrother Building Services Ltd v Frogmore Investments Ltd [2001] CILL 1762 at [31–32]
Pegram Shopfitters Ltd v Tally Wiejl (UK) Ltd [2003] EWCA Civ 1750 at [9–12]
RBG Ltd v SGL Carbon Fibers Ltd [2010] CSOH 77 at [22]
Rodgers Contracts (Ballynahinch) Ltd v Merex Construction Ltd [2012] NIQB 94 at [4–6]
ROK Building Ltd v Celtic Composting Systems Ltd (No 2) [2010] EWHC 66 (TCC) at [23–24]
SG South Ltd v Swan Yard (Cirencester) Ltd [2010] EWHC 376 (TCC) at [5]
Sherwood & Casson Ltd v Mackenzie [2000] CILL 1577 at [24; 30]
VHE Construction plc v RBSTB Trust Co Ltd (as trustee of the Mercury Property Fund) [2000] BLR 187 at [45]
Williams (t/a Sanclair Construction) v Noor (t/a India Kitchen) [2007] EWHC 3467 (TCC) at [15–19]

13.3 TCC enforcement procedure

13.3.2 The nature of summary judgment applications in adjudication

A.T. Stannard Ltd v James Tobutt and Thomas Tobutt [2014] EWHC 3491 (TCC) at [14]
Able Construction (UK) Ltd v Forest Property Development Ltd [2009] EWHC 159 (TCC) at [15]
Beck Interiors Limited v Dr Mario Luca Russo [2009] EWHC 3861 (TCC) at [42–45]
Canary Riverside Development (Private) Ltd v Timtec International Ltd [2000] All ER (D) 1753 at [28–29]
Fileturn Ltd v Royal Garden Hotel Ltd [2010] EWHC 1736 (TCC) at [7]
Galliford Try Building v Estura Ltd [2015] EWHC 412 (TCC) at [40–43]
Geris Handelsgesellschaft GmbH v Les Constructions Industrielles de la Mediterranée S.A. [2005] EWHC 499 (TCC) at [28–29]
Glencot Development & Design Co Ltd v Ben Barrett & Son (Contractors) Ltd [2001] All ER (D) 384 (Feb) at [34–35]
PC Harrington Contractors Ltd v Tyroddy Construction Ltd [2011] EWHC 813 (TCC) at [22–27]
Pilon Ltd v Breyer Group plc [2010] EWHC 837 (TCC) at [66]
Primus Build Ltd v Pompey Centre Ltd & Anor [2009] EWHC 1487 (TCC) at [35]

VHE Construction plc v RBSTB Trust Co Ltd (as trustee of the Mercury Property Fund) [2000] BLR 187 at [68–74]
Williams (t/a Sanclair Construction) v Noor (t/a India Kitchen) [2007] EWHC 3467 (TCC) at [20]

13.3.3 Options for commencing the claim

Bovis Lend Lease Ltd v Triangle Development Ltd [2002] EWHC 3123 (TCC) at [20–24]
Lloyd Projects Ltd v John Malnick [2005] AdjLR 07/22 at [6–7]
William Verry Ltd v North West London Communal Mikvah [2004] EWHC 1300 (TCC) at [3]

13.3.4 Commencing the claim

MBE Electrical Contractors Ltd v Honeywell Control Systems Ltd [2010] EWHC 2244 (TCC) at [2; 39]
Nickleby FM v Somerfield Stores [2010] EWHC 1976 (TCC) at [27–33]
Redworth Construction v Brookdale Healthcare [2006] EWHC 1994 (TCC) at [38–41]

13.3.5 Directions

City Basements Ltd v Nordic Construction UK Ltd [2014] EWHC 4817 (TCC) at [7–12]

13.3.10 Judgment in default and setting aside

Coventry Scaffolding Company (London) Ltd v Lancsville Construction Ltd [2009] EWHC 2995 (TCC) at [13–18]
M. Rohde Construction v Nicholas Markham-David [2006] EWHC 814 (TCC) at [40–51]
The Mayor and Burgesses of the London Borough of Camden v Makers UK Ltd [2009] EWHC 605 (TCC) at [20–28]

13.3.12 Timetable to a decision

Pochin Construction Ltd v Liberty Property (G.P.) Ltd [2014] EWHC 2919 (TCC) at [5]

13.3.14 The effect of the court's decision

HS Works Ltd v Enterprise Managed Services Ltd [2009] EWHC 729 (TCC) at [46]
Michael John Construction Ltd v St Peter's Rugby Football Club [2007] EWHC 1857 (TCC) at [35–46]

13.3.15 Setting aside a summary judgment

Nageh v Richard Giddings & Another [2006] EWHC 3240 (TCC) at [11–14]

13.3.16 Costs: basis of assessment

A.T. Stannard Ltd v James Tobutt and Thomas Tobutt [2014] EWHC 3491 (TCC) at [20]
Able Construction (UK) Ltd v Forest Property Development Ltd [2009] EWHC 159 (TCC) at [21]
Allied P&L Ltd v Paradigm Housing Group Ltd [2009] EWHC 2890 (TCC) at [48–51]
CG Group Ltd v Breyer Group plc [2013] EWHC 2959 (TCC) at [2–6]
Donal Pugh v Harris Calman Construction Ltd [2003] Adj.C.S. 06/30 at [1–5]
Enterprise Managed Services Ltd v Tony McFadden Utilities Ltd [2010] EWHC 1506 (TCC) at [7–14]
Eurocom Ltd v Siemens plc Ex Tempore at [1–4]
Fenice Investments Inc v Jerram Falkus Construction Ltd [2009] EWHC 3272 (TCC) at [49–50]
Fenice Investments Inc v Jerram Falkus Construction Ltd [2011] EWHC 1678 (TCC) at [68]
Gipping Construction Ltd v Eaves Ltd [2008] EWHC 3134 (TCC) at [13–19]
Gray & Sons Builders (Bedford) Ltd v Essential Box Company Ltd [2006] EWHC 2520 (TCC) at [7–16]
Harlow & Milner Ltd v Linda Teasdale (No 1) [2006] EWHC 54 (TCC) at [12–13]
Harris Calnan Construction Co Ltd v Ridgewood (Kensington) Ltd [2007] EWHC 2738 (TCC) at [22–25]
Linaker Ltd v Riviera Construction [1999] AdjLR 11/04 at [8–10]
Mead General Building Ltd v Dartmoor Properties Ltd [2009] EWHC 200 (TCC) at [22–24]
NAP Anglia v Sun-Land Development Co Ltd (No 2) [2012] EWHC 51 (TCC) at [10–13]
O'Donnell Developments Ltd v Buildability Ltd [2009] EWHC 3388 (TCC) at [58–69]
Outwing Construction Ltd v H Randell and Son Ltd [1999] BLR 156 at [7–13]
Pochin Construction Ltd v Liberty Property (G.P.) Ltd [2014] EWHC 2919 (TCC) at [11]
Savoye and Savoye Ltd v Spicers Ltd [2015] EWHC 33 (TCC) at [5–10]
SG South Ltd v Swan Yard (Cirencester) Ltd [2010] EWHC 376 (TCC) at [34]
SG South Ltd. v King's Head Cirencester LLP & Anor [2009] EWHC 2645 (TCC) at [47–48]
Supablast (Nationwide) Ltd v Story Rail Ltd [2010] EWHC 56 (TCC) at [37–40]
Working Environments Ltd v Greencoat Construction Ltd [2012] EWHC 1039 (TCC) at [38]

13.3.17 Costs: assessment of the bill of costs

Allen Watson Ltd v RNR London Ltd [2013] All ER (D) 181 (Aug) at [1–8]
Allied P&L Ltd v Paradigm Housing Group Ltd [2009] EWHC 2890 (TCC) at [52–53]
Amber Construction Services Ltd v London Interspace HG Ltd [2007] EWHC 3042 (TCC) at [18–25]

Balfour Beatty Engineering Services (HY) Ltd v Shepherd Construction Ltd [2009] EWHC 2218 (TCC) at [84–86]

Bryen & Langley Ltd v Martin Boston [2005] EWCA Civ 973 at [48–55]

Camillin Denny Architects Ltd v Adelaide Jones & Company Ltd [2009] EWHC 2110 (TCC) at [43–48]

CG Group Ltd v Breyer Group plc [2013] EWHC 2959 (TCC) at [7–10]

Devon County Council v Celtic Bioenergy Limited [2014] EWHC 309 (TCC) at [8–11; 14–17]

Donal Pugh v Harris Calman Construction Ltd [2003] Adj.C.S. 06/30 at [1–5]

Fenice Investments Inc v Jerram Falkus Construction Ltd [2009] EWHC 3272 (TCC) at [49–50]

Fenice Investments Inc v Jerram Falkus Construction Ltd [2011] EWHC 1678 (TCC) at [68]

Gary Kitt and EC Harris LLP v The Laundry Building Ltd and Etcetera Construction Services Ltd [2014] EHWC 4250 (TCC) at [41]

Gray & Sons Builders (Bedford) Ltd v Essential Box Company Ltd [2006] EWHC 2520 (TCC) at [17–20]

Harlow & Milner Ltd v Linda Teasdale (No 1) [2006] EWHC 54 (TCC) at [13]

Harris Calnan Construction Co Ltd v Ridgewood (Kensington) Ltd [2007] EWHC 2738 (TCC) at [26–28]

Imtech Inviron Ltd v Loppingdale Plant Ltd [2014] EWHC 4109 (TCC) at [3–12]

Jacques (t/a C & E Jacques Partnership) v Ensign Contractors Ltd [2009] EWHC 3383 (TCC) at [54–60]

Ledwood Mechanical Engineering Ltd v Whessoe Oil and Gas Ltd & Anor [2007] EWHC 2743 (TCC) at [41–44]

Linaker Ltd v Riviera Construction [1999] AdjLR 11/04 at [11–12]

Mead General Building Ltd v Dartmoor Properties Ltd [2009] EWHC 200 (TCC) at [25–27]

NAP Anglia v Sun-Land Development Co Ltd (No 2) [2012] EWHC 51 (TCC) at [14–34]

Outwing Construction Ltd v H Randell and Son Ltd [1999] BLR 156 at [14]

Pochin Construction Ltd v Liberty Property (G.P.) Ltd [2014] EWHC 2919 (TCC) at [12–14]

Savoye and Savoye Ltd v Spicers Ltd [2015] EWHC 33 (TCC) at [14–24]

SG South Ltd v Swan Yard (Cirencester) Ltd [2010] EWHC 376 (TCC) at [35]

SG South Ltd. v King's Head Cirencester LLP & Anor [2009] EWHC 2645 (TCC) at [49]

Supablast (Nationwide) Ltd v Story Rail Ltd [2010] EWHC 56 (TCC) at [41]

Working Environments Ltd v Greencoat Construction Ltd [2012] EWHC 1039 (TCC) at [39]

13.3.18 Costs: ATE insurance and conditional fee arrangements

Redwing Construction Ltd v Charles Wishart [2011] EWHC 19 (TCC) at [11–22]

13.3.19 Costs: interest

> Able Construction (UK) Ltd v Forest Property Development Ltd [2009] EWHC 159 (TCC) at [20]
> Fenice Investments Inc v Jerram Falkus Construction Ltd [2009] EWHC 3272 (TCC) at [49–50]
> Linaker Ltd v Riviera Construction [1999] AdjLR 11/04 at [7]
> McConnell Dowell Constructors (Aust) Pty Ltd v National Grid Gas plc (formerly Transco plc) [2006] EWHC 2551 (TCC) at [48]
> Ringway Infrastructure Services Ltd v Vauxhall Motors Ltd (No 2) [2007] EWHC 2507 (TCC) at [16–17]
> SG South Ltd. v King's Head Cirencester LLP & Anor [2009] EWHC 2645 (TCC) at [50]
> Working Environments Ltd v Greencoat Construction Ltd [2012] EWHC 1039 (TCC) at [37]

13.3.20 Costs: settlement reached before summary judgment

> Rokvic v Peacock [2014] EWHC 3729 (TCC) at [7–10]
> Southern Electric v Mead Realisations [2009] EWHC 2947 (TCC) at [13–19]

13.3.22 Staying enforcement proceedings where there is an arbitration agreement

> AMEC Capital Projects Ltd v Whitefriars City Estate Ltd [2003] EWHC 2443 (TCC) at [12 to 16]
> Cygnet Healthcare plc v Higgins City Ltd (2000) 16 Const LJ 394 at [20–26]
> Macob Civil Engineering v Morrison Construction Ltd [1999] All ER (D) 143 at [24–30]
> MBE Electrical Contractors Ltd v Honeywell Control Systems Ltd [2010] EWHC 2244 (TCC) at [26–37]
> Shaw v MEP Foundations Piling Ltd [2009] EWHC 493 (TCC) at [16–20]
> Speymill Contracts Ltd v Eric Baskind [2009] No 9LV 22750 at [119–125]
> Walter Llewllyn & Sons Ltd and Rok Building Ltd v Excel Brickwork Ltd [2010] EWHC 3415 (TCC) at [21–25]

13.4 Other procedures for enforcement

13.4.2 Pre-emptory order

> Macob Civil Engineering v Morrison Construction Ltd [1999] All ER (D) 143 at [31–40]
> MBE Electrical Contractors Ltd v Honeywell Control Systems Ltd [2010] EWHC 2244 (TCC) at [38]
> Outwing Construction Ltd v H Randell and Son Ltd [1999] BLR 156 at [6]

13.4.3 Mandatory injunction

Macob Civil Engineering v Morrison Construction Ltd [1999] All ER (D) 143 at [35]
MBE Electrical Contractors Ltd v Honeywell Control Systems Ltd [2010] EWHC 2244 (TCC) at [38]
Multiplex Constructions (UK) Ltd v Mott MacDonald Ltd [2007] EWHC 20 (TCC) at [47]

13.4.4 Statutory demand

Alexander & Law Ltd v Coveside (21BPR) Ltd [2013] EWHC 3949 (TCC) at [18-22]
George Parke v The Fenton Gretton Partnership [2001] CILL 1713 at [11-18]
Guardi Shoes Ltd v Datum Contracts [2002] CILL 1934 at [15-22]
Harlow & Milner Ltd v Linda Teasdale (No 1) [2006] EWHC 54 (TCC) at [15-16]
Jamil Mohammed v Dr Michael Bowles [2002] 394 SD 2002 at [31-35]
Lee v Chartered Properties (Building) Ltd [2010] EWHC 1540 (TCC) at [12]
Re A Company (number 1299 of 2001) [2001] CILL 1745 at [14-20]
Shaw v MEP Foundations Piling Ltd [2010] EWHC 9 (Ch) at [47-62]
Towsey v Highgrove Homes Ltd [2013] BLR 45 at [37-48]
William Oakley & David Oakley v Airclear Environmental Ltd and Airclear TS Ltd [2002] CILL 1824 at [63-65]

13.4.5 Scottish procedure

Atholl Developments (Slackbuie) Ltd, Re Application for Judicial Review [2010] CSOH 94 at [22]
The Construction Centre Group Ltd v The Highland Council [2002] ScotCS CSOH_354 at [2-3]
Vaughan Engineering Ltd v Hinkins & Frewin Ltd [2003] ScotCS 56 at [31-33]

13.5 Complying with an order of the court

13.5.2 Time for payment

Gipping Construction Ltd v Eaves Ltd [2008] EWHC 3134 (TCC) at [10-12]
SG South Ltd. v King's Head Cirencester LLP & Anor [2009] EWHC 2645 (TCC) at [46]
Treasure & Son Ltd v Martin Dawes [2007] EWHC 2420 (TCC) at [27]

13.5.4 Failing to comply

Anglo Swiss Holding Ltd & Ors v Packman Lucas Ltd [2009] EWHC 3212 (TCC) at [25-31]
Harlow & Milner Ltd v Mrs Linda Teasdale (No 3) [2006] EWHC 1708 (TCC) at [8-26]

Harlow & Milner Ltd v Teasdale (No 2) [2006] EWHC 535 (TCC) at [5–13]
Kier Regional Ltd (t/a Wallis) v City and General (Holborn) Ltd & Ors (No 2) [2008] EWHC 2454 (TCC) at [51–71]

14 Enforcement: insolvency, stay and severability

14.2 Insolvency avoids summary judgment

14.2.2 Liquidation

Alexander & Law Ltd v Coveside (21BPR) Ltd [2013] EWHC 3949 (TCC) at [18–22]
Bouygues (UK) Ltd v Dahl-Jensen (UK) Ltd [2000] EWCA Civ 507 at [29–36]
Enterprise Managed Services Ltd v Tony McFadden Utilities Ltd [2009] EWHC 3222 (TCC) at [61–79]
Hart Investments Ltd v Fidler & Anor [2006] EWHC 2857 (TCC) at [65–75]
Integrated Building Services Engineering Consultants Ltd trading as Operon v PIHL UK Ltd [2010] CSOH 80 at [17–35]
Joinery Plus Ltd (In Administration) v Laing Ltd [2003] EWHC 3513 (TCC) at [108]

14.2.3 Administration

A Straume (UK) Ltd v Bradlor Developments Ltd [1999] CILL 1520 at [9–16]
Connaught Partnerships Ltd v Perth and Kinross Council [2013] CSOH 149 at [15–21]
Gibraltar Residential Properties Ltd v Gibralcon 2004 SA [2010] EWHC 2595 at [16]
Joinery Plus Ltd (In Administration) v Laing Ltd [2003] EWHC 3513 (TCC) at [102–120]
Straw Realisations (No 1) Ltd (formerly known as Haymills (Contractors) Ltd (in administration)) v Shaftsbury House (Developments) Ltd [2010] EWHC 2597 (TCC) at [89–97]

14.2.4 Administrative receivership

Baldwins Industrial Services plc v Barr Ltd [2002] EWHC 2915 (TCC) at [25–40]
Melville Dundas Limited (in receivership) and others George Wimpey UK Limited and others [2007] UKHL 18 at [14].
Rainford House Ltd v Cadogan Ltd [2001] BLR 416 at [15–20]

14.2.5 CVA

Pilon Ltd v Breyer Group plc [2010] EWHC 837 (TCC) at [47–62; 64]
Tate Building Services Ltd v B & M McHugh Ltd [2014] EWHC 2971 at [37–43]
Westshield Ltd v Whitehouse [2013] EWHC 3576 (TCC) at [20–33]

14.3 Stay of execution

14.3.2 Court's discretion to order a stay

> Absolute Rentals Ltd v Gencor Enterprises Ltd (2001) 17 Const LJ 322 at [17]
> Alexander & Law Ltd v Coveside (21BPR) Ltd [2013] EWHC 3949 (TCC) at [24–36]
> AWG Construction Services Ltd v Rockingham Motor Speedway Ltd [2004] EWHC 888 (TCC) at [185–187]
> Berry Piling Systems Ltd v Sheer Projects Ltd [2012] EWHC 241 (TCC) at [15–17]
> Bouygues (UK) Ltd v Dahl-Jensen (UK) Ltd [2000] EWCA Civ 507 at [29–36]
> FG Skerritt Ltd v Caledonian Building Systems Ltd [2013] EWHC 1898 (TCC) at [12]
> Herschell Engineering Ltd v Breen Property Ltd (No 2) [2000] AdjLR 07/28 at [3–20]
> Mead General Building Ltd v Dartmoor Properties Ltd [2009] EWHC 200 (TCC) at [10–12]
> Pilon Ltd v Breyer Group plc [2010] EWHC 837 (TCC) at [46]
> Rainford House Ltd v Cadogan Ltd [2001] BLR 416 at [15–20]
> Rodgers Contracts (Ballynahinch) Ltd v Merex Construction Ltd [2012] NIQB 94 at [14–23]
> Sutton Services International Ltd v Vaughan Engineering Services [2013] NIQB 63 at [5]
> Total M&E Services Ltd v ABB Building Technologies Ltd (formerly ABB Stewarts Ltd) [2002] EWHC 248 (TCC) at [52]
> Wimbledon Construction Company 2000 Ltd v Derek Vago [2005] EWHC 1086 (TCC) at [12–26]

14.3.3 Insolvency procedure pending or not concluded

> *(A) Insolvency procedure pending – liquidation*
> Alexander & Law Ltd v Coveside (21BPR) Ltd [2013] EWHC 3949 (TCC) at [24–36]
> FG Skerritt Ltd v Caledonian Building Systems Ltd [2013] EWHC 1898 (TCC) at [29–32]
> Harwood Construction Ltd v Lantrode Ltd [2001] AdjLR 11/24 at [10–20]
> Humes Building Contracts Ltd v Charlotte Homes (Surrey) Ltd [2007] AdjLR 01/03 at [30]
> Maguire and Co v Mar City Developments [2013] EWHC 3503 (TCC) at [22–29]
> SL Timber Systems Ltd v Carillion Construction Ltd [2001] ScotCS 167 at [30]
> Volker Stevin Ltd v Holystone Contracts Ltd [2010] EWHC 2344 (TCC) at [26–28]
> *(B) Insolvency procedure pending – CVA*
> Mead General Building Ltd v Dartmoor Properties Ltd [2009] EWHC 200 (TCC) at [13–20]
> Pilon Ltd v Breyer Group plc [2010] EWHC 837 (TCC) at [47–62; 64]
> Westshield Ltd v Whitehouse [2013] EWHC 3576 (TCC) at [20–33]

14.3.4 Financial difficulty

(A) Financial difficulties – stay granted
>Ashley House plc v Galliers Southern Ltd [2002] EWHC 274 (TCC) at [18–23]
>Baldwins Industrial Services plc v Barr Ltd [2002] EWHC 2915 (TCC) at [25–40]
>Barry D Trentham Ltd v Lawfield Investments Ltd [2002] ScotCS 126 at [13–15]
>Coleraine Skip Hire Ltd v Ecomesh Ltd [2008] NIQB 141 at [29–31]
>FG Skerritt Ltd v Caledonian Building Systems Ltd [2013] EWHC 1898 (TCC) at [52–59]
>Jacques (t/a C & E Jacques Partnership) v Ensign Contractors Ltd [2009] EWHC 3383 (TCC) at [34–39]
>JPA Design and Build Ltd v Sentosa (UK) Ltd [2009] EWHC 2312 (TCC) at [29–46]
>London Borough of Camden v Makers UK Ltd [2009] EWHC 2944 (TCC) at [11–19]
>NAP Anglia Ltd v Sun-Land Development Co Ltd [2011] EWHC 2846 (TCC) at [62–72]
>Pioneer Cladding Ltd v John Graham Construction Ltd [2013] EWHC 2954 (TCC) at [9–38]
>Rainford House Ltd v Cadogan Ltd [2001] BLR 416 at [15–20]
>Rodgers Contracts (Ballynahinch) Ltd v Merex Construction Ltd [2012] NIQB 94 at [24–26]
>Speymill Contracts Ltd v Eric Baskind [2009] No 9LV 22750 at [113–118]
>Sutton Services International Ltd v Vaughan Engineering Services [2013] NIQB 63 at [20–23]

(B) Financial difficulties – stay not granted
>Absolute Rentals Ltd v Gencor Enterprises Ltd (2001) 17 Const LJ 322 at [10]
>Air Design (Kent) Ltd v Deerglen (Jersey) Ltd [2008] EWHC 3047 (TCC) at [27–28]
>Ale Heavylift v MSD (Darlington) Ltd [2006] EWHC 2080 (TCC) at [95–102]
>All in One Building and Refurbishments Ltd v Makers UK Ltd [2005] EWHC 2943 (TCC) at [57–66]
>Anrik Ltd v As Leisure Properties Ltd Unreported, 8 January 2010 at [29–35]
>Avoncroft Construction Ltd v Sharba Homes (CN) Ltd [2008] EWHC 933 (TCC) at [21–29]
>AWG Construction Services Ltd v Rockingham Motor Speedway Ltd [2004] EWHC 888 (TCC) at [188]
>Berry Piling Systems Ltd v Sheer Projects Ltd [2012] EWHC 241 (TCC) at [18–26]
>Bewley Homes v CNM Estates [2010] EWHC 2619 (TCC) at [28–35]
>Broughton Brickwork Ltd v F Parkinson Ltd [2014] EWHC 4525 (TCC) at [30]
>CSK Electrical Contractors Ltd v Kingwood Electrical Services Ltd [2015] EWHC 667 (TCC) at [29–31]
>Farrelly (M&E) Building Services Ltd v Byrne Brothers (Formwork) Ltd [2013] EWHC 1186 (TCC) at [90–92]
>Herschell Engineering Ltd v Breen Property Ltd (No 2) [2000] AdjLR 07/28 at [15–20]
>J and A Construction (Scotland) Ltd v Windex Ltd [2013] CSOH 170 at [3–14]

JW Hughes Building Contractors Ltd v GB Metalwork Ltd [2003] EWHC 2421 (TCC) at [41–46]
Knight Build Ltd v Urvasco Ltd [2008] EWHC 3056 (TCC) at [44–47]
Lovell Projects Ltd v Legg & Carver [2003] BLR 452 at [42]
McConnell Dowell Constructors (Aust) Pty Ltd v National Grid Gas plc (formerly Transco plc) [2006] EWHC 2551 (TCC) at [50–54].
Michael John Construction Ltd v Golledge & Ors [2006] EWHC 71 (TCC) at [78–87]
Multiplex Constructions (UK) Ltd v West India Quay Development Company (Eastern) Ltd [2006] EWHC 1569 (TCC) at [43–44]
Nolan Davis Ltd v Catton 2000 TCC No 590 at [32–33]
Partner Projects Ltd v Corinthian Nominees Ltd [2011] EWHC 2989 (TCC) at [52–72]
SG South Ltd. v King's Head Cirencester LLP & Anor [2009] EWHC 2645 (TCC) at [39–43]
Shaw v MEP Foundations Piling Ltd [2009] EWHC 493 (TCC) at [39]
Solland International Ltd v Daraydan Holdings Ltd [2002] EWHC 220 (TCC) at [18]
Tera Construction Ltd v Yuk Tong Lam [2005] EWHC 3306 (TCC) at [38–49]
The Mayor and Burgesses of the London Borough of Camden v Makers UK Ltd [2009] EWHC 605 (TCC) at [41–46]
Total M&E Services Ltd v ABB Building Technologies Ltd (formerly ABB Stewarts Ltd) [2002] EWHC 248 (TCC) at [53–54]
Treasure & Son Ltd v Martin Dawes [2007] EWHC 2420 (TCC) at [54–55]
True Fix Construction Ltd v Apollo Property Services Group Ltd [2013] EWHC 2524 (TCC) at [12–14; 26–33]
Volker Stevin Ltd v Holystone Contracts Ltd [2010] EWHC 2344 (TCC) at [26–28]
Wimbledon Construction Company 2000 Ltd v Derek Vago [2005] EWHC 1086 (TCC) at [35–42]

14.3.5 Imminent resolution of other proceedings

Alexander & Law Ltd v Coveside (21BPR) Ltd [2013] EWHC 3949 (TCC) at [13–14]
Harlow & Milner Ltd v Linda Teasdale (No 1) [2006] EWHC 54 (TCC) at [9]
Herschell Engineering Ltd v Breen Property Ltd [2000] All ER (D) 559 at [23]
Kier Regional Ltd (t/a Wallis) v City and General (Holborn) Ltd & Ors (No 2) [2008] EWHC 2454 (TCC) at [68–71]
William Verry Ltd v North West London Communal Mikvah [2004] EWHC 1300 (TCC) at [54–60]
Workspace Management Ltd v YJL London Ltd [2009] EWHC 2017 (TCC) at [40–44]

14.3.6 Manifest injustice

Galliford Try Building v Estura Ltd [2015] EWHC 412 (TCC) at [53–55; 78–101]

14.3.7 Other circumstances in which an application for a stay has failed

AJ Brenton t/a Manton Electrical Components v Jack Palmer [2001] AdjLR 01/19 at [8]
Avoncroft Construction Ltd v Sharba Homes (CN) Ltd [2008] EWHC 933 (TCC) at [27]
Alstom Signalling Ltd v Jarvis Facilities Ltd (No 2) [2004] EWHC 1285 (TCC) at [20]
ART Consultancy Ltd v Navera Trading Ltd [2007] EWHC 1375 (TCC) at [21–26]
Balfour Beatty Construction Northern Ltd v Modus Corovest (Blackpool) Ltd [2008] EWHC 3029 (TCC) at [14–21]
DGT Steel and Cladding Ltd v Cubitt Building and Interiors Ltd [2007] EWHC 1584 (TCC) at [51]
D G Williamson Ltd v Northern Ireland Prison Service [2009] NIQB 8 at [35–36]
Henry Brothers (Magherafelt) Ltd v Brunswick (8 Lanyon Place) Ltd [2011] NIQB 102 at [17–19]
Hillview Industrial Developments (UK) Ltd v Botes Building Ltd [2006] EWHC 1365 (TCC) at [33–35]
Interserve Industrial Services Ltd v Cleveland Bridge UK Ltd [2006] EWHC 741 (TCC) at [48–52]
Knight Build Ltd v Urvasco Ltd [2008] EWHC 3056 (TCC) at [48–50]
Management Solutions & Professional Consultants Ltd v Bennett (Electrical) Services Ltd (No 2) [2006] EWHC 1720_2 (TCC) at [4–5]
McConnell Dowell Constructors (Aust) Pty Ltd v National Grid Gas plc (formerly Transco plc) [2006] EWHC 2551 (TCC) at [50–54]
MJ Gleeson Group plc v Devonshire Green Holding Ltd [2004] AdjLR 03/19 at [24]
SG South Ltd v Swan Yard (Cirencester) Ltd [2010] EWHC 376 (TCC) at [13–15]
SG South Ltd. v King's Head Cirencester LLP & Anor [2009] EWHC 2645 (TCC) at [37]
Sir Robert McAlpine v Pring & St Hill Ltd [2001] All ER (D) 484 (Oct) at [14]
Westshield Civil Engineering Ltd v Buckingham Group Contracting Ltd [2013] EWHC 1825 (TCC) at [30–35]

14.3.8 Partial stay

Galliford Try Building v Estura Ltd [2015] EWHC 412 (TCC) at [53–55; 78–101]
Jacques (t/a C & E Jacques Partnership) v Ensign Contractors Ltd [2009] EWHC 3383 (TCC) at [34–39]
NAP Anglia Ltd v Sun-Land Development Co Ltd [2011] EWHC 2846 (TCC) at [62–72]

14.3.9 Conditions imposed on the stay of execution

Allen Wilson Joinery Ltd v Privetgrange Construction Ltd [2008] EWHC 2802 (TCC) at [32]
Anglo Swiss Holding Ltd & Ors v Packman Lucas Ltd [2009] EWHC 3212 (TCC) at [25–31]

Baldwins Industrial Services plc v Barr Ltd [2002] EWHC 2915 (TCC) at [39]
Coleraine Skip Hire Ltd v Ecomesh Ltd [2008] NIQB 141 at [31]
FG Skerritt Ltd v Caledonian Building Systems Ltd [2013] EWHC 1898 (TCC) at [35; 60–67]
McConnell Dowell Constructors (Aust) Pty Ltd v National Grid Gas plc (formerly Transco plc) [2006] EWHC 2551 (TCC) at [52–53]
Rainford House Ltd v Cadogan Ltd [2001] BLR 416 at [20]
Rodgers Contracts (Ballynahinch) Ltd v Merex Construction Ltd [2012] NIQB 94 at [23–26]
Speymill Contracts Ltd v Eric Baskind [2009] No 9LV 22750 at [118]

14.4 Severability

Adonis Construction v O'Keefe Soil Remediation [2009] EWHC 2047 (TCC) at [49–50]
Allied P&L Ltd v Paradigm Housing Group Ltd [2009] EWHC 2890 (TCC) at [34–35; 44]
AMEC Group Ltd v Thames Water Utilities Ltd [2010] EWHC 419 (TCC) at [99–100]
AWG Construction Services Ltd v Rockingham Motor Speedway Ltd [2004] EWHC 888 (TCC) at [171–179]
Barr Ltd v Law Mining Ltd [2001] ScotCS 152 at [5]
Beck Interiors Ltd v UK Flooring Contractors Ltd [2012] EWHC 1808 (TCC) at [32–33]
Bovis Lend Lease Ltd v The Trustees of the London Clinic [2009] EWHC 64 (TCC) at [69–70]
Cantillon Ltd v Urvasco Ltd [2008] EWHC 282 (TCC) at [58–65; 78]
Carillion Construction Ltd v Devonport Royal Dockyard Ltd [2005] EWCA Civ 1358 at [51]
Carillion Construction Ltd v Devonport Royal Dockyard Ltd [2005] EWHC 778 (TCC) at [55]
Carillion Utility Services Ltd v SP Power Systems Ltd [2011] CSOH 139 at [39–44]
Cleveland Bridge (UK) Ltd v Whessoe-Volker Stevin Joint Venture [2010] EWHC 1076 (TCC) at [107–124]
CSC Braehead Leisure Ltd and Capital & Regional (Braehead) Ltd v Laing O-Rourke Scotland Ltd [2008] CSOH 119 at [35–40]
Estor Ltd v Multifit (UK) Ltd [2009] EWHC 2108 (TCC) at [38]
Eurocom Ltd v Siemens plc [2014] EWHC 3710 (TCC) at [119]
Farebrother Building Services Ltd v Frogmore Investments Ltd [2001] CILL 1762 at [32]
Geoffrey Osborne Ltd v Atkins Rail Ltd [2009] EWHC 2425 (TCC) at [18]
Highlands and Islands Authority Ltd v Shetland Islands Counsel [2012] CSOH 12 at [41–47]
Hillcrest Homes Ltd v Beresford & Curbishley Ltd [2014] EWHC 280 (TCC) at [53]
Hitec Power Protection BV v MCI Worldcom Ltd [2002] EWHC 1953 (QB) at [89–93]
Homer Burgess Ltd v Chirex (Annan) Ltd (No. 1) (1999) 71 ConLR 245 at [5–9]

Homer Burgess Ltd v Chirex (Annan) Ltd (No. 2) [1999] ScotCS 264 at [5–9]
Interserve Industrial Services Ltd v Cleveland Bridge UK Ltd [2006] EWHC 741 (TCC) at [60]
Ken Griffin (t/a K&D Contractors) v Midas Homes Ltd (2000) 78 ConLR 152 at [23]
KNS Industrial Services (Birmingham) Ltd v Sindall Ltd (2001) 75 ConLR 71 at [24]
Lidl UK GmbH v RG Carter Colchester Ltd [2012] EWHC 3138 at [57–61]
Pilon Ltd v Breyer Group plc [2010] EWHC 837 (TCC) at [39–42]
Quartzelec Ltd v Honeywell Control Systems Ltd [2008] EWHC 3315 (TCC) at [39–42]
RSL (South West Ltd) v Stansell Ltd (No 1) [2003] EWHC 1390 (TCC) at [38]
Shimizu Europe Ltd v LBJ Fabrications Ltd [2003] EWHC 1229 (TCC) at [29–30]
Tera Construction Ltd v Yuk Tong Lam [2005] EWHC 3306 (TCC) at [18–19]
Whyte and Mackay Ltd v Blyth & Blyth Consulting Engineers Ltd [2013] CSOH 54 at [66–73]
Working Environments Ltd v Greencoat Construction Ltd [2012] EWHC 1039 (TCC) at [32–34]
WSP Cel Ltd v Dalkia Utilities Services plc [2012] EWHC 2428 (TCC) at [96]

15 FINAL DETERMINATION

15.2 Finalising the adjudicator's decision

15.2.2 Adjudicator's decision made final by contract

Anglian Water Services Ltd v Laing O'Rourke Utilities Ltd [2010] EWHC 1529 (TCC) at [13–32]
Castle Inns (Stirling) Ltd t/a Castle Leisure Ltd v Clark Contracts Ltd [2007] CSOH 21 at [12–20]
Jerram Falkus Construction Ltd v Fenice Investments Inc (No 4) [2011] EWHC 1935 (TCC) at [20–27]
Lafarge (Aggregates) Ltd. v London Borough of Newham [2005] EWHC 1337 (Comm) at [17–30]
Midland Expressway Ltd & Ors v Carillion Construction Ltd & Ors (No. 3) [2006] EWHC 1505 (TCC) at [85–89]
Scrabster Harbour Trust v Mowlem plc t/a Mowlem Marine [2005] CSOH 44 at [21–25]
Straw Realisations (No 1) Ltd (formerly known as Haymills (Contractors) Ltd (in administration)) v Shaftsbury House (Developments) Ltd [2010] EWHC 2597 (TCC) at [35–49]
Van Oord ACZ Ltd And Harbour & General Works Ltd Joint Venture v The Port Of Mostyn Ltd [2003] BM350030 TCC at [95]
Westshield Civil Engineering Ltd v Buckingham Group Contracting Ltd [2013] EWHC 1825 (TCC) at [18–26]

15.2.3 Adjudicator's decision made final by agreement

> Bracken and another v Billinghurst [2003] EWHC 1333 (TCC) at [28-30]
> Jerram Falkus Construction Ltd v Fenice Investments Inc (No 4) [2011] EWHC 1935 (TCC) at [13-32]
> RSL (South West Ltd) v Stansell Ltd (No 1) [2003] EWHC 1390 (TCC) at [37]

15.3 Adjudication and Other Proceedings

15.3.2 Final determination at the same time as enforcement proceedings

> AC Plastic Industries Ltd v Active Fire Protection Ltd [2002] All ER (D) 61 (Aug) at [1-2]
> Alstom Signalling Ltd v Jarvis Facilities Ltd (No 2) [2004] EWHC 1285 (TCC) at [19-20]
> Caledonian Modular Ltd v Mar City Developments Ltd [2015] EWHC 1855 (TCC) at [12-13]
> D G Williamson Ltd v Northern Ireland Prison Service [2009] NIQB 8 at [3]
> Dalkia Energy and Technical Services Ltd v Bell Group UK Ltd [2009] EWHC 73 (TCC) at [44]
> Geoffrey Osborne Ltd v Atkins Rail Ltd [2009] EWHC 2425 (TCC) at [10-18]
> GPS Marine Contractors Ltd v Ringway Infrastructure Services Ltd [2010] EWHC 283 (TCC) at [64]
> Hillcrest Homes Ltd v Beresford & Curbishley Ltd [2014] EWHC 280 (TCC) at [81-96]
> HS Works Ltd v Enterprise Managed Services Ltd [2009] EWHC 729 (TCC) at [46]
> Laker Vent Engineering Ltd v Jacobs E&C Ltd [2014] EWHC 1058 (TCC) at [124-129]
> Leeds City Council v Waco UK Ltd [2015] EWHC 1400 (TCC) at [63-66]
> St Austell Printing Company Ltd v Dawnus Construction Holdings Ltd [2015] EWHC 96 (TCC) at [1]
> Walter Lilly & Co Ltd v DMW Developments Ltd [2008] EWHC 3139 (TCC) at [6-21]

15.3.3 Final determination at the same time as adjudication

> Alstom Signalling Ltd v Jarvis Facilities Ltd (No 2) [2004] EWHC 1285 (TCC) at [19-20]
> Connex South Eastern Ltd v MJ Building Services Group plc [2004] EWHC 1518 (TCC) at [35]
> GPS Marine Contractors Ltd v Ringway Infrastructure Services Ltd [2010] EWHC 283 (TCC) at [64]
> Herschell Engineering Ltd v Breen Property Ltd [2000] All ER (D) 559 at [15-20]
> Northern Ireland Housing Executive v Healthy Buildings Ltd [2013] NIQB 124 at [1; 26-27]
> The Construction Centre Group Ltd v The Highland Council [2003] ScotCS 114 at [15]
> Twintec Ltd v Volkerfitzpatrick Ltd [2014] EWHC 10 (TCC) at [7]

15.3.4 Final determination without complying with the adjudicator's decision

> Anglo Swiss Holding Ltd & Ors v Packman Lucas Ltd [2009] EWHC 3212 (TCC) at [25–31]
> Cygnet Healthcare plc v Higgins City Ltd (2000) 16 Const LJ 394 at [20–27]

15.3.5 Final determination in breach of the contractual dispute resolution procedure (including an agreement to adjudicate)

> Cubitt Building and Interiors Ltd v Richardson Roofing (Industrial) Ltd [2008] EWHC 1020 (TCC) at [72]
> DGT Steel and Cladding Ltd v Cubitt Building and Interiors Ltd [2007] EWHC 1584 (TCC) at [5–12]
> Herschell Engineering Ltd v Breen Property Ltd (No 2) [2000] AdjLR 07/28 at [3–20]
> Impresa Castelli SpA v Cola Holdings Ltd [2002] EWHC 1363 (TCC) at [100–108]
> J.T.Mackley v Gosport Marina Ltd [2002] EWHC 1315 at [35–38]
> Peterborough City Council v Enterprise Managed Services [2014] EWHC 3193 (TCC) at [37–43]
> Sam Abbas and Anthony Hayes (t/as AH Design) v Rotary (International) Ltd [2012] NIQB 41 at [10–26]

15.4 Commencement, onus of proof and costs

15.4.2 Cause of action and limitation period for commencing final determination

> Aspect Contracts (Asbestos) Ltd v Higgins Construction plc [2015] UKSC 38 at [18–33]
> Aspect Contracts (Asbestos) Ltd v Higgins Construction Plc [2013] EWCA Civ 1541 at [16–20]
> Aspect Contracts (Asbestos) Ltd v Higgins Construction plc [2013] EWHC 1322 (TCC) at [26–50]
> Bovis Lend Lease Ltd v Triangle Development Ltd [2002] EWHC 3123 (TCC) at [37]
> David McLean Housing Contractors Ltd v Swansea Housing Association Ltd [2001] All ER (D) 519 (Jul) at [14–17]
> Glencot Development & Design Co Ltd v Ben Barrett & Son (Contractors) Ltd [2001] All ER (D) 384 (Feb) at [33]
> Jim Ennis Construction Ltd v Premier Asphalt Ltd [2009] EWHC 1906 (TCC) at [11–31]
> Ringway Infrastructure Services Ltd v Vauxhall Motors Ltd (No 2) [2007] EWHC 2507 (TCC) at [14–17]
> VHE Construction plc v RBSTB Trust Co Ltd (as trustee of the Mercury Property Fund) [2000] BLR 187 at [38–55]
> Walker Construction (UK) Ltd v Quayside Homes Ltd and Others [2014] EWCA Civ 93 at [58–64]

15.4.3 Delaying the final determination

A v B [2002] ScotCS 325 at [7–11]

Enterprise Managed Services Ltd v East Midland Contracting Ltd [2008] EWHC 727 (TCC) at [32–36]

Jerram Falkus Construction Ltd v Fenice Investments Inc (No 4) [2011] EWHC 1935 (TCC) at [13–32]

Yuanda (UK) Co Ltd v WW Gear Construction Ltd [2010] EWHC 720 (TCC) at [42–51]

15.4.4 Onus of proof in subsequent proceedings

Absolute Rentals Ltd v Gencor Enterprises Ltd (2001) 17 Const LJ 322 at [9]

Alstom Signalling Ltd v Jarvis Facilities Ltd (No 2) [2004] EWHC 1285 (TCC) at [20]

Castle Inns (Stirling) Ltd t/a Castle Leisure Ltd v Clark Contracts Ltd [2007] CSOH 21 at [13]

Citex Professional Services Ltd v Kenmore Developments Ltd [2004] ScotCS 20 at [14–16]

City Inn Ltd v Shepherd Construction Ltd [2001] ScotCS 54 at [54–58]

Walker Construction (UK) Ltd v Quayside Homes Ltd and Others [2014] EWCA Civ 93 at [48–52]

15.5.5 Final decision different to the adjudicator's decision

Castle Inns (Stirling) Ltd trading as Castle Leisure Group v Clark Contracts Ltd [2005] CSOH 178 at [13–14]

15.5.6 Recovery of adjudication costs as part of the costs of a final determination

Castle Inns (Stirling) Ltd trading as Castle Leisure Group v Clark Contracts Ltd [2005] CSOH 178 at [15–21]

Fenice Investments Inc v Jerram Falkus Construction Ltd [2011] EWHC 1678 (TCC) at [16–62]

National Museums and Galleries on Merseyside v AEW Architects and Designers Ltd [2013] EWHC 2403 (TCC) at [124–130]

Sam Abbas and Antony Hayes (T/As A H Design) v Rotary (International) Ltd [2012] NIQB 41 at [10–26]

Walker Construction (UK) Ltd v Quayside Homes Ltd and Others [2014] EWCA Civ 93 at [71–99]

Yuanda (UK) Co Ltd v WW Gear Construction Ltd [2010] EWHC 720 (TCC) at [124–130]

16 The adjudicator's jurisdiction

16.3 Options when a jurisdictional issue arises

16.3.2 Option 1: Determination by the court

> ABB Zantingh Ltd v Zedal Building Services Ltd [2001] BLR 66 at [13]
> Aceramais Holdings Ltd v Hadleigh Partnerships Ltd [2009] EWHC 1664 (TCC) at [40–52]
> Banner Holdings Ltd v Colchester Borough Council [2010] EWHC 139 (TCC) at [1–6]
> Bovis Lend Lease Ltd v Cofely Engineering Services [2009] EWHC 1120 (TCC) at [1–2]
> Carillion Construction Ltd v Stephen Andrew Smith [2011] EWHC 2910 (TCC) at [1]
> Comsite Projects Ltd v Andritz AG [2003] EWHC 958 (TCC) at [24–26]
> Dalkia Energy and Technical Services Ltd v Bell Group UK Ltd [2009] EWHC 73 (TCC) at [7–12]
> Dorchester Hotel Ltd v Vivid Interiors Ltd [2009] EWHC 70 (TCC) at [12–17]
> Forest Heath District Council v ISG Jackson Ltd [2010] EWHC 322 (TCC) at [28–31]
> Glendalough Associated SA v Harris Calnan Construction Co Ltd [2013] EWHC 3142 (TCC) at [56]
> Gotch v Enelco Ltd [2015] EWHC 1802 (TCC) at [23–31; 58–65]
> Jim Ennis Construction Ltd v Combined Stabilisation Ltd [2009] EWHC B37 (TCC) at [1; 28]
> Re W. H. Malcolm Ltd [2010] CSOH 152 at [24–27]
> ROK Building Ltd v Bestwood Carpentry Ltd [2010] EWHC 1409 (TCC) at [1]
> Vitpol Building Service v Michael Samen [2008] EWHC 2283 (TCC) at [13–19]
> William Naylor t/a Powerfloated Concrete Floors v Greenacres Curling Ltd [2001] ScotCS 163 at [9–11]
> WW Gear Construction Ltd v McGee Group Ltd [2012] EWHC 1509 (TCC) at [16–28]

16.3.3 Option 2: Determination by the adjudicator

> Aedifice Partnership Ltd v Shah [2010] EWHC 210 (TCC) at [21]
> Amec Capital Projects Ltd v Whitefriars City Estates Ltd [2004] EWCA Civ 1418 at [41]
> Ballast plc v The Burrell Company (Construction Management) Ltd [2001] ScotCS 159 at [40–42]
> Christiani & Nielsen Ltd v The Lowry Centre Development Company Ltd [2000] AdjLR 06/16 at [14–20]
> CJP Builders Ltd v William Verry Ltd [2008] EWHC 2025 (TCC) at [73–74]
> Dalkia Energy and Technical Services Ltd v Bell Group UK Ltd [2009] EWHC 73 (TCC) at [33–37]
> Enterprise Managed Services Ltd v Tony McFadden Utilities Ltd [2009] EWHC 3222 (TCC) at [98–99]
> Farebrother Building Services Ltd v Frogmore Investments Ltd [2001] CILL 1762 at [27–32]

Fastrack Contractors Ltd v Morrison Construction Ltd & Anor [2000] All ER (D) 11 at [32]
Grovedeck Ltd v Capital Demolition Ltd [2000] All ER (D) 317 at [31]
Homer Burgess Ltd v Chirex (Annan) Ltd (No. 1) (1999) 71 ConLR 245 at [32]
Hortimax Ltd v Hedon Salads Ltd (2004) 24 Const LJ 47 at [21–38]
IDE Contracting Ltd v RG Carter Cambridge Ltd [2004] EWHC 36 (TCC) at [22]
JW Hughes Building Contractors Ltd v GB Metalwork Ltd [2003] EWHC 2421 (TCC) at [16]
Nolan Davis Ltd v Catton 2000 TCC No 590 at [27; 30]
Nordot Engineering Services Ltd v Siemens plc [2001] CILL 1778 at [11–30]
OSC Building Services Ltd v Interior Dimensions Contracts Ltd [2009] EWHC 248 (TCC) at [22–24]
Pegram Shopfitters Ltd v Tally Wiejl (UK) Ltd [2003] EWCA Civ 1750 at [10–13]
Pegram Shopfitters Ltd v Tally Wiejl (UK) Ltd [2003] EWHC 984 (TCC) at [25]
Pilon Ltd v Breyer Group plc [2010] EWHC 837 (TCC) at [11–16]
Project Consultancy Group v Trustees of the Gray Trust [1999] All ER (D) 842 at [15]
Thomas-Fredric's (Construction) Ltd v Wilson [2003] EWCA Civ 1494 at [29–34]
Watson Building Services Ltd [2001] ScotCS 60 at [28]
Whiteways Contractors (Sussex) Ltd v Impresa Castelli Construction UK Ltd (2000) 75 ConLR 92 at [24–27]

16.3.5 Option 4: Reserve the position and proceed with the adjudication

Aedifice Partnership Ltd v Mr Ashwin Shah [2010] EWHC 2106 (TCC) at [15–27]
Air Design (Kent) Ltd v Deerglen (Jersey) Ltd [2008] EWHC 3047 (TCC) at [20]
Ale Heavylift v MSD (Darlington) Ltd [2006] EWHC 2080 (TCC) at [55–56]
All Metal Roofing v Kamm Properties Ltd [2010] EWHC 2670 (TCC) at [21]
Allied P&L Ltd v Paradigm Housing Group Ltd [2009] EWHC 2890 (TCC) at [32–33; 43–44]
Bothma (t/a DAB Builders) v Mayhaven Healthcare Ltd [2007] EWCA Civ 527 at [6; 14]
Bothma (t/a DAB Builders) v Mayhaven Healthcare Ltd [2006] EWHC 2601 (QB) at [35–38]
City Basements Ltd v Nordic Construction UK Ltd [2014] EWHC 4817 (TCC) at [24–26]
CJP Builders Ltd v William Verry Ltd [2008] EWHC 2025 (TCC) at [72]
CN Associates (a firm) v Holbeton Ltd [2011] EWHC 43 (TCC) at [33; 37–38]
CSK Electrical Contractors Ltd v Kingwood Electrical Services Ltd [2015] EWHC 667 (TCC) at [18–20]
Dalkia Energy and Technical Services Ltd v Bell Group UK Ltd [2009] EWHC 73 (TCC) at [33–37]
Durham County Council v Jeremy Kendall (trading as HLB Architects) [2011] EWHC 780 (TCC) at [39]
Euro Construction Scaffolding Ltd v SLLB Construction Ltd [2008] EWHC 3160 (TCC) at [28–29]

GPS Marine Contractors Ltd v Ringway Infrastructure Services Ltd [2010] EWHC 283 (TCC) at [38–43]
Harris Calnan Construction Co Ltd v Ridgewood (Kensington) Ltd [2007] EWHC 2738 (TCC) at [4–8]
IDE Contracting Ltd v RG Carter Cambridge Ltd [2004] EWHC 36 (TCC) at [22]
Laker Vent Engineering Ltd v Jacobs E&C Ltd [2014] EWHC 1058 (TCC) at [31–32]
OSC Building Services Ltd v Interior Dimensions Contracts Ltd [2009] EWHC 248 (TCC) at [22–24]
Project Consultancy Group v Trustees of the Gray Trust [1999] All ER (D) 842 at [14–15]
R Durtnell & Sons Ltd v Kaduna Ltd [2003] EWHC 517 (TCC) at [46]
RC Pillar & Son v The Camber (Portsmouth) Ltd [2007] EWHC 1626 (TCC) at [9–14]
SG South Ltd v Swan Yard (Cirencester) Ltd [2010] EWHC 376 (TCC) at [9–14]
Specialist Insulation Ltd v Pro-Duct (Fife) Ltd [2012] CSOH 79 at [24–38]
Thomas-Fredric's (Construction) Ltd v Wilson [2003] EWCA Civ 1494 at [29–34]
VGC Construction Ltd v Jackson Civil Engineering Ltd [2008] EWHC 2082 (TCC) at [64]

16.3.6 Option 5: Withdraw

IDE Contracting Ltd v RG Carter Cambridge Ltd [2004] EWHC 36 (TCC) at [3]

16.3.7 Option 6: Injunction

ABB Power Construction Ltd v Norwest Holst Engineering Ltd (2000) 77 ConLR 20 at [21]
Aceramais Holdings Ltd v Hadleigh Partnerships Ltd [2009] EWHC 1664 (TCC) at [40]
Ericsson AB v EADS Defence and Security Systems Ltd [2009] EWHC 2598 (TCC) at [34–60]
Glendalough Associated SA v Harris Calnan Construction Co Ltd [2013] EWHC 3142 (TCC) at [53–56]
Herschell Engineering Ltd v Breen Property Ltd [2000] All ER (D) 559 at [15–22]
John Mowlem & Company plc v Hydra-Tight Ltd (2001) 17 Const LJ 358 at [50 et seq.]
Lanes Group plc v Galliford Try Infrastructure Ltd (No. 2) [2011] EWHC 1234 (TCC) at [3–6]
Lanes Group plc v Galliford Try Infrastructure Ltd [2011] EWHC 1035 (TCC) at [28–32]
Matthew Harding (t/a M J Harding Contractors) v Paice and Springall [2014] EWHC 3824 (TCC) at [47]
Mentmore Towers Ltd v Packman Lucas Ltd [2010] EWHC 457 (TCC) at [29–38]
Midland Expressway Ltd v Carillion Construction Ltd & Ors (No. 2) [2005] EWHC 2963 (TCC) at [81]
RG Carter Ltd v Edmund Nuttall Ltd Unreported, 21 June 2000 at [50]

T Clarke (Scotland) Limited v MMAXX Underfloor Heating Limited [2014] CSIH 83 at [32–37]

T Clarke (Scotland) Limited v MMAXX Underfloor Heating Limited [2014] CSOH 62 at [16–22]

Twintec Ltd v Volkerfitzpatrick Ltd [2014] EWHC 10 (TCC) at [88–89]

Workplace Technologies plc v E Squared Ltd and Mr J Riches HT 00 34 at [45–55]

16.4 Losing the right to challenge the adjudicator's jurisdiction

16.4.2 Waiver

Bovis Lend Lease Ltd v Cofely Engineering Services [2009] EWHC 1120 (TCC) at [45–49]

Brims Construction Ltd v A2M Development Ltd [2013] EWHC 3262 (TCC) at [25–30]

CJP Builders Ltd v William Verry Ltd [2008] EWHC 2025 (TCC) at [73–74]

RWE Npower plc v Alstom Power Ltd [2009] EWHC 1192 (QB) at [32–40]

Speymill Contracts Ltd v Eric Baskind [2009] No 9LV 22750 at [19–29]

16.4.3 No reservation or late reservation

Allied P&L Ltd v Paradigm Housing Group Ltd [2009] EWHC 2890 (TCC) at [43–44]

A.T. Stannard Ltd v James Tobutt and Thomas Tobutt [2014] EWHC 3491 (TCC) at [16–17]

Aedifice Partnership Ltd v Mr Ashwin Shah [2010] EWHC 2106 (TCC) at [15–27]

Brims Construction Ltd v A2M Development Ltd [2013] EWHC 3262 (TCC) at [25–30]

C&B Scene Concept Design Ltd v Isobars Ltd [2001] CILL 1781 at [24–30]

CJP Builders Ltd v William Verry Ltd [2008] EWHC 2025 (TCC) at [73–74]

CSK Electrical Contractors Ltd v Kingwood Electrical Services Ltd [2015] EWHC 667 (TCC) at [18–20]

Glendalough Associated SA v Harris Calnan Construction Co Ltd [2013] EWHC 3142 (TCC) at [14–16]

GPS Marine Contractors Ltd v Ringway Infrastructure Services Ltd [2010] EWHC 283 (TCC) at [36–37]

Harris Calnan Construction Co Ltd v Ridgewood (Kensington) Ltd [2007] EWHC 2738 (TCC) at [4–8]

Nickleby FM Ltd v Somerfield Stores Ltd [2010] EWHC 1976 (TCC) at [19–40]

Specialist Insulation Ltd v Pro-Duct (Fife) Ltd [2012] CSOH 79 at [24–38]

16.4.4 Abandoning the reservation

Christiani & Nielsen Ltd v The Lowry Centre Development Company Ltd [2000] AdjLR 06/16 at [29–37]

Hortimax Ltd v Hedon Salads Ltd (2004) 24 Const LJ 47 at [21–38]

16.4.5 Initial consent before objection

Cowlin Construction Ltd v CFW Architects (A Firm) [2002] EWHC 2914 (TCC) at [59–68]

16.4.6 Approbation and reprobation

AMEC Group Ltd v Thames Water Utilities Ltd [2010] EWHC 419 (TCC) at [94–98]
Galliford Try Construction Ltd v Michael Heal Associates Ltd [2003] EWHC 2886 (TCC) at [45–54]
Highlands and Islands Authority Ltd v Shetland Islands Counsel [2012] CSOH 12 at [54–60]
Joinery Plus Ltd (In Administration) v Laing Ltd [2003] EWHC 3513 (TCC) at [91–96]
Laker Vent Engineering Ltd v Jacobs E&C Ltd [2014] EWHC 1058 (TCC) at [33–36]
Linnett v Halliwells LLP [2009] EWHC 319 at [112–117]
Macob Civil Engineering v Morrison Construction Ltd [1999] All ER (D) 143 at [27–29]
Nickleby FM Ltd v Somerfield Stores Ltd [2010] EWHC 1976 (TCC) at [19–40]
Pilon Ltd v Breyer Group plc [2010] EWHC 837 (TCC) at [35]
PT Building Services Ltd v ROK Build Ltd [2008] EWHC 3434 (TCC) at [18–30]
R Durtnell & Sons Ltd v Kaduna Ltd [2003] EWHC 517 (TCC) at [47–48]
Redding Park Development Company Limited v Falkirk Council [2011] CSOH 202 at [54–62]
Redworth Construction Ltd v Brookdale Healthcare Ltd [2006] EWHC 1994 (TCC) at [38–41]
RJ Knapman Ltd v Richards [2006] EWHC 2518 (TCC) at [20–26]
RWE Npower plc v Alstom Power Ltd [2009] EWHC 1192 (QB) at [32–40]
Shimizu Europe Ltd v Automajor Ltd [2002] EWHC 1571 (TCC) at [26–30]
Thameside Construction Co Ltd v Stevens [2013] EWHC 2071 (TCC) at [13; 27]
VGC Construction Ltd v Jackson Civil Engineering Ltd [2008] EWHC 2082 (TCC) at [64]
Wales and West Utilities Ltd v PPS Pipeline Systems GmbH [2014] EWHC 54 (TCC) at [42–44]

16.4.7 Consequence of losing the right: ad hoc jurisdiction

GPS Marine Contractors Ltd v Ringway Infrastructure Services Ltd [2010] EWHC 283 (TCC) at [36–37]

16.5 Threshold jurisdiction challenges

16.5.2 No contract

> Cross refer to Section 4.3.2 in this appendix

16.5.3 Contract is not a construction contract

> Cross refer to Section 4.4 in this appendix

16.5.4 Construction contract is not in writing

> Cross refer to Section 4.8 in this appendix

16.5.5 No dispute

> Cross refer to Section 7.2 in this appendix

16.5.6 More than one dispute

> Cross refer to Section 7.3 in this appendix

16.5.7 Substantially the same dispute

> Cross refer to Section 7.4 in this appendix

16.5.8 Dispute not under the contract

> Cross refer to Sections 7.5 and 7.6 in this appendix

16.6 Process jurisdiction challenges

16.6.2 Incorrect parties named

> A.T. Stannard Ltd v James Tobutt and Thomas Tobutt [2014] EWHC 3491 (TCC) at [18]
> AJ Brenton t/a Manton Electrical Components v Jack Palmer [2001] AdjLR 01/19 at [3–7]
> Andrew Wallace Ltd v Artisan Regeneration Ltd & Anor [2006] EWHC 15 (TCC) at [33–40]
> Belgrave Developments (Poole) Ltd v Vaughan & Anor [2005] AdjLR 06/30 at [86–89]
> Concrete & Coating (UK) Ltd v Cornelius Moloney [2004] ADJ LR 12/06 at [1 to 8]

Durham County Council v Jeremy Kendall (trading as HLB Architects) [2011] EWHC 780 (TCC) at [38]
Estor Ltd v Multifit (UK) Ltd [2009] EWHC 2108 (TCC) at [24–26]
Estor Ltd v Multifit (UK) Ltd [2009] EWHC 2565 (TCC) at [41–42]
Gibson v Imperial Homes [2002] EWHC 676 (QB) at [50–55; 59–64]
Michael John Construction Ltd v Golledge & Ors [2006] EWHC 71 (TCC) at [44–48]
Redworth Construction Ltd v Brookdale Healthcare Ltd [2006] EWHC 1994 (TCC) at [46–47]
ROK Build Ltd v Harris Wharf Development Company Ltd [2006] EWHC 3573 (TCC) at [11–19]
Thomas-Fredric's (Construction) Ltd v Wilson [2003] EWCA Civ 1494 at [10–15]
Total M&E Services Ltd v ABB Building Technologies Ltd (formerly ABB Stewarts Ltd) [2002] EWHC 248 (TCC) at [17–23]
Westdawn Refurbishments Ltd v Roselodge Ltd [2006] AdjLR 04/24 at [45–54]
Williams (t/a Sanclair Construction) v Noor (t/a India Kitchen) [2007] EWHC 3467 (TCC) at [48–58; 73–80]

16.6.3 Adjudicator not correctly appointed

AMEC Capital Projects Ltd v Whitefriars City Estate Ltd [2003] EWHC 2443 (TCC) at [8–11]
AMEC Capital Projects Ltd v Whitefriars City Estates Ltd (No 3) [2004] EWCA Civ 1418 at [10–13]
Aveat Heating Ltd v Jerram Falkus Construction Ltd [2007] EWHC 131 (TCC) at [12]
Bennett v FMK Construction Ltd [2005] EWHC 1268 (TCC) at [7–10]
Bovis Lend Lease Ltd v Cofely Engineering Services [2009] EWHC 1120 (TCC) at [39–44]
C&B Scene Concept Design Ltd v Isobars Ltd [2001] CILL 1781 at [21–23]
CJP Builders Ltd v William Verry Ltd [2008] EWHC 2025 (TCC) at [64–76]
Dalkia Energy and Technical Services Ltd v Bell Group UK Ltd [2009] EWHC 73 (TCC) at [65–88]
David McLean Housing Contractors Ltd v Swansea Housing Association Ltd [2001] All ER (D) 519 (Jul) at [5–7]
Ecovision Systems Ltd v Vinci Construction UK Ltd [2015] EWHC 587 (TCC) at [70–78; 83–93]
Eurocom Ltd v Siemens plc [2014] EWHC 3710 (TCC) at [57–79]
IDE Contracting Ltd v RG Carter Cambridge Ltd [2004] EWHC 36 (TCC) at [9–11]
Impresa Castelli SpA v Cola Holdings Ltd [2002] EWHC 1363 (TCC) at [109–116]
John Mowlem & Company plc v Hydra-Tight Ltd (2001) 17 Const LJ 358 at [41–45]
Lead Technical Services v CMS Medical Ltd [2007] EWCA Civ 316 at [6–15]
Lee v Chartered Properties (Building) Ltd [2010] EWHC 1540 (TCC) at [15–19]
London & Amsterdam Properties Ltd v Waterman Partnership Ltd [2003] EWHC 3059 (TCC) at [75–84]

Makers UK Ltd v The Mayor and Burgesses of the London Borough of Camden [2008] EWHC 1836 (TCC) at [28–29]
Palmac Contracting Ltd v Park Lane Estates Ltd [2005] EWHC 919 (TCC) at [30–36]
Pegram Shopfitters Ltd v Tally Wiejl (UK) Ltd [2003] EWCA Civ 1750 at [30–34]
Pegram Shopfitters Ltd v Tally Wiejl (UK) Ltd [2003] EWHC 984 (TCC) at [16; 25–31]
Pring & St. Hill Ltd v C J Hafner t/a Southern Erectors [2002] EWHC 1775 (TCC) at [17–22]
Profile Projects Ltd v Elmwood (Glasgow) Ltd [2011] CSOH 64 at [51–52]
RG Carter Ltd v Edmund Nuttall Ltd Unreported, 21 June 2000 at [38–50]
Sprunt Ltd v London Borough of Camden [2011] EWHC 3191 (TCC) at [44–51]
Twintec Ltd v Volkerfitzpatrick Ltd [2014] EWHC 10 (TCC) at [57–61]
University of Brighton v Dovehouse Interiors Limited [2014] EWHC 940 (TCC) at [75–98]
Vision Homes Ltd v Lancsville Construction Ltd [2009] EWHC 2042 (TCC) at [51–57]
Watson Building Services Ltd [2001] ScotCS 60 at [21–41]

16.6.4 Referral notice served out of time

Cross refer to case Section 10.2.2

16.6.6 Defective Service

Costain Ltd v Wescol Steel Ltd [2003] EWHC 312 (TCC) at [14–18]
IDE Contracting Ltd v RG Carter Cambridge Ltd [2004] EWHC 36 (TCC) at [9–11]
M. Rohde Construction v Nicholas Markham-David [2006] EWHC 814 (TCC) at [31–38]
Nageh v Richard Giddings & Another [2006] EWHC 3240 (TCC) at [25–26]
Primus Build Ltd v Pompey Centre Ltd & Anor [2009] EWHC 1487 (TCC) at [9–26]
University of Brighton v Dovehouse Interiors Limited [2014] EWHC 940 (TCC) at [69–74]
Willmott Dixon Housing Limited (formerly Inspace Partnerships Limited) v Newlon Housing Trust [2013] EWHC 798 (TCC) at [46–56]

16.6.7 New material during the adjudication

Volker Stevin Ltd v Holystone Contracts Ltd [2010] EWHC 2344 (TCC) at [10–14]

16.6.8 Other procedural improprieties

Aveat Heating Ltd v Jerram Falkus Construction Ltd [2007] EWHC 131 (TCC) at [15–17; 23]
Ballast plc v The Burrell Company (Construction Management) Ltd [2001] ScotCS 159 at [31–34]

London & Amsterdam Properties Ltd v Waterman Partnership Ltd [2003] EWHC 3059 (TCC) at [96–116]

Rydon Maintenance Ltd v Affinity Sutton Housing Ltd [2015] EWHC 1306 (TCC) at [98; 106]

University of Brighton v Dovehouse Interiors Limited [2014] EWHC 940 (TCC) at [62–68]

16.7 Decision based jurisdiction challenges

16.7.2 Lien over the decision

Cubitt Building & Interiors Ltd v Fleetglade Ltd [2006] EWHC 3413 (TCC) at [77–81]

Mott MacDonald Ltd v London & Regional Properties Ltd [2007] EWHC 1055 (TCC) at [75–78]

St Andrews Bay Development Ltd v HBG Management Ltd and Mrs Janey Milligan [2003] ScotCS 103 at [19]

16.7.3 Failure to reach the decision within the required timetable

Cross refer to case Section 11.4

16.7.4 Signing the decision

Treasure & Son Ltd v Martin Dawes [2007] EWHC 2420 (TCC) at [45–48]

16.7.5 Sufficiency of written reasons

Atholl Developments (Slackbuie) Ltd, Re Application for Judicial Review [2010] CSOH 94 at [17; 19]

Balfour Beatty Construction Northern Ltd v Modus Corovest (Blackpool) Ltd [2008] EWHC 3029 (TCC) at [36–43]

Balfour Beatty Engineering Services (HY) Ltd v Shepherd Construction Ltd [2009] EWHC 2218 (TCC) at [45–49; 76–81]

Carillion Construction Ltd v Devonport Royal Dockyard Ltd [2005] EWCA Civ 1358 at [80]

Carillion Construction Ltd v Devonport Royal Dockyard Ltd [2005] EWHC 778 (TCC) at [81]

CSC Braehead Leisure Ltd and Capital & Regional (Braehead) Ltd v Laing O-Rourke Scotland Ltd [2008] CSOH 119 at [53–55]

Gillies Ramsay Diamond and Gavin Ramsay and Philip Diamond v PJW Enterprises Ltd [2003] ScotCS 343 at [29–31]

Gillies Ramsay Diamond v PJW Enterprises Ltd [2002] ScotCS 340 at [82–83]

Greentherm Mechanical Services v KDJ Developments Ltd [2012] EWHC 3525 (TCC) at [31–33]
HS Works Ltd v Enterprise Managed Services Ltd [2009] EWHC 729 (TCC) at [55–57]
Joinery Plus Ltd (In Administration) v Laing Ltd [2003] EWHC 3513 (TCC) at [38–44]
Miller Construction (UK) Ltd v Building Design Partnership Ltd [2014] CSOH 80 at [4–12]
Multiplex Constructions (UK) Ltd v West India Quay Development Company (Eastern) Ltd [2006] EWHC 1569 (TCC) at [34–39]
NAP Anglia Ltd v Sun-Land Development Co Ltd [2011] EWHC 2846 (TCC) at [31–34]
SW Global Resourcing Limited v Morris & Spottiswood Limited [2012] CSOH 200 at [33]
Thermal Energy Construction Ltd v AE & E Lentjes UK Ltd [2009] EWHC 408 (TCC) at [21–29]
Vision Homes Ltd v Lancsville Construction Ltd [2009] EWHC 2042 (TCC) at [47–50]

16.7.6 Scope of decision

(A) Scope of decision – principles

A&D Maintenance and Construction Ltd v Pagehurst Construction Services Ltd [1999] 64 Con LR at [21–22]
AMEC Group Ltd v Thames Water Utilities Ltd [2010] EWHC 419 (TCC) at [87–88]
C&B Scene Concept Design Ltd v Isobars Ltd [2002] EWCA Civ 46 at [30]
Fastrack Contractors Ltd v Morrison Construction Ltd & Anor [2000] All ER (D) 11 at [19]
McAlpine PPS Pipeline Systems Joint Venture v Transco plc [2004] EWHC 2030 (TCC) at [128–140]
Quietfield Ltd v Vascroft Construction Ltd [2006] EWCA Civ 1737 at [33]
RBG Ltd v SGL Carbon Fibers Ltd [2010] CSOH 77 at [28]
Wales and West Utilities Ltd v PPS Pipeline Systems GmbH [2014] EWHC 54 (TCC) at [27]
Workspace Management Ltd v YJL London Ltd [2009] EWHC 2017 at [20–27]

(B) Scope of decision – applications for payment, certification, final account

A&D Maintenance and Construction Ltd v Pagehurst Construction Services Ltd (2000) 16 Const LJ 199 at [22–24]
Barr Ltd v Law Mining Ltd [2001] ScotCS 152 at [20–22; 31–34]
Baune and another v Zduc Ltd [2002] All ER (D) 55 (Aug) at [1–2]
Bickerton Construction Ltd v Temple Windows Ltd [2001] AdjLR 06/26 at [18–19]
Brims Construction Ltd v A2M Development Ltd [2013] EWHC 3262 (TCC) at [29]
CG Group Ltd v Breyer Group plc [2013] EWHC 2722 (TCC) at [21–24]
Chamberlain Carpentry & Joinery Ltd v Alfred MacAlpine Construction Ltd [2002] EWHC 514 (TCC) at [19]
Charles Henshaw & Sons Ltd v Stewart & Shields Ltd [2014] ScotSC 59 at [19–26]
CJP Builders Ltd v William Verry Ltd [2008] EWHC 2025 (TCC) at [77]

David McLean Housing Contractors Ltd v Swansea Housing Association Ltd [2001] All ER (D) 519 (Jul) at [13]
Fastrack Contractors Ltd v Morrison Construction Ltd & Anor [2000] All ER (D) 11 at [33–38]
FW Cook Ltd v Shimizu (UK) Ltd [2000] BLR 199 at [14–20]
JG Walker Groundworks Ltd v Priory Homes (East) Ltd [2013] EWHC 3723 (TCC) at [20–30]
Karl Construction (Scotland) Ltd v Sweeney Civil Engineering (Scotland) Ltd [2002] SLT 312P/872/00 at [18–26]
KNS Industrial Services (Birmingham) Ltd v Sindall Ltd (2001) 75 ConLR 71 at [25]
LPL Electrical Services Ltd v Kershaw Mechanical Services Ltd [2001] AdjLR 02/02 at [8–10]
OSC Building Services Ltd v Interior Dimensions Contracts Ltd [2009] EWHC 248 (TCC) at [25–33]
PT Building Services Ltd v ROK Build Ltd [2008] EWHC 3434 (TCC) at [56–57]
Roe Brickwork Ltd v Wates Construction Ltd [2013] EWHC 3417 (TCC) at [23–37]
Roland Horne v Magna Design Building Ltd and Marcus Build Décor Ltd [2014] EWHC 3380 (TCC) at [16–18]
Watkin Jones & Son Ltd v Lidl UK GmbH (No 2) [2002] EWHC 183 (TCC) at [18–26]
Workspace Management Ltd v YJL London Ltd [2009] EWHC 2017 (TCC) at [20–27]
YCMS Ltd (t/a Young Construction Management Services) v Grabiner & Anor [2009] EWHC 127 (TCC) at [52–56]

(C) Scope of decision – delay and prolongation

Balfour Beatty Engineering Services (HY) Ltd v Shepherd Construction Ltd [2009] EWHC 2218 (TCC) at [49–62]
Cantillon Ltd v Urvasco Ltd [2008] EWHC 282 (TCC) at [67–75]
Edmund Nuttall Ltd v R G Carter Ltd [2002] EWHC 400 (TCC) at [32–40]
Herbosch-Kiere Marine Contractors Ltd v Dover Harbour Board [2012] EWHC 84 (TCC) at [24–34]
McAlpine PPS Pipeline Systems Joint Venture v Transco plc [2004] EWHC 2030 (TCC) at [141–148]
Quietfield Ltd v Vascroft Construction Ltd [2006] EWCA Civ 1737 at [26–38]
R Durtnell & Sons Ltd v Kaduna Ltd [2003] EWHC 517 (TCC) at [42–45]
Sindall Ltd v Solland and Others [2001] All ER (D) 370 (Jun) at [16–21]
WSP Cel Ltd v Dalkia Utilities Services plc [2012] EWHC 2428 (TCC) at [90–93]

(D) Scope of decision – contract and contract interpretation

Curot Contracts Ltd, T/A Dimension Shopping v Castle Inns (Stirling) Ltd T/A Castle Leisure Group [2008] CSOH 178 at [9–10]
Dalkia Energy and Technical Services Ltd v Bell Group UK Ltd [2009] EWHC 73 (TCC) at [38–44]
Nolan Davis Ltd v Catton 2000 TCC No 590 at [27–30]

Viridis UK Limited v Mulalley and Company Limited [2014] EWHC 268 (TCC) at [100–105]

(E) Scope of decision – other

AMEC Group Ltd v Thames Water Utilities Ltd [2010] EWHC 419 (TCC) at [89–93]

AWG Construction Services Ltd v Rockingham Motor Speedway Ltd [2004] EWHC 888 (TCC) at [147–153]

Barr Ltd v Klin Investment Ltd [2009] ScotCS CSOH 104 at [40–42]

Buxton Building Contractors Ltd v The Governors of Durand Primary School [2004] EWHC 733 (TCC) at [18–21]

Carillion Construction Ltd v Devonport Royal Dockyard Ltd [2005] EWCA Civ 1358 at [92–94]

Carillion Construction Ltd v Devonport Royal Dockyard Ltd [2005] EWHC 778 (TCC) at [83–88]

Dean & Dyball Construction Ltd v Kenneth Grubb Associates Ltd [2003] EWHC 2465 (TCC) at [46–47]

HS Works Ltd v Enterprise Managed Services Ltd [2009] EWHC 729 (TCC) at [55–57]

Humes Building Contracts Ltd v Charlotte Homes (Surrey) Ltd [2007] AdjLR 01/03 at [15–18]

ISG Retail Ltd v Castletech Construction Ltd [2015] EWHC 1443 (TCC) at [13–28]

Karl Construction (Scotland) Ltd v Sweeney Civil Engineering (Scotland) Ltd [2000] ScotCS 330 at [28–30]

Letchworth Roofing Company v Sterling Building Company [2009] EWHC 1119 (TCC) at [31–34]

Martin Girt v Page Bentley [2002] EWHC 1720 (TCC) at [10–14]

Mecright Ltd v TA Morris Developments Ltd [2001] AdjLR 06/22 at [26–29]

Northern Developments (Cumbria) Ltd v J & J Nichol [2000] All ER (D) 68 at [29–31]

Shimizu Europe Ltd v LBJ Fabrications Ltd [2003] EWHC 1229 (TCC) at [41–43]

Tera Construction Ltd v Yuk Tong Lam [2005] EWHC 3306 (TCC) at [17–22]

Vision Homes Ltd v Lancsville Construction Ltd [2009] EWHC 2042 (TCC) at [60–67]

Watson Building Services Ltd [2001] ScotCS 60 at [25–26]

Windglass Windows Ltd v (1) Capital Skyline Construction Ltd (2) London and City Group Holdings Ltd [2009] EWHC 2022 (TCC) at [18–27]

WSP Cel Ltd v Dalkia Utilities Services plc [2012] EWHC 2428 (TCC) at [37]

(F) Scope of decision – exceeded

AWG Construction Services Ltd v Rockingham Motor Speedway Ltd [2004] EWHC 888 (TCC) at [147–153]

Baune and another v Zduc Ltd [2002] All ER (D) 55 (Aug) at [1–2]

Bickerton Construction Ltd v Temple Windows Ltd [2001] AdjLR 06/26 at [18–19]

Buxton Building Contractors Ltd v The Governors of Durand Primary School [2004] EWHC 733 (TCC) at [18–21]

Edmund Nuttall Ltd v R G Carter Ltd [2002] EWHC 400 (TCC) at [32–40]

FW Cook Ltd v Shimizu (UK) Ltd [2000] BLR 199 at [14–20]

Herbosch-Kiere Marine Contractors Ltd v Dover Harbour Board [2012] EWHC 84 (TCC) at [24–34]
McAlpine PPS Pipeline Systems Joint Venture v Transco plc [2004] EWHC 2030 (TCC) at [141–148]
Mecright Ltd v TA Morris Developments Ltd [2001] AdjLR 06/22 at [26–29]
Pilon Ltd v Breyer Group plc [2010] EWHC 837 (TCC) at [24–31]
R Durtnell & Sons Ltd v Kaduna Ltd [2003] EWHC 517 (TCC) at [42–45]
Shimizu Europe Ltd v LBJ Fabrications Ltd [2003] EWHC 1229 (TCC) at [41–43]
Vision Homes Ltd v Lancsville Construction Ltd [2009] EWHC 2042 (TCC) at [60–67]
Watkin Jones & Son Ltd v Lidl UK GmbH (No 2) [2002] EWHC 183 (TCC) at [18–26]

(G) Scope of decision – did not exceed

A&D Maintenance and Construction Ltd v Pagehurst Construction Services Ltd (2000) 16 Const LJ 199 at [22–24]
Balfour Beatty Engineering Services (HY) Ltd v Shepherd Construction Ltd [2009] EWHC 2218 (TCC) at [50–63]
Barr Ltd v Klin Investment Ltd [2009] ScotCS CSOH 104 at [40–42]
Barr Ltd v Law Mining Ltd [2001] ScotCS 152 at [20–22; 31–34]
Brims Construction Ltd v A2M Development Ltd [2013] EWHC 3262 (TCC) at [29]
Cantillon Ltd v Urvasco Ltd [2008] EWHC 282 (TCC) at [67–75]
Carillion Construction Ltd v Devonport Royal Dockyard Ltd [2005] EWCA Civ 1358 at [92–94]
Carillion Construction Ltd v Devonport Royal Dockyard Ltd [2005] EWHC 778 (TCC) at [83–88]
CG Group Ltd v Breyer Group plc [2013] EWHC 2722 (TCC) at [21–24]
Chamberlain Carpentry & Joinery Ltd v Alfred MacAlpine Construction Ltd [2002] EWHC 514 (TCC) at [19]
CJP Builders Ltd v William Verry Ltd [2008] EWHC 2025 (TCC) at [77]
Curot Contracts Ltd, T/A Dimension Shopping v Castle Inns (Stirling) Ltd T/A Castle Leisure Group [2008] CSOH 178 at [9–10]
Dalkia Energy and Technical Services Ltd v Bell Group UK Ltd [2009] EWHC 73 (TCC) at [38–44]
David McLean Housing Contractors Ltd v Swansea Housing Association Ltd [2001] All ER (D) 519 (Jul) at [13]
Dean & Dyball Construction Ltd v Kenneth Grubb Associates Ltd [2003] EWHC 2465 (TCC) at [46–47]
Fastrack Contractors Ltd v Morrison Construction Ltd & Anor [2000] All ER (D) 11 at [33–38]
HS Works Ltd v Enterprise Managed Services Ltd [2009] EWHC 729 (TCC) at [55–57]
Humes Building Contracts Ltd v Charlotte Homes (Surrey) Ltd [2007] AdjLR 01/03 at [15–18]
ISG Retail Ltd v Castletech Construction Ltd [2015] EWHC 1443 (TCC) at [13–28]
Jacques (t/a C & E Jacques Partnership) v Ensign Contractors Ltd [2009] EWHC 3383 (TCC) at [28]

JG Walker Groundworks Ltd v Priory Homes (East) Ltd [2013] EWHC 3723 (TCC) at [9–30]

Karl Construction (Scotland) Ltd v Sweeney Civil Engineering (Scotland) Ltd [2000] ScotCS 330 at [28–30]

KNS Industrial Services (Birmingham) Ltd v Sindall Ltd (2001) 75 ConLR 71 at [25]

Letchworth Roofing Company v Sterling Building Company [2009] EWHC 1119 (TCC) at [31–34]

LPL Electrical Services Ltd v Kershaw Mechanical Services Ltd [2001] AdjLR 02/02 at [8–10]

Martin Girt v Page Bentley [2002] EWHC 1720 (TCC) at [10–14]

Nolan Davis Ltd v Catton 2000 TCC No 590 at [27–30]

Northern Developments (Cumbria) Ltd v J & J Nichol [2000] All ER (D) 68 at [29–31]

OSC Building Services Ltd v Interior Dimensions Contracts Ltd [2009] EWHC 248 (TCC) at [25–33]

PT Building Services Ltd v ROK Build Ltd [2008] EWHC 3434 (TCC) at [56–57]

Quietfield Ltd v Vascroft Construction Ltd [2006] EWCA Civ 1737 at [26–38]

Roe Brickwork Ltd v Wates Construction Ltd [2013] EWHC 3417 (TCC) at [23–37]

Roland Horne v Magna Design Building Ltd and Marcus Build Décor Ltd [2014] EWHC 3380 (TCC) at [16–18]

Sindall Ltd v Solland and Others [2001] All ER (D) 370 (Jun) at [16–21]

Tera Construction Ltd v Yuk Tong Lam [2005] EWHC 3306 (TCC) at [17–22]

Viridis UK Limited v Mulalley and Company Limited [2014] EWHC 268 (TCC) at [100–105]

Wales and West Utilities Ltd v PPS Pipeline Systems GmbH [2014] EWHC 54 (TCC) at [32–41]

Watson Building Services Ltd [2001] ScotCS 60 at [25–26]

Windglass Windows Ltd v (1) Capital Skyline Construction Ltd (2) London and City Group Holdings Ltd [2009] EWHC 2022 (TCC) at [18–27]

Workspace Management Ltd v YJL London Ltd [2009] EWHC 2017 (TCC) at [20–27]

WSP Cel Ltd v Dalkia Utilities Services plc [2012] EWHC 2428 (TCC) at [90–93]

YCMS Ltd (t/a Young Construction Management Services) v Grabiner & Anor [2009] EWHC 127 (TCC) at [52–56]

(H) Scope of decision – failure to exhaust jurisdiction

Atholl Developments (Slackbuie) Ltd, Re Application for Judicial Review [2010] CSOH 94 at [19]

Ballast plc v The Burrell Company (Construction Management) Ltd [2001] ScotCS 159 at [42]

Ballast plc v The Burrell Company (Construction Management) Ltd [2002] ScotCS 324 at [16–20]

Barr Ltd v Law Mining Ltd [2001] ScotCS 152 at [20–22; 31–34]

Bouygues E&S Contracting UK Ltd v Vital Energi Utilities Ltd [2014] ScotCS CSOH 115 at [6–8]

Britcon (Scunthorpe) Ltd v Lincolnfields Ltd [2001] AdjLR 08/29 at [8–14]

CSC Braehead Leisure Ltd and Capital & Regional (Braehead) Ltd v Laing O-Rourke Scotland Ltd [2008] CSOH 119 at [31–34]
HS Works Ltd v Enterprise Managed Services Ltd [2009] EWHC 729 (TCC) at [55–57]
Pilon Ltd v Breyer Group plc [2010] EWHC 837 (TCC) at [17–31]
RBG Ltd v SGL Carbon Fibers Ltd [2010] CSOH 77 at [24–29]
SGL Carbon Fibres Ltd v RBG Ltd [2011] CSOH 62 at [37–47]
SW Global Resourcing Limited v Morris & Spottiswood Limited [2012] CSOH 200 at [22]
Vaughan Engineering Ltd v Hinkins & Frewin Ltd [2003] ScotCS 56 at [38]

16.7.7 Errors

(A) Errors of law

Allen Wilson Shopfitters and Builders Ltd v Buckingham [2005] EWHC 1165 (TCC) at [28–30]
Allied London & Scottish Properties plc v Riverbrae Construction Ltd [1999] ScotCS 224 at [14–18]
AMEC Group Ltd v Thames Water Utilities Ltd [2010] EWHC 419 (TCC) at [25–34]
Ballast plc v The Burrell Company (Construction Management) Ltd [2001] ScotCS 159 at [40–42]
Ballast plc v The Burrell Company (Construction Management) Ltd [2002] ScotCS 324 at [16–21]
Barr Ltd v Law Mining Ltd [2001] ScotCS 152 at [6–10]
Bouygues (UK) Ltd v Dahl-Jensen (UK) Ltd [1999] All ER (D) 1281 at [30–37]
Bouygues (UK) Ltd v Dahl-Jensen (UK) Ltd [2000] EWCA Civ 507 at [14–20]
C&B Scene Concept Design Ltd v Isobars Ltd [2001] CILL 1781 at [32–41]
C&B Scene Concept Design Ltd v Isobars Ltd [2002] EWCA Civ 46 at [21–32]
Dean & Dyball Construction Ltd v Kenneth Grubb Associates Ltd [2003] EWHC 2465 (TCC) at [46–47]
Deko Scotland Ltd v Edinburgh Royal Joint Venture & Anor [2003] ScotCS 113 at [15]
Ecovision Systems Ltd v Vinci Construction UK Ltd [2015] EWHC 587 (TCC) at [82]
Geoffrey Osborne Ltd v Atkins Rail Ltd [2009] EWHC 2425 (TCC) at [21–25; 43–75]
Gillies Ramsay Diamond and Gavin Ramsay and Philip Diamond v PJW Enterprises Ltd [2003] ScotCS 343 at [32–44]
Gillies Ramsay Diamond v PJW Enterprises Ltd [2002] ScotCS 340 at [72–83]
GPS Marine Contractors Ltd v Ringway Infrastructure Services Ltd [2010] EWHC 283 (TCC) at [56–67]
Joinery Plus Ltd (In Administration) v Laing Ltd [2003] EWHC 3513 (TCC) at [51–61; 77–78]
Karl Construction (Scotland) Ltd v Sweeney Civil Engineering (Scotland) Ltd [2000] ScotCS 330 at [28–30]
KNS Industrial Services (Birmingham) Ltd v Sindall Ltd (2001) 75 ConLR 71 at [24–25]
London & Amsterdam Properties Ltd v Waterman Partnership Ltd [2003] EWHC 3059 (TCC) at [189–209]

Macob Civil Engineering v Morrison Construction Ltd [1999] All ER (D) 143 at [14–23]
Maymac Environmental Services Ltd v Faraday Building Services Ltd [2000] All ER (D) 1406 at [47–48]
Mott MacDonald Ltd v London & Regional Properties Ltd [2007] EWHC 1055 (TCC) at [62–67]
Northern Developments (Cumbria) Ltd v J & J Nichol [2000] All ER (D) 68 at [33–36]
Pegram Shopfitters Ltd v Tally Wiejl (UK) Ltd [2003] EWCA Civ 1750 at [30–34]
Pegram Shopfitters Ltd v Tally Wiejl (UK) Ltd [2003] EWHC 984 (TCC) at [17–24]
Tim Butler Contractors Ltd v Merewood Homes Ltd (2002) 18 Const LJ 74 at [31–35]
Watson Building Services Ltd [2001] ScotCS 60 at [21–26]
Westwood Structural Services Ltd v Blyth Wood Park Management Company Ltd [2008] EWHC 3138 (TCC) at [13–19]
William Verry Ltd v North West London Communal Mikvah [2004] EWHC 1300 (TCC) at [54–60]
Viridis UK Limited v Mulalley and Company Limited [2014] EWHC 268 (TCC) at [96–99;106–110]

(B) Errors of fact

AJ Brenton t/a Manton Electrical Components v Jack Palmer [2001] AdjLR 01/19 at [3–7]
AMEC Group Ltd v Thames Water Utilities Ltd [2010] EWHC 419 (TCC) at [78–80; 87–92]
Atholl Developments (Slackbuie) Ltd, Re Application for Judicial Review [2010] CSOH 94 at [14–15; 21]
Jerome Engineering Ltd v Lloyd Morris Electrical Ltd [2002] CILL 1827 at [21–22]
Nolan Davis Ltd v Catton 2000 TCC No 590 at [28–29]
ROK Building Ltd v Celtic Composting Systems Ltd (No 2) [2010] EWHC 66 (TCC) at [23–29]
SG South Ltd v Swan Yard (Cirencester) Ltd [2010] EWHC 376 (TCC) at [16]
Shimizu Europe Ltd v Automajor Ltd [2002] EWHC 1571 (TCC) at [23–25]
SW Global Resourcing Limited v Morris & Spottiswood Limited [2012] CSOH 200 at [30–32]
Thomas-Fredric's Construction Ltd v Keith Wilson [2003] EWCA Civ 1494 at [16; 26–31]
Whyte and Mackay Ltd v Blyth & Blyth Consulting Engineers Ltd [2013] CSOH 54 at [72–73]

16.7.8 *Correcting minor errors in the decision*

Cross refer to case Section 12.5

17 Natural justice

17.1 Overview

AMEC Capital Projects Ltd v Whitefriars City Estates Ltd (No 3) [2004] EWCA Civ 1418 at [14]

AMEC Group Ltd v Thames Water Utilities Ltd [2010] EWHC 419 (TCC) at [54]

Balfour Beatty Construction Ltd v The Mayor & Burgesses of the London Borough of Lambeth [2002] EWHC 597 (TCC) at [20; 28–30]

Balfour Beatty Construction Northern Ltd v Modus Corovest (Blackpool) Ltd [2008] EWHC 3029 (TCC) at [51–53]

Camillin Denny Architects Ltd v Adelaide Jones & Company Ltd [2009] EWHC 2110 (TCC) at [39]

Cantillon Ltd v Urvasco Ltd [2008] EWHC 282 (TCC) at [56–57]

Carillion Utility Services Ltd v SP Power Systems Ltd [2011] CSOH 139 at [17–26]

CG Group Ltd v Breyer Group plc [2013] EWHC 2722 (TCC) at [31]

Charles Henshaw & Sons Ltd v Stewart & Shields Ltd [2014] CSIH 55 at [17]

Costain Ltd v Strathclyde Builders Ltd [2003] ScotCS 352 at [15–24]

Dean & Dyball Construction Ltd v Kenneth Grubb Associates Ltd [2003] EWHC 2465 (TCC) at [52–53]

Discain Project Services Ltd v Opecprime Development Ltd (No 2) [2001] All ER (D) 123 at [68]

Farrelly (M&E) Building Services Ltd v Byrne Brothers (Formwork) Ltd [2013] EWHC 1186 (TCC) at [27–36]

Fileturn Ltd v Royal Garden Hotel Ltd [2010] EWHC 1736 (TCC) at [p9–13]

Lanes Group plc v Galliford Try Infrastructure Ltd [2011] EWCA Civ 1617 at [38–61]

Paton, Re Judicial Review [2011] CSOH 40 at [72]

PC Harrington Contractors Ltd v Tyroddy Construction Ltd [2011] EWHC 813 (TCC) at [18–20]

Rankilor (Dr Peter) & Perco Engineering Service Ltd v Igoe (M) Ltd [2006] AdjLR 01/27 at [28]

RSL (South West Ltd) v Stansell Ltd (No 1) [2003] EWHC 1390 (TCC) at [31–33]

Try Construction Ltd v Eton Town House Group Ltd [2003] EWHC 60 (TCC) at [50–57]

17.1.2 Materiality

Cantillon Ltd v Urvasco Ltd [2008] EWHC 282 (TCC) at [57]

Carillion Construction Ltd v Devonport Royal Dockyard Ltd [2005] EWHC 778 (TCC) at [81]

Discain Project Services Ltd v Opecprime Development Ltd (No 1) [2000] BLR 402 at [Addendum]

Kier Regional Ltd (t/a Wallis) v City & General (Holborn) Ltd [2006] EWHC 848 (TCC) at [42–44]

Try Construction Ltd v Eton Town House Group Ltd [2003] EWHC 60 (TCC) at [50]

17.3 Options when a natural justice point arises

> Bovis Lend Lease Ltd v The Trustees of the London Clinic [2009] EWHC 64 (TCC) at [68]
> Costain Ltd v Strathclyde Builders Ltd [2003] ScotCS 352 at [30–33]
> CSK Electrical Contractors Ltd v Kingwood Electrical Services Ltd [2015] EWHC 667 (TCC) at [21–22]
> Dalkia Energy and Technical Services Ltd v Bell Group UK Ltd [2009] EWHC 73 (TCC) at [45]
> Dorchester Hotel Ltd v Vivid Interiors Ltd [2009] EWHC 70 (TCC) at [18–22]
> Farrelly (M & E) Building Services Ltd v Byrne Brothers (Formwork) Ltd [2013] EWHC 1186 (TCC) at [27–36]
> Paice and Springall v Matthew Harding (t/a M J Harding Contractors) [2015] EWHC 661 (TCC) at [55–57]

17.4 Bias and apparent bias

17.4.2 Actual bias

> In Re Medicaments [2000] EWCA Civ 350 at [37–38]
> Lanes Group plc v Galliford Try Infrastructure Ltd [2011] EWCA Civ 1617 at [46]

17.4.3 Apparent bias

> AMEC Capital Projects Ltd v Whitefriars City Estates Ltd (No 3) [2004] EWCA Civ 1418 at [15–18]
> Balfour Beatty Engineering Services (HY) Ltd v Shepherd Construction Ltd [2009] EWHC 2218 (TCC) at [44]
> Gillies v Secretary of State for Work and Pensions [2006] UKHL 2 at [17]
> Glencot Development & Design Co Ltd v Ben Barrett & Son (Contractors) Ltd [2001] All ER (D) 384 (Feb) at [14–20]
> In Re Medicaments [2000] EWCA Civ 350 at [35–40; 83–86]
> Lanes Group plc v Galliford Try Infrastructure Ltd [2011] EWCA Civ 1617 at [44–52]
> Locabail (UK) Ltd v Bayfield Properties Ltd and others [1999] EWCA Civ 3004 at [25]
> Magill v Porter [2001] UKHL 67 at [95–105]
> Makers UK Ltd v The Mayor and Burgesses of the London Borough of Camden [2008] EWHC 1836 (TCC) at [30–32]

17.4.4 Prior involvement in project or in a separate dispute

> Andrew Wallace Ltd v Jeff Noon [2009] BLR 158 at [24–28]
> Fileturn Ltd v Royal Garden Hotel Ltd [2010] EWHC 1736 (TCC) at [20–33]
> Lanes Group plc v Galliford Try Infrastructure Ltd [2011] EWHC 1035 (TCC) at [31]

London & Amsterdam Properties Ltd v Waterman Partnership Ltd [2003] EWHC 3059 (TCC) at [85–95]

Pring & St. Hill Ltd v C J Hafner t/a Southern Erectors [2002] EWHC 1775 (TCC) at [23–29]

17.4.5 Appointment of same adjudicator

AMEC Capital Projects Ltd v Whitefriars City Estates Ltd (No 3) [2004] EWCA Civ 1418 at [19–33]

Ecovision Systems Ltd v Vinci Construction UK Ltd [2015] EWHC 587 (TCC) at [99]

Edmund Nuttall Ltd v R G Carter Ltd [2002] EWHC 400 (TCC) at [29]

Edmund Nuttall Ltd v RG Carter Ltd (No 2) [2002] BLR 359 at [19–21; 29]

Michael John Construction Ltd v Golledge & Ors [2006] EWHC 71 (TCC) at [65–70]

Pring & St. Hill Ltd v C J Hafner t/a Southern Erectors [2002] EWHC 1775 (TCC) at [23–29]

Willmott Dixon Housing Limited (formerly Inspace Partnerships Limited) v Newlon Housing Trust [2013] EWHC 798 (TCC) at [68–76]

17.4.6 Communication between the adjudicator and one party: pre-appointment

AMEC Capital Projects Ltd v Whitefriars City Estates Ltd (No 3) [2004] EWCA Civ 1418 at [35–37]

Makers UK Ltd v The Mayor and Burgesses of the London Borough of Camden [2008] EWHC 1836 (TCC) at [33–36]

Paice and Springall v Matthew Harding (t/a M J Harding Contractors) [2015] EWHC 661 (TCC) at [32–45]

Pring & St. Hill Ltd v C J Hafner t/a Southern Erectors [2002] EWHC 1775 (TCC) at [23–29]

17.4.7 Communication between the adjudicator and one party: post-appointment

CRJ Services Ltd v Lanstar Ltd (trading as CSG Ltd) [2011] EWHC 972 (TCC) at [31–33]

Dean & Dyball Construction Ltd v Kenneth Grubb Associates Ltd [2003] EWHC 2465 (TCC) at [48–54]

Discain Project Services Ltd v Opecprime Development Ltd (No 1) [2000] BLR 402 at [9–11]

Discain Project Services Ltd v Opecprime Development Ltd (No 2) [2001] All ER (D) 123 at [64–70]

17.4.8 Evidence

A&S Enterprises Ltd v Kema Holdings Ltd [2004] EWHC 3365 (QB) at [36–41]
Arcadis UK Ltd v May and Baker Ltd (t/a Sanofi) [2013] EWHC 87 (TCC) at [31–36]
Aveat Heating Ltd v Jerram Falkus Construction Ltd [2007] EWHC 131 (TCC) at [25]
Balfour Beatty Engineering Services (HY) Ltd v Shepherd Construction Ltd [2009] EWHC 2218 (TCC) at [73–75]
Barr Ltd v Klin Investment Ltd [2009] ScotCS CSOH 104 at [43–46]
Camillin Denny Architects Ltd v Adelaide Jones & Company Ltd [2009] EWHC 2110 (TCC) at [40]
CRJ Services Ltd v Lanstar Ltd (trading as CSG Lanstar) [2011] EWHC 972 (TCC) at [31–32]

17.4.9 Failure to make information available to parties

Ecovision Systems Ltd v Vinci Construction UK Ltd [2015] EWHC 587 (TCC) at [96]
Woods Hardwick Ltd v Chiltern Air Conditioning Ltd [2001] BLR 23 at [26–31; 37–39]

17.4.10 Failure to carry out a site visit

Gipping Construction Ltd v Eaves Ltd [2008] EWHC 3134 (TCC) at [7–9]

17.4.11 Organisation of meetings and hearings

Barrie Green v GW Integrated Building Services Ltd & Anor [2001] AdjLR 07/18 at [30–38]
Rydon Maintenance Ltd v Affinity Sutton Housing Ltd [2015] EWHC 1306 (TCC) at [105–106]
Vaultrise Ltd v Paul Cook [2004] Adj. C.S. 04/26 at [4 to 6]

17.4.12 Quasi-mediator

Glencot Development & Design Co Ltd v Ben Barrett & Son (Contractors) Ltd [2001] All ER (D) 384 (Feb) at [21–27]

17.4.13 Without prejudice communications

Arcadis UK Ltd v May and Baker Ltd (t/a Sanofi) [2013] EWHC 87 (TCC) at [35]
Ellis Building Contractors Ltd v Vincent Goldstein [2011] EWHC 269 (TCC) at [25–29; 35–39]
Specialist Ceiling Services Northern Ltd v ZVI Construction UK Ltd [2004] BLR 403 at [18–26]

Volker Stevin Ltd v Holystone Contracts Ltd [2010] EWHC 2344 (TCC) at [17–25]

17.4.14 Preliminary view

Lanes Group plc v Galliford Try Infrastructure Ltd [2011] EWCA Civ 1617 at [55–59]
Lanes Group plc v Galliford Try Infrastructure Ltd [2011] EWHC 1679 (TCC) at [34–79]

17.5 Procedural fairness

17.5.2 Referring party's conduct pre-adjudication

CIB Properties Ltd v Birse Construction [2004] EWHC 2365 (TCC) at [176–179; 190–193]

17.5.3 Abuse of process

Benfield Construction Ltd v Trudson (Hatton) Ltd [2008] EWHC 2333 (TCC) at [56]
Connex South Eastern Ltd v M J Building Services Group plc [2005] EWCA Civ 193 at [38–45]
Connex South Eastern Ltd v MJ Building Services Group plc [2004] EWHC 1518 (TCC) at [33–34]
Dalkia Energy and Technical Services Ltd v Bell Group UK Ltd [2009] EWHC 73 (TCC) at [13–31]
Discain Project Services Ltd v Opecprime Development Ltd (No 1) [2000] BLR 402 at [7]
Emcor Drake & Scull Ltd v Costain Construction Ltd & Skanska Central Europe AB (t/a Costain Skanska Joint Venture) [2004] EWHC 2439 (TCC) at [20–21]
Galliford Try Construction Ltd v Michael Heal Associates Ltd [2003] EWHC 2886 (TCC) at [52–53]
Lanes Group plc v Galliford Try Infrastructure Ltd [2011] EWHC 1679 (TCC) at [43–53]
T Clarke (Scotland) Limited v MMAXX Underfloor Heating Limited [2014] CSIH 83 at [30–31]

17.5.4 Ambush/no opportunity or insufficient opportunity to respond

Austin Hall Building Ltd v Buckland Securities Ltd [2001] All ER (D) 137 at [38]
AWG Construction Services Ltd v Rockingham Motor Speedway Ltd [2004] EWHC 888 (TCC) at [154–170]
Balfour Beatty Construction Ltd v The Mayor & Burgesses of the London Borough of Lambeth [2002] EWHC 597 (TCC) at [36]

Balfour Beatty Construction Northern Ltd v Modus Corovest (Blackpool) Ltd [2008] EWHC 3029 (TCC) at [51–57]

Bovis Lend Lease Ltd v The Trustees of the London Clinic [2009] EWHC 64 (TCC) at [50–51; 66–68]

CIB Properties Ltd v Birse Construction Ltd [2004] EWHC 2365 (TCC) at [180]

CSC Braehead Leisure Ltd and Capital & Regional (Braehead) Ltd v Laing O-Rourke Scotland Ltd [2008] CSOH 119 at [56–61]

CSK Electrical Contractors Ltd v Kingwood Electrical Services Ltd [2015] EWHC 667 (TCC) at [14–17]

Dorchester Hotel Ltd v Vivid Interiors Ltd [2009] EWHC 70 (TCC) at [23–34]

Ecovision Systems Ltd v Vinci Construction UK Ltd [2015] EWHC 587 (TCC) at [96–98]

Edenbooth Ltd v Cre8 Developments Ltd [2008] EWHC 570 (TCC) at [17]

Enterprise Managed Services Ltd v Tony McFadden Utilities Ltd [2009] EWHC 3222 (TCC) at [91–99]

Gary Kitt and EC Harris LLP v The Laundry Building Ltd and Etcetera Construction Services Ltd [2014] EHWC 4250 (TCC) at [31]

Gibson (Banbridge) Ltd v Fermanagh District Council [2013] NIQB 16 at [28 – 29]

Harlow & Milner Ltd v Linda Teasdale (No 1) [2006] EWHC 54 (TCC) at [9]

JW Hughes Building Contractors Ltd v GB Metalwork Ltd [2003] EWHC 2421 (TCC) at [18–37]

Lee v Chartered Properties (Building) Ltd [2010] EWHC 1540 (TCC) at [24]

London & Amsterdam Properties Ltd v Waterman Partnership Ltd [2003] EWHC 3059 (TCC) at [178–186]

M. Rohde Construction v Nicholas Markham-David (No 2) [2007] EWHC 1408 (TCC) at [17–20]

McAlpine PPS Pipeline Systems Joint Venture v Transco plc [2004] EWHC 2030 (TCC) at [150–155]

RSL (South West) Ltd v Stansell Ltd [2003] EWHC 1390 (TCC) at [32–33]

Volker Stevin Ltd v Holystone Contracts Ltd [2010] EWHC 2344 (TCC) at [10–14]

William Verry (Glazing Systems) Ltd v Furlong Homes Ltd [2005] EWHC 138 (TCC) at [51–62]

17.5.5 Christmas claims

Bovis Lend Lease Ltd v The Trustees of the London Clinic [2009] EWHC 64 (TCC) at [51]

CSK Electrical Contractors Ltd v Kingwood Electrical Services Ltd [2015] EWHC 667 (TCC) at [14–17]

Devon County Council v Celtic Composting Systems Ltd [2014] EWHC 552 (TCC) at [24]

Dorchester Hotel Ltd v Vivid Interiors Ltd [2009] EWHC 70 (TCC) at [23–29]

Twintec Ltd v Volkerfitzpatrick Ltd [2014] EWHC 10 (TCC) at [67–73]

17.5.6 Dispute is too large or complex

> AMEC Group Ltd v Thames Water Utilities Ltd [2010] EWHC 419 (TCC) at [55–61]
> AWG Construction Services Ltd v Rockingham Motor Speedway Ltd [2004] EWHC 888 (TCC) at [123–124]
> Balfour Beatty Construction Ltd v The Mayor & Burgesses of the London Borough of Lambeth [2002] EWHC 597 (TCC) at [30]
> Balfour Kilpatrick Ltd v Glauser International SA [2000] Adj.C.S. 07/27 at [5]
> CIB Properties Ltd v Birse Construction [2004] EWHC 2365 (TCC) at [21–27]
> Dorchester Hotel Ltd v Vivid Interiors Ltd [2009] EWHC 70 (TCC) at [23–29]
> Emcor Drake & Scull Ltd v Costain Construction Ltd & Skanska Central Europe AB (t/a Costain Skanska Joint Venture) [2004] EWHC 2439 (TCC) at [20–21]
> Enterprise Managed Services Ltd v Tony McFadden Utilities Ltd [2009] EWHC 3222 (TCC) at [91–99]
> Gibson (Banbridge) Ltd v Fermanagh District Council [2013] NIQB 16 at [27]
> HS Works Ltd v Enterprise Managed Services Ltd [2009] EWHC 729 (TCC) at [47–50;54]
> London & Amsterdam Properties Ltd v Waterman Partnership Ltd [2003] EWHC 3059 (TCC) at [146]
> Whyte and Mackay Ltd v Blyth & Blyth Consulting Engineers Ltd [2012] ScotCS CSOH_54 at [45–48]
> William Verry (Glazing Systems) Ltd v Furlong Homes Ltd [2005] EWHC 138 (TCC) at [11; 51–62]

17.5.7 Failing to address an issue, part of a submission or evidence

(A) Failing to address an issue, part of a submission or evidence – principles

> All in One Building and Refurbishments Ltd v Makers UK Ltd [2005] EWHC 2943 (TCC) at [52–55]
> AMEC Group Ltd v Thames Water Utilities Ltd [2010] EWHC 419 (TCC) at [81–88]
> Ballast plc v The Burrell Company (Construction Management) Ltd [2001] ScotCS 159 at [39–43]
> Bouygues (UK) Ltd v Dahl-Jensen (UK) Ltd [1999] All ER (D) 1281 at [35]
> Cantillon Ltd v Urvasco Ltd [2008] EWHC 282 (TCC) at [57]
> Carillion Construction Ltd v Devonport Royal Dockyard Ltd [2005] EWHC 778 (TCC) at [81]
> CJP Builders Ltd v William Verry Ltd [2008] EWHC 2025 (TCC) at [78–86]
> Humes Building Contracts Ltd v Charlotte Homes (Surrey) Ltd [2007] AdjLR 01/03 at [21]
> HS Works Ltd v Enterprise Managed Services Ltd [2009] EWHC 729 at [51]
> Jacques (t/a C & E Jacques Partnership) v Ensign Contractors Ltd [2009] EWHC 3383 (TCC) at [26]
> Kier Regional Ltd (t/a Wallis) v City & General (Holborn) Ltd [2006] EWHC 848 (TCC) at [39–44]

Paul Broadwell v k3D Property Partnership Ltd [2006] Adj.C.S. 04/21 at [17]
Pilon Ltd v Breyer Group plc [2010] EWHC 837 (TCC) at [17–23]
Quartzelec Ltd v Honeywell Control Systems Ltd [2008] EWHC 3315 (TCC) at [27–33]
Thermal Energy Construction Ltd v AE & E Lentjes UK Ltd [2009] EWHC 408 (TCC) at [21–30]

(B) *Failing to address an issue, part of a submission or evidence – breach*
Ballast plc v The Burrell Company (Construction Management) Ltd [2001] ScotCS 159 at [39–43]
Buxton Building Contractors Ltd v The Governors of Durand Primary School [2004] EWHC 733 (TCC) at [16–21]
Paul Broadwell v k3D Property Partnership Ltd [2006] Adj.C.S. 04/21 at [17]
PC Harrington Contractors Ltd v Tyroddy Construction Ltd [2011] EWHC 813 (TCC) at [21]
Pilon Ltd v Breyer Group plc [2010] EWHC 837 (TCC) at [24–31]
Quartzelec Ltd v Honeywell Control Systems Ltd [2008] EWHC 3315 (TCC) at [27–33]
Quietfield Ltd v Vascroft Construction Ltd [2006] EWCA Civ 1737 at [30–38]
Quietfield Ltd v Vascroft Construction Ltd [2006] EWHC 174 (TCC) at [44–51]
RBG Ltd v SGL Carbon Fibers Ltd [2010] CSOH 77 at [28]
Rupert Cordle v Vanessa Nicholson [2009] EWHC 1314 at [20–22]
Steve Domsalla (t/a Domsalla Building Services) v Kenneth Dyason [2007] EWHC 1174 (TCC) at [99–100]
Thermal Energy Construction Ltd v AE & E Lentjes UK Ltd [2009] EWHC 408 (TCC) at [21–30]
Whyte and Mackay Ltd v Blyth & Blyth Consulting Engineers Ltd [2013] CSOH 54 at [30–35]

(C) *Failing to address an issue, part of a submission or evidence – no breach*
AMEC Capital Projects Ltd v Whitefriars City Estates Ltd (No 2) [2004] EWHC 393 (TCC) at [110–135]
AMEC Capital Projects Ltd v Whitefriars City Estates Ltd (No 3) [2004] EWCA Civ 1418 at [38–43]
AMEC Group Ltd v Thames Water Utilities Ltd [2010] EWHC 419 (TCC) at [89–93]
Arcadis UK Ltd v May and Baker Ltd (t/a Sanofi) [2013] EWHC 87 (TCC) at [38–39]
Balfour Beatty Construction Northern Ltd v Modus Corovest (Blackpool) Ltd [2008] EWHC 3029 (TCC) at [44–49]
Bouygues E&S Contracting UK Ltd v Vital Energi Utilities Ltd [2014] ScotCS CSOH 115 at [6–8]
Broughton Brickwork Ltd v F Parkinson Ltd [2014] EWHC 4525 (TCC) at [28–29]
Camillin Denny Architects Ltd v Adelaide Jones & Company Ltd [2009] EWHC 2110 (TCC) at [40]
Carillion Construction Ltd v Devonport Royal Dockyard Ltd [2005] EWCA Civ 1358 at [71–81]
Carillion Construction Ltd v Devonport Royal Dockyard Ltd [2005] EWHC 778 (TCC) at [89–106]

David McLean Contractors Ltd v The Albany Building Ltd [2005] TCC101/05 at [22–24]

Farebrother Building Services Ltd v Frogmore Investments Ltd [2001] CILL 1762 at [9–32]

Farrelly (M&E) Building Services Ltd v Byrne Brothers (Formwork) Ltd [2013] EWHC 1186 (TCC) at [73–77]

Fleming Buildings Ltd v Mr and Mrs Jane Forrest [2008] CSOH 103 at [104]

Gillies Ramsay Diamond and Gavin Ramsay and Philip Diamond v PJW Enterprises Ltd [2003] ScotCS 343 at [26–28]

Gillies Ramsay Diamond v PJW Enterprises Ltd [2002] ScotCS 340 at [71]

HS Works Ltd v Enterprise Managed Services Ltd [2009] EWHC 729 (TCC) at [51–52; 55–57]

Humes Building Contracts Ltd v Charlotte Homes (Surrey) Ltd [2007] AdjLR 01/03 at [20–28]

Jacques (t/a C & E Jacques Partnership) v Ensign Contractors Ltd [2009] EWHC 3383 (TCC) at [29–33]

Kier Regional Ltd (t/a Wallis) v City & General (Holborn) Ltd [2006] EWHC 848 (TCC) at [39–44]

KNN Coburn LLP v GD City Holdings Ltd [2013] EWHC 2879 (TCC) at [50–54]

Lee v Chartered Properties (Building) Ltd [2010] EWHC 1540 (TCC) at [23]

Letchworth Roofing Company v Sterling Building Company [2009] EWHC 1119 (TCC) at [17–34]

Multiplex Constructions (UK) Ltd v West India Quay Development Company (Eastern) Ltd [2006] EWHC 1569 (TCC) at [39–41]

NAP Anglia Ltd v Sun-Land Development Co Ltd [2011] EWHC 2846 (TCC) at [25–46]

South West Contractors Ltd v Birakos Enterprises Ltd [2006] EWHC 2794 (TCC) at [30–37]

Speymill Contracts Ltd v Eric Baskind [2009] No 9LV 22750 at [88–90]

Speymill Contracts Ltd v Eric Baskind [2010] EWCA Civ 120 at [40–43]

SW Global Resourcing Limited v Morris & Spottiswood Limited [2012] CSOH 200 at [13; 17]

Urang Commercial Ltd v (1) Century Investments Ltd (2) Eclipse Hotels (Luton) Ltd [2011] EWHC 1561 (TCC) at [30–37]

Viridis UK Limited v Mulalley and Company Limited [2014] EWHC 268 (TCC) at [97–98]

William Verry (Glazing Systems) Ltd v Furlong Homes Ltd [2005] EWHC 138 (TCC) at [59–62]

WSP Cel Ltd v Dalkia Utilities Services plc [2012] EWHC 2428 (TCC) at [38–39]

17.5.8 Failure to permit a further submission or information

AMEC Group Ltd v Thames Water Utilities Ltd [2010] EWHC 419 (TCC) at [60; 62–75]

Balfour Beatty Construction Northern Ltd v Modus Corovest (Blackpool) Ltd [2008] EWHC 3029 (TCC) at [54–57]

CJP Builders Ltd v William Verry Ltd [2008] EWHC 2025 (TCC) at [78–86]

Fleming Buildings Ltd v Mr and Mrs Jane Forrest [2008] CSOH 103 at [109–112]

GPS Marine Contractors Ltd v Ringway Infrastructure Services Ltd [2010] EWHC 283 (TCC) at [90–109]

Mecright Ltd v TA Morris Developments Ltd [2001] AdjLR 06/22 at [36]

Pring & St. Hill Ltd v C J Hafner t/a Southern Erectors [2002] EWHC 1775 (TCC) at [33–35]

Quartzelec Ltd v Honeywell Control Systems Ltd [2008] EWHC 3315 (TCC) at [27–33]

17.5.9 Failure to follow the agreed procedure

Dean & Dyball Construction Ltd v Kenneth Grubb Associates Ltd [2003] EWHC 2465 (TCC) at [53]

Rydon Maintenance Ltd v Affinity Sutton Housing Ltd [2015] EWHC 1306 (TCC) at [100–102; 106]

17.5.10 Adjudicator's timetable unfair

NAP Anglia Ltd v Sun-Land Development Co Ltd [2011] EWHC 2846 (TCC) at [12–24]

17.5.11 Documents received late or not at all

Edenbooth Ltd v Cre8 Developments Ltd [2008] EWHC 570 (TCC) at [15–18]

JW Hughes Building Contractors Ltd v GB Metalwork Ltd [2003] EWHC 2421 (TCC) at [18–37]

M. Rohde Construction v Nicholas Markham-David (No 2) [2007] EWHC 1408 (TCC) at [17–20]

17.5.12 Failure to inform the parties about an approach taken or methodology used

ABB Ltd v Bam Nuttall Ltd [2013] EWHC 1983 (TCC) at [5; 37–48]

All in One Building and Refurbishments Ltd v Makers UK Ltd [2005] EWHC 2943 (TCC) at [30–33]

Arcadis UK Ltd v May and Baker Ltd (t/a Sanofi) [2013] EWHC 87 (TCC) at [37]

Ardmore Construction Ltd v Taylor Woodrow Construction Ltd [2006] CSOH 3 at [43–48]

Balfour Beatty Construction Ltd v The Mayor & Burgesses of the London Borough of Lambeth [2002] EWHC 597 (TCC) at [28–39]

Barr Ltd v Klin Investment Ltd [2009] ScotCS CSOH 104 at [43–46]

Berry Piling Systems Ltd v Sheer Projects Ltd [2012] EWHC 241 (TCC) at [8–14]

Brims Construction Ltd v A2M Development Ltd [2013] EWHC 3262 (TCC) at [31]
Broughton Brickwork Ltd v F Parkinson Ltd [2014] EWHC 4525 (TCC) at [23–27]
Cantillon Ltd v Urvasco Ltd [2008] EWHC 282 (TCC) at [76]
Carillion Construction Ltd v Devonport Royal Dockyard Ltd [2005] EWHC 778 (TCC) at [104–105]
Carillion Utility Services Ltd v SP Power Systems Ltd [2011] CSOH 139 at [27–33]
CG Group Ltd v Breyer Group plc [2013] EWHC 2722 (TCC) at [16; 31]
Ellis Building Contractors Ltd v Vincent Goldstein [2011] EWHC 269 (TCC) at [30–34]
Farrelly (M&E) Building Services Ltd v Byrne Brothers (Formwork) Ltd [2013] EWHC 1186 (TCC) at [58–64]
Greentherm Mechanical Services v KDJ Developments Ltd [2012] EWHC 3525 (TCC) at [20–24]
Herbosch-Kiere Marine Contractors Ltd v Dover Harbour Board [2012] EWHC 84 (TCC) at [24–34]
Hillcrest Homes Ltd v Beresford & Curbishley Ltd [2014] EWHC 280 (TCC) at [61–73]
Humes Building Contracts Ltd v Charlotte Homes (Surrey) Ltd [2007] AdjLR 01/03 at [20–28]
Hyder Consulting Ltd v Carillion Construction (UK) Ltd [2011] EWHC 1810 (TCC) at [71–74]
Karl Construction (Scotland) Ltd v Sweeney Civil Engineering (Scotland) Ltd [2002] SLT 312P/872/00 at [8]
Lidl UK GmbH v RG Carter Colchester Ltd [2012] EWHC 3138 at [62–73]
Multiplex Constructions (UK) Ltd v West India Quay Development Company (Eastern) Ltd [2006] EWHC 1569 (TCC) at [28–30]
Palmac Contracting Ltd v Park Lane Estates Ltd [2005] EWHC 919 (TCC) at [37–41]
Primus Build Ltd v Pompey Centre Ltd & Anor [2009] EWHC 1487 (TCC) at [36–44]
Rankilor (Dr Peter) & Perco Engineering Service Ltd v Igoe (M) Ltd [2006] AdjLR 01/27 at [28–32]
Roe Brickwork Ltd v Wates Construction Ltd [2013] EWHC 3417 (TCC) at [21–37]
Shimizu Europe Ltd v LBJ Fabrications Ltd [2003] EWHC 1229 (TCC) at [45]
Straw Realisations (No 1) Ltd (formerly known as Haymills (Contractors) Ltd (in administration)) v Shaftsbury House (Developments) Ltd [2010] EWHC 2597 (TCC) at [29–34]
Try Construction Ltd v Eton Town House Group Ltd [2003] EWHC 60 (TCC) at [58–59]
Vision Homes Ltd v Lancsville Construction Ltd [2009] EWHC 2042 (TCC) at [64–70]

17.5.13 Failure to inform the parties about advice from a third party

BAL (1996) Ltd v Taylor Woodrow Construction Ltd [2004] All ER (D) 218 (Feb) at [31–38]

Balfour Beatty Construction Ltd v The Mayor & Burgesses of the London Borough of Lambeth [2002] EWHC 597 (TCC) at [41]

Baune and another v Zduc Ltd [2002] All ER (D) 55 (Aug) at [1–2]

Bouygues E&S Contracting UK Ltd v Vital Energi Utilities Ltd [2014] ScotCS CSOH 115 at [12–15]

Costain Ltd v Strathclyde Builders Ltd [2003] ScotCS 352 at [21–27]

Highlands and Islands Authority Ltd v Shetland Islands Counsel [2012] CSOH 12 at [20–34]

RSL (South West Ltd) v Stansell Ltd (No 1) [2003] EWHC 1390 (TCC) at [32–34]

Try Construction Ltd v Eton Town House Group Ltd [2003] EWHC 60 (TCC) at [60–66]

Woods Hardwick Ltd v Chiltern Air Conditioning Ltd [2001] BLR 23 at [26–31; 37–39]

17.5.14 Failure to inform the parties about use of own knowledge and expertise

All in One Building and Refurbishments Ltd v Makers UK Ltd [2005] EWHC 2943 (TCC) at [30–33]

Ardmore Construction Ltd v Taylor Woodrow Construction Ltd [2006] CSOH 3 at [43–48]

Balfour Beatty Construction Ltd v The Mayor & Burgesses of the London Borough of Lambeth [2002] EWHC 597 (TCC) at [28–39]

Berry Piling Systems Ltd v Sheer Projects Ltd [2012] EWHC 241 (TCC) at [8–14]

Bouygues E&S Contracting UK Ltd v Vital Energi Utilities Ltd [2014] ScotCS CSOH 115 at [17–19]

Carillion Utility Services Ltd v SP Power Systems Ltd [2011] CSOH 139 at [27]

Costain Ltd v Strathclyde Builders Ltd [2003] ScotCS 352 at [20(6)]

Ellis Building Contractors Ltd v Vincent Goldstein [2011] EWHC 269 (TCC) at [30–34]

Hyder Consulting Ltd v Carillion Construction (UK) Ltd [2011] EWHC 1810 (TCC) at [71–74]

Karl Construction (Scotland) Ltd v Sweeney Civil Engineering (Scotland) Ltd [2002] SLT 312P/872/00 at [8]

Miller Construction (UK) Ltd v Building Design Partnership Ltd [2014] CSOH 80 at [13–18]

Multiplex Constructions (UK) Ltd v West India Quay Development Company (Eastern) Ltd [2006] EWHC 1569 (TCC) at [28–30]

Paton, Re Judicial Review [2011] CSOH 40 at [72–85]

Primus Build Ltd v Pompey Centre Ltd & Anor [2009] EWHC 1487 (TCC) at [36–44]

Rankilor (Dr Peter) & Perco Engineering Service Ltd v Igoe (M) Ltd [2006] AdjLR 01/27 at [28–32]

SGL Carbon Fibres Ltd v RBG Ltd [2011] CSOH 62 at [11–13; 28–36]

Straw Realisations (No 1) Ltd (formerly known as Haymills (Contractors) Ltd (in administration)) v Shaftsbury House (Developments) Ltd [2010] EWHC 2597 (TCC) at [29–34]

17.5.15 Failure to inform the parties about preliminary view

> Ardmore Construction Ltd v Taylor Woodrow Construction Ltd [2006] CSOH 3 at [43–48]
> Barr Ltd v Klin Investment Ltd [2009] ScotCS CSOH 104 at [47–48]
> Berry Piling Systems Ltd v Sheer Projects Ltd [2012] EWHC 241 (TCC) at [8–14]
> Carillion Construction Ltd v Devonport Royal Dockyard Ltd [2005] EWHC 778 (TCC) at [81(3); 114–115]
> Humes Building Contracts Ltd v Charlotte Homes (Surrey) Ltd [2007] AdjLR 01/03 at [20–28]
> Rankilor (Dr Peter) & Perco Engineering Service Ltd v Igoe (M) Ltd [2006] AdjLR 01/27 at [28–32]
> Rydon Maintenance Ltd v Affinity Sutton Housing Ltd [2015] EWHC 1306 (TCC) at [103–104; 106]
> Shimizu Europe Ltd v LBJ Fabrications Ltd [2003] EWHC 1229 (TCC) at [45]

17.5.16 Sufficiency of written reasons

> Balfour Beatty Engineering Services (HY) Ltd v Shepherd Construction Ltd [2009] EWHC 2218 (TCC) at [48]
> HS Works Ltd v Enterprise Managed Services Ltd [2009] EWHC 729 (TCC) at [55–57]
> Multiplex Constructions (UK) Ltd v West India Quay Development Company (Eastern) Ltd [2006] EWHC 1569 (TCC) at [34–39]
> Pihl UK Ltd v Ramboll UK Ltd [2012] CSOH 139 at [23–31]
> ROK Building Ltd v Celtic Composting Systems Ltd (No 2) [2010] EWHC 66 (TCC) at [32]
> Whyte and Mackay Ltd v Blyth & Blyth Consulting Engineers Ltd [2013] CSOH 54 at [30–35]

18 Further grounds for resisting enforcement

18.2 Fraud or deceit

> Andrew Wallace Ltd v Artisan Regeneration Ltd & Anor [2006] EWHC 15 (TCC) at [44–52]
> Eurocom Ltd v Siemens plc [2014] EWHC 3710 (TCC) at [57–75]
> GPS Marine Contractors Ltd v Ringway Infrastructure Services Ltd [2010] EWHC 283 (TCC) at [69–89]
> Pro-Design Ltd v New Millennium Experience Co Ltd [2001] AdjLR 09/26 at [5–10]
> SG South Ltd. v King's Head Cirencester LLP & Anor [2009] EWHC 2645 (TCC) at [19–37]
> Speymill Contracts Ltd v Eric Baskind [2009] No 9LV 22750 at [100–105]
> Speymill Contracts Ltd v Eric Baskind [2010] EWCA Civ 120 at [33–38; 44]

Straw Realisations (No 1) Ltd (formerly known as Haymills (Contractors) Ltd (in administration)) v Shaftsbury House (Developments) Ltd [2010] EWHC 2597 (TCC) at [31]

18.3 Duress

Capital Structures plc v Time & Tide Construction Ltd [2006] EWHC 591 (TCC) at [16–30]
Shepherd Construction Ltd v Mecright Ltd [2000] BLR 489 at [16–21]

18.4 UTCCR

Allen Wilson Shopfitters and Builders Ltd v Buckingham [2005] EWHC 1165 (TCC) at [41–45]
Bryen & Langley Ltd v Martin Boston [2004] EWHC 2450 (TCC) at [27–49]
Bryen & Langley Ltd v Martin Boston [2005] EWCA Civ 973 at [39–47]
Cartwright v Fay [2005] AdjLR 02/09 at [15–22]
Lovell Projects Ltd v Legg & Carver [2003] BLR 452 at [24–31]
Picardi v Cuniberti [2002] EWHC 2923 (TCC) at [97–111; 125–133]
Speymill Contracts Ltd v Eric Baskind [2009] No 9LV 22750 at [73–80]
Steve Domsalla (t/a Domsalla Building Services) v Kenneth Dyason [2007] EWHC 1174 (TCC) at [23–97]
Westminster Building Company Ltd v Andrew Beckingham [2004] EWHC 138 (TCC) at [29–32]

17.5 HRA

Austin Hall Building Ltd v Buckland Securities Ltd [2001] All ER (D) 137 at [13–78]
Edmund Nuttall Ltd v RG Carter Ltd (No 2) [2002] BLR 359 at [30]
Elanay Contracts Ltd v The Vestry [2001] BLR 33 at [16–17]
Whyte and Mackay Ltd v Blyth & Blyth Consulting Engineers Ltd [2013] CSOH 54 at [37–65]

Appendix 9
Alphabetical case index

A Straume (UK) Ltd v Bradlor Developments Ltd [1999] CILL 1520; [1999] AdjLR 04/07 [2000] BCC 333] 34–35, 37–8, 39, 122, 585, 597, 638
A v B [2002] ScotCS 325; [2002] AdjLR 12/17 .... 585, 601, 625, 629, 647
A&D Maintenance and Construction Ltd v Pagehurst Construction Services Ltd (2000) 16 Const LJ 199; [1999] CILL 1518; [1999] AdjLR 06/23
.... 46, 117, 354, 587, 593, 657, 660
A&S Enterprises Ltd v Kema Holdings Ltd [2004] EWHC 3365 (QB); [2005] BLR 76; [2004] CILL 2165; [2004] AdjLR 07/27 .... 373, 597, 667
A.T. Stannard Ltd v James Tobutt and Thomas Tobutt [2014] EWHC 3491 (TCC); [2014] All ER (D) 314 (Oct) 253, 344, 607, 632, 634, 651, 653
ABB Ltd v Bam Nuttall Ltd [2013] EWHC 1983 (TCC); [2013] All ER (D) 224 (Jul); [2013] BLR 529; (2013) 149 ConLR 172; [2013] CILL 3401 .... 392, 601, 673
ABB Power Construction Ltd v Norwest Holst Engineering Ltd (2000) 77 ConLR 20; (2001) 17 Const LJ 246; [2000] AdjLR 08/01 .... 61–62, 330, 589, 590, 650
ABB Zantingh Ltd v Zedal Building Services Ltd [2000] All ER (D) 2243; [2001] BLR 66; (2000) 77 ConLR 32; (2001) 17 Const LJ 255; [2000] AdjLR 12/12
.... 61, 323, 590, 648
Able Construction (UK) Ltd v Forest Property Development Ltd [2009] EWHC 159 (TCC); [2009] All ER (D) 176 (Feb); (2009) 25 Const LJ 449
.... 255, 272, 588, 632, 634, 636
Absolute Rentals Ltd v Gencor Enterprises Ltd (2001) 17 Const LJ 322; [2000] CILL 1637; [2000] AdjLR 07/16 .... 291, 639–640, 647
AC Plastic Industries Ltd v Active Fire Protection Ltd [2002] All ER (D) 61 (Aug)
.... 645
AC Yule & Son Ltd v Speedwell Roofing & Cladding Ltd [2007] EWHC 1360 (TCC); [2007] All ER (D) 100 (Jul); [2007] BLR 499; [2007] CILL 2489; [2007] AdjLR 05/31
.... 222–223, 623–624
Aceramais Holdings Ltd v Hadleigh Partnerships Ltd [2009] EWHC 1664 (TCC)
.... 323, 331, 592, 648, 650
Acsim (Southern) v Danish Contracting (1989) 47 BLR 55 191
Adonis Construction v O'Keefe Soil Remediation [2009] EWHC 2047 (TCC); [2009] All ER (D) 217 (Oct); [2009] CILL 2784 .... 116, 587, 594–595, 597, 611, 643

Alphabetical case index

Aedifice Partnership Ltd v Mr Ashwin Shah [2010] EWHC 2106 (TCC); [2010] All ER (D) 65 (Aug); (2010) 132 ConLR 100; [2010] CILL 2905 .... 325, 327–328, 648–649, 651

Air Design (Kent) Ltd v Deerglen (Jersey) Ltd [2008] EWHC 3047 (TCC); [2008] All ER (D) 97 (Dec); [2009] CILL 2657; [2008] AdjLR 12/10 .... 118, 296, 611–612, 640, 649

AJ Brenton t/a Manton Electrical Components v Jack Palmer [2001] AdjLR 01/19 .... 300, 642, 653, 663

Ale Heavylift v MSD (Darlington) Ltd [2006] EWHC 2080 (TCC); [2006] AdjLR 07/31 .... 592–3, 619, 640, 649

Alexander & Law Ltd v Coveside (21BPR) Ltd [2013] EWHC 3949 (TCC); [2013] All ER (D) 148 (Dec); (2013) 152 ConLR 163 ...... 32, 40, 280, 292–294, 298, 637–9, 641

All in One Building and Refurbishments Ltd v Makers UK Ltd [2005] EWHC 2943 (TCC); [2005] All ER (D) 289 (Dec); [2006] CILL 2321; [2005] AdjLR 12/19 .... 99, 104, 602–3, 605–6, 640, 670, 673, 675

All Metal Roofing v Kamm Properties Ltd [2010] EWHC 2670 (TCC) 328, 593, 649

Allen Watson Ltd v RNR London Ltd [2013] All ER (D) 181 (Aug) 634

Allen Wilson Joinery Ltd v Privetgrange Construction Ltd [2008] EWHC 2802 (TCC); (2008) 123 ConLR 1; [2008] AdjLR 11/17 .... 71, 73, 593–4, 622, 642

Allen Wilson Shopfitters and Builders Ltd v Buckingham [2005] EWHC 1165 (TCC); [2005] All ER (D) 109 (Jul); (2005) 102 ConLR 154; [2005] CILL 2249; [2005] AdjLR 05/27 .... 358, 591, 595, 597, 662, 677

Allied London & Scottish Properties plc v Riverbrae Construction Ltd [1999] ScotCS 224; [1999] BLR 346; (1999) 68 ConLR 79; [1999] CILL 1541; [1999] AdjLR 07/12 .... 622, 662, 679

Allied P&L Ltd v Paradigm Housing Group Ltd [2009] EWHC 2890 (TCC); [2009] All ER (D) 240 (Nov); [2010] BLR 59 .... 99–101, 268, 270, 303, 602–5, 608, 634, 643, 649, 651

Alstom Signalling Ltd v Jarvis Facilities Ltd (No 2) [2004] EWHC 1285 (TCC); [2004] AdjLR 05/28 .... 249, 251, 307, 315, 631, 642, 645, 647

Amber Construction Services Ltd v London Interspace HG Ltd [2007] EWHC 3042 (TCC); [2008] BLR 74; [2007] AdjLR 12/18 .... 271, 634

AMEC Capital Projects Ltd v Whitefriars City Estate Ltd [2003] EWHC 2443 (TCC); [2003] AdjLR 09/19 .... 597, 636, 654

AMEC Capital Projects Ltd v Whitefriars City Estates Ltd (No 2) [2004] EWHC 393 (TCC); [2004] All ER (D) 461 (Feb); (2004) 20 Const LJ 338; [2004] AdjLR 02/27 .... 345, 597, 671

AMEC Capital Projects Ltd v Whitefriars City Estates Ltd (No 3) [2004] EWCA Civ 1418; [2005] All ER 723; [2005] BLR 1; (2004) 96 ConLR 142; (2005) 21 Const LJ 249; [2005] CILL 2177; [2004] AdjLR 10/28 ..... 324, 371–2, 388, 597, 648 654, 664–6, 671

AMEC Civil Engineering Ltd v Secretary of State for Transport [2004] EWHC 2339 (TCC); [2004] All ER (D) 443 (Oct); [2005] CILL 2189; [2004] AdjLR 10/11 .... 100–1, 103, 602–5

AMEC Civil Engineering Ltd v Secretary of State for Transport [2005] EWCA Civ 291; [2005] All ER (D) 280 (Mar); [2005] BLR 227; (2005) 101 ConLR 26; (2005) 21 Const LJ 640; [2005] CILL 2228; [2005] AdjLR 03/17 .... 102, 603–5
AMEC Group Ltd v Thames Water Utilities Ltd [2010] EWHC 419 (TCC); [2010] All ER (D) 267 (Oct) 52, 54, 78, 118, 335, 337, 354, 360, 383, 389, 588, 595, 600, 611–12, 631, 643, 652, 657, 659, 662–4, 670–2
Ameycespa v Taimweser [2014] EWHC 4638 (TCC) 614–5, 618–9
Andrew Wallace Ltd v Artisan Regeneration Ltd & Anor [2006] EWHC 15 (TCC); [2006] All ER (D) 57 (Jan); [2006] AdjLR 01/10 .... 343, 401, 653, 676
Andrew Wallace Ltd v Jeff Noon [2009] BLR 158 .... 369, 665
Anglian Water Services Ltd v Laing O'Rourke Utilities Ltd [2010] EWHC 1529 (TCC); [2011] All ER (Comm) 1143; (2010) 131 ConLR 94; [2010] CILL 2873 ...... 597, 644
Anglo Swiss Holding Ltd & Ors v Packman Lucas Ltd [2009] EWHC 3212 (TCC); [2009] All ER (D) 125 (Dec); [2010] BLR 109; (2009) 128 ConLR 67; (2010) 26 Const LJ 204 .... 309, 637, 642, 646
Anrik Ltd v As Leisure Properties Ltd, Unreported, 8 January 2010 .... 298, 596, 640
Arcadis UK Ltd v May and Baker Ltd (t/a Sanofi) [2013] EWHC 87 (TCC); [2013] All ER (D) 228 (Jan); [2013] BLR 210; [2013] CILL 3305
.... 114, 601, 609–10, 667, 671, 673
Ardmore Construction Ltd v Taylor Woodrow Construction Ltd [2006] CSOH 3; [2006] CILL 2309; [2006] AdjLR 01/12 .... 394, 397, 414, 673, 675–6
ART Consultancy Ltd v Navera Trading Ltd [2007] EWHC 1375 (TCC); [2007] All ER (D) 157 (Jul); [2007] AdjLR 05/31 .... 593, 597, 642
Ashley House plc v Galliers Southern Ltd [2002] EWHC 274 (TCC); [2002] AdjLR 02/15 640
Aspect Contracts (Asbestos) Ltd v Higgins Construction Plc [2015] UKSC 38; [2015] CILL 3696 .... 312, 646
Aspect Contracts (Asbestos) Ltd v Higgins Construction Plc [2013] EWCA Civ 1541; [2013] All ER (D) 339 (Nov); [2014] BLR 79; (2013) 151 ConLR 72; [2014] CILL 3449 .... 225, 625, 646
Aspect Contracts (Asbestos) Ltd v Higgins Construction Plc [2013] EWHC 1322 (TCC); [2013] All ER (D) 296 (May); [2013] B.L.R. 417; [2013] CILL 3369
.... 625, 646
Atholl Developments (Slackbuie) Ltd, Re Application for Judicial Review [2010] CSOH 94 .... 351, 415, 417, 631, 637, 656, 661, 663
Attorney General v Barker [2000] 1 F.L.R. 759 .... 380, 423
Austin Hall Building Ltd v Buckland Securities Ltd [2001] All ER (D) 137; [2001] BLR 272; (2001) 80 ConLR 115; (2001) 17 Const LJ 325; [2001] CILL 1734; [2001] AdjLR 04/11 .... 215, 405, 597, 622, 625, 668, 677
Aveat Heating Ltd v Jerram Falkus Construction Ltd [2007] EWHC 131 (TCC); [2007] All ER (D) 13 (Feb); (2007) 113 ConLR 13; [2007] CILL 2452; [2007] AdjLR 02/01 ..... 147, 176, 220, 222, 229, 349, 374, 597, 606, 615, 617, 618, 623–4, 626, 654–5, 667
Avoncroft Construction Ltd v Sharba Homes (CN) Ltd [2008] EWHC 933 (TCC); [2008] All ER (D) 411 (Apr); (2008) 119 ConLR 130; [2008] AdjLR 04/29
.... 297, 299, 597, 629, 640, 642

Alphabetical case index

AWG Construction Services Ltd v Rockingham Motor Speedway Ltd [2004] EWHC 888 (TCC); [3004] All ER (D) 68 (Apr); [2004] AdjLR 04/05
.... 291, 296, 381, 585, 600, 603, 627, 639–40, 643, 659, 668, 670

BAL (1996) Ltd v Taylor Woodrow Construction Ltd [2004] All ER (D) 218 (Feb); [2004] AdjLR 01/23 .... 395, 674

Baldwins Industrial Services plc v Barr Ltd [2002] EWHC 2915 (TCC); [2003] BLR 176; [2003] CILL 1949; [2002] AdjLR 12/06
.... 58, 62, 289, 301, 589–90, 638, 640, 643

Balfour Beatty Construction Ltd v Serco Ltd [2004] EWHC 3336 (TCC); [2004] All ER (D) 348 (Dec); [2005] CILL 2232; [2004] AdjLR 12/21 .... 242, 245–6, 437, 629

Balfour Beatty Construction Ltd v The Mayor & Burgesses of the London Borough of Lambeth [2002] EWHC 597 (TCC); [2002] All ER (D) 60 (Apr); [2002] BLR 288; (2002) 84 ConLR 1; (2002) 18 ConstLJ 405; [2002] CILL 1873; [2002] AdjLR 04/12
.... 216, 394–5, 424, 597, 620, 622, 631, 664, 668, 670, 673, 675

Balfour Beatty Construction Northern Ltd v Modus Corovest (Blackpool) Ltd [2008] EWHC 3029 (TCC); [2008] All ER (D) 157 (Dec); [2009] CILL 2660; [2008] AdjLR 12/04 .... 300, 384, 390, 598, 629, 642, 656, 664, 669, 671

Balfour Beatty Engineering Services (HY) Ltd v Shepherd Construction Ltd [2009] EWHC 2218 (TCC); [2009] All ER (D) 125 (Oct); (2009) 127 ConLR 110
...... 204, 271, 352, 355, 374, 398, 603, 609–10, 621, 635, 656, 658, 660, 665, 667, 676

Balfour Beatty Ltd v Speedwell Roofing and Cladding Ltd [2010] EWHC 840 (TCC)
.... 235, 626–7, 631

Balfour Kilpatrick Ltd v Glauser International SA [2000] Adj.C.S. 07/27
.... 601, 608, 670

Ballast plc v The Burrell Company (Construction Management) Ltd [2001] ScotCS 159; [2001] BLR 529; [2001] AdjLR 06/21
.... 116, 359, 418, 597, 611, 615, 622–3, 625, 648, 655, 661, 662, 670–1

Ballast plc v The Burrell Company (Construction Management) Ltd [2002] ScotCS 324; [2002] AdjLR 12/17 .... 615, 661, 662

Banner Holdings Ltd v Colchester Borough Council [2010] EWHC 139 (TCC); [2010] All ER (D) 226 (Oct); (2010) 131 ConLR 77 .... 85, 100, 597, 603, 648

Barnes & Elliot Ltd v Taylor Woodrow Holdings Ltd & Anor [2003] EWHC 3100 (TCC); [2004] All ER (D) 142 (Apr); [2004] BLR 111; [2003] AdjLR 06/20
.... 222, 419, 598, 624

Barr Ltd v Klin Investment Ltd [2009] ScotCS CSOH 104; [2009] CILL 2787
.... 374, 598, 609–10, 659–60, 667, 673, 676

Barr Ltd v Law Mining Ltd [2001] ScotCS 152; (2001) 80 ConLR 135; [2001] CILL 1764; [2001] AdjLR 06/15 .... 46, 587, 600, 608, 631, 643, 657, 660, 661–2

Barrie Green v GW Integrated Building Services Ltd & Anor [2001] AdjLR 07/18
.... 58, 231, 376, 589, 623, 626, 667

Barry D Trentham Ltd v Lawfield Investments Ltd [2002] ScotCS 126; [2002] AdjLR 05/3 .... 297, 640

Baune and another v Zduc Ltd [2002] All ER (D) 55 (Aug) 657, 659, 675

Beck Interiors Limited v Dr Mario Luca Russo [2009] EWHC 3861 (TCC); [2010] BLR 377; (2009) 132 ConLR 56 .... 255, 632

Beck Interiors Ltd v Classic Decorative Finishing Ltd [2012] EWHC 1956 (TCC); [2012] All ER (D) 152 (Jul) 244, 629

Beck Interiors Ltd v UK Flooring Contractors Ltd [2012] EWHC 1808 (TCC); [2012] All ER (D) 31 (Jul); [2012] BLR 417
.... 103, 233, 302–3, 341, 603, 605, 608, 626, 643

Beck Peppiatt Ltd v Norwest Holst Construction Ltd [2003] EWHC 822 (TCC); [2003] BLR 316; [2003] AdjLR 03/20 .... 274, 603, 605

Belgrave Developments (Poole) Ltd v Vaughan & Anor [2005] AdjLR 06/30
.... 344, 653

Bell Building Projects Ltd v Carfin Developments Ltd [2010] ScotSC 19
.... 114, 609–10

Bell Building Projects Ltd v Carfin Developments Ltd [2010] ScotSC 68 611

Benfield Construction Ltd v Trudson (Hatton) Ltd [2008] EWHC 2333 (TCC); (2009) 25 Const LJ 319; [2008] CILL 2633; [2008] AdjLR 09/17
.... 195, 380, 598, 609–10, 620, 668

Bennett (Electrical) Services Ltd v Inviron Ltd [2007] EWHC 49 (TCC); [2007] AdjLR 01/19 .... 74, 587, 593–5

Bennett v FMK Construction Ltd [2005] EWHC 1268 (TCC); [2005] All ER (D) 377 (Jun); (2005) 101 ConLR 92; [2005] AdjLR 06/30 .... 121, 598, 613, 654

Berry Piling Systems Ltd v Sheer Projects Ltd [2012] EWHC 241 (TCC); [2012] All ER (D) 140 (Feb); (2012) 140 ConLR 225 .... 293, 296, 397, 639–40, 673, 675–6

Bewley Homes v CNM Estates [2010] EWHC 2619 (TCC) 640

Bickerton Construction Ltd v Temple Windows Ltd [2001] AdjLR 06/26
.... 598, 657, 659

Birmingham City Council v Paddison Construction Ltd [2008] EWHC 2254 (TCC); [2008] BLR 622; [2008] AdjLR 09/25 .... 114, 610

Bloor Construction (UK) Ltd v Bowmer & Kirkland (London) Ltd [2000] BLR 314; [2000] CILL 1626; [2000] AdjLR 04/05 .... 240, 598, 627

BNY Corporate Trustee Services Ltd v Eurosail-UK 2007–3BL Plc [2013] UKSC 28; [2013] 1 W.L.R. 1408; [2013] 3 All E.R. 271; [2013] 2 All E.R. (Comm) 531 32

Bothma (t/a DAB Builders) v Mayhaven Healthcare Ltd [2006] EWHC 2601 (QB); [2006] AdjLR 11/16 .... 109, 608–9, 649

Bothma (t/a DAB Builders) v Mayhaven Healthcare Ltd [2007] EWCA Civ 527; (2007) 114 ConLR 131; [2007] AdjLR05/14 .... 608–9, 649

Bourne v The Charit-Email Technology Partnership LLP [2009] EWHC 1901 (Ch) .. 34

Bouygues (UK) Ltd v Dahl-Jensen (UK) Ltd [1999] All ER (D) 1281; [2000] BLR 49; (2000) 70 ConLR 41; [2000] CILL 1566; [1999] AdjLR 11/17
.... 241, 601, 627, 632, 662, 670

Bouygues (UK) Ltd v Dahl-Jensen (UK) Ltd [2000] EWCA Civ 507; [2001] 1 All ER (Comm) 1041; [2000] BLR 522; (2000) 73 ConLR 135; [2000] CILL 1673; [2000] Adj.L.R 07/31 .... 287, 291, 357, 359–60, 385, 585, 601, 625, 627, 632, 638–9, 662

Bouygues E&S Contracting UK Ltd v Vital Energi Utilities Ltd [2014] ScotCS CSOH
.... 426, 661, 671, 675

Bovis Lend Lease Ltd v Cofely Engineering Services [2009] EWHC 1120 (TCC); [2009] All ER (D) 23 (Sep) 324, 598, 648, 651, 654

Alphabetical case index

Bovis Lend Lease Ltd v The Trustees of the London Clinic [2009] EWHC 64 (TCC); [2009] All ER (D) 240 (Jan); (2009) 123 ConLR 15; [2009] CILL 2672 .... 99, 105, 181, 365, 381, 598, 602-3, 605, 608, 643, 669

Bovis Lend Lease Ltd v Triangle Development Ltd [2002] EWHC 3123 (TCC); [2002] All ER (D) 155 (Nov); [2003] BLR 31; (2002) 86 ConLR 26; [2003] CILL 1939; [2002] AdjLR 11/02 .... 256, 598, 628, 630, 632-3, 646

Bracken and another v Billinghurst [2003] EWHC 1333 (TCC); [2003] All ER (D) 488 (Jul); (2004) 20 Const LJ T75; [2003] CILL 2039; [2003] AdjLR 06/10 .... 306, 598, 607, 645

Branlow Ltd v Dem-Master Demolition Ltd [2004] ScotCS A904/03; [2004] AdjLR 02/26 .... 592, 598

Bridgeway Construction Ltd v Tolent Construction Ltd; [2000] CILL 1662; [2000] AdjLR 04/11 .... 235, 419, 601, 627

Brims Construction Ltd v A2M Development Ltd [2013] EWHC 3262 (TCC); [2013] All ER (D) 317 (Oct) 333-4, 355, 392, 651, 657, 660, 674

Britcon (Scunthorpe) Ltd v Lincolnfields Ltd [2001] AdjLR 08/29 .... 621, 661

British Waterways Board (Judicial Review) [2001] ScotCS 182; [2001] AdjLR 07/05 605

Broughton Brickwork Ltd v F Parkinson Ltd [2014] EWHC 4525 (TCC); [2014] All ER (D) 367 (Oct) 640, 671, 674

Bryen & Langley Ltd v Martin Boston [2004] EWHC 2450 (TCC); [2004] All ER (D) 61 (Nov); [2005] BLR 28; (2004) 98 ConLR 82; [2004] AdjLR 11/01 .... 404, 586, 677

Bryen & Langley Ltd v Martin Boston [2005] EWCA Civ 973; [2005] All ER (D) 507 (Jul); [2005] BLR 508; [2005] CILL 2261; [2005] AdjLR 07/29 .... 269-70, 404, 586, 595, 598, 635, 677

BSF Consulting Engineers Ltd v MacDonald Crosbie [2008] All ER (D) 171 (Apr); [2008] AdjLR 04/14 594

Buxton Building Contractors Ltd v The Governors of Durand Primary School [2004] EWHC 733 (TCC); [2004] All ER (D) 89 (Apr); [2004] BLR 374; (2004) 95 ConLR 120; [2004] AdjLR 03/12 .... 387, 621, 659, 671

C&B Scene Concept Design Ltd v Isobars Ltd [2001] CILL 1781; [2001] AdjLR 06/20 .... 585, 588, 597, 611, 651, 654, 662, 682

C&B Scene Concept Design Ltd v Isobars Ltd [2002] EWCA Civ 46; [2002] BLR 93; (2002) 82 ConLR 154; (2002) 18 Const LJ 139; [2002] CILL 1829; [2002] AdjLR 01/31 .... 358, 585, 588, 611, 657, 662, 682

Cable & Wireless PLC v IBM United Kingdom Ltd [2002] EWHC 2059 (Comm) ... 310

Cain Electrical Ltd v Richard Cox t/a Pennine Control Systems [2011] EWHC 2681 (TCC) 593, 615

Caledonian Modular Ltd v Mar City Developments Ltd [2015] EWHC 1855 (TCC); [2015] All ER (D) 16 (Jul); 160 ConLR 42 .... 133, 135, 308, 614, 645, 682

Camillin Denny Architects Ltd v Adelaide Jones & Company Ltd [2009] EWHC 2110 (TCC); [2009] All ER (D) 117 (Aug); [2009] BLR 606 .... 118, 611, 635, 659, 664, 667, 671

Canary Riverside Development (Private) Ltd v Timtec International Ltd [2000] All ER (D) 1753; (2003) 19 Const LJ 283; [2000] AdjLR 11/09 .... 255, 632

Cantillon Ltd v Urvasco Ltd [2008] EWHC 282 (TCC); [2008] BLR 250; (2008) 117
ConLR 1; [2008] CILL 2564; [2008] AdjLR 02/27 .... 99, 123,
301–2, 353, 363, 385, 392, 393, 598, 602, 603, 618, 632, 643, 658, 660, 664, 670, 674
Capital Structures plc v Time & Tide Construction Ltd [2006] EWHC 591 (TCC);
[2006] All ER (D) 98 (Mar); [2006] BLR 226; [2006] CILL 2345; [2006] AdjLR 03/08
.... 47, 402, 587, 598, 611, 677
Captiva Estates Ltd v Rybarn Ltd (In Administration) [2005] EWHC 2744 (TCC);
[2006] BLR 66; [2006] CILL 2333; [2005] AdjLR 11/11 .... 66, 591
Carillion Construction Ltd v Devonport Royal Dockyard Ltd [2003] BLR 79; [2003]
CILL 1976; [2002] AdjLR 11/27 .... 69, 72, 101, 592, 594, 603, 604
Carillion Construction Ltd v Devonport Royal Dockyard Ltd [2005] EWCA Civ 1358;
[2005] All ER (D) 202 (Nov); [2006] BLR 15; (2005) 104 ConLR 1;
[2005] AdjLR 11/16
.... 149, 155, 209, 215, 250, 415, 429, 615–6, 618, 622, 632, 643, 656, 659–60, 671
Carillion Construction Ltd v Devonport Royal Dockyard Ltd [2005] EWHC 778
(TCC); [2005] All ER (D) 366 (Apr); [2005] BLR 310; (2005) 102 ConLR 167; [2005]
CILL 2253; [2005] AdjLR 04/26
...... 206, 250, 351, 385, 398, 415, 621–2, 632, 643, 656, 659–60, 664, 670–1, 674, 676
Carillion Construction Ltd v Stephen Andrew Smith [2011] EWHC 2910 (TCC);
[2011] All ER (D) 121 (Dec); (2011) 141 ConLR 117; [2011] CILL 3097
.... 324, 602, 610, 648
Carillion Utility Services Ltd v SP Power Systems Ltd [2011] CSOH 139; [2012]
BLR 186 .... 424, 621, 643, 664, 674–5
Cartwright v Fay [2005] AdjLR 02/09 .... 169, 617, 626, 677
Castle Inns (Stirling) Ltd t/a Castle Leisure Ltd v Clark Contracts Ltd [2007] CSOH 21;
[2007] AdjLR 02/06 .... 306, 644, 647
Castle Inns (Stirling) Ltd trading as Castle Leisure Group v Clark Contracts Ltd [2005]
CSOH 178; [2005] AdjLR 12/29 .... 232, 315, 318, 626, 647
CG Group Ltd v Breyer Group Plc [2013] EWHC 2722 (TCC); [2013] All ER (D) 73
(Oct); [2013] BLR 575; (2013) 150 ConLR 1 .... 262, 657, 660, 664, 674
CG Group Ltd v Breyer Group Plc [2013] EWHC 2959 (TCC) 268, 634–5
Chamberlain Carpentry & Joinery Ltd v Alfred MacAlpine Construction Ltd [2002]
EWHC 514 (TCC); [2002] AdjLR 03/25 .... 148–9, 598, 608, 615, 657, 660
Channel Tunnel Group Ltd v Balfour Beatty Construction Ltd [1993] AC 334 310
Charles Brand Ltd v Donegall Ltd [2010] NIQB 67 .... 437, 598, 629, 631
Charles Henshaw & Sons Ltd v Stewart & Shields Ltd [2014] CSIH 55
.... 416–7, 612, 632, 664
Charles Henshaw & Sons Ltd v Stewart & Shields Ltd [2014] ScotSC 59 .... 612, 657
Christiani & Nielsen Ltd v The Lowry Centre Development Company Ltd [2000]
AdjLR 06/16 .... 116, 326, 588, 596, 612, 648, 651
CIB Properties Ltd v Birse Construction [2004] EWHC 2365 (TCC); [2004] All ER (D)
256 (Oct); [2005] BLR 173; [2004] AdjLR 10/19
.... 102, 198, 216, 221, 240, 379, 381–3, 585, 603–5, 620–3, 627, 668–70
Citex Professional Services Ltd v Kenmore Developments Ltd [2004] ScotCS 20; [2004]
AdjLR 01/28 647

Alphabetical case index

City Basements Ltd v Nordic Construction [2014] EWHC 4817 (TCC) 120, 260, 606, 613, 633, 649

City Inn Ltd v Shepherd Construction Ltd [2001] ScotCS 54; [2001] AdjLR 07/17 .... 315, 598, 647

CJP Builders Ltd v William Verry Ltd [2008] EWHC 2025 (TCC); [2008] All ER (D) 190 (Oct); [2008] BLR 545; [2008] CILL 2609; [2008] AdjLR 08/15 .... 328, 333, 390, 598, 618, 648–9, 651, 654, 657, 660, 670, 673

Clark Electrical Ltd v JMD Developments (UK) Ltd [2012] EWHC 2627 (TCC); [2012] All ER (D) 181 (Sep); [2012] BLR 546 .... 81, 596

Cleveland Bridge (UK) Ltd v Whessoe-Volker Stevin Joint Venture [2010] EWHC 1076 (TCC); [2010] All ER (D) 206 (May); [2010] BLR 415; (2010) 130 ConLR 159; [2010] CILL 2876 .... 51, 60–1, 86, 588, 589, 590, 616, 643

CN Associates (a firm) v Holbeton Ltd [2011] EWHC 43 (TCC); [2011] All ER (D) 217 (Jan); [2011] BLR 261; [2011] CILL 2969 649

Coleraine Skip Hire Ltd v Ecomesh Ltd [2008] NIQB 141; (2009) 25 Const LJ 36 .... 56, 240, 436, 589, 627, 640, 643

Collins (Contractors) Ltd v Baltic Quay Management (1994) Ltd [2004] EWCA Civ 1757; [2004] 2 All ER 982; [2005] BLR 63; (2004) 99 ConLR 1; [2005] CILL 2213; [2004] AdjLR 12/07 .... 102, 598, 603–4, 605

Comsite Projects Ltd v Andritz AG [2003] EWHC 958 (TCC); [2003] All ER (D) 64 (May); (2004) 20 Const LJ 24; [2003] AdjLR 04/30 .... 62, 590, 648

Concrete & Coating (UK) Ltd v Cornelius Moloney [2004] ADJ LR 12/06 ..... 592, 653

Connaught Partnerships Ltd v Perth and Kinross Council [2013] CSOH 149 .... 421, 638

Connex South Eastern Ltd v M J Building Services Group plc [2005] EWCA Civ 193; [2005] 2 All ER 871; [2005] BLR 201; (2005) 100 ConLR 16; [2005] CILL 2201; [2005] AdjLR 03/01 .... 380, 613, 668

Connex South Eastern Ltd v MJ Building Services Group plc [2004] EWHC 1518 (TCC); [2004] All ER (D) 318 (Jun); [2004] BLR 333; (2004) 95 ConLR 43; [2004] AdjLR 06/25 .... 70, 122, 309, 592, 595, 645, 668

Conor Engineering Ltd v Les Constructions Industrielles de la Mediterranee SA [2004] EWHC 899 (TCC); [2004] All ER (D) 75 (Apr); [2004] BLR 212; [2004] AdjLR 04/05 .... 244–5, 590, 629

Cornhill Insurance plc v Improvement Services Ltd [1986] 1 WLR 114 32

Costain Ltd v Strathclyde Builders Ltd [2003] ScotCS 352; (2003) 100 ConLR 41; [2003] AdjLR 12/17 .... 19, 365–6, 416, 585, 621, 664–5, 675

Costain Ltd v Wescol Steel Ltd [2003] EWHC 312 (TCC); [2003] AdjLR 01/24 .... 110, 348, 598, 603, 606, 608, 655

Cott UK Ltd v FE Barber Ltd [1997] 3 All ER 540 310

Coventry Scaffolding Company (London) Ltd v Lanscville Construction Ltd [2009] EWHC 2995 (TCC); [2009] All ER (D) 93 (Dec) 262, 633

Cowlin Construction Ltd v CFW Architects (A Firm) [2002] EWHC 2914 (TCC); [2003] BLR 241; 2003] CILL 1961; [2002] AdjLR 11/15 .... 99, 105, 335, 586, 588, 593, 602, 606, 652

CPL Contracting Ltd v Cadenza Residential Ltd [2005] AdjLR 01/31 .... 598, 606

CRJ Services Ltd v Lanstar Ltd (trading as CSG Ltd) [2011] EWHC 972 (TCC); [2011] All ER (D) 122 (May) 374, 666, 667
CSC Braehead Leisure Ltd and Capital & Regional (Braehead) Ltd v Laing O-Rourke Scotland Ltd [2008] CSOH 119; [2009] BLR 49; [2008] AdjLR 08/19
.... 301, 623, 643, 656, 662, 669
CSK Electrical Contractors Ltd v Kingwood Electrical Services Ltd [2015] EWHC 667 (TCC); [2015] All ER (D) 167 (Mar) 158, 365, 606, 616, 640, 649, 651, 665, 669
Cubitt Building & Interiors Ltd v Fleetglade Ltd [2006] EWHC 3413 (TCC); (2006) 110 ConLR 36; [2007] CILL 2431; [2006] AdjLR 12/21
.... 168, 175, 221–3, 350, 597, 598, 617–8, 623, 624, 656
Cubitt Building and Interiors Ltd v Richardson Roofing (Industrial) Ltd [2008] EWHC 1020 (TCC); [2008] All ER (D) 106 (May); [2008] BLR 354; (2008) 119 ConLR 137; [2008] CILL 2588; [2008] AdjLR 05/09 .... 120, 312, 595, 598, 613, 646
Curot Contracts Ltd, T/A Dimension Shopping v Castle Inns (Stirling) Ltd T/A Castle Leisure Group [2008] CSOH 178; [2008] AdjLR 12/16 .... 658, 660
Cygnet Healthcare plc v Higgins City Ltd (2000) 16 Const LJ 394; [2000] AdjLR 09/06
.... 309, 613, 636, 646
D G Williamson Ltd v Northern Ireland Prison Service [2009] NIQB 8
.... 248, 428, 432, 592, 615, 631, 642, 645
Dalkia Energy and Technical Services Ltd v Bell Group UK Ltd [2009] EWHC 73 (TCC); [2009] All ER (D) 273 (Feb); (2009) 122 ConLR 66
.... 110, 116, 323, 346, 356, 380, 597, 608, 612, 645, 648–9, 654, 658, 660, 665, 668
David McLean Contractors Ltd v The Albany Building Ltd [2005] EWHC B5 (TCC); [2005] AdjLR 11/10 .... 586, 601, 611, 629, 672
David McLean Housing Contractors Ltd v Swansea Housing Association Ltd [2001] All ER (D) 519 (Jul); [2002] BLR 125; [2002] CILL 1811; [2001] AdjLR 07/27
.... 208, 246, 608–9, 621, 629, 646, 654, 658, 660
Dean & Dyball Construction Ltd v Kenneth Grubb Associates Ltd [2003] EWHC 2465 (TCC); [2003] All ER (D) 457 (Oct); (2003) 100 ConLR 92; [2003] CILL 2045; [2003] AdjLR 10/28
.....72, 77, 99, 102, 373, 391, 594, 595, 602–3, 605–6, 608, 659–60, 662, 664, 666, 673
Debeck Ductwork Installation Ltd v T&E Engineering Ltd [2002] AdjLR 10/14 592
Deko Scotland Ltd v Edinburgh Royal Joint Venture & Anor [2003] ScotCS 113; [2003] CILL 1999; [2003] AdjLR 04/11 .... 601, 627, 662
Devon County Council v Celtic Bioenergy Limited [2014] EWHC 309 (TCC); [2014] CILL 3465 .... 271, 635
Devon County Council v Celtic Composting Systems Ltd [2014] EWHC 552 (TCC); [2014] CILL 3501 .... 116, 601, 603, 612, 669
DGT Steel and Cladding Ltd v Cubitt Building and Interiors Ltd [2007] EWHC 1584 (TCC); [2007] All ER (D) 43 (Jul); [2007] BLR 371; (2007) 116 ConLR 118; [2007] CILL 2492; [2007] AdjLR 07/04 .... 120, 300, 310, 611, 613, 642, 646
Director General of Fair Trading v First National Bank plc [2001] UKHL 52; [2002] 1 A.C. 481; [2001] 3 W.L.R. 1297; [2002] 1 All E.R. 97; [2001] 2 All E.R. (Comm) 1000
.... 404

Alphabetical case index 687

Discain Project Services Ltd v Opecprime Development Ltd (No 1) [2000] BLR 402; [2000] CILL 1676; [2000] AdjLR 08/09
....363, 606–7, 620, 664, 666, 668
Discain Project Services Ltd v Opecprime Development Ltd (No 2) [2001] All ER (D) 123; [2001] BLR 285; (2001) 80 ConLR 95; [2001] CILL 1739; [2001] AdjLR 04/11
....203, 373, 612, 621, 664, 666
Donal Pugh v Harris Calman Construction Ltd [2003] Adj.C.S. 06/30 634–5
Dorchester Hotel Ltd v Vivid Interiors Ltd [2009] EWHC 70 (TCC); [2009] All ER (D) 264 (Feb); [2009] BLR 135; (2009) 122 ConLR 55; [2009] CILL 2676
.... 323, 364, 598, 648, 665, 669–70
Dumarc Building Services Ltd v Mr Salvador - Rico [2003] Adj.C.R. 01/31 .....598, 629
Durham County Council v Jeremy Kendall (trading as HLB Architects) [2011] EWHC 780 (TCC); [2011] BLR 425; [2011] CILL 3017 .... 586, 592, 649, 654
Earls Terrace Properties Ltd v Waterloo Investments Ltd [2002] CILL 1889; [2002] AdjLR 02/14 588
Ecovision Systems Ltd v Vinci Construction UK Ltd [2015] EWHC 587 (TCC); [2015] All ER (D) 160 (Mar); [2015] BLR 373; (2015) 159 ConLR 84; [2015] CILL 3657
.... 167, 181, 346, 359, 615, 618, 654, 662, 666–7, 669
Edenbooth Ltd v Cre8 Developments Ltd [2008] EWHC 570 (TCC); [2008] All ER (D) 20 (Apr); [2008] CILL 2592; [2008] AdjLR 03/13 .... 62, 64, 590, 591, 669, 673
Edinburgh Royal Joint Venture, Petition of [2002] ScotCS P762/02; [2002] AdjLR 08/02
....629
Edmund Nuttall Ltd v R G Carter Ltd [2002] EWHC 400 (TCC); [2002] All ER (D) 325 (Mar); [2002] BLR 312; (2002) 82 ConLR 24; [2002] CILL 1853; [2002] AdjLR 03/21
.... 99, 104, 107, 598, 603, 606–7, 658–9, 666
Edmund Nuttall Ltd v RG Carter Ltd (No 2) [2002] BLR 359; [2002] AdjLR 04/18
.... 598, 666, 677
Edmund Nuttall Ltd v Sevenoaks District Council [2000] AdjLR 04/14 .... 627, 629
ERDC Group Ltd v Brunel University [2006] EWHC 687 (TCC) 45
Elanay Contracts Ltd v The Vestry [2001] BLR 33; [2000] CILL 1679; [2000] AdjLR 08/30 .... 405, 677
Ellis Building Contractors Ltd v Vincent Goldstein [2011] EWHC 269 (TCC); [2010] CILL 3049 .... 197, 377, 667, 674–5
Emcor Drake & Scull Ltd v Costain Construction Ltd & Skanska Central Europe AB (t/a Costain Skanska Joint Venture) [2004] EWHC 2439 (TCC); [2004] All ER (D) 426 (Oct); (2004) 97 ConLR 142; [2005] CILL 2181; [2004] AdjLR 10/29
.... 598, 611, 668, 670
Enterprise Managed Services Ltd v East Midland Contracting Ltd [2008] EWHC 727 (TCC); [2008] AdjLR 03/27 ....120, 314, 613, 647
Enterprise Managed Services Ltd v Tony McFadden Utilities Ltd [2009] EWHC 3222 (TCC); [2009] All ER (D) 126 (Apr); [2010] BLR 89
.... 33, 103, 107, 118, 138, 285, 287, 294, 602, 605–8, 614, 638, 648, 669–70
Enterprise Managed Services Ltd v Tony McFadden Utilities Ltd [2010] EWHC 1506 (TCC) 269, 612, 634

Epping Electrical Company Ltd v Briggs and Forrester (Plumbing Services) Ltd [2007] EWHC 4 (TCC); [2007] All ER (D) 116 (Jan); [2007] BLR 126; (2007) 113 ConLR 1; (2007) 23 Const LJ 239; [2007] CILL 2438; [2007] AdjLR 01/19 ..... 95, 601, 623, 626

Ericsson AB v EADS Defence and Security Systems Ltd [2009] EWHC 2598 (TCC); [2009] All ER (D) 294 (Oct); [2010] BLR 131; (2009) 127 ConLR 168 .... 120, 331, 613, 650

Estor Ltd v Multifit (UK) Ltd [2009] EWHC 2108 (TCC); [2009] All ER (D) 119 (Oct); (2009) 126 ConLR 40 .... 594, 643, 654

Estor Ltd v Multifit (UK) Ltd [2009] EWHC 2565 (TCC); [2009] All ER (D) 202 (Nov); [2010] CILL 2800 .... 343–4, 654

Euro Construction Scaffolding Ltd v SLLB Construction Ltd [2008] EWHC 3160 (TCC); [2009] CILL 2679; [2008] AdjLR 12/19 .... 72, 594, 649

Eurocom Ltd v Siemens Plc [2014] EWHC 3710 (TCC); [2015] BLR 1; (2015) 157 ConLR 120; [2014] CILL 3593 .... 156–8, 267–8, 345, 610, 616, 643, 654, 676

Eurocom Ltd v Siemens Plc Ex Tempore 634

Faithful & Gould Ltd v Arcal Ltd and Ors. [2001] AdjLR 05/25 .... 163, 617, 626

Farebrother Building Services Ltd v Frogmore Investments Ltd [2001] CILL 1762; [2001] AdjLR 04/20 .... 301, 325, 601, 632, 643, 648, 672

Farrelly (M&E) Building Services Ltd v Byrne Brothers (Formwork) Ltd [2013] EWHC 1186 (TCC); [2013] All ER (D) 131 (May); [2013] CILL 3378 .... 365, 393–4, 601, 640, 664–5, 672, 674

Fastrack Contractors Ltd v Morrison Construction Ltd & Anor [2000] All ER (D) 11; [2000] BLR 168; 75 ConLR 33; (2000) 16 Const LJ 273; [2000] CILL 1589; [2000] AdjLR 01/04 .... 33, 109, 136, 603, 607, 609, 614–5, 621, 649, 657–8, 660

Fence Gate Ltd v James R Knowles Ltd [2002] All ER (D) 34 (May); (2001) 84 ConLR 206; [2001] CILL 1757; [2001] AdjLR 05/31 .... 50–1, 58, 588–9, 596

Fenice Investments Inc v Jerram Falkus Construction Ltd [2009] EWHC 3272 (TCC); [2010] All ER (D) 47 (Jan); (2009) 128 ConLR 124 634–6

Fenice Investments Inc v Jerram Falkus Construction Ltd [2011] EWHC 1678 (TCC); [2011] All ER (D) 103 (Jul); (2011) 141 ConLR 206; [2011] CILL 3068 .... 230–1, 317, 626–7, 634–5

Ferson Contractors Ltd v Levolux AT Ltd [2003] EWCA Civ 11; [2003] 1 All ER (Comm) 385; [2003] BLR 118; (2003) 86 ConLR 98; [2003] AdjLR 01/22 .... 242–3, 626, 628

FG Skerritt Ltd v Caledonian Building Systems Ltd [2013] EWHC 1898 (TCC); [2013] All ER (D) 366 (Jul) 292, 294, 301, 598, 639–40, 643

Fileturn Ltd v Royal Garden Hotel Ltd [2010] EWHC 1736 (TCC); [2010] All ER (D) 128 (Jul); [2010] BLR 512; (2010) 131 ConLR 118; (2011) 27 Const LJ 191; [2010] CILL 2912 .... 253, 370, 632, 664, 665

Flannery Construction Ltd v M Holleran Ltd [2007] EWHC 825 (TCC) 594

Fleming Buildings Ltd v Mr and Mrs Jane Forrest [2008] CSOH 103; [2008] AdjLR 07/15 .... 78, 595, 619, 628, 672–3

Fleming Buildings Ltd v Mr and Mrs Jane Forrest [2010] CSIH 8 586

Forest Heath District Council v ISG Jackson Ltd [2010] EWHC 322 (TCC); [2010] All ER (D) 16 (Nov) 322, 598, 648

FW Cook Ltd v Shimizu (UK) Ltd [2000] BLR 199; [2000] CILL 1613; [2000] AdjLR
02/04 . . . . 601, 658–9
Galliford (UK) Ltd t/a Galliford Northern v Markel Capital Ltd [2003] EWHC 1216
(QB); [2003] All ER (D) 303 (May); [2003] AdjLR 05/12 . . . . 226, 601, 626
Galliford Try Building Ltd v Estura Ltd [2015] EWHC 412 (TCC); [2015] All ER (D) 01
(Mar); [2015] BLR 321; (2015) 159 ConLR 10 . . . . . 30, 133, 299, 585, 614, 632, 641–2
Galliford Try Construction Ltd v Michael Heal Associates Ltd [2003] EWHC 2886
(TCC); [2003] All ER (D) 07 (Dec); (2003) 99 ConLR 19; [2003] AdjLR 12/01
. . . . 73, 80, 337, 587, 595, 596, 652, 668
Gary Kitt and EC Harris LLP v The Laundry Building Ltd and Etcetera Construction
Services Ltd [2014] EHWC 4250 (TCC); [2014] All ER (D) 180 (Dec); [2015] BLR
170; [2015] CILL 3616 . . . . 137, 149–50, 229, 615, 618, 626, 635, 669
Geoffrey Osborne Ltd v Atkins Rail Ltd [2009] EWHC 2425 (TCC); [2010] BLR 363
. . . . .308, 643, 645, 662
George Parke v The Fenton Gretton Partnership [2001] CILL 1713; [2001] AdjLR 08/02
. . . . 225, 625, 637
Geris Handelsgesellschaft GmbH v Les Constructions Industrielles de la Mediterranee
S.A. [2005] EWHC 499 (TCC); [2005] AdjLR 02/11 . . . . 246, 628, 630, 632
Gibraltar Residential Properties Ltd v Gibralcon 2004 SA [2010] EWHC 2595 638
Gibson (Bainbridge) Ltd v Fermanagh District Council [2013] NIQB 16
. . . . 103, 436, 439, 600, 603, 605, 669–70
Gibson Lea Retail Interiors Ltd v Makro Self Service Wholesalers Ltd [2001] All ER (D)
333 (Jul); [2001] BLR 407; [2001] AdjLR 07/24 . . . . 57–8, 588–9
Gibson v Imperial Homes [2002] EWHC 676 (QB); [2002] All ER (D) 367 (Feb); [2002]
AdjLR 02/27 . . . . .585, 654
Gilbert-Ash (Northern) Ltd v Modern Engineering (Bristol) Ltd [1974] A.C. 689;
[1973] 3 WLR. 421; [1973] 3 All E.R. 195; BLR 73 . . . . .4, 191
Gillies Ramsay Diamond and Gavin Ramsay and Philip Diamond v PJW Enterprises
Ltd [2003] ScotCS 343; [2004] BLR 131; [2003] AdjLR 12/24
. . . . 116, 202, 209, 388, 587–8, 612, 622, 625, 656, 662, 672
Gillies Ramsay Diamond v PJW Enterprises Ltd [2002] ScotCS 340; [2003] BLR 48;
[2002] CILL 1901; [2002] AdjLR 06/27
. . . . 49–50, 116, 587–8, 612, 620, 622, 656, 662, 672
Gillies v Secretary of State for Work and Pensions [2006] UKHL 2; [2006] 1 All ER 731
. . . . 368, 665
Gipping Construction Ltd v Eaves Ltd [2008] EWHC 3134 (TCC); [2008] AdjLR 12/11
. . . . 267, 281, 375, 634, 637, 667
Glencot Development & Design Co Ltd v Ben Barrett & Son (Contractors) Ltd [2001]
All ER (D) 384 (Feb); [2001] BLR 207; (2001) 80 ConLR 14; (2001) 17 Const LJ 336;
[2001] CILL 1721; [2001] AdjLR 02/13 . . . . 376, 621, 632, 646, 665, 667
Glendalough Associated SA v Harris Calnan Construction Co Ltd [2013] EWHC 3142
(TCC); [2013] All ER (D) 230 (Oct); [2014] CILL 3441
. . . . 71, 73, 323–4, 593, 595, 648, 650–1
Goldspan Ltd, Re [2003] B.P.I.R. 93 39
Gotch v Enelco Ltd [2015] EWHC 1802 (TCC); [2015] All ER (D) 50 (Jul) 648

GPN Limited (In Receivership) v 02 (UK) Limited [2004] EWHC 2494 (TCC) 587
GPS Marine Contractors Ltd v Ringway Infrastructure Services Ltd [2010] EWHC 283 (TCC); [2010] All ER (D) 232 (Oct); [2010] BLR 377
.... 327, 390, 607, 609, 612, 621, 645, 650–2, 662, 673, 676
Gray & Sons Builders (Bedford) Ltd v Essential Box Company Ltd [2006] EWHC 2520 (TCC); [2006] All ER (D) 285 (Oct); (2006) 108 ConLR 49; [2006] CILL 2395; [2006] AdjLR 10/11 .... 267, 270, 634–5
Greentherm Mechanical Services v KDJ Developments Ltd [2012] EWHC 3525 (TCC)
.... 657, 674
Grovedeck Ltd v Capital Demolition Ltd [2000] All ER (D) 317; [2000] BLR 181; [2000] CILL 1604; [2000] AdjLR 02/24 .... 593, 612, 649
Guardi Shoes Ltd v Datum Contracts [2002] CILL 1934; [2002] AdjLR 10/28
.... 278, 637
Habas Sinai v Sometal SAL [2010] EWHC 29 (Comm) 47
Harding (t/a M J Harding Contractors) v Paice and Springall [2014] EWHC 3824 (TCC); [2014] All ER (D) 237 (Nov); (2015) 157 ConLR 98
.... 112, 129, 131–2, 610–1, 614, 619, 650
Harding (t/a M J Harding Contractors) v Paice and Springall [2014] EWHC 4819 (TCC) 48, 587
Harlow & Milner Ltd v Linda Teasdale (No 1) [2006] EWHC 54 (TCC); [2006] AdjLR 01/16 .... 248, 631, 634–5, 637, 641, 669
Harlow & Milner Ltd v Mrs Linda Teasdale (No 3) [2006] EWHC 1708 (TCC); [2006] BLR 359; [2006] AdjLR 07/07 .... 282, 637
Harlow & Milner Ltd v Teasdale (No 2) [2006] EWHC 535 (TCC); [2006] All ER (D) 382 (Mar); [2006] AdjLR 03/15 .... 282, 638
Harris Calnan Construction Co Ltd v Ridgewood (Kensington) Ltd [2007] EWHC 2738 (TCC); [2007] All ER (D) 284 (Nov); [2008] BLR 132; [2007] CILL 2525; [2007] AdjLR 11/15 .... 74, 595, 596, 634–5, 650, 651
Hart (t/a D W Hart & Son) v Smith & Anor [2009] EWHC 2223 (TCC) 630
Hart Builders (Edinburgh) Ltd v St Andrew Ltd [2002] A69/02 Edinburgh; [2002] AdjLR 08/20 619
Hart Builders (Edinburgh) Ltd v St Andrew Ltd [2003] ScotSC 14; [2003] AdjLR 01/10
.... 619
Hart Investments Ltd v Fidler & Anor [2006] EWHC 2857 (TCC); [2007] BLR 30; (2006) 109 ConLR 67; [2006] CILL 2397; [2006] AdjLR 11/03
.... 34, 68, 175, 285, 591, 618, 638
Harwood Construction Ltd v Lantrode Ltd [2001] AdjLR 11/24 .... 294, 619, 639
Hatmet Ltd v Herbert (t/a LMS Lift Consultancy) [2005] EWHC 3529 (TCC); [2005] All ER (D) 243 (Nov); (2005) 115 ConLR 95; [2005] AdjLR 11/18 592
Henderson v 3052775 Nova Scotia Limited 2006 SC (HL) 85 414
Henry Brothers (Magherafelt) Ltd v Brunswick (8 Lanyon Place) Ltd [2011] NIQB 102
.... 437, 598, 630, 642
Herbosh-Kiere Marine Contractors Ltd v Dover Harbour Board [2012] EWHC 84 (TCC); [2012] All ER (D) 187 (Jan); [2012] BLR 177; (2012) 140 ConLR 97
.... 102, 356, 394, 603, 605, 658, 660, 674

Alphabetical case index 691

Herschell Engineering Ltd v Breen Property Ltd (No 2) [2000] AdjLR 07/28
....291, 310, 639–40, 646
Herschell Engineering Ltd v Breen Property Ltd [2000] All ER (D) 559; [2000] BLR 272; (2000) 70 ConLR 1; (2000) 16 Const LJ 366; [2000] CILL 1616; [2000] AdjLR 04/14
.... 120, 298, 613, 615, 641, 645, 650
HG Construction Ltd v Ashwell Homes (East Anglia) Ltd [2007] EWHC 144 (TCC); [2007] All ER (D) 210 (Feb); [2007] BLR 175; (2007) 112 ConLR 128; [2007] CILL 2453; [2007] AdjLR 02/01 ....598, 610
Highlands and Islands Authority Ltd v Shetland Islands Counsel [2012] CSOH 12
....336–7, 395, 422, 643, 652, 675
Hillcrest Homes Ltd v Beresford & Curbishley Ltd [2014] EWHC 280 (TCC); [2014] All ER (D) 124 (Feb); (2014) 153 ConLR 179; [2014] CILL 3506
....110, 116, 308, 609, 612, 643, 645, 674
Hills Electrical & Mechanical plc v Dawn Construction Ltd [2003] ScotCS 107; [2003] AdjLR 04/07 ....418, 597
Hillview Industrial Developments (UK) Ltd v Botes Building Ltd [2006] EWHC 1365 (TCC); [2006] All ER (D) 280 (Jun); [2006] AdjLR 06/07 ..... 248, 286, 602, 631, 642
Hitec Power Protection BV v MCI Worldcom Ltd [2002] EWHC 1953 (QB); [2002] AdjLR 08/15 ....104, 605, 643
Holt Insulation Ltd v Colt International Ltd [2001] AdjLR 01/09 ....114, 610–11
Homer Burgess Ltd v Chirex (Annan) Ltd (No.1) (1999) 71 ConLR 245; [1999] AdjLR 11/10 .... 61, 224, 588, 590, 625, 643, 649
Homer Burgess Ltd v Chirex (Annan) Ltd (No.2) [1999] ScotCS 264; [2000] BLR 124; (1999) 71 ConLR 245; (2000) 16 Const LJ 242; [2000] CILL 1580; [1999] AdjLR 11/17 644
Hortimax Ltd v Hedon Salads Ltd (2004) 24 Const LJ 47; [2004] AdjLR 10/15
....58, 61, 334, 589, 590, 649, 651
HS Works Ltd v Enterprise Managed Services Ltd [2009] EWHC 729 (TCC); [2009] All ER (D) 241 (Apr); [2009] BLR 378; (2009) 124 ConLR 69
.... 247, 385, 606, 610, 630, 633, 645, 657, 659–60, 662, 670, 672, 676
Humes Building Contracts Ltd v Charlotte Homes (Surrey) Ltd [2007] AdjLR 01/03
.... 388, 394, 397, 639, 659–60, 670, 672, 674, 676
Hurley Palmer Flatt Ltd v Barclays Bank Plc [2014] EWHC 3042 (TCC); [2014] All ER (D) 162 (Sep); [2014] BLR 713; (2014) 156 Con LR 213; [2014] CILL 3577
....54, 588
Hyder Consulting Ltd v Carillion Construction (UK) Ltd [2011] EWHC 1810 (TCC); [2011] All ER (D) 163 (Jul); (2011) 138 ConLR 212 .... 218, 393, 396, 623, 674–5
IDE Contracting Ltd v RG Carter Cambridge Ltd [2004] EWHC 36 (TCC); [2004] All ER (D) 224 (Jan); [2004] BLR 172; (2004) 102 ConLR 102; [2004] AdjLR 01/16
....155, 329, 616, 649–50, 654–5
Image Decorations Ltd v Dean & Bowes (Contracts) Ltd [2004] ADJ CS 03/65
....598, 622
Impresa Castelli SpA v Cola Holdings Ltd [2002] EWHC 1363 (TCC); [2002] All ER (D) 78 (May); (2002) 87 ConLR 123 .... 310, 598, 646, 654

Imtech Inviron Ltd v Loppingdale Plant Ltd [2014] EWHC 4006 (TCC); [2014] All ER (D) 55 (Dec); [2015] BLR 183; [2015] CILL 3613 .... 47, 586–7, 609

Imtech Inviron Ltd v Loppingdale Plant Ltd [2014] EWHC 4109 (TCC) 193, 270, 619, 635

Integrated Building Services Engineering Consultants Ltd trading as Operon v PIHL UK Ltd [2010] CSOH 80; [2010] BLR 622 .... 288, 421, 585, 638

Interserve Industrial Services Ltd v Cleveland Bridge UK Ltd [2006] EWHC 741 (TCC); [2006] All ER (D) 49 (Feb); [2006] AdjLR 02/06 .... 230, 242, 247, 602, 626, 628, 630, 642, 644

Irvin v Robertson [2010] EWHC 3723 (TCC) 586, 596

ISG Construction Ltd v Seevic College [2014] EWHC 4007 (TCC); [2014] All ER (D) 72 (Dec); [2015] BLR 233; (2015) 157 ConLR 107; [2014] CILL 3598 .... 132,134, 610, 614, 619

ISG Retail Ltd v Castletech Construction Ltd [2015] EWHC 1443 (TCC); [2015] All ER (D) 217 (May); [2015] CILL 3680 .... 116, 612, 659–60

J and A Construction (Scotland) Ltd v Windex Ltd [2013] CSOH 170 .... 421, 608, 640

J.T.Mackley v Gosport Marina Ltd [2002] EWHC 1315; [2002] All ER (D) 39 (Jul); [2002] B.L.R. 367 .... 311, 600, 646

Jacques (t/a C & E Jacques Partnership) v Ensign Contractors Ltd [2009] EWHC 3383 (TCC) 270–1, 300, 386, 626, 635, 640, 642, 660, 670, 672

Jamil Mohammed v Dr Michael Bowles [2002] 394 SD 2002; [2003] AdjLR 03/14 .... 279, 598, 637

Jerome Engineering Ltd v Lloyd Morris Electrical Ltd [2002] CILL 1827; [2001] AdjLR 11/23 .... 148, 598, 615, 663

Jerram Falkus Construction Ltd v Fenice Investments Inc (No 4) [2011] EWHC 1935 (TCC); [2011] BLR 644; (2011) 138 ConLR 21; [2011] CILL 3072 .... 614, 644–5, 647

JG Walker Groundworks Ltd v Priory Homes (East) Ltd [2013] EWHC 3723 (TCC); [2013] All ER (D) 85 (Dec) 355, 658, 661

Jim Ennis Construction Ltd v Premier Asphalt Ltd [2009] EWHC 1906 (TCC); [2009] All ER (D) 29 (Aug); (2009) 125 ConLR 141; [2009] CILL 2745 646

Jim Ennis Construction Ltd v Combined Stabilisation Ltd [2009] EWHC B37 (TCC) 648

John Cothliff Ltd v Allen Build (North West) Ltd [1999] CILL 1530; [1999] AdjLR 07/29 627

John Mowlem & Company plc v Hydra-Tight Ltd (2001) 17 Const LJ 358; [2000] CILL 1649; [2000] AdjLR 06/06 .... 92, 161, 330, 597, 601, 617, 650, 654

John Roberts Architects Ltd v Parkcare Homes (No. 2) Ltd [2005] EWHC 1637 (TCC); [2005] All ER (D) 341 (Jul); [2005] BLR 484; [2005] CILL 2288; [2005] AdjLR 07/25 .... 602, 620, 627

John Roberts Architects Ltd v Parkcare Homes (No. 2) Ltd [2006] EWCA Civ 64; [2006] All ER (D) 131 (Feb); [2006] BLR 106; (2006) 105 ConLR 36; (2006) 22 Const LJ 343; [2006] CILL 2323; [2006] AdjLR 02/09 .... 194, 602, 620, 627

Joinery Plus Ltd (In Administration) v Laing Ltd [2003] EWHC 3513 (TCC); [2003] All
ER (D) 201 (Jan); [2003] BLR 184; (2003) 87 ConLR 87; [2003] AdjLR 01/15
.... 35, 37–8, 238, 252, 288, 336, 357–8, 598, 627, 638, 652, 657, 662
Joseph Finney plc v Gordon Vickers and Gary Vickers t/a Mill Hotel (A Firm) [2001]
All ER (D) 235 (Mar); [2001] AdjLR 03/07 607
JPA Design and Build Ltd v Sentosa (UK) Ltd [2009] EWHC 2312 (TCC); [2009] All
ER (D) 06 (Oct) 631, 640
JW Hughes Building Contractors Ltd v GB Metalwork Ltd [2003] EWHC 2421 (TCC);
[2003] AdjLR10/03 .... 391, 606, 641, 649, 669, 673
Kammins Ballroom Co v Zenith Investments [1971] AC 850; [1970] 3 W.L.R. 287;
[1970] 2 All E.R. 871 332
Karl Construction (Scotland) Ltd v Sweeney Civil Engineering (Scotland) Ltd [2000]
ScotCS 330; (2002) 18 Const LJ 55; [2000] AdjLR 12/21 .... 585, 659, 661–2
Karl Construction (Scotland) Ltd v Sweeney Civil Engineering (Scotland) Ltd [2002]
SLT 312P/872/00; (2002) 85 ConLR 59; (2002) 18 Const LJ 55; [2002] AdjLR 01/22
.... 603, 658, 674–5
Ken Biggs Contractors Ltd v Norman [2004] All ER (D) 20 (Aug); [2004] AdjLR 08/20
.... 591, 598
Ken Griffin (t/a K&D Contractors) v Midas Homes Ltd (2000) 78 ConLR 152; (2002)
18 Const LJ 67; [2000] AdjLR 07/21 .... 147, 603, 606, 626, 644
Khatri v Cooperative Central Raiffeisen-Boerenleenbank BA [2010] EWCA Civ 397;
[2010] I.R.L.R. 715; (2010) 107(18) L.S.G. 15 46
Khurana and another v Webster Construction Ltd [2015] EWHC 758 (TCC); [2015] All
ER (D) 262 (Mar); [2015] BLR 396; (2015) 159 ConLR 208 80
Kier Regional Ltd (t/a Wallis) v City & General (Holborn) Ltd [2006] EWHC 848
(TCC); [2006] All ER (D) 64 (Mar); [2006] BLR 315; [2006] CILL 2353; [2006]
AdjLR 03/06 .... 385, 389, 598, 664, 670, 672
Kier Regional Ltd (t/a Wallis) v City and General (Holborn) Ltd & Ors (No 2) [2008]
EWHC 2454 (TCC); [2008] All ER (D) 189 (Oct); [2009] BLR 90; [2008] CILL 2639;
[2008] AdjLR 10/17 .... 282, 298, 638, 641
Knight Build Ltd v Urvasco Ltd [2008] EWHC 3056 (TCC); [2008] All ER (D) 146
(Nov) 300, 641–2
KNN Coburn LLP v GD City Holdings Ltd [2013] EWHC 2879 (TCC); [2013] All ER
(D) 33 (Oct) 176, 223, 611, 618, 624, 672
KNS Industrial Services (Birmingham) Ltd v Sindall Ltd [2000] All ER (D) 1153; (2001)
75 ConLR 71; (2001) 17 Const LJ 170; [2000] CILL 1652; [2000] AdjLR 07/14
.... 215, 599, 607, 615, 618–9, 644, 658, 661–2
Kosmar Villa Holidays Plc v Trustees of Syndicate 1243 [2008] EWCA Civ 147; [2008] 2
All E.R. (Comm) 14; [2008] Bus. L.R. 931 332
L Brown & Sons Ltd v Crosby Homes (North West) Ltd [2005] EWHC 3503 (TCC);
[2005] All ER (D) 63 (Dec); [2005] AdjLR12/05 .... 52, 72, 589, 599, 612
Lafarge (Aggregates) Ltd. v London Borough of Newham [2005] EWHC 1337 (Comm);
[2005] All ER (D) 30 (Jul); [2005] AdjLR 06/24 .... 305, 600, 644
Laker Vent Engineering Ltd v Jacobs E&C Ltd [2014] EWHC 1058 (TCC); (2014) 154
ConLR 77 .... 61, 308, 336, 590, 645, 650, 652

Lanes Group plc v Galliford Try Infrastructure Ltd (No.2) [2011] EWHC 1234 (TCC)
.... 46, 330, 587, 600, 618, 650
Lanes Group plc v Galliford Try Infrastructure Ltd [2011] EWCA Civ 1617; [2011] All ER (D) 179 (Dec); [2012] BLR 121; (2011) 141 ConLR 46
.... 160, 367, 368, 600, 616, 664–5, 668
Lanes Group plc v Galliford Try Infrastructure Ltd [2011] EWHC 1035 (TCC); [2011] All ER (D) 10 (May); [2011] BLR 438; [2011] CILL 3028
.... 597, 600, 616, 618, 650, 665
Lanes Group plc v Galliford Try Infrastructure Ltd [2011] EWHC 1679 (TCC); [2011] All ER (D) 105 (Jul); [2011] BLR 553; (2011) 137 ConLR 1; [2011] CILL 3052
.... 378, 600, 617, 668
Lathom Construction Ltd v Brian Cross & Anor [2000] CILL 1568; [1999] AdjLR 10/29
.... 589, 599
Lead Technical Services v CMS Medical Ltd [2007] EWCA Civ 316; [2007] All ER (D) 270 (Jan); [2007] BLR 251; (2007) 116 ConLR 192; (2007) 23 Const LJ 547; [2007] AdjLR 01/30 .... 345–6, 585, 594, 601, 654
Leander Construction Limited v Mulalley and Company Limited [2011] EWHC 3449 (TCC); [2012] BLR 152 .... 234, 627
Ledwood Mechanical Engineering Ltd v Whessoe Oil and Gas Ltd & Anor [2007] EWHC 2743 (TCC); [2007] All ER (D) 294 (Nov); [2008] BLR 198; [2007] AdjLR 11/20 .... 242, 248, 628, 631, 635
Lee v Chartered Properties (Building) Ltd [2010] EWHC 1540 (TCC); [2010] All ER (D) 112 (Jul); [2010] BLR 500; [2010] CILL 2896
.... 222–3, 419, 604, 607–9, 615–6, 623–4, 637, 654, 669, 672
Leeds City Council v Waco UK Ltd [2015] EWHC 1400 (TCC); [2015] All ER (D) 219 (May); 160 ConLR 58; [2015] CILL 3682 .... 308, 614, 645
Letchworth Roofing Company v Sterling Building Company [2009] EWHC 1119 (TCC); [2009] CILL 2717 .... 388, 599, 616, 619, 623, 625, 659, 661, 672
Levolux A.T. Ltd v Ferson Contractors Ltd [2002] BLR 341; [2003] CILL 1956; [2002] AdjLR 06/26 628
Liberty Mercian Ltd v Dean & Dyball Construction [2008] EWHC 2617 (TCC) 29
Lidl UK GmbH v RG Carter Colchester Ltd [2012] EWHC 3138; [2012] All ER (D) 113 (Nov); (2012) 146 ConLR 133; [2013] CILL 3276 .... 108, 302, 353, 608, 644, 674
Linaker Ltd v Riviera Construction [1999] AdjLR 11/04 634–6
Linnett v Halliwells LLP [2009] EWHC 319; [2009] BLR 312; (2009) 123 ConLR 104; [2009] CILL 2704 .... 77, 169, 175, 229–30, 336–7, 594–5, 599, 617–8, 626, 652
Lloyd Projects Ltd v John Malnick [2005] AdjLR 07/22 .... 68, 591, 593, 633
Locabail (UK) Ltd v Bayfield Properties Ltd and others [1999] EWCA Civ 3004; [2000] 1 All ER 65 .... 368, 665
London & Amsterdam Properties Ltd v Waterman Partnership Ltd [2003] EWHC 3059 (TCC); [2003] All ER (D) 391 (Dec); [2004] BLR 179; (2003) 94 ConLR 154; (2004) 20 Const LJ 215; [2003] AdjLR 12/18
.... 203, 349, 359, 370, 381, 604, 606, 618, 621, 626, 654, 656, 662, 666, 669–70
London Borough of Camden v Makers UK Ltd [2009] EWHC 2944 (TCC)
.... 613, 640–1

Lovell Projects Ltd v Legg & Carver [2003] BLR 452; [2003] CILL 2019; [2003] AdjLR 07/01 .... 64, 76, 78, 244, 404, 591, 595, 599, 604, 607, 628, 630, 641, 677

Lownds v Home Office [2002] EWCA Civ 365 at [31] 269

LPL Electrical Services Ltd v Kershaw Mechanical Services Ltd [2001] AdjLR 02/02 .... 658, 661

M. Rohde Construction v Nicholas Markham-David (No 2) [2007] EWHC 1408 (TCC); [2007] AdjLR 03/26 .... 620, 669, 673

M. Rohde Construction v Nicholas Markham-David [2006] EWHC 814 (TCC); [2006] BLR 291; [2006] AdjLR 03/20 .... 222, 263, 348, 624, 633, 655

Macob Civil Engineering v Morrison Construction Ltd [1999] All ER (D) 143; [1999] BLR 93; (1999) 64 ConLR 1; (1999) 15 Const LJ 300; [1999] CILL 1470; [1999] AdjLR 02/12 ...... 5, 249, 254, 275, 277, 335, 357, 429, 457, 585, 625, 636–7, 652, 663

Magill v Porter [2001] UKHL 67; [2002] 1 All ER 465 .... 368, 665, 692

Maguire and Co v Mar City Developments [2013] EWHC 3503 (TCC) 295, 639

Makers UK Ltd v The Mayor and Burgesses of the London Borough of Camden [2008] EWHC 1836 (TCC); [2008] All ER (D) 378 (Jul); [2008] BLR 470; (2008) 120 ConLR 161; [2008] CILL 2618; [2008] AdjLR 07/25 ...... 158, 189, 372, 599, 616, 655, 665–6

Malcolm Charles Contracts Ltd v Mr Crispin and Mrs Zhang [2014] EWHC 3898 (TCC); [2014] All ER (D) 289 (Nov); (2015) 159 ConLR 185 .... 64, 586, 591, 607

Management Solutions & Professional Consultants Ltd v Bennett (Electrical) Services Ltd (No 1) [2006] EWHC 1720 (TCC); [2006] AdjLR 07/10 594

Management Solutions & Professional Consultants Ltd v Bennett (Electrical) Services Ltd (No 2) [2006] EWHC 1720_2 (TCC); [2006] AdjLR 08/23 .... 594, 642

Martin Girt v Page Bentley [2002] EWHC 1720 (TCC); [2002] AdjLR 04/12 .... 659, 661

Mast Electrical Services v Kendall Cross Holdings Ltd [2007] EWHC 1296 (TCC); [2007] All ER (D) 327 (Jul); [2007] AdjLR 05/17 .... 587, 594

Maymac Environmental Services Ltd v Faraday Building Services Ltd [2000] All ER (D) 1406; (2000) 75 ConLR 101; [2000] CILL 1685; [2000] AdjLR 10/16 ..... 82, 596, 663

MBE Electrical Contractors Ltd v Honeywell Control Systems Ltd [2010] EWHC 2244 (TCC); [2010] BLR 561 .... 258–9, 275, 277, 625, 633, 636–7

McAlpine PPS Pipeline Systems Joint Venture v Transco plc [2004] EWHC 2030 (TCC); [2004] All ER (D) 145 (May); [2004] BLR 352; (2004) 96 ConLR 69; [2004] AdjLR 05/12 .... 204, 585, 604, 621, 657–8, 660, 669

McConnell Dowell Constructors (Aust) Pty Ltd v National Grid Gas plc (formerly Transco plc) [2006] EWHC 2551 (TCC); [2006] All ER (D) 27 (Oct); [2007] BLR 92; [2006] AdjLR 10/03 .... 52, 273, 297, 301, 589, 601, 608, 636, 641–3

Mead General Building Ltd v Dartmoor Properties Ltd [2009] EWHC 200 (TCC); [2009] BLR 225; [2009] CILL 2686 .... 270, 289, 295, 634–5, 639

Mecright Ltd v TA Morris Developments Ltd [2001] AdjLR 06/22 .... 111, 207, 609, 616, 622, 659–60, 673

Mel Davidson Construction v Northern Ireland Housing Executive [2014] NIQB 110 .... 114–15, 439, 611

Melville Dundas Ltd v Hotel Corporation of Edinburgh Ltd [2006] CSOH 136; [2006] BLR 474; [2006] AdjLR 09/07 .... 53, 288–9, 589

Melville Dundas Limited (in receivership) and others George Wimpey UK Limited and others [2007] UKHL 18; [2007] 3 AllER 889; [2007] BLR 257 .... 289, 599, 638

Mentmore Towers Ltd v Packman Lucas Ltd [2010] EWHC 457 (TCC); [2010] All ER (D) 236 (Oct); [2010] BLR 393; [2010] CILL 2846 .... 120, 330, 613, 650

Michael John Construction Ltd v Golledge & Ors [2006] EWHC 71 (TCC); [2006] All ER (D) 140 (Feb); [2006] AdjLR 01/27 .... 110, 371, 599, 609, 611–2, 641, 654, 666

Michael John Construction Ltd v St Peter's Rugby Football Club [2007] EWHC 1857 (TCC); [2007] All ER (D) 458 (Jul); (2007) 115 ConLR 134; [2007] AdjLR 07/30 .... 265, 599, 633

Midland Expressway Ltd & Ors v Carillion Construction Ltd & Ors (No. 3) [2006] EWHC 1505 (TCC); [2006] All ER (D) 105 (Jun); [2006] BLR 325; (2006) 107 ConLR 205; [2006] CILL 2386; [2006] AdjLR 06/13 .... 194, 305, 606, 620, 644

Midland Expressway Ltd v Carillion Construction Ltd & Ors (No. 2) [2005] EWHC 2963 (TCC); (2005) 106 ConLR 154; [2006] CILL 2313; [2005] AdjLR 11/24 .... 607, 650

Miller Construction (UK) Ltd v Building Design Partnership Ltd [2014] CSOH 80 .... 396, 416, 657, 675

Millers Specialist Joinery Company Ltd v Nobles Construction Ltd [2001] CILL 1770; [2001] AdjLR 08/03 .... 62, 70–1, 591–3, 619, 625

Mivan Ltd v Lighting Technology Projects Ltd [2001] Adj.C.S. 04/09 611

MJ Gleeson Group plc v Devonshire Green Holding Ltd [2004] AdjLR 03/19 .... 244–5, 599, 629–30, 642

Mondel v Steel (1841) 8 M&W 858 191

Morphuse Framing Solutions Ltd v Bracknell Property Ltd HT-14–206 ..... 613–4, 630

Motor Oil Hellas (Corinth) Refineries SA v Shipping Corporation of India [1990] 1 Lloyd's Rep 391 332

Mott MacDonald Ltd v London & Regional Properties Ltd [2007] EWHC 1055 (TCC); [2007] All ER (D) 431 (May); (2007) 113 ConLR 33; [2007] CILL 2481; [2007] AdjLR 05/23 .... 222–3, 350, 592–3, 595, 621, 624, 656, 663

Multiplex Constructions (UK) Ltd v Mott MacDonald Ltd [2007] EWHC 20 (TCC); [2007] All ER (D) 133 (Jan); (2007) 110 ConLR 63; [2007] AdjLR 01/10 .... 116, 277, 606, 612, 637

Multiplex Constructions (UK) Ltd v West India Quay Development Company (Eastern) Ltd [2006] EWHC 1569 (TCC); (2006) 111 ConLR 33; [2006] CILL 2446; [2006] AdjLR 06/08 .... 398, 599, 641, 657, 672, 674–6

Murray Building Services v Spree Developments [2004] AdjLR 07/30 ...... 68, 591, 594

Nageh v Richard Giddings & Another [2006] EWHC 3240 (TCC); [2007] CILL 2420; [2006] AdjLR 12/08 .... 266, 348, 633, 655

NAP Anglia Ltd v Sun-Land Development Co Ltd [2011] EWHC 2846 (TCC); [2011] All ER (D) 172 (Nov); [2012] BLR 110 .... 262, 300, 391, 640, 642, 657, 672–3

NAP Anglia v Sun-Land Development Co Ltd (No 2) [2012] EWHC 51 (TCC); [2012] BLR 195; (2012) 141 ConLR 247 .... 634, 635

National Museums and Galleries on Merseyside v AEW Architects and Designers Ltd [2013] EWHC 2403 (TCC) 316, 647

Alphabetical case index

Naylor Construction Services Ltd v Acoustafoam Ltd [2010] All ER (D) 138 (Apr); [2010] BLR 183 .... 71, 242, 247, 592–4, 628, 630
Nickleby FM Ltd v Somerfield Stores Ltd [2010] EWHC 1976 (TCC); [2010] All ER (D) 07 (Aug); (2010) 131 ConLR 203 .... 258, 592, 633, 651–2
Nolan Davis Ltd v Catton 2000 TCC No 590; [2001] All ER (D) 232 (Mar) 627, 641, 649, 658, 661, 663
Nordot Engineering Services Ltd v Siemens plc [2001] CILL 1778; [2000] AdjLR 04/14 .... 79–80, 325, 596, 649
North Midland Construction plc v AE & E Lentjes UK Ltd [2009] EWHC 1371 (TCC); [2009] All ER (D) 194 (Aug); [2009] BLR 574; (2009) 126 ConLR 213; [2009] CILL 2736 .... 51, 59–61, 588–90
Northern Developments (Cumbria) Ltd v J & J Nichol [2000] All ER (D) 68; [2000] BLR 158; [2000] CILL 1601; [2000] AdjLR 01/24 .... 207, 607, 622, 627, 659, 661, 663
Northern Ireland Housing Executive v Healthy Buildings Ltd [2013] NIQB 124; (2013) 153 Con LR 87 .... 435, 601, 645
Nottingham Community Housing Association Ltd v Powerminster Ltd [2000] BLR 309; 75 ConLR 65; (2000) 16 Const LJ 499; [2000] AdjLR 06/30 .... 58, 589, 591
O'Donnell Developments Ltd v Buildability Ltd [2009] EWHC 3388 (TCC); [2010] BLR 122; (2009) 128 ConLR 141 .... 599, 627, 634
Orange EBS Ltd v ABB Ltd [2003] EWHC 1187 (TCC); [2003] BLR 323; (2004) 20 Const LJ 30; [2003] AdjLR 05/22 .... 106, 599, 604–7
OSC Building Services Ltd v Interior Dimensions Contracts Ltd [2009] EWHC 248 (TCC); [2009] CILL 2688 .... 108, 325, 608, 616, 649–50, 658, 661
Outwing Construction Ltd v H Randell and Son Ltd [1999] BLR 156; (1999) 64 ConLR 59; (1999) 15 Const LJ 308; [1999] CILL 1482; [1999] AdjLR 03/15 .... 599, 634–6
Paice and Springall v Harding (t/a MJ Harding Contractors) [2015] EWHC 661 (TCC); [2015] All ER (D) 188 (Mar); [2015] BLR 345; [2015] CILL 3668 ..... 372, 610, 665–6
Palmac Contracting Ltd v Park Lane Estates Ltd [2005] EWHC 919 (TCC); [2006] All ER (D) 186 (Jan); [2005] BLR 301; [2005] AdjLR 03/17 .... 38, 107, 155, 599, 607, 616, 655, 674
Palmers Ltd v ABB Power Construction Ltd [1999] All ER (D) 1273; [1999] BLR 426; (1999) 68 ConLR 52; [1999] CILL 1543; [1999] AdjLR 08/06 .... 58, 62, 589–91
Parkwood Leisure Ltd v Laing O'Rourke Wales and West Ltd [2013] EWHC 2665 (TCC); [2013] All ER (D) 221 (Aug); [2013] BLR 589; (2013) 150 ConLR 93; [2013] CILL 3413 .... 50, 53, 587–9
Parsons Plastics (Research & Development) Ltd v Purac Ltd [2002] EWCA Civ 459; [2002] All ER (D) 44 (Apr); [2002] BLR 334; (2002) 93 ConLR 26; (2002) 18 ConstLJ 494; [2002] CILL 1868; [2002] AdjLR 04/12 .... 243, 596, 619, 628
Parsons Plastics (Research and Development) Ltd v Purac Ltd [2001] AdjLR 08/13 .... 596, 619, 628
Partner Projects Ltd v Corinthian Nominees Ltd [2011] EWHC 2989 (TCC); [2011] All ER (D) 232 (Nov); [2012] BLR 97 .... 209, 290, 297, 599, 622, 641
Paul Broadwell v k3D Property Partnership Ltd [2006] Adj.C.S. 04/21 ..... 385, 599, 671
Paul Jensen Ltd v Staveley Industries plc [2001] AdjLR 09/27 .... 617, 626

PC Harrington Contractors Ltd v Systech International Ltd [2012] EWCA Civ 1371; [2013] All ER 69; [2013] BLR 1; (2012) 145 ConLR 1 .... 168, 170, 231–2, 617, 626
PC Harrington Contractors Ltd v Tyroddy Construction Ltd [2011] EWHC 813 (TCC); [2011] All ER (D) 162 (Apr) 253, 619, 632, 664, 671
Pearson v Dublin Corporation [1907] AC 351 401
Pegram Shopfitters Ltd v Tally Wiejl (UK) Ltd [2003] EWCA Civ 1750; [2004] 1 All ER 818; [2004] BLR 65; (2003) 91 ConLR 173; [2003] AdjLR 11/21
.... 326, 346, 359, 585, 597, 632, 649, 655, 663
Pegram Shopfitters Ltd v Tally Wiejl (UK) Ltd [2003] EWHC 984 (TCC); [2003] 3 All ER 98; [2003] BLR 296; (2003) 87 ConLR 39; [2003] CILL 1990; [2003] AdjLR 02/14
.... 597, 612, 618, 649, 655, 663
Persimmon Homes (South Coast) v Hall Aggregates (South Coast) Ltd [2009] EWCA Civ 1108; [2009] N.P.C. 118 332
Peterborough City Council v Enterprise Managed Services [2014] EWHC 3193 (TCC); [2014] All ER (D) 150 (Oct); [2014] BLR 735; (2014) 156 Con LR 226 ...... 311, 646
Petition of Mitsui Babcock Energy Services Ltd [2001] ScotCS 150; [2001] AdjLR 06/13
.... 62, 590
PHD Modular Access Services Ltd v Seele GmbH [2011] EWHC 2210 (TCC)
.... 198, 620
Picardi v Cuniberti [2002] EWHC 2923 (TCC); [2003] All ER (D) 322 (Jan); [2003] BLR 487; (2002) 94 ConLR 81; (2003) 19 ConstLJ 350; [2003] CILL 1980; [2002] AdjLR 12/19 .... 404, 591, 677
Pihl UK Ltd v Ramboll UK Ltd [2012] CSOH 139 676
Pilon Ltd v Breyer Group plc [2010] EWHC 837 (TCC); [2010] All ER (D) 197 (Apr); [2010] BLR 452; (2010) 130 ConLR 90; [2010] CILL 2865 .... 137, 150, 183, 254, 292–3, 302, 337, 384, 387, 416, 616, 618, 632, 638–9, 644, 649, 652, 660, 662, 671
Pioneer Cladding Ltd v John Graham Construction Ltd [2013] EWHC 2954 (TCC); [2013] All ER (D) 38 (Oct); (2013) 29 Const LJ T179; [2014] CILL 3445
.... 226, 297, 597, 626, 640
Pochin Construction Ltd v Liberty Property (G.P.) Ltd [2014] EWHC 2919 (TCC)
.... 264, 268, 633–5
PP Construction Ltd v Geoffrey Osborne Ltd [2015] EWHC 325 (TCC); [2015] All ER (D) 243 (Feb) 595, 627
Prentice Island Ltd v Castle Contracting Ltd [2003] ScotCS 61; [2003] AdjLR12/15
.... 610, 626
Primus Build Ltd v Pompey Centre Ltd & Anor [2009] EWHC 1487 (TCC); [2009] All ER (D) 14 (Jul); [2009] BLR 437; (2009) 126 ConLR 26; [2009] CILL 2739
.... 147, 254, 348, 394, 602, 615, 632, 655, 674–5
Pring & St. Hill Ltd v C J Hafner t/a Southern Erectors [2002] EWHC 1775 (TCC); (2004) 20 Const LJ 402; [2002] AdjLR 07/31
.... 119, 164, 609, 613, 617, 621, 655, 666, 673
Pro-Design Ltd v New Millennium Experience Co Ltd [2001] AdjLR 09/26
.... 401, 676
Profile Projects Ltd v Elmwood (Glasgow) Ltd [2011] CSOH 64
.... 418, 420, 597, 613, 627, 655

Project Consultancy Group v Trustees of the Gray Trust [1999] All ER (D) 842; [1999] BLR 377; (1999) 65 ConLR 146; [1999] CILL 1531; [1999] AdjLR 07/16 ....80, 596, 649–50
PT Building Services Ltd v ROK Build Ltd [2008] EWHC 3434 (TCC) 70, 105, 176, 337, 422, 592, 606, 609, 618, 652, 658, 661
Pynes Three Ltd v Transco Ltd [2005] EWHC 2445 (TCC); [2005] AdjLR 07/22 ....142, 615
Quality Street Properties (Trading) Ltd v Elmwood (Glasgow) Ltd [2002] CILL 1922; [2002] AdjLR 02/08 608
Quartzelec Ltd v Honeywell Control Systems Ltd [2008] EWHC 3315 (TCC); [2009] BLR 328; [2009] CILL 2665 ....301–2, 385, 618, 644, 671, 673
Quietfield Ltd v Vascroft Construction Ltd [2006] EWCA Civ 1737; [2006] All ER (D) 331 (Dec); [2007] BLR 67; (2006) 114 ConLR 81; [2007] CILL 2425; [2006] AdjLR 12/20 .... 112, 353, 585, 610–1, 657–8, 661, 671
Quietfield Ltd v Vascroft Construction Ltd [2006] EWHC 174 (TCC); [2006] All ER (D) 17 (Feb); (2006) 109 ConLR 29; [2006] CILL 2329; [2006] AdjLR 02/02 ....225, 611, 625, 671
R (Prudential plc and another) v Special Commissioner of Income Tax and another [2013] UKSC 1 196
R and C Electrical Engineers Ltd v Shaylor Construction Ltd [2012] EWHC 1254 (TCC); [2012] All ER (D) 129 (May); [2012] BLR 373; (2012) 142 ConLR 129 ....243, 247, 601, 628, 630
R Durtnell & Sons Ltd v Kaduna Ltd [2003] EWHC 517 (TCC); [2003] All ER (D) 281 (Mar); [2003] BLR 225; (2003) 93 ConLR 36; [2003] AdjLR 03/19 .... 104, 328, 335, 596, 599, 605, 609, 650, 652, 658, 660
Rainford House Ltd v Cadogan Ltd [2001] All ER (D) 144 (Feb); [2001] BLR 416; [2001] CILL 1709; [2001] AdjLR 02/13 .... 289, 291, 297, 301, 585, 599, 638, 639–40, 643
Rankilor (Dr Peter) & Perco Engineering Service Ltd v Igoe (M) Ltd [2006] AdjLR 01/27 .... 170, 396–7, 600, 617, 627, 664, 674–5
RBG Ltd v SGL Carbon Fibers Ltd [2010] CSOH 77; [2010] BLR 631 .... 354, 415, 601, 632, 657, 662, 671
RC Pillar & Son v The Camber (Portsmouth) Ltd [2007] EWHC 1626 (TCC); [2007] All ER (D) 319 (Jul); (2007) 115 ConLR 102; [2007] AdjLR 03/15 .... 586, 595–6, 650
Re A Company (number 1299 of 2001) [2001] CILL 1745; [2001] AdjLR 05/15 ....280, 637
Re Goldspan Ltd [2003] BPIR 93 (Ch) 39
Re L [1997] A.C. 16; [1996] 2 W.L.R. 395; [1996] 2 All ER. 78 196–7
Re Medicaments [2000] EWCA Civ 350; [2000] All ER (D) 2425 .... 367, 368, 665
Re Paton, Mr and Mrs [2011] CSOH 40 ....396, 664, 675
Re W. H. Malcolm Ltd [2010] CSOH 152 .... 322, 417, 601, 611, 648
Redding Park Development Company Limited v Falkirk Council [2011] CSOH 202 ....422, 652
Redwing Construction Ltd v Charles Wishart [2010] EWHC 3366 (TCC); [2010] All ER (D) 305 (Dec); (2010) 135 ConLR 119; [2011] CILL 2964 .... 114, 610–11, 628

Redwing Construction Ltd v Charles Wishart [2011] EWHC 19 (TCC); [2011] All ER
(D) 101 (Jan); [2011] BLR 186; (2011) 27 Const LJ 209; [2011] CILL 2997
....272, 635
Redworth Construction Ltd v Brookdale Healthcare Ltd [2006] EWHC 1994 (TCC);
[2006] All ER (D) 04 (Aug); [2006] BLR 366; (2006) 110 ConLR 77; [2006] AdjLR
07/31 ....258, 607, 633, 652, 654
RG Carter Ltd v Edmund Nuttall Ltd Unreported 116, 338, 599, 604, 612, 650, 655
Ringway Infrastructure Services Ltd v Vauxhall Motors Ltd (No 2) [2007] EWHC 2507
(TCC); [2007] All ER (D) 444 (Oct); (2007) 115 ConLR 149; [2007] CILL 2532;
[2007] AdjLR 10/30 ....599, 636, 646
Ringway Infrastructure Services Ltd v Vauxhall Motors Ltd [2007] EWHC 2421 (TCC);
[2007] AdjLR 10/23 ....106, 599, 603, 604, 607
Ritchie Brothers (Pwc) Ltd v David Philp (Commercials) Ltd [2004] ScotCS 94; [2004]
BLR 379; [2004] AdjLR 04/14 ....618, 624
Ritchie Brothers (Pwc) Ltd v David Philp (Commercials) Ltd [2005] ScotCS CSIH_32;
[2005] BLR 384; [2005] CILL 2244; [2005] AdjLR 03/24 .... 419, 623, 624
RJ Knapman Ltd v Richards [2006] EWHC 2518 (TCC); [2006] All ER (D) 349 (Oct);
(2006) 108 ConLR 64; [2006] CILL 2400; [2006] AdjLR 10/12 ....599, 630, 652
RJT Consulting Engineers Ltd v DM Engineering (Northern Ireland) Ltd [2002] All ER
(D) 108 (Mar); [2002] BLR 217; (2002) 83 Con LR 99; (2002) 18 Const LJ 425; [2001]
CILL 1766; [2001] AdjLR 05/09 ....68, 69–70, 72, 591, 593
RJT Consulting Engineers Ltd v DM Engineering (Northern Ireland) Ltd [2002] EWCA
Civ 270; [2002] BLR 217; (2002) 83 ConLR 99; (2002) 18 Const LJ 425; [2002] CILL
1841; [2002] AdjLR 03/08 .... 66, 67, 73–4, 585, 591–3, 595
Rodgers Contracts (Ballynahinch) Ltd v Merex Construction Ltd [2012] NIQB 94
....297, 632, 639, 640, 643
Roe Brickwork Ltd v Wates Construction Ltd [2013] EWHC 3417 (TCC); [2013] All ER
(D) 105 (Nov) 355, 393–4, 658, 661, 674
ROK Build Ltd v Harris Wharf Development Company Ltd [2006] EWHC 3573 (TCC);
[2006] AdjLR 12/15 .... 599, 604, 605, 654
ROK Building Ltd v Bestwood Carpentry Ltd [2010] EWHC 1409 (TCC); [2010] All
ER (D) 194 (Jun); (2010) 26 Const LJ 670 .... 73, 594–5, 648
ROK Building Ltd v Celtic Composting Systems Ltd (No 2) [2010] EWHC 66 (TCC);
[2010] All ER (D) 107 (Feb); (2009) 130 ConLR 74 ...... 240, 602, 628, 632, 663, 676
ROK Building Ltd v Celtic Composting Systems Ltd [2009] EWHC 2664 (TCC); [2009]
All ER (D) 65 (Nov); (2009) 130 ConLR 61; [2010] CILL 2797 .... 242, 601, 628–9
Rokvic v Peacock [2014] EWHC 3729 (TCC); [2014] All ER (D) 232 (Nov)
....273, 636
Roland Horne v Magna Design Building Ltd and Marcus Build Décor Ltd [2014]
EWHC 3380 (TCC); [2014] All ER (D) 246 (Oct) 616, 619, 658, 661
Rossco Civil Engineering Ltd v Dwr Cymru Cyfyngedic [2004] EWHC HT-03–190
(TCC); [2004] All ER (D) 339 (Jul); [2004] AdjLR 07/15 596
RSL (South West Ltd) v Stansell Ltd (No 1) [2003] EWHC 1390 (TCC); [2003] CILL
2012; [2003] AdjLR 06/16
.... 202, 301, 306, 381, 395, 599, 621, 625, 644, 645, 664, 669, 675

Rupert Cordle v Vanessa Nicholson [2009] EWHC 1314 .... 46, 587, 671
Rupert Morgan Building Services (LLC) Ltd v Jervis & Anor [2003] EWCA Civ 1563; [2004] 1 All ER 529; [2004] B.L.R. 18; (2004) 91 Con LR 81 .... 194, 619
Ruttle Plant Hire Ltd v Secretary of State for the Environment, Food and Rural Affairs [2004] EWHC 2152; [2005] All ER (D) 182 (Dec) 58, 589
Rush & Tompkins Ltd v Greater London Council [1988] UKHL 7; [1988] 3 All ER 737, [1989] AC 1280 .... 139, 197
RWE Npower plc v Alstom Power Ltd [2009] EWHC 1192 (QB); (2010) 133 ConLR 155; [2010] CILL 2835
.... 78, 106, 139, 595, 607, 609, 614, 630, 651, 652
Rydon Maintenance Ltd v Affinity Sutton Housing Ltd [2015] EWHC 1306 (TCC)
.... 656, 667, 673, 676
Sam Abbas and Antony Hayes (T/As A H Design) v Rotary (International) Ltd [2012] NIQB 41 .... 311, 646–7
Samuel Thomas Construction v J&B Developments [2000] CILL 1637; [2000] AdjLR 01/28 .... 591, 599
Savoye and Savoye Ltd v Spicers Ltd [2014] EWHC 4195 (TCC); [2014] All ER (D) 224 (Dec); [2015] BLR 151; (2015) 159 ConLR 120; [2015] CILL 3620
.... 49, 56–7, 588, 589
Savoye and Savoye Ltd v Spicers Ltd [2015] EWHC 33 (TCC); [2015] CILL 3629
.... 268–9, 271, 634, 635
Scrabster Harbour Trust v Mowlem plc t/a Mowlem Marine [2005] CSOH 44; [2006] BLR 176; [2005] AdjLR 03/23 .... 600, 644
SG South Ltd v Swan Yard (Cirencester) Ltd [2010] EWHC 376 (TCC); [2010] All ER (D) 04 (Mar)
.... 71, 593, 632, 634–5, 642, 650, 663
SG South Ltd. v King's Head Cirencester LLP & Anor [2009] EWHC 2645 (TCC); [2009] All ER (D) 120 (Nov); [2010] BLR 47; [2010] CILL 2793
.... 116, 401–2, 599, 612, 619, 634–6, 637, 641–2, 676
SGL Carbon Fibres Ltd v RBG Ltd [2011] CSOH 62
.... 178, 397, 424, 601, 610, 662, 675
Shaw v MEP Foundations Piling Ltd [2009] EWHC 493 (TCC); [2010] CILL 2831
.... 585, 591, 636, 641
Shaw v MEP Foundations Piling Ltd [2010] EWHC 9 (Ch); [2010] All ER (D) 71 (Jan)
.... 637
Shepherd Construction Ltd v Mecright Ltd [2000] BLR 489; [2000] AdjLR 07/27
.... 108, 117, 589, 608, 612, 677
Sherwood & Casson Ltd v Mackenzie [2000] CILL 1577; [1999] AdjLR 11/30
.... 113, 610–1, 632
Shimizu Europe Ltd v Automajor Ltd [2002] EWHC 1571 (TCC); [2002] All ER (D) 80 (Jan); [2002] BLR 113; (2002) 18 Const LJ 259; [2002] CILL 1831; [2002] AdjLR 01/17 .... 336, 357, 359–60, 601, 628, 652, 663
Shimizu Europe Ltd v LBJ Fabrications Ltd [2003] EWHC 1229 (TCC); [2003] All ER (D) 60 (Jun); [2003] BLR 381; [2003] CILL 2015; [2003] AdjLR 05/29
.... 244, 397, 601, 629, 644, 659, 660, 674, 676

Simons Construction Ltd v Aardvark Developments Ltd [2003] EWHC 2474 (TCC); [2003] All ER (D) 482 (Oct); [2004] BLR 117; (2003) 93 ConLR 114; [2003] CILL 2053; [2003] AdjLR 10/29 .... 216, 599, 623–4
Sindall Ltd v Solland and Others [2001] All ER (D) 370 (Jun); (2001) 80 ConLR 152; [2002] CILL 1808; [2001] AdjLR 06/15 .... 599, 602, 606, 658, 661
Sir Robert McAlpine v Pring & St Hill Ltd [2001] All ER (D) 484 (Oct); [2001] AdjLR 10/01 .... 599, 619, 642
Skanska Construction UK Ltd v ERDC Group Ltd & Anor [2002] ScotCS 307; [2002] AdjLR 11/28 .... 198, 611, 620
SL Timber Systems Ltd v Carillion Construction Ltd [2001] ScotCS 167; [2001] BLR 516; (2001) 85 ConLR 79; [2001] CILL 1760; [2001] AdjLR 06/27 ...... 194, 619, 639
Solland International Ltd v Daraydan Holdings Ltd [2002] EWHC 220 (TCC); [2002] All ER (D) 203 (Feb); (2002) 83 ConLR 109; [2002] AdjLR 02/15
.... 619, 625, 630, 641
South West Contractors Ltd v Birakos Enterprises Ltd [2006] EWHC 2794 (TCC); [2006] All ER (D) 63 (Nov); [2006] AdjLR 11/07 .... 606, 672
Southern Electric v Mead Realisations [2009] EWHC 2947 (TCC); [2009] All ER (D) 26 (Dec) 273, 636
Specialist Ceiling Services Northern Ltd v ZVI Construction UK Ltd [2004] BLR 403; [2004] AdjLR 02/27 .... 377, 667
Specialist Insulation Ltd v Pro-Duct (Fife) Ltd [2012] CSOH 79; [2012] BLR 342
.... 650–1
Speymill Contracts Ltd v Eric Baskind [2010] EWCA Civ 120; [2010] All ER (D) 285 (Feb); [2010] BLR 257; (2010) 129 ConLR 66; [2010] CILL 2828
.... 47, 401, 585, 587, 591, 599, 612, 672, 676
Speymill Contracts Ltd v Eric Baskind [2009] No 9LV 22750
.... 591, 599, 609, 636, 640, 643, 651, 672, 676–7
Sprunt Ltd v London Borough of Camden [2011] EWHC 3191 (TCC); [2011] All ER (D) 87 (Dec); [2012] BLR 83; (2011) 140 ConLR 111
.... 71, 85, 154, 202, 418, 592–3, 597, 616, 621, 625, 655
Squibb Group Ltd v Vertase FLI Ltd [2012] EWHC 1958 (TCC); [2012] All ER (D) 151 (Jul); [2012] BLR 408 and [2013] BLR 11 .... 246, 628, 630
St Andrews Bay Development Ltd v HBG Management Ltd and Mrs Janey Milligan [2003] ScotCS 103; [2003] AdjLR 03/20 .... 350, 624, 656
St Austell Printing Company Ltd v Dawnus Construction Holdings Ltd [2015] EWHC 96 (TCC); [2015] All ER (D) 167 (Jan); [2015] BLR 224; [2015] CILL 3625
.... 136–7, 604, 607, 614, 616, 645
Starbev GP Ltd v Interbrew Central European Holding BV [2013] EWHC 4038 196
Staveley Industries plc v Odebrecht Oil & Gas Services Ltd [2001] All ER (D) 359 (Feb); [2001] AdjLR 02/28 .... 52, 57, 588, 589
Stein v Blake (No.1) [1996] A.C. 243; [1995] 2 W.L.R. 710; [1995] 2 All E.R. 961
.... 33, 39, 294
Steve Domsalla (t/a Domsalla Building Services) v Kenneth Dyason [2007] EWHC 1174 (TCC); [2007] All ER (D) 255 (May); [2007] BLR 348; (2011) 112 ConLR 95; [2007] CILL 2501; [2007] AdjLR 05/04 .... 76, 77–8, 595, 596, 671, 677

Stiell Ltd v Riema Control Systems Ltd [2000] ScotCS 174; [2000] AdjLR 06/23
....602, 625
Stirling (t/a M&S Contracts) v Westminster Properties Scotland Ltd [2007] CSOH 117; [2007] BLR 537; [2007] AdjLR 07/09 ....101, 599, 604, 606
Stork Technical Services (RBG) Ltd v Marion Howitson Ross [2015] CSOH 10A
.... 168, 601, 617
Straw Realisations (No 1) Ltd (formerly known as Haymills (Contractors) Ltd (in administration)) v Shaftsbury House (Developments) Ltd [2010] EWHC 2597 (TCC); [2010] All ER (D) 196 (Oct); [2011] BLR 47; (2010) 133 ConLR 119
....285, 288, 421, 638, 644, 674, 675, 677
Stubbs Rich Architects v W H Tolley & Son Ltd [2001] AdjLR 08/08
....168, 170, 599, 617, 627
Supablast (Nationwide) Ltd v Story Rail Ltd [2010] EWHC 56 (TCC); [2010] All ER (D) 136 (Jan); [2010] BLR 211
....118, 600, 612–3, 634–5
Surplant Ltd v Ballast plc (T/A Ballast Construction South West) [2002] EWHC TC33/02; [2002] AdjLR 10/28..599, 605–6, 619
Sutton Services International Ltd v Vaughan Engineering Services [2013] NIQB 63
....297, 438, 639, 640
SW Global Resourcing Limited v Morris & Spottiswood Limited [2012] CSOH 200
....415, 611, 657, 662, 663, 672
Systech International Limited v PC Harrington Contractors Limited [2011] EWHC 2722 (TCC); [2012] All ER (Comm) 381; [2012] BLR 47; (2011) 139 ConLR 102
....623, 627
T Clarke (Scotland) Limited v MMAXX Underfloor Heating Limited [2014] CSIH 83
....651, 668
T Clarke (Scotland) Limited v MMAXX Underfloor Heating Limited [2014] CSOH 62; [2014] BLR 341...331, 423–4, 651
T&T Fabrications Ltd (A Firm) v Hubbard Architectural Metal Work Ltd [2008] EWHC B7 (TCC); [2008] AdjLR04/21... 594
Tate Building Services Ltd v B & M McHugh Ltd [2014] EWHC 2971 .... 289, 638
Tera Construction Ltd v Yuk Tong Lam [2005] EWHC 3306 (TCC); [2005] All ER (D) 359 (Nov); [2005] AdjLR 11/28.........................599, 616, 641, 644, 659, 661
Thameside Construction Co Ltd v Stevens [2013] EWHC 2071 (TCC); [2013] All ER (D) 206 (Jul); [2013] BLR 543; (2013) 149 ConLR 195; [2013] CILL 3392
.... 246, 337–8, 628, 630, 652
The Construction Centre Group Ltd v The Highland Council [2002] ScotCS CSOH_354; [2002] BLR 476; [2002] CILL 1906; [2002] AdjLR 08/23
.... 280, 416, 600, 625, 629, 637
The Construction Centre Group Ltd v The Highland Council [2003] ScotCS 114; [2003] AdjLR 04/11 .... 585, 600, 630, 645
The Highland Council v The Construction Centre Group Ltd [2003] ScotCS 221; [2003] AdjLR 08/05 ....600, 630
The Mayor and Burgesses of the London Borough of Camden v Makers UK Ltd [2009] EWHC 605 (TCC); (2009) 124 ConLR 32; [2009] CILL 2720 ....613, 633, 641

Thermal Energy Construction Ltd v AE & E Lentjes UK Ltd [2009] EWHC 408 (TCC); [2009] All ER (D) 271 (Jan) 351–2, 384–5, 387, 601, 628, 657, 671

Thoburn v Sunderland City Council and Others [2002] EWHC 195 (Admin) at [61] 237

Thomas Vale Construction PLC v Brookside Syston Ltd [2006] EWHC 3637 .... 599, 629

Thomas-Fredric's (Construction) Ltd v Wilson [2003] EWCA Civ 1494; [2003] All ER (D) 341 (Oct); [2004] BLR 23; (2003) 91 ConLR 161; [2003] AdjLR 10/21 .... 81, 359, 596, 649, 650, 654, 663

Three Rivers DC v Bank of England (Disclosure) (No.4) [2004] UKHL 48 at [50] 195, 197

Tim Butler Contractors Ltd v Merewood Homes Ltd (2002) 18 Const LJ 74; [2000] AdjLR 04/12 663

Total M&E Services Ltd v ABB Building Technologies Ltd (formerly ABB Stewarts Ltd) [2002] EWHC 248 (TCC); [2002] All ER (D) 349 (Feb); (2002) 87 ConLR 154; [2002] CILL 1857; [2002] AdjLR 02/26 .... 343, 594, 627, 631, 639, 641, 654

Towsey v Highgrove Homes Ltd 279–80, 637

Treasure & Son Ltd v Martin Dawes [2007] EWHC 2420 (TCC); [2008] BLR 24; [2007] CILL 2533; [2007] AdjLR 10/25 .... 77, 216, 351, 594, 596, 599, 623, 637, 641, 656

True Fix Construction Ltd v Apollo Property Services Group Ltd [2013] EWHC 2524 (TCC); [2013] All ER (D) 112 (Aug) 297, 641

Trustees of the Harbours of Peterhead v Lilley Construction Ltd [2003] ScotCS 91; [2003] AdjLR 04/01 .... 225, 625

Trustees of the Marc Gilbard 2009 Settlement Trust v OD Developments and Projects Ltd [2015] EWHC 70 (TCC); [2015] All ER (D) 194 (Jan); [2015] BLR 213; (2015) 159 ConLR 150 .... 121, 614

Trustees of the Stratfield Saye Estate v AHL Construction Ltd [2004] EWHC 3286 (TCC); [2004] All ER (D) 77 (Dec); [2004] AdjLR 12/06 592–3

Try Construction Ltd v Eton Town House Group Ltd [2003] EWHC 60 (TCC); [2003] All ER (D) 284 (Jan); [2003] BLR 286; (2003) 87 ConLR 71; (2003) 19 ConstLJ 477; [2003) CILL 1982; [2003] AdjLR 01/28 .... 363, 600, 664, 674, 675

TSG Building Services Plc v South Anglia Housing Ltd [2013] EWHC 1151 (TCC); [2013] All ER (D) 102 (May); [2013] BLR 484; (2013) 148 ConLR 228; (2013) 29(4) Const LJ 314 609

Twintec Ltd v Volkerfitzpatrick Ltd [2014] EWHC 10 (TCC); [2014] All ER (D) 177 (Jan); [2014] BLR 150; [2014] CILL 3476 .... 47, 308, 329–30, 587, 595, 613, 645, 651, 655, 669

Universal Music Operations Ltd v Flairnote Ltd & Others [2000] All ER (D) 1182; [2000] AdjLR 08/24 586

University of Brighton v Dovehouse Interiors Limited [2014] EWHC 940 (TCC); [2014] All ER (D) 52 (Apr); [2014] BLR 432; (2014) 153 ConLR 147 .... 121, 146, 347, 349, 614, 615, 655–6

Urang Commercial Ltd v (1) Century Investments Ltd (2) Eclipse Hotels (Luton) Ltd [2011] EWHC 1561 (TCC); [2011] All ER (D) 138 (Jun); (2011) 138 ConLR 233; [2011] CILL 3061 .... 130, 193, 388, 620, 672

Van Oord ACZ Ltd And Harbour & General Works Ltd Joint Venture v The Port Of
  Mostyn Ltd [2003] BM350030 TCC; [2003] AdjLR 09/10 644
Vaughan Engineering Ltd v Hinkins & Frewin Ltd [2003] ScotCS 56; [2003] AdjLR
  03/03 .... 280, 417, 637, 662
Vaultrise Ltd v Paul Cook [2004] Adj. C.S. 04/26 .... 208, 376, 662, 667
Vertase FLI Ltd v Squibb Group Ltd [2012] EWHC 3194; [2012] All ER (D) 187 (Nov);
  [2013] BLR 352 .... 112, 600, 610
VGC Construction Ltd v Jackson Civil Engineering Ltd [2008] EWHC 2082 (TCC);
  [2008] All ER (D) 148 (Aug); (2008) 120 ConLR 178; [2008] CILL 2627; [2008]
  AdjLR 08/15 .... 100, 107, 600, 603, 607, 650, 652
VHE Construction plc v RBSTB Trust Co Ltd (as trustee of the Mercury Property
  Fund) [2000] [2000] All ER (D) 23; BLR 187; (2000) 70 ConLR 51; [2000] CILL 1592;
  [2000] AdjLR 01/13 .... 86, 241, 597, 600, 611, 620, 625, 628, 630, 632–33, 646
Viridis UK Limited v Mulalley and Company Limited [2014] EWHC 268 (TCC);
  [2014] All ER (D) 160 (Feb) 118, 356–7, 389, 587, 612–3, 619, 659, 661, 663, 672
Vision Homes Ltd v Lancsville Construction Ltd [2009] EWHC 2042 (TCC); [2009] All
  ER (D) 68; [2009] BLR 525; (2009) 126 ConLR 95; [2009] CILL 2750
  .... 109, 115, 149, 161, 345, 393, 609, 611, 616, 655, 657, 659–60, 674
Vitpol Building Service v Michael Samen [2008] EWHC 2283 (TCC); [2008] All ER (D)
  185 (Nov); [2008] AdjLR 09/16 .... 252, 322, 596, 600, 648
Volker Stevin Ltd v Holystone Contracts Ltd [2010] EWHC 2344 (TCC); [2010] All ER
  (D) 82 (Oct) 290, 349, 377, 601, 621, 639, 641, 655, 668, 669
Wales and West Utilities Ltd v PPS Pipeline Systems GmbH [2014] EWHC 54 (TCC);
  [2014] All ER (D) 215 (Jan); [2014] BLR 163 .... 336, 353, 601, 652, 657, 661
Walker Construction (UK) Ltd v Quayside Homes Ltd and Others [2014] EWCA Civ
  93; [2014] All ER (D) 71 (Feb); [2014] BLR 215; (2014) 153 ConLR 26
  ....315, 646–7
Walter Lilly & Co Ltd v DMW Developments Ltd [2008] EWHC 3139 (TCC); [2008]
  AdjLR 12/11 645
Walter Lilly & Co Ltd v Mackay [2012] EWHC 649 (TCC) 41, 196–7
Walter Llewllyn & Sons Ltd and Rok Building Ltd v Excel Brickwork Ltd [2010] EWHC
  3415 (TCC); [2010] All ER (D) 288 (Dec) 274, 636
Watkin Jones & Son Ltd v Lidl UK GmbH (No 2) [2002] EWHC 183 (TCC); [2002] All
  ER (D) 340 (Feb); [2002] CILL 1847; [2001] AdjLR 12/27
  .... 132–3, 600, 604, 614, 620, 658, 660
Watkin Jones & Son Ltd v Lidl UK GmbH [2002] CILL 1834; [2001] AdjLR 12/21
  .... 600, 610
Watson Building Services Ltd [2001] ScotCS 60; [2001] AdjLR 03/13
  .... 585, 612, 622, 649, 655, 659, 661, 663
Westdawn Refurbishments Ltd v Roselodge Ltd [2006] AdjLR 04/24
  .... 68, 73, 585, 591, 594, 615, 654
Westfields Construction Ltd v Lewis [2013] EWHC 376 (TCC); [2013] All ER (D) 328
  (Feb); [2013] BLR 223; (2013) 147 ConLR 148; [2013] CILL 3332 .... 63–4, 591

Westminster Building Company Ltd v Andrew Beckingham [2004] EWHC 138 (TCC); [2004] All ER (D) 343 (Feb); [2004] BLR 163/[2004] BLR 265; (2004) 94 ConLR 107; [2004] AdjLR 02/20 .... 117, 404, 589, 600, 612, 677

Westshield Civil Engineering Ltd v Buckingham Group Contracting Ltd [2013] EWHC 1825 (TCC); [2013] All ER (D) 10 (Jul); (2013) 150 ConLR 225; [2013] CILL 3395 .... 300, 306, 600, 642, 644

Westshield Ltd v Whitehouse [2013] EWHC 3576 (TCC); [2013] All ER (D) 292 (Nov); [2014] CILL 3457 .... 38, 289, 295, 638, 639

Westwood Structural Services Ltd v Blyth Wood Park Management Company Ltd [2008] EWHC 3138 (TCC); [2009] All ER (D) 80 (Jan); [2009] CILL 2666; [2008] AdjLR 12/09 .... 600, 663

Whiteways Contractors (Sussex) Ltd v Impresa Castelli Construction UK Ltd [2000] All ER (D) 1171; (2000) 75 ConLR 92; (2000) 16 Const LJ 453; [2000] CILL 1664; [2000] AdjLR 08/09 .... 600, 620, 649

Whyte and Mackay Ltd v Blyth & Blyth Consulting Engineers Ltd [2012] ScotCS CSOH_89 .... 415, 422, 631

Whyte and Mackay Ltd v Blyth & Blyth Consulting Engineers Ltd [2013] CSOH 54 .... 387, 425–6, 644, 663, 670–1, 676, 677

William Naylor t/a Powerfloated Concrete Floors v Greenacres Curling Ltd [2001] ScotCS 163; [2001] AdjLR 06/26 .... 585, 610, 648

William Oakley & David Oakley v Airclear Environmental Ltd and Airclear TS Ltd [2002] CILL 1824; [2001] AdjLR 10/04 .... 596, 637

William Verry (Glazing Systems) Ltd v Furlong Homes Ltd [2005] EWHC 138 (TCC); [2005] All ER (D) 407 (Nov); [2005] CILL 2205; [2005] AdjLR 01/13 .... 138, 183, 386, 604, 608, 614, 619, 669, 670, 672

William Verry Ltd v North West London Communal Mikvah [2004] EWHC 1300 (TCC); [2004] All ER (D) 80 (Jun); [2004] BLR 308; (2004) 96 ConLR 96; [2005] CILL 2185; [2004] AdjLR 06/11 .... 175, 256, 298, 600, 606, 618, 633, 641, 663

William Verry Ltd v The Mayor and Burgesses of the London Borough of Camden [2006] EWHC 761 (TCC); [2006] All ER (D) 292 (Mar); [2006] AdjLR. 03/20 .... 224, 243 -4, 585, 600, 625, 628–9

Williams (t/a Sanclair Construction) v Noor (t/a India Kitchen) [2007] EWHC 3467 (TCC); [2007] All ER (D) 51 (Dec); [2007] AdjLR 11/29 .... 147, 615, 632–3, 654

Willmott Dixon Housing Limited (formerly Inspace Partnerships Limited) v Newlon Housing Trust [2013] EWHC 798 (TCC); [2013] All ER (D) 42 (Apr); [2013] BLR 325; (2013) 147 ConLR 194; [2013] CILL 3364 .... 109, 371, 602, 604, 609, 613, 618, 655, 666

Wimbledon Construction Company 2000 Ltd v Derek Vago [2005] EWHC 1086 (TCC); [2005] All ER (D) 277 (Jun); [2005] BLR 374; (2005) 101 ConLR 99; [2005] CILL 2257; [2005] AdjLR 05/20 .... 291–2, 300, 437–8, 639, 641

Windglass Windows Ltd v (1) Capital Skyline Construction Ltd (2) London and City Group Holdings Ltd [2009] EWHC 2022 (TCC); [2009] All ER (D) 17 (Aug); (2009) 126 ConLR 118 .... 659, 661

Witney Town Council v Beam Construction (Cheltenham) Ltd [2011] EWHC 2332 (TCC); [2011] All ER (D) 141 (Sep); [2011] BLR 707; (2011) 139 ConLR 1; [2011] CILL 3090 ....110–11, 604, 609, 616
Woods Hardwick Ltd v Chiltern Air Conditioning Ltd [2001] BLR 23; [2001] CILL 1698; [2000] AdjLR 10/02 ....375, 585, 620, 631, 667, 675
Working Environments Ltd v Greencoat Construction Ltd [2012] EWHC 1039 (TCC); [2012] All ER (D) 23 (May); [2012] BLR 309; (2012) 142 ConLR 149
.... 106, 184, 302, 604, 607, 619, 620, 634, 635, 636, 644
Workplace Technologies Plc v E Squared Ltd and Mr J Riches HT 00 34.....330–1, 651
Workspace Management Ltd v YJL London Ltd [2009] EWHC 2017 (TCC); [2009] All ER (D) 119 (Aug); [2009] BLR 497; [2009] CILL 2758
.... 248, 298–9, 354, 631, 641, 657, 658, 661
WSP Cel Ltd v Dalkia Utilities Services Plc [2012] EWHC 2428 (TCC); [2013] CILL 3317.. 356, 601, 613, 644, 658, 659, 661, 672
WW Gear Construction Ltd v McGee Group Ltd [2012] EWHC 1509 (TCC); [2012] All ER (D) 16 (Jun); [2012] BLR 355 ....323, 600, 648
Yarm Road Ltd v Costain Ltd [2001] AdjLR 07/30.........................53, 588, 589
YCMS Ltd (t/a Young Construction Management Services) v Grabiner & Anor [2009] EWHC 127 (TCC); [2009] All ER (D) 19 (Apr); [2009] BLR 211; (2009) 123 ConLR 202; [2009] CILL 2692................................. 241, 600, 628, 631, 658, 661
Yuanda (UK) Co Ltd v WW Gear Construction Ltd [2010] EWHC 720 (TCC); [2011] All ER (Comm) 550; [2010] BLR 435; (2010) 130 ConLR 133; [2010] CILL 2849
.... 234, 235, 237, 314, 418, 420, 597, 601, 627, 647

Index

1996 Act *see* Housing Grants Construction and Regeneration Act 1996
1997 Order *see* Construction Contracts (Northern Ireland) Order 1997
1998 Scheme *see* Scheme for Construction Contracts (England and Wales) Regulations 1998
1998 Scottish Scheme *see* Scheme for Construction Contracts (Scotland) Regulations 1998
2009 Act *see* Housing Grants Construction and Regeneration Act 1996
2011 Act *see* Construction Contracts (Amendment) Act (Northern Ireland) 2011
2011 Scheme *see* Scheme for Construction Contracts (England and Wales) Regulations 1998 (Amendment) (England) Regulations 2011
2011 Scottish Scheme *see* Scheme for Construction Contracts (Scotland) Amendments Regulations 2011
2013 Act, Ireland 461–72

abandonment, reservations 334–5, 651
abatement *see also* set-offs…
   generally 191–4, 619–20
abuse of process
   fairness 379, 380, 423–4, 439–40, 667–8
   Northern Ireland 439–40
   Scotland 423–4
the Act *see* Housing Grants Construction and Regeneration Act 1996…
actual bias
   see also bias
   definition 202, 362–3, 367, 665

ad hoc adjudications
   by choice 79–80
   by mistake ad hoc jurisdiction 80–2
   case index 596
   definition 9–10, 43, 75, 79–80, 538
   emails 81–2
   generally 75, 79–82, 83–4, 309, 338, 344–5, 538, 596
   issue-based ad hoc jurisdiction 82
   on issues 82
   letters 80–1
   reservations 81–2
   'reserving the position' protests 82, 327–8, 649–50
ad hoc jurisdiction
   by mistake ad hoc jurisdiction 80–2
   issue-based ad hoc jurisdiction 82
   losing the right to challenge the adjudicator's jurisdiction 338, 652
adjudicating nominating bodies (ANBs)
   appointment of adjudicator 152–8, 165–72, 345–6
   critique 22, 158–62
   definition 10, 20, 158–9, 531–2, 538
   fees 571–7
   generally 10–11, 20–1, 22, 24, 87–8, 144–5, 152–8, 165, 187, 531–2, 538, 570–7, 616
   list of ANBs in the UK 158–9, 571–7
   quality issues 22, 144–5, 158–62
   Scheme adjudications 87–8, 152–8
   statistics 24, 571–7
the adjudication
   checklists 171–2, 212–13, 360–1
   confidentiality issues 173–4, 189, 200, 558–60, 569

A Practical Guide to Construction Adjudication, First Edition. James Pickavance.
© 2016 James Pickavance. Published 2016 by John Wiley & Sons, Inc.

the adjudication (*Continued*)
  definitions 10–11, 173–4, 215–16, 251–2, 526–9
  disclosure of documents 189, 198–9, 210–13, 620
  dropped heads of claim 188, 194–5, 620
  generally 173–213, 250–2, 286–7, 526–9, 617–22
  intimidation problems 188, 190–1, 213
  overview 173–4
  'pay now, argue later' rubric 251–2
  reckoning of time 189, 201, 528–9
  service of documents 189, 200–1, 343, 348–9, 391–2, 528–9, 620, 655–6
  set-offs 183–4, 188–9, 191–4, 227–8, 236–8, 241–8, 284, 437–8, 619–20, 628–31
  settlements 187, 189, 197–8, 199
  staying adjudication proceedings 189, 199, 310–11
  withdrawals 188, 195, 227, 321, 328–9, 364–5, 620, 650
adjudication procedures *see* procedures
adjudication strategy
  see also commencement
  case index 614
  cherry-picking/sampling/pruning approaches 136–8, 177–80, 614
  concurrent adjudications 125–6, 161
  contractual interpretations 128
  deploying arguments 139–41, 148–52, 343–9
  dispute-referral selection criteria 126–39, 150
  generally 123–43, 146–52, 614
  getting-in-there-first factors 124–5
  large disputes 137–8, 150, 180–1, 379, 382–4, 614
  multiple adjudications 125–6, 161, 173–4, 188–9, 247–8, 299, 321–61, 630
  other party's willingness/ability to pay 141–3, 151–2, 614
  overview 123
  pecuniary and declaratory claims 127–43
  preparation needs 123–6
  removal of procedural uncertainties 142–3
  reverse ambush 140–1
  save-the-best-until-last approaches 139–40
  secured assets 141–2, 614

  'smash and grab' adjudications 129–36, 614
  starting times 123–5
  timescales 123–43, 149–52, 180–1
adjudicators
  see also adjudicating nominating bodies; appointment...; challenges...; decisions; duties...; fees; jurisdiction...; natural justice; powers...
  assistance-seeking powers of adjudicators 205–6, 219, 395, 424–5, 674
  bad faith factors 11, 85, 168, 170–2, 210, 227, 359, 367–9, 423, 468, 495, 527, 537, 558
  capability assessments 164–6, 172
  case management skills 166–7
  checklists 171–2, 212–13, 360–1
  communications 176, 180–1, 186–90, 200–1, 206–7, 212–13, 214–26, 348–61, 366, 371–3, 399, 531–7, 620–2, 666
  conflicts of interest 10, 145, 155, 156–8, 163, 171–2, 617
  costs 168–72, 210–13, 217, 227–33, 315–18, 527–9, 557–60, 567–9, 647
  court judgments 164–5, 307–12, 645–7, 648
  critique 12, 21–2, 145–6, 150, 158–60, 170–2, 173–4, 183–4, 201–13, 227, 232–3, 239–41, 250–2, 265, 284, 301–2, 319–61, 362–99, 471–2, 648–76
  CVs 164–5
  definition 10–11, 215–16, 405
  error corrections 227, 239–41, 350–1, 360–1, 527, 567–8, 627–8
  expertise/quality of adjudicators 10, 21–2, 95, 126–8, 144–5, 152–72, 232–48, 250–2, 284, 301–2, 357–61, 395–7, 465–8, 471–2
  extension requests 223–6, 355–6, 382–4, 404–5, 422–3, 439–40, 469–72, 624–5
  fees 168–72, 210–13, 217, 227–33, 304, 315–18, 336–7, 365, 367–9, 408–11, 419–26, 457–60, 480–6, 495–500, 516–20, 533–7, 555–60, 565–9, 626–7, 647
  finalising the adjudicator's decisions 305–7, 644–5
  generally 10–12, 20–1, 22–3, 32–3, 45–6, 51–2, 67–8, 85–96, 108–15, 126–43,

144–72, 173–213, 214–26, 227–48, 276–7, 304–18, 319–61, 362–99, 404–5, 408–26, 453–60, 464–72, 512–20, 526–9, 531–7, 617–22, 626–31, 644–7, 648–76
immunity of adjudicators 209–10, 622
intimidation problems 188, 190–1, 213
jurisdiction issues 12, 32–3, 80–2, 108–15, 145–6, 151–2, 182, 183–4, 187–8, 201–13, 238–48, 250–2, 257–60, 265, 284, 301–2, 319–61, 415–26, 499–500, 648–63
multiple disputes 108–15, 125–6, 161, 230–1, 338–42, 564, 608–11
obiter dicta remarks 73, 114, 170–2, 194–5, 298, 315, 336–7
overview 10–11, 152, 173–4
parallel correspondence 186
pre-emptory orders 249, 276–7, 636
procedural capabilities 165–6, 172
referral notice 180–1
removals 145, 170–2
resignations 90, 111–12, 179, 180–1, 205, 210–13, 216, 228–31, 321–61, 364–5, 367–9, 408–11, 533–7, 564–5
sets of directions 181, 204–5, 212–13, 529, 555–60, 621
substantially the same dispute 110–15, 125–6, 151, 210–13, 338–42, 439–40, 609–11
technical capabilities 165–6, 172, 250–1
terms of the contract 171–2, 178–80, 200–1, 215–26, 232
third-party advisers 205–6, 219, 395, 424–6, 674
third-party liabilities 209–10
adjudicator's agreement 167–9, 557–60
administration
see also compulsory...; insolvency; voluntary...
definition 36, 287–8, 295
generally 36–7, 287–9, 295, 421, 586, 638
administrative receivership
see also insolvency
definition 37, 289, 295
generally 37–8, 283, 289, 295, 434–40, 586, 638
advantages of construction adjudications 3–4, 18–21, 42, 43–4, 443–5

adversarial proceedings, generally 196–7
advisers
see also consultants; experts
assistance-seeking powers of adjudicators 205–6, 219, 395, 424–5, 674
consultants 49–50
deciding to adjudicate 14–17, 25, 142–3
advocates 263–4
after the event insurance (ATE) 272, 635
agreements
appointment of adjudicator 167–9, 557–60
written contracts 68–74, 526, 593–5
ambush
see also timescales and no dispute
fairness 379, 380–2, 668–9
reverse ambush 140–1
risk of 23, 28, 104, 124–6, 380–2, 668–9
amounts in dispute
deciding to adjudicate 15–17, 24, 28, 31–2
statistics 24
an exchange of written submissions in adjudication proceedings, written contracts 70–1, 593
ancillary agreements, construction contracts 52–4, 69–71, 110–11, 117, 308–12, 588–9
apparent bias
see also bias
definition 202, 362–3, 368–9
appeals, TCC 273–4
appendices 7, 44, 84, 177, 182, 215, 521–701
applicability of the Act 84–6, 142–3, 596–7
applicability of Scheme adjudications 84–6, 142–3, 147–52, 596–7
application of the Act to contracts 51, 142–3, 202, 588
application notice forms
enforcement of decisions 257, 258–60, 431–40
TCC documents 257, 258–60
appointment of adjudicator
see also initiating the adjudication
acceptance issues 166, 172
adjudicating nominating bodies 152–8, 165–72
agreement considerations 167–9, 557–60
appointment-acceptance assessments 166, 172
bias 366, 370–1

appointment of adjudicator (*Continued*)
  capability assessments 164–6, 172
  checklists 171–2, 360–1
  defective appointments 154–5, 170–2, 230–1, 342–9
  forum shopping 160–1, 616
  generally 10, 12, 85–8, 90, 126–8, 144–5, 152–72, 174–6, 181, 319, 342–9, 366, 370–1, 408–11, 447, 453–5, 465–7, 479–80, 531–7, 557–60, 563–4, 616–17, 654–5
  named individuals in the contract 161–2, 345, 616
  natural person requirements 163, 617
  objections 154–5, 163–4, 171–2, 205–6, 617
  overview 152
  post-appointment pre-referral issues 167–8
  procedures 152–72, 344–9, 563–4, 616
  referring party checklist 171, 360–1
  responding party checklist 171–2, 360–1
  revocation issues 145, 170–2, 230–1, 342–9, 408–11, 565, 617
  Scheme adjudications 152–72, 175–6, 531–7, 615–17
  timescales 152–3, 168–9, 172, 174–5, 181
  unwilling/unable/busy appointees 162, 169
approbation and reprobation
  losing the right to challenge the adjudicator's jurisdiction 335–8, 421–2, 652
  Scotland 421–2
arbitration
  see also final determination
  costs 19, 22–3, 27–8, 443
  definition 27–8, 215
  enforcement of decisions 255, 262, 265, 274–6, 282–4, 296–300, 636
  fast track 27-28
  generally 19, 22–3, 27–8, 275–6, 304–18, 336–7, 408–11, 443, 568–9
  long timescales 4, 13–14, 18, 21
  set-offs 243, 248
  staying enforcement proceedings 274–6, 282–4, 310–12, 636
  temporary finality aspects of adjudicator decisions 224–6, 625–6
Arbitration Act 1996 262, 274–7, 408–11, 527, 536, 568

architects 40, 49–50, 156–60, 355, 469–70, 523–9, 571–7
  see also consultants
arguments
  deploying arguments 139–41, 148–52, 343–9
  skeleton arguments 261–2
assembly, installation, erection, demolition in connection with certain activities, excluded operations 60–2, 590
assessments of costs 238–9, 264, 266–76, 419–26, 533–7, 633–7
assigned contracts 116–17
assistance-seeking powers, powers of adjudicators 205–6, 219, 395, 424–5, 674
Association of Independent Construction Adjudicators 571
'at any time'
  conclusivity clauses 121–2, 613
  generally 20, 119–22, 126, 613
  preconditions and restrictions 119–22, 613
ATE *see* after the event insurance
attachment of earnings orders, enforcement methods 282–3, 434–40
audi alteram partem maxim 362, 399
  see also natural justice
Australia
  adjudications 443, 446–60, 579–83
  appeal rights 458–60
  appointment of adjudicator 453–5
  background 443, 446–60, 579–83
  Building and Construction Industry Security of Payment Act 1999 (NSW Act) 401–2, 446–60
  case law statistics 460
  challenges to decisions 458–60
  claimable variation and excluded amounts in Victoria 451
  commencement requirements 449–53
  conduct of the adjudication 455
  construction work generally 449–53
  costs 457–60
  decisions 456–60
  east–west coast divide 448–60, 579–83
  enforcement of decisions 458–60
  Federal Royal Commissioner 448–9
  historical background 443, 446–9
  judicial reviews 458–60

legislation 401–2, 446–60, 579–83
natural justice 459–60
New South Wales 446–60
overview of legislation in each State/Territory 447–9
procedures 449–60
processes 453–60
reference dates 451–3
referring parties 453–60
rollout across the States/Territories 447–9
timescales 451–60
authorised nominating authority (ANA), Australia 453–60
awards
see also pecuniary...
adjudicator's costs 232–3
arbitration 243, 248, 296–7, 631
decisions 218–26, 227–48, 401–5, 428–40, 456–60, 469–72, 482–6

bad faith factors, adjudicators 11, 85, 168, 170–2, 210, 227, 359, 367–9, 423, 468, 495, 527, 537, 558
Bailii *see* British and Irish Legal Information Institute
balance sheet tests of insolvency 31–2, 295, 421
bankruptcy 31, 38–9, 278–80, 283, 285–6, 288, 290, 420–1
Bankruptcy Court 35, 283
barristers 40–2, 263–4, 465–6, 571–7
bespoke rules, procedures 96
bias
see also actual...; apparent...; impartiality requirements; natural justice
appointment of the same adjudicator 366, 370–1, 399, 665–6
checklist 399
definition 12, 146, 202, 362–3, 366–9, 399
disclosures 370
evidence bias 366, 373–5, 666
generally 12, 146, 157, 202, 362–78, 399, 665–7
information consideration/dissemination duties of adjudicators 366, 375, 399, 666
meetings and hearings 376, 667
in a nutshell 366–7

post-appointment communications with one party 366, 373, 399, 666
pre-appointment communications with one party 366, 371–3, 399, 666
preliminary views 366, 377–8, 397–9, 667, 675
prior involvement of the adjudicator 366, 369–70, 399, 665
quasi-mediators 366, 376, 667
site visits 366, 375, 667
without prejudice material 366, 377, 667
bill of costs assessments, TCC 269–76, 634–5
binding aspects of decisions 214–16, 218–19, 223–6, 265–6, 276, 304–18, 320–61, 410–26, 435–40, 444–5, 457–60, 470–2, 474–86, 517–20, 527–9, 567–8, 633
see also temporary finality aspects of decisions
Books of Council and Session, Scotland 417, 540
breaches of natural justice 362–99
British and Irish Legal Information Institute (Bailii) 8, 584
Building and Construction Industry Security of Payment Act 1999 (NSW Act), Australia 446–60, 501–2
Building and Construction Industry Security of Payment Act (Cap 30B) 2004 (the 2004 Act), Singapore 501–20
Building and Construction Industry Security of Payment Regulations 2006 (the Regulations), Singapore 502–20
buildings, construction operations definition 55–8, 436–7, 524–5, 589–90
by choice ad hoc adjudications 79–80
by mistake ad hoc jurisdiction 80–2

call-off contracts, framework contracts 54, 69–70
capability assessments
see also expertise/quality of adjudicators
appointment of adjudicator 164–6, 172
capacity of adjudicators 10
case law
see also courts; *individual cases*; judgments; judicial precedent; legislation
access methods 8

case law (*Continued*)
  generally 3–4, 6–8, 222, 472, 584–677, 678–701
  information sources 8
  list of cases 7–8, 584–677
  points of principle 7–8, 29, 353
  statistics 6–7, 460, 584
  uses 6–8, 472
case management conferences (CMCs) 323
case management skills, adjudicators 166–7
'cash flow' tests of insolvency 31–2, 278–9, 292–3, 295, 421
cash-flow advantages of construction adjudications 18–19, 77–8
CEDR Solve
  generally 88–9, 95–6, 376, 562–9, 602
Centre for Effective Dispute Resolution 158–9, 187, 571
certificates 105–8, 114–15, 121–2, 140–1, 192–3, 242, 244, 355–61, 606–7, 657–8
CFAs *see* conditional fee arrangements
challenges to decisions
  see also duress; fraud; Human Rights Act...; insolvency...; jurisdiction issues; natural justice; unfair...
  Australia 458–60
  checklist 284, 360–1
  generally 12, 47, 145–6, 150, 157–8, 173–4, 179, 183–4, 187–8, 201, 204–5, 219, 222, 249–84, 319–61, 364–99, 400–5, 415–26, 435–40, 458–60, 499–500, 518–20, 567–9, 648–77
  losing the right to challenge the adjudicator's jurisdiction 319, 331–8, 421–2, 651–3
  Malaysia 482–6
  New Zealand 499–500
  Northern Ireland 435–40
  overview 12, 145–6, 319–20, 362–3, 400–1, 663–4
  reasons 12, 47, 145–6, 150, 157, 173–4, 179, 183–4, 187–8, 201, 204–5, 219, 222, 250–1, 284, 319–61, 364–99, 400–5, 415–26, 435–40, 459–60, 482–6, 518–20, 648–77
  Scotland 415–26
  Singapore 502, 512–20
  statistics 214, 460

charging orders, enforcement methods 282, 434–40
Chartered Institute of Arbitrators (CIArb) 158–9, 465–6, 572
Chartered Institute of Building (CIOB) 573
cherry-picking/sampling/pruning approaches, adjudication strategy 136–8, 177–80, 614
choice-of-decision-maker advantages of construction adjudications 20, 161
Christmas claims, fairness 379, 382, 529, 669
CIC *see* Construction Industry Council
citations
  see also case law
  generally 8, 530, 584
civil engineers 159–60, 571–7
Civil Liability (Contribution) Act 1978 229
Civil Procedure Rules (CPRs) 13, 29, 35, 45–6, 54, 141–2, 198–9, 221–2, 238–9, 252–84, 286, 291–3, 307–8, 322–3, 329–31, 337–8, 540
  see also Part...
claim forms, TCC documents 257–60
claim/case success assessments, deciding to adjudicate 14–17, 24, 42, 142–3
claiming parties *see* referring parties
claims
  see also enforcement...; preconditions...; referring parties
  abandoned claims 107, 607
  Christmas claims 379, 382, 529, 669
  communications 99–100, 104–8, 152–3
  definition 97–100, 104–5
  dropped heads of claim 188, 194–5, 620
  generally 14–17, 24, 42, 97–122, 123–43, 148–52, 249–84, 401–5, 436–40, 479–86, 504–20, 542–60, 602–13, 633–7
  letters 98–100, 104–8, 147–8, 177–80, 605–6
  timescales 102–4, 124–5, 145, 503–20, 605
  written claims 98–100
claims consultants *see* consultants
Code of Practice, Ireland 461–72
collateral warranties, ancillary agreements 52–4, 278
commencement
  see also adjudication strategy; initiating the adjudication; notice of adjudication

final determination 312–18, 646–7
  generally 10, 97–8, 102, 123–43, 144–5, 256–60, 312–18, 338–61, 430–40, 449–53, 462–4, 474–8, 488–90, 502–4, 614, 633
  TCC 256–60, 633
Commercial Court 47–8, 411–26
Commercial Division of the High Court, Ireland 471–2
commercial intimidation problems 4, 188, 190–1, 213
common law, negligence claims 23, 97, 110, 116
the Commonwealth 443–5, 473
  see also international...
communications
  see also documents; meetings
  adjudicators 176, 180–1, 186–90, 200–1, 206–7, 212–13, 214–26, 348–61, 366, 371–3, 399, 531–7, 620–2, 666
  claims 99–100, 104–8, 152–3
  decisions 214–26, 349–61, 535–7, 566–7, 624–6
  duties of adjudicators 176, 180–1, 186–8, 189–90, 206–7, 212–13, 214–26, 348–9, 371–3, 399
  methods 152–3, 164, 173–4, 178–80, 186–8, 189–90, 200–1, 214–26, 528–9
  parallel correspondence 186
Companies Court 32, 35, 36, 283
company voluntary arrangements (CVAs) 38, 286–7, 289–90, 295, 586, 638–9
  see also insolvency
  definition 38, 289, 295
compensation clauses 128, 179–80
compliance
  court orders 280–4, 637
  decisions 11, 223–6, 260–2, 280–4, 320–61, 625–6, 637
  delaying by contract 225–6, 625–6
  enforcement of decisions 249, 260–2, 280–4, 637
  extending the time for payment 281–4, 469–72, 482–6, 637
  generally 11, 223–6, 249, 260–2, 280–4, 309–12, 320–61, 512–20, 565–6, 625–6, 637, 646–7
  time for payment 280–4, 456–60, 469–72, 482–6, 637
  timescales 280–4, 637
compliance failures
  see also enforcement of decisions
  court orders 281–4, 637
  declarations 283, 637
  final determination without complying with adjudication 309–12, 646–7
  money judgments 282–4
  Scheme adjudications 84–6, 596–7
compulsory administration
  definition 36–7, 287–8
  generally 36–7, 287–9
compulsory liquidation
  definition 34–5
  generally 33, 34–5, 294–5
conclusivity clauses
  'at any time' construction adjudications 121–2, 613
concurrent adjudications, adjudication strategy 125–6, 161
conditional fee arrangements (CFAs) 272, 635
confidentiality issues
  see also privacy...
  the adjudication 19–20, 90, 173–4, 189, 200, 558–60, 569
conflicts of interest, adjudicators 10, 145, 155, 156–8, 163, 171–2, 617
consent before objection, losing the right to challenge the adjudicator's jurisdiction 335, 652
consideration, construction contracts 45–8
construction contracts
  see also adjudications; construction operations; Scheme...
  ancillary agreements 52–4, 69–71, 110–11, 117, 308–12, 588–9
  application of the Act to contracts 51, 202, 588
  definitions 48–54, 338–42, 403, 436, 449–50, 459–60, 462–3, 474–5, 502–4, 523–6, 653
  evidenced in writing 66–8, 70–4, 340–2, 475–8, 503–4, 526, 592–5
  excluded agreements 62–6, 74, 525–6, 591, 593–5

construction contracts (*Continued*)
    existence and terms of the contract 44–8, 67–74, 115–17, 145, 178–213, 215–26, 232, 304–18, 338–42, 356–61, 400–5, 586–8
    generally 3–4, 13–14, 43–74, 75, 80–2, 85–96, 152–3, 161–3, 178–213, 338–42, 436–40, 449–53, 462–4, 474–86, 487–500, 501–20, 523–9, 530–7, 586–95, 653
    interpretations 47–8, 128, 356–61, 658
    multiple contracts 117–19, 338–42, 612–13
    named adjudicators in the contract 161–3
    non-contractual claims 23, 43–4, 116–17
    oral contracts 66–74, 77, 340–2, 593–5
    reasonableness interpretations 47–8, 128
    requirements 43–74, 586–95
    rescinded contracts 46–8
    rights 3–4, 13–14, 44–74
    termination of contract 46–8, 117, 131–6, 356–61, 587
    terms of the contract 45–8, 67–74, 85–96, 115–17, 145, 178–213, 215–26, 232, 304–18, 338–42, 356–61, 400–5, 586–95
    'under' the contract disputes 115–17, 151, 342, 611–13
    void/voidable contracts 45, 46–8, 115, 116–17, 314, 587
    written contracts 43–8, 66–74, 76, 77, 338–42, 526, 591–5
Construction Contracts Act 2002 (the 2002 Act), New Zealand 487–500
Construction Contracts (Amendment) Act (Northern Ireland) 2011 (the 2011 Act) 427–40
Construction Contracts Amendment Bill, New Zealand 500
Construction Contracts (England and Wales) Exclusion Order 1998 (SI 1998/648) 63–6, 339–42
Construction Contracts (England and Wales) Exclusion Order 2011 (SI 2011/2332) 63–6
Construction Contracts (Northern Ireland) Order 1997 (the 1997 Order) 427–40
Construction Contracts Regulations 2003, New Zealand 494–5
Construction Industry Council (CIC) 77, 88–9, 94–5, 562–9, 573, 601–2
    generally 94–5, 562–9, 573, 601–2

Construction Industry Payment And Adjudication Act 2012, Malaysia 473–86
construction operations
    see also construction contracts
    definitions 48–53, 55–8, 436, 449–50, 523–6, 589–90
    excluded operations 55, 58–62, 76, 339–42, 450–1, 524–5, 579–83, 590–1
    generally 48–74, 76, 339–42, 436–40, 449–53, 459–60, 462–4, 474–8, 488–90, 502–4, 523–6, 588–95
    types 55–6, 523–6
Construction Plant-hire Association 573
consultants
    see also advisers; team…
    generally 14–16, 40–2, 49–50, 159–60, 523–9, 588
    fees 40–1
    legal advice privilege issues 41, 173, 188–9, 195–6
contempt of court 283
content/structure considerations, decisions 214, 216–17, 349–61
Contracts (Rights of Third Parties) Act 1999 (The 1999 Act), ancillary agreements 52, 54, 169–70
contractual adjudications
    see also adjudications
    checklist 74
    court treatments 77–9
    definition 9, 43, 74, 75–6, 83–4, 88–9, 538
    enforcement of decisions 252
    generally 9, 43, 74, 75–9, 83–4, 88–96, 126, 151, 174–5, 252, 403–4, 538, 595, 597–602
    procedures 9–10, 83–4, 88–96, 126, 174–5, 597–602
contractual set-off rights 242–4, 628–9
    see also set-offs
corrections, errors by adjudicators 239–41, 350–1, 360–1, 527, 567–8, 627–8
cost apportionments
    assessments 238–9, 419–26, 533–7
    generally 11, 22–3, 28, 210–13, 217–18, 227–33, 237–8, 533–7
    in a nutshell 237
    statistics 238–9
    timescales 237–8
cost budgets, TCC 261, 264

Index

costs
  see also fees
  adjudicators 168–72, 210–13, 217, 227–33, 315–18, 527–9, 557–60, 567–9, 647
  advantages/disadvantages of construction adjudications 11, 19, 22–3, 27–8, 42, 142, 443–5
  arbitration 19, 22–3, 27–8, 443
  assistance-seeking powers of adjudicators 206, 219
  ATE 272, 635
  bill of costs assessments 269–76, 634–5
  CFAs 272, 635
  enforcement of decisions 179, 266–76, 633–7
  final determination 312–18, 646–7
  generally 168–72, 210–13, 217, 227–33, 261, 264, 266–76, 304, 312–18, 433–40, 457–60, 469–72, 482–6, 515–20, 527–9, 557–60, 633–7
  indemnity basis to assess costs 266–76
  interest on moneys 272–3, 430–1, 635–6
  irrecoverable costs 22–3, 138, 142, 195, 206, 227–39, 304, 315–18, 419–20, 433–40, 457–60, 495–500, 516–20, 647
  issues/proportionate-based assessments of costs 267–76
  litigation 19, 22–3, 28, 40–1, 142–3, 261, 264, 266–76, 443, 633–7
  Northern Ireland 433–40
  post decisions 227–33, 626–7
  proportionate-based assessments of costs 267–76
  reasonableness 267–76
  Scotland 419–26
  settlement reached before summary judgment 273–4, 636
  standard basis to assess costs 266–76
  summary/detailed assessments of costs 268–76
  taxes 433–4
  TCC 261, 264, 266–76, 633–7
  Tolent clauses 234–5, 419–20
  without prejudice material 198, 199, 336–7
cost-benefit analysis
  see also fees; resources; time...
  deciding to adjudicate 14, 15–17, 19, 42
counterclaims 11, 127–8, 248, 414, 420–1
County Courts 280, 282–3, 539

Court of Sessions 354, 411–26, 540–1
courts
  see also Bankruptcy...; case law; Companies...; County...; enforcement...; High...; *individual cases*; judicial precedent; legal jurisdictions; litigation; Northern Ireland; Scotland; Technology and Construction Court
  compliance with court orders 280–4, 637
  contractual adjudication treatments 77–9
  discretion to order a stay of execution 290–3, 639
  dispute definition approaches 98–108, 142–3, 602–8
  excluded operations approaches 59–62, 590
  orders 280–4, 637
  removal of procedural uncertainties 142–3
  types 539
Courts Reform (Scotland) Act 2014 411
creditors' voluntary liquidation (CVL) 33, 36
creep between crystallisation and referral, preconditions and restrictions 108, 136–7, 140, 148–9, 177–80, 183–4, 341–2, 607–8
criminal sanctions 283
cross-claims 4–5, 11, 29, 33–4, 127–8, 191–2, 241–8, 278–80, 286, 299–300, 458–60
  see also counterclaims; set-offs
  historical background 4–5
crystallisation generally
  creep between crystallisation and referral 108, 136–7, 140, 148–9, 177–80, 183–4, 341–2, 607–8
  definitions 148–9, 436
  notice of adjudication 148–9, 343–9
CVAs *see* company voluntary arrangements
CVs, adjudicators 164–5

damages 29, 116–17, 118, 209, 242–3, 313–18, 622, 629–30
debts
  generally 11, 129–30, 208–9, 233, 235–9, 278–80, 282–4, 417–26, 622
  Late Payment of Commercial Debts (Interest) Act 1998 11, 129–30, 208–9, 233, 235–9, 317, 430–1, 439–40
deceit *see* fraud

deciding to adjudicate
- advantages of construction adjudications 3–4, 18–21, 42
- checklist 42
- claim/case success assessments 14–17, 24, 42, 142–3
- generally 13–42, 142–3, 320, 338–42, 586
- cost-benefit analysis 14, 15–17, 42
- disadvantages of construction adjudications 21–3, 42
- dispute resolution alternatives 24–9, 42, 120–1
- dispute resolution methods 14, 16, 18–29
- evidence 14–15, 18, 21, 29, 41–2
- insolvency issues 14, 30–9, 42
- liquidation 29, 32–9
- loss assessments 14–17, 42
- overview 13–14
- relationship challenges 17, 18
- team-selection considerations 14, 15, 17, 40–2

decision-based jurisdiction challenges 319–20, 349–61, 656–63

decisions
- *see also* adjudications; challenges…; determination; enforcement…; insolvency; international…; post…; Technology and Construction Court; United Kingdom…
- Australia 456–60
- awards 218–26, 227–48, 401–5, 428–40, 456–60
- binding aspects 214–16, 218–19, 223–6, 265–6, 276, 304–18, 320–61, 410–26, 434–40, 444–5, 457–60, 470–2, 474–86, 517–20, 527–9, 567–8, 633
- communications 214–26, 349–61, 535–7, 566–7, 624–6
- compliance and effects 11, 223–6, 260–2, 280–4, 309–12, 320–61, 456–60, 469–72, 482–6, 493–500, 512–20, 536–7, 625–6, 637, 646–7
- content/structure considerations 214, 216–17, 349–61
- definition 214–16, 222–6, 554–60
- delaying by contract 225–6, 625–6
- 'draft for comment' conclusions 216
- extended timetables 85–96, 214, 218–22, 223–6, 382–4, 404–5, 422–3, 469–72, 624–5
- final determination conflicts 315, 647
- finalising the adjudicator's decisions 305–7, 644–5
- generally 11, 18–21, 39, 51, 76–9, 85–96, 109–15, 145–6, 165–72, 173–4, 212–13, 214–26, 227–48, 250–84, 286–303, 304–18, 320–61, 408–26, 456–60, 469–72, 482–6, 527–9, 535–7, 554–60, 566–9, 582–3, 622–31, 644–7, 656–63
- insurance claims 226, 626
- Ireland 469–72
- lien on decisions 232, 350–61, 656
- Malaysia 474–5, 482–6
- New Zealand 487–8, 493–500
- Northern Ireland 428–40
- overview 214–15
- purpose and nature 214–16, 622–3
- reasons for the decision 214, 217–18, 350–61, 398–9, 623, 656–63, 675–6
- receipt of the decision 218–19, 227–48, 349–61, 623
- requirements 214–18, 349–61, 656–63
- revised decisions 227–8, 239–41, 627–8
- rigidity of the decision time limit 222, 350–61, 418–26, 624, 656
- scope of what the adjudicator can decide 207–8, 212–13, 217–26, 319–61, 408–11, 416–26, 621–2, 648–63
- Scotland 415–26
- severability 286, 301–3, 331–8, 643–4
- signed decisions 216–17, 351–61, 656–7
- Singapore 501–2, 515–20
- statistics 214, 238
- TCC 262–84
- temporary finality aspects 224–6, 625–6
- timescales 11, 13–14, 18–19, 20–1, 43–4, 85–96, 145, 212–13, 214–15, 219–26, 252–5, 264–5, 286–7, 304, 306, 312–14, 349–61, 382–4, 404–5, 418–26, 469–72, 474–86, 501–2, 535–7, 566–9, 623–4, 633
- *ultra vires* challenges 12, 276, 331–2

declaratory claims
- adjudication strategy 127–8
- compliance failures 283, 637

declaratory relief remedy, Northern Ireland 435

default notices 141
defective appointments
   appointment of adjudicator 154–5, 170–2, 230–1, 342–9
   revocation issues 145, 170–2, 230–1, 342–9, 408–11, 565, 617
defective work disputes 19, 24, 41, 127–8, 248, 437–40
defences 10–12, 139–43, 144–5, 148–52, 173–4, 181–213, 259–84, 320–61, 362–99, 400–5, 412–26, 432–40, 618–22, 676–7
   see also challenges...; responses
   generally 10–11, 173–4, 181–4, 261–84, 320–61, 362–99, 400–5, 618–19, 676–7
   impermissible defences 183–4, 191–3, 386–9
defendants 249–84, 290–303, 431–40, 540
   see also enforcement of decisions; responders; Technology and Construction Court
delaying by contract, compliance 225–6, 625–6
delaying issues, final determination 314, 647
deploying arguments, adjudication strategy 139–41, 148–52, 343–9
determination 3–5, 9, 10–11, 12, 18–19, 22, 51, 76–7, 85–6, 127–43, 165–72, 194–5, 285–303, 304–18, 320–61, 408–26, 428–40, 456–60, 469–72, 482–6, 493–500, 515–20, 644–7, 648–51
determination by the adjudicator, jurisdiction issues 320–1, 324–7, 648–9
determination from another adjudicator, jurisdiction issues 326–7, 364
determination from the court, jurisdiction issues 320–3, 364, 648
development agreements 66
development companies 64–6, 403
'difference' generally, disputes 97, 99, 102, 526–7, 604
directions
   requests/direction-making powers of adjudicators 181, 204–5, 212–13, 529, 555–60, 621
   sets of directions from adjudicators 181, 204–5, 212–13, 529, 555–60, 621
   TCC 260–1

disadvantages of construction adjudications 21–3
disclosure of documents
   see also privilege
   the adjudication 189, 198–9, 210–13, 620
disclosures, bias 370
dismissed claims, TCC 264–84
dispute resolution procedures
   see also adjudication; arbitration; construction adjudications; early neutral evaluations; expert determinations; fast-track arbitration; interim...; litigation; mediation; Part 8 claims; winding-up petitions
   alternative types 24–9, 42, 120–1
   generally 3–8, 13–14, 16, 18–29, 43–74, 97–8, 120–1, 214–26, 250, 586–95
dispute settlement/compromised scenario, preconditions and restrictions 108, 187, 199, 338–42, 607
dispute type statistics 24
   see also defective work...; interim payment...; prolongation...; valuation...
disputes
   see also international...; United Kingdom...
   causes 3–12, 443
   courts' approaches 98–108, 142–3, 602–8
   definitions 97–9, 100–8, 142–3, 147, 149–52, 177–80, 241–8, 338–42, 436–40, 526–9, 602–8
   'difference' generally 97, 99, 102, 526–7, 604
   dispute-referral selection criteria 126–39, 150
   exchanges of correspondence 98–100, 104–8, 148–50, 152–3, 177–86, 605–6
   generally 3–12, 97–122, 123–43, 214–26, 304–18, 338–42, 436–40, 443–5, 446–60, 461–72, 473–86, 487–500, 501–20, 526–9, 543–60, 602–13
   historical background 4–5, 443–4
   letters 98–100, 104–8, 177–80, 605–6
   overview 3–12, 443–5
   scenarios 104–8, 605–8
   scope 144–52, 177–80, 183–4, 187–8, 207–8, 212–13, 217–26, 341–61, 618–22
   statutory limitations 122

disputes (*Continued*)
  timescales 10–11, 23, 28, 102–4, 121–2, 123–43, 145, 146–7, 149–53, 168–9, 173–4, 180–1, 201, 212–13, 214–15, 219–26, 304, 306, 312–14, 342–9, 380–4, 391–2, 411–26, 439–40, 451–60, 465–72, 501–2, 526–9, 605, 617–22, 623–4, 673
  'under' the contract disputes 115–17, 151, 342, 611–13
  without prejudice material 106, 139, 172, 188–9, 197–8, 336–7, 366, 377, 607, 614, 667
disregarded submissions/witnesses 204–5, 374–5, 384–9, 670–2
documents
  see also evidence; notice of adjudication; referral notice; responses
  Books of Council and Session 417, 540
  correctly served documents 107, 152–3, 189, 200–1, 391–2, 607, 620
  destruction 569
  disclosure of documents 189, 198–9, 210–13, 620
  referral notice supporting documents 178–80, 189, 200–1, 210–13
  response supporting documents 183–4, 189, 200–1, 210–13
  service of documents 31–2, 107, 152–3, 189, 200–1, 343, 348–9, 391–2, 528–9, 607, 620, 655–6
  TCC 257–60
dormant companies 300
'draft for comment' conclusions, decisions 216
drafting tips 3, 123–5, 146–52, 173–4, 177–80, 182–4
drainage work 62, 65–6
drilling and extraction, excluded operations 58–62, 524–5
duress 12, 47, 145, 284, 400, 402–3, 676
  see also void/voidable contracts
  definition 402–3
duties of adjudicators
  see also jurisdiction issues; natural justice
  communications 176, 180–1, 186–8, 189–90, 206–7, 212–13, 214–26, 348–9, 371–3, 399
  generally 10–11, 173–4, 176, 180–200, 201–13, 214–26, 232–48, 319–61, 362–99, 408–26, 467–8, 512–20, 531–7, 620–2
  impartiality requirements 201–2, 216, 232, 362–78, 534–7, 620–1
  information consideration/dissemination duties 206–7, 212–13, 301–2, 348–9, 366, 375, 384–9, 399, 621, 655, 666, 670–6
  referral notice 180–1
  responses 183–4
  scope of the dispute 207–8, 212–13, 217–26, 352–61, 408–11, 416–26, 621–2
dwellings, residential occupiers excluded agreements 63–6, 80, 339–42, 403, 500, 525–6, 591

early neutral evaluations (ENEs)
  advantages 25
  definition 24–5
east–west coast divide, Australia 448–60, 579–83
economic recessions 4, 461, 472
emails 81–2, 104–8, 153, 164, 178–80
employment contracts, generally 50
Employment Rights Act 1996 50, 523
enforcement of decisions
  see also challenges . . .; commercial actions; decisions; insolvency; mandatory injunctions; pre-emptory orders; statutory demands; stay of execution; summary enforcement procedure; Technology and Construction Court; timescales
  arbitration 255, 262, 265, 274–6, 282–4, 296–300, 636
  Australia 458–60
  commencement of the claim 256–60, 430–40, 633
  compliance 249, 260–2, 280–4, 309–12, 567–9, 637, 646–7
  compliance failures 281–4, 309–12, 637, 646–7
  contractual adjudications 252
  costs 179, 266–76, 633–7
  definition 11, 215–16
  documents 257–60
  final determination 307–12, 645–7
  generally 3–4, 11–12, 19–21, 29, 32–3, 35, 39, 46, 98, 122, 179, 215–16, 222, 233,

249–84, 285–303, 307–12, 320–61,
    400–5, 407–26, 429–40, 458–60, 484–6,
    518–20, 567–9, 631–7, 638–44, 676–7
Ireland 470–2
key statements and court policy 249–52,
    631–2
Malaysia 484–6
methods of enforcing judgments 249,
    276–84, 434–40, 458–60, 484–6, 631–7
New Zealand 487–8, 496–500
Northern Ireland 428–40
overview 11, 249
'pay now, argue later' rubric 251–2
problems 39
Scotland 280, 284, 289, 400, 405, 407–26,
    637
severability 286, 301–3, 331–8, 643–4
Singapore 518–20
staying enforcement proceedings where
    there is an arbitration agreement 274–6,
    282–4, 636
TCC Guide 256–60, 322–3, 633
TCC summary enforcement procedure
    252–76, 284, 285–303, 306, 308–12,
    632–6, 638–44
Enforcement of Judgments Office (EJO),
    Northern Ireland 434
enforcement officers 282–4
Enterprise Act 2002 38
errors by adjudicators 21–2, 77–9, 85–96,
    112–13, 149, 150, 183–4, 205, 227,
    239–41, 250–2, 265, 301–2, 320–61,
    389–99, 499–500, 527, 567–8, 627–8,
    662–3
    corrections 239–41, 350–1, 360–1, 527,
        567–8, 627–8
    in a nutshell 239, 357–60
    types 239, 357–60, 662–3
essential terms of the contract 45–8, 67–74,
    85–96, 115–17, 178–80, 304–18, 338–42,
    356–61, 400–5
    see also construction contracts
European Convention on Human Rights
    (ECHR) 404, 422–3, 425
    see also Human Rights Act 1998
evidence
    see also witnesses
    bias 366, 373–5, 666

deciding to adjudicate 14–15, 18, 21, 29,
    41–2
disadvantages of construction
    adjudications 21, 23
dispute definition 99–100, 104–8, 149–52,
    605–8
exchanges of correspondence 98–100,
    104–8, 148–50, 152–3, 177–86,
    605–6
exhibits 180
failures to address
    issues/submissions/evidence 384–9,
    670–2
hearsay evidence 179–80
insolvency 31–2, 292–5
oral submissions 187–8
payments 105–8, 606–7
preconditions and restrictions 99–100,
    104–8, 152–3, 177–80, 338–42,
    605–8
TCC 255–6, 262
types of evidence 104–8, 149–50, 152–3,
    178–80
without prejudice material 106, 139, 197–8,
    336–7, 366, 377, 607, 614, 667
evidence not under oath, disadvantages of
    construction adjudications 23, 188
evidenced in writing
    see also 'otherwise than in writing'
        provisions; written contracts
    construction contracts 66–8, 70–4, 340–2,
        475–8, 503–4, 526, 592–5
excluded agreements
    construction contracts 62–6, 74, 525–6,
        591, 593–5
    residential occupiers 63–6, 80, 339–42, 403,
        500, 525–6, 591
excluded operations
    construction operations 55, 58–62, 76,
        339–42, 450–1, 524–5, 579–83, 590–1
    courts' approaches 59–62, 590
exhibits, evidence 180
existence and terms of the contract 44–8,
    67–74, 115–17, 145, 178–213, 304–18,
    338–42, 356–61, 400–5, 586–8
expert determinations
    advantages 25–6
    definition 25–6

expertise/quality of adjudicators 10, 21–2, 95, 126–8, 144–5, 152–72, 232–48, 284, 301–2, 357–61, 395–7, 424–6, 465–8, 471–2
see also capability assessments
experts
see also advisers; team…
assistance-seeking powers of adjudicators 205–6, 219, 395, 424–5, 674
generally 25–6, 41–2, 125–39, 179–80, 196–7, 205–6, 292–3, 424–6
fees 16–17, 22–3, 419–20
external lawyers
see also lawyers
generally 40–1
extraction of minerals, excluded operations 58–60, 76, 339–42, 524–5

'fair-minded and informed observer' test 368–78
see also bias; natural justice
fairness
see also natural justice
abuse of process 379, 380, 423–4, 439–40, 667–8
ambush perceptions 379, 380–2, 668–9
checklist 399
Christmas claims 379, 382, 529, 669
definition 12, 362–3, 378–9, 399, 403–4
documents received late/not at all 391–2, 673
failures to address issues/submissions/evidence 384–9, 670–2
failures to follow agreed procedures 390–1, 672–3
failures to inform parties about an approach taken/methodology used 392–4, 673
failures to inform parties about own knowledge/expertise 395–7, 424–5, 674–5
failures to inform parties about preliminary views 397–9, 675
failures to inform parties about third-party advisers 395, 424–6, 674
failures to permit further submissions/information 389–90, 672

large/complex disputes 379, 382–4, 422–3, 669–70
referring party's pre-adjudication conduct 379–80, 667
sufficiency of reasons 398–9, 675–6
unfair timetables 391, 673
UTCCR 12, 64, 145, 232, 400, 403–4, 676–7
familiarity advantages
construction adjudications 20
Scheme adjudications 86–7
fast-track arbitration
amounts in dispute 27–8
definition 27–8
timescales 28
fast-track dispute processes 4–5, 9–10, 27–8
see also timescales
definition 27–8
historical background 4–5
fax communications 153, 178–80
Federal Royal Commissioner, Australia 448–9
fees
see also costs
adjudicators 168–72, 210–13, 217, 227–33, 304, 315–18, 336–7, 365, 367–9, 408–11, 419–26, 457–60, 480–6, 495–500, 516–20, 533–7, 555–60, 565–9, 626–7, 647
ANBs 571–7
consultants 40–1
counsel 16–17, 40–1, 261, 264, 269–70, 272, 635
experts 16–17, 22–3, 419–20
generally 11, 16–17, 22–3, 40–1, 90–6, 138, 168–70, 210–13, 227–33, 261, 264, 269–70, 272, 304, 408–11, 533–7, 555–60, 626–7, 635
liabilities 229–33, 304
post decisions 227–33, 626–7
reasonableness 229–33, 269–76
solicitors 16–17, 40–1, 261, 264, 269–70, 272, 635
types 16–17, 168–70, 261
FIDIC Silver Book 311, 443–4, 519–20
final certificates 121–2, 140–1, 242, 244, 355–61, 629, 657–8
generally 121–2, 140–1, 242, 244, 629
set-offs 242, 244, 629

final determination 12, 18–19, 22, 85–6, 285–303, 304–18, 438–40, 444–5, 483, 644–7
  see also arbitration; determination; insolvency; litigation
  adjudication costs recovery 315–18, 647
  adjudications and other proceedings 307–12, 645–6
  adjudicator decision conflicts 315, 647
  commencement 312–18, 646–7
  costs 312–18, 646–7
  delaying issues 314, 647
  enforcement of decisions 307–12, 645–7
  financial difficulties 296–8, 438–40, 519–20, 640–1
  generally 12, 18–19, 22, 85–6, 296–8, 304–18, 438–40, 644–7
  limitation periods 304, 312–14, 646–7
  onus of proof 312–18, 646–7
  overview 12, 304–5
  stay of execution 296–303, 438–40
  timescales 304, 312–14, 646–7
  without compliance with the adjudication 309–12, 646–7
finalising the adjudicator's decisions 305–7, 644–5
finance and insurance, exclusion orders 63–6
financial difficulties, stay of execution 296–8, 438–40, 519–20, 640–1
fixtures, construction operations definition 55, 58, 524–5
flats, residential occupiers excluded agreements 63–6, 403, 525–6, 591
flexibility advantages of construction adjudications 19, 150
food and drink, excluded operations 58, 61–2, 339–42, 524–5
formation generally, construction contracts 45–8, 67–74, 586–7
forming part of the land, construction operations definition 55, 57–8, 436–7, 524–5
forming, or to form, part of the land, construction operations definition 55, 57–8, 436–7, 524–5
formulation issues, set-offs 242, 247, 630
forum shopping, appointment of adjudicator 160–1, 616

framework contracts, ancillary agreements 52, 54, 69–71
fraud 11, 12, 47, 116–17, 145, 157–8, 168–9, 284, 400, 401–2, 482–3, 676

getting-in-there-first factors, adjudication strategy 124–5
government construction contracts
  Malaysia 477–8
  Singapore 504
Government of Ireland Act 1920 427

hearing bundles, TCC 261–3
hearsay evidence 179–80
  see also evidence…
highways, exclusion orders 63–6
Highways Act 1980 65
historical background, statutory adjudications 4–5, 443–4
Hong Kong 443
Housing Grants Construction and Regeneration Act 1996 (the 1996 Act)
  see also case…; excluded…; legislation; Scheme…; Section…; statutory adjudications
  2009 Act (commencement 1 October 2011) 5–6, 28, 44, 53, 66–74, 76, 130–1, 140–1, 188–9, 193, 228–48, 523–9, 627–31
  commencement dates (1 May 1998 and 1 October 2011) 5–6, 44, 53, 66–7, 76–7, 84, 446
  definition 3, 5, 43–4, 523–9
  generally 3, 5, 7, 9–11, 18–20, 23, 43–74, 84, 109, 126, 130–43, 173–213, 228–48, 319, 403, 419–20, 427–8, 444–5, 476–7, 501–2, 523–9, 530, 579–83, 584
  historical background 4–5, 7, 44
  introductory provisions 523–6
  requirements 43–74, 403, 523–9
  section 104 of the Act 44, 48–54, 74, 339–42, 427–8, 523–4, 529, 587–8
  section 105 of the Act 44, 49, 55–62, 74, 76, 339–42, 524–5, 529, 579–80, 589–90
  section 106 of the Act 44–45, 55–8, 62–6, 74, 525–6, 529, 579, 591
  section 106A of the 2009 Act 63–65
  section 107 of the Act 66–74, 76, 77, 340–2, 427–8, 476–7, 526, 579, 591–5

Housing Grants Construction and
Regeneration Act 1996 (*Continued*)
section 108 of the Act 76, 80, 84–9, 90–6,
97–122, 151–72, 173–213, 219–26,
228–48, 276, 305, 341–2, 383–4, 410–11,
418, 419–20, 526–7, 530–1, 579, 582–3,
596–7, 602–13, 617–22, 623–31
section 108A of the 2009 Act 228-229, 233,
237
section 108(3)(A) of the 2009 Act 239–240
section 109 of the Act 579, 581
section 110 of the Act 130–1, 135–6, 141,
251–2, 531, 581
section 110A of the 2009 Act 130, 141
section 110B of the 2009 Act 141, 192, 194
section 111 of the Act 130–1, 251–2, 530,
536, 581
section 111 of the 2009 Act 130, 135, 141
section 112 of the Act 583
section 113 of the Act 581
section 114 of the Act 76, 84–8, 418, 528,
529, 596–7
section 115 of the Act 200–1, 221–6, 348,
528
section 116 of the Act 201, 221–6, 528–9
section 117 of the Act 529, 579
section 146 of the Act 529
UK and international statutory regimes'
comparisons 579–83
Human Rights Act 1998 (HRA)
definition 400, 404
generally 400, 404–5, 422–3, 425–6, 677
right to enjoy possessions (Article 1) 400,
405, 422–3, 425–6
right to a fair trial (Article 6) 400, 404–5,
422–3
Scotland 400, 405, 408, 422–3, 425–6

ICC *see* Infrastructure Conditions of
Contract
ICE *see* Institution of Civil Engineers
IChemE procedures (Grey Book) 88–9, 91–2,
562–9, 573
identities of the parties, essential terms of the
contract 45–8, 68–74, 110–11, 178–80,
342–9, 653–4
imminent resolution of other proceedings,
stay of execution 298–9, 641

immunity of adjudicators 209–10, 622
impartiality requirements
see also bias; natural justice
definition 362–3, 367–9, 534
duties of adjudicators 201–2, 216, 232,
362–78, 534–7, 620–1
impermissible defences 183–4, 191–3, 386–9
see also defences; set-offs
implied terms of contracts 73, 208, 443–4,
594–5
in-house lawyers
see also lawyers
generally 40
incorporation of terms, terms of the contract
47–8, 356–61, 587
indemnity basis to assess costs, TCC 266–76
independent third parties
see also adjudicating nominating bodies;
construction adjudications
definition 3, 9
generally 3–8, 9–12, 13–14, 25–7, 205–6,
219
individual voluntary arrangements (IVAs),
definition 39, 290
information consideration/dissemination
duties of adjudicators 206–7, 212–13,
301–2, 348–9, 366, 375, 384–9, 399, 621,
655, 666, 670–6
bias 366, 375, 399, 666
Infrastructure Conditions of Contract (ICC)
88–9, 90–1, 600
see also Institution of Civil Engineers
generally 90–1, 600
initiating the adjudication
see also appointment of adjudicator; notice
of adjudication
generally 10, 144–72, 615–17
overview 144–5, 146–7
scope of the dispute 144–52, 347–9
injunctions
see also mandatory…
definition 278, 283, 329–30, 539
generally 249, 277–8, 364, 539, 636–7,
650–1
jurisdiction issues 321, 329–31, 364
successful injunctions 330
unsuccessful injunctions 330–1
inquisitorial proceedings, generally 196–7

insolvency
   see also administration; administrative receivership; bankruptcy; company voluntary arrangements; individual voluntary arrangements; liquidation; stay of execution; winding-up petitions
   against insolvent parties 30–2, 39, 42, 122, 233, 286–303, 420–1
   on behalf of insolvent parties 30–2, 39, 42, 122, 284, 286–303, 420–1
   deciding to adjudicate 14, 30–9, 42
   definition 30–2, 286–7
   enforcement of decisions 32–3, 39, 122, 233, 278–80, 285–303, 420–1, 434–40, 520, 638–44
   evidence 31–2, 292–5
   insurance issues 30–1, 226, 297–8, 438–9
   overview 11, 285–6
   Scotland 420–1
   self-executing insolvency set-offs 285–7
   timescales 286–7
   triggers 30–2
Insolvency Act 1986 30–2, 35–9, 122, 286–303, 421
Insolvency (Northern Ireland) Order 1989 434
insolvency proceedings pending or not included, stay of execution 293–5, 639
Insolvency Rules 32–3, 286–303
Institution of Chemical Engineers (IChemE) 573
   see also IChemE...
Institution of Civil Engineers (ICE) 28, 88–9, 90–1, 311, 437, 444, 562–9, 574, 600
   see also Infrastructure Conditions of Contract
   Arbitration Procedure 2012 fast-track arbitration 28
   generally 90–1, 437, 444, 562–9, 574, 600
Institution of Engineering and Technology (IET) 574
Institution of Mechanical Engineers 574
insurance issues
   ATE 272, 635
   decisions 226, 626
   insolvency 30–1, 226, 297–8, 438–9
intention to occupy, residential occupiers excluded agreements 63–6, 525–6, 591

interest on moneys
   see also costs; money
   costs 272–3, 430–1, 635–6
   disadvantages of construction adjudications 23
   powers of adjudicators 208–9, 233, 235–9, 622
Interim Applications 106, 134–5
interim certificates, set-offs 242, 244, 629
interim payment disputes
   definition 224–6
   evidence 105–8, 606–7
   statistics 24
intimidation problems, the adjudication 188, 190–1, 213
Ireland
   2013 Act 461–72
   adjudications 461–72, 579–83
   appointment of adjudicator 465–7
   background 443, 461–72, 579–83
   case law shortfalls 472
   Code of Practice 461–72
   commencement requirements 462–4
   Commercial Division of the High Court 471–2
   conclusions 471–2
   costs 469–72
   decisions 469–72
   economic recession from 2007 461, 472
   enforcement of decisions 470–2
   historical background 443, 461–2
   legislation 461–72, 579–83
   notice of adjudication 464–6
   overview 461–2
   Panel of Adjudicators 465–7
   powers/duties of the adjudicator 467–8
   procedures 462–72
   processes 464–72
   referring parties 464–72
   timescales 465–72
irrecoverable costs 22–3, 138, 142, 195, 206, 227–38, 304, 315–18, 419–20, 433–40, 457–60, 495–500, 516–20, 647
Isle of Man 443
issue-based ad hoc jurisdiction 82
issues/proportionate-based assessments of costs, TCC 267–76
IVAs see individual voluntary arrangements

JCT 4, 27, 64, 77, 89–90, 121–2, 131–6, 148, 175–6, 276, 345–6, 358–9, 390, 403, 562–9, 597–600
  DOM 1 4
  DOM 2 148, 390
  form of contract 1998 77, 88–90, 121, 175–6, 403, 562–9
  generally 89–90, 131–2, 175, 276, 345–6, 403, 562–9, 597–600
  form of contract 2005 121–2
  suite of contracts 2011 27, 131–6
joinder provisions 23, 87–8, 91
judgment in default, TCC 262–3, 266, 633
judgments 262–84, 304–18, 434–40, 539–41
  see also case law; decisions; litigation; Technology and Construction Court
  information sources 8
  set aside judgments 262–3, 266, 518–20, 633
Judgments Enforcement (Northern Ireland) Order 1981 (the 1981 Order) 434–40
Judicature Amendment Act 1972, New Zealand 499–500
Judicature (Northern Ireland) Act 1978 430–40
judicial precedent
  see also case law; *individual cases*
  generally 4, 7–8
judicial reviews
  Australia 458–60
  New Zealand 499–500
  Scotland 416–17, 541
  Singapore 517–20
jurisdiction
  see also challenges…; legal…; powers…; scope of the dispute
  ad hoc jurisdiction 338, 652
  adjudicators 12, 32–3, 80–2, 108–15, 145–6, 151–2, 182, 183–4, 187–8, 201–13, 238–48, 250–2, 257–60, 265, 284, 301–2, 319–61, 415–26, 499–500, 648–63
  approbation and reprobation 335–8, 421–2, 652
  awareness needs 319–20, 364
  checklists 360–1

  consent before objection 335, 652
  decision-based jurisdiction challenges 319–20, 349–61, 656–63
  definitions 145–6, 319–20, 538
  determination by the adjudicator 320–1, 324–7, 648–9
  determination from another adjudicator 326–7, 364
  determination from the court 320–3, 364, 648
  generally 319–61, 538, 648–63
  injunctions 321, 329–31, 364
  losing the right to challenge the adjudicator's jurisdiction 319, 331–8, 421–2, 651–3
  options 319, 320–31, 648–51
  overview 319–20
  process jurisdiction challenges 319–20, 342–9, 364–5, 653–6
  reservations 81–2, 320–1, 327–8, 333–8, 364–6, 649–52
  threshold jurisdiction challenges 319–20, 338–42, 364, 653
  timescales 319–20, 338–61
  waivers 331–8, 365
  withdrawals 321, 328–9, 364–5, 650

'kitchen sink' final account adjudications 138

the land, construction operations definition 55, 57–8, 436–7, 524–5
large disputes
  adjudication strategy 137–8, 150, 180–1, 379, 382–4, 614
  disadvantages of construction adjudications 22, 137–8, 150, 379, 382–4, 422–3, 614, 669–70
  fairness 379, 382–4, 422–3, 669–70
Late Payment of Commercial Debts (Interest) Act 1998 11, 129–30, 208–9, 233, 235–9, 317, 430–1, 439–40
  conflicts 236–7
  definition 235–6
  generally 233, 235–7, 317, 439–40
late reservations 333–4, 651–2
law reports, generally 8
lawyers
  see also barristers; solicitors; team…

generally 15–17, 25–6, 40–2, 156–8, 173, 188–9, 195–6, 261, 263–4, 571–7
legal advice privilege issues 41, 173, 188–9, 195–6
legal advice privilege issues
  definition 188, 195–6
  generally 41, 173, 188–9, 195–6
legal jurisdictions
  see also case law; courts; international ...; judicial precedent; jurisdiction ...; legislation; procedures; United Kingdom ...
  generally 3–4, 12, 145–6, 151–2, 182, 183–4, 187–8, 201–13, 238–48, 250–2, 257–60, 265, 284, 301–2, 319–61, 400, 499–500, 538, 648–63
legislation
  see also case ...; Housing Grants Construction ...; *individual Acts of Parliament*; international ...; legal jurisdictions; primary ...; Scheme ...; secondary ...; statutory ...; United Kingdom ...
  generally 3–6, 406–7, 427–9, 447–9, 473–4, 476–7, 487–9, 501–2, 523–9, 530–7, 578–83
  historical background 4–6, 406, 427–8, 443–4
  UK and international statutory regimes' comparisons 578–83
letters
  ad hoc adjudications 80–1
  claims 98–100, 104–8, 147–8, 177–80, 605–6
  dispute definition 98–100, 104–8, 605–6
  evidenced in writing 71–2
  notice of adjudication 147–8
letters of intent, written contracts 73–4, 595
liabilities, fees 229–33, 304
lien on decisions 232, 350–61, 656
Limitation Act 1980 313–14
limitation periods
  final determination 304, 312–14, 646–7
  statutory limitations 122, 313–14
liquidated damages 29, 118, 242–3, 245–6, 629–30
  see also damages
liquidation 29, 32–9, 107, 294–5, 586, 638–9

  see also compulsory ...; creditors' voluntary ...; insolvency; members' voluntary ...
  definition 32–6
  generally 32–9, 107, 294–5, 638–9
  types 33–6
litigation
  see also case ...; courts; final determination; Technology and Construction Court
  costs 19, 22–3, 28, 40–1, 142–3, 261, 264, 266–76, 443, 633–7
  definition 215–16, 304
  generally 215–16, 304–18, 443, 472
  historical background 4–5
  long timescales 4, 13–14, 18, 21
  privilege 188–9, 195, 196–7
  set-offs 243, 248, 631
  temporary finality aspects of adjudicator decisions 224–6
  timescales 304
Local Democracy, Economic Development and Construction Act 2009 (Commencement No. 2) (Scotland) Order 2011 407
Local Democracy, Economic Development and Construction Act 2009 (LDEDC) 5–6, 44, 275, 428, 523–9, 538
  see also ... Housing Grants Construction and Regeneration Act 1996
Lord Ordinary 412
losing the right to challenge the adjudicator's jurisdiction 319, 331–8, 421–2, 651–3
loss assessments, deciding to adjudicate 14–17, 42

machinery/equipment, structures 56–7
Malaysia
  adjudications 473–86, 579–83
  administration of the adjudication 481–2
  appointment of adjudicator 479–80
  background 443, 473–86, 579–83
  challenges to decisions 482–6
  commencement requirements 474–8
  conclusions 485–6
  Construction Industry Payment And Adjudication Act 2012 (the 2012 Act) 473–86

Malaysia (*Continued*)
  costs 482–6
  decisions 474–5, 482–6
  direct payments from principal 485–6
  enforcement of decisions 484–6
  government construction contracts 477–8
  historical background 443, 473–4
  Kuala Lumpur Regional Centre for Arbitration (KLRCA) 473–86
  legislation 473–86, 579–83
  Malaysia Regulations 2014 473–86
  natural justice 482–6
  overview 473–4
  payment-claim process step 479–80
  powers/duties of the adjudicator 480–1
  procedures 473–86
  processes 474–81
  retrospective effect of the 2012 Act 478
  submissions 480–1
  suspension/reduction in the work pace 484–5
  timescales 474–86
mandatory injunctions 650–1
  definition 277, 539
  generally 249, 277–8, 539, 636–7, 650–1
manifest injustice, stay of execution 299, 641
manufacture, delivery, installation operations, excluded operations 59, 62, 525, 590–1
materiality thresholds, natural justice 363–4, 416–17, 664
mediation 13–14, 16, 24–7, 120–1, 300, 369–70, 472, 482, 508–20
  see also non-binding voluntary dispute resolution forums
meetings
  see also communications; minutes
  the adjudication 10–11, 178–80, 186–8, 212–13, 217, 376
  benefits 187
  bias 376, 667
  generally 10–11, 178–80, 186–8, 376
  settlements 187
members' voluntary liquidation (MVL) 33, 35–6, 294–5
minutes of meetings, evidenced in writing 70, 178–80
misrepresentation 116, 157–8
Misrepresentation Act 1967 116

money judgments, compliance failures 282–4
multiple adjudications
  adjudication strategy 125–6, 161, 173–4, 188–9, 247–8, 299, 321–61, 630
  set-offs 243, 247–8, 630
multiple contracts
  preconditions and restrictions 117–19, 338–42, 612–13
  Scheme adjudications 119, 612–13
multiple disputes
  connected issues 109–15, 149, 608–11
  generally 97–8, 108–15, 125–6, 149, 151–2, 161, 230–1, 338–42, 608–11
  preconditions and restrictions 97–8, 108–15, 149, 151–2, 338–42, 608–11
  Scheme adjudications 111–15, 119, 609
  substantially the same dispute 110–15, 125–6, 151, 210–13, 338–42, 439–40, 609–11

named adjudicators in the contract 161–3
Nationwide Academy of Dispute Resolution (NADR) 159, 160, 574
natural justice
  see also bias; challenges…; fairness
  Australia 459–60
  awareness needs 364
  breaches 362–99
  checklist 399
  definition 12, 145–6, 362–3, 399, 539
  generally 12, 145–6, 150, 155, 179, 183–4, 188, 201–2, 204–7, 218–19, 228, 232–3, 250–2, 265, 284, 301–2, 352–61, 362–99, 400, 415–26, 459–60, 539, 663–76
  Malaysia 482–6
  materiality thresholds 363–4, 416–17, 664
  New Zealand 492–3
  Northern Ireland 439–40
  options when points arise 364–6, 664
  overview 12, 145–6, 362–3, 663–4
  'reserving the position' protests 364–6
  Scotland 365–6, 396, 415–26
  Singapore 512–20
  waivers 365
natural persons
  appointment of adjudicator 163, 617
  generally 163, 400, 403–5, 425–6, 617
NEC2 procedures 88–9, 92–3, 346, 601

NEC3 procedures 83, 88–9, 92–3, 305, 346, 562–9, 574, 601
negligence claims
see also non-contractual claims
common law 23, 97, 110, 116
negligent misstatement 110–11, 116–17
nemo judex in causa sua maxim 362, 399
see also natural justice
neutral citations, generally 8, 584
New South Wales (NSW) 446–60, 501–2, 579–83
see also Australia
New Zealand
adjudications 448, 487–500, 579–83
appointment of adjudicator 490–3
background 443, 448, 487–500, 579–83
challenges to decisions 499–500
commencement requirements 488–90
Construction Contracts Act 2002 (the 2002 Act) 487–500
Construction Contracts Amendment Bill 500
Construction Contracts Regulations 2003 494–5
costs 493–500
decisions 487–8, 493–500
determination 493–6
enforcement of decisions 487–8, 496–500
historical background 443, 487–8
Judicature Amendment Act 1972 499–500
judicial reviews 499–500
legislation 487–500, 579–83
natural justice 492–3
overview 487–8
procedures 487–500
processes 490–500
proposed amendments 500
rights of a non-respondent owner 496
timescales 497–500
Wages Protection and Contractors' Lien Act 1939 487–8
NHS developments, exclusion orders 63–6
'no dispute' challenges 347–8, 382, 436–40
nominating bodies 8, 10–11, 20–1, 22, 24, 87–8, 144–5, 152–8, 165–72, 187–8, 189–90, 345–6, 371–3, 465–6, 490–1, 531–2, 538, 570–7, 616
see also adjudicating...

non-binding voluntary dispute resolution forums 13–14, 24–9, 42, 76–7
see also early neutral evaluations; mediation
non-contractual claims 23, 43–4, 97–8, 116–17
see also negligence...
disadvantages of construction adjudications 23
Northern Ireland
see also individual topics; United Kingdom...
abuse of process 439–40
adjudications 428–40
application hearings 432–3
application for summary judgment 431–2
background 3–4, 6–7, 311, 427–40
case law statistics 6–7
challenges to decisions 435–40
commercial actions 430–40
costs 433–40
decisions 428–40
declaratory relief remedy 435
enforcement of decisions 428–40
enforcement of judgments 434–5
England and Wales similarities 427–8
judicial consideration 435–40
natural justice 439–40
overview 427–9
procedures 428–40
taxation of costs 433
writ of summons 430–1
Northern Ireland Act 1998 427
Northern Ireland Assembly 427
Northern Ireland Parliament 427
Northern Ireland (Temporary Provisions) Act 1972 427
Northern Territory (NT) 447–60
see also Australia
notice of adjudication
see also commencement; initiating the adjudication; scope...
checklists 151–2
creep between crystallisation and referral 108, 136–7, 140, 148–9, 183–4, 343–9, 607–8
crystallisation generally 148–9, 343–9

notice of adjudication (*Continued*)
  definition 10, 110, 123–4, 144–5, 146–7, 530–1, 539, 542–5
  drafting considerations 123–5, 146–52, 343–9
  dropped heads of claim 188, 194–5, 620
  generally 10, 85–8, 102–3, 108, 110, 113, 121, 123–5, 136–7, 144–5, 146–52, 174–6, 177–80, 188, 194–5, 219, 343–9, 391–2, 416–26, 464–6, 490–3, 508–12, 528, 531–7, 539, 542–5, 615–16
  letters 147–8
  referring party checklist 151
  responding party checklist 151–2
  timescales 123–5, 146–7, 149–52, 174–6, 201, 391–2
  withdrawals 188, 195, 620
notification of intention to refer the dispute 10, 80–1, 85–8
  see also notice of adjudication
  definition 10
novation agreements, ancillary agreements 52–4, 110–11, 308–12
nuclear processing, excluded operations 58, 61–2, 339–42, 524–5

oath, evidence not under oath 23, 188
obiter dicta remarks 73, 114, 170–2, 194–5, 298, 315, 336–7
objections to the appointment of adjudicator 154–5, 163–4, 171–2, 205–6, 617
objects or installations, construction operations definition 55, 58, 524–5
offer and acceptance, construction contracts 45–8
official receivers 34–7, 38–9, 283
  see also bankruptcy; liquidation
oil and gas, excluded operations 58–60, 76, 339–42, 524–5
'omissions defence' 301–2
on behalf of insolvent parties 30–2, 39, 42, 122, 286–303, 420–1
  see also insolvency; referring parties
on-demand bonds 255
onus of proof, final determination 312–18, 646–7
oral contracts 66–74, 77–9, 340–2, 593–5
  see also construction contracts

oral submissions 187–8, 255–6
orally-varied contracts 66–74, 594–5
  generally 66–74, 594–5
  scenarios 72–3, 594–5
order of sale, enforcement methods 282, 434–40
Orders in Councils 427
orders of the court 280–4, 637
other party's willingness/ability to pay
  see also insolvency
  adjudication strategy 141–3, 151–2, 614
'otherwise than in writing' provisions
  see also evidenced in writing
  written contracts 69–74, 592
Outer House of the Court of Sessions 354
overview of the book 3–12

parallel correspondence 186
Part 7 claims 29, 256–60, 322–3, 539
  see also Civil Procedure Rules
Part 8 claims 29, 133, 256–60, 284, 307–12, 322–3, 337–8, 407, 539
  see also Civil Procedure Rules
  advantages/disadvantages 29, 284
  definition 29, 539
  timescales 29
Part 23 claims 329–31
Part 24 claims 253–60, 277–8
particulars of claim in litigation 174
parties' costs 233–9, 568–9, 627
  see also costs; referring parties; responders
pay less notices
  generally 129–36, 182–4, 192–4, 242–3, 244–5, 629
  set-offs 242–3, 244–5, 629
'pay now, argue later' rubric 251–2
payees
  see also referring parties
  definition 4
  generally 18–19, 24, 128–43, 296–303, 614
  historical background 4–5
  'smash and grab' adjudications 129–36, 614
payers 4–5, 18–19, 128–43, 296–303, 614
  see also responders
  definition 4
  generally 18–19, 128–43, 296–303, 614
  historical background 4–5
  'smash and grab' adjudications 129–36, 614

payment certificates as evidence 105–8, 114–15, 192–3, 606–7
payment notices, reverse ambush 140–1
payments
   see also interim ...
   compliance with time for payment 280–4, 456–60, 469–72, 482–6, 637
   evidence 105–8, 606–7
   extending the time for payment 281–4, 469–72, 482–6, 637
   lien on decisions 232, 350–61, 656
   other party's willingness/ability to pay 141–3, 151–2, 614
   Part II of the Schemes - Payment 84, 406–7, 530–7
   regimes 130–6
pecuniary claims 29, 116–17, 118, 127–43, 148–52, 209, 218–26, 227–48, 355–61, 456–60, 463–72, 533–7, 622
   see also damages; money; payments
   adjudication strategy 127–43
PFI (private finance initiative) projects, exclusion orders 63–6
pharmaceuticals, excluded operations 58, 61–2, 339–42, 524–5
pipework, excluded operations 60–2, 524–5
planning, exclusion orders 63–6
plant and machinery, excluded operations 60–2, 524–5
points of principle, case law 7–8, 29, 353
post decisions
   see also decisions
   cost apportionments 11, 22–3, 28, 210–13, 217–18, 227–33, 237–9, 533–7, 626–7
   costs 227–33, 626–7
   error corrections 227, 239–41, 350–1, 360–1, 527, 567–8, 627–8
   fees 227–33, 626–7
   generally 11–12, 227–48, 320–61, 626–31
   Late Payment of Commercial Debts (Interest) Act 1998 11, 129–30, 208–9, 233, 235–9
   overview 11, 227–8
   parties' costs 233–9, 568–9, 627
   revised decisions 227–8, 239–41, 627–8
   set-offs 227–8, 236–7, 241–8, 628–31
   severability 286, 301–3, 331–8, 643–4

post-appointment communications with one party, bias 366, 373, 399, 666
post-appointment pre-referral issues, appointment of adjudicator 167–8
power generation, excluded operations 58, 61–2, 339–42, 524–5
powers of adjudicators
   see also decisions; jurisdiction ...; natural justice
   assistance-seeking powers 205–6, 219, 395, 424–5, 674
   damages 209, 622
   generally 10–11, 173–4, 184–200, 201–13, 227–48, 276–7, 319–61, 467–8, 512–20, 531–7, 565–6, 620–2
   immunity 209–10, 622
   interest on moneys 208–9, 233, 235–9, 622
   pre-emptory orders 249, 276–7, 636
   requests/direction-making powers 181, 204–5, 212–13, 621
   scope of the dispute 207–8, 319–61, 408–11, 416–26, 621–2, 648–63
   taking the initiative 202–4, 621
Pre-Action Protocol for Commercial Actions, Northern Ireland 430–1
Pre-Action Protocol for Construction and Engineering Disputes (Protocol) 256–60
pre-appointment communications with one party, bias 366, 371–3, 399, 666
pre-emptory orders 249, 276–7, 636
preconditions and restrictions
   see also claims; disputes; evidence ...; referring parties; statutory adjudications
   'at any time' construction adjudications 119–22, 613
   claim abandoned 107, 607
   conclusivity clauses 121–2, 613
   correctly served documents 107, 152–3, 391–2, 607, 620
   creep between crystallisation and referral 108, 136–7, 140, 148–9, 177–80, 183–4, 341–2, 607–8
   dispute settlement/compromised scenario 108, 187–8, 199, 338–42, 607
   exchanges of correspondence 98–100, 104–8, 148–50, 152–3, 177–86, 605–6
   generally 10, 97–122, 148–9, 151–3, 338–42, 360–1, 602–13

preconditions and restrictions (*Continued*)
  multiple contracts 117–19, 338–42, 612–13
  multiple disputes 97–8, 108–15, 149, 151–2, 338–42, 608–11
  overview 10, 97–8
  scenarios 104–8, 605–8
  statutory limitations 122
  timescales 102–4, 121–2, 605
  'under' the contract disputes 115–17, 151, 342, 611–13
  without prejudice material 106, 139, 172, 197–8, 336–7, 607, 614, 667
  wrong parties 107, 607
preliminary views, natural justice 366, 377–8, 397–9, 667, 675
preparation needs, adjudication strategy 123–6
prices
  see also money
  essential terms of the contract 45–8, 68–74, 127–8, 178–80
primary legislation
  see also Housing Grants Construction and Regeneration Act 1996...; legislation; United Kingdom...
  generally 3–8, 428
privacy advantages of construction adjudications 19–20, 90, 200
  see also confidentiality issues
privilege
  see also disclosure of documents; legal...; litigation...; without prejudice...
  definition 188–9, 195
  generally 41, 106, 139, 172, 173, 188–9, 195–8, 584, 607, 614
process jurisdiction challenges 319–20, 342–9, 364–5, 653–6
  see also adjudication...; commencement...; initiating...; jurisdiction issues
processes 3–8, 9–10, 27–8, 123–43, 144–72, 173–213, 453–60, 464–72, 474–81, 503–7, 508–20, 617–22
  see also adjudication; commencement; notice of adjudication; procedures
project teams
  see also team...
  generally 41–2

prolongation disputes 19, 24, 41, 115–17, 127–8, 218–26, 245–6, 354–61, 658–9
  statistics 24
proportionate-based assessments of costs, TCC 267–76
Protocol *see* Pre-Action Protocol for Construction and Engineering Disputes
prudent approaches, settlements 261

quality of submissions/evidence disadvantages of construction adjudications 21
quantification issues, set-offs 242, 246, 630
quantity surveyors 40, 49–50, 156–60, 523–9, 571–7
  see also consultants
quasi-mediators, bias 366, 376, 667

reasons for the decision 214, 217–18, 350–61, 398–9, 623, 656–63, 675–6
reasons given, Scheme adjudications 88
receipt of decisions 218–19, 227–48, 349–61, 623
reckoning of time, the adjudication 189, 201, 528–9
recovery
  adjudication costs recovery 315–18, 647
  historical background 4–5
  irrecoverable costs 22–3, 138, 142, 195, 206, 227–39, 304, 315–18, 419–20, 433–40, 457–60, 495–500, 516–20, 647
rectification orders 116
redress/remedy 142–52, 177–213, 215–26, 227–48, 257–84, 313–18, 343–9, 434–40, 543–60
  see also decisions; notice of adjudication; pecuniary...
referral notice 10, 90–6, 108, 110–11, 113, 121, 123–5, 136–7, 148–9, 151–3, 173–213, 219–26, 342–9, 350–1, 418–26, 528, 532–7, 539, 545–8, 564, 617–22, 655
  adjudicator actions 180–1
  creep between crystallisation and referral 108, 148–9, 177–80, 183–4
  definition 10, 110–11, 123–4, 173–5, 532–3, 539, 545–8
  drafting considerations 123–5, 148, 173–4, 177–80, 343–9, 532–3

duties of adjudicators 180–1
  generally 10, 173–213, 219–26, 342–9, 532–7, 539, 545–8, 564, 617–22, 655
  practical considerations and strategy 177–80
  supporting documents 178–80, 189, 200–1, 210–13
  timescales 10, 123–5, 151–3, 173–6, 180–1, 201, 205, 212–13, 219–22, 342, 347–9, 350–1, 391–2, 418–26, 617–18, 655
  witness evidence 179–80, 188, 196–7
referring parties
  see also adjudication strategy; appointment of adjudicator; costs; initiating the adjudication; notice of adjudication; on behalf of insolvent parties; payees; preconditions...; referral notice; replies; sur-rejoinders
  appointment of adjudicator checklist 171, 360–1
  creep between crystallisation and referral 108, 136–7, 140, 148–9, 177–80, 183–4, 341–2, 607–8
  deploying arguments 139–41, 148–52, 343–9
  fairness 379–80
  information consideration/dissemination duties of adjudicators 206–7, 212–13, 301–2, 348–9, 366, 375, 384–9, 399, 621, 655, 666, 670–6
  insolvency issues 14, 30–9, 42, 420–1
  intimidation problems 188, 190–1, 213
  pre-adjudication conduct 379–80, 667
  receipt of the decision 218–19, 227–48, 349–61, 623
  statistics 24
  withdrawals 188, 195, 620
regimes, statutory adjudications 5–6
registering decisions, Scotland 417
rejoinders 10–11, 173–4, 184–6, 539
  see also responders
  definition 10, 173, 184–5, 539
  generally 10–11, 173–4, 184–6, 539
  practical considerations and strategy 184–6
relationship challenges, deciding to adjudicate 17, 18
'relief from sanctions' 266

removal of procedural uncertainties, courts 142–3
removals, adjudicators 145, 170–2
replies 10–11, 21–2, 98–9, 124–5, 139–41, 151–2, 173–4, 184–6, 480, 539
  see also referring parties
  definition 10, 173, 184–5, 539
  practical considerations and strategy 184–6
representation, TCC 263–4
requests/direction-making powers, powers of adjudicators 181, 204–5, 212–13, 621
rescinded contracts 46–8
reservations
  abandonment 334–5, 651
  ad hoc jurisdiction 81–2
  jurisdiction 81–2, 320–1, 327–8, 333–8, 364, 649–52
  late reservations 333–4, 651–2
  losing the right to challenge the adjudicator's jurisdiction 333–5, 651–2
  'reserving the position' protests 82, 327–8, 364–6, 649–50
residential occupiers, excluded agreements 63–6, 80, 339–42, 403, 500, 525–6, 591
resignations of adjudicators 90, 111–12, 179, 180–1, 205, 210–13, 216, 228–31, 321–61, 364–5, 367–9, 408–11, 533–7, 564–5
resources 11, 15–17, 42
  see also costs...; fees; time...
  deciding to adjudicate 17
responders
  see also against insolvent parties; appointment of adjudicator; costs; defendants; payers; rejoinders; responses
  ambush perceptions 23, 28, 104, 124–6, 140–1, 341–2, 379, 380–2, 668–9
  appointment of adjudicator checklist 171–2, 360–1
  defences 10–12, 139–43, 144–5, 148–52, 173–4, 181–213, 259–84, 320–61, 362–99, 400–5, 618–22, 676–7
  disadvantages 23, 28, 104, 124–6, 380–2, 438–40
  documents received late/not at all 391–2, 673

responders (*Continued*)
  generally 10–11, 21–2, 23, 30–9, 100–22, 124–43, 144–72, 177–8, 218–19, 223–6, 227–48, 260–84, 304–18, 360–1, 438–40
  information consideration/dissemination duties of adjudicators 206–7, 212–13, 301–2, 348–9, 366, 375, 384–9, 399, 621, 655, 666, 670–6
  insolvency issues 14, 30–9, 42, 233, 420–1
  intimidation problems 188, 190–1, 213
  notice of adjudication checklists 151–2
  receipt of the decision 218–19, 227–48, 349–61, 623
  secured assets 141–2, 614
  silence 101–3, 148–9, 261, 262–3, 268
responses
  see also defences; rejoinders
  adjudicator duties 183–4
  definition 10–11, 100–8, 173–4, 181–3, 539, 549–51
  drafting considerations 182–4
  generally 10–11, 100–22, 139–43, 173–4, 181–4, 260–84, 439–40, 539, 549–51, 604, 618–22
  nature 101–2, 181–4, 260–1, 604
  practical considerations and strategy 182–4
  scope of the defence 183–4
  supporting documents 183–4, 189, 200–1, 210–13
  TCC 260–84
  timescales 10, 23, 28, 102–4, 124–5, 145, 173–4, 181–4, 212–13, 380–2, 391–2, 439–40
  witness evidence 183–4, 188, 196–7
restitution (unjust enrichment) remedy 116, 313–14
reverse ambush, adjudication strategy 140–1
revised decisions 227–8, 239–41, 627–8
revocation issues, defective appointments 145, 170–2, 230–1, 342–9, 408–11, 565, 617
RIBA *see* Royal Institute of British Architects
RICS *see* Royal Institution of Chartered Surveyors
right to enjoy possessions (HRA Article 1) 400, 405, 422–3, 425–6
right to a fair trial (HRA Article 6) 400, 404–5, 422–3
'rough justice' aspects, dispute resolution 250

Royal Incorporation of Architects in Scotland (RIAS) 576
Royal Institute of British Architects (RIBA) 88, 370, 372, 576
Royal Institution of Chartered Surveyors (RICS) 88, 156–7, 159–60, 166–7, 190–1, 333, 575
Rule 4.90, Insolvency Rules 32–3, 287–303
rules *see* procedures
Rules of the Court of Judicature (Northern Ireland) 1980 (RCJ (NI) 1980) 430–40

save-the-best-until-last approaches, adjudication strategy 139–40
scaffolding, excluded operations 60–2, 524–5
Scheme adjudications
  adjudicating nominating bodies 87–8, 152–8
  applicability 84–6, 142–3, 147–52, 596–7
  appointment of adjudicator 152–72, 175–6, 531–7, 615–17
  benefits 86–7
  certainty benefits 86–7
  compliance failures 84–6, 596–7
  conclusivity clauses 121–2, 613
  confidentiality issues 189, 200, 569
  definitions 6–7, 9–10, 83–5, 530–7
  familiarity advantages 86–7
  generally 83–6, 96, 111–15, 119–20, 135, 144–5, 147–53, 174–213, 216–26, 313–14, 376–7, 406–26, 444–5, 527–9, 530–7, 596–7, 609, 612–13, 615–17, 618–22, 623–6
  joinder provisions 87
  multiple contracts 119, 612–13
  multiple disputes 111–15, 119, 609
  nominating bodies 87–8
  powers/duties of adjudicators 201–13
  procedures 9–10, 83–8, 96, 111–15, 147–52, 174–213, 411–26
  reasons given 88
  statistics 86
  uncontroversial aspects 86–7
  variants 87–8
Scheme for Construction Contracts (England and Wales) Regulations 1998 (Amendment) (England) Regulations 2011 (the 2011 Scheme)

see also Part...; procedures
commencement date (1 October 2011) 84–5, 96, 530
definitions 6-7, 84-5, 410-11, 530-7
generally 6-7, 83-9, 96, 142, 147-52, 165-72, 175-6, 210-13, 407-26, 527-9, 530-7
historical background 6-7, 84-5
paragraph 7(1) 175-176
paragraph 7(2) 175-176
paragraph 7(3) 175-176
paragraph 9 210-211
paragraph 11(1) 170
paragraph 11(2) 170
paragraph 19 219-222
paragraph 22A 239-240,
paragraph 23 224-225
paragraph 25 228
Scheme for Construction Contracts (England and Wales) Regulations 1998 (the 1998 Scheme)
see also Part...; procedures
commencement date (1 May 1998) 6, 84, 530
definitions 6-7, 84-5, 530-7
generally 10, 54, 76, 78, 83-96, 142, 147-72, 176, 211-13, 220-6, 228-48, 275, 276-7, 344-61, 406-26, 428-40, 527-9, 530-7, 562-9, 615-17, 623-31
paragraph 1(1) 54, 147, 209
paragraph 1(2) 54, 147
paragraph 1(3) 147, 349
paragraph 2 153-155
paragraph 3 153-155
paragraph 4 163, 367
paragraph 5 153-155
paragraph 6 153-155
paragraph 7(1) 149, 152-153, 175-176
paragraph 7(2) 152-153, 175-176
paragraph 7(3) 152-153, 175-176
paragraph 8(1) 111
paragraph 8(2) 119
paragraph 8(3) 111, 119
paragraph 8(4) 111, 119, 230
paragraph 9 111-112, 115, 210-212, 230, 231, 342, 353
paragraph 10 164

paragraph 11(1) 170, 230, 439
paragraph 11(2) 168, 230
paragraph 12(a) 202
paragraph 12(b) 232
paragraph 13 187, 202-204, 205-206, 384, 395
paragraph 14 204-205
paragraph 15 198, 204-205
paragraph 16(1) 376
paragraph 16(2) 187
paragraph 17 206-207
paragraph 18 200
paragraph 19 219-222
paragraph 20(a) 111, 122, 135, 184, 207-208, 254
paragraph 20(b) 207-208
paragraph 20(c) 208-209
paragraph 21 225
paragraph 22 217
paragraph 23(1) 224-225, 276-277, 353
paragraph 23(2) 224-225
paragraph 24 276-277
paragraph 25 228-229
paragraph 26 209-210
historical background 6-7, 84-5, 406-7
Scheme for Construction Contracts in Northern Ireland (Amendment) Regulations (Northern Ireland) 2012 428-40
Scheme for Construction Contracts (Scotland) Amendments Regulations 2011 (the 2011 Scottish Scheme) 407-26
paragraph 25(2) 411
Scheme for Construction Contracts (Scotland) Regulations 1998 (the 1998 Scottish Scheme) 406-26
paragraph 9(4) 408-409
paragraph 11(1) 409
paragraph 20 409-410
paragraph 24 410, 417-418
paragraph 25 410
scope of the dispute
see also jurisdiction issues
initiating the adjudication 144-52, 347-9
powers/duties of adjudicators 207-8, 212-13, 217-26, 319-61, 408-11, 416-26, 621-2, 648-63

scope of what the adjudicator can decide 207–8, 212–13, 217–26, 319–61, 408–11, 416–26, 621–2, 648–63
scope of the work, essential terms of the contract 45–8, 63, 68–74, 78, 115–17, 178–80, 338–42, 356–61
Scotland
  see also individual topics; United Kingdom...
  abuse of process 423–4
  adjudications 407–28, 488
  approbation and reprobation 421–2
  background 3–4, 280, 284, 289, 400, 405, 406–26, 540–1
  Books of Council and Session 417, 540
  case law statistics 6–7
  challenges to decisions 415–26
  civil/Roman law 407
  commercial actions 411–26, 540
  costs 419–26
  counterclaims 414, 420–1
  decisions 415–26
  divergence issues 418–26
  enforcement of decisions 280, 284, 289, 400, 405, 407–26, 637
  England and Wales contrasts 400, 404–5, 406–26, 677
  glossary 540–1
  HRA 400, 405, 408, 422–3, 425–6
  insolvency 420–1
  judicial reviews 416–17, 541
  natural justice 365–6, 396, 415–26
  overview 406–7
  procedures 407–26
  registering decisions 417
  timescales 411–26
Scotland Act 1998 406
Scott Schedules, submissions 186
Scottish Minister 65
Scottish Parliament 406, 526
secondary legislation
  see also legislation; Scheme for Construction Contracts...; United Kingdom...
  generally 4, 6–8, 428
Secretary of State 63, 64–6, 427, 523–9, 530–7
Secretary of State for Northern Ireland 427

secured assets, adjudication strategy 141–2, 614
self-executing insolvency set-offs 285–7
Senior Courts Act 1981 277, 283, 318
service of documents
  the adjudication 189, 200–1, 343, 348–9, 391–2, 528–9, 620, 655–6
  generally 31–2, 107, 152–3, 189, 200–1, 343, 348–9, 391–2, 528–9, 607, 620, 655–6
  correctly served documents 107, 152–3, 189, 200–1, 343, 348–9, 391–2, 528–9, 607, 620, 655–6
set aside judgments 262–3, 266, 518–20, 633
  see also challenges...
set-offs
  see also cross-claims
  the adjudication 183–4, 188–9, 191–4, 227–8, 236–8, 241–8, 284, 437–8, 619–20, 628–31
  arbitration awards 243, 248, 631
  contractual set-off rights 242–4, 628–9
  definition 188–9, 191–2, 241–3
  formulation issues 242, 247, 630
  general rule and exceptions 241–3, 628
  interim/final certificates 242, 244, 629
  liquidated damages 242–3, 245–6, 629–30
  litigation on foot 243, 248, 631
  multiple adjudications 243, 247–8, 630
  pay less notices 242–3, 244–5, 629
  post decisions 227–8, 236–7, 241–8, 628–31
  quantification issues 242, 246, 630
  withholding notices 242, 244–6, 629
sets of directions, adjudicators 181, 204–5, 212–13, 529, 555–60, 621
settlements
  the adjudication 187, 189, 197–8, 199, 306
  ancillary agreements 52–4
  costs 273–4, 636
  dispute settlement/compromised scenario 108, 187, 306, 338–42, 607
  generally 189, 199, 261–2, 273–84, 304–18, 338–42, 507–8
  meetings 187
  prudent approaches 261
  TCC 261–2, 273–4, 306, 636

severability
  definition 286, 301
  generally 286, 301–3, 643–4
shareholders, insolvency 35–9, 294–5
signed decisions 216–17, 351–61, 656–7
signed statements of truth 180
silent responders 101–3, 148–9, 261, 262–3, 268
Singapore
  adjudications 501–20, 579–83
  background 443, 501–20, 579–83
  Building and Construction Industry Security of Payment Act (Cap 30B) 2004 (the 2004 Act) 501–20
  Building and Construction Industry Security of Payment Regulations 2006 (the Regulations) 502–20
  challenges to decisions 502, 512–20
  commencement requirements 502–4
  conclusions 520
  conduct of the adjudication 514–15
  contracting out 503–4
  costs 512–20
  crystallisation and dispute settlement periods 507–8
  decisions 501–2, 515–20
  determination 517–20
  enforcement of decisions 518–20
  government construction contracts 504
  historical background 443, 501–2
  judicial reviews 517–20
  legislation 501–20, 579–83
  mediation 508–20
  natural justice 512–20
  notice of adjudication 508–12
  overview 501–2
  payment regime 504–7
  procedures 501–20
  processes 503–7, 508–20
  responses 511–12
  role of the adjudicator 512–15
  timescales 501–2, 503–20
Singapore Mediation Centre (SMC) 508–20
site visits 10–11, 186–8, 212–13, 366, 375, 667
skeleton arguments, TCC 261–2
slip rule, error corrections 239–41, 567
'smash and grab' adjudications 129–36, 614

Society of Construction Arbitrators (SCA)
  100 Day Arbitration Procedure 2004 fast-track arbitration 27–8
  Construction Industry Model Arbitration Rules 1998 (CIMAR) fast-track arbitration 27–8
solicitors
  see also lawyers
  generally 40–2, 157, 263–4
  fees 16–17, 40–1, 261, 264, 269–70, 272, 635
  legal advice privilege issues 41, 173, 188–9, 195–6
  TCC 263–4
South Australia (SA) 447–60
  see also Australia
special resolutions, members' voluntary liquidation 35–6
specific performance 116
standard basis to assess costs, TCC 266–76
starting times, adjudication strategy 123–5
State Administrative Tribunal, Australia 458–60
statement of case in an arbitration 174
statistics 24, 86, 214, 238, 428, 571–7
statutory adjudications
  see also adjudication...; construction...; deciding to adjudicate; dispute resolution...; *individual Acts of Parliament*; insolvency; international...; legislation; preconditions...; United Kingdom...
  advantages 3–4, 18–21, 42, 43–4, 443–5
  checklist 74, 360–1
  definitions 5, 9–10, 18–19, 25–6, 43–4, 74, 76, 215–16, 304, 526–9, 539
  disadvantages 21–3, 42
  dispute type statistics 24
  generally 4–12, 13–42, 43–74, 76, 77–8, 83–4, 97–122, 126, 142–3, 173–213, 214–26, 304, 319–61, 443–5, 461–72, 473–86, 526–9, 530–7, 539, 578–83, 586–95, 602–13, 617–22
  historical background 4–5, 443–4
  intentions 5
  overview 3–12, 443–5
  regimes 5–6
  statistics 24, 214, 238, 428

statutory adjudications (*Continued*)
   UK and international statutory regimes' comparisons 578–83
statutory demands 29, 31–2, 249, 278–80, 637
   see also enforcement of decisions; insolvency; winding-up petitions
   definition 278–9
   service methods 31–2, 189
statutory limitations, preconditions and restrictions 122
stay of execution 11, 135–6, 286, 290–303, 402, 438–40, 520, 639–43
   see also insolvency
   conditions 301–3, 642–3
   court's discretion 290–3, 639
   definition 286, 290–2
   financial difficulties 296–8, 438–40, 519–20, 640–1
   imminent resolution of other proceedings 298–9, 641
   insolvency proceedings pending or not included 293–5, 639
   manifest injustice 299, 641
   overview 11, 286, 290–1
   partial stay orders 291–2, 300, 438–40, 642
staying adjudication proceedings, the adjudication 189, 199, 310–11
staying enforcement proceedings, arbitration agreements 274–6, 282–4, 310–12, 636
steel, excluded operations 58, 60–2, 524–5
strategy *see* adjudication strategy
structural engineers 159–60
structures, construction operations definition 55–8, 436–7, 524–5, 589–90
subcontracts, definitions 49–54
'subject to contract' letters of intent 74, 595
submissions
   see also referral notice; rejoinders; replies; responses; sur-rejoinders
   the adjudication 177–86, 204–5, 212–13, 347–9, 361
   disregarded submissions/witnesses 204–5, 374–5, 384–9, 670–2
   failures to address issues/submissions/evidence 384–9, 670–2
   oral submissions 187–8
   Scott Schedules 186

substantially the same dispute 110–15, 125–6, 151, 210–13, 338–42, 439–40, 609–11
sufficiency of reasons
   see also reasons for the decision
   natural justice 398–9, 675–6
summary comparison of adjudication rules 561–9
   see also procedures
summary enforcement procedure 252–76, 284, 285–303, 306, 308–12, 428–9, 436–40, 458–60, 540, 632–6, 638–44
   see also insolvency
summary/detailed assessments of costs, TCC 268–76
Supreme Court Act, Section 37 141
sur-rejoinders
   see also referring parties
   definition 10, 173, 539
   generally 10–11, 124–5, 151–2, 173–4, 184–6, 539
   practical considerations and strategy 184–6

taking the initiative, powers of adjudicators 202–4, 621
Tasmania 447–60
   see also Australia
taxes, costs 433–4
TCC *see* Technology and Construction Court
team-selection considerations 14, 15, 17, 40–2, 125–6, 160–1
   see also consultants; experts; lawyers; project…
   deciding to adjudicate 14, 15, 17, 40–2
TECBAR *see* Technology and Construction Court Bar Association
technical abilities, adjudicators 165–6, 250–1
Technology and Construction Court Bar Association (TECBAR) 159–60, 562–9, 577
Technology and Construction Court (TCC)
   see also enforcement of decisions; *individual cases*
   appeals 273–4
   application notice forms 257, 258–60
   assessments of costs 264, 266–76, 633–7
   bill of costs assessments 269–76, 634–5
   claim forms 257–60
   commencement of the claim 256–60, 633

cost budgets 261, 264
costs 261, 264, 266–76, 633–7
decisions 262–84
definition 35, 252–3
directions 260–1
dismissed claims 264–84
documents 257–60
effect of the court's decision 265–6, 633
evidence 255–6, 262
generally 20–1, 25, 35, 217, 249–84, 307–12, 322–3, 430–1, 631–7, 645–7
Guide 256–60, 322–3, 633
hearing bundles 261–3
judgment in default 262–3, 266, 633
key statements and court policy 249–52, 631–2
mediation services 27
powers 20–1, 35, 249–84
representation 263–4
response types 260–1
responses to the claim 260–84
roles 35, 249, 252–3
set aside judgments 262–3, 266, 633
settlements 261–2, 273–4, 306, 636
skeleton arguments 261–2
standard/indemnity bases to assess costs 266–76, 633–4
staying enforcement proceedings where there is an arbitration agreement 274–6, 282–4, 636
summary enforcement procedure 252–76, 284, 285–303, 306, 308–12, 632–6, 638–44
timescales 252–5, 258–62, 633
witness statement forms 257, 259–60
Technology and Construction Solicitors Association (TeCSA) 22, 83–4, 87–9, 93–4, 156–60, 333, 346–7, 376, 562–9, 577, 601
see also adjudicating nominating bodies
TeCSA *see* Technology and Construction Solicitors Association
telephone conferences 10–11, 173–4, 186–7
temporarily-binding
advantages/disadvantages of construction adjudications 18–19, 22, 224–6, 304–18

temporary finality aspects of decisions 224–6, 625–6
see also binding aspects of decisions
termination of contract 46–8, 117, 131–6, 356–61, 587
terms of the contract
see also construction contracts
adjudicators 171–2, 178–80, 200–1, 215–26, 232
breach of contract 116–17, 127–8, 209, 309–12, 313, 646–7
choice of terms 47
essential terms of the contract 45–8, 67–74, 85–96, 115–17, 178–80, 304–18, 338–42, 356–61, 400–5
implied terms of contracts 73, 208, 443–4, 594–5
incorporation of terms 47–8, 356–61, 587
unfair contract terms 12, 64, 145, 232, 400, 403–4
Third Parties (Rights Against Insurers) Act 1930 226
third-party advisers, adjudicators 205–6, 219, 395, 424–6, 674
third-party debt orders, enforcement methods 282, 434–40
third-party liabilities, adjudicators 209–10
threshold jurisdiction challenges 319–20, 338–42, 364, 653
see also preconditions...
timescales
see also enforcement; fast-track...
adjudication strategy 123–43, 149–52
advantages/disadvantages of construction adjudication 20–1, 23, 43–4
appointment of adjudicator 152–3, 168–9, 172, 174–5, 181
claims 102–4, 124–5, 145, 503–20, 605
compliance 280–4, 637
compliance with time for payment 280–4, 456–60, 469–72, 482–6, 637
cost apportionments 237–8
decisions 11, 13–14, 18–19, 20–1, 43–4, 85–96, 145, 212–13, 214–15, 219–26, 252–5, 264–5, 286–7, 304, 306, 312–14, 349–61, 382–4, 404–5, 418–26, 469–72, 474–86, 501–2, 535–7, 566–9, 623–4, 633

timescales (*Continued*)
  essential terms of the contract 45–8, 68–74, 115–17, 178–80
  extension requests 223–6, 281–4, 355–6, 382–4, 404–5, 422–3, 439–40, 469–72, 624–5, 637
  extensions 85–96, 214, 218–22, 223–6, 355–6, 382–4, 404–5, 422–3, 439–40, 469–72, 624–5
  fast-track arbitration 28
  final determination 304, 312–14, 646–7
  generally 3–21, 43–4, 45–8, 85–96, 102–4, 121–2, 123–43, 145–6, 149–53, 168–9, 172, 180–1, 189, 201, 203–4, 212–13, 214–15, 219–26, 264–5, 304, 312–14, 391–2, 439–40, 528–9, 530–7, 566–9, 617–22, 623–4, 633, 673
  getting-in-there-first factors 124–5
  historical background 4–5
  insolvency 286–7
  jurisdiction issues 319–20, 338–61
  litigation 304
  notice of adjudication 123–5, 146–7, 149–52, 174–6, 201, 391–2
  orders of the court 280–3
  Part 8 claims 29
  reckoning of time 189, 201, 528–9
  referral notice 10, 123–5, 151–3, 173–6, 180–1, 201, 205, 212–13, 219–22, 342, 347–9, 350–1, 391–2, 418–26, 617–18, 655
  responses 10, 23, 28, 102–4, 124–5, 145, 173–4, 181–4, 212–13, 380–2, 391–2, 439–40
  rigidity of the decision time limit 222, 350–61, 418–26, 624, 656
  Scotland 411–26
  TCC 252–5, 258–62, 264–5, 633
  unfair timetables 391, 673
  withdrawals 188, 195, 227, 620
Tolent clauses, costs 234–5, 419–20
Town and Country Planning Act 1990 65
Treaty of Union 1707 406–7
tried-and-tested advantages of construction adjudications 20
triggers, insolvency 30–2
trivial terms, written contracts 73, 594

ultra vires challenges, decisions 12, 276, 331–2
uncontroversial aspects, Scheme adjudications 86–7
'under' the contract disputes 115–17, 151, 342, 611–13
unfair contract terms 12, 64, 145, 232, 400, 403–4
Unfair Terms in Consumer Contracts Regulations 1999 (UTCCR) 12, 64, 145, 232, 400, 403–4, 676–7
unfair timetables 391, 671
unreviewable error doctrine 77–9, 149
unwilling/unable/busy appointees, appointment of adjudicator 162, 169
UTCCR *see* Unfair Terms in Consumer Contracts Regulations 1999

valuation disputes 24, 105, 110–11, 130–6, 141
variants, Scheme adjudications 87–8
Victoria 447–60
  see also Australia
void/voidable contracts 45, 46–8, 115, 116–17, 284, 587
  see also duress; fraud
voluntary administration 36–7, 287–90
  definition 36–7, 287–8
  generally 36–7, 287–9

Wages Protection and Contractors' Lien Act 1939, New Zealand 487–8
waivers
  by election 332–3
  by estoppel 332–3
  definition 332–3
  losing the right to challenge the adjudicator's jurisdiction 331–8, 365, 651
  natural justice 365
warrants of execution 282
water or effluent treatment, excluded operations 58, 61–2, 339–42, 524–5
Water Industry Act 1991 65
Western Australia (WA) 447–60, 579–83
  see also Australia
winding-up petitions 29, 31–3, 34–6, 226, 278–80, 283, 285–6, 288, 294–5, 300
  see also insolvency; liquidation

withdrawals
   the adjudication 188, 195, 227, 321, 328–9, 364–5, 620, 650
   timescales 188, 195, 227, 620
withholding notices
   generally 105–8, 114–15, 129–39, 141, 182–4, 192–4, 242, 244–6, 302–3, 606–7, 629
   set-offs 242, 244–6, 629
without prejudice material
   bias 366, 377, 667
   costs 198, 199
   definition 197 8
   generally 106, 139, 172, 188–9, 197–8, 199, 336–7, 366, 377, 667
witness statement forms, TCC documents 257, 259–60
witnesses
disregarded submissions/witnesses 204–5, 374–5, 384–9, 670–2
   generally 179–80, 196–7, 204–5, 257, 259, 373–5
   referral notice evidence 179–80, 188, 196–7

response evidence 183–4, 188, 196–7
writ of fieri facias, enforcement methods 282
writ of summons, Northern Ireland 430–1
written claims 98–100
   see also claims
written contracts
   see also construction contracts
   2009 Act 66, 67–74, 76, 526
   certainty benefits 67–8
   generally 43–8, 66–74, 338–42, 476–8, 503–4, 526, 591–5
   implied terms 73, 208, 443–4, 594–5
   letters of intent 73–4, 595
   'otherwise than in writing' provisions 69–74, 526, 592
   requirements 43–4, 66–74, 526, 591–5
   scenarios 71–4, 593–5
   trivial terms 73, 594
written submissions in adjudication proceedings, written contracts 70–1, 593
wrong parties, preconditions and restrictions 107, 607

Printed in Great Britain
by Amazon